DATE DUE			

THE GREAT MOVIE STARS
THE GOLDEN YEARS

THE GREAT MOVIE STARS
THE GOLDEN YEARS

DAVID SHIPMAN

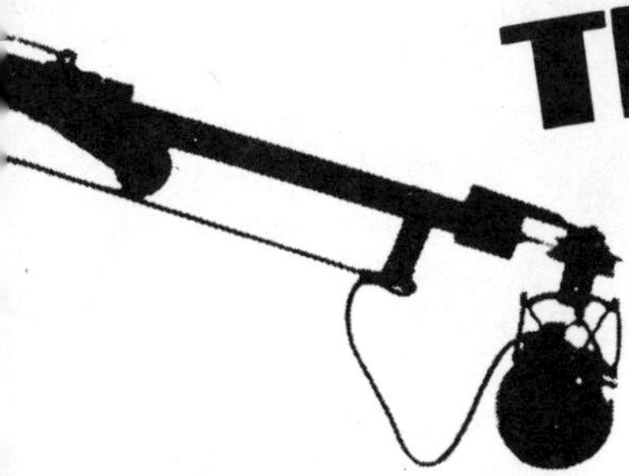

CROWN PUBLISHERS, INC.
NEW YORK

Special Picture Research by John Kobal

Published in the USA by
Crown Publishers, Inc.
419 Park Avenue South
New York, N.Y. 10016

In association with
The Hamlyn Publishing Group Limited

Library of Congress Catalog Number 78–133803

Printed in England
by Jarrold and Sons Limited, Norwich

INTRODUCTION

The stars and the system

The first film players worked on both sides of the camera and were uncredited; but as some of them became familiar to audiences there was a buzz of recognition. Most nickelodeons and variety halls hired their films from the same film-exchanges which relied in turn on the same film suppliers. It wasn't long before all these businessmen began to appreciate that a familiar face could be a definite asset.

Already there were film studios – in sheds or properties that had been warehouses – turning out sometimes several films a week. In 1908 Edison was in The Bronx and Vitagraph in Flatbush; Biograph, probably the oldest company, was on 14th Street in New York. Selig and Essanay were in Chicago. These five companies and five others formed, in 1909, the Motion Picture Patents Co., claiming the exclusive right to photograph, print and develop motion pictures. Edison himself was involved and the patent was quite legal. But when they attempted to control the exchanges and nickelodeons they came up against opposition from the entrepreneurs who were making huge fortunes from distribution, like Carl Laemmle of the Laemmle Film Service. He fought the monopoly in court and out – by ridicule in the trade press and by producing his own movies (the first was a one-reel *Hiawatha*). For his Independent Motion Picture Co. (IMP) he was determined to get one of the best-known personalities in pictures, 'The Biograph Girl.'

This lady had already been identified as Florence Lawrence. She and her husband, Harry Salter, had started with Vitagraph and had moved on to D. W. Griffith's Biograph when she was offered an extra $10 a week – to $25. By 1910 she was sufficiently popular for Laemmle to offer her the violently excessive sum of $1,000 a week. Then she vanished. Laemmle planted a story in the press to the effect that she had been run down and killed by a trolley car in St Louis, and then asserted in an advert in the trade press that the story was an invention of his enemies. Miss Lawrence appeared in St Louis to prove that she was alive – and was mobbed. All of this focused much attention on her and on IMP, proving not only the vast popularity of film-players but underlining their value as commercial properties.

Miss Lawrence the following year went to the Lubin Co., one of the patents group, where she teamed with Arthur Johnson for some popular comedies. Fame didn't last. In the 20s she was in Britain working in minor parts when Marion Davies heard of her plight and sent her the fare to come to Hollywood, plus the offer of a small part in a movie. She became an extra and committed suicide in 1938, completely forgotten. Her rival, Florence Turner 'The Vitagraph Girl', fared little better. When her career began to wane around 1912 she went to Britain with Vitagraph co-star Larry Trimble and they formed their own company in conjunction with Cecil M. Hepworth and were successful for a while. By 1924 her parts were few and small. She returned to the US and played a few more brief roles, such as Buster Keaton's mother in *College* (27).

Mary Pickford was on the scene by 1909, and there were other melting heroines like Blanche Sweet, Clara Kimball Young and Norma Talmadge; romantic heroes like Francis X. Bushman and Maurice Costello; cowboy stars Tom Mix, Broncho Billy Anderson and William S. Hart; and the comedy team of Flora Finch and John

Bunny. It occurred to Adolph Zukor, another exhibitor, that if the public would turn up to see these people, they might be curious to see the great stars of the stage.

The idea was not entirely his. In France Sarah Bernhardt had been persuaded to commit her Camille to two reels of celluloid for the sake of posterity, and as a reprise she was a four-reel *Queen Elizabeth*. Zukor had invested some money in the latter when it got into difficulties during production and therefore held the American rights. He discovered that Bernhardt gave cinemas not only respectability but huge receipts. He conceived the idea of 'Famous Players in Famous Plays' and many Broadway names were cajoled into movies. Few of them stayed because Zukor's prestige pictures were dreary (if worthy): those who did had lucrative careers.

Artists were coming in from vaudeville. Mack Sennett directed his first film for Biograph in 1910 and not long afterwards the variety halls began to be raided for comics – and for acrobats. Pearl White, who became the queen of the serials in *The Perils of Pauline* (14), had been an aerialist. It was essential for all these film-players to have, if not striking good looks, some great *physical* characteristic such as agility or a funny walk or funny expressions or a dimple. (In the Talkies an actor with a strongly individual voice would find this an asset above and beyond looks or physical presence.)

During the First World War Mary Pickford and Chaplin knew an undreamed-of world-wide popularity and by 1920 the studios were fashioning most of their pictures around one individual personality – a personality who was considered to be, commercially, that film's major attraction. Under no circumstances was there more than one star to a film. No matter who in the public's estimation was a star, the billing required only one name above the title – that of the 'official' star: much publicity accrued when contract players were hoisted to 'official' stardom. The contract lists were a huge source of pride, even if the players were like caged animals – to be petted and pampered and exhibited before admiring multitudes, but starved of space in which to fly and move: unable to move artistically. In the early 30s the rules were changed. Said Picturegoer with some awe in 1932: 'It looks as though the two-star film is here to stay – at least for the time being.' Very soon MGM set the fan-magazines buzzing when they announced that *Grand Hotel* would have *six* stars – but it didn't often make sense, economically, to put several stars in one film, when the public would turn up just as eagerly to see one or two.

So much effort went into making and then maintaining a star. In the star-vehicles which constituted the major output of all the studios, infinite care and skill went into costumes and lighting so that the star appeared to best advantage; great care was taken over the first entrance, over the choice of leading man or leading woman; and when the star was undisguisedly ageing, even that fact was turned to advantage.

But if the Hollywood factories were adept at packaging these enticing products called stars, an examination of the 181 stars in this book proves that few careers had much in common. Getting to the top seems to have been a question of chance, with hazards not unlike those encountered on the 'Monopoly' board. For every vital and intelligent talent that makes it several others fail: the history of films is strewn with the names of people who seemed to have the requisite looks, personality and talent but yet who somehow fell down a hole. At the same time there are artists deficient in all three who became world-wide favourites. Youth can be an asset, and so can familiarity – when audiences become conditioned to certain looks and mannerisms; and you can even be taken in by the aura. It has been frequently claimed that the relationship between star and public is like a love-affair – but it is an affair with an element of harlotry: the public will only pay out its money for stars with sufficient skill and personality to sustain the relationship.

Actual acting ability can be minimal, though no screen actor survived who didn't quickly acquire at least a technical proficiency. Considering the elements involved in creating a star performance and the fragmented way a film is made, it is surprising how consistent most artists were/are – variously good from film to film but seldom variable within a film. John Gielgud was once asked to define the basic requirements of an actor. He replied: 'Imagination, self-discipline, industry, a sense of humour if possible. And certain basic qualities of appearance, of authority, of originality. Sort of commonplace prettiness is not very interesting, you know. Just good looks aren't interesting; but interesting looks can be used – a malleable, flexible body and face, and voice. Voice, of course, I think is very important.' Gielgud was not asked to differentiate between screen and stage acting, but it might be noted that very few stage-trained actors have failed in films (the reverse is not the case). A stage-trained actor is equipped with certain advantages such as the ability to play to other actors, to build a scene to a climax, and even – on an elementary level – to handle dialogue. His effectiveness – on stage or screen – can depend on physical conditions like co-stars and climate, and in films it can depend largely on what happens in the cutting-room.

Which is just as well. Film actors in the past had more to cope with than mere acting. Just being a star must at times have been overwhelming. They were well-paid and they were protected from scandal (in most instances) but photographic sessions, interviews and personal appearances usually took precedence over acting. The amount of publicity that they once had to cope with is staggering. And something else was required: the will to survive. One can discount most of the stories about temperament. Many stars had to fight – every step of the way. They fought for better parts, better movies, better terms. If there were signs of public apathy the firing-squad were on stand-by in the morning. The studios protected their interests by the contract with options, but the star had no recourse if he thought the studio was sabotaging his standing with poor films. Talent was his sole ally. Some artists did triumph over every adversary placed in their way by the studios. It is not a coincidence that most of the female stars who had long careers also had strong masculine qualities, but even a Bette Davis can, after years of fighting, become, in Robert Aldrich's words 'a strange lady. She has been misled so many times, and placed her confidence so many times in situations and/or people that didn't pay off, that she's naturally terribly hesitant to trust anybody.' (He added: 'Once she trusts you, she's marvellous.')

The system was firmly rigged against the individual in favour of the machine, and it is hardly surprising that it destroyed talents who never knew how to come to terms with it, like Marilyn Monroe and Judy Garland. Some artists returned to the stage, always a much saner operating ground – and those artists who were equally stage stars usually found it easier to weather the cinematic storms than the others. It was and is a hazardous business: even Charlton Heston – in a TV interview – once confessed that he was insecure 'like all actors' (though as at that time he was being paid $750,000 per film it was difficult to sympathize). Actors, not unreasonably, tend to be extrovert, vain and emotional, and the enclosed, self-centred and fantasy world of Hollywood exaggerated these qualities without being beneficial to them either as artists or individuals.

The drives of an actor are not like yours or mine, but it is essential to bear in mind through the following pages that most stars started out as very ordinary beings simply trying to earn a living. This rather trite observation is worth making if only as an antidote to the general conception that stars are glamorous creatures who do little but get divorced and re-married. In the circumstances it wouldn't be surprising if that were true; but in this book both scandals and personal relationships have been mentioned only when they seem to have some bearing on an artist's career. Fame via the casting-office couch is always a possibility (there are good reasons why this object is not so mythical) but an examination of the way most people got to the top in this particular field proves it to have been rather by industry, integrity and intelligence. Perhaps some later stars did it more by wheeling and dealing, but most of the pre-war stars were of a different breed. This Hollywood generation was extraordinarily blessed with talent, and from all that was written about them there emerges much to admire and little to dislike. In interviews most of them appear to have been realistic and frank (it is only the second-raters who brag of minor successes and gloss over failures – the same tactics that are used by politicians). But what matters of course is what was up there on that screen, and when you see it – the best of it – you're in no doubt as to why movie-stars are the twentieth century's contribution to mythology.

The question of what constitutes star quality must detain us briefly. David Lean said once that he preferred to direct stars because two of them together accept each other as a challenge. They strike sparks. As long as films depended on the theatre (or novels) those with a genuine star player started with an advantage of sorts. It's in the nature of that particular beast. The performing arts generally have always been dependent on star performers. In larger than life-size roles you must have performers to fit. You simply cannot do 'King Lear' or 'Macbeth' without stars, or 'Tosca' or 'Private Lives'; but you can do 'The Three Sisters' or 'The Importance of Being Earnest' or 'Look Back in Anger'. (In the theatre the rapport between star and audience or the current charging between them is, of course, much more palpable than anything comparable in the cinema). In film terms, despite the overall mastery of, say, Hitchcock, his movies were always more effective when he had strong leading players. It is the way of the Hollywood system: virtually no Hollywood director is at his best with unknowns or mere actors. The habit is too ingrained; and Hollywood takes much of its material from plays and books which in turn were influenced by Hollywood. Elsewhere there have been films where you couldn't have had any sort of star – Ray's *Apu* trilogy, Olmi's *Il Posto*, Ichikawa's *Alone on the Pacific* and, even, his *An Actor's Revenge*. Ichikawa's *Tokyo Olympiad* didn't even have actors. To this writer these films are masterpieces, but as I've found it extremely unlikely to encounter a masterpiece every time I go to the cinema I'll settle for something else – like Garbo, if I'm lucky. Her performances are the sole justification of the films in which she appeared. In *Camille*, labouring under every disadvantage that any player ever faced – except direction and perhaps dialogue – she provides an experience as potent as, if different from, that of *Tokyo Olympiad*. The nature of that experience has been analysed by virtually every writer on films – and it remains unfathomable. Of lesser artists one can be more certain: beauty, magnetism, personality, ability – one of these or a combination of these to a degree that is not ordinarily encountered in one's friends or in other actors. The great stars were all great originals and any description more precise founders on their individuality. James Mason tried in *A Star Is Born* with the aid of Moss Hart's script: 'It's that little something extra that Ellen Terry talked about.' It must remain undefined; but you know it when you see it.

A note on the films

It was clear from the outset that motion pictures of ordinary life were not going to be enough, and the film pioneers looked primarily to the stage for inspiration. It was the first mistake they made, for the stage, in the early years of this century, was a sick subject for emulation, inundated as it was with barn-storming melodramas (melodrama: 'a variety of drama, commonly romantic and sentimental' – Webster). True, these plays, transcribed, proved ideal for cinema audiences, but thus the pall of melodrama was to settle on films for more than 50 years. Technical inadequacy – including of course the lack of speech – caused further strait-jacketing, and it was some time before it was revealed that movies could be told *technically* – not only via images but by the arrangement of same, by cutting and the rhythm of cutting, by the camera's own motivation. D. W. Griffith was the greatest of the innovators and the most successful film-maker of his day; but his taste in stories was unsophisticated, with all characters and situations polarized into black and white. His very success may have daunted any spirit who saw life in more sober terms – though certainly his taste in screen fiction was in key with both his audiences and the moguls, whose attitudes were likely to have been moulded by the same factors. In Europe the plots were equally melodramatic, but there were sometimes compensations of atmosphere or feeling; and when Hollywood seduced the best continental directors most of them were forced to conform with patterns already established. A few overcame the handicap of Silence, but if the essence of all drama is conflict – the clash of opinion, motives, personalities – there were few who could portray it in other than simplistic terms. In Russia, Eisenstein, with the prerogative of genius, solved the problem when dealing with the greatest conflict of the age: the motives and behaviour of his protagonists (*October*, *Strike*, etc) are told wholly and satisfactorily in moving picture terms.

Chaplin and Keaton also knew how to reach an audience visually – perhaps because (like Griffith) they came from theatrical backgrounds. They turned the lack of Sound to their advantage (and not only that, but the primitive cameras, film-stock, etc.). Their films dealt in conflict, and *The General* indeed is about opposing factions in the War between the States: there isn't a single facet of the struggle (Keaton on his train and the enemy on theirs) which Keaton couldn't handle with visual wit. With Harold Lloyd, the two great comics rival Eisenstein as a visual writer. It is not a coincidence that these three were comedians. They knew instinctively that you couldn't do drama with only a camera and a splicer – at least not the sort of drama that the Silents wanted to show (*Zabriskie Point*, however, might well have been better with no dialogue at all).

Few other Silent films yield much except to buffs (in which respect of course they're like pre-Elizabethan drama). The so-called classics were lauded for what they attempted rather than achieved – both because this was a medium which, for the first time in history, could communicate to millions and because it was denied the privilege of Sound. There was a further drawback due to the fact that at the start all films were of one-reel or less: although they increased in length it was not until the late 20s that many directors were able to sustain a mood or impose any consistency. Plots were often a series of episodes built round a central theme, and in a film like the 1920 *Mark of Zorro* the scenes could have been shifted without any loss to logic. Everything – not only the sets – seemed made of cardboard and if there was any character development it was in the crudest terms.

Many of the early Talkies were no better: they spoke but didn't say anything. Titles still abounded, and as late as 1935 *Clive of India* was little more than a series of conversations with the plot developments explained by lengthy titles. Films were still constructed with little regard for logicality, though some adaptations of plays and novels were impressive, such as John Ford's *Arrowsmith* (31), where the dialogue and situations of Sinclair Lewis's novel were handled by a director with both a feeling for these and a sense of the medium's potentialities. Ford could bring conviction to almost any environment – despite, say, painted settings and poor dialogue. There was always a feeling of real life. His best films are a physical experience.

In France René Clair used music and dialogue to enhance his fond and witty view of the (Parisian) universe: he, rather than Hollywood, ushered in the inconsequence – the ordered chaos – which was to mark the films of the next decade. In Hollywood and Britain also the introduction of Sound brought in music, and in American films the dialogue was often sharp, fast and slangy. The writers and directors, if left to themselves, went untrammelled by convention. Sound was the *modus vivendi* and inexperience in itself a virtue. They had no failures behind them. It was an era of great confidence. These were to be the golden years – in directing, in screenwriting and in performing. Certainly, at least in comedy.

In the 30s films had an incredible gaiety. Consider this lot: *Duck Soup*, *The Awful Truth*, *Nothing Sacred*, *A Slight Case of Murder*, *True Confession*, *A Hundred Men and a Girl*, *Ninotchka*, *Sing Baby Sing*, *Star of Midnight*, *The Adventures of Robin Hood*, *She Done Him Wrong*, *Bringing Up Baby*, *Mr Deeds Goes to Town*, *Swing Time*, *It's a Gift*, *Snow-White and the Seven Dwarfs*. Mainly comedies: most of them knowing, some of them innocent, all of them insouciant, elegant, confident, captivating. In the world of the dictators, in the shadow of war, Hollywood knew how to make the world forget its troubles.

The vast film factories were churning out chunks of entertainment like these as from an assembly line. All studios aimed at a programme of diverse amusements: musicals, Westerns, gangster thrillers, detective thrillers, smart comedies, folksy comedies, historical dramas, women's dramas, etc. No taste was uncatered for. The films had a different surface gloss, but the products of individual studios were otherwise interchangeable. Certain predilections are discernable – Warners, for instance liked anything that smacked of a social conscience while the more conservative MGM definitely didn't; but a pattern only emerges in that all the studios were willing to repeat a success and therefore seemed to specialize in a certain genre. The overall product did reflect, if not the taste of the front office, the level of its brow and its insatiable quest for conformity.

Whatever the genre, the films were much of a muchness: they fed on each other and not on life. It didn't matter if in comedy the mirror held up to life was distorted – it had its own validity – but in drama it was stifling: stock characters in stock situations. And the star vehicles were hardly conducive to originality, even though there is, clearly, a magic about the best of them; and, because these were the important films, you can often discern a lot of good ideas and themes trying to get loose.

The big budgets were saved for these – the prestige pictures, adaptations of worthy best-sellers and Broadway hits: when they don't work today it is usually because of their Olympian view of the human race. They were supposed to educate the public – the lowest common denominator of it, and Thalberg, for instance, for all his insistence on the best stories and the best writers, demanded absolute conformity in the dénouements. In the 40s Jean Renoir brought some of his humanity to Hollywood, but his films still seemed to end with a Selznick sunset; and Fritz Lang, later, said that he resigned his Hollywood sinecure because the battles weren't worth the ulcers.

Few stars, in any case, wanted to be associated with anything that might be termed 'experimental'. The studios didn't care to have the reputations of their players jeopardized, and the stars hesitated because they knew they were held personally responsible for the success or failure of their films. After the system had broken down, in the 50s, certain stars were willing to back new talent and new ideas – but by this time it was no longer accepted that any individual performer decisively affected a film's performance at the box-office.

The changes of the 50s and 60s are outside the province of this book, but there

No survey of Holly-wood's golden years could be complete without a reference to the work of Walt Disney, represented here by Mickey's Gala Première *(33). Among those who attended the grand event were (left) Laurel and Hardy and (right) Maurice*

should be noted (1) the end of the long-term contract (2) the rise of the actor-impresario (3) the growth of internationalism and, not with sorrow (4) the passing of the B-picture or second feature. These in the early 30s supplanted the shorts and two-reelers which had preceded the feature movie – though by the end of the decade shorts, newsreels and cartoons were filling in time between features. In this book all B-features are designated as such, and these can be taken to mean films of low-budget, with a running time of about one hour and destined for the lower half of the programme. The expression 'programmer' - or programme-filler – refers to those films without pretence to art or huge grosses made merely to keep cinemas busy, and a 'dualler' was the same thing, only in this case it was not considered strong enough to play with a B-picture but needed another film like itself. Few duallers were made as such – they just turned out that way.

Some more trade jargon which should prove useful: a 'sleeper' is a low-budget picture which does unexpectedly well; an 'indie' is an independent production made away from one of the big studios – though sometimes released by one of their distribution companies; a 'sudser' is a species of 'soap-opera' – sometimes a 'weepie' – aimed primarily at the distaff half of the audience; a 'biopic' is a film biography (an invariably depressing species); a 'melo' is obviously a melodrama; and a 'road show' or 'block-buster' a film of huge budget designed to play separate performances at legitimate theatre prices.

The fan-magazines

The fan-magazines were originally house-magazines, like the British 'Pictures', founded in 1912 and later evolving into Picturegoer. In the US the Vitagraph Co. started a magazine to publicize its own stars and films, and both at first were not unlike the trade-journals, with their news of showmen's campaigns and advice to the pianists in the pit. It was soon realized that there was a vast public interest in the off-set activities of its favourites, who were then pictured at home by log-fires or welcoming European royalty to the set. The pose of being infinitely glamorous had to be maintained, and the more prosaic information about current and forthcoming films was interspersed with articles on the romances of their leading players. The fan-magazines of the 20s believed, probably rightly, that their chief readers were women and they bolstered their

Chevalier and Eddie Cantor. Disney's early short cartoons remain perhaps the most charming and inventive work in the field, despite formidable world-wide competition in later years – during which time his own shorts were increasingly mechanical.

contents with items such as beauty hints and fashion notes. The (American) Photoplay of the 20s had a concerned and critical attitude towards films, but its articles on personalities were devoid of any real matter; and by the end of the 30s its film reviews, also, had succumbed to the requirements of the studios. The Picturegoer of the 20s was without character but when it went from monthly to weekly in 1931 it became both informative and responsible. (Both magazines have been drawn upon for much of the material of this book, plus certain trade journals, notably the indispensable Variety).

By the beginning of the Talkie period the fan-magazines were forces to reckon with. In the US they were monthly; and though the number fluctuated there were seldom less than half-a-dozen. In Britain in the 30s there were four weeklies – Picturegoer and Film Weekly, Picture Show and Film Pictorial. They combined into two at the outbreak of war and continued as a duo till the late 50s, when they each folded after a brief attempt at jazzing-up. Film Weekly and later Picturegoer had the finest writer ever to make a living from studying Hollywood, W. H. Mooring, a liberal and kindly man who was more interested in films than in personalities and scandals.

The American magazines only appeared to have the same freedom. They and the studios were mutually dependent: the magazines wanted information – exclusive if possible – and the studios wanted favourable mention of their films and stars. So the magazines were content to reprint the 'copy' turned out by the studio pubmills and by the mid-40s were depicting a never-never (even neverer) land which was later to degenerate into a morass of make-believe scandal. They seemed to be about only plastic people in a plastic world. Nor must one overlook the immense power of the syndicated and broadcasting gossip-columnists, who at their worst were vicious and at their best patronizing; and, with the exception of Hedda Hopper, singularly lacking in humour – if not without their insights. Most stars viewed the columnists as parasites, and the uneasy relationship between them has elements of pathos, with some stars desperately anxious for publicity and the columnists forever fending off a series of imagined snubs. But the columnist always won: it was too simple to write a piece repeating every unfavourable rumour and opinion, finishing with a sop like 'But we believe none of it: we believe he can do it.'

Two more scenes from Mickey's Gala Première: *Marie Dressler, Wallace Beery and Lionel Barrymore; Mickey and Greta Garbo. Disney returned to this idea in* 1938 *in* Mothe Goose Goes Holly-

Such pieces were, however, uncommon until the post-war years when a harsher light was cast and stars were deglamorized. Until then, too, perhaps only Garbo and Chaplin were remarked by the more serious sections of the press, and it wasn't till the 50s, with the advent of Brando and Monroe, that star-gazing was accepted as a worthwhile occupation for the higher brow. It wasn't till then that the serious movie magazines were much interested in stars. For sanity on all such matters one turned to the British Film Institute's two magazines, Sight and Sound and The Monthly Film Bulletin (referred to in the text as the MFB).

Elsewhere the cinema has not been particularly lucky in its commentators. The majority of books on movies are riddled with errors and that includes all but a few listed at the back as sources. The best non-academic textbook on the American film is still Griffith and Mayer's 'The Movies'. The magazine and newspaper critics most often quoted in this book are those whom I feel were and are the masters of their craft. All references in the text to 'the critics' and to 'the press' means the majority unless specifically stated; quotes are used solely to evoke critical response to a particular star – but there were some fine artists who had long careers without kindling any great critical fires.

The industry has never cared for critics, which it sees as sourpusses determined to prevent the public from turning out for the latest million-dollar masterpiece: but the two sides have lived together so long that it is rather like the Trojan War, with moments of bitterness and fury but a general feeling of something to be lived with. The enthusiasm by the best critics for the medium has been under-rated by the industry, though it has been quick to use their good opinions in its advertisements. The critics never made a star, but, like the fan-magazines, they could create a setting where a new personality or a particular performance became a landmark to be seen; and there have been artists of little commercial value who have been utilized by producers because they could be relied upon to bring in favourable notices.

The box-office

Public acceptance has been the surest and perhaps most satisfying barometer of success, and the box-office lists were always carefully studied by studio chiefs. They had other ways of telling, but an appearance in the annual list of top money-makers in the Motion Picture Herald *wood, where there appeared, among others, Katharine Hepburn, Clark Gable, Charles Laughton, Spencer Tracy, Freddie Bartholomew, Edward G. Robinson, W. C. Fields and the Marx Brothers.*

considerably increased that actor's power and/or earning capacity: to head the list was commercially on a par with winning an Oscar.

The statistics can be deceptive. Exhibitors are asked to vote for those artists who bring most money into their tills during one calendar year, so that someone with three successful films to his credit appears more advantageously than another with only one; and many exhibitors are unable to assess the actual appeal of any film so that they credit – or blame – the star at whim. British exhibitors have been wont to vote for any star appearing in a hit, so the British lists have contained a freakish proportion of artists who otherwise didn't mean a thing to patrons. All references in this book to box-office popularity refer to the lists as printed in the Motion Picture Herald. Popularity polls – such as that conducted by Sydney Bernstein for the patrons of his Granada circuit – are all clearly designated as such.

As far as the films are concerned, the figures have been culled from both the Motion Picture Herald and Variety. Variety annually lists the all-time grossers, i.e. all films that took over $4 million, but as very, very few in the 20s and 30s took as much as this the earlier figures are taken from the Motion Picture Herald. Rising seat prices should be kept in mind when considering all details of finance, including salaries: for instance, in 1930 a film with a take of $1 million was a giant hit, while in 1970 a film will expect to take $5 million before beginning to recover its costs. (It might be generally accepted that before the Second World War, £1 sterling equalled $4, and after it $3.

A word of caution on salaries: these are reprinted in good faith from Variety, Picturegoer, etc., and are included as guide-lines, failing more complete statistics – but like dates of birth, details of wages (and contracts) were not something about which either studios or agents were scrupulously honest.

The awards

The Academy of Motion Picture Arts and Sciences was founded by Louis B. Mayer in 1927 in an attempt to prevent unionization of actors and artisans. It has an elected membership of some 3,000 film-workers considered to have reached the top in the industry or in their own particular branch of it. Of these, specialists in 13 sections determine the award nominations, normally five in each category. The winners receive their awards, a gold statuette known as

Oscar, in an annual ceremony in Los Angeles.

The first ceremony in 1929 was a private affair, but the publicity value of the awards was soon apparent. Televised live today, the Oscar ceremony traditionally draws the largest audience of the American viewing year. Both to audiences and within the industry Oscar is the supreme award. To receive one is to enter a golden hall of fame. Books have been written about it. It has been reviled and admired and fought for. Both James Mason and Spencer Tracy are on record as saying that it is invidious to pick *one* performance from the year's best and that to be nominated is sufficient honour. But to receive one is considered the peak of a film actor's career: his fee goes up, and the major awards (Best Film, Best Actor and Best Actress) are reckoned to add as much as $1 million to the film's gross.

However, both in terms of the award itself and its effect on any career, the Oscar is a dazzling enigma. Some have not benefited from it and to some it has merely been a crystallization of the high regard in which they are held by their fellow-artists. Just when you despair as to how some films and players even got nominated something perfectly right happens like the awards to Simone Signoret and Rod Steiger. Who on earth voted for *The Greatest Show on Earth* as Best Film of 1952? – over *High Noon* and *The Quiet Man*, not to mention *Moulin Rouge* and *Ivanhoe* (or *The River* and *Singin' in the Rain*, which weren't even nominated). But then John Ford won the Best Director award that year for *The Quiet Man*, his fourth Oscar. Elizabeth Taylor has two and Marlon Brando only one; neither *Paths of Glory* nor *2001 A Space Odyssey* were even nominated when the winners were, respectively, *The Bridge On the River Kwai* and *Oliver!* – but *Midnight Cowboy* won and *Anne of the Thousand Days* didn't.

There is no doubt that voters are influenced by fine reviews *plus* big business. Sentiment plays a part; and so does publicity – that is just a fact of the Hollywood way of life and the intense campaigning on the part of certain artists should not reflect on their talent or popularity. Also, certain rules are observed: it is easier to win in drama than in comedy, and still easier if the character portrayed is (1) living in sin or penury (2) neurotically afflicted or (3) noble and uplifting. Even with fine critical notices it is difficult to get nominated for a performance in a flop movie. The nominations in themselves are interesting, but because of the waywardness of the system and because of their uncertain value to the nominee's career they have not as a general rule been noted in this book.

Other awards in recent years have proliferated to the point of idiocy. Some are given merely to ensure a personal appearance, supposing that everyone benefits from the mutual publicity: these often have names like 'Middletown Women's Guild Star Mother of the Year Award'. Clearly the law of diminishing returns becomes relevant, and while the Golden Globe awards (decided by the Hollywood correspondents of the foreign press) have been growing in prestige only one other award has major prominence – the New York Critics award, given annually since 1935. Its winners generally become the favourites in the Oscar sweepstakes.

In Britain for years the only award of consequence was the Picturegoer Gold Medal, voted by its readers: so often it was won by major talents that it had considerable prestige for most of the life of the journal. The British Film Academy began giving acting awards in 1952, and so that Hollywood wouldn't sweep the board the four awards were divided into Best British and Best Foreign. The growing internationalism within the British film industry finally made the distinction untenable and it was dropped in 1969. But the acting awards remained four in number, with the adoption of two Best Supporting awards, after the Hollywood pattern. These British awards have generally been more pleasing than their Hollywood counterparts but are knee-high to a grasshopper in prestige, a situation unlikely to change until the ceremony has more weight (the 1970 one plumbed new depths).

About the book

This book does not, could not, tell the whole story of the stars of the golden years and you might well look for all those fine players who supported the stars and contributed so much to that era. We have managed to include some who achieved star-billing and for the rest, their presence is felt. The choice has been guided by the box-office figures, by popularity polls and by the reputation that remains. There are some box-office stars who do not appear (Charles Farrell, Joe E. Brown, Jane Withers, Gene Autry and Roy Rogers) mainly because their entire careers do not seem to justify inclusion, nor have we included stars from radio and the stage who made only occasional forays into films.

For similar reasons the Silent stars included are only those who are remembered today. There is enough to be written on the stars of the Silent screen to make a book twice this length – enough heartbreak and triumph – but for the most part they remain unseen, their films gathering dust in the corners of warehouses, or disintegrating. And some of them, when seen, are very dubious contenders for a pantheon of great stars. The continental stars of the period, unless they worked in Hollywood, have been left to a later volume, on the understanding that from the introduction of Talkies until well after the Second World War even the best of these players were known outside their own countries only to film societies or to the patrons of 'specialized' cinemas.

This survey therefore includes those artists who achieved stardom before and in some cases during World War II. The selection has had to be arbitrary: John Wayne was not a major star until after the war and yet he seems to belong to this period; while Rex Harrison, David Niven and a few others who were in starring roles before the war seem to belong to the post-war period. Care has been taken to examine the stars and their films in the light of their own era, and to balance contemporary opinion against recent showings of the same films. Because of institutions like New York's Museum of Modern Art and London's National Film Theatre, and old movies on television, it is possible to re-examine and discover the films of the past – but one should note, in passing, that this was not always so. Until the 50s the majority of movies were dead and forgotten the day after by all but the public: neither fan-magazines nor critics nor the producers nor the stars themselves ever expected cinemagoers to remember more than six months back.

Each individual entry lists all feature films made by that particular star – i.e. all films of four reels and over. In the case of Silent stars who made one- and two-reelers a selection only has been included, and shorts made by Talkie actors have not normally been included. For space reasons we have neither attempted a separate filmography nor tried to list the co-star and producing company of each film. All films are set down in release order except where otherwise stated (in these cases it seemed that readers sufficiently interested as to which film followed which by a month or two would know where to research such facts). The dates given in parentheses are for the first film *reviewed* in any calendar year per the Film Daily Yearbook – i.e. January to December, and all films following that date were reviewed the same year. (Films are sometimes dated by year of copyright and sometimes by the year of release; because the records of the Film Daily are complete it seems to me best to take their review date i.e. the date when the film was complete and shown to exhibitors). It should be borne in mind that many films are not premièred till some months after the star has finished filming, by which time he or she might well have made several stage appearances, etc.

All film titles are given as in the country of origin and an appendix lists the titles of American films that were re-named for the British market and vice-versa. The appendix also lists a few continental films which were re-titled for the British or American market. In the text, when a foreign title is followed by a stroke and an English language title this indicates that the film is known equally by both titles.

Apart from the published sources listed I am extremely grateful to the following, all of whom read the manuscript, or most of it, and offered invaluable help and comment: Felix Brenner, David Holland, Lee Serjeant, Michael Stapleton, James Tinline and André Vannier: between us I think we can claim to have seen 99% of the films mentioned in this book. My especial gratitude is due to James Tinline who, when he was supposed to be teaching me English literature in the tropical heat of Singapore preferred to talk about this golden age of movies. It was he who first fired me with enthusiasm for artists I hadn't then seen, like Garbo and the Marx Brothers. My thanks are also due to the following for help above and beyond the call of duty: Honor Blair, Janet Faulds, Van Phillips, Roy Seaman, Lita Torgersen-Sherman, Barbara and Jay Williams, Fred Zentner and Paul Welti, who designed the book. I am also deeply indebted to the staff of the British Film Institute Library and Information Section, who were unfailingly courteous even in answering what must have seemed to them many footling questions.

Bud Abbott (left) and Lou Costello as they were when they met the Invisible Man (50)–one of their series of unhistoric meetings.

Abbott and Costello

Bud Abbott was the straight man. Lou Costello was the funny one, a roly-poly little man liable to mishap and misunderstanding. They were a comedy team of the 40s and early 50s and astonishingly popular. Their humour was mainly verbal, too immediate, and it doesn't revive.

Abbott was born in Asbury Park, New Jersey, in 1895; Costello in Paterson in the same state in 1908. Costello started out as a salesman in a hat shop, became a prize-fighter and saved enough to try his luck in Hollywood. The only job he could get at first was labouring at MGM but later he was a stunt man: he once doubled for Dolores del Rio. Then he tried vaudeville. Abbott came from a show business milieu–his parents were part of a circus troupe. He became a sailor at 15, then worked as a box-office clerk in a burlesque theatre: he was selling tickets and Costello was on the bill, and Costello's straight man didn't turn up ... thus the act was formed. This was in Brooklyn in 1930. They formed a team and played on the bump-and-grind circuit without success for seven years, until a New York booking led to an appearance on Kate Smith's radio show. They became radio favourites and in 1939 were in a Broadway revue with Carmen Miranda, 'Streets of Paris'.

Their film career began with *One Night in the Tropics* (40), a Universal musical starring Allan Jones and Robert Cummings. Abbott and Costello's cross-talk was of secondary interest to the romantics, but audience response was enthusiastic, and Universal signed them to a long-term contract. They put them in the Army, *Buck Privates* (41), and *In the Navy*, had them *Hold That Ghost* and *Ride 'em Cowboy*, made them join the Air Force, *Keep 'em Flying*: the second and third of this quintet were among the year's big grossers, and at the end of the year Abbott and Costello were No. 3 at the box office. The following year they were top, thanks to play-off dates and three new ones: *Rio Rita* (42), on loan to MGM; *Pardon My Sarong* and *Who Done It?*. The formula seldom varied. The two comics followed the traditional pattern: they were put in a specific setting (an army installation, a department store) where the utmost havoc could be wrought, relieved now and then by a love story involving two of the studio's more innocuous players. Sometimes artists were brought in to bolster them (such as Martha Raye, playing twin sisters in *Keep 'em Flying*).

Thereafter they normally made two films a year: *It Ain't Hay* (43) and *Hit the Ice*; *Lost in a Harem* (44) and *In Society*; *Here Come the Co-Eds* (45), *The Naughty Nineties* and, on loan again to MGM, *Abbott & Costello in Hollywood*; *Little Giant* (46) and *The Time of Their Lives*, a ghost story; *Buck Privates Come Home* (47) and *The Wistful Widow of Wagon Gap* (who was Marjorie Main); *The Noose Hangs High* (48), *Mexican Hayride* and *Abbott & Costello Meet Frankenstein*. By this time their popularity had fallen off drastically and the films played double bills in most situations; but it had been noticed that the public still responded to Costello–who was nothing if not a coward–when confronted with a ghost or another evil force. The Frankenstein film had perked up their box office a bit so Boris Karloff was re-engaged for *Abbott & Costello Meet the Killer* (49). *Africa Screams* and *Abbott & Costello in the Foreign Legion* (50) returned to the old formula, but *Abbott & Costello Meet the Invisible Man* played safe and used the new one. *Comin' Round the Mountain* had them caught in a Kentucky feud, but Variety declared that their 'fun-making routines have become decidedly wearing'.

By now, *Lost in Alaska* (52), the pictures had become poverty-row efforts and the two tired comedians were entoured by some of the tiredest talents in Hollywood. A half-hearted attempt was made to elevate their status when they moved to Warners for *Jack and the Beanstalk*, filmed in a horrendous process called SuperCinecolor. It didn't get the kids or anybody. Also at Warners

Abbott & Costello Me(e)t Captain Kidd, and then they moved back to Universal: *Abbott & Costello Go to Mars* (53), *Abbott & Costello Meet Dr Jekyll and Mr Hyde*, *Abbott & Costello Meet the Keystone Cops* (55) and *Abbott & Costello Meet the Mummy*. Their last one, *Dance With Me Henry* (56), was made at UA and produced by themselves. Commercially, it was a real fizzle-out. In 1957 the team split, after some TV work. Abbott announced his retirement, but Costello was offered as a single. In 1959 he made another picture, *The Thirty-Foot Bride of Candy Rock*, but died of a heart attack before it was shown (which was hardly anywhere; it was never shown in Britain).

At the time of Costello's death Abbott was suing him for over $222,000 which he claimed were owing to him from their TV series; a while later the Internal Revenue hounded Abbott for back taxes, and he was left badly off. In 1964 he had a mild stroke and still walks with a stick. Sadly he is unlikely to see a revival of interest in the films which he and Costello made together. Buffs and critics never found them funny nor, today, do TV-viewers. But it should be remembered that in 1941–4 inclusive, and 1948–51 they were among the top 10 draws.

Don Ameche

Don Ameche's screen work is not highly regarded today, mostly because he appeared in so few first-class films; further, his reputation has been dogged by his once inventing the telephone. But he was a very cheery fellow, and at least once–in *Heaven Can Wait*–he gave a light comedy performance as good as any done in that genre.

He was born in Kenosha, Wisconsin, in 1908, and read law at the University of Wisconsin. He made a name in college dramatics, and was persuaded by a friend to substitute for one of the leads in a stock company production of 'Excess Baggage' when the actor concerned didn't show up–and that decided him to abandon law. He worked in stock, and got the juvenile lead in 'Jerry for Short' in New York; he did a vaudeville tour with Texas Guinan; then was in radio for five years. He married in 1932 (they have five children). In 1935 MGM tested him and were unimpressed, but a year later 20th signed him for *two* important roles in *The Sins of Man* (36) as the sons of Austrian sexton Jean Hersholt. He impressed the critics and was signed to a long-term contract.

There followed a series of romantic leads.

Alice Faye and Don Ameche were teamed in several films in the late 30s and early 40s. This one is Hollywood Cavalcade *(39).*

In *Ladies in Love* Janet Gaynor got him and he was 'brilliant' said Picturegoer; then there was *One in a Million* with Sonja Henie; and three consecutive movies with Loretta Young: *Ramona*–he was a brave, she a squaw; *Love Is News* (37)–only he lost the girl (as he was to do frequently) to Tyrone Power (whom he had known since his radio days); and *Love Under Fire*, in which she was a suspected jewel thief and he a Scotland Yard inspector, a crazy comedy set against the Spanish Civil War (top marks for that one). His roles didn't vary much: *50 Roads to Town* with Ann Sothern; *You Can't Have Everything* with Alice Faye; *In Old Chicago* (38) with Faye and Power; *Happy Landing* with Henie; and *Alexander's Ragtime Band* where he sang, and actually married Faye before surrendering her to Power–a very good performance in a difficult role.

In *Josette* he vied with Robert Young for Simone Simon, then on her way out as a star at 20th. In *Gateway* Arleen Whelan was on her way in, via Ellis Island, as an Irish immigrant; Ameche was a war correspondent. In *The Three Musketeers* (39) he was D'Artagnan and the Ritz Brothers were the Three, and they all sang. Then came the telephone film, with Young and Henry Fonda, *The Story of Alexander Graham Bell*, by no means the least of the Hollywood biopics of that era; and another such, but with music, *Swanee River* (40), in which he was a Stephen Foster dying of drink. In between was a happier occasion, with Faye, *Hollywood Cavalcade* (39), where he was an

Don Ameche and Betty Grable are admonished by Henry Stephenson in Down Argentine Way *(41). Equally involved is J. Carroll Naish, a fine actor here serving as the comic relief.*

old-time movie director; and she was the focal point of another biopic, *Lillian Russell* (40).

These were the peak years of Ameche's screen career. He was suspended for refusing a loan-out to Paramount for *The Night of January 16*, but he was normally amenable. Thus he got clobbered with *Four Sons*, the remake of a Silent success about a Czech family torn apart by war and now updated and anti-Nazi, with Mary Beth Hughes and Eugenie Leontivitch; and even less interestingly, the 'nothing' romantic leads of three musicals, *Down Argentine Way* (41) with Betty Grable, *That Night in Rio* with Faye and *Moon Over Miami* with Grable. But a couple of pictures on loan-out restored a flagging reputation: *The Feminine Touch*, a comedy at MGM with Rosalind Russell, and more notably, *Kiss the Boys Goodbye*, at Paramount. This was a musical based on Clare Boothe Luce's play sending up the search for Scarlett O'Hara, and he and Oscar Levant had a witty script, trying *not* to discover Mary Martin. In *Confirm or Deny* he and Joan Bennett fell in love in the blackout and in *The Magnificent Dope* (42) he and Fonda were contrasted as city slicker and country cousin. Joan Bennett was his *Girl Trouble* and *Something To Shout About* at Columbia wasn't, but he sang 'You'd Be So Nice To Come Home To' and other Cole Porter ditties to Janet Blair.

Then came *Heaven Can Wait* (43), the supreme example of the later Lubitsch touch, from a Broadway play called 'Birthday'. Ameche got his best notices, playing, as Dilys Powell put it, 'with unexpected range of mood'. The piece was fantasy, about a dead man (Ameche) who tries to explain to the devil (Laird Cregar) why he should be sent to hell, but is sent back to earth for a bit. This was a theme in common with the next one, *Happy Land*, about a ghost returning to say why he died and why we should go on fighting. It seemed like a good idea at the time. Ameche did an indifferent musical, *Greenwich Village* (44), and then had little to do in his last movie for 20th, a (true) heroic story set on an aircraft carrier, *Wing and a Prayer*.

Free-lancing, he distinguished himself by asking for a guest spot in Fred Allen's *It's in the Bag* (45), but most of his subsequent films were distinctly weak: *Guest Wife*, a comedy with Claudette Colbert; *So Goes My Love* (46), another, in period dress, with Myrna Loy, in which he was again an inventor. He had a financial interest in both of these, but a third announced along the same lines was never made. Instead he did *That's My Man* (47), a soggy drama about a gambler who's a wow in the stables but a drop-out in the boudoir. Catherine McLeod played the long-suffering wife, one of two expensive efforts by Republic to make her into a big star (the other was *Concerto* with Philip Dorn). After that, not unexpectedly, Ameche turned to murder in a lower-case thriller, *Sleep My Love* (48): wife Colbert was the intended victim and he was very suave about it. His last film in a long while was the minor–but good–*Slightly French* (49) with Dorothy Lamour.

In 1951 Ameche turned to TV, and he later did a Broadway show, 'Holiday for Lovers'; and in 1955 had a big hit in New York with Cole Porter's 'Silk Stockings': audiences found him in person a master of the light comedy/songs business. He was even better in 'Goldilocks' (58), a delightful spoof on Silent movies with Elaine Stritch. For a long time he ran a TV programme on international circuses, and he appeared in a documentary on same called *Rings Around the World* (66). In 1960, looking terribly distinguished, he had a featured role in *A Fever in the Blood*, which wasn't a success, and in 1966 he graced a silly little B chiller, *Picture Mommy Dead*. Much more welcome were his 1970 appearances in *Suppose They Gave a War and Nobody Came* and Disney's *The Boatniks*.

This scene could have been in any number of early Arbuckle films. He usually chased the girl until she got interested – but then he was bewildered.

Fatty Arbuckle

Roscoe 'Fatty' Arbuckle was the victim of the first major scandal involving cinema-stars. Had he been tall, dark and handsome, it is just conceivable that he might eventually have weathered it, but he was round and clumsy and rather foolish on the screen. He was not unlovable, and his fun, if not subtle, was inventive; but whereas Fatty on the screen chasing a girl was coy and endearingly vulgar, Fatty in real life at the same game – in admittedly more lurid circumstances – was quite unforgivable. Thus the moon-faced, gentle loon faded away.

Arbuckle was born in 1887 in Smith Center, Kansas; the family moved to Santa Ana, California, and the boy Arbuckle sang at local socials and, stage-struck, worked with a touring company in nearby San José. He would have done anything to stay in show business, and he did; he collected tickets, sang ballads in a nickelodeon, did a black-face act in vaudeville; he had a double act with Leon Errol for a year, and when it broke up, he struggled on solo and turned to other things when he couldn't get bookings. About 1907 he appeared in some one- and two-reelers for the Selig Co., and little is known of this time except that in his first film he supported Tom Santchi. He returned to vaudeville, and in 1913 applied to Mack Sennett for a job in his Keystone comedies, just then in their first flush of fame. Sennett wasn't impressed; Arbuckle danced a bit and did some back flips, but Sennett had an odd fancy that the public might find a fat policeman funny, so he made him a Keystone Cop at $3 a day: *In the Clutches of the Gang*. After that, Sennett liked him enough to feature him in a funny bucolic comedy, *Passions He Had Three*.

The company Arbuckle joined consisted of popular comics such as Mabel Normand, Fred Mace, Ford Sterling, Al St John and Minta Durfee (to whom Arbuckle was later married); among the later arrivals was Chaplin, who quickly went to the fore. Arbuckle can be seen in several Chaplin shorts, e.g. *Tango Tangles*, *His Favourite Pastime* and *The Rounders* (14). When Chaplin left the studio, Sennett decided to promote the team of Arbuckle and Normand as a replacement, and they quickly became popular. Here are some of the many titles: *Fatty and Mabel's Simple Life* (15), *Mabel and Fatty's Wash Day*, *Mabel and Fatty's Married Life*, *The Little Teacher*, *Fatty's Flirtation*, *Fatty and Mabel Adrift* (16) and *Fickle Fatty's Fall*. The last film they did together was *The Bright Lights*.

In 1917 Joseph Schenck lured Arbuckle away by promising him his own company, and in the two-reelers he now made Arbuckle went on to a greater popularity. Buster Keaton, who joined him during this time, found him 'conscientious, hard-working, intelligent and eager to please.... He would invent priceless routines and also had a well-developed directorial sense.' Most of these Arbuckle produced and directed: *A Reckless Romeo*, *Rough House* (17), *His Wedding Night*, *Oh Doctor!*, *Out West*, *The Bell Boy* (18), *A Desert Hero* and *The Garage* (19). There are others: many are primitive, and the quality varies. Now Schenck was to lose Arbuckle to Famous Players-Lasky (who had been distributing the Arbuckle films): giving him the same creative freedom, they offered him features at $7,000 a week. The first (not full-length) was *The Round-Up* (20) and it was followed by *The Life of the Party* (cruelly ironic title), *Brewster's Millions* (21), *Dollar a Year Man, A Traveling Salesman*, and *Gasoline Gus*.

Then in September, 1921, Arbuckle went to a party in a San Francisco hotel and a girl died, a bit-player and girl-around-Hollywood called Virginia Rappe. Arbuckle was accused of rape and worse, on the evidence of something the girl said while dying in hospital ('He hurt me. Roscoe hurt me'). Arbuckle claimed that he had merely placed some ice on her thigh after she was taken sick. His friends believed him. And so did the juries: he was tried three times for manslaughter and eventually acquitted. The press victimized him and the public wrote abusive letters to his studio. Exhibitors boycotted his films in the US and Britain; feeling was so strong that his studio–although it had $500,000 bound up in unshown Arbuckle films–was powerless. Friends stood by him, like Lew Cody; Schenck paid his legal fees and Keaton later offered him a directing job (Keaton, in his memoir, finds the gentle Arbuckle innocent of any suspicion); his wife stood by him, but divorced him in 1925. Arbuckle returned to vaudeville, but only curiosity-mongers and friends went to see him. Keaton sadly recalls that he wasn't funny any more.

It was in 1924 that Keaton engaged him to direct *Sherlock Jr*, but he found the changed Arbuckle so difficult that he got him off the lot by persuading Marion Davies to take him on to direct *The Red Mill*. Arbuckle's name was still such anathema to the public that the film (and a couple of others he did) was credited to William B. Goodrich–a corruption of the punning Will B. Good. In 1927 Arbuckle toured in a farce, 'Baby Mine', and in 1928 he was booed in Paris. He remarried, and in 1932 contracted with WB to make 12 short comedies. Some were made and shown without opposition in the US but British exhibitors had longer memories and banned the first to arrive, *Hey Pop!*. They were very bad, however, and the series might have been abandoned had Arbuckle not died in 1933.

George Arliss

In 'The Movies', Griffith and Mayer put down George Arliss thus: 'Brought back to the screen by the Talkies, George Arliss was hailed as a distinguished actor by nice old ladies and other such judges. According to Arliss, Disraeli, Voltaire, Richelieu, and even Alexander Hamilton all looked exactly alike, except for details of costume, and all were crafty but benevolent gentlemen who spent most of their time uniting unhappy lovers.' More justly, admirers of Arliss's art were not confined to nice old ladies: everyone thought he was the cat's whiskers. He was generally referred to as 'The First Gentleman of the Screen' and not merely because of the aristocratic manner and the monocle he sported. Today, the rare Arliss films which get revived by film societies are greeted with not very kind laughter. It is ham, and ripe ham at that, not so much (perhaps) in the tradition of Irving as of some saloon-bar declaimer; that he should have been accepted above virtual contemporaries such as Edmund Gwenn or H. B. Warner must remain among the miracles of the movies.

Arliss was born in London in 1868, the son of a printer-publisher. He worked for his father for a while, but was so keen on the stage that he started his own amateur company; turned pro as a super in a production at the Elephant and Castle of 'Saved From the Sea'. His first West End appearance was in 'Across Her Path' (90); he worked in musical comedy for a while and was later engaged by Mrs Patrick Campbell for her company. He made his first West End success in 'Mr and Mrs Daventry' in 1900, but the following year accompanied Mrs Pat to the US, and stayed there. He had successes in 'The Second Mrs Tanqueray' and 'The Notorious Mrs Ebbsworth'; worked for David Belasco in 'The Darling of the Gods' and with Mrs Fiske's company in 'Becky Sharp' (as Steyne) and 'Hedda Gabler' (as Brack), among other plays. His first starring role was in Ferenc Molnar's 'The Devil' in New York in 1908; and he had other great hits: 'Disraeli' (11), 'Paganini', 'Alexander Hamilton' (17); and 'The Green Goddess' (21) which he played in both London and New York. He was persuaded to immortalize some of these earth-shattering portrayals: *The Devil* (21), *Disraeli*, and *The Green Goddess* (23). He also made a couple of films in 1922, *The Ruling Passion*, a lesson that work is more beneficial to millionaires than medicine, and *The Man Who Played God*, about a musician who, suddenly becoming deaf, assumes a phoney, God-like philanthropy which finally becomes sincere. In *Twenty Dollars a Week* (24) he was a man who disguises himself as a clerk in order to make a man of his son: but in all these films his presence was more prestigious than effective.

George Arliss in Disraeli *(29), the film that established him as the Finest Actor of the Talking Screen and as a top box-office draw.*

In 1924, he scored again on the stage in 'Old English' and a few years later was an admired Shylock. It was his last stage appearance.

In 1929, among the slew of photographed plays thrown up by Sound, WB came up with *Disraeli* (29), with Arliss re-creating his famous part and his wife, Florence Montgomery (or Arliss), also cast. The film was a great artistic and financial success (it ran a record 10 weeks in London) and was awarded the Photoplay Gold Medal as the year's outstanding film; it also brought Arliss an Oscar for the year's Best Actor. Because of the way the Oscar voting was then done, he also got some votes for *The Green Goddess* (30), as the wily potentate into whose hands fall a party saved from an air-crash–both film and performance ludicrous, but such was the thrall of the 'Theatre' that this ageing trouper was accepted as 'The Finest Actor on the Screen' by the readers of Movie Fan magazine, who voted him such. Readers of John Bull magazine voted him Second Most Popular Cinema Artist, after Chaplin (and before, in descending order, Ronald Colman, Marie Dressler, Janet Gaynor, Norma Shearer, Clive Brook and Garbo). WB paid him a salary of $10,000 a week, a figure only equalled by Marion Davies, and enthusiastically rushed him into: *Old English*, as Galsworthy's hedonist; *The Millionaire* (31), a remake of *The Ruling Passion*, with his wife; *Alexander Hamilton*; and, another remake, *The Man Who Played God* (32). There followed: a comedy, *A Successful Calamity*; *The King's Vacation* (33), a Ruritanian story with his wife; *The Working Man*, about a tycoon who anonymously gets a job in his rival's factory and straightens things out; and *Voltaire*. At this point WB announced that they were releasing Arliss from his contract due to the difficulties of finding subjects, but that they hoped he would work for them again.

When Darryl F. Zanuck left Warners to found his own company, 20th, he took Arliss with him for three films, and as if to prove that you can't have too much of a good thing, cast him as two members of *The House of Rothschild*, which had a last sequence in colour and was one of the top hits of 1934. But critics were now carping. Lionel Collier: '. . . he is apt to be mannerized and, in every characterization he gives, presents a good deal of Arliss.' Still, he was *The Last Gentleman* for 20th. He went to Britain to make a film for Gaumont-British, *The Iron Duke* (35), and as Wellington he was, it was generally agreed, 'mis-cast'. After a trip to Hollywood for *Cardinal Richelieu*, he returned to Britain to take up his career there, on a two-year GB contract.

Sir Michael Balcon, then head of GB, has stated in 'A Lifetime of Films' that this was against his wishes. 'Bluntly, he [Arliss] had that exaggerated self-importance which is just pomposity . . . and he certainly tried to convey the idea that he was conferring a great favour on us to be working at all. His contract called for very substantial payments, in fact, more than we had ever paid to an artist, yet by the time he came to us the Arliss novelty was beginning to wear off. . . .' Sir Michael admits that he resented the favourable conditions of the Arliss contract; he also states that the GB films were not good: *The Guv'nor* (Arliss was unconvincing as a tramp), *The Tunnel* (special 'courtesy artist') and *East Meets West* (36), a virtual repeat of his performance in *The Green Goddess*, right up to the jewel in the turban. He started on a historical film called *The Nelson Touch*, but it was abandoned–just before Picturegoer said: 'The Arliss historical portrait gallery has become an international joke.' Instead, he did the minor *The Man of Affairs*, *His Lordship* (in a dual role) and *Dr Syn* (37), a picturization of Russell Thorndike's novel with a parson-by-day/smuggler-by-night hero. Few of these were widely distributed in the US (as GB had hoped, when agreeing to Arliss's terms) and as his star had set in Britain, too, the contract was not renewed. He refused further offers as his wife was going blind and he preferred to stay with her. He died in 1946, monocled to the last.

Jean Arthur

The coming of the Talkies brought into Hollywood an influx of stage-trained actors and actresses, more 'real' not only because they spoke. That they wise-cracked inevitably made them seem more in touch with modern life; and the mood of the Depression required stars who were tough, resilient and supremely capable. This new breed of stars was a remarkable event in the history of Hollywood–indeed, today it looks miraculous. Yet, amidst the brightest new names imported from Broadway were three girls who had been in films for years without getting any specific where. They were Myrna Loy, Carole Lombard and Jean Arthur. They were not at all alike–except in skill–and it would be impossible to confuse them. The thing about the great stars is that they were/are all highly individual; at the same time these three shared attributes with each other and with the other fine comediennes of the time. They were warm and loyal to their leading men but never taken in; were more at ease in restaurants and honking city streets than in night-clubs or boudoirs; they moved quickly to keep up with their men and spoke to them crisply and incisively; they were men's equals, but regarded the world with less illusion.

Loy never lost her cool–Lombard did. Lombard delighted in outraging people–Loy never. Jean Arthur didn't abide by such rules. She was Miss Average American, usually a shop girl or secretary, with blonde good looks and a ready smile; and above all, perhaps, a fetching husky voice, childishly querulous at one moment, deeply reassuring the next. It never left you in doubt and was curiously touching when she was sentimental or wistful; and very cheering when she was in high spirits. (It might be noted that she had a noticeably attractive personality in her Silent pictures.)

She was born in New York in 1905. Her father was a professional photographer and while still at school she began modelling for photographers. Inevitably, one advert came to the attention of a Fox talent scout, and she was screen-tested. A year's contract followed–and 10 years of small parts. At Fox, initially, she was the heroine's best friend in John Ford's *Cameo Kirby* (23), but was sufficiently unimpressive to be demoted from a leading role to a mere apparition as a bathing beauty in the next, *The Temple of Venus*. She finished the contract on the receiving end of a series of custard pies, uncertain whether to stay in Hollywood–but she found work easily in slapstick shorts and in B Westerns produced by minor companies like Artclass and FBO: *Fast and Fearless* (24), *The Drugstore Cowboy* (25), *Tearin' Loose*, *A Man of Nerve*, *Thundering Through* (26), *The Hurricane Horseman*, *The Fighting Cheat*, *The Cowboy Cop* and *Twisted Triggers*. She was also in *The College Boob* and *The Block Signal*. 1927 saw a certain amelioration, with leading parts in two for Tiffany – *Husband Hunters* and *Broken Gates* – and three for Pathé – *Horse Shoes* and *Flying Luck*, in both as Monty Banks's girl, and *Born to Battle*. And in *The Poor Nut* that year, cast as a co-ed, she was spotted by Paramount and placed under contract. Before arriving there she was in *The Masked Menace*, a serial, and *Wallflowers* (28).

Stills of her at this time show her to be a squirrel-like creature, with a timid expression and dark bobbed hair. She was certain she couldn't act, and her early parts at Paramount were of little consequence, starting with *Warming Up* as Richard Dix's love interest; as ditto for George K. Arthur in MGM's *Brotherly Love*; as Jannings's daughter in *Sins of the Fathers* (29); *The Canary Murder Case*, made in Silent and Talkie versions; and *Stairs of Sand*, a Western. Through *The Mysterious Dr Fu Manchu*, (with Warner Oland in the title role), *The Greene Murder Case* (as a murderess –a part intended for Ruth Chatterton) and Clara Bow's *The Saturday Night Kid* (a good comedy about salesgirls), she accustomed herself to filming with Sound. She went on marking time through *Half-Way to Heaven*, where she and Charles 'Buddy' Rogers were partners on a tight-rope; a melodrama called *Street of Chance* (30) in a subsidiary role; William A. Wellman's *Young Eagles*; *Paramount on Parade* and *The Return of Dr Fu Manchu*. She was not good. In most of her parts she was at best insipid, and films like *The Silver Horde* were no help: she was the priggish ingénue who loses Joel McCrea to Evelyn Brent at her most worldly and Barbara-Stanwyckish in this fishing drama. Also at RKO she was in *Danger Lights*; then she returned to Paramount for two last films, a comedy with Jack Oakie, *The Gang Buster* (31) and a melo with Clive Brook, *The Lawyer's Secret*. There was an offer to do

The face of Jean Arthur in the 20s . . .

d in the 30s.

two comedies at Universal, *The Virtuous Husband* ('Jean Arthur has all the requisite "It" as a disappointed wife' said Picturegoer) and *Ex-Bad Boy*. The latter was based on the silent *The Whole Town's Talking*, about a blameless man (Robert Armstrong) who invents a past to impress his fiancée; Lola Lane played a movie star called Letta Larbo.

Arthur thought it essential to learn to act if she wanted to stay in the business, and went back to New York to do stage work, announcing that she was quitting films. She later said that these years were the happiest of her life. She also did stock. Among these East Coast plays were 'Foreign Affairs', 'The Man Who Reclaimed His Head' with Claude Rains, and 'The Curtain Rises', and she received nice notices for all of them. Hence, perhaps, she returned to the screen with greater assurance, but *Get That Venus* (33) gave very few patrons a chance to find out: a cheap (in every sense) comedy, made by a company called Regent, it got almost no bookings. At RKO she played an actress, a supporting role, in *The Past of Mary Holmes*, a remake of *The Goose Woman*, and at Columbia she was Jack Holt's daughter in a melodrama, *Whirlpool* (34). The latter won her a long-term contract with Columbia. Her intention not to return to Hollywood was apparently changed when she married Frank J. Ross Jr (but the marriage didn't last).

The first two for her new studio sank without trace: *The Defense Rests* as the assistant of lawyer Holt; and *The Most Precious Thing in Life*, a drama of mother-love, (she's a cleaning woman at a boys' school and guess who's in one of the dormitories). But *The Whole Town's Talking* (35) was one of the year's funniest comedies. John Ford directed, with Edward G. Robinson in the dual role of mild little clerk and ruthless mobster. Arthur was the clerk's self-reliant co-worker, who starts by pitying him, then encourages him, and finally falls in love with him. It was the sort of part she was to make her own–and this was the first occasion she showed her mature comedy style. Columbia found her less easy to handle thereafter; she had script and director approval, and exercising this privilege led to tears and tantrums, fights and suspensions. There can be no doubt that she was right: her early Columbia films weren't a patch on those she elected to do for other studios and the later ones, when she was Queen of the Lot, are classics of the period. *Public Hero No. 1* (MGM) was an exciting G-man thriller, with Arthur as a gangster's sister who falls for the cop, Chester Morris; *Party Wife* was a bland small-town picture, co-starring Victor Jory; *Diamond Jim* was a Universal biopic, with Edward Arnold as Jim Brady and Arthur in a dual role as two of the women in his life; *The Public Menace* was a programmer–gangsters and George Murphy; and *If You Could Only Cook* a mild Depression comedy about a penniless girl and a sad tycoon (Herbert Marshall) who masquerade as domestic servants.

Next, she was a cynical sob-sister out to 'get' country cousin Gary Cooper on his first visit to New York. Charmed by his naïvety, sickened by the opportunism of his opponents, she changed sides. The result was amusing and in every way memorable: *Mr Deeds Goes to Town* (36). She was *The Ex-Mrs Bradford* (RKO), a polished comedy-mystery, matched with William Powell, and she was very hot property, but the best Columbia could do for her was *Adventure in Manhattan*, a crook comedy with Joel McCrea, and *More Than a Secretary* with George Brent. Between these two she was Calamity Jane at Paramount in *The Plainsman*, with Cooper as Wild Bill Hickok. At UA, she was a bored wife in love with head-waiter Charles Boyer in a delicious ship-board comedy, *History Is Made at Night* (37)–but the history made was a shipwreck which changed the farce to tragedy. *Easy Living* (Paramount) was 100 per cent farce, a witty concoction by Preston Sturges about a penniless stenographer who is installed in a penniless hotel because the hotel management think she is wealthy Edward Arnold's mistress.

Then she quarrelled bitterly with Columbia and was off the screen for almost a year: the matter was resolved with a new three-year contract, two films a year. Her comeback film was outstanding: *You Can't Take It With You* (38), a Broadway comedy about a crazy family, bought for a record sum by Columbia and entrusted to *Deeds* director, Frank Capra. It won a Best Picture Oscar, and was one of 1938's biggest grossers. Around this time, she told an interviewer that though she loved acting, she hated being a star. Stars, she said, owed a duty to the public: 'It's a strenuous job to have to live up to the way you look on the screen every day of your life.'

Only Angels Have Wings (39) was another big success, an aviation drama directed by Howard Hawks at his most adroit, with Arthur as a stranded showgirl at first indifferent towards Cary Grant and later almost sick with yen–she was at her most independent, tender and entrancing. Capra again directed her in *Mr Smith Goes to Washington*, and this time she rooted for

Bored society wife Jean Arthur falls in love with headwaiter Charles Boyer in Frank Borzage's History Is Made at Night (*37*).

hick politician James Stewart the way she had rooted for Gary Cooper. It was a huge box-office success, and so was a Western, *Arizona* (40). Between the two she had done *Too Many Husbands* (40), a beguiling version of Somerset Maugham's farce, 'Home and Beauty', with Melvyn Douglas and Fred MacMurray. *The Devil and Miss Jones* (41) was yet another good comedy, about a salesgirl who reforms crotchety boss Charles Coburn (not, of course, knowing who he is). She made two comedies for George Stevens, *The Talk of the Town* (42) and the better *The More the Merrier* (43), about over-crowded Washington, with Joel McCrea – for which she received her sole Oscar nomination; director Stevens later described her as 'one of the greatest comediennes the screen has ever seen'. She then did the hilarious *A Lady Takes a Chance* with John Wayne at RKO, and *The Impatient Years* (44) with Lee Bowman, the one about the wartime couple who marry and are strangers when re-united. She was 'rather tiresome' said Picturegoer, but who wouldn't have been?

That completed her contract, and according to Bob Thomas in his biography of Columbia boss Harry Cohn, the day her contract finished, she ran around the set whooping with joy. Thomas also said of her: 'Miss Arthur's was an evanescent personality, shining with brilliance before the cameras and fading into timidity in her private life.' It had been known for some time that she was considering retiring; she had been uncooperative with the press and difficult about personal appearances. It would appear that, at the height of her career, shyness did overcome all other considerations, though she has made intermittent public appearances. During the remainder of the 40s, she took extensive courses in such subjects as philosophy, anthropology and sociology – and did one film and one play. The play was 'Born Yesterday' (45) but during the out-of-town tour she became ill, and the part went to Judy Holliday. The film was Wilder's fine *A Foreign Affair* (48), in which she was a prim Congresswoman investigating GI morale in Berlin, and especially John Lund's. She out-classed Dietrich as her rival and Paramount were encouraged to offer her a three-picture contract.

In 1950 she had a great success on Broadway in 'Peter Pan', in which she invested; there was an Equity dispute when she insisted on a holiday after a bout of voice trouble. In 1954 she was on a pre-Broadway tour of 'Saint Joan', but it never got there. Simultaneously, she was seen in cinemas in *Shane* (53), which was the only script Paramount could get her to accept – presumably because Stevens was directing. The contract was later cancelled by mutual agreement. After years of silence, she did an episode in TV's 'Gunsmoke' and apparently liked it so much that she agreed to do a TV series. She played a lawyer in 'The Jean Arthur Show' in 1966 but it didn't run. The following year she invested and was about to star in 'The Freaking out of Stephanie Blake', but a few days before the Broadway opening, the project was cancelled without

Only Angels Have Wings (*39*). *Jean Arthur listens, with Thomas Mitchell and Allyn Joslyn, as airline operator Cary Grant radios instructions to a pilot in difficulty.*

adequate explanation.

Of the many rumours of a screen come-back, the most persistent has been in Paul Gallico's 'Mrs 'arris Goes to Paris'.

Fred Astaire

Within a couple of years of making his first movie, Fred Astaire had acquired legendary status. Gene Kelly has called him 'one of the blessed', and on another occasion prophesied that '50 years from now, the only one of today's dancers who will be remembered is Fred Astaire'; and while Kelly's own contribution to the screen musical has been superlative, Astaire has usually been just that much in front. He is a pleasing light comedian and a convincing actor; all his work has been informed by charm, elegance, precision and grace, but nothing so much as his dancing – once described by The New York Times as 'not only an aesthetic excitement but comedy of a unique and lofty order'. He sings in a thin, reedy voice, but to some observers, like Oscar Levant, 'he is the best singer of songs the movie world ever knew'; certainly, no one, except Ethel Merman, has had as many classic popular songs written expressly for him.

His name has also found its way into dozens of songs, usually as a synonym for lightness and ease – 'the nimble tread of the feet of Fred Astaire' (Cole Porter's 'You're the Top'), but a different approach was made by Lorenz Hart ('Do It the Hard Way' from 'Pal Joey') – 'Fred Astaire just works so hard....' Astaire's rehearsing is famous: probably no Hollywood actor worked so hard. 'Puttin' on the Ritz', for instance, in *Blue Skies*, demanded five weeks of back-breaking physical work. He has been a life-long professional.

His father was in the beer business, an ex-Viennese called Austerlitz, in Omaha, Nebraska, when Fred was born in 1899. Fred began dancing lessons at five, along with his sister, Adele, and they acquired a renown in local church halls. Two years later, their mother took them to New York and enrolled them in a bigger dancing school, and via school recitals, the two Astaires were offered their first pro engagement, in Keyport, NJ. Over the next few years, they toured in vaudeville (their mother schooled them), till in 1916 they were offered a job in a Broadway musical, 'Over the Top'. They were part of 'The Passing Show of 1918', and had their first hit in 1922 in a show written for them, 'For Goodness Sake', which they took to London under the title 'Stop Flirting'. Gershwin wrote 'Lady Be Good' and then 'Funny Face' (27) for them and both shows had happy seasons in both cities. After a so-so effort, 'Smiles' (30), they had another hit, 'The Band Wagon' (31), but Adele was preparing to marry into the British aristocracy and planned to retire. Fred alone – and not without qualms – went into Cole Porter's 'The Gay Divorce', and then asked his agent to negotiate for a film contract. (Paramount at one time had been mulling over 'Funny Face' as a film, with the Astaires; and they had done a Vitagraph short in 1931.)

Goldwyn signed Astaire but released him after a few months. RKO jumped at the chance of getting the illustrious Astaire; they were planning a spectacular musical, *Flying Down to Rio*, for which the second leads would be Astaire and Ginger Rogers, whom he had known as a showgirl in New York. However, it wasn't ready, and RKO let him go to MGM to appear as himself in a spot with Joan Crawford, the *Dancing Lady* (33). His reviews were good, and they were, too, for *Rio* during a record-breaking three-week run at the Radio City Music Hall. RKO placed him under contract and recalled him from London where he was doing 'The Gay Divorce', and they filmed that (34) with Rogers and him heading the cast. The reception was warm enough to cause a third teaming, in Jerome Kern's *Roberta* (35) with Irene Dunne, and again later that year, in Irving Berlin's *Top Hat*. C. A. Lejeune wrote: 'The tonic appearances of young Mr Fred Astaire in dancing comedy–top hat, white tie, tails, and all the rest of it–are, to me, amongst the greatest joys of the modern cinema. It doesn't much matter where, why, or in what story he happens along . . . the engaging thing about Mr Astaire's dancing is the effect of spontaneity. No one, of course, can round off a formal dance number like "Top Hat" or "Isn't This a Lovely Day?" with more neatness and style. . . . Fred Astaire may not be in the leading ranks of the screen's great lovers, its foremost thespians, or even its golden-voiced singers. He is, however, one of the most talented and tonic personalities with a genius for making people happy, and the cinema would be poorer without him by a very long way.'

The public concurred with the critics: *Divorcee* was one of the top money-makers in 1934, and *Top Hat* and *Roberta* were second and third respectively the following year, when the Astaire-Rogers team were voted the fourth biggest draw. As a team, they balanced each other: he was debonair, an unassuming and somewhat innocent man-about-town, bent on winning her chivalrously if possible, but if not, not. She was bright, sassy and suspicious, her chorine background somewhat shaded by his interest. He gave her class, and she gave him sex-appeal (as a studio executive admitted). Both seemed delightful people, humorous, intelligent and charming; but what made the films so popular with contemporary audiences was their gaiety: the ease and imagination of the plots and the dance routines (it has been suggested that the cinema screen was invented expressly for Astaire to gambol on it). When he whisked her into a dance, it was in a natural way: they didn't need a back-stage excuse, or a hundred grand pianos whirling in the background. Their artistry was considerable, and so were the songs. None of this has dated. The plots creak today, with their mistaken identities and disguises, but aided or hindered by the likes of Helen Broderick, Eric Blore and Edward Everett Horton, they pass the time between the dances.

The two for 1936 were Berlin's *Follow the Fleet* and Kern's *Swing Time*, the latter directed by George Stevens and probably the best of all their films (so went contemporary opinion, though Astaire, according to his memoir, 'Steps in Time', 1959, does not agree). Gershwin wrote the songs for the next two, *Shall We Dance?* (37) and *A Damsel in Distress*: but the *Damsel* wasn't Ginger. Although in 1936 (and in 1937) the team were again among the top 10 draws (in the US *and* Britain) there had been a distinct audience falling-off; so Astaire petitioned for a film without Ginger. A non-dancer, Joan Fontaine, was chosen, and Burns and Allen were joyfully included to bolster the box office. P. G. Wodehouse had written the story, Stevens again directed – and of its kind, it was a masterpiece.

Although Astaire and Rogers were now getting $150,000 each per film it was only a matter of time before they split; but first came Berlin's *Carefree* (38) and *The Story of Vernon and Irene Castle* (39). The latter differed from the others in that it utilized a true story, old songs and a backstage plot; also it ended sombrely, with Astaire killed. Despite that, it was an amicable note to end on. Rogers turned 'straight' and Astaire looked for a new partner. It wasn't going to be easy, because he was, in Rogers's own words, 'a hard taskmaster, a perfectionist. He always got a little cross with me because my concentration was not as dedicated to the projects as his was.' (Their producer Pandro S. Berman described their years together as 'six years of mutual aggression' and dance director Hermes Pan observed: 'Except for the times Fred worked with real professional dancers like Cyd Charisse, it was a 25-year war.')

The new girl wasn't found at RKO, but at MGM–Astaire's contract was up, and he moved over to that studio for one film, *Broadway Melody of 1940*. The girl was Eleanor Powell. Then he did an indie (released by Paramount), *Second Chorus*: the girl was Paulette Goddard but they had only one brief dance together. He went to Columbia, for *You'll Never Get Rich* (41) with Cole Porter music and Rita Hayworth,

The most famous dancing partners of the 30s impersonate the couple who, a generation earlier, had been the idols of café society: Ginger Rogers and Fred Astaire as Irene and Vernon Castle (39). Both couples brought the public interest in ballroom dancing to new heights, but the Castles' influence was if anything, greater – as their steps were not choreographed to film requirements. Bottom left: Fred Astaire and Judy Garland in Easter Parade *(48). Astaire regards this as one of the 'high spots of enjoyment' in his career. Bottom right: Leslie Caron was ballet-trained, and one of Astaire's favourite partners.* Daddy Long Legs *(55).*

and its success was such that Columbia had them repeat, this time to Kern's music: *You Were Never Lovelier* (42). Earlier that year he was at Paramount's *Holiday Inn* with Bing Crosby, mostly dancing solo. It was a big success, but *The Sky's the Limit* (43), back at RKO, wasn't. Harold Arlen wrote the score, Joan Leslie was the girl. James Agee took the occasion to write: '. . . Fred Astaire has a lot, besides his Mozartian abilities as a tap-dancer, which is as great, in its own way, as the best of Chaplin. It is in the walk, the stance, the face, the voice, the cool, bright, yet shadowless temper and it would require the invention of a new character, the crystallization of a new cinematic form, to be adequately realized.'

Astaire says (in his memoirs) that there now were no offers, but at MGM producer Arthur Freed (responsible for more good musicals than any other individual) had long cherished a desire to have Astaire under contract there, and got him. The first was *Ziegfeld Follies*, a series of 'turns', of which Astaire had four, one with Gene Kelly, and another to the tune of 'Limehouse Blues', which was a big leap forward towards screen ballet (at MGM, Astaire's style moved considerably nearer the balletic): his partner this time, Lucille Bremer, danced with him again in *Yolanda and the Thief* (45) (Minnelli directed both). It was released before the *Follies*, and though much of it was imaginative, the whole concept was too whimsical for wide appeal. Some sourpusses were commenting on Astaire's age, and while at Paramount for *Blue Skies* (46), a reunion with Crosby, he announced his retirement: he thought this would be a big one to finish on (it was). MGM released him on condition that if he ever decided to return, he would fulfil his commitment to them.

In fact, MGM yelled for him when Kelly broke an ankle during rehearsals for *Easter Parade* (48); it had a Berlin score, and Astaire jumped at the chance of working with Judy Garland. The picture was a smash, and *The Barkleys of Broadway* (49) was prepared for the same team; but Garland fell ill, and Rogers was proposed as a replacement. Their reunion was box-office dynamite, and there could be no question of Astaire returning to idleness. In 1949 he was given a special Oscar for 'raising the standard' of screen musicals, and he made *Three Little Words* (50), ostensibly the story of song-writers Kalmar and Ruby (Red Skelton was the other), with Vera-Ellen as his partner. At Paramount he did *Let's Dance* which, said Lejeune, 'effectively cancels out Betty Hutton's natural ebullience by teaming her with Fred Astaire, and just as effectively cancels out Fred Astaire's natural elegance by teaming him with Betty Hutton'.

Jane Powell was his partner in *Royal Wedding* (51), and Vera-Ellen again in *The Belle of New York* (52)–re-activated; a version with Judy Garland had been postponed at the time of his retirement: Astaire says he enjoyed making it, but that it was a disaster with press and public–due to its fantasy and thin plot (curiously, its very inconsequence today is one of its charms, and at times–particularly when the stars are dancing–it looks suspiciously like his most enchanting work). The next one, however, *The Band Wagon* (53), was by general consent one of the best musicals made till then, a modest, Minnelli-directed backstage musical, with Cyd Charisse, and the Astaire role based very loosely on himself. It was the end of his contract, and he considered retiring again.

Eventually he signed for two at Paramount on the strength of there being one with Crosby; but this fell through, and the other, *Papa's Delicate Condition*, was eventually done with Jackie Gleason. Twentieth planned *Daddy Long Legs* (55) especially for him, and it was popular; but though he liked working with Leslie Caron, they didn't jell, they were both too elfin; and the film was meagre with its undoubted charms. The May-September romance was tried again with *Funny Face* (56) fulfilling his commitment to Paramount. The girl was Audrey Hepburn – the tunes were the Gershwins', and Stanley Donen directed. It was received with rapture and so, to a lesser extent, was *Silk Stockings* (57), directed by Mamoulian from a Broadway show (Cole Porter's), based on *Ninotchka* – in which part Charisse was considerably out of her depth. It didn't do too well, and with musicals supposedly out of fashion, Astaire turned to TV, and did a series of spectaculars which, despite a touch of coyness, won every award in the TV book.

In 1959 he accepted a (dramatic) supporting part in *On the Beach* which starred Gregory Peck, and he did a comedy at Paramount, *The Pleasure of His Company* (61), appropriately titled, but when he danced a few steps, you knew they were mad not to give him a whole number. He supported Jack Lemmon in a comedy, *The Notorious Landlady* (62), and then he went into semi-retirement, emerging for an occasional TV show, and in 1968 for Francis Ford Coppola's invigorating version of an old Broadway musical, *Finian's Rainbow*; the role was suited to his years, the old magic worked, but he danced little. In 1969 he had a part in another straight film, *The Midas Run/A Run on Gold*, starring Anne

Finian's Rainbow (*69*)

Heywood, but no one involved emerged with any credit.

He has said that he has no plans for a complete retirement, but it is doubtful whether he will make another musical. This hardly matters, provided his films from 1933 to 1957 are on permanent display.

Mary Astor

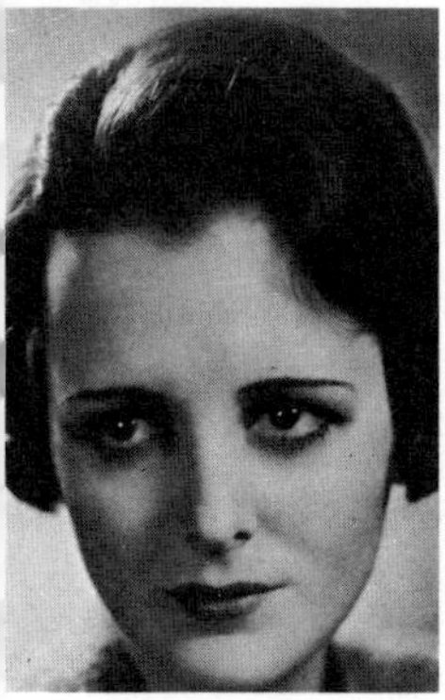

Among buffs at least, Mary Astor's reputation today stands second to none. During a very long career she made many films that have been much-revived, and her acting, incisive but delicate, is not the least factor in their reappearance. Inevitably, in over 100 pictures, she played the same part countless times, with a neat line in bitches at one end of the scale and syrupy moms at the other. The only consistent elements in her portrayals were her beauty and a brittleness; she was never less than competent and frequently more. She chose to be a featured player, which meant that her parts were often small and non-sustaining: she had to make the maximum effect in a few minutes. It is known that she cared little for her craft, but much thought and sensibility went into her best interpretations. Given a big–and sometimes difficult–role, as in *Dodsworth* or *The Maltese Falcon*, she achieved greatness.

She was born in Quincy, Illinois, in 1906 of a German immigrant father and an American mother who both, at various times, were teachers. Her father set his mind on her becoming a movie star, and left no stone unturned in pursuit of this aim. She was still at school, but Father was fired by the success of young artists like Mary Pickford and Mae Marsh. The family moved to Chicago and then New York in attempts to get the child nearer the studios. In New York Father became friendly with Charles Albin, a photographer who knew Lillian Gish (as he was well aware): Albin thought the child had a Madonna quality (which she retained at least till Talkies) and a screen test was arranged with Griffith, who turned her down; but Father did get her tested again while ostensibly arranging with Famous Players-Lasky to translate texts of German imports. She was signed to a six-month contract and dropped at the end of it, having had only three bits: in *Sentimental Tommy* (21) with Gareth Hughes; a propaganda short, *Bullets or Ballots*, and *Bought and Paid For* (22) with Agnes Ayres.

Albin then got her the title part in a two-reeler, *The Beggar Maid* (21), with Reginald Denny, based on 'King Cophetua and the Beggar Maid', and she made some more shorts for the same company, Tri-Art (*The Young Painter*, *Hope*, etc.), and then some features, *John Smith*, *Second Fiddle* with Glenn Hunter, *The Bright Shawl* (23) and *The Rapids*. Her work in these attracted the attention of Famous Players, and she signed with them again, this time for one year at $500 per week. With her mother she went to Hollywood to star in *To the Ladies*, but instead was put into minor programmers: *Success*, *Her Primitive Mate* and *The Scarecrow*, a historical tale with Hunter; and was in *Woman Proof* at Paramount; *The Fighting Coward* (24), a version of Booth Tarkington's 'Magnolia'; and *The Good Bad Girl*–Anna Q. Nilsson in the title role. John Barrymore had been impressed with her on screen, and asked Warners to let him have her as his leading lady in *Beau Brummel*. To her father's delight, she was paid $1,100 a week for this. And was a name. At Paramount she was in *Unguarded Women* with Richard Dix and at Universal in *Oh Doctor!* with Reginald Denny. But it was First National who now offered a contract, and Astor played a sweet young thing in a diverse batch of movies: *Inez From Hollywood*; *Enticement* (25) and *Playing With Souls*, both with Clive Brook; *Don Q Son of Zorro* at UA, starring Douglas Fairbanks; *The Pace That Thrills* with Ben Lyon, *The Scarlet Saint*, a lurid melodrama with Lloyd Hughes; and *The Wise Guy* (26) with Betty Compson and James Kirkwood.

At the end of 1925 she was one of the Wampas babies (which indicated a promising future), and in 1926 again with Barrymore (who had been her lover–according to her memoirs, 'My Story', 1959) in *Don Juan*. She starred in the films that followed: *Forever After* and *High Steppers*, both with Hughes; *The Rough Riders* (27) at Paramount, with George Bancroft and Charles Farrell; *The Sea Tiger* with Milton Sills; and *The Sunset Derby*. Most of these she thought 'drivel'; she begged for good parts, 'instead of perpetually playing the insipid ingénue in third-rate pictures'–such as *Lost at the Front*, a Cohen-Kelly comedy with George Sidney and Charles Murray, and the next, *Rose of the Golden West*, starring Gilbert Roland. She liked *Two Arabian Knights* at UA, where she was an exotic beauty involved with a couple of war buddies (William Boyd and Louis Wolheim), and was quite happy with a comedy, *No Place to Go*, Mervyn Le Roy's first picture; after which came *Sailors' Wives* (28), a title which bore no relation to the plot, and a couple more with Hughes, *Three Ring Marriage* (they were Wild West riders in a circus) and *Heart to Heart*.

A few months earlier she had been loaned to Fox to play in *Dressed to Kill*, where she was a 'sultry but angel-faced girl who actually packed a gun'. When her First National contract expired, Fox made another attractive offer, to do a bright, sophisticated comedy set in Paris, *Dry Martini*. A contract was drawn up with that studio, paying her $3,750 weekly for 40 weeks, a top salary, she said, 'for anyone below full star rating'. She made three more for Fox: *Romance of the Underworld* (29), *New Year's Eve* with Earle Fox, and *The Woman From Hell*; then expected Fox to pick up her option, advancing her to $4,000 per week for 52 weeks. But she flunked the test for Talkies and the studio lost interest, though it did offer to keep her on at half her usual salary (a better deal than many of the newly imported stage-trained actors were getting – sometimes a mere $500 per week). Astor turned down the offer.

No other studio was interested. She spent some months being refused jobs, till Florence Eldridge helped to get her a part in a local production of Victor Lawrence's 'Among the Married' with Edward Everett Horton. She scored a success with the Los Angeles critics, and soon had five movie offers. She accepted *Ladies Love Brutes* (30) at Paramount, with George Bancroft and Fredric March, from a play by Zoë Akins. (During its making, her husband, director Kenneth Hawks, was killed in a plane accident while on location; along with the other widows Astor sued, but she lost her case when it was revealed she had remarried.)

At Pathé/RKO she was in *The Runaway Bride* and then *Holiday*, starring Ann Harding. Warners gave her three good parts: *Misbehaving Ladies* as one of them with Louise Fazenda; *The Lash* (31) opposite Richard Barthelmess; and *Other Men's Women*, where Grant Withers and Regis Toomey fought over her. RKO offered a contract and she made a series of forgotten films for them: *The Sin Ship*, with Wolheim, who also directed – with poor results; *The Royal Bed* – Lowell Sherman working in the same double capacity, but with more success – it was an enjoyable Ruritanian satire; *Behind Office Doors* with Robert Ames; *White Shoulders* with Ricardo Cortez; and *Smart Woman*, again with Ames, who had drunk himself to death before it was released. In *Men of Chance* (32) she portrayed the perils of being a gambler's wife, again with Cortez, and in *The Lost Squadron* she was an actress called Follette Marsh, who had betrayed Richard Dix while he was at the front, and was now unhappily married to a vicious film

Mary Astor and Ann Harding in the first film version of Philip Barry's Broadway comedy Holiday *(30), reckoned to contain 'the best dialogue yet heard from the screen'.*

director played by Erich von Stroheim.

She says in her memoirs: 'RKO wanted to give me a starring contract, but I made the right decision and turned it down. Once your name *goes above* the title of a picture, it must never come down or your prestige is gone.' Instead, Astor decided to free-lance. She had proved beyond doubt to have a clear voice for Talkies, and she had established herself: now she determined to keep the bidding high by signing only for two or three pictures at a time. She continued to make about half a dozen a year, playing parts big and small. She became regarded as a not quite run-of-the-mill feature player. What set her apart was the fact that she was too chic, too worldly, to get lost among the supporting players, and that she never allowed herself to be type-cast.

She was in *Those We Love*, as the Other Woman in this drama at Tiffany with Kenneth MacKenna and Lilyan Tashman; *A Successful Calamity* at WB, as George Arliss's wife; and *Red Dust* at MGM, as the puritan wife tempted to yield to the lust of Clark Gable. It was at this point that her parents decided to sue her for maintenance; and she signed a three-year deal with Warners. She was the society lady who befriends ex-gangster

While George Brent was lost in the Amazon Bette Davis and Mary Astor fabricated The Great Lie (*41*)*: one bore his son, the other brought him up as her own. Before George knew what was happening the girls had fought it out: Bette won the baby and Mary stole the show.*

Edward G. Robinson in *The Little Giant* (33); aged from 20 to 65 with Paul Muni in *The World Changes*; went to Paramount to support Sylvia Sidney as *Jennie Gerhardt*; and solved with William Powell *The Kennel Murder Case*. She went to *Convention City* with Adolphe Menjou, found him *Easy to Love* (34), and lost Warren William to Ginger Rogers in *Upper World*; loved Robinson again in *The Man With Two Faces*, a version of George S. Kaufman's 'The Dark Tower'; experienced with Lyle Talbot the *Return of the Terror*; and helped Warren William, as Perry Mason, solve *The Case of the Howling Dog*.

Most of her next pictures were Bs in which she starred: *I Am a Thief* (35) with Cortez; *Red Hot Tires* with Talbot; *Straight From the Heart* at Universal with Baby Jane Quigley and Roger Pryor; *Dinky*, as Jackie Cooper's imprisoned mother; *Man of Iron* with Barton MacLane; *Page Miss Glory*; and *The Murder of Dr Harrigan* (36) with Cortez. She moved over to Columbia on a two-year deal: *And So They Were Married*, co-starring Melvyn Douglas, *Trapped by Television* with Talbot and *Lady From Nowhere* with Charles Quigley. She made no more films for that studio, perhaps because 1936 also saw the Astor name featured prominently in the world press: she had not contested her second husband's divorce case, but she did fight when custody of the child arose. Her personal diary was used against her, and certain pages came into the possession of the press. Apart from some minor indiscretions disclosed there, most of what was printed was rumour-mongering, but the affair was perhaps the biggest Hollywood scandal (not hushed up) of the decade. One thing the diary revealed: 'I don't like the work and I hate Hollywood.'

Her career might have suffered had it not been for Goldwyn's *Dodsworth*, where she gave a tender, glowing performance as the widow Walter Huston turns to when wife Ruth Chatterton becomes unbearable; and she followed it, after an interval, with an equally sympathetic one in Selznick's *The Prisoner of Zenda* (37), as the pathetic Antoinette de Mauban. She had another second lead in another big one, *The Hurricane*, playing the disillusioned wife of Raymond Massey. Each of these three important performances should have made her a hot property again, but instead she was in, at MGM, *Paradise for Three* (38) with Frank Morgan and Robert Young; at Columbia, *No Time to Marry*, a good funny B, with Richard Arlen, in which she was a

Mary Astor and Humphrey Bogart in John Huston's The Maltese Falcon *(41): one of the screen's classic teamings. He was tough and cynical; she was cool and treacherous.*

sob-sister, and *There's Always a Woman*, in support of Douglas and Joan Blondell; at MGM again, *Woman Against Woman*, as Herbert Marshall's bitchy wife; and *Listen Darling*, as Judy Garland's mother. Concurrently, she had been getting good notices for a second stage attempt, in the West Coast production of 'Tonight at 8.30'; and in 1939 she toured in 'The Male Animal', but decided not to accompany it to New York because of her child. Instead, she did *Midnight* (39) with Claudette Colbert, a comedy in which she was an evil-tongued society bitch; *Turnabout* (40) from Thorne Smith's novel, in support; and *Brigham Young*, as an amalgamation of the wives of that character.

Despite (most recently) her marvellous work in *Midnight*, WB insisted that she test for *The Great Lie* (41)–to play another bitch, contrasting with the Bette Davis character. It was Davis who wanted Astor–ironically, for it was the only time in her career that any player stole a film from her. About this, Astor wrote: 'Davis handed it to me on a silver platter. Bette has always had the wisdom, rare in this business, to know that a star cannot stand alone; she appears to much better advantage if the supporting actors are good.' Astor, venomous in a shingle, got a Best Supporting Oscar, and another plum part at WB, in *The Maltese Falcon*. She was the lovely, frightened Brigid O'Shaughnessy, the prototype of all frail ladies who turn out to be two-faced and lethal. She and Bogart followed it with *Across the Pacific* (42), where she was equally enigmatic. At Paramount she gave another brilliant comic portrayal as the feckless, garrulous heiress of *Palm Beach Story*–at which point she signed an advantageous contract with MGM, who announced that they would launch Astor as a fully fledged star, but instead they gave her nothing but kindly mothers to play: *Young Ideas* (43), a comedy with Herbert Marshall; *Thousands Cheer*, partnered with John Boles in the 'story' part of that semi-revue; *Meet Me in St Louis* (44), matched with Leon Ames; and *Blonde Fever*, a triangle story with Philip Dorn and Gloria Grahame. In 1944 she was in a poor New York play, 'Many Happy Returns'; and then she mothered again: *Claudia and David* (46) at 20th, *Cynthia* (47), *Fiesta* ('a do-nothing mother role, of course') and *Cass Timberlane*. She clamoured for better parts, and did at least get a good bad-mother role in *Desert Fury* (48) on loan-out to Paramount; and in Zinnemann's *Act of Violence* (49) she gave a harrowingly good performance as a middle-aged trollop. But–predictably as Marmie–*Little Women* broke her spirit: 'My bitterness grew, my resentment built higher and higher. The hot lights, the long waits, the heavy woollen costumes, trying to be patient with the silliness of Mlles Allyson, Leigh, Taylor and O'Brien–it wore me down.' She asked for her release–and after a very small role in *Any Number Can Play* MGM let her go.

The 50s were unkind professionally. Her autobiography speaks candidly of a drinking problem (it had begun in the days of *Zenda*), but she says that it didn't impair her work–besides, drinking problems were and are a Hollywood commonplace. The rare film work she did was as polished as ever; she turned to TV ('The Women', 'Sunset Boulevard', 'The Ninth Day' among many) and to the stage–'Biography' in stock, tours of 'The Time of the Cuckoo' and 'Don Juan in Hell', and a flop Broadway venture with Eva Le Gallienne called 'The Starcross Story'. But, mostly, the movies didn't want to know. An agent got her a minute part in WB's *So This Is Love* (53), but she was turned down two years later by the same company for the part of Jane Wyman's mother in *Miracle in the Rain*.

In 1956, 'a week's work in a picture at 20th; a trashy story, and no part at all, but the $300 looked wonderful'. This is presumably *A Kiss Before Dying*, finally released by UA. Her superb cameo of a fond mother brought some offers: MGM's *The Power and the Prize*; Cornel Wilde's *The Devil's Hairpin* (57); *This Happy Feeling* (58); and a silly melo, *A Stranger in My Arms* (59) where she did another obsessed-mother stint. In 1961 she suddenly landed a large role in 20th's *Return to Peyton Place*, and stole the notices. Sight and Sound found it 'watchable for Miss Astor's exemplary job of scene-stealing, and some fanciful notions about how best-sellers get written'. This description might also apply to the next, another fat part, as a benefactress in *Youngblood Hawke* (64), an inept version of Herman Wouk's novel about a budding novelist. She had two sequences of *Hush Hush Sweet Charlotte* and looked very old–but her ability was clearly unimpaired.

Following the success of her memoirs, she turned to novel-writing, and produced several modestly successful works, including 'Image of Kate', and, in 1969, 'A Place Called Saturday'.

Lew Ayres

Because he starred in one of the most famous films ever made, *All Quiet on the Western Front*, the name of Lew Ayres has been well known for 40 years. His career has been disappointing, however, and consists mainly of B pictures. When better things were offered, he proved with comfort that he was worthy of them.

He was born in Minneapolis in 1908, and studied medicine at the University of Arizona. He played the banjo, guitar and piano and joined Henry Halstead's orchestra; later was with Ray West's orchestra at the Cocoanut Grove, LA, and there was spotted by Pathé executive Paul Bern which resulted in a six-month contract with that company–and one part, a bit in a silent called *The Sophomore* (29). He was dropped, but when Bern moved over to MGM he thought of Ayres for *The Kiss*, as the boy who demands just that from Garbo while her lover was away; there were good notices, and Bern recommended him for Universal's *All Quiet*... (30) and a Universal contract. The film was directed by Lewis Milestone from Erich Maria Remarque's novel; it was (and remained) unique among US films in that it saw the War from the German side, and from the point of view of a group of *boy* soldiers whose enthusiasm and patriotism gradually change into resignation (towards death) and disillusionment (about military glory). Its impact was tremendous and in 1930 it was among the top five box-office pictures; a world-wide reissue in 1950 and recent TV showings have again proved its validity.

Lew Ayres as the young German soldier in All Quiet on the Western Front *(30): one of the most impressive starts to any film career.*

Ayres had the principal part and it got his career off to a terrific start. Hollywood immediately saw him as a great new actor, and Warners borrowed him to play a desperate gangster in *Doorway to Hell*, but he was much too young and boyish to be believable; he was more convincing at Fox as Constance Bennett's seducer in *Common Clay*, and, back on his home lot, as a society boy involved with Chinatown Charlie (Edward G. Robinson) and Ming Toy (Lupe Velez) in *East Is West*, a version of the old melodrama. *Many a Slip* (31) was well-named, a tasteless comedy about whether Joan Bennett was or was not pregnant: neither she nor Ayres were at ease with the wise-cracks and they both slipped. He sank lower with *The Iron Man*, *Up for Murder* and *Heaven on Earth*, a romance of the Mississippi, but *The Impatient Maiden* (32) was a slight improvement–Mae Clarke had the title role, intended for Clara Bow before her disgrace, and Ayres was a doctor. His

Young Dr Kildare (*39*): *Lew Ayres in the title role in the first of that series, with Lionel Barrymore as Dr Gillespie, permanent representative of the Old Guard.*

salary was now $1,750 a week, and he was battling for better pictures than *The Spirit of Notre Dame* and *Night World*, the latter a night-club drama with Clarke again. Critics commented that if Ayres made more like that, he'd soon be through. But he did one even worse: *Okay America*. Fox borrowed him for *State Fair* (33) to play opposite Janet Gaynor, and he had another good chance there opposite Lillian Harvey in her first Hollywood film, *My Weakness* (though she failed to duplicate in the US her European success and was soon winging her coy way back to home ground). Ayres returned to Universal for *Cross Country Cruise* and *Let's Be Ritzy*, a poverty-stricken comedy about a ditto-couple who try to live above themselves; Fox then took over his contract and put him with Alice Faye in *She Learned About Sailors* and Gaynor again in *Servants Entrance*.

In *Lottery Lover* (35) with Pat Patterson he was a shy cadet trying to return a garter to a famous actress; it was a B, and the new management at Fox–now 20th Century-Fox –kept him in B pictures: *Spring Tonic* with Claire Trevor and *Silk Hat Kid* with Mae Clarke. He left Fox and could see little future as an actor; he wanted to change to directing, and Republic agreed to let him direct a couple of films provided he would act in one: *The Leathernecks Have Landed* (36). He directed *Hearts in Bondage* with Clarke and James Dunne, but Republic reneged on the second one and Ayres returned to second features–a couple at Columbia, *Panic on the Air* with Florence Rice and *Shakedown* with Joan Perry; and a bevy at Paramount: *Lady Be Careful* as a shy sailor with Mary Carlisle; *Murder With Pictures* and Gail Patrick; *The Crime Nobody Saw* (37); *Last Train From Madrid* with Dorothy Lamour; *Hold 'em Navy*; and *Scandal Street* (38) with Louise Campbell. He made *King of the Newsboys* at Republic, but he was virtually forgotten until he was allotted the part of Katharine Hepburn's brother, a casual, hard-drinking layabout, in *Holiday*.

Interest was rekindled, and Ayres told an interviewer: 'Hollywood, quick to acclaim, soon washed its hands of me. And let me tell you, the snubs you get sliding down aren't nearly as pleasant as the smiles going up.' He thought he was in some measure to blame for his fall by thinking he could coast along on a personality performance. He now was signed to a contract by MGM who cast him in *Rich Man Poor Girl*, supporting Ruth Hussey and Robert Young, and *Spring Madness* with Burgess Meredith; then as one of Joan Crawford's suitors in *Ice Follies of 1939* and as Jeanette MacDonald's romantic interest in *Broadway Serenade*. He was in a college comedy with Lana Turner, *These Glamour Girls* and with Robert Taylor and Greer Garson in *Remember?*; but he had, at the same time, again been consigned to Bs: this time, however, it was in a very popular series, playing an idealistic young doctor, who is opposed by a crotchety old one, Lionel Barrymore. The girl was Laraine Day, the title character Dr Kildare, whom Ayres played with an eager, simple sincerity. Here are the (abbreviated) titles:

n Crawford is known to k back on Ice Follies *1939 with much pondency: it would be ange if James Stewart l Lew Ayres didn't feel same way.*

Young Dr K (38), *Calling Dr K* (39), *The Secret of Dr K*, *Dr K's Strange Case* (40), *Dr K Goes Home*, *Dr K's Crisis*, *The People vs Dr K* (41), *Dr K's Wedding Day* (which was tragic; Laraine Day gets killed on the eve – a way of writing her out of the series), and *Dr K's Victory*. Ayres was also in three other Bs, *The Golden Fleecing* (40), *Maisie Was a Lady* (41) and *Fingers at the Window*, also with Day.

Hardly surprisingly, considering that he had once made *All Quiet*, he registered as a conscientious objector rather than serve in the war. He left films and went to work in a lumber camp, but the public were not appeased. Exhibitors boycotted his films and they were withdrawn from circulation. Ayres volunteered for non-combatant duties, and served as a medic, and later a chaplain's aide. He returned from his experiences thinner, lined and moustached: an altogether more interesting actor. With *The Dark Mirror* (46), starring Olivia de Havilland, he finally bounded to the front of Hollywood leading men, but the offers were few. Hollywood seldom forgives or forgets, and Ayres hadn't returned as a war hero like Gable or Taylor. Warner Brothers did give him a long-term contract, but he did only two parts for them, both sympathetic: with Ann Sheridan in *The Unfaithful* (47), and the kindly doctor in *Johnny Belinda* (48), which he played quite beautifully.

He made *The Capture* (49) with Teresa Wright and *New Mexico* (50) with Marilyn Maxwell, followed by two even lesser ones, *No Escape* (53) with Sonny Tufts and *Donovan's Brain*. He told interviewers that he was semi-retiring from the screen and studying world religions: in 1955 he presented a film he had made about them, called *Altars of the East* after a book he had published of the same name. For a long time his only work in front of the cameras was in occasional TV shows, but he made a welcome comeback among the many old stars in *Advise and Consent* (61), playing the Vice-President. In 1964 he made *The Carpetbaggers*, his last film to date – and that year he married again, after a bachelorhood of 24 years; he had previously been married to Lola Lane and Ginger Rogers.

Lucille Ball

Lucille Ball is far better known for her TV work than for films, though she has been in more than 50. Her sensational success in that other medium has always been considered as some sort of judgment on Hollywood, who failed to develop her, failed to give her adequate vehicles or failed to utilize her rich comic talent; in reality, her success in TV illustrates rather the different standard operating around CBS, NBC, ABC, etc. For Lucy, though she *was* wasted for years, did have some great chances in films; but the cinema public never really took to her in a big way. She was always one of Hollywood's better comediennes, always professional, always predictable, always welcome, and always pretty; more accomplished than, say, Marilyn Monroe, but much less extraordinary; never quite as funny as Judy Holliday and definitely less subtle.

She is still a delight, even in the pasteboard surroundings of her TV series. She mugs and is mechanical; no one is more technically adept at getting a laugh, and certainly TV's gain is the cinema's loss.

She was born in 1910 in either Butte, Montana or Jamestown, New York. At 15 she entered the John Murray Anderson Dramatic School, but she knew she wasn't good and left after a year and got a job in a tour of 'Rio Rita'. It lasted five weeks (she was sacked). She next worked at a soda fountain in New York, but persevered with her show biz ambitions, and eventually became a model for Hattie Carnegie. With several other Carnegie models she went to Hollywood to appear in Goldwyn's *Roman Scandals* (33) and, unlike them, she stayed. She got another brief bit in *Nana* (34) and a few films later Columbia offered a contract (at $75 a week). She made some more appearances, still uncredited, in, among others, *Broadway Bill* and *Fugitive Lady*. Her first credit was as 'nurse' in *Carnival* (35), starring Lee Tracy and others. Columbia dropped her, and she had a bit in RKO's *Roberta*, which resulted in a contract at that studio (at $50 a week). Her parts, by degrees, began to get bigger: *Old Man Rhythm*; *I Dream Too Much*; *Chatterbox* (36), starring Ann Shirley; *Follow the Fleet*; *The Farmer in the Dell*; *Bunker Bean*, a B farce starring Owen Davies Jr that had been filmed twice as a Silent, with the prefix *His Majesty*; *That Girl From Paris*, starring Lily Pons; and *Don't Tell the Wife* (37) with Guy Kibbee and Una Merkel. There was a Broadway offer, 'Hi Diddle Diddle', and though she got good reviews RKO were still not too interested. It was Ginger Rogers (her mother, Leila, was Ball's dramatic coach) who recommended her for a leading part in *Stage Door*: she was conspicuous among the aspirants in that film. It led to better parts: in *The Joy of Living* (38); a B, *Go Chase Yourself*, co-starring with Joe Penner; and *Having Wonderful Time* – second lead to Rogers, and partnered with Red Skelton.

Now RKO rushed her from film to film,

Lucille Ball with two clowns: Red Skelton in DuBarry Was a Lady *(43) and Bop Hope in* The Facts of Life *(60*
Although she has often been teamed with comedians, her dominan style is more effective

but real stardom was still a couple of years off: *The Affairs of Annabel*, as a temperamental star whose PR – Jack Oakie – gets her into stunts; *Room Service*; *Next Time I Marry* with Lee Bowman – she 'played in a delightfully provocative spirit' – Picturegoer; *Annabel Takes a Tour*; *Beauty for the Asking* (39) with Patric Knowles; *Twelve Crowded Hours*; *Panama Lady* – she starred as a showgirl in this B melo with Allen Lane; *Five Came Back* with Chester Morris; and *That's Right You're Wrong*, a Kay Kyser musical. In *The Marines Fly High* (40) she was leading lady to Richard Dix and Chester Morris. There followed *You Can't Fool Your Wife* (in a dual role) and then *Dance Girl Dance*, where she and Maureen O'Hara fought over Louis Hayward. She was top-billed in *Too Many Girls*, a campus musical with Ann Miller, Richard Carlson, Eddie Bracken and Desi Arnaz (whom she married). Though Harold Lloyd produced it, *A Girl, A Guy and a Gob* (41) was poor stuff; *Look Who's Laughing* threw her in with Edgar Bergen and Charley McCarthy and Fibber McGee and Molly; *Valley of the Sun* (42) was a Western with James Craig and Dean Jagger; *Seven Days' Leave* a minor musical with Victor Mature. The only one with pretensions above double bills was the one before that, *The Big Street*, with Henry Fonda, a Damon Runyon story about a temperamental, crippled actress and the bellhop who adores her. Said James Agee in Time: 'Pretty Lucille Ball, who was born for the parts Ginger Rogers sweats over, tackles her "emotional" role as if it were sirloin and she didn't care who was looking.'

The performance brought Ball to the attention of MGM, who were having difficulty finding a star for the title role in *DuBarry Was a Lady* (43). MGM signed her and announced they were going to build her up. She then took over from the pregnant Lana Turner the role of the movie star in another Broadway stage hit, *Best Foot Forward*; then she was in the all-star 'revue' *Thousands Cheer* and in another musical, *Meet the People* (44), with Dick Powell – but in the latter she 'supplies glamour and little else' (Picturegoer). Usually her verve was winning – but the films weren't. MGM blamed her, and she was off the screen for a year before taking a very supporting role (to Hepburn and Tracy) in *Without Love* (45). Then she sat out her contract in an office at MGM (with Buster Keaton) – except for her turn in *Ziegfeld Follies*, not shown until 1946. She was better served by *Easy to Wed* (46), a surprisingly successful remake with music of *Libeled Lady* – and stole the notices cleanly from Esther Williams and Van Johnson. She was loaned to 20th for *The Dark Corner*, a straight heroine part in a not-very-straight thriller, and then, with John Hodiak, made *Two Smart People*, a lighthearted drama which Jules Dassin directed. With that one, MGM and she called it quits.

She free-lanced. At Universal she sparkled in a weak marital comedy with George Brent, *Lover Come Back*, but she had more difficulty trying to carry *Lured* (47) at UA, a whodunnit with George Sanders; *Her Husband's Affairs* with Franchot Tone; *Easy Living* (49) with Victor Mature; *Miss Grant Takes Richmond*, a comedy with William Holden, and *The Fuller Brush Girl* (50), a comedy with Eddie Albert. The only bright spots were when – before the last three – Paramount employed her, at Bob Hope's request, to star with him in *Sorrowful Jones* (49) and – after them – in *Fancy Pants* (50); once again, her notices were excellent. Meanwhile, she toured with her husband in a sketch, 'Cuban Pete', and in Elmer Rice's 'Dream Girl'. She had had a three-film deal with Columbia at $85,000 each: that studio wanted to get out of the last one, and offered a Sam Katzman cheapie, *The Magic Carpet* (51), thinking she would turn it down. She knew the reason and didn't – a woeful experience. Paramount again offered

when supported by a straight man – as her TV partners have been. However, in The Facts of Life *both she and Hope played relatively straight, and it was a peak in both their careers.*

resurrection: de Mille wanted her for *The Greatest Show on Earth*, but at the last minute she became pregnant, and the part went to Gloria Grahame

Realistically, her thoughts had already turned to TV, and in 1951 she began 'I Love Lucy' with Arnaz. Discussing once why she had made it where other girls had failed, she said: 'Maybe because they turned down more working jobs or social opportunities and I did just the opposite. As a result, I've never been out of work in this town except for two hours once between contracts.' TV was just such a move. It brought her undreamed-of popularity, and more – MGM came begging for a couple of films. The first, *The Long Long Trailer* (54), was a comedy with gorgeous moments directed by Vincente Minnelli, but the second, *Forever Darling* (56), was a soggy thing. Arnaz was in both; they were divorced some time later, and he retired from the TV series – but not before they had both become very, very wealthy. They had bought the old RKO studios and founded their own corporation, Desilu. Ball now owns 51 per cent of it and runs it. TV continued for her solo – often because whenever she spoke of retiring, the networks came up with bigger and bigger offers. Everyone really did love Lucy. Even in a flop Broadway musical, 'Wildcat' (61).

Madam Executive-Impresario Ball has taken time off from TV to do only three films in the last decade: two hits and a miss. *The Facts of Life* (60) was an agreeable comedy with Bob Hope, but a reunion three years later, in the film of Ira Levin's play, *Critics Choice* (63), was suitable for neither of them. Then came *Yours Mine and Ours* (68) where she and Henry Fonda, widow and widower, had almost a score of kids between them. She was never better, never funnier, and the film went on to make a small fortune for her (needless to say, she produced).

Tallulah Bankhead

'Miss Bankhead's personal life had such flair that in recent years, when she did so little stage work, there was a tendency to under-estimate her talent by a generation that had never seen her as the eternal prostitute, Sabrina, in Thornton Wilder's "The Skin of Our Teeth", or as the mercenary Regina in Lillian Hellman's "The Little Foxes": so wrote Murray Schumach in The New York Times on the occasion of Tallulah Bankhead's death. And just as her reputation as *bonne vivante* overshadowed her stage work, so both eclipsed her film career. As a star of the silver screen she didn't, as the saying goes, make it: but for a brief while she was a name to conjure with, and her film performances do convey something of the vibrancy of her personality.

She was born in 1902 in Huntsville, Alabama, into a wealthy family (her father was a Congressman); as a child her tantrums were famous and she moved from school to school. She herself decided that the Theatre was the best outlet for her temperament. She got a small part in 'Squab Farm' in 1918, another in 'Footloose', and succeeded Constance Binney in '39 East'. She did get two film chances, *When Men Betray* (18), and *30 a Week* with Tom Moore for Goldwyn. She had garnered a small following by the time of 'The Exciters' (22), but it wasn't enough, she thought, and she jumped at an offer by C. B. Cochran to play London. She caused a sensation on her first night – 'The Dancers' (23) – and became one of the brightest lights on Shaftesbury Avenue. Among the plays: 'Conchita' (24), 'Fallen Angels', 'The Green Hat' (25), 'They Knew What They Wanted', and 'Let Us Be Gay' (30). She appeared in a sketch at the London Palladium ('The Snob') and as Nina in a film version of Pinero's *His House in Order* (28) with Ian Hunter. She also

The Devil and the Deep (*32*). *'You didn't know there was a woman aboard, did you?' Charles Laughton and Cary Grant fascinated by Bankhead, but she's thinking about Gary Cooper.*

scaled the heights of the international celebrity set: gossip columnists wrote her up, women aped her hairdos, her clothes, and the husky inflexions of her voice.

When Talkies came, Paramount tested her in a scene from her current London play, 'The Lady of the Camellias', and signed her. This was Dietrich's studio, and she was seen as a home-grown rival to that lady – with more than a dash of Norma Shearer. She went to Hollywood to play the same sort of parts she had done on the stage – sophisticated, jaded, and very glamorous. The titles are indicative: *Tarnished Lady* (31), deserting husband Clive Brook for a no-good lover, under Cukor's direction; *My Sin* (drugs and murder); and the remake of a Pola Negri vehicle, *The Cheat*. The notices were so dreadful that she lost *Rain* to Joan Crawford. She was inclined to pose, but otherwise the failure of these films was hardly her fault. It was thought that one of the troubles was that at Paramount, Dietrich was on the inside track. Paramount then despoiled her of her luxurious surroundings and dumped her in a more masculine environment; and she remained detached while Charles Bickford and Paul Lukas fought over her in *Thunder Below* (32). Said Picturegoer: '. . . no better and no worse than her other three starring vehicles . . . hopelessly artificial triangle plot.' Charles Laughton and Gary Cooper fought over her in *The Devil and the Deep*. It didn't work. Paramount dropped her and she went to MGM to make *Faithless* with Robert Montgomery, running 'the gamut of sex and degradation' (Picturegoer) in her quest for luxury. MGM wanted her to sign a contract, but she didn't care to be trapped in any more such parts and turned it down. She returned to the stage in 'Forsaking All Others' (33).

She soon achieved in New York the eminence she had known in London, though some of the things she did flopped: 'Dark Victory', 'The Circle' and a particularly despised Cleopatra in Shakespeare's play. She had a small successs in a revival of 'Rain' and in 1939 gave one of the great performances of the American theatre, in 'The Little Foxes'. She made a guest appearance in *Stage Door Canteen* (43) and then Alfred Hitchcock asked her to play the journalist in *Lifeboat* (44), a cunning thriller which took place entirely on same: it was a commanding performance and in the end affecting, and it brought her the New York critics' citation as the year's Best Actress. Twentieth, who produced, were so pleased that they invited her back for *Czarina* (45), a Lubitsch comedy (Preminger directed) about Catherine the Great (and, coincidentally, once done by Pola Negri). It did only fair business and Bankhead made only one subsequent film in Hollywood, *Main Street to Broadway* (52), playing herself.

Meanwhile, her theatre work varied – in quality and content: among several were 'The Eagle Has Two Heads' (47) and an attempt to revive the 'Ziegfeld Follies' (56). She appeared in cabaret and became a familiar figure guesting on TV; earlier (in the late 40s) she had acquired her greatest fame, on radio as the hostess of 'The Big Show': she insulted her guests and her catch-phrase, 'Hello Daaahlings', became nationally famous. That she was a genuinely witty woman was revealed by a best-selling autobiography, 'Tallulah' (52), and that most of the revelations in it were likely to be true was confirmed by a court case which followed publication (her secretary was accused of blackmail). In 1964 she appeared in New York in 'The Milk Train Doesn't Stop Here Anymore' and that summer she toured in 'Glad Tidings'. In 1965 she returned to Britain for a minor Hammer horror, as a religious *Fanatic* and murderess; it revealed that her once great beauty had completely gone. She was reported as saying: 'They used to shoot Shirley Temple through gauze. They should shoot me through linoleum.'

She died of pneumonia in New York in 1968, and that city was the less gay for her death.

Theda Bara

There was a film which went like this: (1) A happily-married young diplomat learns that he is being sent on a special mission to Europe (scenes of felicity, tinged with sadness). (2) On the voyage over, he meets the Vamp, not entirely by chance on her part (scenes of wiles and resistance). (3) He succumbs (scenes of seduction). (4) The family learns of his Fall (scenes of grief). (5) The diplomat and the Vamp disport themselves in Europe (scenes of debauchery). (6) They return to New York (scenes of ostracism). (7) The Vamp leaves him (scenes of finding solace with the Bottle) for other men and pastures new (more scenes of debauchery). (8) His wife attempts to reclaim him (scenes of heart-rending pathos). (9) She is about to win when the Vamp returns: 'Kiss me, my fool,' she cries and he, drunken, drug-addicted, dying, cannot resist (scenes of Nemesis).

Such was (or is) *A Fool There Was*, made in 1914, virtually the only one of Theda Bara's films to survive–which, on this evidence, is no deprivation. The scenes of debauchery consist of little more than couples dancing or lolling about in over-stuffed salons, with a few bottles and packs of cards around; the scenes of seduction consist of a bit of arm-flinging and back-arching on Miss Bara's part, and much hard staring–unrecognizable today as any sort of come-hither look. Yet she was the first glamour-girl, sex-queen, whatever: *A Fool There Was* gave the word 'vamp' to the language ('the only permanent contribution of the Fox-Theda barrage to the world', accurately predicted Terry Ramsaye).

The barrage consisted of some 40 films and publicity which is still remembered. Her name was supposedly an anagram of 'Arab Death', but was in fact a contraction of her Christian name, Theodosia (Goodman) plus a bit of her grandfather's middle name (Baranger). She was supposedly born in the shadow of the Sphinx (actually in Cincinnati, Ohio, in 1890), the offspring of either an Italian or French artist and an Arabian princess (or a sheik and a European princess). She was weaned on serpents' blood, was 'a crystal-gazing seeress of profoundly occult powers', came to films via stardom on the Paris stage, and spent her spare time driving men mad with love. She was frequently photographed with skeletons and always with strings of pearls and jewels, peering intensely at the camera, eyes rimmed with eye-shadow and looking years older than she was. 'The motion-picture public went to the theater to see about all this promisingly snaky stuff and found that the effect on the screen was up to the advance notices. Theda Bara of the screen, working her willowy way with men, became the vicarious and shadowy realization of several million variously-suppressed desires' (Terry Ramsaye). Audiences believed they were sharing a way of life they knew nothing about. How deliciously sinful it was! But as far as can be judged (from *Fool*) her emoting was ludicrous even by the then standards of screen acting.

She had, however, been a stage actress (as Theodosia de Coppet); little is known of her beginnings, though Hedda Hopper records having met her while she was appearing in a tour of 'The Quaker Girl', and she appeared in New York in 1908 in 'The Devil' by Ferenc Molnar. By 1914 she hadn't got as far as she wanted to, and began to haunt movie studios (whether she was or wasn't an extra is debatable; she herself said not). Though 'circumspect and demure', she immediately struck director Frank Powell as being a likely candidate for the female lead in *Fool*, the film version of a London and New York success, in its turn inspired by Rudyard Kipling's poem, 'The Vampire' ('A fool there was and he made his prayer / [Even as you and I] / To a rag and a bone and a hank of hair / [We called her the woman who did not care]'). Bara became famous overnight and the film the box-office rage; the publicity boys got busy and Bara proceeded to make a fortune for the film's producer, William Fox (it is also estimated that he made her–that she was the first star created by publicity). He formed his own company on the profits from *Fool*.

She was seldom permitted to play anything but the vamp: parts wildly different

'The barge she sat in. . . .' Theda Bara in Cleopatra, *a super-production of 1917. Gazing up in adoration is Antony – Art Acord.*

(such as Shakespeare's Juliet) were angled in that direction – partly because a few tentative touches of niceness were found to be unacceptable to the public; even when she did have a sympathetic part, her style of playing and the public's predisposition to find her evil combined to make it seem not so. In time there were copy-vamps (Valeska Suratt, Virginia Pearson, Louise Glaum, Barbara La Marr) – some of them at the Fox studio itself, kept as threats. Her second picture starred Nance O'Neil, with Bara as the sister who steals her husband; *The Kreutzer Sonata*, from the Tolstoy story. She was an unfaithful wife in *The Clemenceau Case* (15); a vengeful vampire in *The Devil's Daughter*; a murderess in *Lady Audley's Secret*. . . . They were all like that. Frequently, she died a ghastly death at the end. An average of one Bara film per month was released over the next three years. The other 1915 titles: *The Two Orphans* (remade as *Orphans of the Storm*); *Sin* (the adverts described the star as 'Destiny's Dark Angel'); *Carmen*, released at the same time as the Geraldine Farrar version for de Mille, which was much better; *The Galley Slave* (the adverts this time said 'Destiny's Dark Archangel') and *Destruction*.

In 1916 there were *The Serpent*, *Gold and the Woman*, *The Eternal Sappho*, *East Lynne* (as Lady Isobel), *Under Two Flags* (as Cigarette), *Her Double Life*, *Romeo and Juliet* with Harry Hilliard (released at the same time as a rival version with Beverley Baine and Francis X. Bushman) and *The Vixen*. There were fewer in 1917: *The Darling of Paris* (based on 'The Hunch-back of Notre Dame'), *The Tiger Woman* ('The Champion Vampire of the Season' said the legend), *Her Greatest Love* (from a novel by Ouida, 'Moths'), *Heart and Soul*, *Camille*, *The Rose of Blood* and *Cleopatra*. The latter was road-shown and a symphony orchestra accompanied prints to the more important bookings: it was one of Bara's biggest hits. (Her Antony, Art Acord, was in movies till Talkies revealed his high-pitched voice; he subsequently and briefly became a miner and finally committed suicide in a cheap Mexican hotel.) She was *Madame Dubarry* (18) and begged to be allowed to widen her range, but when Fox permitted her to film a story she had written herself it turned out to be the same old thing – Javanese priestess renounces her vows to lure a Scotsman to

Theda Bara in When a Woman Sins *(18). She was Poppaea, a trained nurse who becomes a notorious wanton, but reforms when she falls for a young divinity student.*

death and destruction: *The Soul of Buddha*.

Other films she made that year: *The Forbidden Path*, *Under the Yoke* (advertised as 'A volcanic drama of the Philippines–She scorched her Soul to Save an American Cavalry Officer'), *When a Woman Sins* ('The Greatest Woman's Story Ever Filmed–the Regeneration of a Modern Vampire'), inevitably *Salome*; and *The She-Devil*. In 1919: *The Light* (but hers was failing), *When Men Desire*, *The Siren's Song* and *A Woman There Was*. All of them (indeed, all her films since *Under Two Flags*) were directed by J. Gordon Edwards. But now there was to be a new director, Charles J. Brabin–and a new type of part, that of a pure young colleen in *Kathleen Mavourneen*. Fox had bought the property (it was a play by Boucicault) and Bara asked for the title role. Who knows, thought Fox, it might boost her sagging popularity. It did the reverse: she was hopelessly miscast, and Hibernian societies caused chaos at many theatres because an Irish girl was being played by a Jewish girl. Brabin also directed the next, *La Belle Russe*, in which she had a dual role; then *The Lure of Ambition* brought her Fox contract to an end. She had gone from $75 a week to $4,000–and if Fox were inclined to renew, it was more likely to be nearer the lower figure.

In fact, there were no takers. She waited more than a year, and then decided that the theatre might restore her to glory. She toured with 'The Blue Flame' to SRO business but New York quickly let it die out. In 1921 she married Brabin, and became a noted Hollywood hostess. Some plans were announced by her in the early 1920s but came to nothing. Then a small outfit called Chadwick signed her to appear in *The Unchastened Woman* (25), as a neglected wife who goes a-vamping to win back her husband. Hal Roach proposed that she guy her old image in a short, *Madame Mystery* (26), directed by Richard Wallace and Stan Laurel (Hardy was in the cast). Neither did much business. The days of the vamp were over. A remake of *A Fool There Was* (with Estelle Taylor) in 1922 was a complete flop, and Bara's place had been usurped by more sophisticated–and more believable–sirens like Gloria Swanson. Still, she wasn't entirely forgotten: when in 1932, US critics were polled to find the greatest all-time female star, she was third (Garbo was first, Pickford second, Constance Bennett fourth, Swanson fifth and Marion Davies sixth).

She did a few plays without success; and burlesqued herself in more shorts. But her marriage was happy and enduring. All the same, as Griffith and Mayer note, 'almost to her death, she advertised that she was "at liberty" in the Hollywood casting directory'. She died of cancer in 1955.

John Barrymore

The legacy of the Barrymores, John, Lionel and Ethel, is, as it is available to us today, for the most part singularly unimpressive. They have a golden name. Surviving colleagues still speak of them with awe, and the raves they had in their lifetimes are sometimes called into play. Their work in the theatre may have been magnificent, but on the evidence of their screen work, there is little to be said for any of them. True, they were past their prime: all we know of Ethel and Lionel are a series of cantankerous old people, who always have hearts of gold. Lionel was adept at grandfathers, uncles, old bankers, doctors, any aged but authoritative old man. Ethel was the matriarch par excellence, dispensing wisdom with a trowel. But their performances are invariable: from Ethel–*None But the Lonely Heart*, *Pinky*,

That Midnight Kiss and *Young at Heart*, etc.; and Lionel–*Grand Hotel*, *Dinner at Eight*, *David Copperfield*, *Camille*, *Three Wise Fools*, *Key Largo* and others. To get the measure of Ethel as a film actress one need only compare her with Helen Westley, say, or Florence Bates. Lionel was simply an old bore, but for comparison, for openers, there's Guy Kibbee, there's Albert Basserman, there's Reginald Owen....

John is a different matter. Throughout his lifetime he was regarded, quite simply, as a great actor. He was reputedly a great Hamlet and a front-rank light comedian. As a film-star, unlike his brother and sister, he was a big draw–a name that really meant something. His performances were much more varied than those of the others, and he carried a lot of films. Some of his work is impressive, giving credit to the reputation, but some of it, like his Mercutio in *Romeo and Juliet*, is over-cooked, thickly cut ham. At the time there was controversy about this performance: there were those who claimed that he was the only one in the film who knew what his character was about–and there are still critics who would excuse him on the grounds that he was acting in an older Shakespearian tradition. But one has only to compare that performance with Olivier's equally fiery Orlando in *As You Like It*, filmed around the same time–and Olivier is also a traditional actor. However, Barrymore was sometimes capable of giving a fairly naturalistic performance on film.

He was born in Philadelphia in 1882, a few years after Ethel (1879) and Lionel (1878). They came from theatre parents (on both sides). Ethel began acting while young, as did Lionel; but the latter gave it up for a while and went to study with John at the Beaux Arts in Paris. They both intended to become journalists, painters or commercial artists. John succumbed first, in 1903 (Lionel didn't return to the theatre till 1907). He wasn't making a success of journalism, and Ethel got him a part in a play in which she was appearing, 'Captain Jinks of the Horse Marines'. Later that year, he made his Broadway debut in 'Glad of It' at the Savoy. His biographer, Gene Fowler ('Goodnight, Sweet Prince', 1944), says that he was already drinking heavily. The play that established him was 'The Fortune Hunter' in 1909: thenceforward, he was considered the leading light comedian of the New York stage–in plays like 'Princess Zim-Zim', 'Half a Husband', 'The Affairs of Anatole' and 'Believe Me, Xantippe'.

He made his first film in 1913, as the lead in *An American Citizen*, adapted from a stage success. He said: 'The film determines an actor's ability, absolutely, conclusively. It is the surest test of an actor's qualities. Mental impressions can be conveyed by the screen more quickly than vocally. The moving picture is not a business, it is an art.' The following year, he signed a contract with Famous Players-Lasky, and over the next four years made a series of comedies, including *The Dictator* and *On the Quiet* (18), both of which he had done on the stage earlier, on tours in Britain, Australia, etc. Other titles: *The Man From Mexico* (14), *Are You a Mason?* (15), *The Incorrigible Dukane*, *Nearly a King* (16), *The Lost Bridegroom* and *The Red Widow*. The plot of the latter is typical: Barrymore, the groom, is knocked out by a thug and, forgetting his identity, joins a gang who are burgling his fiancée's home. Another clout on the head brings things back to normal. Barrymore and his family looked on these two-reelers as fun. His serious energies were saved for the stage –'Kick In', 'Peter Ibbetson' with Lionel, Galsworthy's 'Justice', Tolstoy's 'Redemption' and 'The Jest', again with Lionel, and reckoned to be the biggest non-musical hit the Broadway theatre had then, 1919, known.

In 1917, while appearing in 'Peter Ibbetson' at night, he made *Raffles The Amateur Cracksman* for an independent company; in 1918 he signed another contract with Famous–*Here Comes the Bride* and *Test of Honor* (19) and then *Dr Jekyll and Mr Hyde* (20), which brought him world acclaim: Agate, eight years later, commented that the Talkies could not improve on 'this masterpiece of acting'. Meanwhile his Broadway career was reaching a zenith–in 1920, after a flop play, 'Claire de Lune', by his second wife, Michael Strange, he had essayed a much admired 'Richard III'. *The Lotus Eater* (21) was a desert-island drama about a playboy who rejects (at first) the advances of a native girl because he loves the unfaithful wife he left behind. The filming was extremely slow, due to the drinking bouts that Barrymore shared with Marshall Neilan, the director, but Colleen Moore, who played the girl, remembered Barrymore as 'charming and witty and ever so debonair, and I adored him'.

In 1922 he was *Sherlock Holmes*–it was made in Britain, and Roland Young was his Watson. He had abandoned screen comedy. And this year he first did his 'Hamlet', which broke records. He also toured with it, and took it to London with success in 1924. The only film that he did was *Beau Brummel* (24) at Warners. Overall it is a poor, even ludicrous performance, especially in the culminating mad scene: but he does brilliantly as the proud poverty-stricken

John Barrymore demonstrating why he was known both as 'The Great Lover' and 'The Great Profile'. In The Sea Beast *(26), left, the lady was Dolores Costello, who later married him and changed her professional name to Dolores Costello Barrymore. The other lady receiving his favours is Garbo, in* Grand Hotel *(32).*

Brummel in Calais. The film was so successful that WB signed him to a contract, at the huge fee of $76,250 per picture, plus $7,625 per week if it wasn't completed within seven weeks; *plus* all expenses paid (film-making had now moved almost completely from New York to Hollywood, but as Barrymore, officially, hadn't, that meant house, servants, car, chauffeur, etc., each time he was in Hollywood). His billing, furthermore, read: 'Mr John Barrymore'. He consented to Don Juan provided that he could play Ahab in a film of 'Moby Dick'. The result was called *The Sea Beast* (26), and Barrymore's initial objection to the introduction of a love interest was much assuaged when it turned out to be Dolores Costello. They later married and he wanted her cast in *Don Juan* instead of Mary Astor, for whom his love had grown cold (according to her memoirs). He didn't get his way. The film was billed 'The World's Greatest Actor as the Greatest Lover of all Ages'; and his next picture would be advertised with the tag 'The Greatest Lover of the Screen'. The latter designation he took particularly seriously in life, when he wasn't drinking.

Don Juan did spectacularly well because it was the first feature to be released with Sound (music only, synchronized on disc). But the reviews were, as Hollis Alpert says in 'The Barrymores', mostly 'unfavourable, and some downright abusive'. Alpert quotes from a couple: 'Artistically, the only thing we could say about Mr Barrymore's performances is that he brings to them remnants of his tricks and mannerisms that stiffen them slightly and perhaps convey the sense of acting to a public that has seen but little of it' (Stark Young in The New Republic), and 'Mr Barrymore himself is almost as bad, at times, as he was in *The Sea Beast*... the movie Barrymore, with a few flashes of brilliance and a great many glints of supreme silliness.' (Robert E. Sherwood in Life magazine). Part of the trouble was that his Fairbanks-like bravado was totally artificial. Nor was there a kinder reception for *When a Man Loves* (27), which was 'Manon Lescaut' re-titled: Costello was Manon, and Barrymore played des Grieux. This was the last of his three pictures for WB, and he decided to move over to UA for $100,000 per film plus a share of the profits;

after two films the sum was upped to $150,000 to offset the fact that there hadn't been any profits till then, plus the loss of living expenses. Still, it looked like a good investment when Barrymore came top of one of the first U.S. box-office surveys (the others, in descending order: Harold Lloyd, Colleen Moore, Gloria Swanson, Richard Dix, Thomas Meighan, Tom Mix, Lon Chaney, Buster Keaton and Rin-Tin-Tin). The three films he made for UA were *The Beloved Rogue* which was, literally, another version of *If I Were King/The Vagabond King* (François Villon); *The Tempest* (28), an epic about the Russian Revolution; and *Eternal Love* (29) directed by Lubitsch, which cast him and Camilla Horn as ill-fated lovers killed in an avalanche.

Don Juan had paved the way for Talkies, and now Barrymore returned to WB for his first Sound feature. His contract was for five films at $30,000 per week, plus a percentage of the profits, a sum owing much to the current studio infatuation for stage actors. *General Crack* required of him no more than to wear a white powdered wig as an officer of the Austrian Emperor; in the all-star *The Show of Shows* he did 'Now is the winter of our discontent' from 'Richard III'; *The Man From Blankleys* (30) was a mild comedy which cast him as an English lord; *Moby Dick* found him as Ahab again, with Joan Bennett as the girl; *Svengali* (31) had him hypnotizing Marian Marsh; and *The Mad Genius* was practically a reprise of the Svengali idea.

He then signed a contract with MGM, where Lionel was a star. It was non-exclusive, and brought him $150,000 per film, a sum not justified by his box-office pull. *Arsene Lupin* (32), with Lionel, did something to re-establish him, and the next, the all-star *Grand Hotel*, was one of the year's top money-makers. (Garbo permitted herself to be photographed on the set with him during the making, a rare gesture). He then moved over to RKO for a thriller with Helen Twelvetrees, *State's Attorney*, and there he was Hepburn's father in *A Bill of Divorcement*, returning to MGM for a film with his brother and sister, *Rasputin and the Empress*. Lionel was the mad monk, Ethel the Czarina, and John played a character clearly based on Prince Felix Youssoupoff: Diana Wynyard was his wife, and in the film was raped by Rasputin. The Youssoupoffs sued for libel in the English courts in 1934, and were awarded £25,000 plus huge costs. In Britain, the film was withdrawn from circulation which was no loss to historical studies or the art of the cinema – it was much inferior to the still current Conrad Veidt *Rasputin*. He then starred, again with Wynyard, in *Reunion in Vienna* (33), from Robert E. Sherwood's play; it was not a success. *Dinner at Eight* had the brothers together again, with Harlow, Beery, etc.; so did *Night Flight*, this time with Clark Gable, Helen Hayes, Robert Montgomery and Myrna Loy. (Thus the two of them were in all of the new MGM 'all-star' films which destroyed the old one-star-one-film policy.) In *Dinner at Eight* John was the fading matinée idol hooked on drink. In life, it had begun seriously to affect his work: his memory began to falter, and cue cards had to be held up round the set. For the moment, however, his name was big enough for the studios to tolerate the delays which his drinking caused.

Caricature by Otis Shepard.

He did *Topaze* (33) at RKO: 'As a non-admirer of John Barrymore, I was all the more agreeably surprised to find myself completely won over by his charmingly subdued (for him) performance as Pagnol's French Schoolteacher, bluffed and bewildered by big business, who himself becomes a business tycoon.' (Peter John Dyer in 1967.) He made *Counsellor-at-Law*, Elmer Rice's play, at Universal ('One of his few screen roles that reveal his measure as an actor; his fabulous "presence" is apparent in every scene; so are his restraint, his humour and his zest.' – Pauline Kael) and *Long Lost Father* (34) – Helen Chandler's – at RKO. He should have then made *Hat, Coat and Glove* at the same studio, but had trouble with his lines and was taken off the film. Of the next, Gene Fowler wrote that Barrymore's talent 'flared brilliantly'. The film was *Twentieth Century*, from the play by Ben Hecht and Charles MacArthur, generally regarded as the first of the screwball comedies; Barrymore played the egomaniac producer trying to lure temperamental actress Carole Lombard into signing a contract.

Around this time there were two plans to film Barrymore's *Hamlet*. Selznick wanted to do it in Technicolor, financed by John Hay Whitney, but the tests made in 1935 were not sufficiently encouraging for the project to go ahead. A year later Barrymore signed with Korda to do it, while on a visit to London, but later decided that he was too old and too portly. He did make his Hollywood return in a Shakespeare film, the Shearer-Howard *Romeo and Juliet* (36), and when his drinking brought his brief participation to a stop the role was offered to William Powell (who refused because Barrymore had given him his start in films). He finally completed it and MGM, ever ready to help, announced that he would appear in *Camille* (in the role that

The first screen teaming of the Barrymores was reckoned to be one of the cinematic events of 1932: Rasputin and the Empress. *Lionel (left) and Ethel had the title roles, and John was the slightly fictitious Prince Paul. The boy in Rasputin's arms is the Tsarevitch; the man at the back a member of the Imperial Guard.*

One of the several pathetic self-parodies Barrymore did towards the end of his life – Playmates *(42) with Patsy Kelly, one of the screen's funniest supporting players.*

Henry Daniell eventually – and superbly – played); instead, he entered a clinic for alcoholics. When he came out, he played a similar role, that of Jeanette MacDonald's protector in *Maytime* (37). It was not a star part, nor was his role in *True Confession* – which he was given on the insistence of Lombard, who starred. The press made much of the fact that the great Barrymore had been demoted to feature billing. His other 1937 films were Bs: *Bulldog Drummond Comes Back*, *Night Club Scandal*, co-starring Lynn Overman, and *Bulldog Drummond's Revenge* (John Howard was Drummond, and Barrymore played his boss). In 1938 there was another, *Bulldog Drummond's Peril*; he had supporting roles, to Gladys Swarthout and John Boles in *Romance in the Dark* and in *Spawn of the North*. He was 'excellent' (Agate) as Louis XV in the first few minutes of *Marie Antoinette* and 'magnificent' (Steven H. Scheuer) in his only lead of the year, *Hold That Coed*, a B comedy, as a politician on the campus.

He made *The Great Man Votes* (39), a superior B-picture directed by Garson Kanin, and *Midnight*, and spent the rest of the year in a dreadful play, 'My Dear Children', with his fourth wife, Elaine Barrie. It toured (notably in Chicago where it ran 34 weeks) and finally opened in New York in January, 1940: its success was widely believed to be due to audiences flocking to see Barrymore making a spectacle of himself (forgetting his lines, sometimes falling over). He was fully aware of this; and when he abandoned the play, at the behest of 20th, it was to appear in a thinly disguised parody of his own decline – and a B at that – *The Great Profile* (40). He had a similar role – that of a broken-down old ham, usually drunk – in Rudy Vallee's radio show throughout 1941. His films were negligible: *The Invisible Woman* (41), at Universal; *World Première* with Frances Farmer; and *Playmates*, a musical with Kay Kayser and Lupe Velez. He died not long after completing the latter, in 1942. He was penniless.

His daughter (by Michael Strange), Diana Barrymore, had a brief film career – notably *Between Us Girls* (43) – and later became an alcoholic. Her biography was filmed in 1958, two years before she died (aged 38); in the film – *Too Much Too Soon* – Errol Flynn played John Barrymore. His son, John Drew Barrymore, has had a mild career in Hollywood, mostly in B actioners.

Alpert's book on the Barrymores has these words by Ethel as a foreword: 'We who play, who entertain for a few years, what can we leave that will last?'

Richard Barthelmess in Tol'able David *(21), directed by Henry King, and probably the least crude, the most fresh and moving, of any silent melodrama.*

Richard Barthelmess

It is improbable that many people, looking at a photograph of him, would agree that Richard Barthelmess 'had the most beautiful face of any man who ever went before the camera', as Lillian Gish asserts in her memoirs. His face is round, pasty, and undistinguished, though he had large, sombre eyes and good blunt features . . . at least, he was and is unprepossessing in stills. But the motion-picture camera caught the beauty, an inner beauty, spiritual; not always, but certainly in *Tol'able David* and *Broken Blossoms*, Barthelmess gave startlingly beautiful performances: he was *pure*. His character in some of his later films has affinities with Scott Fitzgerald's Anson Hunter ('The Rich Boy'). He was not Galahad or Prince Charming, though he played variations of both parts. Normally, he was the champion of the oppressed, almost a Dickens hero: realistic, involved in a recognizable world, but elusive. His was a remarkable talent on a minor scale.

He was born in New York City in 1895, and educated at Hudson River Military Academy at Nyack and Trinity College, Hartford, Connecticut. His father had died when he was a baby, and his mother earned her living on the stage; therefore, from his early days, he worked in theatres between schooling–ASM, or walk-ons. He graduated in 1913, acted that year in 'Mrs Wiggs of the Cabbage Patch', and began in films as an extra. He was in Billie Burke's *Gloria's Romance* in 1916, and had his first important part later that year in *War Brides*, based on Nazimova's vaudeville sketch and starring her (his mother was Nazimova's English coach, and they were friends). He was also in *Camille* (17) with Nazimova and in *Snow White*; then had more important parts in: *The Moral Code* with Anna Q. Nilsson; *The Eternal Sin*, a historical piece in which he was disconcerted on finding that his mother was Lucrezia Borgia; and *The Valentine Girl*, who was Marguerite Clark. He was her leading man again in *Bab's Diary*, *Bab's Burglar*, *The Seven Swans* (18) and *Rich Man Poor Man*, all made for Famous Players. Betweenwhiles he was in *The Soul of Magdalen* with Olga Petrova; *The Streets of Illusion* (they were New York's); *For Valor*, as a Canadian conchie; *Sunshine Nan* with Ann Pennington; *Hit-the-Trail-Haliday*, a comedy with George M. Cohan about Billy Sunday; and *The Hope Chest* (19), a story of young marrieds, opposite Dorothy Gish.

That was the first of several co-starring vehicles with Dorothy and the beginning of a rewarding association with both Gish sisters, and with their mentor D. W. Griffith. Griffith at this time was looking for a successor to his usual leading man, Raymond Harron. (Harron shot himself in New York the following year.) He wanted someone more robust – but equally sensitive – and he tried out Barthelmess in *The Girl Who Stayed at Home*. Griffith signed him to a personal contract for three years, going from $300 to $450 a week; and when he wasn't working for him, he was with Paramount, who released the Griffith films. In *Boots* he was a Secret Service man and Dorothy a London waif; in *Three Men and a Girl*, with Clark, he was a misogynist; he was a doctor in *Peppy Polly* and a reporter in *I'll Get Him Yet*, both with Dorothy. Griffith then co-starred him with Lillian in *Broken Blossoms*, the story of a tragic Limehouse friendship between a Chinese and a slavey ill-treated by step-father Donald Crisp. Karel Reisz wrote years later: 'Richard Barthelmess plays The Yellow Man with a restraint and tenderness rare in the silent cinema.' The film's success firmly established Barthelmess. He was in a couple with Clarine Seymour, *Scarlet Days* and *The Idol Dancer* (20), in the latter as a beachcomber involved with a South Seas beauty. A melodrama, *The Love Flower*, was one of Griffith's least successful movies up to that time, but this next was a huge grosser, and an accepted classic for some years: *Way Down East* with Lillian, who has declared that Griffith 'transformed a crude melodrama into a compelling masterpiece'. (She was the farmhand whose past was betrayed by her wicked seducer and Barthelmess was the farmer's son who rescued her from the snow into which she had been cast.)

Richard Barthelmess in 1931.

Barthelmess then made *Experience* (21) with Nita Naldi, and was invited by Charles H. Duell to form his own company in partnership, for the purpose of exploiting Barthelmess's talent. The company was called Inspiration and the pact was for five years. Its end coincided with a lawsuit involving Lillian which completely discredited Duell, but those five years produced one masterpiece, and at least two other remarkable films, most of them directed by Henry King. The masterpiece is the first, *Tol'able David*, Joseph Hergesheimer's story of a Southern boy called upon to take on a man's responsibilities, defending the US Mail. There followed *The Seventh Day* (22); *Just a Song at Twilight*, an outside studio attempt to dramatize a popular song; the excellent *Sonny*, with Barthelmess in a dual role and his wife, Mary Hay, in the cast; *The Bond Boy*, resisting the advances of his step-mother; *The Bright Shawl*, another Hergesheimer story, with D. Gish, and, as background, the Cuban Revolution; and *Fury* (23). Like *Sonny*, this has affinities with *Tol'able David*: Barthelmess is the gentle son of a stern sea captain (Tyrone Power Sr), who avenges his mother's ruin, and ends up with his faithful Limehouse waif (Dorothy Gish). In *The Fighting Blade* he was a member of Cromwell's army: the leading lady in this, and in *Twenty-One*, was Dorothy Mackaill. And it was May McAvoy in the next, *The Enchanted Cottage* (24), from Pinero's romantic play. Then he did *Classmates* as a West Point cadet; *New Toys* (25), a poor comedy; *Soul-Fire* as a musician who finds fulfilment in the South Seas with Bessie Love; *Shore Leave*, a version of the musical, 'Hit the Deck'; *The Beautiful City*, as an Italian in love with Irish Dorothy on New York's East Side; *Just Suppose*, as an English prince visiting the US and meeting Lois Moran (in Britain the subtitles changed him to a Ruritanian prince, but the new title, *Golden Youth*, still managed to suggest the Prince of Wales). *Ranson's Folly* was an unconvincing period piece about American army life with Mackaill and *The Amateur Gentleman* was more period stuff, from Jeffrey Farnol's novel. *The White Black Sheep* with Patsy Ruth Miller found Barthelmess as an English gentleman ranker at a desert outpost, and in *The Dropkick* (27) he was at college.

Since *Shore Leave*, the Inspiration product had been released through First National, and with the disgrace of Duell, Barthelmess decided to sign a contract with that company, at the reputed (but improbable) figure of $375,000 per film. The first film of the association was *The Patent Leather Kid*, the stock tale of a cocky prize-fighter unwilling to go to war; it was so highly regarded that it was road-shown when first released: it ran 16 weeks in New York and, following this run of mediocre films, re-established Barthelmess as one of the screen's leading actors. In *The Noose* (28) he was in prison for a murder he didn't commit; in *The Little Shepherd of Kingdom Come* (the famous old bestseller) in the title role; in *The Wheels of Chance* Russian twins separated in childhood; in *Out of the Ruins* a French officer; and in *Scarlet Seas* in love with Betty Compson.

With the coming of the Talkies, he was made to sing – in *Weary River* (29), as a boot-legger who got framed. More importantly, he talked well, though a certain withdrawal

Helen Chandler, Walter Byron and Richard Barthelmess in The Last Flight *(31), a remarkable film that lay forgotten until 'rescued' by London's National Film Theatre in 1968.*

was revealed which called for more careful casting. But his popularity held at least for a couple of years (he appears sixth on one of the box-office polls for 1931). He made *Drag* at MGM, a newspaper story; *Young Nowheres*, a 'modern' story; *The Show of Shows*, introducing a turn; *Son of the Gods* (30), in which he, Constance Bennett and the audience all discovered at the end that he wasn't Chinese, as they thought; and *The Dawn Patrol*, as an English pilot, a much-admired and popular war movie–and probably the most famous of his Sound films. Forgotten now are *The Lash* (31), a Western, and *The Finger Points*, in which he was a crusading journalist out to get racketeer Clark Gable, among others. But rescued from oblivion a few years ago was *The Last Flight*, a film damply received by press and public when first shown: a study of a group of ex-flyers in post-war Paris and the girl (Helen Chandler) they briefly pick up. Directed by William Dieterle, written by John Monk Saunders, it outclasses Hemingway's portrait of the Lost Generation at every point: except technically, it is invincibly modern (nonsequential, flip, witty, pessimistic), the rare example of a film years in advance of its time (one can only speculate on the consequences had it been successful). Barthelmess is rightly dour as the leader of the group.

Nor were his subsequent pictures at First National (now Warners) very popular: *Alias the Doctor* (32), a gruesome hospital melodrama with Marian Marsh; *Cabin in the Cotton*, as a cotton picker who wanted to better himself but became involved with tramp Bette Davis; *Central Airport* (33), as a pilot, directed by William A. Wellman; and *Heroes for Sale*, again as a disillusioned war veteran, curing himself of drugs but losing wife Loretta Young in an accident. *Massacre* (34) found him as an Indian rodeo performer, championing his race against exploitation; and in *A Modern Hero* (directed by G. W. Pabst, not very well) he had a rare unsympathetic role, as a heel–and he stayed that way for *Midnight Alibi*, as New York's leading racketeer. The toll of the Talkies took him at last. WB didn't renew his contract (he left at the same time as William Powell and Ruth Chatterton).

Free-lancing for the first time in his 16 years as a star, Barthelmess stayed mean for *Four Hours to Kill* (35, at Paramount), as a crook handcuffed to a cop: it didn't resuscitate his Hollywood career. He went to Britain to play a French aristocrat in *A Spy of Napoleon* (36) with Dolly Haas. And that year he appeared on Broadway in 'The Postman Always Rings Twice'. He retired, but a couple of years later mentioned to an interviewer that he would like to make a film, and was offered a featured role in *Only Angels Have Wings* (39), as Rita Hayworth's failed, cowardly husband. It was a brilliant performance, and Hollywood talked of a comeback. It was reported that he would sign with 20th, but he made only three more pictures: *The Man Who Talked Too Much* (40, at WB) as a gangster, with George Brent;

Greta Garbo as Anna Karenina *(35) and Freddie Bartholomew as her son.*

The Mayor of 44th Street (42, at RKO) as a racketeer, with George Murphy; and *The Spoilers* (42, at Universal) as the sad-eyed, limping barman. He joined the Naval Reserve, and after the war didn't return to acting. He lived on Long Island with his second wife, and died of cancer, after a long illness, in 1963. He left over a million dollars.

Freddie Bartholomew

To Hollywood, Freddie Bartholomew represented a very young scion of the British aristocracy, but in fact he came from a fairly humble (London) home. Born in 1924, he was brought up by his grandparents in Wiltshire, where he made a local name for himself reciting at socials and church bazaars. With his parents' consent, his Aunt Cissie 'managed' him, getting him amateur jobs as well as bits in films locationing locally: *Fascination* (30) and *Lily Christine* (32). He was taken to London to study under Italia Conti, who recommended him to George Cukor and David O. Selznick, in Britain looking for a David Copperfield. They liked him, but due to British government restrictions on child actors, he was reluctantly let go. Auntie and Freddie then (1934) travelled to the US, ostensibly to visit relatives, but they wound up in Hollywood – fortuitously, as Cukor and Selznick, having examined more than 10,000 applicants, were again fighting Louis B. Mayer's choice of Jackie Cooper for the part. Tested again, Freddie of course proved to have histrionic ability, and he played the boy David (35). He was under a seven-year contract starting at $175 and going to $500 a week: but after playing Garbo's son in *Anna Karenina* the contract was revised to stand at $1,000 a week.

He was borrowed by 20th for *Professional Soldier* (36), where Victor McLaglen had the title role as a retired colonel plotting to kidnap a European king (Freddie); and by Selznick (who had now left MGM) for *Little Lord Fauntleroy*, the first of several films in which Mickey Rooney was to appear somewhere in order to point up Freddie's gentility and bearing; and he was in *The Devil is a Sissy* with both Rooney and Cooper. When 20th wanted to borrow him again MGM agreed provided he got top billing – though in *Lloyds of London* he was only in the first part (he grew up to be Tyrone Power). He surprised the critics by giving a good performance in *Captains Courageous* (37): as the spoilt little hero his prissiness and petulance were apt, and his change under the tutelage of Spencer Tracy was well done. He was borrowed by 20th again for the lead in Robert Louis Stevenson's *Kidnap(p)ed* (38) and was then *Lord Jeff*, an orphan boy exploited by grown-ups conniving with Rooney. He had his first teen-age role in *Listen Darling* with Judy Garland.

His popularity had distinctly declined. MGM had no plans for him and he made only one film in 1939: *The Spirit of Culver* at Universal, once again teamed with Jackie

Cooper. It was announced that he would do 'The Boy David' on Broadway, but it didn't materialize. To make things worse, life was troubled by legal battles between his Aunt Cissie and his parents over custody and salary: the case went to court 27 times in all, and whoever was legally or morally right, Bartholomew sided with his aunt–and lost, in lawyers' fees, altogether, almost every penny he had. He was loaned to RKO for two weak versions of English classics, *The Swiss Family Robinson* (40) and *Tom Brown's Schooldays* and then to Columbia for a B, *Naval Academy* (41). He then supported Rooney, now a very big star, in *A Yank at Eton* (42)–indeed, he was billed fourth, after Ian Hunter and Edmund Gwenn. One of the troubles was, as Picturegoer pointed out, that 'Hollywood had developed with vigour the qualities of lordliness and preciousness always inherent' in his character. After another B for Columbia, *Junior Army* (43), and an indie, *The Town Went Wild* (44), he joined the USAAF. He was 18. When he returned there was little work for him: only *Sepia Cinderella* (47), a Billy Daniels starrer for RKO, and *St Benny the Dip* (51). When movies wouldn't have him, he went into TV in 1949, hosting an afternoon show about films; from there he passed on to directing TV shows, to TV commercials, and finally to Madison Avenue, definitely retired from acting. Whether he regrets the past is not known, but he is one of the few child stars to have married happily, and is settled with his second wife in New Jersey.

Warner Baxter

'He is the beau ideal, a Valentino without a horse and the costume of a sheik. He is the fellow the girls meet around the corner, that is, if the fellow were Warner Baxter. He is the chap the lonely woman on the prairie sees when she looks at the men's ready-to-wear pages in the latest mail order catalogue': this appraisal by Jim Tully appeared in Picturegoer in 1936. Baxter was certainly the inspiration for artwork in mail-order catalogues and adverts for pipes, the prototype for men modelling cardigans or pullovers or tweeds. During the early Sound period he was one of Hollywood's leading actors. There was no éclat with him: no scandals, no Hollywood careering. Women liked him because he was mature and reliable. He was a good work-horse of an actor, often at the mercy of his material When it was good, he gave positive, likeable performances. It was a long career but he is hardly remembered today.

He was born in Columbus, Ohio, in 1892; his father died when he was five months old. In 1905 his mother moved to San Francisco and they lost all their possessions in the great earthquake the following year; he went to the Polytechnic High School in that city and in 1908 returned to Columbus where he started work as an office boy. He sold typewriters, cars and agricultural implements, then began his stage career in Louisville, Kentucky, when a friend recommended him to Dorothy Shoemaker when her vaudeville partner fell ill. The engagement didn't last long. He later trained as an insurance salesman, then invested all his money in his brother-in-law's garage in Tulsa–but it went broke. At that point, 1914, he determined to fulfil his acting ambition and got a job with a touring company: his first part was as the juvenile in 'Brewster's Millions'. In 1918 he married his second wife, Winifred Bryson. He joined Morosco's stock company in Los Angeles, alternating leads with Richard Dix and Edmund Lowe. There was also a film part, in *All Woman* (18), starring Mae Marsh. Morosco sent him to New York in the hit 'Lombardi Ltd' and afterwards Baxter toured in it for two years. During this time he made another film *Cheated Hearts* (21), starring Marjorie Daw. As a result of his success in this he had another film offer–from Ethel Clayton to appear opposite her in *Her Own Money* (22). She re-engaged him for *If I Were Queen* at FBO and he then had an offer to be featured in *The Tailor Made Man** starring Wanda Hawley. Morosco was reclaiming his services but Baxter preferred to be in pictures and falsely claimed the studio lights had affected his sight–enough to keep him off the stage, for the moment; so he left Morosco and made the Hawley picture. He then went *In Search of a Thrill* (23) with Violet Dana, was a destitute war veteran in *Blow Your Own Horn*, and got involved in the *Alimony* (24) problems of Grace Darmond. He should have been part of Lubitsch's *The Marriage Circle* at Warners along with Florence Vidor, but after some days shooting was replaced by Monte Blue. However, he managed to get into a couple at First National, *Those Who Dare* and *Christine of the Hungry Heart* with Florence Vidor as its much-married heroine. And he was in *Her Market Value* with the fading Agnes Ayres which got some bookings two years later.

Paramount liked him enough to offer a contract: *The Female*, a South African romance, and *The Garden of Weeds*, both with Betty Compson. De Mille chose him to play Lillian Rich's playboy lover in *The Golden*

Warner Baxter was normally a sobersides executive-type actor, but from time to time in the 30s he played a romantic Mexican bandit, the Cisco Kid – here in the film of that name, with Conchita Montenegro.

Bed (25) – he ungratefully deserts her and she has to seek forgiveness from husband Henry B. Walthall. He got leading roles but not star billing: *The Air Mail* with Billie Dove; *Welcome Home*; *Rugged Water*; the remake of *A Son of His Father*; *The Best People* with Margaret Livingstone; *Mannequin* (26) from Fannie Hurst's story, playing with Alice Joyce the parents of the title character, Dolores Costello; *Miss Brewster's Millions* starring Bebe Daniels; and *The Runaway*. His best chance came when chosen to play opposite Gilda Gray in *Aloma of the South Seas*, as the educated native chieftain who falls for his pagan bride. He was loaned to First National for *Mismates*, then had the title role in a version of a recent best-seller, F. Scott Fitzgerald's *The Great Gatsby*. After *The Telephone Girl* (27) – Madge Bellamy – he was loaned to Fox for *Singed* with Blanche Sweet; then did his last for Paramount, *Drums of the Desert*. He free-lanced: *The Coward* at Radio, *A Woman's Way* at Columbia, *The Tragedy of Youth* (28) at Tiffany, and *Three Sinners* at Paramount. Then he got the part which made him for virtually the first time seem like star material: the noble Indian, Alessandro, in the third of the four screen versions of *Ramona*, opposite Dolores del Rio. He played the long-suffering husband in the first of three screen versions of *Craig's Wife*, with Irene Rich in the title role. He then did *Danger Street* at FBO and supported Lon Chaney in *West of Zanzibar* (29) at MGM.

His great chance came by chance. Raoul Walsh had been set by Fox to direct and star in the first 'outdoor all-Talkie', *In Old Arizona*, based on O. Henry's 'The Caballero's Way', but he was involved in an accident after some weeks' shooting (that's when he lost his eye) and replacements were needed. Irving Cummings took over direction and some dozen actors were tested for the part of the Cisco Kid. Baxter got it, starring alongside Edmund Lowe, and he later won an Oscar for the year's best male performance. Fox hastened to sign him. Baxter had meanwhile done a production for an independent company, *Linda*, but now in a series of Fox pictures he obtained at last screen fame and popularity: *Through Different Eyes*, with Lowe and Mary Duncan; *Behind That Curtain*, with Lois Moran, a Charlie Chan mystery (E. A. Park was Chan); *Far Call*, made as a Silent and released with a music track; *Romance of the Rio Grande* with Mary Duncan and Antonio Moreno – whose star was fading now – as the villainous don who tries to cheat him of his heritage; *Happy Days* (30), Fox's all-star revue; and *Such Men Are Dangerous*. He returned to the part of the Cisco Kid in *The Arizona Kid* and then did a Foreign Legion story, *Renegades*.

He made *Doctors' Wives* (31) with Joan Bennett and then co-starred with the studio's top star, Janet Gaynor, in *Daddy Long Legs*, giving a performance as her 'elderly' benefactor which melted every female heart in the audience. Then he was loaned to MGM to play the role undertaken by Dustin Farnum in 1914 and Elliott Dexter in 1918, *The Squaw Man* – directed by de Mille for the third time (one of the two films he made away from Paramount after a quarrel): in support were Lupe Velez and Eleanor Boardman, and Baxter did very well as the aristocratic Englishman who flees to the American West when his honour is besmirched. He returned to Fox for *Their Mad Moment*; *The Cisco Kid*, another sequel; and *Surrender*. Then followed: *Amateur Daddy* (32) with Marian Nixon, a sentimental piece about a man who mothers a brood of orphans; *Man About Town* with Karen Morley; *Six Hours to Live* as a man brought back from the dead to serve his country; *Dangerously Yours* (33) with Miriam Jordan again; *42nd Street*, on loan to Warners, as the tired but tyrannical stage director; *I Loved You Wednesday*; and *Paddy the Next Best Thing*, which reunited him with Gaynor. Most of his Fox pictures were mediocre, and he got into a good one again on a second loan-out that year: *Penthouse*, with Myrna Loy, a sophisticated thriller, as a society lawyer.

The next was poor: *As Husbands Go* (34), wisely saving wife Helen Vinson from the clutches of a European admirer. Then he did another musical, *Stand Up and Cheer*, playing a State Secretary of Amusement who cheers the nation with a show including John Boles, Aunt Jemima and Stepin Fetchit. The ads offered '1,001 suprises!' plus '1,000 Dazzling Girls! 5 Bands of Music! Vocal Chorus of 500! 4,891 Costumes! 1,200 Wild Animals! 1,000 Players! 335 Scenes! 2,370 Technical Workers!' Baxter was back in more familiar territory with *Such Women Are Dangerous*, the sort of film Fox fashioned for him, about a young girl (Rochelle Hudson) whose infatuation for an older man leads to her suicide. And he was ideal as a doctor in *Grand Canary*, from a novel by A. J. Cronin, with Madge Evans.

He was loaned to Columbia for Capra's delightful *Broadway Bill* (35) with Loy; and then did a feeble war picture about flying: *Hell in the Heavens*. He was with Gaynor again in *One More Spring*, as a victim of the Depression, living with her and Walter King in a shed in Central Park, a film 'fairly dripping with sweetness and light' (Photoplay). There followed: *Under the Pampas Moon*, again in gaucho garb, romancing Ketti Gallian; *King of Burlesque*, in the title role, a musical with Alice Faye; and on loan to MGM, *Robin Hood of Eldorado* (36) as Juan Murietta, who was more factual than the other Robin. The next is probably his best picture, John Ford's *The Prisoner of Shark Island*, as the unfortunate Doctor Mudd who set the broken leg of John Wilkes Booth as he was fleeing from the scene of the crime, and who was, despite his innocence, imprisoned for life: an unbearably tense picture, beautifully told, and beautifully acted by Baxter. It was his first film under the new regime at Fox (now 20th Century) and the next two were also fine: *The Road to Glory*, a war picture with Fredric March, and *To Mary With Love*, a romantic drama with Loy. However, *White Hunter* with June Lang was no great shakes. He was the captain of *Slave Ship* (37), involved with the African slave trade of 1850 until a last reel reformation, and then a couturier in Wanger's *Vogues of 1938*, again married to Helen Vinson. Loretta Young and Virginia Bruce were the other title-rolers of *Wife Doctor and Nurse* (38), and it was Freddie Bartholomew who was *Kidnap(p)ed*, with Baxter as Alan Breck (for which he was some years too old). *I'll Give a Million* was formula Baxter stuff, as a millionaire who disguises himself as a hobo because he wants to be loved for himself: the girl was Marjorie Weaver. It did poorly, and Baxter's days as a top star were drawing to a close. *Wife Husband and Friend* (39) co-starred him with Young again, as a woman who wants a singing career, and he as the husband who achieves success at same, encouraged by prima donna/vamp Binnie Barnes. It was a funny film, but these didn't help: *Return of the Cisco Kid*, yet another in that series, with Cesar Romero in a small role (he later played the title role in a B series based on the same character); *Barricade* (40) with Alice Faye; and *Earthbound*, an appropriately named whimsy about a man who returns from the dead (again!) to put things right on earth. It was his last film for his old studio. He moved over to Columbia for a stong drama about a modern Lear, *Adam Had Four Sons* (41), co-starring Ingrid Bergman.

Warner Baxter in 1941

He was off the screen two years; returned in the first two of a B series for Columbia, in the title role, *Crime Doctor* (43) and *Crime Doctor's Strangest Case*, both of which he ignored when giving an interview on the set of his next, *Lady in the Dark* (44): he said then that he had been absent from the screen because of a nervous breakdown (he blamed years of intensive work rather than being dropped by 20th) and expressed an anxiousness to return as a character actor. His part in *Lady in the Dark* was hardly a character one – he was Ginger Rogers's elderly admirer – but it was certainly small. He spent the rest of his career in Bs for Columbia: *Shadows in the Night*, *The Crime Doctor's Courage* (45), *Just Before Dawn* (46), *The Crime Doctor's Manhunt*, *The Millerson Case* (47), *The Crime Doctor's Gamble*, *A Gentleman From Nowhere* (48), *Prison Warden* (49), *The Devil's Henchman*, *The Crime Doctor's Diary*, and *State Penitentiary* (50).

During these latter years he had been active in civic affairs in Malibu, where he lived; and had suffered from chronic arthritis. He died of bronchial pneumonia in 1951.

* *According to an interview in Picturegoer in 1935. Warner Baxter was not in the film of this title released that year with Charles Ray, but I have been unable to trace the film he meant.*

Wallace Beery

Wallace Beery started in films in low comedy; became typed as a villain, and was given a new lease of life as such by the Talkies, whereupon he did an about-turn, and specialized in bluff, lovable rogues with, as one writer put it, 'a heart of gold functioning on all six cylinders'. Physically, if he wasn't going to be the baddie, this was the only solution. 'Like my dear old friend, Marie Dressler,' he said once, 'my mug has been my fortune.' For a long while he was extremely popular, and occasioned such comments as this in Picturegoer by Frank Shaw in 1931: 'He is of the salt of the earth, and is a son of the earth.' He could be *cabotin*, or he could coast along in formula Wallace Beery films as befitted the veteran he was; and he could, when he felt like it, act.

The facts concerning his early life are difficult to sort out, if only because most later studio biographies give his birth date as 1889. But taking an earlier source giving 1886, the following seems the most likely. He was born in Kansas City, Missouri, half-brother to Noah Beery (1884–1946) who went into films not long after he did, and had a more or less parallel career, but without the same fame. Their father was a policeman, and the family, which was numerous, was not well-off. Wallace ran away from home when he was 16 and joined the Ringling Bros. Circus, assisting the man who looked after the elephants. He is supposed to have quit after two years, but he was certainly in New York in 1903 as a chorus boy in the shows of Henry W. Savage – in, among others, 'The Prince of Pilsen'. He had a big role in 'The American Tourist' (04). For the next few years he did stock in the summer, and sang for Savage in the winter; eventually he garnered a small renown playing 'grotesque old woman' parts. He was in Chicago in 1913 and signed with Essanay at $75 a week to act and direct. He steered Ben Turpin through many of his comic cut-ups, and when he himself appeared before the camera it was as a dumb Swedish housemaid – the 'Sweedie' series. Broncho Billy Anderson, one of the founders of Essanay, offered Beery the chance of working for him in California, but this didn't work out and Beery signed with a company planning to make films in Japan; the company went bankrupt before he was due to sail, and he went to Keystone, where he renewed acquaintance with Gloria Swanson – and they were briefly married. He played a variety of comic parts in shorts such as *Teddy at the Throttle* (16) and *Cactus Nell* with Turpin and Chester Conklin. Like most film-makers at that time he worked when and as he could; he reputedly signed a deal to act and direct at Universal in 1916, but was also doing small parts and was in *Patria* (16) at First National, starring Irene Castle, and in Mary Pickford's *The Little American* (17). The first time he made any sort of mark on the filmgoing consciousness was as the Hun who tried to rape Blanche Sweet in *The Unpardonable Sin* (19), and then, at Paramount, he got another break when he replaced his brother in *The Love Burglar*, which starred Wallace Reid and Anna Q. Nilsson. The following list includes only the features in which he appeared: *Life Line* with Jack Holt; *Soldiers of Fortune* with Norman Kerry: *Victory*, from Conrad's novel; *Behind the Door* (20); Tod Browning's *The Virgin of Stamboul*; and *The Mollycoddle*, starring Douglas Fairbanks.

He did *The Round-Up* with Fatty Arbuckle; *The Last of the Mohicans*, directed by Maurice Tourneur, from the novel by J. Fenimore Cooper, with Beery as the wicked Magua; and *The Rookies Return* (21). He was glimpsed briefly in *The Four Horsemen of the Apocalypse* and *The Three Musketeers*; and seen to more advantage in *A Tale of Two Worlds*; *The Golden Snare*, starring Lewis Stone; and *The Last Trail* (22). He supported Lewis Stone again in *The Rosary*; was in *Wild Honey*; *I Am the Law*, starring Alice Lake; *The Man From Hell's River*; *Trouble*; *Alias Julius Caesar* with Charles Ray;

Hurricane's Gal, starring Gertrude Astor; and *The Sage Brush Trail*. He was now established as a useful actor, especially in villainous roles, but it was Fairbanks, he later said, who really gave him his start when he cast him as Richard the Lion Heart in *Robin Hood*. At all events, Beery didn't lack work: *Only a Shop Girl*; *Ridin' Wild*; *The Flame of Life* (23); *Storm Swept* with brother Noah; *I Am the Law*, starring Alice Lake; and *Bava*, starring Estelle Taylor. Beery was in Tod Browning's *Drifting*; Frank Lloyd's *Ashes of Vengeance* with Norma Talmadge; Buster Keaton's *The Three Ages* (23); *The Eternal Struggle* with Barbara la Marr; *Richard the Lion-Hearted*, in the title role (made partly from footage left over from *Robin Hood*); *The Spanish Dancer*, starring Pola Negri and Antonio Moreno; and *The White Tiger*.

He made: *Drums of Jeopardy* (24); Clarence Brown's *The Signal Tower*, starring Virginia Valli; *Unseen Hands*, a study of a total villain, played by himself; *Another Man's Wife* with Lila Lee; Rafael Sabatini's novel *The Sea Hawk*, as a free-booter, starring Milton Sills, the top box-office picture of the year; *The Red Lily*, starring Enid Bennett and Ramon Novarro; *Dynamite Smith* with Charles Ray; and *Let Women Alone* (25) with Wanda Hawley. In February three films with Beery were released: *The Lost World*, as Professor Challoner in this adaptation of Conan Doyle, with its unconvincing monsters; *The Great Divide*, a Western with Conway Tearle and Alice Terry; and *The Devil's Cargo* with William Collier Jr. These were his last as a free-lance: he signed a featured contract with Paramount, and appeared in the following: *Coming Through* with Thomas Meighan (Picturegoer said Beery made 'a glorious ruffian'); *Adventure*; *The Night Club*, starring comedian Raymond Griffith; *In the Name of Love* with Ricardo Cortez; *Rugged Water*; *The Wanderer*, starring William Collier Sr; and *The Pony Express* with Cortez. He was loaned to First National to appear in Colleen Moore's *So Big* and then Paramount teamed him with another actor mainly associated with villainy, Raymond Hatton, for an army comedy, *Behind the Front* (26). It was a wild success, and Beery's activity decreased under the stress of new-found stardom: *Volcano* with Bebe Daniels; James Cruze's *Old Ironsides* with Charles Farrell and Esther Ralston; and *Casey at the Bat* (27) in the title role, with Zazu Pitts. Paramount, meanwhile, were preparing a series of comedies for him and Hatton: *We're in the Navy Now*, probably the best of the series; *Fireman Save My Child*; *Now We're in the Air*; *Wife Savers* (28); *Partners in Crime*; and *The Big Killing*, a satire on Western feuds. But a

Wallace Beery and kids: in The Champ *(31), his Oscar-winning performance with Jackie Cooper, and in* Bad Bascomb *(46) with another MGM tot,*

big killing wasn't made at the box-office: Beery and Hatton suffered both from over-exposure and from the cheapness of the later ones – they did disastrously at the box-office. Paramount lost interest in him, but William A. Wellman gave him a good part – a return to villainy – in *Beggars of Life* with Louise Brooks, and he used him again in *Chinatown Nights* (29), a story of a Tong War with Florence Vidor, made in Silent and Talkie versions. He was in *The Stairs of Sand*, a Zane Grey Western with Phillips Holmes and Jean Arthur, and, way down the cast list, in *River of Romance*.

Paramount were convinced that Beery was not going places with Talkies, and dropped him. MGM were, however, interested: they considered teaming him with Buster Keaton in *Free and Easy*, but instead used him in a part intended for Lon Chaney before he died: *The Big House* (30), as the thug who leads the prison revolt, a thug without a single redeeming feature. Beery's ferocious performance brought raves and a long-term MGM contract; all the same, MGM couldn't have guessed at this point that this ugly character actor would become one of their biggest money-makers over the next 20 years. Real stardom was only a step away. He was P. T. Barnum in *A Lady's Morals* (they were Grace Moore's, as Jenny Lind), and Pat Garret, the implacable foe of *Billy the Kid* (Johnny Mack Brown). Then the studio had the good sense (and good luck for all concerned) to cast him and Marie Dressler as sparring partners, *Min and Bill*: in the era of the Depression, these two old soaks making do and making up were a tonic, and the film hit the astonishing gross of $2 million.

Margaret O'Brien. The lady singing hymns is Marjorie Main, who partnered Beery in a dozen films at the end of his career.

He was put into John Gilbert's *Way for a Sailor* in order to bolster Gilbert at the wickets; he did a strong gangster melo, *The Secret Six* (31) and then *The Champ*, playing his usual role, a dirty rogue: but nothing could shake the devotion to him of boy star Jackie Cooper, and this time Beery had a heart of gold. Under King Vidor's direction he was more lovable than he had been with Dressler. Audiences cried buckets: enough of them to put this one, too, among the year's top grossers. Beery won a Best Actor Oscar (in a tie with Fredric March for *Dr Jekyll and Mr Hyde*) and at the end of 1932, when the film played off, found himself for the first time among the year's top 10 box-office draws. There were some more big ones in the immediate future: a submarine drama, *Hell Divers*; *Grand Hotel* (32), a fine performance as the nasty little financier; and *Flesh*, as a German champion wrestler, with Karen Morley and Ricardo Cortez–which was a flop.

Tugboat Annie (33) was the second–and last–picture he did with Dressler: more sentiment and laughs (his resource in getting liquor, hers in managing the tug), and more good film-making and big box-office. MGM signed Beery to a new starring contract. Dressler was also in *Dinner at Eight*, but this time Beery, as the tough, uncouth tycoon, was concerned only with the carryings-on of his tarty wife, Jean Harlow. He was then loaned to 20th Century, the new production company formed by Darryl F. Zanuck and Joseph M. Schenck, releasing through UA, for their first film, *The Bowery*, with George Raft and again Jackie Cooper; then he had what was probably his best part –and he gave a superb performance–Pancho Villa in *Viva Villa!* (34), a good account of the Mexican Revolution. He was Long John Silver in *Treasure Island*, with Jackie Cooper as his Jim Hawkins in this adaptation of Stevenson, and then he played P. T. Barnum again in 20th's *The Great Barnum*. 1935 was his last year in the top 10 box-office list: *West Point of the Air*, as a sergeant, with Robert Young; *China Seas* with Clark Gable and Harlow; *O'Shaughnessy's Boy*, again with young Cooper; and *Ah Wilderness!*, as the Uncle. He was loaned to 20th again for another Mexican subject, *A Message to Garcia* (36) with Barbara Stanwyck, and was officially 'demoted' from the roster of top MGM films. He increasingly made programmers–'mush and muscle' pictures as they were called: *Old Hutch*, as an incorrigible loafer; *The Good Old Soak* (37); 20th's good, stark melo, *Slave Ship*, co-starring Warner Baxter; *Bad Man of Brimstone* (38) with Virginia Bruce; *Port of Seven Seas* with Frank Morgan, beautifully directed by James Whale; *Stablemates* with Mickey Rooney; *Stand Up and Fight* (39) with Robert Taylor; *Sergeant Madden*; and *Thunder Afloat*, which the Daily Mail (London) thought 'the best performance Wallace Beery has given since *Min and Bill*'. But it was formula Beery stuff: captain of a tugboat who joins the Navy to get revenge on the Germans who sank his boat, resisting discipline under former rival Chester Morris, and becoming a hero after chasing the German subs.

Beery made a surprise reappearance in the top money-making stars in 1940: *The Man From Dakota*, a Western; *Twenty-Mule Team*, paired with Marjorie Rambeau in an attempt to find a partner that might have the same sort of lure as Marie Dressler; and *Wyoming*, where small-part actress, Marjorie Main, was effectively cast as a blacksmith. It was Main who seemed most to fit Dressler's boots; Beery and MGM were delighted, and she was signed to a long-term contract. After he had done *The Bad Man* (41) with Ronald Reagan, they were teamed several times: *Barnacle Bill*, *The Bugle Sounds* (42) and *Jackass Mail*. He was off the screen for a while, returned in *Salute to the Marines* (43), with Fay Bainter as his wife, and then suffered *Rationing* (44) with Main. They were not as popular as Beery and Dressler; Main, a fine character actress, lacked some of Dressler's 'heart'–she was altogether more predictable; but then the scripts were never as good. Main recalled later that she didn't find it easy working with Beery, because he wouldn't rehearse and kept changing his dialogue and business.

He did *Barbary Coast Gent*; *This Man's Navy*

(45) with Tom Drake–it was in fact about airships; *Bad Bascomb* (46) with Main and Margaret O'Brien; *The Mighty McGurk*; and, after a long interval, *Alias a Gentleman* (48). He got out of the dualler slot and into tails for a musical with Jane Powell and Carmen Miranda, *A Date With Judy*. His last picture, *Big Jack* (49), was released posthumously; he died of a heart attack in 1949, just as he was about to start *Johnny Holiday* (William Bendix replaced him). He married Areta Gilman in 1924 and they separated in 1939.

Constance Bennett

Although Constance Bennett specialized at one time in sob-and-sex dramas where she was morally somewhat soiled–usually an unmarried mother–she is remembered best as a glamorous light comedienne. She is in fact remembered extremely well considering that she was a top star only during the early part of a long career. But then she was special in comedy–one of the specialists–with a subtle, worldly-wise approach, never ruffled, always one step ahead. Said Picturegoer of her in 1931, when she was returning to films after an absence: 'Fans raved over her elegance, her perfect manners, her personality. Her voice was intriguing to a degree. It was the last word in sophistication.'

She was born in 1905 in New York City, into a theatrical family; her father was Richard Bennett, a well-known stage actor and later a supporting player in movies (he appeared in Connie's *Bought*). There were two younger sisters, Barbara, who had a short career in movies starting as a child, and Joan, who became as famous as Constance. Because father Bennett was directing movies around 1921, Constance was seen around movie sets and got parts in three minor pictures: *Reckless Youth* (22), *Evidence* and *What's Wrong With Women?*, but her career didn't get started for another two years, when she met Goldwyn socially and he suggested a screen test. As a result he starred her in *Cytherea* (24) with Lewis Stone: she played a movie star in this melodrama noted more for its two two-colour sequences than for the coherence of its plot (from a novel by Joseph Hergesheimer; it was Goldwyn's third independent production). Next she did a Pathé serial, *Into the Net* (also released as a feature), followed by a quickie that got few bookings, *Married?*, as a wild flapper succumbing to calm Owen Moore.

It was *The Goose Hangs High* (25), directed by James Cruze–a funny small-town piece about a flapper daughter (Bennett)–which

Constance Bennett had established herself as a comedienne in the Silent era, but her early Talkies were maudlin melodramas, often with Joel McCrea. Like Born to Love *(31).*

first attracted attention to her, and the next made her a star: *Code of the West* as a flirtatious flapper being tamed again by cowboy Owen Moore. There followed *My Son* (from Martha Stanley's hit play) and the son was Nazimova's–Jack Pickford, being tempted by Bennett. In *My Wife and I* she stole Irene Rich's husband, and in Clarence Brown's *The Goose Woman* was involved with Pickford again –a fine film about a has-been opera-singer (Louise Dresser) who entangles her son in a murder for the sake of publicity. MGM cast her, Joan Crawford and Sally O'Neill as *Sally Irene and Mary*, and liked her well enough to offer a long-term contract; in the meantime she did two indies, *Wandering Fires* and *The Pinch Hitter* (26). Instead of reporting to Metro, she asked for an annulment of the contract. As a contemporary report put it: 'About this time she eloped with a young millionaire, Philip Plant, and gave up film work. She lived mostly abroad. Obtained a divorce and subsequently returned to the screen.'

But she did not return to MGM, who had first call on her services: she signed with Pathé, doubtless due to the influence of one of their executives, the Marquis de la Falaise, soon to be Gloria Swanson's ex- and Bennett's next husband. The contract stipulated three months' vacation: said she, 'Hollywood is pretty painful even in small quantities.' Her comeback film was a hit comedy with Edmund Lowe, *This Thing*

Constance Bennett and millionaire Wilfred Lawson in Ladies in Love *(36), the first flowering of 20th Century-Fox's perennial about three girls in search of wealthy husbands.*

Called Love (29), a Talkie. She was borrowed by WB for *Son of the Gods* (30), and promptly stole it from co-star Richard Barthelmess; was in *Rich People* with Regis Toomey, discovering that wealth was a bar to happiness; and MGM's *Common Clay*, as the housemaid seduced by the son of the house (Lew Ayres) and battling in the courts for their bastard. This, one of the year's most popular films, led to a run of similar parts – though thereafter she was more ambitious: her sinning was done strictly in the cause of luxury. First there was a melo with Erich Von Stroheim, *Three Faces East*; a comedy with Kenneth MacKenna, *Sin Takes a Holiday* – he paid her a salary to marry him and thus avoided being named in a divorce scandal; then *The Easiest Way* (31) – she took it; *Born to Love* – Joel McCrea, the first of several teamings, this time as the mother of his son in an artificial war romance; *The Common Law*, as a kept woman in love with McCrea; and *Bought* – she was illegitimate herself this time. Ben Lyon was in it, and they were re-teamed in a comedy, *Lady With a Past* (32) – called *Reputation* in Britain, and very good for hers, too ('Connie Bennett as a real person this time,' said Photoplay). *What Price Hollywood?* was a comedy-melo about a Brown Derby waitress who becomes a big star and marries another (Neil Hamilton): *A Star Is Born* later borrowed much of this, though here the drunk was a director (Lowell Sherman) and it was her understanding of his problem which provided the climax – break-up of marriage and flight from stardom. A brilliant film by any standards, directed by George Cukor, and possibly Bennett's best performance.

These were her peak years. In 1931 she was second only to Garbo in a poll of US exhibitors and in 1932 she was second to Norma Shearer in a poll of British cinemagoers (the Bernstein questionnaire). Her salary reflected this: agent Myron Selznick had got $30,000 a week for her for *Bought* at WB – the highest salary paid up to that time – in what was ostensibly her vacation. When she returned to WB for *Two Against the World* (Hamilton was an attorney in love with her despite her unsavoury past) her salary again broke records: $150,000 for four and a half weeks' work. The money was some consolation for not getting Jo in *Little Women*, which went to Pathé/RKO's new star, Katharine Hepburn, but the studio did let her have her way over *Rockabye*, a project they weren't keen on. She played a stage-star, again in love with McCrea. Cukor directed it and the next, *Our Betters* (33), a static version of the Maugham play. Both were conspicuous flops. In *Bed of Roses* (with McCrea) she was a hooker working the Mississippi, and in *After Tonight* a Russian spy: co-star was Gilbert Roland, upped from a minor role in *Our Betters* (as a kept man) and later in life her husband.

Her contract expired, and Pathé weren't anxious to renew. Bennett signed a new long-term deal with 20th, but there were only two films, *Moulin Rouge* (34) with Franchot Tone, and *The Affairs of Cellini*, a good film in which she was superb – but it was stolen from her and Fredric March by Frank Morgan. She moved on to MGM on a three-year contract but, again, there were only two films: *Outcast Lady*, another – poor – version of 'The Green Hat', originally intended for Norma Shearer, and *After Office Hours* (35), a comedy with Clark Gable. Publicity still referred to her as 'the highest paid actress in the world', but after three years of mainly conveyor-belt films her popularity had gone and Hollywood was unwilling to pay. After a year of inactivity she went to Britain to make *Everything Is Thunder* (36), playing a Berlin whore ('on a note of concentrated sweetness and light' – Picturegoer) who helps an escaped p.o.w. (Douglass Montgomery). It was an unhappy experience, and she returned to Hollywood no longer a big star.

Twentieth asked her to play in the multi-star *Ladies in Love*, but alas she lost millionaire Paul Lukas to precocious Simone Simon; then Hal Roach offered her a contract and the two films for which she is best remembered: *Topper* (37), in which she and Cary Grant were ghosts, and, even funnier, *Merrily We Live* (38), a variation on *My Man Godfrey*, with Brian Aherne. She did a weak comedy at Universal, *Service de Luxe*, and then the last under her Roach contract, *Topper Takes a Trip* (39). In 20th's *Tailspin*, a silly film about women flyers, she was billed below Alice Faye. She did a couple of duallers, *Escape to Glory* (40) with Pat O'Brien, and at Warners (for a fee of $10,000), *Law of the Tropics* (41), a re-make of *Oil for the Lamps of China*; and got below-the-title billing in *Two-Faced Woman* – Garbo was in it and there were critics who thought Bennett outshone her. After three Bs, *Wild Bill Hickok Rides* (42), *Sin Town* (a part intended for Mae West) and *Madame Spy*, Bennett did more war-work (from the beginning of the war in Europe she had worked tirelessly for refugees) and toured in 'Without Love' by Philip Barry. She went into fashion and cosmetics and had a radio show.

Under UA's auspices, she produced herself and Gracie Fields in *Paris Underground* (46): a neat little picture, but the public were long since tired of Resistance dramas. The same year she played a glamorous aunt in 20th's *Centennial Summer*, with Jeanne Crain as her niece (and Dorothy Gish as her sister), and Claude Rains's sidekick in *The Unsuspected* (47). The next were Bs: *Smart Woman* (48) at Monogram, with Brian Aherne and *Angel on the Amazon* (49) at Republic, with George Brent. But *As Young As You Feel* (51) gave her a good part alongside Marilyn Monroe, David Wayne and others. In the 50s she appeared on TV, did a brief bit as herself in *It Should Happen to You* (54), had a night-club act for a while and toured in 'Auntie Mame' (58). She toured briefly in 'Toys in the Attic' (61) and did a good featured part in *Madame X* (65) as Lana Turner's mother. Not long before, a fan magazine had written: 'Temperament plus a rather hectic personal life were responsible for hampering her professional success', but the truth was rather that she was too intelligent and independent to play the game except her way. Not long afterwards (1965) she died of a cerebral haemorrhage; her fifth husband was with her.

Joan Bennett

Joan Bennett was always glamorous and capable, the epitome of the film-star. It has been a standard Hollywood story: fresh blonde newcomer and then star – with jet black hair ('Let's talk of Lamarr, that Hedy so fair / Is it true that Joan Bennett wears all her old hair?' ran a lyric in a New York revue), impeccable professional reputation as she aged and the inevitable decline set in; three marriages, one scandal. In Bennett's case, no apparent pretensions: workmanlike – from her days as a demure and distinctly dewy-eyed heroine, a more virginal edition of her elder sister, Constance, to her emergence, especially under the direction of Fritz Lang, as one of the more memorable of the species *femme fatale*.

She was born in Palisades, NJ, in 1910 and expensively educated – there was a finishing school in Versailles. At 16 she ran away with the son of a millionaire and at 17 was a mother (later, of course, she became 'Hollywood's youngest and most beautiful grandmother'). The marriage didn't last and she was briefly a Hollywood extra in *The Divine Lady* (28), before getting a small part in *Power*; then her father, actor Richard Bennett, engaged her to support him at the Longacre, New York, in 'Jarnegan' by Jim Tully. They were an acting family, and, above all, Father wished Joan to have the same screen success as Connie. She appeared again in New York in 'The Pirate' in a small role and then left for Hollywood. Father had talked around, and Joan was tested by Goldwyn – and given a role in his *Bulldog Drummond* (29) with Ronald Colman. It was not an outstanding debut, but she had no difficulty getting work: *Three Live Ghosts*; *Disraeli*; *The Mississippi Gambler* (Universal) with Joseph Schildkraut (more or less a reprise of his part in *Show Boat*); *Puttin' on the*

Joan Bennett as a blonde: the winsome heroine of The Pursuit of Happiness *(34) with Francis Lederer.*

Joan Bennett as a brunette: the tramp known as Lazy-Legs in Scarlet Street *(46) with Dan Duryea.*

Ritz (30) at UA, a backstage drama with Harry Richman; *Crazy That Way* at Fox as a girl with three suitors, including Kenneth MacKenna; John Barrymore's *Moby Dick*, where, clearly, she was an interpolation; and *Maybe It's Love* with Joe E. Brown and the All-American Football Team. She played leads, and being Connie's sister was not detrimental.

UA planned to star her in a new version of *Smilin' Through*, but MGM had their eyes on that property for Norma Shearer. Bennett instead signed a two-year contract with Fox: *Scotland Yard* with Edmund Lowe; *Doctors' Wives* (31), as one of them, neglected by Warner Baxter; *Hush Money*, as mistress of racketeer Owen Moore; *Many a Slip* at Universal with Lew Ayres – 'another of the "unwanted baby" type of picture' said Picturegoer; *She Wanted a Millionaire* (32) – which she got, wishing she'd stuck with Spencer Tracy; *Careless Lady*, as a small-town girl who gets sophistication, with John Boles; *The Trial of Vivienne Ware* with Donald Cook; and *Weekends Only* with Ben Lyon. She was off the screen several months due to a riding accident, then returned with *Wild Girl*, a pioneer drama with Charles Farrell and Ralph Bellamy; *Me and My Gal*, wisecracking with Tracy (the Motion Picture Herald thought her 'a sheer delight'); and *Arizona to Broadway* (33), a gangster burlesque with James Dunn. At this point, Fox dropped her because – they now decided – she was not yet ready for stardom. She announced that she was going to free-lance and after some months got a smaller part than she was used to, but in a good film for once, *Little Women* (34). This brought her to the attention of independent producer Walter Wanger, who signed her, which meant that he loaned her around, usually to his distributing company, Paramount, for whom she did an engaging comedy about the American Revolution, called appropriately *The Pursuit of Happiness*. She was in *The Man Who Reclaimed His Head* (35) at Universal with Claude Rains and was sung to twice by Bing Crosby, in *Mississippi* and *Two for Tonight*; in between whiles, she supported (not very well) Claudette Colbert and Charles Boyer in *Private Worlds*.

There was a comedy with George Raft, *She Couldn't Take It* (she was excellent), and then one with Ronald Colman, *The Man Who Broke the Bank at Monte Carlo*; and some programmers – *Thirteen Hours by Air* (36) with Fred MacMurray, *Big Brown Eyes* with Cary Grant, *Two in a Crowd*, a racetrack comedy with Joel McCrea, and *Wedding Present*, again with Grant. Wanger now had made a new distributing arrangement with UA, and he began putting Bennett in his own films – *Vogues of 1938* (37), which had Warner Baxter, colour, lots of fashion parades and very little else; *I Met My Love*

Again (38), a poor romantic drama with Henry Fonda; *The Texans* at Paramount with Randolph Scott ('They faced a thousand frontier terrors for love'); and *Trade Winds*, where detective Fredric March chased her round the world, only to fall in love with her. She wore a black wig, and it was the start of the new, more interesting Bennett. The now-brunette Bennett marked time in *Artists and Models Abroad* with Jack Benny, and in *The Man in the Iron Mask* for Edward Small-UA. Louis Hayward had the dual-title role – at this time he was thought to be going places – and later Small re-teamed them in another adaptation of Dumas, *Son of Monte Cristo* (40). For UA-Hal Roach she did the amusing *The Housekeeper's Daughter* (39) with Adolphe Menjou and for Universal *Green Hell* (40) with Douglas Fairbanks Jr.

She was now divorced from second husband, writer Gene Markey, and Wanger celebrated the event by casting her in *The House Across the Bay*. Fritz Lang directed, and George Raft and Walter Pidgeon co-starred – a good thriller. Bennett and Wanger were married in 1941, but she was free of her contract and signed with both Columbia and 20th, the latter calling for two pics a year; these were middle-budgeters, and some went out as Bs. The first of this batch was the most interesting, *The Man I Married*, who was Francis Lederer, a German-American; Bennett watches him fall under the spell of Nazidom on a visit to Germany, and the film emerged as strong anti-Nazi propaganda. There was a brief return to escapism with the *Monte Cristo* picture; then *She Knew All the Answers* (41) and Franchot Tone asked all the questions, after which she did another anti-Nazi piece, Fritz Lang's thriller, *Man Hunt*, playing a Cockney tart (not stated, but she wore the regulation mac and beret): it could not be said that she was remotely convincing, but it was a gallant try. The others: *Wild Geese Calling* with Fonda, *Confirm or Deny* with Don Ameche, *Twin Beds* (42) at UA with George Brent, *The Wife Takes a Flyer* at Columbia with Tone, *Girl Trouble* again with Ameche, and *Margin for Error* (43), a pre-TV attempt to make a screen star out of Milton Berle, as a New York Jew involved with pre-war German Consul Otto Preminger (who also directed).

The Bennett career was diminuendo when after nearly a two-year gap Fritz Lang cast her as *The Woman in the Window* (44), the pretty girl with whom Professor Edward G. Robinson gets involved. How guilty is she? This was a version of the treacherous Mary Astor character of *The Maltese Falcon*, and a staple of the 40s. Bennett was one of the best. She moved up in the social scale, to *Nob Hill* (45), enticing George Raft from saloon singer Vivian Blaine. *Colonel Effingham's Raid* (46), with Charles Coburn, was a B, but then Bennett was reunited with Lang, Robinson and Dan Duryea again for *Scarlet Street*; her floozie this time was much less equivocal. She was satanic again in *The Macomber Affair* (47), cuckolding Robert Preston with Gregory Peck, and up to the same tricks in Lang's *Woman on the Beach*, deceiving Charles Bickford with Robert Ryan. The film, however, was preposterous, and so was Jean Renoir's *The Secret Beyond the Door* (48) with Michael Redgrave. After *The Scar* she worked under a third fine European director coincidentally below his best, Max Ophuls: *The Reckless Moment* (49) with James Mason. But all three films were more interesting than most she made – certainly more than *The Scar*, a silly film with Paul Henried as a gangster at Eagle-Lion (the company part-owned by the British Rank Organization).

In 1948 (and 1951) Bennett toured in 'Susan and God'; in films she suddenly became middle-aged, married to Robert Cummings in a dire whimsical comedy, *For Heaven's Sake* (50) and better, but older, to Spencer Tracy for *Father of the Bride* and *Father's Little Dividend* (51). She made *The Guy Who Came Back* with Paul Douglas; and also in 1951 her husband, Wanger, took a pot-shot at her agent, Jennings Lang, when he was talking to her in a parking lot. Wanger admitted jealousy, but no allegations were made other than that Bennett preferred Lang's professional advice to Wanger's. Wanger was convicted, and served a short jail sentence; he and Bennett were reconciled in 1953 when he was released (and remained married until he died in 1968).

In 1953 she toured in 'Bell Book and Candle'. Her subsequent few films do not indicate much good advice on the part of any agent: *Highway Dragnet* (54) for Allied Artists with Richard Conte; Humphrey Bogart's *We're No Angels* (55), which was a good film, but Bennett had only featured billing and a small part as the shop proprietor's wife; *There's Always Tomorrow* (56), a sudser co-starring two others who had seen better days, Barbara Stanwyck and Fred MacMurray; *Navy Wife* with Gary Merrill; and *Desire in the Dust* (60), a well-named Southern drama co-starring Raymond Burr. She did some TV, and worked in the theatre; apart from 'Love Me Little' in 1958, in New York, she was content to tour: 'Best Foot Forward', 'Anniversary Waltz', 'Janus', 'Once More With Feeling', 'The Pleasure of His

Company' and 'Never Too Late'. In the latter she made her London stage début (63) but the play got dreadful notices. In 1968 she began in a TV series, 'Dark Shadows', and she made a film of it (70).

Jack Benny

It is part of Jack Benny's routine that he was a flop in pictures: which is not the case. He wasn't an outstanding success, either, certainly not in the same class as his friend and rival Bob Hope. Their styles were much alike. Benny was cowardly, inept, boastful and, of course, mean. In one thing Benny is/was right: *The Horn Blows at Midnight* was a horrendous film and certified box-office loser.

Benny (Benny Kubelsky) was born in 1894 in Waukegan, Illinois. On leaving school he worked in his father's haberdashery, and played the violin in the local theatre band. He served four years with the Navy during World War I, and it was while trying to decide whether to play classical music to his fellow gobs at a concert that his 'act' was born. After the war he went into vaudeville (and flopped on his first two dates in New York City). His act was caught by Harry Rapf of MGM and he was signed to a long-term contract, two pictures a year at $1,500 a week. Talkies had just come in and Benny was basically a stand-up (talk) comedian. They put him into *The Hollywood Revue of 1929* (29) in a sketch, and *Chasing Rainbows* (30), as the stage manager. Due to his film success he was a smash hit at the London Palladium, and he also had a success in 'The Earl Carroll Vanities' (30) in New York. MGM, on the other hand, had no plans for him and Benny asked for his release. His film career thereafter was distinctly chequered. He was *The Medicine Man* with Betty Bronson for Tiffany; there was a Vitaphone short, *Bright Moments*, and another called *The Song-Writers Revue*, released by Metro-Movietone; and *Mr Broadway* (33), released by the Broadway-

Jack Benny and all-star co-stars. The line-up is from Chasing Rainbows *(30) and includes Benny (third from left), Bessie Love, Eddie Phillips, George K. Arthur, Marie Dressler and Polly Moran. One of the musicals MGM made to cash in on the success of* Broadway Melody.

Hollywood Co. But his great success and fame came with radio: on CBS in the 30s with his wife Mary Livingstone and stalwarts such as Eddie 'Rochester' Anderson.

Encouraged by his national following, UA (Edward Small) put him in *Transatlantic Merry-Go-Round* (35), a melodrama with music, Nancy Carroll and Mitzi Green. And MGM signed him again: *Broadway Melody of 1936* (35), and *It's in the Air*, with Una Merkel, in which he's seeking to find a way to avoid paying taxes. Then Metro let him go again. Paramount tried, and had more success: *The Big Broadcast of 1937* (36), *College Holiday* (37) with radio colleagues and personal friends Burns and Allen, *Artists and Models* and *Artists and Models Abroad* (39). The latter was the first of a new Paramount contract, calling for two films a year at $100,000 each. *Man About Town* was a moderate success, but both *Buck Benny Rides Again* (40) and *Love Thy Neighbour* were big hits, and Benny was riding high as a screen star, in Britain as well as the US. He was much too old for *Charley's Aunt* (41), at 20th, but he is an ingratiating actor and thus one believed in him as an undergraduate (just as, for his sake, when he protests against his reputation for meanness, one tries – hard – to believe him). The film anyway was great fun and included some unusual examples of Benny doing visual gags. As a result of its success, 20th announced that Benny was contracted to do three pictures over the next four years.

At UA he co-starred with Carole Lombard in *To Be or Not To Be* (42), easily his best film: 'Jack Benny's sublimely egotistical actor is a beautiful low-key comedy performance,' said Peter Barnes in 1968. He had another good one that year, at Warners, *George Washington Slept Here*, with Ann Sheridan. But the only other film he made for 20th was a 57-minute effort with Priscilla Lane and Rochester, *The Meanest Man in the World* (43) – and considering this script, also the most unfortunate. But that was nothing: *The Horn Blows at Midnight* (45) was next, a whimsy that began in heaven but was hellish in every respect. WB had let him fiddle a bit and give some indication of his vaude act, as himself in *Hollywood Canteen* (44), but it was too slight a bit to compensate. Benny had also guest-starred in one marvellous sequence in *It's in the Bag* (45), starring a comedian even more rarely in films (and another friend and radio favourite), the great Fred Allen. Benny's subsequent film appearances were merely in guest spots unbilled, such as *Somebody Loves Me* (53) and *The Seven Little Foys* (55). Instead of worrying about films, he went on to conquer TV. His last guest appearance was in *A Guide for the Married Man* (67).

Ingrid Bergman

'Say,' went a joke in New York in 1945, 'today I saw a picture without Ingrid Bergman in it.' *Saratoga Trunk*, *The Bells of St Mary's* and *Spellbound* were playing simultaneously and the point is that *everyone* was going to see them. She was the uncrowned Queen of Hollywood, on a tide of popularity that looked like rolling on forever. Then came the most unexpected scandal in Hollywood's history, and banishment.

Few stars had evoked such praise and fervent admiration: since she had arrived from Sweden in 1939 Bergman represented ideal womanhood to millions of Americans; she was so much more attainable than her great compatriot, Garbo, that comparisons were rarely made. Like Garbo, she was born in Stockholm. In 1915. Her mother died when she was two; her father when she was 12, and the spinster aunt who had raised her died a few months later. She went to live with an uncle, and with her inheritance, later, studied at the Royal Dramatic Theatre in Stockholm. In 1934 she went into films, with the encouragement of Dr Peter Lindstrom, who became her husband in 1937. In her first film, *Munkbrogreven* (34) she was a hotel maid, and she had small parts in *Bränninger* and *Valborgsmässaoaften* (35). The latter starred Lars Hansen, and after a lead in *Dollar*, she was co-starred with him in two consecutive pictures, *Pa Solsidan* and *Swedenhielms* (36). *Intermezzo* followed, a romantic drama directed by Gustaf Molander about a famous violinist (Gosta Ekman) and his adulterous affair with a young pianist (Bergman). Molander had already directed her twice, and he directed her again in *En Enda Natt* and *En Kvinnas Ansikte* (37), remade by MGM as *A Woman's Face*. Bergman went to Germany for *Die Vier Gesellen* in 1937; her other Swedish films: *Med Livet Sominats* and *Juninatten*.

A print of *Intermezzo* found its way to New York and was seen by Katharine Brown, Selznick's story-buyer. She recommended this one, along with Bergman, but Selznick wasn't impressed with Bergman and took her only because Brown insisted that her qualities were essential to the film. He signed her for seven years, just in case, and when the film – *Intermezzo A Love Story* (39) with Leslie Howard as the violinist – came out he exercised his option and recalled her from Sweden. Hollywood had never

Ingrid Bergman and Leslie Howard in Intermezzo: A Love Story *(39), re-titled in Britain* Escape to Happiness, *suggesting somewhat its seven-year-itch theme–on which it was a very romantic variation.*

seen anything like her, and much publicity accrued from her naturalness, her lack of both sophistication and make-up (Joan Fontaine has recalled that she and Vivien Leigh were then chastised by Selznick for using lipstick). Picturegoer said: 'She is intelligent, natural and wholly charming without being beautiful'–the reservation was one which no one else shared. Bergman *was* different from the standard Hollywood star: there was about her a curious, unique freshness. Possibly it was specifically Nordic–a combination of directness/gentleness/good health/sex (it made plausible and even palatable *Intermezzo*'s thesis on marital infidelity).

Selznick, however, had no immediate plans for her, so he let her do 'Liliom' on Broadway, and then loaned her out for a couple of strong dramas: *Adam Had Four Sons* (41), as a governess in love with her charge's father (Warner Baxter), and *Rage in Heaven*, as the unfortunate wife of Robert Montgomery, at MGM. MGM then offered her the ingénue in *Dr Jekyll and Mr Hyde*, but she begged to be allowed to play the floozie, swopping parts with Lana Turner. Her performance was only partially successful, but The New York Times (Theodore Strauss) said it proved again that 'a shining talent' could make something of a poor part–in contrast to Turner and the rest of the supporting cast, who moved 'like well-behaved puppets'. She sought the role of Maria in *For Whom the Bell Tolls*, but even with Hemingway's blessing Paramount turned her down–in favour of Vera Zorina, and Bergman went to Warners who were desperate for a continental heroine after Hedy Lamarr had turned them down. The film was *Casablanca* (42) and Humphrey Bogart was the star; they were memorable together, the film was a solid-gold hit, and it made Bergman a sure box-office draw. That fact, coupled with the rushes of Zorina non-emoting in *For Whom the Bell Tolls* (43) caused Paramount to beg Bergman to take over the part. Her love scenes ('Did you not feel the earth moving?') with Gary Cooper were beautiful, though she was an unlikely Spanish peasant. Still, as James Agee wrote: 'Miss Bergman not only bears a startling resemblance to an imaginable human being; she really knows how to act, in a blend of poetic grace with quiet realism which almost never appears in American pictures.'

Bergman as saint and sinner: as saint in The Bells of St Mary's *(45) and* Joan of Arc *(48) and as sinner in* Arch of Triumph *(48, with cigarette) and* Saratoga Trunk *(44). There is no question that audiences preferred her as a good woman.*

The Bergman fervour was on, and all studios scrambled to employ her; and, though it wasn't foreseen at the time, this was the beginning of the end for the star-contract system. Selznick owned her, but she was available for loan – and was a better box-office proposition than almost any other female star you could name. However, neither of the next two was originally intended for her: *Gaslight* (44) had been bought by Columbia for Irene Dunne and then sold to MGM who wanted it for Hedy Lamarr. Either might have done as well as the frightened wife (of Charles Boyer), but nothing could prevent Bergman getting the 1944 Best Actress Oscar for her performance. At Warners, *Saratoga Trunk* had been turned down probably by Bette Davis and certainly by Vivien Leigh: either would have been better than Bergman as a creole adventuress chasing Gary Cooper. Release was delayed until just after the next two. Selznick himself produced *Spellbound* (45), Hitchcock directed and Gregory Peck co-starred: Bergman was a psychiatrist and the New York Critics thought hers the Year's Best Female Performance. The other was at RKO as a nun opposite Bing Crosby's priest: *The Bells of St Mary's* and Selznick got $175,000 for her services plus the rights to two properties – *Little Women* and *A Bill of Divorcement* – reckoned to be worth another $50,000. Bergman herself got less than $40,000. Selznick and Hitchcock were responsible for *Notorious* (46) with Cary Grant. She was once more unconvincingly cast, as a lady prone to alcohol and casual affairs. Selznick, in fact, sold the film to RKO for $800,000 and half the profits. It was her fourth consecutive box-office smash, and in 1946 she was the biggest female attraction in the US (she was also in the top 10 in 1947 and 1948). No one could have guessed that *Notorious* would be her last successful movie for 10 years.

Her contract was up and Selznick offered another, for seven years, with favourable terms (it carried with it *The Farmer's Daughter* and *To Each His Own*, both of which earned Oscars for their eventual stars). Bergman's husband vetoed the idea and she free-lanced. As a change of pace she played a prostitute in Milestone's version of Erich Maria Remarque's *Arch of Triumph* (48), with Boyer and Charles Laughton, but the public didn't want to see their beloved Bergman in such a part (its failure doomed Enterprise Productions, the new studio which had produced it). She went back to being good, in *Joan of Arc*, a heroine on whom she was fixated – indeed, she had played the part on

Bergman with one of her favourite co-stars, Cary Grant, in Stanley Donen's Indiscreet *(57), based on Norman Krasna's Broadway comedy, 'Kind Sir'. She played an actress, he an American diplomat and the film delightfully detailed their bumpy romance.*

Broadway the previous year and had been voted the year's Best Actress by theatre critics. The film was based on the play ('Joan of Lorraine' by Maxwell Anderson), but this time there were no laurels flying about; the press loathed it, and although it didn't do badly at the box-office, it failed to recover its costs (and also perhaps hastened the death of its director, Victor Fleming). *Under Capricorn* (49) found Bergman in the Australia of 100 years ago, an Irish dipsomaniac; neither she nor director Hitchcock seemed happy with their material and no one flocked to see it.

The truth was–and it was just beginning to dawn on people–that Bergman's ambitions far outweighed her talent. She was beautiful and bewitching and patently sincere in everything she did, she had a radiance which was special to her; but time and again her resources failed her and she was forced back on the same old gestures. There were hundreds of Hollywood actresses more limited, but they did not try to play *everything*. She was unbelievable as a bad woman, but that was a role that she was about to be cast in, by the press and vast sections of the public because of her private life.

The furore now seems incredible–the acres of newsprint used, the amount of indignation (mostly on the part of the American women's clubs) expended (cf the relatively minor fuss made over Vanessa Redgrave or Mia Farrow, in similar circumstances, but 20 years later). What happened was that Bergman fell in love with Italian film director Roberto Rossellini. She had seen his *Open City* and, like everyone else at that time, had been impressed. Seeking a refuge from the standardized Hollywood product, she begged him to let her work with him and as they began locations in Italy for *Stromboli* (50) he began to woo her; when the film was over, she gave birth to his baby. As Jean Renoir said, she is 'so honest that she will always prefer a scandal to a lie'. Facing a barrage of world-wide criticism, she claimed that her marriage had been over for years and as soon as it was possible, she and Rossellini were married; but the public–particularly the American public–were not about to forgive her. *Stromboli* was banned or ostracized, and although its news value did attract some spectators it was not a very good film and soon faded into semi-oblivion.

In 1952 Rossellini directed her in *Europa '51* with Alexander Knox, an ambitious allegory in which she takes the troubles of the world on her shoulders. Seen today, it is far from negligible, but at the time it got few bookings outside Italy. The next four marked a serious decline: an episode in *Siamo Donne* with a quarrelsome chicken; *Viaggio in Italia* (53), a muddled marital drama with George Sanders; *Jeanne au Bucher*, a static film version of the Honegger concert-piece that she and Rossellini had carted round European capitals; and *Angst* (54), a melodrama made in Germany. None of them were at all successful, and it was also clear to Bergman that her marriage was working out as badly as their professional collaboration.

They were bankrupt, and her confidence as an artist had completely gone. Luckily, Renoir had something planned for her; he felt that no film had quite captured her gaiety and designed *Elena et les Hommes* (56) to showcase it. In the event, it did little else and was too slight and wayward to do much on its few US showings (as *Paris Does Strange Things*). While she was making it, Hollywood, in the form of 20th, said 'Come home all is forgiven', offering her $200,000 and the title role of *Anastasia* (57), from a successful play about the pretender to the Czarist fortune. She made it in Britain and returned to Paris, to do 'Tea and Sympathy' on the stage. *Anastasia* opened and Bergman was welcomed back everywhere with great enthusiasm. She won a second Oscar and a second New York Critics Award, tokens of appreciation for herself rather than for her performance.

In Britain, she made two more films for American companies: *Indiscreet*, with Cary Grant, one of the friends who had loyally stood by her in bad times; and *The Inn of the Sixth Happiness* (58), a touching story of a Chinese missionary. After that, none of the announced projects worked out, and she was off the screen until 1961 when she starred in the film of Françoise Sagan's *Aimez-Vous Brahms?* ('Brahms, oui' went the text of one French review). Again she was unsuitably cast, as a forty-year-old woman afraid of losing looks, husband and lover. Said Playboy: '[She] walks away with honours for The Old Bag We'd Most Like to Be Saddled With.' A nebulous English title–*Goodbye Again*–and draggy playing by Yves Montand and Anthony Perkins served the piece ill; but *The Visit* (64) attracted even fewer audiences, and after a disastrous reception 20th gave it a severely limited release. From a play by Dürrenmatt which the Lunts had done on London and Broadway, it was one of those international co-productions with staff literally from all countries and the result partially dubbed. Ironically, as the vengeful, vicious millionairess, Bergman was for the first time convincing in an unsympathetic part; but she was ludicrous for most of her episode of *The Yellow Rolls Royce* (65), as a bad-tempered American tourist converted to love and charity by Yugoslav peasant Omar Sharif. It was a dire film but presumably because of its 10 stars a big hit. She did another episode film, *Stimulantia* (67): her episode was directed by Molander (and the others by Ingmar Bergman, Jörn Donner and Vilgot Sjöman). It doesn't seem to have been shown outside Sweden.

It seems likely that her further absence from the screen was involuntary: in interviews she has said that she is as ambitious as she ever was, and several projects have been announced only to fizzle out. She has done a certain amount of prestige TV work–'Hedda Gabler', 'The Human Voice', etc.; and has appeared on the stage: as Hedda, in Paris in 1963; in Britain in 'A Month in the Country' (65) and in the US in Eugene O'Neill's 'More Stately Mansions'. In that she scored a gigantic personal success, underlining her position as one of the lode-stars of the business; as a result Columbia signed her to a two-picture deal: a film version of a stage success, *Cactus Flower* (69) with Walter Matthau (billed over her except on the Continent) and the marvellous Goldie Hawn, and *A Walk in the Spring Rain* (70), a *Brief Encounter*-type story with Anthony Quinn. The former was a huge personal success for her and became a hit everywhere, but the other wasn't and didn't.

It was more than 20 years since she had filmed in Hollywood. She lives in France with third husband, theatrical impresario Lars Schmidt.

Elizabeth Bergner

Her fans compared her with Garbo. C. B. Cochran proclaimed her 'the greatest actress in the world' and many critics agreed–but then such has been the happy lot of several middle-European actresses. In films, Elizabeth Bergner, with her pixie features and gurgling infectious laughter, was pure dirndl.

She was born in Vienna in 1900, and studied at the Convervatoire from 1915 to 1919. She made her stage début in Zurich, and there played Ophelia and Rosalind, a part she soon was playing in Vienna. She played in Munich and Berlin, achieving a mighty reputation in the German-speaking countries, especially in classic plays. Among her parts: Viola, Katherine ('The Shrew'), Nora in 'A Doll's House', Marguerite Gautier, Hannele, St Joan (Shaw's), Miss

Elizabeth Bergner in As You Like It *(36), directed by her husband, Paul Czinner, in Britain.*

Julie, Portia – and 'The Last of Mrs Cheyney', Tessa in 'The Constant Nymph' and Nina in 'Strange Interlude'. She made her first film: *Der Evangeliman* (23) and loathed it. But director Paul Czinner persuaded her to make others: *NJU* (24), *Der Geiger von Florenz* (26), masquerading as a boy, *Liebe* (27), *Dona Juana* (28), *Fraulein Else* (29) with Albert Basserman and *Traümunde Munde* (31). In 1928 she toured Holland, Denmark, Sweden, Germany and Austria in a variety of plays, and her fame was by now international. In 1930 under Max Reinhardt she was Juliet to Francis Lederer's Romeo; in 1931 she married Czinner and did 'Amphytrion 38': but with the advent of the Nazis, she and her husband quit Vienna. In France they made *Ariane* (32), and also an English language version, *The Loves of Ariane*, with Percy Marmont as the older man who falls in love with her – but that, like the earlier *NJU*, had trouble with the British censor. (It was remade as *Love in the Afternoon*.)

There was considerable interest in the show biz world when it was announced that Korda had signed Bergner to a long-term contract: he later tried to flog it to Paramount in a deal which required them to finance the uncompleted *The Private Life of Henry VIII* – the money had run out, but Paramount was interested in neither *Henry* nor Elizabeth. In the event, Bergner made only one film for Korda, *Catherine the Great* (33), and she was, if anything, even less convincing than Dietrich in her concurrent version (and the film itself was inferior). She made her stage bow in London in Margaret Kennedy's 'Escape Me Never' (33), a trite and artificial tale about a waif's devotion to a heel: it ran almost a year and in 1935 duplicated its success in New York. Her husband directed her in a British film version for which she was reported to get a fee of £20,000. She won the Picturegoer Gold Medal, and in the US Photoplay described the film as 'lighted by the magic of Elizabeth Bergner's divine acting'. Flushed with this triumph, Bergner and Czinner got 20th to back their pretty-pretty version of *As You Like It* (36), usually referred to as 'Elizabeth and Her German Garden'. One of the kindest reviews of her Rosalind was Sydney W. Carroll's in the Sunday Express (London): 'It is too nervous, too restless.... There is too much Barrie in the conception and too little Shakespeare.' Barrie, as it happened, admired Bergner inordinately, and wrote a play for her – and the title role, 'The Boy David'. It was religious. And a fiasco. And his last play.

Bergner signed a five-year contract with United Artists – the films to be made in Britain; the first was to have been a version of Jack London's 'The Little Lady of the Big House', but instead she did a version of her last German film, now called *Dreaming Lips* (37), a tragic triangle drama; Raymond Massey played the lover. Picturegoer thought it 'inferior' to the earlier manifestation, and noted that 'Bergner's mannerisms are apt to become irritating' in her usual part of 'the little, lovable, clinging young woman'. She played St Joan at the 1938 Malvern Festival, and then did a film that Margaret Kennedy wrote specially for her, *A Stolen Life* (39), with Michael Redgrave. She played twins, but Picturegoer this time thought '... the fact is that Bergner is Bergner in both parts'. Paramount, not UA, released it.

In 1940 she contracted to make *49th Parallel* (with Olivier, Leslie Howard, etc.) but after doing the locations in Canada did not return to Britain for interiors and went to the USA. The film was re-started with Glynis Johns. Bergner's action was interpreted in Britain as ingratitude, but a few calm minds pointed out that had Hitler invaded, Bergner would have been one of the first to be marched off to a concentration camp – but then, so might the people who had sheltered her and given her work. In

Hollywood she did the truly appalling *Paris Calling* (42), as a patriotic society girl, 'Little Wipers' – the name bestowed upon her by Nazi protector Basil Rathbone. Then she went to New York and played in 'The Two Mrs Carrolls'; she confined her US work to the stage thereafter, though in the late 40s she did some TV. In 1950 she toured Australia in 'The Two Mrs Carrolls', and reappeared in Britain, in Manchester and London, in a version of 'Le Malade Imaginaire': but both reviews and business indicated that the British had not forgiven her. Nevertheless, she and Czinner settled quietly in Britain again, though she didn't attempt to re-start her career there for almost 20 years. She worked intermittently in Germany and Austria during that time, and Czinner occasionally directed films of stage performances using a TV technique. In 1968 she did a play in Oxford and a TV play; then accepted a role in a British Vincent Price vehicle, *Cry of the Banshee* (70).

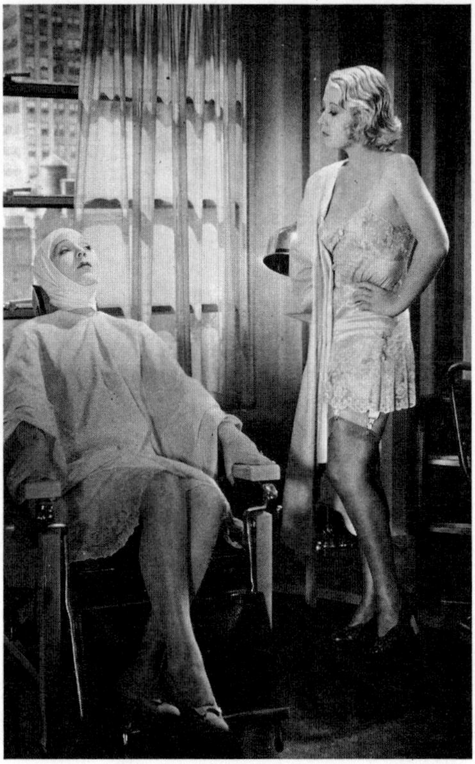

Ina Claire and Joan Blondell in The Greeks Had a Word for Them (*32*).

Joan Blondell

Joan Blondell had an expressive face with slightly pop eyes and a snappy way with a line. She was loyal, cynical and cuddlesome – the wise-cracking broad with the heart of gold. It was a type very common in the 30s, essayed by, among others, Thelma Todd, Lucille Ball, Gladys George, Ginger Rogers, Ann Sheridan and Glenda Farrell. Some of them were sometimes teamed, a conglomeration of gold diggers – Americans striking back at the Depression, dames after money first and men second. The type went out of fashion at the end of the decade; during the war heroines became anaemic and blondes became cheaper (and more venal). Later attempts to revive it – even with the talent of a Gloria Grahame – never quite caught on, though most of the 30s' blondes were still in there pitching (of course), if blowsy now, like Ann Sothern and Blondell herself. None of them were great stars in the accepted sense, but Blondell combined reliability and versatility with an overall attractive personality: to anyone believing that professionalism is the greatest of show biz virtues, it is difficult to overpraise her.

She came from a professional background: her parents were vaude troupers. She was born in New York City in 1909 and was with her parents' act from kid to soubrette, sometimes billed as the original Katzenjammer Kid. The act toured not only in the US, but throughout Europe, in China and Australia. In the latter country Blondell launched out on her own, then returned to the States, and worked in stock in Dallas. She was a Miss Dallas, and with that achievement tried her luck in New York. Eventually she got a part in 'The Trial of Mary Dugan' (27), starring Ann Harding; was also in 'Tarnish' and did a season in the 'Follies'. She was in two plays with James Cagney, and when Warners bought the second of them for filming, they took the two stars along with the rights. The film was called *Sinner's Holiday* (30) and showing concurrently was Blondell's second picture, *The Office Wife*, a drama starring Lewis Stone and Dorothy MacKaill. She had already begun to churn them out. A month later she and Cagney were featured in *Other Men's Women* (also known as *The Steel Highway*): she was WB's favourite second lead.

She supported Barbara Stanwyck in *Illicit* (31), Bebe Daniels and Ben Lyon in *My Past*, Helen Twelvetrees in *Millie* at Radio (as a gold digger), MacKaill and Conrad Nagel in *The Reckless Hour*, Loretta Young and Ricardo Cortez in *Big Business Girl*, and Stanwyck again in *Night Nurse*. She had also supported Cagney in *Public Enemy*, as a gangster's moll, and was, as Tynan once observed, 'a perfect punch-bag for his clenched, explosive talent'. One of the

Model Wife (*41*), *one of the ubiquitous marital comedies of the period. Joan Blondell in the title role, with Dick Powell, her real-life husband.*

reasons she was perfect was that she was never taken in by him. Press and public liked the combination and she got her first lead opposite him, in *Blonde Crazy*. In her nine 1932 pictures she had the lead or top-billing in most of them: *Union Depot* with Douglas Fairbanks Jr; *The Crowd Roars* with Cagney; *The Famous Ferguson Case* with Leslie Fenton; *Miss Pinkerton*, a cooler role than usual in this conventional crime melo with George Brent; *Big City Blues*, befriending hick Eric Linden during his three disillusioning days in New York; and *Make Me a Star* at Paramount, befriending Stuart Erwin in this remake of *Merton of the Movies*. She went to Goldwyn for *The Greeks Had a Word for It*, a title which horrified the censor and became *The Greeks Had a Word For Them*, though the 'it' was the way in which gold digger Ina Claire managed to pinch the admirers of Madge Evans and Blondell – a very funny film. Blondell also snaffled the cameraman, George Barnes, in real life and they married later. The *Three on a Match* were her, Ann Dvorak and Bette Davis, in that order, and then she was a small-town girl in New York, *Central Park*.

It was she and Ginger Rogers who were *Broadway Bad* (33), fighting Ricardo Cortez for the custody of her child; William Powell was her *Lawyer Man* and she was *Blondie Johnson*, a gun moll, with Chester Morris at Fox. She was one of the *Gold Diggers of 1933* and then Warren William said *Goodbye Again* to her. And in a second of the year's big musicals, *Footlight Parade*, she was more than merely decorative, she was nuts for Cagney – only he didn't know it. She didn't show it – because she had his number, the tyrant! Slang-bang, bang-slang when they met, but it ended in a clinch. She and Glenda Farrell were *Havana Widows*, the first of several films teaming them; and then she went to *Convention City* to tempt Adolphe Menjou; Dick Powell was also there – he and Blondell were later married, and the film, a comedy, was a big success.

Her reviews were always good: 'as good as usual', 'excellent', 'worth watching'. Warners did not consider her one of their top stars, but she was officially raised to stardom at last in *The Kansas City Princess* (34) with Farrell. Warren William and Edward Everett Horton fought over her in *Smarty*, and Pat O'Brien and Allen Jenkins in *I've Got Your Number* in which she was a brunette hello girl. It was the first of several with O'Brien. *He Was Her Man* was Cagney, and she was one of the *Dames*, giving that musical 'the snap it needs' (Photoplay). She was *The Traveling Saleslady* (35) with Farrell, and Powell was the *Broadway Gondolier*, a New York taxi-driver in Venice – an enjoyable comedy with music; it was Farrell with Blondell proclaiming *We're in the Money*, and acclaiming her *Miss Pacific Fleet*. Lionel Collier commented that the teaming of the two of them 'was something of a stroke of genius, and the pictures they have made together always reach a level of infectious mirth that it is impossible to resist'. Ruby Keeler was *Colleen* (36), and Powell was in it, an overlong drama where gold digger Blondell's cracks were doubly welcome. Joe E. Brown was one of the *Sons o' Guns*, and she was a French mamzelle; she was a moll once more, a good-hearted one, in *Bullets or Ballots*. *Stage Struck* has one of her most brilliant performances, as a tippling, temperamental leading lady losing her place to newcomer Jeanne Madden, perhaps the wettest ingénue of all time. The plot had Powell loathing her and loving Madden, underlining WB's inability to see them as a romantic team, which could hardly have pleased her. She was also pretty terrific in the fine filmization of the hit farce, *Three Men on a Horse*, teamed with Sam Levene and Frank Hugh; and in *Gold Diggers of 1937*.

The King and the Chorus Girl (37) – Fernand

Gravet was the king–started life as *A Royal Romance*, a tale by Groucho Marx and Norman Krasna about a king who marries a commoner: one of the movies' oldest themes. But this was 1937 and Warners got cold feet; it didn't turn up in Britain until 1939, further re-titled *Romance Is Sacred*. *The Perfect Specimen* was Errol Flynn, then she was *Back in Circulation* with Pat O'Brien; and she got a big fillip when Lesie Howard asked for her for his co-star in *Stand-In* at Wanger-UA. It was her usual part, the knowing blonde, in this case a stand-in who guides innocent Howard through the Hollywood jungle, but she invested it with more depth than even her most devoted fans expected. She got raves, mostly of the what-have-Warners-been-hiding variety. She said later: 'I wasn't such a tremendous star I could afford to revolt', but from this point on she was more than ever discontented with the Warner lot. A good comedy at Columbia with Melvyn Douglas, *There's Always a Woman* (38), was followed by a programmer that she particularly loathed making: *Off the Record* with O'Brien. She was determined to leave Warners. She told reporters that she had read a book called 'May Flavin' and wanted to play the title role: 'I'd like to show that I can do things besides girl reporters and girl detectives.' She was permitted to go to Universal for *East Side of Heaven* (39), but was then in *The Kid From Kokomo*, an unbelievable melo with Wayne Morris. It was the end. She and Powell left at the same time.

Columbia had liked her teaming with Melvyn Douglas and was anxious to reunite them: *Good Girls Go to Paris* and *The Amazing Mr Williams* were the first of a three-pic deal. She free-lanced with success: *Two Girls on Broadway* (40) Lana Turner was the other; *I Want a Divorce* with Powell, a very serious film–and a very poor one; *Topper Returns* (41), as a sexy ghost (Constance Bennett's old part) in one of the creepie comedies popular at that time; *Model Wife* with Powell, a comedy; *Three Girls About Town* at Columbia, with Binnie Barnes and Janet Blair; and *Lady for a Night* (42), a corny costumer, top-billed over John Wayne. When the US entered the war she entertained the troops without waiting for the formation of organized tours, and her film activity was cut considerably. *Cry Havoc* (43) was a war melo superbly acted by her, Ann Sothern and Margaret Sullavan. That year she went to New York to play in 'The Naked Genius', presented by Mike Todd, whom she married not long after her divorce from Powell.

The part of Aunt Cissy in *A Tree Grows in Brooklyn* (44) had originally been intended for Alice Faye as a 'straight' venture; Blondell played it as a character part and there was much talk of a comeback, which it wasn't, but she did steal the notices. She did a programmer with William Bendix, *Don Juan Quilligan* (45); and then *Adventure*, billed below the title for the first time in 12 years–but the stars were Gable and Garson so it didn't seem too face-losing. Especially as she again stole the notices. She starred with George Brent in *The Corpse Came COD* (47), destined for double bills; and had a good part–which she played superbly–as Tyrone Power's first patroness, a much-lived carny queen, in *Nightmare Alley*. *Christmas Eve* was an indie effort with several (then) doubtful box-office names.

She was out of the news for three years, except for a back-stage fracas involving Todd at the Princeton Drama Festival–cause unknown; but it was known that Todd, still a minor theatre impresario, resented reporters paying more attention to her than to him. They were divorced in the early 50s. As a comeback picture, she could have done better than *For Heaven's Sake* (50), with Joan Bennett and Clifton Webb. The notices were dire, but Variety said she had 'been absent from the screen far too long: she's that good'. She had an excellent part in *The Blue Veil* (51) and got a Best Supporting nomination for it. It wasn't enough. During the 50s she toured in a variety of roles–those of Shirley Booth in 'Come Back Little Sheba' and the musical version of 'A Tree Grows in Brooklyn' (as Aunt Cissy); in Helen Hayes's part in 'Happy Birthday' and Merman's in 'Call Me Madam'; in 'The Dark at the Top of the Stairs', and, in 1961, 'Bye Bye Birdie'. There was a Broadway appearance: 'The Rope Dancers'. In 1956 she returned to Hollywood to do three outstanding featured performances for MGM: *The Opposite Sex*, *Lizzie* (57) and *This Could Be the Night*; and there were two for 20th in 1958, back where she started as heroine's sidekick: *The Desk Set* (58) with Katie Hepburn and *Will Success Spoil Rock Hunter?* with Jayne Mansfield. In 1961 she had a good part in *Angel Baby*, where George Hamilton and Mercedes McCambridge were revivalists; but with the exception of *The Cincinnati Kid* (65), where she had a few striking scenes with another Warner alumnus, Edward G. Robinson, her other recent films have been undistinguished: *Company of Cowards?* (63), *Paradise Road* (66), *Ride Beyond Vengeance*, *The Spy With the Green Hat* (a 'Man From Uncle' effort), *Waterhole No. 3* (67), Elvis Presley's *Stay Away Joe* (68), and *The Phynx* (70). In 1968–70 there was a

Blondell deals the cards The Cincinnati Kid (*65*).

successful TV series, 'Here Come the Brides', based very loosely on *Seven Brides for Seven Brothers.*

Humphrey Bogart

Humphrey Bogart's place in the legends of Hollywood is assured; every two-bit reporter who ever got near him has a fund of stories, and some of them (as well as some good ones) have written books about him. No Hollywood figure has been more biographed, and few (Garbo, Chaplin and Monroe) have been so extensively analyzed and studied. Everyone has pronounced, from John Crosby ('Off screen, Bogart didn't diminish, which is more than you can say for most movie stars') to Stanley Kramer ('He had the damnedest façade of any man I ever met in my life. He was playing Bogart all the time, but he was really a big, sloppy bowl of mush'). Other stars have been the subject of cults (Garbo again, W. C. Fields, the Marx Bros.), but no cult has been bigger than the Bogart one – and considering the qualities which the screen Bogart exemplified, this particular cult can only be a very healthy thing.

He was much acclaimed while he was alive, but his intrinsic appeal seems to be stronger now: interest centres not on his ability or even on the overall Bogart, but on the screen character he played in his middle years. Still, even after he had remarkably extended his range, he was always Bogart: he took all sorts of characteristics and varying situations, and made them fit the Bogart persona. That persona gave him a head-start as an actor, because it was a compound of opposing qualities, mixed sometimes ambiguously. He was wiry and not handsome, but women found him attractive; he behaved towards them courteously and at the same time contemptuously. He was both cavalier and dependent. His voice was something between a rasp and a lisp, and he seldom beamed at people or smiled except with reluctance (he went through some films with a single expression of thundering pessimism), but he had an odd, private and mirthless chuckle which he used mostly for scoffing at authority. He looked out for phonies; any opposition roused the cynic in him (it was easily roused). He could be avaricious and mean but stubbornly heroic – when he was on the right side of the law he went after his man with dogged determination. He was true to himself, and in his sympathetic parts, to his friends. Tynan summed him up best: 'We trusted him because he was a wary loner

The Petrified Forest (*36*). *Humphrey Bogart as Duke Mantee, a vicious gangster who holes up in a gas station-café in the Arizona desert. Bette Davis, Leslie Howard and Dick Foran are his prisoners.*

who belonged to nobody, had personal honour . . . and would therefore survive. Compared with many of his Hollywood colleagues, he seemed an island of integrity, not perhaps very lovable but at least unbought.' Said Pauline Kael in 1968: 'There isn't an actor in American films today with anything like his assurance, his magnetism or his style.'

Yet the object of all this interest almost never made it. When stardom came, virtually by chance, he had been in films 12 years: he was always good, though almost alone the Warner Brothers didn't know it. He became a star despite them.

Accounts differ as to his date of birth, but it was around 1900, in New York City. His parents were wealthy – his father was a doctor, who was disappointed when Bogart failed to get the sort of marks which would have got him to Yale. Bogart served briefly in the US Navy at the end of World War I; and began acting in 1920, via knowing Alice Brady's brother Bill: Miss Brady offered him a job as company manager for 'Experience' and he had two lines in it. He had a small part in 'Drifting' with Miss Brady, and Alexander Woollcott wrote: 'The young man who plays the sprig is what is usually and mercifully described as inadequate.' All the same, Bogart began to work non-stop, usually as the romantic juvenile: 'Meet the Wife' (23), 'Cradle Snatchers' (25), 'Saturday's Children' and others. He made a short film in 1930, *Broadway's Like That*, around the time he was spotted in 'It's a Wise Child' by a Fox talent scout. He was signed at $750 a week, made five pictures for Fox and one on loan-out to Universal: *A Devil With Women* (30), in the sort of role he had done on Broadway; *Up the River*, starring Spencer Tracy, both playing prisoners; *Body and Soul* (31), a war story; *Bad Sister* at Universal, playing a meanie, with Bette Davis also in the cast; *Women of All Nations* with Victor McLaglen; and *A Holy Terror*, with George O'Brien.

Fox then dropped him, so he went back to New York and appeared in John Van Druten's 'After All'; he returned to the Coast to make a film for Columbia, *Love Affair* (32) co-starring Dorothy Mackaill; and did two featured parts for WB, *Big City Blues* and *Three on a Match*, both with Joan Blondell. Still nothing happened, so he returned to New York for good, and did a play called 'I Loved You Wednesday' with Henry Fonda also in the cast. He worked regularly; he made a film in New York for Universal: *Midnight* (34), starring Sidney Fox. In 1935 Bogart auditioned for a part in Robert E. Sherwood's 'The Petrified Forest', and to his surprise was cast as a gangster, a small-time hoodlum who holes up in a lonely Arizona inn, his gun at the ready. The play's star, Leslie Howard, promised Bogart that if the play was filmed, he would do his utmost to get him repeating as Duke Mantee. WB bought the play but were unimpressed by Bogart's New York success: didn't they have Edward G. Robinson under contract for such parts? Howard fought for Bogart and WB reluctantly signed him.

If WB were aware of critical and public reaction to Bogart's film performance (36), they didn't show it. Apart from Robinson, they also had Cagney under contract, and the best they could do was to put Bogart in support of them, either as one of their gang or one of their enemies or (with a midway switch) both. WB's billing policy was erratic, but no matter how big his part, Bogart was mostly below the title: *Bullets or Ballots*, opposing Robinson as a cop; *Two Against the World*, starring in this B remake of *Five Star Final*; *China Clipper*; *Isle of Fury*; *The Great O'Malley* (37), who was Pat O'Brien, a cop–Bogart was a waspish petty crook; and *Black Legion*, starring in an A that didn't click. *San Quentin* was his first WB film in the pen; now he was in deep in crime: *Marked Woman* and *Kid Galahad*, both with Robinson (and Bette Davis), playing more

A flashback in Casablanca *(43) establishing the pre-war Paris love affair between Humphrey Bogart and Ingrid Bergman, and their favourite song, 'As Time Goes By', played by Dooley Wilson.*

rat-faced crooks. 'In my first 34 pictures,' Bogart told George Frazier (quoted in Richard Gehman's good little monograph, 1965), 'I was shot in twelve, electrocuted or hanged in eight, and was a jailbird in nine. I was the Little Lord Fauntleroy of the lot.' Gehman adds that Bogart told him: 'I played more scenes writhing around on the floor than I did standing up.'

Two good loan-outs cut no ice at WB: another gangster in Wyler's distinguished *Dead End*, and a disgruntled hard-drinking film director in *Stand-In* with Howard. But *Swing Your Lady* (38) he thought the worst film he ever made, and in his opinion, there was plenty of competition. A hillbilly farce, it was considered too American for foreign tastes and got only a limited distribution. *Men Are Such Fools* was the first after a battle over salary, and was perhaps the Brothers' revenge. *Crime School* starred Bogey, but was a B; he was its principal–but was back toting a gun in *The Amazing Dr Clitterhouse*. Of *Racket Busters* he said: 'I made so many pictures like that, I used to get the titles mixed up. People would ask me what I was working on, and I'd have to think about what it was called.' But with *Angels With Dirty Faces* both title and film were memorable: Bogart got his from fellow-gangster Cagney. He made *King of the Underworld* (39) and *The Oklahoma Kid* (and he and Cagney were improbable in stetsons). Bette Davis's *Dark Victory*, unconvincing as an Irish

Bogart and Lauren Bacall in To Have and Have Not *(44): they were the right chemistry on screen, and off it she became his fourth wife.*

groom; *You Can't Get Away With Murder* as a crook who finally gets his in the Chair; *The Roaring Twenties* with Cagney; and *The Return of Dr X* as Dr X, a B, and referred to by its star as 'this stinking movie'. Then came *Invisible Stripes* (40) with George Raft, one of the studio's new acquisitions; a second Western, *Virginia City*, with Errol Flynn (an actor he particularly despised); *It All Came True*, hiding out in a boarding house of eccentrics, and forcing Ann Sheridan to choose between him and nice Jeffrey Lynn. In *Brother Orchid* he supported Robinson, and in *They Drive by Night* Raft again.

The turning point came when Paul Muni and then Raft turned down *High Sierra* (41): Raoul Walsh directed from a novel by W. R. Burnett, and Bogart gave one of his best performances, as a tired, ageing gangster wanting to retire. Ida Lupino got top-billing, but in the next, *The Wagons Roll at Night*, a circus story, Bogart was top-billed. Raft also turned down *The Maltese Falcon*, and Bogart became Sam Spade, sardonic private eye. Made uncertainly between an A and a B budget, with former script-writer John Huston directing for the first time, the studio had little confidence in it, but it was a critical triumph for all concerned. Said Bogart: 'I had a lot going for me in that one. First, there was Huston. He made the Dashiell Hammett novel into something you don't come across too often. It was practically a masterpiece. I don't have many things I'm proud of . . . but that's one.' He did *All Through the Night* (42, Nazis) and *The Big Shot* (gangsters); then the *Falcon* team (Huston, Bogart, Mary Astor, Sidney Greenstreet) was reassembled for *Across the Pacific*, and that too was a pretty good one. James Agate summed up at this point: 'Bogart is always the same, but he always delights me. He has charm and he doesn't waste energy by pretending to act. He has a sinister-rueful countenance which acts for him. He has an exciting personality and lets it do the work. His expression never changes, whether he is looking on his mistress, the dead body of a man he has murdered, or a blackbeetle. He acts even less than Leslie Howard. And I like him.'

The hoodlum parts were now behind him, and he was the man who had been biffed-about, conceivably the best hero the American cinema ever produced. *Casablanca* (in which he didn't say 'Play it again, Sam') found him the proprietor of a bar there, still in love with ex-flame Ingrid Bergman, now married to Paul Henried: probably the best bad film ever made. It won a Best Picture Oscar and made a mint, and Bogart was king of the Warner lot. From then on, he only made what he wanted to, and got a hike in salary. At the end of 1943 he entered the top 10 list and stayed there until 1949 (and was thereafter never far out of it). There were a couple of war films, *Action in the North Atlantic* and *Sahara* (at Columbia) and a guest appearance in *Thank Your Lucky Stars*; then a couple of imitations of *Casablanca*. *Passage to Marseilles* (44), was hokey, but the other, *To Have and Have Not*, superb, a distortion of Hemingway's novel, but well directed by Howard Hawks. A new girl, Lauren Bacall, said to Bogart: 'If you want anything, just whistle.' He did and she became his fourth wife. They made three more films together: Hawks's *The Big Sleep* (46), a minor masterpiece, after Chandler, who considered him 'so much better than any other tough-guy actor'; *Dark Passage* (47); and *Key Largo* (48), which Huston enjoyably directed from Maxwell Anderson's play. Less interestingly, he menaced Alexis Smith in *Conflict* (45) and Barbara Stanwyck in *The Two Mrs Carrolls* (47), and signed (46) a new record-making 15-year agreement with WB.

At the same time, he was no longer tied down, and formed his own producing company, Santana, releasing through Columbia, where he had recently done a loan-out, *Dead Reckoning* (47). The four films it made were variable, and only moderately successful. The proficient, goodish ones were *Knock on Any Door* (49) and *In a Lonely Place* (50), both directed by Nicholas Ray, and the bad ones *Tokyo Joe*

After Bacall, few of Bogart's screen partners seemed quite right for him; but Gloria Grahame, in In a Lonely Place *(50), had the requisite quality of having lived – or been around – as long as he had. It was a murder mystery set in Hollywood.*

(49) and *Sirocco* (51), though in the latter he was at his cynical peak, casually sharing the joke with the audience. Preceding this quartet was *The Treasure of Sierra Madre* (48). It was made in Mexico, and away from the studio Bogart encouraged Huston to make it the way he wanted – much to the consternation of WB, viewing the rushes. It turned out to be one of Warners' biggest prize-winners, a gripping tale of gold-lust, an 'artistic' triumph, but a no-no at the US box-office. 'Bogart is excellent; already realistically dishevelled and depraved at the start, he grows more insanely selfish and suspicious as the film develops, until he becomes frighteningly inhuman at the end.' (Peter Ericsson in Sequence.) Bogart himself was very fond of the film. In *Chain Lightning* (50) he was a test pilot; then *The Enforcer* (51), in an account of 'Murder Inc.' with a plot unspoilt by romantic intrusions. It was (as it happened) his last film for WB.

Huston then put him in *The African Queen*, from C. S. Forester's novel about a gin-sodden old boatman and the prissy spinster (Katharine Hepburn) who falls reluctantly in love with him: it was a huge success all round, and Bogart's performance surprised even his most fervent admirers. He pinched a Best Actor Oscar from under Marlon Brando's nose, and the British readers of Picturegoer voted him the year's best actor. From then till his death, he flexed his acting muscles as never before, most notably in a startling performance as the psychopathic captain in *The Caine Mutiny* (54). Despite a propensity for alcohol and a not unfounded reputation for living it up, Bogart took his profession very seriously indeed; he once said, 'The only thing you owe the public is a good performance', and he took pains to ensure it, with the maximum of professionalism.

His last films, however, were a mixed bunch: Richard Brooks's *Deadline USA* (52) was a cliché-ridden newspaper story, with Kim Hunter; *Battle Circus* (53) was just that; and *Beat the Devil* was a crime spoof, written by Truman Capote and directed by Huston, with Jennifer Jones, Robert Morley, Gina Lollobrigida and all. It just broke even, and was considered a mess by Bogart (though it had – and has – a cult appeal). He followed with *The Caine Mutiny* (54), a big hit from Herman Wouk's best-seller; and was a last-minute replacement for Cary Grant in *Sabrina*, from Samuel Taylor's play – not improved under Billy Wilder's direction, with William Holden (whom Bogart loathed) and Audrey Hepburn. He was in Mankiewicz's *The Barefoot Contessa*, as a film director for the second time in his career; *We're No Angels* (55), from another play, as a convict – but a fairly amusing one; *The Left Hand of God*, a heavily panned effort, as a priest; and *The Desperate Hours*, from yet another play

In some ways Bogart's best-ever partner was Katharine Hepburn, a personality as trenchant as he but–unlike Bacall–a completely contrasting one. The African Queen *(51) was, among other things, one of the screen's great love stories.*

(by Joseph Hayes) and directed by William Wyler, as a really evil hoodlum menacing Fredric March and family. In his last movie, *The Harder They Fall* (56), Bogart returned to a more typical part, as a broken-down journalist, a bit on the wrong side of the law, who gets integrity in the last reel.

He became somewhat obstreperous during his last years, a period well covered by reporters (the accounts of his happiness with Bacall are touching to read). He died of throat cancer in January 1957. Huston spoke at the funeral: 'He is quite irreplaceable. There will never be anybody like him.' But he left a fine legacy, four or five films which are classics and a score which can be watched over and over. And are.

Clara Bow

The 20s would have been quite different without Clara Bow: she was totally representative of the era, but to what extent she created the flapper and how much derived from her could probably never be calculated. With her bob, her cupid's-bow lips, her saucer eyes, her beads and bangles and her jiggle, she shook up cinema audiences everywhere: she was the bee's knees, she was the cat's pyjamas. She was gay and vivacious, as befitted the new emancipated woman; she had enormous enthusiasm for life and more especially for the opposite sex. She seldom looked at men straight, but had a variety of roguish expressions and stances which resulted in the end as only one message, come-and-get-me. Despite this, she was invariably shocked when taken advantage of–but audiences were titillated. She had only to spot an unattached male, as Alexander Walker has pointed out, and she started to freshen her make-up and pat her hair and primp in his direction; and she liked to touch her men–to flick a finger on his lapel or fix his tie or chuck him under the chin. All this presumably sprang from her off-screen character, restless, jazzy and nimble; it is recorded that she was seldom still. To the extent that the age was vulgar, she was vulgar, and was dismissed as such by Anita Loos, who considered that she 'succeeded in being at one and the same time innocuous and flashy'.

This was hardly the opinion of another eminent literary lady, Elinor Glyn, who discovered in Clara Bow the epitome of 'It' (how typical of the period that having or not having 'It' was almost a *cause célèbre*). Among Madam Glyn's endless definitions of 'It' was this: 'a strange magnetism which attracts both sexes . . . there must be a physical attraction but beauty is unnecessary.' Probably the nomination of Bow as the 'It' Girl was a studio scheme with which Elinor Glyn was happy to comply, but in the founding of the whole silly syndrome, Bow was an entirely worthy centrepiece. Even if the whole thing, including what she did on the screen, was evolved from the sort of girl she was, her life and career still seem to have been dreamed up by one of her script-writers.

She was born in Brooklyn in 1905, into extreme poverty. Her father was an occasional waiter, her mother a semi-invalid with neurotic tendencies. Her first job was as a telephone receptionist for a doctor, but it didn't last long because she won a beauty contest–a 'Fame and Fortune' competition run by three magazines: she was the national winner, and the prize included a screen test and a small part in *Beyond the Rainbow* (22). That got left on the cutting-room floor (though after Bow's success the scenes were restored and the film reissued). None of the other New York studios were interested, but director Elmer Clifton chanced upon Bow's picture in one of the fan mags at the time when he was looking for cut-price talent for *Down to the Sea in Ships* (23): it was a secondary role and required Bow to

Clara Bow as My Lady of Whims *(26), one of the earlier films in which she outflapped all the other flaming flappers of the period. With her is Francis MacDonald.*

masquerade as a boy, but was a fine film and she got some fairly nice notices. A New York agent took her on and got her a contract with B. P. Schulberg's company at $50 a week plus her fare to Hollywood.

Schulberg was then turning out programme-fillers under the name 'Preferred' (which was monumentally untrue) and much of his money came from loaning out his contract-artists to other studios. Bow progressed very slowly – though she quickly lost the virginal appearance with which she arrived in Hollywood, due possibly to the rate at which she worked: 14 Bow pictures were released in 1925. She began with small parts in *Enemies of Women*, which starred Lionel Barrymore, *Maytime* and *Daring Years*; but had a star role in *Grit* (24), about the New York underworld and an unimportant film even if it was written specially by Scott Fitzgerald. She had a featured role in *Black Oxen* which starred Corinne Griffith and concerned glandular rejuvenation – but it was the first of the flapper roles. *The Poisoned Paradise* was Monte Carlo, with an attempt to break the bank there, and the *Daughters of Pleasure* were Bow and Marie Prevost, with Prevost's dad (Wilfred Lucas) offering jewels to her chum (Bow). *Wine* was a topical bootlegging tale, and the 1924 consignment finished off with *Empty Hearts*, *This Woman* (a melo with Irene Rich and Ricardo Cortez) and *Black Lightning*, which starred Thunder, the dog.

The 14 Bow films of 1925 were: *Capital Punishment*, some premature propaganda against; *Helen's Babies*, a vehicle for Baby Peggy; *The Adventurous Sex*; *My Lady's Lips*; *Parisian Love*, as an apache, with Donald Keith; *Eve's Lover*, as a bright relief from the sombre doings of Irene Rich; Lubitsch's *Kiss Me Again*, a good French farce with Marie Prevost and Monte Blue; *The Scarlet West*, a mediocre Western; *The Primrose Path*, as a night-club dancer; *The Plastic Age*, which gave her her best chance to date, a 'moral' tale showing how jazz parties and other vices almost ruin the academic career of Donald Keith; *Keeper of the Bees*, miscast in a shoddy version of the Gene Stratton Porter novel; *Free to Love*, as a wrongly convicted prisoner; *The Best Bad Man*, a Tom Mix Western; and *Lawful Cheaters*, posing as a boy again. By this time Bow had achieved her first popularity, and was liked, whether in the poor Schulberg films or the secondary parts she did on loan-out. She was in *The Ancient Mariner* (26) purportedly based on the Coleridge poem and then was *My Lady of Whims*, flouting her family by living in Greenwich Village with a very masculine sculptress and going for rides in old men's yachts – but finally succumbing (unconvincingly) to Donald Keith, who has been employed to spy on her. *Shadow of the Law* and *Two Can Play* were both quickies made before moving on to the Paramount lot.

Schulberg was (re)joining that company, and Paramount, as part of the agreement, took on some of his contract-artists (Bow was, in fact, the lure). Her first, in a supporting role (as Kittens Westcourt), was *Dancing Mothers*, starring Alice Joyce and Conway Tearle; she starred in her next, *The Runaway*, in the title role, as a film-star in the Kentucky mountains, meeting Warner Baxter and William Powell; and the next one, *Mantrap*, was her first big hit. Directed by Victor Fleming from a story by Sinclair Lewis, it was the old one about the old man (Ernest Torrence), the young wife and the stranger from out of town (Percy Marmont): the whole thing came up quite fresh and Bow put more depth into her characterization than was usual. Paramount were so pleased that after a stint bolstering Eddie Cantor in his first film, *Kid Boots*, a film was built around her: *It* (27). Madam Glyn even appeared in it, to explain to Antonio Moreno what 'It' was. Naturally Bow had buckets of it, getting her department-store boss all in a tizzy over her and winning him despite his prejudices. The film was a big success and

William A. Wellman's Wings *(27) was the first film to win an Academy Award, and some campus showings in 1969–70 have indicated that it stands up well; but Clara Bow was seldom as out of the picture as here–looking particularly doleful as Charles Buddy Rogers congratulates fellow-flier Richard Arlen.*

millions of girls began to ape her make-up and fashions.

Identification was easier in that Bow's screen occupations were resolutely humdrum: 'She was a manicurist, usherette, waitress, cigarette girl, taxi dancer, swimming instructress and salesgirl generally found round the lingerie department. All were roles in the range of promiscuous but legal employment where a girl can flirt with an ever-changing male clientele' (Walker) –and they were also roles which gave her plenty of opportunities to wear a swimsuit or strip to her drawers (so that the appeal was not only to the distaff side). The 'It' girl tag now replaced the earlier one of 'The Brooklyn Bonfire' and more than ever Bow was the honeypot round which the bees clustered. Schulberg now sold her contract to Paramount, having made a considerable profit from renting her services. In *Children of Divorce* with Gary Cooper, however, sex didn't bring happiness and she committed suicide; in *Rough House Rosie* she was a girl from the East Side trying to make it in the Park Avenue Set and not in the most orthodox way. She was in *Wings* rather to bolster the box office than for any other reason, but *Hula* was all her, plus a bit of Clive Brook. Fleming directed, in a Hawaii setting. *Get Your Man*–Charles 'Buddy' Rogers was a French aristocrat and she did; and was an equally unabashed gold digger in *Red Hair* (28)–though she reformed when she fell in love. Picturegoer felt there was no need to describe to readers 'the way she struts her stuff'. Glyn wrote it, and the opening sequence was in colour to justify the title. (Bow had a famous limousine to match her hair; and she drove down the street in an open car with two red chows, dyed to match.) She was one of the *Ladies of the Mob* (with Richard Arlen) and, as a Frisco dance hostess, delighted to learn that *The Fleet's In!* (with James Hall). Glyn again provided the scenario of *Three Weekends*, with Bow as a showgirl pursuing married Neil Hamilton.

It could not be said that Bow was everywhere popular: one of the most persistent arguments (especially in Britain) against talking-pictures was the thought of vulgar, gum-chewing, little Clara talking. Her nasal tones were anticipated, but, in fact, she made the transition easily (though her penchant for darting about the set had to be curbed because mikes at first couldn't follow her). *The Wild Party* (29) found her as the school's bad girl in pursuit of Professor Fredric March (it was shown in Britain only as a Silent–perhaps to placate Picturegoer); in *Dangerous Curves* she was in a circus with Arlen; and in *The Saturday Night Kid* again in

a department store. In *Paramount on Parade* (30) she sang 'I'm True to the Navy Now', and that provided the title for the next, *True to the Navy*–only she was only true to March (the plot had him trying to believe it). *Love Among the Millionaires* was perhaps a more agreeable idea to her (but the brightest spot was Mitzi Green), and *Her Wedding Night* was fun: she shared it with Ralph Forbes. At this point she was getting $5,000 a week–considerably less than she was worth (but more than the $2,800 of a year earlier) and less than rivals like Alice White and Colleen Moore were getting (and a national US poll in 1929 found she was the most popular female star and Colleen Moore was second). But suddenly she was no longer worth even a tenth of that amount.

Already in 1930 there had been two scandals. The first was when she admitted paying off the wife of a Dallas physician who was suing her for alienation of affection; and the other when she refused to settle some gambling debts (with Will Rogers at a casino in Nevada she signed blank cheques until she realized the amount was in the thousands and stopped the cheques). And it was widely believed her engagement to stage star Harry Richman was a stunt to get him known outside New York. Early in 1931 she sued her former secretary, Daisy de Voe, for embezzling $16,000. The sacked de Voe had attempted to blackmail Bow and the latter in retaliation sued her. De Voe was convicted on only one of the 37 larceny charges and went to jail for a year; and hers was the victory: her revelations in court (drink, gigolos and drugs) brought down on Bow's head a barrage of criticism from newspapers and magazines. The two Bow pictures which followed the trial, *No Limit* (31), as an usherette put in charge of a gambling saloon with Dixie Lee, and *Kick In*, with Regis Toomey, did no business. The latter was her first attempt at drama in many years, and Picturegoer described it as a 'valiant' one; but, it went on, 'the public decided to have none of her'. Bow suffered a nervous breakdown, and was replaced in *The Secret Call* by Peggy Shannon and in *City Streets* by Sylvia Sidney. She returned to work in *Manhandled*, but work was stopped, and her contract was dissolved with less than a year to run (reports vary on this: Bow said that she suddenly decided to quit movie-making, but some commentators suggested that Paramount had dropped her due to the complete lack of public support). It was announced that she had retired through ill-health.

She married Rex Bell, who had had a bit in *True to the Navy*, and who was to become a successful cowboy star in B pictures; and they retired to his ranch in Nevada. A year later, in 1932, it was announced that she was going to become a director, and there were rumours that she would play in *Red-Headed Woman* at MGM–but the part went to Jean Harlow. Mary Pickford wanted her for the role of her sister in *Secrets* and impressed Hollywood when she issued a statement defending Bow: 'She is a very great actress and her only trouble has been that she hasn't known enough about life to live it the way she wanted to live it.' Instead, she made two films for Fox, at a reported $125,000 each: *Call Her Savage* (32), in which she was a half-caste and Gilbert Roland played someone called Moonglow, and *Hoopla* (33, not released till 35) as a carnival dancer in this adaptation of Kenyon Nicholson's 'The Barker'. Both were poor and both indicated that she was having a weight problem. In 1934 she said that she planned to make a film in Britain, but nothing came of it and early in 1937 it was announced that she had been approached to take over Simone Simon's part in *Under Two Flags* when the latter's English proved not up to it: but presumably she couldn't diet in time (in 1939 she was reputed to be 200 lbs.)

Bow and Bell left Nevada in 1937 to open a cabaret–called 'It'–in Hollywood, but it didn't last long. She was out of the news until 1947 when she appeared on TV as Mrs Hush, the mystery guest in 'Truth and Consequences'; and in 1960 she made news when she told Hedda Hopper: 'I slip my old crown of "It" Girl not to Taylor or Bardot but to Monroe.' Bell died in 1962; they had been separated–though not divorced–for several years. Bow was a chronic insomniac and seems to have spent several sessions in rest homes. She became a recluse in her later years, painting and reading. In 1965 she died of a heart attack. Ann Pacey commented in The Sun (London): 'Hollywood is ruthless with its victims, but it owes much to personalities like Clara Bow, who helped to create the glamour it has never entirely lost.'

Charles Boyer

The French don't usually transplant. Hollywood has looked world-wide in its search for talent, but somehow the French never make it. Germans and Austrians have thrived here but the French wither and die. Danielle Darrieux took one look, made one film, and returned; Hollywood has never managed to harness the huge resources of talent at large in the French film industry. Renoir, Clair, Duvivier and so on right down to Henri Verneuil didn't manage to come to terms with the Hollywood system for more than a film or two; Michele Morgan, Jean Gabin and Jeanne Moreau have done their least interesting work in US movies; Belmondo and Bardot have held out. The shining exception (Chevalier perhaps apart) is Charles Boyer, and he only made it in Hollywood after a bitter struggle.

He was born in Figeac (Lot) in south-west France in 1899; wanted to be an actor from childhood and after a course at the Sorbonne studied drama at the Paris Conservatoire. He was still there when given a small part in a film, Marcel L'Herbier's *L'Homme du Large* (20), and was then on the stage in 'Les Jardins de Murcie'; he was seldom thereafter out of work – in the theatre. After several small roles he made a success in 'Le Voyageur' in 1922 and was an idol of the *théâtre de boulevard* for the rest of the decade. His film parts got bigger – via *Chantelouve* (22), *L'Esclave* (24), *Le Grillon du Foyer* (25) – to his notable performance in *Le Capitaine Fracassé* (27). *La Ronde Infernale* (28) was another big hit for him, and that year he was in the long-running 'Mélo', which first brought Hollywood attention to him. But he had already signed with UFA to make French versions of German movies in Berlin. He had done *La Barcarolle d'Amour* (30) when MGM approached UFA to buy up his contract: they wanted him for the French versions of their movies. In Hollywood he did *Le Procès de Mary Dugan* and a French *Big House* before it was decided to abandon separate different-language versions for subtitles. He hung around doing nothing till loaned to Paramount for a French subject, *The Magnificent Lie* (31), starring Ruth Chatterton, then returned to UFA for the French version of *Sturm der Leidenschaft*, called *Tumultes* (31) with Florelle. He went back to Hollywood for a lead with Claudette Colbert, *The Man From Yesterday* (32).

He wasn't very good, and he was unhappy; he liked Hollywood no more than it liked him, a feeling confirmed when MGM cast him in a very small part (as a chauffeur) in Jean Harlow's *Red-Headed Woman*. They promised to delete his footage if the film was shown in France, but he was bitter and asked release from his contract. MGM let him go, and he returned to UFA once more, for French versions of two Conrad Veidt vehicles: *F.P.I. Ne Répond Pas* and *Moi et L'Impératrice* (33), with Lilian Harvey. He also appeared in the English version of the latter, *The Only Girl* (*Heart Song* in the US) and then returned to Paris, where he was an undisputed star. He made *L'Epervier* with Natalie Paley and *Le Bonheur* (which he had just done on the stage) with Gaby Morlay. He had also done *La Bataille* (34) on the stage, in a small part, back in 1921: now he played the lead, the Japanese naval commander, that Sessue Hakayawa had done in the Silent version; Anabella co-starred, and there was an English version, *The Battle* (*Thunder in the East* in the US). Twentieth saw it and invited him back to Hollywood; encouraged by Ruth Chatterton, he took the plunge after *Liliom*, from Molnar's play (one of several French movies made by German refugees passing through: Pommer produced; Fritz Lang directed).

Twentieth announced that they had signed Boyer to play in a series of 'romantic European yarns of the Valentino type'. They thought, said Boyer later, 'they might make capital of a man whose eyes could look as though they mirrored all the sorrow in the world'; so they made him a gypsy violinist, caught between Countess Loretta Young and fellow gypsy Jean Parker in *Caravan*: it was a well-deserved flop and Boyer bought up his contract. Walter Wanger thought he would give Boyer a chance – in a featured role with Claudette Colbert in *Private Worlds* (35): for the first time American audiences were impressed and Wanger signed him to a personal contract, with permission to do one film a year in France. He then played opposite Katharine Hepburn in *Break of Hearts* when Francis Lederer walked out during the first week's shooting; and did another film with Young, *Shanghai*, as a Eurasian. In Paris he was the Crown Prince Rudolph in *Mayerling* (36) for Anatole Litvak, with Darrieux, which was probably the peak of his popularity in his native land – and which was much adored on its showings elsewhere. More than anything that had gone before, this established Boyer in the eyes of Anglo-Saxons as the great 'lovair'.

He was dark and handsome, and it had already been proved that when he spoke English he had a fascinating accent: where Chevalier had been cute he was sombre. He was something of a rogue, something of a dilettante; his eyes were dreamy, but they could spark *or* melt when a woman was near, which she invariably was. In *The Garden of Allah* it was Dietrich. By virtue of its being in Technicolor and much publicized it was talked-about if not a big success; and his moody monk, though romancing on the sands of Sahara, typed him as a sheik of the boudoir. He didn't act other than to look pained, but as on other of these lesser occasions, he got by on a compelling sincerity. That he could act and had a sense of humour was established ably by *History*

Conquest (*38*). *Charles Boyer as Napoleon and Garbo as his Polish mistress Marie Walewska. With no guidance from the script he managed to suggest the ambition, the greatness and the pettiness of the Emperor without abandoning the romantic allure that audiences expected.*

Is Made at Night (37), with Jean Arthur, and amply by *Tovarich* with Colbert. Indeed, Boyer was proficient at whatever he turned his hand to: his Napoleon to Garbo's Marie Walewska in *Conquest* was, considered The New Yorker, 'the first time she has had a leading man who contributes more to the interest and vitality of the film than she does'. British readers of Picturegoer voted him the year's Best Actor.

But it was after another French film, *Orage* with Michele Morgan, that he made the film that made him the most famous (and imitated) screen lover of his era: *Algiers* (38). He didn't actually say 'Comm wiz me to the Casbah', but that was the general idea–the fatal attraction a society beauty has for underworld chief Pépé Le Moko (which was the title of the original Jean Gabin version, bought up by Wanger for this remake). Despite Boyer's following, Wanger dropped him because exhibitors warned him that they wouldn't book foreign players. Boyer continued to work and his pictures remained popular; and Wanger reputedly remained indignant for years about the matter. Both of Boyer's 1939 films were successful, and both co-starred Irene Dunne: *Love Affair*, a superb romantic comedy, and the much less enjoyable *When Tomorrow Comes*, a sudser. He returned to France to make *Le Corsaire*, but it was abandoned on the outbreak of war. Boyer joined the French army, but the French Government thought he would be more useful as a propagandist in the US. He did notable work for the Free French, but became an American citizen in 1942.

His films of this period were all superior novelettes: *All This and Heaven Too* (40), secretly in love with Bette Davis; *Back Street* (41), secretly in love with Margaret Sullavan; and *Hold Back the Dawn*, discovering he loves Olivia de Havilland after all. The *Appointment With Love* was also with Sullavan and was also superior. He was effective in Duvivier's two episode pictures, *Tales of Manhattan* (42) and *Flesh and Fantasy* (43) but neither repeated the critical success of that director's earlier episoder, *Un Carnet de Bal*. *Flesh and Fantasy* was co-produced by Boyer and Duvivier, the first under a new actor-producer pact that Boyer had signed with Universal–and the last: presumably its failure caused that studio to annul the deal. Just before that one he was at Warners with *The Constant Nymph*, Joan Fontaine, as the egotistical musician loved by her; and later he was suave and sinister driving wife Ingrid Bergman into insanity by *Gaslight* (44). But he and Irene Dunne *Together Again* was hardly up to the occasion.

Confidential Agent (45) with Lauren Bacall was a not too terrible attempt to film Graham Greene's novel; Boyer was a tired, ageing Spanish loyalist, and though, said Pauline Kael later, his performance was also tired, he was 'still better than almost any actor in the business'. Greene liked his performance and thinks the film is the best Hollywood attempt to film his work. Boyer was a Czech refugee involved with plumber's niece Jennifer Jones in the Lubitsch *Cluny Brown* (46), and was then off the screen till *A Woman's Vengeance* (47) and it was Aldous Huxley who might have felt vengeful about this version of his play 'The Gioconda Smile'. It didn't help Boyer's career, nor did *Arch of Triumph* (48), again with Bergman. As a free-lance Boyer could hardly afford such flops; and in 1948 he left Hollywood to do 'Red Gloves' (Sartre's 'Les Mains Sales') in New York.

When he returned to the screen it was as a character actor–his toupee abandoned, gleefully attacking any elderly part which came his way. *The Thirteenth Letter* (51), a remake of Clouzot's *Le Corbeau*, also found him bearded–and some of the magic had undoubtedly gone; he has remained a persuasive actor, but seldom a memorable one. *The First Legion*, *Thunder in the East* (52),

Charles Boyer and Hedy Lamarr in Algiers *(38). He didn't actually say 'Comm wiz me to the Casbah', but that was the general idea.*

with Alan Ladd, and *The Happy Time* were not, in any case, remotely distinguished, and Boyer was much better served by Ophuls's *Madame de . . .* (53, in France), an elegant triangle tale with Darrieux and Vittorio de Sica. He filmed mainly in France over the next 10 years, but appeared notably in the US on TV: he was one of the originators of 'Four Star Playhouse', was in a series called 'The Rogues' and did 'There Shall Be No Night' with Katharine Cornell. On Broadway he was in 'Kind Sir' (53, filmed as *Indiscreet*) with Mary Martin, 'The Marriage-Go-Round' (58) with Claudette Colbert and 'Lord Pengo' (63). His pictures were not too hot: *Nana* (54) with Martine Carol; *La Fortuna di essere Donna* (55) with Sophia Loren; in Hollywood *The Cobweb* and *Around the World in 80 Days* (56), a cameo appearance; *Paris Palace Hotel* with Françoise Arnoul; *Une Parisienne* (57) with Brigitte Bardot; in Hollywood *The Buccaneer*; *Maxime* (58) with Michele Morgan; the Hollywood *Fanny* (60); *Les Démons de Minuit* (61) with Pascale Audret; and *Adorable Julia* with Lili Palmer, a dire Franco-Austrian emasculation of Somerset Maugham's 'Theatre'.

In 1964 Boyer made his London stage debut in Rattigan's 'Man and Boy'. In films he continued to play character parts, sometimes billed below the title, and usually in Hollywood made-in-Europe products: *The Four Horsemen of the Apocalypse* (61); *Love Is a Ball* (62; director David Swift spoke in awe of his 'professionalism'); *A Very Special Favor* (64); *How To Steal a Million* (65) and *Is Paris Burning?*; *Barefoot in the Park* (67), in Hollywood; *The Day the Hot Line Got Hot* (68); *The Madwoman of Chaillot* (69); and *The April Fools*.

He has been married since 1934 to British-born actress Pat Patterson.

Louise Brooks

In 1957 Ado Kyrou wrote in 'Amour-Eroticisme et Cinéma' that Louise Brooks was 'the only woman who had the ability to transfigure–no matter what the film–into a master-piece. . . . Her vivid beauty, her absolutely unique acting (I do not know of a greater tragedienne on the screen) predisposed her to the top rank. Not one woman exerted more magic, not one had her genius of interpretation. Nevertheless she disappeared in 1931 in a manner altogether inexplicable, at the age of 24. . . .'

When she disappeared, hardly anyone noticed. She is revered today, but in the 20s neither she nor anyone else thought her a good actress, let alone a goddess. *That* is what is inexplicable.

She was born in Cherryvale, Kansas, in 1906. From 1921 to 1924 she danced with Ruth St Denis and Ted Shawn and their company; she transferred to George White's 'Scandals' and thence to the 'Ziegfeld Follies' (25). Ziegfeld promised to star her, but her looks had attracted Paramount, who signed

Louise Brooks is remembered best for the two films she made in Germany for G. W. Pabst: Pandora's Box *and* Diary of a Lost Girl *(both 29). Two scenes from* Diary of a Lost Girl, *left with Kurt Gerron.*

her and gave her a bit part in *The Street of Forgotten Men* (25). She preferred to be a star in movies, and was a beauty-contest winner in *The American Venus* (26), starring Esther Ralston. Most of the time she was a shop-girl, in bangs and a beret: *A Social Celebrity* (26), starring Adolphe Menjou; *It's the Old Army Game*, a W. C. Fields vehicle, directed by Eddie Sutherland (to whom she was married, 1926–8); the film of George Kelly's Broadway hit, *The Show-Off*, starring Ford Sterling; and *Just Another Blonde* with William Collier Jr. Around this time Picturegoer noted her subtle vamping: 'She is extraordinarily vital and alive. The sheer, sharp grace of face and figure, the very chic of her bob, combine to draw struggling heroes into her net.' There followed: *Love 'em and Leave 'em*; *Evening Clothes* (27) with Virginia Valli; *Rolled Stockings*, a collegiate story with Richard Arlen; *The City Gone Wild*, directed by James Cruze, an underworld story with Thomas Meighan; and *Now We're in the Air*, a Beery-Hatton comedy, in a dual role.

She was loaned to Fox to play a circus high diver in Hawks's *A Girl in Every Port* (28), being fought over by Victor McLaglen and Robert Armstrong, and is magical–as she is in William A. Wellman's moving *Beggars of Life*, dressed as a boy and riding the freight trains with Arlen.

G. W. Pabst, at any rate, saw the magic. After he had seen the Hawks film he wanted her at once for his long-planned *Die Büchse van Pandora/Pandora's Box* (29), adapted from Wedekind's 'Lulu'. Paramount refused. Later there arose the question of their option on Brooks, and because of the arrival of Sound, they gave her the chance of sticking at her old salary or quitting. She quit, and immediately advised Pabst that she was free–just as he was about to take the then little-known Dietrich (who said later: 'Imagine Pabst choosing Louise Brooks when he could have had me'). Thus Brooks became the most entrancing nymphomaniac in film history. Said Paul Rotha: '... the performance he [Pabst] extracts from Brooks is one of the phenomena of the cinema'. She stayed on in Germany to make, for Pabst, *Das Tagebuch einer Verlorenen/Diary of a Lost Girl*, and, against his advice, returned to her homeland.

Her incredible, incandescent performances were somewhat overlooked outside Germany and certainly in the US, where Silent films were *démodé*. Paramount asked her to dub *The Canary Murder Case* (William Powell as Philo Vance), which she had made before her German trip, so they could release a synchronized version, but she refused (Margaret Livingstone substituted). She also turned down *Bad Girl*, which Paramount offered her, and returned to Europe where she was idolized. For Augusto Genina, in France, she made her first Talkie (from an idea by Pabst), *Prix de Beauté* (30), a lush, exquisite melodrama about a shopgirl who found tragedy when she won a beauty contest.

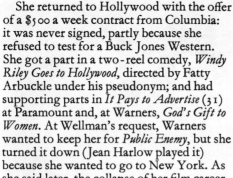

She returned to Hollywood with the offer of a $500 a week contract from Columbia: it was never signed, partly because she refused to test for a Buck Jones Western. She got a part in a two-reel comedy, *Windy Riley Goes to Hollywood*, directed by Fatty Arbuckle under his pseudonym; and had supporting parts in *It Pays to Advertise* (31) at Paramount and, at Warners, *God's Gift to Women*. At Wellman's request, Warners wanted to keep her for *Public Enemy*, but she turned it down (Jean Harlow played it) because she wanted to go to New York. As she said later, the collapse of her film career was mostly her own fault.

uise Brooks: in mage to her Jean-Luc dard made Anna rina wear her hair in Brooks bob in Vivre Vie *in 1962.*

She also claimed that she had never behaved like a movie star, but nevertheless or therefore she was declared a bankrupt in 1932. In 1933 she went back to dancing, mostly in night-clubs, but in 1936 was back in Hollywood, broke again, and desperate to work. She did a minor part in a Western, *Empty Saddles*, and then Columbia offered her a test for a star part if she would appear in the chorus of Grace Moore's *When You're in Love* (37). She did, and stills were issued with captions thus: 'Louise Brooks, former star, who deserted Hollywood at the height of her career, has come back to resume her work in pictures. But seven years is too long for the public to remember, and Louise courageously begins again at the bottom.' The only results from this were a bit part in *King of Gamblers* and the lead in a B Western with John Wayne, *Overland Stage Raiders* (38).

In 1943 she returned to New York and worked intermittently in radio, in publicity offices and finally as a salesgirl, until in 1948 she became a recluse. In 1955, two years before Kyrou's tribute was written, James Card, the Curator of Motion Pictures at Eastman House in Rochester, NY, sought her out and found her oblivious to the fact that she had been re-discovered by film-buffs: after 25 years in limbo she found, like Buster Keaton, that she was not forgotten. Remembrance was limited to film societies, but it was intense. The Paris Cinémathèque had this programme note: 'Those who have seen her can never forget her. She is the modern actress *par excellence* because, like the statues of antiquity, she is outside time.... It is sufficient to see her to believe in beauty, in life, in the reality of human beings....' Brooks herself began taking an interest in films, and has written superbly on screen acting and other subjects. James Card wrote in 1958: '... from the day the preservation of great films began, the petty plotting of small and selfish men to wipe out the record of beauty and truth that has sometimes been achieved in spite of them, was forever frustrated. The return of Louise Brooks to the screens of the world is a portent: the art of the film has its own immortality.'

Jack Buchanan

Jack Buchanan was no Fred Astaire, but he put a strictly limited song-and-dance talent to almost as great advantage. He sang or rather crooned with an attractive, nearly nasal casualness; and danced or rather tapped with an easy elegance. He was the epitome of that 20s/30s hero, the debonair man-about-Mayfair, and, as such, was often satirized and imitated. What the others lacked was his svelte charm. The British theatre has seldom seen anyone as good in that particular line, and though it wasn't a great talent, the British cinema had no one else at all. His films are probably remembered less by his contemporaries than his stage appearances, but many of them are rather charming in an awful sort of way.

He was born in Helensburgh, near Glasgow, in 1891, the son of an auctioneer. Stage-struck, he had no training, but in 1912 made an unsuccessful debut in a small part at the Grand, Glasgow. Later that year he had a walk-on in London at the Apollo in 'The Grass Widow'; got a good job understudying Vernon Watson in a revue, 'All the Winners', and had his first taste of success touring (15–17) in 'Tonight's the Night'. That proved his forte was light comedy. He attracted attention in London in 'Bubbly'; and was really established by Charlot's 'A to Z' revue in 1921, along with Bea Lillie and Gertrude Lawrence. The three of them went to New York in 1924 ('The Charlot Revue of 1924') and became the rage of the Great White Way. Other successes of the 20s included 'Battling Butler' in 1923, 'Toni' in 1924, 'Sunny' in 1927 and 'That's a Good Girl' in 1928.

He started in films in 1917 with *Auld Lang Syne*; after *Her Heritage* (19), he had leading roles in some very bad films: *The Audacious Mr Squire* (23); *The Happy Ending* (25) and a triangle drama, *Settled Out of Court* (26), both with Fay Compton; and *Bulldog Drummond's Third Round*. The first successful one was *Confetti* (27)–at least, he was good in a serious part. The following year he brought *Toni* to the screen, but he seemed forced and the film was unfunny. When Talkies arrived, he got the Hollywood call, and made *Paris* (29) there in colour, co-starring with Irene Bordoni; also for First National he had a guest spot in *The Show of Shows*. He went to

New York for 'Wake Up and Dream' with Jessie Matthews, and then returned to Hollywood for *Monte Carlo* (30), a Lubitsch frolic in which he was an aristocrat posing as a hairdresser (a part intended for Chevalier) for the benefit of Jeanette MacDonald. By the time that had gone the rounds, the all-singing, all-talking, all-dancing craze was on its way out and his plans to produce his own films in Hollywood came to nothing. Instead, he became involved in stage production and real estate. In Britain, he built the Leicester Square Theatre, originally to house his own musicals. It opened in 1931, but that year he starred at the London Hippodrome in 'Stand Up and Sing'. Despite earlier scorn directed at the British film industry, he also appeared in a British movie for Paramount called *Man of Mayfair* (it was 20 years before he filmed again in Hollywood).

His British films were light-hearted concoctions, aimed mostly at capitalizing on the genial and gracious Buchanan image, (UA released in the US). After *Goodnight Vienna* (32) the emphasis was on farce rather than romance, though today the humour is very coy, way behind the early Astaire films (which a couple of them resemble). In 1933 he began to direct as well as star: *Yes Mr Brown* (an adaptation of the German *Ein Bisschen Liebe*) and *That's a Good Girl*, both with his favourite leading lady, Elsie Randolph. *Girl* is a minor triumph in that it successfully opened out a stage show which he had done (as star and producer) – a knockabout farce about a rich ne'er-do-well and his even richer aunts, set on the Riviera. It also contains one of the most evocative 30s numbers, 'Fancy Our Meeting'.

Later in 1933 he was starring in 'Mr Whittington'; when its run finished he made a new version of the old farce, *Brewster's Millions* (35), followed by *Come Out of the Pantry*. *When Knights Were Bold* (36) – a dream sequence took the hero back to the Middle Ages with Fay Wray – was one of his most successful films; and *This'll Make You Whistle* (37) was unique in that both show and film were running in London at the same time at one point (the film was made during the early part of the run): as so often in the past, Buchanan was the toast of the town. Van Phillips, who was his musical director over the next few films, said: 'No one was as much loved – for his position – as Johnny B, as we all called him. He was meticulous, but nothing and no one were too unimportant for him to give time and trouble to.' Buchanan was his own producer on these films: *Smash and Grab*, a straight picture à la *The Thin Man*; *The Sky's the Limit*, obviously about aeroplanes; *Sweet Devil*, with Bobby Howes, which he produced only; *Break the News* (38), directed by René Clair, in which Maurice Chevalier co-starred (Adele Astaire was the heroine till, halfway through shooting, she was replaced by June Knight); and *The Gang's All Here* (39), again playing the debonair insurance-agent hero of *Smash and Grab*, and at one point impersonating a Bogart-like gangster. For ABPC he did *The Middle Watch*, a version of a naval farce by Ian Hay and Stephen King-Hall, and *Bulldog Sees It Through* (not Drummond).

In 1940 he had a setback when a big show on tour, 'Top Hat and Tails', collapsed – at the same time as France, and the two events were not simply coincidental. Britain, during the first year of the war, had no time for top hats and tails, and Buchanan became merely a memory, along with 'Stop Me and Buy One' and street-lighting. He enter-

Jack Buchanan and Lili Damita in Brewster's Millions *(35), an oft-filmed farce about a young man who has to spend a fortune within 24 hours.*

tained the troops, and continued to act on the stage under his own management, notably in a revival of 'The Last of Mrs Cheyney' and in 'Canaries Sometimes Sing'.

It was Hollywood which restored him to public favour. Minnelli co-starred him with Fred Astaire in *The Band Wagon* (53): the character was unsympathetic – a temperamental and egotistical producer, reputedly based on Minnelli himself – but Buchanan played with some tongue-in-cheek and had several fine numbers with Astaire and Nanette Fabray. Back in London, he had his longest run for some time in a feeble farce, 'As Long As They're Happy' – and was a cinch to repeat on film (54). In 1955 he appeared with Glynis Johns and Peter Finch in *Josephine and Men*, and in France in the sad, botched last film of Preston Sturges, *Les Carnets de Major Thompson*. It was only exported in a heavily cut version, by which time both Sturges and Buchanan were dead. Buchanan died in 1957, after a long battle with cancer.

Billie Burke with Thomas Meighan in The Land of Promise (*17*), *directed by Joseph Kaufman from Somerset Maugham's play about settlers in Canada and one of Miss Burke's rare serious pictures.*

Billie Burke

Ginger Rogers, among others, refers to the 30s as Hollywood's Golden Years. It isn't just looking back through rose-coloured glasses, though to artists like Rogers there must have been in herself and around the studios an atmosphere of self-confidence, of success and all's-right-with-the-world. The big studios pampered and protected their stars; and they churned out film after film without a consideration of losing money. They were the Golden Years because there were so many really funny comedies and because there was, behind them, a glittering assembly of supporting players whom the public knew and loved almost as much. In the Astaire-Rogers pictures, there were stalwarts like Edward Everett Horton, Eric Blore, Helen Brodrick and the great Alice Brady.

Billie Burke, like Alice Brady, was a considerable stage actress doomed to playing the same part in pictures: that of the fluttery, irresponsible older lady whose lack of logic induced despair in the rest of the cast and hilarity in the audience. Burke wrote in her memoirs ('With a Feather on My Nose', 1949): 'These characters, these bird-witted ladies whom I have characterized so often that I presume you know them – how could you escape? – derive from my part in "The Vinegar Tree". I am neatly typed today, of course, possibly irrevocably typed, although I sincerely hope not, for I should like better parts.' She didn't get them and audiences perhaps should be grateful: Billie Burke's bird-witted lady was one of the perfect things in an imperfect world.

Prior to taking on this part, she had been a great beauty and a great stage favourite on both sides of the Atlantic. She was born in Washington in 1885, into a family of entertainers. Her father brought his company to Europe, and Burke toured in Russia, France, Germany, etc.; they arrived in Britain where she sang 'coon songs' at Birkenhead, and appeared in panto at Glasgow and Sheffield. Her first major legit role was in 1903 at the London Pavilion, in 'The School Girl', singing 'Mamie, I Have a Little Canoe'. After which she had important roles, at one point taking over the lead in 'The Belle of New York'. One of the great impresarios of the period, Charles Frohman, took her back to New York to co-star with

John Drew in 'My Wife', in 1907, and she worked with him for a number of years – in plays such as 'Love Watches', Maugham's 'Mrs Dot' and 'The Land of Promise', and Pinero's 'The Mind-the-Paint Girl' and 'The Amazon'. It was Maugham who introduced her to Florenz Ziegfeld, recently divorced from Anna Held, and she married him (her memoirs are mostly an account of marriage to that legendary showman).

Triangle (Thomas H. Ince) made picture overtures, and in what was already Hollywood, she made *Peggy* (15), playing a Scots maid, with William Desmond as her leading man. She got $10,000 a week, the highest sum yet paid to a movie artist. Ince offered her a five-year contract, but she realized the difficulty of being a movie star and remaining Mrs Ziegfeld, and declined; however, she made an indie in Florida, *Gloria's Romance* (16) with David Powell. The film companies remained insistent and Burke finally signed with Paramount (Famous Players-Lasky) because they had a New York studio and she would not have to be parted from her philandering husband. She made: *The Mysterious Miss Terry* (17), *Arms and the Girl*, *The Land of Promise* with Thomas Meighan, *Eve's Daughter* (18), *Let's Get a Divorce*, *The Make-Believe Wife*, and *Good Gracious Annabelle!*, one of her biggest hits. There followed *The Misleading Widow*, *Sadie Love*, *Wanted a Husband*, *Away Goes Prudence* (20), *The Frisky Mrs Johnson* (21) and *The Education of Elizabeth*. Most of them were very poor, and she lost interest. She continued to appear on Broadway – Booth Tarkington's 'Intimate Strangers' (21), Noël Coward's 'The Marquise' (27) among others – but was mainly Mrs Ziegfeld. Ziegfeld, by 1930, was penniless – partly due to some flops, partly via poor speculation, and partly because of the circumstances caused by the Depression; and Burke returned to the stage, in her first character role, in Ivor Novello's 'The Truth Game'; that led to an offer to appear in the Los Angeles production of 'The Vinegar Tree' (31) by Paul Osborne, which led in turn to a Hollywood offer.

In 1930 she appeared in some Pathé-Rodeo (short) comedies; but *A Bill of Divorcement* (32) is usually listed as her Talkie debut. The invitation came from director George Cukor, and she played the pretty but thoughtless wife of mentally ill John Barrymore. Originally she was co-starred with Barrymore, but as it became apparent that the film belonged to the debuting Katharine Hepburn, the billing was changed

The Young in Heart (*38*): *Janet Gaynor and Billie Burke (right) playing cards with Minnie Dupree, and fleecing her. They were two of a family of con-artists, and the film amusingly told of their regeneration because of their kindness.*

and Hepburn's name added: Burke then went below the title to keep her company. She followed with another with Hepburn, *Christopher Strong* (33), and then at MGM was Lionel Barrymore's wife, the vapid hostess giving the *Dinner at Eight* (in New York revivals her outburst when things finally get too much for her is greeted with applause). She was already type-cast: *Only Yesterday* (34) at Universal; at RKO *Finishing School* starring Frances Dee and Bruce Cabot; *Where Sinners Meet*; and *Now We're Rich Again* with Marian Nixon and Reginald Denny; and at MGM, two Clark Gable vehicles, *Forsaking All Others* (35) and *After Office Hours*; and *Society Doctor* with Chester Morris.

MGM offered her a contract – mainly as the result of her cooperation over *The Great Ziegfeld* which they were preparing (Myrna Loy played her). She continued to work for other studios and her parts continued to be both starring and supporting. She co-starred with Will Rogers, then Fox's – and the US's – top box-office star, in *Doubting Thomas*, an ingratiating comedy about a plain man whose silly wife has stage aspirations; and then went on to gurgle but briefly as a Duchess at the ball on the Eve of Waterloo in *Becky Sharp*. She made: *A Feather in Her Hat*, starring Pauline Lord and Basil Rathbone; *She Couldn't Take It* with Joan Bennett; *My American Wife* (36) with Ann Sothern; *Piccadilly Jim* with Robert Montgomery; *Craig's Wife* with Rosalind Russell; and *Parnell* (37). Then Hal Roach was inspired to cast her as Mrs Topper in *Topper*. Roland Young was Topper, and they were an irresistible combination: both well-meaning and both vague, but where he bumbled, she dithered.

After it came *The Bride Wore Red*, starring Joan Crawford; *Navy Blue and Gold* with Lionel Barrymore and Robert Young; *Everybody Sing* (38) with Judy Garland; and again for Hal Roach (MGM released) *Merrily We Live*. This had the classic virtues of the period: a crazy comedy about a crazy family. Burke was the daffy mother who insisted on adopting a fake tramp (Brian Aherne) and making him the chauffeur. Said the New Statesman: 'Billie Burke's mother attains (like Parsifal) to a foolishness so pure that it verges on beauty.' Clarence Kolb was the father, but Burke was back with Roland Young in the equally delightful *The Young in Heart*, with Douglas Fairbanks Jr and Janet Gaynor, and in *Topper Takes a Trip*. The New Statesman again enthused: 'Here I must pay tribute to Billie Burke who . . . excels all her previous studies in good-natured imbecility, her every word

Spencer Tracy, as the Father of the Bride *(50), drinks to the groom's father, Moroni Olsen.* *Billie Burke was the groom's mother and Joan Bennett the bride's.*

proceeding from a wonderfully complete inner vacuum.' Also for Roach she was in *Zenobia* (39), after which she was Robert Young's flighty mother in *Bridal Suite* and Glinda the Good Fairy in *The Wizard of Oz*, her favourite film part she has said, and the nearest to her stage roles. She was in the Taylor-Garson *Remember?*, the Niven-Loretta Young *Eternally Yours*; *The Ghost Comes Home* (40) with Frank Morgan and *And One Was Beautiful* with Robert Cummings and Laraine Day; and starred, with several fine contemporaries (Charles Coburn, Beulah Bondi, Helen Brodrick, Helen Westley, Marjorie Main), in *The Captain Is a Lady*. *Dulcy* was an Ann Sothern vehicle in which Roland Young appeared with her; she starred again in a B with Frank Morgan, *Hullabaloo*. She and Young were *not* married in *Irene* and had only a couple of scenes together; she spent *One Night in Lisbon* (41) with Fred MacMurray and Madeleine Carroll; and was back starring with Young in *Topper Returns* and with Frank Morgan in *The Wild Man of Borneo*, the last under her MGM contract. She was ideally cast as the mother of the house in *The Man Who Came to Dinner* with Bette Davis, and after *What's Cookin'* at Universal, was light relief and mother again in a heavier Davis film, *In This Our Life* (42). The Joan Crawford-Melvyn Douglas *They All Kissed the Bride* was the last she did with Roland Young. She supported Don Ameche and Joan Bennett in *Girl Trouble* and was featured in the amusing *Hi Diddle Diddle!* (43), after which she starred in a clutch of Bs: *Gildersleeve on Broadway*, one of a series that starred Harold Peary; *Laramie Trail* (44), a Republic Western with Smiley Burnette; *So's Your Uncle* with Donald Woods, and *Swing Out Sister* (45), which has Rod Cameron as a classics composer with a secret passion for swing. It was no wonder that she tried Broadway in two not-too-successful comedies, 'This Rock' (43) and Zoë Akins's 'Mrs January and Mr X' (44).

The Cheaters was a Republic programmer which reprised threads from other, better Burke pictures: how ham actor Joseph Schildkraut reforms a well-to-do and somewhat crooked New York family. Burke, of course, was the mother, selfish, spoilt and unthinking; it was a straight performance but audiences wanted to laugh at her. She was unacceptable now except in comedy, partly because, as she grew older, her voice more than ever was–so appropriately–like the twittering of birds. Alas, her activity decreased: *Breakfast in Hollywood* (46) with Bonita Granville; *Bachelor Daughter* (47); *The Barkleys of Broadway* (48); *And Baby Makes Three* (49) with Robert Young and Barbara Hale. She was groom Don Taylor's mother in *Father of the Bride* (50) and in the sequel, *Father's Little Dividend* (51), and in between was one of several talents wasted in *Three Husbands* (50) and *Blaze of Glory*. After that she did varied TV work, had a small part in *Small Town Girl* (53) and then retired. She was induced out of retirement for a couple of plays in stock (including 'The Solid Gold Cadillac') and for very small parts in *The Young Philadelphians* (59), *Sergeant Rutledge* (60) and *Pepe* playing fluttery old ladies. She died in 1970.

James Cagney

Cagney the actor has been, perhaps inevitably, overshadowed by Cagney the gangster. He was the best gangster there was. He came from the back streets, with a square trilby clapped on his grinning head. The clothes marked his new affluence; he was dapper, assured, smug. Like someone's pet terrier: bouncing, eager. He moved on the balls of his feet, the fists ready. Otherwise, only the eyes betrayed the necessary wariness–a quick glance, a quick frown; then the snarling and the yelping. But not pitiful, rather defiant. Come the three corners of the world in arms and he would, still, shock them. He was convinced of his own invincibility. They would never get him. That was his charm. He never asked–he commanded, but in a voice that itself was a wheedler, skitting breathlessly, high-pitched, on its sentences, like the butter-covered knife he jabbed in the air, accompanying the words between mouthfuls. Women kept their place around him. He was convinced of his appeal: so what they didn't like it, there was another broad someplace. Said Kenneth Tynan in 1952: '. . . but he possessed, possibly in greater abundance than any other name star of his time, irresistible charm. . . . Even the most ascetic cinéaste will admit that it is impossible to forget how he looked and talked at the height of his popularity.'

But C. A. Lejeune earlier (in 1946, reviewing *Blood on the Sun*) admired the talent: 'James Cagney is one of the best screen actors of our time, with gifts of pathos and an impish humour second to none. . . . With no hint of a four-dimensional character to work from, little material to suggest the hero's past and background, or even his tastes and way of living, Mr Cagney is content to convey all the immediate reactions of a man who is exuberantly alive today and expects to be

Angels with Dirty Faces *had the same plot idea as* San Francisco *two years earlier. That it all seemed fresh was due partly to Cagney's effervescent personality and a cast that included henchman Bogart.*

terribly dead tomorrow. It is a lesson to all young film actors to study how he does this.... Few heroes of melodrama can claim that so much skill of such a high order has been spent in bringing their poor bones to life.'

The persona, of course, was tremendously strong. Cagney was *always* dynamic, alert, tough and fast-moving, as if some ferocious inner energy was carrying him along. He could have played few of the roles that someone like Burt Lancaster regards as 'acting' but while he was active his versatility was much admired. The key lies in his own words: 'There's not much to tell you about acting but this: never settle back on your heels. Never relax. If you relax, the audience relaxes. And always mean everything you say.'

He was born in 1904, on New York's lower East Side, and although he studied briefly at Columbia, family circumstances compelled him initially to such jobs as a department-store wrapper, a waiter and a racker in a pool room. To earn more he applied for a job in vaudeville and was in 'Every Sailor', which seems to have been a 1914–18 equivalent of 'Soldiers in Skirts': he was one of the chorus-girls, and then he moved over–in a double sense–to the chorus of 'Pitter-Patter' (20); later in its run he was given a specialty dance. He toured in vaude with his wife, occasionally getting a break in short-lived Broadway musicals. He made his mark in 'Outside Looking In' and had a small role in a Mary Boland vehicle, 'Women Go On Forever', and another in 'Grand Street Follies'. A big part in 'Maggie the Magnificent' with Joan Blondell led to another co-starring assignment, in 'Penny Arcade': he was a weak little murderer prepared to let someone else take the rap.

Warners bought the rights and brought the two players to Hollywood to film it, rechristened *Sinner's Holiday* (30); the billed stars were Grant Withers and Evalyn Knapp and it was a mild success. WB took up their option on Cagney's services, at $400 a week. He was billed fifth on *Doorway to Hell*, as one of Lew Ayres's (double-crossing)

Cagney's own sister, Jeanne, made one of her rare appearances as his screen sister in Yankee Doodle Dandy *(42), a tribute to George M. Cohan – for which Cagney won the Oscar.*

hoodlums, and had a small role, with Blondell, in *Other Men's Women*, a railroad drama. He was a fast-talking insurance man in *The Millionaire* (George Arliss) and was then given the second lead in *Public Enemy* (31): after three days' shooting producer Darryl F. Zanuck and director William A. Wellman made him and lead Eddie Woods swop parts. They played brothers with a taste for luxury and Cagney in particular had a complete disregard of any honest means of achieving it: till he ended up dead, riddled with bullets, on their mother's doorstep. These mobsters were 'detailed with a realism new to the screen. In danger more from rival gangsters than from the police, they moved uneasily from apartment to apartment, their surroundings at once luxurious and sordid, their women women and nothing more' (Rotha and Griffith, 'The Film Till Now'). A new era of gangster pictures was ushered in and Cagney was in most of them, now a star, flashing away with his gat but not, thereafter, pushing half a grapefruit into Mae Clarke's physog.

This wasn't high cinematic art. Cagney's early pictures were made cheaply and quickly, and weren't considered important – though the deliberately implied social criticism of many of them was recognized. Today they are still entertaining: they move jump-jump-jump through the clichés and are at least emotionally honest. It's ironic that the early Warner Talkies, less expensive and ballyhooed than those of other companies, should stand up best today.

The other great Warner gangster was the already established Edward G. Robinson. Cagney became his henchman in *Smart Money*, but they didn't appear again as rivals, colleagues or enemies: there was no advantage to studio finances to put them both in the same film. After *Blonde Crazy* Cagney fought for a salary raise – to $1,000 – the first of a series of bitter battles with the brothers Warner. He made *Taxi* ('. . . an outstanding performance', thought Picturegoer, 'he gets under the skin of his role as a tough of the goodhearted but hot-to-anger type'); Hawks's *The Crowd Roars* (32) as a track driver, and *Winner Take All* as a prize-fighter.

He was now earning $1,250 weekly, considerably less than some other Warner stars (before they took salary cuts because of the Depression, Ruth Chatterton and William Powell got $6,000, Robinson, Fairbanks Jr and Kay Francis $4,000, and Loretta Young $1,000). At the onset of shooting *Blessed Event* Cagney walked out (Lee Tracy took over), claiming he was doing too many pictures for too little. He offered to do three for nothing, provided that at the end of the year he was given his real due. He told an interviewer: 'My stand is based on the fact that my pictures, for the time being, are big money-makers – and that there are only so many successful pictures

The title, presumably, referred to prison-life – and suggested gloom and tragedy: but the way they played it, it was rather a thrill a second.

in a personality. And don't forget that when you are washed up in pictures you are really through. You can't even get a bit, let alone a decent part. . . . I don't care if I never act again. If I never had to do another scene, it would be all right with me. I have no trace of that ham-like theatrical yen to act all the time no matter what. I shan't miss trouping.' WB eventually offered \$3,000 a week; it was later to go to \$4,500.

He returned for the appropriately named *Hard to Handle* (33), as a press agent organizing a dance marathon; *The Picture Snatcher*, ex-con turned photographer; *Mayor of Hell*, prison governor; and *Footlight Parade*, theatre producer. In that one he sang and danced ('Lookin' for My Shanghai Lil') and hustled the cast like a whirlwind: a performance which would be exhausting were it not so captivating. Large audiences were captivated: the film grossed the then outstanding sum of \$1¾ million. In *Lady Killer* (34) he was a hood turned film-star, dragging Mae Clarke across the floor by her hair; and then he was *Jimmy the Gent*. Said Mordaunt Hall in The New York Times: 'a swift-paced comedy in which he gives another of his vigorous, incisive portrayals'; but *He Was Her Man* was soggy. The her was Blondell again, as a hooker, and he was an ex-con. *Here Comes the Navy* was the first of several in which Pat O'Brien was his rival or sparring partner: they went virtually through the same story – in the Marine Corps – the following year in *Devil Dogs of the Air*. It was the second of the six Cagney films released in 1935 and later in the year O'Brien was a cop and Cagney his wastrel brother in *The Irish in Us*. Cagney was also *The St Louis Kid*, a truck driver, and the *Frisco Kid*, a dock-rat: Picturegoer thought it 'rather much to ask one's sympathy' for a murderer, but that Cagney 'has a magnetism' which let him get away with it. He was on the other side of the law in *G-Men* (which Robinson had turned down), a terrific anti-gangster piece in which he said, 'I seen too many back alleys as a kid to want to go back to them'.

There followed the film that Warners claimed was 'Three Centuries in the Making', *A Midsummer Night's Dream* and Cagney was Bottom. John Marks found him 'so sensitive, so dramatic, and so sure of his rendering . . . that it is worth sitting through the whole ordeal once for the sake of his scene with Titania and the sweet fooling of his fellows'. Robert Forsythe lamented the collapse of the comedy: 'Since I would rather die than admit that Mr Cagney is not a great actor, I must blame it on Shakespeare or Reinhardt. Something is wrong and it isn't me and it isn't Cagney.' What was wrong was that Reinhardt's basic conception was vulgar, but the damp reviews were offset by a gigantic publicity campaign and the Motion Picture Herald listed its gross as a surprising \$1½ million.

Ceiling Zero (36) was more – indeed, very – conventional, with Cagney and O'Brien doing their Flagg and Quirt act again, as commercial airline pilots, Cagney as a fast-talking Don Juan: Howard Hawks directed and it was great fun. But not to Cagney: it was his fifth film within a year, despite the contracted four. He looked for a technical point to break his contract and found it when a cinema bannered O'Brien's name above his for *Devil Dogs of the Air* – a film which, he added gratuitously, 'had no reason for being filmed under any circumstances'. The case went to court, but pending the outcome he signed a contract with a small indie firm, Grand National: *Great Guy* (36) on the side of the law, and *Something to Sing About* (37), a musical. Neither was outstanding, and he couldn't have been sorry when the case went against him and he returned to Warners.

The studio had learnt something and so had he. That they needed each other is shown by the record of the top 10 draws: he had crept into the list in 1935, at 10th, returned in 1939 at 9th, and was solidly entrenched again 1940–3 inclusive, until he left the studio. His first film was good: *Boy Meets Girl* (38),

Cagney's early fans loved the caveman way he treated his women. Here's an example from a later film, Blood on the Sun *(46). The stoic lady is Sylvia Sidney.*

from the Spewacks' Broadway hit about Hollywood, with O'Brien and Marie Wilson (and for some reason not shown in Britain till 1940). And the second, which he had planned to do at Grand National, was even better, *Angels With Dirty Faces*: the one about the boys who grow up together and part–Cagney a hood and O'Brien a priest. A fine cast included Humphrey Bogart and Ann Sheridan, and the New York Critics voted Cagney the year's Best Actor. He and Bogart were pitted against each other in *The Oklahoma Kid* (39), mainly memorable because they both felt incongruous in chaps and sent the whole thing up; *Each Dawn I Die* was a superior pen epic, with George Raft as a fellow con; and *The Roaring Twenties*, almost the last major gangster film Warners made, ended the series with a bang. Said Graham Greene: 'Mr Cagney, of the bull-calf brow, is as always a superb and witty actor. Mr Bogart is, of course, magnificent.'

Cagney's contract finished in 1940 and he wanted to start his own company, but because of the world situation he signed on for two years more with Warners. *The*

Fighting 69th (40, recruits in World War I) and *Torrid Zone* (rivals for Ann Sheridan) were the last two with O'Brien. *City for Conquest* was New York: Cagney was a boxer and Arthur Kennedy his composer kid-brother. This was a powerful melodrama directed by Anatole Litvak with a much admired poetic touch – the very quality which has dated it more than most in the Cagney canon. Almost undated is *Strawberry Blonde* (41), a small-town romance with Olivia de Havilland. *The Bride Came C.O.D.* was a fairly unhappy excursion into comedy for him and Bette Davis, and *Captains of the Clouds* (42), a tribute to the Royal Canadian Air Force: both contributed to Cagney's being the second highest paid US citizen in 1941 (Louis B. Mayer was first). Earlier, another citizen had officially accused him of Communism. The charge was dismissed, but Cagney was determined to show publicly where his feelings lay, and chose to do a biopic of composer George M. Cohan, *Yankee Doodle Dandy*. It took the vast sum of $4 million in the US and was equally popular in Britain, so clearly for 1942 the ingredients were perfect: sentiment, nostalgia, patriotism and music – but it badly needed the salt-and-pepper of Cagney's performance, which brought him another New York Critics award and a much-applauded Oscar.

He spent the war years selling bonds and touring with USO; formed his own company with his brother William, releasing through UA, but audiences were not taken by *Johnny Come Lately* (44) about a vagabond helping a dear old lady to run a town's paper, or by Saroyan's *The Time of Your Life* (48). *Blood on the Sun* (46) was perhaps the most popular, because it was most like the standard Cagney vehicle, and *13 Rue Madeleine* (also 46) was an efficient 'real life' spy story at 20th made in the new 'documentary' manner. None of the Cagneys' other plans came to anything, and he accepted an offer from WB to play a gangster again in *White Heat* (49), one with a fixation on mother Margaret Wycherly, the head of the gang. In other ways, times had changed: the film was bloodier and more brutal than of yore, but Raoul Walsh handled it with the same brilliance he'd brought to *The Roaring Twenties*. Cagney stayed with his old studio a couple of years: Variety found him 'a delight' in *The West Point Story* (50), 'particularly his bombastic, temperamental storming, his hoofing and cocky personality whether making love or directing a stage show'. He did another and lesser gangster film, *Kiss Tomorrow Goodbye*; a likeable drama about an ex-alcoholic journalist, *Come Fill the Cup* (51); a guest appearance in *Starlift*; plus

Still tough in his last picture, One Two Three *(62), Cagney berates his personal assistant Hanns Lothar for a scheme that went wrong.*

A Lion in the Streets (53), which came too soon after *All the King's Men* to claim serious attention – nor was his stab at the Huey Long-type part anything but superficial.

Earlier, the John Ford remake of the Silent classic *What Price Glory?* (52) had been an out-and-out flop: its sentiment had dated and both Cagney and Dan Dailey were miscast; and with *Run for Cover* (55), although a good Nicholas Ray Western, his career really was in low gear. There had been so little critical and public attention during these years that his burst of activity in late 1955 was talked of as a comeback: as The Gimp, Doris Day's racketeer husband in *Love Me or Leave Me*; the neurotic captain in *Mister Roberts*; and George M. Cohan, an effective guest appearance in Bob Hope's *The Seven Little Foys*. In 1956 he took over from Spencer Tracy the lead in an indifferent Western, *Tribute to a Bad Man*, and again at MGM was involved in a minor domestic drama with Barbara Stanwyck, *These Wilder Years*. He gave a sympathetic performance as Lon Chaney in *The Man of a Thousand Faces* (57), notable otherwise only for the perfect reconstructions of Chaney's make-up; and then directed competently a remake of *This Gun for Hire* called *Short Cut to Hell*. A Universal musical with Shirley Jones, *Never*

Steal Anything Small (58), utilized his talents well–he was a crooked labour boss–but in most other departments it was deficient; and he was also well cast in *Shake Hands With the Devil*, a melo about the Irish troubles, but the acting generally, like the dialogue, was platitudinous.

He returned to independent production, in conjunction with Robert Montgomery who directed *The Gallant Hours* (59), a sober tribute to World War II Admiral William F. Halsey Jr: Cagney did his best to give dimension once more to a character written without any, but the film was too sober, too well-intentioned. He retired, but Billy Wilder coaxed him back for *One Two Three* (62), to play a Coca-Cola executive in Berlin whose boss's daughter falls in love with a young Red: he rattled off his lines in his own invincible fashion–a virtuoso display in a well-nigh perfect comedy. But a certain audience coolness indicated that he no longer had his old hold. He reputedly turned down the role of Dolittle in *My Fair Lady* and lives quietly on one of his ranches. He doesn't ever do TV, even guesting (though he did make three appearances in the mid-50s).

Eddie Cantor

There was a generation of performers who seem to have become immortal; they came at that point when American show business was at its most confident: vaudeville had become the most popular art form the world had yet known, and, allied to it but slightly higher up the social scale, the musical theatre was in the hands of great showmen and great songwriters. The artists thrown up during these years are legendary: Fanny Brice, W. C. Fields, Helen Morgan, Al Jolson, Sophie Tucker, Eddie Cantor and so on (Cantor writes warmly and revealingly about many of the others in his two memoirs, 'My Life Is in Your Hands', 1929, and 'Take My Life', 1957.) Movies and records increased their popularity (in most cases) and perpetuated it. Cantor, small, dapper, Jewish, 'Banjo-eyes', was for some years one of the most popular of screen comedians (though the Motion Picture Almanacks of the time do warn that the huge grosses listed for his films were 'supplied by Mr Cantor himself'). Today, many of his effects look forced, but let him skip around (and sing) as he did in his vaudeville act, and there is some magic.

He was born in the heart of the ghetto in New York in 1893. His parents died while he was a child and he left school early to become an office boy. He began performing at amateur nights till there wasn't one within miles he hadn't covered. His first pro job was in a burlesque show, 'Indian Maidens', and in 1912 he was in Gus Edwards's 'Kid Kabaret'; in 1914, he was in London in Charlot's 'Not Likely'. Ziegfeld put him in the 'Follies' in 1917, 1918 and 1919. They quarrelled and Cantor worked for other managements in 'The Midnight Rounders' and 'Make it Snappy' among others; but they made it up and Ziegfeld had one of his greatest hits with Cantor in 'Kid Boots' (23). The plot concerned an officious (but lovable, of course) golf caddie who bootlegs on the side and can't be sacked because he knows too much. Paramount decided to film it: *Kid Boots* (26) with Cantor and Clara Bow and a different plot. It was a big success, but a follow-up film he did for that studio was a flop: *Special Delivery* (27).

His next film appearance was guesting in an early film musical to which Ziegfeld lent his name for promotion purposes, *Glorifying the American Girl* (29). Meanwhile, he had given Ziegfeld another giant hit, 'Whoopee' (28): it was taken off (after a year) only because Ziegfeld was broke and needed the money Goldwyn had offered for the screen rights. And Goldwyn had signed Cantor as star and consultant. The film (30) was no more than a photographed stage show–the adventures of a hypochondriac out West; it was a great hit and Goldwyn exercised his option on Cantor's services: *Palmy Days* (31) was a lot of brouhaha set in a sweet factory, with a tasteless musical finale involving kids, ice-cream and early colour. Its success caused Goldwyn to sign Cantor for five pictures, to be spread over five years. They were *The Kid From Spain* (32)–comic bull-fighting with the Goldwyn Girls and Lyda Roberti; *Roman Scandals* (33) with the GGs and Ruth Etting; and *Kid Millions* (34) and *Strike Me Pink*, both with Ethel Merman. According to the figures supplied by Cantor, all but the last two did sensational business. He meanwhile had become a big star on radio in New York–a fact which Goldwyn blandly refused to appreciate; Cantor resented sitting around on the Coast, losing his radio fees, while Goldwyn tinkered with the scripts and made other changes. The last film of the contract was not made.

Cantor moved over to 20th on long-term contract and had another success with *Ali Baba Goes to Town* (38), but there was some dispute between them as to how financially successful it was; there were also disagreements over material, and the contract was dissolved. He went to MGM for one but

Eddie Cantor, full flight, in Strike Me Pink *(35), his last film for Goldwyn.*

this thudded badly: a (straight) sentimental comedy with Judith Anderson, *Forty Little Mothers* (39). He went back to Broadway – 'Banjo Eyes' (41) – but he returned to films in *Thank Your Lucky Stars* (43) as part of the plot which tied together all the star acts. In 1944 he did *Show Business*, a cozy and not unlikeable collection of all the clichés in the backstage book; aided by Joan Davis, George Murphy and Constance Moore, it did very well – so well, that Cantor was asked to do another one with Davis: *If You Knew Susie* (48). He adored working with her, and she was an extremely funny lady in her own right – but the script was poor and the film flopped. Cantor didn't actually appear in his next flop: *The Eddie Cantor Story* (53) – Keefe Braselle played him. In 1956, he was given a special Oscar 'for distinguished service to the film industry'. During his later years he worked mostly in TV. He died in 1964.

Madeleine Carroll

Madeleine Carroll belonged to that unselect band of ladies whose beauty was more immediately apparent than her acting ability. In 1937 James Montgomery Flagg said that he considered her the most beautiful woman in the world. However, few of her parts demanded much more of her than to be cool and lovely while embroiled in creakily melodramatic situations: it is not surprising that Hitchcock used her twice in the 30s, and her greatest claim to fame may well be as the first of his blondes.

She was born in West Bromwich in 1906, studied at Birmingham University (hence the later publicity which emphasized that she was a beauty with brains), where she acted; began teaching at Hove, but abandoned it to try her luck as a professional actress. For a while she modelled hats but she eventually got a part in a tour of 'Mr What's His Name' starring Seymour Hicks, which led to her West End début, 'The Lash' (27). She applied for the female lead in a war picture, *The Guns of Loos* (28) and was chosen from 150 girls. It gave her few chances, but enabled her to get into another three West End plays (all at the Vaudeville) and brought more film offers: in *The Firstborn* she was married to a degenerate Miles Mander, in *What Money Can Buy* persecuted by a merciless philanderer, and she was again with Mander in *The Crooked Billet* (29). She went to France to make *L'Instinct*, but because it was a Silent it was never seen in Britain or the US. Her first Talkie was *The American Prisoner*, a period piece set on Dartmoor, followed by *Atlantic* and *Young Woodley* (30), the second film version of John Van Druten's play (a Silent had been made a year or so previously but because of the craze for Talkies was never shown). She did *The W Plan* with Brian Aherne, Galsworthy's *Escape* with Gerald du Maurier (who took over the lead from Clive Brook after several weeks of shooting), and *French Leave* and *The School for Scandal*, which premièred simultaneously. The former was a comedy that she had done on the stage (she had also recently been in 'The Constant Nymph' and 'Beau Geste') and the latter a shabby version of Sheridan made by Maurice Elvey; Carroll was Lady Teazle and the cast included the charming Dodo Watts, considered by many to be Carroll's likely successor.

Carroll was by now the biggest female star in British films, though her popularity by no means approached that of the American stars. She was not very much beyond being charming and pretty–in a mousy way–certainly not the sleek creature of the Hollywood years. The first time she was unmistakably blonde was in *Madame Guillotine* with Aherne. In 1931 she made *Kissing Cup's Race*, *Fascination* and *The Written Law* and then officially retired from the screen–due, she complained, to the quality of these films. She had also married an army officer, but she continued to work on the stage. Gaumont-British finally offered her a generous contract (a reported £650 per week) and starred her in two of the better British films of the period, *Sleeping Car* (33) with Ivor Novello and *I Was a Spy*.

Hollywood had not been unaware of her during these years, and Fox negotiated to borrow her for John Ford's *The World Moves On* (34), co-starring Franchot Tone, a two-part saga (early nineteenth century and modern) and a flop. Back in Britain she was loaned out to Toeplitz for the film which marked Clive Brook's return after years in Hollywood, a period piece called *The Dictator* (35): it also flopped, and was variously re-christened *Loves of a Dictator* and *The Love Affair of a Dictator*. In 1935 she made her last London stage appearance in 'Duet for Floodlight'. Hitchcock cast her in *The 39 Steps* and *Secret Agent* (36, with John Gielgud, based on Somerset Maugham's 'Ashenden') and she was ideal. These were by far the best films she had made, but she fretted in the British studios which she found far less efficient than those in Hollywood. No one was surprised when it was announced that 20th and Walter Wanger had signed her to contracts.

Madeleine Carroll in two of the films which established her as the perfect storybook heroine–frail but brav and very beautiful: wit

Carroll, during her Hollywood years, became many a man's dream girl: she seemed to be made of sugar and spice–good enough to eat. And she appeared in some of the more notable films of the period. This was not a phrase, however, which could be applied to the first, *The Case Against Mrs one Power (left) in* yds of London *) and with Ronald* *man in* The soner of Zenda *). Both were period* *mas.*

Ames (36) with George Brent; but *The General Died at Dawn*, with Gary Cooper and Akim Tamiroff (as the General), was a strange, moody and excellent adventure story. And two she did at 20th were both popular: a historical saga with Tyrone Power, *Lloyds of London*, and a musical with Dick Powell, *On the Avenue* (37) – she wasn't called upon to sing or dance; Alice Faye took care of that side of things. *It's All Yours* was a comedy at Columbia with Francis Lederer and then she was the heroine *par excellence* of *The Prisoner of Zenda* with Ronald Colman. Wanger put her into one of his own films, *Blockade* (38) with Henry Fonda, intended as peace propaganda and negligible as entertainment.

Carroll then signed a long-term contract with Paramount, and did three in a row with Fred MacMurray, *Café Society* (39), the funny *Honeymoon in Bali* and *Virginia* (40).

Her best performance is probably in *My Son My Son* with Brian Aherne, a moving (and popular) drama of a wastrel son (Louis Hayward): proving that, given the material, she was more than a pretty face. But she could do nothing with the routine jungle piece, *Safari*, with Douglas Fairbanks Jr, nor with her role in de Mille's *North West Mounted Police*, though she looked better than ever in colour. She and MacMurray then had *One Night in Lisbon* (41), an up-dating of Van Druten's 'There's Always Juliet' and with husband Sterling Hayden she took the *Bahama Passage* (42), a seeming excuse to show them both off in their blonde and very tanned (half-) nakedness. Indeed, the film's sole virtue was its colour, though audiences roared when Carroll invited Hayden to make love and he replied: 'No, let's fish.' After a gallant gambol with Bob Hope as his *(My) Favorite Blonde* (42) she asked Paramount to release her in order to devote herself to the war effort: she and Hayden changed their names in order to avoid publicity.

She did much for the Allied Relief Fund and was active in the Red Cross; she didn't return to films till 1946 in a weak British weepie, *White Cradle Inn*, co-starring the then almost unknown Michael Rennie. It was announced that she had formed a company to make semi-documentaries 'to promote a better understanding between the peoples of the world' but nothing emerged. In 1948 she appeared on Broadway in 'Goodbye My Fancy', and that may have re-awakened Hollywood's interest. At all events, she made a couple more films: *Don't Trust Your Husband* (48) and *The Fan* (49) as Mrs Erlynne in this heavy version of Oscar Wilde. Both were flops. Since then she has kept out of the limelight – working at one time for UNESCO. But that she hasn't entirely abandoned show business was proved when she accepted a part in the Broadway-bound 'Beekman Place' in 1964: however she left the cast before it hit town – wisely, as it turned out. Her fourth marriage, to Life magazine publisher Andrew Heiskel, ended after 15 years in 1965. Since then she has spent her time in London and Paris.

Lon Chaney

In the Silent era, audiences loved to be thrilled by Lon Chaney. They sat aghast as he clambered about the screen as one monster or freak after another: 'The Man of a Thousand Faces'. His make-up and disguises were sources of wonder: part of his success was due to audience curiosity as to what weird guise he would materialize in next. He took painstaking hours over preparation, and in private suffered for it; during the last years of his life it was a living martyrdom, with permanently aching limbs, headaches and eye-strain. It is difficult to say to what extent Chaney, beneath the

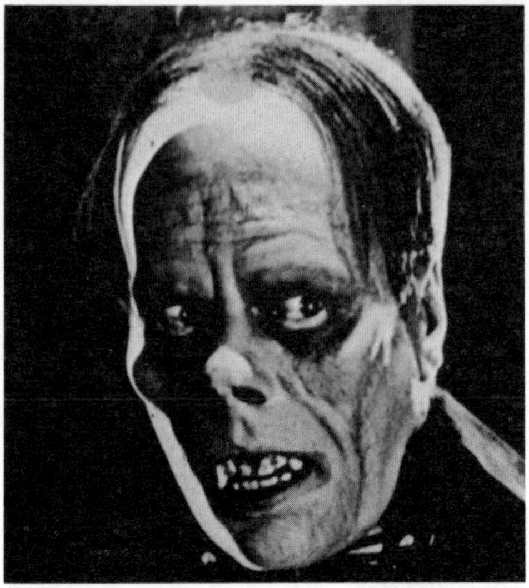

Four of the many face
of Lon Chaney: All t
Brothers Were Vali
(*23*), The Phantom

make-up, was an actor in the technical sense: these were physical creations. But that he was a cathartic figure, there is no doubt. His creatures were vulnerable and sympathetic, immensely powerful and real; though considering the extent to which they were maimed and mutilated–armless, legless, one-eyed, hunchbacked–*and* his 'fabulous popularity . . . one might be moved to speculate on the peculiar tastes of the mass audiences of the 20s' (Pauline Kael).

Chaney was born in Colorado Springs in 1883 of deaf-mute parents. He started on the stage as a boy because his brother owned a theatre, but his father had him taught paper-hanging and carpet-laying. He returned to the stage, however, working as prop man, actor, transportation agent. In 1899 he and his brother produced 'The Little Tycoon'; they did one-night stands. Chaney became second comic in 'The Red Kimono' and a song-and-dance man. He decided to quit travelling when he divorced his wife and was given custody of the child; like many another travelling actor at this time he sought a job in films.

He began as an extra and small-part player in two-reelers. His first credit was *Poor Jake's Demise* (13), followed by about seventy shorts, mostly Westerns, and usually he was the villain. Many of them were directed by Tod Browning, who was to be so significant in Chaney's career. Indicative of things to come was one called *The Lion the Lamb and the Man* (15), where Chaney was a grotesque and hairy primitive man. He himself directed some two-reelers that year; signed a contract with Universal and became a general-utility actor for them: his first important part in a feature was in *Hell Morgan's Girl* (17). There were other small parts, many of them for Universal's subsidiary, Bluebird: *The Flashlight*, *The Vengeance of the West*, *A Doll's House* (from Ibsen's play), *The Fires of Rebellion*, *The Rescue*, *Pay Me*, *The Girl in the Checkered Coat*, *The Empty Gun*, *Anything Once*, *The Scarlet Car*, *The Grand Passion*, *Broadway Love* (18), *Fast Company* and *Broadway Scandal*. He was loaned out to play the villain in William S. Hart's *Riddle Gawne*, and that was his first success. A month later he scored in *That Devil Bateese*, but Universal were unimpressed by this notable double and kept him in poor parts. *The Talk of the Town*, *Danger Go Slow* and *The Wicked Darling* (19), directed by Browning. His contract was about to be renewed but his (second) wife persuaded him to freelance: *False Faces* and *A Man's Country*. He heard that Paramount were looking for a contortionist to play a bogus cripple in *The Miracle Man* (19) and applied. It was a low budgeter–$120,000–but it grossed world-wide over $3 million and made stars of Chaney and his fellow-players, Betty Compson and Thomas Meighan.

Universal now offered a contract on favourable terms, and Chaney was much in demand at other studios. His films over the next few years: 1919: *When Bearcat Went Dry*, *Paid in Advance*, and *Victory*, from Conrad's novel. 1920: *Treasure Island* (Paramount; as Pew, the blind pirate), *The Gift Supreme*, *Nomads of the North*, *The Penalty* (Goldwyn; as a legless criminal). 1921: *Outside the Law* (directed by Browning; in a dual role–a gangster and a Chinaman), *Bits of Life* (a three-part story–as another Oriental in the last sequence), *Night Rose* and *Ace of Hearts*, both starring Leatrice Joy, and *For Those We Love*. 1922: *The Trap*, *Voices of the City* (a gangster), *Flesh and Blood*

e Opera (*25*), The
nholy Three (*25*) *and*
'est of Zanzibar (*28*)

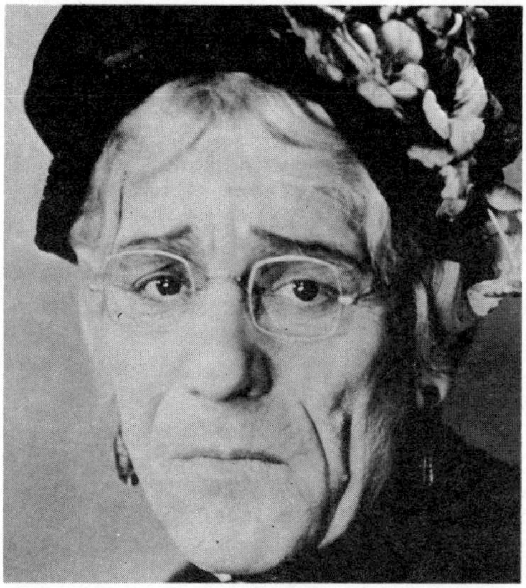

(a deranged and crippled crook), *The Light in the Dark* (the villain), *Shadows* (a Chinese laundryman), *Oliver Twist* (First National; Fagin to Jackie Coogan's Oliver), *Quincy Adams Sawyer* (the heavy) and *A Blind Bargain* (mad scientist and ape-like man). 1923: *All the Brothers Were Valiant* (as one of the brothers; the other–the star–was Malcolm McGregor), *While Paris Sleeps* (made in 1920; as another mad scientist), *The Shock* and *The Hunchback of Notre Dame*.

Chaney's performance as Quasimodo, the hunchback, in this version of Hugo's novel, was much admired and it is perhaps his most famous part: in the US it grossed \$1½ million, one of the year's top films. It also concluded his contract, and there were lots of offers. He did *The Next Corner* (24) at Paramount, and then signed a lucrative deal with MGM. His first film there was *He Who Gets Slapped*, from Leonid Andreyev's tragic play about a circus clown; Norma Shearer was the object of his Pagliacci passion and Victor Sjöstrom directed. The second was *The Monster* (25)–yet another demented scientist. Picturegoer commented that Chaney didn't need sound: '. . . he makes such a palpable, menacing reality out of every shadowy movement that no audible "atmosphere" is necessary to bring gasps of horror from spectators.'

Then Browning came to MGM. For the last two years he had been drinking heavily, but Chaney talked Thalberg into signing him for *The Unholy Three* (three crooks; Chaney was a ventriloquist who spent much of the movie as a sinister old woman): it was a huge success, and the start of the Browning-Chaney partnership (Browning was responsible for roughly half the Chaney films to come). After *The Tower of Lies*, Victor Sjöstrom's fine study of tragedy in a Swedish village, Chaney returned to Universal (on loan) to play *The Phantom of the Opera* (25), from Gaston Leroux's novel about a musician, his face scarred by acid, who haunts the subterranean passages of the Paris Opéra. Mary Philbin was the girl he secretly loved. In the US this was another Chaney triumph, but in Britain it wasn't seen. As a publicity gimmick, the cans of film were met at Southampton Dock by a brigade of guards and escorted to the railway station. Questions were asked in Parliament; it was never disclosed who had 'loaned' the guards to Universal's publicity outfit, but the film was banned as a result (the ban was lifted in 1929, when some Sound sequences were added, but it was too late: it was not a success).

Browning was responsible for the next two: in *The Blackbird* (26) Chaney was a Limehouse criminal who disguises himself as a crippled bishop; in *The Road to Mandalay* he was Singapore Joe, an evil saloon-keeper with a cataract eye. He looked like himself for the first time in years in *Tell It to the Marines* (27). There followed *Mr Wu*, in the title role; *The Unknown* as an armless knife-thrower in a Madrid circus, with Joan Crawford; *The Mockery* as a dim-witted Russian peasant; *London After Midnight* in another dual role–a police inspector and a vampire; *The Big City*; and *Laugh Clown Laugh* (28), where he again eschewed his sinister make-up and gave a 'perfect' characterization and 'his best work since *The Unholy Three*' (Photoplay); *While the City Sleeps*, as a detective; and *West of Zanzibar* (29), as a paralytic trader.

The last one Browning did was *Where East Is East*, a Malayan story, with Lupe

Velez, and Chaney as a man who traps animals for circuses. Then there was *Thunder*. Early in 1930 Chaney signed a new five-year pact with MGM which stipulated Talkie remakes of most of his old hits. A new version of *The Unholy Three* (30) was first; it was almost completed when Chaney died of throat cancer. Browning paid him this tribute: 'He was the hardest working person in the studio.'

His son, Creighton Chaney, just then beginning in films, soon changed his name to Lon Chaney Jr. Apart from a fine performance in *Of Mice and Men* (40) he did little of interest, but he has worked consistently to the present day, mainly in horror films. He did not play his father in a biopic, *Man of a Thousand Faces* (57): James Cagney did.

Charlie Chaplin

Charlie Chaplin has lived long enough to see his supremacy challenged by Buster Keaton. Because Keaton's reputation was under-privileged for so long and because Chaplin's appeared unassailable, the re-discovery of Keaton brought the Chaplin-knockers. Jacques Tati, for instance, felt it incumbent upon him to praise Keaton at Chaplin's expense; and it can be said that the taste of the 60s found Keaton more palatable: it responded at once to his fantasies rather than to Chaplin's, to his battles with mechanisms, to his lack of sentimentality. Chaplin's art, unlike Keaton's, is rooted in Victorian melodrama and sentiment.

Keaton himself said of Chaplin: 'At his best, and Chaplin remained at his best for a long time, he was the greatest comedian who ever lived.' Chaplin must not be under-estimated. Here are some quotes, from his peers and others: 'I believe . . . that Charles Chaplin is a genius' (Beatrice Lillie). 'Oh well, he's just the greatest artist that ever lived' (Mack Sennett). 'Chaplin will keep you laughing for hours on end without effort; he has a genius for the comic. His fun is simple and spontaneous. And yet all the time you have a feeling that at the back of it all is a profound melancholy' (Somerset Maugham). 'But the best comics are also good actors. Chaplin is a wonderful actor' (Zero Mostel). 'But when Chaplin talked about pictures we all sat still and listened hard. We knew very well what we had among us. The greatest actor of our time, unique, irreplaceable. He stood quite outside the jurisdictions or embroilings of Hollywood. He was beyond jealousy. He was an absolute' (Agnes de Mille). 'The man who has made more people laugh than any other man who ever lived and who may be truly called a genius' (Theodore Huff). 'I think he is the greatest of all film stars' (Ruby M. Ayres). 'Of all comedians he worked most deeply and most shrewdly within a realization of what a human being is, and is up against. The Tramp is as centrally representative of humanity, as many-sided and mysterious, as Hamlet, and it seems unlikely that any dancer or actor can ever have excelled him in eloquence, variety and poignancy of motion' (James Agee). '. . . the greatest clown the world has ever seen, magnificent egotist, trampler on conventions, unique, lonely, loved and unforgettable, the wittiest, most sophisticated, the most graceful, the most moving actor on the screen, and possessed of a unique capacity to confer these gifts on all who work with him' (Michael Powell). 'I don't think there's any greater in the business or ever will be. He's the greatest artist that was ever on the screen' (Stan Laurel). 'Chaplin is not only the greatest theatrical genius of our time, but one of the greatest in history. . . . If I were to recall the three greatest performances I've ever seen on the screen, all of them would be performances by Charlie Chaplin' (Charles Laughton). '. . . in addition to being a great actor, [he] is a great producer' (Arnold Bennett). 'The son of a bitch is a ballet dancer. . . . He's the best ballet dancer that ever lived, and if I get a good chance I'll kill him with my bare hands' (W.C. Fields).

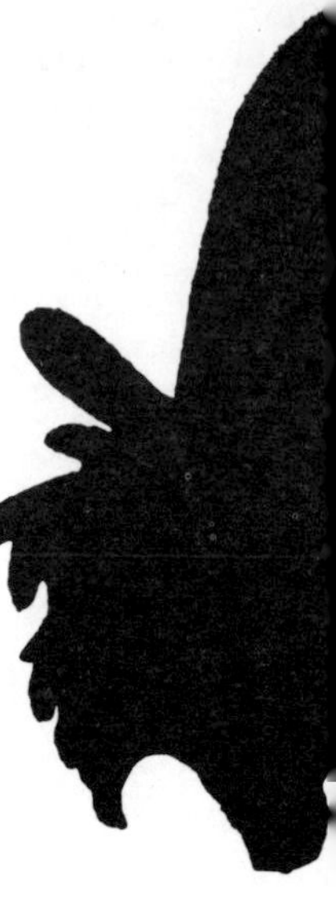

There has been more serious comment on Chaplin than any other screen artist, star or director, and most of it is good. Like Proust, Chaplin seems to inspire his commentators. But then, there is hardly an adjective that doesn't apply: Chaplin's Tramp, as Agee said, was universal. He could be jaunty, malicious, soppy, wistful, cunning, crass, observant, beautiful, painstaking, annoying, mean, innocent. . . .

He was born in 1889 in Lambeth, in South London. His parents were music-hall entertainers, though not particularly successful ones: his father died while he was a child and his mother was committed to an infirmary. Much of his boyhood was spent in poverty. He made his first stage appearance at the age of five, at Croydon, deputizing for his mother: he sang one of her songs. When he was eight, he joined a music-hall act, 'The Eight Lancashire Lads' and from then on worked non-stop, all over Britain as well as in Paris; he was in a play at the London Hippodrome called 'Giddy Ostend' in 1900; he played Billy, the

office boy in 'Sherlock Holmes' and was a wolf in 'Peter Pan'. When he was 17, he joined Fred Karno's company, first of all to play in a sketch called 'The Football Match'. He progressed with the company, until he was one of the leading comedians; and as such he played in 'Mummingbirds', or–its US title–'A Night at an English Music Hall' on a tour of the US in 1910–11. On a second and longer tour in 1912–13, he was seen by Adam Kessel and Mack Sennett of the Keystone Co. who invited him to replace Ford Sterling, whose popularity was waning. Thus he joined Keystone for $150 per week (twice his Karno salary), to make mainly one- and two-reelers with already established artists like Sterling, Mabel Normand, Chester Conklin, Fatty Arbuckle and Mack Swain.

He arrived in Los Angeles in December 1913 (Keystone was in the vanguard of the studios to location in California) and his first one-reeler, *Making a Living*, was released in February, 1914. The studio was not enthusiastic about it. During 1914 he made 35 films: from *Twenty Minutes of Love*, made in one afternoon, to *Dough and Dynamite*, made in nine days at a cost of $1,800 (which was $800 over the budget). Most of them were made in one week. They were crude stuff and only the Chaplin name has kept them from oblivion. Mostly Charlie was the villain or some kind of blundering intruder thinking himself just the thing for Mabel Normand, though she was not prepared to go beyond a mild flirtation. They were full of slapstick among cardboard sets, and they all ended with what seemed to be wild drunken chases. In the second one, *Kid Auto Races in Venice*, Chaplin wore his famous costume for the first time on screen, but in most of them he was made up with the vestiges from his music-hall act–top hat, frock coat, a masher's moustache; similarly, they merely hint at the comic genius to come, as he worked towards mastery of the medium. Robert Payne, in his 1952 biography, observes of this time: 'Charlie is at home in the empty streets and the crowded doss-houses; most of all he is at home when he has a mop and pail in his hand, and goes about his business. He was born to be a nightwatchman or a janitor . . . erratic as a chauffeur, incompetent as a boxing referee, awkward as a lover, a perverse scene-shifter, he is at full powers as a janitor.'

After four or five films, he was anxious to write and direct his own: he was assigned to one that Mabel Normand was directing–probably *Caught in a Cabaret* (actually, his 12th film), and there was some altercation but the next one, *Caught in the Rain*, he directed himself, and he later directed Normand (and himself) in *The Fatal Mallet*, *Mabel's Busy Day*, *Mabel's Married Life*, etc. Others of the Keystone films: *Laughing Gas*, *The Face on the Bar Room Floor*, *The New Janitor*, *His Trysting Place* and *Tillie's Punctured Romance*, the latter a six-reeler with Marie Dressler. It was this one that really made him famous. His last picture for Keystone, *His Prehistoric Past*, was a burlesque of de Mille's *Man's Genesis*, in which he wore his bowler (and a leopard skin). He was now getting $175 a week, and though Keystone were prepared to up this considerably, Chaplin preferred an offer from Essanay at $1,250 weekly, plus bonuses.

Essanay's announcement that they had signed Chaplin pulled no punches: 'the world's greatest comedian,' it said. The first Essanay picture (made in Chicago; the rest were made in San Francisco and then Los Angeles) was *His New Job* (February 1915), which was set in a film studio: it was still Keystonian slapstick, but the setting gave Chaplin some opportunities for satire; he followed it with *A Night Out*–he and Ben Turpin were drunks; it was also the first picture in which appeared Edna Purviance, who was to be his leading lady over the next eight years (and was on salary with the Chaplin studio till she died). Then: *The Champion*, *In the Park*, *The Jitney Elopement* and *The Tramp*, 'generally considered to be Chaplin's first real masterpiece' (Theodore Huff)–and also the first 'in which he injects a note of pathos'. He was now permitted to take more care and trouble, and after *By the Sea* only one Chaplin appeared per month–*Work*, *A Woman*, *The Bank* (perhaps the most popular as well as the most accomplished of the Essanay period), *Shanghaied*, *A Night in the Show*, *Carmen* (a burlesque on de Mille's *Carmen*: Chaplin played Darn Hosiery) and *Police* (March 1916). Another Essanay two-reeler, *Triple Trouble*, released in 1918, consisted only of unused bits from these films.

Chaplin's popularity was by now enough to justify several imitators (e.g. Billie West, 'Billie' Richie), though few of them were accepted by the public. There was also a Charlie Chaplin cartoon created by Pat Sullivan, as well as numerous songs about him. Further, no less than Mrs Minnie Madden Fiske wrote an article in Harper's Bazaar entitled 'The Art of Charlie Chaplin': it referred to him as an 'extraordinary artist'. He thought his Essanay salary was inadequate, both because he wrote, directed and starred, and because they sold their

M-ALET
N.Y.
137
N.Y.

Chaplin's early career divides naturally into three periods, each corresponding to the company for whom he was working: Keystone (1914–15), Essanay (1915–16) and Mutual (1916–17). One of the best of the Mutual films is The Immigrant *(17) with Edna Purviance.*

product in 'blocks' on the strength of his films being among them. He went to Mutual who offered him $10,000 a week, plus a $150,000 bonus. He made 12 films for Mutual (May 1916–October 1917), a remarkable outburst of creativity. He was permitted more preparation; the advance on his Essanay work is considerable (just as the First National films were to be an advance on these)–the slapstick may be just as beautifully timed, but it is gradually becoming more inventive, less mechanical. Chaplin, in fact, is becoming daring both as comic and director and he is finding his way towards the emotionalism he was to exploit so miraculously in his feature films. Neither of the first two, *The Floorwalker* or *The Fireman*, were as good as the later ones, but Chaplin notes himself in his memoirs that after the first, 'I was in my stride'. He said that this was the happiest period of his career, because he was unencumbered by financial considerations. The third Mutual, *The Vagabond*, was an almost straight film; *One A.M.* has him in pantomime, drunk, a solo performance; *The Count* has him impersonating same in order to win Miss Moneybags–Edna Purviance; and *The Pawnshop* has Charlie getting a gag from everything in sight and foiling a robbery at the end. *Behind the Screen* takes place in a film studio again, and has some outrageous camp humour; *The Rink* is Charlie at his most inventively graceful; and *Easy Street* finds him at his most ingratiating–trying to rob the Mission poor-box, and then, with great ingenuity, foiling the crooks. He arrives for *The Cure* with aplomb and a case of booze, and promptly falls foul of gouty, black-bearded Eric Campbell, the heavy of many of this series. And as *The Immigrant* he is arriving in the USA, a funny film which veers startlingly into poignancy and is as good as anything he did; while as *The Adventurer* he was merely back at slapstick, though the level of inventiveness is much higher than in, say, *The Floorwalker*.

Public admiration and esteem–everyone everywhere was singing a song, 'The Moon Shines Bright on Charlie Chaplin'–was tempered by the fact that Chaplin had not gone to war: this was the first of those curious attacks on him that were to mark his career. Later his first two divorces made screaming and hostile headlines.

Early in 1918, his brother, now his manager, arranged for him to go to First National to make eight two-reel comedies at $150,000 each. The first three, *A Dog's Life* (18), *Shoulder Arms* and *Sunnyside* (19) are, according to Robert Payne, 'more magical than any he composed before or afterwards . . . one dealt with poverty, another with war and the third with paradise'. *Sunnyside*, in fact, was almost a ballet, as befits paradise. There followed *A Day's Pleasure* and then *The Kid* (21), in which the Tramp–or The Little Fellow, as Chaplin himself referred to his character–found the baby Jackie Coogan, a miniature version of his own pathos and artfulness. The film was a six-reeler (there were rows with the studio over this); it took 18 months to film and cost $500,000–but it was more profitable than any movie made up to that time, with the exception of *The Birth of a Nation* (an estimated $3½ million against *The Kid's* $2½). First National therefore didn't balk when, after *The Idle Class*–the Tramp samples the pleasures of the rich–and *Pay Day* (22)–the Tramp's working day–Chaplin asked to do another feature–i.e. a four-reeler, which would replace the final two shorts contracted for. He was finding the company 'inconsiderate, unsympathetic and short-sighted', despite the fact they gave him a guarantee of $400,000 and an interest in the profits. The film was *The Pilgrim* (23), in which Charlie, as an escaped convict, is forced to pose as a priest. There are, as usual, marvellous gags, and the ending–Charlie skipping on the frontier between American Law and Mexican Banditry–is tremendous.

He was now free to join United Artists, which he had formed with Mary Pickford and Douglas Fairbanks: the idea was that they kept the profits from their films (at First National, lesser stars had got higher salaries than Chaplin, clearly paid from the receipts of his films). His first film was a starring vehicle for Edna Purviance, *A Woman of Paris* (23), which he directed only. The film is reputed to be masterly, but remains unseen in 40 years (Chaplin, who owns all his later films, has refused to let it out). He took two years to prepare *The Gold Rush* (25), the Tramp in the Frozen North. He said at the time: 'This is the film I want to be remembered by' (he said it about *The Kid*, and would say it about *Monsieur Verdoux*)–and in Sight and Sound's 1952 poll of the world's movie critics it was judged the second-best film ever made (*Bicycle Thieves* was first); in the same poll 10 years later it had slipped to 10th. It was an episodic piece, reaching a peak perhaps in the dance of

The Gold Rush (*25*). *It is New Year's Eve and the heroine (Georgia Hale) has forgotten that Charlie asked her to dinner. He falls asleep waiting and dreams that he is entertaining her with the ballet of the buns. The pit-piano player was instructed to play 'The Oceana Roll'.*

the rolls on New Year's Eve: in 1925 the world laughed and cried at this, and the gross was $2½ million against a probable cost of $650,000.

The Circus appeared in January, 1928: Chaplin played a trapeze artist. Robert Payne finds it 'so coldly calculated, so elaborately chilling' but 'the most homogenous and the most deftly constructed of all Chaplin's films'. Chaplin did not permit it to be re-issued till 1969, and doesn't mention it at all in his memoirs. He was awarded a special Oscar, however, at the first Oscar ceremony for 'versatility and genius in writing, acting, directing and producing *The Circus*'.

As he prepared his next film, it became clear that Sound was here to stay: Chaplin's only compromise was to compose a score for the soundtrack (though he did announce

Jew Süss as a Talkie, starring himself). UA, as distributors, were apprehensive, and many predicted failure: but *City Lights* (31) grossed $1 million, the fourth biggest money-maker of the year. It is perhaps his most sentimental film – the Tramp has a crush on a blind girl, pays for her operation and is rejected by her when she is cured – but it has some funny sequences with a millionaire who is friendly with the Tramp when drunk, and knows him not when not.

A further Silent came along in 1935, though Chaplin did speak a few words of gibberish: *Modern Times* borrowed freely from *A Nous la Liberté* in its satire on mechanics and machines, but refined the jokes. It was equally a showcase for Paulette Goddard, with whom the Tramp is in love. Press criticism was guarded (for the first time) but the public stayed faithful – it took $1,800,000, being beaten that year only by *San Francisco*.

He had toyed with many ideas since he had begun making features, and during the 30s many projects were put into motion, not to get very far; one that didn't come to fruition, though some meetings were held, was a Napoleon story, with Chaplin as Bonaparte, Garbo as the female lead, and Jean Renoir directing. But his 1940 film, *The Great Dictator*, was ambitious enough: he played a dual role, as a Jewish barber and as a dictator clearly based on Hitler. Jack Oakie was Mussolini, and Paulette Goddard was the Barber's girl-friend. The film had some mammoth statements to make about tyranny and freedom, and is incomparably the most adult and most bitter of the anti-Nazi films. The press raved. The New York Critics voted Chaplin the year's Best Actor (he refused to accept the award) and its gross of $2 million made it the top money-spinner of 1941. Pro-German forces in the US were unlikely to forgive Chaplin for this film; and he managed to alienate a good many more American citizens by his championship of Russia's cause during the war. After the war a paternity suit – though he was patently innocent and was finally cleared – sent his stock sinking.

Then, in 1947, he had the effrontery to make a comedy about murder, *Monsieur Verdoux*, based on Landru, the mass-murderer. The thesis of the – very wordy – script was that Landru/Verdoux's crimes were no worse than war; the sets were amateurishly painted, and much of the film technically inept. Howard Barnes of the New York Herald Tribune said: 'It has little entertainment weight, either as somber symbolism or sheer nonsense. . . . It is also something of an affront to the intelligence.' The onslaught by the American press determined its future: in places where it wasn't banned, no one went to see it. Yet there were critics who liked it. Agee wrote: 'It is permanent if any work done during the past 20 years is permanent'; and of Chaplin's own performance as the fastidious, foppish Verdoux: 'the best piece of playing I have ever seen'. Chaplin himself believes that *Verdoux* 'is the cleverest and most brilliant film I have yet made'. It did better in Britain and Europe than in the US, but Chaplin quickly withdrew it; its only subsequent showings have been at a short special season at London's NFT in 1956. Calmly considered, after all the shouting had died, Chaplin and Agee are right: it had the feel, the shape – that undefinable something – of a masterpiece, not only very funny, but more moral than any of 10,000 other Hollywood products.

His next picture, *Limelight* (52), was a portrait of an ageing clown, Calvero. Once again, the settings were perfunctory so that the whole film seemed quaint and old-fashioned. But in Europe at least the press was in ecstasy. Gavin Lambert wrote of Chaplin the actor (just voted the year's best by a rare London critics poll): '. . . it is Chaplin's dramatic performance that is the film's most lasting achievement. He shows a range and mastery of effect that one might, perhaps, have suspected, but are no less breathtaking when one sees them.' In Britain, the film was big box-office, but it did only so-so business in the US: Chaplin's stock there was even lower, due partly to his refusal to take out American citizenship and to a hostile press which hadn't forgotten a disastrous press conference at the time of the *Verdoux* showings. When he announced his intention of going to Europe with *Limelight* to première it there, he was informed that he might not be permitted a re-entry visa. In the event, he didn't apply for one, but settled in Switzerland with his family and his fourth wife, Oona, daughter of Eugene O'Neill. He has never been back to the USA, and he refused to allow his next film, *A King in New York* (57), to be shown there. (To most people outside the USA, the existence of anti-Chaplin pressure groups is inexplicable, the attitude of the American press beneath contempt – though in recent years, some Chaplin revivals have done something to redress the balance.)

A King in New York, made in Britain, had some fun at the expense of American advertising and commercialism, but it was a disappointment by even journeyman standards and critics were baffled; it seems, however, a gem beside *A Countess From*

Chaplin and Marilyn Nash, 'one of his discoveries', in Monsieur Verdoux (*47*).

Hong Kong (66), made in Britain, and backed by Universal. Brando and Loren starred, and Chaplin himself did a cameo as a steward. The best thing about it was that it was reminiscent of 30s comedies, a not disagreeable anachronism. Despite massive interest, the reviews killed it at the box-office. In 1970 he planned to make a film with his children.

In 1942 Chaplin re-issued *The Gold Rush* with an unctuous commentary and a music track; and he has subsequently revived most of his features, plus *A Dog's Life*, *Shoulder Arms* and *The Pilgrim* in a compilation called *The Chaplin Revue* (60). Between these infrequent re-issues he rigorously denies showings, even to film societies. Public reception of these revivals appears to be spotty: in France and Germany, for instance, the audiences are as large as for new products; in other places there appears to be something not much bigger than a cult following. BBC TV paid a record sum for a Christmas showing of *The Gold Rush*–the only major Chaplin to be shown on TV–but the price wasn't justified by the viewing figures. The question for the future is whether these mainly black-and-white silent flickering images will hold the vast public and the place to which genius entitles them, or whether they will be hived off into a minority enthusiasm.

Ruth Chatterton

Among the actresses consistently given material unworthy of them, Ruth Chatterton holds a high place. Her films were True Magazine stuff, and she suffered nobly in them, caught–indeed trapped–in the wicked ways of the world. She was put-upon but resigned, sensitive but mature (physically–being in her mid-30s when she started in films, no one tried to keep her young) and usually upper-bracket: she was the sort of woman with whom all women could identify, if not necessarily sympathize. Men liked her because she was a woman of experience, because she had a 'class' rare at that time, and for an intriguing blend of serenity and humour in her eyes. There were no mannerisms or histrionics: she was completely believable and made almost compelling the most dishonest dialogue. She dominated the screen and was in advance of her time, though contemporary appreciation was not lacking. James Agate said once: 'as an actress La Chatterton seems to me to knock La Garbo silly', and in 1931 the readers of Movie Fan voted her the 'Finest Actress on the screen'. She was often referred to as the First Lady of the Screen.

Her spell in Hollywood, however, was but a brief interlude in a long career. She was born in New York City in 1893; her parents separated, and to earn money at 14 she got a job as a chorus girl in a play in Washington (Helen Hayes played the same girl, younger, in Act I). From there she went into stock, and in 1911 made her Broadway bow in 'The Great Name'; had her first success the following year in 'The Rainbow' under Henry Miller's management. Most of her subsequent plays were for him; among them: 'Daddy Long Legs' (as Judy), 'Come Out of the Kitchen', 'Mary Rose' (which she also directed) and 'The Little Minister'. She became one of New York's leading Leading Ladies and the movie people were interested –but she either wanted too much money or script approval. However, she went to Hollywood in 1925, accompanying her husband who had been offered a part in *Beau Geste*. (He was Ralph Forbes, a Britisher and some years her junior, who was successful during the late 20s and early 30s; a sleek moustached actor with slightly watery eyes. They were divorced in 1932; he died in 1951.)

Chatterton did a couple of plays on the Coast, and in one of them, 'The Devil's Plum Tree', she was seen by Emil Jannings. Although Paramount had already tested her unsuccessfully for *The Docks of New York*, he insisted on their taking her on to play his second (and worthless) wife in *Sins of the Fathers* (28). She was good and Paramount signed her: her stage training was an asset with the advent of Talkies. She was a faithless wife again in *The Doctor's Secret* (29), with H. B. Warner, but true to Fredric

Lionel Barrymore and Ruth Chatterton welcome her husband Ralph Forbes to the set of the classic tearjerker Madame X *(29). Barrymore directed.*

March in *The Dummy*. However, in *Madame X* (29), she ditched her husband again and was paid the wages of sin in various parts of the world, finally standing trial for the murder of a man who planned to blackmail her husband – and defended by a young lawyer who doesn't know she is his mother (all the same, he concludes: 'She was a good woman, whoever she was'). This old stage weepie was a big one for MGM who produced and Chatterton's performance was, considered Picturegoer, 'the most poignant thing the Talkies have given us to date'.

She returned to her home lot as a big attraction and did *Charming Sinners* (from Maugham's 'The Constant Wife') and *The Laughing Lady*, both with Clive Brook, in the latter as a divorcee falling unwillingly in love with her husband's attorney. It was considered notable mainly for her performance, as (even more so) was *Sarah and Son* (30) – as a German immigrant returning disgraced to the Fatherland, becoming a famous diva and going back to the US to reclaim her son. March co-starred, and they did a sketch together in *Paramount on Parade*. MGM borrowed her to play Nancy in *Oliver Twist*, but when this was cancelled she was their *Lady of Scandal*; then at Paramount she was *Anybody's Woman*, but Brook's in particular (as a downtown chorus girl reforming him, a lawyer, after he had married her one alcoholic night).

It had become customary to regard Chatterton as one of the few screen actresses able to absorb herself completely in her character, and her next role was considered a *tour de force*, playing both Mother and Daughter in *The Right to Love* (31). The man in question was Paul Lukas, and Chatterton then proceeded to be *Unfaithful* with him – but that made three wretched films in a row. She listened to the advances made by WB

George Brent and Ruth Chatterton play husband and wife in The Crash *(32). At this time they were husband and wife in real life as well.*

(it was said she was annoyed at the money being spent to publicize Dietrich which – if it worked – would presumably entail her own demotion from queen of the lot). There was a fourth horror, *The Magnificent Lie* (31), about a cabaret singer who deceives a blind doughboy into believing she is the woman he once loved (Françoise Rosay). After that, she did sign with Warners, and Picturegoer commented that if her films there weren't an improvement, her days as a star were numbered. The last two for Paramount were appalling: *Once a Lady*, as a Russian, with Ivor Novello; and *Tomorrow and Tomorrow* (32), as a bored wife who turns to doctor Lukas to get herself a baby.

She certainly hoped for better films. WB gave her $6,000 a week and a say-so on material; and they advertised her with the tag: 'Acting from a contented actress'. The first was a mildly amusing comedy, *The Rich Are Always With Us* (32), co-starring George Brent, who soon became her second husband (too soon: the rapidity of their marriage less than 24 hours after her decree final created a sensation in the summer of 1932). The studio cast them together again to capitalize on their romance, in *The Crash*, even if the plot had her being unfaithful to him. It was well-named as far as receipts went and Chatterton, all too conscious of being in a rut, wanted to leave Hollywood. She stayed because of Brent, whose career was just beginning, and fought against making *Frisco Jenny* (33), which was a doing-over of *Madame X* with the Earthquake thrown in. She was miscast in both *Lilly Turner* (as a cooch dancer) and *Female* (as a career woman who sexes herself up in a bid for love). Brent was in both of these, but by the end of 1934 the marriage was over and so was WB's contract. The last one might have been better had it been directed by G. W. Pabst, as intended, *Journal of a Crime* (34): the crime was hers, shooting the mistress of husband Adolphe Menjou and letting someone else die for it. The crime was also the Warners', who had given her even worse films than Paramount (she had walked out of one, *Mandalay* – Kay Francis replaced her); she was now dead at the box-office, and MGM, who had pursued her eagerly over the years, suddenly lost interest.

Chatterton also collided with Holly-

Chatterton and Paul Lukas in The Right to Love, *one of several films they made together.*

A saga of mother-love in which she aged cleverly and ended up playing her own daughter.

wood's obsession with youth: outside of star character actors like Marie Dressler, she was easily the oldest lady star of the time. After almost two years absence from the screen, Columbia starred her in some more mother-love nonsense, *Lady of Secrets* (36), and 20th gave her what was basically a supporting role in the naïve *Girls' Dormitory* (she lost fellow-teacher Herbert Marshall to Simone Simon). And Goldwyn cast her as the vapid, self-centred Fran, who finds European culture and men more exciting than husband Walter Huston in *Dodsworth*–an untypical part, but considered by many to be the best performance of her career. It should certainly have led to more Hollywood offers, and Goldwyn did announce his intention of starring Chatterton in *Stella Dallas*, but he changed his mind in favour of the more popular Barbara Stanwyck.

Instead she went to Britain, to co-star with Anton Walbrook in *The Rat* (38) and with Pierre Blanchar in *The Royal Divorce*–an unconvincing Josephine to his Napoleon. Neither was of a quality to resuscitate her screen career. She told a reporter, explaining why she had left Hollywood: 'But I don't feel inclined to fight against bad parts in plays or films; it isn't worth it; and even if it were, I'm just too lazy.' In London she also appeared in a revival of 'The Constant Wife' and got poor notices; in the US she toured in 'West of Broadway', and got there again in 1940 in 'Leave Her to Heaven'. She married again (Barry Thomson) and did stage work, TV and radio in the 40s and 50s, including tours of 'Pygmalion' (40–41), and 'Private Lives' (42), a City Center revival of 'Idiot's Delight' in New York in 1951 and a TV Gertrude to Maurice Evans's Hamlet. Her last appearance was in St Louis in 1956 in 'The Chalk Garden' And between 1950 and 1958 she published four novels, notably 'Homeward Borne'. She died in 1961, of a cerebral haemorrhage, in Redding, Connecticut.

Apart from *Dodsworth*, her films are mainly forgotten and seldom revived, and practically the only important contemporary reference to her is by American critic Pauline Kael, who spoke of her as 'the great Ruth Chatterton'.

Maurice Chevalier has Jeanette MacDonald on his lap and sex on his mind in Lubitsch's deliciously risqué One Hour With You *(32)*.

Maurice Chevalier

'Every little breeze seems to whisper Louise....' Maurice Chevalier sang it in his first American film, and even during the years of partial eclipse it remained (on disc) one of the most easily identifiable sounds in the world. Maurice: debonair, the eternal boulevardier, with his cane and *canotier*: one of the great show-biz figures, even in his latter-day renaissance as a twinkle-eyed French uncle. On the stage he remains one of the best one-man shows (if not *the*). On film, his best work was in his early American Talkies – gems which glitter as brightly now as they did then. Under (mainly) the direction of Lubitsch, Chevalier starred in a series of farces with music which effectively presented him as a ne'er-do-well whose interests seldom wandered far from the bedroom. But, as Lubitsch put it: 'Chevalier can make even the most scabrous situation acceptable.' By less than a wink, less than a grin, he was more suggestive than another actor ripping off a girl's blouse; and he showed a mastery of boudoir comedy which other actors could only try to imitate.

He described his career once thus (The Times, London, 1968, to Peter Daubeny): 'My career consists of low comedian with red nose; low comedian without red nose; going elegant with straw hat and jacket; music-hall comedies; Hollywood; return with straw hat and jacket to Paris; one-man show; return to America and dramatic actor.' He was born in Menilmontant, a quartier of Paris, in 1888, the ninth of 10 children – of which three survived. His father was a house-painter and drunk: he died when Maurice was 11. The boy was at one time in an institution; started work as an electrician and was later apprenticed to a metal engraver, but didn't like this and at the age of 12 tried to get up an acrobatic act with his brother. He entertained in the cafés of the quartier for some years, until accepted by the Casino de Tourelles (06), and at their café-concerts imitated famous stars for 12 francs a week. Subsequently he was a *boxe-boy* in vaudeville; and then Mistinguett's dancing partner at the Folies-Bergères. He was in the army during the war, was wounded and captured (he learnt English from a fellow-prisoner), and after the war (in February 1919), made his first London appearance succeeding Owen Nares in a revue, 'Hullo America' – the start of a career as '*la plus typiquement (et conventionelle-ment) "parisienne" des vedettes internationales*' (Seghers's 'Dictionnaire du Cinéma', 1962).

He returned to Paris and Mistinguett, but they split soon after it was clear that he could make it as a solo performer: he had a great Paris success in an opérette, 'Dedé' – which he also did briefly in the US. In 1927 he appeared with his then (and only) wife, Yvonne Vallee, in a London revue, 'White Birds': it was not a success. Back in Paris, Thalberg of MGM offered Chevalier a screen test (he had done a few shorts since 1911, e.g. *L'Affaire de la rue Lourcine*, *Jim Bougne Boxeur*): the test was negative, but Chevalier kept it and showed it to Lasky of Paramount, who was also interested. Lasky signed him.

Chevalier's first Hollywood movie, *Innocents of Paris* (29), was tawdry and sentimental, but he was an instant world hit: with his second picture, *The Love Parade*, he was a world sensation. Jeanette MacDonald co-starred and Lubitsch directed, with a visual wit and gaiety which made it a model for subsequent musicals; but above all it was a triumph for Chevalier, with his roguish smile and ver' Frainch accent. His salary had been tripled after *Innocents*, but Paramount now offered a fabulous $8,000 a week and dumped him in *The Big Pond* (30), pursued across the Atlantic by a determined Claudette Colbert for a satire on American big business (vs European charm and know-how); concurrently he could be seen in a guest spot in the poor *Paramount on Parade*. Also in 1930 he was to be found in person singing in New York and in London – in the latter city at a reported £4,000 a week, but over-publicity spoiled the occasion and he did a concert to a virtually empty Albert Hall.

But cinemas were full and Paramount signed him to a new contract: four films for $1 million. Photoplay said of the first, *The Playboy of Paris*, 'Maurice Chevalier deserves better than this light farce, which is amusing only in spots' – and he got it in spades with the next three. Lubitsch directed *The Smiling Lieutenant* (31), a version of 'The Waltz Dream' with a hapless Chevalier caught between Colbert and Miriam Hopkins, and he supervised *One Hour With You* (32; Cukor directed, uncredited), considered later by Theodore Huff to represent 'Lubitsch and Chevalier at the peak of their form'. This time Chevalier was caught between MacDonald and Genevieve Tobin, in rhyming couplets, and even more enchantingly. Rouben Mamoulian directed *Love Me Tonight* with the same vivacity: Chevalier was involved in more risqué situations with MacDonald. But off the screen he was unhappy, fighting (well-publicized) battles against his material. He lamented years later ('With Love', 1960): 'Paramount and I were still miles apart, too. I was still asking their top people why every picture I made must be in the same mould, why every character I played must be debonair and cute and devoid of emotional depth, and I was still receiving the same answer – that my films were making too much money to risk a change of pattern.'

But there were already signs of a falling box-office, and *A Bedtime Story* (33) matched the star and Helen Twelvetrees in a conscious attempt to emulate the maudlin success of the early Jolson pictures; and *The Way to Love*, with its synthetic Paris, did even more poorly. Audiences were tired of the cuteness. But at MGM both Lubitsch and Thalberg had faith in Chevalier, and he moved over to MGM on long-term contract, starting with a new Lubitsch version of *The Merry Widow* (34): a sparkling film, great reviews – but business didn't meet its astronomical cost. The Widow was MacDonald, against Chevalier's opposition (he was uncertain as to how much the success of 'his' films was due to her); Grace Moore had been originally engaged, but there was a dispute about billing, and MacDonald replaced her. He was loaned to 20th for *Folies Bergere* (35), with Ann Sothern and Merle Oberon, a gay dual-identity skit, but receipts were only so-so. As a second MGM venture, the studio again proposed a Chevalier-Moore teaming, but this time he insisted on

Chevalier and MacDonald worked winningly together several times under Ernst Lubitsch. But Rouben Mamoulian directed Love Me Tonight *(32), which was almost as risqué and just as delightful.*

MacDonald. Now *she* demurred, and as a result of this and some dispute over the subject of the film with Metro, the contract was dissolved by mutual consent. Chevalier left Hollywood declaring that he would rather top the bill at the Montparnasse Casino at 100 francs a day than be second at the Palace, New York, at $1,000 a day (thus almost confirming James Agate's downbeat assessment of the Chevalier persona when reviewing his first American film; Agate pointed out: 'Nevertheless this French star has the one quality which transcends all others – the quality of being a success').

In London Chevalier did another revue, 'Stop Press', and in Paris played an engagement at his old haunt, the Casino de Paris. He made two films, Duvivier's *L'Homme du Jour* (as an electrician with stage ambitions; in one sequence he meets himself playing himself) and *Avec le Sourire* (36); then tried to retrieve his international reputation with the remake of *The Beloved Vagabond*, made in Britain in both English- and French-speaking versions: a picaresque tale of a tramp and a waif, it no longer had great appeal. René Clair then directed him and Jack Buchanan in *Break the News* (37), playing chorus boys who fake a murder for

Count Your Blessings (*59*) *was a romantic drama starring Deborah Kerr and* Rosanno *Brazzi, but was memorable mainly for Chevalier's presence.*

publicity purposes; and in 1939 in France Robert Siodmack directed him in *Pièges*, a serious film at last (a murder mystery).

During the war he sang in the non-occupied zones, and was tainted with collaborationist suspicions because he had sung to German troops: later it was proved that he had done this to try to help some Jewish friends. He returned to films in 1946 when Clair cast him in a character part–an old-time movie director–for *Le Silence Est d'Or*: its charm was too quiet. He sang in New York and in London over the next couple of years–the beginning of the hit one-man shows which he has since done all over the world. But only the French cinema offered him movie-work: *Le Roi* (49), *Ma Pomme* (50) and *J'avais Sept Filles* (54). Paramount did announce (in 1950) that he would be returning to star in *A New Kind of Love*, but nothing came of this, and it wasn't till 1956 that he was recalled to Hollywood, by Billy Wilder, who wanted him to play Audrey Hepburn's father in *Love in the Afternoon*: a small part but, in his hands, not a negligible one. However, it was *Gigi* (58), as a charming and dapper old roué, that brought him back with a bang: he had a small triumph.

Hollywood, ever to make amends for neglect (provided the artist has proved again to be commercial), in 1958 presented Chevalier with a special Oscar; and in between stage, night-clubs and TV appearances, he has brightened a not inconsiderable number of pictures–most of which were in dire need of same: *Count Your Blessings* (59), *Can-Can* (in a limp re-play of his *Gigi* double-act with Louis Jourdan), *Pepe* (as himself), *A Breath of Scandal*, *Fanny* (61), *Jessica* (as a priest), Disney's *In Search of the Castaways* (62), *A New Kind of Love* (63, as himself), *I'd Rather Be Rich* (64), *Panic Button* and Disney's *Monkeys Go Home* (66). In 1969 he put an advert in Variety saying that his one-man shows were over, but that he was looking for a film or TV part.

Chevalier lives near Paris in a home full of memorabilia, which he would like to be a Chevalier museum. As well as 'With Love' he has published several volumes of reminiscences and is reportedly working on a ninth. There have been several proposals to make a film of his life, mostly by himself, and in 1956 Danny Kaye was announced to play the part.

Claudette Colbert

Claudette of the bangs and apple cheeks, with her saucer eyes and her throaty laugh, once likened to a cat's purr: Claudette with whom half the world was once in love. Throughout the 40s and before, she enjoyed a huge popularity, as the always controlled Miss Above-Average America. Hers wasn't a spectacular personality – nor was she a lady inclined to make headlines – so the fan-magazines were reduced to writing copy like this: 'In private life Claudette is Mrs Norman Foster, and their marital experiment of living in separate houses is one of the wonders of Hollywood' (it didn't work, apparently – they were divorced; but for more than 35 years, until she was widowed in 1969, she was happily married to a doctor). Dated that sort of gubbins may be, but Colbert's way of playing comedy hasn't. Like so many of her contemporaries, it remains stunning.

She didn't play only comedy: at one point in her career she was a sexy vamp, but she did, later, sensibly restrict her dramatic work to long-suffering wives. She played a strumpet or two, but courtesans – or frumpish spinsters – these were not for her. She ran her career with great acumen. In her autobiography, Gracie Fields records that she was once surprised by Constance Bennett's preparations for a scene (lighting, etc.). Replied Bennett: 'If you think I'm bad, you should see Claudette Colbert. Mind you, that's why she is Claudette Colbert.'

Colbert was born in Paris in 1905, but was educated mainly in New York, whither her parents emigrated when she was six. She became a stenographer, but wanted to be an actress, an ambition realized with 'The Wild Westcotts' (23) after a chance meeting with the play's author. Her notices weren't sensational, but they were good enough to ensure that (apart from a later starry production of 'Leah Kleshna') she thereafter appeared only in leading roles. Broadway producer Al Woods put her under contract, and over the next few years she appeared in some half-dozen plays, including 'We've Got the Money', 'The Cat Came Back', 'A Kiss in a Taxi' (25), 'The Ghost Train' and 'The Barker' (27), with Walter Huston and Foster. It was her biggest hit, and she later did it in London. Meanwhile she made her first movie, *For the Love of Mike* (27), at First National, a tale of three bachelors – Jewish, Irish, German (George Sidney, Ben Lyon, Ford Sterling) – who adopt a boy and send him to Yale. Capra directed; but Colbert's ingénue part got her nowhere. She was in Eugene O'Neill's 'Dynamo' when film companies started combing Broadway for new talent for the Talkies: Paramount negotiated to buy her contract from Al Woods.

Her first movies were made in New York: *The Hole in the Wall* (29) as a child kidnapper, and *The Lady Lies* (by night she was appearing in 'See Naples and Die', her last play for over 20 years); *L'Enigmatique Mr Parkes* with Adolphe Menjou, the French version of *Slightly Scarlet*, and one of the few 'foreign' versions to get a US showing; and *The Big Pond* (30), which she got because she was bi-lingual (it was made in two versions). Chevalier was the star, and he had admired her on the stage ('She was lovely, brunette, talented and a delicious comedienne, and her English was perfect'). Then she starred in *The Young Man of Manhattan*, as a gossip columnist married to sports-writer Foster: they quarrel and he takes to drink. Picturegoer, later, found it ironic that he was her weakest leading man: 'he did not seem to get any sincerity into his love scenes'.

Colbert's first really serious film was very stark indeed, a remake of Leatrice Joy's old melo, *Manslaughter*, about a girl convicted of same by her fiancé, Fredric March – the first of several together. There was *Honor Among Lovers*, with March, but it was the next which really made the customers sit up: as a mousy violinist, she demonstrated that she knew how to hold her man better than Queen Miriam Hopkins. The man was Chevalier, *The Smiling Lieutenant*, and Colbert hands him over to Hopkins with some bizarre sung advice about winning him over: 'You've got to jazz up your lingerie'.

It was another year before she got another prize part, but Paramount kept her busy: *Secrets of a Secretary*, a conventional marital drama with Herbert Marshall; *His Woman*; *The Wiser Sex* (32) – politicians and racketeers; *The Misleading Lady*, a comedy with Edmund Lowe; and *The Man From Yesterday*, a modern version of the Enoch Arden theme, with Clive Brook and Charles Boyer as the two men in her life. The big one was de Mille's *The Sign of the Cross*, playing Poppaea and taking her famous bath in asses' milk and, gosh, she was mean and evil. This Roman antique was re-issued during the war with a modern commentary, but in 1932 it was not especially hot box-office (Eddie Cantor's spoof, *Roman Scandals*, did far better).

The Phantom President was George M. Cohan, in a double role, with Colbert quite miscast as his wife; and *Tonight Is Ours* (33) was a Noël Coward frivolity with March. *I Cover the Waterfront* found her as a fisherman's daughter (the 'I' was Ben Lyon), and *Torch Singer* found her in more murky doings, going from maternity home to stardom in cabaret – but eventually marrying the father of her bastard. After which she must have welcomed *Three Cornered Moon*, a delicately done Depression comedy, in which she goes to work to support mother Mary Boland. De Mille then cast her in *Four Frightened People* (34) – others were Herbert Marshall, Mary Boland and William Gargan, on a desert island – one of his few 'modern' stories during the Talkie period, and one of his rare flops. She did not welcome *It Happened One Night* on loan to Columbia (like co-star Gable, she was being punished for not playing ball with her studio, and, like him, she was not the first choice: Myrna Loy was). This was a comedy about a runaway heiress and the reporter who pursues her and it became one of filmdom's milestones; it had a great effect on film comedy, and won several Oscars, including Best Actress for Colbert (the story runs that she was about to board a train at the time of the ceremony because she thought so little of her chances).

For de Mille again she did *Cleopatra*, in the title role, a *papier mâché* epic enlivened fitfully by its dialogue ('Poor Calpurnia! – of course, the wife is always the last to know') and the Colbert sense of merriment. Henry Wilcoxon was Anthony and Warren William Caesar. Then she began to alternate between comedy and drama, and in the end the latter won: there was a clutch of good comedies in her future. The dramas were tear-jerkers like

De Mille's The Sign of the Cross *(32). Charles Laughton was Nero and Claudette Colbert Poppaea. She had an uncontrollable passion for Captain of the Guard Fredric March, seen here defying Nero for love of Christian girl Elissa Landi.*

Fannie Hurst's *Imitation of Life* (mother-love) on loan to Universal; and the comedies were all rather like *The Gilded Lily* (35), the first of several with Fred MacMurray. There was another drama, *Private Worlds* (mental hospitals) with Boyer, which was 'panned unmercifully' (in the words of its producer, Walter Wanger); then *She Married the Boss* with Melvyn Douglas, brilliantly directed by Gregory La Cava, and one of the year's top successes; and *The Bride Comes Home* with MacMurray. Most of these were hits, and Colbert was voted one of the top 10 money-makers in both 1935 and 1936. In 1936 her contract expired, and Paramount signed her to a new one, calling for seven pictures over a two-and-a-half-year period. She succeeded Carole Lombard as the highest paid star.

She was called in by 20th to play Cigarette in Ouida's *Under Two Flags* (36) when Simone Simon's English proved inadequate (it was said). In 1937 she was the *Maid of Salem* (a tepid piece about witch-hunting, directed by Frank Lloyd), and then was with Douglas in *I Met Him in Paris*. At WB she did *Tovarich*, with Boyer, from a stage success about White Russians working as domestic servants in Paris. Anatole Litvak directed, and there was trouble when he sacked Colbert's own cameraman. Prevailed upon eventually to accept a replacement, she insisted again on her own after she had seen the rushes, offering to waive her salary if the film went over schedule. (*En passant*, it can be noted that Colbert was seldom seen in left profile.) After that, *Bluebeard's Eighth Wife* (38), where her tongue-in-cheek was nicely countered by Gary Cooper's blink. Chance played a hand again and she was summoned to play *Zaza*, when Paramount were having their own difficulties with an imported actress, Isa Miranda. Despite Cukor's direction, this remake was a flop with both critics and public. It was the last 'naughtee girl' role Colbert played (vaude artist falls in love with Herbert Marshall, discovers he is married, revenges herself by becoming the toast of Paris).

Also in 1939 she did *Midnight*, playing a gold digger. She made the character scatterbrained but cagey, a characteristic touch; a soft but not mushy centre in a hard (and hilarious) film. With the same aplomb she moved west, as a pioneer woman in John Ford's beautiful *Drums Along the Mohawk*. In 1940 she turned down a seven-year contract worth $200,000 a year because she could free-lance more profitably: her fee during the 40s was $150,000 per film (she always had good advice – her brother was her manager). At MGM she did *It's a Wonderful World* (40) with James Stewart and *Boom Town* with Gable (as his loving wife).

Back at Paramount, Colbert did a couple with Ray Milland, *Arise My Love* (41), a Wilder-Brackett script that begins with a crackle but soon runs into war-angled bathos, and *Skylark* (41), a completely forgettable marital comedy. She moved to 20th to play a schoolteacher in *Remember the Day*: Agate found it sloppily sentimental throughout, 'but once again Claudette Colbert is her clever, witty and typically Parisian self: indeed, there are moments when she reminds one of any French actress and thus gives us that distinction, at once so brittle and so elegant. . . .' Preston Sturges's *The Palm Beach Story* (42) is a strong contender for the most satisfying comedy film ever made and Colbert was captivating as the would-be divorcee (from Joel McCrea). After that,

The happy ending of It Happened One Night *(34) – after it had all happened. There was an even happier one later, when both Clark Gable and Miss Colbert won Oscars (the only time the Best Actor and Actress awards went to performers in the same film).*

Joel McCrea and Claudette Colbert in Preston Sturges's very funny The Palm Beach Story *(42).*

Even the superstars posed for fashion stills.

No Time for Love (43) with MacMurray was small fry and so was *So Proudly We Hail*, a tribute to the nursing service.

She took top-billing in Selznick's big, big (and synthetic) drama about the women that waited at home, *Since You Went Away* (44). It was helped to success by drum-beating, but no one was fooled that the typical American wife was like Claudette Colbert. Her last for Paramount was *Practically Yours*, with MacMurray. At war's end she was in Sam Wood's comedy, *Guest Wife* (45), and then two cruddy soap operas, *Tomorrow Is Forever* (46) and *The Secret Heart*. Richard Winnington said of the latter: 'There never was a screen heroine who carried so bravely and girlishly and irritatingly such a burden of idiotic sacrifice as does Claudette Colbert through the longuers. . . . I noticed in her last film that she has developed a maddening flutter, a sort of half-embarrassed dither, doubtless occasioned by the inanities that encircle her. She has let it grow on her in this film, and though the poor girl has every excuse, she is very hard on the nerves.'

In truth, even her comedy playing now seemed mechanical: in *Without Reservations*– released before *The Secret Heart*–with John Wayne, and in a truly horrible bucolic piece, *The Egg and I* (47), with MacMurray. Audience weakness for slapstick (tripping over in farmyard, etc.) carried this to box-office success, Colbert's last. She and MacMurray did something similar with *Family Honeymoon* (48), but it played double bills. So did, in the interim, *Sleep My Love* (48, Don Ameche trying to murder her), and *Bride for Sale* (49). It was unfortunate that Colbert missed out on two good films. She had signed for *State of the Union* to be done with Gary Cooper, but when Spencer Tracy was cast in the lead, it became impossible to fulfil her contractual requirement of finishing at 5 p.m. instead of 6. It was not a Hollywood secret that Katharine Hepburn wanted to play the part. The other film was *All About Eve*, which she lost when she broke her back. But *Three Came Home* was a popular war film, even if she was miscast. Neither *The Secret Fury* nor *Thunder on the Hill* (51, as a nun–it was a thriller set in a convent) nor *Let's Make It Legal* were interesting. Of the latter Frank Quinn in the New York Daily News opined that Colbert, 'a capable farceur', couldn't make it merry: 'While she is on the Roxy screen the comedy skips along, but when her co-stars take over the plot labours.' Co-stars included Macdonald Carey and Zachary Scott.

Colbert travelled to Britain for a drama of the Malayan troubles, *The Planter's Wife* (52), with Jack Hawkins; topicality and chauvinism took it to success in Britain, but the US (rightly) ignored it. And outside France, the two films she made there were hardly seen. *Destinées* (53) was an episoder, with Michele Morgan as Joan of Arc, Martine Carol as Lysistrata, and Colbert a modern woman coping with the same problem (war); *Si Versailles m'était Conté* (54) was a historical panorama, which gave her another bit. In 1956 she did a programmer, *Texas Lady*, playing a crusading lady editor.

In 1956 she returned to Broadway, taking over the lead in 'Janus' from Margaret Sullavan (earlier, in Westport, she had done Coward's 'Island Fling'–later called 'South Sea Bubble'); and two years later, she and Boyer kept 'The Marriage-Go-Round' running for 450 performances. TV appearances include 'The Royal Family of Broadway' (with March and Helen Hayes) and 'Blithe Spirit' (with Coward and Lauren Bacall). She continues to do occasional stage work. In 1961 WB suddenly asked her to play Troy Donahue's mother in *Parrish*: the press was glad to see an old friend, but few cinemagoers knew she was in it; it did poor business and the ads played her down for the teenage 'stars' who, as it turned out, were merely passing through.

When a reporter asked her some years later why she didn't make more films, she replied: 'Because there have been no offers.' A report (the Evening News, London, 1968) said there had been offers for TV situation comedies and unsuitable films, and added that Colbert had asked her agent to stop untrue press reports of offers and come-backs. She said they embarrassed her before her friends. The agent said: 'In all my years in this very tough business, it was the closest I ever came to shedding tears, to hear that grand lady say that.'

Ronald Colman

In 1927, 1928 and 1932 Ronald Colman was voted the top male star in the Bernstein Questionnaire; in 1932 the readers of a British women's magazine voted him their No. 1 favourite. He was a heartthrob for almost three decades–he was in his 50s in *Random Harvest* (42), and women everywhere were falling for him all over again. He is almost the only major Silent male star (except Chaplin) who remained a star well into the Talkie era (curiously enough, two others who survived, William Powell and Richard Barthelmess, were intimates of Colman). Colman was the dream lover: calm, dignified, trustworthy. Although he was a lithe figure in adventure stories, his glamour–which was genuine–came rather from his respectability: he was an aristocratic figure without being aloof. In Talkies, he proved to have a voice not quite classless, not quite transatlantic, but authoritative, gentle . . . the perfect voice for the face. In his great romantic roles it had the ring of an Irving while being completely right in film terms. And there was a charm, a formidable charm. He was not always an inspired actor, but he was never bad or dull. Like all great stars he left his imprint very firmly on all his films. A Colman performance lingered in the memory.

He was born in 1891 in Richmond, Surrey, the son of a silk importer. His father died when Colman was 16, and he became an office boy in the British Steamship Company; he was with them five years, during which time he became an enthusiastic amateur actor (and he started out as a professional with a tenth-rate concert party, 'The Mad Medicos'). In 1914 he joined the London Scottish Regiment, and served in France until 1916, when he was invalided out, with a fractured ankle. He managed to get a part in a Lena Ashwell sketch at the Coliseum (wearing blackface) and having by now had some experience as a light comedian, was offered a small part in 'The Misleading Lady' starring Gladys Cooper. In 1918 he had the lead in a production of 'Damaged Goods'.

His first film was a two-reeler made over a garage which apparently never saw the light of day; he had other odd work in films and on the boards. He was in *The Toilers* (19); *A Son of David*, a star role as a Jewish pugilist, with Poppy Wyndham, who was drowned not long afterwards; *Snow in the Desert*, directed by Walter West; *The Black Spider* (20), made in Monte Carlo; and Cecil Hepworth's *Anna the Adventuress*. His lead in *A Son of David* had led nowhere, and he decided to try the USA. He emigrated in 1920. His first American job was a walk-on in 'The Dauntless Three', there were more small parts, including 'East Is West', which starred Fay Bainter, and two films, *Handcuffs or Kisses* (21) and *The Eternal City* (23, un-billed). Colman got a good role in a play starring Ruth Chatterton, 'La Tendresse', and Lillian Gish saw it: her director, Henry King, confirmed her choice of Colman as her next leading man.

The film was *The White Sister*, after which

Colman got a part in *Twenty Dollars a Week* (24). Then Goldwyn signed him to a starring contract. His first picture was *Tarnish*, a triangle story with May McAvoy and Marie Prevost; and he was then loaned to First National (at that time Goldwyn's distributing company) for *Her Night of Romance* – Constance Talmadge's, and he was a nobleman disguised as a doctor. Next to be released was *Romola*, a reunion with Gish and King. Public reaction was more than favourable, and Goldwyn started to plan a series of Colman vehicles (during Colman's time with him, he presented 30 films, of which 18 starred Colman): *A Thief in Paradise* (25) in Samoa, with Doris Kenyon, *His Supreme Moment* and *The Sporting Venus*, both with Blanche Sweet (the latter at MGM). He was loaned again to First National for *Her Sister From Paris*, with Constance Talmadge as twins, one impersonating the other to woo back husband Colman. Then came two of Goldwyn's four-handkerchief efforts, and two of his all-time hits: *The Dark Angel*, in which Colman's love for Vilma Banky is all but destroyed by his being blinded in the war; and *Stella Dallas*, as the bounder who married beneath him and then deserted her – an unforgettable performance by Belle Bennett. From a novel by Olive Higgins Prouty, it was one of 1925's top successes.

Colman went to WB for Lubitsch's version of Wilde's *Lady Windermere's Fan*, to play Lord Darlington; with McAvoy, Irene Rich and Bert Lytell, it was a *tour de force*, 'capturing the Wildean spirit without the use of a single Wildean epigram' (Herman G. Weinberg). At First National, he was Norma Talmadge's leading man in *Kiki* (26) and at Paramount in the popular and much-liked version of *Beau Geste*, from P. C. Wren's novel about the Foreign Legion. Dashing and determined, Colman was the ideal Beau. Meanwhile, Goldwyn had prepared *The Winning of Barbara Worth*, a Western, co-starring Banky. Again, it was a popular success, and Colman and Banky were reunited to become one of the great love teams of the 20s: *The Night of Love* (27), a swashbuckler built around the *droit de seigneur* idea with Colman as the gypsy hero; *The Magic Flame*, in a dual role as a circus clown and a prince; and *Two Lovers* (28), more of same. But Lily Damita starred with Colman in *The Rescue* (29), from Conrad's story.

Then Goldwyn prepared his prize property for his Talkie debut. Richard Griffith has written on this: 'Striking good looks were perhaps the basis of his Silent fame, but from the moment he spoke it was apparent that here was an actor who not only understood his craft but was far ahead of his time. . . . It was also clear from his performance that restraint, underplaying, and the ability to react in pauses between lines of dialogue were to be the essentials of acting in the new medium.' The film was *Bulldog Drummond*, and it was directed lightly. Critics sat up and cheered, and queues for it became a permanent feature of London and New York and other cities for months. It was also soon clear that Colman was the pre-eminent Talkie actor. Said Elinor Glyn: 'Undoubtedly the greatest male personality in present-day pictures'; and Goldwyn satisfied overwhelming public demand for him by rushing him into a series of movies. Banky got left behind in the

Ronald Colman and Vilma Banky in Two Lovers *(28), a drama of the Spanish Netherlands and one of the five movies they made together. They were perhaps the most famous co-starring team of the 20s, but the Hungarian-born Miss Banky did not survive the coming of Talkies.*

Talkies did give a new lease of life to Colman's career, and this one was particularly good: Arrowsmith *(31), directed by John Ford from the novel by Sinclair Lewis. Myrna Loy was the Other Woman.*

rush. There was *Condemned* with Ann Harding; *Raffles* (30), E. W. Hornung's novel about an amateur cracksman; *The Devil to Pay*, with Loretta Young, a good comedy by Frederick Lonsdale, specially written for Colman, who played a black sheep; and *The Unholy Garden* (31) with Fay Wray, a love story set in the Sahara which Goldwyn made against his better judgment (it was a great flop).

He gave a sensitive performance in John Ford's *Arrowsmith* (from Sinclair Lewis's novel), a film that has dated but little, and was even better in *Cynara* (32), as the lawyer drawn to a young girl while still in love with his wife. He had a dual role in a thriller, *The Masquerader* (33). During its making, in 1932, the Goldwyn publicity department issued some statements, purportedly by Goldwyn himself, to the effect that Colman looked better on screen when mildly dissipated, and that he played his love scenes better after several drinks. Colman sued for $2 million damages. The case was settled out of court, and Colman didn't work for Goldwyn again.

He signed a contract with 20th, who cautiously put him into *Bulldog Drummond Strikes Back* (34) and *Clive of India* (35), both with Loretta Young. The new 20th company was having some success with historical figures, and films extolling the virtues of British Colonialism were a commercial staple of Hollywood at that time. Of its type, *Clive* was okay, and Colman was fine–though many sob-sisters used up newsprint in mourning the loss (for the first time) of the famous moustache. But it returned when Colman became *The Man Who Broke the Bank at Monte Carlo*, a pleasant comedy.

At MGM, he was Sidney Carton, holding together the spectacular but meandering *A Tale of Two Cities*. The Times thought his performance 'subtle . . . Dickens created in Carton the most psychologically complicated of all his characters, and Mr Colman, who has never acted so well before, has realised it'. After *Under Two Flags* (36) from Ouida's adventure novel, he free-lanced with success. No studio planned things for him, as was happening with Gable at MGM, or was soon to happen to Tyrone Power at 20th, so he reduced his activity and took the few plum films that were offered. At Columbia he was the hero who found love and wisdom in Shangri-La, *Lost Horizon* (37), from James Hilton's novel, directed by Frank Capra. It cost so much that even a great box-office performance was not enough: but prestige accrued (today, it has a lingering charm). Then Selznick cast Colman in the famous dual role, *The Prisoner of Zenda*, from Anthony Hope's novel, which gave the world Ruritania. Of the three film versions, Colman's is the definitive one. He made a short commitment with Paramount and starred as François Villon in *If I Were King* (38), one of the four movie versions of that tale (two with music as *The Vagabond King*). The Villon of the 1920 version, William Farnum, had a small part. At Paramount Colman also did *The Light That Failed* (40), Kipling's story, that had once been mooted for Gary Cooper and Ray Milland.

He had had a remarkable run, but his stock fell somewhat with three weakish comedies: *Lucky Partners* with Ginger Rogers; *My Life With Caroline* (41), whose failure is perhaps due to the inadequacy of Anna Lee in the co-starring role; and *The Talk of the Town* (42) with Jean Arthur and Cary Grant. But Colman returned in force with *Random Harvest*, James Hilton's novel that MGM had bought for Spencer Tracy. As the amnesiac who marries Greer Garson twice without realizing it, Colman's quiet weight and charm made it all seem almost plausible – one of the best examples of that sort of sleight of hand in the history of cinema acting. MGM retained his services for the remake of *Kismet* (44), but his deft spoofing touch was not equalled by other participants in this Arabian Nights extravaganza.

He appeared in a civilized film version of John P. Marquand's *The Late George Apley* (47), silver-haired now; and in *A Double Life* (48), written by Garson Kanin and directed by Cukor, a medium melodrama about a Shakespearian actor who takes to doing 'Othello' off-stage – with fatal consequences to waitress Shelley Winters. It brought Colman's fourth Oscar nomination, and his first win: but it was hardly his most notable performance, and the film is much less well-remembered than *Champagne for Caesar* (49) which played on dual bills. It was a funny film about quiz programmes, and his last film role of any importance. He had guest spots in *Around the World in 80 Days* (56) and *The Story of Mankind* (57), and guested on TV, notably with his wife in a Jack Benny show, which was conceivably the drollest 30 minutes in the history of that medium. They also appeared in a series, 'The Halls of Ivy'. She was his second wife, a charming English actress, Benita Hume, whom he married in 1938 (during the 20s, a long separation from his first wife caused fan-magazines to label him 'The Man of Mystery'). He died in 1958, just as his type was going out of fashion – but his style doesn't date.

Gary Cooper

Agent-turned-producer and old Hollywood hand Arthur P. Jacobs has no doubt: 'He was the greatest film star there has ever been – and that includes Gable.' He, Gary Cooper, was certainly on all counts one of the most successful. His career spanned 35 years and, except at the very beginning and during the last few years, he was one of the biggest attractions in films (during the period 1936–57 he missed the Exhibitors' top 10 list on only three occasions, and he was first in 1953, second in 1944 and 1952). He won two Oscars, and for the same two films, *Sergeant York* and *High Noon*, the New York Critics designated him Actor of the Year. Early in his career John Barrymore said: 'That fellow is the world's greatest actor. He can do, with no effort, what the rest of us spent years trying to learn: to be perfectly natural.' And Charles Laughton admired him: 'I knew in a flash he'd got something I should never have . . . that boy hasn't the least idea how well he acts.' After his death Robert Preston spoke of him: 'Now, Cooper doesn't have the reputation as a great actor except with us who knew him as an actor. But he was great. People used to comment on what they called his idiosyncrasies, his little foibles. But Cooper never made a move that wasn't thoroughly thought out and planned. He is probably the finest motion picture actor I ever worked with.'

The strange thing is that Cooper (as his TV interviews showed) had in life a number of rather effeminate mannerisms. However, on the screen he was virility personified, all that was required of a hero: honest, courageous and determined – determined to do what must be done at whatever the cost. The image was fixed quite early, though he did, with surprising elasticity, manage from time to time less admirable qualities: mawkishness, craftiness, hesitancy. But he could never be villainous. He himself considered that his consistent popularity stemmed from the fact that he always played 'the part of Mr Average Joe American. Just an average guy from the middle of the USA.'

The middle of the USA was actually Helena, Montana, but Cooper's parents were British immigrants; his father was a judge. Cooper was born in 1901. He was educated in Britain for some years before World War I; at college he became known for his cartoons and caricatures, and intended to make a career from drawing. But in Los Angeles, where his father worked, he couldn't get a job. Through friends he got work as an extra in movies, including *The Eagle* (25). Because he could ride, most of these films were Westerns, and he occasionally had a line. He acquired an agent, who got him a small part in a Goldwyn Western, *The Winning of Barbara Worth* (26) – but only because the actor cast for it was held up on another film. Still, it was a good part – he had to die in Ronald Colman's arms. Goldwyn offered him $65 a week, but Paramount bettered it.

At Paramount they gave him a miniscule part in *It* (27) with Clara Bow, but he was promoted to her leading man in *Children of Divorce*. According to Hedda Hopper, who was also in it, he was stiff and gave a 'horrible' performance – but he was learning to relax, and the studio had faith in him. He had the lead in *Arizona Bound* and a small

Gary Cooper and Fay Wray *in* One Sunday Afternoon (*33*), *a gentle small-town story about a dentist who can't help loving the Other Woman.*

but vital part in *Wings*. Mostly, he was in actioners: *Nevada*, *The Last Outlaw* and *Beau Sabreur* (28); *The Legion of the Condemned* with Fay Wray ('Paramount's Glorious Young Lovers'); and *Doomsday*. He was shipwrecked on a desert island with *Half a Bride*, Esther Ralston, having abducted her; gave *The First Kiss* to Wray; and was loaned to First National for the cheerless *Lilac Time* with Colleen Moore, an aviation drama. He was a naïve young soldier drawn to kept woman Nancy Carroll, *The Shopworn Angel* (29), and another nice young man drawn to Lupe Velez in *Wolf Song*; he supported Emil Jannings in the unsuccessful *The Betrayal*; and then starred in his first all-Talkie, *The Virginian*, from Owen Wister's novel. It was a hit, and made him a top draw (he remained fond of the film though in later years was irritated that the laconic dialogue–'yip' and 'no'–was forever associated with him). He was officially raised to stardom with *Seven Days' Leave* (30), co-starring Beryl Mercer, and called in Britain *Medals*, being a slushy version of Barrie's 'The Old Lady Shows Her Medals'. The other 1930 movies were mostly actioners: *Only the Brave*, with Mary Brian, a Civil War story; *Paramount on Parade*; *The Man From Wyoming*, an artificial war romance with June Collyer; O. Henry's *The Texan* with Wray; the first of the three Talkie versions of Rex Beach's *The Spoilers* (there had been two Silent ones), with its famous climactic saloon brawl with William Boyd; and *Morocco*, with Marlene Dietrich.

In 1931 there was *Fighting Caravans*; Mamoulian's fine *City Streets*, as a Westerner unwillingly drawn into the Underworld, with Sylvia Sidney and one of the year's top money-makers; *I Take This Woman*, as a cowhand courting Carole Lombard; *His Woman*; and *The Devil and the Deep* (32) with Tallulah Bankhead and Laughton. He was unlucky with *If I Had a Million*, being in one of the three poor episodes, and it was indifferently received and played the lower half of double bills (its later reputation was due to two episodes and the cast). But thereafter, for a good many years, Cooper made very few clinkers. *Today We Live* (33) would certainly come into that category, an MGM drama of flyers and patriotism (British variety) with Joan Crawford, from a William Faulkner story; but the one that preceded it, Hemingway's *A Farewell to Arms* (32), with Helen Hayes as the doomed light o'love, is fondly remembered today by all who saw it (it was certainly remembered by critics reviewing the 1957 remake). And Dilys Powell remembered *One Sunday Afternoon* (33) when reviewing its remake (*Strawberry Blonde*): 'Mr Cooper, abandoning

Jean Arthur and Gary Cooper in De Mille's The Plainsman *(36), one of the many films about Calamity Jane and Wild Bill Hickok, and perhaps the best.*

for once his role of the laconic scout, cowboy, or Deadeye Dick, appeared as a dentist: an honest, insensitive lout, pursued through life by an adolescent passion for a beauty who fooled him, and hatred for her husband; the audience saw him grow from booby to domestic cynic . . . the natural deliberation of Mr Cooper's playing gave the simple story character and truth.'

There were four poor ones. *Design for Living* found him not yet ready for drawing-room comedy; *Alice in Wonderland*, unrecognizable as the White Knight; *Operator 13* (34), at MGM in the arms of Marion Davies; and *Now and Forever*, gooey-eyed over Shirley Temple. Goldwyn's *The Wedding Night* (35) was better, though heavy, and Cooper's popularity couldn't save it from box-office disaster. During these same months, however, the public was flocking to see him, moustached and heroic, with Franchot Tone and Richard Cromwell, in *Lives of a Bengal Lancer*, under Henry Hathaway's direction Cooper's most popular picture to date. Hathaway directed *Peter Ibbetson*, with Cooper and Ann Harding as the ill-fated lovers who meet in dreams after their separation: a curious piece, not sufficiently Victorian-Gothic, filmed because a Broadway version of the old novel had been a success. The film wasn't. Cooper returned to more congenial circumstances with Borzage's *Desire* (36), underplaying to good effect as an innocent American conned by the worldly Dietrich; and he was in his element in Capra's *Mr Deeds Goes to Town*, as the country boy who is taken for a ride by, but finally routs, the city slickers. Graham Greene said his performance was 'subtle and pliable . . . it must be something of which other directors have only dreamed.' The film itself won prizes (the Picturegoer Gold Medal for Cooper), made a mint, and is today hardly less funny or relevant than it was then.

Cooper followed with a spate of adventure films: Lewis Milestone's tortuous but exciting *The General Died at Dawn* with Madeleine Carroll; *The Plainsman*, as Wild Bill Hickok to Jean Arthur's Calamity Jane – one of de Mille's better epics, and another giant grosser; and Hathaway's indifferent *Souls at Sea* (37). He was now under contract to Goldwyn. That producer, peeved at losing him years ago, had made a favourable offer (three pictures a year at $100,000 each) in 1936 when Paramount had been tardy in taking up their option on Cooper's services. Paramount took the case to law, with the result that when Goldwyn didn't need Cooper, they had the first call on him. The first under the Goldwyn contract was the hysterical *Adventures of Marco Polo* (38). Dramatist Robert E. Sherwood had been commissioned to provide a none too serious look at the great explorer, but had not foreseen audiences rolling in the aisles during scenes like the one where Marco Cooper teaches the Chinese princess (Sigrid Gurie) how to kiss. He returned to Paramount for *Bluebeard's Eighth Wife* with Claudette

Colbert, and it confirmed the *Mr Deeds* impression of a new comedy skill. So did *The Cowboy and the Lady* (she was Merle Oberon) before he went back into action: the popular and sympathetic remake of *Beau Geste* (39) – though you had to shut your ears to believe he was British; *The Real Glory*, a well-timed but absurd tribute to British colonialism; *The Westerner* (40), Wyler's leisurely story of a brave man and Cooper's first performance for a couple of years that didn't rely mainly on mannerisms and his reticent charm; and some forgettable but successful de Mille stuff, *North West Mounted Police*. For this period (1939–40), Cooper was the highest salaried actor, at just under $500,000.

He did another for Capra, *Meet John Doe* (41): crusading it was and Christ-like he was, but it didn't repeat the success of *Mr Deeds*. His partner was Barbara Stanwyck, and they were teamed again, more happily, in Howard Hawks's *Ball of Fire*, where she was a hard-boiled cabaret dancer and he an absent-minded professor. Meanwhile, Cooper had started a short series of tributes to all-American heroes: *Sergeant York* under Hawks's direction at WB (loaned by Goldwyn in exchange for Bette Davis); Lou Gehrig in *The Pride of the Yankees* (42), one of the very few hit baseball pictures; and de Mille's *The Story of Dr Wassell* (44), based on an episode in the Pacific war, only the real Dr W. was an eldery man – truths twisted 'to be regretted beyond all qualification' (James Agee). And a fourth (autobiographical?) hero was Hemingway's *For Whom the Bell Tolls* (43). The author was insistent that Cooper should play Robert Jordan; Ingrid Bergman was Maria; and the film, like all this batch, was synthetic and a roaring success.

Cooper was now free of a long-term contract, and it was said that he would be involved with a new concern, International; but like the other big names involved in independent production companies in the immediate post-war period, his association was brief: a pleasant comedy with Teresa Wright, *Casanova Brown* (44; released by RKO), a remake of *Little Accident*; and *Along Came Jones* (45), a Western actually produced by himself. His films over the next few years were mainly undistinguished: *Saratoga Trunk*, a cotton-wool epic by Edna Ferber in which his part was subsidiary to Bergman's; Fritz Lang's *Cloak and Dagger* (46), a wartime espionage story; de Mille's long and boring *Unconquered* (47) with Paulette Goddard; *Variety Girl* (a guest spot); and *Good Sam* (48), a sentimental Leo McCarey comedy with Ann Sheridan.

Both during production and after release For Whom the Bell Tolls *(43) was one of the most publicized films of its time; and the public certainly lined up to see Ingrid Bergman and Gary Cooper. Greek actress Katina Paxinou (right) won a Best Supporting Actress Oscar for her performance.*

All was not well. He signed a six-picture deal with WB, but it didn't rescue him from the doldrums: Ayn Rand's *The Fountainhead* (49) with Patricia Neal; *Dallas*; *Task Force*; *Bright Leaf* (50) with Neal and Lauren Bacall, a rambling saga of the tobacco industry which did poorly; and *USS Teakettle* which did so badly that it was withdrawn and re-issued (successfully) as *You're in the Navy Now*. He also had guest spots in two Doris Day musicals (*It's a Great Feeling* and *Starlift*) and went to MGM for the all-star *It's a Big Country* (51). In 1952 his WB deal expired and he did three Westerns: *Distant Drums*, *High Noon* and *Springfield Rifle*: when in doubt, always fall back on a Western. The first and third got by, but *High Noon* streaked ahead. Under Fred Zinnemann's direction, it was taut and intelligent. There were raves and those, plus its theme music, brought in the crowds. Cooper's own reputation soared again, and he had a run of acceptable films: *Return to Paradise* (53), based on some James A. Michener stories; *Blowing Wild* with Stanwyck; *Garden of Evil*, a Western; and – best of all – *Vera Cruz* (54) pitted against a grinning Burt Lancaster.

There followed three duds: *The Court Martial of Billy Mitchell* (55), Wyler's *Friendly Persuasion* (56) and Billy Wilder's *Love in the*

Cooper with Audrey Hepburn in Love in the Afternoon *(57), a comedy about a young French girl who spends her afternoons in the Ritz Hotel apartment of an elderly and wealthy American: under Billy Wilder's direction it was an acceptable situation.*

Afternoon (57). The latter couple were produced by Allied Artists in a bid to move from minor to major status. Cooper apart, both directors were among the most-admired in the business, but critical opinion was divided. The Wyler film, a gentle comedy about Quakers and pacifism (from a novel by Jessamyn West), did do good business in certain territories (it won a Grand Prix at Cannes) and finally did well due to a hit theme tune. Wilder's picture concerned an affair between the fifty-ish Cooper and teenager Audrey Hepburn: treated with the director's customary wit, delicacy and melancholy but the public just didn't want to know. Cooper then blundered into a similar tale, John O'Hara's *10 North Frederick* (58), but the director was no Wilder and Suzy Parker no Hepburn: it thudded.

Two Westerns did better: *Man of the West* and *The Hanging Tree* (59), and there were two adventure stories, Robert Rossens's *They Came to Cordura* with Rita Hayworth, one of Cooper's rare masochistic performances, and the entertaining *The Wreck of the Mary Deare* (60) with Charlton Heston. He then made *The Naked Edge* (61), in which wife Deborah Kerr spent most of the time wondering whether he was a murderer. The film was implausible in other ways, too, but it did good business. By the time it came out 'Coop' was dead, of cancer, in 1961 (leaving as widow his wife of 30 years, Sandra Shaw), and audiences went to see it for a last, sad look at their old favourite. He had been awarded an honorary Oscar for services to the industry in 1960.

Cicely Courtneidge

Cicely Courtneidge is not everyone's cup of tea. The ebullience which is her stock-in-trade a minority find alienating–and some find her vitality enervating. No one could deny her a professionalism of a very high order: in the consistently poor stage material with which she has landed herself in recent years her way with a line or a piece of business can be joyous, and with first-class stuff she can be very droll indeed. Her films were modest affairs, usually made in tandem with her husband, Jack Hulbert, and not startlingly original, not very witty. But they are (still) funny: Hulbert is a likeable if languid leading man and light comedian, and Cis is–well Cis: uninhibited, infectious, a top lady clown.

She was born in Sydney in 1893, the daughter of Robert Courtneidge, a famous theatrical manager who was touring Australia at the time. She made her stage debut in 1901 as Peaseblossom in 'A mid-summer Night's Dream' at Manchester, returned to Australia with her father; reappeared in Britain at the same Manchester theatre in 'Tom Jones' (07), the start of a short and inglorious career as ingénue in musical comedy–some half-dozen shows, including 'The Pearl Girl' (which provided her first meeting with Hulbert; they were married in 1919) and 'The Cinema Star'. Later, when she tried to get work outside her father's management, agents scoffed at her, so she turned to the (Music) Halls, and began singing comic songs. Her success was almost instantaneous; she played panto and became a music-hall topliner (songs and sketches) before venturing back into the West End–'Ring Up' (21). In 1926 she made her New York debut in 'By-the-way', a revue that had been a great success in London; other hit shows of the period included 'Lido Lady', 'Clowns in Clover' (27), and 'The House That Jack Built' (29). She and Hulbert were among the top half-dozen draws in the West End.

In 1930 the Hulberts were invited to appear in *Elstree Calling*, a revue styled after the Hollywood film revues of the period but supposedly a series of turns in a television station; they did 'Folly to Be Wise' (31) at the Piccadilly, and then went whole-heartedly into films. The first one was *The Ghost Train* (31), based on a hit comedy-thriller by Arnold Ridley, with Hulbert as the lead, and Courtneidge as a middle-aged spinster; they subsequently did *Jack's the Boy* (32) and *Happy Ever After*, the latter an English version of a UFA vehicle for Lilian Harvey – Courtneidge had only a supporting role. But both Hulberts were, for a few years, box-office attractions in their own right. With Edward Everett Horton she did one of her biggest successes, *Soldiers of the King* (33) as both mother and daughter; then teamed with Hulbert again for *Falling for You*. The formula was simple; to get Courtneidge into as many scrapes and disguises as possible, helped out of difficulties by an indifferent Hulbert, but getting him in the last reel. She was on her own in *Aunt Sally* (34), a gangster comedy, and *Things Are Looking Up* (35), in the latter, hilariously, as a games mistress and a circus acrobat; and in *Me and Marlborough*.

The partnership being temporarily disbanded, MGM sent for Courtneidge to co-star with Frank Morgan in *The Perfect Gentleman*. According to her memoirs, 'Cicely' (1953), the part was quite wrong for her, and the first few days' work 'shockingly unfunny'. To her astonishment she found that the film's producer had no knowledge of her previous work, but later he ran through some of her earlier films and as a result built up her part: 'I did not think the result very good. I will go further, I thought it was rubbish. We remade the rubbish, twice with different directors.' The film was a gigantic flop on both sides of the Atlantic – in Britain it was re-christened. 'They call it *The Imperfect Woman* and, by gosh, it is,' said C. A. Lejeune, noting that MGM had failed to capture her 'unique brand of bubbly'.

Back in Britain Courtneidge made *Everybody Dance* (36) as a cabaret singer called Lady Kate; and with Jack, *Take My Tip* (37), possibly their best film. He was still filming when she was offered a stage show, 'Hide and Seek'; and in 1938 the two of them were reunited on stage in 'Under Your Hat': it ran for two years and in 1940 they filmed it. In 1945 came 'Under the Counter' in London, which she subsequently played

Cicely Courtneidge's vehicles always required her to wear funny costumes – often disguises – and usually to do a comic dance or so: here's one with Jack Hulbert from Under Your Hat *(40).*

in New York (it failed), Australia and on TV; she did 'Her Excellency' (49) and 'Gay's the Word' (51). The British industry was not making comedies of their kind, but Courtneidge played the title role in *Miss Tulip Stays the Night* (55), though it was in fact a vehicle for Diana Dors. She had a featured role in a terrible Agatha Christie effort, *Spider's Web* (60), with Glynis Johns, and toured with the original play, in the leading role, off and on for many years afterwards. There had been very few stage hits for a long while, but Courtneidge had appeared regularly on TV. In a way, all the stage failures were compensated for by *The L-Shaped Room* (62): Courtneidge had a featured role, playing an ageing and lonely Lesbian, and by any standards it was an outstanding performance. She subsequently had bits in *Those Magnificent Men in Their Flying Machines* (65) and *The Wrong Box* (66); and in 1967 she, with her husband, got glowing notices in a West End revival of 'Dear Octopus'.

Joan Crawford more or less as audiences first knew her – the jazz-mad flapper of Our Dancing Daughters *(28). Her partner is Johnny Mack Brown and behind to the left are Dorothy Sebastian and Nils Asther.*

Joan Crawford

'Movie stars? I don't like the name. . . . The words "movie stars" are so misused they have no meaning. Any little pinhead who does one picture is a star. Gable is a star, Cooper is a star, Joan Crawford, as much as I dislike the lady, is a star. But I don't think the so-called others are. To be a star you have to drag your weight into the box-office and be recognized wherever you go.' Humphrey Bogart said that once to reporter Ezra Goodman, and his grudging admiration for Miss Crawford reflects contemporary opinion – colleagues and critics – over the past half-century (almost).

The length of Crawford's career is awesome, especially as she has never been considered much of an actress – nor has she made a habit of appearing in good films. Yet she remains the only major female player surviving from the Silent era. She must be, as she looks, as tough as old boots. Her life, as with many others, might be fashioned after one of her scenarios: struggle, fight, get to the top, stay there. . . . Some accounts reckon that she survived because she changed her style, adapted herself to new fashions: but only in the physical sense did she adapt – new hairstyles, modes. The essential Crawford didn't change, whether as dancing daughter, sophisticated heroine or tragic lady. She has played one sort of American woman all these years. She admits that she has worked hard at the acting game – but she has achieved little beyond the projection of that woman. Her repertory of gestures and expressions is severely limited. Scott Fitzgerald years ago complained in a letter of the difficulties of fashioning a script for her: 'She can't change her motions in the middle of a scene without going through a sort of Jekyll and Hyde contortion of the face, so that when one wants to indicate that she is going from joy to sorrow, one must cut away and then back. Also, you can never give her such a stage direction as "telling a lie" because if you did she would practically give a representation of Benedict Arnold selling West Point to the British.'

Yet Michael Redgrave wrote almost 20 years later (in 1955): 'How splendid that she can still outstare us all!' Perhaps that is the clue: the big eyes, the determination, the conviction she seemed to feel, even in the egregious melodramas in which she played. The worse the film, the more mesmerizing she is, stalking through the jungle of clichés like a tigress, burning brightly: the working girl from the wrong side of the tracks, clawing her way to the top. Depending on the whim of her scriptwriters, she defended her honour or gave it away, and generally suffered the vicissitudes of the damned – only to suffer a bit more, when she reached the top, the agony of the guilty and/or the lonely. A pile of men lay at her feet discarded, as she defiantly faced the future, her shoulders flung back – those shoulders, draped by Adrian or Orry-Kelly, that were always so much more eloquent than her face.

Picturegoer in 1932 wondered whether, as a Silent star, she could survive much longer. A few months later, it wrote: 'Joan wants to stay in pictures until she is 40 and believes that she has nowhere near reached the peak of her career yet.' Her career started in 1906, in San Antonio, Texas, though she didn't arrive in Hollywood till 1925, when she was 19. Betweenwhiles she had been a waitress, a shopgirl in Kansas City, and had won a Charleston contest. Her first professional appearance as a dancer was in what she has described as an 'out-of-the-way' café in Chicago, and that led to the chorus-line of a Detroit club, which led to a Shubert revue on Broadway, 'Innocent Eyes'. She had been on the stage three years when MGM executive Harry Rapf discovered her: she was still in the chorus (of 'The Passing Show of 1924'). She was tested and sent out to Hollywood.

Her first job was doubling for Norma Shearer, playing a double role, in *Lady of the Night* (25), in long-shots, and then she was a chorine covered in imitation snow in *Pretty Ladies* (Myrna Loy also had a bit). There was a walk-on in *The Only Thing*, but then the ingénue part in a Jackie Coogan vehicle, *Old Clothes*. This was better: it was very important to succeed, to show the people of Kansas City, who 'had never believed in my talent'. MGM sponsored a contest in a fan-magazine to find a new name, and so Lucille Le Sueur became Joan Crawford in time for her first big part, in *Sally Irene and Mary*. MGM took up her option, embarked on a publicity campaign, put her into *The Boob* (26). She was voted a Wampas Baby Star. However, she was not pleased to be loaned out for Harry Langdon's *Tramp Tramp Tramp*, because valuable properties were not loaned. Most of her films were rush jobs: *Paris* with Charles Ray; *The Taxi Driver* (27) with Owen Moore – re-christened in Britain *The Taxi Dancer*; *Winners of the Wilderness* with Tim McCoy; *The Understanding Heart*; *The Unknown*, starring Lon Chaney; *Twelve Miles Out*, starring John Gilbert; and two William Haines vehicles, *Spring Fever* and *West Point* (28). She was a silent *Rose Marie*, singing mutely while the pit piano played from a score provided by MGM. Also that year: *Across to Singapore*, *The Law of the Range*, *Four Walls* (described by Variety as 'another underworlder') and *Dream of Love*, top-billed over Nils Asther and Aileen Pringle in this Ruritanian romance.

But that one followed *Our Dancing Daughters*: 'I'd read the story. . . . I'd stolen the script, gone to producer Hunt Stromberg, begged for it and was given it.' It was a Clara Bow part (Bland Johaneson in the New York Mirror thought she had 'beauty, charm and more refinement than the trim-legged Bow'): 'I was the flapper, wild on the surface, a girl who shakes her wind-blown bob . . . and dances herself into a frenzy while the saxes shriek and the trombones wail, a girl drunk on her youth and vitality.' This film, more than any of Bow's up to that time, showed the sticks what the jazz babies were all about. It made Crawford. MGM doubled her salary, and her name went up on marquees: 'I'd drive around with a small box camera taking

Stills like these poured forth from MGM to herald each new Crawford opus: no matter where the characters came from in reel one they would certainly be in evening dress by the end. With Clark Gable in Possessed *(31).*

pictures of "Joan Crawford" in lights.' There was another film with Haines, *The Duke Steps Out* (29), and then a sequel, *Our Modern Maidens*, with Crawford's fiancé, Douglas Fairbanks Jr in the cast. It was one of the few Silents that did well in a market avid for Talkies, so Metro didn't rush to make Joan speak.

But she did sing (and dance – 'Gotta Feeling for You') in *Hollywood Revue of 1929*, and she sang two songs in *Untamed*, in which she was a dusky maiden. There was *Montana Moon* (30), and then another flapper picture, *Our Blushing Brides*. But Crawford had had enough of bright young things: she wanted the sort of big meaty roles that went to Garbo and Norma Shearer, and when Shearer couldn't do *Paid* because she was pregnant Crawford went after it. Already filmed twice (as *Within the Law* with Alice Joyce and then Norma Talmadge) it was again a hit, and led to more of same for Crawford. In *Dance Fools Dance* (31) she was a socialite who, rendered penniless, becomes a top reporter: Clark Gable was featured, and he was her co-star in her next, *Laughing Sinners* (she was a blonde prostitute), and, later that year, in *Possessed*, one of the year's top grossers. Picturegoer, hower, found Crawford 'prone to strive for effect to the point of artificiality', and that magazine wasn't kind about the one just before, *This Modern Age*, 'so obviously a concession to the present vogue of screen sensationalism'. Another critic called it 'a shopgirl's delight', a description aptly describing *Letty Lynton* (32), based on Mrs Belloc-Lowndes's novel based on the Madeleine Smith case.

According to contemporary reports, she was not pleased to be *just one* of the stars in *Grand Hotel*, and reputedly delayed filming by playing records of Dietrich (supposedly Garbo's rival) to get herself into the right mood. But she had no scenes with Garbo. However, exposure in it did her no harm (the ex-chorine among so many proved talents) and certain critics thought she stole the film (today, only the Garbo scenes stand up). In a way, the laugh was hers: she was voted the third top money-maker at the end of the year and Garbo was fifth (for 1933 Crawford came 10th, and Garbo was 31st).

Her Sadie Thompson in *Rain* (UA), a fairly hysterical performance, wasn't much liked, nor was she better as an English girl in *Today We Live* (33). She confessed later: 'The whole picture missed. I missed most of all.' It flopped, but *Dancing Lady*, re-teamed with Gable, helping her get to the top, was the success she needed. Married now to Franchot Tone, she played with him in *Sadie McKee* (34), formula stuff, as a servant girl who is married by Edward Arnold while he's drunk. Then there were two triangle stories with Gable, *Chained*, in which the third side was Otto Kruger, and a comedy, *Forsaking All Others* (35), in which it was Robert Montgomery. This one, in particular, was a great success. After *No More Ladies* (with Montgomery) and *I Live My Life* (with Brian Aherne), she wanted to break from formula, and asked for *The Gorgeous Hussy* (36), her only period film: she was Peggy Eaton, an actress married to a member (Tone) of Andrew Jackson's administration. Frank S. Nugent (New York Times) found her 'gorgeous, but never a hussy . . . sweet, demure, trusting. . . .' The film did well despite studio scepticism; and Crawford had more hits with *Love on the Run*, with Gable and Tone, and *The Last of Mrs Cheyney* (37), with William Powell and Montgomery.

MGM had always backed Crawford with potent male leads, and the grosses of her films had justified this; but her tremendous popularity had abated somewhat by now: in 1937, for the first time for years, she didn't appear among the top money-making stars. It could be that the novely had worn off: it is tempting to assume that her popularity had much to do with her cooperation with the press, even her monotonous habit of baring her soul to the fan-magazines. In 1937 she even talked about seeing herself on the screen: 'And then I wish I could crawl away and die. Because it appears to me that I haven't given a thing–that not the faintest spark of emotion has been picked up.' (Earlier, in 1934, when she had spoken of the new Metro contract to be signed the following year, she had announced that it would give her six months off annually for stage work; thereafter she was able to announce regularly that she had not found the right vehicle.)

Then *The Bride Wore Red* (with Tone and Robert Young) failed at the box-office, though it was no better nor worse than most of her films–still, it was pretty bad, a comedy set in Austria with a very heavy performance by its star. Said Howard Barnes in the New York Herald Tribune: 'Your enjoyment of it will depend on how much of Miss Crawford you can take at a stretch.' Nor was *Mannequin* (38), with Spencer Tracy, very popular (said Picturegoer: 'Joan Crawford plot No. 1, with the star as an ambitious factory girl . . .'). However, MGM had just signed Crawford for five more years, at $1½ million and five pictures a year, and they weren't immediately alarmed when she appeared on the list of stars declared box-office poison in the famous full-page ad in the Hollywood Reporter, placed there by exhibitors 'tired of losing money on the glamour stars detested by the public'. To counter that, the press department noted that Crawford had just received her 900,000th fan letter–she had kept count of every one. However, when *The Shining Hour* (Crawford was backed by a strong cast, including Margaret Sullavan) didn't do too well, MGM worried. The executives started believing the fan-magazines which persisted in the cry that Crawford was through, which was poetic justice, because she had always ardently believed in them. So they ditched her in *Ice Follies of 1939* (39), which she has described as trash, echoing contemporary opinion.

'At this critical moment I set my sights on the part of Crystal, the hard-boiled perfume clerk who uses every wile to catch another woman's husband in *The Women*.' In this, Crawford did well, a delicious vixen, over-playing with precision. (According to

'Do you like music?' asks Conrad Veidt. 'Symphonies? Concertos?' Joan replies, 'Some symphonies, most concertos.' A Woman's Face (*41*).

The years roll by and Crawford is still in jewels and furs, even in Nazi-occupied Paris. Reunion in France (*42*), *with Philip Dorn, as her No. 1 admirer.*

Bosley Crowther in 'The Lion's Share', she did the part off-screen, bitching Shearer and being bawled out by director George Cukor for unprofessionalism.) The decline was halted, if temporarily, and Crawford got Gable back as her leading man in *Strange Cargo* (40) – but her part was much subsidiary to his, even though she was top-billed. It was one of her least typical and best performances, even though hampered by lines like 'As for going any place with you, I still pick my own gutters.' *Susan and God* did poorly (Crawford's performance was a poor imitation of the one that Gertrude Lawrence had given on the stage), but *A Woman's Face* (41) was a big success, the remake of a melodrama that Ingrid Bergman had done in Sweden. Cukor directed, and Crawford was at her least mannered.

When Ladies Meet was considered much inferior to the earlier version, and another comedy, *They All Kissed the Bride* (42), did poorly (it was made at Columbia, and had been planned for Carole Lombard: Crawford gave her salary for it to the Red Cross, who had found Lombard's body). Then she helped the Resistance in mink: *Reunion in France* ('You are France,' says Philip Dorn. 'Whenever I think of France I think of you') and *Above Suspicion* (43). 'Undiluted hokum,' said Crawford. 'If you think I made poor pictures after *A Woman's Face*, you should see the ones I went on suspension not to make!' (One of them was *Cry Havoc*.)

She left MGM. 'The consensus of opinion among the top brass was that I was washed up again,' and, indeed, it had been a long run by the prevailing standards. WB signed her at a third of her MGM salary, but apart from a brief appearance as herself in 1944's *Hollywood Canteen* (GI Dane Clark, glassy-eyed, danced with her) didn't use her. Worried about rumours that they wanted to drop her, Crawford got hold of a script that Bette Davis had turned down, *Mildred Pierce* (45), and talked producer Jerry Wald into giving it to her rather than Barbara Stanwyck. She seized her chance: as the waitress turned restaurateur who killed for her cherished but vicious daughter ('I don't know whether it's right or whether it's wrong but that's the way it's gotta be') she won a Best Actress Oscar.

WB capitalized on the demand for her by casting her as the Society woman who takes up humble violinist John Garfield in *Humoresque* (46), though playing second fiddle to him: 'Bad manners,' she says admiringly, 'the infallible sign of genius.' WB now signed her for seven years at $200,000 per film, anxious perhaps to punish Bette Davis, who might have been their greatest glory but was also the biggest thorn in their flesh. Variety said, 'Crawford's back and MGM hasn't got her', and WB prepared to let their phoenix fly in the sort of stuff which had been Davis's dramatic beef: *Possessed* (47, not a remake) with Van Heflin, *Daisy Kenyon* (at 20th; 'I've got to be going somewhere, somewhere interesting – even if it's to the moon'), *Flamingo Road* (49) and *The Damned Don't Cry* (50). At Columbia she was the overbearing house-proud *Harriet Craig* (the remake of *Craig's Wife*) and back at WB, was in a dud comedy, *Goodbye My Fancy* (51). *This Woman Is Dangerous* (52) she has described as 'a cheap and corny one', the tale of a gangster's moll who is redeemed by the doctor (Dennis Morgan) who saves her life. Bosley Crowther's review referred to Crawford's 'stony charm' and thought 'the incredibly durable star' had 'a theatrical personality' which had 'now reached the ossified stage'.

Be that as it may, Crawford now asked to be released from her contract, she says, and she went to RKO for *Sudden Fear*, a thriller so successful that it confounded the scoffers.

Amidst a fanfare of trumpets she returned to MGM for *Torch Song* (53, her first in colour apart from a guest spot in 1949's *It's a Great Feeling*), a rather trying effort about a Broadway actress who doesn't know what she does want and lives in solitary splendour stubbing out cigarettes all over the place. She danced, but her singing was dubbed by India Adams. She went to Republic for a Freudian Western, *Johnny Guitar* (54) with Mercedes McCambridge, who records that the technicians applauded her at the end of one scene, which made Crawford 'mad – and she *was* the star of the picture. I guess if I were Joan Crawford I'd be mad if some Mamie Glutz horned in on my territory that way.' In 1955 Crawford turned up in two classics, the hysterically grim *Female on the Beach*, in which she thinks her lover (Jeff Chandler) is out to murder her; and the more deliberately funny *Queen Bee*, in which writer-director Ranald McDougall brilliantly exploited every aspect of the screen Crawford in her 'bitch' hat (this time *all* the characters wanted to murder her – with some justification).

She did another at Columbia, *Autumn Leaves* (56), as a spinster in love with a younger man, and in 1957 was in Britain to make *The Story of Esther Costello*, from Nicholas Monsarrat's novel. None of these made much of a splash, and though Crawford's place in the star hierarchy was unassailable, it wasn't surprising that she was offered nothing worthwhile till *The Best of Everything* (59) at 20th – and that was hardly the biggest part.

Then in 1962 something unexpected happened: Robert Aldrich cast her and Davis as two ex-movie queens holed up in eccentric isolation: *Whatever Happened to Baby Jane?*. It was a box-office triumph, partly because of its 'horror' content. As a result Crawford was offered several similar pieces: *The Caretakers* (63), a melo about mental hospitals, as a Senior Nurse who taught her underlings judo (she was billed third, after Robert Stack and Polly Bergen!); and *Straightjacket* (64) and *I Saw What You Did* (65), both programmers for William Castle. In the latter she played an axe-murderess. In 1964 she and Davis began a follow-up to *Baby Jane* called *Hush Hush Sweet Charlotte*, but Crawford was taken ill and was replaced

A lesson in indestructibility: Berserk *(67) with Crawford and Diana Dors, of whom a wag once wrote (unjustly), 'Forgotten but not gone.' Crawford makes certain it could never be said of her.*

by Olivia de Havilland. Davis didn't hide her glee, and the production stills showed the cast ostentatiously drinking Coca-Cola (Crawford had been a great propagandist for the rival, Pepsi-Cola, since marrying its head in 1956 – her fourth husband; she has since been widowed, but still does much for Pepsi in a PR capacity).

In 1967 Crawford injudiciously appeared in two silly films: in one of the UNCLE films, *The Karate Killers* (a guest spot but wasted) and a British horror film, *Berserk*. She becomes annoyed when journalists refer to her recent work as 'horror' films, but it's a question of definition: the British *Trog* (70) was supposed to be sci-fi. But there is no question: these are all programmers.

It is unlikely that she will retire. She may enjoy tub-thumping for Pepsi, but filming is her life. She adores meeting her fans: Spencer Tracy once observed that she likes to have them follow her when she goes shopping. In her memoir ('Portrait of Joan', 1962), she says of a visit to England in the 30s that her fans 'tore my evening coat off my back and I basked in their fond affection'. Hedda Hopper once said: 'She's cool, courageous and thinks like a man. She labours 24 hours a day to keep her name in the pupil of the public eye.' It certainly won't be Crawford's fault if she doesn't make another 50 films before she dies.

Laird Cregar

Laird Cregar was one of the screen's best villains, a burly, stylish actor with a remarkable range; but his girth and height typed him. His studio saw him as a Junior Sydney Greenstreet, but he brought compassion and understanding to the hackneyed roles he played. He never played a hero, and he was only 28 when he died. He was born in Philadelphia in 1916, one of six brothers (fully grown, at 6 foot 3 inches, he was the smallest of them). He was educated at Winchester Academy, UK, as well as various US schools; ran away from home at 13, and later did a variety of jobs – theatre bouncer, book salesman, etc. He won a scholarship to the Pasadena Community Playhouse but when, later, money ran out, he slept in a parked car and depended on friends for food. He got bit parts in Warners' *Granny Get Your Gun* (40), and Universal's *Oh Johnny How You Can Love*. In 1940 he managed to persuade a local company to put on 'Oscar Wilde' with himself as Oscar: the Los Angeles press gave him rave notices. Twentieth signed him and began to build him – it didn't need much: from his first entrance in *Hudson's Bay*, as a French fur-trapper, here was clearly an actor of authority. He had a small part in *Blood and Sand* (41), as an aficionado of the bull ring, then demonstrated a fine comedy technique as Mr Spettigrew in *Charley's Aunt*; but he first came into his own on the screen as the sinister detective in *I Wake Up Screaming*, with his pathetic crush on the murdered girl (Carole Landis). He was loaned to RKO for *Joan of Paris* (42); played a confidence trickster in *Rings on Her Fingers*; was loaned to Paramount for *This Gun for Hire*, as the double-crossing bossman who hires the gun (Alan Ladd); and was one of the *Ten Gentlemen From West Point*.

In *The Black Swan* he was Captain Henry Morgan, Tyrone Power's arch-enemy, and he brought more accomplishment than it deserved to *Hello Frisco Hello* (43), playing the hero's friend, an adventurer whose sudden fortune at the end brings smiles all round; but he was at home in the elegance of Lubitsch's *Heaven Can Wait*, as the devil, with Don Ameche. He was bearded in *Holy Matrimony*, with Monty Woolley, and was *The Lodger* (44) – otherwise Jack the Ripper – in a creepy adaptation of Mrs Belloc-Lowndes's thriller, loping through the gaslit fogbound streets of a Hollywood Whitechapel in search of his prey. As a follow-up 20th took Patrick Hamilton's novel *Hangover Square* (45), set it back to the turn of the

Laird Cregar in The Black Swan (*42*), *one of his highly individual villains.*

Linda Darnell and Laird Cregar in Hangover Square *(45), a study of a schizophrenic composer compelled to murder every time he hears a wrong note. It was Cregar's last film.*

century and cast Cregar (top-billed) as a schizophrenic, with Linda Darnell in a performance almost as masterly as his.

He died in 1945, after reducing (too much) for surgery: his heart was fatally weakened. W. H. Mooring in a nice tribute in Picturegoer described him as 'somewhat eccentric' as a person.

Bing Crosby

It could be argued that no one in the history of mankind has given so much pleasure to so many people as Bing Crosby, not even Chaplin (who was perhaps the pioneer of popularity when the era of mass-communications began). During the 10-year peak of Crosby's film career he was consistently voted the most popular actor, and nine of his films remain in Variety's all-time grossers, a record unequalled till these recent years of exorbitant seat prices – and smaller audiences. He was also for 15 years one of the very top attractions of radio, and from *circa* 1930 onwards the greatest seller of records of his time: 20 of his discs have sold a million copies or more, and one of them, 'White Christmas', is far and away the biggest seller of the century at 30 million copies – out of a total Crosby sale of 300 million. (It is possible that his success in this field will be overtaken by either Elvis Presley or the Beatles, but neither he nor they have yet had such wide general acceptance.)

Crosby himself attributes most of his success to good fortune. He is modest about his singing and of his acting he said (in a memoir, 'Call Me Lucky', 1953): 'Once or twice I've been described as a light comedian. I consider this the most accurate description of my abilities I've ever seen. That's just about all I am, a light comedian. I'm not a very funny fellow and I'm not a very serious fellow either. Nor do I give off a terribly romantic aura' – a summing-up of his screen image which is totally in keeping with it: amiable, unassuming, casual, charming. Maybe what attracted people to him was that they wanted to be like that, just as easy. Or maybe, as Ella Fitzgerald once said, there is nothing as relaxing as watching Bing Crosby. James Agee wrote in 1945: 'I would enjoy Crosby . . . probably even if he did nothing more than walk across a shot.'

This epitome of niceness was born in Tacoma, Washington, in 1901. He studied at Gonzaga University, but there was nothing he fancied so much for a living as singing, and in 1921 he teamed up with Al Rinker, 'Two Boys and a Piano – Singing Songs Their Own Way'. Some years later they were taken up by Paul Whiteman,

In his early films Crosby always serenaded the heroine: here she's Marion Davies in Going Hollywood *(33). The brunette onlooker is Fifi D'Orsay.*

who added Harry Barris to the act and rechristened it 'Paul Whiteman's Rhythm Boys'. Crosby also did some solo recordings and made a Pathé short, *Two Plus Fours*: on the strength of both factors he was signed by Mack Sennett to make some shorts built around songs he was making popular ('Please', 'Just One More Chance', 'I Surrender Dear'). Around the same time, 1930, he made his feature debut in *King of Jazz*, with the Rhythm Boys (he should have had a big solo number, 'Song of the Dawn', but when it was due to be filmed he was in gaol for drunken driving and it went to John Boles). He appeared as one of the Rhythm Boys in *Check and Double Check* and sang solo, unbilled, in *Reaching for the Moon*; and became famous overnight when he was given his own radio show (1931). That, coupled with a crowd-pulling season at the Paramount, New York, and favourable reviews for the Sennett shorts, caused Paramount to offer him a three-year contract at $300,000 for five films. He played a crooner in *The Big Broadcast* (32) and The New York American said: 'Bing Crosby is the star, make no mistake about it. The "Blue of the Night" boy is a picture personality, as he demonstrated in his two-reelers. He has a camera face and a camera presence. Always at ease, he troupes like a veteran.'

Two years later he was voted for the first time one of the 10 biggest draws in films. He made an average of three films a year during the 30s, mainly distinguishable now by their songs (which were good, but not of the calibre Astaire was getting at RKO) and by some first-class supporting talent, something that he insisted upon. Jack Oakie, Burns and Allen, Mary Carlisle and Richard Arlen supported him in *College Humor* (33), fortunately for Picturegoer, who thought his 'screen personality and histrionics negligible'. He improved: through *Too Much Harmony* with Oakie; *Going Hollywood*, on loan to MGM and Marion Davies; *We're Not Dressing* (34), with Carole Lombard, Ethel Merman and Burns and Allen, as 'Crichton' in this totally revamped version of the Barrie play; *She Loves Me Not* with Miriam Hopkins; *Here Is My Heart* with Kitty Carlisle; *Mississippi* (35) with W. C. Fields, a new version of Booth Tarkington's 'Magnolia'; *Two for Tonight*; *The Big Broadcast of 1936*, with Oakie, Burns and Allen and another roster of guest stars; *Anything Goes*, an enjoyable version of the Cole Porter musical with Merman, directed by Lewis Milestone; and *Rhythm on the Range*. He was loaned to Columbia for *Pennies From Heaven*, one of his biggest early successes, with Madge Evans and Louis Armstrong; and with *Waikiki Wedding* and *Double or Nothing*

Bing Crosby and Marjorie Reynolds in Holiday Inn *(42), a genial musical with a score of Irving Berlin songs including, for the first time, 'White Christmas', here being reprised for the finale.*

Crosby as he appeared in The Bells of St Mary's *(45), one Hollywood religious film that got by with the critics as well as being a huge success with the public.*

in 1937 he made it to fourth in the box-office 10. *Doctor Rhythm* (38) was a very good one (based on an O. Henry story) with Crosby involved with an heiress and aunt Beatrice Lillie; Louis Armstrong was again in the cast. Between songs in *Sing You Sinners* he had some straight acting to do and did it very well. Otherwise he was polishing up his comedy technique: *Paris Honeymoon* (39) with Franciska Gaal and Shirley Ross; or doing a bit of both: in *East Side of Heaven*, a sentimental comedy at Universal with Joan Blondell, and *The Star Maker*, a biopic of Gus Edwardes.

Crosby needed everything he knew about comedy in 1940 when he came up against Bob Hope. They had been friends for some time, but their teaming came about by chance, when Fred MacMurray refused a vehicle for him and George Burns: *Road to Singapore*. A fairly nondescript script with the two of them in pursuit of Dorothy Lamour, it became rather funny due to the empathy of Hope and Crosby, a spontaneity and free-wheeling in their playing, and according to the Motion Picture Herald, it was the year's most popular film. *If I Had My Way* at Universal and *Rhythm on the River* with Mary Martin did well, and Crosby came in again in the Golden Ten. Paramount reunited him with Hope and Lamour for *Road to Zanzibar* (41) and this time there were no holds barred, a deliberately silly story that was a spoof of the jungle films that Lamour usually made and a zany, funny film. Bing and Bob ad-libbed much more: and the film gave them a sharp push towards the stratospheric popularity that was to be theirs for more than a decade. *Birth of the Blues* with Mary Martin is one of Crosby's own favourites, and then came a real big one, *Holiday Inn* (42), with Fred Astaire and a fine Irving Berlin score, including 'White Christmas', ubiquitous in the autumn of that year, and every Christmas since. In between entertaining the troops, Crosby's box-office held with the third *Road* film (*to Morocco*, 43); *Star Spangled Rhythm*, guesting but top-billed, and singing the 'Old Glory' number at the climax; and his first in colour, *Dixie*, a biopic of Dan Emmett with Lamour.

In 1943 he was No. 4 at the box-office; in 1944 he was top (a position he clung to with monotonous regularity in both Britain and the US). The film that did it was *Going My Way*, the story of a singing priest in a slum community. Although the reliable Leo McCarey produced and directed, no one at Paramount had faith in the project. Perhaps its most popular aspect was the antagonism between the young priest and an older one – Barry Fitzgerald at his most cantankerous. Both of them won Oscars, and the Academy and the New York Critics thought it the year's Best Picture. Crosby's acting ('there is nothing . . . to remind us of the crooner or

Every studio made musicals about show-biz stars being drafted and putting on a patriotic entertainment for the other guys on the installation. Here Come the Waves *(44) was one of the more enjoyable: Crosby, Betty Hutton and Sonny Tufts.*

the comedian' – Forsyth Hardy) was further endorsed by the year's Picturegoer Gold Medal. McCarey wanted to do a sequel, and under the terms of the deal Crosby moved over to his studio, RKO, for *The Bells of St Mary's* (45); Ingrid Bergman, as a nun, played opposite him: 'If you're ever in trouble dial O for O'Malley,' he told her. The film did even better than the first one, and they wound up at third and fourth among the most successful films yet made (beaten only by *Gone With the Wind* and *This Is the Army*).

Between the two Crosby was in one of the better Service musicals, *Here Come the Waves* (44), and he did a sketch and sang one song in *Duffy's Tavern* (45). Variety gave him one of the rare front-page banner headlines devoted to a performer: 'Bing's Bangup Box Office in '45' and called him 'the hottest guy in show biz today'. Paramount negotiated a new seven-year deal with Crosby's manager, brother Everett, who until this peak had kept Crosby tied for only three years at a time – and he was to get considerably more per film than the $125,000 he got for *Going My Way*. But 1946 was even bigger: both *Road to Utopia* and *Blue Skies* (with Astaire; music by Berlin – a '$3 million technicolored exhibition of Old Masters' in Time's words) were huge grossers; and so was *Welcome Stranger* (47) with Fitzgerald, as opposing doctors. And so again (after guesting in *Variety Girl*) were *Road to Rio* and *The Emperor Waltz* (48), a Billy Wilder piece with Crosby as an American at the court of Franz Joseph. Then he was *A Connecticut Yankee in King Arthur's Court* (49), his first poor film for years. An Irish comedy with Fitzgerald, *Top of the Morning*, was even worse, but there was a return to form with two that Capra directed, *Riding High* (50, a remake of *Broadway Bill*) and *Here Comes the Groom* (51, with Jane Wyman). Between the two was *Mr Music* (50, a remake of *Accent on Youth*, with Nancy Olsen), a title that Crosby disliked, and so, apparently, did the public. He had slipped from the top slot – but not far. In 1952 Crosby did a medium musical with Wyman, *Just for You*, and then the old team had a hit when they hit the *Road to Bali*: but more than one critic pointed out that it was rather like two indulgent uncles and an aunt dressed up for a children's party.

To the horror of Marghanita Laski, Crosby was cast in the film of her novel about an American searching for his son in Europe years after the war, *Little Boy Lost* (53), but after she had seen it, she magnanimously admitted she'd been wrong (even though he still sang four songs). After an interval, he sang a lot of songs, and they were Berlin's, in *White Christmas* (54): his sidekick was Danny Kaye, and there must have been something right about the

Two award-winning performances: Bing Crosby and Grace Kelly in The Country Girl *(55), for which she won a Best Actress Oscar and he the New York Critics Best Actor citation.*

teaming, for the public flocked to it and it still gets huge ratings on TV in the US (other countries found the mawkish patriotism considerably embarrassing). For Crosby, the leading role in the film of Odets's *The Country Girl* (55) was changed from has-been actor to broken-down musical star: he acted with considerable emotional depth, got great notices, and a second New York Critics Best Actor award. Grace Kelly was in it, and William Holden, and it was a hit; but his last for Paramount, a remake of *Anything Goes* (56) with Mitzi Gaynor and Donald O'Connor, was weak in every respect. Then came what was to be his last film success: *High Society* (56), and his last big record hit, 'True Love'; there was a Cole Porter score and a lot more going for it–Grace Kelly, Sinatra, Celeste Holm. And as with *The Country Girl*, his co-stars were considered bigger factors in its success than he–by exhibitors.

Perhaps he should have capitalized on its success, but instead he did a serious film (he sang only over the credits): *Man on Fire* (57), as a divorced man squabbling with his ex-wife over their son. It was generally disregarded by the press and lit no fires at the box-office, which was a pity, for Crosby's naturalistic work here was comparable to that of Spencer Tracy. But if 1957 marked a low in his professional life, privately things were better when he married starlet Kathryn Grant. In a later interview he admitted that the previous years had been tough. His wife since 1930, ex-star Dixie Lee, had died, an alcoholic, in 1953; his grown sons had reputations as roisterers; and it was believed he was morose about the course his career had taken. He had, he said, been reading deeply and learning languages; and then his new wife presented him with a family.

His film career, however, never again got moving. He produced and starred in two films for 20th: *Say One for Me* (59) as a priest again and *High Time* (60) as a middle-aged college freshman; there was nothing to tempt old admirers from fireside TV, and the young players in both didn't attract young cinemagoers. His marvellous lazy singing style was out of fashion, pushed out by the frenetic phrasing of Sinatra; but it was curious that Crosby, a millionaire several times over, hadn't commissioned better material. It must have seemed a good idea to do *Road to Hong Kong* (62) and indeed the public went to it, but it was a pale shadow of past glories.

There had been guest appearances in 1960

in *Let's Make Love* and *Pepe*; and though he was working often in TV he wanted to film again, and asked Sinatra for a small role in *Robin and the Seven Hoods* (64), a comedy about Chicago in the Prohibition days. He had three songs, in one of which Sinatra and Dean Martin chided him for not having 'Style': but he showed them, leaving them further back than was intended – right at the starting post. He was also the best thing about the re-make of *Stagecoach* (66), as the tippling doctor: but when he wasn't on-screen it wasn't worth watching and the reviews killed any box-office potential it may have had.

On TV, ageing but still admirable, he has his own specials and hosts the 'Hollywood Palace' from time to time. Film offers are not lacking: he turned down the Lee Marvin part in *Paint Your Wagon* because he didn't like the prospect of long locations and didn't care for the subject. His voice isn't what it was, nor is he the American institution he was; but his contribution to popular music is greater than any other male singer of the century, and his contribution to films is deceptively high: he always made it look so easy.

Bebe Daniels

Bebe Daniels had a long career in Silent pictures and made the transition to Talkies with ease, though Talkies hardly utilized her talent. She was not yet 30, but in the roles they gave her she was usually somewhat passé: a grande dame, an adventuress. Her playing was incisive, but she was able only to hint at the impishness and warmth that had made her such an appealing Silent comedienne.

She was born in Dallas, Texas, in 1901, of a Scottish father and Spanish mother; both were on the stage, and at three Bebe was appearing in her father's stock company, as one of the Princes in 'Richard III', billed as 'The World's Youngest Shakespearian Actress'. Two years later she was on the Los Angeles stage in 'The Squaw Man'; at seven she was in 'The Common Enemy', and repeated in the film version (08) for Selig-Polyscope. She continued to work in pictures, mainly in Westerns, between her stage work. She was considered to have 'kid-appeal'. She also found time to get some education at the Sacred Heart Convent in LA; when she left there – she was 13 – she signed a contract with Pathé (Hal Roach) to appear in two-reel comedies with Snub Pollard and Harold Lloyd: she was in over 200 altogether – in most of the 'Lonesome Luke' series with Lloyd, featured as 'the charming little comedienne'. She and Lloyd were often seen together socially, and won several dancing contests. Cecil B. de Mille saw them win at Santa Monica and offered Daniels a contract, but she refused because her contract with Roach had a year to run. When it expired (her last short with Lloyd was either *Just Neighbors* or *Captain Kidd's Kids*) she approached de Mille, who signed her to a four-year contract; most of her films during that period were made for Realart, a subsidiary of Paramount, for whom de Mille worked. When the deal expired, Paramount signed Daniels to a long-term contract: thus, in effect, she worked for that company from 1919 to 1928. Her first picture for de Mille was *Male and Female* (19) and she had only a tiny bit as Thomas Meighan's concubine in the Babylon sequence. She was Vice in *Everywoman*, a modern morality tale, and the Other Woman in *Why Change Your Wife?* (20) with Meighan and Gloria Swanson. Then she achieved star status, or at least was the leading woman: Sam Wood's *The Dancin' Fool* and *Sick Abed*, both with Wallace Reid; *The Fourteenth Man*, based on 'The Man From Blankley's'; *You Never Can Tell*, which had no connection with the Shaw play; *Oh Lady Lady*, as a small-town girl who makes it on Broadway; *Two Weeks With Pay* (21), in a dual role; *She Couldn't Help It*, a remake of Mary Pickford's *In the Bishop's Carriage*; *Ducks and Drakes*, *The March Hare* and *One Wild Week*, a trilogy of comedies directed by Maurice Campbell, in which she was a madcap heiress; and de Mille's *The Affairs of Anatol* (21), based on Schnitzler's play, with Reid, and playing a character called Satan Synne.

In 1921 she was caught speeding by the county police and spent 10 days in gaol, which occasioned a bonanza of publicity, not all of it unfavourable: it turned out to be a rather luxurious 10 days, and Realart capitalized on the event by rushing her into a movie about a movie queen who goes to gaol, *The Speed Girl*. She was an orphan in *Nancy From Nowhere* (22) and a señorita in *A Game Chicken*. *North of the Rio Grande* was a Western with Jack Holt, and *Nice People* a version of a play by Rachel Crothers: ironically, it cast Daniels as a hard-drinking flapper and Reid as the innocent Westerner – one of his last pictures before dying of drug addiction. She did *Pink Gods* with James Kirkwood; *Singed Wings* with Conrad Nagel; and *The World's Applause* (23), whose plot bore more than a passing resemblance to another recent scandal – the murder of William Desmond Taylor, with Daniels as the star who, like Mary Miles Minter, was ruined thereby. She was increasingly cast as a playgirl, a cross between Gloria Swanson of a year or two before, and Joan Crawford or Clara Bow to come – not too flippant, not too worldly: *The Glimpses of the Moon*, from Edith Wharton's novel, hunting romance in Europe with Nita Naldi; *The Exciters* with Antonio Moreno; and *His Children's Children*, with Dorothy Mackaill as her equally jazz-mad sister.

She then did a Zane Grey Western, *Heritage of the Desert* (24); was loaned out for *Daring Youth*; and did *Unguarded Women* with Dix, a study of a 'reckless, anchorless girl of today' (Picturegoer). She was Valentino's leading lady in *Monsieur Beaucaire* and was stuck on a desert island with Richard Dix in *Sinners in Heaven*. There followed: *Dangerous Money* – she inherited it – with Tom Moore; *Argentine Love* with Ricardo Cortez, a romance of what the fan-mags called 'tango-land'; *Miss Bluebeard* (25) with two husbands plus Raymond Griffith; *The Crowded Hour*, from a play about an actress who leaves her career for the man she loves – fighting in France; *The Manicure Girl*, who discovers that wealth isn't everything; *Wild Wild Susan* with Rod La Rocque; *Lovers in Quarantine* with Alfred Lunt and Harrison Ford; *The Splendid Crime* with Neil Hamilton; *Miss Brewster's Millions* (26), the old comedy with a sex-change to accommodate her; *Volcano*, a tropical melodrama with Cortez; *The Palm Beach Girl*, a silly comedy about a first visit to the sea; *The Campus Flirt* and *Stranded in Paris*, both with James Hall.

Gloria Swanson and Pola Negri remained Paramount's top two stars: but Daniels made a good third. Like them, she was photographed in all manner of exotica – lace, feathers, jewels. 'Let who will be good but Bebe will be beautiful' said one caption. But she was warmer, more approachable – almost like middle-period Myrna Loy, but more reckless, and often in risqué situations. Picturegoer at one point was worried that she was becoming 'the screen's leading male impersonator'. She was certainly Paramount's principal light comedienne, and got the pick of the comic scripts. All of them were directed by Clarence Badger and some were very good: *A Kiss in a Taxi* (27); *Senorita* at one point as a fiery Spaniard, and *Swim Girl Swim*, both with Hall; *She's a Sheik* (28), kidnapping Foreign Legionnaire Richard Arlen; *The Fifty-Fifty Girl*, sharing ownership of a mine with Hall; and *Hot News* with Neil Hamilton and Paul Lukas. Then: Gregory La Cava's *Feel My Pulse* with Arlen; and *Take Me Home* and *What a Night!*, both with Hamilton. With the coming of Talkies her star at Paramount tottered and fell: other studios wanted to nurture their stars through the Talkie period, but Paramount wanted to drop theirs, whom they considered overpriced, in favour of the stage talent they were importing. They didn't put Daniels in a Talkie, nor even test her; after some months of inactivity, she bought up the remaining nine months of her contract.

At RKO erstwhile Paramount producer William Le Baron was in charge of production. He had heard Daniels sing privately at parties and signed her for the lead in a production that tried to transfer to the screen the lavishness and glamour of a Ziegfeld show – it was a Ziegfeld musical, *Rio Rita* (29), opposite John Boles. Hollywood thought it an impetuous step as Daniels was considered all washed up; but it turned out that she not only spoke effectively, but had a soprano voice of warmth and charm. The film was one of the year's biggest grossers, at $2 million. As Hollywood hastened to congratulate Daniels and RKO, Paramount executives sat red-faced. 'You didn't tell us you could sing,' they said reprovingly to Daniels. 'You never asked me,' she replied. She began a new career at RKO: *Love Comes Along* (30) with Lloyd Hughes, where she sang; and *Alias*

Bebe Daniels in Rio Rita *(29), which established her as the singing queen of the Talking screen – but her reign was, regrettably, all too brief.*

French Gertie, an agreeable crook melodrama where she and Ben Lyon were partners in crime–until they went straight. In life, they were married, and columnists predicted it wouldn't last: he had just reached the top after years as a feature player and she, despite *Rio Rita*, was considered part of the former generation. Also, the very happiness of the marriage conflicted with the public image: stars like Daniels were not (yet) expected to settle for domesticity. She did another big musical, *Dixiana*, and then a sophisticated melo directed by and co-starring Lowell Sherman, *Lawful Larceny*.

She moved over to United Artists to be Douglas Fairbanks's leading lady in *Reaching for the Moon* (31), and then Warners signed her to play the fading beauty who falls in love with young Lyon in *My Past*: most of her past consisted of being Lewis Stone's mistress (it was from a best-seller called 'Ex-Mistress'), and it was all very unconvincing, despite her alluring appearance. Warners liked her, however, and signed her to a contract: *The Maltese Falcon* with Cortez, in the part later played by Mary Astor; *The Honor of the Family* with Warren William, a modern adaptation of a Balzac story; *Silver Dollar* (32), as a platinum blonde comforting tycoon Edward G. Robinson; and *42nd Street* (33), as the temperamental has-been actress whose inability to go on brings stardom to chorine Ruby Keeler–it was hardly the sort of part liable to keep her career going at full throttle. Her last film for Warners was a programmer, *Registered Nurse*, whose release was held up for over a year. She went to Columbia for *Cocktail Hour* with Randolph Scott, then accepted a British offer: *The Song You Gave Me*, a musical with Victor Varconi. It got some Stateside bookings, but *A Southern Maid*, which she stayed on to make–she had a dual role–didn't. She returned to Hollywood to play the faithful secretary in *Counsellor at Law* (34), starring John Barrymore, but her good work there elicited no further offers. After an interval Fox signed her for a reprise of her role in *42nd Street*, only this time she played a has-been movie star touring in vaudeville: Alice Faye was the girl who replaced her when she had the chance of a movie comeback and the film was *Music Is Magic* (35). Also in 1935 she toured in a comedy 'Hollywood Holiday'. In 1936, when Lyon's Hollywood career had also come to a halt, they accepted a London engagement at the Palladium, and stayed on touring the Halls. They also accepted another offer from the British studios, *Murder in the Stalls*, finally shown in 1939 as *Not Wanted on Voyage*–and not wanted was its eventual fate. Daniels did make another British picture and it was a slight improvement, *The Return of Carol*

Bebe Daniels was John Barrymore's secretary in Counsellor-at-Law *(33), based on Elmer Rice's play about a hectic day in the life of same.*

Dean (39), a mystery story.

By this time she and Lyon were established headliners in British music halls, and in 1939 they did a revue at the Holborn Empire called 'Haw Haw!', which took them into the days of the blitz. During this period they began a BBC radio show, 'Hi Gang!' with Vic Oliver, and their snappy American style and their expertise made other comic shows look slow. Their publicity then and subsequently made much of the fact that, as American citizens, they had stayed to entertain the British during the dangerous days of the blitz, but there is no doubt that (*a*) the British became genuinely fond of them and (*b*) they became genuinely fond of their adopted country. They also worked for ENSA, trooped round factories doing a comedy act and singing; and Daniels's work for US servicemen, as organizer and entertainer, brought her in 1946 the US Medal of Freedom. She and Lyon and Oliver made a film based on their radio programme, *Hi Gang!* (41), about the same time as the Lyons were in a West End revue, 'Gangway'. Later Daniels appeared in the British edition of Cole Porter's 'Panama Hattie'.

They returned to Hollywood in 1945 when Lyon took up an executive position with 20th; in 1948 Daniels produced a low-budget comedy for Hal Roach, *The Fabulous Joe*. But they were homesick for Britain and Lyon negotiated a British job with 20th. In 1949 they began a second series of 'Hi Gang!' but it did not repeat its earlier success; in 1950 they began a popular series, 'Life With the Lyons', whose cast included daughter Barbara and adopted son Richard. Daniels wrote most of the scripts, and it became a TV series as well as spawning a couple of weak pictures, *Life With the Lyons* (53) and *The Lyons in Paris* (55): but it was in any case a dreadful series, unworthy of their work in the past.

In 1963 she had a stroke and was a long time in convalescence; but in the last year or so has occasionally been glimpsed at premières.

Marion Davies

'And Marion never looked lovelier!' The line is reiterated by T. C. Jones in an otherwise unfunny sketch about Hollywood in the 30s. Jones is taking off Louella Parsons, ace film gossip of the Hearst press, and in that one line he evokes the whole bizarre saga of Parsons, William Randolph Hearst and Marion Davies, who was Hearst's protégée, mistress and life-long companion. In this campy way–or as the original of the character played by Dorothy Comingore in *Citizen Kane*–is she remembered today. W. A. Swanberg writes in his biography of Hearst: '. . . it was Hearst's considered intention to make Miss Davies the greatest star in the nation'. Hearst lost, it was estimated, over $7 million in the attempt. He loved her with great devotion, and would certainly have married her had his wife consented to a divorce; it was his penchant for romance–as well as glory–which prompted him to try to impose Davies on the public. Only a handful of her films made money. And yet she was an actress of considerable charm and a comedienne of some talent. She might well have gone further without Hearst. Swanberg writes: 'Her friends, then and now, are unanimous in judging her an incredibly warm and winning personality–fun-loving, joyous, a born comedienne, wildly sentimental and generous.'

The Hearst-Davies relationship would presumably be accepted today by fans as it was accepted at the time by Hollywood society and by the distinguished guests at their home, San Simeon; but the press of the period–not only Hearst's–never linked their names. The official publicity line on her was that she was Hollywood's leading bachelor girl.

She was born in Brooklyn in either 1897 or 1900, and educated in a convent, from where, apparently, she went straight into the chorus-line of 'Chu Chin Chow'; she was in the chorus of 'Oh Boy!' (17), where Ziegfeld saw her and invited her to be in 'The Ziegfeld Follies of 1917'; she was also in 'Miss 1917' and a movie, *Runaway Romany* (17). Picturegoer enthused: 'Miss Davies is petite, winsome, and altogether charming, at times a little reminiscent of Mary Pickford.' It is uncertain when the showgirl and budding movie star made the acquaintance of newspaper tycoon Hearst, but by the beginning of 1918 he had decided that she was to become a great movie star–the greatest. He tutored her himself and had her tutored, and 'arranged' for her first starring vehicle, *Cecilia of the Pink Roses* (18), a domestic drama. The Hearst press, which till then had evinced only a mild interest in films, was transformed overnight: all of Hearst's papers discovered 'a movie masterpiece' and they hailed a fabulous new star, 'a vision of loveliness', 'a bewitching beauty'. The other papers were markedly less enthusiastic.

In 1919 Hearst formed an agreement with Adolph Zukor to release Marion Davies pictures through Paramount: the producing company was called Cosmopolitan, and though it was to make other pictures through the years apart from those with Davies, it was around her that the whole operation revolved. Her second starring movie was *The Belle of New York* (19), from the stage success. She was a Salvation Army lass. Tom Milne has written (1967): 'She is the only thing worth watching in a creaky melodrama: her exquisite beauty shines through soulfully, and she acts with a restraint and repose rare at the time.' But this is mild praise compared to that of the Hearst columnists; instructions went out to all Hearst papers that Davies's name was to be mentioned in some way at least once in every issue.

The films that followed: *Getting Mary Married*, *The Dark Star*, *The Cinema Murder* (20), *April Folly*, *The Restless Sex*, *Buried Treasure* (21), *Enchantment*, *The Bride's Play* (22), *Beauty's Worth* and *The Young Diana* (currently, Photoplay was praising her as 'a lively Venus of common sense'). They all lost money, though one of the reasons was that Hearst insisted on the best for Davies, down to the smallest detail. *When Knighthood Was in Flower* cost the extraordinary sum of $1½ million, and Hearst commissioned Victor Herbert to write two special songs for cinemas that were playing the film: one was called 'The Marion Davies March'. Davies played Mary Tudor, sister of Henry VIII (Lynn Harding), in a generally lively historical romp. It was good, but not quite as good as the Hearst press maintained: 'Marion Davies soars to new heights', 'Superlative performance by the talented star'. By some fluke it turned a profit, but the next one didn't: *Adam and Eva* (23), a silly film with Biblical and modern sequences.

Marion Davies as Mary Tudor (the one who married Louis XII of France) with Ruth Shepley in a successful historical film of 1922, When Knighthood Was in Flower.

Hearst and Zukor now split, and Cosmopolitan moved over to the Goldwyn Co., where it made *Yolande* (24), a not unsuccessful attempt to repeat the success of *Knighthood* with Harding this time as Charles the Bold; *Janice Meredith*, another historical drama; *Zander the Great* (25), a triangle story built round a magician; and a backstage story, *Lights of Old Broadway*. This, too, netted Hearst a profit, though, according to Bosley Crowther in his book on MGM, it was the only one to do so during the Cosmopolitan-MGM tie-up. Goldwyn had amalgamated with M and M to become MGM, whose head, Louis B. Mayer, made a proposal to Hearst, and it was a staggering one: MGM would finance Cosmopolitan's films *and* pay Davies the unprecedented salary of $10,000 per week. Further, Hearst would get a percentage of the profits. It was tacitly understood that all MGM films would be getting as much publicity in Hearst's 22 papers as Davies (and certainly Hearst was also to contribute financially in some way).

Davies had, in fact, accumulated quite a following, and they turned up in reasonable numbers to see her in the Ruritanian – or Graustarkian – *Beverley of Graustark* (26), – where she masqueraded as a boy – originally made in 1916; *The Red Mill* (27), an awful 'Dutch' effort; *Tillie the Toiler* as a girl torn between love and the lure of wealth; *The Fair Coed*; and J. M. Barrie's *Quality Street*, with Conrad Nagel. A propos that one and the Hearst columnists, Swanberg notes 'regardless of how colossal her previous pictures were, the latest ones were always greater'. (In Britain, of course, no one told Picture-

Playing a would-be movie star, Marion Davies mimics the grand manner of a screen queen in Show People *(28), one of the the films which exploited her comic ability. Watching her are, left, William Haines (who retired from films and became a successful interior decorator) and Dell Henderson.*

goer to describe the Davies performance as 'adorable'.) All the same, not enough people agreed. The trouble was that Davies was not suited to the virginal heroines, the dainty country maidens, the Mary Pickford parts, that Hearst wanted to see her in: her forte was light comedy, as she had demonstrated in *The Fair Coed*. That was sufficiently well received for Hearst to reluctantly agree to three more comedies. *The Patsy* (28) was based on a comic-strip, a satire on family life with Davies as a flapper, doing very funny impersonations of Pola Negri, Mae Murray and Lillian Gish. King Vidor directed, and the film did more for Davies than her last 10 films put together. She did well again in *The Cardboard Lover* with Nils Asther, and better in Vidor's *Show People*, designed as a burlesque on Gloria Swanson's career from slapstick to dramatic actress: it ended without much pungency, but Davies was amusing, especially with some more facial clowning.

Talkies were going to be a problem, because she stuttered–but this, too, was overcome: *Marianne* (29), perhaps wisely, gave her little to do, but she sang a couple of songs. Already she had sung in *The Hollywood Revue of 1929*–and danced on a drum. She was ineffectual in most of her Talkies. 'She has too few chances' was a constant plaint of reviewers, or else she was much too old for the roles in which she was cast: *Not So Dumb* (30) with Donald Ogden Stewart; *The Floradora Girl*, from the old musical; *The Bachelor Father* (31), from a big stage hit; *It's a Wise Child* with Lester Vail; *Five and Ten* with Leslie Howard; and *Polly of the Circus* (32), an updated version of an old favourite, with Clark Gable. She was also *Blondie of the Follies* with Robert Montgomery, and *Peg o' My Heart* (33), a Barriesque piece of whimsy done years before by Laurette Taylor, and now updated and musicalized. Once again the public greeted the Davies movies with indifference, so to boost her appeal Paramount was raided for Bing Crosby and Gary Cooper, to co-star in *Going Hollywood* and *Operator 13* (34) respectively. Crosby says in his memoir that filming–only a little every day–was accompanied by dance bands and much drinking and a good deal of fun. Davies's hospitality in her studio bungalow was famous.

But the bungalow was now to be dismantled and carted from Culver City to Burbank. The Hearst-Mayer rift began with *The Barretts of Wimpole Street*. Hearst and

This was the sort of part which William Randolph Hearst preferred to see Miss Davies in: Operator 13 *(34)* with *Gary Cooper. In Britain it was called* Spy 13.

Davies insisted that it was just the ticket for her, but MGM (Thalberg and Mayer) had earmarked it for Norma Shearer. Davies insisted on testing, in a black wig, but Shearer played it. After the one with Cooper, Davies and Hearst took off for Europe, and while they were 'doing' Versailles they decided that Marie Antoinette should be Davies's next role. Coincidentally, Thalberg had the same idea for Shearer. This time the dispute was acrimonious, and Mayer decided to settle it by offering the subject to Hearst, providing he would pay the production costs. Hearst considered, and declined. He approached WB with what Jack L. Warner described as 'a multimillion-dollar proposition': he gives no details, but Davies, Hearst, Cosmopolitan and bungalow settled on the Burbank lot.

Shearer's name was not mentioned in the Hearst press (nor for some years to come). It was announced that Davies would be making strong dramatic pictures, among them a life of Marie Antoinette, and probably a *Twelfth Night* (Hollywood was Shakespeare-happy at this time), but three of the four films she made at WB were certainly comedies and the other is a doubtful: *Page Miss Glory* (35) with Dick Powell, about a chambermaid who wins a beauty contest; *Hearts Divided* (36), again with Powell, a love story set in Napoleonic times; *Cain and Mable* with Gable (loaned by MGM to show there was no hard feeling, along with Montgomery–but in exchange for Paul Muni and Leslie Howard); and *Ever Since Eve* (37) with Montgomery, about a girl who puts on glasses to stop men making passes (but the film still belonged to Patsy Kelly). Said Warner: 'It may surprise the dour prophets to know that they all brought in a solid profit.' However, Davies made no more pictures for WB or anyone else. Hearst in 1937 found himself in considerable financial difficulties, and Davies came to his aid, dipping into her own hefty private fortune. It is not known whether either of them continued to nourish hopes of movie fame–she, probably not, for she had never had much ambition in that direction, but had humoured the old man.

He died in 1951, and within 24 hours the instructions regarding the daily mention of Davies's name were rescinded (it is doubtful whether, by this time, many readers remembered who she was). Four months later, she married: 'for the first time' said one paper significantly. She died in 1961.

Bette Davis

Provided you're taking the retrospective view, that old tag 'The First Lady of the Screen'–after examining all the contenders–belongs decisively and firmly to Bette Davis. Speaking of her great years, when she was not only gilt-edged box-office but in a variety of roles a wonder to the critics, Gene Ringgold has written ('The Films of Bette Davis') that her films 'comprise an admirable record, one that may never be equalled by another film actress'. When everything has been said against her–and much has been said–she remains unrivalled as a screen actress. She broke the old mould for female stars: she didn't want to get up on that screen and be decorative, to be glamorous like Garbo, to be sympathetic like Janet Gaynor, to pose as an actress like Norma Shearer: she wanted to *act*, to illuminate for audiences all the women she found within her–waitresses, dowagers, spinsters, harridans, drunks. She fought to play them. All subsequent screen stars owe her a debt, in that she proved that an actress could be an excellent judge of material, and her dedication destroyed a lingering belief that stage acting was 'superior' to film acting. She once told a reporter that one of the reasons she worked so hard was because there were so few real actresses in films.

She never disappeared inside a part: she was too intense, too electric, too mannered (increasingly, as time went on), but she shaped her roles to herself, burying as much of herself as she could. The end result then – this 'admirable record' – is a bewildering gallery of screen portraits, a total of 10 Oscar nominations (beaten only by Katharine Hepburn), a reputation that a mostly latent tendency to ham can't tarnish, and an undiminishing army of admirers.

It has been a long career, and she has written a ferociously intelligent book about it ('The Lonely Life', 1962). It all began in Lowell, Massachusetts, in 1908. She decided at school that she wanted to be an actress and studied at the John Murray Anderson school; from there she was employed with a stock company in Rochester, until its director, George Cukor, fired her. She got a job with the Provincetown Players, 'The Earth Between' (28), and then did a tour alternating 'The Wild Duck' (as Hedwig) and 'The Lady From the Sea' (as Boletta). After a spell in rep, her agent got her a leading role in 'Broken Dishes', a mild domestic comedy and a success; then she had another good part in 'Solid South'. During the first play she flubbed a Goldwyn screen test, but then she passed one for Universal, whose boss, Carl Laemmle, thought she might be right for the daughter in *Strictly Dishonorable*. He hadn't met her; when he did, he observed that she had 'as much sex-appeal as Slim Somerville'. This confirmed her fears that she wouldn't fit into a Hollywood deeply committed to glamour and beauty. Still, she was getting $300 a week, and did her best in the film they did put her into, *Bad Sister* (31), as the good sister. The response to this mousy little girl didn't surprise Universal: there wasn't any. They gave her bits in *Seed* and *Waterloo Bridge*, loaned her out for a truly horrendous bucolic comedy, *Way Back Home* (32), and a routine Edgar Wallace melo, *The Menace*.

But she was getting wised-up: she dyed her hair blonde for *The Menace*. According to most versions, a friend of George Arliss saw her in this and recommended her for the lead opposite him in *The Man Who Played God*; but Jack L. Warner insists that she was recommended to him by a Warner talent scout when Universal dropped her. At all events, after a B for Capital, *Hell's House*, she was cast in the Arliss film and signed by Warners. Being Arliss's leading lady gave her status, but beyond that she clearly was talented. She supported Barbara Stanwyck in *So Big* and Ruth Chatterton in *The Rich Are Always With Us*; was Warren William's leading lady in *The Dark Horse* and Richard Barthelmess's in *Cabin in the Cotton*, as a teenage tramp: Warner said there first appeared 'the magic quality that transformed this bland and not beautiful little girl into a great artist when she was playing bitchy roles'. *Three on a Match* gave her little to do, but *20,000 Years in Sing Sing* (33) showcased her with Spencer Tracy; *Parachute Jumper* was a Fairbanks Jr programmer about the Depression; *The Working Man* a fair comedy with Arliss.

She worked – very hard: much later she observed that the MGM stars were treated like queens and the Warner players like factory workers. She must have thrived on it. In each picture there was a little more confidence, a little more mastery. However, in what was to have been her first official starring picture, blonded-up again, most critics found her inadequate: *Ex-Lady*, 'a piece of junk', she said, 'my shame was only exceeded by my fury'. Nor did the public like it (having seen it two years earlier as *Illicit*). Studio publicity started to play her down again; but they kept her churning out programmers: *Bureau of Missing Persons*, a fast-paced thriller with Pat O'Brien; *Fashion Follies of 1934* (34), a musical – neither she nor William Powell sang; *The Big Shakedown*, a poor racketeer drama with Ricardo Cortez and Charles Farrell; *Jimmy the Gent*, a small role but she liked working with Cagney; and *Fog Over Frisco*, one of her best early performances, as a 'fence'.

Director John Cromwell at RKO wanted to borrow her for *Of Human Bondage*, but Warners refused. Davis fought; she was desperate to do it. And did. As the vicious, grasping waitress who enslaves Leslie Howard, she gave 'probably the best performance ever recorded on screen by a US actress' (Life). Warners were delighted with the general acclaim and cast her in *The Case of the Howling Dog*. She flatly refused to do it, and her hand was strengthened by the two films she had in the can (the second of them was in fact made before *Bondage*). Her performance as the *Housewife* (Ann Dvorak was her rival) was admired, but she got raves again for her work in *Bordertown* (35), as the two-timing wife who goes all to pieces under the stress of having murdered (with dialogue like 'I thought I told you to stay out of my life' and 'We're riff-raff you and I. We belong together'); her mad scene in court, done more realistically than was usual, was particularly appreciated.

She petitioned John Ford for the role of Elizabeth in the *Mary of Scotland* he was preparing but he refused. She and Warners

Bette Davis with Leslie Howard in Of Human Bondage *(34), the film that established her as one of the cinema's outstanding actresses: there was considerable surprise when she wasn't even nominated for an Oscar for it.*

made it up, and they 'officially' starred her for the first time again: *The Girl From Tenth Avenue*. Like *Front Page Woman* (she was a reporter) and *Special Agent* (a quickie with Farrell) it did nothing for her, but then came *Dangerous*, a tenuous tale about a dipso ex-actress who throws a jinx on anyone who comes near her. She says she found the script maudlin and mawkish, but went to work on it: the performance today is both powerful and subtle, suggesting she would have been a great Hedda. The Oscar she got for it she (and others) thought was a consolation prize for not getting one the previous year (she thinks it should have gone to Hepburn for *Alice Adams*).

Surprisingly, the next was also first-rate: *The Petrified Forest* (36), as the girl in the sticks with a yen for France and poetry. Frank S. Nugent thought it 'demonstrates that she does not have to be hysterical to be credited with a grand portrayal', and it was also a landmark for Bogart and Leslie Howard. After that, the critics thought she made much out of little with *Golden Arrow*, a comedy with Geroge Brent, but she could do little with *Satan Met a Lady*, the second and worst of the three filmizations of 'The Maltese Falcon'. Her dissatisfaction with her material increased when the studio refused her a part in *Anthony Adverse* and instead cast her in *God's Country and the Woman*. God's country, she decided, could do without this particular woman. She was suspended and taken off salary ($5,000 a week), at which point Ludovic Toeplitz, one of the money-men in British films, approached her with an offer: a movie to be made in Italy with Douglass Montgomery, and one in France with Chevalier–plus script approval.

She sailed to England to begin work, but Warners issued an injunction. She filed suit, and the moguls in Hollywood waited anxiously for the verdict. She lost: her contract bound her to Warner Bros and only Warner Bros until 1942. They, generously, paid her share of the damages – and had also, in her absence, prepared some better scripts. *Marked Woman* (37) marked a turning point in more ways than one, even if her performance in this underworld melo was over-illustrious; she had a similar role in *Kid Galahad*, as Edward G. Robinson's moll, not caring to look back on her past or daring to look to the future. *It's Love I'm After* was a literate crazy comedy with Leslie Howard, and *That Certain Woman* a sudsy remake of *The Trespasser*, with Henry Fonda. Photoplay found 'Bette Davis exerting every ounce of her undeniable ability to turn sheer melodrama into legitimate emotion'.

Then, with *Jezebel* (38), began the great series of Davis vehicles, as smooth as limousines, elegantly crafted, designed to display every facet of her talents. Whether or not she chose *Jezebel* in order to urge herself to the forefront in the Scarlett O'Hara sweepstakes, the two parts have much in common: this was another beguiling novelette about a wilful Southern belle, directed for considerably more than it was worth by William Wyler. To him and Fay Bainter (superb as an aunt) Davis gave credit for her performance. Said Freda Bruce Lockhart: 'By the pure power of imaginative acting she gives a performance as vivid and inspiring as any star display of personality – and an infinitely deeper level of truth.' James Shelley Hamilton commented that Davis was 'growing into an artistic maturity that is one of the wonders of Hollywood'. She won a second Oscar, and so, coincidentally, did Spencer Tracy, which prompted The New York Times to refer to them as the King and Queen of American films.

She was still battling for material; she was suspended again for refusing two scripts, but was satisfied with *The Sisters*, a period piece with Errol Flynn, bought originally for Kay Francis; and she loved *Dark Victory* (39), a hollow but likeable story about a spoiled society girl going blind, and a

Davis did get an Oscar for Jezebel *(38). Here, in the ballroom scene, with Henry Fonda and George Brent, she wears the red dress that so scandalized New Orleans society: even filmed in black and white it worked.*

Picturegoer Gold Medal winner for her; but she didn't care for *Juarez* after Paul Muni had cut down her part and Brian Aherne's, as Maximilian, and beefed up his own. Still, she was impressive as Carlotta. Then she did the title role in Edith Wharton's *The Old Maid*, with Miriam Hopkins. Graham Greene wrote: 'Great actresses choose odd mediums and perhaps Miss Davis is a great actress. Her performance . . . is of extraordinary virtuosity – as the young girl, as the secret mother, and the harsh prim middle-aged woman. . . .' The film was one of the year's top money-makers. She was with Flynn again in her first (and only, till the 50s) colour picture, *The Private Lives of Elizabeth and Essex*. It has odd conceits (the Queen visiting Essex in the Tower), but with entirely the wrong-shaped face Davis managed an uncanny resemblance to the Queen, and she dominated the film as Elizabeth had her court. Peter John Dyer observed that by this time her 'mannered emotionalism had acquired an added dimension of more disciplined restraint. She had become the mistress of the dry, disillusioned inflection and telling, angular gesture, and it is these qualities, together with a ribald wit, that makes this story of Elizabeth and Essex so compulsively viewable.'

Fortune Magazine's popularity poll noted that Davis had supplanted Shirley Temple as America's favourite star, and the exhibitors' poll confirmed it; in 1940 she was voted the Queen of Hollywood (Mickey Rooney was King). These triumphs made it easier to get her own way, and what she got was pretty good: an outstanding film version of Rachel Field's best-selling sob-story, *All This and Heaven Too* (40), about a governess in love with the Master (Charles Boyer); *The Letter*, also improved from book to film, a superb melodrama from Maugham's pot-boiler, with Wyler getting from Davis 'what is very likely the best study of female sexual hypocrisy in film history' (Pauline Kael); and *The Great Lie* (41), more women's magazine stuff, but put over superlatively well with the aid of Mary

The Private Lives of Elizabeth and Essex *(39): Bette Davis presides at the conference table. Left to right, Henry Daniell, Henry Stephenson, Ralph Forbes, Errol Flynn, Leo G. Carroll.*

The protagonists of Old Acquaintance*(44): Bette Davis and Miriam Hopkins. Davis wrote 'literary' books and lost the man she loved to Hopkins, who wrote trashy best-sellers: at the end, they drink a toast to the prospect of middle-age.*

Astor. Davis then did a footling comedy with Cagney, *The Bride Came C.O.D.*

Goldwyn borrowed her – at a fee of $385,000 – for *The Little Foxes*, with Wyler directing. Later he told the New York World Telegram: 'I am not knocking Bette for she is a great actress but I am relieved the picture is done. Maybe she is just as relieved.' They fought because he insisted on an imitation of Tallulah Bankhead's stage performance. Dilys Powell (ignoring this?) thought he was 'enormously helped by his chief player: Bette Davis has never given a finer performance than as the cold murderess. . . .' It was one of the year's top grossers, and remains today the classic example of its kind (passions in Southern mansions) and type (photographed plays – in this case Lillian Hellman's). Davis did another filmed play, *The Man Who Came to Dinner* (Monty Woolley), and showed herself a surer mistress of comedy than the year before; then played another bitch – quite unlike all the others – wreaking havoc all around her *In This Our Life* (42), quite justifying the ad-line: 'No one is as good as Bette when she's bad.' *Now Voyager* was more sob-stuff ('Oh Gerry don't let's ask for the moon – we have the stars'), but somewhat compelling, due to the transformation of put-upon frump to soignée woman of the world – but even Davis couldn't sustain the second half, cosseting the weird child of lover Paul Henried. The Manchester Guardian observed that 'Bette Davis has no superior in the matter of emotional film acting', and Picturegoer readers voted her another Gold Medal.

These were the confident years, too: there was a directness of emotion seldom equalled in films, and, as Laurence Olivier once commented, at climactic moments she never failed you; and, throughout, you could never be sure how she'd react. Her luck held in 1943: she amused everyone by croaking her way through 'They're Either Too Young or Too Old' in *Thank Your Lucky Stars*; and gave a self-effacing portrayal in Hellman's *Watch on the Rhine* with Paul Lukas. And she was fine again with Hopkins as her rival in the film of John Van Druten's *Old Acquaintance* (44). C. A. Lejeune called it bosh, but thought Davis almost saved it: 'With her intimate command of detail in gesture and expression, her sensible way with lines, and her positive genius for being in the right place on the set at the right moment, she does manage to keep you consistently interested. . . . There is no actress in Hollywood more expert at giving an intelligent reading of a part that need never have been written in the first place.' She then did some hugely enjoyable hokum about a selfish woman whose beauty is fading, *Mr Skeffington*, with Claude Rains, and put in an appearance in *Hollywood Canteen* (a servicemen's rendezvous which in life she had been instrumental in founding).

Both are considerably more viewable now than *The Corn Is Green* (45) from Emlyn Williams's play about a village school-mistress, a serious subject (the education of

All About Eve (*50*). *The moment when Margo Channing (Davis) realizes that she will miss Monday's performance, leaving the stage clear for her understudy, Eve. Celeste Holm and Hugh Marlowe have arranged for the car to run out of gas, as a favour to Eve.*

the industrial poor at the turn of the century) betrayed by novelettish writing and Hollywood earnestness. James Agee wrote of Davis's performance: 'It seems to me that she is quite limited, which may be no sin but is a pity, and that she is limiting herself beyond her rights by becoming more and more set, official and first-ladyish in mannerism and spirit, which is perhaps a sin as well as a pity. . . . I have a feeling that Miss Davis must have a great deal of trouble finding films that seem appropriate, feasible and worth doing. . . . For very few people in her position in films mean, or could do, so well.' She chose the next subject (and produced it) but it was hardly appropriate, feasible, or worth doing: the remake of *A Stolen Life* (46)–though it gave her a chance for virtuosity as twins. Later that year she was involved in *Deception*, again with Rains and Henried. Cecelia Ager's comment was: 'It's like grand opera, only the people are thinner. . . . I wouldn't have missed it for the world.' She was still either just in or just out of the box-office lists, but the decline had begun. She took a year's vacation (and had a baby), but returned inauspiciously with *Winter Meeting* (48), a talkie-talkie piece about a poetess and a naval officer: in Britain it got poor notices and after a brief West End run disappeared for good. *June Bride*, a comedy with Robert Montgomery, did well, but *Beyond the Forest* (49) was sneaked into flea-pits some years later: a ludicrous small-town drama, directed by King Vidor: he and Davis fought. She wore a Dracula-like wig and was described as 'a twelve o'clock girl in a nine o'clock town'. She says that during the making she asked for release from her contract and Warner granted it; Warner's version is that he could no longer take the entourage from MCA (her agents) so 'I told Bette I was through.' In 1948 she had been the highest paid star, at $365,000.

RKO offered her a choice role in a conventional divorce drama with Barry Sullivan, *Payment on Demand*, but withheld release pending the one that she was doing at 20th, *All About Eve* (50). The script had been turned down by Gertrude Lawrence, and was scheduled for Claudette Colbert, who became ill (it was based on an incident that happened to Elizabeth Bergner and not Tallulah Bankhead, as was generally supposed). Twentieth offered it to Davis–and probably never did a wiser thing. James Monahan wrote: 'Bette Davis as an ageing star who has heart, mind and temper, has perhaps never had so richly human a part to play: she plays it magnificently', while Winnington observed that she 'is always in command of a very great talent'. In the US, Alton Cook: 'Bette Davis, for nearly two decades one of our greatest actresses and worst performers, finally is shaken out of her tear-jerking formula and demonstrates what a vivid, overwhelming force she possesses.' Some critics felt this saga of a Broadway star and her would-be usurper (Anne Baxter) too talky, but it has the highest quotient of (verbal) wit of any film made before or since. It won a Best Picture Oscar, was a triumph for writer-director Joseph L. Mankiewicz and a box-office smash. Davis won the New York Critics award, but the Oscar went to Judy Holliday.

She was back on top with a vengeance, and might have stayed there had she not elected to go to Britain for *Another Man's Poison* (51). Frank Hauser wrote in the New Statesman: 'It is fascinating watching Bette Davis, a superb screen actress if ever there was one, play everything in a blaze of breath-taking absurdity. From beginning to end, there is not a life-like inflection, a plausible reaction . . . it is like reading Ethel M. Dell by flashes of lightning.' Her co-star was fourth husband Gary Merrill, and he was also in *Phone Call From a Stranger*, an episoder: her part was short, but showy. Still at 20th, she was again a fading star, this time of movies, *The Star* (52). Winnington wrote: 'The career of Bette Davis has been a 20 years battle to protect her talent from the effects of Hollywood processing. As the result of travelling the hard way her status as a film actress is unique and unassailable. But with the long battle won the two-edged nature of victory is manifest. Miss Davis with more say than most stars as to what films she makes seems to have lapsed into egoism. The criterion for her choice would appear to be that nothing in the film must compete with the full display of each polished facet of the Davis art. Only bad films are good enough for her.'

In 1955, hearing that 20th were to make a film about Sir Walter Raleigh, Davis asked to play Elizabeth. The part was built up and the film renamed *The Virgin Queen*. Her dialogue was a brilliant pastiche of Elizabeth's letters and speeches, and she was even better than she had been in 1939. However, whenever the Raleighs appeared (Richard Todd and Joan Collins) the film delved into insipidity; and failed at the box-office. Nor was there much popular welcome for *Storm Center* (56), a modest drama about a small-town librarian, or *The Catered Affair* (56), a Paddy Chayevsky piece where Davis was merely overblown as an Irish-Bronx mother. In 1959 she did a cameo (Catherine the Great) in a produced-in-Spain biopic, *John Paul Jones* (Robert Stack): but she didn't come on till the end, and wise spectators had left long before. She was no luckier with *The Scapegoat*, made in Britain from a dreary Daphne du Maurier suspenser: she quarrelled with co-star Alec Guinness during filming and her part later was cut to ribbons (it also wasted Irene Worth and Pamela Brown).

During the 50s she had done some stage work: 'Two's Company' (52), a revue; 'An Evening With Carl Sandburg', readings with Merrill, starting in 1954; and in 1961, 'The Night of the Iguana': it wasn't the leading role but she did it to please author Tennessee Williams, who had created many of his heroines with her in mind. She returned to films with *A Pocketful of Miracles* (61), at the behest of Glenn Ford (who, years earlier, she had chosen for *A Stolen Life*). Capra directed from an old film of his, and it was a misjudged venture; Davis was conscientiously tearful as 'Apple Annie', the lady for a day; and she and Ford quarrelled: its failure at the box-office confirmed the warning of those who had advised Ford not to use her.

No other offers were forthcoming, so she took full-page adverts in the trade press asking for work, adding that she had 'had' Broadway. Newspapers picked up the story, but offers were forthcoming: Aldrich's *Whatever Happened to Baby Jane?* (62), a chiller about two grotesque old dears living in crumbly isolation. Joan Crawford was the other. Davis's fee was a derisory $25,000, but she got a share of the profits and eventually made over a million: it took the world by storm. She followed with a minor but expert thriller, playing twins again, *Dead Ringer* (64), directed by Henried. Time said: 'And her acting, as always, isn't really acting; it's shameless showing-off. But just try to look away.' In Italy she did *The Empty Canvas*, directed by Damiani from a novel by Moravia; making it was, she said, a nightmare: just so for audiences–acres of boredom (Horst Buchholz and Catherine Spaak) punctuated by her. The same could be said of *Where Love Has Gone*, where her authority and verve were in somewhat greater supply. There was a dispute about interpretation: '. . . so I said to them, if she has to be shown as a monster at least give me one scene being really monstrous to the daughter so that people will really believe it. Unfortunately Miss what's-her-name didn't see it that way, and she did get top billing, so . . .' (interview in Sight and Sound).

Hush Hush Sweet Charlotte (65) was a follow-up, and superior, to *Baby Jane*. Tynan wrote: 'An accomplished piece of Grand Guignol is yanked to the level of art by Miss Davis's performance as the raging, ageing Southern belle: this wasted Bernhardt with her screen-filling eyes and electrifying vocal attack, squeezes genuine pathos from a role conceived in cardboard. She has done nothing better since *The Little Foxes*, 24 years ago.' Her subsequent films have been made in Britain, for Hammer, which

Bette Davis in her last film to date, Connecting Rooms *(70), made in Britain. With her is Alexis Kanner.*

specializes in pallid horror films. *The Nanny* (65) was better than most of their products, thanks to Davis's equivocal performance in the title role, but *The Anniversary* (67) ranks as one of the most squalid films ever made: a monster-mother's birthday party, with no cohesion (the original director was replaced during the first week's shooting) and Davis at her most baroque. She had done nothing worse since *Another Man's Poison*. Somewhat better was *Connecting Rooms* (70) co-starring Michael Redgrave.

She told an interviewer, Rex Reed, in 1968: 'You want to know what's ruined this business? Actors. They'll walk across the screen for anything, but I'm the only one of those dames who kept her price. My price for putting my name on that marquee is $200,000 and 10 per cent of the gross and I won't even talk to anybody for less because when they see me on screen they're seeing 37 years of sweat. They pay for my experience and if that loses its importance I might as well get lost.' She added that the greatest recent disappointments of her career were not getting her stage part in the film of *The Night of the Iguana* and the lead in *Who's Afraid of Virginia Woolf* which author Albee had wanted her to play. Later that year she was further disappointed in not getting the lead in *The Killing of Sister George*.

Olivia de Havilland

The appeal of Olivia de Havilland was never better expressed than by James Agee in his review of *The Dark Mirror* in 1946: 'She has for a long time been one of the prettiest women in movies; lately she has not only become prettier than ever but has started to act, as well. I don't see any evidence of any remarkable talent, but her playing is thoughtful, quiet, detailed, and well-sustained, and since it is founded, as some more talented playing is not, in an unusually healthful-seeming and likeable temperament, it is an undivided pleasure to see.' At that time she had just won a long struggle, the basis of which was to prove that she was not just a pretty face, and was getting, at last, parts worthy of her abilities. She went on to win a couple of Oscars and to a reputation as one of the most prestigious of film actresses; but one thinks of her less as a tragedienne than as a player whose delicacy and daintiness were enormously winning.

She was born in Tokyo in 1916 of British parents. They separated when she was five, and Mother took the two daughters to live in California (the other became Joan Fontaine). De Havilland's entrée into films was fortuitous and simple. While still at college she was in a local (Saratoga) production of 'A Midsummer Night's Dream', as Puck, and was seen by a talent scout who recommended her to Max Reinhardt, then preparing both a production of the play for the Hollywood Bowl and a film of it for Warners. Without great enthusiasm de Havilland became first an understudy and on the first night Hermia in the play; and was cast in that role in the film. She showed inexperience but was the best of the quartet of lovers (a poor compliment). Warners had signed her to a seven-year contract and made her Joe E. Brown's stooge in *Alibi Ike* (35) and James Cagney's adored-one in *The Irish in Us*, both released before the *Dream*. She was to become accustomed to standing on the sidelines looking pretty.

Mostly as Errol Flynn's leading lady. It was a combination that was to bring a lot of money into the Warner coffers (though he was to overtake her in popularity and for a while was billed solo above the title, with her featured below). They first co-starred in

Olivia de Havilland as the sweet young heroine of Captain Blood *(35), in which her loving looks were directed towards Errol Flynn.*

Captain Blood, a Caribbean sea story: the dashing Flynn and the demure de Havilland complemented each other in a fairy-tale way. His lack of experience may have inspired her to an assured performance, but her inexperience showed again in *Anthony Adverse* (36), unable to cope with being both Fredric March's lovelight and Napoleon's concubine. She was with Flynn again in the mammoth *The Charge of the Light Brigade*, courted equally by Patric Knowles; the ingénue in *Call It a Day* (37), an English family piece by Dodie Smith with Ian Hunter; in *The Great Garrick* with Brian Aherne as the actor; supporting Bette Davis and Leslie Howard in *It's Love I'm After*; and involved with George Brent in a technicolor adventure story, *Gold Is Where You Find It* (38). None of them did much for her, but at the very least she must have melted the hearts of a million schoolboys when she was Maid Marian to Flynn's Robin in *The Adventures of Robin Hood*. Years later she saw it again and said she 'was enchanted with the gaiety and charm of it and its excellence on its own terms' – which was the way it was then, in 1938. She was a spoiled heiress in a couple of comedies, the witty and sophisticated *Four's a Crowd* with Flynn, and the routine *Hard To Get* with Dick Powell; was given little to do in *Wings of the Navy* (39), a dim aviation drama with Brent and John Payne; but was effective as a crusading newspaper woman in *Dodge City*, with Flynn. Bette Davis was her rival for same in *The Private Lives of Elizabeth and Essex*, and though a Queen, lost out to maid-of-honour de Havilland (not that it mattered in the end).

Amidst all the brouhaha about the casting of *Gone With the Wind* (40) de Havilland was quickly thought of as Melanie. It was an impossible part, butter-wouldn't-melt-in-her-mouth (Amelia to Vivien Leigh's Becky), and audiences can only sympathize with Scarlett's contempt. That de Havilland, honey-tongued, made this ninny not only real but enormously moving was proof that she was 'a born actress', as Mervyn Le Roy called her later. It had been prophesied that after working on the Selznick lot, plus the eventual acclaim, she would no longer be content at WB: and she now joined the distinguished battle line who fought the brothers Warner for better parts. The films she made were not in themselves disagreeable: *Raffles*, on loan to Goldwyn; *My Love Came Back*, a breezy comedy with Jeffrey Lynn; *Santa Fe Trail*, a Flynn biggie; *Strawberry Blonde* (41), as the gentle wife who keeps on losing Cagney to Rita Hayworth; and at Paramount, an impressive soap opera written by Brackett and Wilder, *Hold Back the Dawn*, as a shy schoolteacher wooed and married by suave refugee Charles Boyer in order to get a US visa. She was nominated for an Oscar but lost to sister Fontaine.

They Died With Their Boots On was her last with Flynn and was good. Not so good was *The Male Animal* (42) with Henry Fonda, a saccharine version of a hit Broadway play, but *In This Our Life* was a superior melo in which sister Davis bitched her and every other member of the family. In *Thank Your Lucky Stars* (43) she and Ida Lupino had a guest spot doing a boogie-woogie, shaking their legs; and her Warner contract finished with two medium comedies, *Princess O'Rourke* with Robert Cummings, and on loan to RKO *Government Girl* with Sonny Tufts (Sonny Tufts?). At least, she thought her contract was finished, but WB claimed an extra six months for times she had been on suspension. She filed suit against the studio and was later backed by the Screen Actors Guild; after long legal wrangles the case was settled and seven years became the upper limit for any film contract (including suspensions where necessary), an important decision in the history of studio and player relationships. 'Hollywood owes Olivia a great deal,' said her sister admiringly, in a TV interview, going on to pooh-pooh the reputed feud between them.

While her suit was being settled, de Havilland couldn't film; she toured the war zones and sold war bonds. In 1946, however, Warners released (or let escape) a film she had made three years earlier: *Devotion*. It never made clear who was devoted to whom or what, unless it was curate Paul Henried, an object of passion for Charlotte (de Havilland), Emily (Lupino) and Anne (Nancy Coleman). They all wrote novels and had a drunken brother called Branwell. (*N.B.* this film contains one of the screen's immortal exchanges – as Charlotte is walking with Sydney Greenstreet they meet a man: 'Good morning Mr Thackeray', 'Good morning Mr Dickens'.) Concurrently de Havilland was able to work again, and signed a three-picture pact with Paramount. She did a comedy with Ray Milland, *The Well-Groomed Bride* (46), and a drama of (unwed) mother love, *To Each His Own*: John Lund played both father and son, fliers in both wars ('I got a glimpse up there – of what it could be like between you and me'). For her performance she won a Best Actress Oscar. At Universal she did an efficient thriller with Lew Ayres, *The Dark Mirror*, as twins, one nice and one nasty (natch). Also in 1946 she married Marcus Goodrich the novelist ('Delilah') and emerged from the sheltered life she had led; she said later that she had until then lived an incredibly quiet life for a movie star.

The peak of her career was approaching. At 20th she was a patient in a mental home, *The Snake Pit* (48), a brave and unusual film, well made by Anatole Litvak. The reviews were almost unanimously favourable, and included this by Peter Ericsson in Sequence: '*The Snake Pit* will always be remembered for Olivia de Havilland's performance. . . . Looking back over a number of years there is no other performance in a comparably developed part to equal it. One has almost to go back to the Silent period to find acting which combines intelligence and feeling, insight and variations of mood in the same moving way. Olivia de Havilland, one feels, is intuitively aware of the whole complexity of her part at all times. She plays all her scenes with an appreciation and subtlety which counteract the occasional clumsiness in the direction, and overcome the inadequacy of those who play opposite her. . . .' The film was a big box-office success, and de Havilland's performance was

De Havilland as the plain, awkward Catherine Sloper – The Heiress *(49), a film adaptation of a play based on Henry James's 'Washington Square'. She won her second Oscar for it.*

considered the year's Best on the distaff side by the New York Critics; which august body gave her the palm again the following year, for *The Heiress* (49); and she won a second Oscar as well. There were dissenters – she was said to be too attractive despite the make-up; but in her gaucheness and clumsiness this was an honest attempt at an Ugly Duckling, in some ways an improvement on Wendy Hiller's Broadway performance and Peggy Ashcroft's London one (the play was based on Henry James's 'Washington Square'). William Wyler directed, and the film was not a great popular success.

At this point she decided to establish herself as a stage actress and played Juliet and Candida on Broadway: neither performance increased her reputation, though the Candida was the better of the two. She returned to the screen as *My Cousin Rachel* (52), from one of Daphne du Maurier's lesser best-sellers, and was away again until 1955 when she played the one-eyed Princess of Eboli in *That Lady*, with a silky sweetness that was entirely inappropriate. Gilbert

Hush Hush Sweet Charlotte (*64*). *Olivia de Havilland and Bette Davis in a superior piece of Grand Guignol, which de Havilland only did as a favour to long-time friend Davis.*

Roland was the hero and Terence Young directed; Young said later that the film would have been better had the leads been Olivier and Ava Gardner, but added 'I made a mess of it.' Concurrently, de Havilland was miscast as a blonde Swedish nurse in *Not As a Stranger* (56).

She had married, in 1955, Pierre Galante, the editor of Paris Match, and went to live in France; and she indicated to interviewers that she was no longer very interested in filming – something that was sometimes apparent from her (few) subsequent performances, where her ladylike manner was somewhat disconcerting, though in *The Ambassador's Daughter* (filmed in Paris, 56) she was more like her younger, gayer self, and in *Proud Rebel* (58), with Alan Ladd, she gave a remarkably beautiful performance as a pioneer woman. She was an English milady in the British *Libel* (59), with Dirk Bogarde, and an American mother in *The Light in the Piazza* (61), a much underrated piece, set in Florence, about a woman intent on marrying her mentally retarded daughter (Yvette Mimieux) to a wealthy young Italian (George Hamilton). She made two films in Hollywood in 1964, both chillers: *Lady in a Cage* and *Hush Hush Sweet Charlotte*, taking over the latter – most reluctantly – from Joan Crawford when she fell ill (director Aldrich said that co-star Bette Davis vetoed alternatives such as Vivien Leigh and Katharine Hepburn, and that de Havilland's name was the only one agreeable to all; earlier, de Havilland had told a reporter that Davis was perhaps the only close friend remaining from her Hollywood days). She returned to the screen to play a philandering wife in *The Adventurers* (70), a hunk of Harold Robbins commerce.

In 1961 she appeared on Broadway with Fonda in 'A Gift of Time'; in 1963 published a book on her life in Paris, 'Every Frenchman Has One' (a liver); and still lives there, though separated from her husband. She has appeared on TV, notably in a good adaptation of Katherine Anne Porter's 'Noon Wine' (67), a performance quite as good as any of her best on film.

Dolores del Rio

Dolores del Rio was one of the screen's early exotics, Latin-style, 'the first of the Mexican mamas'. She played the highly emotionally charged young foreign girl, alternatively either a vamp or a saint. She was exceptionally beautiful – 'orchidaceous' – with dark eyes, an oval face and jet-black hair; but her screen presence was somewhat shadowy. Her career has lasted till today, but her greatest period was at the beginning, in the late 20s.

She was born in Durango, Mexico, in 1905, in comfortable circumstances (her father was a bank manager) and convent-educated. She was a second cousin of Ramon Novarro. At 16 she married the wealthy Jaime del Rio and she lived the life of a wife appropriate to her station: until they were visited by film director Edwin Carewe and his wife on a visit to Mexico City for the wedding of Claire Windsor and Bert Lytell. Carewe thought Dolores should be in pictures, and persuaded her to take a small part in *Joanna* (25) which he was directing, as a rival to its heroine Dorothy Mackaill. Carewe put her under personal contract, and directed her again in *High Steppers* (26) supporting Mary Astor, and *Pals First*; then loaned her to Universal for an Edward Everett Horton vehicle, *The Whole Town's Talking*; then to Fox for *What Price Glory* with Edmund Lowe and Victor McLaglen. Del Rio was a girl of dubious morals called Charmaine (the song called that was written to be played in cinemas at the time) and made a deep impression with her beauty. The film was the year's second biggest, with $2 million taken at the domestic box-office. Carewe then directed her in an adaptation by himself and Count Ilya Tolstoy of Count Leo's *Resurrection* (27) with Rod La Rocque as Prince Dimitri: her

The beautiful Dolores del Rio, at the beginning of her Hollywood career . . . towards the end of her stardom, in Lancer Spy *(37) . . . and as she looked in 1961, for* Flaming Star.

performance in this was for some years considered her best.

Then Walsh directed her in *The Loves of Carmen* (Don Alvarado was Don José and McLaglen was Escamillo); she was loaned out to Fox again for *The Gateway to the Moon* (28), as a native girl; to MGM for *The Trail of '98*, as a dance-hall hostess; to Fox again for *No Other Woman* and *The Red Dance* (*The Red Dancer of Moscow* in Britain). Meanwhile Carewe had provided her with one of her most famous roles, and another song hit, in *Ramona*, the third film version of Helen Hunt Jackson's novel of old California. Warner Baxter co-starred. Carewe also directed her in *Revenge*, as a proud and tempestuous gypsy girl tamed by James Marcus. In an attempt at another hit song, Carewe commissioned none other than Al Jolson to write the one for *Evangeline* (29), adapted from the poem by Longfellow–only this time del Rio would sing it on the screen (despite a recent pronouncement: 'Nevair, nevair, will I make a Talkie. I zink zey are tairibble'). She serenaded the hero at the end of the film, and as she finished, he died–not surprisingly, said the critics. It was a heavy film, and not very popular. It marked the end of the artistic association of Carewe and del Rio: his wife divorced him at the same time as del Rio's husband left her. The Carewes later re-married, in 1931–while Carewe was making *Resurrection* as a Talkie with Lupe Velez and John Boles; Mr del Rio not long after died in Germany, and fan-magazines were highly critical of the loving cable that del Rio had sent him on his deathbed. The widowed Dolores soon married MGM art director Cedric Gibbons.

She signed a contract with UA (Carewe sued: the matter was settled out of court) at $9,000 a week and made *The Bad One* (30) her first all-Talkie, as the señorita sailor Edmund Lowe breaks ship for. But her contract lapsed when she was taken ill with what was probably a nervous breakdown (at the time it was said to be acute pyelitis); recovered, she signed with RKO who put her into *The Girl of the Rio* (32), an adaptation of Willard Mack's play 'The Dove', which UA had been preparing for her a year earlier. And for this studio she made King Vidor's *The Bird of Paradise*, with Joel McCrea, as the Polynesian girl who sacrifices herself to a volcano: she probably never looked more beautiful. Next, she starred in *Flying Down to Rio* (33), but Astaire and Rogers of course stole the film. RKO dropped her.

She now signed with WB who realized that her greatest talent was her beauty; and it was that that they utilized in *Wonder Bar* (34) with Al Jolson; *Madame Du Barry*, directed by William Dieterle, one of his lighter looks at history; two more musicals, *In Caliente* (35) and *I Live for Love*; and *The Widow From Monte Carlo* with Warren William. Then she went to Britain to appear in Douglas Fairbanks Jr's *Accused* (36); back in Hollywood, Columbia announced that the first picture under her contract with them would be *Continental*, but the only one she made there was a programmer with Richard Dix, *The Devil's Playground* (37). At 20th, there were two with George Sanders, *Lancer Spy* and *International Settlement* (38). She was off the screen for two years, till MGM offered her the part of Wallace Beery's leading lady in *The Man From Dakota* (40). A while later she was seen around much with Orson Welles, and she appeared in his *Journey into Fear* (42), but only in the first two reels. Realizing at last that her Hollywood career was a lost cause, she returned to Mexico, where she signed a deal that gave her a percentage of the profits.

She immediately made four pictures under the direction of Emilio Fernandez, co-starring her masterly compatriot, Pedro Armendariz (also just returned from Hollywood, after failing to make a go of it as Armen Dariz): *Flor Silvestre* (43) as a peasant girl, *Maria Candelaria*, *Bugambilia* (44), and *Las Abandonadas*. Only the second, re-titled *Portrait of Maria*, was widely seen outside Mexico, when MGM distributed it some years later, a common tale of a girl who loves too much and gets stoned to death by her neighbours. In 1945 she made *La Selva de Fuego* and in 1946 *La Otra* (from the same novel which became Bette Davis's *Dead Ringer*). In 1947 she co-starred with Henry Fonda in *The Fugitive*, which was made mainly on location in Mexico. She signed to appear in Abel Gance's *Giselle*, to be made in Spanish, French and English, but it wasn't made in any of them. In 1948 she went to Argentina to make a local version of 'Lady Windermere's Fan', called *Historia de una Mala Mujer*, and then confirmed her position as Mexico's leading star with: *La Malquerida* (49), *La Casa Chica*, *Dona Perfecta* (50), *Deseada* (51), *Reportaje* (53) and *El Niño y la Niebla*. She had also become one of her country's leading stage actresses. In 1954 she was offered a part in *Broken Lance* by 20th, but her visa did not come through in time, and Katy Jurado took over; instead del Rio went to Spain and made *Señora Ama*.

In 1956 she did return to the US, and played 'Anastasia' in stock; in 1958 she did two Mexican films, *La Cucaracha* and *A Donde van Nuestros Hijos*; in 1959 she married Lewis A. Riley Jr, an American impresario working in Latin America. They live today in a suburb of Mexico City. Del Rio accepted a Hollywood offer in 1960, as Elvis Presley's mother in *Flaming Star*, and later another, in Ford's *Cheyenne Autumn* (64)–in the first she played a Red Indian (Hollywood never forgets); in both she still looked very beautiful. She began appearing occasionally on US TV and did some more Mexican films, *La Dama del Alba* (66), *Casa de Mujeres* and *Rio Blanco* (67). At the same time as the latter she made *C'era una Volta* (68): it was only a small role, but Carlo Ponti was particularly anxious to have del Rio play Sophia Loren's mother. She was one of the many stars appearing in *The Phynx* (70).

Marlene Dietrich

Marlene! the name has magic. She is the living legend. She has been much-hymned: by Hemingway ('If she had only her voice, she would break your heart'), by Cocteau ('Your beauty is its own poet, its own praise') and by scores of lesser lights. Curtis Harrington wrote in 1952: 'Like Garbo, she transcends any period, though some of her films do not. Her style throughout remains constant, within little characteristic variations, and as a personification of sexuality her lustre never dims.' From our first glimpse of her in *The Blue Angel* ('I can only say that she makes reason totter on her throne'–James Agate) to her last concert, the world has been at her feet. She has fascinated three generations or at least part of them. She is fêted, she is renowned, she is one of the most famous women of the century–perhaps its second goddess, or its third. Age does not wither her, nor custom stale her infinite sameness.

Her witchery would seem to work from a combination of opposites and from qualities which, on examination, offer only a blank. She is as enigmatic (and as graceful) as a cat. Like a cat, she invites love and then disdains it. She is a solitary. She is beautiful but her looks have been rendered by the addition of too much make-up, crazy eyelashes, feathers, furs and male-drag: dolled up, she is the apotheosis of chorus-girl glamour, but beneath is discernible a really glamorous, mysterious woman. She offers a parody, both conscious and unconscious, of sex, suggesting, as she gets her men to commit mighty mayhem for her or as she leads them, steely-hearted, to destruction, that it's all a delusion after all. She is witty about it and then on other things–herself–singularly humourless; she is both androgynous and feminine, practical and scatty. Jacques Feyder once said of her: 'She has great charm. She uses it with stunning virtuosity', and that is what Dietrich the artist is all about: spontaneous and mechanical–sometimes, unbelievably, at the same time, intuitively right and then agreeably ridiculous, calculating and as phoney as a feline.

Her comments on herself are rarely

Dietrich unforgettably chanting 'They call me naughty Lola in The Blue Angel *(30).*

consistent. She has said on occasion that she made no films before *The Blue Angel* and in her cabaret act she claims that she was a student when Von Sternberg discovered her, but she had in fact been in Show Business for at least 10 years. Due to admiring research in recent years, her early career is well documented. Someone even dug up her birth certificate. The year is given as 1901, the place Berlin. It seems that she studied at the Max Reinhardt Drama School and may have begun in films as early as 1918 as an extra. She certainly had a line in *Die Freudlosse Gasse* (25), though her first real part appears to have been in *Die Tragödie der Liebe* (23). In 1925 she was in Vienna in a play with Albert Basserman, followed by a revue, 'Es Liegt in der Luft', in Berlin and a leading role in the Abbott-Dunning 'Broadway'; at the same time she had feature roles in *Manon Lescaut* (26) starring Lya de Putti; *Eine Dubarry von Heute*; *Der Juxbaron*, as the female lead; *Gefahren der Brautzeit* (27) and *Sein Grösster Bluff*. Her first starring part was in *Wenn ein Weib den Weg Verliert* (28), made in Vienna, followed by *Prinzessin Olala*, *Ich Küsse Ihre Hand Madame* (29), *Die Frau nach der Man sich Sehnt* (also known as *Drei Lieben*) and *Das Schiff der Verlorenen Menschen*, both opposite Fritz Kortner. She also was in a stage production of Shaw's 'Misalliance', and it was in a revue, 'Zwei Kravatten', that Von Sternberg discovered her.

He had been working in Hollywood when Emil Jannings asked him to direct *The Blue Angel* (30). He has said that she was unprepossessing but he could see she had something. According to John Kobal, 'even without Von Sternberg Dietrich would, sooner or later, have become a success in German films. Everything pointed to it. . . . But it is doubtful whether she could have become a legend on her own.' Between them they fashioned one of the screen's perfect performances – Lola-Lola, good-time girl, insolently enslaving poor professor Jannings. The part was older than Theda Bara, but Dietrich was new: top-hatted, silk-stockinged, white thighs gashed by black

In each succeeding Von Sternberg film Dietrich was more outrageously gowned and coiffeured: this costume is one of the lesser efforts in The Devil Is a Woman *(35), which – fortunately perhaps – was their last together. With her is Lionel Atwill, 'protector' obsessed with her.*

suspenders, she lolled back, sensual, promising, indolent, 'falling in love again' – with Hans Albers, leaving poor old Jannings to the birds. She herself disliked the part and thought it would ruin her, but before the film was premièred Von Sternberg had shown a rough-cut to Paramount (his American employers), who signed her for one film: *Morocco*. She was again a cabaret entertainer, the older man this time Adolphe Menjou, the younger one French legionnaire Gary Cooper, for whom in the end she sacrificed everything, trekking after him in the desert in evening dress. It was premièred in New York about the same time as the English-language version of *The Blue Angel* and the furore was such that Paramount wanted her to stay at any price.

This was $125,000 per film, Von Sternberg directing, and the right to okay publicity. There are conflicting statements on these Paramount contracts, but it seems that each was for two or three films at a time. According to Arthur Knight, Paramount spent a reputed $5 million on publicity – which, initially, emphasized a rivalry with Garbo. Garbo was making *Mata Hari*, and Paramount, not afraid of the comparison, made Dietrich a spy in *Dishonored* (31). She was also a shady lady ('It took more than one man to change my name to Shanghai Lily') in *Shanghai Express* (32), a slight tale of international intrigue which was her and Von Sternberg's biggest American success with a gross of over $3 million. Unlike the Garbo vehicles, Dietrich's films were mainly from original stories concocted especially for her – but they all seemed to have come from the same mould as the Garbo films. *Blood and Sand* was announced for her, unsuitably *A Farewell to Arms* and more appropriately *R.U.R.*, but instead she was the *Blonde Venus*, working in Gary Grant's club in order to pay for an operation which will save the life of husband Herbert Marshall – who, ungratefully, tells her to choose between them: she runs away and sinks from poverty to prostitution until in the end all is discovered and forgiven. Despite the fact that in a musical number, 'Hot Voodoo', she emerged from a gorilla skin, the film was far from the anticipated success, and Paramount decided to separate star and director: speculation about their artistic association crescendoed when Von Sternberg's wife sued for alienation of affection and libel (Dietrich won). On Von Sternberg's advice, Dietrich accepted Rouben Mamoulian for *The Song of Songs* (33), a remake of *Lily of the Dust*, described by the Sunday Express (London) as 'a field-day of hokum' and liable today to drive audiences into hysteria – there's a climax with a blazing house and the star being chased through the woods by (1) husband Lionel Atwill, (2) true love Brian Aherne, and (3) a casual love, a game-keeper on the estate. Replicas of the nude statue used in the film were exhibited in cinema foyers.

Rumours persisted that Dietrich would return to Germany – and indeed Hitler had ordered her to do so (she refused and her films were banned there). Instead, she played Catherine the Great (hadn't Garbo played Queen Christina? Catherine, after all, had been a German princess) in *The Scarlet Empress* (34). She was considered foolish to compete with Elizabeth Bergner, then making a British film about Catherine, and was roundly trounced: C. A. Lejeune said her performance 'suggests a lady with a good pair of legs and few other resources at all'. The film was a box-office disaster (so was Bergner's) despite an all-pervading atmo-

The film that changed the Dietrich image – profitably, for all concerned: Destry Rides Again *(39), with James Stewart as the shy sheriff who tames her, but loses her to a killer's bullet.*

sphere of eroticism, and a triumphant finale with the soundtrack blending 'The Ride of the Valkyries' and the '1812 Overture'. After Russia, Spain: *The Devil Is a Woman* (35), and it's Atwill she ensnares again, with Cesar Romero as the younger competitor (after Joel McCrea sensibly walked out). This is her own favourite film: 'Because I looked more lovely in that film than in any other of my whole career' – certainly she was accoutred in as many feathers and in as much lace as was possible. Von Sternberg had been increasingly decorating his films beyond a reasonable standard of the exotic and now went too far: more than ever Dietrich was simply a prop among the décor. Paramount no more liked seeing their investment reduced to this than they liked Von Sternberg's no-holds-barred expenditure. The film failed, and Paramount didn't protest when the Spanish government, claiming misrepresentation, asked them to withdraw it from circulation. Von Sternberg announced that he had brought Dietrich as far as he could.

Paramount tried to pick up the pieces: her films now might be less visually stunning, but they would be, mostly, less banal. It was decided that Lubitsch should handle her, and he produced and Frank Borzage directed *Desire* (36), a romantic comedy with Gary Cooper: she was a con-woman and he the conned, and they pursued each other through most of Europe. It appeared that comedy was her forte and the film succeeded in its attempt in reviving interest in her. However, she began a remake of *Hotel Imperial*, now called *I Loved a Soldier*, with Charles Boyer: but after a few days shooting it was abandoned (reputedly because Dietrich refused to continue after Lubitsch had made changes; it was re-started with Margaret Sullavan, but didn't make it to the screens of the world till 1940 with Isa Miranda as the star). Selznick grabbed both stars for the Technicolor remake of *The Garden of Allah*, ditching on the way Merle Oberon, who sued for the $25,000 she should have got for the part – as opposed to Dietrich's $200,000 fee (earlier, Garbo had turned it down). Boyer and Dietrich mooned about the desert and she was never more beautifully photographed; aware of this, perhaps (she always kept a pier-glass on the set), she acted less than ever. Korda then offered her a fee with expenses that worked out at almost $450,000 to make in Britain *Knight Without Armour* (37) with Robert Donat, a story set in the aftermath of the Russian revolution; and then Lubitsch fashioned *Angel* for her, another cunning, candy-floss comedy, with Melvyn Douglas and Herbert Marshall. She was superb, but it didn't turn the tide. Rumours had been emanating from the studio that she had quarrelled with both Borzage and Lubitsch, and Picturegoer reported that Lubitsch and Mitchell Leisen had refused to direct her in *French Without Tears* (like *Midnight*, also bought for her, it went to another actress). At the end of 1937, it was discovered that she rated 126th at the box-office, so Paramount bought up her contract, at a variously reported $200,000 or $250,000–the price of the one film to come. It was not surprising that she was prominent on the list of stars said to be box-office poison–thus did America repay her for becoming naturalized about this time.

There was immense speculation on her screen future. Critics and fan-magazines liked her, if the public didn't. MGM were interested, but in the end she signed deals for one picture each with Columbia (to play George Sand) and Warners (a remake of *One-Way Passage*). Both were postponed and the studios collected her commitments later on other properties. Thus she had been off the screen more than two years when she was advised to accept–at a fee reputed to be less than $50,000–the part of the brawling, strident Frenchie in a spoof Western, *Destry Rides Again* (39): it was really a variation of Lola-Lola but a public accustomed to the Von Sternberg Dietrich, aloof and slinky, now enjoyed her. Universal signed her to a contract, but, in Arthur Knight's words, 'all her new employers could see was a sleazy, sexy hussy for strong men to fight over'. *Seven Sinners* (40) was no more than an attempt to satirize South Seas films in the way that *Destry* had Westerns, but Dietrich did her Sadie Thompson act with aplomb. She was more in command and more compelling than the old Dietrich. René Clair tried to combine old and new Dietrichs in *The Flame of New Orleans* (41), but it was one of his lesser efforts. Edward G. Robinson and George Raft brawled over her in *Manpower*; she was a musical comedy actress in a weak farce at Columbia, *The Lady Is Willing* (42); and John Wayne and Randolph Scott were the antagonists in both *The Spoilers* and *Pittsburgh*. It was said that she was dissatisfied with her roles and considered retiring–but instead she went off on long and valiant tours entertaining the troops.

She let Orson Welles saw her in half in a guest spot in *Follow the Boys* (44), and she was painted gold all over for a dance sequence in MGM's *Kismet*, an agreeable send-up of that old play, with Ronald Colman. Then it was announced that she and off-screen friend Jean Gabin would appear in *Les Portes de la Nuit*, to be directed by Marcel Carné, at that time the most prestigious director in French films. At the last minute Dietrich withdrew because she disliked her role, and Gabin with her. There was an outcry in the French press and the film they subsequently did together, *Martin Roumagnac* (46), was a boom neither in France nor anywhere else (other French projects included the *Dédée d'Anvers* that Simone Signoret eventually played, and Death in Cocteau's *Orphée*). Dietrich returned to Paramount, unconvincing as a gypsy in the silly *Golden Earrings* (47), but ideal as a Berlin cabaret entertainer in Billy Wilder's brilliant *A Foreign Affair* (48), though her role was subordinate to Jean Arthur's. A grandson was born around this time, and she became tagged as 'the world's most glamorous grandmother'.

The rest of her movie career indicates mutual wariness: she wanted to make films because films meant the big money and prestige, but she was exacting about parts, co-stars, billing, etc. (two she turned down were *Gigi* and *Pal Joey*). Hollywood needed her only because she was one of its legendary names: her value at the box-office continued to be, at the most, doubtful. She played a stage-star in *Stage Fright* (50), a flashy if minor role in a minor-league Hitchcock, and she was a famous movie star in *No Highway* (51) with James Stewart, which was a big success. Her last good part was out West again in Fritz Lang's masterly *Rancho Notorious* (52). Lang's comments are revealing: he says that they could only get a small budget for the film, that Dietrich resented moving into the category of more mature parts and that on the set she was a trouble-maker and increasingly difficult. In *The Monte Carlo Story* (57), an Italo-American effort with Vittorio de Sica, she was a confidence trickster–shades of *Desire* (shades indeed!). She wasted her time even more grievously with an unconvincing guest appearance in Welles's *Touch of Evil* (58) and also *Witness for the Prosecution*, where her Cockney impersonation gave the whole game away. Further, she looked gaunt and seemed to be afraid to smile: but in her spot

Seven Sinners (*40*), *a title that referred not to any of the cast, but to the sailors' rendezvous where Dietrich sang, among other things. The British title was* Café of Seven Sinners. *With her are John Wayne and Broderick Crawford.*

in the coloured *Around the World in 80 Days* (57) she had vaulted time with years to spare. Her last film was *Judgement at Nuremberg* (61), where she was 'a stagy Junker widow' (Dwight Macdonald).

In the early 50s she had a radio series, 'Café Istanbul' (espionage tales), but she has evinced no interest in TV. Her real life's work, she has said, began during the war when she sang to the troops, and she has aimed ever since to become a *chanteuse* like Piaf–telling a story in song. In 1954 she appeared in cabaret in London, at a reported $6,000 a week, and for equally fabulous sums, in equally stunning gowns, she has appeared regularly in Las Vegas. She has appeared in clubs or in concerts in most countries in the world from Russia to Australia, notably in Germany where, because of her noted anti-Nazi stand, she was not expected to be entirely welcome; but she played to the same packed houses, at the same high prices as elsewhere, and her German recording of 'Where Have All the Flowers Gone?' became one of the all-time best-selling records in Europe. She did not make her New York debut till 1967. Her success in Paris she found particularly pleasing, for her art is a French art. Among other quoted remarks are that she works only for money and that she loathed being a film-star. She told Rex Reed: 'I am an international theatre star now. It's so boring, all that talk about the legendary Marlene and the legendary films of Von Sternberg.... Those films were all right, but keep them in their place. Don't make them important. I do not like to be interviewed any more by pansy film-fan writers, because all they want to know about is *Blonde Venus* and *Shanghai Express*.' It is a curious remark since most of her act–which has altered by hardly a syllable or even an intonation over the past 15 years–consists of references to her Hollywood years, and the songs she sings now are the songs she sang then.

Richard Dix

Today only older filmgoers know the name Richard Dix, and most of them will remember him as a stalwart of second features in the late 30s and 40s; but before that he had been successful for a good number of years. Indeed, other than Richard Barthelmess and Ronald Colman, he was the only male *star* to survive from the early Silent era well into the Talkie period. He was not an inspired actor, but he was an honest one, projecting a certain degree of masculine charm.

He was born in St Paul, Minnesota, in 1894; he studied medicine at the University of Minnesota, and acted with the University drama group. A travelling troupe one day advertised for a local to play a football player in 'The College Widow' and Dix applied: he had the bug, and thereafter gave up medicine. He worked in stock in Philadelphia, Dallas and Montreal; spent the war years in the army, returned, and got his New York break: in 'The Hawk' in 1919. He did some other plays (including 'The Song of Songs', Gorki's 'A Night's Lodging') and was then offered star parts with an LA stock company: which inevitably led to screen tests. On the second, he was offered two star parts in *Not Guilty* (21)–twins; whereupon Goldwyn offered him a contract: *The Sin Flood*; *Dangerous Curve Ahead*, marital difficulties with Helen Chadwick; *All's Fair in Love*; *Poverty of Riches* with Leatrice Joy; *The Glorious Fool* (22) and *Yellow Men and Gold*, both with Helen Chadwick. Other leading ladies: Colleen Moore in *The Wallflower*; Claire Windsor in *Fools First*; and Betty Compson in *The Bonded Woman*. He was then sent to Britain for the film of Sir Hall Caine's *The Christian* (23), directed by Maurice Tourneur, playing a minister in love with an actress (Mae Busch) but giving her up when he thinks that Doomsday is nigh. *Souls for Sale* was his last for Goldwyn, a story of the movies, with Busch again, and Eleanor Boardman, Barbara La Marr, Lew Cody, William Haines and Aileen Pringle.

It was rumoured that he would do *Ben Hur* eventually, but Paramount had just lost Wallace Reid (his death from the too enthusiastic use of drugs was a scandal that shook Hollywood) and they anxiously needed a replacement. Dix, though considerably unlike, would be able to do the same sort of he-man roles, thought Paramount, and they made him an attractive offer. His first films there had been intended for Reid: *Racing Hearts* with Agnes Ayres; *The Woman With Four Faces*, ironically–but topically–about a DA who breaks up a dope ring; and two from Zane Grey novels, *To the Last Man* and *Call of the Canyon*, both with Lois Wilson. Between these two he was in the modern half of de Mille's all-star *The Ten Commandments*, the second biggest grosser of 1923 (at $2½ million, a million behind *The Covered Wagon*). He made *The Stranger* (24) from Galsworthy's 'The First and the Last', *Icebound*, *Unguarded Women* (Bebe Daniels and Mary Astor); *Sinners in Heaven* with Daniels; *Manhattan*, as a bored society boy who seeks thrills in the underworld with Jacqueline Logan; *A Man Must Live* (25), a newspaper story again with Logan, from I. A. R. Wylie's 'Jungle Law'; *Too Many Kisses* with Frances Howard; *Men and Women*; *The Shock Punch*; *The Lucky Devil*, an uproarious comedy about a car with the voodoo; and Zane Grey's *The Vanishing American*, a notable performance as a Red Indian. There followed *Womanhandled* (26)–Esther Ralston doing the handling; *Let's Get Married* with Lois Wilson again and Edna May Oliver; *Say It Again*, a Ruritanian comedy with Alice Mills; *The Quarterback* with Ralston; *Paradise for Two* (27), a comedy about a bachelor who must marry or lose an inheritance, with Betty Bronson; *Knockout Reilly* as a boxer on the comeback trail; and *Man Power* as a luckless youth who makes good–and *Shanghai Bond*, both with Mary Brian.

Most of these had been filmed in New York, which Dix preferred to Hollywood, and when Paramount closed its NY studio he complained; he wanted out of his

Esther Ralston and Richard Dix in The Lucky Devil (*25*), *one of the auto-racing pictures popular at that time. The public also liked this teaming so much that they played together on three more occasions. Ralston was one of Paramount's biggest stars of the 20s.*

contract, and as a further lever complained about Paramount's re-release of an indie he had made in 1923, *Quicksands*. He complained later: 'I made my name in a few good parts, then they gave me a series of walk-throughs in shoddy productions.' Paramount retaliated by upping his salary to $4,500 a week. Dix went on to make *The Gay Defender* (28), a biopic of the bandit later played by Warner Baxter in *Robin Hood of El Dorado*; *Sporting Goods*, a remake of Fatty Arbuckle's 'The Traveling Salesman'; *Easy Come Easy Go* with Nancy Carroll; *Warming Up* with Jean Arthur; *Moran of the Marines*, a far-fetched adventure story; *Redskin* (29), in the title role–it had some colour sequences; and *Nothing But the Truth*, his first Talkie. He followed with *The Wheel of Life* (moustached as a British officer, in love with Esther Ralston) and *The Love Doctor*, a farce (his studio saw him mainly as a comedian).

The quarrel with Paramount had not really been fixed up, and Dix was not considered by them to be ideal for Talkies; as with many of their other stars, they dropped him. He signed a new deal with RKO, who starred him first in one of the numerous pic versions of George M. Cohan's old thriller, *Seven Keys to Baldpate*. After *Lovin' the Ladies* (30) with Lois Wilson again and *Shooting Straight*, as a racketeer, he made *Cimarron* (31), Edna Ferber's epic of the Oklahoma land-rush days, directed by Wesley Ruggles and co-starring Irene Dunne as the faithful wife. It was highly praised and a big grosser. RKO took great trouble to find the right properties, but as far as Dix was concerned, *Cimarron* was a temporary halt in a career which had begun a gentle decline. He had difficulty in controlling his girth. All the same, he was fighting for more salary. Most of his films were programmers: *Young Donovan's Kid*, from a Rex Beach story with Jackie Cooper in the title role; *The Public Defender* (he turned crook to trap some dishonest financiers); *Secret Service*, a Civil War story; *The Lost Squadron* (32) as a disillusioned war hero;

Irene Dunne and Richard Dix in Cimarron (*31*), *the film that put her on the map and was certainly the most important and successful of the hundred that he made.*

and *The Roar of the Dragon* with Gwili Andre. *Hell's Highway* is a short, stark film about convicts: (the framed) Dix attempts to escape. He moved back to A picture status with *The Conquerors*, with Ann Harding, but it did not repeat the success of *Cimarron*, which it somewhat resembled. After it he made another, similar, period drama, *The Great Jasper* (33), with Florence Eldridge; *No Marriage Ties*, as a hard-drinking reporter; *Day of Reckoning*, another marital drama – at MGM, with Madge Evans; *The Ace of Aces*, an aviation drama; *Stingaree* (34), another big one with Irene Dunne but almost incredibly bad; *His Greatest Gamble*, sacrificing all for his daughter's happiness; *West of the Pecos*, a good Western from a novel by Zane Grey; and *The Arizonian* (35) with Margot Grahame and a screenplay by Dudley Nichols.

In 1935 in Britain he made *The Tunnel*, a drama with an Anglo-American cast handicapped by the poor direction of Maurice Elvey; back in Hollywood he finished his RKO contract with *Yellow Dust* (36) and *Special Investigator*, both Bs. He did four Bs for Columbia, *Devil's Squadron*, *The Devil's Playground* (37), *The Devil Is Driving* (no connection between them, despite the titles) and *It Happened in Hollywood*, a B about a Western star who fails at first in Talkies, but triumphs later: as a gimmick lots of 'doubles' played stars. He returned to RKO for *Blind Alibi* (38), *Sky Giant* with Joan Fontaine and *Twelve Crowded Hours* (39) with Lucille Ball. At Republic he did one of their bigger ones, *Man of Conquest*, a biopic of Sam Houston, and at 20th *Here I Am Stranger*, as alcoholic father to Richard Greene. He went back to RKO, to Paramount, Universal, etc., making a decent living in programmers – most of them, coincidentally, of above-average quality: *Reno* (40) with Gail Patrick; *The Marines Fly High* with Chester Morris; *Men Against the Sky*; *Cherokee Strip*; the remake of Fatty Arbuckle's *The Roundup* (41), an A budget picture with Patricia Morison; *Badlands of Dakota* as Wild Bill Hickok, billed under Robert Stack and Ann Rutherford; *Tombstone the Town Too Tough to Die* (42); *American Empire*; *Eyes of the Underworld* (43); and *Buckskin Frontier* and *The Kansan*, both with Jane Wyatt, Albert Dekker and Victor Jory. He had a change as the father of *Top Man* Donald O'Connor, but returned to the action stuff with Val Lewton's *The Ghost Ship* (directed by Mark Robson), as a homicidal captain. Then Columbia signed him to a series of low-budgeters, based on CBS's long-running 'The Whistler' programme: *The Whistler* (44), *The Mark of the Whistler*, *The Power of the Whistler* (45), *The Voice of the Whistler* (46), *The Mysterious*

Intruder, *The Secret of the Whistler* and *The Thirteenth Hour* (47).

Dix died, a wealthy man, in 1949 after a series of heart attacks. He married twice–in 1931 and 1934.

Robert Donat

The story of Robert Donat, though not overly-dramatic, is a heart-rending one. He was a highly gifted actor, one of the aristocrats of his craft, notable for a beautiful speaking voice and a quiet and diffident charm. Charles Laughton once referred to him as 'the most graceful actor of our time'. Most of his stage-work was admired, and in films he enjoyed a popularity and prestige in the US (at least for a time) on the level of that of Olivier and Leslie Howard: but Donat only ever made one film in Hollywood and few in Britain. His tragedy was that the promise of his early years was never fulfilled, and that he was haunted by agonies of doubt and disappointment (which probably were the cause of his chronic asthma). For most of the last years of his life he was unable to work, to function as an actor.

He was born in Withington, Manchester, in 1905. His father (Polish by birth) loathed the office work which he himself did and planned to send the boy to Canada for an adventurous life (as he had sent the elder sons); but Donat's mother thought he was too shy. To help overcome this, and to cure a stammer, he was given elocution lessons. His teacher gave recitals with Donat accompanying him, which led to his stage debut in Birmingham in 1921 in a small part in 'Julius Caesar'. He became private secretary to his tutor and through him met Sir Frank Benson and was taken on by him. The Benson Company toured the provinces in the classics–the famous business of 'bringing culture to the hicks'. It was not an especially distinguished company, but Donat learned his craft, over a four-year period, and later referred to this as the happiest period of his life. In 1928 he joined Liverpool Rep for a season and moved on to Cambridge, working with Flora Robson and Tyrone Guthrie. Then he decided to try London and was offered a part in 'Knave and Queen' (30). It flopped. So did the next half-dozen plays, but in 1931 he did a good Dunois in 'Saint Joan', and in 1932 made his mark in an adaptation of 'Precious Bane' put on in a peripheral London theatre (the Embassy, Swiss Cottage): he made sufficient mark for MGM to make approaches about his doing *Smilin' Through*, but he wasn't interested in Hollywood. As a struggling actor he did several screen tests in Britain, and Korda signed him for three years: one of his first discoveries. Korda put him in a story of Oxford undergraduates, *Men of Tomorrow* (32), directed by Leontine Sagan, *That Night in London* and *Cash* (33), a feeble comedy with Edmund Gwenn, as a bank clerk who embezzled just that. By an odd stroke (Korda was having distribution difficulties) these films were much more widely shown in the US than in their country of origin. He did a play, 'When Ladies Meet' and in his next film became an international name, though he had only a supporting role: that of Culpeper, the man who cuckolded a king (Charles Laughton) in *The Private Life of Henry VIII*. And by the time it was shown, Donat had scored a great West End success in James Bridie's 'The Sleeping Clergyman' in two different parts.

Hollywood beckoned, and Korda loaned him for *The Count of Monte Cristo* (34). The indie company making the film had Donat forced on them by the director, Rowland V. Lee, but they liked him well enough later to double the budget. Said The Sunday Times (London): 'a striking performance . . . his part is a long one. It has many difficult scenes, but he handles it with superb assurance, an ease and a certainty that mark him as a finished actor.' Beyond that, the film was a good version of Dumas and very popular. In London, he did a play with Flora Robson, 'Mary Read'; and then was loaned to GB to play Richard Hannay in Hitchcock's exciting version of Buchan's *The Thirty-nine Steps* (35), considered then the ultimate in screen thrillers and later accepted as a classic. C. A. Lejeune observed: 'For the first time on our screens we have the British equivalent of a Clark Gable or a Ronald Colman playing in a purely national idiom.' There followed another hit, René Clair's *The Ghost Goes West* (36), in a dual role, as the ghost accompanying the castle being removed brick by brick to the US by millionaire Eugene Palette, and as his modern descendant. Donat next decided to do another Hitchcock, *Sabotage*, at a salary of £30,000, but Korda balked. He had, he complained, bought several properties for Donat: 'Precious Bane', a piece about Nelson, and was preparing a film *Hamlet*. He had also bought *Knight Without Armour* (37), by James Hilton, and Donat did that instead, co-starring with Dietrich in a far-fetched tale of the Russian revolution. (During filming his asthma attacks worsened. and Laurence Olivier was on standby to replace him if necessary.)

Indecision was Donat's great failing. For some time now he had been plagued with

Robert Donat as the gentle schoolteacher, Mr Chipping, introducing to the school the wife he has met and wooed while away on a walking tour: Goodbye Mr Chips *(39) with Greer Garson.*

Robert Donat as The Young Mr Pitt *(42) – ageing. Carol Reed's study of the man who became Prime Minister at the age of 24.*

asthma, and it was a deadly combination. After *Monte Cristo* the Warner Brothers had negotiated for Donat's services in Hollywood, but he never arrived to make the important films they had announced for him: *British Agent*, *Anthony Adverse*, *Captain Blood* and *Robin Hood*. Other things he didn't do during this stage of his career included: Marco Polo, Chopin, the Squire in *South Riding*, *Peter Ibbetson*, Lawrence of Arabia, *Romeo* (to Shearer's Juliet), Mr Darcy of *Pride and Predjudice*, The Old Pretender in A. E. W. Mason's *Clementina*, *The Son of Monte Cristo*; during the war he dithered over playing the Chorus in Olivier's *Henry V* – but MGM appear to have frowned on that project.

MGM signed Donat to a six-picture contract at £25,000 each (with the period unspecified because of his health). The first was *The Citadel* (38) from A. J. Cronin's best-seller about the local GP who loses his idealism when he becomes a Mayfair specialist. Donat did the part with candour and enthusiasm, and the film restored the reputation of King Vidor, who directed. The next was an even bigger triumph, James Hilton's story of a gentle schoolmaster and his dedication to his pupils: in 1939 the world cried at this grossly sentimental picture, *Goodbye Mr Chips*. It won Donat a Best Actor Oscar and the Picturegoer Gold Medal. Hollywood clamoured for him, and, turned down for military service, he might have gone. Instead, he planned an Old Vic season (aborted by the war) and in London in 1940 he played Dick Dudgeon in 'The Devil's Disciple'. His next film was a contribution to the war effort, *The Young Mr Pitt* (42), and he managed to express Pitt's fervour and single-mindedness; Carol Reed directed. In *The Adventures of Tartu* (43) he was a dandified secret agent. The same year he did Shotover in Shaw's 'Heartbreak House'. *Perfect Strangers* (45) was his last for MGM (Korda produced for that company) and the last of his films (except the final one) to have any wide showing in the US. Deborah Kerr co-starred.

He had leased a London theatre, and had gone into management, but this was a venture which, in the end, went sour on him. Perfectionist he may have been but he was also finicky and vacillating: for this reason, a film of *Precious Bane* for Rank (who now held the rights) came to nothing. But he was disappointed at being turned down for Sykes in *Oliver Twist* after testing. Later, he pondered a film of 'The Sleeping Clergyman' (filmed as *Flesh and Blood*) which he revived at this time. He also played Benedick in 'Much Ado'.

Thus he was not on the screen again until 1947, a brief cameo as Parnell in an Irish story, *Captain Boycott*. The following year, at

Deborah Kerr and Robert Donat in Perfect Strangers *(45) – their separation and war service has rendered them somewhat more glamorous to each other.*

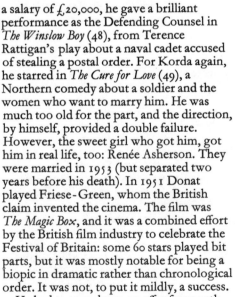

Robert Donat in The Winslow Boy *(49) as the fashionable KC hired to clear the name of the naval cadet accused of stealing a postal order.*

a salary of £20,000, he gave a brilliant performance as the Defending Counsel in *The Winslow Boy* (48), from Terence Rattigan's play about a naval cadet accused of stealing a postal order. For Korda again, he starred in *The Cure for Love* (49), a Northern comedy about a soldier and the women who want to marry him. He was much too old for the part, and the direction, by himself, provided a double failure. However, the sweet girl who got him, got him in real life, too: Renée Asherson. They were married in 1953 (but separated two years before his death). In 1951 Donat played Friese-Green, whom the British claim invented the cinema. The film was *The Magic Box*, and it was a combined effort by the British film industry to celebrate the Festival of Britain: some 60 stars played bit parts, but it was mostly notable for being a biopic in dramatic rather than chronological order. It was not, to put it mildly, a success.

He had to turn down an offer from 20th to do *No Highway*, but in 1953 he returned to the stage as Becket in Eliot's 'Murder in the Cathedral' for the Old Vic; he was very ill, and cylinders of oxygen were kept in the wings. No indication of his difficulties was visible to the audience, but later that year he had to abandon plans to play Mossop in *Hobson's Choice* with Charles Laughton. John Mills took over. However, a year later he did manage to do a leading role, a parson, in a pleasant rural picture, the aptly named *Lease of Life* (54). The Times (London) said: 'It is legitimate to infer that he takes great pains with his parts, and he knows how, scrupulously and decently, to subdue himself to his part, to adapt his personality without abandoning it.' During his last years he was desperately ill. So much money was spent on treatment that it was known widely that Donat was broke when 20th signed him for a supporting role in Ingrid Bergman's *The Inn of the Sixth Happiness* (58). As a Chinese mandarin, his last words on the screen were: 'We shall not see each other again, I think.' It was the impeccable performance expected, but he had worked himself into a complete total and physical wreck; while in hospital, his left lung collapsed. He left only his fee for the film, £25,000. C. A. Lejeune saluted him: 'An actor of honour, a man of courage'.

Melvyn Douglas

In the 30s Melvyn Douglas was one of the screen's most accomplished farceurs. Dapper and invariably frivolous, he chased after, or was chased by, all the comediennes of the time. He was a prop for the girls, unlike, say, William Powell, who was a star in his own right. Later, like Powell, he was always married. Lionel Collier observed that he was cast only in marital comedies: 'The movie moguls seem to have discovered that Melvyn has a suave manner, a way with the ladies and an enigmatical smile which can be used only in a certain kind of production.' Douglas himself has said: 'I earned what became an international reputation for being one of the most debonair and witty farceurs in Hollywood.' And yet he wasn't happy; he returned to the stage and when he came back to films it was as a character actor.

He was born in Macon, Georgia, in 1901, the son of concert pianist Edouard Hesselberg. He got the acting bug in High School, and made his stage debut in Chicago in 1919; he worked in stock and toured in everything from Shakespeare to Broadway hits, until 1928, when he made his New York bow in 'A Free Soul' with Fay Bainter. There were other plays, and in 1930 he was in a big success, 'Tonight or Never', which brought him marriage (to Helen Ganagan, who was in the cast) and a Hollywood offer. Gloria Swanson persuaded Sam Goldwyn in his capacity as production head of United Artists (as he was at that time) to buy the play for her, and Goldwyn signed Douglas along with it, at a starting fee of $900 a week. The film (31), however, did nothing for Douglas – as the young man adored by temperamental prima donna Swanson (despite the fact that she believes he's being kept by Alison Skipworth, who is really his aunt). Then, of all incredible things, he was chosen to play Garbo's lover in *As You Desire Me* (32), an accolade that led nowhere. It was released after the next three: *Prestige* with Ann Harding; *The Wiser Sex* with Claudette Colbert; and *The Broken Wing* with Lupe Velez. In none of these films did he get very good notices. Goldwyn loaned him out for drearier and drearier parts: *The Old Dark House*; *Nagana*, a jungle tale that was expected to make a star out of Tala Birell; and *The Vampire Bat* (33) with Fay Wray at Majestic. He asked to be released from his contract and did one as a free-lance, *Counsellor-at-Law*, supporting John Barrymore. Then he returned to New York for a comedy, 'No More Ladies'.

Melvyn Douglas was a young actor fresh from Broadway and not established in films when Garbo chose him to be her leading man in As You Desire Me (*32*).

However, his wife was offered the lead in *She*, virtually the only film she made, and Douglas accompanied her back to the Coast. He did three B pictures: *Dangerous Corner* (34), J. B. Priestley's play, filmed by RKO with Conrad Nagel and Virginia Bruce; *Woman in the Dark* (Fay Wray); and *The People's Enemy* (35), an old-hat melodrama, as an attorney, with Preston Foster. He was really a back number when Columbia had difficulty in getting a big draw to star with Claudette Colbert in *She Married Her Boss* and took him to play the boss who finds out his perfect secretary doesn't make a perfect wife. They liked him so much that they signed him to a seven-year contract. He was loaned out: to RKO to play Colonel Cody in *Annie Oakley*; and to Paramount for the excellent *Mary Burns Fugitive* (36) with Sylvia Sidney; he did *The Lone Wolf Returns* with Gail Patrick; *And So They Were Married*; and then Columbia gave him another fine chance, with Irene Dunne, in *Theodora Grows Wild*. They loaned him to MGM for *The Gorgeous Hussy*, starring Joan Crawford and three other names above his, but most critics thought him the best thing in the film. So, presumably, did MGM, and taking into account his fine notices for *Theodora*, they negotiated with Columbia to share his contract. According to Douglas, both contracts had the usual options and he expected to be dropped before they ran their full terms.

And so, he also said, he became 'a run-of-the-mill leading man'. Maybe; but one who was instantly at home, stylish and nimble. With a player of his own class he could bat back dialogue like a champion ping-pong player. He was well-mannered and deferential; his look was quizzical rather than sarcastic (or enigmatic)–not that his skill was much needed in either *Women of Glamour* (37) with Virginia Bruce or *I'll Take Romance* with Lily Pons. But *I Met Him in Paris* was a fairly good Colbert comedy with Robert Young; and *Angel* a delightful one, with Dietrich and Herbert Marshall. He had only a supporting role, as Freddie Bartholomew's father, in *Captains Courageous*.

He was the French gentleman crook who came back in *Arsene Lupin Returns* (38) and an authority on rare books in *Fast Company* with Florence Rice, one of the several *Thin Man* imitations that he made around this time. He was with Luise Rainer in *The Toy Wife*, and then did another one, *There's Always a Woman*–and she was Joan Blondell. *The Shining Hour* was Joan Crawford's, and it was Deanna Durbin at *That Certain Age*, with a crush on him. *There's That Woman Again* (39) was a singularly unfortunate title, for while it was a sequel, Blondell had been replaced by Virginia Bruce; after which it was *Tell No Tales*–to Louise Platt, a B at MGM. Douglas's skill by this time was equally as good as William Powell's, but he had never achieved Powell's eminence at MGM; however, the latter's illness at this time gave Douglas the chance of playing opposite Garbo again in *Ninotchka*–though in fact he plays against her: he is flippant where she is solemn, cheaply insincere where she has great glooms of feeling. It was a perfect mating. He found working with her 'an extraordinary experience', and he enjoyed working with Lubitsch, who had done *Angel* with him already. 'Of all the movies I made, I liked just two or three, and that was chiefly because of the directors.' (He also liked Richard Boleslawski, who directed *Theodora*.)

He did *Good Girls Go to Paris* and *The Amazing Mr Williams* with Blondell, and then romanced Jean Arthur in *Too Many Husbands* (40); Loretta Young in *He Stayed for Breakfast*, a satire on Communism, *Ninotchka* in reverse; Rosalind Russell in the remake of *This Thing Called Love*; Myrna Loy in *Third Finger Left Hand*; Merle Oberon in Lubitsch's *That Uncertain Feeling* (41); Joan Crawford in *A Woman's Face*, as her surgeon and lover, his only straight picture in this batch; Ruth Hussey in *Our Wife*; Garbo in *Two-Faced Woman*; Norma Shearer in *We Were Dancing* (42); Crawford again in *They All Kissed the Bride*; and Ann Sothern in *Three Hearts for Julia*.

He combined film-making at this period

She fell hook, line and sinker but then played hard to get in Third Finger Left Hand *(40), a comedy whose banalities were offset by the playing of Myrna Loy and Melvyn Douglas.*

After a long absence from movies, Douglas returned as a character actor, in Hud *(63), and promptly won a Best Supporting Actor Oscar.*

(41–42) with Defence work in Washington; enlisted in the US Army as a private, was demobbed in 1946 as a major.

He was happier in the army than back in Hollywood: *Sea of Grass* (47) at MGM, supporting Tracy and Hepburn; *The Guilt of Janet Ames* at Columbia with Russell, as a drunken reporter. Then, according to his own account, his lawyer found a loophole in his contract and he made only a couple of films before leaving Hollywood. In fact, he was in: *Mr Blandings Builds His Dream House* (48) with Loy, *My Own True Love* (Phyllis Calvert), *A Woman's Secret* (49) with Maureen O'Hara, *The Great Sinner* with Gregory Peck, *My Forbidden Past* (51), and *On the Loose* with Lynn Bari. But he was back on Broadway in 1949, in 'Two Blind Mice'; and subsequently in such plays as 'Time Out for Ginger' (52, including tours in the US and Australia), 'Inherit the Wind', 'The Waltz of the Toreadors', 'The Gang's All Here' and 'The Best Man' (60, winning a Tony for his performance). He has described this time as 'except for my early years, the most productive and most satisfying of my life'. He also worked in TV.

Douglas returned to the screen in *Billy Budd* (62), as the Dansker; and the following year was the grandfather in *Hud* (63), for which he won a Best Supporting Oscar. He has since done *A Company of Cowards?*, *The Americanization of Emily* (64) where his comic mastery showed through in a funny delineation of an eccentric admiral, *Rapture* (65), *Hotel* (67) and *Questions* (70), the screen version of Robert Anderson's 'I Never Sang for My Father'.

Marie Dressler

In 1933 the Motion Picture Herald and the Hollywood Reporter both named the same lady at the top in their annual polls to discover the biggest draws in films. She wasn't young or glamorous – a Garbo or a Shearer or a Gaynor – but an ageing, ugly and bulky lady whose speciality was low-life drunks: Marie Dressler. She had been a has-been for most of the 20s, but had returned to fame with the coming of the Talkies, and within a year had achieved a great popularity (in 1931 the first female star in a John Bull poll of favourites; in 1932 third in the Bernstein Questionnaire, top of the Motion Picture Herald list).

At that time the private lives of stars were common property, to a degree far surpassing that of the current PR-angled show business scene, and every cinemagoer knew that Dressler had triumphed over adversity: thus she had a very special meaning during the years of the Depression. It was once said that she was the Heart of America, just as Douglas Fairbanks Sr was the son of America and Mary Pickford its girl next door. But Doug and Mary (apart from the fact that they had been around so long) were out of tune with the times, with their optimism and high spirits, their gracious living and innocence: the public wanted rather to see the pessimistic and worldly-wise Dressler. Her normal expression was one of extreme scepticism – she of course being the only sane person around.

However, she was a mistress of facial expression. She was a considerable actress and a prodigious comedienne (her popularity was in no way a freak), with much experience in vaudeville. Most of the early humour she had generated had been crude references to her girth. She realized early, she said in her memoirs, 'The Life Story of an Ugly Duckling', that she 'was too homely for a prima donna and too big for a soubrette'.

She was born in Coburg, Ontario, in 1869, and made her first public appearance as a Cupid in a church hall pageant. She never went to school, and, at 14, after answering a newspaper ad, joined a roving light opera troupe and worked mostly in the chorus. Her first major appearance was in a minor version of 'Under Two Flags', as Cigarette, out in the wilds, in 1886; by 1892 she had progressed to New York, and made her debut there in 'Robber on the Rhine', a play by and with Maurice Barrymore. It was Barrymore who realized her potentialities as a comic: in 1896, still in her 20s, she played Mrs Malaprop, and then Barrymore persuaded her to go into vaudeville, where she was featured with Weber and Fields. In 1901 Weber (with Ziegfeld) featured her in a revue, 'Higgledy-Piggledy'. She became one of the nation's leading artists, and scored also big successes in London in 1907 and 1909, though on the latter occasion she collapsed from an ulcerated throat, the show closed, and she lost all the money that she had put into it. She recouped her losses with 'Tillie's Nightmare' the following year, probably her biggest New York success. In 1913 came 'Marie Dressler's All-Star Gambol' and in 1914 she was in 'A Mix-Up'.

She was in Los Angeles that year when Mack Sennett talked her into making a film version of 'Tillie'. No expense was spared: it was going to run to an unprecedented six reels instead of the usual one or two, and have a shooting schedule of 14 weeks; and Dressler was to be supported by two of Sennett's star attractions, Charlie Chaplin and Mabel Normand. Audiences everywhere

They were the public's favourite screen lovers in the early Talkie period: Wallace Beery and Marie Dressler in Min and Bill *(30). It was one of the year's outstanding successes.*

roared at the antics of these three: the mercenary Chaplin pursuing alternately the pretty Mabel and the formidable–but now suddenly wealthy, his ex-sweetheart–Dressler. The film was called *Tillie's Punctured Romance* (14) and has been re-issued countless times (sometimes re-titled *For the Love of Tillie* or *Tillie's Millions*) both in Britain and the US, right up to the present. But two that Dressler did without her co-stars and for other producers, *Tillie's Tomato Surprise* (15) and *Tillie Wakes Up* (17), had little success. In 1917, for Goldwyn, she was *The Scrublady*, and in 1918 she had the title role again in a mixture of slapstick and patriotism, *The Cross Red Nurse*.

Dressler's main centre of activity remained vaudeville, but at the same time as her Hollywood career failed to get off the ground, that turned sour on her. In 1917 she was one of the champions of the chorus-girl strike (which led to the founding of Equity), and after it she was persona non grata with most important managements. She was in a Broadway show in 1923, 'The Dancing Girl', and did some one-reel comedies in France: but by 1926 she was on the bread-line. She had a small part in Fox's *The Joy Girl* (27), starring Olive Borden, but was considering taking a job as a housekeeper on Long Island when MGM scenarist Frances Marion came to the rescue. Dressler had shown great kindness to Marion at the time of *Tillie Wakes Up*, and in return now Marion fashioned a screenplay for her and 'sold' the idea to Irving Thalberg. Dressler was signed at $1,500 per week, and another comedienne, Polly Moran, co-starred: *The Callahans and the Murphys*. After a few showings, however, various Irish pressure groups worked militantly against it and MGM withdrew it.

Marion persuaded Dressler to stay in Hollywood, and Dressler got a part in *Breakfast at Sunrise* which starred Constance Talmadge; then Marion found another part for her–and Moran–in *Bringing Up Father* (28), an adaptation of George McManus's popular comic strip; and again at MGM Dressler had a supporting part in Marion Davies's *The Patsy*. Then there were no more film offers and she joined Edward Everett Horton's stock company in LA. When she found herself in demand due to the need for stage-trained performers, she left Horton flat, much to his indignation. She took to Talkies with ease: *The Divine Lady* (29) at First National–Corrine Griffith as Lady Hamilton; *Dangerous Females* at Paramount, co-starring again with Moran; and *The Vagabond Lover* (Rudy Vallee) at RKO. At MGM she did a turn in *Hollywood Revue of 1929*, as Venus rising from the sea, and she played a passé actress in *Chasing Rainbows*: Moran was also in it, but it was basically a

starring vehicle for Charles King and Bessie Love, who had been in *Broadway Melody*.

Dressler was established as a funny supporting woman. Marion persuaded Thalberg to let Dressler test for the part of Marthy in *Anna Christie* (30) – a serious part: the old harridan who welcomes Garbo when she returns looking for her father. Garbo was reputedly impressed; so were the critics and MGM, who now offered Dressler a contract. She was loaned out for *One Romantic Night*, playing Lillian Gish's mother and a Queen – she hardly sounded or behaved like one – and put into *The Girl Said No*, a comedy that starred William Haines. Audiences still talked about her in *Anna Christie*, and MGM tried again a teaming with Moran, *Caught Short*, with Dressler as a boarding-house dragon. The studio had doubts because of the lack of love-interest, but it was a big success.

Still in 1930 Dressler was the highlight of both Norma Shearer's *Let Us Be Gay* and Ramon Novarro's *Call of the Flesh*; and the star, with Wallace Beery, of *Min and Bill*, an adroit mixture of slapstick and sentiment: it was a huge hit in both Britain and the US and brought Dressler a Best Actress Oscar. She became, officially, a star, and was paid a salary of $5,000 a week. Dressler and Moran were teamed again: *Reducing* (31) – getting thin – and *Politics* – municipal variety – still and always as bosom pals, incessantly fighting and bickering. Although she clowned, Dressler's was a serious character study: Moran was more robust and much less sensitive. In 1931 she signed a new long-term contract, while making *Emma* (32), in which she was Jean Hersholt's indispensable maidservant and (in the last reel) bride. This was a Picturegoer Gold Medal performance and the film was, again, big box-office. There was a reunion with Moran, *Prosperity* – Dressler was the prez of a small-town bank – and one with Beery, *Tugboat Annie* (33). The Times (London) reported that the stars played 'with finished technical cunning and an immense communicable energy of joy in the job. She is a game old woman, the captain of a tugboat, who is inordinately proud of her son (the captain of a liner) and has an ineradicable fondness for her husband (the tugboat's chief liability), "who has never struck me except in self-defence" . . . both Miss Dressler and Mr Beery have that exceptional power of making a comic point with complete certainty, of isolating it, and the next moment of making with the same certainty an effect that wins a sympathetic response deeper than laughter. Always – and it is their supreme merit – they have abounding life.'

MGM billed Dressler as 'The World's Greatest Actress', and fan-magazines referred to her as 'that grand old trouper'; it was agreed (probably truthfully) that she was the most beloved star on the lot. She dispensed homely philosophy (but kept quiet about the two broken marriages in her past). In films she brought her fine common touch to the role of the actress down on her luck in *Dinner at Eight*, and to that of the housekeeper in *Christopher Bean*. She died in 1934, of cancer, while still topping popularity lists. Said Photoplay in memoriam: 'It is the greatest of all tributes to Marie Dressler to say that her appeal was universal. . . . I do not care what your status in life may be, of one thing I am certain: if you ever saw

Marie Dressler on the screen she went straight to your heart. That was because the shining qualities that made her so beloved by everyone that knew her personally, were revealed–every word, gesture, and facial expression–in her film interpretations.'

Irene Dunne

Irene Dunne's forte was indestructible dignity. In the slushy melodramas she made at the start of her career she suffered with patience: she was noble in *Cimarron*. When she turned to comedy she was invincibly ladylike–it is hardly a coincidence that Deborah Kerr inherited two of her old parts. Kerr is possibly a better actress, but you can't tell for sure: a different sensitivity was required in the well-oiled Dunne vehicles of the 30s than is needed in the more realistic (supposedly) films that Kerr makes. Dunne perhaps had more lightness, more humour. Few actresses could play comedy as she did: there is a brief sequence in *The Awful Truth* where, her back to the camera, she is contemplating the antics of Cary Grant–her gurgling, smothered laugh is more eloquent than many another's close-ups. She was airy and rather super.

She was born in Louisville, Kentucky, in 1904, the daughter of a government official, and educated there at the Loretta Academy. She graduated from the Chicago College of Music, with a local reputation as a fine singer, and was quickly taken on to play Irene in the touring company of the musical of that name. Her first New York appearance was in 'The Clinging Vine' (23). She also appeared in 'Lollipop' (24), 'Sweetheart Time' (26), 'Yours Truly' (27), 'Luckee Girl', 'She's My Baby' (starring Beatrice Lillie and Clifton Webb), etc.; in 1929 she was chosen to play Magnolia in the road company of 'Show Boat', and that led to Hollywood and a starring contract with RKO.

First she was tucked away in a cheerful army musical (from Broadway's 'Present Arms') with Eddie Foy Jr and a host of comics, *Leathernecking* (30), and might have languished had Richard Dix (who had seen her on the stage) not recommended her for the lead opposite him in *Cimarron* (31), as wife Sabra Cravat in Edna Ferber's story. She ended up a Congresswoman and an Oscar-nominee; the film won a Best Picture Oscar and, at $2 million, was 1931's biggest money-maker (in Britain, too). Dunne was now a big star. RKO put her into *Bachelor Apartment*, with Lowell Sherman directing and co-starring; loaned

When a woman loves a man . . . she will live in Back Street *for him, welcoming his nightly visits before he goes home to his wife. Irene Dunne and John Boles in one of the big hits of 1932. There were two later versions.*

her to MGM for *The Great Lover*, a backstage romance with Adolphe Menjou finally sacrificing his own happiness for the sake of hers and Neil Hamilton's; involved her with Pat O'Brien, on the rebound, in a *Consolation Marriage*; and made her make the supreme sacrifice for fashionable Jewish doctor Ricardo Cortez in *Symphony of Six Million* (32) in order to bring him to his senses–and back to the ghetto. This was a much-praised movie, directed by Gregory La Cava, from a novel by Fannie Hurst. Dunne was one of the *Thirteen Women*, the only one not bumped off by Myrna Loy; but there was *No Other Woman* (33) for Charles Bickford.

Meanwhile, she lived in *Back Street* (32), another Hurst novel, as the mistress of married man John Boles, one of the weepies by which other weepies are measured. And more handkerchiefs were required for *The Secret of Madame Blanche* (33), a wartime story with Dunne as a Frenchwoman standing trial for a murder committed by a British Tommy–the son she lost to his British father at birth: MGM borrowed her for this, presumably because none of their own stars would do it. She was at least a bit more positive in *The Silver Cord*, opposing a possessive mother-in-law (Laura Hope Crews) in this version of Sidney Howard's play: Joel McCrea was in the midst of the tug-of-war. And there was more of same: *Ann Vickers* with Walter Huston; *If I Were*

Women the world over wept when Irene Dunne, blind, was loved by Robert Taylor in The Magnificent Obsession *(35).*

Later Miss Dunne was one of the screen's perfect wives: notably in Penny Serenade *(41) with Cary Grant.*

Free, a John Van Druten story with Clive Brook and Nils Asther; *This Man Is Mine* (34), a triangle drama with Ralph Bellamy and Constance Cummings; and *The Age of Innocence*, with Boles, which contrived to make Edith Wharton's novel as much like *Back Street* as possible.

Earlier in 1934, however, Dunne had been reunited with Dix for *Stingaree*, an Australian drama about an outlaw and a singer who finally make for peace in the outback. Reminded that Dunne could sing, WB borrowed her for the film of Jerome Kern's stage hit, *Sweet Adeline* (35), with Donald Woods; and RKO co-starred her in Kern's *Roberta*, with Astaire and Rogers. It was a welcome touch of levity, but Dunne said: 'Heavy dramatic roles are essential for an actress of my type. I know definitely that the status I have achieved has been achieved through tears. So for my career I cry.' Her contract was up, and she signed short-term deals with Universal and Columbia. Universal starred her in another sudser, Lloyd C. Douglas's *The Magnificent Obsession*, as the woman blinded by playboy Robert Taylor in an accident (he makes amends by–secretly–caring for her); and *Show Boat* (36), done as a straightforward melo with songs, with Allan Jones and Dunne superb in her old stage part. Columbia, however, took a risk and put Dunne into *Theodora Goes Wild*, a sunny, harum-scarum comedy about a small-town girl who writes a hot best-seller and is humanized by Melvyn Douglas. She got great notices and the film was popular: with that and *Show Boat*, her stock soared.

She continued to free-lance, picking her vehicles with care, with an almost rigid alternation between comedy and drama (she was announced for lives of Madame Curie and Mary Baker Eddy, but nothing came of either project). There was another comedy, the delicious *The Awful Truth* (37) with Cary Grant, a will-she-won't-she-divorce-him; which was sandwiched between two musicals, both with Kern music: *High Wide and Handsome* with Randolph Scott at Paramount, and *Joy of Living* (38) with Douglas Fairbanks Jr at RKO. Wrote Fairbanks: 'One of the more civilized women. She's a dream, an absolute dream, one of the most professional women I've ever known. Nothing is instinctive, everything she does is carefully thought out, she knows every movement, every intonation, every nuance. She's a first-class craftswoman. Her hours are like office hours, she's never late, she never slips, but instead of being dull and perfect, she's absolutely enchanting and perfect.'

In 1939 Dunne had a very successful *Love Affair* with Charles Boyer, but *Invitation to Happiness* (society girl marries boxer Fred MacMurray) was hardly that as far as audiences were concerned. *When Tomorrow Comes* was another four-handkerchief effort with Boyer in love with her and keeping from her the fact that he has a wife who is loco. There were two more with Grant: *My Favorite Wife* (40), a fair comedy, and George Stevens's *Penny Serenade* (41), a series of vignettes of married life–relentlessly sentimental, but exquisitely done and perfectly acted. Neither *Unfinished Business* nor *Lady in a Jam* (42) were memorable, but, moving on to MGM, Dunne did two of the biggest wartime weepies, *A Guy Named Joe* (43) with Spencer Tracy, and *The White Cliffs of Dover* (44) with Alan Marshall, an account of a British family in two world wars. It was clearly inspired by *Mrs Miniver* and the ads blatantly aimed it at the same public. 'Antiquity and quaintness are the keynotes,' observed Forsyth Hardy, noting that Dunne, as an American learning to understand the British, 'plays with a generous warmth of feeling'.

Then she and Boyer were *Together Again*, she as a prim mayoress and he as a sculptor: the outcome was predictable. *Over 21* (45), with Alexander Knox, was even less agreeable, but Dunne was offered three big ones in a row. *Anna and the King of Siam* (46) was a successful, if not very good, version of Anna Leonowens's book. Richard Winnington commented: 'The indomitable Victorian governess is a smart, witty, resourceful woman, in fact, Miss Irene Dunne, and nobody but.' The other two were both from Broadway successes, both 'memory' pieces: *I Remember Mama* (47) and *Life With Father* (48). *Mama* was made by Stevens, a tender story of a Norwegian community in the US at the turn of the century, and *Father* (William Powell) was upper-class New York in the 90s: the latter was funnier, and one of the year's biggest money-makers.

Dunne then made a mistake: 20th, taken in by the matriarchal image she had now assumed, cast her in *The Mudlark* (50), the tale of a Cockney kid who visits Queen Victoria (Dunne). The British press resented an American actress being imported for this part, and maybe that's why British audiences stayed away–despite the presence of the then-potent Alec Guinness in the cast. American audiences stayed away too–maybe because they didn't want to see Dunne padded and in a rubber mask. Two modestly budgeted comedies did nothing to restore her to favour–the inaptly titled *Never a Dull Moment* (52) with MacMurray, and *It Grows on Trees* with Dean Jagger. She hasn't filmed since.

In 1956 she appeared in a TV drama, and the following year, presumably abandoning the hope of a good movie offer, she became an Alternative Delegate at the 12th Session of the UN General Assembly. In 1965 her husband of almost 40 years died. Occasionally her picture appears in the press, taken at some Hollywood function. In 1966, when Leslie Halliwell did a British TV programme on the Oscar Ceremony, he wrote in Films and Filming that of all the celebrities he had met in Hollywood, Dunne was by far the most unaffected and most charming.

Deanna Durbin

In 1942 there was a unique programme playing the Odeon circuit throughout Britain: 'The Durbin Festival–designed to give the public seven Happy Days with Deanna. . . . From the child of our hearts to the woman we love.' Each of the films played for one day only, but it was the same film in all the cinemas; and there were second features. A considerable feat of organization (transporting prints, etc.): but the Festival played to packed cinemas. Durbin's popularity was considerably greater in Britain than the US; in Britain during the four years 1939–42 she was easily the top female box-office draw, but she was liked everywhere and was a critics' pet. The qualities they praised in her–charm, spontaneity, naturalness, her artlessness and her singing voice–were more highly prized then than they are now, but she was probably the most agreeable child who ever starred in movies.

In private life she was extremely self-assured, and there are touches of wit and acerbity in her performances which place her easily in the forefront of those girls who have made a career out of playing Cinderella. These qualities were matched, in the almost perfect vehicles of her early period, by the cynicism of some of the supporting cast: 'She's not going to *sing*?' says her cousin in *First Love*, half-contemptuously, half-despairingly.

She was born in Winnipeg, Canada, in 1921 or 1922 (studios lied about the age of child stars), of émigré-Lancashire parents, who moved to Los Angeles soon after. Her remarkable singing voice attracted attention and brought an MGM talent scout to her

Deanna Durbin grows up. She was one of the most appealing of child stars. But as she grew up the studio tried to turn her into the standardized Hollywood glamour girl.

school to hear her; his studio planned a life of opera singer Eva Schumann-Heink and Durbin was signed with a view to playing her as a child. The film was abandoned, and she was put into a short with Judy Garland, *Every Sunday* (36); then, at the end of six months, dropped (legend has it due to a misunderstanding: Louis B. Mayer said 'Drop the fat one', meaning Garland). Universal producer Joe Pasternak ran the short with a view to signing Garland for a movie he was making about three teenage girls who reunite their divorcing parents, but Garland had just been loaned to 20th, and Pasternak ran the short again to see whether Durbin could substitute; and Universal signed her. By this time her parents had found an agent to handle her, and he got her a job singing on the Eddie Cantor Radio Hour–so that she was nationally famous by the time *Three Smart Girls* (37) was shown. But Universal knew they had a gold-mine when they saw the rushes: apart from the voice, the child had high spirits and warmth. Her part was padded and the meagre budget of $150,000 doubled. Public response was immediate and a gross of $2 million poured into Universal's empty coffers (they had been floundering in the red for a couple of years).

Bankruptcy averted, Universal gratefully gave Pasternak what he wanted for their new asset, some 'highbrow' music: the plot of *One Hundred Men and a Girl* had Durbin persuading an unwilling Stokowski to conduct an orchestra of Depression-hit musicians. Said The New Statesman (P. Galway): 'Useless to pretend that I am tough enough to resist the blandishments of Miss Deanna Durbin. The candid eyes, the parted lips, the electric energy, the astonishing voice; if they bowl over 50 million or so, surely a critic may be pardoned for wobbling a little on his professional cynical base. For this is pure fairy tale; but it comes off.' Universal proffered a new contract, going from $1,500 to $3,000 a week, plus a bonus of $10,000 per film, and they got a bargain. Pasternak noted independently at this time that a top star was worth $10 million, adding (significantly) that every bad film caused a $2 million depreciation.

No need to worry: he had an uncanny knack of selecting the right vehicles. In her 1938 films she brought romance in the shape of Herbert Marshall to unhappy mother–*Mad About Music*–and had a schoolgirl crush on Melvyn Douglas in *That Certain Age*. Said the Sunday Express: 'These Deanna Durbin pictures–and this is the fourth–are the miracle films of today. They never put a wrong foot forward. They never overreach themselves. They never for a moment lose that sparkle. They never miss.' And Punch said: '. . . in her other films her ability often struck me as miraculous; now it seems to me instinctively perfect.' Hollywood concurred: she was awarded a special juvenile Oscar. In 1939 her enthusiastic followers watched *Three Smart Girls Grow Up* and then saw, with trepidation, their idol receive her

In It's a Date *Deanna played at matchmaking between Kay Francis and Walter Pidgeon. It was a role often given to juvenile stars and she was much less saccharine than most.*

first screen kiss (from Robert Stack), an event covered by the presses of the world without moderation, in *First Love*, an undisguised modern rendering of 'Cinderella'. In 1940 a new contract was negotiated, at $400,000 per film. The skill – and big business – continued through *It's a Date* (40); *Spring Parade*, a Viennese tale; *Nice Girl?* (41); and *It Started With Eve*, a delightful teaming with Charles Laughton.

She married; and the transition to adult star having been successfully accomplished, Pasternak took up an offer from MGM. Immediately the lack of guidance began to show, and she was suspended for refusing *Boy Meets Baby*; she returned only when given story and director approval. But things didn't go well on *The Amazing Mrs Holliday* (43): the Wilder-Brackett script wasn't used and Jean Renoir (no less) gave up the direction because Durbin 'was unable to escape from the style that made her famous'. No matter: she 'maintains her fetching naturalness' (News Chronicle) and 'has never given a more natural or lovelier performance' (Daily Mail). *Hers to Hold* was another – loose – sequel to *Three Smart Girls*, with Joseph Cotten and some patriotism; *His Butler's Sister*, an escapist light comedy with Franchot Tone. But Durbin wanted to become a dramatic actress, and to appease her Universal cast her in *Christmas Holiday* (44), and although she wasn't, as in Maugham's novel, a Russian whore working in Paris but a night-club singer in New Orleans, the public refused to accept her in the part. The film was a considerable box-office hit, but the outcry was such that Universal refused to consider a similar experiment, at which point Durbin lost all interest in films.

Pasternak had prophesied that Durbin was one of 'those personalities which the world . . . insists on regarding as its personal property', and her public stayed faithful through divorce and re-marriage and attempts to publicize her as just another cutie; but they blenched a little at the harsh make-up and the blonde curls of *Can't Help Singing*, even if she was in colour for the first time and had songs by Jerome Kern. It was the last real Durbin hit, though a comedy-thriller, *Lady on a Train* (45), and a reunion with Charles Laughton, *Because of Him* (46), didn't do badly. She had matured into a polished light-comedy player, but where her old co-star Judy Garland (their careers and private lives had run parallel for some time) was being given colour and the best talent MGM could afford, Durbin was enmeshed in feeble plots with lacklustre leading men: *I'll Be Yours* (47, a remake of *The Good Fairy*) with Tom Drake, *Something in the Wind* with John Dall and *Up in Central Park* (48) with Dick Haymes: the latter, a Sigmund Romberg Broadway hit, didn't even rate colour. Universal argued that it couldn't be otherwise after her salary had been set against the budget: in 1945 and 1947 she was the highest paid woman star in Hollywood. In 1949 with one film–*For the Love of Mary*–waiting to be released, they announced that due to 'increasing public apathy' they were paying her the salary due to her for three more films and releasing her. There were reports of other offers–Pasternak dreamed for years to come of getting her to MGM–but she announced her retirement and left Hollywood: she had wanted to quit at the time of her first marriage but had been persuaded to stay because it was wartime and she was an entertainer. She was 27.

Shortly afterwards she married a French film technician and settled near Paris. Unlike Judy Garland, her money had been invested wisely and she is a very wealthy woman. She refuses to see the press, but has emerged from retirement to squash rumours of a comeback. She told Eddie Cantor: 'I don't want to have anything to do with show business ever', and in one announcement made it clear that she had disliked Hollywood and stardom and, what is more, had loathed 'the concocted Durbin personality' which 'never had any similarity to me, not even coincidentally'.

Nelson Eddy

The phenomenal success of the Jeanette MacDonald-Nelson Eddy operettas owed more to her than to him. In commercial terms, he was always some paces behind (she was one of the top 10 draws in Britain 1937–42 inclusive; he trailed behind on three occasions, 1939–41) and although he could sing manfully–in his own way as stolidly good as she in her way–he hadn't much facility with a line and his presence on the screen wasn't unlike that of a cold suet pudding at a children's tea-party. Most of what he was given to do was, of course, impossible, even within the conventions, but the same is true of her material and she is much less risible today.

He was born in Providence, Rhode Island, in 1901, and as a boy sang soprano in church choirs. He moved to Philadelphia in his teens and worked there as a switchboard operator and shipping clerk. Through a friend, he got a job writing obits on a local paper and worked his way up in journalism; but he had the urge to sing and appeared in an amateur musical, 'The Marriage Tax', and in Gilbert and Sullivan; and won a competition to sing with the Philadelphia Civic Opera. His first role was Amonasro in 'Aïda' (24) and he made his New York debut, at the Met, when the Civic Opera visited there with 'Pagliacci': he was Tonio. In New York in 1931 he played the Drum Major in Berg's 'Wozzeck', but from 1928 onwards concentrated on recitals and concerts. These, and radio work, made him quite well known: MGM, when they got hold of him, tried to render him anonymous again. Ida Koverman had seen him in concert in Los Angeles and had persuaded the studio to sign him, but for a couple of years all he did were guest stints, singing one song each, in *Broadway to Hollywood* (33), *Dancing Lady* and a terrible Jimmy Durante vehicle, *Student Tour* (34).

He languished, in fact, while MGM searched for a leading man for MacDonald for *Naughty Marietta* (35). It was a pet project of Mayer's, and it was he who finally insisted that Eddy be given his chance. The result was box-office pow, and Eddy was assigned to co-star with Grace Moore in *Rose Marie* (36). However, she would not be ready till he had left on a concert tour so MacDonald replaced her. The box-office this time was pow-wow, and when the Moore and Eddy schedules once more conflicted over *Maytime* (37), MGM had no hesitation in once more casting MacDonald. He sang, however, with Ilona Massey in *Rosalie*, a lavish (Cole Porter) musical built around the dancing of Eleanor Powell, but was back with MacDonald in *Girl of the Golden West* (38–*most* unlikely as a dashing Mexican bandit–and *Sweethearts*. He was without her in the next two: *Let Freedom Ring!* (39), a gird-our-loins patriotic drama that fell by the wayside despite Virginia Bruce's rendi-

When Austrian composer Nelson Eddy can't sell his operas he and his English debutante wife Jeanette MacDonald take to performing in the streets of Vienna: a scene from MGM's distortion of Noël Coward's Bitter Sweet *(40).*

tion of 'The Star Spangled Banner', and *Balalaika* (from a West End musical), that was heard of for a few years hence. The leading lady here was Massey, who had been kept in the wings by MGM as a threat to the sometimes recalcitrant Jeanette: but to fans this was something akin to adultery, and they were delighted to have the Singing Sweethearts together again in *New Moon* (40) and *Bitter Sweet*, even if they were perceptibly ageing.

Metropolitan star Risë Stevens was his co-star in *The Chocolate Soldier* (41), which was not a version of that stage musical, but of 'The Guardsman'–the stars, however, played actors appearing in 'The Chocolate Soldier': it was successful. MacDonald and Eddy were back again in *I Married an Angel* (42)–for the last time, just as MGM had announced before it went into production. Some mystery surrounds the break: the receipts of the series had decreased but slightly; the most likely explanation is that Hunt Stromberg, who had produced most of them, was leaving to set up his own company, plus the fact that the studio felt that the very high production costs had become risky in the changed world situation. MacDonald's contract was almost up, and Eddy's was allowed to lapse.

After an interval, he turned up at Universal in *The Phantom of the Opera* (43), with hair dyed black and a pencil-line moustache, supposedly transformed into a Frenchman: the film was a huge success but it took him a year to find another role, in the film version of the Weill-Anderson *Knickerbocker Holiday* (44), with Constance Dowling and Charles Coburn. It broke agreeably from back-stage conventions and he was much more animated than hitherto, but it wasn't what you'd call popular. RKO dickered with the idea of a MacDonald-Eddy musical, and both were agreeable despite an animosity which hadn't lessened with the years; but the executive who'd favoured it died and the project was shelved. After a longer silence, broken only by his dubbing of Willie the Whale in Disney's *Make Mine Music* (46), he was reduced to working at Republic, with Massey, in *North West Frontier* (47), which the British distributors prophetically re-named *End of the Rainbow*–and had difficulties getting bookings for.

Eddy did concerts and records, and then had a rather unexpected success on the night-club circuit, with a girl called Gale Sherwood: most of the act consisted of reprises of songs from his film musicals. While appearing in Australia, in 1967, he collapsed on stage and died of a stroke. He left a widow, Anne Franklin, whom he had married in 1939.

Douglas Fairbanks

The elder Fairbanks inspired one of the most moving tributes ever penned by a critic to a star. This is C. A. Lejeune, the week he died: '[His death] has robbed the movies of a bit of themselves–a drop of the life-blood that first made them gay, and great, and indomitable. . . . Fairbanks never really knew how good he was. Behind those acrobatic stunts and that schoolboy exuberance, there was real genius. His leaps, and fights, and swift, violent trajectories were thrilling to watch, but they were inventive, too; they had about them the quality of beauty and surprise. He was an unconscious harlequin. Everything he did had poise and rhythm.... We may have forgotten the names of the pictures, but that tough, stocky little figure, that friendly grin, and the sense of almost illimitable mastery of space and time stays with us.'

And his friend, Chaplin (in his memoirs): 'It was not for naught that Douglas captured the imagination and love of the public. The spirit of his pictures, their optimism and infallibility, were very much to the American taste, and indeed to the taste of the whole world. He had extraordinary magnetism and charm and a genuine boyish enthusiasm which he conveyed to the public.' The word used by Oscar Levant in an odd moment was 'magical'. He was unique and greatly loved. Fans merely smiled indulgently when learning that his hobby was listed as 'Doug'.

Fairbanks was born in Denver, Colorado, in 1883, the son of a lawyer. He was expensively educated, and spent some months at Harvard before deciding to bum around Europe for the sake of experience; at one point he worked in Paris as a labourer, but back in New York he had more suitable ambitions. He toyed with stockbroking and the law, but was most strongly drawn to the theatre. He had acted (as a lackey) in a play in Richmond, Virginia, in 1900; in 1902 he had a small part in a Broadway play ('Her Lord and Master') and, finally, later that year, he decided to make the stage his career. He was in the chorus of 'Fantana' when producer William A. Brady heard of him from his wife, Grace George, and decided that his exuberance would lead to stardom. He signed Fairbanks for five years, and during that time Fairbanks played juveniles in New York and on tour. His first starring part was 'All for a Girl' in 1908; after that, he toured in 'A Gentleman From Mississippi' and did a sketch in vaudeville; by 1914 he had become a popular Broadway actor, and as such was sought by Triangle (D.W. Griffith, Thomas H. Ince and Mack Sennett), as represented by Harry E. Aitken, who noted later that Fairbanks was picked 'because of the splendid humanness that fairly oozed out of him'. The film industry's new gambit of signing stage names was chiefly in a bid for respectability (huge grosses had been registered by films starring the likes of Sarah Bernhardt, which the curious went to see). Fairbanks hesitated, but was swayed by the cash ($2,000 a week), by the thought that he was merely another ageing juvenile and, finally, by the concept of a new movie era ushered in by the showing of *The Birth of a Nation* (his own first movie was also to have a swank première with Paderewski as guest of honour, and was to play New York at theatre prices – $3 a seat). Typically, he was fascinated by the risk involved in beginning a new career. When the run of 'The Show Shop' was over, he entrained to Hollywood to make *The Lamb* (15).

His exuberance on-set alienated many on the unit, including the supervising Griffith, who thought Fairbanks might do better in two-reel comedies with Mabel Normand; but both film and performance were a hit with critics and public (it was based on 'The New Henrietta' in which Fairbanks had starred on Broadway; it later became Keaton's *The Saphead*). Griffith directed *Double Trouble* and then Fairbanks was turned over to director John Emerson and scenarist Anita Loos who are usually credited with harnessing his huge smiling energy; from their creation was to come the eventual Fairbanks persona. In the 11 films he made for Triangle in 1916, he was 'a young vigorous man as uncompromising as his splendid physique, unfazed by tricky problems of taste and class behaviour, gallant to women, with an affection for the American scene tempered by a wink' (Alistair Cooke in a Museum of Modern Art monograph, 1940). The films debunked the phoney and pretentious, leavened with some even healthier athleticism: *His Picture in the Papers*, *The Habit of Happiness*, *The Good Bad Man* (a Western with Bessie Love), *Reggie Mixes In* (as a playboy saving Bessie from gangsters), *Flirting With Fate*, *The Half-Breed* (in which he braved a forest fire) and *The Case of the Leaping Fish* (where he took on with both hands another element, Water).

Of the next one, *Manhattan Madness*, Fairbanks's biographers, Ralph Hancock and Letitia Fairbanks ('Douglas Fairbanks: The Fourth Musketeer', 1953), note that a contemporary critic commented that it was 'really nothing more than St Vitus' Dance set to ragtime'. And David Robinson (in 'Hollywood in the Twenties', 1968) finds that Fairbanks's back-slapping 'looks nowadays a ludicrous caricature of the extrovert personality'. But *Manhattan Madness* was a wow at the time; hardly less so were *American Aristocracy* (also with Jewel Carmen), *The Matrimaniac* (with Constance Talmadge) and *The Americano* (down South as 'an all-round chap, just a regular American'). With this one (December 1916) his contract was up; he was now getting $10,000 a week, but considered this chicken-feed compared with what his pictures were earning: thus was set up the Douglas Fairbanks Pictures Corp., with distribution through Artcraft (later Famous Players –

Douglas Fairbanks in his early days as a star.

Lasky). With him went Emerson and Loos, and director Alan Dwan, though Fairbanks himself worked increasingly on the creative side of his pictures.

In Again Out Again (17) was the first: 'Doug again, too–sounds like him, doesn't it?' said Picturegoer. It was a modest effort which sent up the pacifist movement (the US had just gone to war; and it should be noted that the Fairbanks character was especially acceptable to Americans during the uneasy period of neutrality, and now, war). *Wild and Wooly* marked a further refinement of the character: here he was chained to a desk, but hung up on shooting Red Indians out west: henceforward he was to represent a free spirit, at odds with that Brooks Brothers suit mentality. In *Down to Earth* he sent up hypochondriacs–a scenario he wrote, as he did the next one, *The Man From Painted Post*. *Reaching for the Moon* rounded out his 1917 releases (in all but the first of which Eileen Percy was his leading lady). In 1918 came *A Modern Musketeer* (a young chap inspired by reading about D'Artagnan); *Headin' South*, *Mr Fix-It*, *Say Young Fellow*, *Bound in Morocco*, *He Comes Up Smiling* and probably his worst film, *Arizona* – the only one he directed himself. His leading lady this year (except in *Morocco*) was Marjorie Daw, and she was also with him in his last under his contract, *The Knickerbocker Buckaroo* (19).

During much of this time, Fairbanks, with Mary Pickford and with Chaplin (three heroes such as American history had never known), sold millions of dollars worth of war bonds. Now the war was over, the three of them (with Griffith) founded UA to produce and distribute their own pictures. His first two for that company reflect his own post-war optimism – *His Majesty the American* and *When the Clouds Roll By* – a mood enhanced by his love for Miss Pickford. Both were afraid of the effect of the respective divorces on their popularity, but their marriage (1920) was the most natural thing that could have happened, 'the logical finale of the Fairbanks role as popular philosopher. . . . [They] came to mean more than a couple of married film stars. They were a living proof of America's chronic belief in happy endings' (Cooke). They honeymooned in Europe, and the cities where they stopped were never quite the same again. Simultaneously *The Mollycoddle* was released, a tale of an effete young American bred on the Riviera who finds real red blood in his veins when he returns to his native west.

A similar idea was employed in the next one, *The Mark of Zorro* (20) – Zorro was an indolent fop by day and a dashing Robin Hood by night, but otherwise it marked an entirely new departure, with the emphasis on swashbuckling rather than on social comedy. It was already clear that the disillusioned, more permissive post-war world found Fairbanks the 'do-gooder' somewhat dated, and the actor was anxious to break the mould: nor should his eager desire to please the public be underestimated. He did one more like that – *The Nut* (21) – in case *Zorro* failed; but on the contrary, it was a smash. Fairbanks immediately put *The Three Musketeers* into production. It was a long-cherished dream; he admitted that D'Artagnan had influenced all his film roles (and friends believed that he consciously or subconsciously lived the part in private throughout his life, and he kept thereafter the moustache he had grown for the role). The film's success was such that at last he rivalled Pickford and Chaplin as an earner. Next was *Robin Hood* (22), with the biggest sets and cast assembled in Hollywood up to

The Thief of Bagdad (24): *Fairbanks was just over 40 when he made it, and still at the height of his athletic powers.*

that time – and although it wasn't evident from his Ariel-like presence on the screen, Fairbanks had become absorbed by producing, and these costume spectacles would have been notable without his (very) physical participation. This was one of the most expensive films made up to that time, but it made a profit. Kevin Brownlow thinks it 'the most awe-inspiring' of the Fairbanks costume epics, '. . . unique in every respect. Nobody connected with it ever achieved anything quite like it again.' These were the golden years: Doug was unrivalled, the uncrowned King of Hollywood.

Either *Robin* or *The Thief of Bagdad* (24) was the peak of Fairbanks's career: *Thief* was certainly the most financially successful and the most praised ('An entrancing picture, wholesome and beautiful, deliberate but compelling, a feat of motion picture art which has never been equalled' said a contemporary review) – not that there was any noticeable descent with the next few, though they were somewhat less extravagant, and the actor himself gradually lost a little of his agility: *Don Q, Son of Zorro* (25) with Mary Astor; *The Black Pirate* (26) – in colour – with Billie Dove; and *The Gaucho* (27). In 1929 a silent *The Iron Mask* appeared, to do well amidst the more vogueish Talkies: but it was a farewell to the Fairbanks fans

For years fans had been clamouring to see 'Doug' and Mary co-starring. With the coming of Talkies they gave in to their fans and chose–unwisely– The Taming of the Shrew (*29*).

knew: playing in this D'Artagnan again, he played him as an old man, and died for the first and only time in a film. A few months later he and Pickford, co-starring at last, came out with his first Talkie, *The Taming of the Shrew*: there were theatre prices and separate performances, but the public weren't deceived into thinking that it was better than a third-rate rep production. Its failure didn't help an already shaky marriage –due, apparently, to some casual infidelity on the part of the husband. There is reason to believe that (in the manner of great romances) they continued to love each other, and the melancholia of his last years seems to be due as much to the divorce (in 1935) as to the demise of the career.

In 1931, tired of producing, but still at UA, he accepted a fantastic salary of $300,000 (or $5,000 a day) to do *Reaching for the Moon*, a satire on big business, with Bebe Daniels, which had only a fair success; then *Around the World in 80 Minutes*, which he co-directed with Victor Fleming. It was virtually a travelogue–and like the next, *Mr Robinson Crusoe* (32), was disastrously unworthy of him. He now had shares in Korda's London Films and it was announced that he would make several British films. But the first was a great flop: *The Private Life of Don Juan* (34)–one of Korda's several attempts to emulate the success of his *Henry VIII*. Fairbanks again proved himself competent as a Talkie actor but his accent grated and the old magic had gone. There were no others.

During his last years, he lived frequently in Europe, and after his divorce was married to Sylvia, Lady Ashley (who later briefly nabbed Clark Gable). In 1936 he publicly announced that he had retired from acting. Two years later in London he announced that he had formed Fairbanks-International, a new producing company, with capital of £500,000 sterling. He was planning *The Californian* to star his son, Doug Jr, when he died in his sleep of a heart attack in December, 1939. A folk-hero had departed.

Douglas Fairbanks Jr

Douglas Fairbanks Jr was the first instance of the second generation in movies. He never achieved anything like his father's renown, and maybe because he was his father's son he was always underrated. They were hardly comparable, except on those few occasions when Doug Jr turned swash-buckler, when he was equally as athletic as his father and just as debonair. He had even more charm than his father, and attempted with ease a wider range of parts; but in a generally unsatisfactory career he was less overshadowed by Senior than by other actors of his own very gentlemanly type. Watching him, one is aware of a host of other actors – Ronald Colman, John Barrymore, Errol Flynn, William Powell, even on occasion Gary Cooper and Cary Grant. He explained once why he never really cared for acting: 'I began to be embarrassed that the interpretation was really someone else's creation . . . realizing my own limitations, I became aware that I could never be a creative actor. I would only be an interpretative one or an imitator' (quoted by his biographer, Brian Connell, 'Knight Errant', 1955). As for following in his father's footsteps, they 'were so light that they left no trace for anyone to follow. My respect for his work is so considerable that I don't believe *anyone* could successfully emulate him.' But if Junior's talent was neither individual nor varied, it was always singularly refreshing.

He was born in New York in 1909, of his father's marriage to Beth Sully. After the divorce, the boy lived with his mother. The first film offer came to them when he was 13, from Jesse Lasky of Paramount, who frankly admitted that his aim was to exploit the Fairbanks name. The film in which he starred the boy, *Stephen Steps Out* (23), was carefully carved from Richard Harding Davis's 'The Grand Cross of the Crescent', and told of Stephen's adventures in the wicked Orient; but despite kind reviews, it was a miserable failure. Senior, whose views on Junior's film career were widely publicized, took some consolation from that fact; later, he accepted that Junior wanted and could have a successful career, and in the early 30s they became at last quite close friends. At the moment, however, a career seemed out of the question: the youngster was petitioning Paramount for work (because the Sully family fortunes were in a bad way and he was the only one likely to make much money) and that studio, because of the failure of *Stephen*, weren't much interested.

Finally he was given a contract at a minute sum, and expected to work as an extra and do any jobs as well as acting in any parts that might seem suitable. Among the films: *The Air Mail* (25) with Warner Baxter and *Wild Horse Mesa* with Jack Holt. Goldwyn cast him as the young lover in *Stella Dallas* and he got good notices but nothing much to follow-up – only small parts in *A Texas Steer*, Rex Beach's *Padlocked* (26) with Lois Moran, *Broken Hearts of Hollywood* starring Patsy Ruth Miller, *Manbait* (27) starring Marie Prevost, *Women Love Diamonds*, *Is Zat So?* with George O'Brien, *The Brass Band*, *Dead Man's Curves* (28), *Modern Mothers* and *The Toilers*. At the same time he was so hard-up that he eked out his pay by writing titles for some Ronald Colman-Vilma Banky pictures as well as for his father's *The Gaucho*. He also acted on the stage – in LA – in 'Young Woodley' and 'Saturday's Children', and this attracted favourable attention to him; but his career didn't take a real upward swing until he met Joan Crawford. Egged on by her, he became more ambitious – they were engaged and the darlings of the fan-magazines. At the end of 1928 he had a good part in Capra's *The Power of the Press* at Columbia, and another immediately afterwards in *The Barker* at WB, turning up to remind Milton Sills, in the title role, of the responsibilities of fatherhood – that was his first Talkie. MGM cast him in Garbo's (silent) *A Woman of Affairs* (29) and he at last began to emerge as a name in his own right and not merely as his father's son.

At Radio he and Marceline Day represented *The Jazz Age* in a part-Talkie. This was the sort of picture Crawford was making. He was her husband by now, and MGM cashed in on public interest by casting them together in *Our Modern Maidens* (the marriage lasted four years, until 1933). Released around the same time were four co-starrers with Loretta Young: *The Careless Age*, *The Fast Life*, *The Forward Pass* and *Loose Ankles*: WB produced these melodramas of little consequence, and Fairbanks also appeared in the WB revue, *The Show of Shows*. He went to Tiffany to do *Party Girl* (30), then returned to WB to appear in *Moby Dick* – but instead did *The Dawn Patrol* with Richard Barthelmess, a change he leapt at. His work was so impressive that WB at last put him under long-term contract. He did a couple with Dorothy Revier, *The Way of All Men* and *Sin Flood*, and one with Billie Dove, *One Night at Susie's*; and was loaned to Universal to play opposite Anita Page in *The Little Accident*, a farce in which he was excellent. But it was supporting Leslie Howard in *Outward Bound* and Edward G. Robinson in *Little Caesar* (31) as the gigolo, that he really made his mark. WB re-wrote his contract, reducing his output to four films a year, and giving him the sort of supervisory powers his father had – over script, direction, costumes, etc. There was no appreciable improvement in quality: *Chances*, *I Like Your Nerve* (32), falling in love with Loretta Young again; *Union Depot*, a personal hit for him, with Joan Blondell; *It's Tough to Be Famous* with Mary Brian, based on the national adulation for

Lindbergh but by a sad coincidence released at the time of the kidnapping of the Lindbergh baby and withdrawn for a while; *Love Is a Racket* with Ann Dvorak, Frances Dee and Lee Tracey – Fairbanks was poor as a chatter columnist; and *Scarlet Dawn* with Nancy Carroll, a drama of the Russian revolution. Around this time he had a story published in Liberty magazine called 'Gay Love'.

He was one of the multitude of unemployed in *Parachute Jumper* (33) along with Bette Davis and Frank McHugh (though he did get work as the title explains), but more fortunate on loan to the RKO *Morning Glory* (as Katharine Hepburn's fiancé). He was a boxer accused of murder hiding out with Young and Aline MacMahon in *The Life of Jimmy Dolan*; and then *Captured!* (a war drama) with Leslie Howard. After *The Narrow Corner* (from Somerset Maugham's sea story, 'freely adapted' said the credits, a huge understatement) he really was unemployed – indeed his quarrel with WB caused them to release his last film without his name on the credits. WB were unhappy because the veto power he had over his material was not being compensated for by any big box-office interest, and because he had wangled them out of the profit they should have made when they loaned him to RKO; at the same time he refused to re-sign with them unless his salary was restored to its pre-Depression level (at one point WB had halved most salaries as a temporary measure). In the event, WB didn't offer him a further contract. He did some stage work, including 'No More Ladies'.

Paramount offered him *Design for Living*, but he was ill and Fredric March played the part; then with his father he went to Britain, where they both acted for Alexander Korda, who had impressed them as a film-maker of international potential. Fairbanks Jr played the mad Czar in *Catherine the Great* (34) and was fairly good while neither film nor Catherine (Elizabeth Bergner) were. He returned to the US and RKO for *Success at Any Price*, one of Colleen Moore's last films, throwing her over for the ritzy Genevieve Tobin in his ruthless scramble to the top. But Britain held his attention for the next few years; his name was linked privately with that of Gertrude Lawrence, and professionally in two plays, 'The Winding Journey' and 'Moonlight Is Silver' and a film, *Mimi* (35), an unsuccessful version of 'La Bohème'. When he needed money, in 1936, he did a quota quickie for WB-

A bench in Central Park during the Depression: Bette Davis and Douglas Fairbanks Jr in Parachute Jumper *(33). At the moment he's a chauffeur but he'll take to the skies in reel nine.*

The younger Fairbanks made some swashbucklers quite as good as his father's: The Corsican Brothers *(41). Between them/him is J. Carroll Naish as the faithful retainer.*

British, *Man of the Moment*, set in Monaco and co-starring Laura La Plante; then, ambitiously, decided to found his own production company. Partnered by, among others, Marcel Hellman, Fairbanks turned out four flops – well, the first, *The Amateur Gentlemen* (36, from Jeffrey Farnol's Regency novel, with Elissa Landi), wasn't at all bad; but *Accused* (with Dolores del Rio) was a feeble court-roomer and *Jump for Glory* (37, with Valerie Hobson) a dull actioner. Fairbanks wasn't in the fourth, *Crime Over London* (it starred Paul Cavanaugh). The company was dissolved with some bitterness, and Fairbanks, disillusioned, said that the films, 'for what they are, have been disastrously expensive', and he considered his career had been 'devaluated beyond recognition'.

He returned to Hollywood, and Selznick offered him the part of the laughing villain, Rupert of Hentzau, in *The Prisoner of Zenda*: it was not the leading role, but it firmly re-established him, and he signed a contract with Selznick for one film a year. He followed up wisely with a couple of comedies at RKO, *Joy of Living* (38, with Irene Dunne) and *Having Wonderful Time* (with Ginger Rogers), and two more good ones. The first was *The Rage of Paris*, which made Danielle Darrieux briefly the rage of the US (she loathed Hollywood and returned to France); despite the title, it was set in New York, and concerned a gold digger and the man who saw through her, but got caught all the same. The other was *Young in Heart*, and Fairbanks was one of the family of cons (his only other picture for Selznick). Then came a bevy of action pictures, most of them – to Fairbanks's satisfaction – incorporating much pro-British propaganda: George Stevens's *Gunga Din* (39); *The Sun Never Sets*, a silly Colonial drama; *Rulers of the Sea*, about the first Atlantic steamship; *Green Hell* (40) and *Safari*, both jungle melodramas. He was in the city jungle with *Angels Over Broadway* (41); then was both of *The Corsican Brothers* (42) in a fairish version

That Lady in Ermine (*48*) *was an unsuccessful attempt to get away from the Betty Grable formula film: but Douglas Fairbanks made a very dashing Prince Charming. It was about a man who falls in love with a portrait and then meets her modern-day descendant.*

of the Dumas swashbuckler. He joined the US Navy; became a Lt-Commander, and perhaps the most honoured of the stars who served.

After four years away, he was greeted by Joan Crawford at a party: 'Darling, of course you're so behind the news, aren't you? I suppose you haven't even heard that I'm no longer with MGM. I'm with Warner Brothers now' (quoted by Connell). Hollywood had not changed; RKO was eager for him to play *Sinbad the Sailor* (47) and he did–it was the most financially successful film of his career. Encouraged, he again formed his own production company, releasing through Universal, and did a couple of similar films, *The Exile* (Charles II's adventures after the Battle of Worcester) and, in 1949, *The Fighting O'Flynn* (Irish soldier of fortune agin Napoleon). The first did so-so business, the second hardly any (it was in black and white and all the–heavy–competition were in colour). In between, in 1948, Fairbanks played opposite Betty Grable in *That Lady in Ermine*, a Lubitsch frou-frou that didn't please her public. Two flops and Fairbanks's career was in jeopardy.

The British knighted Fairbanks in 1949 (one of some 70-odd Americans to be so honoured) for his work in promoting Anglo-US relations, and it was the British who offered him his next film, and one of his best–an exciting political thriller, *State Secret* (50), but it played only unimportant houses in the US. The next was a fantasy about a duck who lays a uranium egg, and so did the film: *Mr Drake's Duck* (51, one of a few films made by director Val Guest to promote his wife, the American Yolande Donlan–an engaging talent, but like the film, too slight). It was Fairbanks's last full-length film. He went back to the US, and, Connell says, 'made every attempt to pursue his professional career . . . [but] it became clear that film production in Britain provided the only outlet'. (Two of Fairbanks's projects were made by other studios, *Knights of the Round Table* and *Elephant Walk*.)

In the event, his British production company began producing TV films, screened as 'Douglas Fairbanks Presents'. He starred in some; and some were shown as featurettes in cinemas (where they looked even more junky than they had on TV). Living mostly in Britain with his second wife, he became a social lion. His interests diversified; and in the 60s his only active show business work has been guesting on TV and some successful stock appearances in the US in 'My Fair Lady'.

Frances Farmer

Beauty and the Beast: the Beauty was Frances Farmer, and the Beast was Alcohol. It was a short and not dazzling career, but it's a shame what happened to her because she was talented, intelligent and gorgeous to look upon. She made very few films, and most of them were rotten: but she is unforgettable in the good ones.

She was born in Seattle, Washington, in 1914, the daughter of an attorney. Whether he was a wealthy attorney is not known, but Farmer worked her way through college (the University of Washington) by waiting on tables and ushering in cinemas, a very serious girl with a keen interest in Little Theatre activities. She won a contest organized by a Seattle newspaper for 'the most marriageable girl'–and the prize was a trip to Europe. During the voyage she met a man with influence in the film world: he arranged a screen test and Paramount signed her. They started her off in a couple of Bs, *Too Many Parents* (36), a military-school yarn with Colin Tapley, and *Border Flight* with John Howard. The reaction was strong and she was upped to being Bing Crosby's leading lady, an heiress, in *Rhythm on the Range*. More impressively, Goldwyn wanted to borrow her for *Come and Get It*, a conventional Edna Ferber story of lumberjack country, directed by Howard Hawks and William Wyler (Wyler took over during shooting at Goldwyn's request). The sparring pair are Joel McCrea and Edward Arnold, and the girl is Farmer–playing mother and daughter. The daughter is not too interesting, but the mother in the early part of the film, a brassy saloon singer, knocks spots off Dietrich's similar role in *Destry Rides Again*.

Farmer became a sensation, the hottest tip for the next big star. Photoplay reported

Frances Farmer with singing waiters in Come and Get It *(36), a performance that seemed to prelude a brilliant career.*

that 'her studio says she is now too precious to play a mere lead, as planned, opposite Gary Cooper'. But her studio was also finding her a thorn in their flesh, as 'difficult' as Hepburn or Maggie Sullavan, having as little truck with the Hollywood silliness. In the end her parts in her next three films were hardly spectacular: *The Toast of New York* (37), with Arnold again (as Jim Fiske) and Cary Grant; *Exclusive*, a newspaper story with Fred MacMurray, and *Ebb Tide* with Ray Milland. None of these made her happy, and she then made Paramount *very* unhappy by insisting on going to New York to do the Group Theater's 'Golden Boy': her lack of stage-training showed, and her looks signalled her out as a Hollywood beauty whether she would or no: but she was happy with the Group.

Paramount considered the momentum had been lost, and when she returned put her into a programmer, *Ride a Crooked Mile* (38), a silly prison drama with Akim Tamiroff and her husband, Lief Erikson. She rebelled again: she preferred to be in New York and she wanted good scripts. Finally, to punish her, she was loaned to United Artists to play a saloon girl in a crass jungle film, *South of Pago Pago* (40) with Jon Hall. She insisted on doing *Flowing Gold* at Warner Brothers, with the Group's John Garfield, but Paramount threw her into three Bs in a row after that: *Badlands of Dakota* (41) at Universal, as Calamity Jane, with Robert Stack; *World Premiere* (John Barrymore at the end of his decline); and *Among the Living* with Albert Dekker. Her career might still have been saved by *Son of Fury* (42)–it was more jungle stuff, and demanded little of her, but it cast her with stars like Tyrone Power and Gene Tierney (Farmer was George Sanders's daughter): but she was copped that year on a charge of drunken driving. Early in 1943 she broke probation and was ordered to a sanatorium.

'From then on,' went a later newspaper report, 'Frances Farmer's epic was one of drinking bouts, nervous breakdowns, and mental homes. With a fair amount of clatter she disappeared.' In 1944 it was reported that she had had another breakdown and had entered an institution. What is certain is that Hollywood turned its back on her and the fan-mags had already forgotten her.

In 1957 Farmer was discovered in a San Francisco hotel working as a receptionist; shortly afterwards she appeared on the Ed Sullivan Show, singing one song. She said that she hoped to restart her career, and in 1958 was fourth-featured in *The Party Crashers*, a teenage drama made for Paramount, and starring Mark Damon, Connie Stevens and another Hollywood lost one, Bobby Driscoll. It was Grade Z stuff, and they didn't get around to distributing it in Britain until 1969. Also in 1958, Farmer married her third husband, Leland Mikesell, a Frisco consultant. She died in 1970.

Alice Faye

Alice Faye belongs absolutely to the 1930s. If the quintessential star of that period was one of those up-and-at-'em dames, Faye, better than anyone, represents the other heroines, the gentle, yielding ones. She was blonde, cuddly, shapely and kind–almost bovine. When men crossed her, she didn't start throwing things (as Betty Grable did later) but quietly left the room, her eyes welling with tears. She smiled a lot. Men in particular adored her. She had a warm contralto voice and, invariably leaning against a pillar with palm-trees and a moon behind, she was given some remarkably fine songs to sing ('Wake Up and Live', 'Now It Can Be Told', 'This Year's Kisses', 'You Turned the Tables on Me', 'There's a Lull in My Life', 'You'll Never Know'). She was no great shakes as an actress, but hers is the supreme example of an amiable temperament caught by the camera. She was/is always a pleasure to see and her position in the constellation can't be overlooked. It was for years, but TV showings of her movies have brought her a new army of fans.

She was born in New York's 'Hell's Kitchen' in 1915, and at 14 joined the Chester Hale Dance Group, touring the Atlantic Coast resorts; later got a job in the chorus of 'George White's Scandals'. The star, Rudy Vallee, heard her sing at a cast party, and gave her a weekly song on his radio show. When Fox arranged to film the Scandals (34), Faye was to have one song in it: but when Vallee's co-star, Lilian Harvey, withdrew (reputedly because her part was too small), Vallee persuaded Fox to give Faye the lead. Her vivacity impressed and Fox also gave her a contract.

She was just another blonde at first. In *Now I'll Tell* she got involved with big-time gambler Spencer Tracy and was killed in an auto accident; then *She Learned About Sailors* (a weak effort with Lew Ayres) and spent *365 Nights in Hollywood* (also originally intended for Harvey). After *George White's 1935 Scandals* (35), she reported to Paramount *Every Night at Eight* with George Raft, and discovered that *Music Is Magic*. Warner Baxter was the *King of Burlesque* (36), in a plot that was entirely typical of Faye's films. Up to that time she was a sub-Harlow blonde, peroxided, with plucked eyebrows and a brassy front, but Zanuck thought she had something better and decided to groom her. Afterwards, she was nice enough to be around Shirley Temple in *Poor Little Rich Girl* and *Stowaway*, between which she was an aspiring actress in *Sing Baby Sing* whose PR man got her involved with drunken has-been actor played by Adolphe Menjou–a hilariously funny comedy. However, she lost Dick Powell to the more classy Madeleine Carroll in *On the Avenue* (37) and wound up herself with a sugar-daddy.

Faye really imposed herself in three pleasant musicals: *Wake Up and Live*, *You Can't Have Everything* and *You're a Sweetheart*, on loan to Universal. She had improved out of all recognition. Freda Bruce Lockhart noted in Film Weekly at the end of 1937 that Faye 'has emerged as a personality of rare charm, a singer whose

A moonlit balcony and the sea beyond: the perfect setting for 30s romance and certainly a constant in Alice Faye's films. It's Tyrone Power here who's just realized he loves her. Alexander's Ragtime Band (*38*).

Alice Faye in Little Old New York (*40*). *Said the ads: 'A spirited belle of the brawling water-front, headlong in love with handsome Robert Fulton, fighting the whole town to win his heart and share his glory. . . .'*

acting touches a deeper level of sincerity than any previous musical comedy artist'. Now she was a fully fledged star, someone you built musicals around. But first she was in two big hits, both with Tyrone Power and Don Ameche, *In Old Chicago* (38), some fiction tagged on to the great conflagration, and *Alexander's Ragtime Band*, some fiction built round more than 20 Irving Berlin songs–a peach of a musical, and her own favourite film. In 1938 she also did a musical remake of the Constance Bennett movie about chorus girls, *Sally Irene and Mary* (Joan Davis had Joan Crawford's old part); and she made the top 10 money-makers that year. She stayed there in 1939, with a straight film, *Tailspin* (as an aviatrix), and a couple of musicals trading on nostalgia: *Rose of Washington Square*, with Power, a thinly disguised account of Fanny Brice's first marriage; and *Hollywood Cavalcade*, with Ameche, her first in colour, a story of the Silent days. Another straight film, *Barricade*, was filmed in hunks over a 16-month period and inevitably a hodgepodge–about a cabaret singer fleeing a murder rap and a drunken reporter (Warner Baxter) holed up in a mission in China besieged by rebel forces: filmed in one month it would still have been a fiasco.

There were two more 'historical' pieces: *Little Old New York* (40), a tale of the first steamship, with Richard Greene as Robert Fulton–she was a saloon keeper; and *Lillian Russell*, a poor performance in the title role, with Edward Arnold playing Diamond Jim Brady for the second time. There was also *Tin Pan Alley*, in which she and Grable had a sister act, and a musical look at the early days of radio, *The Great American Broadcast* (41), plus her first in 20th's series of gay escapist colour musicals, *That Night in Rio* and *Weekend in Havana*. Carmen Miranda was in both and in most that followed, but Faye was replaced by that other blonde, Grable, who had rapidly overtaken her in popularity. Faye wasn't very interested: two parts intended for her–*Roxie Hart* and Aunt Cissie in *A Tree Grows in Brooklyn*–were eventually offered to other actresses. After a year's absence, she did two hit musicals, *Hello Frisco Hello* (43) and *The Gang's All*

Here, but she seemed bored, especially in the second of them. In 1944 her only movie was a guest spot in *Four Jills and a Jeep*. There was talk of retirement but she signed a new contract, one picture a year with story approval. She said that she was tired of doing the same plot over and over, and in the event she made only one film, a murder mystery, *Fallen Angel* (45), in which she was a wealthy spinster 'taken' by Dana Andrews, who had the more glamorous Linda Darnell on the side. 20th begged her to stay on to do *The Dolly Sisters* with Grable, but they had to replace her with June Haver.

Faye wanted to devote herself to husband and family: she had married Phil Harris in 1941 (after a brief union with singer Tony Martin). With Harris she has done occasional radio and TV shows, notably in 'Hollywood Palace': she does it, she says, just for fun. She looks back on her Hollywood career similarly, as great fun. When she did make a movie comeback in 1962 in the otherwise uncharming remake of *State Fair* she made it quite clear that she wasn't back permanently. She told the Evening Standard (London) in 1970 that she would like to make another movie, 'but what in God's name would they want me for now?' The interviewer found her 'natural, relaxed, untroubled by a need to retain the image as it was, completely undisappointing to meet'. And genuinely surprised she should be so affectionately remembered.

Gracie Fields

In their study of the inter-war years, 'The Long Weekend', Robert Graves and Alan Hodges quote a conservative writer, Major Rawdon Hoare, on the subject of Gracie Fields. He described her in 1934 as the only outstanding personality providing healthy entertainment. 'In her own way she has done a tremendous amount of good. In the cinemas there is an absence of healthy amusement, there is too much sex-appeal: but in the performance of Gracie Fields we get a breath of fresh air and an opportunity for some real laughter. This all helps to keep the right spirit of England together–clean-living, with a total absence of anything bordering on the unnatural.' Graves and Hodges go on to say: 'Indeed, Gracie Fields's Lancashire accent and humorous, long-suffering but optimistic sentiment more truly represented contemporary England than slick Americanistic film comedies or heavily modern problem plays.'

This paragon–as 99 per cent of the population of Britain in the 30s could have told you–was born in Rochdale, Lancashire. In 1898. Over a fish-and-chip shop. She started her career by singing in a local cinema, and then joined troupes of various child performers, such as Charburn's Young Stars (at 4*s*. a week). She later toured the halls as a solo act and made her only pantomime appearance as the Princess in 'Dick Whittington' (14) at the Grand, Oldham, before being booked into a revue at Manchester, 'Yes, I Think So'. One of the cast was Archie Pitt, and he later put together another revue, 'Mr Tower of London', and asked Gracie to join it. It toured the provinces, with tremendous success, from 1918 to 1922, when it was finally brought to London: and she conquered London as easily as she had captured the rest of Britain. She went on to do a straight play with Gerald du Maurier, 'SOS' (28), by which time she was a music hall top-liner. In the meantime she had married Pitt, and in 1931 he arranged a film for her, a cheap little effort adapted from a North Country comedy called 'The Likes of 'er'. It was called *Sally in Our Alley*, and Gracie only glimmered, but it was a thumping big success.

She didn't like filming, but the demand was there: by 1934 she was the biggest female draw in British cinemas, and most of the decade she was the biggest draw–period. She made *Looking on the Bright Side* (32) and *This Week of Grace* (33), the latter for the British branch of Radio Pictures, at a fee of £20,000. Gaumont British now offered a contract at £25,000 per film to start with *Love, Life and Laughter* (34) in which she was a village pageant Nell Gwynn falling in love with Ruritanian king John Loder. She didn't of course, get him. Basil Dean, who directed most of her early films, saw her less as a heroine than as a clown, and she was normally lovelorn, only to lose the man to an ingénue in the end. Most of the humour was broad caricature. The pattern was followed in *Sing As We Go*, in which she was a factory girl on holiday in Blackpool. Dorothy Hyson got Loder, and Fields didn't even get comic cop Stanley Holloway. J. B. Priestley wrote it, perhaps the best work he did for the screen. It was a tremendous success and its title song became a theme song for the Depression years in Britain. A snub, however, was administered by C. A. Lejeune: 'We have an industrial north that is bigger than Gracie Fields running round Blackpool Fun Fair.' Priestley also wrote *Look Up and Laugh* (35), which surrounded Fields with a flock of music-hall comics, and that also packed them in.

Gracie Fields in The Show Goes On *(37). Here it's going on backstage, with Queenie Leonard, Isobel Scaife and Elsie Wagstaffe.*

Dean didn't want to direct the next, and asked Monty Banks, a one-time Hollywood Silent comic, to do it. In *Queen of Hearts* (36) he gave her something approaching Hollywood glamour, in an attempt to interest the American market. Dean directed her next, *The Show Goes On* (37), about a North Country girl who, via the halls, becomes a famous cinema star, having been 'moulded' by a prominent impresario. It was suspiciously autobiographical, especially as she later divorced Pitt and married Banks (though she makes it clear in her memoirs that she was more in awe of Pitt than in love with him).

She didn't just make films; her records sold like hot cakes, her stage appearances played to SRO, and when she made a rare radio appearance, all of Britain stayed home. Parliament was once adjourned because she was about to broadcast. Later, in 1939, when she was seriously ill, multitudes gathered outside the hospital, waiting, and the press gave it as much coverage as a Royal sickness. And everyone knew her simply as 'Our Gracie'.

Hollywood had watched her with interest, but was afraid. In 1936 MGM's British boss, Sam Eckman, compared her to Will Rogers: 'two of the greatest comedians of their time, but their humour is strictly national'. However, two years later, Darryl F. Zanuck of 20th decided to take the plunge. He offered £200,000 for four films, 'the highest salary ever paid to a human being', with the option of two more at £60,000 each (some reports speak also of a percentage). Amidst great fanfare, she went to Hollywood, but she didn't like it, and asked whether her first 20th film could be made in Britain. The studio complied; however, they gave her the beauty treatment, and two US leading men, Brian Donlevy and Victor McLaglen, to fight over her. But the film, *We're Going To Be Rich* (38), set in a South African mining community, had a poor plot. Fields said: 'I thought we were going to get something fancier like, so that we could show American audiences what I can do. This film won't do it.' Twentieth tried again, with *Keep Smiling*, but that laid an even bigger egg in the US. Fields returned to Hollywood, but without publicity this time. She still refused to film there: 'I have always been afraid that if I came to Hollywood to work, they'd make me half an' half, sort of, and they mightn't use the right halves either.' So, in their dilemma, 20th left the handling of the next two films to Banks, as if by some miracle he could make Fields in British films an American star. In 1939 she made *He Was Her Man* and *Shipyard Sally*. The four films were entertaining, and did nothing to impair her popularity in Britain–or impose it in the USA.

'Our Gracie' after she had received the 20th Century-Fox glamour treatment.

Then came the war. In the autumn of 1939 Gracie went to sing to the BEF in France, with a great morale-booster, a song called 'Wish Me Luck As You Wave Me Goodbye'. In 1940, when Italy entered the war, Banks was declared an alien (born in Italy, he had in fact lived in the US since he was 10) and Gracie decided that her place was with her husband: he became an American citizen later, but in the meantime, 'the storm broke. Every British newspaper screamed that I had deserted my own country and taken all my money.... I was a traitor.... I'd run away.' Overnight, the national heroine was a dead duck. True, she had settled in Beverly Hills, but she continued to give concerts in Canada and the US, donating all the proceeds to the British war effort (she estimates that she earned £1½ million), and she toured the world entertaining Commonwealth troops; she came to Britain, and sang at munitions factories. Most of the time, when singing in Britain, she met an initial hostility; and eye-witnesses report how, after two songs, she had–movingly–won over her audience. Her war effort went mostly unnoticed in the British press.

There were film offers in Hollywood: she turned down a Laughton picture, *The Man From Down Under*, despite his pleas (Binnie Barnes played it), but accepted an offer from 20th to co-star with Monty Woolley in *Holy Matrimony* (43), a much-liked adaptation of Arnold Bennett's 'Buried Alive'. Twentieth looked around for a follow-up and came up with *Molly and Me* (45), a story based on a hypothetical incident in Marie Dressler's life by her friend Frances Marion, and once announced by MGM for Sophie Tucker, when they had plans to turn her into a big movie star. Woolley co-starred again and Fields was again a housekeeper–this time taking a group of out-of-work actors under her wing. She had a guest spot in the all-star *Stage Door Canteen* (44), but her version of The Lord's Prayer was cut for British showing. She played with Constance Bennett in *Paris Underground* (46)–its British title, *Madame Pimpernel*, explains the plot: it was a poor film, but Gracie's portrait of an ageing but energetic Scottish spinster was first-class.

She hasn't made another film. In 1947 she won Britain back via a BBC radio series and a hit song, 'Now Is the Hour', and in 1950, at the London Palladium, to cheers, she showed a new generation what all the fuss was about. She has been semi-retired since the early 50s, living on Capri with her third husband. Unlike many American 'light' entertainers she has hardly reached legendary status, but she was as good as the best of them. She sang comic songs and sad songs with equal skill, but her magic came mostly from a personality which was 101 per cent natural. She loved her audiences, she loved entertaining, she loved to make people laugh; she was joyously irreverent and if she had any artifice, it never showed. In British Show Business, there has never been anyone like her: none of the subsequent British girl singers come up to her big toenail. Just as Gertrude Lawrence was way out in front as a star of revues and musicals, so Fields easily outclassed all other stars of the Music Hall. When it comes to filming her life-story, it will need the sort of magic casting that was employed when Julie Andrews was engaged to tackle the Lawrence portrayal.

W. C. Fields

The world owed a living to W.C. Fields. He was set upon and put upon by friend and foe alike and even by inanimate objects–even things like socks, telephones, dustbins and golf-clubs. His family (usually) despised him, strangers distrusted him, his employers (if any) disregarded him; he was fair game for cops, an American small-town Lear, permanently encouraged by several large whiskies. 'He played,' said Kenneth Tynan, 'straight man to a malevolent universe which had singled him out for destruction.' He proceeded warily, gingerly side-stepping some pitfalls, tumbling into others with the air of resignation which was his habitual mien. He is not, in *The Man on the Flying Trapeze*, remotely astonished that he can commit a motoring offence while parked–indeed several; and he accepts his tickets from the cops with an almost devil-may-care air of obsequiousness. There was no point in protesting his innocence. On the few occasions he tried, he did it half-heartedly and never got beyond one sentence. If you looked carefully into his puffy little eyes you saw a glimmer there of revolt: the gaze was baleful and there was a dream of revenge. Otherwise his sole defence was to mutter some misanthropic comment out of the side of his mouth. His self-esteem remained unharmed and his confidence unshaken in the belief that he was the sole sane member of the community; and when he found a like-minded crony he didn't complain, but invented some implausible tale of which he was the shining hero: in *Mississippi* he boosts his ego with some valorous deed in the struggle against the Indians: muttering continuously of the way he cut his way through a wall of human flesh. There is a famous instance in *My Little Chickadee* where he boasts of knocking down Waterfront Nell to a barman, who angrily wants the credit for that deed. Unfazed, Fields replies, 'Well, I started kicking her first.'

He was as much a coward as he was a braggart; he cheated at cards; he lied; he drank. In *Poppy* he sold a talking dog (he was a ventriloquist) to a barman; in *The Bank Dick* he tried to persuade his son-in-law to steal some money from the bank where he worked for some fake scheme; and in that same film he tried very hard to persuade a small child to pick up a brick and throw it at its mother. His philosophy was perhaps best expressed in his well-known remark: 'Any man who hates small dogs and children can't be all bad.'

Yet James Agee thought him not only the toughest but 'the most warmly human of all screen comedians'. His perversity and his low opinion of humanity was appealing, and he was consistent, like all great comics, in his approach to adversity. And, like all great comics, his universe is uniquely his own.

It is reckoned that a childhood of exceptional hardship contributed to his comedic beliefs. Certainly, off-screen, he was remarkably like the character he played–if perhaps more aggressive. He was born in Philadelphia in 1879, the son of a British immigrant. When he was 11 he ran away from home after a row with his father, and for several years lived rough (his rasping, wheezy voice was said to be the result of the colds he experienced at this time, just as his bulbous nose was the result of fights with other yobs). He did odd jobs, and took up juggling, which was a vaudeville feat he much admired. At 14, he got a job juggling in an amusement park near Norristown, Pennsylvania, and for the next few years he lived a hand-to-mouth existence in one seedy vaudeville outfit after another. However, vaudeville was prospering and so was he, and by the time he was 20 he was getting top billing. (He married in 1900.) In 1901 he went to London to appear at the Palace; later he toured Europe, South Africa and Australia. In 1907 his act was incorporated in a 'book' show, 'The Ham Tree'; in 1914 he was in a Dillingham show, 'Watch Your Step', doing his billiard act, but after the first night he was cut. However, one of Ziegfeld's aides had seen him, and he joined the 'Ziegfeld Follies', where he stayed until 1921. During the run of his first 'Follies' he made a short, *Pool Sharks* (15), which was mostly his stage act.

In 1923 he had the lead in 'Poppy', a musical about a carny man and the pretty ward he carts round the country with him. All of Fields's subsequent roles stemmed from this one–a conniving but good-natured juggler. During its run he had a small part–comic relief–in a Marion

Davies costume epic, *Janice Meredith* (24). Paramount bought *Poppy* as a vehicle for Carol Dempster and eventually decided to have Fields in his stage role, now somewhat reduced. Alfred Lunt was the juvenile lead; D. W. Griffith directed (it was not one of his major efforts) and for some reason it was re-titled *Sally of the Sawdust* (25). Fields was a great success and Paramount signed him to a contract; he played Dempster's father in another Griffith picture, *That Royle Girl* (26) – he was supposed to be a light relief in what was protracted melodrama. The next one was a star vehicle for Fields, a series of gags built round him as a village druggist, his mishaps and the unlikely things that happen to him, *It's the Old Army Game*. It set a pattern which almost all subsequent Fields films followed – including its reception by the public, which was cool. Most of Fields's movies were liked by the critics, and he had a healthy following, mostly among men, mostly in urban areas; but there were numerous people who did not see him as a star attraction, and for them Paramount kept the running time of his films short enough to constitute a supporting film; and the shorter time also kept costs down.

Fields then made *So's Your Old Man*, *The Potters* (27), *Running Wild*, in all of which he was at odds with his family and/or the local townsfolk; and *Two Flaming Youths* and *Tillie's Punctured Romance* (28), which had carnival and circus backgrounds respectively. Louise Fazenda had the Marie Dressler role in this revised version. Fields tried to con Chester Conklin, as a rich oil man; they made a third consecutive film together, *Fools for Luck*, but were not a notable team. This terminated his contract. He wanted more money and his price was too high – it included the right to insert into his films any material he thought necessary. Indeed, he was difficult to work with, and his celebrity made him impossible. He returned to the stage, in 'Ballyhoo' but continued to think of himself primarily as a screen comic.

His first sound film, *The Gold Specialist* (30), was a two-reel re-enactment of one of his stage routines. He made four more shorts in 1932–3 for Mack Sennett (at an amazing $5,000 a week) – *The Dentist*, *The Fatal Glass of Beer*, *The Pharmacist* and *The Barber Shop*. Paramount distributed, and it was with Paramount again that he eventually signed, after casting around Hollywood to see who would pay him most. His first two Talkies for Paramount were on a picture-by-picture basis and it wasn't until the success of *International House* that they put him under contract. First, at WB he did *Her Majesty Love* (31), as the disreputable father of a Marilyn Miller aiming at high society.

Paramount suffered under him, as Tynan

If I Had a Million (*32*): *Alison Skipworth and W. C. Fields in a sequence that required every ounce of their comic gifts – deliberately and philanthropically wrecking the cars of road hogs.*

Cukor's David Copperfield *(35): some who saw the 1970 British version thought longingly of this earlier version and especially of Fields's Micawber. Freddie Bartholomew was David.*

put it, until 1938, but the majority of the films he made were classic. With Sound, Fields had come into his own, and the critics' approval became adoration–but public reception remained as it had been. The series consisted of: *Million Dollar Legs* (32), a delicious comedy with Jack Oakie and no discernible plot or logicality; *If I Had a Million*, an episode in which he and Alison Skipworth, the perfect feminine counterpart in guile, deliberately wrecked the cars of road-hogs; *International House* (33), which was just as inconsequential as *Legs*; *Tillie and Gus*, with Skipworth, as a card-sharper who takes over a decrepit river boat; and *Alice in Wonderland* found him unrecognizable as Humpty Dumpty. The *Six of a Kind* (34) were Fields, Skipworth, Burns and Allen, Mary Boland and Charlie Ruggles–only they weren't, really: Fields and Skipworth were not the sort of crooks the other four innocents ever expected to tangle with, on this trip out west or anywhere else. They don't appear until towards the end of the film, but the other four were marvellous: this might well be the funniest film ever made. *You're Telling Me* was a remake of *So's Your Old Man* and *The Old-Fashioned Way* was from a story by Fields himself, about a bunch of theatrical troupers in the sticks, whose leader, the Great McGonicle, always needs to keep one step ahead of the sheriff. *Mrs Wiggs of the Cabbage Patch* was a historic sudser about Mrs Wiggs (Pauline Lord) living in happy squalor, made bearable only by Zazu Pitts as a spinster neighbour and by Fields in a last-minute appearance as her (Pitts's) eye-to-the-main-chance suitor. *It's a Gift* is quintessential Fields, trying to cope with Baby LeRoy and nagging wife Kathleen Howard. André Sennwald wrote in The New York Times: 'Perhaps if the W.C. Fields idolators continue their campaign on his behalf over a period of years his employers may finally invest him in a production befitting his dignity as a great artist. In the meantime such comparatively journeyman pieces as *It's a Gift* will serve very adequately. . . .' It hardly looks journeyman today.

Fields was now reaching the peak of his popularity and idolators must have been happy when Paramount loaned him to MGM for *David Copperfield* (35). Blessed with good direction (Cukor's) and a fine cast (Edna May Oliver, Basil Rathbone, Roland Young, Lewis Stone, Elsa Lanchester, etc.) it was in every way a good reflection of the original, and press approval carried it into the Motion Picture Herald's list of the year's top money-makers. Fields played Micawber, and was very flattered at being asked; but he did not play the part with an English accent as his contract stipulated and he reputedly tried to insert a sequence where he did some juggling. The result, however, was a true and touching Micawber.

Mississippi came from an old Booth Tarkington story, dusted off the shelf as a vehicle for Bing Crosby, with Fields as a standby. The result was something of a shambles, because Crosby and all concerned let Fields have his way with most of his scenes; but among the magnolia and crinolines, Fields's humour was welcome. The Times (London) thought his Commodore 'a glorious creation, and he can, from the audience's point of view, never tell too often of his deeds against the Indians'. *The Man on the Flying Trapeze* was a meaningless title: Fields was henpecked and how! It's one of his funniest films. Then *Poppy* (36) was remade, under its rightful name. He was seriously ill during much of the shooting, and it was completed with a sometimes clearly visible double. He was off

One of the great comic teamings of all time: Mae West and W. C. Fields (plus Indian) in My Little Chickadee *(40). But the film, alas, wasn't very funny.*

the screen for two years, for a year of which he gave up drinking (which proved to his friends how ill he was); and in *The Big Broadcast of 1938* (38) he looked considerably older. But he was not too ill to fight with Paramount or to seek a new studio which would pay him more money. He went to Universal.

His biographer, Robert Lewis Taylor, states that 'he was at the height of his powers. His illness, his troubles, his suspicions, his worries and frights had only served to sharpen his genius. He was at once at the twilight and at the climax of his career.' At Universal he got $125,000 per film, plus $25,000 for contributing the story, which was usually merely an outline on a scrap of paper. Taylor remarks that Universal, like Paramount, deserve great credit not only for their forbearance with an extremely difficult man, but their courage in permitting him 'to turn out products of his that defied every law of the industry, and sometimes netted a minute financial return'. The Fields cult was by this time quite large and vociferous; and his four films with Universal were greeted hysterically. Truth to tell, only one is very good.

You Can't Cheat an Honest Man (39) co-starred him with Edgar Bergen, the ventriloquist, and his dummy Charlie McCarthy (Fields did a radio programme with them). Officially directed by George Marshall, Fields's sequences were directed by old friend Edward Cline, because Marshall was incapable of handling Fields – and Cline found it little easier. *My Little Chickadee*, the historic meeting with Mae West, was no better – again perhaps due to internal dissensions: they were supposed to have collaborated on the script, but Fields was non-cooperation personified. West said: 'There is no one quite like Bill. And it would be snide of me to add, "Thank God". A great performer. My only doubts about him come in bottles.' However, *The Bank Dick* (40) worked. Fields wrote story and screen-play (under the name Mahatma Kane Jeeves) which was why, perhaps, Time was able to describe it as '74 minutes of almost clear Fields'. James Agee bracketed it later with *It's a Gift*, 'fiendishly funny and incisive white-collar comedies, [which] rank with the best comedies (and best movies) ever made'. At the time William Whitebait wrote: 'Fields is a comedian of almost Shakespearian

The Bank Dick (*40*)*: Fields as Egbert Souse (pronounced Sousé he insists) held up by bandit Al Hill on his first day as bank guard.*

mould. He is loud-voiced, dauntless, self-sufficient–one of those human balloons no amount of puncturing can deflate.' The title of the next one came from P. T. Barnum's famous dictum, already used to advertise one of Fields's silent pictures, *Never Give a Sucker an Even Break* (41). It has marvellously droll moments and bits of the best of Fields, including a lack of plot (contributed by him). Agee felt that backstage bickering may have marred it.

Certainly there were then no takers in Hollywood. Fields cast around for new deals without success. Ill with polyneuritis, he also stepped up his drinking. In 1942, 20th put him with Margaret Dumont in one episode of *Tales of Manhattan*, but it was cut from the final print; his other three film performances were as himself in grade B musicals: he did his pool-hall act in *Follow the Boys* (44); reopened his feud with Charlie McCarthy in one short scene of *Song of the Open Road*; and was one of several turns (Cab Calloway, Sophie Tucker, etc.) in *Sensations of 1945*. He died on Christmas Day, 1946–ironically, for he pretended to loathe Christmas. His friends put an ad in the Hollywood Reporter which described him as 'the most authentic humorist since Mark Twain'.

He did not lack for panegyrists during his lifetime–and has certainly not since his death. Taylor's excellent biography (49) paints a vivid picture of a great artist and impossible man, and there have been good books on his films by Donald Deschner and on his art by William K. Everson. His films, after a lag in the late 40s and early 50s, have been constantly revived, and by the late 60s he had become a cult figure. A record of soundtrack clippings was issued in the US in 1968. His voice is aped by comics as often as those of James Cagney and Peter Lorre. All the same he *is* one of the immortals, arguably the best comic since Talkies came in.

Errol Flynn

Errol Flynn's notoriety considerably out-stripped his fame even at its height, and his fame way outstripped his talent. He blamed his studio, claiming that the run of stereotyped roles caused him to lose faith in himself as an actor. He might have been a poor actor, but as a personality–in those stereotyped roles–he was unique. More recent actors in tights just aren't in the running; and, in the Talkie period, no actor swashed so blithe a buckle. When Flynn stopped fighting and fencing, costume films became much less fun. As Richard Schickel remarks, he was 'a laughing cavalier'. He was also handsome, and his screen work gave just the impression of the real-life peccadilloes for which a big movie star might be forgiven: vanity, impatience, lechery, sauvity. Sometimes it seemed he belonged in a scented boudoir rather than in the Warner studio, but there were some memorable occasions on screen. Said Jack L. Warner in his memoirs: 'As a matter of fact, he had mediocre talent, but to the Walter Mittys of the world he was all the heroes in one magnificent, sexy, animal package. . . . Actor or no actor, he showered an audience with sparks when he laughed, when he fought, or when he loved.' He was, said Warner, 'one of the most charming and tragic men I have known'.

Flynn was born in 1909 in Hobart, Tasmania, into a family more respectable then he was ever to be (his father was a professor). Before he arrived in films he was a professional adventurer: he had worked passage on ships, prospected for gold,

Robin Hood has a midnight tryst with Maid Marian (Olivia de Havilland) in her room at Nottingham Castle – for the most innocent of reasons. But then there is a knock on her door. The Adventures of Robin Hood (*38*).

managed a plantation, hunted tropical birds, smuggled diamonds and served with the New Guinea Constabulary. He once stood trial for the murder of a native marauder on a jungle camp. Or so he claimed in an early memoir, 'Beam Ends'. There was a grain of truth in some of it: but certainly in 1926–7 he was a shipping clerk. Later he accompanied an expedition to New Guinea, and his appearance in a film of that trip led to an offer to play Fletcher Christian in a local semi-documentary, *In the Wake of the Bounty* (33). MGM bought it and used bits in their own *Bounty* film. The producer, Charles A. Chauvel, advised Flynn to leave Australia if he wanted to act, and Flynn went to Britain and landed a job with the Northampton Rep. A couple of their productions found their way to London, and Flynn was offered a job in *Murder in Monte Carlo* (34) – a film he hoped would remain in obscurity. WB produced, and at the end of the first day's shooting, he was offered a contract at $150 a week.

Transferred to Hollywood, he was 11th-billed playing a corpse in a Perry Mason story, *The Case of the Curious Bride* (35), and he supported Warren William again in a comedy, *Don't Bet on Blondes*. Then WB decided to take a chance on him when Robert Donat failed to turn up for *Captain Blood* (according to one version there was a dispute over the fee, but more likely Donat had not definitely committed himself): the sets were waiting, and Flynn became Rafael Sabatini's pirate-hero. Much of the early shooting was scrapped because of his inadequacy, but he began to acquire authority – and the charm was there (not that acting was required with dialogue like 'Follow me, m'hearties' and all). Olivia de Havilland co-starred, and they were re-teamed in *The Charge of the Light Brigade* (36), a stirring tribute to British gallantry set in India (except for the finale–otherwise it was our old friend, the Bengal Lancers picture). The contrast between the prim and pretty de Havilland and the assured, gallant Flynn was a happy one and it made happy box-office; and they liked each other. Says de Havilland's friend, Bette Davis, in her memoirs: 'But it was Olivia de Havilland whom he truly adored and who evaded him successfully in the end. I really believe that he was deeply in love with her.'

Flynn made four movies before they were re-teamed: *The Green Light* (37), a soppy weepie by Lloyd C. Douglas about a playboy who reforms; *The Prince and the Pauper*, top-billed but appearing late and briefly–the Mauch twins were in the title roles; *Another Dawn*, a triangle melo with Kay Francis and Ian Hunter; and *The Perfect Specimen*, a very funny comedy–*It Happened One Night* in reverse, with Joan Blondell as the reporter and Flynn as the wealthy scion. De Havilland was Maid Marian to his Robin, *The Adventures of Robin Hood* (38), a storybook come to life, in colour; a 'magnificent entertainment' (Photoplay) and a box-office winner. *Four's a Crowd* included them (and Rosalind Russell and Patric Knowles)–a funny comedy. His next co-star was Davis, who didn't care for him, ('but handsome, arrogant and utterly enchanting, Errol was something to watch'); however, she thought him right as the newspaperman in *The Sisters*, though the MFB thought the film was not helped by his 'superficial and unintelligent acting'. Davis was 'appalled' at the prospect of Flynn as Rhett Butler, when it was proposed that WB lend them both as a package to Selznick for *Gone With the Wind*, and she fought for Laurence Olivier as against Flynn for *The Private Lives of Elizabeth and Essex* (39)–nor was she happy about the title, which was changed from the original *Elizabeth the Queen* because Flynn's contract required there to be a reference to him. Still, if a beardless Flynn made no attempt to look or act the part, he was easily the jewel of the court.

With the two pictures that preceded this, 1939 was Flynn's biggest year (he made the box-office 10; was in the British list for some years further): these were the remake of *The Dawn Patrol* and a coloured Western with de Havilland, *Dodge City*. She wasn't in *Virginia City* (40), nor another Rafael Sabatini swashbuckler, *The Sea Hawk*, but was in *Santa Fe Trail*, which had Raymond Massey as John Brown. Brenda Marshall was Flynn's co-star in *Footsteps in the Dark* (41)–he was a detective–and Alexis Smith in *Dive Bomber!*; then Flynn and de Havilland were paired for the last time in *They Died With Their Boots On*, where her quiet gentle Mrs Custer seemed to dominate his reckless, headstrong General: but it is one of his most winning performances. The title of that film proved a boon to jokers a while later when it was learned in court that Flynn made love with his socks on. Stories of Flynn's amatory escapades now culminated in a trial for

Flynn made a number of Westerns, which was just as well because he wasn't very convincing except as a man of action: Virginia City *(40), with Randolph Scott and Miriam Hopkins.*

statutory rape. He was acquitted, and it would become clear that the revelations had not harmed his box-office.

The Aussie accent had long since gone; the Irish charm was to take some years to fade, but after de Havilland departed Flynn was never quite the same. Also in 1941 he quarrelled with Michael Curtiz, who had directed most of his films. It could be coincidental, but the adventure melos he made thereafter were pallid in comparison. *Desperate Journey* (42) was panned: a melo about the RAF and the sabotaging of German war plants, a victorious Flynn at the end cries: 'Now for Australia and a crack at those Japs!' The outcry was so fierce that Hollywood resolved to be more circumspect in its depicture of war (it wasn't). In *Gentleman Jim* he was boxer Jim Corbett, in *Edge of Darkness* (43) a member of the Norwegian underground. He did a Cockney sailor routine in *Thank Your Lucky Stars*, and was in three more war melos: *Northern Pursuit*, *Uncertain Glory* (44) with Paul Lukas, and *Objective Burma* (45). The latter, in particular, reinforced the view that Flynn was winning the war single-handed, and the lack of any obvious British participation in the Burma campaign caused it to be withdrawn from British cinemas.

Jokes about these war exploits coupled with poor films caused a falling-away of the box-office: *San Antonio*; *Never Say Goodbye* (46), a comedy with Eleanor Parker; *Cry Wolf* (47), being sinister to Barbara Stanwyck; and *Escape Me Never*, a weepie with Ida Lupino. Jack Warner suggests that Flynn's disintegration began in 1946, adding that in the final years of his Warner contract he was drinking more than heavily. (During the early 50s Flynn was rehabilitated briefly by marriage to a WB starlet, Patrice Wymore; he had been married twice before: the second wife was Lily Damita, the mother of Sean Flynn who, during the 60s, had a so-so career in routine French and Spanish products.)

A distinctly soggy saga, *Silver River* (48), with Ann Sheridan, did nothing for anyone; but he returned to something like his old favour with *The Adventures of Don Juan*, a jolly piece. And MGM borrowed him to play Soames in *That Forsyte Woman* (49), an efficient performance. He was in *Montana* (50) and *Rocky Mountain*, and back at MGM for *Kim* (with Dean Stockwell as Kipling's boy hero). At Republic he made *The Adventures of Captain Fabian* (51), for which he had written the original screenplay, and his WB contract wound up with a dull adventure story, *Mara Maru* (52). There were three more swashbucklers, but it was apparent that his old zest had gone: *Against All Flags* at Universal; *The Master of Ballantrae* (53), an indie in the UK, from Stevenson's novel; and, in Italy, *Crossed Swords/Il Maestro di Don Giovanni* with Gina Lollobrigida. This was a venture he had assembled himself and was not a success; then he lost every penny he had in an ill-fated attempt to film *William Tell* in Switzerland. The money ran out, and no new backing was forthcoming; the film was never finished, but Herbert Wilcox offered to rescue Flynn from his debtors provided he would co-star with Anna Neagle in a couple of pictures.

Wilcox thought the combination would be box-office – *Lilacs in the Spring* (54) and *King's Rhapsody* (55, Wymore was the ingénue in the latter) but the reverse was true. Wilcox later admitted that Flynn's fans weren't Neagle's and vice versa – and neither went; he makes no mention of Flynn in his memoirs (after all, one of the few top stars he directed). In Britain Flynn also made, for Allied Artists, *The Dark Avenger* and, back home, another routine film, *Istanbul* (56). He was not otherwise in demand, and by all accounts sat around drunk and bitter; he made a cheap little programmer called *The Big Boodle* (57). It got very few bookings anywhere.

However, not long afterwards 20th asked him to play Mike Campbell in *The Sun Also Rises*. This wastrel was his first good part in years, and he got good notices. Warners

A familiar sight in his later films: Flynn and bottle. This one is The Roots of Heaven *(58)*.

took him back for something similar, the boozy John Barrymore in *Too Much Too Soon* (58), the film of Diana Barrymore's autobiography (Dorothy Malone played her; Flynn's own memoirs, 'My Wicked Wicked Ways', were published a year earlier). The film got downbeat reviews and flopped. He then got a stage offer, and found himself on tour in 'Jane Eyre', but left after two weeks and was suspended by Equity: the real reason for his departure was that he couldn't memorize his lines. He did his third screen drunk in a row, in Huston's *The Roots of Heaven* and was again favourably noticed; but there were no further offers, and he became involved in a messy little indie film, a semi-documentary called *Cuban Rebel Girls* (59), which featured his current flame, the teen-aged Beverly Aadland. There were virtually no bookings, despite more sensational revelations unleashed after his death, of a heart attack, in Vancouver, in October 1959. The coroner observed that the body was that of an old, tired man, and Jack Warner says that during the making of *Too Much Too Soon* 'he was one of the living dead'. It is a sad epitaph on the man who was the screen's gayest, sprightliest and most disarming Robin Hood.

Henry Fonda

Other stars come and go, but Henry Fonda goes on forever, with none of the ups and downs that milestone most long careers. It has been a career without éclat, though there was at one time a tendency to regard him as a giant among film actors. The view is hardly tenable, though there are ample reasons why he has endured when so many have fallen by the wayside; and it is a relief to find him still with us in these years of the psychotic and/or cocksure leading man. He is Honest Joe, deliberate, intelligent, slow to anger, chary: as a Western hero, brother to Gary Cooper, the antithesis of men of action like Gable or John Wayne. He speaks quietly with a deliberately (although he himself believes it limits him) flat, unaccented, unemotional voice. As a young man he was rather Caspar Milquetoast, a pleasing light comedian, a patient and finally successful rebel. He really is that dependable likeable actor that so many others have aspired to be.

He was born in Grand Island, Nebraska, in 1905, and started acting as an amateur (with Marlon Brando's mother) with the Omaha Community Playhouse; he became a full-time professional in 1928 and played with the Provincetown Players and later the University Players Guild (Joshua Logan, James Stewart, Margaret Sullavan, Bretaigne Windust, etc.). His first New York appearance was a walk-on in 1929 ('The Game of Life and Death'); he did stock and was for a while a scene designer. He was in New York in 'I Loved You Wednesday' (32) and 'Forsaking All Others' (33); his big chance came as one of the 'New Faces of 1934' and he acquired an agent, who persuaded him to sign a contract with Walter Wanger–two pictures a year starting at $1,000 a week. Before going to Hollywood he did 'The Farmer Takes a Wife'. Twentieth/Fox bought the rights, and Wanger decided that would be his first film (35), generously giving him another $2,000 per week from the $5,000 he was getting for the loan. Janet Gaynor co-starred, and Fonda was seen as the natural successor to her old partner, Charles Farrell. They should have been teamed again in *Way Down East*, but she had an accident and Rochelle Hudson replaced her. He then went to RKO for *I Dream Too Much* with Lily Pons (wags called it 'I Scream Too Much').

Wanger then reclaimed him for three–most notably *The Trail of the Lonesome Pine* (36), the first outdoor Technicolor picture and a huge success: it was his performance as a backwoods mountaineer which established the Fonda persona–idealistic, resolute (Al Capp later admitted that it had inspired L'il Abner). He then did a comedy with ex-wife Sullavan, *The Moon's Our Home*, and the trifling *Spendthrift*, in the title role, with Pat Patterson. His quiet, insistent approach to his parts made him almost unique among *jeunes premiers*; never very different, he fitted wherever he was slotted: a horse-racing story, *Wings of the Morning* (37), with Annabella, filmed partly in Ireland and the first British Technicolor film; a drama, *You Only Live Once* with Sylvia Sidney, Fritz Lang's moving story of an out-of-worker turned criminal; and a rowdy triangle drama, *Slim*, as a telephone linesman, with Pat O'Brien and Margaret Lindsay. He said: 'It was a C picture . . . but there was something about it that was good.' He stayed on at Warners for *That Certain Woman*, a tear-jerker with Bette Davis, and after a Wanger romance with Joan Bennett, *I Met My Love Again* (38), was back there again with Davis in a period piece, *Jezebel*, as the steady but strong-willed beau who will take only so much from her. There was Wanger's ambitious but silly story of the Spanish Civil War, *Blockade*, with Madeleine Carroll; an actioner with George Raft, *Spawn of the North*; a madcap comedy, *The Mad Miss Manton*, with Barbara Stanwyck, which he

Henry Fonda as the ultimate home-spun hero: in John Ford's The Young Mr Lincoln *(39). With him is Spencer Charters.*

Fonda as the wealthy innocent taken by cardsharp Barbara Stanwyck, with ship's steward, in The Lady Eve *(41), one of Preston Sturges's ageless comedies.*

considered 'trashy'; a Western, *Jesse James* (39), as Tyrone Power's brother and partner-in-crime; a grim little drama, *Let Us Live*, with Maureen O'Sullivan; a biopic, *The Story of Alexander Graham Bell*, which he stole from Don Ameche; and another, *The Young Mr Lincoln*, this time in the title role. Its critical reception firmly established him, though it wasn't a great success, a leisurely bucolic piece directed by John Ford at 20th. Ford directed the next two: the huge-grossing and engrossing pioneer piece, in colour, *Drums Along the Mohawk*, with Claudette Colbert; and *The Grapes of Wrath* (40) from Steinbeck's novel about Dustbowl migrants who refuse to be depressed by the Depression: 'Can't nobody wipe us out. Can't nobody lick us. We'll go on forever, Pa. We're the people,' said Jane Darwell, whose performance really made the film (she got a Best Supporting Oscar). Many considered it the first honest, non-sentimental film about poverty. To get it, Fonda (his Wanger contract up) had to sign a seven-year deal with 20th.

This was not a happy time professionally; he had liked Wanger and had at least not minded most of the films he'd been loaned out for; but he hated most of his 20th films: *Lillian Russell* with Alice Faye; *The Return of Frank James*, reprising a character he'd played the year before; *Chad Hanna*, a circus drama–Walter D. Edmonds's best-seller; *The Lady Eve* (41), which he did love–Preston Sturges's brilliant comedy at Paramount, with Stanwyck; another filmed best-seller, Stewart Edward White's *Wild Geese Calling*–he had wanderlust; and *You Belong to Me* at Columbia, a third comedy with Stanwyck, but not up to the earlier two. Along with *The Lady Eve*, he has mentioned liking the Thurber-Nugent *The Male Animal* (42) at Warners; and *The Big Street* with Lucille Ball at RKO wasn't bad either. Of the next, its director, Rouben Mamoulian, at least is on record as disliking it: *Rings on Her Fingers*, a tinny comedy; and it would be hard to feel much affection for the Fonda-Ginger Rogers episode in *Tales of Manhattan*, or a comedy with Don Ameche, *The Magnificent Dope*. The 20th Front Office loathed William A. Wellman's *The Ox-Bow Incident* (43), until it started winning prizes and critical plaudits all over the place; and Fonda objected to *The Immortal Sergeant*, a war story, because the studio had him deferred in order to make it; then he joined the Navy.

He owed 20th three pictures, but much to his satisfaction he only did two: *My Darling Clementine* (46), John Ford's contribution to the Wyatt Earp mythology (Victor Mature was Doc Holliday); and *Daisy Kenyon* (47), a silly Joan Crawford novelette. Between them Fonda took on the Gabin role in *The Long Night*, Litvak's remake of *Le Jour se Lève*: rebel against society. It was critically scorned at the time, but later considered superior to the original. Then he did another for Ford, *The Fugitive*, an attempt to film Graham Greene's 'The Power and the Glory' that was never less than misguided–

Four of Hollywood's most likeable actors in one film: James Cagney, Fonda, Jack Lemmon and William Powell in Mister Roberts *(55). The title role had been a great success for Fonda on Broadway – he played it three years.*

but, hemmed in by political and religious difficulties during the Mexican location work, Ford lost interest. Fonda did an episode of *On Our Merry Way* (48) with James Stewart, and then played a martinet – his first unsympathetic part – in Ford's fine *Fort Apache*.

Then – he was 43 – he turned his back on Hollywood and went to re-establish himself on Broadway. He was in three hits-and-(long) runs: 'Mister Roberts', a likeable study of the crew of a World War II cargo ship, which he played 1,670 times; 'Point of No Return' (51) for another two years; and 'The Caine Mutiny Court Martial' for one year. Warners had bought *Mister Roberts* (55) for filming, and favoured for the title role either William Holden or Marlon Brando (who actually accepted). Fonda was no longer box-office, but Ford, directing, refused to go ahead without him: ironically, they fought over interpretation and even came to blows. Ford's illness removed him from the battle zone (Mervyn Le Roy took over) and Fonda has said that he would never work with him again. The finished film was the year's biggest hit (apart from *Cinerama Holiday*, a special case).

That Fonda had been missed was apparent from the flurry of offers: he was Pierre in the

US-Italo *War and Peace* (56). There was again disagreement about interpretation – with producer de Laurentiis this time: Fonda fought to play the part as written. The result, said Time, was that he seemed to be 'the only cast member who had read the book'. He was still blatantly miscast. Then he had the title role in Hitchcock's documentary-keyed *The Wrong Man*. It was a box-office dud, and so was *Twelve Angry Men*, which he set up himself after being impressed by it as a TV play, a drama about jurymen: but it was a critical success and he has said that he is prouder of that than anything he has done. His performance won a BFA Best Actor award. Sidney Lumet (his debut) directed, and he also helmed *Stage Struck* (57): a remake of *Morning Glory* with Fonda in the Menjou role, it was fatally injured by Susan Strasberg's inability to fill Hepburn's old shoes. Fonda then did a couple of Westerns, *The Tin Star* and *Warlock* (58).

He returned to Broadway in 'Two for the Seesaw' (58), and his film appearances since have been scattered between some more long runs – 'Silent Night Lonely Night' (59), 'Critic's Choice' (60), 'A Gift of Time' (62), etc. He also had a successful TV series, 'The Deputy', in the late 50s. He has said that he does films less for love than money, and to keep his name before the public. The results recently have not been spectacularly interesting, being almost equally divided between ageing sheriffs and ageing politicians (or public officials of some sort). But they have all been chock-a-block with typical Fonda qualities: *The Man Who Understood Women* (59), which he connived to do because he liked Nunnally Johnson's script – but he thought the result a mess and that Johnson shouldn't have directed it (it's a strong contender for the worst film ever made); *Advise and Consent* (61), from Allen Drury's political novel; the Cinerama *How the West Was Won* (62); *The Longest Day*, one of the myriad guest stars in this big-budgeted and successful version of Cornelius Ryan's story of D-Day; the folksy *Spencer's Mountain*, which he disliked; *The Best Man* (63), Franklin Shaffner's version of Gore Vidal's absorbing account of a political convention; *Fail-Safe* (64), Lumet's nightmarish 'hot-line' drama, with Fonda as the President on the phone to Moscow; and *Sex and the Single Girl*, another of Fonda's pet dislikes, mainly because director Richard Quine reneged on several promises (including one to build his and Lauren Bacall's parts till they were as big as Tony Curtis's and Natalie Wood's). There were signs that things were faltering: *The Rounders* (65), with Glenn Ford, was thrown away by MGM on the lower half of double bills; Preminger's *In Harm's Way* did poorly, though buttressed by John Wayne; *A Big Hand for the Little Lady* (66), a comedy-Western, was poorly received, and although in some markets *The Battle of the Bulge* did well, another 'starry' international piece, *La Guerre Secrète*, got very few bookings in the US (as *The Secret Agents*) or Britain (as *The Dirty Game*). Fonda was a master spy in his sequence, filmed in Britain by Terence Young. *Welcome to Hard Times* (67) shared the same fate as *The Rounders*. Don Siegel's *Madigan* was a first-class thriller with Richard Widmark, somewhat flawed by dull sequences involving police-chief Fonda, who didn't help them by letting his integrity tipple over into sanctimoniousness; nor was he very good as the baddie in another poor Western, *Firecreek* (68), with James Stewart. But *Yours Mine and Ours*, a comedy with Lucille Ball, was a big hit, and so was *The Boston Strangler* with Tony Curtis in the title role and Fonda again as a police chief. He elected to do an Italian Western, Sergio Leone's overlong and pretentious *Once Upon a Time in the West* (69), as a double-dyed villain, billed *after* Claudia Cardinale; and he got $50,000 for a two-day guest stint in Robert Aldrich's *Too Late the Hero* (70); then was with Stewart once again in *The Cheyenne Social Club;* and *There Was a Crooked Man*.

Fonda has been married five times; second-generation stars Jane and Peter are the children of second wife, Frances Seymour Brokaw, who committed suicide. He said a few years ago: 'I remember when I first started, working with Fred MacMurray in *The Trail of the Lonesome Pine*. We had both sort of fallen into this, and we were talking about this fantastic money we were making and how, if we could only last two more years and put it in the bank, we could say the hell with 'em'. And [Henry] Hathaway [the director] just laughed, saying we'd still be at it in – I don't recall, 20 years or something like that, and we both thought he was absolutely insane. But here we are, both of us. I think it's incredible.'

Joan Fontaine

As a young woman, Joan Fontaine was one of the loveliest of stars. She looked – as she still does – so right. In her early movie roles she was angelic and unaffected, and later, when she became sophisticated in a typical movie-star way, she remained fetching. Like her sister, Olivia de Havilland, she was

'It's Rebecca's body lying there on the cabin floor': Laurence Olivier and Joan Fontaine in Hitchcock's Rebecca *(40), from Daphne du Maurier's novel.*

impeccably genteel, without seeming either inhibited or formidable. And her acting wasn't bad either.

She was born in Tokyo a year after Olivia, in 1917, of parents who were divorced shortly after. The children went with their mother to the US, where they settled in Saratoga; mother remarried in 1925 (a man called Fontaine, hence the eventual stage name). In her teens Joan paid a visit to her father in Tokyo: when she returned, Olivia was a successful actress. She started towards the same goal, as Joan Burfield: first with a little theatre group in San José, then in a production of 'Kind Lady' starring May Robson. MGM tested her and cast her as Joan Crawford's sophisticated rival in *No More Ladies* (35), but it was a minute role and nothing came of it. She returned to the stage (as Fontaine) in Dodie Smith's 'Call it a Day' – the same role her sister played in the film version. This was in LA and someone at RKO caught a performance. She was signed to a contract.

She had an insignificant role in *Quality Street* (37), and was then starred in a B with Preston Foster, *You Can't Beat Love*. RKO liked her work, and cast her as leading lady in two musicals, *Music for Madame* with Nino Martini and *A Damsel in Distress* with Fred Astaire. There had been much speculation as to who would succeed Ginger Rogers as his partner, and Astaire had turned down Ruby Keeler as being unsuitable to play an English aristocrat: Fontaine was right for that; she was unlike Rogers in many ways – and was given only one dance so that comparisons weren't invited. But she caused little comment whatever and returned to Bs: *Maid's Night Out* (38), *Blonde Cheat*, *The Man Who Found Himself* with John Beal, and, more importantly, *Sky Giant* with Richard Dix and *The Duke of West Point* with Louis Hayward. She was Fairbanks Jr's love interest in *Gunga Din* (39), directed by George Stevens, and was loaned to Republic to play Dix's first wife in *Man of Conquest*, her first bitchy part. RKO then dropped her, but she was tested by Cukor for Scarlett O'Hara, as a result of which she had the only sympathetic part (if you discount Norma Shearer) in *The Women*.

Having progressed nowhere and being on the point of marrying Brian Aherne, she decided to abandon her career – but sat next to David O. Selznick at a dinner party and was invited to test for *Rebecca* (40) – she had been urging Margaret Sullavan on him. Selznick had a hunch there and then that she might be perfect. She was. As the shy, mousy, uncertain second wife of Laurence Olivier her poignancy added immeasurably to the drama and suspense: Hitchcock, said W. H. Mooring, 'has succeeded in transforming Joan Fontaine from an unsatisfying feminine decoration into a great screen

Joan Fontaine was probably never more beautiful than in the Technicolor Frenchman's Creek *(44). Here she entertains her pirate lover, Arturo de Cordova, 'the scourge of the Cornish coast', with the aid of butler Cecil Kellaway.*

actress'. Picturegoer readers voted her their Gold Medal. Selznick had her under contract, but he found her difficult to handle. She refused to go to Universal for *Back Street*, claiming it was an unworthy follow-up to *Rebecca*; part of the trouble was that he saw her as a defenceless, very feminine heroine, while she considered herself more the Constance Bennett type. He won: she was another uneasy wife (Cary Grant's) in *Suspicion* (41), loaned with Hitchcock to RKO, for this version of Francis Iles's 'Before the Fact': the performance brought her an Oscar and the New York Critics award, though observers considered these were compensations for not winning with *Rebecca*. In *This Above All* (42) she and Tyrone Power made a very solemn couple, oh-so-British, with her showing him the way to patriotism in the end; the British atmosphere was sillier than most. She was a teenager in the film of Margaret Kennedy's *The Constant Nymph* (43), and Charles Boyer was the composer (a part played by husband Aherne in the British version of 1935). Then she was *Jane Eyre* (44) among studio-bound Yorkshire moors, and much too pretty, but by sheer will she managed to project some of the right innocence before the film rolled downhill. *Frenchman's Creek* found her as another Daphne du Marurier heroine, a Restoration milady on vacation with pirate Arturo de Cordova: lush and silly. At a cost of $4 million it was the most expensive film yet made in the US (concurrent with MGM's *Ziegfeld Follies*), and not the hoped-for box-office sensation.

Fontaine's appearance in it was extremely glamorous, and she now got a chance to play the sort of part for which she yearned: *The Affairs of Susan* (45)–it was also her first film in years not set in Britain. She was a woman seen through the eyes of four different suitors (George Brent, Dennis O'Keefe, Don Defore and Walter Abel) and it was quite funny: but in appearance she had become interchangeable with any other Hollywood female, and was, into the bargain, developing a fey quality that had once been incipient. Meanwhile, relations with Selznick had worsened: she resented his getting huge sums for loaning her out (he had paid her $11,500 for *Rebecca*, $17,000 for *Suspicion*) and she refused the role that Ginger Rogers eventually played in *I'll Be Seeing You*. After being suspended for most of the year, they decided to call it quits and she returned to RKO for *From This Day Forward* (46) with Mark Stevens, a story of young marrieds in the Bronx.

She was in Edwardian costume for the next three. *Ivy* (47) was the first of a four-pic deal with Universal and had originally been offered to her sister: the story of an ambitious lady, who didn't shrink from using poison as a means to the wealthiest possible husband. The artificial streak in Fontaine's acting sat easily on this character. Later, stronger directors would curb it (and when they didn't, she was uninteresting): it was not countenanced by Billy Wilder on *The Emperor Waltz* (48) – but she was merely decorative in this Bing Crosby musical – nor by Max Ophuls on *Letter From an Unknown Woman* (produced by second husband William Dozier). Of the latter, William Whitebait praised 'the enchantment of the whole piece and especially of Joan Fontaine's performance in it': it is possibly her best work, a beautiful piece of kitsch, young love lost/remembered. Stefan Zweig wrote the original story and Louis Jourdan was the lover who *didn't* remember. Universal disliked it so much they sold it off in Britain to another distributor, who cast it out into the flea-pits, from whence it was rescued by a couple of British critics; but it was never very popular. Fontaine's other Universal pictures were both conventional, *Kiss the Blood Off My Hands*, a phoney domestic drama with Burt Lancaster, and *You Gotta Stay Happy*, a runaway-heiress comedy with James Stewart.

She hit the wicked-lady trail again in one that had originally been announced for her by Selznick, *Born To Be Bad* (50), and it lived up to its title; then signed a three-picture deal with Paramount. *September Affair* was an astute and ingratiating mixture of Kurt Weill's 'September Song', Rachmaninoff, Joseph Cotten and Italian locations: a poor girl's *Brief Encounter*. It was popular, but the other two disappeared on completion: *Darling How Could You!* (51), a predictably feeble adaptation of Barrie's 'Alice-Sit-By-the-Fire', with John Lund; and George Stevens's *Something to Live For* (52). Stevens was a talked-about name because of *A Place in the Sun*, but Paramount threw this away, an intelligent if over-glamorous study of alcoholism. She was a budding actress bent for the skids and Ray Milland an ex-lush from AA sent to help her. She was infinitely touching, proving again that she had no peers when she really tried. With one exception it was her last good film.

Ivanhoe wasted her – she was Rowena; *Decameron Nights* (53), with Jourdan, a four-part film based on Boccaccio, was misbegotten from the start and she was arch in all her parts; *Flight to Tangier* was a programmer and she was an FBI agent; *The Bigamist* a serious but sentimental look at that subject; and in *Casanova's Big Night* (54) she was little more than Bob Hope's feed. She was Mario Lanza's society 'protector' in *Serenade* (56), once offered to Tallulah Bankhead and in the original novel a man; was in one of the late and lesser Fritz Langs, *Beyond a Reasonable Doubt*; and had the 'daring' role of the woman loved by Harry Belafonte in *Island in the Sun* (57), though most audiences were asleep by the time the clinch came. Still, there were many of them, perhaps influenced by the original novel's best-seller status. Her one good picture was Robert Wise's evocation of wartime New Zealand, *Until They Sail*: she played the eldest sister with much of her old skill and warmth.

A Certain Smile (58) with Rosanno Brazzi and *Voyage to the Bottom of the Sea* (61) with Walter Pidgeon were uneasy versions of popular French novels: in the latter she got an overdose of radiation and was then eaten by a shark. She had a supporting role but star billing in *Tender Is the Night* (61), and her brittle limning of Nicole's sister was the only thing in the film that critics liked. After an absence she appeared in one of the better Hammer horror pictures, *The Witches* (66), but her own performance was unremarked upon.

In 1954 she replaced Deborah Kerr in the Broadway production of 'Tea and Sympathy', and has done occasional stage work since, mainly in stock. She married for the fourth time in 1964, and lives in New York, a lady of some wealth and considerable social achievement. She doesn't need to make pictures, she says, and is content to wait until a part comes along which she likes: most of the current parts for women of her age were parts she definitely did *not* want to play. She did begin an Italian picture (*A Girl Called Jules*) in 1970, but there was disagreement over the contracted salary terms and she walked out.

George Formby

The character played by George Formby wasn't original: the gormless North Country boy, tolerated or despised by everyone in the film until the last reel when – more by luck than good judgment – he ousts the baddies and daringly wins the heroine, the girl who all along had been aware of his simple faith and preferred it to his more flashy rivals. At some point he would cause the contents of a shop to fall about its customers, at some point he would unwittingly cross a local dignitary or innocently disclose the secret plans to the villains: then, realizing, he would scream 'Ooooh Mother' and flee. The films always ended with a chase.

It was a character assumed in the 50s by another British Music Hall comic, Norman Wisdom. Both used certain characteristics: the shy grin, the slapstick, the chirpy self-confidence, the resignation over their lack of sex-appeal. But Formby never played for sympathy, and the worst of Wisdom's faults, like the cringe-making attempts at pathos, were never hinted at; and the admittedly rudimentary humour of the Formby vehicles eschewed the sort of unfunny falling over in which Wisdom indulges himself. What made Formby so endearing and ultimately unique was the air with which he carried his naïvety. He had a ukelele which he strummed in moments of stress or with which he serenaded the girl and most of his songs had a quota of crude double entendres: his expression, when he came to those lines, was perfect, a combination of 'Look what a naughty boy I am' and 'It's all in your minds'.

Like Wisdom, Formby never broke the American market, but in Europe, in the then British Empire and in Britain both held sway. For ten years, 1936 to 1945, Formby was one of the top money-makers for British exhibitors. He was top of the British artists from 1938 to 1942 and during that time the only Britisher able to pull his weight with the Tracys, Durbins and Gables. That his appeal was insular–beyond the fact that at that time you couldn't sell in the US a Lancashire accent–was due less to his abilities than his vehicles, which were simple-minded and somewhat frowsy compared with the Hollywood product (West End audiences never liked them). Everybody else liked him because they thought they knew him.

His expertise undoubtedly came from a solid music-hall background. He was born in Wigan in 1904, the son of a popular North Country comedian. He became a jockey, but apparently decided to become a comic after hearing another comedian using his father's material: his first pro appearance was at the Hippodrome, Earlestown, under the name of George Hoy. Later, he paid a local impresario £300 to learn the pantomime business. It wasn't until he was topping the bill that he felt able to take on his real name–his father's name. He later dropped the Jr. His career was managed by his wife, known simply as 'Beryl': he was a shy man and almost certainly would not have bothered but for her.

Originally, he toured the North of England, but as he ventured South he discovered that he was equally appreciated there (which was rarely the case: another North Country comedian, Frank Randle, operating in the 40s, used to film at Manchester little comedies for release in the North, where they were widely successful; the South never took to them at all). Formby's first film, *Boots Boots* (34), was set mainly in the kitchen Below Stairs where he was the humblest servant. Beryl co-starred to save costs–they were exactly £3,000–and it was made in a converted garage in two weeks and looked like it. It was successful enough for the budget to be upped somewhat on the next, *Off the Dole*. Again it did nice business, and at the same time he was becoming nationally famous via radio and records. Ealing Studios, then called ATP, offered him a contract and starred him in *No Limit* (35), an unpretentious story about a young man mad on motor bikes and determined to make his name by winning the Isle of Man TT. The smarties sneer at him and, just as obviously, he overcomes all obstacles (in this case, literally) and wins. There was a girl to encourage him (Florence Desmond) as there was to be in all his films (as in life: when he was earning £30,000 per film, he was allowed only five shillings a day pocket-money). The Ealing films are rather attractive, with some broad and good-hearted satire at the expense of some easy targets. Like Will Hay at a rival studio, like Wisdom later (and like most American comics), the milieu was clearly defined. He followed a readily recognizable craft–thus in *Keep Your Seats Please* (36) he was a bus conductor. There followed: *Feather Your Nest* (37); *Keep Fit*, a send-up of the then current League of Health and Beauty, with Kay Walsh; *I See Ice* (38), ice-skating; *It's in the Air*, the RAF; *Trouble Brewing* (39), from a comic novel by Joan Butler, with Googie Withers; *Come on George* as a jockey; *Let George Do It* (40) with Phyllis Calvert; *Spare a Copper*–as a would-be policeman; and *Turned Out Nice Again* (41). His scriptwriters knew how to exploit him–from these same talents came most of the best post-war comedies–but once the war came, circumstances changed and Formby was no longer the cornerstone of Ealing economics: the last two films at least show a marked decline as though the heart had gone out of the production team (Michael Balcon in his memoir discloses that he cared little for Formby as a person, suggesting he was dumb rather than difficult). Will Hay had left Gainsborough and joined Ealing, and Formby in turn moved on to Columbia-British.

The films he made there continued the decline, though the plots were more amorphous, less constraining: *South American George* (42) with frizzled hair and

George Formby was hardly a hair-cream ad but he had only to strum his ukelele and sing a saucy song for the heroine to capitulate. This one is Googie Withers, later one of Britain's best actresses. Trouble Brewing *(39)*.

a gigolo moustache, the inevitable wartime spy comedy; *Much Too Shy*; *Get Cracking* (43), about rival Home Guard units; *Bell Bottom George*, in the Navy; and *He Snoops to Conquer* (44), as an odd-job man elected to the local council. During this time he travelled throughout Africa, etc., entertaining troops, but his film popularity sank. Both *I Didn't Do It* (45) and *George in Civvy Street* (47) played double bills.

Formby's rejection by the British film industry was complete, and it wasn't due to merely ailing box-office. The industry, during the war, had discovered that it could make more important films than George Formby comedies. It was a portent when James Mason replaced Formby as the biggest British draw, and there began a wholesale rejection of the lighter people who had made the country laugh in the tense pre-war days; in the immediate post-war period there was no laughter from the British studios, only turgid, phoney dramas with titles like *When the Bough Breaks* and *Good Time Girl*. It must have come as quite a shock to their perpetrators – so keen on turning out Hollywood imitations and chunks of British 'art' – to find that the homely cut-ups of pre-war comedy stand up much better in later years.

With the collapse of his film career, Formby went back to the Halls, and the South heard little of him until he appeared at the Palace Theatre, London, in 1951, in a musical, 'Zip Goes a Million' – a belated West End success. He left the cast after a heart attack, but knowing that he had retained the affection of the public. Eighteen months later, in an era dominated by American stars, he topped the bill at the Palladium; and he had another success in London, in panto in 1956, as Idle Jack in 'Dick Whittington'. He did summer seasons and occasional TV and was plagued by ill health. In the winter of 1960–1 he was forced to leave the panto he was doing at Bristol. Simultaneously his wife died; and there was much comment in the press when it was announced that Formby plannned to marry at once a young schoolteacher. He felt called upon to inform the press that the marriage believed to be ideally happy had been killed years earlier by his wife's drinking. Suddenly the British public became sentimental over him, and wished him happiness; but he died of a heart attack in February, 1961, not long before the wedding date.

Kay Francis

Wavishing Kay Fwancis (she had trouble with her Rs) was not one of the greater talents, but she had beauty and intelligence; and in the early 30s–her heyday–her fashions and make-up were eagerly watched by women the whole world over. She was always on the lists of the best-dressed stars. For the men, a good plus was a suggestion that underneath the chic was a nice warm heart.

She was born in 1906 in Oklahoma City. Her mother was stage and vaudeville artist Katherine Clinton, but Kay tried stenography, real estate, PR and marriage before deciding on a stage career; a certain New York socialite fame got her the offer of a stage part, that of the Player Queen in a modern dress 'Hamlet' (25) starring Basil Sydney. She acted under her own name of Katharine (it didn't become Kay till after she was in pictures). Some parts followed, both in stock and in New York, culminating in a feature part in 'Elmer the Great' starring Walter Huston: which led to a good part with that actor in *Gentlemen of the Press* (29). She played a vamp, and Paramount liked her enough to offer a contract. She had only a small part in *The Cocoanuts*, as a shady lady outwitted by the Marx Bros; and was equally slinky and little more important in *Dangerous Curves*, *The Illusion* (with Charles 'Buddy' Rogers and Nancy Carroll) and *The Marriage Playground*, though it was generally conceded that in the first of these she stole the film from Clara Bow. However, after driving William Powell to his doom in *Behind the Makeup* (30) she had her first sympathetic part (with Powell) in *The Street of Chance*. They became a popular team. She was loaned out for *A Notorious Affair* (trying to snaffle Basil Rathbone from Billie Dove) and *Raffles*; offered as a prop for Jeanette MacDonald and Jack Oakie in *Let's Go Native*; and teamed again with Powell *For the Defense*.

Francis took her final step to stardom with *The Virtuous Sin*. It was the first of a series of pulsating romances where she was either forbidden or forgiving (in that particular one she gave herself to Huston in order to save scientist husband Kenneth MacKenna, who became her husband in life): *Passion Flower* at MGM with Charles Bickford and *Scandal Sheet* (31) with George Bancroft and Clive Brook, both triangle dramas; *Ladies' Man* with Powell; *The Vice Squad* with Paul Lukas; *Transgression* at RKO, as a lonely wife turning to Ricardo Cortez for comfort; *Guilty Hands* at MGM as a murder suspect (only prosecuting attorney Lionel Barrymore really did it); *24 Hours*, the bored wife of dipsomaniac Clive Brook; *Girls About Town* (the other was Lilyan Tashman); and *The False Madonna* (32) which was she, posing as a dead woman in the hope of collecting a fortune. *Strangers in Love*, with Fredric March, confirmed earlier hints that she could play comedy, but it was her last for Paramount. That company was having money troubles, and WB made a generous approach to agent Myron Selznick to get three of his big Paramount clients: Francis, Powell and Ruth Chatterton. There was a court battle, resolved by Warners offering to lend her to Paramount when required. WB celebrated their acquisition by offering this as official publicity: 'Has very tender vocal chords and is unable to scream when called upon to do so; to save her throat has somebody else to scream for her.' And by putting her into a couple of stinkers: *Man Wanted* (David Manners as her secretary) and *Street of Women*, whose sole enlivenment was Roland Young.

But then they teamed her with Powell: first in a tricky but gay comedy, *The Jewel Robbery* (she was a baroness, he a burglar), and then in the romantic *One Way Passage*. It has become a classic of the genre, and at the time was respectfully received; but as with most of the straight films that Francis made earlier, some spectators went into wild laughter over it. Laughter was more in order for Lubitsch's *Trouble in Paradise*, for which she returned to Paramount, though resentful that Miriam Hopkins was top-billed over her. It went over schedule, and WB refused to delay the start of *42nd Street*, so Bebe Daniels was given the part intended for Francis, to the latter's annoyance. But it meant that she was free to answer an urgent call from Goldwyn when his socialite discovery, Dorothy Hale, didn't make it before the cameras; the film was *Cynara*, and as Ronald Colman's wife Francis gave one of her most lovely, most typical performances. There were three murky dramas: *The Keyhole* (33) with George Brent; *Storm at Daybreak* (at MGM, with Huston); *Mary Stevens MD*; and then a good one, *I Loved a Woman*, though it was basically a vehicle for Edward G. Robinson. In both *The House on*

Kay Francis and William Powell in One-Way Passage *(32). The reason it was one way was because she had an incurable disease and he was being escorted home for the Chair.*

56th Street (34) and *Mandalay* she bumped off Ricardo Cortez; the former was a not-unenjoyable period melodrama where she sacrificed herself for her daughter after 20 years in prison, but she was miscast in *Mandalay*. Both had been rejected by Chatterton, whose place as Queen of the Lot Francis was slowly usurping.

Wonder Bar–an Al Jolson musical and a big box-office film–was the cause of a well-publicized quarrel with WB, when her part was chopped down to make way for that of new contract player, Dolores del Rio: it was the beginning of a mutual disenchantment that was to end tragically for her. Meanwhile, *Doctor Monica* gave her a good part, and *British Agent*, with Leslie Howard, gave her perhaps her best film. Three consecutive pictures with George Brent, *Living on Velvet* (35), *Stranded* (both directed by Frank Borzage) and *The Goose and the Gander*, indicated that they were not the public's favourite screen team, and of her films that year, only the four-handkerchief *I Found Stella Parrish* (with Ian Hunter) found much favour at the box-office. Warners hoped for better results from *The White Angel* (36)–Francis as Florence Nightingale. After all, director William Dieterle had just done wonders with Paul Muni as Louis Pasteur. But the press considered both film and star antiseptic, and when they died the death at the box-office, Francis was on her way out. It was, said Variety later, the 'final crusher' and WB decided against putting her into *Tovarich*, which they had bought for her. They borrowed Claudette Colbert for the part and Francis threatened a lawsuit. The real trouble was that her huge salary ($227,500 in 1937) was not justified by public response and there were others on the payroll breathing down her neck–like Bette Davis, whose salary was one-fifth of Francis's.

The studio persevered for a while longer: *Give Me Your Heart* with George Brent, from a stage weepie, 'Sweet Aloes', *Stolen Holiday* (37) with Claude Rains, and *Confession* with Basil Rathbone, a shot-by-shot remake of Pola Negri's recent (German) *Mazurka*–in turn based on Gloria Swanson's *The Coast of Folly*, about a mother who kills her ravisher when she learns he is about to lead her daughter down the same primrose path. Filming was marred by battles between Francis and director Joe May. Ian Hunter was also in it, and he was in *Another Dawn*, just another triangle drama, with Errol

Flynn. It was too late for Francis to refer to this batch of films as 'real stinkeroos', too late for producer Hal Wallis's gallant statement: 'It is the producer's business to gauge his public; it is the star's business to trust the producer's judgment. Kay Francis is possibly the only star in the entire history of Warners who has realized this fact and who has been ready to meet us more than half-way.' She said: 'Even if it was me the public so kindly went to see, there was a limit to the number of times a certain type of story or motif could be repeated.'

Warners could not be held entirely to blame. There was a point in the career of virtually every star, no matter how popular and talented, when they failed to draw. Some were lucky – a change of formula or a change of studio worked. There was no public antipathy towards Francis; people were simply tired of the sort of films she made, and when the formula was changed not enough of them heard about it. Maybe they would have if she had co-starred with Flynn again, when he became big box-office, or Cagney, or Gable, but the salaries of the mighty men stars, along with her own, could not be fitted into the budgets. There were two comedies: *First Lady*, as a wise-cracking society dame in a part that had been a hit for Jane Cowl on Broadway, and *Women Are Like That* (38), a marital romp with Pat O'Brien as her drunken husband. 'Poor Kay Francis certainly got a dirty deal in this. Unbelievably gauche and tiresome. . . . Maybe we'd better pretend we didn't know about it' (Photoplay). A couple of duallers were no better liked: the sentimental *My Bill* (she had six children) and *Secrets of an Actress* with George Brent. Francis begged for the part of the Empress Carlotta in *Juarez*, but instead WB announced that Francis would work out her contract in Bs – at $4,000 a week! Tradesters were shocked, and the fact that the move was announced was a professional blow to Francis. She put on a good face and told reporters that she was tired of being a star and looking forward to retiring (now divorced from Kenneth MacKenna, she was expected to marry a German baron), but W. H. Mooring wrote later that Warners almost broke her heart.

Comet Over Broadway, with Hunter, had been turned down by Davis, who got the important *The Sisters*, bought for Francis. *King of the Underworld* (39) was a remake of *Dr Socrates*, with a sex-change: it had been intended as a big one for Francis, but was made on a B budget, and Francis was billed *below* the title, in letters one-half the size of Humphrey Bogart, starred above. After

Women in the Wind – she was an aviatrix, with William Gargan – she left the Warner lot and Davis moved into her bungalow.

Carole Lombard helped her off the skids by getting her into *In Name Only*, as the unhappy wife (emoting heavily) in this triangle drama, and Francis had another good featured part as Deanna Durbin's mother in *It's a Date* (40). She got top-billing again in *Little Men*, as Jo at RKO, but it was a cheap little film. There were more such: *When the Daltons Drove*, a Randolph Scott Western; *Playgirl*, an unsavoury piece about an older woman passing on the tricks of the trade to a young girl now that she's past it; *The Man Who Lost Himself* (41) with Brian Aherne – and then the title role in Jack Benny's *Charley's Aunt*. She played with style and spirit, but it was a part easily overlooked. With equal zeal she supported Don Ameche and Rosalind Russell in *The Feminine Touch* and scored a great success: enough for WB to agree to Huston's wish that she return to co-star with him in *Always in My Heart* (42). At Universal she starred with Diana Barrymore (*her* bid for screen stardom) and Robert Cummings in a comedy, *Between Us Girls*.

When the US entered the war she joined USO and toured with Martha Raye, Carole Landis and Mitzi Mayfair; in 1944 20th decided to star the four of them (as Themselves) in a film about it, *Four Jills in a Jeep*.

Always in My Heart (*42*): *Kay Francis involved with another convict, Walter Huston. She was his unfaithful wife, here visiting him in prison.*

In 1945 she toured in 'Windy Hills'; then co-produced with Jeffrey Bernerd three low-budgeters at Monogram in which she starred: *Divorce* (45), *Allotment Wives* and *Wife Wanted* (46, as a fading movie star). None of them were successful (they do not appear to have reached Britain). She went to New York and replaced Ruth Hussey in 'State of the Union' (46) and toured with it. In 1948 in Columbus, Ohio, she was taken to hospital after an overdose of pills, said to have been caused by the strain of the tour. She was drinking not heavily but more than moderately. She appeared in stock in the East for four years and then retired.

During her years as a big star she had been uncooperative with the press; had she been otherwise, the columnists might have tried to help her during her decline (as they had for others). In her later years she refused to see journalists or discuss her career. She was reputedly extremely bitter on that subject. She died of cancer in 1968, leaving a sum very little short of $2 million, most of it for guide dogs for the blind.

Clark Gable

Clark Gable once said to David O. Selznick: 'The only thing that kept me a big star has been revivals of *Gone With the Wind*. Every time that picture is re-released a whole new crop of young movie-goers gets interested in me.' The 1967–9 revival of *GWTW* easily re-confirmed Gable's place among the immortals. His reputation, having been unassailable throughout the first phase of his screen career, fluctuated in the post-war years and after his death (unlike the reputations of Cooper or Bogart or Tracy) went into diminuendo. But in 1967 Joan Crawford could write, without fear of contradiction: 'Clark Gable was the King of an empire called Hollywood. The empire is not what it once was – but the King has not been dethroned, even after death.'

Gable was born in Cadiz, Ohio, in 1901, and began working in stock companies in his teens, mostly as a handyman. At one point, stranded during a tour, he worked as a lumberjack, and no one, certainly not his colleagues, took seriously the odd acting chores he did. He did some 'extra' work in Hollywood in 1925 (including *The Merry Widow*) but no studio evinced the interest he hoped for. He went to New York, and began to be noticed in small parts in Broadway plays, such as 'Machinal', 'Hawk Island' and 'Love Honor and Obey' (30), which starred Alice Brady. While in the latter he was offered the West Coast lead in 'The Last Mile', Killer Mears, the part that Spencer Tracy was playing on Broadway. In Los Angeles an old friend, Lionel Barrymore, got him a test at MGM: for some reason he appeared in a Polynesian get-up, with a flower behind his ear. Thalberg said no, and he was also thumbsed-down by WB, who tested him for the lead in *Little Caesar*. His agent, however, got him a part (as a heavy) in a Pathé Western, *The Painted Desert* (31), and then MGM changed its collective mind and gave him a contract, for two years with six-monthly options, starting at $350 per week.

He started at eighth on the cast list: in *The Easiest Way*, as star Constance Bennett's brother-in-law, a milkman; moved up one place for *The Secret Six*, a gangster melo; was loaned to WB for another gangster movie, *The Finger Points*, and for an effective bit in *Night Nurse*. By this time the word was out: MGM had a new star. He was rushed from film to film (seven more Gable pictures were released in 1931) to capitalize on the furore, though at one point interest waned so quickly that MGM were prepared to drop him. It was Thalberg who insisted on keeping him. There was *Sporting Blood* and *Dance Fools Dance* with Joan Crawford: the studio was so impressed with the Gable-Crawford sequences in this that a film she had just made with Johnny Mack Brown was scrapped, and Brown's scenes re-shot with Gable. The revised effort was called *Laughing Sinners*: the team was hot box-office and they were soon reunited in *Possessed*. Said James R. Quirk in Photoplay: 'He's everybody's big moment'; but not in Britain – the censor banned it (it was about a politician's illicit affair). Meanwhile, Gable had starred with MGM's other goddesses: slapping Norma Shearer about in a supporting role in *A Free Soul*, and featured opposite Garbo in *Susan Lenox: Her Fall and Rise*, a part destined for John Gilbert, with whom she, reputedly, refused to work. And, as the year ended, fans crowded to see him in *Hell Divers*.

MGM needed a new male star more than somewhat. Their two biggest bets, John Gilbert and Ramon Novarro, were, with the coming of the Talkies, very much on the wane (some vehicles designed to refurbish their he-men images were later re-assigned to Gable): and ever since Cagney had pushed a grapefruit in Mae Clark's face, a new type of leading man was in fashion. The 20s' idols had been suave, slick and attentive towards women. Cagney wasn't. And Gable was better-looking than Cagney and, in a word not current then, more sexy. He had – at first, anyway – little natural instinct for acting, but he was manly and magnetic. He was not courtly. He pushed women around, traded insults with them, pinched their behinds; he pretended to despise them, while secretly adoring. And just as he was every woman's ideal lover (they now realized), he was every man's man, at home in a garage or in a fishing boat; almost a heel, but too considerate; boisterous, unafraid and casual. However, for the moment, he was labelled the second Valentino.

Thrilled as MGM were by the money he was minting, they (according to a biographer, Charles Samuels) 'kept on insisting that Gable was a freak box-office attraction who would disappear once the public was tired of gangster pictures'. When Gable asked for a rise, they offered $50 a week. So he stayed away from the set of *Polly of the Circus* (32, as a priest!) with Marion Davies; until the studio was forced (by the volume of fan-mail) to give in. A year later he was getting $2,500 per week.

He was paired with Shearer again, in the decent film of O'Neill's *Strange Interlude*; and then with Jean Harlow in *Red Dust*. The formula of the latter wasn't new: he chased prim, newly-wed Mary Astor while the tarty Harlow chased him. But the wise-cracks were fresh and the finish classic: while he is recuperating after the now-smitten Astor has tried to kill him, Harlow reads him an especially inane children's story – and his hand creeps up her leg. At the end of 1932 he appeared on the list of the top 10 money-makers, and he was to stay there till the war interrupted his film work. Most of the time he was at second position: somehow

Clark Gable as Fletcher Christian, the unwilling leader of the mutineers (all rebels in Hollywood films started by being unwilling): Mutiny on the Bounty *(35), with Charles Laughton.*

he was overtaken by Shirley Temple, Mickey Rooney or Abbott and Costello.

After that he was loaned to Paramount for *No Man of Her Own*, with Carole Lombard, and then did the remake of *The White Sister* (33) with Helen Hayes. He made *Hold Your Man* with Harlow ('They're at it again,' said Film Daily, 'a sure-fire hit'); *Night Flight* with Hayes and Myrna Loy; *Dancing Lady*, as Crawford's dance-director; and *It Happened One Night* (34). Frank Capra was directing for Columbia (curiously, MGM had once owned the property) and that studio, having failed to get Fredric March, had negotiated with MGM for Robert Montgomery; but on the eve of filming MGM released *Fugitive Lovers*, also a cross-country tale, also with Montgomery. Columbia indignantly refused him and demanded Gable – and MGM complied (to punish Gable, who had just balked at another gigolo-type role opposite Crawford). Both Gable and co-star Claudette Colbert were gloomy about the script and resentful at being farmed out to this minor studio; Capra coaxed them until they finally enjoyed making it, but neither suspected that it would bring them an Oscar apiece, and win another as 'Best Film' – as well as make enough money for Columbia to transform itself into a major studio. (Gable also won a Picturegoer Best Actor Medal.) Another sidelight: because Gable was seen to be wearing no undershirt it was acknowledged that sales of said garment fell almost to zero in the US (till the exigencies of World War II brought in the T-shirt).

Myrna Loy was now Gable's leading lady in *Men in White* (doctors) and *Manhattan Melodrama* (gangsters): she became the third of his three staple co-stars of the period; then he was with Crawford in *Chained* and *Forsaking All Others*; with Constance Bennett in another comedy, *After Office Hours* (35); with Loretta Young at 20th for Jack London's *Call of the Wild*. It was Harlow in an adventure melo, *China Seas*, and Harlow and Loy in the scintillating *Wife Versus Secretary* (36), which came along between his most popular films – two of MGM's big box-offices of the 30s. Coincidentally, he had resisted doing both: *Mutiny on the Bounty* (35) because it was a costume film, and *San Francisco* (36) because he thought he would play second fiddle to prima-donna Jeanette MacDonald. *Mutiny* found him (for the last time without his moustache) opposing the wicked Captain Bligh (Charles Laughton) in a first-rate sea-story, and *San Francisco* as a nogoodnik becoming heroic in an earthquake, one of his strongest, most likeable performances, and with an admirable new sparring partner in Spencer Tracy (in private life he admired Tracy enormously, but was somewhat wary of him, because he was so much better an actor).

Also in 1936 he was in two comedies, *Love on the Run* with Crawford, and *Cain and Mabel* (at WB) with Davies, but in 1937 he cut down his activity, around the same time as he and Loy were voted the King and Queen of Hollywood (the title stuck to him). The 1937 pair were in the disastrous *Parnell*, probably the worst biopic ever made (and the only pre-war Gable film to lose money) and a horse-racing story, *Saratoga*, which was Harlow's last film. He and Tracy were again a first-rate team in *Test Pilot* (38): the girl was Loy, and she was his co-star in his other film that year, *Too Hot to Handle*, an adventure melo about rival news cameramen. He was reunited with Shearer, in the sparkling screen version of Robert E. Sherwood's *Idiot's Delight* (39): he delighted as a song-and-dance man.

Then came *Gone With the Wind* (40). When Selznick first bought the book for filming he announced briefly that the leads would be taken by Tallulah Bankhead and Ronald Colman; but as Margaret Mitchell's novel became the decade's best-seller, the casting of the movie became, apparently, a major concern to all literate Americans. Bosley Crowther writes in his history of MGM: 'On the casting of Rhett, there was no question. Although there was some mention of Gary Cooper, the overwhelming sentiment was that Gable *must* play the role.' There were two snags: Selznick released through UA and MGM would not loan Gable unless they had distribution rights; and Gable didn't want to play Rhett. He said later that he only read the book to find out why everyone clamoured for him to play Rhett– and he still didn't want to. However, the decision was not up to him; and Selznick, to get him, postponed production until his agreement with UA expired, in order to make a deal with Metro (the delay was providential because of the difficulty of casting Scarlett). Two years after buying the book, a year after signing Gable, production commenced, with George Cukor directing. He was soon fired, and it was later admitted that Gable had had him removed because of his preferential treatment of the female stars (Vivien Leigh, Olivia de Havilland); the crunch came when Cukor insisted that Gable cry (on hearing of his daughter's death): Gable felt this would hurt his screen image. However, public opinion had been right; the casting of Gable as Rhett Butler was one of the most right things in the

Before the earthquake: San Francisco (*36*). *Gable ran a gambling saloon, much to the mocking disapproval of diva Jeanette MacDonald. He mocked her too, but he loved her really.*

history of films, and it contributed then, and still does, more than somewhat to the success of that film. In 1942 MGM acquired Selznick's interest in the picture, and have made huge sums on periodic re-issues: during Gable's lifetime it was (by far) the most financially successful film ever made (today it runs neck-and-neck with *The Sound of Music*), and one of his many grudges against MGM when he left them was that they had never offered him even a token gift for bringing the film their way in the first place.

After *GWTW*, it was back to running-the-mill at his own studio, but he carried at least the first two into the year's biggest money-grabbers. The *Strange Cargo* was Ian Hunter as Christ (perhaps) in an allegorical but otherwise routine effort about escaping cons, with Crawford; and *Boom Town* was an overlong epic drama about oil-wells, bolstered by Tracy and Colbert. But MGM at last conceded the right to top-billing, contractually, so it was finis to Gable-Crawford and Gable-Shearer, and when Tracy in turn insisted on top-billing, the Gable-Tracy team was no longer possible. Gable got some new leading ladies: Hedy Lamarr in *Comrade X*, a *Ninotchka*-like comedy; Rosalind Russell in *They Met in*

'Those famous lovers we'll make them forget/From Adam and Eve to Scarlett and Rhett': so ran a song Judy Garland once sang. Gable and Vivien Leigh in Gone With the Wind *(40): he isn't taken in by a show of grief on her widowhood.*

Bombay (41), a spectacularly silly piece of pro-British propaganda – Gable is a con-man who joins the British army to escape justice and becomes a hero; and Lana Turner in both *Honky Tonk* and *Somewhere I'll Find You* (42). In the former he was a saloon keeper insistent that she would appeal to him more in black lace and feathers, and in the latter a reporter following her out to the Pacific war zone. It was, as everyone knew, his last film before he joined the army, and to many moviegoers that was a deprivation on a level with meat-rationing.

Gable himself suffered a loss when his third wife, Carole Lombard, was killed in a wartime air-crash. Earlier he had been married to two ladies considerably older than himself, a cause of much pain to the MGM publicity department; later he married, briefly, Sylvia Lady Ashley who had been married to the elder Fairbanks; and finally a non-professional, Kay Spreckles, who bore him his only child, a son, after his death.

His return film, *Adventure* (45), had originally been planned as a vehicle for Freddie Bartholomew. His co-star was Greer Garson, who had risen to a Queen of the Lot in his absence. He didn't like her (he distrusted clever women) and loathed the slogan 'Gable's Back and Garson's Got Him' (even less did he like one critic's jibe, 'and they deserve each other'). He told the press that he thought the film 'lousy' (and the critics agreed with him), and he also disliked *The Hucksters* (47), a goodish drama of the advertising world. (Indeed, he stalled so long that at one point Errol Flynn was about to start it, borrowed from Warners in exchange for William Powell.) His presence in both ensured them places in the top grossers of their years, but thereafter his appeal began to falter and then plummet. MGM tried hard, but the formula was never quite right: *Homecoming* (48), a wartime romance with Turner; *Command Decision*, an excellent if static war drama where he was over-grim as a general; *Any Number Can Play* (49), with Alexis Smith, a confused gambling melo; *Key to the City*, with Loretta Young, a comedy for most of whose length he gamely trotted about in a Fauntleroy suit and garters; *To Please a Lady* (50) – Barbara Stanwyck – a poor car-racing drama; and, like garters for a sagging box-office, two Westerns, *Across the Wide Missouri* and *Lone Star* (51). They held up at the wickets, but *Never Let Me Go* (52) didn't. It was an Iron Curtain melo, cruelly titled, because Metro had decided not to renew Gable's contract.

He was making *Mogambo* (53) on location in Africa, a remake of *Red Dust* under John Ford's direction. Hugely enjoyable, it proved that in the right film Gable was still the

Gable's last film, The Misfits *(61), with Thelma Ritter and the incomparable Marilyn Monroe.*

All gone: as is a fourth principal of the cast, Montgomery Clift.

King; and, as the returns rolled in, MGM changed its mind. He wasn't staying, however: he had made more money for them than any other individual and was bitter that they wanted him out. The actual parting film, *Betrayed* (54, another war drama with Turner), found him dispirited. It didn't do well.

He signed with 20th for two, for $100,000 each against a percentage of the profits. *Soldier of Fortune* (55) did fair business, but a Western, *The Tall Men*, 'the Gable picture the women have been waiting for during the past 10 years' (Hollywood Reporter), copped a huge $6 million. And Gable came in at 10th on the list of top money-makers. There was an indifferent Western at UA, *The King and Four Queens* (56) and a Southern at WB, *Band of Angels* (57), and then the tide began to turn: *Run Silent Run Deep* (58), in a submarine with Burt Lancaster, and then three comedies for Paramount, all of which did nice business – *Teacher's Pet* with Doris Day; *But Not for Me* (59), a flat remake of *Accent on Youth*; and *It Started in Naples* (60) with Sophia Loren. The King was looking his age – but he was still the King (concluded the fan-magazines, having examined some odd contenders, such as Richard Egan) – even if he was regarded less an actor than an institution. His playing could still be incisive, but he was more tolerant, and the old *désinvolture* had a hint of sadness.

His last film was sad: *The Misfits* (61), written by Arthur Miller for Marilyn Monroe. 'But,' said producer Frank Taylor, 'we felt there was only one actor in the world who expressed the essence of complete masculinity and virility that we needed for the leading role – and that was Gable.' Hedda Hopper disclosed that he was paid $750,000 for it, plus $58,000 for each week's overtime. He died a few weeks after completion of shooting (in November 1960), due possibly to the strenuous location work. Hopper suggests unkindly that his desire for the fee overcame health considerations, and it is probable that he would have liked to have gone out on what looked like a hit. But it is sad that he could not have seen his reviews – overwhelmingly the best of his career: a beautiful and indeed moving performance. Said The New York Times obituary: 'Gable was as certain as the sunrise. He was consistently and stubbornly all man.'

Greta Garbo

She is, ultimately, the standard against which all other screen actresses are measured. Since the time of her second, if not her first, Hollywood film she has not been surpassed. For over 40 years the mystery, the enigma of Garbo has been a statutory feature of magazine journalism, her ability a source of wonder to critics: 'After much brooding and re-appraisal I still cannot make up my mind whether Garbo was a remarkable actress or simply a person so extraordinary that she made everything she did, even acting, seem remarkable' (Isabel Quigley in The Spectator). Writers have speculated, eulogized, have written rhapsodies to her; just as Hollywood itself has never got over her, neither have critics. Here are three more, taken at random over the years. Tully Marshall in Vanity Fair, 1927: 'This affectedly sad, languid, indifferent girl is vibrant with inner life. She has the power to charm men and women. Thousands have called her the Sarah Bernhardt of the films, but Garbo is one of the few who deserve to be mentioned in the same breath.' Life magazine in 1928: 'She is the dream princess of eternity–the knockout of the ages.' André Sennwald in The New York Times in 1934: 'She is the most miraculous blend of personality that the screen has ever seen'; and in 1936 Alistair Cooke despaired: 'When you start to write about Garbo, you are reminded more forcibly than ever that practically all the criticism of emotional acting we have reads like a fourth form essay on the character of Napoleon.'

'La Divine' the French call her. When she was sad there was all the sadness in the world; when she was happy, never such self-indulgence. Fatalistic, enslaving, tough but never bitter, wary but never un-passionate.... Art? Instinct? No one has solved the mystery, not least, it is said, the lady herself. She stands apart from every other star.

She was born in 1905 in Stockholm, the daughter of a labourer. Her first job was soaping men's faces in a barber shop, and later she worked in the PUB department store. She was chosen for a PUB advertising short (21), which led to her doing another, for the Co-op Society's Bakery department, and that led, indirectly, to a comic short called *Luffar-Peter*, made by and with Erik A. Petschler. She cavorted in a bathing suit, but was encouraged to try for a scholarship to the Royal Stockholm Theatre School; while there, she was recommended to Mauritz Stiller, who was looking for an ingénue for *The Atonement of Gosta Berling* (24). Thus began an association considered for years to be akin to that of Trilby and Svengali.

The film wasn't a great success, nor was Garbo noticed: but it did well enough in Germany for its distributor there, Trianon, to offer to Stiller and Garbo a four-year joint contract, and they went to Istanbul to

Garbo's second American film, The Temptress *(26): when her husband invites old pal Antonio Moreno to dinner he lives to regret it....*

make *The Odalisque from Smyrna* (or *Smolna*), a tale of White Slavery during the Crimean conflict. Trianon, however, went bankrupt before filming began, and Stiller and Garbo returned to Berlin to look for work. Through the intervention of fellow-Scandinavian Asta Nielsen, Garbo was signed for the film that she was making for Pabst, *Die Freudlosse Gasse* (25), a gloomy portrait of post-war Vienna. Garbo again was the ingénue (if contemplating–because or poverty–streetwalking). At the same time Louis B. Mayer was in Europe looking for talent: he had seen *Gosta Berling*, and wanted Stiller, but Stiller wouldn't go without his protégée. Mayer thought her too fat but finally agreed to sign her to get Stiller; she was given a three-year contract starting at $350 a week.

Garbo arrived in Hollywood frizzy-haired and dopey-eyed, and MGM didn't know what to do with her. They photographed her with automobiles and animals and hopefully labelled her 'The Norma Shearer of Sweden'. It was Stiller who arranged a striking photo of her in Vanity Fair, and that prompted the studio to use

Garbo and Gable at the end of Susan Lenox Her Fall and Rise *(31). She had been a woodman's daughter and he a promising architect; now she's a barroom tramp and he a drunken construction worker – but she had sought him across two continents.*

her. Stiller got her salary upped to $500, and if Thalberg remained unimpressed by Garbo, there was a part available which he didn't consider good enough for Shearer, that of a Spanish peasant who becomes a prima donna and is thereupon ravished by childhood sweetheart Ricardo Cortez: years later, now a vamp, she revenges herself. Garbo thought the part silly. The film was *The Torrent* (26) and when it opened, she was acclaimed (said Variety: 'This girl has everything, with looks, acting ability and personality').

MGM had realized what they had after the first few rushes, and Stiller, still smarting from not being assigned to her first film, began preparing *The Temptress*; but the studio removed him during shooting (he later made three films for Paramount, returned to Sweden in 1928 and died there not long afterwards). This time Garbo was a Paris hostess who pursues lover Antonio Moreno to South America, destroying him and a lot of other men en route (she ends, appropriately enough, back in Paris as a hooker – at least in Europe: in the version shown in the US she and Moreno were miraculously reunited). She balked at playing another demi-mondaine in *Flesh and the Devil* (27), but enjoyed filming with director Clarence Brown and co-star John Gilbert. Audiences were thrilled by the way Garbo loved Gilbert: no screen actress had ever loved as she did, hungrily, passionately. . . . This was an even bigger success than the first two and, unlike them, was liked in Europe.

But she refused a fourth such part, in *Women Love Diamonds*; and encouraged by Stiller, she stayed at home until her salary was increased from $600 per week to $5,000. It took MGM seven months to capitulate and then, to placate her, they made her Anna Karenina in *Love*. Tolstoy had been modernized and Garbo thought her character had been loused-up by the script as well, but she played it – with Gilbert as Vronsky. MGM then decided that she should play Sarah Bernhardt, but after the script had been re-written eight times, it bore little resemblance to the play about Sarah that they had bought – indeed, *The Divine Woman* (28, with Lars Hanson) was the *n*th Hollywood variation on the 'Nana' theme. In *The Mysterious Lady* (with Conrad Nagel) Garbo was a Russian spy who shoots her chief after she has fallen for an enemy officer. The returns weren't as good as expected, so Gárbo was co-starred again with Gilbert (much was being written about a reputed off-screen romance): *A Woman of Affairs* (29), allegedly based on Michael Arlen's best-seller, 'The Green Hat'. It was a popular film but little else. In *Wild Orchids* Javanese prince Nils Asther challenged husband Lewis Stone for her favours; and in *The Single Standard* she found redemption in the arms of Johnny Mack Brown after a fling with Asther. *The Kiss* re-hashed similar themes, but was given some distinction by Jacques Feyder's direction.

These last four films had been rushed through before the public completely rejected silents, and it was clear that Garbo would eventually have to 'talk'. MGM delayed as long as possible, and interest in her Talkie debut continued to mount: by the time it finally appeared, Talkies had been in for over two years, and virtually every star of Continental origin had gone or was going. MGM advertised *Anna Christie* (30) with the slogan 'Garbo talks!', a phrase that lives on today. After 34 minutes of screen-time, she did: 'Gimme a visky with chincher aile on the saide–and don't be stingy, baby.' The world breathed again, and the film's reception 'proved that Garbo talking was an even more magical figure than Garbo mute' (John Bainbridge in 'Garbo', 1955). A German version was made at the same time, by Feyder, and Garbo reputedly much preferred that version (it couldn't have been difficult; the US version is a literal transcription of the O'Neill play, and very dull). MGM and Garbo relaxed: the studio began to cater to what were regarded as her whims: her distaste for publicity, her insistence on 'closed' sets. The stories of her aloofness were legion, but she was liked and respected by her co-workers.

Her other 1930 movie, *Romance*, cast her again as an opera singer, and again with Stone (this time, her protector), and Stone was also with her in *Inspiration* (31), which critics found neither inspired nor inspiring. Lionel Collier thought Garbo's temperament in it 'so consistently unhappy that it is apt to exhaust the average person's patience'. Anyway, they had seen it all before: Garbo in her familiar role of the tarnished lady who finds true love and suffers when he (Robert Montgomery this time) deserts her 'on hearing of her lurid past'. The presence of new heart-throb Clark Gable did give a lift to the formula in *Susan Lenox: Her Fall and Rise*, and helped to make it one of her biggest successes–an absurd thing about a wood sprite who, spurned by him after a misunderstanding, rises to being one of New York's leading courtesans (seen today, it is not only believable but moving–a remarkable demonstration of her powers).

She had a hankering to play Shaw's St Joan, she told reporters, but MGM cast her instead as that other great lady of war, *Mata Hari* (32) with Ramon Novarro. The Hollywood Reporter found her 'so ravishing, so glamorous and so radiant that her previous performances fade by comparison'. Garbo herself said in a delightful interview in Picturegoer: 'Screen vamps make me laugh tremendously. The fact that I am considered one makes me laugh even more' (presumably an authentic interview, though a later issue of this magazine says she gave her last interview in 1928, i.e. four years earlier).

The formula was shattered when she played the ballerina in *Grand Hotel*, notable also because it broke with a vengeance the rule of one star = one film. There were five stars! One of them, John Barrymore, issued this statement: 'Greta is simple and that is her greatest quality. She's also extraordinarily dexterous. She has a very powerful personality which gives her command of everything she does, but she never depends on it, never considers it an asset. What she does consider is that acting is her job, and she keeps everlastingly at it. It is because she is so completely simple that Garbo bears the unmistakable mark of greatness. Modjeska had it, that same simplicity, so that when she came on stage you expected to see the theatre catch fire. Ellen Terry was another who made it felt, a sudden arrestation, a strange power that held you. Garbo has only to flash on the screen to seize our attention. Her brilliance dispels our dullness. She takes us out of ourselves by the mere accident of her presence. It isn't acting; it has nothing to do with acting; it is something which holds us in its spell–a kind of magic. This magic is Garbo.' *Grand Hotel*'s author, Vicki Baum, on Garbo's performance, thought it better than expected, 'and I expected the utmost'. The author of the next one, *As You Desire Me*, Pirandello, thought Garbo 'at the highest peak of her art'–though he disliked the film of his play. Still, although cast as 'an amnesiac Budapest cabaret artist', Garbo's embroilments were less puerile than usual, and she was able to give her most polished performance so far.

1932 was certainly Garbo's peak as a commercial property: for the last two or

Garbo in the first role she played that was at all worthy of her: Queen Christina *(33)*.

'Garbo Loves Taylor in Camille' *said the posters and ads in 1936. It is impossible to believe in her as a* demi-mondaine*; and impossible not to be moved by her.*

three years she had been appearing near the top of popularity polls and box-office lists, but wouldn't again (in the US, at any rate). Her contract had expired, and there were rumours of retirement. MGM was offering $7,000 a week and Garbo was sticking out for $10,000. She went to Europe on vacation, and would only return on her own terms. They were agreed: a two-picture deal, one of MGM's choice and one of Garbo's and that one a picture about Christina of Sweden. *Queen Christina* (33) was extravagantly admired for itself (Rouben Mamoulian directed) and brought Garbo the best personal notices that she had yet had. Said C. A. Lejeune: 'Under the most fearsome battery of close-ups ever given to a star, she remains aloof. Every inch of the Garbo countenance is exposed to the scrutiny of the audience, every eyelash and pore of the skin presented for our consideration. There is a bedroom scene which would have stripped any other actress spiritually naked. But Garbo is still her own mistress at the end of it.' In Britain, readers of Picturegoer voted this the year's best female performance with a huge 42 per cent of the poll.

Despite the praise, *Christina* was only a modified success in the US, and so was MGM's choice, *The Painted Veil* (34), a chunk of Hollywood-orientated Oriental hokum (only in her performance does some of the quality of Maugham's original novel come through; MGM, incidentally, announced that Maugham had been commissioned to write stories especially for Garbo, but nothing ever came of this). The credits refer to the star simply as 'Garbo', and the word is held in white under the other credits. Despite this, MGM executives in Hollywood had decided to drop her. Those in New York were for keeping her: if her name was weak in the US, she was still the biggest draw everywhere in Europe, and

Garbo as Marie Walewska in Conquest *(37).*

her prestige was needed often enough to sell an otherwise indifferent package of films. Variety acknowledged that she was a goodwill asset, and MGM finally agreed to increase her salary to $250,000 per film, but on a one-film-at-a-time basis.

The first under the new arrangement was a serviceable version of *Anna Karenina* (35) for which Garbo won the New York Critics Best Actress award. She rejected an offer to appear on Broadway at a fee of $10,000 a night, holidayed in Europe and returned to Hollywood to play *Camille* (36), generally considered to be her finest performance (under Cukor's direction): again the New York Critics thought her the year's Best Actress (but in Hollywood, the Oscar voters thought Luise Rainer was: *Camille* provided Garbo with her *first* nomination). Garbo's next part was Marie Walewska in *Conquest* (38), opposite Charles Boyer's Napoleon and under Clarence Brown's direction (he directed her several times; in 1939 he said, 'Garbo to me is a never-ending source of wonder'). MGM were more generously lavish than ever: the film cost over $2 million, almost an unprecedented amount, but it didn't get back its cost in the US as was normal (European takings were 'profit'). During its making Garbo was awarded Sweden's highest honour, the medal 'Litterie & Artibus', and named by theatre owners of the US as one of the 'box-office poison' stars.

Again, her career was in peril. She threatened again to retire, and few voices were raised at MGM to gainsay her. The solution was found: comedy. She had begged the studio to buy *Tovarich* for her, without success; and now in 1939 MGM did buy *Idiot's Delight*–but Shearer did it. Yet plans went ahead to make Garbo gayer. It had long been clear that whereas Shearer and the others had to end in a clinch, audiences didn't mind Garbo dying: but those that stayed away from her gloom might find her

attractive in comedy. As the world darkened, it was informed that 'Garbo laughs!'. The film was Lubitsch's *Ninotchka* (39), and, as Kenneth Tynan pointed out, she pleaded the world's cause: 'Bomps will fall, civilizations will crumble–but not yet–give us our moment!' The mood generally was witty and gay (a Communist converted to Western ways by Melvyn Douglas and Paris), and the world queued to see it. Garbo got another Oscar nomination.

Reassured that the home public wanted to see Garbo in comedy, MGM postponed *Madame Curie* (a pet project of studio and star, though Garbo worried whether it wasn't too 'intellectual' for her) and began to prepare another 'light' subject. There are several versions of the salary negotiations which preceded filming, but the most likely story seems to be that Metro asked her whether she would do *two* pictures for her normal fee. After some thought, Garbo agreed to do one for $150,000; MGM came back and asked whether she would do two for twice that sum, but she wouldn't. The result, anyway, was *Two-Faced Woman* (41), and under Cukor's direction, Garbo enjoyed making it: but she disliked the material, suspecting that it was a studio plot to kill her off. MGM was merely misguided. As *Ninotchka* demonstrated, she had no comedy technique, but she had an instinct for funny situations and a sense of humour that had nothing to do with tongue-in-cheek: Myrna Loy or Carole Lombard she was not. This was frivolous, heartless stuff, posing as her twin sister to win back philandering husband Melvyn Douglas. She appeared (briefly) in a swimsuit and danced the Chica-Choca. Critics and public, yelping for their idol, hurled abuse at MGM; to make things worse, it was condemned by the Legion of Decency and banned in Australia. It was withdrawn 'for tidying up' (a line was inserted to suggest that Douglas knew of the impersonation), but, even so, did indifferent business.

Its failure caused Garbo to reject MGM's next offer, and she decided to withdraw until the European market was open again, until she could play the sort of parts she felt were suitable. Her popularity actually declined in the US after *Two-Faced Woman* because she was not seen to take part in wartime fund-raising schemes like other stars: the American public failed to understand that she could not muck in like other stars, and columnists made the situation worse by tut-tutting over her refusal to 'entertain' by filming, adding that her salary demands were excessive in these 'difficult' times. One biographer, Fritiof Billquist, suggests that, at war's end, she considered herself too old to return to film-making: but of all the speculation over her retirement the only definite fact is that she at first regarded it as temporary. In 1945–6 she seriously considered a remake of *Flesh and the Devil* and a Selznick-produced life of Bernhardt and a year later a life of George Sand, involving Cukor and Laurence Olivier (but in this case backing fell through). In 1949 she signed a contract and accepted a salary advance for a US-Italian version of *La Duchesse de Langeais*, to be directed by Max Ophuls, but according to projected co-star James Mason backing was withdrawn when she refused to meet the backers except in a darkened room. In 1951 Dore Schary of MGM interested her in John Gunther's 'Death Be Not Proud', and was sufficiently encouraged to ask Gunther to prepare a treatment; and a year later Cukor persuaded her to do *My Cousin Rachel*, but she changed her mind the next day: 'I can't go through with it. I have not the courage to make another picture.' Later she flirted with the idea of doing *The Deep Blue Sea*.

She had ever been a timorous actress. Lubitsch had described her as 'the most inhibited person I've ever worked with', and Melvyn Douglas has said that she worried at not being a trained actress (her failure in her last film might seem to have confirmed her limitations).

In the first years of her withdrawal, the press hounded her as they had always done, producing unflattering pictures of her hurrying, in big hats, across airport tarmacs. She still is not left entirely alone by a curious world, but little is known of her personal life; and people who claim to have glimpsed her in the flesh can dine out on it for weeks. It is news when she is said to be considering a film offer, but we have given up hoping she would not withhold herself from us; we ask nothing more of her. MGM are the guardians of the legacy.

For over a decade she was away from us: to the post-war generation she was a name and a catchphrase ('I vant to be alone', originally 'I t'ank I go home now'). In London there was only a week of *Ninotchka* in 1949, and brief showings of that and two others at the NFT in the winter of 1953–4. It wasn't till 1955 that MGM obliged and showed *Camille*. In the New Statesman John Freeman wrote: 'in a series of mostly trivial films – unlike Chaplin she never seems to have *bothered* to insist on the setting which could have heightened her lustre – we fell in love with her, until suddenly . . . she disappeared. . . . Was it possible that the light could shine as we remembered it through a 25-year-old melodrama? But we needn't have worried. From the corny melodramatics of the re-issued *Camille* she distils more femininity, more passion, more humanity, more sheer beauty than the post-war generation has ever seen. Emerging again from eclipse, she is a more refulgent star by comparison with the evanescent galaxy of hellcats and cuties who succeeded her. She died, the other afternoon, in a fierce and tearful silence, broken only by the sobbing of two very young women. . . . My generation was vindicated. At least we knew how to jerk a tear.' And Derek Prouse wrote in Sight and Sound: 'One leaves the cinema after *Camille* uncertain for the moment where familiar bus routes pass, unwilling to dissipate the awed and uplifted certainty that one has been in the presence of greatness.'

Since then, MGM have sneaked out occasional revivals in the world's great cities, but they have been niggardly. The films were shown on TV in the US, but were later withdrawn; when they were shown on Italian TV in 1962–3 cinema attendances fell by 75 per cent. In London in 1963 a Garbo festival created the longest cinema queues seen there for years, and the five-week season was repeated twice. Clarence Brown said that year: 'Today, without having made a film since 1940, she is still the greatest. She is the prototype of all stars.' In 1968 the first complete Garbo retrospective in New York was sold out before it opened. The films are not, as films, much to be proud of, but even the MGM of today, changed beyond measure, must feel proud of having been once associated with her. The old MGM was: their London flagship, the Empire, was on occasion hung with English and American flags – and one Swedish flag.

John Garfield

John Garfield was a strong, sympathetic actor too often trapped in run-of-the-mill films. The titles of two of his early films give an indication of the sort of character he was usually called upon to play – *They Made Me a Criminal* and *Dust Be My Destiny*: it was he of course who was made a criminal, he who was searching for destiny. Chronologically, he came after the Henry Fonda of *You Only Live Once* and before the Brando of *On the Waterfront*. He was invariably the boy from the other side of the tracks, the boy with the chip on his shoulder – but idealistic, you know: he often ended up killed or a killer. When he left WB, which had nurtured him, it was clear that a real talent had been obscured: with all his vigour and pugnaciousness there was a real sensitivity.

Clifford Odets once described his rise from the slums of New York to Hollywood fame as illustrating 'one of the most cherished folk-ways of our people'. Odets was a personal friend, and it was his play 'Golden Boy', in a supporting role, which brought Garfield to the attention of Hollywood. He was born in New York City in 1913. He won a scholarship to the Ouspenskaya Drama School, and served his apprenticeship with Eva La Gallienne's company, and later became connected with the Group Theater, founded by Stella and Luther Adler. The Group Theater was, approximately, as influential in New York in the 30s as the Royal Court in London in the 50s, but almost none of its sentimental left-wing plays have stood the test of time (including 'Golden Boy', the story of a slum boy torn between being a violinist or a boxer).

WB signed him and put him into *Four Daughters* (38), a tender Fannie Hurst story

Priscilla Lane and John Garfield in Dust Be My Destiny (*39*). *Said the original caption: 'The story of a boy who went to reform school to forget what environment had taught him . . . he couldn't forget the school-warden's daughter though!'*

about four motherless girls (the Lane sisters and Gale Paige): he was the poor boy who got mixed up with one of them (Priscilla Lane). Its success spawned several follow-ups, but as Garfield had been killed in it, some changes were made to the characters to accommodate him – *Daughters Courageous* and *Four Wives* (39). Neither was considered to be a patch on the original, which had been a considerable critical success. In the interim he had established himself: *They Made Me a Criminal* (the remake of *The Life of Jimmy Dolan*); *Blackwell's Island*, a programmer; a small role in *Juarez*; and *Dust Be My Destiny* with Lane. The subjects he was given to do were strangely predictable, surrounded by people like Ann Sheridan and Pat O'Brien, in these declining years of WB's tough social-conscious melodramas: *Castle on the Hudson* (40) – the remake of *20,000 Years in Sing Sing*; *Saturday's Children*, Maxwell Anderson's piece about a hard-working family; *Flowing Gold* – oil-wells; *East of the River*, described by Steven H. Scheuer thus – 'typical Garfield yarn about the ex-con who, when put to the test, is a nice guy'; *The Sea Wolf* (41), a good adaptation of Jack London's novel; *Out of the Fog*, taken from Irwin Shaws's 'The Gentle People', about gangsters preying on the innocent; and *Dangerously They Live* – spies.

Garfield got out of the rut and into a better film when MGM borrowed him for *Tortilla Flat* (42), and then his gutsy determination seemed ideal for a war film hero: *Air Force* (43); *The Fallen Sparrow* at RKO; and *Destination Tokyo*. But WB refused to lend him to Columbia for *The Adventures of Martin Eden* or to UA for *Jack London*. He was also in, briefly, WB's two wartime revues, *Thank Your Lucky Stars* and *Hollywood Canteen* (44); and in the ineffectual remake of *Outward Bound* called *Between Two Worlds*, as the cardsharper.

He was *The Pride of the Marines* (45), an ex-soldier adjusting himself to blindness; and Lana Turner's lover in *The Postman Always Rings Twice* (46) at MGM, making good chemistry in this version of James M. Cain's diabolical thriller. Then it was back to more standard fare in *Nobody Lives Forever*, setting out to swindle Geraldine Fitzgerald and falling in love with her; and as a back-street violinist, he tolerated dipso patroness Joan Crawford in *Humoresque*, the last under his contract. Warners wanted him to re-sign, but he considered that he had been badly treated: he had either been given the Cagney and Bogart rejects, or stuck behind the eightball in the same old propagandish story. Instead he formed his own production company and did one of the two films generally considered his best – *Body and Soul* (47), playing a boxer with dumb eloquence. At 20th he was the Jewish soldier in *Gentleman's Agreement* with Gregory Peck; and then he did his other good film, Abraham Polonsky's *Force of Evil* (48), a crime story which did poor business at the time it was released. Dilys Powell wrote: 'John Garfield, who for years has been allowed to re-play himself, is returning to solid interpretation; and his quick, cursive delivery of difficult dialogue is worth attention.' Huston's *We Were Strangers* (49, at Columbia), a tale of revolutionary intrigue in Latin America, did little better at the wickets; nor did *Under My Skin* (50, at 20th) from a Hemingway story about racing. Garfield then returned to WB for another Hemingway subject, 'To have and have not': when WB had originally filmed it, with Bogart, they kept little but the title, so now, when they re-filmed it straight, they dreamed up a new title, *The Breaking Point*. It ranks as one of the best screen versions of Hemingway; Garfield's own performance ('A man alone ain't got no chance') was exceptionally true. He chose then to do an undistinguished crime story, *He Ran All the Way* (51) with Shelley Winters.

Because of suspected left-wing sympathies, he was finding it increasingly difficult in this McCarthy era to find work in Hollywood. Years later a Reuter's article quoted 'a writer friend' as saying: '... the tragedy was that Garfield wasn't accused of anything. He was a street boy with a street boy's sense of honour, and when they asked him to give the names of friends at parties he refused. They blacklisted him for that.

'When he wasn't able to work he ran around in a violent, stupid kind of way. In the end he died of a heart attack. The blacklist killed him.' He was in New York preparing for a revival of 'Golden Boy', in the lead this time, when he died in 1952.

Judy Garland

There was a tribute to her on Australian television after she died: not, said the narrator, 'a blow by blow description of the prolonged finale when press agents were doing dreadful things to the human soul, but the way it was for us in the golden Hollywood years when all was tinsel, glitter, bluebirds and rainbows, when the whole apparatus of illusion was the dream factory in full blast producing its masterpiece – Judy'.

Judy Garland was born of vaudeville parents (like her old side-kick, Mickey Rooney), in Grand Rapids, Minnesota, in 1922. She made her stage debut at three, singing 'Jingle Bells' in the theatre her father managed, and was later teamed with two older sisters as 'The Gumm Sisters' (they were born Gumms). As a kiddie act, it wasn't very successful, and broke up when one of the sisters married; but Judy had already established herself as the outstanding talent of the three and, encouraged by her mother, continued solo. Songwriter Lew Brown caught her act and had her screen-tested at Columbia where he worked; Columbia wasn't buying, but Mother Gumm had acquired an agent who got a test at MGM. Her pianist for the test was Roger Edens, who, 20 years later, described her advent as 'the biggest thing to happen to the MGM musical'. She was 13, and her father had just died.

She made a short with Deanna Durbin, *Every Sunday* (36), but nothing else. Edens got her on to the Jack Oakie Radio Hour, where a 20th scout heard her and arranged for her to be borrowed for *Pigskin Parade*, a rah-rah college musical of no particular merit; and Garland, ninth on the cast list, was just another puppyfat kid. Edens wouldn't give up, and wrote a special version of 'You Made Me Love You' for the child to sing to Clark Gable at his birthday party on the lot: Metro, at last enthusiastic, rushed her and song into *Broadway Melody of 1938* (37). Her notices were warm, and she was featured in *Thoroughbreds Don't Cry* with Mickey Rooney; *Everybody Sing* (38) with Allan Jones and Fanny Brice; *Listen Darling* with Freddie Bartholomew and Mary Astor; and *Love Finds Andy Hardy* with Rooney. She had the lead in most of them, but there was front-office opposition when producer Arthur

Freed wanted to cast her as Dorothy in the big-budgeted *The Wizard of Oz* (39): however, when 20th refused to loan Shirley Temple for it ('thank God' said Freed later), Garland it was. It was a miracle film: from L. Frank Baum's story about the Kansas schoolgirl who journeys to the magical land of Oz with the Scarecrow (Ray Bolger), the Tin Man (Jack Haley) and the Cowardly Lion (Bert Lahr). Frank Morgan was the Wizard. A big hit at the time, it has seldom been out of circulation and nowadays nets MGM a cool million annually when it is telecast in the US. It made Garland world-famous, won her a special Oscar, and gave her a hit record and identification-song ('Over the Rainbow', which was at one point deleted from the finished film).

Babes in Arms, with Rooney, consolidated her success, and they were re-teamed in *Andy Hardy Meets Debutante* (40) and *Strike Up the Band*: contemporary critics thought he overshadowed her, but there is something winning about her work–a directness of emotion in her usually unspoken crush on him and her sad little songs, and the

A detour on the yellow brick road to the Land of Oz: Ray Bolger and Judy Garland in The Wizard of Oz (*39*). *Disney apart, it is the screen's most enchanting fairy-tale.*

unforced precocity of her handling of the more typical peppy songs. MGM signed her to a contract worth \$680,000 (\$2,000 per week going to \$3,000 for the last two of the seven years) and she rewarded them by coming in at 10th that year in the top 10 list. Meanwhile her burgeoning talent got a good chance in *Little Nellie Kelly* with George Murphy, where she played both mother and daughter and as the former had a death scene; and in *Ziegfeld Girl* (41), where she, Lana Turner and Hedy Lamarr were aspirants to stardom–and only she made it, which gave the film a conviction it lacked elsewhere.

In 1941 she also did *Life Begins for Andy Hardy* and *Babes on Broadway*, both with Rooney, and married bandleader David Rose. *For Me and My Gal* (42) marked her first solo billing, supported by Murphy and Gene Kelly, a pleasant vaudeville musical with a patriotic finale. Said Howard Barnes in the New York Herald Tribune: 'Miss Garland is someone to reckon with. Of all the youngsters who have graduated into mature roles in recent years, she has the

Judy Garland in her first solo starring role with her two leading men, George Murphy and Gene Kelly: For Me and My Gal *(42). It was one of the year's most popular films.*

surest command of her form of make-believe.' '... and how good *she* is!' said Agate. 'She is no Venus, let us admit it–but how delightful is her smile, how genuine her emotion, how sure her timing, and how brilliantly she brings off her effects....' *Presenting Lily Mars* (43), from a Booth Tarkington story, found her as another stage-struck girl, and *Girl Crazy*, an old Gershwin musical, again with Rooney. She toured with USO and in MGM's starry support for troop morale, *Thousands Cheer*, sang 'The Joint Is Really Jumpin' Down at Carnegie Hall', accompanied by José Iturbi. She looked thin and edgy. To compensate, MGM (Arthur Freed; and against her will) put her into *Meet Me in St Louis* (44), the second miracle film of her career. It was the first screen musical in years not to use some sort of 'backstage' technique to introduce its songs, a slight, gay, utterly enchanting portrait of a well-to-do St Louis family at the time of the world's fair (Leon Ames, Mary Astor, Margaret O'Brien, and Tom Drake as the boy next door). It is as fresh today as the year it was made–when it was the highest grossing film musical up to that time, and MGM's biggest grosser apart from *Gone With the Wind*.

The director was Vincente Minnelli, who replaced Fred Zinnemann on her next (she and Zinnemann didn't get on) and later became her second husband. *The Clock* (45) was a straight film, a New York weekend with a GI on furlough (Robert Walker) and the girl he meets. James Agee said it proved 'beyond anybody's doubt that Judy Garland is a very sensitive actress. She can handle any emotion in sight, in any shape or size, and the audience along with it.' At the end of 1945 she was one of the top 10 money-makers again, but mostly on the strength of *St Louis*. MGM therefore refashioned *The Harvey Girls* (46) as a musical for her (it was originally planned straight for Turner) and it was almost as good: 'nice' waitresses vs saloon girls in the Old West. John Hodiak was the man. Also that year Garland sang 'The Great Lady Grants an Interview' in the revue-format *Ziegfeld Follies*, and she had two songs, guesting as Marilyn Miller, in the otherwise dreary *Till the Clouds Roll By* (47).

Kelly partnered her in Minnelli's crazy musical spoof of swashbucklers, *The Pirate* (48), a neat money-maker but otherwise probably the least successful of her MGM films; and she was with Fred Astaire in Irving Berlin's joyous *Easter Parade*, one of the top half-dozen grossers of 1948. A successor with Astaire was planned, but before shooting began she was replaced by Ginger Rogers. This was the first time that her health troubles were publicized and the beginning of the reputation for unreliability. The reason given then (and afterwards) was 'nervous exhaustion' and it became common to blame MGM for all Garland's subsequent troubles. There is no question that as a youngster she was on a treadmill, regimented in matters of diet, routine, etc., and

Judy Garland looking wistfully at 'The Boy Next Door': a scene from Minnelli's enchanting Meet Me in St Louis *(44).*

she was still very young when she became hooked on sleeping pills and pep pills: after her death it was disclosed that for years she had relied on pills. Mr Harry Ansliger, former Narcotics Commissioner of New York, 'said that he had attempted to help the singer give up morphine'. His recommendation that she be given a year's rest was rejected by a film studio executive on the ground that 'we have $14 million tied up in her' (reported in The Times, London). But whatever caused her to crack then was presumably the cause of all the later difficulties. Witnesses have said that at one point during these years she first suffered from a lack of confidence, and never again recovered it. In later years she believed she had a God-given talent and reviews and audiences testified to it: but she never overcame her fear of performing. Certainly from the late 40s onwards a nervousness is evident in her work, and it is probable that part of her genius sprang from that–the wistfulness, the fleeting smile, the quirky way with a comic line (she had a reputation as Hollywood's wittiest woman), the warmth poised on the brink of sadness.

In 1948 she seemed edgy again in her segment (two songs, one with Rooney) of *Words and Music*, another 'composer' biopic. But she was more her old self with Van Johnson *In the Good Old Summertime* (49), replacing a pregnant June Allyson. This was *The Shop Around the Corner*, now selling sheet music, and transferred to the Chicago of 1904, but in many ways identical. Halfway through filming *Annie Get Your Gun* she walked off the set and didn't return. The property had been bought for her at the then unprecedented price of $700,000 and the film's costs were then $500,000. She was suspended, and Betty Hutton replaced her. After hospitalization, she returned for *Summer Stock* (50) with Kelly. As shooting dragged along he was reported as saying (echoing Van Johnson's comments the previous year): 'I don't care how long I wait for that girl–I'd wait forever for that magic.' Producer Joe Pasternak said: 'It took six months to make . . . but never once did I hear a cross word, a tart comment, a bitter crack . . . they all understood.' When shown the film turned out to be a gay 'putting-on-a-show' musical. Life magazine said: 'The great song-and-dance actress makes this movie a personal triumph.'

Garland later said that she was insufficiently rested (and her marriage was breaking up) when recalled, to replace Allyson again, in *Royal Wedding*: one day she didn't show and was suspended. The papers reported a suicide attempt (the news is said to have prompted Max Ophuls to conceive his *Lola Montez*) and she was again hospitalized. Plans to star her in the new *Show Boat* were suspended, and in June 1950 MGM quietly and reluctantly scrapped her contract. She was 28.

The only offer of work came from Britain, to appear in person at the London Palladium. The season (51) was a modified triumph–she lacked assurance; but by the time she had finished a record-breaking run at New York's Palace Theater later that year she had begun to acquire that authority and command which were to make her the most potent stage performer of her generation. Indeed, if it can be measured by the pitch of excitement in the auditorium, Garland was the greatest artist of the century: no one who was ever at one of her concerts could ever forget the tiny stocky figure on stage, the huge, warm, dramatic voice and the hysteria invoked in the audience. Because of this latter and because she so absurdly embodied so many Show Business myths, commentators later passed her up; but at the times when she was 'fashionable' she probably got better notices than any of her contemporaries.

Hollywood now wanted her back, and Sid Luft (her third husband) arranged a three-picture deal at Warners, starting with a remake of *A Star Is Born* (54). Shooting went over-schedule and over-budget (though director Cukor insists that this was not Garland's fault; early shooting was scrapped and re-done in CinemaScope). The result was, said Time, 'just about the finest one-woman show in modern movie history'. Penelope Houston in Sight and Sound: 'Since Judy Garland temporarily deserted the screen . . . some of us have been grudging about even the best musicals. Whatever they had, they hadn't got Judy Garland, and, although Hollywood may have found singers or dancers more expert, no one has been able to match the high-strung vitality, the tensely gay personality that made Miss Garland such a uniquely stimulating performer. . . . Her comeback picture proves the sort of personal triumph that helps to explain, and justify, the star system. . . . If we are to believe that Vickie Lester has that elusive, indefinable attribute of star quality, then the actress playing her must positively dazzle us with it. But the special fascination of Judy Garland's playing is the way it somehow contrives to bypass technique: the control seems a little less than complete and the emotion comes through, as it were, neat. In this incandescent performance, the actress seems to be playing on her nerves: she cannot but strike at ours.' The New

The third miracle film of her career: Judy Garland and James Mason in A Star Is Born (*54*).

Statesman: 'Miss Judy Garland is a world in herself. A new world . . . [she] really is one of those feminine wonders that scriptwriters are always trying to conjure up out of the relentless tedium of Hollywood's self-intoxication. The film has got something, too, if not quite as much as Miss Garland. . . .' The Spectator: 'In the end, however, it is for Judy Garland to withstand the full torrent of my admiration. She has lost a little in looks but gained enormously in talent. Warm, sensitive, touching, she always was, but now her pathos has a poignancy and her singing a passion. After hearing her sing "The Man That Got Away" and "Born in a Trunk" I felt she had seized the torch I carry for her from my hand and scorched my soul with it!' This performance did not win an Oscar – Groucho Marx described it as the biggest robbery since Brink's, and the omission remains the film city's greatest injustice. The film itself got raves (and so did co-star James Mason) and was one of the year's top 10 grossers. It was among Variety's 100 top money-makers until eased out in 1968, but for years a rumour persisted that it had flopped. At all events, Warners reneged on the other two pictures.

Garland spent the next six years in cabaret and concerts, and in the early 60s was commanding $5,000 nightly. In 1960 at the London Palladium she hit the peak of her form in a concert, which was repeated the following year at Carnegie Hall and described as the greatest night in show business history. A two-record recording of it sold an unparalleled two million copies. Various film projects had come to nothing (*Carousel*, *South Pacific*) and Garland had had weight problems. In the wake of this new wave of adulation, Hollywood tried again. In *Judgment at Nuremberg* (61), she had an effective nine-minute spot as a blowsy German hausfrau defending her marriage to a Jew: she got raves ('tremendously moving' – Dwight Macdonald) and an Oscar nomination. But the two she carried were hardly successful. *A Child Is Waiting* was a box-office disaster: Burt Lancaster co-starred, and he couldn't save it, a quiet, controlled piece, beautifully directed by John Cassavetes, about mongoloid children. Garland was a teacher. She sang, obviously, in *I Could Go On Singing* (63), made in Britain with Dirk Bogarde, but it offered little to non-devotees: the press loved her but trounced the film, a 30s-type sob story about mother-love. It was announced, however, that she was considering three more films; but she returned to personal appearances, records, and a series for CBS TV. In 1965 she was announced as the mother in the Electronic *Harlow* but didn't play it, and in 1967 20th proudly stated that they had captured 'the legendary Judy' for *Valley of the Dolls*, but she could not be persuaded to leave her dressing-room for the set and was sacked. There were débâcles at concerts when she appeared late, as at her last engagement in cabaret in London in 1969: but she was still breaking house records, and, more curiously, was deeply loved backstage. She never lost the great love she had within show business, and when she died in 1969 from an accidental overdose of sleeping pills, shortly after her fifth marriage, hard-boiled journalists were amazed at the huge demonstrations of public affection. Said Ray Bolger: 'Judy didn't die of anything, except

Her last film: I Could Go on Singing (*63*).

wearing out. She just plain wore out.' She had earned during her career $8 million, but left debts of $1 million.

She had said recently: 'What do I do when I'm down? I put on my lipstick, see my stockings are straight and go out there and sing "Over the Rainbow".' Daughter Liza Minnelli spoke of 'the legend', writers spoke of the gaiety of the young Judy, but finally it is tragic. Just how tragic is witnessed by these British reviews for *I Could Go On Singing*: 'Watching Judy Garland, I have a surge of affection.... It is for something beyond acting that one cherishes this vivid, elated little creature.... It is for the true star's quality. The quality of being' (Dilys Powell); 'One of show-business's all-time magical greats' (Dick Richards); 'She is a harrowingly good actress' (Penelope Gilliatt); 'A few great players are alchemists, who can turn corn golden, and Judy Garland is one of the few' (Paul Dehn); 'She is personally as superb as ever, as enchantingly vulnerable, as thrillingly strident.... Always fascinating to watch, she sometimes makes much out of little' (David Robinson); 'She is a star; the genuine outsize article.... She is an actress of power and subtlety; a singer whose way with a song is nothing short of marvellous.... She is a great artist. She is Judy. She is the very best there is' (Philip Oakes).

Greer Garson

Greer Garson arrived at the time when MGM and cinema audiences really needed her. Garbo and Norma Shearer were on the verge of retiring, and Hollywood needed a big suffering lady (emphasis on the word lady). Irene Dunne, Joan Crawford and others were all very well, but no one was as right as Greer for the matriarch in the mansion. To millions of war-weary women she represented an ideal of nobility and matronhood, clear-browed, capable and unruffled: you really felt she could do her own marketing if called upon to do so. Men cared for her less, but when she wasn't being comfy-wifely, she had a bewitching Irish charm. As an actress she is a puzzle, as up and down as they come: in any given scene in, say, *Random Harvest*, she is as wily, as actressy and as self-consciously charming as it's possible to be, and the next minute she'll take your breath away–effortless, sincere and dead right.

She was born in County Down, Ulster, in 1914. The family moved to London and she studied at its University, intending to become a teacher; instead, she went into advertising and spent her evenings at amateur dramatic clubs. A friend gave her an intro to Birmingham rep, and she bowed there in 'Street Scene'. She was there for two seasons; then made her London debut in the 1934 season in Regent's Park Open Air Theatre, after which she was engaged by Olivier to understudy in 'Golden Arrow' (35): but when he couldn't get Carol Goodner for the lead he promoted her. It was her first break and she became a successful West End ingénue–in 'Twelfth Night' and 'The School for Scandal' among others. On TV she was Juliet to Olivier's Romeo. She had the lead in 'Old Music' (38), and Louis B. Mayer was in the audience, under the misapprehension that it was a musical: Garson impressed him so much that he signed her to a contract starting at $500 a week. In Hollywood she collected her pay check and nothing else. She was about to return to London when director Sam Wood saw a test she had done and requested her for *Goodbye Mr Chips* (39) with Robert Donat; so she returned to London anyway, for the filming. She didn't want to play Mrs Chips because the part was too small (she died after 20 minutes): but the film was a great success and made her famous.

She returned to Hollywood to be much less suitably cast in *Remember?*, a comedy with Robert Taylor that she referred to later as 'Forgive and Forget'; but was appropriate enough as Elizabeth Bennett in *Pride and Prejudice* (40), a part originally intended for Norma Shearer: Clark Gable had long ago refused to play Darcy, so Olivier and she found themselves playing together again. She then played Mrs Edna Gladney, a real-life lady who crusaded on behalf of bastards,

Garson and Olivier in MGM's Pride and Prejudice *(40): hardly Jane Austen but entertaining – due to both stars, and Mary Boland, Edmund Gwenn, and Edna May Oliver.*

Greer Garson in Random Harvest *(42) with Ronald Colman as the amnesiac she marries twice. The cherry blossom was much in evidence in the film.*

clearly the *Blossoms in the Dust* (41), an over-sickly piece with Walter Pidgeon. With Crawford she did *When Ladies Meet*: the French called it *Duel de Femmes* and Garson was a runaway victor. Crawford in fact had been hoping to inherit Shearer's queenly place at the studio and was now rather disconcerted to see it going to Garson. Shearer turned down *Mrs Miniver* (42) because she didn't want to play a mother, and it was assigned to Garson who, more reasonably, didn't want to play a mother either. After a fight she gave in (and fell in love with the actor playing her son, Richard Ney; at the studio's request the marriage was delayed till the film had gone the rounds). Pidgeon was her film husband, William Wyler directed, and the film, a stiff-upper-lip drama about the British Home Front, was an enormous success. It is said to have done more for the British cause (the US was not then in the war) than any other single factor; more surprisingly – because, though well-meant, it is phoney – it was a hit in Britain. Garson won a Best Actress Oscar for her performance.

But if *Miniver* was a success, *Random Harvest* was hardly less so, another huge grosser: from James Hilton's novel, with Ronald Colman as an amnesiac and Garson as the faithful wife he marries twice. She did a song and dance in it, in tights, which made news and doubtless helped it break records at the Radio City Music Hall and the Empire, Leicester Square. And she won the Picturegoer Gold Medal for the third consecutive year (the first was for *Blossoms*). MGM negotiated a new contract, a remarkable seven-year one *without options*, and one peak followed another, handsomely mounted square vehicles like *Madame Curie* (43), which James Agate did not think had much merit, but 'I am inclined to think the time has come to recognize Greer Garson as the next best film actress to Bette Davis'.
Mr Miniver was Monsieur Curie. There followed: *Mrs Parkington* (44), a family saga, again with Pidgeon; *The Valley of Decision* (45), more family saga, with Gregory Peck; and when Gable returned after war service, it was to Garson's arms and *Adventure* (46). It was a hit but critically knocked – and her fans didn't care for her much as a sailor's pick-up. Significantly, she disappeared from the top 10 the following year, but the film concerned, *Desire Me* (47), was a disaster.
A while earlier she had been about to do a parody-great-lady number in *Ziegfeld Follies*, but had withdrawn because she thought it undignified (Judy Garland did it): now, in an effort to renew box-office interest, she took pratfalls with Pidgeon in

Julia Misbehaves (48), an unfunny version of Margery Sharpe's sparkling comic novel, 'The Nutmeg Tree'. More suitably, Garson was Irene, *That Forsyte Woman* (49), a poor version of part of Galsworthy's saga. It did well, but MGM were wrong to resurrect the Minivers: *The Miniver Story* (50) was a flop on all counts.

MGM tried another comedy, a remake of *The Last of Mrs Cheyney* called *The Law and the Lady* (51) with Michael Wilding, but it was long-winded and Garson's attempts at vamping in a black wig were disheartening. Apart from what was a cameo role – Calpurnia – in *Julius Caesar* (53) audiences were encouraged to forget her: both *Scandal at Scourie* (52) with Pidgeon and *Her Twelve Men* (54) with Robert Ryan were shop-soiled sentiment. However, MGM did take conscience that the last two at least were unworthy and made some revitalizing plans – *Remembrance Rock*, an American epic written by Carl Sandburg, and a life of opera-singer Marjorie Lawrence. But Garson, in March 1954, asked for release from her contract and was given it. (The Sandburg film was never made and the other went to Eleanor Parker.)

A year later Warners yelled for Garson and she did a Western, *Strange Lady in Town* (55), but it failed to draw. She then went to New York to replace Rosalind Russell in 'Auntie Mame'. Warners yelled again for Garson to play Eleanor Roosevelt in the film of Doré Schary's play, *Sunrise at Campobello* (60): Ralph Bellamy was Franklin. Her make-up was remarkably like and she received her seventh Oscar nomination, but the film did only faint business in the US and was yanked off a West End screen after a week and hasn't been heard of since. The same year she did a guest appearance in *Pepe*. She had married a wealthy Texan, her second husband, in 1949, and didn't need to work; and she certainly didn't need to make *The Singing Nun* (66), a small part as the all-wise Mother Superior. She played with all the old mischievous twinkle, alas. Better was *The Happiest Millionaire* (67), but it wasn't one of Disney's happier efforts and the press hardly bothered to mention that she was in it.

Janet Gaynor

Janet Gaynor was the first woman to win an Oscar – in 1927–8, for three films (the awards were given thus, originally): *Seventh Heaven*, *Sunrise* and *Street Angel*. She was also, and for some subsequent years, one of the biggest stars in the firmament: in 1931–3 trailing only Marie Dressler in popularity polls, in 1934 the Box-Office Queen. She took over Mary Pickford's role as Leading Waif, and her title, 'America's Sweetheart'; and, as befitted the sobriquet, she was winsome and wistful. 'Because she is of Quaker origin she knows how to be demure,' wrote Marjorie Collier in Picturegoer. Sex was merely a potential – despite the fact that the gamins she played were very often ladies of the pavement. She was, of course, more sinned against than sinning. The wholesomeness of her heroines was due to her charm and large eyes, not to mention her naïvety: thespian ability hardly entered into it.

She was born in Philadelphia in 1906. The family moved to Chicago to Florida to San Francisco to Los Angeles, where Gaynor decided she would be happier doing extra work in films (she had worked as a theatre usherette and as a bookkeeper in a shoe store). She did extra work for four years, gradually rising to small parts in two-reelers at the Roach studios; at Universal she was given the lead in a two-reel Western, and then Herb Moulton, a newspaper executive, arranged for a test at Fox (she and Moulton later eloped, but didn't marry). Fox liked her and gave her the second lead in *The Johnstown Flood* (26), which she promptly stole from stars George O'Brien and Florence Gilbert. She was offered a five-year contract at $100 a week, and starred in *The Shamrock Handicap*, *The Midnight Kiss*, John Ford's *The Blue Eagle*, being fought over by O'Brien and William Russell, and *The Return of Peter Grimm* (from the dead: David Belasco's very serious ghost whimsy).

Her work in *Peter Grimm* impressed Fox sufficiently to raise her pay to $300 a week, even though she was still little-known; and pressure was brought on two studio directors to use her in their new films. F. W. Murnau had wanted Lois Moran for *Sunrise* (27), but Gaynor was good in it, as the little wife whose husband abandons her for a city vamp. Until they are reconciled, the film is, in Arthur Knight's words, 'at least one-half of a masterpiece': then it goes off in wild, melodramatic whirls. It was released after Frank Borzage's *Seventh Heaven*, which made Gaynor a star, a sordid little love story about a Paris streetwalker redeemed by and redeeming sewer-rat Charles Farrell: the direction gave it a fairy-tale quality. She then made a comedy, *Two Girls Wanted*, but the returns from *Heaven* were now coming in (it was the second biggest grosser of 1927, behind *The Jazz Singer*) and Fox hastened to re-team Gaynor

Charles Farrell and Janet Gaynor when they were the world's favourite sweethearts. Farrell's films without Gaynor were much less popular than those they did together and he retired from films while still comparatively young. He was never so effective in Talkies.

and Farrell in as similar a story as could be found, *Street Angel* (28). Again business was fantastic, and whenever Fox were in doubt, over the next few years, they co-starred them, 'America's Favorite Lovebirds'. Farrell's popularity never reached the heights of Gaynor's. Her career was personally guided by the production chief of Fox, Winfield Sheehan. She was, said Picturegoer once, 'not only a Winfield Sheehan star, but *the* Winfield Sheehan star'.

Christina (29), *Four Devils* (as a trapeze artist, Murnau again directing) and *Lucky Star* (with Farrell; a sentimental rural drama) were all part-talking; *Sunny Side Up* was Gaynor's first real Talkie, a musical–or 'talkie-singie'–which smashed at the box-office (it took over $3 million). Her voice wasn't too hot, but she enjoyed singing and dancing–for the moment. She was in Fox's contribution to the all-star revue, *Happy Days* (30), and then with Farrell in one concocted to cash in on the success of *Sunny Side Up*: *High Society Blues*, a little-girl-makes-good tale. She fought against doing it (she liked the saccharine parts but not the skittish ones) and begged Fox not to put her in any more musicals. Fox wouldn't promise, so she walked out and the part that they had promised her in *Liliom* went to Rose Hobart. Also, she was fed-up with the Fox publicity, which depicted her as a little darling. The little darling took herself off to Hawaii and waited for Fox to capitulate. She was off-salary for seven months (losing her $1,500 weekly) when she gave in.

As a peace offering, Fox put her in a starkly dramatic piece, in which she was a cabaret queen turned junkie and Farrell was a wealthy scion turned dipso, *The Man Who Came Back* (31). It was a success, but Gaynor said later 'It was positively the worst picture I made', and she was more amenable thereafter. And the next one was a big one, *Daddy Long Legs*, from Jean Webster's best-seller about the orphan girl and the wealthy guardian (Warner Baxter) who falls in love with her. Like *Tess of the Storm Country* (32) with Farrell, it was a remake of an old Mary Pickford vehicle, though Gaynor did refuse to do Pickford's *Rebecca of Sunnybrook Farm* around the same time. Marion Nixon played it, an artist whom Fox hoped might supplant Gaynor in popularity (to this end, she was teamed with Farrell a couple of times). Before *Tess*, Gaynor and Farrell were also teamed in three pictures: *Merely Mary Ann* (31); *Delicious*, another big hit, the story of a fey Scots lassie in a glengarry, in the US; and *The First Year* (32), laughter-and-tears among newly-weds.

But the team was doomed. In 1933 Gaynor signed a new contract with Fox, and thereafter she appeared only once with Farrell. She had, however, another big grosser–though she fought against doing it–*State Fair* (33), sharing starring honours with Fox's No. 1 male star, Will Rogers (as her father). Her co-star in *Adorable* (music by the Gershwins) was Henri Garat, and in *Paddy the Next Best Thing* Warner Baxter. In this load of old Irish whimsy 'she displays more acting ability than usual', said Screenplay, while Picturegoer thought the next, *Carolina* (34), contained her best performance: 'Her simpering affectations are non-existent and she brings real character to the part.' It was also a good film, about a broken-down family in the South, with Robert Young. *Change of Heart* teamed her with James Dunn, and Farrell with Ginger Rogers–at the outset of the film: but it was their twelfth and last together, and much more modern than most of the other ones. There followed *Servants Entrance* with Lew Ayres; *One More Spring* (35) with Baxter, a film she particularly liked; and *The Farmer*

Janet Gaynor and Henry Fonda in The Farmer Takes a Wife *(35). She was a canal-boat girl who ran away from home and he was the boy who befriended her. It was his first film and one of her last.*

Takes a Wife, with Henry Fonda.

But there were now no longer any queues at the box-office. Fox had amalgamated with 20th Century and the new boss, Darryl F. Zanuck, wasn't interested in promoting Gaynor's career. *Banjo on My Knee*, intended for her, was given to Barbara Stanwyck, and perhaps in retaliation, she refused to do the remake of *Seventh Heaven*; nor were strained relations at 20th alleviated when she had an accident and had to leave the remake of *Way Down East* (with Fonda; Rochelle Hudson replaced her). Recovered, she was loaned to MGM for *Small Town Girl* (36), married by city slicker Robert Taylor while he was drunk. It was a comedy.

On her home lot, she learned that it was proposed to star her with Constance Bennett, Loretta Young and newcomer Simone Simon (tipped to take her place) in *Ladies in Love*. Gaynor had no wish to share either title or billing with other luminaries and wanted to sue (she had been, after all, an official 'star' longer than any queen except Garbo); further, her salary for it was to be reduced from her customary $150,000 per film to $115,000 (still one of the best fees in Hollywood). Eventually, she did the film, and then looked around for a new home.

She signed with Selznick for two and MGM for one. Both Selznick movies are fondly remembered. The first was the first version of *A Star Is Born* (37), a moving, literate Hollywood saga (with Fredric March as the star on the wane whose wife, Gaynor, waxes): Gaynor has said she thought it superior to the remake, but despite a good moment impersonating Garbo, Hepburn and Mae West her own work is (inevitably) light years behind Judy Garland's. The MGM film was *Three Loves Has Nancy* (38), a dull antic about a small-town housekeeper and her New York novelist boss Robert Montgomery. The other Selznick picture was *The Young in Heart*, an endearingly funny tale by I. A. R. Wylie about a family of confidence tricksters (Gaynor, Douglas Fairbanks Jr, Roland Young and Billie Burke) and the old lady (Minnie Dupree) for whom they reform.

On this high note Gaynor announced her retirement and her second marriage at the same time – to Adrian, MGM's top dress designer (the first was to a lawyer, Lydell Peck). She said later that she might not have stayed away if the marriage had not been so happy. (It was announced in 1940 that she had bought a property, *Forever*, for herself, but nothing came of it.) In 1957 she did make an appearance as Pat Boone's mother in *Bernadine* (20th), but the occasion somehow garnered little publicity. After her husband's death two years later she was in a short-lived Broadway play, 'Midnight Sun', and throughout that decade she made occasional appearances in TV dramas.

About her reasons for quitting, she told reporter Roy Newquist: 'I really felt that I had had it all. I had all the pleasure and excitement of being at the top and I wanted to know about other things in life. I felt I didn't want to spend my whole life being an actress.' And she added: 'I think I had a wonderful career; I enjoyed it all, and have no sad tales to tell you.'

John Gilbert

John Gilbert is remembered as the classic case of the Silent star ruined by the coming of Sound: there is an element of myth in it, but he was the top male draw of the late 20s; some audiences *did* roar with laughter during his first Talkie and refused to go to see the others, and his death was believed to have been caused by a broken heart. Much has been written about Gilbert's fall from grace: Griffith and Mayer quote an unnamed critic who found it 'embarrassing' to review a John Gilbert Talkie: 'It isn't that Mr Gilbert's voice is insufficient; it's that his use of it robs him of magnetism, individuality, and strangest of all, skill. He becomes an uninteresting and inexperienced performer whose work could be bettered by hundreds of lesser-known players.' That contemporary opinion is substantiated by the only one of Gilbert's performances that most modern audiences have seen, playing opposite Garbo in *Queen Christina*. Like the head of the village drama group who has cast himself as Hamlet, Gilbert is inadequate for the part: he is weedy and prissy, ill at ease in his costumes, and his voice, of course, is light and inexpressive. But in his Silent pictures, he had dash and authority–even if, most of the time, it is difficult to see why he was so highly regarded. For what it is worth, Elinor Glyn thought him 'greater than Valentino'.

He was born in 1897 in Logan, Utah, into a family of strolling players. He was educated as they went along, but after his mother died he was sent to a military school in California–for a while: the money ran out, and he took various jobs, including selling newspapers in the street and one as a rubber goods salesman. He was movie mad, however, and eventually his father contacted an old buddy, Walter Edwards, who worked with the Thomas H. Ince company. Ince-Triangle offered Gilbert a two-year contract starting at $30 a week, and he started in films, playing in bit roles. He was an extra in a Western starring William S. Hart, *Hell's Hinges* (16), and was then billed–as Jack Gilbert, the name he retained for five years–on *Bullets and Brown Eyes*. He was in *The Apostle of Vengeance* starring Hart, *The Phantom*, *The Eye of the Night*, *Shell 43*; and he had his first lead opposite Enid Bennett in *The Princess of the Dark*. Mostly he was cast as the Other Man or in unsympathetic parts for which, Ince thought, his looks qualified him–as in *Happiness*, where he was the rich boy trying to woo Bennett from her poor sweetheart. There followed *The Millionaire Vagrant* starring Charles Ray; *Hater of Men*; *Golden Rule Kate*, a Western with Louise Glaum, with Gilbert as an outlaw who reforms at the end; *The Devil Dodger* starring Belle Bennett; and *Nancy Comes Home* (18).

Triangle dropped him when that company changed hands and he worked mostly for minor companies: *More Trouble*, *Shackled*, *Three X Gordon*, *Wedlock* with Glaum, *The Mask*, *The Dawn of Understanding* and *White Heather* (19) directed by Maurice Tourneur. In *The Busher*, a baseball comedy, he lost Colleen Moore to Charles Ray, but he then had a good part opposite Mary Pickford in *Heart o' the Hills*. He made *The Red Viper*, *Should Women Tell?* with Alice Lake, *Widow by Proxy* starring Marguerite Clark and *The Servant in the House* (20); and *The Great Redeemer* at Metro, a tale about a convict who paints a Crucifixion on the wall of his cell, and the effect on the other inmates. Gilbert wrote the script with Clarence Brown, who directed under Tourneur's supervision; and he played the lead.

Tourneur invited him to work on two he was doing for Paramount, *The White Circle* (from Robert Louis Stevenson's 'The Pavilion on the Links') and *Deep Waters* (21). Gilbert had a hand in the adaptations and starred. These three films together gave him a standing in Hollywood and he had offers to direct. Instead, he signed a three-year acting contract with Fox starting with *Shame* with Anna May Wong. He returned to Paramount briefly for *Ladies Must Live* with Betty Compson and Leatrice Joy (at that time his wife) and then did *Gleam O'Dawn* (22); *Monte Cristo*, after Dumas, in the title role, with Renée Adorée, the first of several together; *Arabian Love*, one of the films which tried to capitalize on the 'Sheik' craze started by Valentino; *The Yellow Stain*; *Honor First* with Adorée; *Calvert's Valley*;

and *The Love Gambler* with Carmel Myers. In 1923 was released Tourneur's *While Paris Sleeps* with Lon Chaney, made three years earlier. The other Gilbert films that year: *Truxten King*; *The Madness of Youth* with Billie Dove; *Saint Elmo* with Barbara La Marr and Bessie Love; and John Ford's *Cameo Kirby* from the play by Booth Tarkington and Harry Leon Wilson about a Mississippi riverboat gambler – the film had some tinted sequences and was very popular. From this point on Gilbert's career was on an upward curve: *A California Romance*; *Just Off Broadway* (24) with Marion Nixon; *The Wolf Man* with Norma Shearer; *A Man's Mate* with Adorée, an Apache romance; *The Lone Chance*; and *Romance Ranch*.

When his contract was up, MGM offered another, convinced that Gilbert could become a very big star with better material than that in which Fox had served him up; also, he was dark and Latin-looking, and that was a positive asset in an industry dazzled by the success of Valentino. Accordingly, he was given parts – often in uniform – in which he could cut a dash. Like Valentino, he was encouraged to use his eyes – and, in fact, he used them better: they were big, dark eyes and he became adept at two expressions in particular – fiery passion and deep compassion. He needed all the former quality chasing Aileen Pringle round the boudoirs in *His Hour*, which King Vidor directed and Elinor Glyn adapted from one of her own steaming novels; and he used the compassion in *He Who Gets Slapped*, a circus drama with Lon Chaney and Shearer. However, of his part in *The Snob*, also with Shearer, Picturegoer commented that 'the screen has never given us a more sustained character portrait of an utter rotter'; and he was only a mite more sympathetic in Vidor's *The Wife of the Centaur* (25), as the Centaur – a modern one – again with Pringle. Then he was cast as the profligate Prince Danilo in *The Merry Widow* with Mae Murray as the widow. This was directed by Erich von Stroheim, and there are von Stroheim touches which set it apart from the other Ruritanian romances that Gilbert made (and it was also the only enjoyable musical filmed without music): the public presumably were titillated, because the film was one of the year's biggest grossers, at an estimated $1½ million. But this was less than half what Gilbert's next clocked up – *The Big Parade*, 1925's most popular film and certainly the most highly regarded. It ran for two years at the Astor in New York and grossed an estimated $15 million world-wide. This was so far the best of the films inspired by the

Neither producers nor audiences approved of John Gilbert without his moustache, but he didn't sport it in his biggest success, The Big Parade *(25). King Vidor directed, and his leading lady was Renée Adorée.*

War, neither pro- nor anti-, but a wry look from the point of view of the average doughboy. King Vidor's direction was masterly and Gilbert was excellent. He started on a new – and his highest – phase of popularity.

Vidor also directed his next two, *La Bohème* (26) – he was Rudolph and Lillian Gish was Mimi – and *Bardelys the Magnificent*, a swashbuckler based on a novel by Rafael Sabatini. In his next, there were love scenes which Photoplay described as 'smolderingly fervent': the lady was Greta Garbo and the film *Flesh and the Devil* (27). A supposed off-screen affair between the two gave this film an aura for the fans (though Garbo in an interview printed by Picturegoer in 1931 said convincingly that there was nothing between them), and MGM hurried to reunite this successful love-team. In the meantime he did *The Show* with Adorée, a melodrama set in Budapest where he was an apache of sorts, and *Twelve Miles Out*, as a rum runner with Joan Crawford; and when Garbo was

One of the less passionate love scenes from Flesh and the Devil *(27). The other love scenes, declared Photoplay, were 'smolderingly fervent', and the supposed fact that Garbo and Gilbert were in love in real life didn't hurt it at the box-office either.*

ready again they did *Love*, a modern version of 'Anna Karenina': he was Vronsky. He starred with Jeanne Eagels in *Man Woman and Sin* (28) and with Adorée again in *The Cossacks*, a handsome production of another Tolstoy story, followed by *Four Walls* with Crawford, *Masks of the Devil*, *A Woman of Affairs* (29) with Garbo, and *Desert Nights*. These all came out while the craze for Sound was sweeping the studios and cinemas, and it was clear that Gilbert could not be silent much longer.

His actual Talkie debut was in *The Hollywood Revue of 1929* in a coloured sequence with Norma Shearer about which no words are too unkind: they did the balcony scene from 'Romeo and Juliet'. But the crunch came with *His Glorious Night* adapted from Molnar's 'Olympia', with Catherine Dale Owen: some audiences sniggered, others fell about. But MGM had just signed a new fantastic four-year million-dollar contract with Gilbert. (Nicholas Schenk had been negotiating to sell MGM to Fox at that time; Fox had insisted on Gilbert as part of the deal and Gilbert, aware of this, had raised his price accordingly.) His first Talkie should have been *Redemption* (30), from Tolstoy's story, but sensibly enough, being heavier stuff, it was postponed until after *His Glorious Night*. But no matter: it died at the box-office. In Britain it was shown first and Picturegoer stoutly informed its readers that as a Talkie actor, 'his success seems assured'. It has been suggested that MGM deliberately tried to hurt Gilbert by recording him badly because he had become unmanageable. However, in an attempt to make audiences forget the voice, he was cast as a tough gob in *Way for a Sailor*, but instead audiences merely forgot the film. MGM, unsuccessfully, asked him to take a salary cut. His misery was not helped by the fact that his current wife, Ina Claire, was a Broadway actress and therefore doing quite well in pictures – they were divorced in 1931, after two years of marriage. Gilbert went on filming: *Gentleman's Fate* (31), which was good; *The Phantom of Paris*, based on Leroux's 'Cheri-Bibi'; *West of Broadway* (32); and *Downstairs* – with Virginia Bruce, to whom he was also married briefly. He wrote the thing and gave himself the part of a totally amoral villain. No one was impressed and soon an advert appeared in the trade press: 'Metro-Goldwyn-Mayer will neither offer me work nor release me from my contract. Signed, John Gilbert.' It was a typical gesture: Gilbert was impetuous, spoiled and quite unable to see that he had no future in films. The studio tried one last time: Tod Browning directed Gilbert in *Fast Workers* (33), but no one went to see that either. MGM, however, breathed again: it was the last film due under the contract. Some months later, surprisingly, they sent for him, to replace Olivier as Garbo's leading man in *Queen Christina*: his performance did less than nothing to re-establish him.

He was finally offered a job by Columbia, interested as ever in getting a cut-price name. Lewis Milestone directed, and the result was quite a decent picture called *The Captain Hates the Sea* (35): Gilbert gave a convincing performance, fourth-billed, as a drunken Hollywood writer. It was not at that point in his life a hard role to assume – his deal with Columbia called for 'star treatment', but after a week on the wagon he was an alcoholic mess throughout filming and difficult to handle. He literally drank himself to death, in 1936, though the official cause was a heart attack. He might more sensibly have sought other fields, but there was in this actor a more than usual element of self-destruction.

Lillian Gish

'I think the things that are necessary in my profession are these: Taste, Talent and Tenacity. I think I have had a little of all three,' Lillian Gish told Sight and Sound in 1957. Most observers seem to think that there was more than a 'little' talent. In her time she was considered to hold in films the sort of place that Bernhardt or Duse had in the theatre, as Bosley Crowther attests in 'The Lion's Share', remarking what a coup it was for MGM to sign her; and a modern critic like Kevin Brownlow, from his studies of the Silent Cinema, can describe her as 'one of the sublimest actresses of the Cinema'.

To most modern (i.e. film-society) audiences, she is at first resistible: a wraith-like heroine in raggedy-Ann clothes gazing passively and innocently at the world which is wronging her so cruelly. But she did admirably everything that was required of her by her directors and her plots – and the demands were heavy. Given the strong Victorian sentiment which inspired D. W. Griffith and some others among her directors, she reacted with a spirituality and charm which not only harmonized with it, but sometimes infected it with a sense of urgency; and while her frail body cowed under the blows inflicted on it in the cause of melodrama, the camera recorded a peculiar and very personal intensity.

Gish was born in 1896 in Springfield, Ohio. Her father was a drifter and drifted away altogether not long after the family (which now included a younger sister, Dorothy) had settled in New York. To pay the rent, Mother Gish sought a job as an actress, but found that it was simpler to let the children act: there were good parts for juveniles in the dramas of the day, if you were not caught up with by one of the societies which wanted to ban child performers. Thus Lillian made her stage bow at the age of five back in Ohio, in a town called Rising Sun, in a play called 'In Convict's Stripes'. In time Mother and both daughters were acting in touring companies, and among their colleagues was the child who became Mary Pickford. They visited Pickford on the Griffith lot after she had gone into movies, and Pickford persuaded Griffith to give the two girls contracts. They debuted together in *An Unseen Enemy* (12). The films they made were one- and two-reelers, and some of them were made in two days or less: like the others (Pickford, Lionel Barrymore, Robert Harron, etc.) in Griffith's company, the Gish sisters played parts of all sizes: among the 20 or so films Lillian made over the next two years are: *The Musketeers of Pig Alley*, *My Baby*, *Gold and Glitter*, *The New York Hat*, *A Cry for Help*, *A Misunderstood Boy*, *The Lady and the Mouse* (13), *The Mothering Heart* (the first role specially written for her), *During the Round Up*, *The Conscience of Hassan Bey* – and *Judith of Bethulia* (14) and *Lord Chumley*, which were Griffith's first feature-length (four-reels) releases. During this period Lillian returned to the stage, but collapsed from lack of food; when she returned to Griffith he upped her salary from $5 a day to $50 a week.

When Griffith left Biograph for Mutual, the Gish sisters went with him. He directed Lillian personally in her first there, *The Battle of the Sexes* (five reels) and in two other features, *Home Sweet Home* (supposedly a biopic of that song's composer) and *The Escape*. The latter two were made in Hollywood, whither Griffith had moved, and where he planned *The Birth of a Nation* (15), the film which changed the whole concept of cinema and cinema-going. He believed in features, and his backers were wary: to complete it when it went over its $25,000 budget, money was raked in from other sources (the total cost was $91,000 which included \$30,000 for exploitation, etc.). Griffith had adapted two novels by Thomas E. Dixon, 'The Clansman' and 'The Leopard's Spots', for this epic of the Civil War. It ran an unprecedented 12 reels and opened in New York at \$2 a ticket: 'The sensation it created was without precedent and has never been duplicated' (Griffith and Mayer). The movies had become Art – and Big Business: its gross is uncalculable, but Variety puts it around the staggering \$50 million, which includes numerous re-issues. Even in the 40s it could play commercially, but its apparent approval of the institution of the Ku-Klux-Klan (regardless of anything else) makes it unwatchable today. As far as Gish was concerned she was considered important enough to be star of it (though Blanche Sweet had been the original choice) and, naturally, it made her world-famous.

While Griffith prepared his next epic, Gish went on working – but only in features from now on, all of them until 1922 for the Griffith company or under his auspices or direction (several producing companies were involved). She was in *The Lost House*, *Captain Macklin*, *Enoch Arden*, *The Lily and the Rose*, *Daphne and the Pirate* (16), *Sold for Marriage*, *An Innocent Magdalene* – and *Intolerance*, as the cradle-rocker who bound the four parts together, a simultaneous telling of stories set in old Babylon, in Christian times, in Huguenot France and in the present day. It ran longer than *Nation*, cost more and was a financial disaster (partly, it was thought, because it was anti-war propaganda – at the wrong time). The next one in which Griffith directed Gish was a happier experience (for the spectator, too): before it she did *Diane of the Follies* in the title role, *Pathways of Life*, *The Children Pay*, *The House Built Upon Sand* (17) and *Souls Triumphant*. *Hearts of the World* (18) was shot in Britain and France, with the cooperation of the British Government; it was the story of a boy (Robert Harron) and a girl in an idyllic village, torn asunder by the war, and reunited in the midst of conflict. Today: crude, obvious and melodramatic, but Gish is splendid in the second half when she can act instead of merely moon. It was a great hit for her and for Griffith.

He directed all the films she made from then until she went to MGM: *The Great Love* and *The Greatest Thing in Life* (19), two more war stories, and *A Romance of Happy Valley*, all reuniting her with her *Hearts* co-star, Harron. In *Broken Blossoms* she played opposite Richard Barthelmess: the quintessential Limehouse story and her own favourite among the Griffith films. James

Henry King directed this version of George Eliot's Romola *in 1924. Lillian Gish was the sweet young heroine and William Powell her wicked husband.*

Agate, re-seeing it some years later, wrote that Gish's performance 'still seems to me surpassingly true and moving. She puts into her scenes of terror as much power and pathos as Sarah ever put into Tosca, and I think that, if I were to hear her cries, she would move me more. As it is, the film scene is the more nearly unbearable. I do not say that this little girl is as great an actress as Sarah. For all I know she may not be able to speak the President's American. What I do know is that in this one picture she ranks with the world's great artists. It is curious that, when she wears her hair down the sides of her pinched woebegone little face, with all the expressiveness of that wistful countenance drawn from the eyes down the long suspense of the nose to come to final meaning in the trembling mouth – it is curious that this plain little American child should give the world an exact image of the great actress in far-off youth.'

Gish was *True-Heart Susie*, another hit, and in *The Greatest Question*, both with Harron, and then in *Way Down East* (20), with Barthelmess and *Orphans of the Storm* (21), with her sister. Both were taken from hoary old plays, and both are awash with reversals and sentiment: *Orphans*, set during

Max Rée's impression of Lillian Gish as Mimi in La Boheme *(26). Puccini–obviously without music.*

Lillian Gish as Hester Prynne in The Scarlet Letter *(26), the third of the three film versions of Nathaniel Hawthorne's novel.*

the French Revolution, works the better of the two with Gish, kindly and heroic, tending sister Dorothy. During this period she signed with a new company which went broke during what should have been her first film for them, *World Shadows*, and she also directed her sister in *Remodelling Her Husband* (20). Her parting with Griffith came when *Orphans* went over budget, and he wouldn't pay her the salary to which she felt entitled: good offers were being made by other companies: Tiffany offered $3,500 a week, but she went to Inspiration at $1,250 plus a percentage of the profits, because they gave her story approval.

For them she made two films in Italy, both directed by Henry King, both with Ronald Colman. *The White Sister* (23) was from Marion Crawford's novel about a girl who takes the veil when she thinks–wrongly–that her lover has been killed in battle. The Women's Clubs of America were outraged at the prospect of this 'sensational' novel being filmed but, because of Lillian's respectability, proposed to lift the ban if she would hold herself 'personally responsible'. The second film was an adaptation of George Eliot's novel about medieval Italy, *Romola* (24). Inspiration then sued her for breach of contract: she had refused to work further when she realized that the president of the company, Charles H. Duell, had been via professed friendship whittling away her contractual rights, and because she thought the profits of *Sister* had been wrongly accounted; amidst the bitterness, Duell alleged that she had promised to marry him. He was later convicted of perjury.

Metro had released the two Inspiration films, and it was to MGM she now moved, with a contract worth $800,000 for six films, and creative approval. She didn't do *Romeo and Juliet* as she had hoped, but with John Gilbert made two other famous lovers, Mimi and Rudolph: *La Bohème* (26). On the strength of *The Big Parade*, she had chosen King Vidor to direct. He said of her later: 'She is the most dedicated actress I have ever known. . . . She makes you believe [a scene] is actually happening.' Fresh from this triumph she insisted on doing Nathaniel Hawthorne's *The Scarlet Letter* against studio opposition (Louis B. Mayer said the book was 'banned for the screen'): she chose Victor Sjöstrom to direct, and Lars Hanson to co-star, thinking that Swedes could get closer to the Puritan New England setting. Pauline Kael in 1968: 'Her Hester Prynne is one of the most beautifully sustained performances in screen history–mercurial, delicate, passionate. There isn't an actress on the screen today, and perhaps there never was another, who can move like Lillian Gish: it's as if no bones, no physical barriers, stood between her intuitive understanding of the role and her expression of it.' Once again it did well, but *Annie Laurie* (27)–a tale built round the massacre of Glencoe–did so badly after poor reviews that the studio re-titled it *Ladies From Hell*. Neither of the next two did well, despite glowing reviews: the pacifist *The Enemy* (28) or *The Wind*. Sjöstrom directed *The Wind*, about a Virginia girl in the Texas prairies, a film amazingly vivid and alive. MGM insisted on a happy ending.

Before it was released, the studio wanted to take her off salary, as they had nothing ready for her–but she considered that their fault and not hers. Commercially she had been a disappointment and to buck up her box-office, Thalberg suggested that the studio invent a scandal for her. She refused. They decided to let her go without making the last film of her contract–for one thing, her fame as a serious actress was now over-shadowed by Garbo's. She signed a contract with UA, at $50,000 plus 50 per cent of the profits, and the first was to be directed in Germany by Reinhardt, about a German peasant girl (then living) with a stigmata: but with the advent of Sound, UA decided that her Talkie debut should be made in Hollywood. So, instead, she did *One Romantic Night* (30) from Molnar's 'The Swan' with Rod la Rocque; it was not a success, even though she had mastered the microphone with ease. ('The Miracle Girl with the Miracle Voice' said the adverts.) Next, she considered a remake of *The White Sister* as well as *Strange Interlude* with Colman–but a plagiarism suit was brought against Eugene O'Neill and that was postponed. In the end, she asked to be let out of her contract.

Thus, as Louise Brooks put it, 'stigmatized as a grasping, silly, sexless antique, at the age of 31, the great Lillian Gish left Hollywood for ever, without a head turned to mark her departure'. In fact, the screen was overrun with actresses very different from Gish, and her sort of film was now old-fashioned. Her talent was undeniable, but continued public acceptance was something else again. She turned to the stage and did three plays, including 'Uncle Vanya' (30) and 'Camille', both on Broadway, and did make another film, *His Double Life* (33), with Roland Young, an adaptation of Arnold Bennett's play, 'The Great Adventure'. Paramount released; Gish made no pictures for RKO, who announced at this time that they had signed her. She did two more plays

After almost 10 years away from films, Miss Gish returned in the early 40s and was soon being driven to drink by Lionel Barrymore in David O. Selznick's expensive Duel in the Sun *(46). With her is Jennifer Jones as the half-breed girl her sons were fighting over.*

on Broadway, and in 1936 toured in Britain in 'The Old Maid' but the play didn't make London; later that year she played Ophelia to Gielgud's Hamlet in New York. In 1937 she did Maxwell Anderson's 'The Star Wagon' and in 1938 'Dear Octopus', both in New York; later she toured in 'Life With Father'. She was asked to play Belle Watling in *Gone With the Wind*; and did return to movies in 1942, in a supporting role in *The Commandos Strike at Dawn*; then she and Richard Dix played Donald O'Connor's parents in *Top Man* (43). She was a spinster running a boarding house in *Miss Susie Slagle's* (46), and the drinking wife of former co-star Lionel Barrymore in *Duel in the Sun*. She found filming 'much less exciting .... Before, I had been responsible for my films; I had involved myself in various facets of production. Now acting in films was largely a matter of doing as you were told and collecting your salary.'

Since 1948 she has kept three careers going: in TV as well as on the stage and in films, invariably playing genteel spinster ladies. TV plays include 'The Trip to Bountiful', 'Morning's at Seven', 'Ladies in Retirement' and in 1969, with Helen Hayes, 'Arsenic and Old Lace'. On the stage she has done 'Crime and Punishment' (47), 'The Trip to Bountiful' (53), 'The Chalk Garden' on tour with her sister, 1956; 'The Family

Reunion' (58) and 'All the Way Home' (60), both in New York; 'A Passage to India' (62) in Chicago; Mrs Mopply in 'Too True to Be Good' (63) in New York; the Nurse in 'Romeo and Juliet' (65); 'Anya', a flop version of 'Anastasia'; and 'I Never Sang for My Father' (67), among other plays. On screen, *Portrait of Jennie* (49), *The Cobweb* (55) and a leading role–beautifully played–in Charles Laughton's *The Night of the Hunter*. She had another chance to show at length her mastery in the British anti-war *Orders to Kill* (58), made by Anthony Asquith. She was the mother of Burt Lancaster in *The Unforgiven* (60); and was in Disney's *Follow Me Boys* (66); *Warning Shot*; and *The Comedians* (67).

In 1932 she published 'Life and Lillian Gish' and in 1969 'The Movies, Mr Griffith and Me'. She has never married. She and her sister Dorothy were very close until the latter died in 1968. Dorothy also had a successful career, parallel to her sister's in many ways, including the fading from films when Sound came; and she was a very agreeable actress in her own right.

Paulette Goddard

When Charles Chaplin Jr published his memoir of his father, Paulette Goddard found herself the heroine. The author wrote that he and his brother 'looked into that friendly face with its mischievous, conspiratorial smile and we lost our hearts at once'; later he added, 'She wasn't just pretty. She was warm and enthusiastic about everything.' Thus did wartime audiences also fall for her. She had no outstanding ability as a dramatic actress, and she played comedy with verve rather than finesse, but she was vivacious, pert and *very* pretty. She would probably have made it to the top even without Chaplin.

They met on Joe Schenck's yacht in 1932: she was a blonde divorcee ex-chorine, aged 21, and a member of Hal Roach's stock company. She was born in Great Neck, Long Island, in 1911; the home broke up and she became a breadwinner at an early age. At 14 she was a Ziegfeld girl, and she had some lines in 'No Foolin'; she had a small role in 'Rio Rita' and then married and retired. When her marriage broke up she and Mother headed for Hollywood, and she got bit parts in *The Girl Habit* (31), *The Mouthpiece* (32) and *The Kid From Spain*. She was a Goldwyn Girl in the latter, and that got her the job at Roach. When Chaplin met her she was about to invest her $500,000 alimony in a phoney film venture. He prevented that; and he bought her contract from Roach and let her hair grow back to its original black. *Modern Times* was conceived as a vehicle for them both: he began the script in 1932, and the film wasn't premièred until 1936 (in which year they were secretly married). Chaplin coached Goddard unceasingly in the part of the gamine, but in the finished film it appears to be a performance of complete spontaneity–and is quite delightful.

Among Chaplin's projects over the next few years were several for his wife (including one with Gary Cooper–a script that eventually saw the light as *A Countess From Hong Kong*), but he worked so slowly that she began to get restless in case the public forgot her. Eventually it was agreed that she might test for the part of Scarlett O'Hara. Selznick liked her enough to sign her, and for a long time she was a favourite for the part. In the meantime he put her in a comedy, *The Young in Heart* (38), with Janet Gaynor, and loaned her to MGM for the undramatic *Dramatic School* with Luise Rainer and then to be one of *The Women* (39). Her first star part was opposite Bob Hope in *The Cat and the Canary* at Paramount. That studio wanted her for another film with Hope, and Selznick didn't want her for Scarlett, so he sold her contract to Paramount. Thus she was again a frightened heroine in *The Ghost Breakers* (40). She had a smallish role, as a gypsy, in *North West Mounted Police*, but then was Fred Astaire's co-star in *Second Chorus*: she had one dance with him and the chance to get to know Burgess Meredith, whom she later married. Intermittently she was working with Chaplin on *The Great Dictator*, which was premièred late in 1940. They worked together now much less harmoniously: she was established and experienced and he was tremendously exacting. In his autobiography he says that he was angered by her agent's demands over billing. At all events, she divorced him in 1942, without, apparently, bitterness on either side (one script that had been planned for her eventually became *A King in New York*).

Meanwhile Paramount loaned her to UA for a dim 'swing' musical with James Stewart, *Pot o' Gold* (41), which was produced by one of Roosevelt's sons; and gave her second lead in *Hold Back the Dawn*, where her brittle gaiety contrasted with the spinster schoolteacher, Olivia de Havilland. But back with Bob Hope in *Nothing But the Truth*, one of the year's top grossers, she was the star; and the studio began to give her more important vehicles. *The Lady Has Plans* (42) with Ray Milland, was a witless spy film, and it was followed by another with Milland, marginally more enjoyable, de Mille's *Reap the Wild Wind*: Goddard's role was clearly designed to compensate her for not getting Scarlett O'Hara, even if it had been offered first to Katharine Hepburn. *The Forest Rangers* was more spectacle – a forest fire – with Fred MacMurray. She did a number with Dorothy Lamour and Veronica Lake in *Star Spangled Rhythm*; was in a comedy with Milland at United Artists, *The Crystal Ball* (43); then a war drama: *So Proudly We Hail* (nurses), with Claudette Colbert and Lake. With MacMurray in 1944 there was *Standing Room Only* in overcrowded Washington, and with Sonny Tufts *I Love a Soldier* – only the trouble was she appeared to love them all.

Goddard was now among the top two or three women stars at Paramount, and she was re-signed to a new seven-year pact. She had a wholesome quality that set her apart from the other wartime pin-ups, but now that she or the studio were bent on making her a dramatic actress, it began to disappear. *Kitty* (45) was from a novel by Rosamund Marshall and it had a plot almost identical to *Forever Amber*, only this gutter-snipe got started by a liaison with a painter, Gainsborough (Cecil Kellaway); then it veered towards Pygmalion, with Milland as the Professor. It was reasonably free of anachronism, handsome to look at, somewhat less dull than *Amber* and a big success. She guested in *Duffy's Tavern*, and then gave probably her best performance, in Renoir's *Diary of a Chambermaid* (46), produced by him and husband Meredith, who also acted

Paulette Goddard and Ray Milland made four films together, of which the first was this one, The Lady Has Plans (*42*). *It was also one of the year's silliest films.*

in it: indeed she is as good as (though different from) Jeanne Moreau in the later Buñuel version of Octave Mirbeau's novel (just as the films are different and excellent: gay-black and grey-grim respectively). There was a weak comedy with MacMurray, *Suddenly It's Spring* (47), a guest spot in *Variety Girl* and then more costume pictures: de Mille's mammoth and boring *The Unconquered*, with Gary Cooper, where she was a slave girl lusted after by Howard da Silva in the New World–probably her worst performance.

She was allowed one outside film a year and she signed a deal with Korda. At first he announced a *Carmen* for her, but instead she did his version of Wilde's *An Ideal Husband* with Michael Wilding: she was Mrs Chevely and one of the few lively things about that film. It didn't do well in the States, and was indeed one of the turkeys which virtually finished Goddard's film career. The others were *Hazard* (48), a so-called comedy with Macdonald Carey; *On Our Merry Way*, an episode comedy with Goddard and Meredith as the link, and a weak link it was; and *Bride of Vengeance* in which she played Lucrezia Borgia. Ray Milland has said that it was the only film he refused to do during his 21 years at Paramount. He added: 'Richard Maibaum was the producer, Mitchell Leisen was the director, John Lund replaced me, Paulette Goddard, John Sutton, Albert Decker.

Paulette Goddard didn't make many good films, but Diary of a Chambermaid *(46) was certainly one of them. With her here, in a character role, is her husband at the time, Burgess Meredith, playing the neighbour who, like every other male in the film, was mad for her.*

Everyone of them was fired after the film was previewed.' This is presumably an over-simplification, but Goddard didn't work for Paramount again.

She made a version of *Anna Lucasta* in which the original Negro community became white, but despite the notoriety which the play had had (Anna was a whore), the film did poor business (the producers had wanted Susan Hayward, but Goddard had had a prior claim on the material); and Goddard's next job was in a Mexican film with Pedro Armendaiz, *The Torch* (50), where 'both [her] appearance and talent [are] out of place' (Variety). Her Hollywood career trailed off in a series of B films with pretensions – *Babes in Baghdad* (52), an Arabian Nights lark with Gypsy Rose Lee produced by the Danziger brothers before they favoured British audiences with their B pictures; *Vice Squad* (53) with Edward G. Robinson; *Paris Model* with Marilyn Maxwell; *The Sins of Jezebel*, in which she was a Biblical queen; and *The Charge of the Lancers* (54) with Jean-Pierre Aumont, in which she was a gypsy girl. She returned to Britain for *The Stranger Came Home*, one of the dreadful second features of the 50s with passé Hollywood names made in an effort to get bookings in the US market (in this case by by the people who later became Hammer films). In 1958 she married Erich Maria Remarque and gave up any serious thought of working, though in 1966 she did play in an Italian film adapted from a Moravia novel, *The Time of Indifference*. Despite a distinguished cast – it includes Rod Steiger – this was never shown in Britain. Whether Goddard will film again is debatable. She wouldn't do it for the money. She doesn't need it: her jewellery collection is famous.

Betty Grable

'Her special forte was the backstage musical in which her famous legs were put on display on the most absurd of pretexts. Miss Grable's beauty – if that is the word for it – was of the common sort. Nor did she offer much in the way of character or maturity. She was, at best, a sort of great American floozie, and her appeal to lonely GIs was surely that of every hash-house waitress with whom they ever flirted': such is Richard Schickel's judgement on Betty Grable in his book 'The Stars'. She herself, looking back, is hardly kinder: 'As a dancer I couldn't outdance Ginger Rogers or Eleanor Powell. As a singer I'm no rival to Doris Day. As an actress I don't take myself seriously. I had a little bit of looks yet without being in the big beauty league. Maybe I had sincerity. And warmth. Those qualities are essential. I don't think I've ever had a good review. My films didn't get them either. Yet they did well at the box-office' (to interviewer James Green of the 'Evening News'). Had she wanted to, Grable might have boasted more of that box-office glow: she really had her contemporaries beat. She was one of the exhibitors' Golden Ten in the US for 10 consecutive years – for four of them the top female draw, with Greer Garson the runner-up. The British preferred Garson, and nowhere outside the US was Grable's home popularity equalled. She was very American, she *was* like a hash-house waitress – but in a nicer way than Schickel intended: she was bright, friendly, brash and comfortable. She was one of the crowd.

Certainly it took Hollywood long enough to distinguish her among the ranks of starlets. She was born in St Louis in 1916, and when she was 12 she went with her mother to Los Angeles to study dancing – and in no time was in the chorus line, blacked-up with 63 other girls, in a film musical called *Let's Go Places* (30). She could be briefly glimpsed in *New Movietone Follies of 1930* and Goldwyn's *Whoopee*. The great Sam noticed her and signed her to a five-year contract, changed her name to Frances Dean, and gave her bits in *Kiki* (31), *Palmy Days*, *The Greeks Had a Word for Them* (32), *Probation* (on loan) and *The Kid From Spain*. Then he dropped her, as being unlikely star material. She was signed by RKO who changed her name back again, and gave her the female lead in a Wheeler and Woolsey comedy, *Hold 'em Jail*. Plans were made to make her a big star, but she wasn't ready and went back to small parts: in *Child of Manhattan* (33) and *What Price Innocence* at Columbia, *Student Tour* at MGM, and at RKO *The Gay Divorcee* (34), duetting 'Let's Knock Knees' with Edward Everett Horton, and *By Your Leave* which starred Frank Morgan. She also sang with a couple of bands, and in 1935 toured with Wheeler and Woolsey; was in their *The Nitwits* (35), which George Stevens directed, and in *Old Man Rhythm* with Charles 'Buddy' Rogers, *Collegiate* (36) starring Joe Penner, *Follow the Fleet*, *Pigskin Parade* at 20th and *Don't Turn 'em Loose*. But RKO did. Grable was now married to Jackie Coogan, the former child star, at this time battling in the courts for possession of his earnings. On a wave of publicity Coogan and Grable did a nation-wide vaude tour.

Back in Hollywood Paramount had a crisis with an unimportant movie called *This Way Please* (37), starring Shirley Ross

Betty Grable made almost 30 films before becoming a star. Here she is, left, in one of them, Man About Town *(39) with Binnie Barnes, Jack Benny, Dorothy Lamour and, behind, Edward Arnold and Phil Harris.*

and Jack Benny's wife, Mary Livingstone. Benny apparently beefed up his wife's part, and Ross walked out: Paramount got Grable to replace her. They liked her so much in this and *Thrill of a Lifetime* that they signed her to a contract and planned a massive publicity campaign to push her into top stardom. She was the ingénue in two Martha Raye vehicles, *College Swing* (38), *Give Me a Sailor* (also with Burns and Allen), and then in *Campus Confessions*, *Man About Town* (39) and *Million Dollar Legs* (not hers, the football team's). Paramount, like Goldwyn, concluded that she wasn't ready for stardom and dropped her.

Grable returned to vaudeville briefly, and then got a part in a minor movie at RKO, *The Day the Bookies Wept*. She went to New York for the second lead in 'Du Barry Was a Lady' – not very enthusiastically, for she had no illusions about her singing voice: but the show was a hit, and so was she. Columnists stopped referring to her as 'Coogan's Ex'. More importantly, 20th now wanted her to sign a contract, feeling they could promote her where the others had failed. She was on tour with 'Du Barry' when Alice Faye came down with appendicitis, and 20th needed her at once for *Down Argentine Way* (40), replacing Faye opposite Don Ameche. It was in colour, and colour greatly enhanced Grable's appeal. Twentieth were pleased, and cast her as Faye's sister in *Tin Pan Alley*, and then as one of three girls seeking millionaire husbands in *Moon Over Miami* (41).

That one was a favourite plot at 20th (Grable later played in one of its remakes), and it established Grable as a fairly mercenary charmer, on-the-make careerwise if nothing else. She was seldom on the level, and the plots had to do with the

'Welcome to the Diamond Horseshoe' sang Betty Grable in a musical set in and around the nightclub of that name. The film was called that too (45).

leading man discovering this the hard way and getting reconciled to it in time for the final fade-out. It was always the same plot–backstage romancing–with almost identical routines. The dialogue was witless, the direction featureless, most of the supporting cast talentless. The same dearth of imagination hit the ads: *Pin Up Girl* was labelled 'The Zenith of Musicals', not capitalizing on Grable's popularity with the troops. But first, there were two straight movies: *A Yank in the RAF* (as Tyrone Power's snappy sweetheart) and *I Wake Up Screaming* (uncovering the murderer of sister Carole Landis); and the next one, *Footlight Serenade* (42), was the last Grable film in black and white. She had just hit the top 10 lists (1942) and a grateful studio promised Technicolor for as long as she was under contract. They also insured her legs with Lloyds of London for £250,000 (cf Fred Astaire's at £200,000, Dietrich's at £175,000).

While the armies of the Allies drooled over those legs, on clippings pinned above their beds, Grable worked in this escapist stuff: *Song of the Islands*, *Springtime in the Rockies*, *Coney Island* (43), *Sweet Rosie O'Grady*, *Pin Up Girl* (44) and *Diamond Horseshoe* (45). Her leading men were innocuous (Victor Mature, John Payne, Dick Haymes, etc.) and were deliberately chosen thus. As the troops came home, Grable and June Haver were *The Dolly Sisters*, one of 1946's top money-makers, even if it turned the true story into the same tired concoction. But 20th seemed to be mindful at last of the poor reviews, and cast Grable in a period piece with rediscovered Gershwin songs, *The Shocking Miss Pilgrim* (47)–shocking because she was a typist. Her character was softened, and there was another untypical vehicle, *Mother Wore Tights*, with her as Mother ('Are you being quite fair, Mikie? Do you think your friends would stop liking you because your parents are on the stage?'). Dan Dailey was Father, and the film was liked by press and public (though its charm is singularly elusive today). A third attempt to get Grable out of the rut, *That Lady in Ermine* (48), was liked by neither; Douglas Fairbanks Jr co-starred, a mock-Ruritanian piece directed by Lubitsch for a week before his death (it was finished–off–by Otto Preminger).

Grable was re-teamed with Dailey three times: *When My Baby Smiles at Me* (49), a going-over of 'Burlesque', *My Blue Heaven* (50) and *Call Me Mister* (51), which jettisoned the best of a Broadway show. In between were: *The Beautiful Blonde From Bashful Bend*–one of Preston Sturges's weakest efforts, *Wabash Avenue* (both 50) and *Meet Me After the Show* (51; 'Grable gams its chief asset', says Steven H. Scheuer). Grable was still a big draw according to exhibitors (No. 3 in 1951), but 20th accountants knew differently: besides, a young girl called Mitzi Gaynor had stolen the notices of *My Blue Heaven* and was having a vehicle called *Golden Girl* built for her. And the 20th musical was a dead duck, killed by what was happening in this field at MGM. Twentieth did take a leaf from Metro's book, and gave Grable a good (Harold Arlen) score, lovely (Lake Erie) locations and *no* backstage plot for *The Farmer Takes a Wife* (53), a remake of the Janet Gaynor film, but the Metro magic was missing, and it was released as the lower half of double bills.

The golden girl at 20th wasn't, in the end, Gaynor, but Marilyn Monroe, and she usurped Grable's position as surely as Grable had earlier usurped Faye's; and it was the still-new Monroe who got top-billing in *How to Marry a Millionaire*. Grable's gold-digger was one of her most endearing performances, but it came third to those of Monroe and Lauren Bacall. Monroe's biographer Zolotow reports that Grable told Monroe: 'Honey, I've had it. Go get

How To Marry a Millionaire (*53*) *was the* nth *version by 20th Century-Fox of the old gold-digger plot – this time notable mainly for the performances of Marilyn Monroe, Grable and Lauren Bacall. The object of their attention is Cameron Mitchell.*

yours. It's your turn now.' Later, Monroe took over her dressing-room.

Twentieth tried once more with Grable, cast again as a wise-cracking showgirl, but the film, a campus comedy, *How to Be Very Very Popular* (55) was a damp squib; and its publicity ignored Grable to focus on co-star Sheree North and how 20th had *her* ready to take Monroe's place should the latter become very, very difficult. Most of the publicity that Grable got was about her being out now in the cold. She was taken in by Columbia, for a musical remake of Jean Arthur's *Too Many Husbands* called *Three for the Show* (55), but reviews and business were poor. Grable decided not to accept any more offers unless they were good ones. They weren't, so she joined husband Harry James in Las Vegas.

After sitting around there for a year or two (the marriage ended after 20 years in 1965), she accepted leads in café-musicals, most notably 'Guys and Dolls'; she also did 'Born Yesterday' and was one of the Broadway Dollies ('Hello Dolly'). In 1969 in London she starred in the disastrous 'Belle Starr' and got warm personal notices (though less for what she did, than what she was). As she also said to James Green: 'All I want to do is please the public. I'm a professional and always set out to do the best I can.'

Cary Grant

In 1935 (he had made more than 20 films and was officially a star) Cary Grant received less than one per cent of the votes cast in the Motion Picture Herald poll to find the year's top attractions. Within two years he had become one of the most sought-after leading men, and in the mid-40s he edged into the list of the top 10 draws. He was in there twice more in that decade and then, after a break, came in at second in 1959; and stayed there throughout eight consecutive years. When he and the century entered their 60s, much was made of his continuing popularity, looks and youthfulness. He was everyone's favourite uncle, brother, best friend and ideal lover: more than most stars he belonged to the public. When his fourth wife divorced him and in court did a thorough character-assassination job on him, no one cared, no one was interested – they looked the other way. He really is, still,

Again Puccini without the music: Sylvia Sidney as Cio-Cio-San and Cary Grant as the unfaithful Pinkerton in a rather foolish film made by Paramount in 1932.

charismatic. He stayed young. We loved Gable, Crosby, Cooper as much, but they aged. The appeal of many of them lay in familiarity: unlike us and the world, Grant was changeless.

It is his elegance, his casualness, his unaccented charm; he is, as Tom Wolfe put it, 'consummately romantic and consummately genteel' – 'the old leathery charmer' in Alexander Walker's words (regretting his earlier, more interesting, existence as a 'hard-eyed cad'). It certainly isn't from acting ability: his range must be the most limited of all the great matinée idols. His gift for light comedy has been much touted, but it's been a mite heavy at times and one can think of half a dozen names who were sometimes better. Katharine Hepburn (interviewed by Roy Newquist) once summed him up: 'Cary Grant, I think, is a personality functioning. A delicious personality who has learnt to do certain things marvellously well. He can't play a serious part or, let me say, the public isn't interested in him that way, not interested in him at all, which I'm sure has been a big bugaboo to him. But he has a lovely sense of timing, an amusing face and a lovely voice.'

Grant was born in Bristol in 1904, into what is known as a 'broken home'. There was a theatrical tradition (one of his grandfathers had been an actor) and he became callboy at Bristol Hippodrome, joining, without parental permission, a company who were appearing there, Bob Pender's troupe of acrobats. With them he sang, danced, juggled, and with them he travelled to the US in 1920. He liked it there and decided to stay; after the troupe had returned home, he did odd jobs (he sold painted neck-ties, did a vaudeville stint with a mind-reading act). In 1923 he went back to Britain and managed to get some small parts in musical comedies. Arthur Hammerstein saw him, and took him back to New York to play the juvenile in 'Golden Dawn', a musical written by Oscar Hammerstein II; then Grant was in 'Polly' with Fred Allen and 'Boom-Boom' with Jeanette MacDonald (they were both screen-tested, but nothing came of it). He did some operettas in St Louis, and then returned to New York to appear in 'Nikki' (based on the same novel as the movie *The Last*

Flight): playing Cary Lockwood (hence the first half of his screen name; his own name was Archie Leach). When it folded he went to Hollywood and was hired by Paramount to feed lines to an actress being tested: he got a contract and she didn't. He started at $450 a week, in a good part in *This Is the Night* (32), a musical starring Charles Ruggles, Lily Damita and Roland Young.

He had supporting roles in *Sinners in the Sun*, *Merrily We Go to Hell*, *The Devil and the Deep* and then was spotlighted as the cause of Dietrich's ruination in *Blonde Venus*. Paramount were excited by Grant: they announced a *Blood and Sand* for him and Tallulah Bankhead, seeing him as a successor to Gary Cooper. Instead he did a couple that Cooper had turned down: *Hot Saturday*, top-billed in this tale about teenagers (playing 'the dour he-man lover somewhat woodenly'–Picturegoer) and *Madame Butterfly*, as Pinkerton to Sylvia Sidney's Madame. Mae West's story that Grant was an extra when she picked him for *She Done Him Wrong* (33) is clearly untrue, but exposure with her didn't harm him any; however, he was not helped by *The Woman Accused* starring Nancy Carroll, which was religiously based on a 10-part magazine serial by 10 different writers (including Zane Grey and Vickie Baum). In *The Eagle and the Hawk* he was an aviator; in *Gambling Ship* a gangster; in *I'm No Angel* another of Mae West's victims; in *Alice in Wonderland* the Mock Turtle; in *30-Day Princess* (34) a publisher; in *Born to Be Bad* (at 20th-UA) a millionaire; and in *Kiss and Make Up*, with Genevieve Tobin, a beauty specialist. From time to time he struck a spark, but he was exceptionally heavy-handed in *Ladies Should Listen*, involved with several of said ladies; then there was *Enter Madame* (35) Elissa Landi; *Wings in the Dark* as a blind man; and *The Last Outpost*, moustached.

RKO borrowed him to play a Cockney con-man in *Sylvia Scarlett* (36) opposite Katharine Hepburn, with Cukor directing. Cukor found Grant 'rather wooden . . . inexperienced, too' but noted that for the first time since Grant had been an actor 'he felt all his talents coming into being . . . he suddenly burst into bloom'. It was a part in which Grant felt at home. MGM borrowed him for Jean Harlow's *Suzy* sandwiched between two on his home lot with Joan Bennett, *Big Brown Eyes*, one of the better imitations of *The Thin Man*, and *Wedding Present*. That concluded his contract. He asked for control over his parts before re-signing, but Paramount wouldn't grant it, so he didn't. He took himself off to his homeland to do the amateurish Sound remake of E. Phillips Oppenheim's *The Amazing Quest of Ernest Bliss*–which flopped. In Britain it was re-titled *A Rich Young Man* and in the US it turned up as *Romance and Riches*. Grant hurried back to Hollywood, where he was surprised to find himself much in demand–mostly as a result of the Hepburn and Harlow movies. He signed joint contracts with RKO and Columbia, with script approval–and few stars ever made a wiser move: from the doldrums of *Ernest Bliss* he went into some of the best films of the period. True, luck played a good part in it, for though both studios were rich in talent, little of it was in the male-star category (Paramount, MGM and Warners had the big actors of the period).

Not that it started auspiciously: Grace Moore's leading man in *When You're in Love* (37) and a conventional part in *The Toast of New York*. But at the Roach studios he was one of the ghosts in *Topper*, with Constance Bennett, giving the first real proof that he had been polishing and indeed burnishing his comic style. Back and forth between his two studios he went, getting better and better: *The Awful Truth*, flippant with Irene Dunne; and a couple with Hepburn, the hilarious, slapstick *Bringing Up Baby* (38)–baby was a leopard–and the quieter *Holiday*. *Baby* had been turned down by Ray Milland, Robert Montgomery and Ronald Colman; and Grant was able to do it when *The Pioneers* with Jean Arthur was cancelled. It was a triumph for him. Said Basil Wright: 'Cary Grant, adept by now at knockabout, adds real wit and acting ability.' There were two super and popular adventure films, *Gunga Din* (39), directed by George Stevens, 'inspired' by Kipling's poem ('Cary Grant makes a perfect Cockney soldier–good-natured, pugnacious, optimistic'–Film Weekly), and Howard Hawks's *Only Angels Have Wings*, batting insults marvellously with Jean Arthur; but the year finished lamely with a conveyor-belt drama, *In Name Only* (Kay Francis was the wife, and Carole Lombard the Other Woman).

More comedy: *His Girl Friday* (40) with Rosalind Russell; *My Favorite Wife* with Dunne; a break for *The Howards of Virginia* with Martha Scott, a hopeless family saga set at the time of the American Revolution and one of Grant's worst late performances; *The Philadelphia Story* with Hepburn at MGM; and the tender *Penny Serenade* (41) with Dunne. Another break for a serious film, Hitchcock's *Suspicion*, silly but successful (you knew damned well he wasn't going to murder Joan Fontaine, whatever *she* thought); then, Stevens's *The Talk of the Town* (42) with Jean Arthur and Ronald

Cary Grant, Jean Arthur and Ronald Colman in The Talk of the Town *(42), directed by George Stevens at Columbia: except at MGM it was rare to see three such big stars together in one film. Grant was the talk of the (small) town, as the man unjustly accused of murder.*

Colman, followed by two even thinner comedies, *Once Upon a Honeymoon* and *Mr Lucky* (43). There was a long, grim war film at Warners, *Destination Tokyo*, and a further comic deterioration, *Once Upon a Time* (44), about a boy with a dancing caterpillar, with Janet Blair (intended for Bogart and Rita Hayworth, till she turned it down). But *Arsenic and Old Lace* was a pippin, a Capra-directed version of Joseph Kesselring's black farce and Broadway hit, with Jean Adair and Josephine Hull as the dear old killers (Warners had made it a while earlier and delayed release; Grant gave his salary for it to War Relief charities).

Grant was anxious to play the Cockney tramp hero of Richard Llewellyn's best-seller *None But the Lonely Heart*, directed and screenplayed by Clifford Odets, and he was Oscar-nominated: but the film didn't click. And Cole Porter was anxious to have Grant play him in his biopic, *Night and Day* (46)–or so he pretended: in fact, he made the suggestion facetiously to WB, but they took him at his word. Grant got $150,000 for a film with almost no relation to fact, some good tunes and indifferent acting. It did well in a year of big musicals, but not as well as Hitchcock's *Notorious*, with government agent Grant, among the plotters of Rio, trying to get Ingrid Bergman on 'our' side. Even more popular was *The Bachelor and the Bobby Soxer* (47), one of the year's top hits. Three more comedies, the mushy *The Bishop's Wife* with Loretta Young; the agreeable *Mr Blandings Builds His Dream House* (48) with Myrna Loy; and *Every Girl Should Be Married*, with Betsy Drake, didn't quite make it into the golden money-makers, but Hawks's *I Was a Male War Bride* (49), with Ann Sheridan, stands on Variety's list as a huge earner. Grant was the bride, and the plot's convolutions caused him at one point to appear in drag: one instance where he skated easily on perilously thin ice.

He was no longer tied to any studio, and his price went up to $300,000 per film, but it's doubtful whether MGM found it worth while for Richard Brooks's gloomy if gripping tale of South American politicking, *Crisis* (50); or 20th for Mankiewicz's *People Will Talk* (51) and how they did! Nor were there any flags out for *Room for One More* (52) with Drake, a comedy about kids. (She was

Chased across the face(s) of Mount Rushmore: Cary Grant and Eva Marie Saint in Hitchcock's North by Northwest *(59). Grant was one of Hitchcock's favourite leading men.*

Whatever he brought to his films, Cary Grant had good luck with most of his scripts and directors. The best of his 60s films was Stanley Donen's Charade *(63), with Audrey Hepburn.*

a discovery of his, a delightful actress, and the longest-lasting of his four wives; earlier Grant had been married to actress Virginia Cherrill, heiress Barbara Hutton, and in the 60s he was briefly hitched to Dyan Cannon.) *Monkey Business* was another Hawks comedy, about rejuvenation, notable only for Marilyn Monroe's cameo; and *Dream Wife* (53) an engaging enough trifle with Deborah Kerr: but it suffered a fate common to films at that time with waning stars – going out without benefit of press-showings, showcasing and ballyhoo. It was MGM that did that to Grant. The fan-magazines decided he was through (though it wasn't known at the time, he had changed his mind at the last minute about doing both *Sabrina* – the Bogart role – and *A Star Is Born*, two of 1954's biggest hits; earlier a one-picture deal with Korda had fallen through, and Grant had thus missed *The Third Man*).

It was Hitchcock who brought him back, making nice music with Grace Kelly in *To Catch a Thief* (55), proving that two years' absence and *Dream Wife* hadn't impaired his appeal. He was absent again for a bit, filming *The Pride and the Passion* (57) in Spain, Stanley Kramer directing from a C. S. Forester novel about the Peninsular War. Grant was disastrously miscast and the film dreary: but it did finally make back its enormous cost. He made up for lost time by immediately making *An Affair to Remember* with Kerr, Leo McCarey's poor but popular remake of his own 1939 *Love Affair*, and *Kiss Them For Me*, a wartime comedy that was the first film of Grandon, the production company set up by Grant and Stanley Donen. It was a bad start: reviews were fair, but antipathy to co-star Jayne Mansfield severely limited bookings.

The next one atoned: *Indiscreet* (58), not a better film, but Bergman was in it and audiences responded warmly; and *Houseboat* (59) was pleasant, though, like most comedies of this time, elongated. Sophia Loren was the girl, and she said that she learnt more from playing with Grant than any other actor. Another big one followed: *North By Northwest*, a classic 'running man' concoction of Hitchcock's – he said he wanted Grant because audiences could identify with him. *Operation Petticoat* (60) was the beginning of Grant's association with Universal, and probably the biggest financial hit of his career; as with most of his subsequent films, most of the profits went to him – and he got nice money, too, from *That Touch of Mink* (62) with Doris Day, and *Charade* (63), a tongue-in-cheek thriller with Audrey Hepburn. Less successful were *The Grass Is Greener* (60) with Kerr, Jean Simmons and Robert Mitchum, which was the last production of Grandon; *Father Goose* (64) with Leslie Caron; and *Walk Don't Run* (66) with Samantha Eggar – *The More the Merrier* remade with Grant in the Charles Coburn part, set against the Tokyo Olympics. The general opinion was that these films weren't worthy of everyone's favourite (old) film-star. Well, he chose them. He can write his own ticket, name his terms. No one else of his generation, except John Wayne, looks so good to the money-men. However, he has become a director of Rayett-Fabergé, and is engrossed, apparently, in big business. Queried about his future in 1969 he said: 'I'm not really making pictures and I don't know whether I'll ever make any – or whether I'll make one or 10.' He doesn't need the money and he probably doesn't expect an Oscar – though in 1970 he was given a special one for sheer 'brilliance' in the acting business. He holds one record that is unlikely to be broken: 28 of his movies have played the Radio City Music Hall, said to have the pick of all films scheduled to play New York, for a total playing time of 113 weeks (runners-up are Katharine Hepburn: 22 pictures and 64 weeks; Fred Astaire: 16 pictures and 60 weeks)

Ann Harding

Ann Harding: once a name to conjure with, now a lingering memory of calm loveliness and great dignity, consummate talent and real artistry. In a series of heavy-breathing melodramas she played without histrionics, too soon taken for granted. But at the outset, when Talkies arrived, she was one of the screen's aristocrats.

She was born in 1902 at Fort Sam Houston, Texas, the daughter of an army officer; and educated at Bryn Mawr, whence she went to work for an insurance company. She also worked in Paramount's reading department, and friends there persuaded her to join the Provincetown Players for recreation: she made her first appearance with them in 'The Inheritors' (21). Her 'recreation' that summer led to a New York offer – 'Like a King', and she embarked on an acting career. She appeared in stock in Buffalo and Detroit, and in 'The Horse Thief' in Chicago. Her first Broadway success was in 'Tarnish' in 1923. At Philadelphia she played leads in three Shaw plays ('Candida', 'Misalliance' and 'Captain Brassbound's Conversion') and in 'The Master Builder', with subsequent New York successes in, among others, 'Stolen Fruit' (25) and 'The Trial of Mary Dugan' (as Mary). In 1929 she toured as Lena in 'Strange Interlude', and then accompanied her husband, Harry Bannister, to Hollywood when he was offered film parts. Harding herself got five offers, and accepted a starring contract with Pathé.

Her first movie was *Paris Bound* (29), Philip Barry's domestic comedy with Fredric March, and the second *Her Private Affair*, an unforgettable performance, conscience-stricken after committing a *crime passionel*, with John Loder. She was loaned to Goldwyn to play opposite Ronald Colman in *Condemned* (and got him in the end in the British version; in the American one he remained on Devil's Island).

She was now getting $2,000 a week, and was worth somewhat more after the success of Philip Barry's *Holiday* (30), a refreshing comedy about two sisters and a man (Robert Ames); her touch was deft, but she went back to suffering nobly in the sextet that followed. At WB she did David Belasco's *Girl of the Golden West* and was then in some more hoary old goulash at Fox, *East Lynne* (31) with Clive Brook and Conrad Nagel, and not too sickly an experience in Frank Lloyd's astute hands (certainly better than a rival, modernized version going the rounds some months later, *Ex-Flame*). In *Devotion* she posed as a Cockney governess to be near the man she loved, Leslie Howard, and in *Prestige* (32) she was out East with Adolphe Menjou. Lionel Collier wrote: 'Although she does not share the glare of the big lights to the same extent as Garbo, Dietrich and Tallulah, she is certainly their equal in acting talent. In fact, I personally put her with Chatterton and Genevieve Tobin, ahead of her perhaps more glamorous rivals.' Harding's own prestige was enormous, but took a severe knock when she divorced her husband: stars in the sweet, innocent Harding mould just did *not* get divorced. Pathé/RKO had planned a sophisticated role (*Bed of Roses*) but decided now would not be an appropriate time to change the image. However, after some deliberation Harding played a divorcee (an innocent, gentle one) in *Westward Passage*, with a cast including a tyro Laurence Olivier, who remembered for

Ann Harding's u[...] filmstar-like appear[...] made her a critic's [...] and she could act as [...]

Ann Harding and William Powell in Double Harness *(33), one of the few films where she was allowed to look glamorous. Said the Kine Weekly: 'This delightful marital drama is intelligent stuff.'*

years Harding's kindness, her consideration and help with his part. Then she did *The Conquerors* with Richard Dix, a big William A. Wellman epic about an American family during the latter part of the last century and a bit of this.

Another Barry stage hit, *The Animal Kingdom*, cast her as the woman Howard preferred to his wife, Myrna Loy: but it was a comedy and another triumph for Harding. The rivalry of Harding and Loy had gone down so well that MGM borrowed Harding for *When Ladies Meet* (33), the first and best of the two versions of Rachel Crothers's play. This time Harding was the wife–of publisher Frank Morgan, whom aspiring writer Loy thinks she wants (till Robert Montgomery dissuades her). It was the first of the 'bitchy' films, so it was perhaps appropriate that it was stolen from both ladies by another, Alice Brady. Harding was now getting $6,000 a week, but planned to retire (she had particularly disliked *Prestige*); she stopped giving interviews. Then, suddenly, she was in *Double Harness* with William Powell (vamping him) and had *The Right to Romance* Nils Asther.

Her contract expired, but she signed on again for two years (three films a year, one of them at an outside studio). *Gallant Lady* at 20th-UA was her own choice, a creditable mother-love piece with Brook; but *The Life of Vergie Winters* (34) with John Boles was merely a re-hash of *Back Street*. *The Fountain* was a version of Charles Morgan's novel, a triangle story with a wartime background, with Brian Aherne as the lover and Paul Lukas as the husband. The Photoplay review gives an idea why Harding's movies were now faltering at the box-office: 'A beautiful, contemplative novel is made into a film exquisite to look at, but moving with measured tread.... Fine restrained acting....' MGM liked her, and tried to revive interest: *Biography of a Bachelor Girl* (35), a version of S.N. Behrman's 'Biography', with Robert Montgomery; and *The Flame Within* with Herbert Marshall. She was a psychiatrist, but it was Harding-formula stuff, and poor at that. *The Enchanted April* was another superior best-seller (by 'Elizabeth') adapted for Harding and Frank Morgan, and business was again disappointing. She went to Paramount for *Peter Ibbetson*, playing the childhood love of Gary Cooper who meets him clandestinely after marriage and goes on meeting him in dreams as he lives out his life incarcerated in prison; she was ideal as the real lady, and suitably ethereal as the dream one. RKO

Some of the cast of the sparkling first version of When Ladies Meet *(33): Myrna Loy, Alice Brady, Robert Montgomery, Ann Harding, Martin Burton.*

tried re-vamping her too dramatic image with a comedy, *The Lady Consents* (Herbert Marshall as a philanderer returning to her, his first wife, at the end), but once again it was too artificial and once again a flop. RKO wound up her contract by shoving her into *The Witness Chair* (36), a B, again as a sorrowing woman, with Walter Abel.

Harding was 'dead' in Hollywood. Like Chatterton earlier and Kay Francis later, she was killed by formula material. Some stars survived by battling for better material like Bette Davis, or prolonged their careers by turning to comedy like Claudette Colbert and Irene Dunne (apart from the fact that they were more entertaining, the values and standards in the comedies reflected more accurately real life than the dramas of the period); only MGM had the knack of keeping interest alive in its Dramatic ladies. Failing Hollywood offers, Harding went to Britain, where she sat around while a long search was made for the right material: finally she was the intended victim of sinister husband Basil Rathbone in Frank Vosper's melo, *Love From a Stranger* (37). She played 'Candida' in London, the play's first West End production, and married Werner Janssen, the orchestra conductor.

She returned to the US and it was reported that due to her British success her Hollywood terms had risen. She didn't make films, but made headlines in several court battles over the custody of her daughter. She toured the Pacific Coast in 'Candida' in 1938; and had a breakdown. She disappeared from view and reappeared in 1942 with the minimum of fuss, as the wife of blind detective Edward Arnold in a B directed by Fred Zinnemann, *Eyes in the Night*. In 1943 she was Walter Huston's wife in *Mission to Moscow*, and she was with him again in Russia in *North Star*. She had featured roles in *Nine Girls* (44), a sorority house mystery tale; *Janie* with Joyce Reynolds; *Those Endearing Young Charms* (45) with Laraine Day, *Janie Gets Married* (46), and had star roles again in *It Happened on 5th Avenue* (47) with Victor Moore and Don Defore, one of Monogram's more ambitious efforts, and in *Christmas Eve*, playing an ageing spinster in this sentimental comedy with the Georges Raft and Brent.

She returned to the theatre: toured in 1949 in 'Yes My Darling Daughter' and took over Ruth Hussey's part in 'Goodbye My Fancy'; then made three films for MGM: *Two Weeks With Love* (50), in the back seat as Jane Powell's mother; *The Magnificent Yankee* (51), as the wife of Oliver Wendell

Holmes (Louis Calhern) in a biopic that was beautifully done but too placid for popular taste; and *The Unknown Man* (51), a confused crime melo with Walter Pidgeon. She didn't film again until 1956 when she did three films: *The Man in the Grey Flannel Suit* as Fredric March's wife; *I've Lived Before* starring Jock Mahoney; and *Strange Interlude* starring Edmund Purdom and Ida Lupino. Theatregoers have been luckier: in 1958 she took over two of the leading parts in Tennessee Williams's one-acters, 'Garden District', and she has toured in 'September Tide' and 'The Corn Is Green'. Her last Broadway performance was in 'Abraham Cochrane' in 1964. She has appeared frequently on TV.

Cedric Hardwicke

He was one of the very few actor-knights ever to use his title professionally, and 'Sir Cedric Hardwicke' on a cast-list was an indication of two aspects of him: he did sell out to the Hollywood vineyards, and he was a remote, aristocratic actor. He never deserted the stage completely and rather despised films, but he is remembered best for his movie work and his capacity as a good supporting player, middle-aged and usually gruff. He always looked somewhat sad, which meant that he seemed understanding when he played kindly old men, and embittered or sardonic when he was villainous. He was not a very sympathetic actor, but he was a fine craftsman and most of the films in which he appeared were the richer for his presence.

He was born in 1893 in Lye, Stourbridge, Worcestershire. He trained for the stage at RADA, and made his first appearance as a walk-on, in 'The Monk and the Woman' in London in 1912. He was in a short, *Riches and Rogues* (13), the result of which was that Vitagraph Co. offered him a contract, but he preferred to stick to the stage. After serving in World War I he joined the Birmingham Rep, and began to make a name for himself, mostly in Shaw: Shaw himself liked his Captain Shotover, but what established Hardwicke with the public were two plays by Eden Phillpotts, 'The Farmer's Wife' (24) and 'Yellow Sands' (28). In 1925 he did a second film, in a supporting part, *Nelson*. His career went upwards: he played Captain Andy in 'Show Boat' at Drury Lane (28), originated the part of Magnus in 'The Apple Cart' (29), and Shaw wrote a part into 'Too True to Be Good' for him. In 1930 he had a big West End success in 'The Barretts of Wimpole Street'.

Not the wittiest of Nells nor the merriest of monarchs: Anna Neagle and Cedric Hardwicke in Nell Gwynn *(34)*.

This led to his having the title role in *Dreyfus* (31), an indifferent view of that affair, and a row of other films: *Rome Express* (32), as the falsely philanthropic millionaire; *Orders Is Orders* (33), as a peppery brigadier general; the weak *The Ghoul*, as a shady lawyer, with Boris Karloff; and *The Lady Is Willing* (34), a comedy with Leslie Howard, as the villain of the piece, a swindling businessman. This was the peak of his career. He was knighted in 1934, while appearing successfully in 'The Late Christopher Bean'. MGM wanted him for *Vanessa* and *David Copperfield*, but much to his annoyance he was committed to a tour of the play. He made some British films instead, *Nell Gwynn*, Charles II to Anna Neagle's pert Nell; *Jew Süss*, a very poor performance as the Rabbi; *The King of Paris*, in the title role of this story of theatrical life; and *Bella Donna* with Mary Ellis and Conrad Veidt. At the end of 1934 he was free to take up a Hollywood offer and went out to play the Marquess of Steyne in *Becky Sharp* (35)–a performance which is by far the best thing in the film. He stayed on to play the Bishop in *Les Misérables*; returned to Britain to play in 'Tovarich'–his last London stage appearance for 10 years. On film he was reunited with Neagle, as David Garrick to her *Peg of Old Drury*. He then did *Things to Come* (36) for Korda; *Tudor Rose*, a very popular picture about Lady Jane Grey (Nova Pilbeam), as the Earl of Warwick, who schemed to have Jane succeed Edward VI, and thus the instigator of her doom; and the spongeing brother-in-law in J. B. Priestley's *Laburnum Grove*.

Warners sent for him to play another Bishop, but a kindly one now, in the nonsensical *The Green Light* (37), and he made his New York stage debut in 'The Promise', under the management of Gilbert Miller, who had directed *The Lady Is Willing*. Apart from a trip to Britain to play Allan Quartermain in *King Solomon's Mines* (37) he was for the next few years on Broadway, notably in 'Shadow and Substance'; but he settled in Hollywood in 1939, while out there to play Mr Brink (his favourite film part) in MGM's *On Borrowed Time*, a goodish piece of whimsy with Lionel Barrymore and Beulah Bondi. He was excellent again as Livingstone in *Stanley and Livingstone* with Spencer Tracy at 20th, and as Frollo in *The Hunchback of Notre Dame* with Charles Laughton at RKO. RKO signed him to a contract, four films a year. Most of them were made on loan-out: *The Invisible Man Returns* (40) at Universal, as the villain; *Tom Brown's Schooldays*, as Dr Arnold; *The Howards of Virginia* at Columbia as a crippled reactionary; and *Victory* at Paramount, from Conrad's book. Said Howard Barnes: 'The Hardwicke characterization of the evil, woman-hating Mr Jones is the only one that comes through with the impact it had in the book. It is superb. Terror stalks the screen from the moment Mr Jones appears and builds into an irresistible crescendo. . . .'

He was established as one of the leading supporting actors in Hollywood, and he no longer aspired to star billing. He took brief bits in both *Suspicion* (41) and *Sundown* and better parts in several poor programmers: *The Ghost of Frankenstein* (42), *Valley of the Sun*, a Western; *Invisible Agent* with Jon Hall; and *The Commandos Strike at Dawn* (43) with Paul Muni. Then came *Forever and a Day*, the story of a London house through several generations, of which he was the begetter. In 1940 he had suggested to RKO an all-star charity film to aid British War Relief, the idea being that British artists in Hollywood should give their services free and RKO provide facilities and distribution. They liked the idea, and asked him to undertake the project as producer. It eventually began filming in 1941; and the several episodes were only completed finally due to the persistence of Hardwicke and directors Frank Lloyd and Herbert Wilcox. Other directors involved were René Clair and Victor Saville, and the cast, if not as starry as at first announced, still had some strong box-office names. Hardwicke himself did slapstick with Buster Keaton. The picture was shown finally in 1943, when its profits were split with American War Relief–but they weren't huge. For Hardwicke it had been a miserable experience. His contract was up and 20th wanted him to play the Nazi commander in Steinbeck's *The Moon Is Down*, the leading role in an important film: to make Hardwicke worthy of it and vice versa–to ensure he didn't do bit roles with other companies–they signed him to a three-year contract. He went to MGM for *The Cross of Lorraine* to play a priest, and then worked exclusively for 20th: *The Lodger* (44), as the householder; *Wing and a Prayer*, as an admiral; *Wilson*, as Henry Cabot Lodge; *The Keys of the Kingdom*, as another high-ranking cleric; and *Sentimental Journey* (46),

Cedric Hardwicke in what was virtually his only leading role in Hollywood, The Moon Is Down *(43), a drama about the Nazi occupation of Norway.*

as a doctor, befriending John Payne.

He didn't film in 1945, but was in a flop play in London, and in New York directed Gertrude Lawrence in 'Pygmalion'. His work over the next few years alternated between the two countries and while his parts in American films became smaller, his British work propped up his career. He was good in the British *Beware of Pity* and good again in one of his studies of bleak, implacable villainy, Ralph Nickleby in *Nicholas Nickleby* (47), an attempt by Cavalcanti at Ealing to film Dickens: some other good eccentrics (Sybil Thorndike, Athene Seyler, Stanley Holloway), but weak leads (Derek Bond, Sally Ann Howes). He returned to Hollywood: *The Imperfect Lady*; *Ivy*, as a Scotland Yard inspector; *Lured*; *Song of My Heart*, a Monogram biopic of Tchaikowsky (Frank Sundstrom); *Tycoon*, in the title role, with John Wayne; *A Woman's Vengeance* and *I Remember Mama* (48). He returned to Britain to play father Winslow in *The Winslow Boy*, then in Hollywood was another father, more tragically, in *Rope* (it was his murdered son in the trunk) and the king in *A Connecticut Yankee in King Arthur's Court* (49).

In London he joined the Old Vic Company for the 1948–9 season, and played the warden in a prison drama, *Now Barabbas* . . ., which starred Richard Greene, and never reached the US. In New York a revival of 'Caesar and Cleopatra' with Lilli Palmer boosted him, but in films his parts were either routine or prestigious five-minute bits: *The White Tower* (50); *Mr Imperium* (51); *The Desert Fox*; *The Green Glove* (52); *Caribbean*, a coloured B pirate picture with John Payne and Arlene Dahl; *Salome* (53), excellent as Tiberius; *Botany Bay*; and *Bait* (54) directed by and starring Hugo Haas. He was recalled to Britain by Olivier to play Edward IV in *Richard III* (55), which renewed his prestige and resulted in a series of cameo parts: *Helen of Troy* (55) as Priam; *Diane*; *Gaby* (56); *The Vagabond King*; *The Power and the Prize*; *The Ten Commandments* and *Around the World in 80 Days*. In 1957 he was in *The Story of Mankind* and *Baby Face Nelson*, excellent as a broken-down and drunken doctor. He said around this time that he would work in anything for the money–and then had economic security for a while on Broadway in a big hit, 'A Majority of One'.

In the 60s he did TV as well as stage work, and wrote an autobiography, 'A Victorian in Orbit': none of these ventures was wildly successful. He was in the film version of *Five Weeks in a Balloon* (62), and had a tiny but effective part in *The Pumpkin Eater* (64). He died later that year in virtual poverty–he had been married three times and it was believed that he was crippled by alimony. His first wife was actress Helena Pickard, and their son Edward Hardwicke has been one of the company at Britain's National Theatre.

Jean Harlow

To those unacquainted with Jean Harlow the oft-made comparisons with Marilyn Monroe must have seemed impertinent. Their personal lives had many similarities, including early deaths, but why should the genuinely attractive Monroe have been constantly compared with Harlow, platinum blonde, cross-legged in her hideous shapeless body-revealing sateen dresses, her smile the genuine toothpaste advert? Monroe was often rumoured to be on the verge of playing Harlow in a film life-story, it is true; but Monroe was like a marshmallow and Harlow was as hard as rock candy. Harlow was coarse, tarty–much more Iris Adrian or Marian Martin; when she wanted something, like Mae West she asked for it straight out. (At one point Metro approached West to write Harlow's dialogue.) She moved with unfettered ease, swaggering before her men, not appraising them but demanding them to appraise her. She vamped, with humour, and when men were indifferent, she didn't shrug like West, or melt like Monroe but shouted and glared. She was never innocent, like Monroe, though the situations that screen-writers got both girls into were frequently similar; audiences were titillated that both girls used sex blatantly, openly enjoying it (cf *Red Dust* and *Clash by Night*), an attitude in the 30s assumed to be extraordinary.

Where the comparison freely stands is that both were outstanding comediennes and both survived early critical hostility, emerging with solid reputations. Here is a selection of Harlow's notices: 1931: André Sennwald in The New York Times: '. . . it is unfortunate that Jean Harlow, whose virtues as an actress are limited to her blonde beauty, has to carry her share of the picture' (*The Iron Man*), and Mordaunt Hall, in the same paper: 'The acting throughout is interesting, with the exception of Jean Harlow' (*Public Enemy*). Irene Thirer in the New York Daily News: 'She is a decorative person but lacks the spark needed to make her shine as a personality' (*Goldie*). 1932: Variety: '. . . does better than might be expected, but she fails to be convincing' (*Three Wise Girls*). Later that year, Richard

Watts Jr in the New York Herald Tribune: 'The flagrantly blonde Miss Harlow, who hitherto has attracted but intermittent enthusiasm from this captious department, immediately becomes one of its favourites by her performance in *Red Dust*. . . . She proves herself a really deft comedienne.' 1933: Watts again: 'For those of us who are enthusiastic for the increasing talents of the distinguished Miss Harlow, *Bombshell* is chiefly important for the fact that it provides the first full-length portrait of this amazing young woman's increasingly impressive acting talent.' Sennwald again: 'Miss Harlow, who simply must be accepted as a fine comedienne in her particular sphere, plays her laughs too shrewdly to warrant the frequently heard opinion that not all her humor is intentional' (*The Girl From Missouri*). 1936: Howard Barnes in the New York Herald Tribune: '... she vitalizes the material throughout. She proves anew that she is a really fine comedienne' (*Libeled Lady*).

Jean Harlow was born in Kansas City, Missouri, in 1911; when she was 16, and still at school, she eloped with a wealthy Chicago boy, but it didn't last. With her mother and step-father, she found herself in Los Angeles, where she began to work as an extra in films: in *Moran of the Marines* (28), in *The Love Parade* (29) and *City Lights*. She appeared in some Christie comedies in 1929–30, and earlier had been quite conspicuous in a couple of Laurel-and-Hardys at Roach, including *Double Whoopee!* She had a fairish sized part in *The Saturday Night Kid* as a salesgirl in the store where Clara Bow and Jean Arthur worked, but was back on the Roach lot afterwards, waiting to be discovered. She was.

Howard Hughes had begun *Hell's Angels* in 1927, a tale of the Royal Flying Corps in World War I; after two years of filming much of the film was scrapped, in order to add sound, and with the salvage went Greta Nissen, whose accent little qualified her to play a British girl. Hughes saw Harlow at the Roach studios and signed her to replace Nissen. It cannot be said that Harlow's own accent sounded even remotely British, nor did those of Ben Lyon and James Hall resemble Oxford undergraduates – not that it matters today, because the film is now extremely dull. In its time, however, it was impressive, and was one of the top 10 money-makers of 1931. Hughes put Harlow under contract at $250 a week.

The new look in screen lovers: she was a cheap tramp who hid her yen under a flow of wise-cracks and he thought women were in the way except when he wanted sex: Harlow and Gable in Red Dust *(32), regarded in 1932 as the height of daring.*

Wallace Beery and Harlow arriving for Dinner at Eight *(33),* nouveau-riche *in a* haut-monde *world. As the film ends Harlow is making small talk with Marie Dressler: 'Do you know that the guy said machinery is going to take the place of every profession?' Dressler: 'Oh my* dear, *that's something* you *need never worry about.'*

Because of her low-cut gowns and equivocal role–she takes on both heroes and has an affair with a third man–Harlow became instantly famous. She was loaned out quickly: to MGM to play a gangster's moll in *The Secret Six* (31), to Universal to play the loose-living wife of boxer Lew Ayres, *The Iron Man*, and to WB for another moll in *Public Enemy*. In Fox's *Goldie*, a remake of *A Girl in Every Port*, the word 'tramp' was used for the first time on screen to describe a woman–but nevertheless, or therefore, Spencer Tracy and Warren Hymer still pursued her. She came into her own at last as Capra's *Platinum Blonde* at Columbia, miscast though she was as a society girl who woos and wins reporter Robert Williams but loses him to Loretta Young because, *inter alia*, she insists he wears garters: an extremely funny film. Still at Columbia (who were paying Hughes $1,750 a week for her services), she was a country girl in New York, and Mae Clarke and Marie Prevost were the others of the *Three Wise Girls* (32).

Her agent then stepped in. Hughes had no further movie plans and she would exist indefinitely on loan-outs. The agent wanted her at a studio who would build her, and he wanted her at MGM; furthermore, MGM wanted her. They bought her for $60,000

William Powell, Harlow and Franchot Tone in Victor Fleming's Reckless *(35). Harlow is a showgirl whose husband, Tone, commits suicide: then it's Powell to the rescue.*

plus the right for Hughes to use her for two pictures within five years at her normal salary: which would be $1,250 weekly up to a ceiling of $5,000 over a seven-year period (though for 52 weeks annually instead of the customary 30 only). She was thrown away, as a gangster's moll again, in *The Beast of the City*, but the second one was a part that Crawford and Shearer had turned down: *Red-Headed Woman* from Katherine Bush's best-seller. She was an unscrupulous vamp and wisely played for laughs, and got her first grudging reviews–but not in Britain. The film was banned because it was 'so tough' (Film Pictorial). *Red Dust* followed, and it did as much for her as she did for it–as the wise-cracking, predatory blonde who wanders into Gable's masculine little world and disrupts it. She was superb. Time magazine spoke of the film's 'brazen moral values' and for a long time it was regarded as the epitome of sexual daring.

She was duoed with Gable again in *Hold Your Man* (33), a comedy, and then cast as a movie sexpot who wanted to be a wife and mother, in *Bombshell*, one of the funniest satires ever on Hollywood life. At the end of the year, she was reckoned one of the top 10 draws in pictures. Appropriately enough then, she was among the distinguished company invited for *Dinner at Eight*, and she practically stole the film from all of them as the tarty, indolent wife, goading tycoon Wallace Beery and amusing herself on the side with Edmund Lowe. She got more good notices with another comedy, *The Girl From Missouri* (34)–who goes millionaire-hunting but falls for his son, Franchot Tone; but in a musical, *Reckless* (35), her dancing wasn't up to much and her singing voice was dubbed. The film was based loosely on the Libby Holman case (Holman, a big Broadway star, had been suspected of murdering her husband) and had been intended till the last minute for Joan Crawford; but William Powell was the co-star, and MGM wished to capitalize on his reported off-screen romance with Harlow (they eloped in 1936 but didn't marry).

China Seas was a variation of the *Red Dust* theme, with Harlow as a tropical trollop called China Doll; Gable co-starred again, and Beery–and the three of them were box-office dynamite. She went into *Riff Raff*, a hard-boiled thriller with Tracy; *Wife vs Secretary* (36), a brittle Faith Baldwin story with Gable and Myrna Loy; and *Suzy*, a silly spy story with Cary Grant. MGM were tentatively trying to broaden her range, to let her play some scenes straight, but *Libeled Lady* was pure comedy, and with her, Tracy, Powell and Loy, pure joy. Which cannot be said about *Personal Property* (37) with Robert Taylor.

During the making of *Saratoga* she became seriously ill, and she died (reportedly of

uraemic poisoning) before it was completed (37). The piece, a horse-racing comedy-drama, again with Gable, has its moments, but it is difficult to guess what it might have been like. Some later sequences are clearly curtailed, and the double used is laughably obvious (she's either hiding her eyes or has her back to the camera). Certainly there's nothing in it to suggest why it should have been the biggest film hit of 1937, with a colossal take of $2 million–unless the public were either anxious or morbidly curious to see Harlow for the last time.

In 1964 a scurrilous biography of her was published, dealing mainly with her second marriage to MGM executive, Paul Bern, who committed suicide (1932) in mysterious circumstances. (His suicide note spoke of impotency and the subsequent newspaper headlines threatened to ruin Harlow and her forthcoming *Red Dust*–they didn't.) The book became a best-seller and was filmed with Carroll Baker. A rival film with Carol Lynley was made simultaneously by a process called Electrovision (which meant that it was filmed, for speed, like a TV play): both were rushed to the market to meet with complete public apathy. Neither book, nor the films, seemed to have anything to do with that jolly girl who traded insults with Clark Gable and Spencer Tracy.

Will Hay

The number of British comics who have made it in the international market can be numbered on the fingers of one hand and Will Hay, fondly remembered in Britain, is not one of them. His films were not exportable when made, and Americans chancing on them on British TV find them slow, laboured and crude. The dialogue does not go snap snap snap as with the American comics, following a vaudeville tradition that was altogether more swiftly paced than the British Music Hall style. The British have laughed at the major US comedians while their own laughter-makers thudded overseas. The films of Will Hay *are* slow, laboured and crude. But they are also genuinely funny: a Will Hay Festival at London's National Film Theatre in the 50s was as well-received as later festivals of the Marxes and W. C. Fields.

Hay was like Fields in that he perfected a certain character that was at its best in situation comedy. The laughs depended on the reaction of that character to what was happening around him, on the follies and foibles of that character. Some comics–as disparate as Bob Hope and Buster Keaton–worked subjectively, through instinct rather than intellect. Chaplin worked both ways, and Jack Benny, for instance, has it both ways: he is not a character comedian, but he gets a hundred laughs out of his meanness.

Will Hay was not instinctively funny, but he constructed a character that was. He was invariably in a position of authority for which he was totally unfitted. He looked seedy and disreputable and indeed was. He had so far advanced through the world by bluffing, bragging and cheating, and the shiftiness of his eyes suggested that it wouldn't be long before he was caught up with. That being so, one more lie, one more dishonesty wouldn't come amiss. His eye was to the main chance where cash or booze were concerned–he seldom began to consider his chances with women; nor was he often seen intoxicated, a state which might suggest that he had abandoned his normal wary stance. His successes were minor and non-lasting and were due mainly to luck–an old flash of cunning that went undetected. He never went soft, was never pitiable.

In parentheses, a later comedian, Tony Hancock, owed something to both Hay and W. C. Fields. The character carefully created for him by his script-writers, Galton and Simpson, had elements of both: he was also a braggart without conviction, a little man who dreamt of glory, of routing his enemies. His first starring picture, *The Rebel* (60), met a hostile reception in the US, and Dwight Macdonald (who was living in Britain at the time and might therefore have been sympathetic) observed drily for the readers of Esquire that he was much admired over there 'for inscrutable reasons'. Yet informed British comment on Hancock at his best, both before and since his tragic death, insists that he was a great clown.

Just as Hancock was at his best with Sid James, so Hay was at his best with his two sidekicks, both of them cynical about his abilities, and otherwise downright contemptuous: Graham Moffat (Albert), the fat boy, insolent, lazy and sarcastic, and Moore Marriott (Harbottle), the senile gap-toothed old codger, ever-hopeful and suspicious. Like Hancock and James, these three matched each other in duplicity. The profound comic invention of their best scenes (Val Guest contributed to most of Hay's best scripts)–Hay arriving at 'his' station in *Oh Mr Porter!*, the business with the station poor-box in *Ask a Policeman*–is as funny as anything on celluloid. But British indulgence over the matter of timing may always restrict revivals to indigenous audiences.

An atmosphere of mutual distrust: Will Hay (centre), Graham Moffat and Moore Marriott in Ask a Policeman *(33) with, at left, Herbert Lomas. One of the film's funniest scenes.*

Hay was born in Aberdeen in 1888. The family moved to Manchester where he was apprenticed as an engineer; reputedly he was fired with ambition to go on the stage when he saw W. C. Fields do his juggling act. He entertained at charity shows till an offer was made to him to turn professional. He made his debut on the Halls in 1909, writing his own sketches, based often on his sister's experiences as a school-teacher. Gradually – after World War I – there evolved 'The Fourth Form at St Michael's' which was to be the prototype for all his future work: the idea of course was that the boys were brighter than he. During the 20s he toured in the US and the then British Empire, and successfully adapted his technique to radio; he also obtained a considerable reputation as a leading amateur astronomer.

He entered films with *Those Were the Days* (34) sub-titled 'A Night at an Old Time Musical': more surprisingly, it was based on Pinero's farce 'The Magistrate', whose plot it mostly jettisoned. Hay was the unfortunate magistrate. He was the D.G. of B.H. (head of the BBC) in *Radio Parade of 1935*, imitating Hollywood models, and was then involved in another adaptation of Pinero, *Dandy Dick* (35). These were made for B.I.P. but he signed a contract with Gainsborough, starting with *Boys Will Be Boys*, which, though the credits claimed it was based on Beachcomber's Narkover College, was in fact an extension of his best-known Music Hall sketch. He was then an incompetent private eye in *Where There's a Will* (36) and an incompetent skipper in *Windbag the Sailor*, his first teaming with both Marriott and Moffat.

There was another school story, *Good Morning Boys* (37), and then *Oh Mr Porter!*, which John Montgomery in 'Comedy Films' lists as the funniest British film of that era. Time hasn't tarnished it. Hay was the station-master of a derelict and probably haunted country station, Buggleskelly, and Moffat and Marriott were his helpmates. In *Convict 99* (38) he became a prison governor via the usual first-reel misunderstanding, and had Moffat as a warder and Marriott as the oldest lag in the business. Basil Wright wrote that Hay 'makes a success of the job partly by mistake and partly by that shady but genteel ability to tell lies and conduct swindles which he invests with so much genuine charm'. He was, alas, bereft of his cohorts in *Hey Hey USA*, perhaps his weakest film, a satire on gangsters. *Old Bones of the River* was a take-off on Edgar Wallace's 'Sanders' stories, and the three of them were again at their best in *Ask a Policeman* (39) and *Where's That Fire?*. Moffat and Marriott continued to be of inestimable advantage but Hay disliked being dependent on them and quarrelled with Gainsborough over it: as a result he left them and moved over to Ealing.

His first film there, *The Ghost of St Michaels* (41), was in the old mould, but distressingly near a boy's comic-book strip in style and content. Thereafter he tried less familiar situations: two war stories, *The Black Sheep of Whitehall* and *The Goose Stepped Out*, are uneven in quality, though they have sequences of moment (similar difficulties were confronting the Marxes in Hollywood). On the former Dilys Powell compared him to other British comics: 'Will Hay with his evasions, chases, absurd disguises, and the inevitable débâcle seems to me streets ahead of the rest.' Hay then did a straight character part in a semi-documentary, *The Big Blockade* (42) with Michael Redgrave and John Mills. His last film, *My Learned Friend* (43), had savage moments, a *comédie noire* with very few let-ups and an irreverence worthy of his best work at Gainsborough (Hay knew he was to be the sixth victim of a homicidal maniac). Ill-health caused a semi-retirement, alas for the laughter of Britain (from 1937 to 1942 he was one of the best draws at the box-office, of British stars trailing only Gracie Fields and George Formby). He did an occasional Music Hall booking, and had a popular radio programme until he died in 1949.

Helen Hayes

It is a distinguished name in the theatre: Helen Hayes. An actress of great resource and impeccable technique, an actress who has spent her life in the business and has been acclaimed (as have several others) 'The First Lady of the American Theatre'. For a brief while she was one of the first ladies of films.

She was born in 1900 in Washington DC, where she made her first stage appearance only five years later, in 'The Royal Family', as Prince Charles. She had a fairly prolific career as a child actress, and made her Broadway debut in 1909 in 'Old Dutch'; the following year she appeared in a Vitagraph two-reeler, *Jean and the Calico Doll* (Jean was a dog); from 1913 to 1916 she was in stock in Washington, and in 1917–18 toured as 'Pollyanna'; but thereafter was seldom away for long from the Broadway scene. Among

In an Italian garden: Gary Cooper and Helen Hayes in the best of the two screen versions of A Farewell to Arms *(32), directed by Frank Borzage.*

her successes: 'Dear Brutus' (18), 'Clarence' by Booth Tarkington (19), 'To the Ladies' (22), 'Caesar and Cleopatra' (25), 'What Every Woman Knows' (26), 'Coquette' (27); and on tour thereafter: when she left the cast to have a baby the management sued. Hayes won, amidst headlines, and had what was known as the Act of God baby. 'Petticoat Influence' (30) was her last play before accepting an MGM contract.

Hayes didn't really want to go to Hollywood, and didn't want to be in films, but husband Charles MacArthur, the dramatist, had had lucrative writing offers. He wrote her first film, not entirely seriously, an incredibly maudlin tale of mother-love – from innocent girlhood to decrepit old whore – *The Sin of Madelon Claudet* (31). Neither of them liked it but it did bring her a Best Actress Oscar. The next two were nothing to be ashamed of, however; both from good novels: *Arrowsmith* at Goldwyn, an imposing performance as Ronald Colman's wife, and *A Farewell to Arms* (32) at Paramount, as Catherine, with Gary Cooper. Had all her pictures been as good, she might not have left Hollywood (she did return to New York briefly in 1931 for

'The Good Fairy'). But the next two were not an improvement on *Madelon Claudet*. In *The Son-Daughter* she and Ramon Novarro were Chinese soulfully in love, with her sacrificing herself to Warner Oland whom she finally strangles with his own pigtail; and *The White Sister* (33), the remake of a Lillian Gish film, was another 'impossible' love story – about a girl who thinks her lover (Clark Gable) has been killed (in war) but meets him again after she has become a nun. Somewhat better were *Another Language*, a dullish version of Rose Franken's play about a dominating mother (Louise Closser Hale) and the one daughter-in-law who opposes her; and *Night Flight*, again with Gable.

She rushed back to New York to appear in Maxwell Anderson's 'Mary of Scotland'; stayed in 'Scotland' for *What Every Woman Knows* (34) with Brian Aherne, a vehicle which MGM chose hoping that it would please her; then toured as Mary. She had told MGM that she had no wish to continue her film career, and made an announcement, part of which ran: 'I am leaving the screen because I don't think I am very good in the pictures and I have a beautiful dream that I'm elegant on the stage.' Long before it appeared, *Vanessa Her Love Story* (35) was publicized as her last film. It was an adaptation of a novel by Hugh Walpole (who much approved of her), and co-starred Robert Montgomery.

At the end of 1935 Hayes scored perhaps her biggest stage success: in the title role of Lawrence Houseman's 'Victoria Regina'. Here is a partial list of subsequent stage work: in Chicago, 'The Merchant of Venice' (38); in New York, 'Twelfth Night' (40) as Viola; 'Harriet' (Beecher Stowe) (43–45); 'Alice-Sit-by-the-Fire' on tour (46); 'The Glass Menagerie' (as Amanda) in London (48); 'The Wistaria Trees' (50); 'Mrs McThing' (52); 'Time Remembered' (57); and 'A Touch of the Poet' (58) in the New York theatre named after her. There were also numerous revivals of 'What Every Woman Knows'. In 1961 she toured Europe in 'The Skin of Our Teeth' (as Mrs Antrobus) and 'The Glass Menagerie' for the State Department; there have been few other appearances: a Shakespeare recital with Maurice Evans and a chronicle play about the wives of the presidents, 'The White House' (64). She has also done much TV, and there have been to date five subsequent film appearances: in *Stage Door Canteen* (43), as herself; *My Son John* (52), Leo McCarey's silly anti-Red film, with Robert Walker; *Main Street to Broadway* (53), again as herself; *Anastasia* (56), as the Grand Duchess; and *Airport* (70), billed as 'Miss Helen Hayes' and playing her cute-old-lady part with the accumulated mannerisms of a lifetime. Her son, James MacArthur, has had an indifferent movie career, after a brilliant start in Frankenheimer's fine *The Young Stranger* (56).

Rita Hayworth

The appellation 'The Love Goddess' has been used about a dozen stars, but mostly about Rita Hayworth. Whatever other girls had – and sexy, desirable girls were never in short supply in films – Rita had more of. She was ravishing in black and white, and breathtaking when (very sensibly) they put her into Technicolor: auburn-haired, brown-eyed, and with the proverbial peaches-and-cream complexion. It wasn't just physical allure. Naturally it's preferable when the woman on the seducing end is attractive – provocation was an early Hayworth speciality – but she did have that special star lustre. One fan-mag-writer in 1963 considered her 'an interesting interval – if not an especially dynamic one – between Jean Harlow and Marilyn Monroe', but her sex-appeal was really somewhat more subtle than either. She was once described as 'the intellectual's glamour girl', presumably implying that a lot of people liked her who weren't expected to. Later in the career the lustre dimmed (in fact quite quickly) and she became less interesting; but the face, still beautiful, suggested an interesting past.

She was born in New York in 1918, the daughter of Eduardo Cansino, a Latin-American dancer (and by virtue of their mothers being sisters, a cousin of Ginger Rogers). She followed in her father's steps (under the name Margarita Cansino) and got a job dancing at the Agua Caliente in LA, then popular with film folk. As she hoped, she was noticed and signed for a Fox contract. She appeared in *Under the Pampas Moon* (35), and in some other films, mostly dancing in the background; but had parts in *Charlie Chan in Egypt*, *Dante's Inferno*, *Paddy O'Day* (which starred Jane Withers) and *Human Cargo* (36). Fox decided she was star material, and planned *Ramona* for her and Gilbert Roland; but when 20th combined with that company and the new management took over, they were replaced by Loretta Young and Don Ameche. After a part in *A Message to Garcia* she was dropped. She got some leading parts in B pictures: *Meet Nero Wolfe* at Columbia, *Rebellion* and *Old Louisiana* (37) both with Tom Keene, *Hit the Saddle* and *Trouble in Texas*.

Her husband, a businessman, decided to

take a hand, and on the strength of that one role at Columbia talked that studio into giving her a contract (for seven years, starting at $250 weekly and going to $1,750). Her first name had already been reduced to Rita, and now she got a new surname, Hayworth. Columbia considered her strictly B-picture stuff: *Girls Can Play*; *The Game That Kills*; *Criminals of the Air*; *The Shadow*; and *Convicted* (38), all with Charles Quigley; *Paid to Dance* (37) with Don Terry; *Who Killed Gail Preston?* (38) with Robert Paige; *Juvenile Court* with Paul Kelly and *Homicide Bureau* (39) with Bruce Cabot. She supported Joan Blondell and Melvyn Douglas in *There's Always a Woman* (38), and Cukor tested her for the role of Hepburn's sister in *Holiday* without success; she played opposite Warren William in *The Lone Wolf Spy Hunt* (39) which wasn't quite a B; was loaned to RKO for *Renegade Ranger* with George O'Brien; and was then cast in an unequivocally good part, the second female lead in *Only Angels Have Wings*, as Richard Barthelmess's philandering wife. Then it was back to Bs: *Special Inspector*, *Music in My Heart* (40) with Tony Martin, and *Blondie on a Budget*. But Cukor recalled the test and at MGM borrowed her for a good part in *Susan and God*. This, and the response to the plethora of pin-up pictures that Columbia had issued, suggested to the studio that she might play the part Jean Arthur had turned down in Ben Hecht's uncertain fable, *Angels Over Broadway*; Douglas Fairbanks Jr and Thomas Mitchell co-starred, and it flopped. However, they then decided to star her in *The Lady in Question*, a remake of the French *Gribouille*, for which Luise Rainer had been considered. In it, Hayworth was on trial for murder, and Brian Aherne co-starred.

On the evidence of both films it seemed that Hayworth was decorative but unlikely to go very far: thus the studio were not averse to loaning her to WB when Ann Sheridan walked out of *Strawberry Blonde* (41). As the other woman, James Cagney's recurrent crush, she was assured and sparkling. WB sagely kept her to add some spice to *Affectionately Yours*, a comedy with Merle Oberon and Dennis Morgan. The word was out: Hollywood had a new star (at last) and 20th jumped in with an offer (and five times her normal salary) to play another temptress in *Blood and Sand*, a part originally destined for Carole Landis. It was in colour and Hayworth was in every way superb.

Columbia then teamed her with Fred Astaire for a Cole Porter musical, *You'll Never Get Rich*; 20th borrowed her again for a colour musical with Victor Mature, *My Gal Sal* (42), a big hit, and the Charles Boyer episode in *Tales of Manhattan*. Hayworth couldn't sing (her singing voice was dubbed), but she went on to make a string of musicals: *You Were Never Lovelier* with Astaire, and the one which will always be associated with her, *Cover Girl* (44). Jerome Kern provided the score and Gene Kelly co-starred: it was lush, inventive and way ahead of most musicals of the period. Business was great, but *Tonight and Every Night* (45), supposedly a follow-up (based on London's Windmill 'We Never Closed' Theatre), didn't have Kelly – or Astaire – and was so-so. *Down to Earth* (47) cast Hayworth as Terpsichore, posing as a mortal for a Broadway show.

Gene Kelly and Rita Hayworth in Charles Vidor's Cover Girl, *the backstage musical that broke the conventions of backstage musicals, and broke box-office records.*

It was preceded by *Gilda* (46): 'There Never Was a Woman Like Gilda!' said the ads. Hayworth was the post-war epitome of screen eroticism, a somewhat déclassé

Rita Hayworth and Glenn Ford in Char. Vidor's Gilda (*46*) *in Burt Kennedy's* T

adventuress who descends on Glenn Ford and George Macready and splits their (surprisingly explicit) liaison. The first hour is keen with mystery, but as C. A. Lejeune observed, there are hints 'subsequently confirmed, that nothing is going to happen except Miss Hayworth'. However, in a clinging black satin dress, in elbow-length gloves, she sang 'Put the Blame on Mame'. Then, as if to confirm her status as a sex-symbol, second husband Orson Welles – they were on the point of divorcing – cast her as a (blonde) treacherous lady in *The Lady From Shanghai* (48). Columbia tried to retrieve the situation with *The Loves of Carmen*, again with Ford (as Don José), but Hayworth just wasn't fiery enough.

At this point she eloped to Europe with, and later married, Prince Aly Khan, a match that occasioned screaming headlines. The union of playboy and movie star didn't conflict with the Hayworth image, but Columbia wanted her back – she was, after all, by far the most popular of their contract players. She came back as the marriage died: and something within her seemed also to have died. The old vivacity had gone. *Affair in Trinidad* (52), with Ford resumed her career, but she and the film were monotonous together and business was only fair. It was followed by a couple of classic vamps, *Salome* (53) and *Miss Sadie Thompson* – Maugham butchered to make a Hayworth holiday. Both films were ludicrous, but it is unlikely that, in kinder circumstances, Hayworth could have measured up to the parts. Married now to Dick Haymes and uncertain of public interest, Hayworth stayed away for three years, returning with an actioner co-starring Robert Mitchum, *Fire Down Below* (57). She was from time to time her old self in *Pal Joey* and appeared to some advantage as the ageing beauty in *Separate Tables* (58), among whose producers was her new husband, James Hill (they were divorced in 1961).

Few of her subsequent films have caused a squeak at the box-office, but it wasn't her fault. Most of them were terrible. The best of them was perhaps *They Came to Cordura* (59), an adventure yarn with Gary Cooper in which she was, personally, excellent; and the most expensive *Circus World* (64) with John Wayne. The others: *The Story on Page One* (59) with Anthony Franciosa; *The Happy Thieves* (61), a so-called comedy with Rex Harrison; *The Money Trap* (65), a reunion with Ford which played the lower half of bills; and *L'Avventurio/The Rover* (67) with Anthony Quinn, a version of Conrad

Money Trap (*65*). *The former was a great success, the latter wasn't.*

directed by Terence Young that hadn't seen the light of day three years later.

In 1969 Hayworth told a reporter that she considered she had a new career, a modest one, and very different from the other one. To prove her point, she was seen in *I Gatti/Sons of Satan* (69), an Italian programmer that Joan Crawford decided at the last moment not to do; *The Grove* (70), an indie, made in Florida; and Georges Lautner's *La Route de Salina.*

Sonja Henie

A Sonja Henie, like an Esther Williams, can, one assumes, only happen once to the film business. They were speciality performers and today TV would probably display their talents to audiences who craved such thrills. Sonja skated. She was undoubtedly a great skater. Beyond that, it was dimples and a mile of kitsch.

She was born in Oslo in 1913; at four she learned dancing and at eight began ice-skating. At 11, she won the Figure-Skating Championship of Norway, and two years later was placed second in the World Championships. The following year she gained the World title, and held on to it for 10 consecutive years. Meanwhile, she began to study ballet under Karsavina. In the Olympic Games of 1928, 1932 and 1936 she broke records and gained Gold Medals; it was after the 1936 Games that she decided to turn professional.

Henie desperately wanted to be in movies. She underwent extensive beauty treatment and Hollywood was certainly interested – but not at her asking price, $75,000 per film. So she hired a rink in Los Angeles so that producers could gauge her appeal; as ever, she was an SRO success. Darryl Zanuck decided to gamble and cast her in *One in a Million* (36), backed by Adolphe Menjou, Don Ameche and the Ritz Brothers. It was so successful that she was hurried into *Thin Ice* (37) with Tyrone Power, and at the end of the year she had zipped into the top 10 money-makers. After *Happy Landing* (38), with Ameche, 20th negotiated a new contract for three films, at $125,000 each, but as that film did continued fine business and edged into the year's top hits, Henie – noted for her keen business sense – demanded revised terms. The contract was amended: five years, three pictures a year at $160,000 per picture – which, working out at $16,000 a week for 10 weeks per film, made her the highest paid of stars.

Sonja Henie in One in a Million*: it was 20th Century-Fox's Christmas present to cinemagoers in 1936.*

The films were all much of a muchness. Most of them were set in winter-sports resorts, with stories devised to keep audiences as mindless as possible between the Henie bouts on skates. They were gay and glamorous, and Henie was invariably chased by the most handsome louts on the 20th lot–like Richard Greene in *My Lucky Star*. None of these gentlemen was a great talent, but they made the lady twinkle a bit, and with the aid of such things as the Irving Berlin score for *Second Fiddle* (39) the films were amiable entertainment. Power and Rudy Vallee were also in that, but it wasn't the expected hit. Ray Milland and Robert Cummings were in *Everything Happens at Night*, and they were journalists involved with the Gestapo–but not too seriously (yet). There was no Henie film in 1940, and her contract was revised again: only one film a year. The novelty had worn off; the trouble was that when she wasn't skating, unassuming and sweet as she was, she was as interesting as a cold potato. Confronted with John Payne in *Sun Valley Serenade* (41) nary a spark flew, but the Glenn Miller Orchestra and two hit songs caused it to more than smoulder at the box-office. However, *Iceland* (42) with Payne and *Wintertime* (43), with Cornel Wilde and Jack Oakie didn't do well, and 20th quietly didn't renew her contract. She signed with International for two films, the first of which was *It's a Pleasure* (45), with Michael O'Shea, but whatever the addition of colour did to the skating scenes, it was ineffective at the box-office. (It was released by RKO who had earlier had their own Henie-rival, Irene Dare; but the only other skater who made it in films–in a very mild way–was Belita.)

International Pictures had amalgamated with Universal, and they released the skating remake of an old Universal property, *The Countess of Monte Cristo* (48). It was a flop and, as Henie insisted on her films being built round her, there were no more takers in Hollywood. But she had always found 'in-person' shows lucrative and most of her subsequent fortune came from them. She had played Madison Square Garden annually for years, and did so until 1952 when there was a row with the management. She 'was considered temperamental' said Variety. She transferred her show to the Knightsbridge Armory in the Bronx, but ticket sales were meagre. She then gave up. She had appeared also in Europe and was a very wealthy lady indeed. But even if she needed films as little as they needed her, in the late 50s she turned up in Britain to make something called *London Calling* with Michael Wilding, apparently some sort of revue: its first showings seem to have been delayed until 1968 when it appeared among some afternoon TV schedules. That same year Henie made news when it was announced that she and her wealthy (third) husband were going to donate most of their fine modern art collection together with a new gallery to the city of Oslo. She died in 1969, of leukaemia, while on a plane journey to that city.

Katharine Hepburn

The longevity of Katharine Hepburn's career must have confounded her early detractors: both in and out of Hollywood she evoked strong feelings for and against, and sometimes only the praise of reviewers saved her from the wrath of producers and exhibitors. The fan-magazines watched from the wings, half-admiring, half-aghast: 'Is Hepburn Killing Her Own Career?' asked Photoplay in 1935, detailing the new exploits of this *enfant terrible* and the bumpy road of her latest movie at the box-office. George Cukor described her: 'a person whose rare charm and strength is her uncompromising individuality. . . . From the beginning, Miss Hepburn chose a direct line and stuck to it. It can frankly be said that Hepburn has not grown up to Hollywood. Hollywood has grown up to her.' She herself has said: 'I suppose when I was a very young actress I was very unsure of myself, and I thought you had to be nice to everybody, so I was. Then I got to be a big star rather quickly, and it occurred to me that you didn't, so then I was difficult with the press and everybody. Then after a while, things didn't go so well, so I decided it was time to be sweet again. And by that time, the press and I had got to be rather old and sweet together. You know, when someone has been around as long as I have, people get fond of you, like some old building.'

'Fond' is hardly an adequate word to describe the current attitude to Hepburn: when, in 1967–9 she returned to films and decided to give a series of interviews, journalists searched in dictionaries for new superlatives, and critics did not so much review her performances as send her love-letters. The fact is that today she is a Very Big Star Indeed, after years of a strictly limited popularity (for instance, since the 30s she has seldom attained top billing).

She was a star from the word go. She had a whacking part in her first film, and the world knew there had arrived a star to be reckoned with, perhaps challenging the supremacy of Garbo (which resulted in a silly fan-magazine rivalry). But it is in the Garbo stratosphere that she belongs (Kenneth Tynan once termed her 'the Garbo of the Great Outdoors').

Hepburn was born in Hartford, Connecticut, in 1909, into a wealthy family. She acted at college and made her pro debut in Baltimore in 1928 in 'The Czarina'; acted for four years without success ('Death Takes a Holiday', 'Art and Mrs Bottle') and was also married (1928–34) with similar results. She was often fired (hence the insecurity) and was at one point dropped from the lead in an up-dating of 'Lysistrata' – 'The Warrior's Husband' (32); but taken on again, she became a Broadway star. Paramount had already offered a test, but Hepburn had preferred to wait: now she went on her own terms, on a one-picture deal at RKO at $1,500 a week. The studio hesitated, however, till Cukor ran a test she

One of the most talked-about and significant debuts in the history of motion pictures: Katharine Hepburn, with Billie Burke, in A Bill of Divorcement *(32). It was based on Clemence Dane's play.*

had done, and he demanded her for *A Bill of Divorcement* (32), as John Barrymore's daughter, fearing she might inherit his mental derangement. RKO saw the rushes and signed her to a five-year contract.

Said the Daily Telegraph (London): 'Miss Hepburn has many limitations. She is not at all beautiful, and her voice is uncommonly harsh, though, thank heaven, not shrill. But give her 10 minutes to work her spell and you forget these things. You realize that here is something new and different – a very young actress with the power of a well-trained tragedienne, a strange, dynamic and moving young person in a profession full of characterless, synthetic blondes.' Such notices brought some reaction by the time *Christopher Strong* (33) was shown. But in the New York Herald Tribune Richard Watts

Jr declared defiantly that she remained 'just as good an actress and just as distinctive a personage'. She played, with the same burning conviction, a celebrated British aviatrix, the sort of resolute part she was to play so often. Co-star Colin Clive told an interviewer: 'There is nobody quite like her in Hollywood – or anywhere else for that matter. . . . She is not just a face, but a terrific personality. I said just now that she is not beautiful and that is true, though she understands the art of acting so amazingly that she can convey the illusion of beauty if the part demands it!' And Paul Muni said, after her third film: 'There's no one to touch her among the younger actresses – the only one approaching her is Margaret Sullavan, but she's soft, charming, lovely. She hasn't Hepburn's drive.'

The third film was *Morning Glory*, and Hepburn was *very* determined as a struggling actress, until Adolphe Menjou said, 'You don't belong to any man now – you belong to Broadway.' Said A. J. Harman of this performance in the London Evening News: 'The most remarkable acting I have ever seen.' In Hollywood she won the Best Actress Oscar. Cukor directed her again in (his favourite among his own films) *Little Women*. She was perfectly cast as Jo, again got great notices, and the film was a huge grosser. *Spitfire* (34) – as a wild girl of the mountains – didn't do so well, and by this time Hepburn received a rebuff in New York that might have sunk a lesser person. It was a play called 'The Lake', and it provided her with a famous line: 'The calla lilies are in bloom again'. It also provoked two more deathless lines: Dorothy Parker's comment on her performance, 'She ran the gamut of emotions from A to B', and George S. Kaufman's (on hearing that she had had sheets put up in the wings), 'She's afraid she might catch acting'.

She limped back to Hollywood, which offered little solace with J. M. Barrie's synthetic and cloying *The Little Minister* (34) – she was Babbie, the gypsy girl – and the weak *Break of Hearts* (35), desperately loving Charles Boyer after a Cinderella romance. Of *Minister* she confessed (in an interview in Sight and Sound) years later: 'I didn't really want to play it until I heard another actress was desperate for the role. Then of course it became the most important thing in the world for me that I should get it. Several of

The beginning of a great screen partnership: Tracy and Hepburn in Woman of the Year *(42). He was a sports columnist and she a commentator on international affairs: her citation as Woman of the Year almost broke up their marriage.*

my parts in those days I fought for just to take them from someone who needed them.' (*Minister* had at one time been bought by Universal for Margaret Sullavan, and at least two Hepburn roles – *Christopher Strong* and *A Woman Rebels* – had been intended for Ann Harding.) It was announced that she would play Joan of Arc, George Sand and Elizabeth I; instead she played *Alice Adams*. Says Pauline Kael (1968): '. . . her beautiful angularity and her faintly absurd Bryn Mawr accent are perfect for Booth Tarkington's desperately pretentious small-town social climber. . . . Hepburn's pantomiming in some of the scenes is as fine as the best American acting I've ever seen – she makes Alice one of the few authentic movie heroines.' The film still looks good today, due as much to the direction of George Stevens, a new man whom Hepburn insisted on having.

Cukor directed her again, in the transcription of a novel by Compton Mackenzie, *Sylvia Scarlet* – 'Father, I'm going to cut my hair off! I'm going to be a boy!'; and John Ford helmed the film of Maxwell Anderson's *Mary of Scotland* (36), a lush and silly picture with memorable solecisms (a soundtrack of Jacobite melodies; Mary in a tartan, and saying to the Confederate lords, 'I'm through!'). Hepburn despised Mary, and was better cast in two more costume dramas: *A Woman Rebels*, a saga of a woman's emancipation in Victorian England with Van Heflin as her lover and Herbert Marshall as the man who stands by her; and better Barrie, *Quality Street* (37), beautifully directed by Stevens with Fay Bainter equally fine as the older sister. And quality was the keynote again with *Stage Door*, directed by Gregory La Cava, with Ginger Rogers and a fine cast in this excellent adaptation of the Ferber-Kaufman stage hit about aspiring actresses; and with *Bringing up Baby* (38), directed by Howard Hawks, with Cary Grant and Hepburn displaying a dazzling aptitude for screwball comedy.

Despite great reviews for most of this batch, they did increasingly badly, and RKO came reluctantly to the conclusion that the appeal of their most prized property had distinctly declined. At this juncture their pessimism was confirmed when a group of exhibitors labelled her box-office poison (for some reason the label stuck to Hepburn longer than to the others on the list). RKO then proposed a property they had had hanging around for some time, *Mother Carey's Chickens*, and rather than submit, Hepburn bought up her contract. She cast around for a job, and had a yen to do *Holiday*, a play she had once understudied; it so happened that Columbia had just bought this for a derisory figure, among a batch of old Pathé properties acquired from RKO. She negotiated with Columbia to do it there, with Cukor directing, and herself getting a fee of $175,000. Cukor and she did their usual accomplished work, but the film was too talky for general acceptance. There were no further film offers, though there was an outside chance that Selznick would cast her as Scarlett O'Hara. He had produced some of her early films, and Cukor was set to direct *Gone With the Wind*; and eventually she was offered Scarlett, one of the three actresses who were. But she sensed that Selznick had only approached her out of desperation, and accepted provisionally: it was widely accepted that she hadn't the requisite sex-appeal, and it was known that Clark Gable didn't want her. She wasn't surprised when Selznick discovered Vivien Leigh at the last minute, and preferred her.

The next offer was from MGM, and involved a mere $10,000: true, it was a Lubitsch film, but she didn't like the script. It was a helluva drop, and Hepburn decided that she needed an exceptional film if she was to continue. She approached Philip Barry, the author of 'Holiday', and asked him to write a play for her. He came up with 'The Philadelphia Story', a comedy about a girl on the eve of her second marriage – and Hepburn also quietly purchased the movie rights. As the spoilt, aristocratic, emotionally indecisive Tracey Lord, she avenged herself with a vengeance for the flop of 'The Lake'. It was the hit of the Broadway season, and Hollywood began bidding for the movie rights. Hepburn's price included herself, and MGM bought this, but they bolstered her at the box-office with Cary Grant and James Stewart. With Cukor directing, the film (40) did as well on the screen as it had on stage, and Hepburn was the New York Critics' Best Actress of the Year because of it.

If on the screen she was intrinsically the same (mannered, extravagant, but now with her technique polished needle-sharp), in private she was more cooperative, less patronizing. She badly wanted an MGM contract and when MGM weren't forthcoming, she offered them another property she had acquired as a co-starring vehicle for Spencer Tracy and herself. MGM bought it, and paid her in addition a salary of $100,000. The first day on the set she said: 'I'm afraid I'm too tall for you, Mr Tracy', and he replied: 'Don't worry, Miss Hepburn, I'll soon cut you down to my size': it was the beginning of an off-screen friendship which was to last until Tracy's death, and an on-screen partnership which may well be the most rewarding in film history. There were 10 films all told. This first one set the pattern: *Woman of the Year* (42), directed by Stevens. They were journalists of opposing interests on the brink of divorce. She was eager, 'intellectual', idealistic; he down-to-earth, mocking, 'tolerant' – presumably reflections of real-life characteristics. They were urbane and completely captivating as a team; and the success of the film caused Metro finally to offer her a long-term contract. It is doubtful whether the studio ever cared much for her: the films she made without Tracy were very poor indeed and the subsequent films they made together were each initiated by themselves rather than by the studio.

For the moment they turned to drama: Cukor's version of I. A. R. Wylie's *Keeper of the Flame*, a novel about a widow and the reporter who makes her admit that her husband was a fascist. Without Tracy she did *Stage Door Canteen* (43) at UA, as herself – one of Hollywood's love-songs to show business; and *Dragon Seed* (44), a melodramatic Oriental charade after Pearl S. Buck in which Hepburn was an improbable Chinese patriot. She and Tracy did *Without Love* (45), a comedy that she had done on stage without him in 1942; then Robert Taylor tried to murder her in a psychological melodrama directed by Vincente Minnelli, *Undercurrent* (46). She was in period costume for *The Sea of Grass* (47), directed by Elia Kazan, with Tracy, and in *Song of Love*, where she and Paul Henried were the Schumanns and Robert Walker a boyish Brahms. Then there were two excellent comedies with Tracy: *State of the Union* (48), a witty political piece directed by Frank Capra – his best post-war film; and *Adam's Rib* (49), directed by Cukor, written by Ruth Gordon and Garson Kanin, about husband-and-wife lawyers who find themselves on opposing sides in a serio-comic attempted murder case. Their lines were good and they batted them back and forth like Wimbledon champions: their mutual admiration remains a pleasure to see. There has been speculation about their off-screen relationship, but the only fact known to outsiders is that Tracy and his wife never divorced. Hepburn, asked once by a reporter whether she loved Tracy, replied: 'Everyone loves Mr Tracy.'

In 1950 she returned to Broadway in 'As You Like It'; in 1951 she played Shaw's 'The Millionairess' in London and New York, and there were several further forays into Shakespeare over the next few years: Portia, Isabella and Katharina ('The Shrew') on an Australian tour for the Old Vic in 1955, and, later, Portia again, Beatrice,

A brief encounter in Venice: Hepburn and Rossano Brazzi in Summer Madness *(55). 'She plays every scene with characteristic attack and insight . . . but she is often simply too fascinating' – Gavin Lambert in* Sight and Sound.

Viola and Cleopatra at the Shakespeare Festival in Connecticut.

She was off the screen for two years, and returned with a bang: as the prissy spinster who found love ('Dear – what's your first name?') on a tramp steamer chugging through the African jungle, *The African Queen* (51). C. A. Lejeune said: 'We always knew that Miss Hepburn was a dab hand with the timing of a comic line, but it is a long while since she gave so much heart and tenderness to a role. To sustain such a long and complex part without a fault is something of a *tour de force*.' Humphrey Bogart was the unshaven and unlikely object of her affections, and John Huston directed from a novel by C. S. Forester: raves all round, her greatest box-office hit to that time – and happy memories (in 1967 the Los Angeles Times found it was the favourite movie among their readers). Hepburn then did another with the *Adam's Rib* team, *Pat and Mike* (52): she was an all-round athlete and Tracy her trainer. Dilys Powell found 'her acting at its most enchanting: spirited, gay, the voice with its curiously attractive flat tones modulating into triumph, the harassed rectangular look melting into affection.' It was her last for MGM.

After another long absence, she played two more ageing spinsters, firstly in the David Lean-directed version of Arthur Laurent's 'The Time of the Cuckoo', *Summer Madness* (55, a British film), as a schoolteacher having her first – and probably last–love-affair, with an Italian adventurer. It was, again, a captivating performance, poised just on the right side of laughing-through-the-tears: but if the combination of Hepburn and Venice was irresistible to aficionados and most critics, the film wasn't popular. *The Rainmaker* (56) was, perhaps because Burt Lancaster was in it, the object of the plain jane's last-gasp love-affair; but when she wasn't doing a useful transformation job, it was pure slodge. However, it was ambrosia beside the British *The Iron Petticoat*, a pseudo-*Ninotchka* comedy: whoever advised her and Bob Hope to cross the Atlantic for it did them a profound disservice.

She and Tracy did *The Desk Set* (57) at 20th, a ponderous CinemaScope version of a good stage comedy; then she was off the screen until 1960, when she did the bereaved mother of *Suddenly Last Summer*: it was a supporting role, but she wiped the floor with the other players and received her eighth Oscar nomination. Two years later she did another screen version of a play, Eugene O'Neill's *Long Day's Journey Into Night*, directed by Sidney Lumet. She played the drug-addicted mother and 'emerges as a superb *tragedienne*' said Dwight Macdonald. Said Pauline Kael: '... the most beautiful comedienne of the 30s and 40s has become our greatest tragedienne ... experiencing the magic in the art of acting, one can understand why the appellation "the divine" has sometimes been awarded to certain actresses.' With Ralph Richardson, Jason Robards and Dean Stockwell, Hepburn won an ensemble acting award at the Cannes Festival, but the film, though critically admired, was of limited appeal (recognizing this, the cast had accepted much less than their normal salaries).

Then she stayed away for five years, neglected, one felt, though notes in the press suggested that she was devoting her time to the increasingly ill Tracy (she certainly turned down *Rosie*, which Universal had bought for her); it was further suggested that she only accepted the uninteresting role of the mother in *Guess Who's Coming to Dinner* (67) to be close to him. (Her fee was $200,000; he got $300,000.) It was their last film together, and a triumph no one could have foreseen: critics who disliked the material talked of the 'alchemy' of this 'legendary' team, and crowds flocked to see them. Aided by the box-office potency of Sidney Poitier, the film made a fantastic $20 million-plus. Hepburn received an Oscar, and if general reaction was that for this performance it was hardly deserved, no one would deny her a second–35 years after the first.

Perhaps in the wake of Tracy's demise, she embarked on two movies. *The Lion in Winter* (68) was another smash, from a Broadway play, with Peter O'Toole as Henry II. Most American critics talked of Oscars, and Hepburn's performance was thought to be the best she had given: 'Katharine Hepburn crowns her career. She is simply stunning'–Judith Christ. In The (London) Times John Russell Taylor: 'Playing the relentlessly intelligent, ambitious, cunning, devious ... human and vulnerable Eleanor of Aquitaine she finds possibilities, both in herself and in the text which we would hardly have guessed at. The script ... offers chances, but such as only a great actress could see and an even greater actress could take ... a growing, developing, still surprising actress.' Hepburn did get an Oscar–the first leading player to get a third (with an almost unparalleled 11 nominations); and in Britain the BFA decreed her Best Actress for this and *Dinner*. The other film was *The Madwoman of Chaillot* (69), from the play by Giraudoux–unlikely screen

The Lion in Winter *(68), a historical charade enlivened by some good performances: Hepburn's brought her her third Best Actress Oscar.*

material and in the event a dreadful film. Even Hepburn's new standing with the public couldn't prevent its being a complete flop.

In late 1969 she did her first musical, 'Coco', on Broadway, at a record salary for a performer in a regular New York show: she is also committed for the movie version. In 1970 it was announced she would play Hecuba in *The Trojan Woman*. She has said of her future: 'I only want to go on being a star. It's all I know how to be.' No one who cares for films would wish it any other way.

Wendy Hiller

Wendy Hiller's screen appearances have been few, presumably because 'she has very strong views on the feminine problem of Home versus a Career. It is her opinion that it is impossible to make a success of both all the time' (Picture Show, 1957). Equally, she has limited her theatre work; and this would seem to be one actress genuinely committed to domesticity (she married dramatist Ronald Gow in 1937). She was born in Bramhall, Cheshire, in 1912; went straight from school into the theatre, studying at Manchester rep – ASM, understudies and small parts. In 1934 she was given the lead in 'Love on the Dole' (by Gow) and took it from the provinces to London and thence to New York in 1936. It established her quite firmly as one of Britain's leading young actresses; and brought her her first film part – another North Country dialect role – *Lancashire Luck* (37). Already she had played the part – Eliza Doolittle – which was to bring her world fame: in 1936 she had done that and Saint Joan at the Malvern Festival, to the delight of Shaw himself; and he recommended her for the film version of *Pygmalion* (38). Her Eliza was very touching, and was an admirable foil for Leslie Howard. Gabriel Pascal produced, and put Hiller under contract. The film's success in the US brought Hollywood offers, which she or Pascal refused.

She did a second Shaw film for Pascal, *Major Barbara* (40), and was again memorable, playing with a steely determination, a wit and a blazing sincerity which have made this part difficult for other actresses. Her particular qualities were utilized nicely by Powell and Pressburger in their Scottish love

Leslie Howard as Higgins and Wendy Hiller as Eliza in Pygmalion *(38).*

story, *I Know Where I'm Going* (45) with Roger Livesey and Pamela Brown. She went to the Bristol Old Vic in 1946 to play in her husband's adaptation of 'Tess of the D'Urbervilles', which she later did in London. Other stage appearances at this time included 'The Heiress' in New York (47) and in London (50), taking over from Peggy Ashcroft. She returned to the screen as Mrs Almayer, the drab, resigned wife, in *An Outcast of the Islands* (52); somewhat less notable were the 20th-backed *Singlehanded* (53) from a novel by C. S. Forester, where she was the mother of Jeffrey Hunter, and a duo in 1957, the American *Something of Value* and a British comedy, *How to Murder Your Uncle*. She went to Hollywood to play the stern, embittered hotelier of *Separate Tables* (58), and won the Best Supporting Actress Oscar. Other stage appearances of the 50s include an Old Vic season (55–56), and New York visits for 'A Moon for the Misbegotten' and 'Flowering Cherry' (the latter she also did in London for a while). In 1963 she appeared in 'The Wings of the Dove'.

She was once again memorable as the sad mother in *Sons and Lovers* (60) – this time Dean Stockwell was the unlikely son; and she was good in Hollywood's *Toys in the Attic* (63), which as a play she had done in the West End, though in a different part. As Thomas More's impatient nagging wife, however, in *A Man for All Seasons* (66), she entirely misjudged her effects. But she was excellent as Mrs Micawber in *David Copperfield* (70).

Hiller has also appeared from time to time on TV in both countries.

Valerie Hobson

Valerie Hobson was – to her disadvantage – ineffably ladylike. The British film industry of the 30s and 40s was a man's world, and the female stars got short shrift. Those British girls who did go to Hollywood were criticized back home for submitting to that town's despised 'glamour treatment'. But whether or not they emerged with their individuality gone – and some did – they were invariably better to look upon.

Hobson's time in Hollywood was not at all worthwhile, and she might have made no stronger mark in the British industry had not she managed to assert her distinctive personality from time to time. It was not until the 60s that British girls got less than a raw deal from their own studios: as the British industry became internationalized, the girls – many of them clearly less talented than Hobson – became more attractive and more sexy. It was not, of course, part of Hobson's function to be sexy, but through three dozen films, she represented British womanhood, and it was, overall, a prospect unlikely to stir the blood in Dallas and Delhi, or even, come to that, in Droitwich.

She was born in Larne, Northern Ireland, in 1917, of English parents (father was a naval officer); she studied at RADA and found stage success early when she appeared in 'Ball at the Savoy', starring Maurice Evans at Drury Lane. Around the same time she had a bit in a film called *Eyes of Fate* (33), and then got leading roles in *Two Hearts in Waltztime* (34) which starred Carl Brisson; *The Path to Glory*, whose cast included Maurice Evans and Henry Daniell, a satire on war that she had done as a radio play; and *Badger's Green*, a cricketing comedy that had been a success on the stage. Then Hollywood – Universal – offered a contract; that studio planned a version of *Great Expectations* and thought Hobson would be ideal as Estella. But they changed their mind; the part went to Jane Wyatt, and Hobson, briefly a platinum blonde, was given a featured part in a domestic comedy, *Strange Wives* (35). There followed: *Rendezvous at Midnight*; *The Mystery of Edwin Drood*; *The Bride of Frankenstein*; *The Werewolf of London*; *Chinatown Squad*; *Oh What a Night*, made in Britain; and *The Great Impersonation* – the Edmund Lowe version. Neither the films nor she were impressive (she had little to do but look afraid and scream), and she was dropped by Universal when it was reorganized (the Laemmles were bought out). She lingered hopefully in Hollywood to make two Bs, *August Weekend* (36), an indie, and *Tugboat Princess* at Columbia supporting Edith Fellows.

In Britain she prepared to start again at zero, but was offered a star part in *Secret of Stamboul* with James Mason, a preposterous little picture based on a novel by Dennis Wheatley; then she got leads in *No Escape*, an air drama with Leslie Perrins, and (as an adventuress) in *Jump for Glory* (37), which Raoul Walsh crossed the Atlantic to direct. It was the first time she had come into her own on the screen. Korda liked her and cast her as the Colonel's wife in *The Drum* (38), a tale of tension on the NW Frontier: she did it as if to the manner born (she was), and was delightful as well. Korda used her again, as a reporter, in *Q Planes* (39); and before that she had been a reporter's wife – Barry K. Barnes's – in a thriller, *This Man Is News* (38). It was a modest success and a sequel was made, *This Man in Paris* (39). The producer was Anthony Havelock-Allen, and he and Hobson were married in 1939. Until they

Kind Hearts and Coronets (*49*) *was that rare thing – a* stylish *British comedy; and it remains delightful. Dennis Price as the murderer, Alec Guinness as his intended victim and Valerie Hobson – who will be widowed by the one and then wooed by the other.*

were divorced in 1952, she certainly enjoyed a privileged position in the British film world.

Also in 1939 she made *A Spy in Black* with Conrad Veidt and *The Silent Battle*, and she was with Veidt again in *Contraband* (40); after which she was decorative while Michael Redgrave forded the ocean with the *Atlantic Ferry* (41), just in case, one day, as the film put it, 'Britain and the United States should be united against a common enemy'. She made *Unpublished Story* (42) and *The Adventures of Tartu* (43) starring Robert Donat. In 1942 it was announced that she had signed a Hollywood contract, but she didn't go to Hollywood; and she didn't film again till she played a woman MP in Daphne du Maurier's *The Years Between* (46) with Redgrave. Her husband, meanwhile, had become Exec-Producer of Cineguild, which released through Rank, using the talents of director David Lean and producer Ronald Neame – which could be why Hobson at last played Estella in *Great Expectations*, a highly praised version of Dickens, with John Mills as the grown-up Pip. The whole cast was memorable, with Hobson the ideal Estella. She had not achieved the popularity of actresses like Margaret Lockwood or Phyllis Calvert but at last was in the fore-front of British stars. She was not too happy in Cineguild's *Blanche Fury* (47) with Stewart Granger, a period melodrama purportedly done in an effort to show rival British studios how. It didn't. Havelock-Allen left Cineguild, and Hobson went with him, to make *The Small Voice* (48), with James Donald and Howard Keel, about the house-hold held to ransom by escaped convicts (an old theme liable to at least three more goings-over during the next few years).

Ealing gave her a couple of rare chances to play elegant comedy: felicitously in *Kind Hearts and Coronets* (49), unhappily in *Train of Events*, an episoder where she was fighting with husband-conductor John Clements. *The Interrupted Journey* was also, more direly, about trains, with Richard Todd; *The Rocking Horse Winner*, with Mills, was a version of a D. H. Lawrence story. After a break, Hobson brought her own special glitter to three comedies – *The Card* (51) with Alec Guinness, and a couple where she was well matched by Nigel Patrick, the unpretentious *Who Goes There?* (52), which was otherwise spoiled by Peggy Cummins in the leading role, and *Meet Me Tonight*, which completely wrecked three of Noël Coward's 'Tonight at 8.30' playlets: weak direction handicapped the stars (who included also Stanley Holloway and Kay Walsh). There were two minor dramas, *The Voice of Merrill* and *Background* (53), and then Hobson's last chance to demonstrate how she could flower under a good director: René Clement's fine *Knave of Hearts* (54) with Gérard Philipe.

Hobson had already announced her retirement. In 1953 she had been chosen to play the Gertrude Lawrence role in the British production of 'The King and I' (and did, beautifully), and she said that she didn't think her career could top this and she wouldn't try. She had married an MP, John Profumo, and proposed to devote her life to being his wife. Whereupon, when 'King' ended, she passed from the headlines – until the scandal of 1963 involving Profumo, by then a prominent Minister of the Crown. Hobson stood by him during his difficulties.

Bob Hope

Bob Hope is probably the best known of all American comedians, and if not the most admired, probably the most liked. As a film-star, these days, he is much less thought of than as Bob Hope, American institution. He seems always to be picking up medals, degrees or citations for his unceasing work. He is, in the word of Time, a 'workaholic'. He planes into Britain for a TV show, a première or a charity performance; the next day he's doing a concert in Dallas or entertaining the troops in Vietnam. He appears at Lambs' banquets, he emcees the Oscar Ceremony, he does a series of Specials on TV and makes one movie a year.

His team of script-writers is legendary, and there are those who grant him little beyond a status as a stand-up comedian, mechanically firing-off high-speed patter. One of the joys of that, though, is in his professionalism, his control of his audience; he clearly gets a kick out of doing it. Certainly he is adept at ad-libs and seems – which is important in his line of comedy – underneath it all a regular guy. His screen counterpart is much less trustworthy. He saunters on in the same way as the stage Hope, primly smug, boyishly audacious, a smart-Aleck supremely in command: but at the first sign of danger his eyes go big and his knees go weak. He is mean and avaricious but above all he is cowardly. He will certainly ditch Crosby and he has been known to ditch Lamour. He fancies himself as a sexpot and isn't sexy. At his best, he is midway between a great comic like W. C. Fields and a fine light comedian like Jack Lemmon; what spoils him is that he is too knowing, especially when he shares it with the audience. James Agee had other reservations: in discussing what comedy had lost since the golden days, he instanced Hope (in *The Paleface*) as the best of the current crop: 'Bob Hope is very adroit with his lines and now and then, when the words don't get in the way, he makes a good beginning as a visual comedian. But only the beginning, never the middle or end. He is funny, for instance, reacting to a shot of violent whisky. But he does not know how to get funnier (i.e. how to build and milk) or how to be funniest (i.e. how to top or cap his gags). The camera has to fade out on the same old face he started with.'

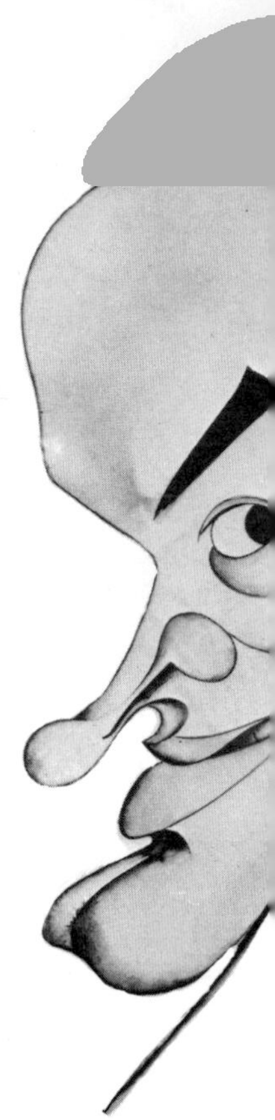

He was born in Eltham in S.E. London in 1904. His father, a stone-mason, took the family to Cleveland when Hope was four. Before trying vaudeville, he had done various jobs – soda-jerk, boxer and newsboy. He had won some Charlie Chaplin impersonation contests and started out professionally, advertising himself as a master of 'Songs, Patter and Eccentric Dancing'. But he gradually worked humour into his act. He played a vaude performer in his first Broadway show, 'Ballyhoo', but didn't make his mark till cast in 'Roberta' (33). He was married around this time to Dolores Reade – one of the proverbially happy marriages of show business. He was featured in the 1936 'Ziegfeld Follies' with Fanny Brice and in 'Red Hot and Blue' with Merman and Durante. He made several shorts for Educational and other companies, e.g. *Going Spanish*, but said he had no interest in movies; he became a radio name, and it was because of that that Paramount signed him for *The Big Broadcast of 1938* (38) with a host of names, including W. C.Fields. Hope was more or less the juvenile lead, with some funny moments and a great duet with Shirley Ross, 'Thanks For the Memory'. Together, they made a film of that title, sandwiched between three Martha Raye vehicles: *College Swing*, *Give Me a Sailor* and *Never Say Die* (39). He and Ross were in *Some Like It Hot*, a poor remake of 1934's *Thank Your Stars* (which had Jack Oakie); then Paramount thought he might be right for the remake of the creepie-funny *The Cat and the Canary* with Paulette Goddard: he made the hero a

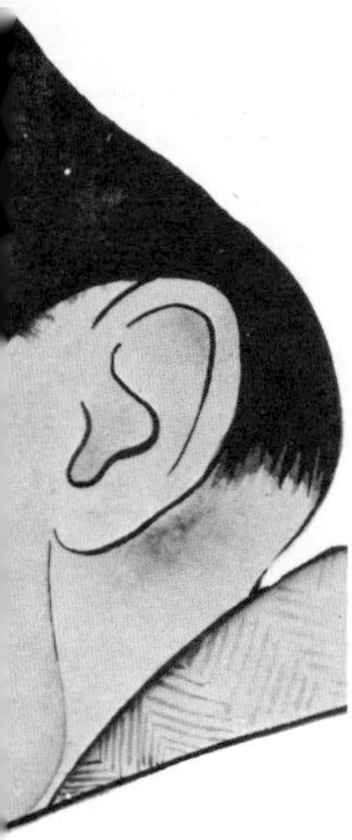

Martha Raye and Bob Hope in College Swing *(38). The cast list read: Burns & Allen, Martha Raye, Bob Hope, Edward Everett Horton, Ben Blue, Betty Grable, Jackie Coogan, Florence George, John Payne, Robert Cummings, Skinnay Ennis–in that order.*

real scaredy-cat. A follow-up was ordered, *The Ghost Breakers* (40).

Hope found his first great popularity, however, with the one before that: *Road to Singapore* (40) with Crosby and Lamour. Though Crosby was one of the studio's top stars, great things were not expected, but the film grossed the sort of money usually taken only by big prestige pictures. A follow-up was called for: *Road to Zanzibar* (41). Now the fun was zany and sometimes witty, and the gross was again around $\$1\frac{1}{2}$ million. Later films in the series–after seat prices had risen–took $\$4\frac{1}{2}$ million, less than some of Crosby's Hope-less films but still huge. The 40s would not have been quite the same without the *Road* films, but they revive variably. The more conventional Hope material has dated, though when his lines are good he is extremely funny. The Crosby-Hope teaming, however, works immaculately with, at their best, a combined sympathy/timing that is unequalled by any other screen partnership.

There were two more hits: *Caught in the Draft*, an army comedy with Lamour, and *Nothing But the Truth*, the old farce remade with Goddard; and at the end of 1941 Hope was among the top 10 money-makers. He stayed there till 1953, usually a place or two behind Crosby. And the next few were popular: *Louisiana Purchase*, in Technicolor, a bowdlerized version of Irving Berlin's Broadway show; *Road to Morocco* (42); *My Favorite Blonde*, a spy comedy with Madeleine Carroll; *Star Spangled Rhythm* in a guest spot; *They Got Me Covered* (43), another spy story, with Lamour out on loan to Goldwyn; *Let's Face It*, another army comedy, with Betty Hutton; *The Princess and the Pirate* (44), a spoof swashbuckler, again at Goldwyn; and *Road to Utopia* (45).

In 1945 he signed a new seven-year contract with Paramount, and after a guest spot in *Duffy's Tavern*, played Valentino's old part in *Monsieur Beaucaire* (45). It did well at the time on the strength of his name but the fun today looks laboured. *My Favorite Brunette* (47) with Lamour was another follow-up, and *Where There's Life* was again a return to the formula of the wartime spy comedies, with Hope in this case the

Road to Morocco (*42*), *perhaps the best of the 'Road' pictures: Hope has just double-crossed Crosby in an attempt to get to grips with Lamour on the couch.*

unknowing heir to a European kingdom being stalked through New York by a motley gang of crooks, agents of his political rivals. There was more guesting, in *Variety Girl*, and then *Road to Rio*; and *The Paleface* (48) – out West and as cowardly as ever, his biggest hit sans Crosby. On the strength of that he overtook Crosby and everyone else and was voted 1949's biggest draw. *Sorrowful Jones* (49) with Lucille Ball was a remake of *Little Miss Marker*, and Hope fitted Damon Runyon's world so well that *The Lemon Drop Kid* was re-done with him in 1951. Before it came *The Great Lover* (49), a ship-board frolic, the mélange as before – a killer (Ronald Young) and a mysterious redhead (Rhonda Fleming); and *Fancy Pants* (50), with Ball again, and out West again, as a butler based more than somewhat on *Ruggles of Red Gap*.

More follow-ups: *My Favorite Spy* (51) with Hedy Lamarr, *Son of Paleface* (52), with Jane Russell again, and not up to the original, and *Road to Bali*. Then, an army comedy again, *Off-Limits* (53) – and somewhere around here the scripts got somewhat weaker: *Here Come the Girls* (54) with Rosemary Clooney, and *Casanova's Big Night*, a period romp with Joan Fontaine. He tried a more serious piece, *The Seven Little Foys* (55), a biopic of vaudevillian Eddie Foy, but it was so cliché-ridden that fewer fans than usual cared; *The Iron Petticoat* (56) with Katharine Hepburn was his first outside Paramount in years and his first in Britain: alas. *That Certain Feeling* raised the standard, but it wasn't vintage Hope. *Beau James* (57) was another biopic, and Hope might have made a convincing Mayor Walker, had the writers not seemed uncertain whether to let the loved American comedian play the all-American heel; also it neglected to suggest that Walker might have been guilty and at no point was astringent enough. Much to-do was made about *Paris Holiday* (58), at UA, a co-starrer with Fernandel, made at Hope's own request, but their styles didn't jell. However, *Alias Jesse James* (59) was in *Paleface*-vein and almost in *Paleface* form. It was his last for Paramount.

The Paleface (*48*): *Jane Russell as Calamity Jane and Hope as dentist Painless Potter–who, much to his horror, is mistaken for Wild Bill Hickok.*

Most of his succeeding films have been produced by his own company for UA. He was more serious again in *The Facts of Life* (60), in which he and Lucille Ball leave their respective spouses in an attempt to commit adultery: delicately handled, delightful together, and if the fun was gentle, it was at least there. Which is more than can be said for: *Bachelor in Paradise* (61, MGM); *Road to Hong Kong*; *Critic's Choice* (62, WB) with Ball, from a play by Ira Levin; *Call Me Bwana* (63) with Anita Ekberg; *A Global Affair* (64); *I'll Take Sweden* (65); *Boy Did I Get a Wrong Number* (66); and *Eight on a Lam* (67) with Phyllis Diller. The latter did well in the US (TV plugs?), but in Britain the press clobbered it and it went out as a second feature. Something similar happened to *The Private Navy of Sgt O'Farrell* (68) and *How To Commit Marriage* (69) with Jackie Gleason and Jane Wyman. Indeed, the low quality of Hope's movies has become a byword: the reviews are sorrowful rather than peeved and one wonders why he bothers. Certainly he has said: 'You do a movie and you have to wait to find out if it's any good. But personal appearance tours, that's instant satisfaction.' It is curious that a seasoned professional should turn out such turkeys–which suggests, perhaps, that the old system wasn't so bad after all.

Miriam Hopkins

In an odd book published in the mid-30s, 'The American Cinema', William H. Rideout claims: 'On all counts, Miss Hopkins is easily the finest actress on the screen today.' It is one of his most curious judgements, even though, at the time, there were executives in Hollywood who shared it. Hopkins was agreeably versatile: she played floozies and *grandes dames* and was sometimes extremely interesting, but most of the time neither her hostessy graciousness nor cracked ice delivery varied much.

She was born in 1902 in Savannah, Georgia. She was educated at Syracuse University and studied ballet–but broke an ankle and became a chorus girl instead: in 'The Music Box Revue' (21) in New York. After some years on the lighter side she moved over to legit: 'An American Tragedy' (26), 'Excess Baggage' (27), 'The Bachelor Father' (29, in London), 'Ritzy' (30), 'Lysistrata' and 'Anatol' (31), among others. She was seldom out of work, but she was not conspicuously successful; nor did films at first treat her more kindly, though Paramount did sign her on a starring contract as the result of her work in 'Anatol'. In *Fast and Loose* (31) with Carole Lombard she was the offspring of indulgent parents, with too much money and too little to do: though adapted by Preston Sturges from Avery Hopwood's play 'The Best People', the film, too, did little–and she was generally considered poor in it. Her second picture, however, made everyone sit up: Lubitsch's *The Smiling Lieutenant* (31), as the Queen-bride of the unwilling Chevalier; then she was a cabaret girl who got murdered in the Clive Brook-Kay Francis *24 Hours*–which put her in line for Ivy the barmaid in *Dr Jekyll and Mr Hyde* (32). She had her sights on the ingénue part but director Mamoulian convinced her that she was the only actress on the Paramount lot capable of playing the drab: and under his tuition she was memorable.

Her stock went soaring, as Mamoulian had promised, though already in the can were three weak programmers: *Two Kinds of Women* with Phillips Holmes; *Dancers in the*

Fredric March, Miriam Hopkins and Gary Cooper in Lubitsch's film version of Noël Coward's Design for Living *(33). Coward's dislike of the picture was not alleviated by a remark of its scriptwriter Ben Hecht: 'There's only one line of Coward's left in the picture – see if you can find it.' Needless to say, the film was not an improvement on the play.*

Dark with Jack Oakie; and *The World and the Flesh* with George Bancroft. She had the lead in Lubitsch's delightful *Trouble in Paradise* with Kay Francis and Herbert Marshall, and the success of that reinforced her position on the lot; she got another important part, in *The Story of Temple Drake* (33), the first, wretched, version of Faulkner's 'Sanctuary'; and then was loaned to MGM for a pointless rural drama, *The Stranger's Return*. Lubitsch directed her again in *Design for Living*, but unnoticeably: not only did it seem unlikely that she could enslave either Gary Cooper or Fredric March, but they all lacked the style for the Coward dialogue. Also in 1933 she returned to Broadway in 'Jezebel' (taking over from Tallulah Bankhead; Bette Davis filmed it some years later). She returned to Paramount for the very funny *All of Me* (34) with March, and *She Loves Me Not*, as Bing Crosby's leading lady, a futile farce which was considered a waste of her talents.

Her contract was up and Goldwyn promptly signed her; but as he had nothing ready he loaned her to RKO for a couple, *The Richest Girl in the World*, in which she was a thinly disguised Barbara Hutton, and *Becky Sharp* (35). This was in fact an RKO release of a Pioneer film, the first feature-length film completely in three-colour Technicolor: the system was not entirely new to cinemagoers and the film was not a great success (unlike the first Talkie, the first in CinemaScope, the first feature in 3-D, etc.). Some forgave it its faults because of the novelty and because of the way Mamoulian used colour; but it curtails the original novel and achieves the feat of making what little is left considerably dull, including the machinations of Becky, played by Hopkins in a wildly conventional way.

She made only four films for Goldwyn. *Barbary Coast*, with Edward G. Robinson, contains perhaps her best performance, as a saloon-keeper, and is a pretty good film; but *Splendor* (a title that does *not* convey the film's quality) was a sudser about a nice Southern girl marrying into a family of broke Manhattanites. In *These Three* (36), directed by William Wyler, she was a schoolteacher caught up in a web of scandal – but not one involving Lesbianism, as in Lillian Hellman's original play, 'The Children's Hour': the Hays Office would not let Goldwyn use either title or subject, but

The Old Maid *(39) was directed by Edmund Goulding from a play by Zoë Akins based on a novel by Edith Wharton. Bette Davis had the title role – here being comforted by Miriam Hopkins after being jilted on her wedding day (and it was Miriam who was responsible for the groom's defection). Bette's bastard – brought up by Miriam – much preferred Bette's mothering.*

Hellman cleverly adapted her own work into a strong conventional triangle story, with Joel McCrea and Merle Oberon. Hopkins was loaned to Korda for a silly British drama, *Men Are Not Gods* (37), where Gertrude Lawrence, as a bitch, was somewhat more sympathetic than she was; and then to RKO for *The Woman I Love*, overacting again with Paul Muni. The director was Anatole Litvak, who became the second of her four husbands. Her last for Goldwyn was a screwball comedy, *Woman Chases Man* with McCrea: Goldwyn considered it a failure, but it was well received. Also in 1937 she did a play, 'Wine of Choice', but it didn't get beyond Chicago.

Goldwyn loaned her to RKO again for *Wise Girl*, with Ray Milland, after which she signed a new contract at Warners with script approval; but her time there was no happier. Great plans were announced, but after some months she co-starred with Bette Davis in *The Old Maid* (39), in a part which was secondary in interest, and tertiary or worse in terms of audience sympathy. And her part in *Virginia City* (40), as a saloon-cutie again, was subsidiary to Errol Flynn's. He hadn't wanted her in the film and there was trouble on the set. Picturegoer commented: 'Miss Hopkins seems to be singularly unfortunate. Most of her pictures have been stormy affairs.' She had a good part in *The Lady With Red Hair* with Claude Rains, as Mrs Leslie Carter, but James Agate wrote: 'I don't feel she is a sufficiently good actress to impersonate one who was, in Mr Shaw's words, "a melodramatic actress of no mean powers".' Further, director Curtis Bernhardt said that Hopkins was 'terribly difficult to work with'. (Also in 1940 the 'Harvard Lampoon' cited her 'the least desirable companion on a desert island'.)

In 1941 Hopkins announced that she had bought a property about Nellie Bly and hoped to find a producer; she turned down *Badlands of Dakota* as unsuitable and instead appeared in a trite sentimental drama at UA, *A Gentleman After Dark* (42), as Brian Donlevy's ruthless wife. She returned to Warners for *Old Acquaintance* (43), but this time was featured below the title. Again Davis was the put-upon heroine and Hopkins the spoilt rival who causes most of the trouble. According to Davis this was a pattern repeated on the set, though she adds that Hopkins was not happy with bitchy parts. She could have been no happier with the notices, which Davis stole again. Said Edgar Anstey in The Spectator: 'Miss Davis has never been better. Miss Hopkins tends to overact.'

Hopkins returned to Broadway, taking over Tallulah Bankhead's part in 'The Skin of Our Teeth', and continued to play in New York and in summer theatres over the next few years; in 1949 she toured as Catherine in 'The Heiress', and the following year Wyler recalled her to Hollywood to play Catherine's aunt in the film version, with Olivia de Havilland. She did supporting stints in *The Mating Season* (51) and *The Outcast of Poker Flat* (52), and then Wyler again used her, as the selfish, nagging wife of Olivier in *Carrie*. Another decade went by, and Wyler sent for her again, for the new version of *The Children's Hour* (62), now with the original title and subject intact: instead of playing Martha, Hopkins was Martha's aunt. Similarly the years had withered either Wyler's talent or the effectiveness of the piece.

A couple of years later Hopkins accepted the star role–that of a Madame–in a tinny German-filmed version of *Fanny Hill* (64), which, when it wasn't banned, was turned down by exhibitors on more aesthetic grounds. She had a bit part in *The Chase* (66), and in 1969 it was announced that she would play an ageing movie star in an independent production, *The Comeback*, with two other revenants, Minta Durfee Arbuckle and Gale Sondergaard. She appears frequently on TV.

Leslie Howard

Leslie Howard was the ideal Englishman–to Americans at least. Hollywood in the 30s was a haven for aristocratic-seeming English actors, and although Howard was a gentleman all right, he was much more approachable than most of his compatriots. He could not have played the squire, like Nigel Bruce and C. Aubrey Smith, or the military commander, like Sir Guy Standing and Clive Brook, or the double-breasted cad, like Lionel Atwill and Herbert Marshall. In fact, Howard could only really play himself, tweedy, idealistic, vague and dreamy, kindly and upright; he seemed to have nostrils as sensitive as a thoroughbred's. He was, in fact, off-screen very much like his vagabond poet in *The Petrified Forest*. He tried a wider range and was seldom unconvincing simply because he was a relaxed and relaxing actor: in his time he was held in more or less unparalleled esteem. Some of his dramatic work looks somewhat effete now, but his sure touch in comedy remains a pleasure.

Curiously, he was an Englishman only by accident of birth. His parents were Hungarian immigrants, and had not long been in Britain when Howard was born in 1893, in London. He studied at Dulwich College and went to work in a bank. In 1917 he was invalided home from the Western Front suffering from shell-shock: to help him recuperate his mother–who was involved in local dramatics–suggested that he try acting. Theatre companies at that time were taking young men with even a modicum of talent, and Howard had little difficulty in getting into a (professional) tour of 'Peg o' My Heart'. He established himself rapidly, and after a good part in 'Mr Pym Passes By' (22) he was offered a leading role in the New York production of 'Just Suppose' by A. E. Thomas. It was there that he achieved real fame, in a sequence of hit plays: 'Aren't We All?', 'Outward Bound', 'The Green Hat' (25) with Ann Harding, 'Her Cardboard Lover' and Galsworthy's 'Escape'. In 1926 he returned to the West End for 'The Way You Look at It' with Edna Best, and in 1928 he crossed the Atlantic again for 'Her Cardboard Lover', appearing in it with Tallulah Bankhead (also that year he produced a play he had written, 'Tell Me the Truth'). He stayed on in London for a revival of 'Berkeley Square' and while there received overtures from WB, who were planning a film of *Outward Bound* (30).

WB payed him $5,000 a week, and the film–a macabre tale about passengers on a liner who gradually realize they are dead–was a success with those audiences who wanted more than mere talk (though the British censor banned it). Howard scored a personal success and was in demand. He moved to MGM for three: *A Free Soul*, somewhat ineffectual in Norma Shearer's big hit; *Never the Twain Shall Meet* ('This girl's of a different race, of a different world. You've got your friends, your position,' says C. Aubrey Smith); and *Five and Ten*, as a young architect in love with pampered department-store heiress Marion Davies. He then made a deal with RKO, and made *Devotion* with Harding; about which time he told a reporter: 'The movie studios are sweat shops killing the best in actors'; and he described his movies as 'drivel'.

Perhaps he would feel differently in Britain: Korda made him an offer to star in the first of his new set-up (while still with Paramount–before founding London Films): *Service for Ladies*, at £500 a week, reckoned to be the highest salary paid in

British films until that time. And Howard scored again, taking on Adolphe Menjou's Silent role as a king of head waiters in this John Van Druten piece. He returned to New York for Philip Barry's 'The Animal Kingdom', which he filmed some months later with Harding, after an interval as Shearer's great love in *Smilin' Through* (32). He was in another lachrymose piece, *Secrets* (33), which took him and Mary Pickford from love at first sight to doddery old age; and also that year made *Captured!* at WB, an incredible war drama with Douglas Fairbanks Jr; the successful and beautiful film version of *Berkeley Square*, of which he was personally fond (a concussion takes him back to the 18th century); and *The Lady Is Willing* (34) with Binnie Barnes, the first picture that Columbia ever made in Britain – a farce which deservedly flopped. He also turned down the role of Garbo's lover in *Queen Christina* because he thought he wouldn't be noticed.

Due rather to prevarication than ill-will Howard was not an easy man to please, and he now signed a contract with WB which was to give him and them several headaches. He was supposed to make three films yearly over a three-year period, but it became extended as he refused most of what they offered him. However, the association began well, with *British Agent*, a thriller in which he was a consul-general in St Petersburg and Kay Francis was Lenin's secretary. He was loaned to RKO for *Of Human Bondage*, as Somerset Maugham's club-footed hero enslaved by the slatternly Bette Davis (it didn't do well, despite good

Leslie Howard and Merle Oberon as Sir Percy and Lady Blakeney in The Scarlet Pimpernel *(34), based on Baroness Orczy's popular novel, first published in 1905. There had been an earlier film version, in 1917, and Korda was to make another Pimpernel film in the late 40s.*

Leslie Howard, with David Niven, in his last picture, The First of the Few *(42): it was one of a fine group of wartime films that seemed to herald a renaissance of the British Cinema. The 'Few' were the Battle of Britain pilots – in the US the film was retitled* Spitfire.

notices) and to Korda for *The Scarlet Pimpernel*, as the foppish, laconic Sir Percy who whisked out the aristos from under the eyes of the Terror. The film cost £81,000 and grossed a nice £420,000 – and Howard's performance brought him the 1935 Picturegoer Gold Medal. Sir Percy had been a role to which his style was admirably suited; and he was even better cast in *The Petrified Forest* (36), with Davis again, only this time she was genteel and yearning. It gave a lift to both careers (and Humphrey Bogart's) and reinforced MGM's choice of Howard to play Romeo after Fredric March had turned it down. Howard was wary, and almost certainly wouldn't have done it had not WB refused to loan him. Thus he partnered Shearer in *Romeo and Juliet* (36). He was too old and violently unsuitable by modern standards, but he spoke the verse beautifully, and was much liked at the time. Later that year he played Hamlet on Broadway, and that did not detract from his prestige although he was considered less good than John Gielgud, also concurrently in New York in that role.

Howard had become ambitious in all directions. He negotiated with WB to form his own company in Britain, releasing through UA. Two pictures were announced, *Riviera* and *Bonnie Prince Charlie*, in Technicolor; but, instead, in Hollywood, he made a couple of likeable comedies: *It's Love I'm After* (37) with Davis as his wife, a couple of squabbling thespians; and *Stand-In*, as a bewildered accountant taking over a film studio: the teaming with the brash Joan Blondell was particularly felicitous. In 1938 his own company did produce a movie, Shaw's *Pygmalion*, one of the few movies of the time that Britain was proud of and able to export with profit. Howard's Higgins was a perfect performance and at least until music was added the definitive one; he co-directed with the difficult Gabriel Pascal, and this uneasy collaboration announced plans for Howard to play both Nelson and Lawrence of Arabia. While Pascal prepared them, Howard returned to Hollywood looking for work. According to his daughter's biography, there were no offers, apart from *Gone With the Wind* (40), which wasn't due to start yet anyway. Jack L. Warner has said that he made Selznick kowtow to him in order to borrow Howard, which was little consolation to Howard, who didn't want to do it anyhow. He boasted that he hadn't read the book and had no intention of doing so; and there was some strife with Vivien Leigh because he wouldn't learn his lines. It is, for all that, a conscientious performance, though the least highly regarded of the four stars'; his dialogue is stilted and priggish (so maybe he was right after all).

A consolation was that Selznick permitted him to co-produce *Intermezzo* (39), a love story with Ingrid Bergman–of superb vintage but somewhat unpalatable today (in the 40s in Britain it had a record three circuit showings). Howard returned to the UK to make *The Man Who Lost Himself*, but the outbreak of war cancelled that project (nor were Pascal's projects more advanced). Howard, however, found himself a leading figure in a British film industry gradually revitalizing itself. As he grew older, he realized that his roots were in London and not in Los Angeles, and he set to work with a will. During 1940–2 he was involved in five films: *Pimpernel Smith*, an anti-Nazi thriller in which he appeared and which he directed; *The 49th Parallel* (41), another fine propaganda piece, with Laurence Olivier, Anton Walbrook and Raymond Massey (financed by the Ministry of Information, the Canadian Government and the head of Britain's Odeon circuit); *The Gentle Sex*, which he co-directed, a film about the ATS; *The Lamp Still Burns*, which he produced, a tribute to nurses; and *The First of the Few* (42) with David Niven, which he directed and in which he played R. J. Mitchell, the inventor of the Spitfire.

The British Film Yearbook 1945, summing up the British industry during the war, observed that Howard's 'presence in England as a producer, director and actor, constituted in itself one of the most valuable facets of British propaganda'. Early in 1943 the British used him for something less overt: afraid that Spain and Portugal might enter the war on the Axis side, Howard was sent there, ostensibly to lecture on the Theatre. His plane was shot down not long after it left Lisbon on the return journey. It was the day that Churchill returned from a conference in Algiers, and the Germans believed that he was on the same plane as Howard. It is no exaggeration to say that no figure in British show business was so deeply mourned, or missed, during this century. A son, Ronald Howard, was a mild success in British films later in the 40s, persuaded into the profession by a strong resemblance to his father.

Walter Huston

Walter Huston was one of the great actors of the first half-century. James Agee wrote of his work in *The Treasure of Sierra Madre*: 'I doubt we shall ever see . . . better acting than Walter Huston's beautiful performance', more or less the culmination of a professional lifetime of praise. Circumstances –he was in his mid-40s before he first appeared on the screen–prevented him from being a top-ranking star except for a brief spell. He was tall, somewhat angular, and usually vaguely amused by what was happening around him. He turned his hand to goodies and baddies with equal facility. Gregory Peck once asked him why he was so good; Huston said: 'Son, always give 'em a good show and travel first class!'

He was born in 1884 in Toronto. He studied engineering and at the same time attended drama classes; he was 18 when he had a chance to appear with a stock company in his native city. He gave up engineering and went touring. In 1905 he reached New York in a melodrama called 'In Convict Stripes'. He appeared in vaudeville also that year; but gave it all up when he married. When his son John was born in 1906 he was working in water and electricity plants in Missouri, but in 1909 (he was 25) he returned to the stage, doing a song-and-dance act with Bayonne Whipple. She became his second wife in 1914.

He stayed in vaudeville until 1924, writing his own acts, but in that year was offered the lead in 'Mr Pitt' in New York. The critics liked him, and (after a Shubert Road Show) he was starred in 'Desire Under the Elms', as the old man. He was made for life. He starred on Broadway until 1928 when a flop play, 'The Commodore Marries', caused him to think about Talkies. He signed a contract with Paramount and made *Gentlemen of the Press* (29), as one of them, and *The Lady Lies*. He had two Broadway successes, 'The Barker' and 'Elmer the Great' (and made three shorts around this time: *The Bishop's Candlesticks*, *The Carnival Man*, *Two Americans*); then headed for Paramount's West Coast studio to play the villain, Trampas, in a classic Western, *The Virginian*. *The Bad Man* (30) at WB was also a Western, but Huston was less convincing as a dashing Mexican bandit. *The Virtuous Sin* was a penny-dreadful: 'Torrid love in frigid

Wyler's Dodsworth *(36). Like the novel on which it was based, the film was basically an account of New World puritanism and plain-speaking* vis-à-vis *European sophistication. Walter Huston represented the former, and Mary Astor was the fellow-countrywoman who comforted him when his wife left him for the latter.*

Russia', said Photoplay, adding that Huston and Kay Francis were 'simply grand'. These two were sandwiched between two good ones, in both of which Huston played men of integrity and authority: *Abraham Lincoln* (30), in Griffith's otherwise undistinguished study (and last film), and the prison governor in Howard Hawks's excellent *The Criminal Code* (31).

He did three for WB: *The Star Witness*; *The Ruling Voice*, where he was required to be shady and noble at the same time; and *A Woman of Monte Carlo* (32), the first Hollywood vehicle for Lil Dagover (only it was a hearse and she returned to Germany); and a couple at Universal, both written by son John, a budding scriptwriter (and described in Dad's studio biography as one of his hobbies). Both were good, if hackneyed. *A House Divided* was a re-hash of 'Desire Under the Elms' with Huston a fisherman under William Wyler's direction, and *Law and Order*, a Western with the plot that was to serve most memorably in *Shane*. He signed a deal with MGM and made six more films in 1932, starting with *The Beast of the City*, scoring a sensational success with his portrait of an over-zealous cop. He was put among the Prohibition problems of Upton Sinclair's *The Wet Parade*, but the chief problem was how to stay in the cinema when his drunken, run-down hotel proprietor wasn't on the screen. He was a judge in *Night Court* (and 'magnificent' – Photoplay) and a humanitarian banker in Columbia's *American Madness*, Capra's fine Depression movie; after which he moved away from contemporary social problems for a bit. In *Kongo* he was the bitter, bestial Deadlegs Flint, a part he had originated on Broadway; it had already been filmed with Lon Chaney as *West of Zanzibar* and there was some discussion as to which was the sillier of the two versions. At UA he was the Reverend Davidson in *Rain* with Joan Crawford – only he wasn't a reverend, but demoted to amateur status to conciliate religious groups.

In 1933 he was a crooked politician who became an idealist on being elected president – *Gabriel Over the White House*. It was a courageous film, and not a big success. He played a brutal submarine commander in *Hell Below*; went down to fifth billing on *The Prize-fighter and the Lady*; but was one of the leading triangle in *Storm at Daybreak*, which started with the assassination at Sarajevo but dropped that event for more exciting things, like the infidelity of wife Kay Francis. He moved over to RKO for *Ann Vickers* with Irene Dunne and *Keep 'em Rolling* (34), about army horses; then returned to the stage to score a great hit in a dramatization of Sinclair Lewis's 'Dodsworth'. Despite his success, the only interesting film offer he got was from Britain, to play the title role in *Rhodes of Africa* (36) – Oscar Homolka was Kruger. While there he was a 'courtesy player' in a remake of a German thriller, *The Tunnel*, playing an American president.

In Hollywood, Goldwyn's film of *Dodsworth* (36) was waiting for him. There is unlikely to be unanimity on Goldwyn's contribution to the screen, but for this one he must be admired. None of the principals (Ruth Chatterton, Mary Astor and Paul Lukas were the others) was box-office, but much money and care was spent on it. Wyler directed, and Huston was magnificent as Sam, impulsive, bewildered, firm and childlike: the New York Critics voted him the year's Best Actor. The film, much-praised, just realized its cost, but by dint of revival finally earned a profit. Huston himself set much store by its success, but no studio rushed to employ him; so he went to Broadway and played Othello – but he didn't let himself go enough, and it folded after three weeks. There was only one film offer, a sentimental Civil War piece at MGM, *Of Human Hearts* (38), so Huston returned again to New York and played in Kurt Weill's 'Knickerbocker Holiday', singing 'September Song'. He reminded reporters that he had once been in vaudeville.

He had a supporting role in *The Light That Failed* and also in 1940 did two plays. And then found himself consistently in demand in the film city. One thing that helped was *All That Money Can Buy* (41) when his performance met with resounding success ('Mr Walter Huston's Devil is a really brilliant performance. This clever actor makes the fellow at once likeable and loathsome – a droll combination of pure logic and stark unreason' – James Agate). Another asset was the success of son John,

Walter Huston in The Treasure of Sierra Madre (*48*). *Said José Ferrer once: 'Certainly Walter is one of the greatest actors who ever lived. . . . Just because every time I saw him do anything he just hit me sort of deeper in the pit of the stomach than most actors ever did.'*

now a director, with films like *The Maltese Falcon* and *In This Our Life* (42), in both of which Dad did friendly walk-ons. He got top billing for a small part in Renoir's dull *Swamp Water* (41), and was in Von Sternberg's silly *The Shanghai Gesture*, *Always in My Heart* (42), a sudser with Kay Francis, and *Yankee Doodle Dandy* (42) as George M. Cohan's father.

In 1941 he was in Howard Hughes's *The Outlaw*, not released until after the war; Huston was warbound himself with *Edge of Darkness* (43) starring Errol Flynn; *Mission to Moscow*, as US Ambassador Joseph E. Davies; Goldwyn's *North Star*; and MGM's incredible *Dragon Seed* (44), in Chinese drag (but one of the film's few believable performances).

In 1946 Huston did his last Broadway play, 'The Apple of His Eye', and there were three supporting stints, none of them among his better work: *And Then There Were None* (45), René Clair's filming of Agatha Christie's 'Ten Little Niggers', *Dragonwyck* (46) and *Duel in the Sun*. He gave a slight, charming performance as the father in *Summer Holiday* (47), and then showed the others How again, in his son's *The Treasure of Sierra Madre* (48): he was really the only choice for the Best Supporting Actor at the Oscar ceremonies. His fee around this time was $40,000 and he got it only twice more, for *The Great Sinner* (49) and *The Furies* (50) as the fond and proud father of scheming Barbara Stanwyck – the first of the Freudian Westerns. He died not long after the latter was completed.

Betty Hutton

The pyrotechnic talent of Betty Hutton was not to everyone's taste, but during her 10 years of stardom she was a valuable asset to Paramount, and all the time she kept improving herself. She first appeared in films as the US entered the war when, in musicals, the jitterbug was replacing the aria. Hutton was as brash and volatile as any weary GI demanded: not for nothing was she known as The Blonde Bombshell (and The Huttentot, The Blonde Blitz and Bounding Betty). Her eagerness was appealing always, but in her early films the exuberance now is merely alienating. She's like a grown-up Shirley Temple. Says Dorothy Lamour in one film, playing her sister: 'I don't like leaving Bobbie alone with all those men.' 'Don't worry,' replies another sister, 'they can probably take care of themselves.' One wonders. Later Hutton simmered down and displayed an unexpected sweetness of disposition and real dramatic ability.

She was born in Battle Creek, Michigan, in 1921; her father died when she was a kid. She became a band-singer while still in her teens and originated her bombshell act during her first important engagement, singing with Vincent Lopez. She graduated thence to vaudeville and then Broadway, notably in 'Panama Hattie' (40); June Allyson was her understudy. Paramount signed her and cast her in *The Fleet's In* (42), as second female/comedy relief, with Eddie Bracken, and in *Happy Go Lucky* (43) she was again uninhibited and man-mad. She was partnered again by Bracken in the plot part of *Star Spangled Rhythm*, and still gave no indication of relaxing. She was only mad for Bob Hope in *Let's Face It*, but again much less selective in Preston Sturges's *The Miracle of Morgan's Creek* (44), getting drunk, married and pregnant all in one night to a GI whose name she couldn't even remember. Eddie Bracken was the faithful village swain, and James Agee found it 'funnier, more adventurous, more abundant, more intelligent and more encouraging' than any Hollywood film in years.

Agee liked Hutton. Reviewing *And the Angels Sing* he found her 'almost beyond good and evil, as far as I am concerned'. The film was somewhat between the two, and quite tasteless, with sisters Hutton and Lamour getting drunk in pursuit of band-leader Fred MacMurray and the money he had conned from them. However, *Here Come the Waves* was agreeable despite its patriotic finale: Bing Crosby was in it, and Hutton was twins – one of them grave and subdued. She did make it seem like two different actresses. There were two programmers, *The Stork Club* with Barry Fitzgerald, and *Cross My Heart* (46) with Sonny Tufts – a remake of *True Confession*; and a guest appearance in *Duffy's Tavern*. And in the midst of these Hutton made a good bid as a dramatic actress, playing Texas Guinan,

'They say that falling in love is wonderful': Howard Keel and Betty Hutton in George Sidney's Annie Get Your Gun *(50).*

the night-club queen, in a musical biopic, *Incendiary Blonde* (45). It was so successful that Paramount came up with something similar two years later, *The Perils of Pauline* about serial queen Pearl White. Also announced for Hutton, but never filmed, were lives of Clara Bow, Theda Bara and Sophie Tucker.

In 1948 Hutton gave a thoughtful performance in the underrated movie of Elmer Rice's *Dream Girl*; and after the noisy *Red Hot and Blue* (49) she had a dream part: MGM borrowed her for *Annie Get Your Gun* (50) when Judy Garland became too ill to carry on. It was a performance good enough for some critics to forget Garland; but Lindsay Anderson in the MFB clearly didn't: 'Played as a series of turns rather than as an acting performance, this predominately hysterical appearance is keyed rather to the requirements of the Hollywood Bowl than to the searching, sensitive eye and ear of the movie camera.' The film was a blaze of colour and song (Irving Berlin's) and a huge grosser in Britain and the US. MGM were so pleased and impressed that they tried to buy her contract from Paramount. But that studio wasn't selling. They put her into *Let's Dance* with Fred Astaire, and gave her the leading role in de Mille's *The Greatest Show on Earth* (52), a multi-star, multi-cliché circus picture that quickly went to second on Variety's list of all-time grossers. It also won a Best Picture Oscar.

Somebody Loves Me (*52*): *Betty Hutton's last major film was a conventional backstage story based on the life and songs of Blossom Seely. Ralph Meeker was the screen husband who resented her success until a last-reel reconciliation.*

Hutton then did another biopic (Blossom Seely), *Somebody Loves Me*. She married her dance director on this, Charles O'Curran, and insisted that he direct her next film. Paramount refused, and Hutton walked out on her contract. It was widely prophesied that she would never work in Hollywood again, and when she did, it was in an unimportant little picture for UA, *Spring Reunion* (57). She gave an excellent account of a spinster scared of marriage, but no more film parts were forthcoming, straight or musical.

She has occasionally announced her retirement, but still works in nightclubs and stock. Curiously, none of her subsequent appearances have been comparable to two in-person triumphs at the London Palladium in 1948 and 1952; yet she has lost none of her energy, which she occasionally uses in headline-making feuds with managers. In 1965 she failed to make an impact in New York, when she substituted for the ailing Carol Burnett in 'Fade In Fade Out' (receipts fell away to nothing); and in 1966 she walked out on *Red Tomahawk*, a B Western which would have reunited her with the partner of her *Annie* triumph, Howard Keel.

She has been married four times; and in 1967 she filed a petition for bankruptcy – she has since been discharged.

Emil Jannings

During the time of his American career and for a long while afterwards Emil Jannings was accepted without question as the screen's greatest actor. In 1941 James Agate repeated his view that he was 'one of the world's great actors . . . is there any film actor living today who is possessed of the sheer power of Jannings, who always in his massivity reminded me of Richter's handling of Wagner?' He had weight, he had authority, he was good at disguises and he played tragic parts. More significantly, he was directed by some of the finest talents in silent pictures. When he died, Richard Winnington, with his customary lucidity, wrote that Jannings 'learned the differing tricks of film acting, but only in the narrowest sense. His ritual, for all the temporary disguises, almost invariably expressed the same figure of pomp, respectability or power, brought low and destroyed by weakness or fate–a routine that fitted like a glove into the German neurosis and incidentally got him spotted at once by Hollywood. Because of his one-track technique he was not and never could have been a great film actor, and many of his films were pathetic, even ludicrous imitations of the *Vaudeville* and *Waxworks* Jannings.'

Jannings was born in Brooklyn in 1886 of German parents, who returned to Germany during his childhood. He was educated at Zürich and Gorlitz, and at Gorlitz he joined a stock company, playing boy's parts and doing odd jobs. He was restless, and the life of a touring actor suited him; he played with companies in Bremen, Leipzig and Mainz, until Werner Krauss, a mutual friend, got him an invitation to participate in the Darmstadt Royal Theatre in Berlin, studying under Max Reinhardt. He made his first films in 1914: *Im Banne der Leidenschaft*, *Passionels Tagebuch* and *Frau Eva*; *Die Ehe der Luise Rohrbach* in 1915; and *Vendetta* in 1916. This was directed by Lubitsch, a fellow-actor, and Lubitsch is generally credited for making Jannings aware of the possibilities of screen acting. He directed him again in *Wenn Vier Dasselbe Tun* (17); after which Jannings was in *Das Leben ein Traum*, *Die Augen der Mumie Mâ* (18), *Bruder Karamazoff* directed by the Polish Dimitri Buchowetsky, *Der Stier von Oliviera* and *Rose Bernd* (18). The great day of the German cinema was just dawning. The government was subsidizing it, having formed UFA as one central producing company; and important theatre talents were flocking to it. Within the next few years it was to make international reputations for directors like Lubitsch, Fritz Lang, G.W. Pabst, Paul Leni, Robert Weine and Paul Wegener; and for artists like Jannings, Pola Negri, Lil Dagover, Conrad Veidt, Werner Krauss, and Fritz Kortner. Jannings himself quit the theatre permanently, though his publicity always insisted that he despised the cinema: whether he really did is not known, but publicists liked to infer that major actors were conferring an honour on films by appearing in them.

The US succumbed to Lubitsch, Negri and Jannings (he was Louis XV) when *Madame Dubarry/Passion* (19) was imported, while in Britain Jannings first became famous as another monarch Teutonized, Henry VIII, in *Anna Boleyn* (20), made by Lubitsch; the film there was renamed after the king, but in the US it kept Anne's name. Most of Jannings's subsequent films got showings in both countries, often re-titled and often delayed. The German titles are *Kohlhiesel's Töchter*; *Danton* in the title role, directed by Buchowetsky; Lubitsch's *Das Weib des Pharao* (21); *Tragödie der Liebe* and *Ratten* (22). Then Jannings hit a new stride in a couple of films: *Othello* (23) though Werner Krauss as Iago overshadowed him, and *Peter der Grosse*. There was a minor picture, *Alles für Geld*, and then he turned up as another emperor, Nero, in the third version of *Quo Vadis?* directed jointly by the German Georg Jacoby and the Italian Gabriellino d'Annunzio. Said Picturegoer: '. . . pompous and cruel, vain and false, repulsive in his utter bestiality he dominates the canvas until one gets heartily sick of what is undisputably a remarkable and wonderful piece of work!' There followed *NJU* (24) with Elizabeth Bergner, and then *Der Letzte Mann/The Last Laugh*, which shook rigid all existing ideas of what film could do: F.W. Murnau directed, Carl Meyer wrote it (there were no sub-titles), Karl Freund photographed it, and by their creative, imaginative work made meaningful the slight tale of an ageing hotel doorman reduced to lavatory attendant. Arthur Knight ('The Liveliest Art', 1957) calls it 'a *tour de force*' but thinks the camera gives as good a performance as Jannings; Liam O'Leary ('The Silent Cinema', 1965) says the film is 'a masterpiece' and that Jannings 'gave his greatest performance'.

The next four were hardly less triumphant: Paul Leni's *Die Wachsfigurenkabinett/Waxworks*, an elaborate three-part fantasy on historical figures with Jannings in one of his few comic portrayals as Haroun al Raschid–and Fritz Kortner as Jack-the-Ripper; Murnau's version of Molière, *Tartuff* (25), with Jannings in the title role; Murnau's *Faust* (26), as much Dürer as Goethe, with Jannings as Mephisto; and E.A. Dupont's *Variete/Vaudeville*. This was a triangle story about three trapeze artists: the out-of-work partnership of Jannings and Lya de Putti, and the handsome and successful Warwick Ward who takes them on, takes de Putti away from Jannings and is murdered because of it. It was a film which had everything: suspense and sex and rave reviews; inevitably it was a smash hit in the US, and Jannings joined the exodus of German artists by signing a Paramount contract for three years, at a reported $10,000 a week.

The studio proceeded to construct 'Emil Jannings vehicles', stories as much as possible like his great German successes,

Emil Jannings in (left to right, top to bottom) Anna Boleyn (*20*), Tragödie der Liebe (*22*), Quo Vadis? (*23*) *and* Der Letzte Mann (*24*). *Josef von Sternberg wrote: '... Jannings had every right to the universal praise that was his for so many years, and his position in the history of the motion picture is secure, not only as a superlative performer but also as a source of inspiration for the writers and directors of the time. This, in my opinion, is the highest compliment within the scope of an actor to earn.'* ('*Fun in a Chinese Laundry*'.)

stories of 'tragic old men broken by fate ... a series of pictures in which tragedy struck in retribution for the old man's sexual peccadilloes. ... Jannings was made to feel every sling and arrow of outrageous fortune that the Paramount script department could devise,' said Arthur Knight, adding that 'his suffering was arbitrarily conceived, his retribution so mechanical that not even the great Jannings could conceal the basic falseness of both the stories and their characters.' All the same, his directors were distinguished: Victor Fleming directed him when, as a bank-clerk, he went *The Way of All Flesh* (27) and Von Sternberg when he heard *The Last Command* (28), a drama of a Hollywood extra who had once been a Russian general. For both performances – it was done differently then – he was voted Best Actor of the year by the Academy (it was the first given, before it was called Oscar). Mauritz Stiller directed *The Street of Sin* in which he was a racketeer, and Lubitsch *The Patriot*, with Jannings playing 'the mad Tsar Paul I in his heaviest ham style' (David Robinson). In Ludwig Berger's *The Sins of the Fathers* (29) he was a bootlegger deserted by wife Ruth Chatterton and cronies at the end. Like all his Hollywood films it was a big success – but the next was a disaster: *The Betrayal* (29), a triangle story with Gary Cooper. Lewis Milestone directed, and he found Jannings 'very difficult to work with'. It was a Talkie; audiences couldn't understand Jannings's strong guttural accent. It had been predicted when he had got his Oscar that he wouldn't be able to do American Talkies, and he had already announced his intention of returning to Germany. It was the loss of such actors which caused so many commentators to be bitter about the coming of Talkies. For, as Lionel Collier wrote in Picturegoer, in 1929: 'Nine people out of 10 if asked to say who is the greatest actor on the screen . . . would unhesitatingly reply Emil Jannings.'

Jannings returned to Germany planning to play Rasputin, but instead did *Der Blaue Engel/The Blue Angel* (30) in both German and English with the latter being generally considered the inferior. Marlene Dietrich co-starred: Paramount took her up, but the film confirmed Jannings's incomprehensible English and he wasn't re-signed. He made two German films, *Liebling der Gotter* (in French as well) and *Stürme der Leidenschaft/The Tempest* (31), the latter with Anna Sten in a part too much like that of Dietrich in *The Blue Angel*. In 1932 he made a weird French effort, *Le Roi Pausole*, a Pierre Louys tale about a king with 365 wives. It was heavily cut by censors, and on its first night in London in an English version, *The Merry Monarch*, was greeted with jeers and catcalls; it was withdrawn the following day and has hardly been heard of since. The reviews said that Jannings himself was bad. It was then announced that he had retired, but he made some German films – some of which were shown abroad: *Der Schwarze Walfisch* (34), *Der Alte und der Junge König* (35), his best Talkie, as Friedrich Wilhelm, the father of Frederick the Great, *Traumulus*, *Der Herrscher* (37), *Der Zerbrochene Krug* and *Robert Koch* (39).

In 1940 the Nazis appointed him head of UFA, and that year he played the Boer leader, *Ohm Kruger*, in an anti-British film. He made *Die Entlassing* (42) and *Altes Herz Wird Wieder Jung*, and was in the process of making *Wo Ist Herr Belling* (45) when the Allies advanced to Berlin. It was not finished. For his work in conjunction with Goebbels's Ministry of Propaganda he was black-listed by the Allies, and he retired to Austria, where he died in 1950, mourned by few other than his fifth wife, the former Mrs Conrad Veidt.

Al Jolson

Jolson is one of the legendary figures of American Show Business. As a vaudeville artist, many considered him the best there was, or would ever be: Jack Benny once said that in the Business he was commonly regarded as such (adding that Judy Garland could have been greater, 'had she wanted to be'); and he has a niche in film history because he was the first person to talk on the screen. Opinions vary as to his gifts. Chaplin, for instance, thought him 'a great instinctive artist with magic and vitality. . . . He personified the poetry of Broadway, its vitality and vulgarity, its aims and dreams.' He added that only a shadow of the real Jolson appeared in films, but Don Herold, reviewing *Go Into Your Dance* in 1935, clearly disagreed: 'Al Jolson, like so many members of his race and several other races, has unbelievable vitality rather than any singing or dancing ability, but his vitality eventually interests me to some extent. It is all no doubt a business with Al, if he were manufacturing pants he would be at it just as hard.' Gavin Lambert, 20 years later, commented (on *Hallelujah I'm a Bum*): 'Even if one cannot really like Al Jolson, his skill is undeniable.'

Jolson was overpowering. He didn't sing songs, he sold them. He seized the limelight, strutting, nimble and magnetic. He had tremendous self-confidence – almost gall; between songs his personality seemed unctious and he was obviously vain. He was a Jewish performer from the top of his head to the soles of his feet, and in his big black Jewish eyes was a deep sensitivity. One might respond or not to his singing, but on the screen, when given the chance, he really could act: you have only to watch his eyes to see that he was a considerable actor.

He was born in what was then St Petersburg in 1888, and brought to the US as a child. It was intended that he should become a cantor, but instead he ran away from home and joined a circus as a ballyhoo man, graduating to cafés and then vaudeville. His vaudeville act evolved with the years: he first wore blackface in 1906. His New York debut was in 'La Belle Paree' in 1911, and later he was in 'Vera Violetta', a Gaby Deslys vehicle. Mae West was also in it. From that time on he was a star – through 'The Honeymoon Express' in 1913, 'Robinson Crusoe Jr' in 1916, 'Sinbad' (in which he first sang 'Swanee') in 1918,

'Bombo' in 1921 and 'Wonder Bar', all on Broadway. He was idolized through the US, partly through his records – probably the first big pop star there was.

In 1923 D. W. Griffith decided that he would try to capture some of Jolson's electrifying personality on film, and they started *Mammy's Boy* together; but Jolson disliked the rushes so much that he refused to finish it, leaving Griffith with a loss of $100,000 (there was no signed contract). Two years later, however, Jolson was happy to make a short – because he could sing, as the short had Sound. The inventor of the system, Dr Lee de Forest, sold the system to WB, who sent for Jolson again; he sang three songs in *April Showers*. It was only one of several Talkie shorts that WB made in 1926: so far, no one thought that Sound films were here to stay.

WB, whose fortunes were failing, decided to risk all on a Talkie feature, and they selected *The Jazz Singer* with George Jessel repeating his Broadway success. It was a mild tale – curiously enough about a Jewish boy who doesn't want to be a cantor, flees from home and becomes a big success in vaudeville. WB were to pay Jessel $30,000. When Jack L. Warner informed Jessel by phone that songs and some dialogue were to be part of the set-up, Jessel asked for another $10,000 and insisted on the offer in writing. Warner said: 'If you can't take my word let's forget the deal.' The film was then offered to Eddie Cantor, who turned it down on the grounds that it was impossible to follow Jessel in the part. It was then offered to Jolson, who asked – and got – $75,000 for his services.

The Jazz Singer opened in New York in October 1927: the sound was recorded on disk, synchronized with the action. It was mostly background music; after 10 minutes, the actor playing Jolson as a boy sings – and then it's back to music. Twenty minutes later, Jolson appears and sings: after the song he says 'You ain't heard nothin' yet,' and sings again. Later in the film, he has a long monologue between songs to his mother. The film, mild as it was, caused a sensation and racked up the then considerable gross of $3½ million. Jolson went on to make another for WB, similarly lachrymose (parents fighting over the custody of their child), *The Singing Fool* (28). It was only part Talkie, but the Silent sequences were few and he sang 'Sonny Boy' to Davey Lee. It was, by the time it was shown, only one of several part-Talkies; but its success was astounding – it made $5½ million, a record unbroken for 10 years (*Gone With the Wind* overtook it in 1939).

'Climb upon my knee Sonny Boy', one of the more maudlin moments from The Singing Fool *(28): Al Jolson and Davey Lee.*

Sonny Boy (29), *Say It With Songs* (more pathos; Davey Lee gets run over), *Mammy* (30) and *Big Boy*, a racing comedy, followed the same formula to such an extent that audiences fell away with dangerous rapidity – particularly dangerous as he was getting (reputedly) $½ million per film. He signed a long-term contract with UA but only one film emerged: *Hallelujah I'm a Bum* (33), directed by Milestone, with Rodgers and Hart rhyming couplets. It was not a success. Then Jolson was involved with a Theatre Guild plan to play the title role in a Jerome Kern musical based on Dubose Hayward's novel, 'Porgy', but someone had second thoughts, and the project was taken over by the Gershwins. Jolson returned to WB for *Wonder Bar* (34) – as a cabaret owner whose wife, Kay Francis, is unfaithful to him; and it was announced that he had signed a new contract for one film a year with certain executive powers. But Jolson was touchy and there were only two (though a third, *Bowery to Broadway*, was announced): *Go Into Your Dance* (35) about a big-headed 'Mammy'-singer down on his luck and saved by Ruby Keeler (his real-life wife); and *The Singing Kid* (36), with Beverly Roberts, the maudlin tale of a big star who loses his voice and goes into the country to recuperate. It started with Jolson singing a medley of his old songs – something with

Wonder Bar (*34*): *Dolores del Rio with four of her leading men: Dick Powell, Ricardo Cortez, Jolson and Robert Barrat. Del Rio and Cortez were a dance team – till she stabbed him. Powell was the man she fell for in the end, and Jolson ran the club – the Wonder Bar.*

which the public were now over-familiar. That didn't prevent 20th from letting him do it all over again throughout *Rose of Washington Square* (39), in a characterization clearly based on himself, Alice Faye's old vaude buddy. It wasn't much of a characterization and it wasn't much of a part, but Jolson was solid gold. He then played E. P. Christy (of the 'Minstrels') in the Stephen Foster biopic, *Swanee River* (40). No more film offers were forthcoming, so he returned to Broadway for the first time in 10 years, in 'Hold on to Your Hats' with Martha Raye. It was a qualified success. In 1944 he played himself in the film about George Gershwin, *Rhapsody in Blue*.

Jolson was a wealthy man, but career-wise, he had been on his uppers for some years (though as one of the biggest egos in the business, he probably didn't recognize it). To general surprise, he regained popularity singing to the troops during the war. As a result, Columbia decided to make *The Jolson Story* (46): Jolson was peeved when he wasn't allowed to play himself, but he dubbed Larry Parks who did. The film was a monumental assembly of backstage clichés, but a new generation was discovering the Jolson voice and the Jolson songs, and it was a huge money-maker; further, it opened up a new career for Jolson on radio and records – there, once again, he was a hot property. Columbia felt called upon to make a sequel to *The Jolson Story*, all about how Jolson made a comeback because of *The Jolson Story*. It was called *Jolson Sings Again*, and had a scene where Parks as Jolson meets Parks playing Parks. Marginally more entertaining than the earlier film, it was one of the top box-office films of 1949. Jolson died the following year, still high on the crest of his second or third wave of popularity.

Boris Karloff

He was, said London's Evening Standard when he died, 'the acknowledged king of Hollywood horror films'. Boris Karloff was/is one of Hollywood's most famous names, but he was not a great star. He found his niche and he stayed there. He was a master of make-up; his monsters and villains were varied but they almost all had a touch of pathos: in life he was a gentle, courteous, thoughtful man and these qualities were always somewhat present in the grotesques he played (he liked gardening and poetry and was a devotee of cricket). His fame obscured the fact that the films in which he starred were invariably unimportant, B pictures and programme-fillers, and that in better films he was merely one of the supporting cast. Almost certainly he could not have widened his range, could not have sustained a real star part: he was one of those actors whom everyone likes while having no illusions about the talent. Karloff could be clumsy on occasion – but then, he seldom worked under first-class directors. He is revered by fans of horror pictures, but the cult for horror films stands quite apart from the mainstream of film appreciation: standards appertain there which would not be tolerated in other genres. Still Karloff was in some of the classics, even if most of them seem quaint and innocuous today. His films had style: there is more style in one reel of *Frankenstein* (31) than the complete output of that British studio which specializes in horror films. And Karloff, for all his shortcomings, had style.

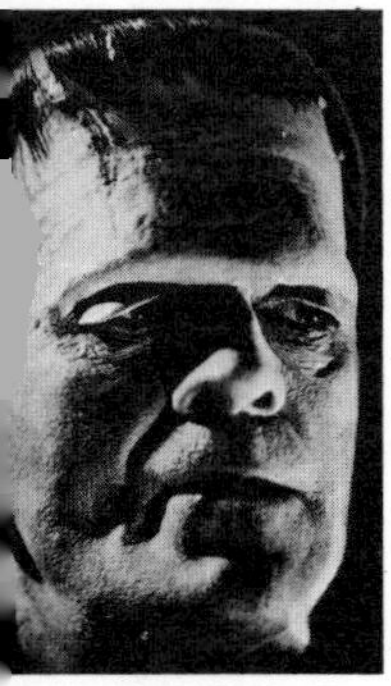

f made up for enstein's monster.

He was born in Dulwich, South London, in 1887, the youngest of nine children (a brother, Sir John Pratt, had a distinguished diplomatic career; their father was in the Indian Civil Service). He was educated at Merchant Taylor's School and at London University; was destined for the consular service but in 1909 emigrated to Canada where in Ontario he worked on a farm. An advert in a newspaper gave him a chance to join a touring company and it was then he adopted the name of Boris Karloff. For 10 years he played the sticks in melodramas, often a different one every night, sometimes doubling as stage manager; he worked for several troupes, perhaps the most distinguished of which was the one which took 'The Virginian' to the West. He was out of work in 1919 in Los Angeles, and thinking about turning to vaudeville. Instead he became a film-extra, starting as a soldier in *His Majesty the American* (19).

His work in Silent pictures was not notable. Occasionally he had a fair-sized part, but his roles were small, and often, to pay the rent, he returned to labouring to make a living. The titles: *The Prince and Betty*; *The Deadlier Sex* (20), starring Blanche Sweet, his first sizeable part, as a fur-trapper; *The Courage of Marge O'Doone*; *The Last of the Mohicans*; *Without Benefit of Clergy* (21); *The Hope Diamond Mystery*, a serial; *Cheated Hearts*; *Cave Girl* (22); *The Man From Downing Street*; *The Infidel*, as a native chieftain; *The Altar Stairs*; *Omar the Tentmaker*, the first picture in which he wasn't evil; *A Woman Conquers* (23); *The Prisoner*; *Dynamite Dan* (24); *Parisian Nights* (25), in a good part as one of Lou Tellegren's apache gang; *Forbidden Cargo*, being mean to Evelyn Brent; *Prairie Wife*; *Lady Robin Hood*; *Never the Twain Shall Meet* with Anita Stewart; *The Greater Glory* (26) with Anna Q. Nilsson and Conway Tearle, from a stage play about the effects of the War on the Viennese; *Her Honor the Governor*; *Flames*; *The Golden Web*; *Flaming Fury*; *The Bells* with Lionel Barrymore in Henry Irving's old part, and Karloff as the mesmerist; *Eagle of the Sea*, a pirate story with Florence Vidor and Ricardo Cortez; *Old Ironsides*; *Man in the Saddle*, starring Hoot Gibson; *Tarzan and the Golden Lion* (27) with James Pierce as Tarzan; *Let It Rain*; *The Meddlin' Stranger*; *The Phantom Buster*; *Soft Cushions*, a comedy at Paramount with Sue Carol and Douglas McLean; *Two Arabian Knights*; *The Love Mart* (28) with Billie Dove; *Little Wild Girl* (29); *The Devil's Chaplain*; *Vultures of the Sea*; *Phantoms of the North*; *Two Sisters*; *Burning the Wind*; and *The Fatal Warning*, a serial.

His first Sound picture was *The Unholy Night*, a melodrama set in London in which he was a Hindu servant. He did a serial for Mascot, *King of the Kongo*, and the following: *Behind That Curtain*; *The Bad One* (30); *The Sea Bat*, notable as Nils Asther's first audible Talkie role; *The Utah Kid*; and *Mother's Cry*, notable for the performance of Dorothy Peterson as the mother. That he had so far achieved no sort of fame in films is made apparent by the fact that Picturegoer thought the next, *The Criminal Code* (31), was his first picture. Some months earlier an offer had come out of the blue to play a small part in the original play, in its Los Angeles production, and that had led to Columbia offering Karloff the same role in the film, as the trusted convict who turns killer. He scored a small success and was immediately much in demand in films: *Cracked Nuts* with Wheeler and Woolsey; *Young Donovan's Kid*; *Smart Money*; *The Public Defender*; *I Like Your Nerve* as a butler; *Five Star Final* as the aide of ruthless editor Edward G. Robinson for whom, literally, he will stop at nothing; *The Mad Genius* as Marian Marsh's vicious father; *The Yellow Ticket*; *The Guilty Generation* as Robert Young's father, a prohibition racketeer; and a serial, *King of the Wild*.

Universal, meanwhile, had had a big success with *Dracula*, starring an actor of Hungarian origin, Bela Lugosi. A follow-up was planned, *Frankenstein*, from Mary Shelley's old novel and Lugosi was set for the lead. Lugosi, however, demurred because he planned a picture called *Quasimodo*

Goings-on in The Old Dark House *(32). Karloff as the butler, with Eva Moore–who for plot purposes was married to Ernest Thesiger.*

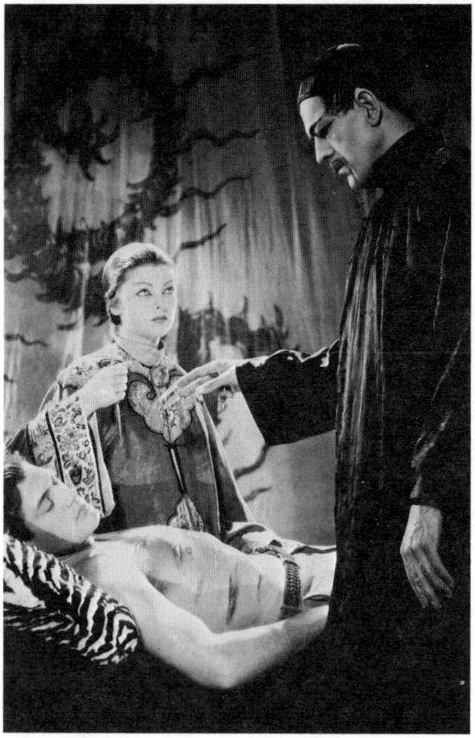

The Mask of Fu Manchu *(32): Karloff as Fu Manchu, Myrna Loy as his equally wicked daughter and Charles Starrett as their victim.*

(it was never made)–and he was, in any case, a difficult man. Karloff was on the Universal lot playing a murderer in *Graft*, starring Regis Toomey and Sue Carol. Director James Whale tested him in the make-up of Frankenstein's monster, a huge automated creature, blind-eyed, and somehow pathetic. Colin Clive had the title role and Mae Clarke was the girl. The film was a huge success and Universal signed Karloff to a seven-year contract. Like Lugosi before him, he was boosted as the successor to Lon Chaney.

Meanwhile, Karloff had several commitments to other studios: *Tonight or Never* in a funny scene as a waiter; *Business and Pleasure* (32) as a sheik whom Will Rogers meets on a trip to the East; *Alias the Doctor* as a misanthropic surgeon; *Scarface* as a rival mobster; *The Miracle Man* with Sylvia Sidney, as a man running a fake mission; and *Behind the Mask* with Jack Holt, one of the year's best chillers. In the first film of his new contract he played himself in one sequence, *The Cohens and Kellys in Hollywood*. He was the nightclub owner, a sympathetic part, in *Night World*, but soon reverted to type: the title role in *The Mummy*, returning to life after 3,700 years in an Egyptian tomb to claim the girl he considers a reincarnation of his dead love, with David Manners and Zita Johann; and *The Old Dark House*, a ferocious performance as the deaf-mute butler/killer. MGM borrowed him to play Fu in *The Mask of Fu Manchu*, the hated enemy of Lewis Stone, Karen Morley *et al.*

Karloff was occasionally billed merely as 'Karloff', but all was not well with him and Universal. He wanted more salary, but they refused and dropped him. He took a holiday and returned to Britain, where he made the inferior *The Ghoul* (33), with Ernest Thesiger and Cedric Hardwicke. Photoplay found 'audiences are apt to be amused when action is intended to be most terrifying'. Karloff returned to Hollywood to two good films: John Ford's *The Lost Patrol* (34) with Victor McLaglen, about British soldiers stuck in the desert, with himself at his most outrageously hammy as the one with religious mania; and *House of Rothschild* with George Arliss, as an anti-semitic baron. He made it up with Universal, who put him at the head of a devil-worshipping cult in *The Black Cat*, with Lugosi in support: Photoplay found 'no great suspense . . . all too unconvincing'. He did a guest appearance in that company's

Gift of Gab, starring Edmund Lowe; went to Monogram to play a kindly detective – the title character – in *The Mysterious Mr Wong* (35); returned to Universal for a good sequel, *The Bride of Frankenstein* – Elsa Lanchester in that part; and *The Raven* with Lugosi, based loosely on Poe and described by Photoplay as an 'absurd mélange'. At Columbia he had a dual role in *The Black Room* with Katharine de Mille; went back to Universal for another with Lugosi, *The Invisible Ray* (36).

There followed: *The Walking Dead* at Warners and *The Man Who Changed His Mind* in Britain with Anna Lee, directed by her husband Robert Stevenson. After that Karloff was in Bs: *Charlie Chan at the Opera* with Warner Oland as Chan; *Juggernaut* (37); *Night Key*, as an inventor whose burglar alarm device is stolen from him and whose subsequent neutralizer is wanted by crooks; *West of Shanghai*; *The Invisible Menace* (38); *The Son of Frankenstein* (39) with Lugosi and Basil Rathbone; *Mr Wong in Chinatown*; *The Man They Could Not Hang*; and *The Tower of London* with Rathbone as Richard III, and Karloff as Mord, the limping headsman. He did: *The Fatal Hour* (40); *British Intelligence*, a remake of *Three Faces East*; *Black Friday* with Lugosi; *The Man With Nine Lives*; *Devil's Island*; *Doomed To Die*; *Before I Hang*; *The Ape*; *You'll Find Out*, sharing the villain role with Peter Lorre and Lugosi in this Kay Kyser musical; *The Devil Commands* (41); and *The Boogie Man Will Get You*. Most of these were poverty row efforts – several were at Monogram. Whether or not he was depressed by the quality of these is not known, though he considered it more important to work than to worry about artistic principles; but at that point he accepted a stage offer, 'Arsenic and Old Lace', playing the old ladies' mad and equally homicidal nephew. One of his lines went: 'I killed him because he said I looked like Boris Karloff.'

This *comedie noire* ran for three years and Karloff returned to Hollywood with renewed prestige. His comeback was in an A, in colour, *The Climax* (44), billed after Susannah Foster and Turhan Bey: it was designed as a follow-up to *The Phantom of the Opera* which had been a big hit for Foster and Universal some months earlier, and had to do with hypnotism at the opera. Karloff then returned to B pictures. *The House of Frankenstein* (45) was a nothing, but Karloff then did three for Val Lewton's famed 'horror' outfit at RKO, the first directed by Robert Wise and the others by Mark Robson: each followed Lewton's dictum that terror can be aroused more by implication than by indication: *The Body Snatcher* (*s*)

In the 40s Karloff often dispensed with heavy make-up: in The Climax *(44) he looked like his off-screen self. The lady in distress is Susanna Foster.*

– the *s*, rightly, was added for Britain, from Robert Louis Stevenson's story based on the case of Burke and Hare – with Lugosi, and Henry Daniell as the anatomist who bought the corpses they collected; *Isle of the Dead* with Karloff as its overlord; and *Bedlam* (46), ditto.

After that Karloff was sometimes in A pictures, in support: *Lured* (47) with Lucille Ball; *The Secret Life of Walter Mitty*; *Unconquered*, as a Red Indian, with Gary Cooper; *Dick Tracy Meets Gruesome* with Ralph Byrd as Tracy, and Karloff as the other title character; *Tap Roots* (48), again as an Indian; and *Abbott & Costello Meet the Killer (Boris Karloff)* (49) – sometimes his name was used as part of the title. In 1948 he returned to Broadway in J. B. Priestley's 'The Linden Tree' – one of his rare 'straight' performances – but the play was not a success. His subsequent films were not distinguished: *The Strange Door* (51) starring Charles Laughton; *The Black Castle* (52) with Richard Greene; *The Hindu*, a weird (in the wrong sense) international effort; *Abbott & Costello Meet Dr Jekyll and Mr Hyde* (53); *Il Mostra dell'Isola*; *Voodoo Island* (57); *Frankenstein 1970* (58) – 'the whole inept effort is a slight on the horrific name of Frankenstein', said the

MFB; and *The Grip of the Strangler*, a neat little chiller with Jean Kent. The last-named was made in Britain, whither Karloff had returned to live, deep in the countryside; there was a companion picture, equally good, *Corridors of Blood*, made around the same time but not shown until four years later. By that time Karloff had acceded to the demand of Roger Corman, then making a series of fairly stylish pictures for AIP: *The Raven* (63), a spoof of the films based on Poe tales, with Vincent Price and Peter Lorre; *The Terror*; *A Comedy of Terrors* (64) with Lorre and Price again, plus Basil Rathbone; and *I Tre Volti della Paura*, a three-part film directed by Mario Bava, with Karloff as a grandfather vampire in an episode based on a Tolstoy story. There were three more for AIP: *Bikini Beach*, *Die Monster Die* (65) and *The Ghost in the Invisible Bikini* (66); *The Venetian Affair* (67) starring Robert Vaughan; and the British *Curse of the Crimson Altar* (68). In 1968 he made four cheapies which have not yet been shown: *Isle of the Snake People*, *The Incredible Invasion*, *The Fear Chamber* and *The Hour of Evil*.

He was also in *Targets* (67), made in fuzzy colour by critic Peter Bogdanovitch, a dual story of an ageing star of horror movies (a tired Karloff virtually playing himself) and a clean-cut American youth who takes to sniping at cars on the free-way because he loves guns. Cruel and gripping, it was more intelligent and more terrifying than anything Karloff had done, and with its gentle self-portrait was an unusual swan-song.

During this period he worked frequently in TV ('Starring Boris Karloff', 'Colonel March of Scotland Yard', etc.) and at one time told bedroom stories to children over the radio. In interviews he never knocked the type of films he made, but did speak wistfully of more 'serious' material: he scored a great success as Mr Darling and Captain Hook to Jean Arthur's Peter Pan (50–51), and later played Cauchon in 'The Lark' to Julie Harris's Joan of Arc. He married twice, and died in 1969.

Buster Keaton

Buster Keaton was not born in a trunk, but it was a near thing. His parents were on tour in Kansas–with a troupe that included Houdini–when Buster was born in 1895. By the time he was three, the child had, at his own insistence, joined the act. Later, 'The Three Keatons' were one of the best-known vaudeville acts, and Buster, following in his father's steps, became a remarkable athlete, adept at pratfalls, handsprings and marksmanship: the star of the act and, before he reached his teens, a celebrity in his own right.

There was a movie offer in 1913 when it was proposed that they should appear in a series based upon the strip-cartoon 'Bringing Up Father', but this Father disapproved of movies. Thereafter things went badly: the famous quarrel between the vaudeville artists and their employers, the owners of the circuits, put the Keatons out of the big time; and Father's drinking threatened the safety of his wife and Buster during the stage acrobatics. In self-defence they ditched the old man and Buster went to New York where he was offered a turn in 'The Passing Show of 1917'. Instead, he went into movies, via a chance street meeting with a vaudeville chum. He was invited to watch Roscoe 'Fatty' Arbuckle filming one of his two-reelers, *The Butcher Boy* (17), and was asked to participate–without rehearsal. During that one day he fell in love with the whole paraphernalia of filming, and he joined Arbuckle at $40 a week–instead of the $250 he would have been paid on Broadway. His salary with Arbuckle was to climb until it reached that figure, but in the meantime he was soon regarded as the second chief member of the company; and he and Arbuckle became friends. He made between 14 and 17 shorts with Arbuckle–in one of which, *Fatty at Coney Island*, can be glimpsed his only on-screen laugh. After *The Cook* (18) he left for military service and when he returned he received two offers at $1,000 a week from Jack Warner and William Fox. He chose to stay with Arbuckle, but Arbuckle was about to leave the company to go to Zukor; their producer, Joseph M. Schenck, proposed to Keaton that he take it over–at $1,000 a week plus 25 per cent of the profits. Metro were to release.

First, however, Metro wanted Keaton for a feature, *The Saphead* (20). It was adapted from 'The New Henrietta' that Douglas Fairbanks had done as play and film, and it was he who suggested Keaton for the lead. The script was re-worked to make Keaton the central character, a foppish man-about-town who, *almost* by chance and much to their surprise, saves the family from ruin. Little of it is typical of his work to come, but he scored a hit and some critics said that Chaplin would have to look to his laurels. The first two-reeler starring Keaton in his own right, *The High Sign*, was already in the can, but release was delayed because he wasn't satisfied with it; thus the first one released was *One Week*, described by Keaton himself as 'a mild parody of Elinor Glyn's "Three Weeks" – only one-third as shocking ... built around my efforts to put together the portable home I'd bought for our love-nest.' There followed *Convict 13*, *The Scarecrow*, *Neighbors*, *The Haunted House* (21) and *The Goat*, all made within the space of a year. Each marked an advance both visual (e.g. the incredible escape leap through the transom window in *The Goat*) and thematic. Keaton had never been a banana-peel/custard-pie comic, but he was beginning to express himself in almost surrealistic terms, with two predominant conceits – Buster caught in the toils of machinery and Buster dogged by misfortune and misunderstanding.

Then came four consecutive masterpieces: *The Playhouse*, with its theatreful of Busters, done by photographic sorcery still not adequately explained; *The Boat* – which pulls down the garage in which it was built and then the house and which, when launched, promptly sinks; *The Paleface* – Buster, chasing butterflies and pursued by Indians; and *Cops* (22), a whole city police force after a Buster who had inadvertently crossed them. The level of visual wit is Everest-high, but *The Boat* and *Cops* suggest a blacker vision, a fatalism – inexorable and absurd.

My Wife's Relations and *The Blacksmith* were, in the words of Keaton's biographer, Rudi Blesh, 'like early Keystones, little more than good slapstick', but *The Frozen North* – intended as a parody of William S. Hart – was wild fantasy. The mechanism of *The Electric House*, naturally, collapses disastrously. *Daydreams* is a bitter piece, juxtaposing the fancies in the letters to the girl back home with the harsh truth. *Balloonatics* again was fantasy with, at fade-out, Buster and his girl paddling their canoe in the sky. There followed *The Love Nest*, and after that Schenck informed Keaton that he could make features under a new deal with Metro, who had released the first half of this batch of shorts (First National had handled the rest).

Keaton was by now world-famous. Though neither he nor Lloyd nor – more debatably – Chaplin had the prestige of the dramatic stars they were hugely popular: they were merely funny men, albeit in what Dilys Powell has called 'the high summer of comedy'. It was to be a long time before Keaton was considered a genius. His behind-the-camera contribution to his own films, as writer, innovator and director, was around 90 per cent – though he shared credit wherever he could (in *The Playhouse* he had ridiculed those Hollywood directors – specifically Thomas H. Ince – who accepted half-a-dozen credits on each movie). From 1923 onwards, when he went into features, he was 'the equal of any director working in Hollywood' (David Robinson).

The Keaton the public saw was a dignified, impressively grave young man, 'the great stone face'. Deadpan, but not inscrutable: 'He was very handsome and generally silent. Most of the emotional work was done by a pair of remarkable eyes and a brave, schooled body. He had his own fashions for expressing feelings' (John Coleman). A slight blink meant bewilderment, a slight frown meant determination, as he struggled against the perversities of his opponents. A long gaze meant ardour, passion for his heroine – usually more a handicap than a help – but his aloofness was really shyness imposed on a sense of his own inadequacies. He needed to have patience and infinite resource, as well, of course, as his body: he was incredibly lithe and strong '... he brought pure physical comedy to its greatest heights. Beneath his lack of emotion he was always uninsistently sardonic; deep below that, giving a disturbing tension and grandeur to the

foolishness of those who sensed it, there was in his comedy a freezing whisper not of pathos but of melancholia. With the humour, the craftsmanship and the action there was often, besides, a fine, still and dreamlike beauty' (James Agee).

Economically, it made sense to go into features: the Keaton shorts were often the biggest attraction on the bill, but they took much less in rentals than the features. His salary went to $2,000 per week (later to go to $2,500) plus his percentage bonus. The features themselves were to cost between $200,000 and $220,000 – about 25 per cent more than most dramatic films, but the cost was justified by much bigger profits. Keaton's features each grossed between $1½ and 2 million, a little less, he estimated, than Harold Lloyd's.

The first of them was *The Three Ages* (23), a burlesque on *Intolerance*, and basically three two-reelers, with a boy-meets-girl, loses, wins, common to each; the ages were the Stone Age, Ancient Rome and the present day. The same year came *Our Hospitality* – an ironic title: he became involved in a family feud in the Deep South. The film contains some of his most outrageous physical feats, including the rescue from the waterfall. *Sherlock Junior* (24) was Buster – in his alter ego: the rest of the time he is a cinema projectionist, roaming, like the film, between dreams and reality; at one time he walks straight into the screen, but that isn't half as magical as the chase sequence, with a motorcyle ride which is pure poetry.

The Navigator has Keaton and his girl-friend on a deserted liner, he, with daffy ingenuity, mastering its mechanics. It was the biggest money-maker of all his films and one of the two most highly regarded (the other is *The General*, and they were Keaton's own favourites). He didn't care for *Seven Chances* (25) which he unwillingly constructed from a play that Schenck had bought for him: to inherit a fortune, he advertises for a bride; 500 turn up at the church – and give chase, almost the best he did, bedevilled later by falling boulders. Blesh says that the chase in *Go West* did not please Keaton, 'but it is an excellent film and in some respects a great one': the idea is good – Buster is besotted with a cow – but the laughter is sparse. *Battling Butler* (26) also has weaknesses, but it causes something nearer the normal laughter quotient, especially the sojourn in the wild with attendant valet; and there is a fine example of Keaton originality – the serious boxing match at the end.

The General (27) came next, a unique contribution to Civil War mythology, and

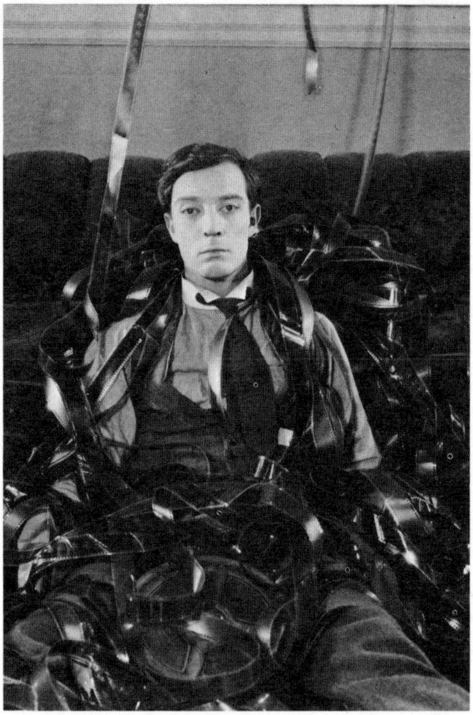

Buster Keaton in She lock Junior, *left*, *an* The Navigator, *the* *films he made in 192*

Keaton's most inspired and hilarious chase; and then *College*, a Keatonish variation on Lloyd's *The Freshman*. *Steamboat Bill Jr* is basically just Buster in a cyclone, 'the most fantastic dithyrambs of disaster ever committed to film' (Blesh). It was previewed with Buster smiling at the end, but the audience wouldn't take it.

Then in 1928, 'I made the worst mistake of my career. Against my better judgement I let Joe Schenck talk me into giving up my own studio to make pictures at the booming MGM lot in Culver City' ('My Wonderful World of Slapstick', 1960). Both Chaplin and Lloyd advised against it. Keaton thought Schenck acted in his best interests, but he did approach Paramount to take on the distribution of his films, retaining autonomy on production, but they had just undertaken to release Lloyd's products and didn't want two comics. Keaton understood that there was an underground conspiracy to get him to MGM, whose boss, Nicholas Schenck, was Joe's brother. He was, at least, to be paid $3,000 a week. The first film was *The Cameraman* (28) and it stands high in the Keaton canon: 'he knew it was fine, perhaps his finest' (Blesh). The trouble was, he had had to fight to make the thing his way. He was not permitted to work with his own team or develop his own story ideas: 'MGM writing staff began descending on us in droves'. Things were even worse on *Spite Marriage* (29). *The Cameraman* was making a

… both remarkable … mples of his unflag- … g comic invention.

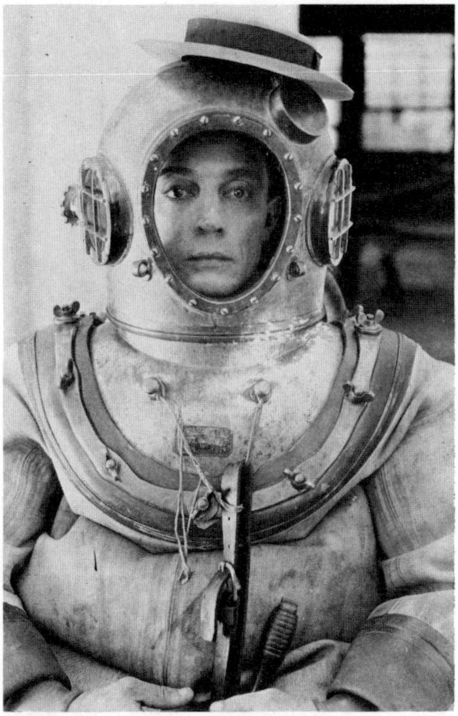

mint, which only proved to MGM how well they could make a Keaton comedy. Thus, 'All the good sequences in *Spite Marriage* represent battles with one MGM executive or another' (Blesh). And this too broke records.

A synchronized version was made of *Marriage*, and Buster made a French version (with Françoise Rosay); and he did a Salome dance in *Hollywood Revue of 1929*; but his first Talkie is reckoned to be *Free and Easy* (30). It was hardly a good Keaton film (he sang 'Conchita!'), but it was successful and Louis B. Mayer gave him a $10,000 bonus and three months holiday. In fact, the public were turning up to see anything that talked, however muffled, and were no longer interested in the visual comedies of the silent screen. Keaton's popularity, however, had continued to grow and was now at its peak: the descent was to come a couple of films later and be rapid and sudden. Blesh says that *Doughboys* is 86 per cent Keaton (he provided its original story), but Dilys Powell has recalled: 'a snigger of amusement, the rest was disaster'. Contemporary critics were commenting favourably, but *Parlour Bedroom and Bath* (31) really marked a decline. Reginald Mortimer wrote in Picturegoer: 'When you consider the brilliant comedies Keaton has given us . . . there is something rather pathetic in his efforts to retain his following in Talkies that frequently remind one of a burnt-out squib.' It was not entirely his fault: he said of *The Sidewalks of New York*, which came next, that the directors 'alternated in telling me how to walk, how to talk, how to stand, and how to fall–where and when, how fast or slow, how loud or soft. . . . It came out such a complete stinker, such an unbelievable bomb.' As grosses tumbled, MGM dickered with the idea of a 'straight' Buster, and he tested for the role Lionel Barrymore played in *Grand Hotel*. Instead, they announced that his new contract called for split-billing–a sure sign that he was on the skids. Jimmy Durante teamed with him in *The Passionate Plumber* (32), a version of *Her Cardboard Lover*, and though the notices were terrible MGM, undeterred, teamed them again: *Speak Easily* and *What No Beer* (33). Filming proceeded badly, with Keaton missing days.

That his drinking–he was an alcoholic by this time–was a contributory factor to the decline of his career cannot be doubted. The Hollywood of the 20s was a heavy-drinking place, but Keaton wasn't hooked until his marriage to Natalie (youngest of the Talmadge sisters) as well as his career went to pieces. Unlike Lloyd and Chaplin, he wasn't a businessman. He was only an artist, a gentle man, never pushing himself forward, always trusting, an innocent in the film jungle that had grown up round him in the last decade. He had only one obsession: to make people laugh. His waking hours were spent devising new ways to create laughter, even in the agony of these days: booze could provide the dreams he needed, for he dreamt of laughter.

When *What No Beer* demonstrated another marked decrease in public interest, MGM decided that they wanted no further truck with their 'difficult' star; and after a minor quarrel (Mayer wanted Keaton to be on the set to greet visitors one Saturday, and Keaton wanted to be at a baseball game) he was told that his services were no longer required. Thalberg asked him to go back some months later ('Aside from Norma Shearer, his wife, I think I was his favourite MGM star') to discuss a spoof version Keaton had planned of *Grand Hotel*, but Keaton was too proud. Instead, broke–the divorce had left him penniless–he went to Florida to make an independent film, but was so appalled by the set-up that he persuaded the backers to abandon the project. It had been widely publicized 'so what I got from it was a couple of weeks' work and another failure on my record'. No Hollywood studio would touch him, so he accepted an offer for a French film, *Le Roi des Champs Elysees* (34), at $15,000,

Keaton had two ambitions in The Cameraman *(28) – to get a newsreel scoop and make his name, and of course to win the girl. For a moment he is diverted from the latter by an unknown buxom beauty he meets on the beach: he appears to be clutching her hand, but she was really the pursuer – and a very determined one.*

and then one in Britain, for Sam Spiegel, *An Old Spanish Custom* (35). Both were skin-flint efforts, and unsuccessful.

Back in Hollywood, and cured of alcoholism (he didn't drink again until 1940, and after that had occasional outbursts; though on doctor's orders he didn't drink during the last years of his life) he approached Educational to let him make comedy shorts: they agreed to pay him $2,500 per short, the things to be shot in three days each. He made 18 for Educational over a three-year period (35–37) and the quality is generally low. In 1939–41 he had a similar arrangement with Columbia for six a year. He begged Columbia to let him make a feature, but there was no interest. However, he did begin to get feature work again in 1939, starting with a four-week stint at 20th on *Hollywood Cavalcade*, where, ironically, he was called upon to heave a custard pie, almost his first. He was in, and worked on the scripts of, two of 20th's Jones family series (*The Jones Family in Hollywood* and *The Jones Family and Quick Millions*), but most of his work was for a day's duration: *The Villain Still Pursued Her* (40) and *Li'l Abner*. In 1940, sick of the 'cheaters' at Columbia, he approached MGM for a job, and was paid $100 a week (and later $300) as gag man and comedy constructionist: he failed to click with either the Marx Brothers or Abbott and Costello. He also began to do stock, touring in 'The Gorilla'.

Dilys Powell, in her introduction to his memoirs: 'He was in fact missed rather than forgotten. Few film-stars have been missed so much and so long. It was with a shock of delight that, one day in the war, one recognized in a film called *San Diego I Love You* (44) the long, sad, glacier face of Buster Keaton.' He was also in *Forever and a Day* (43), *That's the Spirit* (45), *That Night With You* and *God's Country* (46). Then he made a film in Mexico, *El Moderno Barba Azul* (45) and one in France with Bourvil, *Un Duel à Mort* (48); and in 1947 commenced the first of several successful sorties into the Cirque Medrano in Paris, billed as 'L'homme qui rit jamais'. He had featured roles in *You're My Everything* (49), *The Lovable Cheat* and MGM's *In the Good Old Summertime* (in a smaller role and with smaller billing than S. Z. Sakall); and made a wan, if effective,

Keaton in his short, sad, guest appearance in Sunset Boulevard *(50). He said later that he never saw the film.*

appearance in *Sunset Boulevard* (50) and another in one sequence of *Limelight* (52).

It was then that the resurrection began: he had a successful TV show on the West Coast 1950–1, and film societies began to show his films. James Agee's famous Life magazine piece on the great Silent comedians had appeared in 1949; in 1952 his fee in Paris at the circus was $3,500, and afterwards he toured the British provinces with his wife (his third, last, and enduring – since 1940 – marriage). He was honoured by Eastman House, in their Festival of the Arts, as one of the 10 who had contributed most to the art of the movies (the others: Pickford, Lillian Gish, Mae Marsh, Lloyd, Barthelmess, Norma Talmadge, Swanson, Ronald Colman, Chaplin). In 1957 came *The Buster Keaton Story*, with Donald O'Connor as Keaton – an inept biopic, but one which made Keaton a fairly wealthy man for the rest of his life; and *Around the World in Eighty Days* (56), where he, the forgotten star, the one who didn't want to be loved, drew more audience response than any of the other guest stars. In 1959 he was awarded a special Oscar for his contribution to the art of the cinema.

But the real acclaim was to still come. In 1954 Keaton had approached Raymond Rohauer, managing the Society of Cinema Arts in Los Angeles, with an offer of several decomposing reels of his great films. Soon after that a cache was found in James Mason's home (which had once been Keaton's). Rohauer set out to restore to Keaton not only his films, but the glory, and by the time that Keaton died had managed to purchase for him–sometimes saving from destruction–all his best work. The films began to be shown: there was a retrospective at the Venice Film Festival in 1963, and in 1965 Keaton was at the Festival–a 20-minute standing ovation reduced him to tears. In Germany in 1962–63 *The General* broke records in most German cities, and a revival in Paris was also mobbed (the best London could do was to put it in support of a re-run of *The Ipcress File* for two weeks).

Also, there was work: supporting roles in *The Adventures of Huckleberry Finn* (60), the Canadian *Ten Girls Ago* (62), *It's a Mad Mad Mad Mad World* (63) and *The Triumph of Lester Snapwill*; in 1965 Buster appeared in no less than seven films, either in guest spots or in shorts; two of them were made in Canada, *The Railrodder* and *Keaton Rides Again*, a survey of his career. There were Samuel Beckett's *Film* (half-an-hour of the back of Keaton's head!); *Pajama Party*, *Beach Blanket Bingo*, *How to Stuff a Wild Bikini*; there was the Italian *Due Marines e un General*; and there was Lester's *A Funny Thing Happened on the Way to the Forum*. His last films were *The Scribe*, made in Canada, and *Sergeant Deadhead*, which starred Frankie Avalon. He died in 1966.

'But that game, ridiculous little figure in its flat hat, stumping about on stiff short legs, with arms that are inclined to start into sudden motion like a windmill and, at the centre of all the activity, a still face of absurd solemnity and astounding *beauty*, cannot die. Undefeated, he continues to match his ingenious little devices against the Goliaths; and passes into the universal folk heritage, as the supreme clown-poet' (David Robinson in 1968). 'But between 1920 and 1930 he did manage to make a succession of films which we are even now only beginning to appreciate properly. His legacy is resplendent and irreplaceable' (John Russell Taylor, also in 1968).

Ruby Keeler

In 1965 the New York Gallery of Modern Art arranged there and elsewhere showings of the films of Busby Berkeley, who specialized in mammoth girlie routines: girls geometric, girls floral, girls as harps, girls as waterfalls, hundreds of girls playing hundreds of grand pianos. In the midst of this amusing but Freudian old tat can be glimpsed a couple singing, an aggressively grinning juvenile, Dick Powell, and a dark little girl with more than a passing resemblance to a bush baby, Ruby Keeler.

Ruby Keeler came all the way to New York to break into show business–but all she managed was to get a job on showman James Cagney's backstage staff. Until one day . . . Footlight Parade *(33). Watching her are Cagney and his adoring secretary, played by Joan Blondell.*

She danced, too, a spirited but unexpressive tap, a suitable counterpoint to her cracked nasal soprano. At these Cinematheque showings, Berkeley appeared and reminisced about these antique movies, and he was accompanied by Keeler, a slim and attractive middle-aged woman. She disarmed audiences by confessing: 'It's amazing. I couldn't act. I had that terrible singing voice, and now I can see I wasn't the greatest tap dancer in the world either.'

Keeler was born in Halifax, Nova Scotia, in 1909; her family moved to New York when she was three, and in New York at 13 she began her career as a buck-dancer with Patsy Kelly. She was also in the chorus of Broadway shows for four years, till she got a part in 'Bye Bye Bonnie', followed by 'The Sidewalks of New York' (24) and 'Whoopee!'. In 1928 she married Al Jolson, who had met her while she was hoofing in Texas Guinan's club. Ziegfeld then starred her in 'Show Girl' – remembered now because Jolson sometimes wandered into the theatre when his own show was over, and sang 'Liza' to her walking through the stalls. He was already a Warner Bros star but it wasn't until three years later that that studio placed Keeler under contract.

k Powell and Ruby 'er in Frank zage's Flirtation lk *(34). Though they d working together both fought against g teamed because they ght that limited them.*

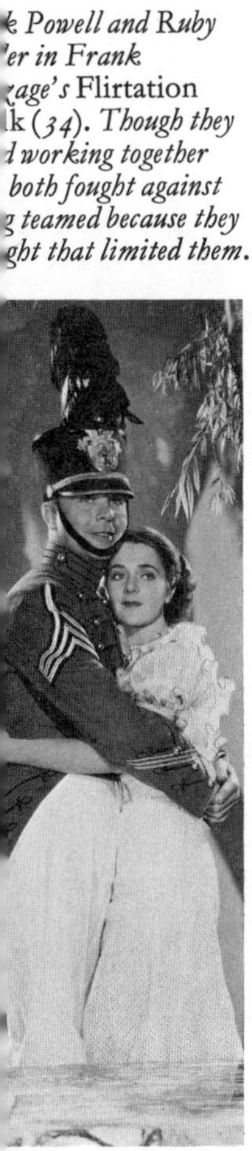

42nd Street (32), directed by Lloyd Bacon (Berkeley did the musical numbers), cast her as the girl picked from the chorus line to replace the ailing, temperamental star (Bebe Daniels): 'You've got to go on and give and give' exhorts Warner Baxter, '. . . and Sawyer, you're going on a youngster, but you've got to come back a star!' Most of her subsequent films seemed to have the same plot, or at least she was always naïve (indeed, downright imperceptive), swimming to success in the hard-boiled, soft-hearted show biz pool. But *42nd Street* was different, hard and fierce and almost melancholy, quick-moving and tuneful: the prototype of the 'new' musical, more realistic than those hitherto. It grossed over $2¼ million, an enormous sum. Hardly less good was *Gold Diggers of 1933* (33), paired again with Dick Powell, a couple of innocents in a world composed of the likes of Aline McMahon, Joan Blondell, Guy Kibbee, Warren William, Ginger Rogers, Una Merkel and Ned Sparkes. And *Footlight Parade*, aided by Cagney's energetic performance, is as enjoyable now as it was then. Powell was in it, and he and Keeler continued their romance through *Dames* (34), *Flirtation Walk* (35), *Shipmates Forever* (36) and *Colleen*. In 1935 she made a film with her husband, *Go Into Your Dance*.

In 1937 she was getting $4,000 a week. In an interview that year with W. H. Mooring she said that she didn't think she was good enough to carry a film and that she was sick of backstage romances. She added: 'This film business isn't my whole life.' She made only three more films. Her last film for Warners was a 'musical extravaganza', *Ready Willing and Able* (37), with Ross Alexander (just before he shot himself during a drinking bout).

About the time it finished shooting, Jolson quarrelled with Warners and walked out, angrily taking Keeler with him. She signed a contract with RKO, who finally dumped her into *Mother Carey's Chickens* (38), already turned down by Ginger Rogers, Katharine Hepburn, and Joan Bennett among others. The contract was quietly allowed to lapse. In 1940 she and Jolson were divorced: she did a B musical at Columbia with Ozzie Nelson, *Sweetheart of the Campus* (41), and that was the last the audience heard of her until she turned up at the Gallery of Modern Art. She refused to let her name be used when Columbia made *The Jolson Story*, around which time she married a Californian land developer; they have four children. In 1970 she made a guest appearance in *The Phynx*.

Alan Ladd

In the hierachy of tough-guy stars, Alan Ladd holds an honoured name: through 50 or so formula pictures he strolled, stone-faced, in roles which fitted him as snugly as the iron strapped to his side. No one ever pretended that he could act. He got to the top, therefore, by a combination of determination and luck.

He was born in Hot Springs, Arkansas, in 1913. His father died when he was three; with his mother and step-father he went to California. At high school he was noted for his athletic prowess and was later a diving champion. He was further noted, if anything, for the variety of jobs he had, including gas-station attendant and life-guard. He was taken on by Universal in 1933 as one of a group of college boys to be groomed for stardom, but was dropped after six months. The experience left a vivid impression on him and he managed to get a job as a grip at Warners. He also worked on a newspaper and owned a hot-dog stand. He did not despair. Finally he got some local stage and radio work and a few 'extra' jobs in films – he can be glimpsed, for instance, in *The Goldwyn Follies*. In 1938 he met Sue Carol, a former movie star (*c.* 1925–33) turned agent (purportedly after she had heard him on the air). She took him under

Neither Alan Ladd nor Veronica Lake were quite so effective without the other: her sulky looks and little-girl-lost voice were ideally complemented by his unsmiling countenance and discourteous manner. Here in This Gun for Hire *(42), the film that made him a star.*

her wing, pushing him with determination and devotion. He married her in 1942, having been divorced from his first wife. Despite his stature (he was 5 ft 6 in.) Carol could sense in his cold, blond looks a certain star potential. She got him a small part in *Rulers of the Sea* (39) and a dozen others, mainly Bs at Republic and Monogram. He was the juvenile lead in the minor *The Goose Step*, but down to 12th on the cast list of Paramount's *Light of Western Stars* (40). The others: *In Old Missouri*, *Those Were the Days*, *Gangs of Chicago*, *The Green Hornet* (a Universal serial), *Captain Caution*, *Wildcat Bus*, *Meet the Missus*, *Her First Romance*, *Petticoat Politics* (41), *Citizen Kane* (as a reporter), *The Black Cat* (where he was first noticed) and *The Paper Bullets* (another lead). He also had a bit in Disney's *The Reluctant Dragon* (a visit to the Disney studio, part cartoon/part live action); was in *Great Guns* and *Cadet Girl*; and his big chance came in RKO'S *Joan of Paris* (42) in which Michèle Morgan helped shot-down airmen, including him, to escape the Nazis.

As a result of that role, Paramount cast him as the hired killer in *This Gun for Hire*, based loosely on Graham Greene's 'A Gun for Sale': it was transferred to a US setting. Billed fourth (after Robert Preston, Veronica

Lake and Laird Cregar), he still had the best and biggest part. On its own terms it was a first-rate thriller, and Ladd was excellent as the hard-boiled gun who gets caught in a trap like a rat; Picturegoer readers voted him their annual Best Actor Gold Medal. Paramount signed him, and put him quickly into another tough film, the remake of Dashiell Hammett's *The Glass Key*. Again it was strong entertainment, again he was good, and again the contrast of the taciturn Ladd and the silky, provocative Lake worked box-office magic. (Apart from a couple of guest appearances, they appeared together twice again only: but were one of the 40s' most celebrated teams. In an interview later he said that he disliked working with her.)

Paramount of course were delighted. The majority of stars were earmarked as such when they appeared on the horizon – from Broadway or from wherever they came; if it seemed unlikely that public acceptance would come with one film they were trained and built-up: the incubation period was usually between two and five years. As far as Ladd was concerned, he was a small-part actor given a fat part *faute de mieux*, and after his second film for them he hadn't merely hit the leading-men category, but had gone beyond it where films were constructed round his personality. In *Lucky Jordan* he was a gangster reformed by the love of a Good Woman (Helen Walker) and a stint in the army. He guested in *Star Spangled Rhythm*, and in *China* (43) was a tough oil man redeemed by Loretta Young and the suffering around him. Bosley Crowther wrote: 'Mr Ladd consumes countless cigarettes and gets into some ludicrous postures in pretending to be a tough, dead-panned guy.' Ladd then did his own hitch in the USAAF, until invalided out some months later. He was with Young again in *And Now Tomorrow* (44), but it was more her vehicle than his – a soap opera about a spoilt woman going deaf and her harsh-seeming doctor. They ended in a clinch. It was a pitch to sell Ladd to women filmgoers, though he hadn't changed one iota, and he didn't have a noticeable romantic aura. But Paramount hoped that women might feel that beneath the rock-like expression there smouldered fires of passion, or something like. His black-lashed eyes, however, gave nothing away: it was 'take me as I am' or 'I'm the boss around here'. He never flirted nor even seemed interested (which was one of the reasons he and Lake were so effective together).

1945.

He was *Salty O'Rourke* (45), a drama about what the ads called 'The Sport of Kings', with Gail Russell, and he guested again in *Duffy's Tavern*, spoofing his image (and a year later was in a similar film, *Variety Girl*, singing 'Talahassee' with Dorothy Lamour). Then he refused to work until a more favourable contract was drawn up. He was on suspension for four months, and returned in three in a rush: *The Blue Dahlia* (46) with Lake and a typical Raymond Chandler script, as a war veteran who returns to find his wife first unfaithful and then dead – one of the classic thrillers of the period; *OSS* with a new type of leading lady, cool and ladylike, Geraldine Fitzgerald; and *Two Years Before the Mast*, a vigorous adaptation of Richard Henry Dana's autobiographical novel, with William Bendix and Barry Fitzgerald, two scene-stealers who lost in this case to Howard Da Silva in a masterly interpretation of the vile captain.

Now – 1946/7 – he was one of the 10 most popular stars in Britain, and in the US he was No. 10 in 1947. This was despite a mouldy couple of pictures that year – *Calcutta* with Gail Russell and *Wild Harvest* with Lamour. Nor were the 1948 trio much better – *Saigon*, the last with Lake, *Beyond Glory* with Donna Reed, and *Whispering Smith*.

Physically, he was perfect as *The Great Gatsby* (49), and his emotional immobility might have worked better in a better film. Critics disliked the picture – though Scott Fitzgerald had not then been rediscovered – and the public didn't go because it wasn't what they expected of a Ladd movie. More popular was his other picture that year, a thriller, *Chicago Deadline*, again with Donna Reed. There followed: *Captain Carey USA* (50) with Wanda Hendrix; *Branded* with Mona Freeman; *Appointment With Danger* (51) with Phyllis Calvert as a nun; *Red Mountain* with Lizabeth Scott; and *Thunder in the East* with Deborah Kerr: all tailored for the action market. The latter, made in 1951, wasn't shown in Britain until 1952 and the US until 1953, an indication perhaps that box-office receipts were falling. Paramount re-negotiated the contract – it had two years to run – for only two more pictures, at $100,000 each. He was also free to sign elsewhere, and made a deal with Warner Brothers (who had recently lost Bogart) for six films over a six-year period at $150,000 against 10 per cent of the gross. His first there was *The Iron Mistress* (52) – the title referring to the Bowie knife he invented and not to co-star Virginia Mayo.

He also signed with Universal for a couple, the first of which was *Desert Legion* (53), with Richard Conte and Arlene Dahl: he was in the Foreign Legion. Then came

George Stevens's Shane *(53): among other things, there was a touching depiction of hero-worship from Ladd and Brandon de Wilde (as the son of pioneers Van Heflin and Jean Arthur).*

Shane at Paramount, in which George Stevens took the second oldest cliché of Western movies and turned it into a beautiful drama of pioneer homesteaders: Ladd was the gunman who rides into town and only rides out when law-and-order have been restored. His monolithic presence made him good casting, though Karel Reisz in the MFB found his performance 'empty' and thought him 'the only box-office concession in an otherwise single-minded film'. It was the only outstanding film he made; it grossed a huge $9 million, and remains the film with which he is chiefly associated. It boosted him at the box-office, and he made the top 10 again in 1953 and 1954; in 1954 he was also the Britons' favourite star. Paramount, however, only had him for one more film, another sea story with another villainous captain, James Mason, *Botany Bay* (54). Already among the British he had made *The Red Beret* (53), the first of a three-pic deal with Warwick/Columbia on a percentage deal; he was a Mountie in *Saskatchewan* (54) at Universal, and then returned to Britain: *Hell Below Zero* with Jill Bennett, from a Hammond Innes novel, and *The Black Knight*, where he was particularly ludicrous as a medieval warrior.

Some of his Warner films were produced by his own company, Jaguar, but none of them were of much interest except to action buffs: *Drum Beat*; *The McConnell Story* (55) with June Allyson; *Hell on Frisco Bay* with Edward G. Robinson; *Santiago* (56) with Rosanna Podesta; *The Big Land* (57) with Mayo; *Boy on a Dolphin* (57) at 20th Century-Fox with Sophia Loren, filmed on location in Greece; and *The Deep Six* (58). He had turned down the role that James Dean played in *Giant*, but did get into another good one, *The Proud Rebel*, a gentle drama about a drifter and his mute son (played by his own son David). His own performance is his best work, sincere and likeable (due perhaps to an odd resemblance in long shot to Buster Keaton), but the film didn't have the success it deserved: Ladd's own fans missed the bang-bang, and de Havilland's fans weren't persuaded that any film she did with Ladd could be that good. After that, it was usually the bottom half of double bills: *The Badlanders*, *The Man in the Net* (59), *Guns of the Timberland* (60), *All the Young Men* (a war picture), *One Foot in Hell* and *13 West Street* (62) – the last was produced by himself in conjunction with Columbia. Before that one he had been to Italy for *Horatio* (61), released finally in the US in 1964 as *Duel of the Champions*. He was distinctly ill at ease as a Roman officer.

In 1962 he was found at his home with gun-shot wounds: it was said to be accidental. He had been drinking heavily for years and when he died in 1964 cause of death was said to be the result of sedatives on top of a high level of alcohol. There was one more picture to come – a sort of come-back – in a key role in *The Carpetbaggers* (64), a razzamatazz tale of sex and skulduggery in old Hollywood. The novel had been a best-seller, and the film raked up giant grosses. Ladd played a cowboy star of the Silent era. He was only one of several names in the cast and went more or less unnoticed.

Veronica Lake

When Veronica Lake was tub-thumping for her autobiography ('Veronica', 1968) some suggestion was advanced that she had been the queen of Hollywood in the 40s. Not so, by any means, though at least in cinemas for some time she held a certain sway. She came in with the decade, and was gone by the end of it. John Russell Taylor once observed (in Sight and Sound) that for him she has always been 'the classic instance of the true 40s vamp. . . . Ah, the tension which would build up in a film as one waited for the invitation in that strangely husky voice, in the provocative swing of the sequinned box shoulder, to reach its consummation at a moment of climactic abandon when the face-obscuring mane of blonde hair would be swept aside in an embrace and reveal the full glory of the large, lustrous eyes, the slightly sunken cheeks and then, heavily made-up lips which marked the apogee of 40s glamour.'

She was born in Brooklyn, New York, in 1919. Paramount publicity had her father alternatively as a college professor and a commercial artist, but in a 1955 interview (and in her book) she said that he had been a German-Danish seaman. The official version also has her studying at McGill University for a while, before moving to California (because of the health of her step-father who *was* a commercial artist), but she appears rather to have been entering beauty contests in Florida. In Los Angeles she joined the dramatic class of the Bliss-Hayden theatre and appeared in some plays. She was interviewed by RKO and under the name of Constance Keane (she was born Constance Ockelman) appeared in *Sorority House* (39), Paramount's *All Women Have Secrets* and *Forty Little Mothers* (40) at MGM. Her agent got her a test there, but that studio wasn't impressed. He showed it to Paramount, who thought her perfect for *I Wanted Wings* (41) – it was the female lead, but she was seventh on the cast list. She was signed to a seven-year contract, starting at $75 a week.

Her second Paramount film was Preston Sturges's *Sullivan's Travels* (41), playing the companion of a film director Joel McCrea while he posed as a bum. It was a notable comedy, and she was effective; but what she had going for her most was the peek-a-boo hair, and a brief partnership with Alan Ladd – *This Gun for Hire* (42) and *The Glass Key*: Bogart and Bacall were better, but Ladd and Lake came first. She was now getting $350 a week – soon to go up. She was also admirable as the witch in Clair's *I Married a Witch*, made on loan-out, but inept doing a song ('A Sweater, a Sarong and a Peek-a-Boo Bang') with Paulette Goddard and Dorothy Lamour in the all-star *Star Spangled Rhythm* (43). It promptly went. The hair, that is. So many girls had emulated Lake's locks that there were many accidents in munitions factories when hair got caught in machines. The US Government made an official request to Paramount to change her style; thus she appeared with it rigidly knotted in *So Proudly We Hail* (43), playing a nurse. As Russell Taylor said: 'Poor Veronica Lake: she was never so exciting once her hair had been reduced to normal proportions.'

The Hour Before the Dawn (44) had been a novel by Somerset Maugham written for the US market (he never allowed it to be published in Britain): Lake played a Nazi spy posing as a refugee in Britain. The film was

Veronica Lake hits the big time – in I Wanted Wings (*41*), *with Ray Milland and William Holden. It was directed by Mitchell Leisen, one of Hollywood's under-rated directors.*

too slow to be good propaganda, and it also marked the end of the Lake vogue. Further, she was difficult to handle: Paramount threw her into three little pictures with the also-fading Eddie Bracken – *Bring on the Girls* (45) – in her own words, 'an inane musical'; *Out of This World*, a take-off on the Swoonatra business: Bracken played the crooner (dubbed by Bing Crosby); and *Hold that Blonde* – 'It was another in Paramount's formula of the moment – put a comic and a popular sexy type together and the folks will come see'. She then did *Miss Susie Slagle's*, a guest spot in *Duffy's Tavern*, and appeared again with Alan Ladd in an excellent melodrama, *The Blue Dahlia* (46). The short-lived Enterprise Co. borrowed her for a Joel McCrea Western, *Ramrod* (47), and her Paramount contract petered out with a guest spot in *Variety Girl* and three duallers: *The Sainted Sisters* (48), *Saigon* with Ladd, and *Isn't It Romantic* (49). She was in a picture at 20th, *Slattery's Hurricane*, and then, she says, there were no offers; in 1950 there was talk of a British film, directed by her then-husband, André de Toth, called *Before I Wake* (a film of that title was made in the UK five years later by Mona Freeman).

In Mexico she made *Stronghold* (51) with Zachary Scott, and not long afterwards the de Toths filed voluntary bankruptcy petitions. She toured or appeared in stock for some years: 'The voice of the Turtle', 'The Little Hut', etc. and then disappeared from view. In 1962 the New York Post discovered her, working in a Manhattan cocktail lounge, and she hit the headlines again a couple of times being convicted of drunkenness. Also in that year she married for the fourth time. But she was offered work again: TV hostess in Baltimore; in the 1964 off-Broadway revival of 'Best Foot Forward'; in stock in Florida in 1965–6, and in a Z-budget movie made in Montreal in 1967, *Footsteps in the Snow*. Her memoirs also focused some attention on her: as a result, she toured in Britain in a flop play, 'Madam Chairman', and played 'A Streetcar Named Desire' in a suburban theatre with Ty Hardin.

Hedy Lamarr

In her autobiography ('Ecstasy and Me: My Life As a Woman', 1966) Hedy Lamarr pauses in an account of some love-making to quote the critics on her first American film performance (in *Algiers*): 'The reviews spoke of "definite artistry", "beauty that enthralls", "a new star shining bright", "alluring like a night horizon of jewels", "a surprising and vital performance for a newcomer" and "Hedy Lamarr is glorious".' Neither the artistry nor vitality were much in evidence afterwards, but – as she points out at least once in every chapter – she was considered the most beautiful woman in films at the time.

She was born in Vienna in 1914. According to her account she was still at school studying design when she gate-crashed one of the studios in Vienna and was selected by director Alexis Granowsky for a bit part in *Sturme ein Wasser Glas* (Silent, 30). She had bit parts in some other films (*Mein Brauchte Kein Geld*, *Die Koffer des Herr O. F. Herne*) and on the stage; in 1933 was offered the star part in *Extase*, a Czech picture directed by Gustav Machaty – and this gave her a certain renown (as Hedwig Kiesler; before MGM changed her name). The plot concerned an impotent old man, his young bride, and the young man who spies her swimming in the old water-hole. The technique was as naïve as the plot, but the point is that young Hedwig was swimming nude, and that and the subsequent run through the wood – still starkers – guaranteed the film a notoriety that has lasted to this day. Soon after completion, its star married an Austrian millionaire, Fritz Mandl, who tried to buy up all copies of the film. He didn't succeed; the film was shown in the US in 1937, the year the couple were divorced.

Kiesler/Lamarr went to London, where her agent introduced her to Louis B. Mayer, but he was not certain whether – because of *Extase* – she was respectable enough to fit into the MGM family. But when he sailed for the US on the 'Normandie' he found Lamarr on board and by the end of the voyage had capitulated, offering her a seven-year contract starting at $500 a week. After some delay, uncertain what to do with her, MGM loaned her to Wanger for *Algiers* (38), at a 200 per cent mark-up on her salary. It was a sensational role (as the society beauty for one last glimpse of whom Charles Boyer leaves the Casbah) and when it was shown her name became synonymous with glamour; the film was a big success. A delighted Mayer decided he would make Lamarr the greatest motion picture star there ever had been – greater than Garbo (who was troublesome, anyway). Dietrich's old director, Josef von Sternberg – thought to be the ultimate in packaging European glamour – was brought in and Spencer Tracy was assigned to co-star. But Mayer interfered; Von Sternberg was fired; *I Take This Woman* stopped and started so often and so much was scrapped (including Walter Pidgeon's part) that studio wags called it 'I Re-take This Woman'. During one lull, when Tracy was otherwise engaged, Lamarr was rushed into *Lady of the Tropics* (39) as a half-caste, with Robert Taylor as a

Clark Gable and Hedy Lamarr in Comrade X *(40), directed by King Vidor. Gable was an American newspaperman in Moscow and she was a streetcar driver.*

millionaire, in case she was forgotten. Said the ads: 'You too will be "Hedy" with delight and your verdict will be "Lamarrvellous"', but Picturegoer's wasn't: 'Hedy Lamarr shows that Sex with a capital S is rather dull.' Such reviews convinced Mayer she could never be a great star and when *Woman* too flopped he lost interest in her.

Her own response was to stop battling with the studio for the first time since *Algiers*. She needed a hit, and *Boom Town* (40) provided it, when she lured Clark Gable away from Claudette Colbert – but with her advent halfway through, the film stopped being interesting; just as in *Comrade X*, again with Gable, her performance in a *Ninotchka*-like part was as unlike Garbo's as possible. Nor was she any more animated in a comedy with James Stewart, *Come Live With Me* (41), or a musical, *Ziegfeld Girl*, though her work in *HM Pulham Esq*, from John P. Marquand's novel, was a distinct improvement. She did *Tortilla Flat* (42) with Tracy, *Cross Roads* (a remake of the French *Carrefour*) with William Powell, and *White Cargo* with Walter Pidgeon: the remake of this old warhorse found her as Tondelayo, 'a half-caste jungle temptress'; 'I thought with some interesting make-up, a sarong and some hip-swinging I would be

Three young ladies of MGM in Ziegfeld Girl *(41): Hedy Lamarr, Judy Garland and Lana Turner (at this time Lamarr was already the veteran of two marriages; between them they would rack up a total of 17 husbands).*

a memorable nymphomaniac.' She wasn't. Then she did a comedy with Powell – he was an astronomer – *The Heavenly Body* (43), but was 'no substitute for Myrna Loy' (Picturegoer); she then took a sabbatical. In fact, she was extremely difficult about her material: she turned down *Casablanca*, *Gaslight* and *Saratoga Trunk* (all of which, coincidentally, were big ones for Ingrid Bergman). At the same time MGM found that she was hardly the draw that her fame implied: so they were happy to loan her to RKO for *Experiment Perilous* (44), a psychological melodrama with George Brent (the picture she likes herself best in) and to WB for *The Conspirators* with Paul Henried. Her MGM contract finished with a comedy with Robert Walker, *Her Highness and the Bellboy* (45).

Lamarr says she asked for release from her contract – which had a short time to run – and was granted it on condition that she make three pictures for MGM over the next five years (in fact, only one was made). She formed her own producing company and did two for UA, *Strange Woman* (46) with George Sanders and *Dishonored Lady* (47) with her then-husband, John Loder. In both she was a *femme fatale*; of the second one she says in her memoirs: 'Again there were critics who pointed out that I had played a dissolute woman, while my nature in real life was different.' (Another remark worth noting in the book: 'I think if I were to compare my style to some actresses, I would say I am a cross between Judy Garland and Greta Garbo.') Neither film did smash business; and her next was a flop, *Let's Live a Little* (48), a comedy for Eagle-Lion with Robert Cummings. Lamarr says that her judgment of scripts brought this decline: 'At MCA, the biggest talent agency in the world, I had the reputation of being hard to handle. . . . I was the highest-priced and most important star in Hollywood, but I was "difficult".'

In fact, she was very much a back-number when Paramount cast her as Delilah in *Samson and Delilah* (50), but by general agreement her box-office risk was compensated for by a beauty that was ideal for the role: audiences might not go and see Lamarr in a comedy, but they would be tempted to see her as the world's most famous temptress. And they did – in huge numbers. It turned out that the combination of Lamarr, Victor Mature as Samson, and the directorial touch of de Mille were ideally suited: critical put-downs didn't prevent it from being the top box-office film of the year. Paramount now offered her a Western with Ray Milland, *Copper Canyon*; and MGM revived their interest and offered her *A Lady Without Passport* with John Hodiak. She got $90,000 for it, and it's doubtful whether it took much more than that at the box-office. Paramount, meanwhile, weren't anxious to have her work for them again (because she had turned down a PA tour for *Delilah*), but at Bob Hope's misguided insistence she co-starred with him, conspicuously out of place, in *My Favourite Spy* (51): she refused to do PAs for that, too, and didn't work in Hollywood again for some years.

In 1953 it was announced that she would make her comeback picture in Britain, *Queen Esther and the King of Egypt*, but nothing came of it; nor of two projects – probably to be made in Italy – *The Loves of Three Women* (as Helen of Troy, the Empress Josephine and someone called Genevieve) and *Femmina* (as Helen and as Mary Queen of Scots). She did play Helen in Italy, in *L'Amante di Parigi* (53) and she did make a film there called *Femmina*, but it was about an ordinary girl. The former got a few Stateside bookings, dubbed, and christened *The Face That Launched a Thousand Ships*, but the latter (after being once abandoned when the money ran out) was never released anywhere. In 1957 Lamarr's interest in playing the famous women of history may have got her the part of Joan of Arc in an episode of *The Story of Mankind*, but the result was generally judged ludicrous. That year Hollywood gave her another chance: at Universal she was *The Female Animal*, as an ageing film-star in love with the same man as daughter Jane Powell: it was a silly picture not helped by the Lamarr histrionics.

But in fact, since *Delilah*, Lamarr's name was in the press less as an actress than as one of those movie stars always getting divorced – the sixth was in 1965; the same year she was on a shop-lifting charge that brought headlines round the world, and was found not guilty. She admitted to journalists that she was broke and lost a part ($10,000-worth) in a B called *Picture Mommy Dead* due, it was said, to the adverse publicity – Zsa Zsa Gabor played it. The following year she published the autobiography, and though in some quarters it was rated 'sizzling' the press was repelled and the industry shocked: at its end Lamarr intimated that she was taking up her career again, but Hollywood is prudish and there were no offers. In 1966 she unsuccessfully sought an injunction against the publication of the book, and three years later she sued her collaborators for $21 million damages for misrepresentation.

Dorothy Lamour

Dorothy Lamour loathed the sarong she was famous for wearing. She begged her studio to let her play more considerable parts, and, ironically, her request was granted as a result of a successful comic picture in which she wore it, *Road to Singapore*. She played it fairly straight, in her dumbly pretty way, but in the enormously successful sequels, with Hope and Crosby in full cry, she developed into a rather pleasing comedienne and a box-office star. If, as a dramatic actress, she was only just on the right side of competent, her work in those *Road* pictures is fondly remembered. She was at her best with Bob Hope: the hint of asperity in her voice always suggested that she knew exactly how to deal with him.

She was born in 1914 in New Orleans. In 1931 she was elected 'Miss New Orleans', but, ungratefully, went to Chicago and worked as an elevator operator at Marshall Field. She wanted to be a singer, however, and after several auditions Herbie Kay took her on to sing with his band and married her. In New York she sang at the Stork Club, which led to a contract with NBC and her own radio show in LA. Paramount, then discovering that she looked as good as she sang, if not better, screen-tested her and signed her; and because her looks were fairly exotic, cast her as *The Jungle Princess* (36). It was a nothing progammer, but the reception at previews persuaded Paramount to release it as an A picture, and it did well. Said Picturegoer: 'The main asset of the picture is the naturalness and unsophisticated charm of Dorothy Lamour who makes the main character as credible as it is possible for it to be.'

For a while she had to be content with big parts in other people's pictures: Carole Lombard's *Swing High Swing Low* (37), Jack Benny's *College Holiday* (his leading lady though) and Irene Dunne's *High Wide and Handsome*. Before that one, she was in a programmer with Lew Ayes, *Last Train to Madrid*, and then she did *Thrill of a Lifetime* starring Eleanore Whitney. Her second big break came when Goldwyn borrowed her to play with Jon Hall as the

John Ford's The Hurricane *(37): Jon Hall as the young man unjustly convicted and Dorothy Lamour as the new bride he keeps escaping for. None of it was very interesting till the climactic hurricane which destroyed the island and most of the characters.*

decorative foreground to *The Hurricane*: she had no dialogue that wasn't monosyllabic and no acting apart from moulding the sarong, but the film's success made her well known. Back home she did a similar stint, *Her Jungle Love* (38)–he was Ray Milland, and *Tropic Holiday* with Bob Burns; was in an action movie with Henry Fonda, *Spawn of the North*; *St Louis Blues* (39); *Man About Town* with Jack Benny; and *Disputed Passage*, from Lloyd C. Douglas's novel, with Akim Tamiroff, in which she gave a somewhat heavy performance.

She was a rather sulky (and plump) moll in *Johnny Apollo* (40) at 20th, transferring her affections from Lloyd Nolan to Tyrone Power; then climbed back into the trees and a sarong in *Road to Singapore*, *Typhoon* and *Moon Over Burma*, all of which were amusing, though only one of them was meant to be. She was loaned to 20th again for *Chad Hanna*, a 19th-century circus story, and then there was *Road to Zanzibar* (41), which really kidded jungle epics. Crosby and Hope double-crossed each other for love of her, and she was hardly less perfidious than they. She was with Hope again when he was *Caught in the Draft*, and then was *Aloma of the South Seas*, immortalized thus by C. A. Lejeune: 'Extensive tour/Of D. Lamour,/Nearly all/Of Jon Hall./ Sudden panic,/Cause volcanic,/And a torso/Or so.' She was more pleased with a hit musical, *The Fleet's In* (42), but *Beyond the Blue Horizon* was real third-rate film-making, unable to be facetious about the plot's idiocies, though looking once or twice in that direction. Lamour herself had the measure of it and also looked very attractive.

Lamour spent the next few years mainly as foil to Hope or Crosby or both: and if she continued to wear the sarong, it was only because Paramount convinced her it was good for wartime morale: *Road to Morocco*; *Star Spangled Rhythm*, guesting; *They Got Me Covered* (43, Hope); *Dixie* (Crosby); *Riding High* with Dick Powell; *And the Angels Sing* (44), a musical with Fred MacMurray; *Rainbow Island* (44), the end of Paramount's sarong fetish, a juvenile musical with Eddie Bracken; and *Road to Utopia* (45). She returned to dramatics with the film of Steinbeck's *A Medal for Benny*, but it was stolen from her and Arturo de Cordova by J. Carroll Naish; and with *Masquerade in Mexico* (46), also with de Cordova. She was *My Favorite Brunette* (Hope's); one of the guest stars in *Variety Girl* (47); with Alan Ladd in *Wild Harvest*; and encountered on the *Road to Rio*.

Her films away from Paramount were a sorry lot, and just about killed her box-office standing: *Lulu Belle* (48), a corny little melo; *A Miracle Can Happen*, kidding the sarong in one sketch; *The Girl From Manhattan*, a small-town comedy; *The Lucky Stiff* (49), a mystery with Brian Donlevy; and–slightly better–*Slightly French* with

Dorothy Lamour at the time when Bing Crosby and Bob Hope were double-crossing each other for her favours: singing 'Personality' in Road to Utopia *(45)*.

Don Ameche. Back at Paramount, another tired mystery, *Manhandled*, did nothing to re-establish her, and she didn't work in films for three years. But Paramount were more generous than some to fallen employees and gave her a big role in de Mille's *The Greatest Show on Earth* (52) and reunited her with the boys in *Road to Bali* (also 52). In 1953 it was announced that she had retired, and indeed she wanted to bring up the sons by her second (happy) marriage to William Ross Howard. During the 50s she very occasionally did nightclub work.

When, for reasons best known to themselves, Hope and Crosby decided in 1961 to make *Road to Hong Kong*, the burning question was whether they were going to bring back Lamour. The female lead went to Joan Collins, and Lamour was offered a guest spot for old times' sake. Somewhat hurt, she agreed, provided it was built up. The film was made in Britain and the press reported that Lamour was snappy on the question of age, and didn't like close-ups: but she looked relatively stunning on film and her part was padded some more. They might have given her the lead and jettisoned Collins, and the finished product was the poorer because they didn't. Lamour later was featured in a lesser John Ford piece, *Donovan's Reef* (63)–she had little to do–and did another guest shot in an innocuous teenage film, *Pajama Party* (65). For a while she enjoyed a big success as the star of one of the numerous touring versions of 'Hello Dolly!' and in 1970 she put in an appearance in *The Phynx*; but she has said that she will not film again unless the offers are more interesting than those she has been getting.

Elissa Landi

Elissa Landi was beautiful, capable and charming. She moved lightly and gracefully, somewhat like a gazelle. She was ladylike and intelligent but there was nothing bluestocking about her, nothing formidable, nothing glacial. But she seemed to be acting behind gauze. Her quality never came through the screen. She wasn't remote, but she was intangible without being quite magical enough: so in the end she was one of Hollywood's most publicized failures.

She was aristocrat by birth, and 'claimed to be' (as her publicity carefully put it) the granddaughter of the Empress Elizabeth of Austria–which conflicts somewhat with the other claim (which is true) that her father was an Italian count and mother was an Austrian countess. She was born in Venice in 1904, was educated in England and studied to be a dancer. While still in her teens she published a novel, 'Neilson', and then she wanted to write a play so joined Oxford rep for experience: she made her stage debut in the Playhouse Theatre in that city in 'Dandy Dick' (23). This determined her on an acting career and she made her first prominent London appearance in 'Storm' at the Ambassadors in 1924. Later she was a successful Desdemona, and also played in 'The Painted Swan', 'Lavender Ladies' (25) and 'The Constant Nymph' (26), among others. She published two more novels and in 1928 married a barrister.

She had a part in Herbert Wilcox's *London* (28) as Dorothy Gish's Mayfair benefactress, but it was Anthony Asquith who gave her her film break with the lead in *Underground*. She had another lead in *Bolibar*, and was then in *The Inseparables* (29); and was, according to Picturegoer, 'much in demand' abroad. In Sweden she made a German picture released in Britain as *Sin*; in France she made two which turned up as *Ecstasy* and *The Parisian*. Also in France she made a bi-lingual Talkie with Adolphe Menjou, *My Kid of a Father* (30) which, again according to Picturegoer, was never shown anywhere. In Britain she made two pictures written and directed by Elinor Glyn, who had, since her return from Hollywood, attempted to establish her own film company: *Knowing Men* with Carl Brisson, made in English and French and distributed by a company called Talkiecolour, and *The Price of Things*. Both were failures, and Landi was hardly better served by *Children of Chance*, made for BIP, with John Stuart and Mabel Poulton (a big British Silent star whose Cockney accent was at this time killing her Talkie career).

Also that year she went to Broadway to appear in 'A Farewell to Arms'. Earlier she had turned down a Fox contract, but Fox were persistent, and after her New York success renewed their blandishments. So she signed a long-term contract with them. They co-starred her with Charles Farrell in *Body and Soul* (31), a melodrama about American flyers in Britain during the war, and memorable mainly because the supporting cast was headed by Humphrey Bogart and Myrna Loy–playing a spy who tries to throw the blame on Landi. Then she did *Always Goodbye*, in which she played a movie star; *Wicked*, a specious mother-love drama with Victor McLaglen; and *The Yellow Ticket* with Laurence Olivier and Lionel Barrymore, a melodrama which she considered her best film. A year later she was to describe herself as 'the miraculous survivor of seven pictures', in defence of the silly tag that Fox had stuck on her, 'The Empress of Emotion'. Fox were seriously worried about her: they had boosted her to the skies and her four films so far had not been box-office smashes. Indeed, the last one had failed, and so did the next two: *The Devil's Lottery* (32) with McLaglen again, which went through the old 'money doesn't bring happiness' routine (they won the Calcutta Sweepstakes) and *The Woman in Room 13*, a dreadful picture in which Landi was a concert singer and all the marriage vs career clichés were dragged in. Ralph Bellamy co-starred and Loy was again in the cast. Fox did not blame themselves for the failure: they announced that Landi would be loaned to other studios or play featured roles until her contract expired. Meanwhile, she was making *A Passport to Hell*, a triangle drama with Paul Lukas, but the critical and the box-office receipts of that did nothing to

retrieve the situation.

Rescue came in the form of Cecil B. de Mille, who borrowed her to play the Christian heroine of *The Sign of the Cross* (33), who enslaves Roman centurion Fredric March (she was billed second to him, above Claudette Colbert). Then 20th-UA borrowed her for the lead opposite Ronald Colman in *The Masquerader*. Fox hoped that two such important films might at last establish Landi and starred her again, in *The Warrior's Husband*, a modern telling of the Lysistrata story, from a play that Katharine Hepburn had done on Broadway, and in *I Loved You Wednesday*, from another play, as a ballerina, with Warner Baxter. Tired of poor films, she refused to do *I Am a Widow*, and Fox took the opportunity to annul the contract.

She was offered a plum part in another filmed play at Universal, *By Candlelight* (34), playing a ladies' maid who masquerades as her mistress and dines with butler Lukas, masquerading as his master. Beautifully directed by James Whale, it did something to revive Landi's fortunes, but she was still suffering from Fox's publicity campaign, which had seriously overestimated her appeal and ability. Her next film co-starred another artist who was also to suffer from over-exploitation, Francis Lederer, direct from his Broadway success, *Man of Two Worlds* at RKO: he was an Eskimo and she the explorer's daughter with whom he falls in love. She moved on to Columbia for *Sisters Under the Skin*, in which Frank Morgan made himself her guardian. Once again she showed a flair for sophisticated dialogue, and she did well in the sentimental *The Great Flirtation* at Paramount, as a girl who becomes a star at the same time as husband Adolphe Menjou loses popularity. At UA she was the heroine of *The Count of Monte Cristo* opposite Robert Donat, and Photoplay thought her 'perfect'.

As a free-lance so far she had been notably successful. Other studios considered that Fox had misused her, but they still couldn't find where her public lay. Paramount gave her a two-picture deal, *Enter Madame* (35), with Cary Grant, in which she was a prima donna, and *Without Regret*, a marital drama with Paul Cavanagh, but were not encouraged to endeavour

Before disaster strikes: Robert Donat and Elissa Landi at the ball celebrating their betrothal. The Count of Monte Cristo (*34*), *the most popular of several film versions.*

further. And then her shaky position was threatened by Madeleine Carroll, also from Britain, and somewhat more regal and beautiful. Landi went to France to make *Koenigsmark* (36), in English and French, not a story of Hanover but of Ruritania, from a novel by Pierre Benoit, with Pierre Fresnay and John Lodge; and then in Britain she co-starred with Douglas Fairbanks Jr in *The Amateur Gentleman*. Said Picturegoer: '... as the heroine, Elissa Landi is somewhat colourless'. She returned to Hollywood, to MGM, where Myrna Loy had recommended her for a supporting role in *After the Thin Man*, though first she starred in a programmer there with Edmund Lowe and Zazu Pitts, *Mad Holiday*. She then did a B there with Dame May Whitty and Madge Evans, *The Thirteenth Chair* (37); but she was a lost cause.

She was divorced in 1936. In 1939 she was lecturing in American colleges, and in 1943 she married again. She also appeared in an independent production, *Corregidor* (43), opposite Otto Kruger. It was a silly film and occasioned no further offers. She made news in 1944 when she gave birth to a daughter; in 1948 she died of cancer in New York.

Harry Langdon

'Harry was called the baby-face comedian,' said Harold Lloyd. 'It was an apt description, for his actions were like that of a little boy. He'd start to do something, then he'd change. Indecision was an integral part of his character. Also innocence.' James Agee had said: 'There was also a sinister flicker of depravity about the Langdon character, all the more disturbing because babies are premoral. He had an instinct for bringing his actual adulthood and figurative babyishness into frictions as crawley as a fingernail on a slate blackboard, and he wandered into areas of strangeness which were beyond the other comedians.' Agee's famous 1949 essay ('Comedy's Greatest Era') re-established Langdon by bracketing him with Chaplin, Keaton and Lloyd; noting that they used much physical comedy, he said 'Langdon showed how little of that one might use and still be a great silent-film comedian. In his screen humour he symbolized something as deeply and centrally human, though by no means as rangily so, as the Tramp. There was, of course, an immense difference in inventiveness and range of virtuosity. It seemed as if Chaplin could do anything, on any instrument of the orchestra. Langdon had one queerly toned, unique little reed. But out of it he got incredible melodies.' From that point on Langdon became accepted by some observers as the fourth big Silent film comic, though it is difficult to be as enthusiastic about his work: perhaps his whey-faced, dolly humour is much too cute for modern taste, and his 'strangeness' still too far ahead of it.

Langdon was born in Council Bluffs, Iowa, in 1884. His parents worked for the Salvation Army, so at an early age he learned to fend for himself: after doing an amateur night in nearby Omaha, he joined a travelling medicine show; and spent the next 20 years in minstrel shows, circuses, burlesque and vaudeville. Early on his baby-faced little man evolved, and it was this physical aspect which so pleased Frank Capra when he first saw him. At that time Capra was working for Mack Sennett; Langdon had just come to Sennett's attention and been signed as a lead comic. Altogether Langdon made some 25 two- and three-reelers for Sennett, starting with *Picking Peaches* (24) and ending with *Soldier Man* (26). A few of the titles in between: *Shanghaied Lovers*, *The Luck of the Foolish*, *Feet of Mud*, *The Sea Squawk*, *Boobs in the Wood*, *His Marriage Wow*, *There He Goes* and *Fiddlesticks*. There was also a feature, *His*

Harry Langdon made only three successful features, of which The Strong Man *(26) was the second and perhaps best: an episodic comedy about the adventures of a weightlifter's meek assistant in cleaning up – unwittingly – a modern Sodom.*

First Flame, released in 1927, after Langdon had left Sennett.

He had become nationally popular, and other companies sought to steal him from Sennett. He went to WB at $6,000 a week plus 25 per cent of the net, provided he could make six films in two years, at $150,000 each. Sennett is caustic about this deal in his autobiography ('King of Comedy', 1954). Noting that Langdon had managed to spend the production cost of the first film before it started, he writes: 'Harry suddenly forgot that all his value lay in being that baby-witted boy on the screen and he decided he was also a business man. His cunning as a business man was about that of a backward kindergarten student and he complicated this with marital adventures, in which he was about as inept as he was on the screen.' Langdon took with him to WB his usual director, Harry Edwards, and his gag man, Capra. Their first film there, *Tramp Tramp Tramp* (26), was 'a beautiful thing in which Harry wins a cross-country walking race, despite imprisonment, a cyclone and infatuation for Joan Crawford' (David Robinson). Capra directed the next two, and they were again triumphs, full of good gags and admirably paced: *The Strong Man* and *Long Pants* (27).

Langdon then, egotistically, decided that he didn't need either Edwards or Capra, and decided to direct himself. The results were disastrous: *Three's a Crowd* was overly sentimental, and although Langdon took note of that and returned more to gags for *The Chaser* (28), they just weren't funny; the third picture, *Heart Trouble*, combined the faults of both and died at the box-office. WB dissolved the agreement; and Langdon had acquired a reputation for being difficult and autocratic – something which took years to live down. He had made important enemies. After an 18-month absence from the screen, Hal Roach (at MGM) boldly announced that Langdon was returning to the shorts which had made him famous: Roach produced him in eight (Talkies) but the arrangement lasted only a year. Also that year Universal teamed him with Slim Summerville in *See America Thirst* (30) and he returned to WB supporting Ben Lyon in a vulgar picture about doughboys, *A Soldier's Plaything* (31): neither was successful, and Langdon returned to vaudeville. In 1931 he filed a petition for bankruptcy.

In 1933 he began to make shorts for Educational, and he subsequently made a few for Paramount; in 1934 he began a similar operation at Columbia and except for the period 1935–8, when he made no films, that continued to his death in 1944, at an average of two a year (some of the later ones were directed by Edwards). He had only a few substantial roles in the features he

After his career nose-dived, Langdon was offered three or four comeback chances, of which the best-remembered is Hallelujah I'm a Bum *(33), with Al Jolson.*

made. In 1933 he supported Al Jolson in *Hallelujah I'm a Bum*, but it did nothing to revive either ailing career, and he played a cupid in *My Weakness* with Lew Ayres and Lilian Harvey. He had small comic parts in *Atlantic Adventure* (35), *He Loved an Actress* (38) and *There Goes My Heart*, then by the kindness of Stan Laurel got a job with Roach as a gag man. This landed him two film roles there: *Zenobia* (39) a charming but unfunny comedy about a rogue elephant (he was its owner) and notable mainly for the teaming of Oliver Hardy and Billy Burke as a country doctor and his wife; and *All-American Co-ed* (41) starring Frances Langford. He also had roles in some products released by Monogram and its kin: *Misbehaving Husbands* (40), *Double Trouble* (41) as a Cockney evacuee in the US, *House of Errors* (42), *Spotlight Scandals* (43), *Hot Rhythm* (44), *Block Busters* (the East Side Kids) and *Swingin' on a Rainbow* (45). He died of a cerebral haemorrhage in December, 1944. He was broke, and left as widow his third wife, whom he had married in 1935.

Charles Laughton

Charles Laughton was a total actor. His range was wide. He was only in mid-career when James Shelley Hamilton wrote in the National Board of Review Magazine: 'Laughton has made an astonishing gallery of screen portrayals. The pitiful little Cockney murderer in *Payment Deferred*, Nero, Henry VIII, Ruggles, Javert, Captain Bligh – no screen actor has come anywhere near so large a compass of characterizations, each one vivid and individual.' One always imagined Laughton seizing these parts with relish, his eyes glinting as he read the scripts, already selecting from his bag of tricks. In performance, you could see him savouring his own artifice. He was a big, brazen, show-off actor. He went overboard sometimes and, in some of the poor films he made, he got near to chewing the scenery; but as well as the bold, daring gesture – the hallmark of the great actor – he could perform with infinite delicacy. His enjoyment – his mastery – of his art was infectious though, paradoxically, he was violently uncertain of his talent. He was one of the few film-stars able to overcome an unprepossessing personal appearance (fat, blubbery) and go on to receive wide audience acceptance. He was reliable box-office for at least half of his 20-year screen career; later, his films faltered, but he was, and is, among the screen's finest artists.

Born in Scarborough, Yorkshire, in 1899 into a family of hoteliers, it was confidently expected that Laughton would go into the family business. But from early childhood he wanted to act; after his war service, he joined a company of amateurs. He does not appear to have been exceptional, but he finally broke down family opposition and was permitted to study at RADA. His mentor there was Komisarjevsky, who gave him a small part in his production of 'Three Sisters' in 1925, and then the more considerable part of Lepihodoff in 'The Cherry Orchard'; and it was in Komisarjevsky's production of 'Liliom' that Laughton made his first definite impression. He went on to success in the West End – in 'The Greater Love', 'The Happy Husband', 'Paul the First', 'The Man With Red Hair', 'Mr Pickwick' (as Pickwick) and others. In one play, Arnold Bennett's 'Mr Prohack', he met a young actress, Elsa Lanchester, who was appearing in a series of comic two-reelers devised (they were Silent) by H. G. Wells. Laughton made his screen debut in one of these (uncredited) – probably *Bluebottles* (28). He was a burglar in that; in *Daydreams* he was an Eastern potentate. He and Miss Lanchester were married in 1929, the year in which he made his 'official' screen bow, a cameo of a piggish diner in E. A. Dupont's *Piccadilly*, written by Arnold Bennett. He also appeared in *Comets*, a 'talkie-review', and later bought the US rights to prevent its being shown there; Wilcox's *Wolves* (30), not shown in the US – despite ads in the American trade press describing Laughton as 'England's greatest character actor' – till 1936, much cut and retitled *Wanted Men*; and *Down River* (31) as the Eurasian skipper of a tramp steamer. Meanwhile, on stage, he had a big success as Tony Perelli in Edgar Wallace's 'On the Spot', and a mild one with C. S. Forester's 'Payment Deferred'. Gilbert Miller took the latter to New York, with Laughton and Lanchester, and when the run finished Laughton revived 'Alibi', which he had done in London (he played Hercule Poirot). His acclaim meant that film offers were inevitable, and Laughton finally accepted a contract from Paramount on his own terms.

Neither husband nor wife were certain how they would make out in Hollywood, and she, petite and birdlike, had to wait a couple of years before having any success (as a character actress). Laughton had always been neurotic about his deficiency in those physical qualities expected of a star; by now he had relaxed, but he felt insecure when watching Gary Cooper act with him in *The Devil and the Deep* (32). He liked Cooper and learned from him – but stole the notices:

'... but Mr Laughton's forceful and resilient portrait is the outstanding histrionic contribution', said The New York Times. It was his second American film: while waiting for it to begin he had been loaned to Universal for a small but effective role as a buffoon who turns heroic in *The Old Dark House*, one in that studio's series of classic horror pix (this one was constructed from J. B. Priestley's 'Benighted)'. He was loaned to MGM to repeat his stage role in *Payment Deferred*, but Lanchester's part as his daughter was taken by Maureen O'Sullivan. The film wasn't a success. De Mille then cast him as Nero in *The Sign of the Cross* (33): he played it for laughs (to De Mille's initial annoyance) with more than a sidelong glance at Mussolini: during the rest of that dictator-prone decade he often looked to Europe for the several species of oligarchs he played (and when playing the Emperor Claudius, he got the key from the abdication speech of Edward VIII).

Paramount kept him busy, though the contract was quietly scrapped: he played the sinister Dr Moreau in an H. G. Wells story, *Island of Lost Souls*, a scientist who turned men into animals. Despite a nation-wide publicity campaign to find a girl to play the Panther Woman, the film was a box-office dud; and the British censor banned it outright. Today, when the goings-on aren't preposterous, they are unpleasant; and Laughton looked back on it with unease. Finally, he had the briefest episode in *If I Had a Million* as the suddenly wealthy clerk who mounts to the executive suite to blow a raspberry at the boss.

In London, Korda was preparing *The Private Life of Henry VIII* (33), an irreverent chronicle of the king's marriages; Lanchester played Anne of Cleves for the film's funniest scenes. It was a totally unexpected wow. It was the first British film in years, if ever, to have a big acceptance in the world market, and its success laid the foundation-stone for Korda's studio and thence the growth of the British film industry. For Laughton it meant an Oscar, a hundred imitators, and–partly because of his resemblance to the Holbein portraits–a common conception that he was more like Henry than Henry (today, his lusty portrayal shines out from a generally anaemic movie). Laughton elected then to go to the Old Vic; among other parts, he played Shakespeare's idea of the same Henry, Prospero, Angelo in 'Measure for Measure', Macbeth, and Wilde's Canon

Korda's The Private Life of Henry VIII *(33) broke the existing records of New York's Radio City Music Hall (it had been open nine months): it was the only British film of the decade to find wide acceptance in the US. (Robert Donat in foreground.)*

Laughton as Ruggles of Red Gap *(35), a part played by Edward Everett Horton in the 1923 silent version.*

There have been at least six film versions of Victor Hugo's 'Les Misérables' *– of which the best is generally considered to be the 1935 film version directed by Richard Boleslawski: with Fredric March, Charles Laughton and John Carradine.*

Chasuble. There were reservations about his handling of the verse.

Back in Hollywood, he played a Cockney king of the river in a rubbishy jungle adventure with Carole Lombard, *White Woman*; the tyrannical Victorian father in *The Barretts of Wimpole Street* (34), a performance long considered the prototype; and he should have stayed at MGM for *David Copperfield*, to play Micawber (Lanchester was to be the Micawber's maid) – but he became increasingly convinced that the only actor who could play the role was W. C. Fields, and persuaded MGM to replace him with Fields. At Paramount he led a superb team of farceurs (Ruggles, Boland, Roland Young, Zasu Pitts), in a classic comedy about an English butler in the Wild West, *Ruggles of Red Gap* (35); and then played Javert against Fredric March's Valjean in *Les Miserables*, which Lanchester considers one of his best performances. But everything he did at this time was outstanding, and when he played Bligh in *Mutiny on the Bounty*, Mark van Doren remarked that this performance 'fixes him in my mind at any rate as by far the best of living actors'. The New York Critics, in the first of their annual awards, cited Laughton for his Bligh and his Ruggles. *Mutiny* was judged by the Hollywood Academy as the year's best film, and it was the year's number one money-maker; *Miserables* was a runner-up.

Laughton at this moment turned his back on Hollywood, which he found artistically stifling: it didn't allow him sufficient latitude – he wanted more sympathetic parts. And his agreement with MGM was dissolved when Thalberg died. In Britain, with Korda he made *Rembrandt* (36), a remarkably sober account of the artist's life – too sober, perhaps, because the public didn't take to it. Laughton's performance, however, held to his standard: he tried hard not to appear to act, and The New York Times gratifyingly noted 'Mr Laughton becomes Rembrandt as nobody else in the world could – of this we are firmly and unmistakably convinced.' Thirteen years later, when the film was revived in London, the Daily Telegraph (Campbell Dixon) said: 'Laughton never again did anything so good.' Still with Korda, he began *I Claudius*, from Robert Graves's novel, under the direction of Joseph von Sternberg. After several weeks' work, shooting was stopped when Merle Oberon was injured in a car crash, and when she was better it wasn't resumed. The reasons remain mysterious. Elsa Lanchester in her book 'Charles Laughton and I' merely remarks that she

Laughton's make-up for Rembrandt *(36) was remarkable: and so was his performance–still the best film about a painter.*

didn't listen to the gossip; and a BBC documentary made in 1965, 'The Epic That Never Was', hardly clarified the matter, though it interviewed the surviving principals, including Merle Oberon and von Sternberg himself. It seems likely that the project was stymied by von Sternberg's callous disregard for costs, and Laughton's temperament–especially directed towards the director. But von Sternberg, speaking of the film in his memoirs, said: 'The well from which a man draws his talents is deep, but Laughton's well had no bottom.' (Two other Laughton projects abandoned by Korda were a *Cyrano de Bergerac* with Vivien Leigh as Roxane, and a life of Diaghilev, with Anton Dolin as Nijinsky.)

Laughton joined up with Erich Pommer (formerly with UFA) to form a company called Mayflower to make films starring Laughton. The first was *Vessel of Wrath* (37) from a Maugham story about a beachcomber and a prissy missionary–Lanchester in a touching and funny performance. There followed *St Martin's Lane* (38), an odd little film about buskers in a London that looked suspiciously like the Berlin of Pommer's UFA films; and the character that Laughton played was like those played by Emil Jannings (Pommer had produced *Vaudeville*). However, Basil Wright in The Spectator, after comparing Laughton with Jannings said: '... Laughton gives quite the finest performance of his career, and it is by sheer acting technique, not to say the electric discharge of his personality, that he forces us ... to examine our own hearts, not his.' Neither of the two movies was a success, despite the fact that *St Martin's Lane* had Vivien Leigh in it and it opened in the US not long after *Gone With the Wind*. An attempt to resurrect the fortunes of Mayflower with a Hitchcock thriller was no more successful: there was a good movie to be made out of Daphne du Maurier's *Jamaica Inn* (39), but this–distorted version–wasn't it. A fourth project–*The Admirable Crichton* (with Lanchester as the tweenie)–was shelved (the rights were sold back to Paramount, but the film was never made) when two things happened simultaneously: war broke out, and RKO offered Laughton the role of Quasimodo in *The Hunchback of Notre Dame* (40). He liked the RKO offer, and had had, in any case, enough of playing an impresario (especially an unsuccessful one). His Quasimodo was a marvellous creation, regardless of make-up, but the film otherwise was flaccid.

He was next the Italian immigrant with a mail-order bride (Lombard) in *They Knew What They Wanted* and then in Deanna Durbin's *It Started With Eve* (41), playing an old man. It was a delightful comedy performance, but the part was less substantial than he was accustomed to. Other parts were negligible–*Tuttles of Tahiti* (42), a family comedy and just one step up from a B picture; a bit in the all-star *Tales of Manhattan*; *Stand-by for Action*; *Forever and a Day* (43), another all-star effort; and *The Man From Down Under*. But the latter was preceded by *This Land Is Mine*, a piece about the French Resistance in which he was a meek schoolteacher. Despite Jean Renoir's clearly deeply felt direction–it is a superficial picture: Laughton's performance, with its impassioned plea for freedom at the end, wasn't liked at the time, but is today one of few effective aspects of the film.

There were now criticisms of the roles he was given, and sometimes of how he played them. He turned his energies towards entertaining the troops (readings, recitals, lectures–work he continued after the war) and took his salary, which remained huge. The next two films proved that he was a better actor than ever: inventive and witty as *The Canterville Ghost* (44), the Wilde story updated for Margaret O'Brien; and *The Suspect*, an Edwardian murder story which was phoney and unconvincing except for his own gentle performance as a man driven to kill his nagging wife (Cora Witherspoon).

1945 found him as *Captain Kidd*, which was mainly for the kiddie market; 1946 again with Durbin in a fallow comedy, *Because of Him*. There was an improvement when he played the judge in Hitchcock's *The Paradine Case* (48), though it was a small part and a poor film, but *The Big Clock* was a first-rate thriller and his tycoon/killer was 'both ludicrous and magnificently repulsive–one of Laughton's most successful characterizations' (Peter Ericsson in 'Sequence'). It wasn't his fault that *Arch of Triumph* was so poor, but his participation in this lot suggests that the heart had gone out of him: *The Girl From Manhattan* with Dorothy Lamour, *The Bribe* (49) with Ava Gardner, *The Man on the Eiffel Tower* (50), as Maigret, a French picture, made in English, and *The Secret Door* (52), an unabashed B. In 1951 in the episodic *The Blue Veil* he gave a touching portrayal of the elderly widower who offers his hand to governess Jane Wyman; and his sketch as the tramp in the *Clarion Call* episode of O. Henry's *Full House* (52) further heartened fans – but a stint in *Abbott and Costello Meet Captain Kidd* shocked and saddened them. He then played Herod in *Salome* (53), an appalling film and a performance which clearly indicates his dilemma as a fine actor offered only poor material: he seems uncertain whether to play the part straight, whether to send it up or just not bother at all. He was more his old self again in another bash at Henry VIII in *Young Bess* with Jean Simmons.

His thoughts increasingly turned away from films. In 1947 he had played Brecht's 'Galileo' on Broadway; in the early 50s he toured extensively in two 'readings' – Shaw's 'Don Juan in Hell' (with Cedric Hardwicke, Agnes Moorehead and Charles Boyer) and Stephen Vincent Benét's 'John Brown's Body' (with Tyrone Power, Raymond Massey and Judith Anderson). Solo readings included Dickens, the Bible, Thurber, etc., and Laughton made recordings, and appeared on TV and radio. Meanwhile, he made a good film, Lean's version of *Hobson's Choice* (54, in Britain), but his own performance was over-exuberant and threw the film off-balance. In 1955 he directed a film for connoisseurs only, *The Night of the Hunter*: it deserved more success than it had, though there were flaws – but it does suggest Laughton might have been a great film-maker. In 1957 he made another good film: as the QC in Wilder's *Witness for the Prosecution*: both he and Lanchester received Oscar nominations.

He now felt ready to tackle Shakespeare again, and at Stratford-upon-Avon appeared – with qualified success – as King Lear and Bottom (the latter production included the then unknown Albert Finney, Vanessa Redgrave and Ian Holm). He and Lanchester then gave, in their different styles, dazzling performances in a dim play, 'The Party', in London.

In *Spartacus* (60) his acting, and that of Olivier and Ustinov, provided the most satisfactory elements of an above-average spectacle; the same year he played an admiral in an undistinguished war film, *Under Two Flags*, made in Italy. His last film was *Advise and Consent* (62) as the wily Southern senator, Sheb Cooley. He died from cancer before it was shown, and Hollywood didn't bother even to nominate him posthumously for an Oscar. But it was far and away the most subtle, the most engaging and most convincing performance of the year, as he intended.

Laughton's film work of the 40s and 50s contains only isolated fine performances: but his last film, Advise and Consent *(62), found him again at his most showily brilliant. With Don Murray.*

Laurel and Hardy

The question of what is funny is so notoriously difficult that it is best left alone. Laurel and Hardy were left alone by critics for most of their careers, and the merit in rehabilitating them is indeed debatable – though the fault there lies less in the action than in the claims made for them: 'They are the most universal of comics, in range as in appeal,' said Charles Barr in 'Laurel and Hardy', his monograph on them, 1968. There were and are people who find them unfunny; it was and is possible to find on one day an audience laughing its head off at Laurel and Hardy and the next day to find another stony-silent–in both cases, in both commercial houses and film societies. The truth is that their work is extremely variable, even in the stuff which their admirers take to be their peak; plus the fact that apparently in order to relish them some prior acquaintance is desirable. David Robinson, writing in Sight and Sound in 1954, commented on their recurring jokes: 'the pleasures of *recognition* which have always been exploited in the music hall–in the use of catchphrases, of dialogue which becomes comic by its very familiarity. . . . Stan's cry, or the frequent sight of Oliver, prostrated and turning up his face in speechless appeal, may seem unfunny at first acquaintance, but gradually grow upon one until they are hilarious, irresistible, looked-for and cherished.'

Non-adherents find the trade-marked gags, obviously, resistible and laboured, the bag of tricks almost empty, the two comics merely like great babies; Hardy's timing invariably seems off, his look of despair (straight into the camera) or his waggling of his tie repeated merely because no other material was available to them. But in fact, Laurel and Hardy never aspired to be anything but simple funny men. Their work is more primitive than that of the great screen clowns, but it never pretended to be otherwise. They never went in for subtlety. They were pals, the rotund, grand, slow-moving Hardy ('Ollie'), with his pretensions to elegance, omniscience and lady-killing; and the wiry, bumbling, crushed, comparatively miniscule Laurel ('Stan'), whose good intentions were the bane of Ollie's life–though he bumbled too. There was seldom any justification for his impatience with Stan. The mistakes they made they made together, each compounding the felony. On occasions their building a gag could be glorious, like their antics delivering a piano in *The Music Box*; but they were even better at sustaining quite simple ideas, like their incompetence as waiters in *From Soup to Nuts* or the foiled attempts to change trousers in *Liberty*. They seldom eschewed a healthy vulgarity–the trouser-tearing sequence in *You're Darn Tootin'*, the hen-pecking wives and cheap broads of their domestic films; but most glorious of all are the mystic orgies of chaos that, united now, they would reap upon the common enemy–the destruction of James Finlayson's villa in *Big Business*, the pie-throwing sequences in *The Hoosegow* and *The Battle of the Century*. At times like these they can stand up and be counted among the screen's great comics.

Stan Laurel was the creative one of the two: 'I don't know what would have happened to the Laurel and Hardy films if it hadn't been for Stan. He was the one that took an idea that [Hal] Roach would have and brought it to life' (John McCabe in his biography, 'Mr Laurel and Mr Hardy', 1961). He was British, being born in Ulverston, Lancashire, in 1890, the son of an actor and theatre manager, and grammar-school educated–for a while. In 1903 he joined 'The Juvenile Pantomime Company' and thereafter played music halls. Later he joined Fred Karno's Company and went with it to the US in 1910, and again in 1913; sometimes he understudied Chaplin, who was also with Karno. He played in vaudeville in the US at one point, imitating Chaplin. Adolph Ramish, who managed a Los Angeles theatre where he played, liked him enough to put him in a two-reeler, *Nuts in May* (18); Universal bought it and signed Laurel for a year to play a character called 'Hickory Hiram', but after three or four shorts he was sacked. He returned to vaudeville but in 1919 did a short for Broncho Billy Anderson, now a producer: *Lucky Dog*. Metro bought it, and Anderson signed Laurel to make a series of spoofs–*Mud and Sand*, *When Knights Were Cold*; and Hal Roach signed him to continue the series at his studio. He moved over to Universal for his own series, 'The Stan Laurel Series', but it wasn't till he signed with Roach again in 1926 that he began to be well known. He had made over 50 shorts when the partnership with Hardy started the following year.

Oliver Hardy was born in Atlanta, Georgia, in 1892; he wanted to be an attorney but instead ran a cinema–from which he went into films, as early as 1913. He was an extra, a bit-player (he was in *Lucky Dog*) and had some success as a heavy in Billy West comedies; he worked in various capacities for several companies, but didn't really come into prominence until he appeared in and co-directed some Larry Semon comedies in the early 20s, by which time he was generally known as 'Babe' Hardy. Later Hal Roach signed him to join his Comedy All-Stars team.

The partnership began this way: Laurel was directing *Get 'em Young*, in which Hardy had a small part as a butler; but Hardy couldn't do it because of illness, and Laurel played it. They acted together in the next one, *Slipping Wives*, and played as part of the company in 10 two-reelers before Roach decided to pair them permanently; coincidentally, the lead in most of these films was Finlayson, who was often to support them later. Their first short was *Putting Pants on Philip* (27), a mild prank with Philip (Laurel)

The Battle of the Century (*27*)*–one of their earliest shorts and one of their most anarchic: it ended with a giant custard-pie battle involving every extra on the lot.*

as a Scotsman in a kilt, embarrassing his American relative (Hardy); it isn't typical of their work, but they were to find their feet very quickly. Over the next three years they turned out almost one short a month (most of them directed by Leo McCarey, who went on to bigger things). The other 1927 titles (generally considered to be 'Laurel and Hardy' rather than the 'All-Stars'): *The Second 100 Years*, *Hats Off* and *The Battle of the Century*. The 1928 ones: *Leave 'em Laughing* (which added Edgar Kennedy, so often their policeman foe), *The Finishing Touch*, *From Soup to Nuts*, *You're Darn Tootin'*, *Their Purple Moment*, *Should Married Men Go Home?*, *Early to Bed*, *Two Tars* (they cause a great traffic jam), *Habeas Corpus* and *We Faw Down*.

These shorts were often divided into two or more sections; thus *Liberty* (29) starts with Ollie and Stan as escaped convicts, has the gag where they're wearing the wrong pants, and concludes with some precarious antics (almost as good as Lloyd's) on some scaffolding at the top of a skyscraper. There followed: *Wrong Again*, *That's My Wife*, *Big Business*, *Double Whoopee*, *Berth Marks*, *Bacon Grabbers*, *Angora Love* (their first 100 per cent Talkie), *Men of War*, *The Perfect Day*, *They Go Boom* and *The Hoosegow*. It was an astonishingly creative period–hardly disturbed by the coming of Sound; sensibly, Laurel and Hardy virtually ignored it–and later, when they depended more upon it, their dialogue exchanges were seldom memorable. For many years they made versions of their films in French, German, Spanish and Italian after the English one was completed–though they spoke these languages only phonetically. They were also in *Hollywood Revue of 1929*. In 1930: *Night Owls*, *Blotto*, *Be Big*, *Brats*, *The Laurel and Hardy Murder Case*, *Below Zero*, *Hog Wild*, *Another Fine Mess* and *The Rogue Song*, made originally as a starring vehicle for Lawrence Tibbett–then MGM decided that they needed comic relief to boost foreign sales, so constructed a sub-plot which was cut in later. It was made in colour. In 1931:

Laurel and Hardy as escaped convicts at Liberty *(29) . . . they had got on each other's trousers and there was many a misunderstanding as they tried to rectify the mistake.*

Laughing Gravy, *Our Wife*, *Come Clean*, *One Good Turn*, *Beau Chumps* and *Helpmates*. But something happened that year: the sets for *Pardon Us* became too expensive for a short subject and it became a feature: it was little more than a series of gags, but the public, accustomed to finding Laurel and Hardy thrown into the programme for good measure, still turned up to see it. Picturegoer, however, though it liked the shorts, thought 'three-quarters of an hour of this comedy team is too much'; nor were contemporary critics kind to their subsequent features.

In 1932 they tried another one, *Pack Up Your Troubles*, and did the following shorts: *Any Old Port*, *The Chimp*, *County Hospital*, *Scram*, *Their First Mistake* and *The Music Box*, which won an Oscar in a category established that year: Short Subjects (Live Action)–Comedy. But although they had always reprised their best routines–often improving upon them–there was now beginning to show a remarkable fluctuation in quality. There were only six shorts in 1933: *Towed in a Hole*, *Twice Two* (they both had dual roles–as the other's wife), *Me and My Pal*, *The Midnight Patrol*, *Busy Bodies* and *Dirty Work*. But they made two features: the second of them, *Sons of the Desert*, Barr thinks is 'the most perfect' of their features; and the first, *Fra Diavolo*, was a follow-up to *The Rogue Song*. Dennis King and Thelma Tod co-starred in this version of Frank Auber's operetta. It was successful enough to bring forth two similar ventures, *Babes in Toyland* (34), from the Victor Herbert musical, and *The Bohemian Girl* (36), from the one by Michael W. Balfe (and in 1934 they did a turn in a revue, *Hollywood Party*, notable only for a sequence provided by Walt Disney).

They did only a few more shorts: *The Private Life of Oliver VIII*, *Going Bye Bye*, *Them Thar Hills* and *The Live Ghost* in 1934; and *Tit for Tat*, *The Fixer Uppers* and *Thicker than Water* (which concluded with each impersonating the other) in 1935. Laurel no

The Laurel & Hardy Murder Case (30), *one of their most popular films – though probably because of its title rather than any intrinsic merit.*

longer wished to do two-reelers, and Roach announced a separation, with Hardy to appear in a family series called *The Hardys*. Instead, they did do a feature, *Bonnie Scotland* (35), and it was successful, as for a few years were their other features; in Britain for a couple of years (36 and 37) they were among the top 10 box-office draws. Laurel was allowed to produce a feature, *Our Relations* (36), but he remained unhappy, and though their quarrel had been considered patched up he issued a statement in 1936 about an intended vacation, considered by the industry to be a challenge to Roach and Hardy. In 1937 the break was considered irremediable and Hardy was announced for a project, *Road House*, with Patsy Kelly and Buster Keaton. Again, the differences were sealed and Laurel produced *Way Out West* (37), though it wasn't until late in 1937 that things went smoothly again. The 1938 pair, *Swiss Miss* and *Blockheads*, were the last for Hal Roach-MGM, for whom they had worked for 11 years. *Flying Deuces* (39) was made for RKO, and *A Chump at Oxford* (40) and *Saps at Sea* for Hal Roach-UA. Said Picturegoer of *Saps*: 'Just a series of gags, which is more likely to please juveniles than any one else.' That was the end of their association with Roach. John McCabe's book gives no indication of the reasons for the break-up, but as Laurel and Hardy were always the best of friends, it would appear that the difficulties were only between Roach and Laurel. In 1940 Laurel and Hardy set up an independent company but nothing was made; they found themselves forced back to the big studios: six pictures for 20th and two significantly for MGM, who had made a lot of money out of them over the years.

In 1940–1 they toured in 'The Laurel and Hardy Revue' with some success, but they were ageing, and their recent film work had been seldom inventive or even funny. In their remaining eight films they were allowed no creative control, and, predictably and justly, these played the lower half of double bills: *Great Guns* (41), *A Haunting We Will Go* (42), *Air Raid Wardens* (43) at MGM, *Jitterbugs*, *Dancing Masters*, *The Big Noise* (44), *Nothing but Trouble* at MGM, and *The Bullfighters* (45). Laurel loathed these films and until he died was bitter at the 20th management for giving them so little freedom. In 1947 they went to Britain for a music-hall tour, and planned a film there that came to nothing. They did make in France in 1951 *Atoll K/Robinson Crusoeland*, but they lost heart as the 12-week schedule stretched out to a year, and it showed: there were only spotty bookings.

They continued to work in music halls when possible: neither were wealthy men. Hardy did a solo film (he had already appeared with Harry Langdon in *Zenobia* in 1939, but that was only Roach's way of using him before his contract expired; Laurel's already had) – *The Fighting Kentuckian*, starring John Wayne, in 1949. He died in 1957 after a heart attack. He had been married twice. Laurel married four times, twice to the same woman. Laurel died in 1965, in poverty, but he had lived long enough to see the team's work restored from semi-oblivion and given its due (or more than its due). He received a special Oscar in 1960 'for his creative pioneering in the field of cinema comedy'. There was much applause when Laurel and Hardy excerpts were included in films like *When Comedy Was King*, and there were later three anthologies devoted to them: *Laurel and Hardy's Laughing Twenties* (65), *The Crazy World of Laurel and Hardy* (66) and *The Further Perils of Laurel and Hardy* (67). Apart from the two books already mentioned, there is a third good one, William K. Everson's 'The Films of Laurel & Hardy', published in 1967.

Vivien Leigh

Even if she had not played Scarlett O'Hara, the most coveted role in movie history, it is probable that Vivien Leigh's striking Dresden Shepherdess beauty would have won her a place among the great stars. She was recognized, even by unbelievers, as one of the beauties of her era: what with that and Scarlett, and being for much of her life Lady Olivier, fame and acclaim rather obscured her actual ability. On a couple of occasions she was breathtakingly good, but much of her screen and stage work was no better than that of any other decent, hard-working and abnormally ambitious actress. James Agate wrote in 1946: 'She's heavenly to look at, and is an exquisite, charming, delightful, witty, entrancing little actress. She is, indeed, everything except what I should call a good actress, and can be played off the screen any time by any number of actresses with one-tenth of her looks, exquisiteness, charm, delightfulness, etc.'

Her parents were living in India when she was born in 1913, in Darjeeling. She was educated in Britain, Germany, France and Italy; and was planning to go to RADA when she met her first husband, a barrister. She did study at RADA for a short while after her marriage, and made her professional debut in a film, *Things Are Looking Up* (34), as one of the schoolgirls; she was also in a couple of quickies, *The Village Squire* (35) and *Gentlemen's Agreement* (top-billed), and in Gracie Fields's *Look Up and Laugh*, with only a few sentences to speak. Her stage debut was in the London suburbs, at the Q Theatre, in 'The Green Sash' (35); four months later, in May, she appeared in the West End in Ashley Dukes's comedy, 'The Mask of Virtue', and became famous over-night. Korda was in the audience, and he signed her to a five-year contract, two films a year, starting at £13,000 for the first year and rising to £18,000. She didn't, however, make a film for over a year; she continued on the stage until cast as a lady-in-waiting, the heroine of *Fire Over England* (37), an Elizabethan adventure with Olivier. Then she was Conrad Veidt's dangerous love interest in a complicated spy story, *Dark Journey*, and the very ingénue lead of a slight comedy, *Storm in a Teacup*; she and Olivier were re-teamed in *21 Days*, a clodhopping melo which wasn't released in Britain until 1939 and the US a year later. MGM-British borrowed her for the lead opposite Robert Taylor in *A Yank at Oxford* (38), but due to Louis B. Mayer's intervention she was replaced by Maureen O'Sullivan and relegated to the part of a minxish don's wife who liked to philander with the students. She was considerably effective, as she was in *St Martin's Lane*, as the self-centred little busker who, helped by Charles Laughton, becomes the toast of Shaftesbury Avenue. At the same time, she continued to enhance her stage reputation: among other parts she played were Titania and Ophelia (to Olivier's Hamlet, in Elsinore).

She was about to start *The Thief of Bagdad* when on a whim she flew to see Olivier in Hollywood, late in 1938. *Gone With the Wind* (39) had started without a Scarlett after two years' search; according to the usual version, Olivier, Leigh and Selznick's agent brother Myron were watching the burning of Atlanta, and Myron turned to David and said: 'I want you to meet Scarlett'. She was tested and cast: there was some furore over the choice of an English girl, particularly among the partisans of the other aspirants. She told 'The Observer' in later years that her performance only satisfied her in a couple of places, and: 'I never liked Scarlett. I knew it was a marvellous part, but I never cared for her. I couldn't find anything of myself in her, except for one line ... it was the only thing in the character I could take hold of. It's in the scene after Frank's funeral, when she gets drunk and tells Rhett how glad she is her mother's dead and can't see her. "She brought me up to be kind and thoughtful and ladylike, just like her, and I've been such a disappointment." I liked her then, and perhaps at the end.' It is difficult to find an endearing trait in Scarlett beyond her determination and, whether Leigh realized it or not, she was basically an unsympathetic actress: this was a perfect mating of artist and character. Fascinating certainly, if far from flawless: but any other Scarlett is inconceivable. John Coleman reviewing the 1968 revival thought her contribution the 'paramount' one. She won the Best Actress Oscar and the New York Critics award.

She was under contract to Selznick and the hottest property in Hollywood. Of this period Wolfe Kaufman wrote years later in Variety: '... she made life hell for everybody near her, unless they did everything she wished, as she wished, and when she wished. Despite which she was surrounded by people who worshipped her and were ready to carry out her whims.' She did not, however, get her way over Olivier as co-star (they were married in 1940). Pre-*GWTW*, she had begged to be Cathy to his Heathcliff, and had been offered Isabella Linton as a sop; now she wanted to be with him in *Pride and Prejudice* or have him with her in *Waterloo Bridge* (40). Instead, Robert Taylor was cast in *Bridge*, a World War I anecdote about an aristocrat and a ballerina; they marry, and while he is away fighting, she becomes a tart (to survive); he recovers her, never learning of her fate, but she abandons him for the sake of the regiment, as personified by C. Aubrey Smith. There was, apparently, a large audience for such things in 1940. Said the Evening News (London): 'Vivien Leigh gives a performance of beauty, inspiration and sensitivity which I do not expect to see surpassed this year.' In New York she and Olivier were 'Romeo and Juliet' to a distinctly unappreciative public, but prestige was regained with *That Hamilton Woman/Lady Hamilton* (41), made by Korda in Hollywood: quickly and cheaply, but it was effective both as romance and propaganda. Leigh's Emma was visually right, and she did not shrink from the less attractive qualities in the lady's character: like most of her screen portraits this one was not withal a one-man woman.

She and Olivier returned to Britain, but apart from a stage appearance as Jennifer Dubedat, illness prevented her from working; a further barrier was Selznick, who refused to let her play the French princess in her husband's *Henry V* because, he said, the part was too small. It was believed, however, that he acted in retaliation for her refusal to leave either Britain or husband. He did loan her to Rank for *Caesar and Cleopatra* (45), Gabriel Pascal's version of the Shaw play and at £1¼ million or $5 million the most expensive movie yet made anywhere in the world. Critics were caustic about the cost, and generally liked only Claude Rains and her (she was appropriately kittenish and wily) in the title roles. In Britain it did good business, but in the US the reviews dampened any curiosity to see Leigh after a four-year absence. In 1945 the Selznick contract was declared invalid by a British court when he tried to stop her doing 'The Skin of Our Teeth' on the stage; she continued to turn down Hollywood offers, but after recovering from TB she agreed to be Korda's *Anna Karenina* (48) under Julien Duvivier's direction: an unsatisfactory film, hindered more than somewhat by an inadequate Vronsky (Kieron Moore). Leigh invited comparison with Garbo, and few critics were kind enough not to make it. Said James Agee: 'Vivien Leigh is lashed about by the tremendous role of Anna like

Laurence Olivier and Vivien Leigh in That Hamilton Woman *(41). Theirs was the most famous show-business marriage of the time and though they frequently acted together on stage this was their only screen appearance together.*

a pussy-cat with a tigress by the tail.' Nor did the public like it.

Meanwhile, with Olivier she was touring Australasia with the Old Vic company; in London in 1949 she played Lady Teazle, Lady Anne in 'Richard III' and Anouilh's 'Antigone'; in 1951, in London and New York, still opposite Olivier, she played Shaw's and Shakespeare's Cleopatras: all to generous appreciation. Also, in 1949 in London she played Blanche in Tennessee Williams's 'A Streetcar Named Desire'; and when Olivia de Havilland declined the film version (51) she was invited to do it, opposite Marlon Brando, and got her best film reviews since Scarlett. Milton Shulman thought 'She just misses pathos. But this is, nevertheless, a performance such as the screen rarely sees.' C. A. Lejeune: 'One would have to be blind not to appreciate the brilliance of Vivien Leigh's performance. It is possible not to be touched by her, inconceivable not to be impressed and dazzled. Her Blanche is a woman shimmering in a sheath of gold, never very clearly seen, but taking glint and radiance from every facet.' For the second time both the Academy and the New York Critics discerned her the year's Best Actress, and the British Film Academy voted her the year's Best British Actress. One of the most touching tributes ever paid to an actress was made by the author, who later told Life magazine that she had brought everything to the part he had intended and much that he had never dreamed of.

In 1953, much to filmland's surprise, Leigh began work with Peter Finch in what was clearly a programmer, *Elephant Walk*; after locations in India and some studio work in Hollywood she had a nervous breakdown and was replaced. Olivier flew to bring her home, which killed, temporarily, speculations about the break-up of the marriage. She recovered to appear with him on stage in Rattigan's 'The Sleeping Prince' (54); a year later they were at Stratford, where her Lady Macbeth and Viola cruelly exposed her limitations as a 'classical' actress. She returned to films with *The Deep Blue Sea* (56), Korda's version of the Rattigan play about a middle-aged woman trying to hang on to her lover, a garish, soupy film, directed by Anatole Litvak; Leigh's austere, carefully modulated performance was outclassed by Kenneth More as the lover. (He later revealed that they hadn't got on, partly because he objected to her insistence on her character's physical beauty.) Business wasn't lucrative.

Stage appearances included 'Duel of Angels' (London and New York), 'Look After Lulu' (a Coward adaptation of Feydeau), and, after the divorce (1960), a

Marlon Brando and Vivien Leigh in Elia Kazan's film of A Streetcar Named Desire *(51): one of the most potent clashes in screen dramaturgy – from Tennessee Williams's play.*

Kenneth More and Vivien Leigh in The Deep Blue Sea *(56), produced by Korda and distributed by 20th Century-Fox – on condition that it was made in CinemaScope (which turned out to be entirely unsuitable for this intimate drama).*

musical 'Tovarich' in New York and 'The Lady of the Camellias', on tour, Australasia and South America. Both her last films included an undue proportion of lines which could be construed as masochistic: in both she was a fading beauty with a lot of past but no future. In *The Roman Spring of Mrs Stone* (61) she was a retired actress (who'd been bad in Shakespeare) involved with an Italian gigolo, and in *Ship of Fools* (65) an embittered divorcee who drank too much. The former was a competent version of Tennessee Williams's only novel; the second transformed Katharine Ann Porter's ambitious best-seller into a pretentious pot-boiler: neither was over-successful.

Her last play, 'La Contessa' (65) folded on tour. She was seriously ill again with TB when she died in 1967. The public, who had increasingly regarded her as a remote deity, were nevertheless shocked and saddened; and it seemed improbable that this most genuinely glamorous of creatures should rest in a London crematorium rather than in some special Nirvana.

Harold Lloyd

Harold Lloyd completes the great triumvirate of the Silent clowns. After Keaton and Chaplin there is no other whose reputation is quite so secure, and at the time he was probably the most popular of the three: certainly he was the best bet at the box-office during the 20s. Lloyd's humour sprang more from plot and situation than the others: he was a very ordinary, indeed conventional young man. Keaton was a loner and Chaplin thumbed his nose at society, but Lloyd was the eager young American, Alger-indoctrinated, dressed in duds which were the 20s equivalent of the grey flannel suit – plus the ubiquitous straw hat, and the glasses, betokening anxiousness and shyness. To what extent he was satirizing the all-American boy is not known, but the public did respond enormously to the character; James Agee is one critic who did find Lloyd 'funny from inside'. After acknowledging what Lloyd had described as his 'unusually large comic vocabulary' he went on: 'more particularly he had an expertly expressive body and even more expressive teeth, and out of his thesaurus of smiles he could at a moment's notice blend prissiness, breeziness and asininity, and still remain tremendously likeable.' In 'Harold Lloyd's World of Comedy' (64) William Cahn went on from there: 'It was Harold's aim to develop a character the public could believe in. His antics and adventures were stretched, but never beyond the post of possibility. . . . An extrovert to the core, Harold was the young man who would not take no for an answer. Evidently, nobody ever told him that anything was impossible. Therefore, he proceeded to do what could not be done.' Tackling the impossible for Lloyd often meant some incredible, perilous feats of daring or athletics, like scaling the skyscraper in *Safety Last* – perhaps the supreme example of its kind. Less imaginative, in the end, than Keaton, he could sustain a gag longer, like his trailing garter in *Movie Crazy* which manages to rip off most of the ladies' clothes and create general havoc.

Lloyd was born in Burchard, Nebraska, in 1893, into a fairly poor family. His first stage job was to cry 'Help' in 'Macbeth' (he was Fleance) with a local touring company; he had further acting experience at school and with another stock company. When he was 17 the family moved to San Diego, and there, in 1912, came the Edison Co. to do locations: Lloyd volunteered and was paid $3 to play a near-naked Red Indian extra. He was movie-besotted – the original, almost, of *Merton of the Movies*. He continued to get intermittent extra work until a fellow-extra, Hal Roach, inherited a few thousand dollars and invited Lloyd to join him in his own company. They experimented with a character called Willie Work, played by Lloyd, but none of the shorts they made

Harold Lloyd and Bebe Daniels in a short made not long after he began what he called his 'glass' character. The man with the droopy moustache behind is Stan Laurel.

found a buyer. One short they did, *Just Nuts* (15), was, however, liked enough by Pathé for that studio to approach Roach: but at this point Lloyd left because he discovered that Roach was paying Roy Stewart (the dramatic star of the little company) $10 a day while he was to get $5. He went to Essanay and did a few small parts, but returned to Roach and Pathé some weeks later when offered $50 a week. They worked out a character called Lonesome Luke. Chaplin was their inspiration (for one thing, distributors preferred other comedians to ape him), only where his clothes were too roomy, Luke's were too tight. Lloyd himself loathed the character, but the films, one- and two-reelers, became very popular: starting in January, 1916, he made over a hundred of them. Sometimes he was making several simultaneously. Lloyd has said: 'The picture always ended with 200 feet of chase. I was pursued by dogs, sheriffs, angry housewives, circus tigers, motor cars, baby carriages, wild bulls, trolley cars, locomotives, and, of course, legions of cops.'

Within a short while Lloyd had worked out a successor to Lonesome Luke. He had the idea of playing a college boy, and on to that was grafted the mild manner (and spectacles) of a screen hero whom he had recently seen, a person who was not so mild when roused. To his surprise Pathé gave their permission to try out the new character, which Lloyd did, in early 1917, in *Over the Fence*, a one-reeler. He continued making the Lonesome Luke shorts till the end of that year, and then Pathé let him drop them. He stuck to one reel only for his Glass character, as he called him: with Roach's cooperation, and sometimes writing and directing himself, he did around half a dozen alongside Luke; but once that character was out of the way, he didn't stop–around 60 were released in 1918, and another 30 in 1919. Almost all of them included two stalwarts from the Lonesome Luke period, Bebe Daniels and Snub Pollard. In 1919 Pathé suggested that Lloyd become more ambitious and do two-reelers. The first was *Bumping into Broadway*, followed by *Captain Kidd's Kids*, after which Bebe Daniels defected, and Lloyd found a new heroine, Mildred Davis: she was featured in all his films until *Safety Last*, when her contract expired. Lloyd married her, and she retired. Meanwhile, she made her debut in *From Hand to Mouth*; and after the next, *His Royal Slyness*, the formula changed slightly when Pollard left. More seriously, during the making of *Haunted Spooks* (20), Lloyd was posing for a publicity photograph with what was thought to be a papier maché prop bomb–only it wasn't; seriously injured, he was hospitalized for six months, and handicapped thereafter by the loss of his right thumb and forefinger and a stiffness in that hand.

The film was finally completed and Lloyd did *An Eastern Westerner* and then *High and Dizzy*, the first time he attempted sky-scraping on a grand scale; followed by *Get Out and Get Under* and *Number Please*, the last one Roach directed. Lloyd moved on to three-reelers: *Now or Never* (21), *Among Those Present*, *I Do* (though that was cut to two reels after previewing) and *Never Weaken*, another successful excursion into the high and dizzy. And then four-reelers: *A Sailor-Made Man*–which proved that the public would accept Lloyd as a feature attraction. *Grandma's Boy* (22) was a five-reeler, and those that followed were six- or more: the new Pathé contract signed in 1922 stipulated six features, and Lloyd welcomed the change. Already he had managed to give his character a variety of professions, and now he was able to develop stronger plot lines. The first premeditated feature was *Dr Jack* (22), in the title role, which was more than a series of gags; but half of *Safety Last* (23) consists of the famous vertical climb (as a store employee he replaces a professional climber in a publicity stunt). Audiences were, in fact, thrilled more than amused–to the tune of making the picture one of the year's top five money-makers. Sam Taylor joined Fred Newmeyer–who

Harold Lloyd out west. He was The Kid Brother *(27), who helped his sheriff father recover the gold that had been entrusted to him.*

Professor Beware *(38): Lloyd has some explaining to do. It wasn't* his *fault he lost his pants and ended up at the police-station.*

had directed the previous features – as co-director, and they worked together on all Lloyd's subsequent pictures.

The new leading lady was Jobyna Ralston: she first appeared in *Why Worry?* in which they were involved in a South American revolution. *Girl Shy* (24) was one of the year's top five money-makers, due possibly to the climactic ride on top of a runaway streetcar. The *Hot Water* he was in was caused by troublesome in-laws and his new 'used' car; then he was *The Freshman* (25) – the shy college boy who scores the winning goal. This took over $2½ million at the box-office, one of the most successful of all Silent pictures. His contract with Pathé was up (he had already parted amicably with Roach) and he approached Paramount to distribute him: as before, he had complete artistic control and the ownership of the negative. The first under this agreement were: *For Heaven's Sake* (26), *The Kid Brother* (27), and *Speedy* (28) about a soda-jerk with an obsession for baseball. About this time Lloyd published an autobiography, 'An American Comedy'. With the advent of the Talkies came *Welcome Stranger* (29), shot as a Silent, but with a few sequences dubbed before release. Lloyd didn't care for the restrictions imposed by early Sound, but it was a success. However, his first real Talkie, *Feet First* (30), was so disappointing at the box-office, despite another high building antic, that Paramount considered cancelling the distribution agreement. *Movie Crazy* (32) with Constance Cummings – Jobyna had fallen by the wayside – was on the contrary much liked and probably his most successful Talkie.

For his next picture he tried to subordinate gags to plot, and bought Clarence Budington Kelland's *The Cat's Paw* (34), the story of an innocent conned into running for mayor by gangsters. It didn't do well for Fox, who released, and Lloyd returned to Paramount for the long-in-filming *The Milky Way* (36) about a milkman who becomes a prizefighter, and *Professor Beware* (38). Neither were vintage Lloyd, but there were good things in them, and his respected position brought respectable box-office. In 1940 he did contemplate another film, but said: 'I had come to the conclusion nobody had any particular use for me as a comedian any more.' He did *produce* a couple of clinkers for RKO soon after, but didn't film again until producer Howard Hughes and director Preston Sturges invited him to do *Mad Wednesday* (47), but by this time that strange decline of Sturges had begun and Lloyd was unhappy with much of the material: the critics didn't like it, and the public shunned it. Lloyd turned down further offers. An extremely wealthy man, he didn't need the money. In 1952 a special Oscar was awarded him, 'Harold Lloyd, master comedian and good citizen'. In 1962 he put together a compilation of his best old stuff, *Harold*

Lloyd's World of Comedy, and it was so popular that he did another one a couple of years later, *Harold Lloyd's Funny Side of Life*. They proved that great comedy is timeless.

Hugh Williams and Margaret Lockwood en route for the sea in Bank Holiday *(38), an enjoyable study of the way some of the British take their pleasures.*

Margaret Lockwood

Margaret Lockwood was not by any means a great screen actress, but she was spirited and likeable: the British public queued to see her until blatant mishandling ruined her career. Possibly (age apart) she might not have retained her popularity: there was something about her South-London-bred personality which suited the 40s, and by the mid-50s she and her fellows (Phyllis Calvert, Patricia Roc, Jean Kent) were passé as far as the cinema was concerned. One can only speculate as to what they might have been like had they ever had good scripts or first-rate directors, though Milton Shulman, in the Evening Standard in 1946, had little doubt; in an open letter to Mr Rank he claimed that he could find five girls as pretty and talented as this bunch by watching the secretaries get off the escalators in Leicester Square Station. He couldn't, of course.

Maggie Lockwood was born in Karachi in 1916. She studied for the stage at the Italia Conti School, and made her first stage appearance as a fairy in 'A Midsummer Night's Dream' in 1928 at the Holborn Empire. She later walked-on in 'Cavalcade'; and studied at RADA. Her first success was in 'Family Affairs' (34) which led to a small part in *Lorna Doone* (34). Victoria Hopper was Lorna and Dorothy Hyson had the second lead. When Hyson fell ill Lockwood took over, and British Lion offered her a long-term contract. She was a starlet of some promise through *The Case of Gabriel Perry* (35), *Some Day* and *Honours Easy*, a 'revenge' drama. Her first leading role was in *Midshipman Easy*, and her biggest early breaks came when she was cast with Douglas Fairbanks Jr in *Man of the Moment*, poor though it was, and then leading lady to Maurice Chevalier in the English version of *The Beloved Vagabond* (a French one was made simultaneously). Variety said she 'had a pleasing personality and a voice that is less British than the average. Her wistfulness reminds me of Janet Gaynor.' She was the fresh young heroine in another half-dozen films: *Jury's Evidence*, *The Amateur Gentleman* (Fairbanks again), *Irish for Luck* (36), *The Street Singer* (Arthur Tracy), *Who's Your Lady Friend?* (Vic Oliver and Frances Day) and *Melody and Romance*. Gainsborough borrowed her for *Dr Syn* (37) with George Arliss, and after a few days negotiated to buy her contract. She was in *Owd Bob* and in Carol Reed's *Bank Holiday* (38), an affectionate look at a British family, which really established her as the white hope of British films. She made another for Reed, *A Girl Must Live*, and Hitchcock's *The Lady Vanishes*, before hitting the Hollywood trail.

She was now earning £6,000 a year. Her studio wanted her to go to the US under a lend-lease scheme they operated with 20th Century-Fox. She did *Susannah of the Mounties* with Shirley Temple, then went to Paramount for *Rulers of the Sea* (39) with Fairbanks Jr again and Will Fyffe. The experience was not a happy one, and she returned to Britain to find herself more in demand than ever: she made two more under Reed's direction, *The Stars Look Down* (40) and *Night Train to Munich*. In the former she gave her best early performance, as the flibbertigibbet who comes near to ruining coalminer Michael Redgrave. She was also in a thriller, *A Girl in the News*, and in a stagey but agreeable light comedy, *Quiet Wedding* (41). That year she ceded her role in *The Young Mr Pitt* to Phyllis Calvert when she found that she was pregnant. After a poor performance in *Alibi* (42), a remake of *L'Alibi* with Raymond Lovell in the Von Stroheim part, she played in *The Man in Grey* (43) and that made her a super-star–in Britain, at any rate. Audiences loved Lockwood as Hesther, who steals her best friend's husband and later murders her. She

Felix Aylmer, Margaret Lockwood and Patricia Roc in The Wicked Lady *(45). Aylmer is dying and there are no prizes for guessing who put the poison in his porridge.*

cornered the British market in feminine deviousness and that lasted her for several years (just as the same film established James Mason as her male equivalent). There were other films – *Dear Octopus*, *Give Us The Moon* (44) and most notably the riotous *Love Story* in which she, a pianist with a fatal disease, fought with Pat Roc over Stewart Granger, an RAF pilot who was going blind. She never did take any of this stuff seriously, but begged for better parts. In 1945 she was given *I'll Be Your Sweetheart*, an Edwardian music-hall tale for which her singing voice was dubbed and *A Place of One's Own*, in which she was a frightened heroine. The same year came her apotheosis as *The Wicked Lady*, with Mason and Roc, as a calculating husband-pinching murderous bitch who, to further amuse herself, takes to playing highwaywoman at night. Audiences then lapped it up, but today the film is too amateurish to be risable. She was also bad in Vera Caspary's *Bedelia* (46) and Norah Lofts's *Jassy* (47), but in the interim was patient and afflicted in Daphne du Maurier's *Hungry Hill* (46) and later in *The White Unicorn* (47). In 1946 she had signed a new seven-year Rank contract.

Her popularity was astonishing. In 1946 she replaced Greer Garson as Britain's favourite female star, and twice again she was in the list of top money-makers in Britain. During the same three years she was overwhelmingly voted Britain's Best Actress by the readers of the Daily Mail. She was in the Britons-only list consistently from 1943 to 1949. Hollywood dangled contracts – she was offered *Forever Amber* – but she wasn't tempted. However, she finally began to quarrel with Rank about her parts and films. She refused to do the role Jean Kent eventually played in *The Magic Bow*, and was later suspended for refusing an innocuous little comedy, *Once Upon a Dream* (which Googie Withers did); but, as was observed at the time, one could feel little sympathy because she promptly accepted an even worse one, *Look Before You Love* (48). Indeed, that bore a strong claim to being the worst film of the year – until *Madness of the Heart* came along to squash all competition. That one had Lockwood as a blind girl whose husband's ex-fiancée keeps trying to murder her. Rank had got the message and didn't show it to the critics. She played Nell Gwynn in *Cardboard Cavalier*, a period comedy which vainly tried to capture the considerable talent of comic Sid Field. She had pleaded for the part, but the best that could be said for her comedy technique was that she was hearty and well-meaning. Rank then promised her a good film. She turned down several subjects which might have been ideal (*The Browning Version* and *The Reluctant Widow*: Jean Kent played both) and several films were announced which never materialized (*Elizabeth of Austria* and *Ann Veronica*). In the end, she made a modest

Cast a Dark Shadow (*55*): *Margaret Lockwood gave a good character study of a wealthy widow who marries Dirk Bogarde. Here's a wedding-day toast from Philip Stainton.*

thriller, *Highly Dangerous* (50): a Hollywood leading man (Dane Clark) was imported, and for the first time in 10 years she was given a director who was better than mediocre (Roy Baker). Eric Ambler wrote the script, and the result was reasonably, if not highly, entertaining.

Her Rank contract was dissolved, and she signed a two-year contract with Herbert Wilcox, who had been churning out a series of very successful vehicles for his wife, Anna Neagle. Neagle had supplanted Lockwood as Britain's No. 1 female star, and thus much was made of this move. Doubtless Lockwood felt that what Wilcox had done for his wife, he could do for her. She couldn't have been more wrong. The first was a dull version of a classic mystery tale, *Trent's Last Case* (52), and the second an inadequate version of a Conrad story, *Laughing Anne* (53), in which she was a gay lady out East. With *Trouble in the Glen* (54), a so-called Scottish comedy, the Lockwood-Wilcox association came quietly to an end. She then accepted a character role in an independent film, *Cast a Dark Shadow* (55): as the blowsy ex-barmaid who marries Dirk Bogarde she got her best notices in years, and might, in a different set-up, have continued her film career as a character actress. But the British film industry seemed no longer interested.

She accepted the decline in her film fortunes with high good humour, and returned to the stage. Already, in 1949, she had toured in 'Private Lives' and in 1950 had played Peter Pan. The plays she has elected to do have been invariably undistinguished, apart from–perhaps–'An Ideal Husband' (65) when she was most accomplished as Mrs Cheveley. The same year she had a successful TV series, 'The Flying Swan', and in 1970 she played in Somerset Maugham's 'Lady Frederick'. Her daughter Julia is also an actress.

Carole Lombard

Very early on, movie stars became confused with gods and goddesses. As the cinema grew up the concept went completely out of fashion, but there's a strong case to be made for the divinity of Carole Lombard. One is certain that, at Olympian banquets, she's right up there next to Zeus. If she's not (invited), she's probably throwing things. Lombard's tantrums were a staple of 30s screwball comedy, though these were the least of her. Catherine de la Roche wrote ('Sight and Sound', 1953) that she was 'the most delicate satirical comedienne the screen has ever had'. Pauline Kael thinks her 'talents were not of the highest, but her spirits were, and in her skin-tight satins she embodies the giddy, absurd glamour of thirties comedy'. Here are two colleagues' views: Barbara Stanwyck (explaining why

Lombard was Hollywood's most interesting person in 1936): '. . . because she is so alive, modern, frank, and natural that she stands out like a beacon on a lightship in this odd place called Hollywood', and Bing Crosby: 'She had a delicious sense of humour; she was one of the screen's greatest comediennes and, in addition, she was very beautiful. The electricians, carpenters and prop men all adored her because she was so regular; so devoid of temperament and showboating. . . . The fact that she could make us think of her as being a good guy rather than a sexy mamma is one of those unbelievable manifestations impossible to explain.'

She was born Jane Peters in 1908 in Fort Wayne, Indiana. Her parents were divorced while she was young, and she moved with her mother and brothers to Los Angeles. Her movie debut came when she was spotted in a neighbour's yard by Allan Dwan, who was visiting that family; he was then directing for Fox and needed just such a high-spirited girl to play Monte Blue's daughter in *A Perfect Crime* (21). She continued at High School, went to a drama school and kept hoping for another movie chance: she was tested for the lead in *The Gold Rush* but another test, at Fox, did get her the female lead opposite Edmund Lowe in *Marriage in Transit* (25), at $75 per week. Fox changed her name to Carole Lombard (though the 'e' on Carol disappeared for a while; returned for good in 1930) and signed her to a five-year contract. However, after *Hearts and Spurs*, a Buck Jones Western, she was involved in an automobile accident, and it was annulled. When she recovered she got a job with Mack Sennett, appearing in two-reelers, including *The Girl From Everywhere* (27), *His Unlucky Night* and *The Swim Princess* (28). During this time she rose from $50 a week to $400 and learnt the timing which was the basis of her comedy technique.

She left Sennett and got small parts in *The Perfect Crime* at FBO with Clive Brook and in Raoul Walsh's *Me Gangster* at Fox: the me was Don Terry. Then Pathé gave her a year's contract. The films weren't much but she had leads: *Power*, starring William Boyd; *Show Folks*, starring Eddie Quillan; *Ned McCobb's Daughter*, a version of Sydney Howard's play, with Irene Rich; *High Voltage*, her first all-Talkie, with Boyd and Owen Moore; Gregory La Cava's *Big News*, as the wife of reporter Robert Armstrong; and *The Racketeer*, again with Armstrong. At Fox she vamped *The Arizona Kid* (30)–Warner Baxter, who fell for her only to discover she was a crook (Mona Maris consoled him); then Paramount cast her as one of the reasons for Charles 'Buddy' Rogers's creed, *Safety in Numbers*. They were delighted with her work and signed her to a seven-year contract, starting at $350 a week.

She had good parts in two comedies, *Fast and Loose* with Miriam Hopkins, and *It Pays to Advertize* (31) soap, with Norman Foster. The *Man of the World* and *Ladies Man* both were William Powell, and they were married not long after meeting on the set. She achieved star status without being thought of as anything extraordinary–effervescent and competent as a super-sophisticated but basically nice girl, noted more for her slinky blonde looks, good legs and daring gowns than for anything else: *Up Pops the Devil*, a marital comedy with Stuart Erwin, Lilyan Tashman and Foster; *I Take This Woman*, pursued by cowhand Gary Cooper; *No One Man* (32) as a pleasure-mad divorcee, with Ricardo Cortez; and *Sinners in the Sun* with Chester Morris, which was little but fashion parades. She was loaned to Columbia for a couple: *Virtue* (she hadn't any; as Pat O'Brien's wife, a lady with a Past) and *No More Orchids* (she didn't want any; in love with Lyle Talbot, she rejected money for love). As a fast-talking showgirl she had *No Man of Her Own* (33) when gambler Clark Gable walked into her life: he pursued and married her (the comic half) and reformed for her (the dramatic half). She put up a fine showing, but her comic abilities continued to be wasted. Still, she maintained a light touch when she could get away with it: *From Hell to Heaven* with Jack Oakie, as a bookmaker's daughter; *Supernatural*, a silly ghost picture with Randolph Scott; *The Eagle and the Hawk*, where she had one brief sequence, with Fredric March; *Brief Moment*, as a night-club singer who marries playboy Gene Raymond to reform him, a poor version of S. N. Behrman's play, at Columbia; and a steamy melodrama, *White Woman*, betraying Charles Laughton with Kent Taylor. And there were fights with the studio when she refused to do *The Way to Love* and refused to be loaned to WB for *Hard to Handle*.

Her roles in *Bolero* (34), where she danced, and *We're Not Dressing*, where she listened, were subsidiary to those of George Raft and Crosby respectively, but it was more than ever clear that here was a witty, sinewy, leading lady; she got a beautiful chance, and took it beautifully, as the temperamental actress courted–for professional reasons–by John Barrymore, on a trip in the *Twentieth Century*. Howard Hawks directed for Columbia and it shot Lombard into the forefront of Hollywood stars. Said Barrymore:

Carole Lombard in the days when she was more noteworthy as a beauty than as an actress.

Gary Cooper and Carole Lombard in Henry Hathaway's Now and Forever *(34). Shirley Temple is not in this still but she was much in evidence in the film.*

'She is perhaps the greatest actress I ever worked with.' It was hardly to be expected that she would be happy playing second fiddle to Shirley Temple in *Now and Forever*, and her battling with Paramount intensified. However, two outside pictures didn't help: *Lady by Choice* at Columbia was really a vehicle for May Robson, who had recently had a hit in *Lady for a Day*: 'Men Who Loved Her Grew Sadder–but Wiser' said the ads, ambiguously. And *The Gay Bride* at MGM cast her as a mercenary showgirl who marries bootlegger Chester Morris. Said Richard Watts Jr in the New York Herald Tribune: 'Miss Lombard achieves the feat of being almost as bad as her picture, and plays her part with neither humour nor conviction.' She didn't care much for *Rumba* (35) with Raft (an attempt to cash in on the success of *Bolero*) but liked *Hands Across the Table*, once more a gold digger, and the first of four co-starring vehicles with Fred MacMurray.

She did two comedies at Universal: *Love Before Breakfast* (36) with Preston Foster; and *My Man Godfrey*, with ex-husband Powell as a Depression-bum taken on as butler by a family consisting of Lombard, Gail Patrick, Eugene Pallatte, Alice Brady and Mischa Auer: they were all wonderful. There were three in a row with MacMurray, two of them almost as good as that: *The Princess Comes Across*–she was a bogus princess and it was the Atlantic she was crossing; *Swing High Swing Low* (37), one of the several screen versions of 'Burlesque' and poor; and *True Confession*, as a congenital liar in a farce about a murder trial. Her third 1937 picture, *Nothing Sacred*, is–if *My Man Godfrey* isn't–the funniest of all 30s comedies: a brilliant satire on press ethics. She is a bogus invalid exploited by Fredric March to boost circulation. Said William Whitebait: 'The acting is superb . . . Carole Lombard has a touch of comic genius.'

She was the highest paid star for 1937, at $465,000. Her contract with Paramount had expired in 1936, when she was getting $3,500 per week. They had signed a new deal, worth $2 million, three films a year, beginning at $150,000 per film, and she was permitted to free-lance: *Nothing Sacred* was the first of three for Selznick at $175,000 per film. She did not in fact ever make another film for Paramount. At the end of 1937 in Film Weekly Freda Bruce Lockhart wrote: '. . . there is one very significant indication of a star's ranking–Hollywood's own opinion. Every visiting Hollywood producer or director I have spoken to this year has mentioned Carole's name with that mysterious professional enthusiasm whose authenticity cannot be mistaken. And they all declare that she is as fine an emotional actress as a comedienne.'

Fools for Scandal (38) was a weak comedy at WB with Fernand Gravet. She said: 'I knew it wasn't a sensation when my friends confined their comments to how beautifully I had been photographed.' Her next four were serious: Selznick's *Made for Each Other* (39), a sentimental marital tale with James

Gregory La Cava's delightful My Man Godfrey *(36): William Powell in the title role and Carole Lombard as the daughter of the house who pursued him – to put it mildly.*

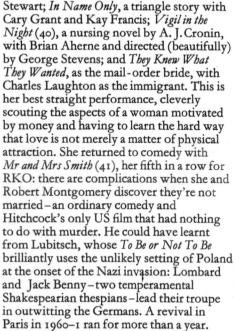

William A. Wellman's Nothing Sacred *(37): Lombard, as the heroine of the hour, participates in a fire-rescue operation. With her, Fredric March and John Qualen.*

Stewart; *In Name Only*, a triangle story with Cary Grant and Kay Francis; *Vigil in the Night* (40), a nursing novel by A. J. Cronin, with Brian Aherne and directed (beautifully) by George Stevens; and *They Knew What They Wanted*, as the mail-order bride, with Charles Laughton as the immigrant. This is her best straight performance, cleverly scouting the aspects of a woman motivated by money and having to learn the hard way that love is not merely a matter of physical attraction. She returned to comedy with *Mr and Mrs Smith* (41), her fifth in a row for RKO: there are complications when she and Robert Montgomery discover they're not married – an ordinary comedy and Hitchcock's only US film that had nothing to do with murder. He could have learnt from Lubitsch, whose *To Be or Not To Be* brilliantly uses the unlikely setting of Poland at the onset of the Nazi invasion: Lombard and Jack Benny – two temperamental Shakespearian thespians – lead their troupe in outwitting the Germans. A revival in Paris in 1960–1 ran for more than a year.

Lombard was killed in an air crash in early 1942, when the plane in which she was travelling flew into a mountain near Las Vegas. She had just sold over $2 million worth of war bonds in Indianapolis, near her home town. She left heart-broken widower Clark Gable (they were married in 1939 after a courtship which deserved all the affectionate publicity it got). President Roosevelt cabled him: 'She brought joy to all who knew her, and to millions who knew her only as a great artist. . . . She is and always will be a star, one we shall never forget, nor cease to be grateful to.'

Myrna Loy

It is widely known that Myrna Loy was an Oriental vamp before becoming the perfect screen wife, but it is less generally realized that she made over 60 films before becoming a star; she served a long apprenticeship in Silents – from leads to walk-ons and back again – without ever quite making it. By the time stardom came, she was an excellent all-round actress, but her forte was comedy. She was an adroit and irresistible comedienne, with a dry-martini voice, calm and measured in the two-piece suits and hats that Adrian designed for her – silly hats like saucers cocked over one eye. She was seldom in the kitchen or even by the fireside: perfect wife she may have been, but more for exchanging barbed comments in the Oak Room at the Plaza. Certainly she *cared* – like all the good actresses of that era she had great warmth–but presumably her appeal lay in the fact that she was more chic and more sophisticated than any real wife could be. Both men and women adored her: somewhere around her 80th film she was the most popular female star in Hollywood. And her expertise was much admired–only two or three of today's girls approach it.

She was born in Helena, Montana, in 1905. Her father died when she was 10. In 1919 the family moved to Los Angeles where for a while she taught dancing; she moved on to the chorus of Grauman's Chinese Theatre, dancing in prologues. A photographer, Harry Waxman, noticed her, and through him she was tested by Valentino for a part in *Cobra*. She didn't get it, but he recommended her to his wife who gave her a brief role in *What Price Beauty* (25, released in 28). Bitten now by the film-bug, Loy tested for the role of the Virgin in *Ben Hur*, but instead they made her the mistress of one of the Senators; also at MGM she was a chorine in *Pretty Ladies* (25), starring Zasu Pitts and Lilyan Tashman.

She haunted the casting offices, and then through Waxman she met Lowell Sherman, who thought she might be useful at Warners: they gave her a five-year contract, but in the first one, *Cave Man* (26) starring Matt Moore, she ended in the chorus again. She made four more films that year: *The Gilded Highway*; *Why Girls Go Back Home*, starring Patsy Ruth Miller; *Across the Pacific* as a native girl in this tale of the Spanish-American War; and *Don Juan*, as a spy of the Borgias. Thereafter, till she became a star, she averaged eight a year. 1927: *Ham and Eggs at the Front*, a Negro army comedy–only the Negroes were 'blackface', including Loy, playing a spy; *The Climbers*, starring Irene Rich; *Simple Sis*, starring Louise Fazenda; *Bitter Apples*, her first lead, as a girl who marries Monte Blue from revenge and learns to love him; *The Jazz Singer* where she was glimpsed but briefly, as a showgirl; and *The Girl From Chicago*, second-billed, after Conrad Nagel, in this Underworlder; 1928: *If I Were Single*, supporting Mae McAvoy; *Heart of Maryland*, starring Dolores Costello; *Beware of Married Men*, starring Irene Rich; *Turn Back the Hours*, on loan-out, as a Spanish Beauty; *Crimson City*, which was Shanghai, second-billed again in her first Oriental role; *Pay As You Enter*, supporting Louise Fazenda; *State Street Sadie*, as Slinky, a cop's daughter, in this melo with Sound sequences; *The Midnight Taxi*, as gangster Antonio Moreno's moll; and the spectacular *Noah's Ark*, starring Dolores Costello and George O'Brien, as a dancer in the modern part, a slave-girl in the Biblical sequences.

Roy del Ruth's Across the Pacific *(26) was a melodrama set in the Philippines starring Monte Blue, who dallied with Myrna Loy between battles.*

1929: *Fancy Baggage*; *The Desert Song*, all-Sound with colour sequences, starring John Boles and Carlotta King, with Loy as Azuri, and generally considered to be the best thing in the film; *The Black Watch*, as an Indian mystery woman at Fox; *The Squall*, in a small part as a gypsy adventuress; *Hardboiled Rose*, as a Southern belle; *Evidence*, as a native girl; and *The Show of Shows*, in two dance sequences. Like many 'Silent' players, Loy was worried by the competition offered by newcomers from the stage, and decided to get as much exposure as she could: when Warners didn't need her she worked elsewhere. Nine Loy pictures were released in 1930: *The Great Divide*, as a Mexican, starring Dorothy Mackaill and Ian Keith; the third film version of *Cameo Kirby*, starring J. Harold Murray; *Isle of Escape*, as a native belle; *Under a Texan Moon*, getting the guy (Frank Fay) in spite of four exotic contenders –the others were Raquel Torres, Armida and Betty Boyd; *Cock o' the Walk*, a real chance as a potential suicide who is married and then insured by gigolo Joseph Schildkraut–but a pretentious piece, made by an indie; *Bride of the Regiment*, back in support, as a camp follower; *The Last of the Duanes*, Zane Grey's Western, starring George O'Brien; *The Truth About Youth*, as Kara 'the firefly', a grasping cabaret artist; and *The Jazz Cinderella*: 'Myrna Loy and

Jason Robards do as well as they can, which isn't much' (Photoplay).

Early in 1931, after *Naughty Flirt*, starring Alice White, Warners dropped Loy, but she was established as one of the most reliable leading women in Hollywood and had no difficulty getting work. Most of the year she spent at Fox, starting with *Renegades*, as one of Bela Lugosi's harem, but betraying him for love of hero Warner Baxter. She sang and danced in a minor Western, *Rogue of the Rio Grande*, returning to Fox for: *Body and Soul* starring Elissa Landi and Charles Farrell; *A Connecticut Yankee*, as Morgan Le Faye; *Hush Money*; *Transatlantic*, a liner drama, and down to sixth on the cast-list; and *Skyline*, as builder Thomas Meighan's girlfriend. At RKO she was the Other Woman in both *Rebound* (Ina Claire and Robert Ames) and *Consolation Marriage* (Irene Dunne and Pat O'Brien). But her best opportunities were in a similar role in two Ronald Colman vehicles, one earlier in the year and the other at its end: the blonde flirt in *The Devil to Pay* and the sympathetic Joyce in *Arrowsmith*.

Critics were asking when Loy was going to be raised to official stardom, but in Hollywood there was only one producer who could see that she had that extra something – Irving Thalberg. He liked her so much in *Skyline* that he signed her to an MGM contract. She was just treading water at first – indeed, her parts got smaller: *Emma* (32) as Marie Dressler's daughter; *The Wet Parade*; *Vanity Fair*, as Becky in an almost unrecognizable modern version, made by an indie and hardly shown; *New Morals for Old*; *The Woman in Room 13* starring Elissa Landi (Fox); *Love Me Tonight*, as a wise-cracking man-hunter; *Thirteen Women*, as a (half-caste) homicidal maniac; and, back at MGM, *The Mask of Fu Manchu*, as Manchu's sadistic daughter, a role she considered virtually unplayable. But there were to be no more Oriental parts, and as with many another player, it was a loan-out which was to show her own studio what she could do, as Leslie Howard's vicious wife in *The Animal Kingdom*: she herself considered this her first real break in pictures. RKO liked her so much they kept her to play the tycoon's kind-hearted mistress in *Topaze* (33).

MGM decided to build Loy and for the first time officially listed her as one of their stars; after an abortive start as Ramon Novarro's mate in *The Barbarian* she was put into the sort of smart roles RKO had proved she could play: *The Prizefighter and the Lady*, a vehicle for boxer Max Baer and re-christened *Every Woman's Man* for Britain – Loy was his wife; *When Ladies Meet*, as the young writer; and *Penthouse*, as Warner Baxter's heart-of-gold mistress (demonstrating, said Picturegoer, what strides she had made in her acting ability). *Nightflight* was the first of several movies with Clark Gable and the first of Loy's Perfect Wives (only here she was William Gargan's). In *Men in White* (34) Gable was a doctor and she a flighty society dame, and in *Manhattan Melodrama* he was a gangster and she a nice girl who deserts him for politician William Powell. (The film gained notoriety – and a quite undeserved popularity – by virtue of the fact that Dillinger the gangster was trapped while watching it and shot while emerging from the cinema).

The director was W. S. Van Dyke, who became convinced that Loy and Powell could be profitably teamed in comedy; MGM saw them both primarily as heavies, but gave the go-ahead for a film version of Dashiell Hammett's light-hearted murder mystery, *The Thin Man*. The result swept the world. It was something quite new: Nick and Norah Charles, affluent private-eye and wife, bantering, and affectionately bitching each other; their chief interest seemed to be alcohol, and neither could be said not to have a philandering nature. She: 'Go ahead see if I care. But I think it's a dirty trick to bring me all the way to New York just to make a widow of me.' He: 'You wouldn't be a widow long.' She: 'You bet I wouldn't.' He: 'Not with all your money.' There was a spontaneous gaiety (it looks fresh today) which had much to do with the understated incisiveness of the stars' playing. Their styles matched perfectly and it is obvious (as Loy has confirmed) that they loved acting together. The team became one of the keystones of MGM in the 30s.

Now a big star, Loy was wasted in one of the manifold screen versions of the 'Fraulein Doktor' tale, *Stamboul Quest* with George Brent, but was Powell's wife again in *Evelyn Prentice*, on trial for murdering a blackmailer, with him defending her. She was loaned to Columbia for Capra's delightful version of Damon Runyan's horse-racing tale, *Broadway Bill*, with Baxter; and to Paramount for *Wings in the Dark* (35) with Cary Grant, playing a stunt flyer. As she emerged into the limelight, Loy was seen to be one of the least typical of movie actessses: a rather shy, quiet girl, living with her mother, working hard without any great ambition to be Queen of the Lot. She considered that she had been working *too* hard, and went to New York and then Europe on an unauthorized vacation, passing up a couple of films with Powell. MGM forgave her, and acceded to her demand for a salary raise. She returned for *Whipsaw* but Powell was not ready, and Spencer Tracy replaced him. She was a jewel thief and he her pursuer. Said Time: '... but Myrna Loy's charm and Tracy's skilful underplaying are assets that no picture can have and be bad.'

Wife vs Secretary (36) had Jean Harlow as the latter and Gable as the husband; *Petticoat Fever* was a farce with Robert Montgomery; Loy was Billie Burke, the wife of *The Great Ziegfeld* (Powell); and at 20th gave one of her best performances opposite Warner Baxter in a tale of marital discord, *To Mary With Love* ('They say the movies should be more like life–I think life should be more like the movies'). After *Libeled Lady* (Powell, Tracy, Harlow) and *After the Thin Man* (it was up to the original), she accepted the part that Joan Crawford turned down in *Parnell* (37)–Katie O'Shea. It harmed neither her nor Gable, and in Ed Sullivan's poll they were voted King and Queen of Hollywood. Loy also entered the exhibitors' top 10 list, trailing Shirley Temple and Sonja Henie as the nation's biggest female draw (in 1937 and 1938). She was happily back with Powell in the screwball *Double Wedding*, but less happy as the spoilt ingénue in *Manproof* (38) with Franchot Tone, an insufferably dull drama. She was admirable as a country girl who marries *Test Pilot* Gable, and as his romantic interest in *Too Hot to Handle*; but neither she nor Robert Taylor found *Lucky Night* (39) very lucky. 'Here's a galloping case of whimsy,' said Photoplay.

In a deliberate attempt to get away from type-casting Loy asked 20th whether she could play the silly socialite who found redemption when *The Rains Came*. Then she did a run with Powell: *Another Thin Man*, *I Love You Again* (40), the deft *Third Finger Left Hand* (partnered instead by Melvyn Douglas), *Love Crazy* (41), a minor classic out of the old divorce game–mad, vulgar, logical and witty, and *Shadow of the Thin Man*. There were rumours of retirement: Loy had been upset over two broken marriages (she married twice again, first to writer-producer Gene Markey, who had been married to Joan Bennett and Hedy Lamarr); she asked MGM for leave-of-absence and spent the war years working full-time for the Red Cross. MGM announced that Irene Dunne would replace her in the next Thin Man movie, but in fact Loy did it, her only wartime picture, *The Thin Man Goes Home* (44). It finished her contract, but she promised MGM she would return if ever they wanted her to do another comedy with Powell. In 1947 she did: *Song of the Thin Man*, but like the 1944 one it was, in her own

Most of the Myrna Loy - William Powell pictures were smart comedies with sophisticated dialogue, but Love Crazy *(41), being mainly slapstick, was a new departure. It was still very funny. They were married at the start of the film–and at the very end–and in-between-whiles dickered with divorce.*

Myrna Loy and Jack Lemmon on the set of The April Fools *(69): Lemmon also produced and it was he who persuaded Loy back before the cameras after a nine-year absence. She and Charles Boyer played a middle-aged couple who encouraged Lemmon and Catherine Deneuve to run off together.*

words, 'very bad indeed'.

In 1945 she attended the inital meetings of the United Nations, and filmed thereafter only occasionally, as a free-lance. She sought to change her image but hardly did: she was soon playing perfect mothers. There was a period comedy at Universal with Don Ameche, *So Goes My Love* (46): said Richard Winnington, 'Myrna Loy is much too lovely and clever for such nonsense'; and then came the apotheosis of her screen wife portrayal, *The Best Years of Our Lives*. The part was built up for her because Goldwyn and Wyler were determined to have her and she considered it too small; Fredric March was the husband and Teresa Wright her daughter. The film was a huge success. RKO released, and Loy had a three-year contract at that studio, but did only two more films there – *The Bachelor and the Bobby Soxer* (47) with Cary Grant, and after the *Thin Man* film Grant and Melvyn Douglas were her leading men in the amusing *Mr Blandings Builds His Dream House* (48). At Republic, under Lewis Milestone's direction, she was the mother in John Steinbeck's *The Red Pony* (49), but, like some other Milestone films, it didn't turn out as well as expected.

She signed a one-picture deal with Korda in Britain, and it was announced as being *Love in Idleness* with Ralph Richardson; instead she did a perfectly dreadful sudser about a woman's affair with her step-daughter's boyfriend (Richard Greene) while her husband goes blind: *That Dangerous Age*. For 20th she played the mother of a large brood in *Cheaper by the Dozen* (50) and its success led to a sequel, *Belles on Their Toes* (52). She accepted an assignment to be one of the US representatives on UNESCO in Paris, and while there took a poor part (but with star billing) in a poor comedy, *The Ambassador's Daughter* (56). Back in Hollywood, she played an alcoholic wife (Robert Ryan's) in *Lonelyhearts* (58) and an alcoholic mother (Paul Newman's) in *From the Terrace* (60). For this and for *Midnight Lace* – as Doris Day's aunt, the best thing in the film – she accepted below-title billing.

She made her stage debut in 1962 in 'There Must Be a Pony' but it didn't reach New York. She came to the Theatre rather late, as she ruefully admits, but enjoys acting, and has since toured in 'Barefoot in the Park'. She would like to film again, she said in 1967, but did not want to play the sort of 'psychotic, disintegrated old bags' which were being offered to the older actresses; other offers 'that have come up have, frankly, not been exciting enough' (they include the Chinese Empress in *55 Days to Peking*, the mother of Lana Turner in *Madame X* which Kay Francis also turned down). In 1969 she did find a part she liked, in *The April Fools*, starring Jack Lemmon.

Paul Lukas

At the outset of his career, in the Silent days, Paul Lukas was cast as the suave Middle-European seducer. As he aged, his thoughts turned otherwise than to women, but he remained villainous – the epitome of that experienced Continental elegance that was always such a bogyman for Hollywood scriptwriters. He did it very well: smooth, sharply shod, upright, moustached and with sleek hair that was always slightly greying. To that extent he did what was required of him. He realized very early on that if he wanted a Hollywood career he was going to be type-cast and he simply played his specious lines as professionally as he knew how. He always regretted that his accent limited him. He did, now and then, get to play sympathetic parts, and for one of these he won his Oscar.

He was born on a train in Budapest in 1895 and received his stage training at the Actor's Academy of Hungary; he made his debut in the title role of Molnar's 'Liliom' in his native city in 1916 and for the next nine years played, says one source, 'every conceivable character in the works of Shakespeare, Chekhov, George Bernard Shaw, Oscar Wilde and Galsworthy'. He was also making films: *Sphynx* (17), *Udvari Levego*, *Sárga Árnyék* (20), *Little Fox*, *Névtelen Vár* (the first one to be shown outside Hungary, as *Castle Nameless*), *Masomód*, *Olavi*, *Szinésznо*, *New York Expresz Kábel* (21), *Hétszázéves Szerelem*, *A Szürkeruhás Hölgy* (22), *Lady Violette*, *Diadalmas Élet* (23) and *Egy Fiunak a Fele*. Max Reinhardt saw him on the Budapest stage and negotiated for him to act in Berlin and Vienna. In Vienna, Lukas made a film for UFA *Samson und Dalilah*, with Maria Corda as the other half of the title; the director was a fellow countryman who later achieved Hollywood success as Michael Curtiz.

Lukas returned to Budapest and was appearing on the stage there in 'Antonia' when he was seen by the head of Paramount, Adolph Zukor, there on a visit to what was his native land also. Zukor offered a Paramount contract and Lukas left for Hollywood. He made his bow in a Pola Negri picture, *Three Sinners* (28), and was then loaned out for the Colman-Banky *Two Lovers*. He made *Hot News* with Bebe Daniels; *The Night Watch* at Warners with Billie Dove; *The Loves of an Actress* and *The Woman From Moscow*, both with Negri; and *Manhattan Cocktail* with Nancy Carroll and Richard Arlen. He was then cast opposite Carroll in *The Shopworn Angel* (29): she had the title role, as the 'kept woman' who falls for the younger Gary Cooper. This was part-Talkie, and so, originally, was the *The Wolf of Wall Street*, but during production the studio liked it so much that the Silent sequences were re-done: Lukas's part was painstakingly dubbed by Lawford Davidson. His role, anyway, was already brief because of his accent: the stars were Carroll and George Bancroft (in the title role).

Lukas's future in the US was now in the balance. He had not reached the front rank of stars and therefore it would not harm his prestige to retire to smaller roles, which was what he did after some months of inactivity, in another Carroll vehicle, *Illusion*. He stayed with Paramount: *Halfway to Heaven* with Charles Buddy Rogers; *Slightly Scarlet* (30) starring Evelyn Brent and Clive Brook; *The Benson Murder Case* starring William Powell; *Young Eagles*, William A. Wellman's follow-up to his own *Wings*, again with Charles Buddy Rogers; *The Devil's Holiday* with Phillips Holmes and Carroll (replacing Jeanne Eagles, who had just died); *Grumpy*, who was British actor Cyril Maude reprising his famous stage role in his screen debut; and *Anybody's Woman*, as Ruth Chatterton's lover before she returned to husband Clive Brook. Lukas's accent had diminished enough to allow him to be Chatterton's leading man in her next two: it was he she had *The Right to Love* (31) and he with whom she was *Unfaithful*. Paramount thought their 'worldliness' well matched. In *City Streets* he was the vicious gang boss with whom Gary Cooper got involved, and in *The Vice Squad* an embassy attaché turned informer loved by Kay Francis. There followed: *Women Love Once*; *Beloved Bachelor*, starring, with Dorothy Jordan; *Strictly Dishonourable*, the film of Preston Sturges's play at Universal with Sidney Fox; *Working Girls* with Charles Buddy Rogers and Frances Dee; *Tomorrow and Tomorrow* (32) as a Viennese psychiatrist, with Chatterton; *No One Man*, one of the idle rich, opposite Carole Lombard; and *Thunder Below* with Tallulah Bankhead.

At this point Lukas left Paramount and began to free-lance. Nevertheless his next picture, *A Passport to Hell*, was like his last – only this time it was Elissa Landi who was the bone of contention in the lonely outpost. He then supported John Gilbert in *Downstairs* and Constance Bennett in *Rockabye* (33). He co-starred with Loretta Young in *Grand Slam* and then had a good part in James Whale's fine *A Kiss Before the Mirror* as the husband who murders his faithless wife, almost prompting Frank Morgan to follow suit with his, Nancy Carroll. Universal produced, and signed Lukas to a loose two-year contract. He did *Sing Sinner Sing* at Majestic; *Captured!* at Warners as a German officer; *The Secret of the Blue Room*, a gumshoe thriller with Gloria Stuart; and *Little Women* (34), as the shy and gentle Professor Bhaer, virtually his first chance in Hollywood to exploit his versatility. With one exception, his next seven pictures were all for Universal: *By Candlelight* with Landi; *The Countess of Monte Cristo* with Fay Wray in the title role, a film extra posing as a countess and unmasking crook Lukas; *Glamour*, an Edna Ferber story with Constance Cummings as the showgirl who becomes a star, and Lukas as her composer husband; *I Give My Love*, a mother-love story with Wynne Gibson, who had been his mistress in *City Streets*; *Affairs of a Gentleman*, a murder mystery, as a thriller-writer; *The Fountain* at RKO, as Ann Harding's German officer husband; and *The Gift of Gab*, a guest appearance in a 'radio' musical whose cast included Ruth Etting, Ethel Waters and Gene Austin.

Universal had done very well by Lukas but had not succeeded in turning him into a top star. Free-lancing again, he was in Bs: Paramount's *Father Brown Detective* (35), G. K. Chesterton's character played by Walter Connolly, and Lukas miscast as his prey; *The Casino Murder Case*, as Philo Vance detective, with Alison Skipworth; and *The Age of Indiscretion*, a divorce story with Madge Evans. He then received an invitation from RKO to play Athos in *The Three Musketeers*, originally planned in colour with a starry cast, but now much less glamorous with Walter Abel (fresh from Broadway) as D'Artagnan, Onslow Stevens and Moroni Olsen: still, it was good if not very popular. At Warners he supported Kay Francis and Ian Hunter in *I Found Stella Parish*, and his

Thunder Below *(32) was one of Paul Lukas's best early performances, but it is impossible to believe that he and Charles Bickford could so easily ignore such a vibrant personality as Tallulah.*

next two parts were small, if telling. In *Dodsworth* (36) he was the Continental charmer with whom Chatterton dallies – he played it beautifully – and in *Ladies in Love* he was Constance Bennett's 'protector'. His only other work at that time was supporting Madge Evans and Edmund Lowe in *Espionage* (37); he then departed for Britain where he stayed long enough to suggest that he was starting a new career.

The British Studios were surprised to find that Lukas's off-screen personality was light-hearted and friendly, in contrast to his screen image; nevertheless, they conspired to re-present the sinister Lukas: *Brief Ecstasy*, a silly melo directed by Edmond T. Greville, and *Mutiny on the Elsinore*. *Dinner at the Ritz*, with Annabella, had moments of gaiety but then came *The Lady Vanishes* (38), where he did for Hitchcock his Continental menace act. He did it again, back in Hollywood, in *Confessions of a Nazi Spy*, with Edward G. Robinson, and still in Hollywood was in *Captain Fury*, in a small part. He returned to Britain for *A Window in London* and the remake of *The Chinese Bungalow* (40) with Kay Walsh, in both of which he was the heavy – but they were good parts. Back in the States he remained nasty but his parts were small: *Strange Cargo* as a fascist, starring Clark Gable, and *The Ghost Breakers* with Bob Hope. After supporting parts in *The Monster and the Girl* (41) and *They Dare Not Love*, a trite anti-Nazi film with George Brent and Martha Scott, he accepted the offer of a play in New York.

This was Lillian Hellman's 'Watch on the Rhine', and he played an undercover agent arrived in Washington, a man whose life was dedicated to fighting the Nazi cause: the character was something of a cipher, but Lukas gave him dimensions that encompassed both his past and future (or lack of it). He got great reviews and there was seldom any doubt that he would repeat in the film version that was inevitable: Warners made it in 1943 with Bette Davis as his wife and Lucille Watson also repeating as his mother-in-law, and Lukas won both the New York Critics Award and the Best Actor Oscar. Star parts were offered him again, even if the next three were all anti-Nazi dramas: *Hostages* with Luise Rainer; *Uncertain Glory* (44), another fine performance as the detective in this Errol Flynn drama; and *Address Unknown*.

His good fortune didn't hold; all he was offered were the sort of melodramas he had done at the start of his career: *Experiment Perilous* (45), very villainous, with Hedy Lamarr; *Deadline at Dawn* (46) with Susan Hayward; *Temptation* with Merle Oberon;

Paul Lukas, Merle Oberon and George Brent in Temptation *(46). It was Universal that was tempted – to re-do this played-out old plot: audiences weren't.*

Whispering City (47); and *Berlin Express* (48) with Oberon. After a two-year absence he headed the supporting cast of *Kim* (50), as a lama. Then he returned to the stage: 'Call Me Madam' (51) and 'Flight into Egypt' (52). He had his last good film role in Disney's *20,000 Leagues Under the Sea* (54), as the professor, though the MFB thought him 'colourless'. He had bits in *The Roots of Heaven* (58); *Scent of Mystery* (60), a film produced by Mike Todd Jr that was supposed to bring the 'smellies' to cinema-going via a device under the seats–but the thing that stank was the film; *The Four Horsemen of the Apocalypse* (61), a bigger part as one of the invading Germans; *Tender Is the Night*, as a psychiatrist; *55 Days at Peking* (63); *Fun in Acapulco*, starring Elvis Presley; *Lord Jim* (65) and *Sol Madrid* (67), a thriller starring David McCallum.

Lukas has been married twice. He was widowed in 1962 and married again the following year.

Ida Lupino

Ida Lupino was a strong, convincing actress who for a brief period looked like a challenger for the Bette Davis crown at Warners. Indeed, she was sedulously built up by that studio as a successor: but somehow she didn't quite get the breaks, and retreated behind the camera where her solid professionalism surprised no one. However, of her blonde cutie period at the beginning, there is very little to be said that is complimentary.

She was born in London in 1918, into a British vaudeville family of Italian origin. Her father was Stanley Lupino, who had left the acrobatic troupe to become a star comedian in revue, pantomime and films. Ida was trained at RADA while still very young; and she had experience at this time in tours and as an extra. Her film chance came when Allan Dwan, filming in Britain, wanted a young girl who seemed a likely trap for a much older, married author: *Her First Affair* (33). She was much less 'trampy' in some of *Money for Speed* starring John Loder, and when Paramount saw these sequences they thought she might be ideal for their *Alice in Wonderland*. Meanwhile, she was making a lot of films: *High Finance* starring Gibb McLaughlin; *Prince of Arcadia*; *The Ghost Camera* with Henry Kendall; and Ivor Novello's *I Lived With You*. Paramount signed her, but she was decidedly too sexy for Alice, so they starred her in *The Search for Beauty* (34) with Larry 'Buster' Crabbe. Then she did two with Richard Arlen,

Ida Lupino and John Garfield in The Sea Wolf *(41), the fifth of the seven movies based on Jack London's novel of that name.*

Come on Marines (she had little to do) and *Ready for Love*, a small-town tale; next she was the ingénue in *Paris in Spring* (35) which was the first of the vehicles intended to make native-born Mary Ellis a star after her successes on the London stage. She was charming, but didn't make the grade.

The studio were as disenchanted with Lupino: through *Smart Girl*, *Peter Ibbetson* and *Anything Goes* (36) her parts got successively smaller, until (fortunately) in the last of these, she is hardly there at all. But she had a good chance in *One Rainy Afternoon* at United Artists, a satirical comedy with Robert Young and Francis Lederer; and then Paramount put her into *Yours for the Asking* starring George Raft. The same UA producers borrowed her again for *The Gay Desperado*, a musical starring Nino Martini: it was a sleeper, and due to

From the publicity desk: 'She paints; is simply out of her mind about lampshades . . . enthusiatic over $16.75 dresses' (*Photoplay*).

Mamoulian's sparkling direction grabbed good notices and business. Paramount loaned out Lupino again: for *Sea Devils* (37) with Victor McLaglen at RKO, where she had little to do; and a B, *Let's Get Married*, with Ralph Bellamy at Columbia. On her home lot, she had an uninteresting part in Jack Benny's *Artists and Models*: so, on the basis of her success on loan, she asked to be released from her contract. Paramount complied; but after a job in RKO's *Fight for Your Lady*, a comedy with John Boles and Jack Oakie, she didn't appear in a picture for over a year, and Picturegoer later reported that she had tried unsuccessfully to get work in Britain. In 1938 she married British-born Louis Hayward.

Finally she got parts in two Bs at Columbia: *The Lone Wolf Spy Hunt* (39) (Variety found her 'at times ridiculous'); and *The Lady and the Mob*, starring Fay Bainter. Her English accent helped her get a part in 20th's *The Adventures of Sherlock Holmes*, and, although it was a wooden performance, it was a contributory factor in Paramount asking her back for *The Light That Failed* (40); they had also been wont to cast her as a tart, and as such in this she gave the first strong indications that she might have talent. Warners thought so, signed her to a long-term contract, and gave her the part of Alan Hale's floozy wife in *They Drive by Night*. According to Jack L. Warner's memoir, Lupino stayed away during filming because an astrologer had told her the film would be bad luck: $½ million had been spent and the crew were put on another picture before she returned. He implies that she was not a very easy star to handle, but she got another fine part, opposite Humphrey Bogart and top-billed, in *High Sierra* (41). Said William Whitebait: 'Ida Lupino gives us the best moll I have ever seen.' She had strong parts in *The Sea Wolf* and *Out of the Fog*, and then went to Columbia with husband Hayward for *Ladies in Retirement*, as the steely housekeeper who murders her employer, a vulgar ex-actress, rather than see her two mental sisters put away. And the next two were on loan-out, at 20th: *Moontide* (42) with Jean Gabin, which turned out to be a re-hash of *Quai des Brumes* set in California. Lupino had the Michele Morgan role of the tramp-waif; there was trouble during production, and Gabin's Hollywood career was killed at the start (he did make *The Imposter* later, also unsuccessful). *Life Begins at 8.30* was a theatrical tale with Monty Woolley and Cornel Wilde.

She returned to Warners to do it *The Hard Way* (43), an ambitious girl who doesn't care how she makes it to the top – a 'Lady Macbeth of the slums' as Picturegoer put it; but at last people took her seriously as an actress: the New York Critics voted her the Year's Best. She was in three starry efforts: RKO's *Forever and a Day*; *Thank Your Lucky Stars*, jitterbugging with Olivia de Havilland; and *Hollywood Canteen* (44); then, more suitably, in *In Our Time*, as an Englishwoman in love with Polish aristocrat Paul Henried at the time of the Nazi invasion. *Pillow to Post* (45) was a minor comedy; and *Devotion* an idiotic biopic on the Brontës (she was Emily). She got better chances in *The Man I Love* (46) – he was Robert Alda and she was a torch singer; *Deep Valley* (47), as a backwoods girl with a speech impediment; and *Escape Me Never*, in Elizabeth Bergner's old part as a European peasant girl weeping over the heel she loves (Errol Flynn). It was her last film for Warners: she had acted conscientiously for them in a series of inferior soap operas, but she ranked after the other three Warner ladies who were making similar films – Davis, Joan Crawford and Ann Sheridan. Of them, only Davis was consistently able to rise above her material, and, having done so often enough, she was in a position (during the time that Lupino was at Warners) to demand the best that was going.

Lupino played another torch singer in an enjoyable mish-mash, *Road House* (48), and that year married a Columbia executive, Collier Young. She appeared in a Columbia Western, *Lust for Gold* (49), and went into TV, writing and producing. Out of this came a film about a pregnancy, *Not Wanted*, which she produced (it starred Sally Forrest and Keefe Brazelle). She was the *Woman in Hiding* (50) at Universal, co-starring with Howard Duff, whom she later married, but she also managed to put together another low-budget film, *Never Fear* – directing this time. The (modest) critical success of her two productions brought her a deal at RKO. She directed and scripted *Outrage* and directed *Hard Fast and Beautiful* (51); still at the same studio she played a blind girl in *On Dangerous Ground* with Robert Ryan, and a woman menaced by a killer (Ryan again) in *Beware My Lovely* (52) from Mel Dinelli's play 'The Man'; and she directed *The Hitchhiker*. In 1953 she appeared in *Jennifer*, and directed *The Bigamist*, which starred Joan Fontaine (now married to Lupino's ex-husband Young). She was in *Private Hell 36* (54) with Duff; *Women's Prison* (55), as its sadistic boss; *The Big Knife* – the only poor performance in an otherwise well-acted picture, as the wife of film-star Jack Palance; Fritz Lang's *While the City Sleeps* (56); and *Strange Intruder* with Edmund Purdom. A middling list. She has continued to direct for movies (*The Trouble With Angels*, 66, etc.) and TV. In the late 50s she and Duff had their own TV series, 'Mr Adams and Eve'.

Jeanette MacDonald

Jeanette MacDonald said that if she ever published her memoirs she would call the book 'The Iron Butterfly': that, she knew, was what some people called her. Like most operetta-ladies, she was a butt for comics and an object of derision to some of those more concerned with the higher reaches of cinema art – which was really getting her all wrong. She was a superb comedienne, and even in that age of great comedy-players she could run rings round most of her rivals: as the daffy heroine of Lubitsch's boudoir comedies, she established a standard which others sought to reach. She was a critics' pet – vivacious, excessively pretty – at the time when she first carried her brand of self-parody to Nelson Eddy. There are indications that after a while she began to take the conventions of operetta seriously, and in her later films it is hard to defend her from charges of coyness and artificiality.

She was born in Philadelphia in either 1907 or 1901 – the latter date seems more likely as she made her New York debut in 1920, in the chorus of 'The Demi-Tasse Revue'. She had been schooled in singing and dancing and followed her sister Blossom into the chorus. By 1923 she had progressed to leading roles, and had her first success with 'The Magic Ring'. The Shuberts signed her to a contract, and gave her the ingénue role in the Gershwin's 'Tip Toes' (25). Among other shows, she starred in 'Bubbling Over' (26), and was in 'Angela' (28) when Richard Dix saw her and wanted her for his leading lady in *Nothing But the Truth*. Paramount tested her, but nixed her as his or anybody else's leading lady. Lubitsch, however, saw the test, and was impressed enough to take train to Chicago to see her in 'Boom Boom', whereupon he knew that she was just the thing for *The Love Parade* (29), as the Queen who would convert rakish consort Maurice Chevalier.

The reception of both film and MacDonald was cordial, and Paramount co-starred her with Dennis King in a coloured (two-tone) version of *The Vagabond King* (30). Picture-goer, one of the dissenters over her first film performance, now said: 'she seems absolutely lost and incapable of rising to the opportunities the part offers'. But Lubitsch still liked her, and put her into *Monte Carlo* with Jack Buchanan, singing 'Beyond the Blue Horizon' in a railway train in her camiknickers. She was then in a Jack Oakie comedy about castaways, *Let's Go Native*, which was nonsense but enjoyable. Paramount then dropped her. At UA she did a pretentious musical, *The Lottery Bride*, arriving at Nome on a ship and belting out a Friml song with gusto; and then did three comedies for Fox: the piquant *Oh for a Man!*; *Don't Bet on Women* (31), starring Edmund Lowe and Roland Young; and *Annabelle's Affairs* with Young and Victor McLaglen, the remake of an old Billie Burke picture.

After a concert tour of Europe (she had aspirations to grand opera), Lubitsch persuaded Paramount to take her back for two more with Chevalier, *One Hour With You* (32) and *Love Me Tonight*, films of immortal facetiousness. However, musicals in 1932 were 10 a penny, and even goodies like these

Jeanette MacDonald sings for her supper in The Firefly (*37*). *The gentleman–glimpsed only this briefly in the film–was Ralph Byrd. Her leading man was not Nelson Eddy but Allan Jones.*

failed to attract. MacDonald was out of work again, and she accepted a British offer from Herbert Wilcox to make *The Queen's Affair* with Herbert Marshall, with the possibility of *Bitter Sweet* to follow. The first was in rehearsal when the stars left: no explanation was ever given. Anna Neagle took MacDonald's parts in both films, and the latter was certainly soon at work again. Musicals were back in vogue, via the success of *42nd Street*, and MGM signed her for two pictures, the first of which was to be *I Married an Angel*, a spicy farce with Rodgers and Hart songs: but the new Production Code turned down the script (and the composers departed with their songs, to make a Broadway hit out of them). MGM offered her two alternatives, the film of Jerome Kern's *The Cat and the Fiddle* and/or *Naughty Marietta*. She loathed the idea of both of them, but agreed finally to do the Jerome Kern film (34), with Ramon Novarro. *Marietta* was postponed because they couldn't find a suitable leading man, though MGM were considering teaming MacDonald with a new star, singer Nelson Eddy, in a (straight) remake of *The Prisoner of Zenda*.

Meanwhile, Chevalier and Lubitsch had moved to MGM to make a new version of *The Merry Widow* with Grace Moore; there was a dispute about billing, and MacDonald stepped in. 'The picture was so expensive that only a box-office miracle could have made it profitable. The miracle did not occur' (Deems Taylor). MGM signed her to a five-year contract, and decided to put Eddy with her in *Naughty Marietta* (35). Then, when Grace Moore couldn't make the schedule for *Rose Marie* (36), they were teamed again. Directed with humour by W. S. Van Dyke, it stands today as their best movie: MacDonald's performance as a petulant prima donna has asperity and style, at least until she succumbs to Eddy and the Indian Love Call. She was also rather terrific in the next, *San Francisco*, a property that she had sold to the studio on the proviso that Gable co-star: he and Jack Holt fought over her–at least until the Earthquake. It was a big hit, and brought MacDonald into the top 10 draws of 1936 (she never made the list thereafter; but in Britain she was one of the top 10 from 1937–42 inclusive).

MGM dusted off another hoary old property, *Maytime* (37), and the Eddy and MacDonald voices again blended in harmony. It was her own favourite film (she liked working under Robert Z. Leonard's direction) and a wow at the time, a banal piece about a singer who marries her impresario (John Barrymore) rather than the student (Eddy) she loves; it ends with an aged MacDonald watching the young spirits of herself and Eddy warbling among the cherry blossoms. As a change of pace, she was given Allan Jones (somewhat less wooden an actor than Eddy) for *The Firefly*: improbably, they were both master-spies ('You're a clever woman, señorita, but not clever enough'), but the film was good of its own crumby kind, and a big success.

However, fans were clamouring for Eddy and MacDonald. It wasn't until now that MGM came to consider them as a permanent team, and they were together in *The Girl of the Golden West* (38), the old Belasco play with a new, non-Puccini score, and in *Sweethearts*, the studio's first all-colour film, and one of the top money-makers of 1938. She had a new (non-singing) co-star, Lew Ayres, for *Broadway Serenade* (39), but was back with Eddy again in the risible *New Moon* (40) and a lavish chocolate-box version of *Bitter Sweet* (Coward loathed it). MGM bought from other studios both *The Vagabond King* and *Show Boat* for the team, among other properties, but instead MacDonald did a new version of *Smilin' Through* (41) with Brian Aherne and her husband, Gene Raymond; then she and Eddy did something much less saccharine, *I Married an Angel* (42) returned with thanks from Broadway; but the public liked not the change. And *Cairo*, a send-up of spy films with Robert Young, was none too successful. MacDonald's contract had been extended by a couple of years in 1940, but now it wasn't. She left the studio. She had at one time been Louis B. Mayer's favourite star, but at the time of *The Firefly* she had gone over his head to the New York office about the dubbing of her own voice in the foreign editions of her films; the quarrel was never patched up and she herself believed that that was why she was dropped.

Nelson Eddy and Jeanette MacDonald in the last picture they made together, I Married an Angel (*42*). *MGM had announced the split before it went into production, but the public did not rush to see them together for the last time–perhaps because this was not a typical vehicle for them.*

Certainly there had been only slight indications that her popularity was waning, even if the changing taste of the war years favoured the younger girls like Lana Turner. MacDonald took the chance of this hiatus to go into grand opera–with Ezio Pinza she sang 'Romeo and Juliet' in Montreal and 'Faust' in Chicago, but the notices were not overwhelmingly favourable. She did a guest spot (singing two songs) in *Follow the Boys* (44) and, at the behest of Joe Pasternak, returned to MGM for two mother-roles, in *The Birds and the Bees* (48) with José Iturbi, and *The Sun Comes Up* (49), a sentimental piece with Lassie and Claude Jarman Jr. Neither did good business, and MacDonald settled into semi-retirement, realizing that her type of movie was out-moded–though she might well have continued in the sort of parts that Ina Claire had once done. But the less sentimental aspect of MacDonald's screen character was virtually forgotten. She did some concerts from time to time, appeared in cabaret, and in stock in musicals like 'The King and I'. She died in 1965.

Her fans stayed remarkably faithful, and when MGM took to reviving her films with Eddy in the 50s, they found they could pack cinemas for limited bookings. In fact, MacDonald's fame well outlasted her career, and should survive as long as there's a market for Palm Court romance.

Aline MacMahon

Aline MacMahon did not want to be a star. After her third picture Warners offered her the chance of stardom but she turned it down and remained a leading character actress. She was, perhaps, not really suitable star material. She was too tall, a little ungainly; her features–her mouth, her eyes–were too big for classical beauty. She had a lovely presence and sharp common sense, which made her ideal for the secretary roles she played several times. In her first film, *Five Star Final*, she was secretary to Edward G. Robinson, and she had every detail right; unlike most film typists she did not merely tap on her machine: it seemed to be part of her. In a couple of sentences she conveyed much of her life outside the office – or what there was of it, for she doted on Edward G. more than somewhat, though her yen was masked under a string of barbed, unfazed comments on his behaviour. She was later publicized as 'the perfect screen secretary', a description which just as effectively concealed her very real abilities. She was one of the screen's few perfect actresses.

She was born in McKeesport, Pennsylvania, in 1899, the daughter of an Irish telegraph operator who wrote stories and articles on the side and later took up journalism as a profession. She was educated at Erasmus Hall and then Barnard College, where she enjoyed acting so much that she decided to take it up professionally. After graduating, she joined a stock company in Yorkville and later got a small Broadway part in 'The Mirage' (21). She joined the Neighborhood Playhouse, where she made a hit in one of their 'Grand Street Follies' with a take-off of Gertrude Lawrence. This led to a contract with the Shuberts and a role in the 1925 edition of 'Artists and Models'. She scored a great success in a revival of O'Neill's 'Beyond the Horizon' (26), and later appeared in 'Spread Eagle', 'Her First Affair', 'Maya' (28) and 'Winter Bound' (29). She was then engaged by Moss Hart to do a play he had written with George S. Kauffmann about the coming of Talkies to Hollywood, 'Once in a Lifetime', specifically to play the passé vaudeville star who teaches Speech to the Silent stars: but the New York management preferred Jean Dixon, and MacMahon was offered instead the West Coast company. On the night after the Los Angeles opening, she was approached by Warners for the role in *Five Star Final* (31). This brought her rave notices and meanwhile she did do 'Once in a Lifetime' on Broadway. Warners were waiting with a contract, which she signed on condition that filming was restricted to certain periods so that she could live in New York where her architect husband practised (Clarence S. Stein; they were married in 1928 and remain married).

Her contract with Warners called for four films a year: *The Heart of New York* (32) with Jewish comedians Dale and Smith, as the tenement janitress; *The Mouthpiece*, as secretary to Warren William, who was carrying on with fellow worker Sidney Fox; *Weekend Marriage*, as Loretta Young's sister; *One Way Passage*, as the bogus countess; *Life Begins*, as a nurse; and Universal's film version of *Once in a Lifetime*. Richard Watts Jr wrote in the New York Herald Tribune: 'She provides the best acting of the picture – a customary occurrence in the films in which Miss MacMahon appears.' She certainly gave a beautiful performance in *Silver Dollar*, as the wife who Understands when Edward G. Robinson dallies with Bebe Daniels. She was with Loretta Young again in *The Life of Jimmy Dolan* (33), and was the most practical of the *Gold Diggers of 1933* – she landed millionaire Guy Kibbee. She played opposite Richard Barthelmess in William A. Wellman's *Heroes for Sale*, comforting him when wife Young is killed; and was Paul Muni's mother in *The World Changes*, ageing throughout the picture. *Heat Lightning* (34) was a melodrama based on a play by Leon Abrams and George Abbot with MacMahon (top-billed) and sister Ann Dvorak running a gas station at a tourist spot suddenly invaded by Reno divorcees and robbers, including Ruth Donnelly, Glenda Farrell, Preston Foster and Lyle Talbot. Dvorak longed for excitement and got it. In *Side Streets* Dvorak was the threat to her marriage; said Photoplay: 'Aline MacMahon's characterization of the love-starved woman who marries a jobless sailor (Paul Kelly) is superb.'

Five Star Final (*31*): *Aline MacMahon, the perfect secretary, gets a shock from a telephone caller about her boss, newspaper editor Edward G. Robinson.*

The Merry Frinks was a modest comedy in which MacMahon was married to Hugh Herbert, and Kibbee was his wealthy uncle who thinks she's too good for him. Warners liked the combination of Kibbee and MacMahon so much that they co-starred them together in four more consecutive films: *Big Hearted Herbert*, with Kibbee as the grouchy husband whom she finally decides to reform; as *Babbitt* and his wife in this competent version of Sinclair Lewis's best-seller; *While the Patient Slept* (35), a murder mystery; and *Mary Jane's Pa*, in which they're married again, part, and come together again. MacMahon liked acting with Kibbee and didn't mind that because he was 13 years older than she, Warners moved her into an older age-group; but she didn't like the sameness of the parts. She asked to be released from her contract, and after some hesitation Warners agreed.

MGM immediately put her into three pictures: *I Live My Life*, supporting Joan Crawford; *Ah Wilderness!*, as the spinster aunt in love with Wallace Beery; and *Kind Lady*, based on a Hugh Walpole story, in the title role, terrorized by Basil Rathbone; MGM also tested her for the lead in *The Good Earth*–and when she didn't get it, she visited China. She was off the screen for more than a year, then returned as Grace Moore's secretary in *When You're in Love* (37). She did 'Candida' in stock, and made occasional stage appearances over the next few years. Her film appearances became rare: *Back Door to Heaven* (39), as a school-teacher in this Paramount programmer; *Out of the Fog* (41), as Ida Lupino's shrewish mother; and *The Lady Is Willing* (42), as stage star Marlene Dietrich's secretary. In *Tish* she and Marjorie Main and Zasu Pitts were three middle-aged ladies constantly getting into hot water. She was in *Stage Door Canteen* (43) and was Walter Huston's wife in *Dragon Seed* (44), had more featured roles in *Guest in the House* and *The Mighty McGurk* (46).

Her best film part in years was in Zinnemann's *The Search* (48), of which Albert Johnson wrote a while later (in Sight and Sound, 1955): 'Here is Aline MacMahon as Mrs Mallory, the careworn directress of this outpost of destitute youngsters. Her uniform somehow enhances a warm, matriarchal sympathy, and although she is a secondary figure, one is curious to know more about her. This is MacMahon's forte, to make everything she does stick in the memory. She brings a nobility to the part, a kind of native sagacity that lingered in my childhood impressions of her as one of the sharp-tongued, brittle *Gold Diggers of 1933*. . . .' After that her film appearances were disappointingly few, and most of them

Fred Zinnemann's The Search *(48) was one of the best pictures of the 40s, and Aline MacMahon was superb as a voluntary officer looking after displaced persons.*

were unworthy: *Roseanna McCoy* (49), a silly Goldwyn melodrama with Farley Granger and Joan Evans; *The Flame and the Arrow* (50), as a crone; *The Eddie Cantor Story* (53), as his grandmother; *The Man From Laramie* (55), as a lonely rancher; *Cimarron* (60), well down the cast list as the newspaper proprietor; *The Young Doctors* (61), as a kindly doctor; and *Diamond Head* (62), as a Hawaiian woman.

She did another lovely job in the small role of Judy Garland's dresser-companion in *I Could Go on Singing* (63): anyone who had coped with Edward G. Robinson, Grace Moore and Dietrich could handle Garland, and MacMahon's attitude of scepticism and affection was entirely right, and unforgettable. She was also fine in *All the Way Home* with Jean Simmons and Robert Preston, as Aunt Hannah, a part that she had played on the stage. Other stage appearances over the last three decades: 'The Eve of St Mark' (42), 'The Confidential Clerk' (54), and 'A Day by the Sea' (55), all in New York; the Nurse in 'Romeo & Juliet' and the Countess in 'All's Well That Ends Well' (59) and Volumnia in 'Coriolanus' (65) in Stratford, Connecticut; and 'The Madwoman of Chaillot' (51) in Los Angeles. She has also done TV.

Fred MacMurray

Fred MacMurray's forte has been playing the all-American go-getter, genial and deceptively lazy–nice, but determined. It is not a characterization that offers much after a couple of viewings, but it has been available on average twice a year for the last 35 years; now and then MacMurray has abandoned it to play a heel–and it is perhaps significant that by far his best performances (and good acting by any standards) are as such in *Double Indemnity* and *The Apartment*.

His pre-Hollywood career isn't unlike the stories in which he used to appear. He was born in Kankakee, Illinois, in 1908, the son of a concert violinist. He was educated at a military academy, among other establishments, and studied for a time at the Chicago Art Institute–but while playing in school bands he decided to become a full-time saxophonist. His peregrinations took him to Hollywood and he worked as an extra–in *Girls Gone Wild* (28) among others; between films he worked with orchestras–sometimes as a vocalist–and recorded with Gus Arnheim. He joined the Californian Collegians, and with them played Broadway in a revue, 'Three's a Crowd' (30): Libby Holman sang 'Something to Remember You By' to him. In two further shows he doubled as saxophonist and featured player: 'The Third Little Show' and 'Roberta' (33).

Then–there were two studio versions–either a Paramount talent scout saw him in 'Roberta', or he went to Hollywood and signed on with Central Casting. But certainly he was under contract to Paramount in 1934: he had been loaned out to RKO for *Grand Old Girl* (35) with May Robson when Claudette Colbert was looking for a leading man for *The Gilded Lily*. She saw his screen test and this became the first of several co-starring comedies–and a big success.

Paramount put him into *Car 99* and *Men Without Names*, a gangster film with Madge Evans: both were programmers, but his success in the Colbert film made him the hottest tip in town. Katharine Hepburn at RKO asked for him for *Alice Adams*; Carole Lombard okayed him as a replacement for George Raft in *Hands Across the Table*; and Colbert wanted him again for *The Bride Comes Home*: it was his seventh film within a year, and by the time it was shown he was established. He did *The Trail of the Lonesome Pine* (36) with Henry Fonda and Sylvia Sidney; *Thirteen Hours by Air*, a comedy with

The Gilded Lily (*35*). *At the time the lady was Queen of the Paramount lot, but these were first leading roles for the two men: Claudette Colbert with Fred MacMurray and Ray Milland. It was directed by Mitchell Leisen.*

Murder on their minds: Barbara Stanwyck and Fred MacMurray plot the destruction of her husband – the perfect murder – in Billy Wilder's classic Double Indemnity *(44).*

Joan Bennett; *The Princess* (Lombard) *Comes Across*; and *The Texas Rangers* with Jean Parker, a good Western directed by King Vidor and originally meant for Gary Cooper.

Apart from this one MacMurray's abilities had so far not been stretched; but he was entirely misplaced as a swashbuckling parson in an historical piece with Colbert, *Maid of Salem* (37); however, he was at ease again in the contemporary settings of *Champagne Waltz*, the third attempt by Paramount to make prima donna Gladys Swarthout into a movie star; *Swing High Swing Low* with Lombard; *Exclusive* with Frances Farmer; *True Confession* again with Lombard; and *Cocoanut Grove* (38), where he crooned a bit, with Harriet Hilliard. He and Ray Milland were the *Men With Wings*, a Technicolored history of aviation told in soap-opera terms; William A. Wellman's direction almost makes it work (he was a specialist in aeroplane pictures) and the characterless playing of the two men is somewhat offset by Louise Campbell as the girl they (naturally) both love. In *Sing You Sinners* Bing Crosby did most of the singing and MacMurray was his no-good brother – not mean, just lazy. He then did the first of several with Madeleine Carroll, *Cafe Society* (39). *Invitation to Happiness* with Irene Dunne took a prize for the year's most deceitful title, but *Honeymoon in Bali* with Carroll made up for it.

In 1940 he renewed his pact with Paramount for another five years, two films a year plus the right to make one outside one. He was not, after all, the big star that had been predicted when he started, but he was a dependable leading man, and this was probably his most popular period. Comedy remained his mainstay, but he did crop up in certain serious situations, such as *Remember the Night* (40), a good sentimental drama about an assistant DA who befriends the shoplifter (Barbara Stanwyck) he has to look after. He was loaned to 20th Century-Fox for *Little Old New York* with Alice Faye, and then to Columbia for *Too Many Husbands*: it was Jean Arthur who had them. There was a feeble Western with Paramount's new bid for the stellar stakes, Patricia Morison, *Rangers of Fortune*, and then two poor ones with Carroll, *Virginia* (41), an historical story, and *One Night in Lisbon*, which was a wartime tale set in Britain (Lisbon at that time was the leading neutral European city). MacMurray went to *New York Town* with Mary Martin and then to Warners for *Dive Bomber* with Errol Flynn. At Columbia he tamed Dietrich in *The Lady Is Willing* (42); then was dictated to by Rosalind Russell: *Take a Letter Darling*. *The Forest Rangers* was a singularly unattractive adventure story, in colour, with Paulette Goddard, not improved by the obtuseness of the character that MacMurray played, nor by a jingly song, 'We've got spurs that jingle jangle jingle'. He guested in *Star Spangled Rhythm* and then he and Russell took a *Flight for Freedom* (43); he and Joan Crawford were *Above Suspicion* at MGM, much heavier histrionics; he and Colbert had *No Time for Love*; and there was *Standing Room Only* (44) for him and Goddard. He stayed on the lighter side in *And the Angels Sing* with Betty Hutton and Dorothy Lamour.

According to director Billy Wilder, neither he nor Barbara Stanwyck wanted to do *Double Indemnity*: 'He in particular was afraid of what it would do to his image'– which was curious, because the shifty insurance agent/murderer of this was in no way less admirable than the bandleader he'd played in *And the Angels Sing*; eleven other actors had turned it down, and it brought MacMurray the best notices of his career. And naturally it boosted it: tradesters now talked of MacMurray as an *actor*. After two mild comedies, *Practically Yours* with Colbert and *Murder He Says* (45) with Helen Walker, he accepted a bid from 20th, much to Hollywood's surprise. He signed a new long-term contract that gave him approval over his films. He was announced for *A Tree Grows in Brooklyn* (for the part that won James Dunn a Best Supporting Oscar) and *Nob Hill*, but he presumably turned them down–certainly he didn't do them. What he did do was *Where Do We Go From Here?*, an historical/musical romp, and *Captain Eddie*, a routine biopic (Captain Richenbacker) with Lynn Bari. His co-star in the first of these was June Haver, who in later years gave up her career and went into a convent –which she left after MacMurray's wife died in 1953; they were married in 1954.

At Columbia he produced and starred in *Pardon My Past* (46)–a venture behind the camera that didn't encourage further efforts– and then did *Smoky* (46), a horsey picture with Anne Baxter. It was his last for 20th. It was announced that he was unhappy there and returning to Paramount on long-term contract. In fact, he did one film there, *Suddenly It's Spring* (47) with Paulette Goddard, and then started to free-lance. As an independent, he started off with a big hit, Universal's *The Egg and I* with Claudette Colbert, but thereafter settled into those programmers–mostly comedies, which were churned out in the late 40s and early 50s and which not only helped to kill the cinema-going habit, but murdered most of the stars as well. MacMurray just survived. The names and co-stars will suffice: *Singapore* with Ava Gardner; *The Miracle of the Bells* (48) with Frank Sinatra and Alida Valli; *On our Merry Way* in the sequence with William Demarest; *Don't Trust Your Husband* with Madeleine Carroll; *Family Honeymoon* with Colbert; *Father Was a Fullback* (49) with Maureen O'Hara; *Borderline* (50) with Claire Trevor; *Never a Dull Moment* with Irene Dunne–and for their second film together, another dishonest title; and *A Millionaire for Christy* (51) with Eleanor Parker. *Callaway Went Thataway* with Dorothy McGuire was a minute improvement, but that his star had definitely waned was evident from his acceptance of a junk vehicle at Republic, *Fair Wind to Java* (52), opposite the lovely Vera Hruba Ralston. *The Moonlighter* (53) with Stanwyck got lost somewhere.

MacMurray came back somewhat with *The Caine Mutiny* (54), fourth-billed as the smarty-pants officer-writer who is the captain's first critic: once again, in an unsympathetic part, he was good; as he was as a crooked cop in *Pushover*. He was in a couple of those 20th Century-Fox pictures which CinemaScoped half a dozen names into one movie, *A Woman's World* and *The Rains of Ranchipur* (55), in between which he did the unimportant *The Far Horizons* (55) supporting Charlton Heston. He now emulated Randolph Scott and Joel McCrea, and kept his career going with budget-price actioners, mostly Westerns: *At Gunpoint*, *There's Always Tomorrow* (56), a soap opera, with Stanwyck, *Gun for a Coward* (57), *Quantez*, *Day of the Badman* (58), *Good Day for a Hanging*, *Face of a Fugitive* (59) and *The Oregon Trail*. But in 1958 Walt Disney had cast MacMurray in one of his early excursions into domestic comedy, *The Shaggy Dog*. Undistinguished in every way, the film–presumably due to the magic of the Disney name–drew huge audiences and was one of the year's top money-makers. Then in 1960 Billy Wilder asked for MacMurray again, for *The Apartment* when Paul Douglas died a week before filming: it was only a featured role, but effective, as Shirley MacLaine's boss/seducer.

In the early 60s MacMurray began a highly successful TV series, 'My Three Sons', but it was undoubtedly Disney who prolonged his film career. He had great faith in MacMurray, and was justified by the box-office returns–especially in the US. In 1961 *The Absent-Minded Professor*; in 1962 *Bon Voyage* (with Jane Wyman); in 1963 *Son of Flubber* (a sequel to the Professor film); in 1966 *Follow Me Boys*; and in 1967 *The Happiest Millionaire*. The last two did less well, especially *Boys*, a comedy about scouts which got terrible notices; and *Kisses for My President* (64) for Warner Brothers with Polly Bergen, really died the death of all bad films.

Fredric March

'I'm just a ham,' said Fredric March once, discussing acting, a modest, depreciatory remark, but accurate on more than one occasion. Still, he is normally quietly excellent, seldom memorable and less affectionately regarded than the other two actors who twice won Best Actor Oscars, Spencer Tracy and Gary Cooper. He did go through a spell of being a Very Romantic Leading Man, but for most of his career he has been a dedicated no-nonsense actor, authoritative and reliable; if you look at publicity stills of March you will find them more direct, less affected, than those of any other leading star: he does not pose. He is direct. And he has managed to be in an above-average number of good movies.

He was born in 1897 in Racine, Wisconsin, and studied at that state's University. He was destined for banking, but during a spell in hospital determined to become an actor; he went to New York and made the rounds of the agents. His appearance–handsome, healthy, middle-class–got him some modelling work, and 'extra' jobs in movies, including *Pay the Piper* with Dorothy Dickson and *The Great Adventure* starring Lionel Barrymore. His first stage appearance was a two-line bit in Granville-Barker's adaptation of Sacha Guitry's 'Deburau' (20), and he progressed until he had a role in 'The Devil in the Cheese' (27) which netted him good notices from the New York press. He has described himself at this period as a 'general-utility' actor, and in that capacity the Theatre Guild sent him on tour ('Arms and the Man', 'The Guardsman', etc.); he was in the West Coast production of 'The Royal Family' as the member of that family based on John Barrymore (Barrymore adored his parody). That led to a Paramount offer of a five-year contract.

March was virtually the first new star of the Talkies, and certainly of the new intake, he was the only one who endured. He was in *The Dummy* (29), opposite Ruth Chatterton, a modest version of a stage melo, and in *The Wild Party* as the professor enticed by student Clara Bow. Few people noticed him, but he was an oasis of sobriety and integrity in an unbelievable, corny film. He made more impression as a philandering movie star in *The Studio Murder Mystery* (his wife, Florence Eldridge, made her film debut in it), but it was on loan-out for Ann Harding's *Paris Bound* that he first got his film career off the ground. Jeanne Eagels asked for him for *Jealousy*: the film had been finished, with Anthony Bushell in the lead, but she demanded that it be re-shot with March. She was seriously ill, and dead before it was released, to indifferent notices and business. Another big star, Colleen Moore, asked for him to be her stage-door johnny in *Footlights and Fools*. He played with Mary Brian in *The Marriage Playground*; with Ruth Chatterton in *Sarah and Son* (30); with most of the Paramount roster in *Paramount on Parade*; Mary Astor in *Ladies Love Brutes*; Clara Bow in *True to the Navy* as a brash gob; and Claudette Colbert in *Manslaughter*, George Abbott's remake of some old de Mille hokum.

He liked doing *Laughter* as the amorous composer yearning for married Nancy Carroll; after which he moved out of the co-star status when he re-did his Barrymore impersonation in the film version, re-titled *The Royal Family of Broadway*, all high spirits and zip: today it seems a very awkward performance. Colbert was his secretary in *Honor Among Lovers* (31)–he lost her and won her back–and Carroll was *The Night Angel* (a part intended for Dietrich, which did much to kill off Carroll's career–the film was a giant flop). March was in a second failure, *My Sin*, playing a degenerate lawyer opposite Tallulah Bankhead, but he came back in force when Mamoulian selected him to play *Dr Jekyll and Mr Hyde*, still the best version of several. In the transformation

Dr Jekyll into Mr Hyde: Fredric March in Rouben Mamoulian's film version (31).

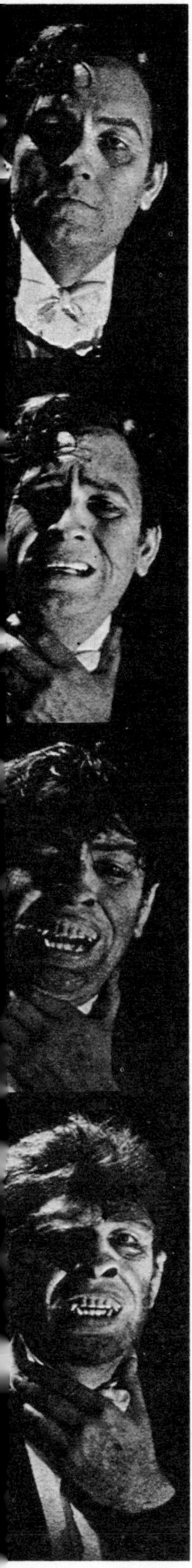

scenes wonders were accomplished with make-up and trick photography, but March's two impersonations were gripping and won a well-deserved Oscar.

Naturally, his parts got better: in a dual role (twins, good and bad) in *Strangers in Love* (32) with Kay Francis; in *Merrily We Go to Hell*, as a hard-drinking journalist; on loan to MGM for *Smilin' Through*; in *The Sign of the Cross*, as the Roman centurion; in *Tonight Is Ours* (33), as the commoner who marries princess Claudette in this poor version of Noël Coward's 'The Queen Was in the Parlour'; in *The Eagle and the Hawk*, as an aviator; and in *Design for Living*, as one of the unholy trio – Gary Cooper and Miriam Hopkins were the others. March liked none of these, nor *All of Me* (34) with Hopkins, but he did like *Death Takes a Holiday* (he still considers it one of his four best films, with *Dr Jekyll*, *A Star Is Born* and *The Best Years of Our Lives*). 'As Death, who mingles with guests at a house party, and finds love with Evelyn Venable, Fredric March is superb' (Photoplay). Thus, after *Good Dame*, a silly programmer thrown together because he and Sylvia Sidney were available when the film of R.U.R. was cancelled, he refused to re-sign with Paramount (also, he hadn't liked the studio publicity which insisted that he was a successor to John Gilbert: he wanted to be a character actor).

He signed a contract with 20th, with the proviso that he had control over his material and could do outside parts. Years later, Hume Cronyn was to refer to him as a total actor, because he could play anything. But not quite yet. Hollywood was at that point embarking on costume epics galore, and March was one of the few native actors who wasn't incongruous: but he was not *always* at home in the parts that followed. He might well have been good in the Damon Runyan story that 20th announced for him, but he was only fair in *The Affairs of Cellini*, which he did instead, bearded. And James Agate said his Robert Browning in *The Barretts of Wimpole Street* 'is just a joke in so far as he must be supposed to resemble the poet. He is a good, straightforward, manly lover, though we feel the intricacies of "Mary had a little lamb" would be beyond him.' He was good in Mamoulian's version of Tolstoy's 'Resurrection', *We Live Again* with Anna Sten, and very good in the best screen version of *Les Miserables* (35, at 20th), but his Vronsky to Garbo's *Anna Karenina* was callow and unconvincing. He was stilted in *Anthony Adverse* (36), WB's big-budgeted and long-winded version of Hervey Allen's best-seller (which often seemed as though Runyan had written the dialogue). It was sandwiched between two 'modern' subjects, the lachrymose *The Dark Angel* (35) and Howard Hawks's very fine war drama, *The Road to Glory* (36). In fact, March was afraid of being typed a costume actor, and he turned down, among others, *The Count of Monte Cristo*, *The Prisoner of Zenda* and *Two Years Before the Mast* (which Republic were contemplating).

Sylvia Sidney and Fredric March – socialite wife and ne'er-do-well reporter husband – in Merrily We Go to Hell *(32), directed by Dorothy Arzner, virtually the only successful woman director.*

He did do *Mary of Scotland* (a spirited but unlikely Bothwell; Eldridge was Elizabeth I) and then signed for two contemporary subjects with Selznick (at $125,000 each – now the fifth-highest paid actor in Hollywood. William A. Wellman steered both, helping to rescue the faltering March reputation. *A Star Is Born* (37) cast him as a falling movie star – a beautiful performance (quite the equal of James Mason's in the remake), and in *Nothing Sacred* he was a newspaper editor, flummoxed by the lies of Carole Lombard: it was her film, but he more than held his own. He then returned to Paramount for *The Buccaneer* (38), with an acceptable French accent: a de Mille spectacular and another big success for March. But he and his wife had decided to return to Broadway, and they did a play about Richard Steele of The Spectator, 'Yr Obedient Husband': it opened to dire notices and closed after a week. The Marches returned to Hollywood.

But Hollywood is a funny place, and yesterday's hero is today's redundancy: the

March's second Oscar was for The Best Years of Our Lives *(46), perhaps the most successful American film of the immediate postwar period. He was a veteran adjusting to civilian life.*

only offers March got were from two independents, at half his usual salary (but plus a share of the profits). For Hal Roach he did a comedy, *There Goes My Heart* (38), as a reporter, with Virginia Bruce as an heiress, and for Wanger a poor adventure tale, *Trade Winds* (39). Hollywood's fickleness didn't distress the Marches, and they have worked since in that city and New York alternately. They like working together, but Eldridge has been unable to command the attention in Hollywood that she can on Broadway; she is clearly less obvious film material than her husband. She was a woefully poor Elizabeth I, but in their Broadway appearances and in the three films they made together in the 40s she was, in talent, his equal. In 1939 they appeared in New York in the Hart-Kaufman pageant of Americana, 'The American Way'; in 1941 in 'Hope for a Harvest'; in 1942 in the successful 'The Skin of Our Teeth'; and in 1946 in 'Years Ago' (Ruth Gordon's play that became *The Actress* for films). March was on his own in 1944's 'A Bell for Adano'.

After their second absence on Broadway (1939), March astonished tradesters by getting $100,000 each for his two return movies: *Susan and God* (40), being driven to drink by Joan Crawford, and *Victory*–Conrad with a happy ending. Then: *So Ends Our Night* (41) with Margaret Sullavan; *One Foot in Heaven*, a meandering but much-liked study of a Methodist minister, with Martha Scott; *Bedtime Story*–famous playwright battling with actress/wife Loretta Young, and vainly, for laughs; René Clair's gay *I Married a Witch* (42), from a Thorne Smith story; *The Adventures of Mark Twain* (44) with Alexis Smith, and with the make-up men literally making up for the deficiencies of the scriptwriters; and *Tomorrow the World* with Betty Field, about an American family who discover the boy they've adopted is a Nazi.

After a two-year absence March returned to the screen as the senior of the three returning war veterans in Wyler's *The Best Years of Our Lives* (46): the press reception was rapturous and helped to make this by far the biggest money-making film that March had been in. It also won seven Oscars, including a second Best Actor for March; but it didn't lead to anything big, partly because in the flood of post-war leading men he was considered a veteran. At Universal he did two films with his wife, *Another Part of the Forest* (48), a cheapjack version of Lillian Hellman's sequel to 'The Little Foxes', and *Act of Murder*, a drama about euthanasia; but good acting didn't bring either to box-office respectability. The

Fredric March, Diane Cilento and Paul Newman in Hombre *(67). Newman was a white man reared by Apaches and returning to the white man's world.*

next was his first major mistake since he had started free-lancing: a trip to Britain for Rank's *Christopher Columbus* (49), an effort, more determined than usual, to capture a share of the American market; with a risible script the Marches (she was Isabella) floundered, until the direction scuttled them.

There were three stage appearances in 1950–1 (including 'An Enemy of the People') and a spot in the all-star, patriotic spot, *It's a Big Country* (51); then March got the much-coveted part of Willy Loman in the film of Arthur Miller's *Death of a Salesman* (52). His performance was prized at the Venice Film Festival, but was unfavourably compared–as being over-hysterical–with those given by Lee J. Cobb in New York and Paul Muni in London. It brought March a fifth Oscar nomination and was a box-office failure. So was Kazan's *Man on a Tightrope* (53), an odd Iron Curtain/Circus melo, proving again that March's name alone couldn't carry a film. However, helped by good reviews and some other big names, he was in three successes: *Executive Suite* (54) with Barbara Stanwyck, William Holden, etc.; *The Bridges at Toko-Ri* with Holden and Grace Kelly; and *The Desperate Hours* (55), splendid as the householder menaced by escaped thug Humphrey Bogart and agonizingly thinking in circles. He had supporting roles (but star billing) in the so-so *The Man in the Grey Flannel Suit* (56) and the flop *Alexander the Great*, unrecognizable–fortunately–as Philip of Macedonia.

After those, he returned to New York with his wife for O'Neill's 'Long Day's Journey into Night' and the general opinion was that this was the most distinguished work of their stage careers (he won the Critics' Best Actor award); its run kept him off the screen until 1958, when he played a middle-aged man prepared to sacrifice everything for Kim Novak in Paddy Chayevsky's *The Middle of the Night*. Said Time magazine: 'What most strikingly meets the eye is the profound performance of Fredric March. Seldom have youth and crabbed age lived together in one face with so much suffering and meaning.' The film failed pitiably–and sadly, because his next performance was knots below, in *Inherit the Wind* (60), with Spencer Tracy. Newsweek, having commented on Tracy's almost motionless performance, kindly said that March 'by contrast achieves a magnificence of over-acting'. He was more his old self in *The Young Doctors* (61), and in the weird international production of Sartre's play *The Condemned of Altona* (63) again indicated the comprehension and authority of which he is capable. His other roles have not been big: *Seven Days in May* (64), *Hombre* (67) and *Tick Tick Tick* (70). On starting the latter he confirmed that he had retired, 'however, not as definitely as Jimmy Cagney'.

Herbert Marshall

Herbert Marshall's co-stars included Garbo, Hepburn and Bette Davis, not to mention Claudette Colbert, Margaret Sullavan, Deanna Durbin, Dietrich, Joan Fontaine, Jean Arthur, Joan Crawford, Barbara Stanwyck, Constance Bennett, Kay Francis, Shirley Temple, Mary Astor, Ruth Chatterton, Miriam Hopkins and Norma Shearer: which suggests that he was a somewhat self-effacing actor. Norma Shearer once explained: 'The first time I saw Mr Marshall on the screen was in a picture with Claudette Colbert. I thought I had never seen a lady so thoroughly and convincingly loved. He is both manly and wistful. He wins the sympathy of women because his face expresses tenderness and silent suffering.' Actually he was urbane, soft-spoken and somewhat distant, but he let the ladies act rings round him–except perhaps in comedy, where his skill added much to the sophistication of some of the screen's best pieces; at the same time he was seldom outmatched and his performances – both as cuckolded husbands – in *The Painted Veil* with Garbo and *The Letter* with Bette Davis give much weight to both films.

He was born in London in 1890, into a theatrical family, was educated at a school in Essex, and afterwards articled to a firm of chartered accountants. He became business manager for impresario Robert Courtneidge, from which it was a short step to acting, making his debut in a rep at Brighton in 'The Adventures of Lady Ursula' (11). Two years later he appeared in London in 'Brewster's Millions' and then toured the US with the Cyril Maude Company in 'Grumpy'. He served with the BEF during the war, and was severely wounded: his right leg was amputated (but apart from a slightly stiff walk this was never apparent to audiences and did not affect his career). He returned to the stage, and soon became a West End favourite; he appeared on Broadway in 'These Charming People' (25); in London in Noël Coward's 'The Queen Was in the Parlour' (26) and in New York again in 'The High Road' (28) with Edna Best. They married, and became one of the most popular teams of the time – in such plays as 'Michael and Mary', 'The Swan' (in both London and New York) and Van Druten's 'There's Always Juliet'. They both preferred Britain (Miss Best came from Hove), but certainly where films were concerned the opportunities were not there: Marshall appeared in two Silents, *Mumsie* (27) starring Pauline Frederick and *Dawn* (Sybil Thorndike as Edith Cavell; it was at first banned for political reasons), but his film career really began with Somerset Maugham's *The Letter* (29), as the lover, playing opposite Jeanne Eagels: Paramount produced, and Marshall was offered a short-term contract.

Prior stage commitments took the Marshalls to Britain, however, and while he was there appearing in 'The Swan' he made *Murder* (30), a brilliant performance as an actor-knight, directed by Hitchcock from Clemence Dane's story, 'Enter Sir John'. He and Best co-starred in two British pictures: *The Calendar* (31), a racing story by Edgar Wallace, and *Michael and Mary*, their stage hit; then he returned to Hollywood for *Secrets of a Secretary* with Claudette Colbert. The Marshalls went home again, to make *The Faithful Heart* (32), a dull family saga; then they crossed the Atlantic again to do 'There's Always Juliet' on Broadway. Meanwhile audience reaction to Marshall in the Colbert film was very strong, especially among the women, and Paramount couldn't wait to have him back. They bought him out of his Broadway play and hurried him into *Blonde Venus*, as Dietrich's husband, and *Trouble in Paradise*, a Lubitsch soufflé in which he and Kay Francis tried to cheat Miriam Hopkins out of her fortune. This film established him as a romantic, mature leading man, and he was given a similar part offering *Evenings for Sale* to Sari Maritza and other women. Paramount saw him as the next 'great lover', and were disappointed when he insisted on returning to Britain to honour three commitments: *Clear All Wires* (33), *The Solitaire Man*, and *I Was a Spy* with Madeleine Carroll.

After that, however, he fretted less in Hollywood – and, indeed, films there occupied him exclusively over the next score of years. The break-up of his marriage lessened his interest in the stage and in Britain; and shortly his name would be romantically linked with Gloria Swanson (a brawl over her in a Hollywood night spot brought headlines). Marshall did not, however, become the great star that Paramount had envisaged: he had another five years as a star actor, but his reserve and age limited him. He was one of the *Four Frightened People* (34) stranded on a desert island for de Mille, from which he went to MGM for three, reputedly at the request of the ladies concerned: *Riptide* with Norma Shearer, as the jealous husband whose suspicions force her into the arms of Robert Montgomery; *Outcast Lady* with Constance Bennett; and *The Painted Veil* with Garbo. M. D. Phillips, in Picturegoer, wrote of his performance in the Bennett picture: 'Marshall is becoming too mannerized and is inclined to walk through his part with too obvious an air of nonchalance.' He was scheduled for a fourth with another big Metro star, *Three Weeks* with Swanson, but it was never made. He was: the attractive older man who wins Margaret Sullavan at the end of *The Good Fairy* (35); the sober industrious older man who waits by while Ann Harding dallies with dipsomaniac Louis Hayward in *The Flame Within*; the attractive older man who is won by secretary Sylvia Sidney in *Accent on Youth*; and the noble older man who waits while Merle Oberon loves Fredric March in *The Dark Angel*.

In two comedies he got out of the rut somewhat: with Ann Harding in *The Lady Consents* (36), as a philanderer, and with Jean Arthur in *If You Could Only Cook*, blueblood in a gangster's pantry. There were two with Gertrude Michael, *Till We Meet Again* (spies, ex-lovers meeting again) and

Richard Boleslawski's The Painted Veil *(34) reduced Maugham's study of the Colonial mentality to a mere regeneration theme. Here's Garbo as the unfaithful wife at the time she's redeeming herself for husband Herbert Marshall, a doctor curing an epic outbreak of cholera.*

Forgotten Faces, described thus by Photoplay: 'Herbert Marshall is superb as the cultured murderer trying to keep his daughter clear of his wife's clutches.' Then it was back to type-casting: the headmaster on whom Simone Simon has a crush in *Girls Dormitory*, and Katharine Hepburn's Old Faithful in *A Woman Rebels*. He made the minor *Make Way for a Lady* with Anne Shirley; and was then Dietrich's husband again and cuckolded again in *Angel* (37). He and Barbara Stanwyck had a comic *Breakfast for Two*; and he was a famous actor adopted by Deanna Durbin as a father to impress her schoolmates in *Mad About Music* (38). He was less congenially trapped in three sudsers: *Always Goodbye* with Stanwyck; *Woman Against Woman*–Mary Astor and Virginia Bruce and divorce and remarriage; and *Zaza* (39), as the man who loves and leaves Claudette Colbert.

In the remake of *The Letter* (40) he was this time the husband; in the remake of *A Bill of Divorcement* he was the man mother Fay Bainter wants to marry; and in Hitchcock's marvellous *Foreign Correspondent*, with Joel McCrea and Laraine Day, her father, sympathetic and the surprise villain. After a tame political drama, *Adventure in Washington* (41), with Virginia Bruce, he was again Bette Davis's suffering husband in another Wyler-directed film, *The Little Foxes*–a strong portrayal of a weak man; he did *When Ladies Meet* with Joan Crawford and Greer Garson, and Shirley Temple's *Kathleen*, and then, memorably, *The Moon and Sixpence* (42), playing the narrator (Somerset Maugham) *vis-à-vis* the 'Gauguin' of George Sanders. It was more or less his last leading role, and the beginning of a period of decreased activity.

In 1943 he did *Flight for Freedom* with Rosalind Russell; *Forever and a Day*; and *Young Ideas* with Astor and in 1944 only

The Foreign Correspondent *(40) was Joel McCrea, in Europe on the eve of war. Among those he becomes involved with is his girl-friend's father, Herbert Marshall, whose peace propaganda campaign is a front for pro-Nazi activities.*

Andy Hardy's Blonde Trouble; he was the understanding blind friend of the lovers in *The Enchanted Cottage* (45)–for the first time appearing on the screen with stick and limp; and was in *The Unseen*.

He repeated his discreet Maugham impersonation in *The Razor's Edge* (46); was in the Pat O'Brien *Crack-Up* and then did another of the gloomy roles in which he was being increasingly cast, as the proud father of Jennifer Jones killed off early in *Duel in the Sun*. Predictably, he was ensnared and cuckolded by the poisonous *Ivy* (47)–Joan Fontaine, but it was not a big role; he had small roles in *High Wall* (48) and in *The Secret Garden* (49), as the child's unfeeling guardian.

The Underworld Story (50), starring Dan Duryea, was almost the first time in his career that Marshall had done an unabashed B product, and not all of his later films were more distinguished: the US-Spanish *Black Jack*; *Anne of the Indies* (51), a pirate drama with Jean Peters and Louis Jourdan; George Stevens's *Something to Live For* (52) with Joan Fontaine; and *Angel Face* with Jean Simmons. In 1952 he did a TV series, 'The Unexpected'. In a couple of low-budget sci-fiers produced by Ivan Tors for United Artists, *Riders to the Stars* (54) and *Gog*, he had conventional 'doctor' roles, and did them impeccably; even reduced to the rubbishy cardboard castles of a Hollywood Merrie England in *The Black Shield of Falworth*, with Tony Curtis, he couldn't help being good. But his name was well down the cast-list, and it was again in *The Virgin Queen* (55), as an ageing Leicester to Davis's Elizabeth. He returned to Britain for a couple of Bs, *Wicked As They Come* (56), which referred to Arlene Dahl, pronounced dull, and *The Weapon* (57) with Steve Cochran and Lizabeth Scott: despite the US names, neither got many bookings Stateside.

Stage Struck (58) with Henry Fonda was more the quality he had been used to, but neither *The Fly* (58) nor *College Confidential* (60) were–though Vincent Price, who co-starred in the former, has recalled that Marshall treated the whole thing as a great joke. Maybe he was as light-hearted about his last pictures: *Midnight Lace*, *A Fever in the Blood* (61), *Five Weeks in a Balloon* (62), *The List of Adrian Messenger* (63), *The Caretakers* and *The Third Day* (65). He died of a heart attack in 1966. He had married five times; he and Edna Best divorced in 1940. Their daughter, Sarah Marshall, has had small roles in a few films (*The Long Hot Summer*) and seems to have inherited more than a fair share of their talents.

Mary Martin

Mary Martin is regarded as one of Hollywood's lost causes. At the time of her Broadway peak ('South Pacific', 49) some publicity was made from her failure in Hollywood some years earlier. It is a failure hard to fathom: she could sing, she was a delightful comedienne, she was pretty–in fact, she comes out fairly high in any assessment of the Musical Ladies of that time. Her voice was her best asset: speaking, it was melodic and nicely Texas-accented; and singing, she could range within her warm soprano from 'Il Bacio' to 'Wait till the Sun Shines Nellie'. Maybe she was just too talented, and too individual to fit into the wartime mould.

She was born in Waterford, Texas, in 1913. She was educated in Nashville, Tennessee, but returned to her home town and taught dancing; she took her troupe (the Martinettes) to Fort Worth for the Centennial Celebrations, but Billy Rose, who was staging it, advised her to return home (some of the Martinettes got engagements, however). Instead, Martin tried Hollywood. She made the rounds and even got screen-tested (by five studios) plus a bit part as Danielle Darrieux's dancing teacher in *Rage of Paris* (38); she eked out a living by singing in clubs–and was caught one night at the Trocadero by Broadway producer Lawrence Schwab. She went to New York,

Bing Crosby and Mary Martin in Birth of the Blues *(41), directed by Victor Schertzinger.*

Happy Go Lucky *(42) wasn't a bad title for a musical about a stenographer (Mary Martin) who spends her life savings on a cruise in an effort to entrap a wealthy husband. It's no surprise when she lands Dick Powell instead.*

but the show Schwab was planning fell through and he loaned her to another producer, Vinton Freely, for a Cole Porter musical, 'Leave it to Me'. It was a minor role, but it included 'My Heart Belongs to Daddy' to a simulated strip-tease, and overnight Martin became the toast of Broadway.

She returned triumphantly to Hollywood with a Paramount contract in her pocket. Her first film was *The Great Victor Herbert* (39), which used tunes from his operettas–and him as a subsidiary character (Walter Connolly)–for an utterly conventional story of a show-biz marriage; Martin, second-billed, made a favourable impression as Allan Jones's long-suffering wife, and she sang a lot. The film was popular; and she went on to play opposite Bing Crosby in *Rhythm on the River* (40) and Jack Benny in *Love Thy Neighbor*, refereeing in the fights with Fred Allen. *Kiss the Boys Goodbye* (41) gave her a fine chance as a would-be Scarlett O'Hara, a funny musicomedy which spoofed the search for the screen Scarlett, and she was again captivating as Crosby's *vis-à-vis* in *The Birth of the Blues. New York Town*–without music–effectively cast her as a hard-working city girl, a sort of lower-case Jean Arthur, but it wasn't good. She duetted with Dick Powell on 'Hit the Road to Dreamland' in *Star Spangled Rhythm* and starred with him in another musical, *Happy Go Lucky* (43), but that, though Technicolored, was again very ordinary. Nor was *True to Life* much improvement. W. H. Mooring in Picturegoer suggested that the trouble was that Martin only got offered the pictures that Claudette Colbert turned down. She left Hollywood, dissatisfied, and no Paramount executive cried over her departure.

She did a show which failed to reach New York, 'Dancing in the Streets', and in late 1943 had another Broadway musical smash, 'One Touch of Venus', which kept her busy for 18 months. She scored such a hit that UA (Mary Pickford) wanted her to repeat for the film version and borrowed her from Paramount, to whom she still owed three films. However, for some reason it was not made (director Gergory la Cava sued UA for his salary). Martin returned to New York and 'Lute Song', and Paramount announced she would do *Alice-Sit-by-the-Fire*–but her only film work was singing 'My Heart Belongs to Daddy' in WB's Cole Porter biopic, *Night and Day* (46). As on Broadway, she stole the notices with this number, and Hollywood renewed its interest–particularly Warners, who had no musical lady to match the appeal of the Garlands and Huttons and Grables at other studios. In 1948 Martin was to have made *Romance on the High Seas*, but as with her first screen tests, she was thought unphotogenic. And she herself, once-bitten, was wary. Meanwhile, in London she had done 'Pacific 1860' by Noël Coward, and in the US toured in 'Annie get your Gun'. In 1949 came 'South Pacific', an undreamt-of success, which placed her (alongside Ethel Merman) as the first lady of the American musical stage. In 1952 she played herself in *Main Street to Broadway*: despite its roster of stars, it got few bookings. She continued to have great successes on the stage: 'Kind Sir' (53), 'Peter Pan' (54), 'The Sound of Music' (59), 'Hello Dolly' (65) on tour and in London; and on TV, in some of the most successful specials in the history of the medium. But, incredibly, she was passed over for the film of *South Pacific*. Joshua Logan, who directed–as he had on stage–said: 'Outside of my own family, I love Mary more than anyone in the world, but I felt I couldn't subject her to the endless adjustments she would have to make in putting her superb performance on film.' The film was inescapably, infinitely, poorer for that decision.

Chico and Harpo in Horse Feathers *(32) which, as far as can be ascertained, concerned a college football match. Groucho was certainly the new head of the college. Harpo was a dog-catcher and Chico had something to do with a speakeasy.*

The Marx Brothers

It should have been an occasion for rejoicing when the Marx Brothers began to enter the realms of mythology. Is there a figure of this century more wholly admirable than Harpo? or Groucho? or even Chico? The reverence accorded them these days is hardly in accordance with their own anarchic attitude to everything, but it does mean that they are often with us and it is possible to keep in touch with them at repertory cinemas; and apart from their myth-status their clowning still makes them immortal. Some of their gags have dated, but they remain on the whole funnier than ever–funnier and more modern than any other comic team (or, indeed, any other comic) which came afterwards. As Allen Eyles says in his excellent study of them (1966), they 'are the heroes of everyone who has suffered from other people's hypocrisy, pomposity, pedantism, and patronage. They settle for none of it. The Marxes assume that we join them on their comic crusade.' Not that the world that the Marxes inhabit is sane to begin with–it is not only the amorous, deluded and indestructible Margaret Dumont who takes them seriously: the connivers and cheats whom they are trying to outwit accept them–with exasperation, perhaps–as rational beings. It really was a world turned upside down into which the Marx Brothers tore with antic delight, tipping it further askew with a wild defiance of logic.

Groucho is generally accepted as the best of them–perhaps because he got most of the (often audacious) wisecracks. He was the one with fake moustache and cigar, with the sardonic asides to the audience, the one who was one-step-up, an aspiring bureaucrat, a parvenu chasing after the ever-ready Mrs Rittenhouse, Mrs Claypool or Mrs Emily Upjohn (whose trains and feathers Dumont inhabited so majestically). Groucho had no illusions though–he was modest enough to accept the others in uneasy alliance whenever he was about to be found out, or before that, if he was in a gullible mood.

Harpo was the one with the hair like Bubbles, the dumb one, the one with the recalcitrant leg and the propensity for collecting things like bicycle horns. To state categorically that Groucho was Harpo's superior (plot exigencies aside) takes into account the softening of the Harpo character in the later films, where he can be found aiding the lovers or entertaining children. The early Harpo was much too bent on lechery and larceny–and between times causing as much chaos as possible ('unregenerate destruction' in Dilys Powell's words)–for such slop: indeed, he pursued his entirely selfish aims as ferociously as a demon. Chico aided and abetted them both, usually with a bias towards Harpo who, after all, was more destructive and less pretentious than Groucho–indeed, Chico himself had no pretensions; he knew his place. Despite his Italian-American punning (or perhaps because of it) he isn't as funny as the others, but his readiness to obstruct is quite endearing.

They were a New York family, of

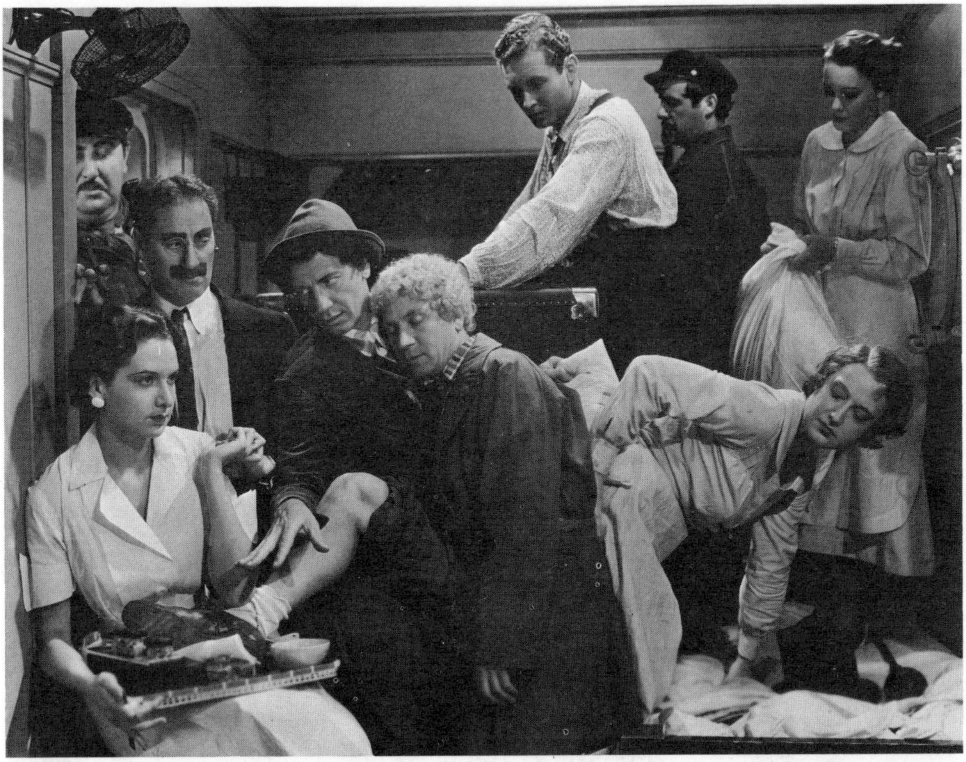

Two scenes from A Night at the Opera *(35). Top, the Ocean crossing–in the Marx's cabin (Allan Jones is the gentleman in the flowered shirt). Bottom, after the 'opera' with Margaret Dumont, who for love of Groucho will bail them out as usual.*

German-Jewish descent. Chico was born in 1891, Harpo in 1893, Groucho in 1895 and Zeppo – the straight man in the early films – in 1901. (Another brother, Gummo, never appeared in films with them.) Their mother – whose brother was Al Sheean, the vaudeville star – pushed them into show business quite early, singly or as a troupe, and Sheean was sometimes called in to help polish the act. With mother and an aunt, they started as 'The Six Musical Mascots'. Bit by bit they evolved the characters that they were to bring to the screen. Their first break came when they left the halls and appeared in a 'book' show, 'I'll Say She Is'; after two years flogging this around the country, they took it to Broadway, and became cult figures overnight. It had a smash run (during which Harpo had a small role in a Richard Dix comedy, *Too Many Kisses*) and was followed by 'The Cocoanuts' in 1925 and by 'Animal Crackers' at the end of 1928.

During the run of 'Cocoanuts' they had made a film privately – for $6,000 – but it was never released; now, while they were in 'Animal Crackers', Paramount and Fox offered them contracts. They signed with Paramount for three films, at $75,000 per film, and made a movie version of *The Cocoanuts* (29) in New York. It was like a primitive TV show, with stage routines and painted settings, no more than a filmed record of the stage show – and with too much plot not involving them. The filmization of *Animal Crackers* (30), which followed, was a bit more cinematic. The plot centres on a fake African explorer – Groucho as Captain Spaulding – and a fake old master.

The next one was made in Hollywood, *Monkey Business* (31), and they were

A Day at the Races (*37*). *Margaret Dumont at her patient best. Said Cecilia Ager in her review of this film: 'There ought to be a statue erected, or a Congressional Medal awarded, or a national holiday proclaimed, to honour that great woman, Margaret Dumont . . . a lady of epic ability to take it, a lady whose mighty love for Groucho is a saga of devotion, a lady who asks but little and gets it . . . once again her fortitude is nothing human. It's godlike.'*

stowaways on a liner, adventitiously involved with gangsters, who include Thelma Todd, a more glamorous but less exacting foil than Dumont. Dumont isn't in the next one, either, *Horse Feathers* (32), but otherwise it has some right ideas, such as casting Groucho as a college dean and the other two as students. Said C. A. Lejeune: 'There is nothing persuasive about the Marx Brothers. They coolly turn their backs on their audience and get on with their business. They never solicit applause and they go out of their way to reject sympathy. Their clowning is an emetic for emotion. They play to one another and criticize one another; Marx is occupied with Marx to the exclusion of the public, the orchestra, the plot and the rest of the cast.' *Duck Soup* (33) had some even brighter ideas, like Groucho as President (of a banana republic), Rufus T. Firefly. His stunning ineptitude, blindly supported by the wealthiest widow in the land (Dumont), leads to friction with a neighbouring state – whose idea of secret agents is Harpo and Chico (not that they stay on one side for very long). In no sense a political satire, though heavily involved with dictators and revolution, it was banned by Mussolini. Eyles says: '*Duck Soup* is the most highly regarded of the Marxes' pictures. Groucho himself thinks it is the craziest' – but at the time it fared badly at the box-office.

At Paramount the success of the Marx Brothers was – according to a biographer, Kyle Crichton – 'solid but not sensational': following the flop of *Duck Soup* and a change of management the studio wasn't interested in renewing the contract. But Irving Thalberg at MGM was keen to have the Marxes, and the contract that Chico and he worked out gave them a salary plus 15 per cent of the gross (which meant, for instance, that the team earned $30,000 from a re-issue of *A Night at the Opera* in 1949). Thalberg in other ways was shrewd – he let the Marxes take the key sequences out on a road-tour to test them before audiences (an idea they welcomed) and he insisted on a love interest (not involving them): the result, *A Night at the Opera* (35) drew big crowds, made more money than any of their other films, and today remains the most famous. Groucho himself considers it the best. The second one at MGM is only a whit less enjoyable, *A Day*

A Night in Casablanca (*46*).

at the Races (37) – again the Brothers tried out on stage the important scenes, and again there was an insipid romance and, bang in the middle of the film, holding it up, a lavish production number; what was more worrying was that a softening of their characters was becoming apparent.

They then moved over briefly to RKO, who had bought – for $225,000, then a record sum – a Broadway hit, with the idea of letting the Marxes loose on it: the result, *Room Service* (38), has them bothering a mite more with plot than usual, but it doesn't diminish them. Back at MGM, *At the Circus* (39) does: Thalberg was dead, and no one now at the studio cared. Groucho's son, Arthur, wrote (in 'Groucho', 1954) that he 'didn't like MGM without Thalberg and apparently MGM was beginning to feel the same way about the Marx Brothers.' The thing most people remember about *Circus* is the symphony orchestra drifting out to sea at the end. The film on the whole was preferable to the next, *Go West* (40), which, after a typically Marxian opening, degenerates into gags which any lesser team could have done.

Groucho himself has written bitterly of this time – the team was unhappy with the material MGM forced on them and they found the atmosphere uncongenial, but they themselves were ageing and less interested. They agreed to go their separate ways but did one more first: *The Big Store* (41), which was funnier than the last two put together (a hackneyed setting, but they made it seem fresh). They changed their minds about retiring in 1946, when they were offered a percentage of the profits on an independent venture, *A Night in Casablanca*: to a post-war world agog for laughter, it was a gas, but their devotees knew that it wasn't up to much. Another comeback, *Love Happy* (49), was greeted sadly and did poor business: the Marxes couldn't give impetus any longer to feeble scripting. Chico and Harpo semi-retired, but appeared now and then for TV or miscellaneous stage work. The three of them appeared, but not together, in a weirdie of a film which came out in 1957, *The Story of Mankind*: Chico was a monk who advised Columbus, Groucho was Paul Minuit and Harpo Sir Isaac Newton. Chico died in 1961 and Harpo in 1964.

Their work separately throughout their career was often varied – e.g. Harpo once played in 'The Man Who Came to Dinner' and Chico once had his own band. But Groucho's work is the most interesting: with Norman Krasna he wrote a screen-play, *The King and the Chorus Girl* (filmed in 1937 with Joan Blondell) and a play, 'Time for

Elizabeth'; he has written several books–mostly memoirs–and has known considerable success on TV, notably with his own quiz show, 'You Bet Your Life'. In 1960 he played Koko in 'The Mikado' on TV. And he has made several films without the others: *Copacabana* (47) with Carmen Miranda; *Mr Music* (50), guest star; *Double Dynamite* (51) with Sinatra and Jane Russell; *A Girl in Every Port* (52) with William Bendix; and, after a long interval, he was in Preminger's flop *Skidoo* (69).

James Mason

There was a considerable outcry when James Mason quit British films for Hollywood not long after the end of the war. It had always irked the British–their journalists if not their filmgoers–that most home-made actors yielded sooner or later to the blandishments of the wealthier and more glamorous American industry. It was beside the point that until the war most British films were tombs for talent: at that point the only British stars of international note were those who had worked for Hollywood or/and Alexander Korda. During the war, however, British films suddenly–and temporarily, as it turned out–improved, and at the same time threw up a whole new crop of stars. Not all these new stellar attractions were in the good films, but for the first time there was more than a handful of Britishers competing with the Americans for the box-office cash. None of them was bigger than James Mason, who from 1944 to 1947 inclusive was easily the top British box-office draw: in 1946 he drew more patrons into cinemas than anyone else, including Bing Crosby. His retreat or escape to Hollywood lost him his special place in Britain, yet almost alone of those wartime stars he has survived. So has Deborah Kerr, who came along a while later, and she also deserted the gloomy skies of Bucks for sunnier climes; but in both cases the reason has less to do with Hollywood than with talent.

Mason was born in Huddersfield in 1909, and was educated at Marlborough and Cambridge. He studied architecture, but the Drama claimed him and he made his first appearance in 'The Rascal' (31) in Aldershot. Two years later he scored a London hit in 'Gallows Glorious', after which he played secondary roles at the Old Vic. Korda saw him as Jeremy in 'Love for Love' and signed him for a part in *The Private Life of Don Juan*: but after a few days decided he was miscast and let him go. For the next three years (34–37) Mason was with the Gate Company in Dublin, but he commuted to Britain, tentatively beginning his film career as the star of quota quickies: *Late Extra* (35) and *Troubled Waters* (36), both with Virginia Cherrill, *Twice Branded*, *Prison Breaker*, *Blind Man's Buff* and *The Secret of Stamboul*. He had an effective small role in Korda's *Fire Over England* (37), but that producer still couldn't see his potential. On stage he was Hannibal in Sherwood's 'The Road to Rome', about the same time as he was Tom Tulliver in a screen transcription of George Eliot's *The Mill on the Floss* (Geraldine Fitzgerald was Maggie). Then he was in two more West End plays, and in *The High Command*, a règimental drama starring Lionel Atwill; *Catch As Catch Can*; and *The Return of the Scarlet Pimpernel*, who returned not as Leslie Howard but as Barry K. Barnes.

With two friends Mason set up *I Met a Murderer* (39), co-scripting as well as starring. It had a brief critical success; and when the friends later divorced, Mason married her (Pamela Kellino; the marriage lasted till 1964). In 1941 he was on the stage again in 'Jupiter Laughs', but it was his last London appearance because films began to claim all his attention (and he is on record as disliking acting in the theatre): *This Man Is Dangerous* (41); *Hatter's Castle*, from A. J. Cronin's novel with Robert Newton as the hatter and Mason as the juvenile lead; *The Night Has Eyes* (42); *Alibi*; *Secret Mission*; *Thunder Rock* starring Michael Redgrave; and *The Bells Go Down* (43), an Ealing tribute to the Fire Service.

Then came the one that made the difference: *The Man in Grey*. Eric Portman had turned it down and Mason took it reluctantly (he recalled later, with glee, Agate's description, 'bosh and tosh'): a preposterous Regency novel, wherein he was terribly mean to Phyllis Calvert while carrying on with her supposed friend, Margaret Lockwood–till she murdered Calvert and he took a horsewhip to her. For this Picturegoer readers voted him Actor of the Year; and when the film arrived in the US Time magazine observed: 'Swaggering through the title role, sneering like Laughton, barking like Gable and frowning like Laurence Olivier on a dark night, he is likely to pick up many a feminine fan.' Gainsborough/Rank, who produced, signed him to a contract.

There were some ordinary chores to be got out of the way: *They Met in the Dark*, *Candelight in Algeria* and *Hotel Reserve* (44): then Mason returned to villainy in *Fanny By Gaslight*, from Michael Sadleir's novel–and the only one of these films to have much

Margaret Lockwood and James Mason in The Man in Grey *(43), which leap-frogged them to the fore of all other British stars.*

After the series of Gainsborough romances Mason finally made a film the critics liked: Odd Man Out *(46). With him is Fay Compton.*

merit. Audiences gloated while he was mean again to Phyllis Calvert, taking it all much more seriously than he did. As a change, he insisted on doing a character part, as a bluff elderly Yorkshireman in the film of Osbert Sitwell's ghost story, *A Place of One's Own* (45). But as World War II ended British audiences were queueing to see Mason up to his neck in Dirty Work: he drove Dulcie Gray to suicide in *They Were Sisters*; out on loan he brought down his stick on the hands of pianist Ann Todd in *The Seventh Veil* (only she loved him after all); and as a highwayman he lusted after Lockwood in *The Wicked Lady*. *The Seventh Veil* was a well-directed, enjoyable farrago of nonsense, and was a big success in the States: 'That Mason,' said D. W. Griffith to Ezra Goodman, 'is the greatest actor.' The Times (London) had earlier commented that Mason had made the character 'attractive in spite of his aberrations and [he] suggests a passion for art that is strong and selfless.'

The next one was a big critical success: Carol Reed's version of a novel by F. L. Green, *Odd Man Out* (46), a sad and almost surrealistic tale of a wounded gunman on the run in Belfast; but *The Upturned Glass* (47) was a psychological thriller of no discernible merit. Mason himself produced, but this concession on the part of his employers didn't mollify him; as he, wife and cats embarked for the USA he patiently explained that he didn't care for the production set-up in Britain and that he had no confidence in an industry dominated by J. Arthur Rank. Further, there were fantastic offers from Hollywood. There were, however, still commitments in Britain (including a two-picture deal with Korda, one of which was to have been *The King's General*, though that was postponed and then cancelled) and once in the US Mason found himself in the midst of litigation and injunctions preventing him from filming. He appeared in a Broadway play that flopped, 'Bathsheba' (47), and appeared on TV where he made a few chance criticisms of Hollywood; so that when he eventually arrived there he was a very much cooler property.

Later he agreed that he had bungled this move, and he considers that he permanently ruined his chances of top Hollywood stardom by playing mainly negative roles – losers, nice guys, weaklings – the sort of parts which attracted him as a change from villainy. Certainly he started badly: trapped in Max Ophuls's *Caught* (49), as the nice doctor keen on Barbara Bel Geddes; as

Flaubert in the curious prologue to Minnelli's *Madame Bovary*; as the white-hearted blackmailer in Ophuls's *The Reckless Moment* with Joan Bennett; as Barbara Stanwyck's playboy husband in *East Side West Side*; and as the disgraced doctor involved with crooks in *One Way Street* (50) with Marta Toren. He returned to Britain to play a ghost in love with Ava Gardner in the beautiful but boring *Pandora and the Flying Dutchman*.

His Hollywood career finally took impetus with two films for 20th, with whom he had a loose contractual agreement: *The Desert Fox* (51), a fine portrayal of Rommel in this good biopic, and Mankiewicz's gripping *Five Fingers* (52), based on 'Operation Cicero', a true account of the valet/spy (Mason) at the British Embassy in Ankara during the war. But as Mason once commented wryly, each time he did what he and the critics considered a good job, there was seldom a follow-up, and there was now a long hiatus – though his position was weakened by *The Lady Possessed*, produced by himself at Republic with his wife and June Havoc. He was fine, again, as Rupert of Hentzau in *The Prisoner of Zenda*, though the role was much smaller than that of Stewart Granger, his erstwhile second lead in a couple of British films. For producer Huntingdon Hartford he played one of Conrad's sea-captains in *Face to Face*, a two-part film which got few bookings; and for himself and his wife he played three parts in a three-part film, *Charade* (53). Roy Kellino directed. The MFB thought it 'an almost embarrassingly amateurish failure' and it does not appear to have been released in the US, though made there.

His row with Korda was by now settled, and Mason appeared in his *The Man Between*, Carol Reed's attempt to do in Berlin what he had done in Vienna in *The Third Man*, but it didn't come off. Back in Hollywood, Mason did a couple of repeats. He did his *Seventh Veil* bit in Episode One of *The Story of Three Loves* with Moira Shearer this time as his ward/victim, and he was Rommel again in *The Desert Rats*. Then Mankiewicz chose him to play Brutus in his excellent version of Shakespeare's *Julius Caesar* ('Greater Than *Ivanhoe*' said the adverts): of a fine cast – Brando, Gielgud, Louis Calhern, Edmond O'Brien, etc. – many critics thought Mason's the best performance. It was probably his best screen work to date, but the only good subsequent offers were *Botany Bay*, as the baddie in this Alan Ladd vehicle; and *Prince Valiant* (54), a comic-strip swashbuckler. Nor were they exactly lining up at his door for *A Star Is Born*: Warners wanted

Perhaps the best screen version of Shakespeare: Julius Caesar *(53); James Mason as 'the noblest Roman of them all'.*

Humphrey Bogart, and Cary Grant was actually signed for the part: but Mason in the end it was, offering in response to Garland's virtuosity some of the best emotional acting the screen had then seen. It was *not* a step up to play Nemo in Disney's *20,000 Leagues Under the Sea*, but he again got good notices and the film was a hit. In 1954 at Stratford, Ontario, he played Angelo in 'Measure for Measure' and 'Oedipus Rex'.

For some years he plodded on without great éclat: in big parts in mainly poor films, and subsidiary roles in some goodish films. He never lost star billing, but once or twice it was a very close thing. He was an angel in a thudding Lucille Ball comedy, *Forever Darling* (56), a film he would rather forget, and he was a drug addict – a superb performance – in *Bigger Than Life*; but this was otherwise a disastrous venture, again produced by himself. Nicholas Ray directed. Another good director (Robert Rossen) let him down with the film of Alec Waugh's best-seller, *Island in the Sun* (57), which turned out to be a tour of the dreariest couples on said island. He had good parts in two modest thrillers made by Andrew and Virginia Stone, *Cry Terror* (58) and *The Decks Ran Red* – but modest was the way MGM pushed them. He stayed at that studio for

Hitchcock's *North by Northwest* (59), and in his small part was so suavely villainous that he outshone Cary Grant; and in Jules Verne's *Journey to the Center of the Earth* he played with a tongue-in-cheek that set new standards for this sort of thing. But in the British *A Touch of Larceny* (60) and the American *The Marriage-Go-Round* (61) he demonstrated, as the press told him, that he couldn't play comedy – at least, not under these directors. In between came *The Trials of Oscar Wilde* (60) with Peter Finch, and some observers informed him that his interpretation of advocate Sir Edward Carson was inferior to Ralph Richardson's in the rival film: a strange verdict.

Perhaps disheartened, Mason took a guest spot (on the cast list but unbilled) in Yul Brynner's *Escape From Zahrain* (62). But he then got his best chance in years, when Noël Coward turned down Stanley Kubrick's film of Nabokov's virtually unfilmable *Lolita*; but as the hapless middle-aged victim of nymphet Sue Lyon his performance divided the press. Dwight Macdonald found it as 'earthbound' as expected from this actor, and of American critics only Pauline Kael liked it: 'Mason is better than (and different from) what almost anyone had expected . . . he really is in command of a comic style.' Sight and Sound in Britain found him 'so much better than American reviews had hinted at as to suggest some sea-change in mid-Atlantic', adding, 'James Mason has been quietly good, or merely quiet, for so long, in so many films, that it is easy to under-estimate his achievement here.' But the most impressive accolade was director Sidney Lumet's, who said that he had read the script and considered that without Mason to pull it together the film would have been a mess. (Mason himself thinks it his best film, with *Odd Man Out* next.)

What is certain is that, despite the critical and popular success of *Lolita*, Mason's career resumed its oscillating pattern, and he went on to this trio: *Hero's Island*, an adventure story which he co-produced; the Rank *Tiara Tahiti* with John Mills; and *Beta Som/Torpedo Bay* (63), an Italian war film with English dialogue. The Rank one was shown on the Rank circuit in Britain, but the three of them were for strictly lower-case bookings, if that. However, he then began to accept supporting roles and in film after film stole the notices: *The Fall of the Roman Empire* ('only James Mason's Timonides emerges with honour and authority undiminished' – Peter John Dyer in the MFB); *The Pumpkin Eater* with Anne Bancroft; *Lord Jim* (65) with Peter O'Toole; and *Genghis Khan*, an 'international' effort with Omar Sharif and Stephen Boyd. The MFB said that Mason 'once again shows up the dreary wastes of acting round him'. But *Les Pianos Mécaniques*, made in Spain by J. A. Bardem with Melina Mercouri and Hardy Kruger, was so badly received in some countries that it surfaced only briefly in the US and not at all in Britain.

Mason then had three hits: *The Blue Max* (66), a World War I aviation story with George Peppard; *Georgy Girl* with Lynn Redgrave; and *The Deadly Affair* with Simone Signoret, a most undeadly thriller, directed by Lumet from John Le Carré's novel. Then three failures: *Stranger in the House* (67), a British remake of Raimu's *Les Inconnus dans la Maison*; *Duffy*, a 'swinging' film with James Coburn; and *Mayerling* (68), another cosmopolitan effort with Sharif as Rudolph, and himself as the Emperor Franz Joseph, but that, for some reason, did well in Britain. Mason's was virtually the only reputation salvaged from poor reviews, and when he played Trigorin for Lumet in his film of Chekhov's *The Seagull*, Variety said: 'And for those who have long admired Mason, even in latter-day roles played, figuratively, with one arm tied behind his back and both eyes closed, this will be rewarding evidence that the original fire still burns brightly, when permitted.'

In Australia he made *Age of Consent* (69)

Vanessa Redgrave and James Mason in Sidney Lumet's film of The Seagull *(68), the first successful filming in English of a play by Anton Chekhov.*

under Michael Powell's direction, and produced by both of them. It was poorly received, and so was *Spring and Port Wine* (70), as a Yorkshire paterfamilias in this film of Bill Naughton's play. He went on to do *The Yin and the Yang*. He seems to have settled to being a good journeyman actor, which is perhaps a pity because he is primarily a great romantic actor. He has for years planned to play Rochester in *Jane Eyre*, but just after the project seemed at last to be viable another British company announced their version: another reversal in a career full of riddles. He has never won a Best Actor Oscar and has only been nominated *once*–for *A Star Is Born*; though in 1967, on the occasion of the Montreal Exposition, he was named 'Cinema Actor of the Century': a curious award–and how did they arrive at *any* conclusion? But not unjust.

Jessie Matthews

'When you've got a little springtime in your heart' warbled Jessie Matthews in *Evergreen*, and it should have been her signature tune; she was Springtime when the movies were young, and she stayed in people's hearts. She was slight, cool, and, when she danced, as light as thistledown. They advertised her as 'The Dancing Divinity'. Not that she didn't have her detractors: some people found her over-cute, and others liked neither the trill in her singing voice nor the ersatz Mayfair accent. Today, almost everything about her early screen performances has dated–in a way that those of, say, Ginger Rogers haven't. But more than any other British artist, Matthews benefits from nostalgia for the period. With that accent, the giggle, the teeth, and those silly high kicks, she fits only into the 30s; you can't begin to imagine her in Technicolor, for instance. For all that, her films do not survive as mere historical relics: many of them have a genuine gaiety–a rare quality in British films–and the impish charm of the star does not fade.

She was born in poverty–one of 11 children–in 1907 in Soho: where she used to dance in the streets for passers-by, or so runs the fable. Certainly as a child she was so interested in dancing that she was sent to study it, though her theatrical ambitions began when she won third prize in an elocution contest. In 1917 she made her first appearance on a stage, at the Alhambra, in 'Bluebell in Fairyland'; a few years later, in 1923, she was in the chorus of 'The Music Box Revue', understudying Gertrude Lawrence. She made her film debut also, in bit parts in *The Beloved Vagabond* (23) and *Straws in the Wind* (24). One night she went on for the star.... Real success came with 'The Charlot Revue of 1926', and stardom with 'One Dam Thing After Another' (27). There were other Cochran shows: 'This Year of Grace' (28) with Sonnie Hale, 'Wake Up and Dream' (29, London and New York) and 'Evergreen' (30).

She was the toast of London. No one, however, believed that she was film material, until she was signed to play the heroine in *Out of the Blue* (31, starring a popular song-and-dance man of the period, Gene Gerrard). She returned to the stage for 'Hold My Hand', and was then offered the lead in a much-liked comedy with Owen Nares, *There Goes the Bride* (32): 'She was hailed by the critics, given a long-term contract with Gaumont British, and made a series of musical films exploiting her talents. Jessie could dance like an angel, sing with point and significance, and she could act' (Michael Balcon). She fulfilled a stage commitment, 'Sally Who?', which flopped, then took up her £7,000 a year contract–a top fee by local standards: it forbade her to do stage or radio work. *The Midshipmaid* was part farce/part musical and crude, but *The Man From Toronto* (33) was a pleasant comedy about a young widow who will inherit a fortune if she marries a Canadian she has never met. And Victor Saville's *The Good Companions* was a beautiful piece of work. It caught exactly J. B. Priestly's best-selling, picaresque novel,

John Mills and Jessie Matthews in The Midshipmaid *(32), the adventures of a soubrette on one of His Majesty's ships.*

and had fine lead performances by John Gielgud, Edmund Gwenn and Matthews (as Susie). For her, The Observer thought it 'a tremendous personal triumph'.

It was now a question to find vehicles for her. After *Friday the Thirteenth*, an all-star thriller, she did *Waltzes in Vienna* (34), though Picturegoer thought her 'out of her depth as a romantic ingénue'. Hitchcock directed, making much of little and Gwenn and Esmond Knight were the two Strausses. The next one was aptly titled *Evergreen*, an enchanting fable about an Edwardian music-hall star blackmailed into retirement, and the daughter who impersonates her to win success for herself. Matthews played both parts, and it was her biggest success. Then came *First a Girl* (35), an attempt to do a transvestism theme with charm.

Mystery surrounds the next step. She left for Hollywood to make a musical with Robert Montgomery at MGM, *This Time It's Love*: it wasn't made, and Picturegoer merely notes laconically that the scripts that MGM had prepared for Matthews were re-tailored for Eleanor Powell. Balcon (among others) testifies to the Hollywood interest during this period, but says that she turned down all offers because she wanted to stay near her family; he also says 'her taut nerves, combined with her passionate involvement with her work, kept her at a dangerous point of strain'. She did have a breakdown in 1937.

MGM sent Robert Young over to appear with her in *It's Love Again* (36) but had no other connection with it. Also in the cast, as usual, was Sonnie Hale, now her husband. (He had earlier been married to Evelyn Laye, and there had been much publicity when he left one lady for the other.) An unprepossessing appearance prevented him from co-starring, and as comic relief he was wearing. As if he knew it, he went behind the cameras for the next three, as director. *Head Over Heels* (37) was a genuine attempt to break away from British film musical conventions, and so was *Gangway*, where the star was involved with American gangsters, including Nat Pendleton. There followed *Sailing Along* (38) and *Climbing High* (39), a (non-musical) farce, co-starring Michael Redgrave, and directed by Carol Reed. These ended her contract.

If Hollywood was now panting more than ever for Matthews she certainly didn't go. Alas! For there began, slowly, the years in the wilderness. In 1939 she toured in 'I Can Take It', but it didn't get to Town. The war came, and in 1940 she had a short run in 'Come Out to Play'. In 1941 there was a Broadway offer, and Matthews started a tour of 'The Lady Comes Across', but she had a breakdown and the show was cancelled.

She suffered from poor health over the next few years and the off-and-on project of a film with Fred Astaire was finally abandoned. She did, however, make a film in Hollywood to please Victor Saville who was involved in the project: *Forever and a Day* (43), an all-star episoder made for war charities. Her only stage work in several years was a suburban London revival of 'Wild Rose' in 1942 and the only other film a B made by a minor British company: *Candles at Nine* (44), which required her to wander through a haunted house, holding a candelabra and singing, wearing only a chic hat, a fox fur and camiknickers.

She reappeared, glory considerably dimmed, in 1948 in 'Maid to Measure' and did another revue, 'Sauce Tartare', the following year: these were her last West End appearances. In her case, the public was fickle. To an austerity Britain she represented pre-war luxury; apart from a brief moment in 1936 when she was the sixth biggest box-office attraction in Britain, she had never been popular with all classes, and she lacked the common touch which enabled Gracie Fields also to come back after years of eclipse. There was work to be had on tour and in the provinces – in plays like 'The Browning Version' and 'Private Lives'. In 1958 she made a welcome return to the screen in *Tom Thumb* (as Tom's mum), and then spent two years visiting her daughter in Australia, working in TV there as well as on the stage. She returned to Britain and toured as the mother in 'Five Finger Exercise'; she was plump now, and cosy – no longer the sylph of memory. But, like a groundswell, the public began to make amends for the neglect, and in club and theatre engagements they cheered the stout lady, doubtless happy to find her charm undimmed. In London and New York there were retrospectives of her films. Matthews herself, though flattered, did not care too much to go on singing 'Dancing on the Ceiling' and 'Over my Shoulder'. She wanted to be a character actress, and spent six years playing the mother in a radio soap opera ('The Dales', 1963–9). Then she returned to the stage. Her third marriage ended many years ago and she lives in London with her family.

Jessie Matthews in I
Love Again (*36*).

Joel McCrea

Joel McCrea was one of the leading Leading Men of the 30s, a tall, good-looking, reliable actor without any great pretensions. Physically, he was not unlike Gary Cooper,

Chance at Heaven (*33*): *Ginger Rogers, right, lost Joel McCrea to Marion Nixon in reel one, but after several reels of unhappy marriage he returned to her in time for the fade-out.*

and they generally played the same sort of roles. Curiously, he was in as many good films as Cooper was, and was hardly less competent, but he hardly had the same allure; there was something just a little bit more forced about his playing. He reached his peak in the early 40s, and thereafter quickly reversed and buried himself in programmer Westerns where he stayed, comfortably, for almost another 20 years. He had no illusions about his ability: 'Acting? I never attempt it. A placid sort of fellow, that's me. . . . So when I face the cameras I just stay placid . . .' (to the Evening Standard, London).

His talent carried him so far; but just as some – a very few – people became great stars simply because they wanted to be, McCrea didn't reach the heights because he didn't really want to.

He was born in South Pasadena, California, in 1905. He graduated from Pomona University, where he had taken part in dramatics, and for the next two years he acted in community theatre plays, often in leading parts. He wanted to be in films and worked during that time as an extra. One day he was picked out when a goodish part in *The Jazz Age* (29) remained uncast; whence he moved over to MGM on contract and was given small parts in *The Single Standard* (with Garbo) and *So This Is College*. Cecil B. de Mille took over his contract and made him the juvenile lead in *Dynamite*, and after some months of inactivity he moved on again to RKO to play the hero in *The Silver Horde* (30): this led to two good parts at Fox, *Lightnin'* with Will Rogers, and *Once a Sinner* (31) with Dorothy Mackaill, in the latter as a nice country boy who can't prevent his wife returning to her old ways. This was the sort of dilemma he was to face in most of his serious films.

It was at RKO that he finally settled. That studio had liked the McCrea-Mackaill teaming, and reunited them in *Kept Husbands*, where they had similar parts, but he found his most consistent partner when Constance Bennett decided that she was *Born to Love* him: he was an aviator. In *The Common Law* he was an American painter in Paris and she his high society model. He was loaned to Paramount for *Girls About Town*, as a small-town boy who bewitches one of them (Kay Francis), and to Fox for *Business and Pleasure* (32). There followed *The Lost Squadron* as a flyer again, with Richard Dix, *Bird of Paradise*, on a desert island with Dolores del Rio; *The Most Dangerous Game*, on an island again, this time with Fay Wray, both as the human prey of mad Leslie Banks and his hounds; *Rockabye* with Bennett; *The Sport Parade*; *The Silver Cord* (33) at MGM with Irene Dunne and Frances Dee (whom he married that year; they were long considered one of Hollywood's happiest couples but split in the late 60s); *Bed of Roses* with Bennett; *One Man's Journey*–Lionel Barrymore's, from obscurity to fame as a country doctor; and *Chance at Heaven*, as an uppercrust boy torn between wealthy Marion Nixon and poor Ginger Rogers. He had a similar part in *Gambling Lady* (34)–Barbara Stanwyck–but a second loan-out, for *Half a Sinner*, found him merely as the juvenile: the star was Berton Churchill, repeating his 'Alias the Deacon' performance. In *The Richest Girl in the World* he was tested by Miriam Hopkins's friends to see whether he was a fortune hunter.

Hopkins was under contract to Goldwyn, and he liked McCrea's work in this enough to sign him to a contract some months later. In the meantime McCrea left RKO and got parts in *Private Worlds* (35), *Our Little Girl*–Shirley Temple–and *Woman Wanted*, an MGM mystery with Maureen O'Sullivan. Goldwyn put him into three pictures in a row: *Barbary Coast*; *Splendor* with Hopkins, where their earlier positions were reversed, and he was now the society boy and she the poor girl–though they were married; and *These Three* (36), the other two of whom were Hopkins again and Merle Oberon. He and Joan Bennett were the *Two in a Crowd*, a horse story; he had an *Adventure in Manhattan*; and then Goldwyn gave him perhaps his strongest role to date, in *Come and Get It*, as a lumberjack, but both his playing of it and the writing were conventional. He was with Stanwyck again in *Banjo on My Knee* at 20th and *Internes Can't Take Money* (37) at Paramount, in the latter playing a Dr Kildare; and with Hopkins again in *Woman Chases Man*. His next for Goldwyn should have been *The Hurricane*, but he didn't want to do it, and he was put into *Dead End* instead–the lead role, but the film was stolen from him by Bogart, Claire Trevor, Marjorie Main, Sylvia Sidney and others. He was loaned again to Paramount for *Wells Fargo*, his first Western and one of the year's top grossers.

He was borrowed by 20th for *Three Blind Mice* (38) opposite Loretta Young and he did *Youth Takes a Fling* at Universal, playing a Kansas hired man who yearns for the sea, with Andrea Leeds. Goldwyn didn't use him: he had taken Gary Cooper under contract–it was reported that McCrea often got roles that he or Cary Grant had turned down. Still, McCrea was in a big one, de

Union Pacific *(39) was a sprawling de Mille film set against the foundation of that railway. Workmanlike performances by Joel McCrea, Barbara Stanwyck and, right, Robert Preston –plus some typical spectacle–made it seem better than it was.*

Mille's *Union Pacific* (39) with Stanwyck; then he did his last for Goldwyn, *They Shall Have Music*, a sort of musical *Dead End* with guest appearance by Jascha Heifitz. McCrea was reported in Picturegoer as saying: 'I've never had star rating because I dislike the responsibility. . . . A picture hangs on a star. When a picture is bad, the star is washed up. A leading man, such as I am, hangs on to a picture.'

He free-lanced: *Espionage Agent* at WB; *He Married His Wife* (40) at 20th; *The Primrose Path* with Ginger Rogers; and Hitchcock's *Foreign Correspondent*, his best role in some time. Then he signed a deal with Paramount: William A. Wellman's *Reaching for the Sun* (41), a sentimental comedy with Ellen Drew; Preston Sturges's funny *Sullivan's Travels*–another good part–with Veronica Lake; Wellman's *The Great Man's Lady* (42), an insufferable pioneering drama with Stanwyck; Sturges's *Palm Beach Story* with Claudette Colbert; and George Stevens's *The More the Merrier* (43) with Jean Arthur. In most of these he played second fiddle to the ladies, but he was the focal point of both Wellman's *Buffalo Bill* (44) at Fox, in the title role, and Sturges's *The Great Moment* with Betty Field, a serious picture about the first dentist to use ether; and *The Unseen* (45), a follow-up to *The Uninvited* and again with Gail Russell. His last picture for Paramount was a remake of *The Virginian* (46), in Gary Cooper's old role.

That was a Western, and so, with two or three exceptions, were all of McCrea's subsequent films: *Ramrod* (47) with Veronica Lake; *Four Faces West* (48) with his wife; *South of St Louis* (49) with Alexis Smith; *Colorado Territory* with Virginia Mayo; and *Stars in My Crown* (50), as a militant parson who tamed a small Southern town first with guns and then with preaching: it was the last of his films to be well-noticed. The rest were duallers: *The Outriders*; *Saddle Tramp*; *Frenchie* with Shelley Winters, a remake of *Destry Rides Again*; *Cattle Drive* (51); *The San Francisco Story* (52) with Yvonne de Carlo, a tale of the honky tonk days; and *Rough Shoot* with Evelyn Keyes, a poor thriller made in Britain. McCrea continued to be among the surest Western draws. He made: *Lone Hand* (53), *Border River* (54), *Black Horse Canyon*, *Stranger on Horseback* (55), *Wichita* (he also did a TV series under this title), *The First Texan* (56), *The Oklahoman* (57), *Trooper Hook* with Stanwyck, *Gunsight Ridge*, *The Tall Stranger*, *Cattle Empire* (58), *Fort Massacre* and *The Gunfight at Dodge City* (59).

Most of these were poor films and in the words of a reviewer in the MFB McCrea played with 'stolid competence'. But he came out of retirement to give a good performance in one of the best Westerns of the 60s, Sam Peckinpah's *Ride the High Country* (62), teamed with Randolph Scott: they were two old-timers taken on to escort gold-dust from the mine to the bank. MGM treated it as just another McCrea (or Scott) Western, but it established Peckinpah's reputation and for McCrea was a fine curtain.

Victor McLaglen

The Beloved Brute was the name of Victor McLaglen's first American film, and it was thus, afterwards, that publicity usually described him. He was a big, grinning man, type-cast throughout a long career as a tough N.C.O. with a heart of gold, a Wallace Beery without the cunning. He won an Oscar for playing a slight variation of this part, in a rather good picture, but was not, overall, an actor of great subtlety.

He was born in Tunbridge Wells in 1886, the eldest of eight brothers (Cyril, Leopold, Clifford, Arthur and Kenneth also worked in films later, with considerably less success). Father was a clergyman. In 1900 Victor joined the Life Guards (lying about his age), hoping to be able to fight in the Boer War: father later bought him out. He went to Canada where he worked on farms and did casual labour, became a professional prize-fighter (he once went six rounds with Jack Johnson, world heavyweight champion), graduated from that to exhibition boxing with Wild West shows and circuses, which led in turn to vaudeville. He toured in the US and in Australia, where he took part in the Kalgoorlie Gold Rush, and was in South Africa (where Father was now Bishop of Claremont) on the outbreak of war in 1914. He returned to Britain, joined the Irish Fusiliers and served in the Middle East: he was Provost-Marshal of Baghdad and was demobbed with the rank of Captain. After the war he took up boxing again and was in the National Sporting Club in London when a producer I. B. Davidson saw him and offered him the lead in *The Call of the Road* (20). He accepted in a non-serious mood, but this costume romance was good, the best British picture of the year, and he found himself somewhat in demand.

He made *Carnival* (21) which starred Matheson Lang and Ivor Novello, *Corinthian Jack*, *Prey of the Dragon* and *The Sport of Kings*; then J. Stuart Blackton engaged him to play the ruffian who abducts Lady Diana Manners in a Jacobean drama, 'The Glorious Adventure' (22). They repeated on the screen – in colour (it was the first British colour film) and designed mainly to exploit the beauty of Lady Diana; but McLaglen's was the most important male role and it reinforced his position as one of Britain's leading male stars. There followed: *A Romance of Old Baghdad*; *Little Brother of God*; *A Sailor Tramp*; a version of Edgar Wallace's *The Crimson Circle* with a 'name'-cast that included Flora le Breton; *The Romany* (23); *Heartstrings*; *M'Lord of the White Road*, another highwayman story; *In the Blood* (24) with Ben Webster and Dorothy Bellew; *Women and Diamonds* (25), a South African story with Madge Stuart and Florence Turner; *The Gay Corinthian*, made for Butchers, and another swashbuckler, in the title role; and *The Passionate Adventure* starring Clive Brook. McLaglen had only a supporting role in the latter, and times were bad for British films generally: there was a slump in 1924 (the release of these last three pictures was delayed over a year).

He was, therefore, delighted to get a Hollywood offer; indeed he was so broke that his fare had to be cabled to him. His rescuer was the same J. Stuart Blackton who had employed him earlier (Blackton was an Englishman who worked mainly in the US). He wanted him for *The Beloved Brute*, a Vitagraph feature, to star along with William Russell and Margerite de la Motte. McLaglen did not lack for further offers. At Fox he was in *The Hunted Woman*, who was Seena Owen; at Pathé in *Percy*, who was Charles Ray; and at MGM one of *The Unholy Three*, along with Lon Chaney and Harry Earl. He went to First National for Frank Lloyd's *The Winds of Chance* starring Anna Q. Nilsson and his work in that brought him a contract there. He returned to Fox for a supporting part in *The Fighting Heart*, which had George O'Brien as a boxer who gives up fame for the love of Billie Dove. John Ford directed, and he was to use McLaglen in numerous pictures over the years.

McLaglen's next were *The Isle of Retribution* (26) and *Men of Steel* with Milton Sills; then he was loaned to Paramount for a supporting role in *Beau Geste*. It was another loan-out which made him a big Hollywood star: *What Price Glory?* This had been a fine anti-war play by Maxwell Anderson and Laurence Stallings done on Broadway some years earlier with Louis Wolheim and William Boyd, but which had aroused no interest in Hollywood. The success of *The Big Parade*, however, had changed that, and Fox had bought it and assigned Raoul Walsh to direct. Edmund Lowe was cast as Sergeant Quirt, and McLaglen was borrowed

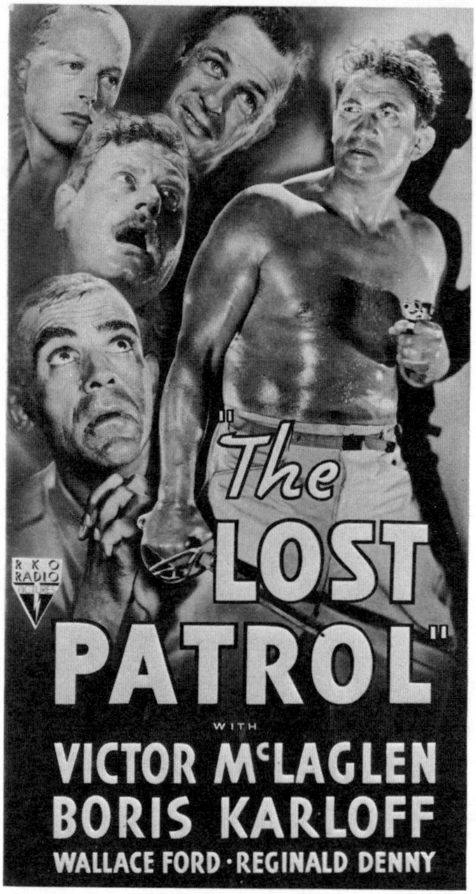

to play Captain Flagg. In the transition to the screen, their amorous exploits somehow took precedence over the bitterness expressed in the title, but the film was a big hit with critics and public (it took over $2 million at the box-office), and before shooting was finished Fox had negotiated to buy McLaglen's contract.

However, Fox did not yet see him as real star stuff, and his next two parts were only featured ones: in Ford's *Mother Machree* and *The Loves of Carmen* (27) with Dolores del Rio. The Ford film was in fact not released until early 1928, while some sequences were tinted (later a music track was added). It starred Belle Bennett, in a reprise of her *Stella Dallas* performance, only in Irish immigrant circumstances and was excessively sentimental. McLaglen followed with another big hit, Howard Hawks's *A Girl in Every Port* (28) top-billed, with Louise Brooks; then Ford's *Hangman's House*, an Irish melodrama; *River Pirate*; *Captain Lash* (29) with Claire Windsor; and Ford's *Strong Boy*, in the title role, a conventional tale about a baggage porter who outwits a gang of train robbers. The last two were released

Victor McLaglen in his Oscar-winning performance in Ford's The Informer *(35), with Wallace Ford.*

with music tracks; McLaglen's first Talkie was *The Black Watch*, directed by Ford, a British army story set in India with McLaglen as an officer thought to be a coward but in fact on a secret mission. It did well, but not as well as Walsh's *The Cock-Eyed World*, a Flagg and Quirt reunion (with Lily Damita) whose gross exceeded all of Fox's wildest hopes: it was third among the year's money-makers.

McLaglen was now one of the two or three sure draws at Fox, and pictures were devised for him which were increasingly decried as McLaglen-formula stuff: *Hot for Paris* and Fifi D'Orsay, with El Brendel as his sidekick thickhead this time; *Happy Days* (30), the studio's all-star revue; *On the Level* with William Harrigan; and *A Devil With Women*, as a mercenary in a banana republic with Mona Maris, who at the end prefers Humphrey Bogart to him. His role in Paramount's *Dishonored* (31) got him somewhat out of the rut, as the bluff but kindly Russian officer who falls in love with, and is betrayed by, Marlene Dietrich. Then he and Lew Cody were *Not Exactly Gentlemen* with Fay Wray; and he was demoted to sergeant to make him the same rank as Quirt in *Women of All Nations*, only they were in the Marines this time and it wasn't as good. He had another change when he became involved in *Annabelle's Affairs*, as a strong and silent Westerner who marries Jeanette MacDonald as a favour and is later wooed by her when they meet again, after he's become a gentleman. He was *Wicked* with Elissa Landi; *The Gay Caballero* (32), with George O'Brien now in support of him; won *The Devil's Lottery*; and was with Helen Mack *While Paris Sleeps*. Paramount borrowed him and Lowe for *Guilty as Hell*, a murder mystery, but it was not up to their earlier teamings; McLaglen was *Rackety Rax* in a college football tale; then Fox teamed him and Lowe for the last time in *Hot Pepper* (33). The girl this time was Lupe Velez and it was some sort of nadir; Picturegoer observed that the series had been growing ever more pointless and licentious.

McLaglen's career was indeed in trouble. He left Fox at that point and there were no Hollywood offers beyond one from Mascot, *Laughing at Life*. So he accepted an offer from Gaumont-British to do the sort of film he had done at the start of his career, *Dick Turpin*. It was not a success. It was Ford who rescued him, by casting him as the Sergeant, the one survivor of *The Lost Patrol* (34), one of his best films. This helped rid McLaglen of the Flagg image, and established him as a reliable supporting player again: *No More Women* at Paramount with Lowe and Sally Blane; *Wharf Angel* with the piquant Dorothy Dell in the title role and Preston Foster; *Murder at the Vanities* with Carl Brisson and Kitty Carlisle; *The Captain Hates the Sea* (35), as a detective with John Gilbert; and at Fox, a couple of programmers with Lowe, *Under Pressure*, in which they were tunnellers, and *The Great*

McLaglen in another Ford picture, Wee Willie Winkie (*37*), *the adventures of a meddling brat* (*Shirley Temple*) *with her grandfather's regiment in India. McLaglen was the tough sergeant who first tolerates her and then befriends her – until he is killed.*

Hotel Murder, in which McLaglen was the dumb house-dick and Lowe a suave thriller-writer guest.

It was as though Ford was McLaglen's guardian angel: he chose him to play Gypo Nolan, *The Informer*, who ratted on a pal because he wanted the £20 reward to buy a steamship ticket to the States. It was set in Dublin in 1922, at the height of the Troubles, and was based on a novel by Liam O'Flaherty; RKO produced, and if they'd had their way, would never have released it. But it won a New York Critics' award at year's end for Ford, and then five Oscars, including a Best Actor one for McLaglen. RKO then began patting themselves on the back. Conversely, today it seems like one of Ford's weakest efforts, and McLaglen's work is not exceptional. He began getting top parts again: *Professional Soldier* (36), in the title role, opposite Freddie Bartholomew; *Klondike Annie*, as the bruiser who falls for, but is not fooled by, Mae West; *Under Two Flags* with Ronald Colman; *The Magnificent Brute*, in the title role, with Binnie Barnes; *Sea Devils* (37), a drama of the Coast Guard patrol with Preston Foster; and *Nancy Steel Is Missing* with Peter Lorre. The momentum had not been maintained. He had a supporting role in *This Is My Affair* starring Barbara Stanwyck. His role in *Wee Willie Winkie* – Ford directing Shirley Temple – was good, but the next two were programmers: *The Battle of Broadway* (38) with Louise Hovick – who was Gypsy Rose Lee at a time when Hollywood was chary of using her 'striptease' name; and *The Devil's Party*.

Twentieth sent him to Britain to play opposite Gracie Fields in *We're Going To Be Rich*, then he took another trip, as the chief engineer, on a *Pacific Liner* (39), hampering doctor Chester Morris in his efforts to cure an outbreak of cholera. He was the menace in Nelson Eddy's *Let Freedom Ring*, then returned to India for *Gunga Din* with Cary Grant and to Australia for a second rip-roaring thriller, *Captain Fury*, where he and Brian Aherne were ex-cons. He was the

Ex-Champ, now a doorman, teaching his old craft to Tom Brown, and then a murderer on his deathbed making a *Full Confession* to a priest – before recovering. There were three more uninteresting films for Universal: *Rio* with Basil Rathbone; *The Big Guy* (40), as a prison warden, with Jackie Cooper; and *Diamond Frontier*. *Broadway Limited* (41) was a comedy set on a long-distance train, with Dennis O'Keefe, and was McLaglen's only film in a year; but he had no intention of retiring, and *Call Out the Marines* (42) actually teamed him with Lowe again, this time rounding up spies. He was the recalcitrant foreman of a munitions plant in *Powder Town*, and then somewhat more devious in *China Girl* with Gene Tierney.

After a guest spot in *Forever and a Day* (43) he was villainous again in *Tampico* (44), starring Edward G. Robinson, and in *The Princess and the Pirate*, as a pirate, starring Bob Hope. Inbetweenwhiles, he was with old co-stars Preston Foster (in the title role) in a B at 20th, *Roger Touhy Gangster* and then with Chester Morris in *Rough Tough and Ready* (45) at Republic. Still at that studio he was with some other faded glories – Virginia Bruce, Nils Asther and Edward Ashley (in real life the Earl of Warwick) – in *Love Honor and Goodbye*. He did: *Whistle Stop* (46) with George Raft; *Calendar Girl* (47) starring Jane Frazee; *The Michigan Kid*, supporting Jon Hall in this his first Western, a B and a poor one at that; and *The Foxes of Harrow*, supporting Rex Harrison. Ford came to the rescue again, and cast him as a sergeant in the three films that make up a trilogy about the U.S. Cavalry, *Fort Apache* (48), *She Wore a Yellow Ribbon* (49) and *Rio Grand* (50) – in the latter two as Sgt Quincannon, a character played in the first one by Dick Foran. Then he was in Ford's *The Quiet Man* (52), followed by *Fair Wind to Java* (53), a Republic adventure in Trucolor; *Prince Valiant* (54) as a faithful retainer of that gentleman (Robert Wagner); the British *Trouble in the Glen*; *Many Rivers to Cross* (55), a Robert Taylor Western; *City of Shadows*, a Republic B in which he starred; *Lady Godiva* (Maureen O'Hara); *Bengazi*, as the owner of an underworld café, with Richard Conte; and *The Abductors* (59), a B directed by his son, Andrew V. McLaglen, in which he was once again an ex-con.

His last picture was made in Britain, Rank's *Sea Fury* (58), with Stanley Baker, and he played a belligerent and hard-drinking captain who at the end realizes that he is too old for his job. McLaglen's colleagues felt similarly about him: he had difficulty remembering his lines and it was believed that he would not film again. He died of a heart attack in 1959. He was married three times; son Andrew was by his first wife, who died in 1942. McLaglen then married his secretary, but that marriage ended in divorce in 1948.

Ray Milland

One of the staples of the old days was the featured leading man – the actor who was never quite starred: he was the hero's brother, the hero's rival or the Other Man, and sometimes – in comedies – the hero's friend. There were dozens of them: John Carroll, John Loder, John Sutton, often Ralph Bellamy. Ray Milland spent a good ten years in such parts before making his mark as a light comedian, cheery and good-natured; and he went on from there to be a highly competent actor. He made some costume films and Westerns, but was most at home in a double-breasted pin-stripe suit. Real life rarely breathed into any of the films that he was given to do, and it is therefore somewhat difficult to assess him as a serious actor.

He was born in Neath, Glamorganshire, in 1905, and educated at King's College, London. He served for a while as a Royal Guardsman, but all accounts of his early career suggest a dilettante existence. He was, apparently, friendly with Estelle Brody, and on a visit to her at the studio was offered a small part in *The Plaything* (29), which starred Lya de Putti. He was billed as Spike Milland. He had some walk-ons in films and toured in 'The Woman in Room 13'; then got another chance in the first, British, version of *The Informer* with de Putti and Lars Hanson. He became the fireman on *The Flying Scotsman* and had the lead in *Goodwin Sands*, but both flopped; he was also in *The Passion Flower*. He was now billed as Raymond Milland. C. B. Cochran offered him a contract, but Milland meanwhile had heard that Anita Loos had recommended him to MGM. He decided to brave Hollywood, and MGM did give him a contract. They put him into Marion Davies's *The Bachelor Father* (31) and into *Just a Gigolo*, but mostly loaned him out: to WB for *Bought* (where he did wrong to Constance Bennett): to Fox for Will Rogers's *Ambassador Bill* and to Warners again for *Blonde Crazy* and *The Man Who Played God* (32). He had an insignificant part in *Polly of the Circus*, and a reasonably good one in *Payment Deferred*, being murdered by Charles Laughton, both at his home studio, which promptly dropped him. He returned to Britain and got parts in an old army farce,

The second of the three film versions of Beau Geste *(39), a story about three brothers who join the Foreign Legion when one of them – Beau – is falsely suspected of robbery. In this early scene Ray Milland is contemplating disgrace, watched by the girl all three brothers love (Susan Hayward).*

Orders Is Orders (33), and *This Is the Life* starring Gordon Harker; and then decided to try his luck again in Hollywood.

Paramount gave him a small part as a gigolo in *Bolero* (34), and then the part of Bing Crosby's supercilious rival in *We're Not Dressing*. They liked him, offered him a long-term contract and cast him as the romantic lead in a very funny Burns and Allen vehicle, *Many Happy Returns*. He was featured in *Charlie Chan in London* (at Fox), *Menace* with Gertrude Michael, and *One Hour Late* (35) with Helen Twelvetrees. His parts were getting bigger and his best chance came as Fred MacMurray's rival for Claudette Colbert in *The Gilded Lily*. He was in *Four Hours to Kill*; was fourth on the cast list of the George Raft *The Glass Key*; and had the lead in a Universal B, *Alias Mary Dow*. That studio liked him enough to keep him on as James Stewart's rival for Margaret Sullavan in *Next Time We Love* (36). He then did *The Return of Sophie Lang*, one of a series that starred Gertrude Michael; *The Big Broadcast of 1937*; *The Jungle Princess*, as a writer discovering Dorothy Lamour in Malaya; *Bulldog Drummond Escapes* (37), somehow considerably miscast as Drummond; and, again at Universal, *Three Smart Girls*, in a very small role. He couldn't protest, especially when that studio retained him once more, this time to co-star with Wendy Barrie in *Wings Over Honolulu*.

His first real impact was made in *Easy Living*, as the millionaire's son trying to make his own way – until Jean Arthur brings the automat crashing down around them; and he ended up with the girl for once.

Frances Farmer was the girl in *Ebb Tide*, and she and Oscar Homolka were billed above him in this Technicolor version of a Robert Louis Stevenson story; and Miriam Hopkins was the *Wise Girl* at RKO. He was now recognized as a fully fledged leading man, but again in the next two the biggest attraction was considered to be the Technicolor: *Her Jungle Love* (38) Dorothy Lamour's; and *Men With Wings* – Fred MacMurray was the other one. He was with Lamour again on a *Tropic Holiday*, and then he did a B again, *Say It in French* with Olympe Bradna. He was with another doomed import, Isa Miranda, in the remake of *Hotel Imperial* (39), and after playing one of *Beau Geste's* brothers was with a third broken-accented lady, Sonja Henie, in *Everything Happens at Night*, at 20th. Paramount then gave him his biggest chance, as the only 'name' in the cast of their British-made version of the Terence Rattigan stage hit, *French Without Tears* (40): his skill with the bright lines was one of the best things about a disappointing film. They announced that Milland was being groomed to be one of the biggest stars on the lot.

He starred in *Irene* at RKO, an Anna Neagle musical which badly needed his elegance; in *The Doctor Takes a Wife*, a slight marital comedy with Loretta Young; and in *Untamed*, a title which referred both to Patricia Morison and the Frozen North (it was a remake of *Mantrap*). Nonchalant, smiling (often, over-smugly), well-tailored, he breezed his way through mechanical pieces: *Arise My Love* and *Skylark* (41), both with Claudette Colbert and intended originally for Joel McCrea and Melvyn Douglas respectively. Earlier in the year he was in one of those films which were Hollywood's way of letting the world know that the USA was not unprepared for war, *I Wanted Wings*; and then he and Paulette Goddard were gallant Americans in wartime Lisbon in *The Lady Has Plans* (42). Goddard was with him again in de Mille's *Reap the Wild Wind*, a big box-office hit, and notable for his battle with a giant squid. He gave his opinion of the film to a reporter years later: 'I thought it was horrible.' There were four comedies: *Are Husbands Necessary?* with Betty Field was pleasant; Billy Wilder's *The Major and the Minor* with Ginger Rogers was somewhat better, though less good than its reputation allows; a sketch in *Star Spangled Rhythm*; and *The Crystal Ball* (43) with Goddard again.

There was more serious stuff in *Forever and a Day*, about a big house in London; and in *The Uninvited* (44), about a big house on the Cornish cliffs which is haunted, with Gail Russell. But *Lady in the Dark* with Rogers was his last escapist entertainment for some time. *Till We Meet Again* was a war story with Barbara Britton, and *The Ministry of Fear* was a thriller set in London during the blitz, Fritz Lang's enjoyable but unsatisfactory version of Graham Greene's 'entertainment'. Marjorie Reynolds co-starred. *The Lost Weekend* (45) had originally been a novel about an alcoholic by Charles Jackson, and Wilder's surprising choice of Milland for this part was due to his satisfaction with his work in *The Major and the Minor*. It was a sympathetic and convincing performance–undoubtedly his best screen work–and it won him a Best Actor Oscar and the New York Critics' award. Wilder directed with perception–the film has dated less than almost any other 40s drama–and it won a Best Picture Oscar and did fine at the box-office.

Few of Milland's next films were worthy of his new status: *Kitty*, a period drama in which he had little to do but shoot super-

Before Ray Milland lost his weekend (45): his brother (Phillip Terry) and his fiancée (Jane Wyman) take away his whisky as they're not going to be there to guard him from it. From then on it's an odyssey in search of more booze.

cilious lines at Paulette Goddard; *The Well-Groomed Bride* (46), a weak comedy with Olivia de Havilland; *California*, a Western with Barbara Stanwyck; and *The Imperfect Lady* (47) and *The Trouble With Women*, a couple of programmers with Teresa Wright, period thriller and marital farce respectively. Indeed, Milland couldn't hold his box-office status either, and after the next two they played double bills. *Golden Earrings* was some nonsense in which, as an escaping British officer, he was disguised as a gypsy with the aid of Marlene Dietrich; but *The Big Clock* (48) was a first-rate thriller directed by John Farrow with Farrow's wife, Maureen O'Sullivan, and Charles Laughton. Milland made *So Evil My Love* in Britain with Ann Todd, another period piece. Then: *Sealed Verdict*, a silly romantic drama; *Alias Nick Beale* (49) with Thomas Mitchell, an interesting crime melo with a Faust theme; *It Happens Every Spring* at 20th with Jean Peters; *A Woman of Distinction* (50) at Columbia with Rosalind Russell; and *Copper Canyon*, a conventional Western. '*Copper Canyon* I loathed,' he said later in an interview. 'I hated working with Hedy Lamarr.'

It was almost his last film for Paramount, and he began to free-lance successfully:

A Life of Her Own with Lana Turner; *Circle of Danger* (51) which he produced in Britain, a muddy little drama with Patricia Roc; *Night Into Morning* with John Hodiak, battling with the Bottle again; *Rhubarb*, some whimsy about a cat; *Close to My Heart* with Gene Tierney; and *Something To Live For* (52), another study in alcoholism but this time Joan Fontaine was a bigger drunk than he. His box-office after this lot was decidedly shaky, but it perked up with a Western, *Bugles in the Afternoon*, and there was considerable interest in *The Thief*, which had the novelty or gimmick of having almost no dialogue. His final film for Paramount came up: *Jamaica Run* (53), a pathetic farewell gift to one of the old reliables.

However, it cannot be said that his work was very distinguished: in *Let's Do It Again* with Jane Wyman he seemed to have congealed; and he looked rather bored throughout his participation in both Hitchcock's *Dial M for Murder* (54) with Grace Kelly and in *The Girl in the Red Velvet Swing* (55), as Stanford White in this account of a famous turn-of-the-century *crime passionel*.

This trio was virtually the end of his First Feature days, but he turned to directing himself with pleasing results, firstly with an unusual Western, *A Man Alone* (56), and then making something out of a routine melo, *Lisbon*. After discouraging results when directed by other people – *Three Brave Men* (57), *The River's Edge* and *High Flight*, a mundane British film about the RAF, he directed himself again in a goodish crime piece, *The Safe-Cracker* (58).

After an absence of four years (he had a TV series in the US, 'Markham') he returned to films, mostly on the horror/science-fiction trail. Some of them are highly regarded by addicts: *Premature Burial* (61), *Panic in Year Zero* (63) which he also directed, and *The Man With the X-Ray Eyes* (64). In 1965 he and Ginger Rogers made a movie in Jamaica, *The Confession*, but it has not yet been shown anywhere. Two years later he journeyed to Britain to direct and appear in *Hostile Witness*, a court-roomer in which he had starred in New York and in Australia; it was also released as a B in 1970. In that year he also did *Love Story*.

He married in 1932 and the marriage has endured happily.

Carmen Miranda

Carmen Miranda was known as The Brazilian Bombshell. Her speciality was Latin-American songs-and-dances, particularly the faster numbers, rumbas and sambas. She came on flamboyantly decorated; her headdresses towered, often with half an orchard and a couple of baskets of fruit; the platforms of her shoes were three inches high (which did nothing to impair her dancing). She was great fun. In between songs there was little that script-writers could find for her to do: she was usually the heroine's friend – or rival – and she was loyal, fast-talking, with a very low tolerance point. She showed occasional skill with a comedy line, and, in other circumstances, might have had a longer career.

She was born in Marco Canavezes, Portugal, in 1909, and taken to Brazil as a child. Later she established a reputation as a night-club entertainer, with her own band and her own radio show, and she made four films: *Alo Alo Brasil* (34), *Estudantes*, *Alo Alo Carnaval* and *Banana da Terra* (38). She was known throughout South America when Marc Connelly brought her to the attention of the Shuberts, who gave her a featured part in a Broadway show, 'Streets of Paris' (39). In it she sang 'South American

Way' and 20th asked her to repeat it for a Betty Grable musical, *Down Argentine Way* (40): she filmed her scenes in New York (the first time she had acted, according to 20th). After a few days' rushes she was signed to a long-term contract. Her success in Hollywood was instantaneous; she was imitated everywhere, both seriously and in parody. She made two more lush musicals, designed partly to encourage America's Good Neighbour Policy: *That Night in Rio* (41) and *Weekend in Havana*. Twentieth reluctantly let her do an Olsen and Johnson, 'Sons o' Fun', but she returned to the west and moved north for *Springtime in the Rockies* (42). By the time of *The Gang's All Here* (43) her limitations were all too painfully obvious.

All the same, after guesting in *Four Jills and a Jeep* (44) she was top-starred over Don Ameche in *Greenwich Village* and was, said the Sunday Chronicle (London), 'dazzlingly dynamic'. The Evening Standard was 'invigorated' by her 'bounding vitality'. She was not, of course, the romantic lead – that was Vivian Blaine, who 20th hoped would replace the decamping Alice Faye. Miranda and Blaine were starred again in *Something for the Boys* (45), a good Broadway musical which 20th standardized with their usual skill; and in both *Doll Face* and *If I'm Lucky* (46), but these two were in black and white, a fair indication that the combined box-office worth of the two ladies couldn't encompass Technicolor. And Miranda in black and white was much less impressive. Twentieth had no further plans for her and she signed a long-term deal with Universal; but she made no films for them and instead turned up opposite Groucho Marx in *Copacabana* (47), a mild little comedy. She herself was fine, and MGM took her up for featured parts in two musicals, *A Date With Judy* (48) and *Nancy Goes to Rio*: neither studio publicity nor box-office returns indicated that this was a new lease of life for

It could be a scene from any *Carmen Miranda film, but it is in fact from* That Night in Rio *(41). The leads were Alice Faye and Don Ameche, but she stole the film.*

her. She turned to nightclubs and personal appearances, including the London Palladium in 1948, and got one last break with featured billing: *Scared Stiff* (53), a Martin and Lewis comedy. She died that same year, it was said of a broken heart (really peritonitis). She had been married in 1947 to David Sebastian.

Maria Montez

The name of Maria Montez brings joy to the hearts of some fanciers of 1940s nostalgia. (Not for nothing is her name sacred to one of 'The Boys in the Band'.) Queen of some wartime dustbin epics, her reign was brief: if talent will out, then so will the lack of it.

Born in 1920 in Barahona, in the Dominican Republic, to the Spanish consul there, she was, needless to say, convent-educated. That over with, she journeyed to Europe where she joined a theatrical troupe; in Belfast (when she was 17) she married an officer in the British army. After the divorce she went to New York and became a model. Her striking Latin beauty led to a screen test with Universal, who signed her at $150 a week. Her first work consisted of bits in *The Invisible Woman* (41) and *Lucky Devils*, and her first real part was opposite Johnny Mack Brown in *Boss of Bullion City*, a B Western; then she was loaned to 20th Century-Fox for *That Night in Rio*. Her demands for better parts got her the leads in the likes of *Raiders of the Desert*, *South of Tahiti* starring Brian Donlevy, *Bombay Clipper* (42) and *The Mystery of Marie Roget*, freely adapted from Poe, with Marie Onspenskaya well cast as her grandmother; while some interest accrued to her because she was almost the only artist on the contract list considered dishy enough to compete on barrack-room walls with the Grables and Hayworths of other studios. It occurred to Universal that she might be showcased (as they were) in some lavish escapist entertainment. As she couldn't sing or dance, the solution was: *Arabian Nights*. She played Scheherazade (and did dance–of sorts) and Jon Hall was Haroun al Raschid. Its success spawned a sequel, *White Savage* (43)–which had been the British title for *South of Tahiti*, so for audiences there this was re-titled *White Captive*. And more . . . all of them remarkable for their Technicolor and dozens of girls with bare midriffs, plus some less ingratiating ingredients–cheap painted sets, grade-school dialogue, and acting which wouldn't have disgraced a cigar-store Indian. As twin sisters in *Cobra Woman* Montez's performance (the plural would be inappropriate)

One of the most curious aspects of wartime entertainment was the proliferation of comic-strip Oriental 'extravaganzas' all starring Maria Montez. The best of them was probably the first, Arabian Nights *(42), produced by Walter Wanger. The gentleman in charge in this picture is Sabu.*

has to be seen to be believed. C. A. Lejeune observed of the film that it 'certainly dragged its slow length along'. The others were: *Ali Baba and the 40 Thieves* (44), *Gypsy Wildcat* and *Sudan* (45). Hall and usually Turhan Bey supported Montez. As public interest waned, the studio tried her in a period musical, *From Bowery to Broadway*; then in a modern drama, *Tangier* (46); then in *The Exile* (47), a Douglas Fairbanks swash-buckler directed by Max Ophuls–in a small part; and then in something called *Pirates of Monterey*. Unsurprisingly, when her contract ran out, it wasn't renewed.

With her husband, Jean-Pierre Aumont, she did an independent, black-and-white throwback to her heyday, *Siren of Atlantis* (48): she got $100,000, but the film didn't get its money back. She and Aumont went to Europe, where she made a motley group of French and Franco-Italian pictures. The titles: *Hans le Marin* (48), *Le Portrait d'un Assassin* (49), *The Thief of Venice/Il Ladro di Venezia* (50, made in English), *Terre de Violence* and *La Vengeance du Corsaire* (51). She had begun to have weight problems, and tried to counter them by taking hot saline baths. She died in one, of a heart attack, in 1951. Her daughter Tina married actor Christian Marquand and has acted in French pictures.

Robert Montgomery

Robert Montgomery is probably remembered less for what he did in his own right than for squiring on-screen the famous ladies of MGM – Garbo, Shearer, Crawford. He was MGM's all-purpose actor, but he was best in light comedy, a *jeune premier* of the Park Avenue set, immaculate, boyish and smooth.

Whether or not he came from the requisite background is not known. MGM publicity insisted that he was born into a wealthy family (in Beacon, New York, in 1904) who became penniless when Montgomery's father died. He became a mechanic's mate and a deck-hand on an oil-tanker. Said a studio blurb: 'He used to write sea stories, having had adventures in a tanker.' Montgomery was still in his teens and trying to make a living as a writer when he was offered five different walk-ons in a near-by Greenwich Village theatre, in 'The Mask and the Face' (21). He was later in rep in Rochester, New York, in over 70 plays in 18 months; and his Broadway appearances included 'Dawn', 'Arlene O'Dare', 'One of the Family' and 'Possession' (28). He was well-noticed in the latter, and Goldwyn announced that he would head the supporting cast of Vilma Banky's *So This Is Heaven*; but after testing him changed his mind. MGM executives in New York saw the test, however, and signed him to a contract at $350 a week. The Hollywood end of the company were dismayed when they saw him – too skinny and fragile and unprepossessing. Eventually he was cast in *So This Is College?* (29) and director Sam Wood had him padded to play a fullback.

Somewhat less desperately he was loaned to UA for a remake of *Three Live Ghosts*, the story of three soldiers returned to London on Armistice Day. But whatever he may have been like in the flesh he photographed well and was cast opposite jungle-flower Joan Crawford in *Untamed*, and then as one of the children, with Leila Hyams, in *Father's Day*: Louis Mann was father.

Our Blushing Brides (*30*). *'You must see Joan Crawford in those lace step-ins,' said Photoplay. Robert Montgomery, however, wasn't impressed.*

His big lift came when cast opposite Norma Shearer in *Their Own Desire* (30), after which he wasn't too happy at being, with Anita Page, the love interest in *Free and Easy*, starring Buster Keaton and Trixie Friganza. He was back with Shearer, seducing her, in *The Divorcee*, and back with the cast of *Father's Day* in a sequel known variously as *The Richest Man in the World* and *Sins of the Children*. His rating advanced again as the yellow welcher in the hit prison melo *The Big House* with Wallace Beery and Chester Morris and, less spectacularly, with *Our Blushing Brides* with Crawford, and *Love in the Rough*, a remake of a 1927 William Haines vehicle, *Spring Fever*. He was also the leading character in *War Nurse*, supported by Robert Ames, June Walker, Anita Page and Marie Prevost, a tribute that Photoplay found 'by turns gruesome and silly'. After that it was back to the Great Ladies: Garbo in *Inspiration* (31) – he was poor as the country boy who loves her; Constance Bennett in *The Easiest Way*, deserting her on hearing of her past; and Shearer in *Strangers May Kiss*. It was Dorothy Jordan in *Shipmates*; then he was *The Man in Possession*, an ex-con turned broker's man in the house of wealthy widow Irene Purcell, from a successful play. *Private Lives* had also been lived out on the stage first, and its author, Noël Coward, thought Montgomery and Shearer played 'charmingly' though on the whole he didn't care for it. Montgomery's acting is perhaps too knowing. The *Lovers Courageous* (32) were him and Madge Evans: 'On her wedding night she ran to the arms of her lover' said the ads, suggesting (erroneously) that the film might be either salacious or dramatic. He did *But the Flesh Is Weak*, an adaptation of Ivor Novello's play 'The Truth Game'; *Letty Lynton* with Crawford again; *Blondie of the Follies* with Marion Davies; and *Faithless* with Tallulah Bankhead.

Hell Below (33) was a submarine drama with Jimmy Durante, Walter Huston and Madge Evans; the girl he *Made on Broadway* was Sally Eilers, a weak satire on publicity methods; he was present *When Ladies Meet*; spoke *Another Language* to Helen Hayes; and took a *Night Flight* with her, Clark Gable and two of the Barrymores. He and Madge Evans were lovers again, not courageous this time, but *Fugitive Lovers*: this made a run of poor parts, but Metro signed him to a new contract, and he was seen to advantage in *Riptide* (34) with Shearer, as the charming, playboy Other Man; *The Mystery of Mr X*, with Lewis Stone and Elizabeth Allen, as the slick playboy thief; and *Hide-Out* with Maureen O'Sullivan, as the smooth-tongued playboy racketeer. He was with Crawford and Gable, *Forsaking All Others*; with Helen Hayes in *Vanessa Her Love Story* (35)–inadequate as Benjie; with Ann Harding in *Biography of a Bachelor Girl*; with Crawford again in a fair version of a hit stage comedy, *No More Ladies*; with Myrna Loy in *Petticoat Fever* (36), as the wireless operator for whom she leaves stuffy fiancé Reginald Owen; and with Rosalind Russell in *Trouble for Two*, from–a long way from–Robert Louis Stevenson's 'The Suicide Club'. *Piccadilly Jim*, from a P. G. Wodehouse story, was one of his best pictures, and the fact that he was not, for once, supporting one of MGM's queens (though it had the underrated Madge Evans) gave him fine chances: he was more or less evenly matched with Crawford in *The Last of Mrs Cheyney* (37). His employers, however, were not very happy with him; he had done sterling work on behalf of the newly formed Screen Actors Guild, and when he asked to play the homicidal maniac in *Night Must Fall* the studio readily bought it for him, thinking it would destroy his popularity. It had been a very successful stage thriller and Montgomery was only too convincing as the maniacal Danny, outwardly sane, with the head in the hat-box: it increased his stature, in fact. The studio, unmollified by his success, loaned him out for the first time

Montgomery and Norma Shearer in Private Lives *(31)–in the midst of the second-act battle.*

Montgomery with Madge Evans, his co-star in four pictures. She retired when she married dramatist Sidney Kingsley.

sincè 1929, to Warners for *Ever Since Eve* with Marion Davies; they then threw him into *Live Love and Learn*, a comedy with his *Night Must Fall* co-star Rosalind Russell – though rumours emanated from the studio that they didn't get on – and then into a couple of programmers with Virginia Bruce, *The First Hundred Years* (38) and the excellent *Yellowjack*.

Montgomery had in any case never had the first choice of the MGM farceur roles (they had gone to William Powell), but was considered the leading young light comedian in films; a situation eroded by Cary Grant, who had come to the fore as *the* leading purveyor of this sort of comedy. MGM lost all interest in Montgomery as an asset: he was virtually in support of Janet Gaynor in *Three Loves Has Nancy*, and he took over a role just vacated by Melvyn Douglas, sleuth Joel Sloan in *Fast and Loose* (39) with Russell as his wife (the Douglas film had been *Fast Company* with Florence Rice and the characters would be played in the next one, *Fast and Furious*, by Ann Sothern and Franchot Tone). Montgomery was back on a better track with *The Earl of Chicago* (40), an enjoyable comedy about a bootlegger who becomes a member of the British aristocracy; and he remained ennobled, as Lord Peter Wimsey in *Busman's Honeymoon* with Constance Cummings – and that was actually filmed in Britain. Shooting was stopped on the outbreak of war and resumed early in 1940: in the interim, as a gesture of friendship, Montgomery visited the BEF in France.

At RKO he was half of the mere *Mr and Mrs Smith* (41) with Carole Lombard as the other half; then he was a paranoic again in *Rage in Heaven*, trying to murder wife Ingrid Bergman and best friend George Sanders because – as far as could be discerned – he had a subliminal crush on Sanders. It was Columbia who proudly announced *Here Comes Mr Jordan*, with Claude Rains as Mr Jordan, helping (dead) boxer Montgomery to find himself a new body – one of the few acceptable film whimsies, and one of the few Montgomery films where he assumed an accent – in this case an effortless Bronx. He was loaned out again to Universal for a comedy with Irene Dunne, *Unfinished Business*, after which he joined the US navy, ending up as a Lieutenant-Commander.

He had a beautiful *rentrée*, Ford's *They Were Expendable* (45) with John Wayne, one of the most lyrical of war films, but MGM had already lined up *Desire Me*: Montgomery in his old role as chief courtier, in this case to Queen Greer. But there was trouble during the shooting, and he was replaced by newcomer Richard Hart (and the film later went out without director credit). *Lady in the Lake* (46) was much talked about. From one of Raymond Chandler's novels, it told the film in first person: Montgomery was Marlowe, seen only in an occasional mirror – but he directed, which put him very much in front. The studio, however, had never quite forgiven him and at that point he left them.

He went to Universal to direct and star in *Ride the Pink Horse* (47) – and did both almost brilliantly; but the confused plot (hoodlum on the revenge trail) and a poor title killed it at the box-office. His career wilted again with *The Saxon Charm* (48), a melodrama at Universal with Susan Hayward and John Payne, in which he played a self-centred, ruthless and nasty theatre producer, but revived with *June Bride*, opposite Bette Davis (who disclosed in her memoirs that she loathed working with him). He directed as well as starred in *Once More My Darling* (49), a comedy about a playboy and a debutante (Ann Blyth); and had the same functions on *Your Witness*, made for Warners in Britain. With that, as he said later, he got out while the going was good: he had had a long and successful career and didn't feel disposed to continue in the sort of weak films he had had since he left MGM.

He turned to TV, first in the 'Lucky Strike Theatre' and then in 'Robert Montgomery Presents', a dramatic series in which he sometimes starred and which he often directed; and for most of the 50s he was consultant to President Eisenhower on all things televisual, including the presentation of said President. He became executive producer of Cagney-Montgomery Productions, but the film in which he directed long-time friend Cagney (and which took three years to set up), *The Gallant Hours*, did poor business. In the 60s his daughter Elizabeth demonstrated that she had inherited much of his comedic skill in a TV series, 'Bewitched'.

Grace Moore

It almost beggars belief that Grace Moore was once a popular film-star, but at the time she was considered an attractive as well as an accomplished artist. True, she was skinny at a time when prima donnas were expected to be obese. Unfortunately, as well as her opera-trained voice, she brought to films too many prima donna characteristics (including tantrums on the set). She was always inappropriate: her face though not uncomely bore an unhappy resemblance to that of comedienne Joan Davis, disqualifying

'Princess or pauper, I love you': Emperor-in-disguise Franchot Tone thinks Grace Moore is an innkeeper's daughter, but she's incognito too and really Elizabeth of Bavaria. The King Steps Out (*36*).

her for the dainty heroines she ventured to play; too often she frisked about the screen, like a horse thinking it was a kitten. But here is a contemporary opinion: 'She is one of the few singers who is easy to look at even when tackling a high C; she acts pleasantly, moves engagingly, has obvious wit and character' (C. A. Lejeune on *One Night of Love*).

She was born in Del Rio, Tennessee, in 1903, and educated at Nashville, where her remarkable voice was first trained; while still a student she sang in a Martinelli concert at the National Theatre, Washington. She went into operetta and had her first important role in 'Up in the Clouds'. She also appeared in some of the Music Box Revues (in the 1924 edition she introduced 'What'll I do?') and was in one of the later 'Hitchy Koo' shows. She continued to study voice–with Maraflot–but really turned her attention to higher things when she was befriended by millionaire music patron Otto Kahn: under his auspices she studied in Europe and began to give concerts. She made her Metropolitan debut in 1928 as Mimi in 'La Boheme'.

MGM signed her to a contract and put her into two films, *A Lady's Morals* (30), an inept concoction based on the life of Jenny Lind, and *New Moon*, with Lawrence Tibbett, which kept the songs but threw away the story of the stage version. Both were resounding failures, and Moore returned to opera and concerts. In 1933 she starred on Broadway in 'The Dubarry', and her success caused Hollywood to look at her again. She desperately wanted to return to MGM, who had dropped her ignominiously three years earlier, and when she heard that they wanted her for *The Merry Widow* she was prepared to waive her fee. But neither she nor Chevalier would accept second billing, and when MGM backed Chevalier, she dropped out and Jeanette MacDonald played the part. She was consoled by a contract from Columbia at $25,000 per film. But Columbia had second thoughts and wanted out. Moore threatened to sue, so they went ahead with *One Night of Love* (34) in which she mixed ballads with bits of grand opera. To everyone's surprise, the public lapped it up (and even more surprising, the star was nominated for an Oscar). Thalberg at MGM now wanted Moore more than ever, and MGM announced that she would appear for them in both *Rose Marie* and then *Maytime*; but she missed the schedule on the first and again MacDonald played both parts; with the death of Thalberg, interest in Moore at MGM ceased.

Columbia, however, had Grace Moore vehicles lined up: *Love Me Forever* (35); and more frou-frou, *The King Steps Out* (36), which had suitable music by Fritz Kreisler. Franchot Tone was an incognito Franz Joseph II enraptured by publican's daughter Moore. It didn't do as well as the earlier two, and grosses dropped on the next couple, *When You're in Love* (37) and *I'll Take Romance*, despite the presence of leading men Cary Grant and Melvyn Douglas respectively – and the fact that in the first of these Moore essayed a much-publicized 'Minnie the Moocher'. Her temperament was a Hollywood byword, and when no further offers were forthcoming, she accepted the lead in Charpentier's *Louise* (39), made in France. Abel Gance directed and it was a monumental bore. She never filmed again, but in 1953 – six years after she was killed in an air crash on a Copenhagen runway – WB made a biopic, *So This Is Love*, with Kathryn Grayson as Moore.

By this time, chunks of opera were accepted screen fare. In 1935 Grace Moore had been a pioneer. The Society of Arts and Sciences had given her a gold medal for 'distinctive service in the arts, especially for conspicuous achievement in raising the standard of cinema entertainment'.

Frank Morgan

There was a time when no MGM film seemed complete without Frank Morgan, a stocky middle-aged man with an air of perpetual surprise: his neigh of astonishment is one of the soundtrack's enduring memories. He dithered, he was just short of being eccentric, he was the beloved family fool: the characteristics had been worked out early in his stage career and MGM at least weren't going to let him lose them. His actual range was much wider, though perhaps it doesn't matter: whatever he did Morgan was one of the most satisfying and endearing performers ever to make movies.

According to The Great Ziegfeld *(36) Ziegfeld started his career running a sideshow in a carnival. Frank Morgan played his chief rival for the public's attention.*

He was an artist with a talent for gauging the tones of co-players and script and acting up or down accordingly.

He was born in New York City in 1890 into a family of importers (Angostura bitters; later, during his film-career, he was Vice-President) and was educated for a time at Cornell University. He sold space for a Boston newspaper, but quit that and went West where he worked as a cowboy. His brother Ralph had taken up acting and Frank decided to follow him and worked up a vaudeville sketch: like his brother, he changed his surname from Wuppermann to Morgan. He was doing his sketch in vaudeville when he was offered the juvenile lead in 'Mr Wu' (14), starring Walter Whiteside. At least, that was the way Studio Biographies had it; but 'Who's Who In the Theatre' (33) says he studied at the AADA and made his New York debut in 'A Woman

Killed With Kindness' and, later, was in stock, playing leads, in Northampton, Massachusetts. Not long afterwards Vitagraph signed him to a contract and when Anita Stewart lost her normal leading man, Earl Williams, Morgan was appointed in his place. His early films: *The Suspect* (16), *The Daring of Diana*, *Light in Darkness* (17), *A Modern Cinderella* with June Caprice, *That Girl Philippa* with Stewart, *Who's Your Neighbour?*, *A Child of the Wild*, *Baby Mine* at Goldwyn starring Madge Kennedy, *Raffles the Amateur Cracksman* starring John Barrymore, *The Knife* (18), *At the Mercy of Men*, *Gray Towers of Mystery* (19) and *The Golden Shower*.

It could not be said that he was conspicuously successful, and his stage work continued to give him more fame and satisfaction. Among his stage appearances: 'Seventh Heaven' (22), 'Lullaby' (23), 'Gentlemen Prefer Blondes' (26) and 'Topaze' (30) in the title role. He had mostly small roles in his other Silents: Gloria Swanson's *Manhandled* (24), *Born Rich* (25) starring Doris Kenyon; *The Man Who Found Himself* starring Thomas Meighan (also in the cast were brother Ralph and Lynn Fontanne); *The Crowded Hour*; *The Scarlet Saint* with Mary Astor; and *Love's Greatest Mistake* (27). He was in 'Rosalie' (28) on Broadway, as the fluttery King. Two years later Paramount starred him in a short, *Belle of the Night*, and as a result signed him to a long-term contract: *Queen High* (30), a musical strung around him and Charles Ruggles as partners in a garter business, gambling on who should buttle for the other for a while; *Dangerous Nan McGrew*, which was a vehicle for Helen Kane; *Laughter*, where he was Nancy Carroll's elderly millionaire husband and *Fast and Loose* with Miriam Hopkins.

The contract ended abruptly when he was offered a part in 'The Band Wagon' with the Astaires, and he was off the screen for almost two years. He returned, free-lancing, and seven Morgan pictures were released within six months: *Secrets of the French Police* (32) co-starring with Gwili Andre; the funny *The Half-Naked Truth* with Lupe Velez and Lee Tracey; *The Billion Dollar Scandal* (33) with Robert Armstrong; *Hallelujah I'm a Bum* starring Al Jolson; *Luxury Liner* at Paramount from a best-seller by Gina Kaus; *Sailor's Luck*, a Sally Eilers-Jimmy Dunn programmer; and *A Kiss Before the Mirror*, in which he was Nancy Carroll's cuckolded husband. At that point MGM signed Morgan to a contract, and he appeared in a further six films that year: *Reunion in Vienna* with John Barrymore; *The Nuisance*; *When Ladies Meet* with Ann Harding, his best Hollywood part so far; *Best of Enemies* at Fox; *Broadway to Hollywood* starring with Alice Brady in a beautifully made and acted story of two vaudeville hoofers, and *The Blonde Bombshell* with Jean Harlow.

Morgan's skill was recognized by Metro, who gave him good parts even if they failed to consider him one of their top stars; and he was doing very well in a town where most actors of his age were considered past their prime. After *The Cat and the Fiddle* (34) MGM acceded to demand and loaned him to virtually every other studio: *Success at Any Price* and *Sisters Under the Skin* at Columbia; *Affairs of Cellini* at 20th-UA; *A Lost Lady* at Warners; *There's Always Tomorrow* at Universal, as a father tired of being taken for granted, with Binnie Barnes; and *By Your Leave* at RKO with Genevieve Tobin. Photoplay said there was 'a gilt-edged guarantee of abundant chuckles. As the husband in his 40s, seeking by a week of wild-oat sowing to re-charge his ego, Frank Morgan gives the most completely inspired portrait yet of that pathetic creature – a man who wants to be naughty, but who has forgotten how.' At Universal he did *The Good Fairy* (35) and at RKO *The Enchanted April*. Then MGM kept him busy: *Naughty Marietta*, *Escapade*, *I Live My Life*, *The Perfect Gentleman*, and *The Great Ziegfeld* (36) as Ziegfeld's showman rival.

Pioneer-RKO borrowed him for *The Dancing Pirate*, which was the third all-Technicolor feature: Charles Collins had the title role and Steffi Duna was the girl, but Morgan was the star by both billing and right, as the befuddled mayor of the village that is invaded by the pirates. He was in *Trouble for Two*; *Picadilly Jim*; *Dimples* at 20th; *The Last of Mrs Cheyney* (37) as a rather assinine suitor of that lady; *The Emperor's Candlesticks*; *Saratoga* as Una Merkel's fond and foolish sugar-daddy of a husband; and *Rosalie* in the part he had done on the stage (only there was a new Cole Porter score). Before that he had one of his few star roles in a good while in *Beg Borrow or Steal*, with Florence Rice. Normally MGM found him more useful to head their supporting casts – which were usually the strongest of all the companies.

He and Rice were co-starred again in *Paradise for Three* (38); there followed *Port of Seven Seas*, MGM's version of the *Fanny* trilogy with Morgan in the Raimu part, happy with Maureen O'Sullivan till the father (John Beal) of the baby tries to break it up; *The Crowd Roars*, as a dipsomaniac father; *Sweethearts*, as an impresario; *Broadway Serenade* (39); *The Wizard of Oz* in the title role; *Balalaika* (40); and *Henry Goes Arizona*, in which he played an ex-vaudevillian inheriting his brother's farm and, along with Virginia Weidler, getting involved with outlaws. It was the first of several Bs in which MGM were to star Morgan over the next few years, and was not improved by changing directors, many re-writes, and the deletion of George Murphy after several weeks' filming. Murphy, in fact, superseded Morgan at the head of the supporting cast of *Broadway Melody of 1940*, which came along just after *The Shop Around the Corner*, in which Morgan was the irascible but kindly store-owner. He was a professor in *The Mortal Storm*; then co-starred with Billie Burke in *Hullabaloo* and *The Ghost Comes Home*; and was the buddy/rival of Gable and Tracy in *Boom Town*. He made *Keeping Company* (41) with Ann Rutherford; *Washington Melodrama* as a kindly do-gooder; *The Wild Man of Borneo*, playing a sponger, with Mary Howard; *Honky Tonk* as Lana Turner's father and killed off in reel one; and *The Vanishing Virginian* with Kathryn Grayson.

Then, just as cinemagoers were forgetting what a fine serious actor he could be, he was cast in a straight role in *Tortilla Flat* (42) and won a second Oscar nomination. He followed with parts in *White Cargo*; *The Human Comedy* (43); *A Stranger in Town*, starring again, as a Supreme Court judge; *Thousands Cheer*; *The White Cliffs of Dover* (44); and two on loan-out, *Hail the Conquering Hero* and *Casanova Brown*. He gave a rich making-bricks-without-straw performance in *Yolanda and the Thief* (45) as a con-man and then did sterling service in the third Lassie picture, *Courage of Lassie* (46). He was in *Lady Luck* at RKO; *The Cockeyed Miracle* as Keenan Wynn's father (they were both ghosts); *Green Dolphin Street* (47); *Summer Holiday* (48) as the tippling uncle, the part done by Wallace Beery in the earlier version, *Ah Wilderness!*; *The Three Musketeers* as the King; *The Stratton Story* (49); *Any Number Can Play*; *The Great Sinner* and *Key to the City*. He was working on *Annie Get Your Gun*, playing Buffalo Bill, when he died in his sleep (1949): the film was re-shot with Louis Calhern in the part. He left a widow, whom he had married in 1914. His brother also had a long career in films, but without the same success.

Rouben Mamoulian's Summer Holiday *(48): the spinster aunt is wooed by the bachelor uncle on the other side–Frank Morgan and Agnes Moorehead.*

Paul Muni

Paul Muni was the 30s idea of a Great Actor: he never looked the same twice. 'King of the Character Actors' says 'The Picture Show Annual for 1939', showing him in eleven of his roles–moustached or bearded (three beards of different shape), hair combed forward or in a mop, centre-parted and slicked down or just curled. He took meticulous care with his make-up. Bette Davis, who acted with him in *Juarez*, said in her autobiography: 'Mr Muni seemed intent on submerging himself so completely that he disappeared. There is no question that his technique as an actor was superb. But, for me, beneath the exquisite petit point of details, the loss of his own sovereignty worked conversely to rob some of his characterization of blood.' He was over-conscientious: in 1937 W. H. Mooring observed admiringly in Film Weekly that Muni was never content to 'walk through' a part. In retrospect, it is a pity: he was an actor of great integrity but his work has badly dated.

Muni was born in Lemberg, (then) Austria, in 1895 into a family of strolling players; they emigrated to the US when he was a child, and in 1918 he joined the Yiddish Theatre stock company in New York, moving on to the Jewish Art Theatre (inbetweenwhiles being educated in New

York and Cleveland). He acted in London in 1924, but it wasn't until 1926 that he made his first appearance in an English-speaking part, taking over from Edward G. Robinson, in 'We Americans' (it was filmed, but Muni was considered unsuitable and was replaced by George Sidney). The following year 'Four Walls' really established him, and when Talkies came in he was immediately considered likely film material. Fox signed him to a long-term contract (and announced him in their early publicity as a new discovery from Russia), but he made only two pictures for them, both failures. The first, *The Valiant* (29), was almost abandoned, because he was considered, after all, to have limited appeal; but it brought him an Oscar nomination–playing a murderer hiding his true identity from his mother. The second, *Seven Faces*, cast him as a concierge in a waxworks (allowing him for some reason to portray seven different characters). Fearing that Fox wanted to make a second Lon Chaney out of him, he took himself back to New York and scored a huge success in Elmer Rice's 'Counsellor-at-Law' (31). Hollywood decided to try again, in the person of Howard Hawks, and cast him in the title role of his searing gangster picture, *Scarface* (32). Then Warners gave him a whirl with *I Am a Fugitive From a Chain Gang*. The success of both films, critically and with

Two sides of a triangle: Paul Muni and Bette Davis in Bordertown *(35). The third was Eugene Pallette–his employee and her husband–soon to be killed by her.*

the public, established Muni and WB offered him a long-term contract. He signed on condition that he could okay his material.

He supplanted George Arliss and for eight years was that studio's most important actor. Cagney and Robinson, and later, Dick Powell, might be more popular, but Muni had Class. He had the pick of parts, although at the same time WB realized that he was too powerful an actor for ordinary roles. *The World Changes* (33), cast him as an immigrant farmer who rises to meat-packing king, with Mary Astor; in *Hi Nellie!* (34) he was a tough newspaperman reduced to doing the sob-sister column; in *Bordertown* (35) he was a failed Mexican lawyer making it big as a café boss – a studied and ebullient performance; in *Black Fury* a miner rebelling against injustice; and in *Doctor Socrates* a decent man drawn into crime. He and Warners fought over scripts, and they opposed him violently over a film which brought them more prestige than anything yet in the history of the studio: *The Story of Louis Pasteur*, a painstaking and sincere portrait of the great French scientist. Muni's performance brought him an Oscar.

The triumphs of 1937 then gave him an unprecedented position in Hollywood: two of the three films he made were among the year's half-dozen top money-makers (with a take of over $1½ million each) and his acting in them was extravagantly praised. The other one was a poor picture at RKO about the Lafayette Esquadrille, *The Woman I Love*, who was Miriam Hopkins – which was sandwiched between the other two. In *The Good Earth*, from Pearl S. Buck's novel, at MGM, Muni was a Chinese, and he was another famed Frenchman in *The Life of Emile Zola*. Said the very dignified ads: 'Warner Brothers takes pride in presenting Mr Paul Muni . . . in one of the few great pictures of all time. . . .' *Zola* won a best picture Oscar and for Muni the Best Actor Award from the New York Critics. It concentrated mainly on Zola's involvement with Dreyfus in terms which today seem plodding and cliché-ridden (as indeed is Muni's interpretation of his role); but to many at the time this series of Warner biographies – all directed by William Dieterle – seemed to grapple nobly with Important Issues. By far the best is *Juarez* (39), which does attempt to explain in real terms the reasons for, and the consequences of, Napoleon III's Mexican adventure; Muni was fine in the title role, the great native patriot, but it might have been better had he not bolstered his own part at the expense of the original conception. All the same, Graham Greene thought 'a quite impressive film has emerged'. Warners had agreed to do *Juarez* against their better judgment and it didn't do well; nor did *We Are Not Alone* (39) from James Hilton's novel, and that was also much praised. WB thought Muni might be more appealing to the public as a gangster in *High Sierra*, but he wanted to do a life of Beethoven. Although they had recently come to a new contract agreement, WB decided they could no longer afford him – he had at no point been the most docile of contract-players – and they settled his contract.

Muni returned to New York and made a great success there in 'Key Largo' by Maxwell Anderson. He went back to

Muni as Juarez *(39). Graham Greene found his make-up 'extraordinarily impressive'.*

Muni in his last film, The Last Angry Man *(59), directed by Daniel Mann.*

Hollywood under contract to 20th, but made only one film: *Hudson's Bay* (40), a pointless historical film not improved by his own tiresome performance as a French fur-trapper. He starred again on Broadway as a has-been actor in 'Yesterday's Magic' (Emlyn Williams's 'The Light of Heart' retitled) and in Hollywood *The Commandos Strike at Dawn* (42), a syrupy tribute to Norwegian resistance fighters. Also for Columbia he did a similar film, *Counter-Attack* (45): '... excellent in his quieter moments he is too often an over-generalized stagey embodiment of Russia' (James Agee). Released a few months earlier was *A Song to Remember* which had been held up because the studio feared that classical music wasn't box-office. This life of Chopin had at one time been a cherished project of Frank Capra (a screenplay prepared for him was eventually used). When Columbia eventually took the plunge, Chopin became top of the pops for a while. The film was, however, 'appallingly silly' (Richard Winnington). Cornel Wilde was Chopin, and Muni, though top-billed, had only a featured role as his professor, 'so buried beneath whiskers and senile whimsy that I had a shock when I read his name on the programme afterwards' (Winnington).

It was virtually the end of his film career. There was an odd fantasy with Claude Rains, *Angel on My Shoulder* (46) which did poorly. In 1949 he went to London to appear there in 'Death of a Salesman' and to Italy in 1951 for a movie with Joan Loring, eventually released under the title *Stranger on the Prowl*: it did nothing to resurrect his career, but in 1955 he had another Broadway hit, 'Inherit the Wind'. This reawakened the interest of Hollywood, and Columbia signed him for *The Last Angry Man* (59) from a best-selling saga about a GP in the Brooklyn slums; Muni did very well as the doctor, cranky, cantankerous, kindly–but proved an unsaleable commodity at the box-office. In Britain it was a Royal Performance selection, and was agreed to be dull but (just about) worthy. Prior to its making he had toured in the US as Kringelein in 'At the Grand', a musical version of 'Grand Hotel', and he had appeared on TV in a 'Playhouse 90' production, 'Last Clear Chance'–that, at least, was a last success for him. He died in 1967, and it was disclosed that he had been virtually blind for the past several years. His wife was Bella Finkle, who married him before his Hollywood days, and was always thought to be the complete guiding light behind his career.

Anna Neagle

'As a box-office star-maker, my masterpiece was, of course, Anna Neagle,' wrote Herbert Wilcox in his autobiography. She was, as he pointed out, Britain's biggest female draw for seven years, which–even taking into account the paucity of such species–remains a record. And four times she won the Picturegoer Gold Medal Award, twice alongside Laurence Olivier. The story of Anna Neagle is not unlike the plots of some of her films, right to the present, being created a Dame of the British Empire (69). Born in 1904, in a working-class district of London (Forest Gate) she decided at an early age that she wanted to be a dancer and went in for Ballroom Championships. At 20 she set out to make her fame and fortune on the stage. She danced in the chorus of a Charlot revue, and later became a Cochran 'Young Lady'. Cochran made her Jessie Matthews's understudy for 'Wake Up and Dream' and though there is no record of the star falling sick and Anna going on in her place, the big break wasn't long in coming: Jack Buchanan selected her as his leading lady for 'Stand Up and Sing' (31) at the London Hippodrome. Herbert Wilcox, then a leading producer-director, happened to drop by the theatre one night to discuss *Goodnight Vienna*, which he was to film with Jack, and he saw Anna and decided that she must be his co-star.

She was not without film experience – pictures had already appeared in the fan-magazines of 'Ann Eagle', and she had had a small part in an old farce, *Should a Doctor Tell?* (30), and another in the remake of *The Chinese Bungalow* (31) with Matheson Lang as an evil Chinese, less a film than a series of stills of him in fancy dress. Neagle's flower girl in *Goodnight Vienna* (32) so impressed Wilcox that he placed her under long-term contract and during the rest of her career she has only twice been directed by other people. The first time was in her next picture, *The Flag Lieutenant* (33) with Henry Edwards. Wilcox directed her again in *The Little Damozel*, and her performance as a sexy cabaret singer was, said Picturegoer, only 'fair'. However, he thought she had world potential and began to build her into a big star. The first attempt, a version of Coward's musical *Bitter Sweet*, was a commercial failure, and Picturegoer thought her 'disappointing'. When Jeanette MacDonald left the cast Wilcox made Neagle the New York shopgirl in *The Queen's Affair* (34), but the film which established her was *Nell Gwynn*. It flopped in the US for whom – to please the Hays Office – Wilcox had added a scene showing Charles (Cedric Hardwicke) and Nell marrying, but the British lined up for miles to see Anna's cockney sparrow act. A sort of sequel was arranged, with Hardwicke again, but Anna was Irish this time: *Peg of Old Drury* (35) as Peg Woffington.

It was then decided that she should dance again, and Wilcox shoved her into three ratty musicals: *Limelight* (36), *The Three Maxims* and *London Melody* (37), the last two with Tullio Carminati. But to compensate for these he had one of the best ideas of his career, a life of Queen Victoria – just in time for Coronation year. The ban on representations of the Queen on stage and screen had just been lifted, so Anna became *Victoria the Great*, suitably kittenish, and surrounded by a fine cast. James Agate called her 'Victoria the Little', but its success all over the world was such that plans were scrapped for Neagle to play 'Nell Gwynn' on Broadway and a Lyons *Nippy* on film, and Wilcox promptly remade it, in Technicolor and using some different incidents, as *Sixty Glorious Years* (38). During the war years the first half of the first one and the second half of the second one were spliced together and patriotically re-issued under the title *Queen Victoria*. The public apparently couldn't get enough of the Saxe-Coburg-Gotha saga, but Wilcox set Anna to play Marie Lloyd, the Queen of the Halls. However, he couldn't get a suitable leading man and instead she played another, and more inspiring British heroine, *Nurse Edith Cavell* (39).

Graham Greene chastised Wilcox: 'We get from his films everything except life, character, truth. Instead we have flags, anthems, leading articles, a tombstone reticence. It would be unfair to call his Way of a Neagle vulgar showmanship . . . for there is seldom anything vital enough to be called vulgar in the successive patriotic appearances of this rather inexpressive actress. Miss Neagle looked nice as Queen Victoria, she looks just as nice as Nurse Cavell: she moves rigidly on to the set, as if wheels were concealed under the stately skirt; she says her piece with flat dignity and trolleys out again – rather like a mechanical marvel from the World's Fair.'

This was made in Hollywood for RKO, who had made a deal with the Wilcox-Neagle team after the success of the *Victoria* films; they stayed on in Hollywood, and Anna danced again, in three old musicals updated, *Irene* (40), *No No Nanette* and *Sunny* (41). *Irene* did well, but the success of the other two was not (to put it mildly) sufficient to hold the team in Hollywood, and after doing their sequence in an Anglo-American effort, *Forever and a Day* (released in 1943), they returned to a blitzed London to make *They Flew Alone* (42), the inspiring story of Amy Johnson with Robert Newton. Then they made their last under their agreement with RKO, *The Yellow Canary* (43), a spy melodrama with Richard Greene; and got married.

During 1944 Neagle toured with ENSA and did a stage version of Jane Austen's 'Emma' under Robert Donat's management. When she returned to the screen it was for another attempt to better Anglo-American relations: *I Live in Grosvenor Square* (45) and she loved both Dean Jagger and Rex Harrison. The success of this, though relative, led to another contemporary story with a London setting, this time with a comparative newcomer, Michael Wilding. *Piccadilly Incident* (46) told how they met in the Blackout, fell in love and married; how war separated them and how he, believing her dead – she was castaway on a desert island – married again; how she came back and after meeting his wife, disappeared – to entertain the troops; and how he found her again, just before she was killed by a bomb. This load of old codswallop (which was based on a story-outline by the star herself) certainly hit the public fancy, and clearly called for a follow-up; so Britishers queued again to see both stars in *The*

Anna Neagle and Michael Wilding, with Josephine Fitzgerald, in Spring in Park Lane *(48). She was a wealthy young lady and he a milord masquerading as a footman. 'Miss Neagle is in the true tradition of screen starriness in that she doesn't act or do anything much. . . . Her chief weapon is the coy, knowing, self-protective smile' (Richard Winnington).*

Courtneys of Curzon Street (47), a tenth-rate if flattering imitation of Coward's 'Cavalcade'. They were thereupon paired a third time, this time in a comedy, *Spring in Park Lane* (48); the critics liked it and the public adored it, so Wilcox thereupon re-made it, in colour, with a few plot changes, and called it *Maytime in Mayfair* (49). It did well, but less well, and the same might be said for one that Neagle did earlier that year without Wilding, *Elizabeth of Ladymead*, an inspiring episode film detailing the effects on four wives of their husbands returning from the Crimea, the Boer and the two World Wars. Apart from the one where the star was, ludicrously, a 20s flapper, it was paralysingly boring.

Nor was Wilding in *Odette* (50), the inspiring story of a war heroine, which Anna agreed to do for her husband only after Michèle Morgan and Ingrid Bergman had turned it down. It was well received and big box-office. Wilding was back with Anna for *The Lady With the Lamp* (51)–Florence Nightingale, who else?–and for *Derby Day* (52), of which Richard Winnington wrote: '. . . the principal jokes consist of gibes at the dire state of the British film industry. Gibes that have an insolent ring in a film that falls well short of accepted Wilcox mediocrity.'

In 1953 she returned to the stage in 'The Glorious Days', recapping some of her famous roles (Victoria, Nell Gwynn, etc.). It was, as Tynan said, 'Anna Neagle anthologized' but it didn't run too long because she had 'film commitments'. The film committed was the screen version of this, re-titled *Lilacs in the Spring* (54). It had the unlikely assistance of Errol Flynn, and so did *King's Rhapsody* (55), a stagey, stultifying film of an Ivor Novello musical: 'Here, beneath these bastions of rock we lay our story . . .' said the foreword. The Neagle-Novello combination might once have been potent, but it was too late. Wilcox, later, commenting on the failure of both films, said that Anna's public wasn't Errol's public. He then put her into an 'up-to-date' story, *My Teenage Daughter* (56), cruelly referred to as 'My Stone-Age Mother', and–in another attempt to re-interest the public–loaned her to ABPC to play a hospital matron in *No Time for Tears* (57). But it was: *The Man Who Wouldn't Talk* (58) played just a week in a small West End cinema and didn't make the circuits; and many cinemas showing her last film, *The Lady Is a Square* (59), omitted her name. It was a harsh verdict on someone who had coined a lot of money for the same houses. At the same time this tired old stuff–

all about a gracious lady converted to pop by her butler, an undiscovered pop singer – indicated that Wilcox no longer had his finger on the public pulse.

The butler was played by a pop singer, Frankie Vaughan, who was under personal contract to Neagle, but the three films she produced with him were failures. Early in the 60s Wilcox was in the bankruptcy courts. She sold her jewels, and went to work with a will. She starred in a critically-panned but much patronized musical, 'Charlie Girl', on the stage. Its long run confirmed her very special place in British show business; although her abilities as actress, singer or dancer are really rather like painting with numbers, her genteel charm is considerable enough to have endeared her to great sections of the public.

Pola Negri

Pola Negri was the first of Hollywood's European imports. She was extravagantly admired in her German films, and every American studio was prepared to meet her price; but despite great fame and publicity, she never really caught on among Anglo-Saxons – which is why, perhaps, she is remembered today less as an actress than as an exotic, a hot-house flower that bloomed briefly in the Hollywood garden. That was the sort of simile that was used about her: 'she has eyes like dark lagoons' went another, 'wherein men drown'. A later reporter dismissed her as 'all slink and mink', and most film histories pass her by, with a frivolous footnote on her titled husbands and the other, similar, publicity. But she was a vivid and, on occasion, convincing film actress. Lotte Eisner has described her as 'The Magnani of the Silent Screen' and she was much admired by contemporary critics. The most fulsome modern assessment is by Theodore Huff, writing on *Madame Dubarry* in 'The Films of Ernst Lubitsch': 'Miss Negri gave a colourful performance almost never equalled for vitality and emotional depth. Never before had a screen star burst on the public in such full bloom. With grace, verve and vivid radiance, she created a living character who was simple, vivacious, a capricious child one minute and the next a restless and passionate woman, carried away by her love of luxury. In spite of the character of Dubarry, Miss Negri made her a fascinating and disturbingly sympathetic figure who was actually pathetic towards the end – a "toy of erratic destiny" in the grip of events beyond her simple and extremely feminine nature.'

It was part of Negri's own extremely feminine nature to live the life of a film-star up to the hilt, and, depending on her caprice, she altered the facts of her pre-US career to provide more drama for reporters. 'Fled from Russian Revolution', says one account, and another, not taken in, 'was a shopgirl in Berlin'. The following, most likely, facts are offered cautiously therefore: She was born in Yanowa, near Lipna, Poland, in 1894; her father died (or disappeared) when she was six, and she was brought up by relatives in Warsaw. She seems to have begun her stage career with the Russian Imperial Theatre in St Petersburg as a dancer, but left there, apparently to go into cabaret – probably playing the violin; in 1913 she made her legit debut in Warsaw in Hauptmann's 'Hannele', and the following year was starring in her first film, financed and written by herself, *Niewolnica Zmysłów/Love and Passion* (14). The director was Aleksander Hertz, who was responsible for all her Polish films: *Bestia* (15), *Czarna Ksiazka* or *Zólty Paszport*, *Pókoj Nr 13* or *Tajemnica Hotelu*, *Arabella* (16), *Jego Ostatni Czyn*, *Studenci* and *Zona*. On the stage she was appearing in an Oriental spectacle, 'Sumurun', when Max Reinhardt saw her and persuaded her to go with him to Berlin (he also changed her name from Apolonia Chalupec – but as Poland's leading film-star, that name was retained for her there right through her Hollywood days).

She did 'Sumurun' in Berlin, and commenced another successful film career: *Nicht Lange Tauschte mich das Glück* (17), *Die Toten Augen*, *Rosen die der Sturm Entblättert*, *Wenn das Herz in Hass Erglüht* (18), *Küsse die Man Stiehlt in Dunkeln*, *Manja* and *Die Augen der Mumie Mâ/The Eyes of the Mummy* – as a temple dancer. The latter was directed at Negri's insistence by a young actor from the German 'Sumurun' company, Ernst Lubitsch: it was the start of a brilliant career. After *Der Gelbe Schein*, she was directed again by Lubitsch in *Carmen/Gypsy Blood*, and its success put him at the head of his profession in Europe. She made *Karussell des Lebens* (19) and *Kreuziget Sie* and after these Lubitsch directed her again in *Madame Dubarry*, with a Louis XV played by Emil Jannings. It was a sensation in Europe, but there were no takers for a while for the US. Finally First National bought it for $40,000 and opened it cautiously – advertised as 'A European Spectacle' because of anti-German feeling – and re-titled *Passion*: it caused a furore in the States as it had done in Europe. Meanwhile, Negri was filming *Comtesse Doddy* and *Vendetta* (the dates of both are uncertain but are believed to belong

to the Lubitsch period); *Die Marchesa D'Arminiani* (20); *Sumurun/One Arabian Night* with Lubitsch directing; *Das Martyrium*; *Die Geschlossene Kette*; *Arme Violetta/The Red Peacock*–'Camille' taken from Verdi rather than Dumas; Lubitsch's *Die Bergkatze/The Mountain Cat*, in the title role; *Sappho/Mad Love*; and Lubitsch's *Die Flamme/Montmartre* (20).

Due to the success of *Passion* most of these were shown very profitably in the US: the public could not get enough of Negri or of Lubitsch, and emissaries from Hollywood waited on the lady offering contracts; she accepted one from Paramount (Lasky) and sailed for Hollywood. Her first film there was *Bella Donna* (23)–after many script revisions on which she insisted. But nothing could change the basic story–that of an adventuress who, finally forsaken by both her lovers and her deceived husband, walks out into the sands of Egypt and is eaten by a panther. The second one wasn't much better: *The Cheat*, already filmed in 1915 with Fannie Ward: she cheated on her Oriental potentate lover (Charles de Roche) and he had her branded in retaliation. It was considered absurd by the critics, and the public stayed away in droves–though partly because her German films were playing off still and the public was satiated with Negri (few fans realized that these films were European in origin).

The next was *The Spanish Dancer*, a part meant for Valentino but re-written for her; curiously, it was from the same play that gave birth to Mary Pickford's *Rosita*, filmed the same year by Lubitsch, who had also crossed the Atlantic. The dancer in question was befriended by Wallace Beery (as Philip IV) and loved by Antonio Moreno. It did somewhat better at the box-office, but Paramount's hoped-for repeat of the success of *Passion* was not repeated. They tried: *Shadows of Paris* (24), as queen of the Apaches, with Adolphe Menjou; *Men* with Robert Frazer and a ludicrous ending ('The woman who pays and makes men pay', said the posters); *Lily of the Dust*, as a girl in a German garrison town, with Ben Lyon, which failed, Photoplay thought, because 'Pola Negri isn't particularly interesting as the Lily'; Lubitsch's *Forbidden Paradise*, 'his most brilliant film' (Paul Rotha), a story of Catherine the Great, with Rod la Rocque and Menjou; *East of Suez* (25), as a half-caste, with Noah Beery Sr, from Somerset Maugham's play, with a happy ending and Raoul Walsh directing; *The Charmer*; *Flower of Night*; *A Woman of the World*, directed by Mal St Clair; *The Crown of Lies* (26), as a boarding-house slavey declared queen of a mythical kingdom; and *Good and Naughty*, a farce with Tom Moore. 'The better she was photographed,' wrote Griffith and Mayer, 'the more lavishly she was coiffed and gowned and sleeked and groomed, the more standardized she became, until in the studied attitudes of stylized acting in her last films nothing was discernible of the highly individual heroine of *Passion* and *Gypsy Blood*.' An exception was the Lubitsch film in the middle of this batch and it was regarded as a comeback: but generally the tigerish Negri had been metamorphosed into a pussycat–at least, on screen. Picturegoer complained that she did too many peasant roles, observing 'the electric energy of a magnetic Pole is usually undisputed'. Off-screen, her battles for better parts gave her a reputation for temperament. 'Everyone knows,' said Picturegoer later, 'how narrowly she escaped artistic annihilation under the Lasky banner.'

But what was basically wrong was that the brooding, remote Negri was out of key with the times; her so-called feud with the other queen of the Paramount lot, Gloria Swanson, might have been fodder for the fan-magazines, but it deprived her of dignity–while robbing Swanson, the all-American girl, of little. Her ostentatious mourning for Valentino provoked giggles instead of sympathy; and worse, she hardly tried to hide her contempt for her films and the cultural level of Los Angeles as compared with Berlin. As with several other Europeans, it was acknowledged that she was in Hollywood for the money and, once she'd got a lot, would return to make the sort of films she wanted to make. However, she did have a big hit in *Hotel Imperial* (27) as a hotel maid who lets an Austrian hussar (James Hall) pose as a valet in order to shield him. Mauritz Stiller directed, as he did the next, *Barbed Wire*, a moving story of a French girl in love with a German prisoner (Clive Brook): but these were respites in a public apathy which was soon to cause exhibitors to leave the Negri name off the bills. Films like *The Woman on Trial*, though directed by Mauritz Stiller, didn't help much either. Next came *Three Sinners* (28), an artificial story about a drab wife who becomes a woman of the world, with Paul Lukas, Warner Baxter and Tullio Carminati; *The Secret Hour* with Jean Hersholt, a version of 'They Knew What They Wanted' which did so badly that it could be remade as a Talkie two years later–ironically as a vehicle for Vilma Banky (but it didn't save her career either, which was also killed by her accent); *Loves of an Actress*, a biopic of the French tragedienne, Rachel, with Nils

Pola Negri as A Woman of the World *(25), married to a playboy husband and considerably worse than he is – until reformed by social worker Holmes Herbert. Here's the reform in action.*

When Pola Negri's American career ended, she made half a dozen films in Germany, but returned to the US during the war. She has filmed only twice since, the first time in 1943: Hi Diddle Diddle, *a farce with Martha Scott.*

Asther; and finally, *The Woman From Moscow*, based on Sardou's play 'Fedora', with Paul Lukas. Negri pocketed her last salary cheque ($8,000 a week) and left the set. Her dressing-room was made over for Clara Bow.

There were no Hollywood offers. And she, in Europe, said she would never return. She began a film in France, but walked out after some weeks. She petitioned Shaw for the rights to 'Caesar and Cleopatra', but he refused to part with them. She did make a British film, *The Woman He Scorned* (29). Paul Czinner directed for Imperial, as a Silent, and it was partially dubbed – but not by its stars. One of the cast, Warwick Ward, sought an injunction because he was dubbed by another artist, and the film was withdrawn in Britain; but in the US, WB gave it a limited release. During her stay, she also appeared in a sketch at the London Coliseum, 'Farewell to Love'. But in 1932 RKO, encouraged by the success of Dietrich in US movies, decided to give Negri another fling: *A Woman Commands* was based on the romantic story of Queen Marie Draga of Serbia and it co-starred Basil Rathbone and Roland Young. Negri had a song, 'Paradise', which she sang beautifully, but her voice was deep and too heavily accented to be acceptable. Besides, it was a rotten film, and its failure killed her Hollywood hopes. She returned to Europe and went to France to make *Fanatisme* (34) with Pierre-Richard Wilm. The following year she was in Germany making *Mazurka* (35). There was some move by MGM to star her in *The Good Earth*, but when this came to nothing, she signed a three-year contract with UFA. She made *Moskau-Shanghai* (36), *Madame Bovary* (37), *Tango Notturno*, *Die Fromme Lüge* (38) and *Die Nacht der Entscheidung*. Goebbels didn't like her, and called her 'the Polish Jewess'; but Hitler did, and had her Aryan origins proved. She returned his admiration, and when asked whether he was responsible for her return to German films, replied: 'Why not; after all, there have been many important men in my life – Valentino for example.'

At the outbreak of war she was on the Côte d'Azur; she joined the Red Cross, but returned to the US only in 1943 after much haggling with the immigration authorities. Hollywood welcomed her, and offered her a comedy with her one-time co-star, Adolphe Menjou, *Hi Diddle Diddle* (43). It led to no further offers. She later retired to San Antonio with a friend, a Texas heiress (she made headlines some years later when the woman married and she threatened to sue – but she didn't; soon after, the heiress divorced and the ladies were reunited). She took an interest in real estate and in writing her memoirs (planned over many years, and announced in 1957, they finally appeared in the spring of 1970). In 1964 Disney, after reading a piece about her in a San Antonio newspaper, signed her to play the enigmatic jewellery expert in *The Moon-spinners*. Accompanied by a cheetah, and outrageously gowned, she gave a small lift to the climax of the film. There may yet be other films: Negri still considers herself a star. A memorable portrait was painted by Rodney Ackland in his memoir, 'The Celluloid Mistress' (1947): 'She had a blind and uncritical admiration of her own genius in the blaze of which her sense of humour evaporated like a dew-drop on a million-watt arc lamp.' She told him that one sequence she had done in *Mazurka* was 'the greatest piece of acting that has ever been seen on the screen'.

Ramon Novarro

Ramon Novarro was one of the 'Latin' actors thrown up in the wake of Valentino's success (others: Ricardo Cortez, Antonio Moreno), and he possessed a similar facility for the same sort of romantic costume parts – though with little of Valentino's peculiar intensity. DeWitt Bodeen says 'he was too audacious, too droll, too impudent to be the "Great Lover" or "The Sheik". Romantically, he never took himself seriously either on screen or off.' However, as the vogue for their type of exotica waned, so did Novarro's career. His studio tried him as an All-American boy, as a comedian. In *Huddle* he was the hero of a Yale football game, in *The Flying Fleet*, a hapless serviceman in his shirt-tails searching endlessly for his stolen trousers, and smiling all the while. He did survive the advent of Sound, and made over a dozen Talkies, but it is as a Silent star that he is remembered.

He was born in Durango, Mexico, in 1899, the son of a dentist. The family fled the country at the time of the Huerta Revolution in 1914 and settled in Los Angeles. When the father died Ramon became the chief breadwinner: he worked as a waiter and also sang in restaurants, did some vaudeville and – more suitable to his ambitions – became a film extra. Among the films he is known to have appeared in are *The Hostage* (17, Wallace Reid), *The Little American* (Mary Pickford), *Joan the Woman* (Geraldine Farrar) and *The Goat* (18). Several name actors (including Moreno) interested themselves in him, and he was tested by D. W. Griffith and Sam Goldwyn among others, but it wasn't until 1921 that vaudeville dance director Marion Morgan (he had danced with her troupe since 1919) helped him to surface above his fellow-extras. She suggested him for the novelty dance in a full-length Sennett comedy with Ben Turpin and Phyllis Haver, *A Small Town Idol*, in turban and loin cloth with Derelys Perdue. He had a featured part in Goldwyn's *Mr Barnes of New York* (22) starring Tom Moore; and the same year was chosen to play the lead in a small independent production, *The Rubaiyat of Omar Khayyam*, directed by Ferdinand Binney Earle. One of Earle's associates was Mary O'Hara, who had written the scenario for Metro's *The Prisoner of Zenda*, and through her its director Rex Ingram got to see *Omar Khayyam* (though no one else did; it wasn't released till three years later, under the title *A Lover's Oath*). Ingram chose Novarro – still under his own name of Ramon Samaniegos – to play Rupert of Hentzau, complete with beard, monocle and long cigarette holder; Lewis Stone was Rudolph and Alice Terry and Barbara La Marr the women.

Ingram had directed *The Four Horsemen of the Apocalypse*, and he saw in Ramon some of the qualities which had made the world's females swoon over Valentino; so he signed him to a personal contract (at $125 per week), changed his name, and gave him a part in *Trifling Women*, again with La Marr and Stone. Then, also for Metro, he put him into the three pictures which made him a star (all co-starring Alice Terry, his wife). *Where the Rainbow Ends* (23) cast him as a native boy in love with the missionary's daughter: in the original he drowned at the end, but exhibitors found audience resentment at the cruel fate awaiting the new screen idol, and Ingram shot an alternative ending in which the boy discovers he's a sun-burnt Caucasian and can thus marry the girl. *Scaramouche* was a highly successful version of Rafael Sabatini's swashbuckler, and *The Arab* (24) an enthusiastic reprise of the mixed romance theme. It made no bones about being also inspired by Valentino's *The Sheik* – only it was actually filmed in North Africa. The Ingrams elected to remain (he made the 1927 *Garden of Allah* there and later became a Muslim) and sent Novarro back to Hollywood, where his $500 a week Ingram contract became, after protracted negotiations, $10,000 a week with Metro-Goldwyn.

He did three pictures before the one for which he is best remembered – *Thy Name Is Woman* with La Marr, *The Red Lily* with Enid Bennett, and *The Midshipman* (25), made at Annapolis with Navy co-operation. *Ben Hur* (26) had been an old pseudo-religious novel by Lew Wallis that had seen sturdy service in stage adaptations: the film was begun in Italy with Charles Brabin directing

Ramon Novarro and Norma Shearer in The Student Prince *(27)–almost the oldest musical comedy plot of them all. This version didn't have songs or even speech, but the direction by Lubitsch compensated–and indeed makes it preferable to the 1954 version.*

George Walsh as Ben Hur. Things had gone badly, and at the moment that Mayer was added to Metro-Goldwyn, Mayer's right-hand-man, Thalberg, elected to start again in California, replacing director and star by Fred Niblo and Novarro respectively. The contemporary estimate of its cost (by Variety) was $6 million, which seems unlikely, but it was certainly the most expensive film made up to that time: fortunately for MGM it was a box-office triumph, ending up on the Variety lists of top grossers at $4 million (though it took years to reach that figure: a version with synchronized sound materialized in 1931 and it was last heard of playing in Paris a couple of years before the 1959 remake opened). Novarro's popularity went to new heights, even if some critics thought that his portrayal was not sufficiently masculine.

He returned to less epic fare: *Lovers?* (27) with Alice Terry, a tale set in Spain, of how gossip united Novarro and his best friend's wife, making the rumours a reality; *The Road to Romance* with Marceline Day, an adaptation of 'Romance' by Conrad and Ford Maddox Ford; and *The Student Prince*, which Lubitsch directed. Said Picturegoer: 'Ramon Novarro and Norma Shearer give of their flawless acting and radiant charm'; but Film Daily was unhappy with his performance in *Across to Singapore* (28), thinking him 'miscast as a tough sea dog'. Joan Crawford was the girl and it was the second of the three screen versions of Ben Ames Williams's 'All the Brothers Were Valiant'. The next two cast Renée Adorée as his leading lady: *A Certain Young Man* (which had been started two years earlier and abandoned for some time), and *Forbidden Hours*, a Ruritanian romance between a king on a clandestine night out and his Premier's daughter. MGM were at a loss to understand why Novarro was not more popular: his pictures did well, but strictly with the distaff side. *The Midshipman* had not been successful, but another attempt was made to 'sell' him as a normal young American: in *The Flying Fleet* (29), as one of six guys training for the Navy Air Corps. It had a soundtrack added, and there was a music score with *The Pagan*, where Novarro retreated to a more primitive existence and only opened his mouth to sing 'Pagan Love Song' to Renée Adorée. A Napoleonic romance, *Devil May Care*, was all-Talkie, and had four songs and some Technicolor sequences; Novarro was again with Dorothy Jordan and also sang–playing a Spanish troubadour both times–in *In Gay Madrid* (30) and *Call of the Flesh*, the latter a re-titling after it looked like flopping as *The Singer of Seville* (Adorée was also in it, in

Garbo as Mata Hari *(32), and Novarro as the Russian officer. Playing opposite Garbo helped prop up Novarro's ailing career.*

Novarro's last major role in a major film was The Night Is Young *(35), a Ruritanian musical with Evelyn Laye as his leading lady. Here he is with second lead* Rosalind Russell.

a supporting role – her last film; Novarro also directed and co-directed the Spanish and French versions respectively).

'Frankly,' said Picturegoer, 'Ramon is one of the disappointments of the Talkies.' He was a disappointment to MGM too, and there were rumours that he would retire or take up opera-singing. He continued, however, with *Daybreak* (31), from Schnitzler's novel about a debt-ridden guardsman saved from suicide by a girl (Helen Chandler); and *Son of India*, another inter-racial romance – with Madge Evans. Jacques Feyder directed both, both were fine: and unpopular. Novarro got a boost by being cast with Garbo in *Mata Hari* (32) – except that her art cruelly exposed the immaturity of his acting style, and the end was in sight. Surprisingly, therefore, MGM announced that he had been signed to a new seven-year contract, to act and direct (but such announcements were not uncommon and were a reiteration of faith rather than the truth). The studio tried Yale – *Huddle*; then another Oriental prince, with the prestigious Helen Hayes, in *The Son-Daughter*; then a remake of *The Arab* called *The Barbarian* (33) – only this time the barbarian's white passion had to have an Egyptian mother before the censor would pass it. None of them worked, and indeed *The Barbarian* became *A Night in Cairo* for British audiences in the hope of making it more attractive. But the studio persevered, and believed that *The Cat and the Fiddle* (34) opposite Jeanette MacDonald would bring back his own public. It didn't. Nor, more understandably, did the next two. The publicity line on *Laughing Boy* was that it had taken a two-year search to find the right actor (no wonder he was laughing): Novarro is a Red Indian brave in love with Slim Girl (Lupe Velez), whom he accidentally kills after she has taken to the Oldest Profession. It was from the Pulitzer-prize-winning novel by Oliver LaFarge. At least it was very different from *The Night Is Young* (34), the result of Hollywood's second flirtation with British stage star Evelyn Laye: they made the most arch screen couple on record, and plans to re-team them in another musical (*Love While You May*) were scrapped.

So was the rest of Novarro's contract. He turned to other fields: he appeared in London at the Palladium and in a flop musical, 'A Royal Exchange', and was bitter about Hollywood when he spoke to reporters; in Hollywood he wrote, produced and directed (but did not star in) a Spanish feature, *Contra la Corriente* (36); and then was signed by Republic for a comeback, *The Sheik Steps Out* (37), which tried to kid the old image. The studio liked it enough to sign him for four more, but *A Desperate Adventure* (38) with Marian Marsh, set in Paris, was desperate indeed, and he asked to be released. In 1940 in Rome he did a French movie, *La Comedie de Bonheur*, with Micheline Presle, Michel Simon and the young Louis Jourdan – and finished directing it himself when Marcel L'Herbier left it. It was popular in Europe but does not appear to have hit the Anglo-Saxon market, possibly due to the war. In Mexico he made *La Virgen que Forjo Una Patria* (42), and towards the end of the decade seems to have made an effort to become accepted as a character actor: *We Were Strangers* (49), *The Big Steal*, *The Outriders* and *Crisis* (50); but as such, he was hardly in the top flight. Ten years later he had a small part in Cukor's *Heller in Pink Tights* (60).

He did not want for money. He never married; and there were rumours throughout his career that he would retire into a monastery. He did, however, show a most unmonklike propensity for alcohol and on numerous occasions was arrested by the Los Angeles police for drunken driving. In 1968 his nude corpse was found, after what appeared to have been a tremendous struggle; his apartment had been ransacked. Later two teenage hustlers were arrested and convicted of the murder.

Merle Oberon

Merle Oberon is a brown-eyed, dark-haired beauty with a long and successful career behind her and possibly another before her. As a young woman her work singularly lacked interest, but her appearances in the 60s show a striking new authority and a beauty which outclasses most of her contemporaries.

She was born in Tasmania in 1911, and was educated in India, where she and a girl-friend gave recitals in the Railway Institute at Lahore. She arrived in the mother country at the age of 17 and under her own name of Queenie O'Brien began to seek theatrical work. She became a dance hostess at the Café de Paris; and got work as a film extra. Alexander Korda noticed her on the set of one of his films (his biographer, Paul Tabori, notes that Oberon's 'extra' file-card read 'A.K. interested') and tested her and signed her for five years. Briefly she was Estelle Thompson before getting her present name. Her early screen credits are uncertain, as she invented some of them in an effort to seem more important ('... I'd not only never been in but never even seen' she admitted in 1969), but she was in *Alf's Button* (30), *Never Trouble Trouble* (31), *Fascination*, *Service for Ladies* (32, presumably when Korda met her), *Ebb Tide* and *Aren't We All?* Korda gave her a biggish part in *Wedding Rehearsal*, followed by a lead (the Other Woman) in *Men of Tomorrow*; then the small but telling part of Anne Boleyn in *The Private Life of Henry VIII* (33), after which she was considered a star – big enough to be sought for a leading part in the English-language version of a Charles Boyer vehicle, *The Battle* (34). She was a Japanese. When she returned from filming this in France, Korda loaned her out for *The Broken Melody* and made her first one of Douglas Fairbanks's entourage in *The Private Life of Don Juan* and then Lady Blakeney in *The Scarlet Pimpernel*.

But Hollywood, impressed by Mistress Boleyn, was offering better things: Oberon became a vamp and one of Maurice Chevalier's leading ladies in *Folies Bergere* (35), and though she was poor in it Goldwyn was offering a contract. Korda, who was in love with her, saw only the advantages of a Hollywood career and agreed to share her; so she did the three Goldwyn dramas which transformed her from a cheap exotic and established her as an international name: *The Dark Angel*, a remake of a Silent weepie, with Fredric March; *These Three* (36) with Miriam Hopkins, a triangle tangle which is perhaps her best early performance; and *Beloved Enemy*, a tale of the Irish troubles with Brian Aherne. She returned to Britain to play opposite Charles Laughton in *I Claudius*, and it was her near-fatal car crash which was the pretext for abandoning that film. When she recovered, Korda put her into two Technicolor comedies with two of his brightest leading men: the sluggish *Over the Moon* (37) with Rex Harrison and the trivial *The Divorce of Lady X* (38) with Laurence Olivier. She was then cast in something else that didn't get made: *Graustark*, with Gary Cooper and Sigrid Gurie. Huge sets had been erected on the Goldwyn lot, but the day before shooting was due to commence he called the whole thing off and Oberon and Cooper instead did a comedy, *The Cowboy and the Lady*. Olivier was her co-star again in *Wuthering Heights* (39), which Goldwyn envisaged as primarily a vehicle for her, an artistic error of major proportions.

In 1939 she was married to Korda (earlier, she had broken off an engagement to Joseph M. Schenck, one-time chairman of UA and head of 20th, on the grounds that her career was more important to her): he starred her in *The Lion Has Wings*, a piece of propaganda turned out quickly in the autumn of 1939 and her last British picture for more than a decade. With the coming of the war they went to Hollywood where she had fortuitously signed a short-term contract with Warners: *Till We Meet Again* (40), with George Brent, a remake of *One-Way Passage* that was even more lachrymose; and *Affectionately Yours* (41), a comedy with Dennis Morgan. Both parts had been destined originally for Bette Davis, and WB were seriously considering Oberon as her successor. Between the two she did the Lubitsch *That Uncertain Feeling* with Melvyn Douglas, and that was all. Then came *Lydia*, in which an ageing lady recalled her four lost loves. It was inspired by Duvivier's *Un Carnet de Bal*, and he again directed. Korda produced: it was the end of his professional relationship with Oberon; he returned to Britain the following year and they were divorced in 1945.

Merle Oberon's best-remembered film, ironically, contains one of her worst performances: Goldwyn's production of Emily Brontë's Wuthering Heights *(39), directed by William Wyler. Here she is as the dying Cathy, being supported literally by her Heathcliff – Laurence Olivier.*

In 1943 she made brief appearances in *Forever and a Day* and *Stage Door Canteen*, and was a Norwegian patriot in the idiotic *First Comes Courage* with Brian Aherne; then she almost became one of the victims of Jack the Ripper (Laird Cregar) in *The Lodger* (44). Said Picturegoer: 'Merle Oberon is rather colourless as Kitty; she performs two can-can dances.' – 'Might one call it the can't-can't?' suggested C. A. Lejeune. She was also threatened in *Dark Waters*, a dim variation of the one about the heroine being driven insane. 1945 was a bad year: only ridicule greeted both her George Sand in the Chopin biopic *A Song to Remember* and a tear-jerker called *This Love of Ours* (with Charles Korvin), a very distant adaptation of Pirandello. It was the first of several for Universal: Wanger's *A Night in Paradise* (46) with Turhan Bey, an Arabian Nights extravaganza that made Purgatory seem attractive; and *Temptation* with George Brent

A Song to Remember *(44): Merle Oberon and Cornel Wilde as George Sand and Chopin. Said Richard Winnington: 'William Bendix being Chopin would have been no less incongruous than Merle Oberon being George Sand in a smart sort of Vesta Tilley outfit.'*

and Paul Lukas, a curious attempt to film–for the sixth time–an Edwardian best-seller, 'Bella Donna'. After which, not surprisingly, Oberon went to the lower half of double bills: *Night Song* (47) with Dana Andrews; *Berlin Express* (48) with Korvin; and *Pardon My French* (51) with Paul Henried.

The British cinema offered a chance back to the top: *24 Hours of a Woman's Life* (52) with Leo Genn and Richard Todd–one of the many filmizations of Stefan Zweig's novel and probably the worst. In 1954 she made a Spanish film with Francisco Rabal, *Todo Es Possible en Granada*, and rather unexpectedly got prime parts in two major Hollywood films: *Desirée*, as the Empress Josephine to Brando's Napoleon; and *Deep in My Heart*, as Sigmund Romberg's lyric writer, Dorothy Donnelly. Both demonstrated conspicuously her major asset as an actress: style. But a stupid melodrama, *The Price of Fear* (56) with Lex Barker, put paid to further ambitions for the time being. After several years she played a nympho who goes bonkers because *Of Love and Desire* (63): its bookings were severely limited. But her work in the next two was widely seen (and admirable), both adaptations of meretricious best-sellers. Stephen Boyd was the actor-heel, a most unlikely candidate for *The Oscar* (65), and Oberon a fading screen star with a couple of minutes' screen time; in *Hotel* (66) she was a duchess who had her jewels stolen.

In life she is renowned for same. A very wealthy woman, she lives with her third husband in four homes–one in California, three in Mexico. In 1969 it was announced that she would leave them to make a British film, *The Private War of Mrs Darling*, but nothing came of it.

Margaret O'Brien can be considered the most successful child actress after Shirley Temple, and the most talented of all the children who attained stardom. Our Vines Have Tender Grapes *(45) contains one of her most delicate performances: a tale of a Norwegian farming community in Wisconsin, with Edward G. Robinson.*

Margaret O'Brien

American children–or at least Hollywood children–are an acquired taste. Non-American audiences have remained immune through the likes of Bobby Breen, Gigi Perreau, the Corcoran sisters and Cora Sue Collins, that child in *Queen Christina* who, incredibly, grew up to be Garbo. An exception was Margaret O'Brien, a one-time gold-mine for MGM and one of the top 10 ranking box-office stars in 1945 and 1946.

She was born in 1937 in Los Angeles (some months after her father's death). MGM chose her for a one-minute shot in a sequence involving war orphans in *Babes on Broadway* (41), and a year later put her into a well-meaning film about the blitz, with Laraine Day and Robert Young, *Journey for Margaret* (42). Her success in that caused MGM to change her name from Maxine O'Brien to Margaret and put her under contract. She appeared in *Dr Gillespie's Criminal Case* (43) and *Thousands Cheer*; was starred in *Lost Angel*, a comedy about a group of scientists involved with a child genius, and had a bit in *Madame Curie*. She was loaned to 20th to play Adèle in *Jane Eyre* (44), where she was fairly dreadful (Peggy Ann Garner, playing the young Jane, was also an exception among child stars). She co-starred with Laughton in *The Canterville Ghost*, which caused James Agee to remark: 'She is an exceptionally talented child, and it is infuriating to see her handled, and gradually being ruined by oafs.' However, she was next in *Meet Me in St Louis*, part of a well-nigh flawless cast, and Agee this time approved, adding, 'many of her possibilities and glints of her achievement hypnotize me as thoroughly as anything since Garbo.' In 1944 she won a special Oscar.

Of the next, *Music for Millions*, C. A. Lejeune wrote: 'This grave little girl, who can give the screen a morning glow by simply stumping into camera range . . . is something out of the ordinary in performing children. She belongs more with the Menuhins and Mozarts than with the Shirley Temples. . . . The child is as formal and old-fashioned as your grandmother's bonnet, but she has something of the same decorum and authority.' Lejeune also considered her the year's best actress for *Our Vines Have Tender Grapes* (45), a folksy tale with Edward G. Robinson as her father.

MGM were now in the position that 20th had been with Temple, of finding suitable star vehicles. They didn't succeed. The child's work continued to be impeccable, with only a hint of artifice, but each film did less business until the company didn't bother to exploit them properly: critical thumbs-downs didn't help. She was cast with Wallace Beery in a Western, *Bad Bascomb* (46); with Lewis Stone, Frank Morgan, Lionel Barrymore and Edward Arnold in the remake of *Three Wise Fools*; and then in a series of weepies: *The Unfinished Dance* (47), a glammed-up remake of *La Morte du Cygne*, *Tenth Avenue Angel* (48) and *The Big City* where she was an orphan adopted jointly by Jew, Catholic and Protestant. After a gap she was in two children's classics, Louisa May Alcott's *Little Women* (49) and Frances Hodgson Burnett's *The Secret Garden*. O'Brien was Beth in the former, and was very touching – the best of the four March girls. The film was a big one for MGM. But they were less pleased when the child refused to go to Disney for *Alice in Wonderland*, then intended to be part live-action. They suspended her.

It was coldly announced that she was leaving MGM for Columbia; there she received her first screen kiss in *Her First Romance* (51): the film was conventional adolescent stuff and passed unnoticed. Sensibly, she retired rather than go the teenage route, but an attempt as a dewy young heroine at RKO in *Glory* (56) – it was about a horse of that name – was doomed by the film's own ineptness. In 1960 she had a small character part – as an unwilling ingénue in a stock company – in *Heller in Pink Tights*. She was rather good but there were, apparently, no more screen offers. She does a lot of TV, and has appeared in stock in plays like 'Barefoot in the Park', 'Under the Yum Yum Tree' and 'A Thousand Clowns'. She has been married and divorced. In 1977 the money that she earned as a child will come to her. It will be well over a million (at the age of nine she was earning $2,500 per week).

Laurence Olivier

Laurence Olivier bestrides his profession in this century as Shakespeare bestrides the art of drama. ('I consider him, in common with my colleagues, the finest actor alive' – Charlton Heston; and Spencer Tracy referred to him as 'the greatest of them all'.) That doesn't make him the biggest box-office draw – far from it – nor of course does it mean that he is a great *film*-actor. However, as a Best Actor Oscar nominee (seven times) he is surpassed only by Tracy; and if an Oscar nomination is a puny thing in the context of his career, this record does give an indication of the quality of his screen work and its recognition.

He was born in Dorking, Surrey, in 1907, the son of a clergyman, into, in his own words, 'an atmosphere of genteel poverty . . . probably the most fertile ground for ambition there can be'. While at school he played Katharine in 'The Taming of the Shrew', and was encouraged to take up a stage career. He studied at the Central School, had his first professional experience as an ASM at Letchworth, and made his debut at the Brighton Hippodrome in a curtain-raiser. He joined a company which did Shakespeare in the London suburbs, in places like Camberwell Baths, and was with Sybil Thorndike's troupe for a while. He was with Birmingham Rep 1926–8, and with that company in a London season which brought an offer to take over a lead in 'A Bird in the Hand'. He did a number of West End plays, and made his New York bow in 'Murder on the Second Floor' which flopped. His film debut was in Germany, in the English version of a murder mystery with Lilian Harvey, *The Temporary Widow* (30) at UFA, in the part Willy Fritsch did in the original. He did four days' work on a quickie, *Too Many Crooks*, and was in *Potiphar's Wife* as the chauffeur heart-throb of the lady of the house.

This was the sort of part for which he was physically ideal, with his marcelled hair and dandy's moustache – but his ambition at that time was only to be a matinée idol. It was recognized that he had talent – Cedric Hardwicke recalled that he was noisy and lacked subtlety, 'but I knew instinctively he'd be a great actor'. Olivier credits Noël Coward, who cast him as Victor in 'Private Lives' (30), for persuading him to move onward as well as upward. However, the route was to be circuitous, and during the New York run of the Coward play his sights were on Hollywood. Several companies tested him, and he accepted a dazzling offer from RKO; but the films weren't dazzling: *Friends and Lovers* (31), in which he and Adolphe Menjou scrapped over Lily Damita; *The Yellow Ticket*, on loan to Fox, a melo with Elissa Landi; and *Westward Passage* (32) with Ann Harding. RKO tested him for the lead opposite Pola Negri in *A Woman Commands*, but didn't use him. Picturegoer reported that the US authorities had refused to renew his work permit, but he had also had a British offer, from Gloria Swanson, filming *Perfect Understanding* (33) in London: the result Olivier considers the worst film he ever made. With Gertrude Lawrence he did a farce, *No Funny Business*, about male and female divorce co-respondents.

Then MGM, having failed to interest Leslie Howard and been unable to contact Ronald Colman, offered him the male lead in Garbo's *Queen Christina*, but he proved inadequate and was replaced after some days by John Gilbert. MGM consoled him with a contract offer worth $1,500 a week, but he refused and went to New York to do 'The Green Bay Tree'. In London he appeared in 'Biography' and other plays, and accepted a Korda contract. He played Lunardi the balloonist in one sequence of *Conquest of the Air*, a semi-documentary directed by John Monk Saunders and written by H. G. Wells – but the film was abandoned when costs mounted (some of it was used in later Korda films and the rest released, under the same title, in 1941). Thus Olivier's first Korda film was *Moscow Nights* (35), starring Harry Bauer. His stock had risen when he and John Gielgud had alternated Romeo and Mercutio on the stage – which probably got him the part of Orlando opposite Elizabeth Bergner in *As You Like It* (36). Picturegoer chastised him for announcing that he preferred plays to films, but the stage didn't claim him entirely: he was romantic again, with Vivien Leigh, and swashbuckling vigorously in *Fire Over England* (37), then romancing Merle Oberon in a comedy, *The Divorce of Lady X* (38). Also in 1937 he and Leigh made *21 Days* (script by Graham Greene from a Galsworthy story), but it wasn't released until 1939 after they had both become very famous – and if they hadn't, it wouldn't ever have been, in his own opinion. They were both unbelievably bad.

He had tired of the West End, and had asked to be taken on at the Old Vic: in 1937–8 he played Henry V, Hamlet, Macbeth, Sir Toby Belch, Iago and Coriolanus, and on screen he and Old Vic colleague Ralph Richardson brought style and attack to an adventure story, *Q Planes* (39); then with some reluctance he returned to Hollywood for Goldwyn's expensive *Wuthering Heights*. He was no happier making it than expected, but director Wyler gradually changed his aloof attitude to films. Richard Griffith wrote later: 'Olivier's Heathcliff, a figure of earth, belongs to the great screen performances'. It was marred only by being too well-spoken. The picture was much admired, but didn't start to make a profit until it was re-shown.

In New York he played 'No Time for Comedy', then returned to Hollywood for Selznick's *Rebecca* (40), directed by Hitchcock from a novel by Daphne du Maurier; as the moody aristocratic Maxim he gave another superb romantic performance. And he was also fine as Mr Darcy in MGM's *Pride and Prejudice*, the only one of the cast whom Jane Austen might have acknowledged. Also in 1940 he and Leigh (now his wife; his marriage to Jill Esmond had been dissolved) did 'Romeo and Juliet' in New York, partly financed by himself from the salary that Warners had paid him for a projected remake of *Disraeli* (it was cancelled, and revived a year later in Britain, with Gielgud). The 'Romeo' was critically roasted and he lost his money. In Hollywood Korda co-starred the two of them in *Lady Hamilton* (41), a jingoistic piece designed to sway Americans to the British side in the European war. Olivier's Nelson brought him a second Picturegoer Gold Medal – the first was for *Rebecca* – and the film rounded out a remarkable Hollywood quartet. All four films have been endlessly revived: in 1942 a poll of New York cinemagoers voted *Rebecca* and *Wuthering Heights* among their ten favourite films, and in Los Angeles in 1967 both were voted in the top 10 films people most wanted to see again.

In film parlance, Olivier was on top of the world. Every studio made him offers (20th offered to delay *How Green Was My Valley* until he was ready), but he did not want to be, he said later, just a film-star, 'like dear Cary'; he also wanted to serve in the war. In Britain he joined the Fleet Air Arm, but was released to make two entertaining propaganda pieces, *49th Parallel* (41) and *The Demi-Paradise* (43). He played a French-Canadian and Russian respectively, perfectly accented – both demonstrating Gielgud's point that Olivier is a great 'observer'.

His biggest propaganda effort was, however, Shakespeare's *Henry V* (44). It was an idea he had considered, but the

Olivier at the time of RKO contract.

(*Top left*) *Olivier and Renée Asherson in* Henry V (*44*). (Right) *Vivien Leigh and Laurence Olivier at the time they were working on* That Hamilton Woman.

(*Bottom*) *Olivier, Anton Walbrook and Leslie Howard in* The 49th Parallel (*41*), *a good British spy film that was intended primarily to swing Americans to Britain's wartime cause.*

'All for Love' was always one of the cinema's pet themes, and it was never more heart-breakingly rendered than by Laurence Olivier *in* Carrie *(52) – perhaps his finest screen acting. These three pictures give only* some *idea of his disintegration (in picture one with Eddie Albert; in picture two with Jennifer Jones – the cause). William Wyler directed, from the novel by Theodore Dreiser.*

an add colours to the meleon. . . .' Olivier Richard III (55).

project became reality under the auspices of Filippo del Giudice, who ran Two Cities Films. Olivier approached Wyler to direct, but he couldn't take it on, nor could Terence Young or Carol Reed, so he took the plunge himself. When the film came out, his undeniably imaginative work as director/producer as well as star caused the word 'genius' to be bandied about. It was a milestone: great chunks of it have been frequently copied, and for the first time screen Shakespeare seemed not only feasible but desirable. But neither Olivier's name nor great reviews helped the box-office at first. It built into a success; in the US it did very well (in New York it ran almost a year) and brought Olivier the New York Critics' award (Best Actor) and a special Oscar. He referred recently to it: '. . . a rather sweet film. I like it. I feel proud of it.'

Back at the Old Vic he did the series of performances which established him as the first actor of his time – Hotspur, Astrov, Lear, Oedipus, Richard III. Films beckoned vainly, but just as he and Leigh were on the point of signing for a Hollywood *Cyrano de Bergerac*, del Guidice proposed a film *Hamlet* (48). Olivier was knighted while it was in production. The film was somewhat less ecstatically received than *Henry V* (and is downcried today mainly because of a too-restless camera), but Olivier's own prestige soared even higher. He won a Best Picture and a Best Actor Oscar, and indeed the prizes copped world-wide for both films were considerable, as Rank (who financed) used to announce in special ads. Financially, *Hamlet* was a palpable hit, especially in the US, and 'made a great deal of money at the moment when the British film industry particularly needed it' (Felix Barker, 'The Oliviers', 1953).

Olivier's chief functioning ground, however, remained the stage; he went into management and presented, *inter alia*, the Shaw and Shakespeare Cleopatra plays, with himself and Leigh. He was one of many stars in cameo parts in *The Magic Box* (51), but as a Cockney policeman stole the notices. That year Leigh was offered a Hollywood film she wanted to do, and Olivier let it be known that he was open to offers. The one he accepted, Wyler's version of Theodore Dreiser's (Sister) *Carrie* contained 'the finest acting of his career' said Richard Winnington, noting 'the refinement with which this actor compels the raptures, miseries and final suicidal despair of an obsessive passion' (for Jennifer Jones). Olivier was not, however, Oscar-nominated, presumably because the film failed at the box-office. His next picture fared worse, and according to Herbert Wilcox, who produced, it was taken off the circuits after one night and compensation paid; the title, *The Beggar's Opera* (53), contained not one but two off-putting words (Olivier himself refused to agree to a post-première change to *Macheath the Highwayman*). Further, it opened in London during Coronation week and got a grudging press reception.

The trouble was that as a film artist Olivier was associated with so-called 'high-brow' stuff, and it was no longer the star of *Rebecca* who sought to immortalize his stage portrayal of *Richard III* (55). Said Gavin Lambert: 'Olivier's performance was brilliant on the stage; here it is even more impressive, the irony sharpened, the arrogance made more breath-taking by the camera's intimacy.' Half-wolf, half-vulture, Olivier dominated this handsome interpretation of one of the less compulsive plays, perhaps the best of his three Shakespeare films. In an attempt to get its costs back quickly, it was premièred on TV in the US, and otherwise did satisfactory business. Korda, who presented it, died, and Olivier failed to get backing for his next Shakespeare venture. Rank wasn't interested, nor were the American majors; he went cap in hand till the last minute, with all preparations made for location-shooting in Scotland two days later. It was to have been *Macbeth*, a part that he had played a year earlier (1956) at Stratford and his greatest performance.

Amidst great publicity, however, the next embarked: *The Prince and the Showgirl* (58), directing and co-starring with Marilyn Monroe (in the part that Leigh had played with him on the stage); the result was, inevitably, an anti-climax, though his own performance as a mittel-European princeling impeccably done. He also did 'John Gabriel Borkman' on TV that year, to date his only post-war British appearance in TV drama (though in the US he won plaudits in two adaptations of novels, 'The Moon and Sixpence' and 'The Power and the Glory'). In 1959 he took a featured role in *The Devil's Disciple*, with Kirk Douglas and Burt Lancaster. It was brave of them rather than him; his stylish General Burgoyne almost saved the day, causing the Evening Standard, uncharacteristically, to blazon their review on their front page, headed 'The Greatest Actor in the World'. But prestige he didn't need, and the film of John Osborne's *The Entertainer* (60) did little to raise his box-office. On the stage he had played Archie Rice, a run-down music-hall comic, and on screen he was even more mesmerizing, *being* rather than acting. But some critics

The screen teaming that made headline news: Olivier and Marilyn Monroe in The Prince and the Showgirl *(58). Olivier directed, and it was a soufflé that failed to rise.*

didn't like Tony Richardson's direction, and the popular press was then waging war on Osborne: few films have been so ridiculously treated. (Olivier's film daughter was played by Joan Plowright, who became his third wife in 1961.)

Show Magazine in 1962, in an article on salaries, said that Olivier was no crowd-drawer, but was worth millions in prestige; he certainly pocketed a huge fee for *Spartacus* (61, in Hollywood) and confessed he only did it for money, with Peter Ustinov and Charles Laughton backing such unlikely Romans as Kirk Douglas and Tony Curtis. This was Olivier the sly one, the senator who calmly awaits his eventual triumph. He played a schoolteacher in the bleak *Term of Trial* (62), whose 'only interest,' said Dwight Macdonald, was 'in confirming, once more, one's opinion that Laurence Olivier is the best actor now going . . . but what a waste of talent'.

As a stage actor, he was the logical choice to head Britain's National Theatre Company which started up in 1963: very quickly it became one of the world's best companies; his own work there included two definitive productions of English-Chekhov, some deliberately chosen supporting parts and two more acting triumphs, in 'Othello' and 'The Dance of Death'. The New Statesman said that a film should be made of his

Olivier in The Entertainer *(60): 'And the movie, if it gave us nothing but Olivier's interpretation of this character, would be a rare and important experience' (Pauline Kael). With Joan Plowright (his third wife), a magnificent stage actress in one of her rare film performances.*

Othello for posterity, but the film that was made (65)–a sort of TV version, in colour and Scope, not directed by him–gave little idea of what it had been like as a theatre experience, and bewildered people who had only read about it. The reviews were poor; Pauline Kael did a favourable one, with this analysis of Olivier: 'Every time we single out the feature that makes Olivier a marvel–his lion eyes or the voice and the way it seizes on a phrase–he alters it or casts it off in some new role, and is greater than ever. It is no special asset, it is the devilish audacity and courage of this man. . . . What is extraordinary is inside, and what is even more extraordinary is his determination to give it outer force. He has never levelled off; he goes on soaring.'

Bunny Lake Is Missing (65) called for no special abilities, an amiable performance as a Scotland Yard inspector, and almost the only one in his later screen-career where he looked like his off-screen self. He returned to blackface as the Mahdi in *Khartoum* (66), a performance not much liked, and didn't film again until 1968 when he embarked on several projects: *The Shoes of the Fisherman*, as the Soviet premier; *The Dance of Death* (69), filmed in a similar way to the *Othello*, but marginally better; and cameo parts as high-ranking officers in two world wars: Sir John French in *Oh! What a Lovely War* and Lord Dowding in *The Battle of Britain*. In both cases reviewers singled him out of the starry casts for special praise. There was another 'all-star' venture, *David Copperfield* (70) where his bit as Mr Creakle was the only Dickensian and indeed enjoyable two minutes. It was made for TV in the US and cinemas elsewhere, and the distinguished participants were on a percentage. Then *The Three Sisters* (70), directing from his own stage production and playing the small part of the doctor. There have been too many small parts, but Olivier no longer enjoys acting: 'Perhaps the responsibility is too great' he has said. In 1970 he was created a Lord, the first actor to be so honoured.

Lilli Palmer

Lilli Palmer is the most cosmopolitan of stars. She has worked in Britain, the United States, France, Germany, Austria and Italy – and apart from Italy (only twice) several times in each country. She projects exactly what you might expect: the elegant, sophisticated, much-travelled and much-experienced *dame d'une certaine age*. She has said in recent years that she is no longer interested in acting, which might account for a recent mechanical streak in the still potent charm; it is to be wondered what she might do with a really good part if it came her way.

She was born in Posen, Germany, in 1914, the daughter of a surgeon; studied at the Ilka Grüning School of Acting in Berlin, after earlier studies there and in Vienna. In 1932 she made her stage debut, in Berlin, in 'Die eiserne Jungfrau' and worked later in stock and in cabaret. When the Nazis took over in Germany she went to Paris and appeared in an operette 'Viktoria et son Hussard', but returned subsequently to Frankfurt and appeared in 'The Gypsy Princess'. Korda saw her and brought her to Britain under contract. However, he dropped her after some months without using her. She got a part in a quickie called *Crime Unlimited* (35) and as a result Gaumont-British signed her. She was usually cast as a continental mantrap: *First Offence* (36) starring John Mills; *Wolf's Clothing*; Hitchcock's *Secret Agent*, in a small supporting part; *Good Morning Boys* (37) starring Will Hay; *The Great Barrier*, as a camp follower in this epic of Canada starring Richard Arlen; and on loan for *Sunset in Vienna* starring Tullio Carminati, which was the first time the critics noticed her favourably. As a result she got leads in *Command Performance* opposite Arthur Tracy, *Crackerjack* starring Tom Walls (then one of Britain's top stars), and *The Man With a Hundred Faces* with Charles Heslop. Her contract expired, but GB asked her back to play a tough Hungarian chorus girl in Carol Reed's *A Girl Must Live* (39); then she made *Blind Folly* and *The Door With Seven Locks* (40), with Leslie Banks. She was also on the stage in, among others, 'Road to Gandahar', 'Little Ladyship', and 'Ladies in Action' (40), as Felicity Van der Loo.

The first time she made any considerable impression was as the Other Woman in 'No Time for Comedy' at the Haymarket in 1941; and in marked contrast to that glittering performance she played a sad-eyed little ghost in *Thunder Rock* (42): now she was accepted as a serious dramatic actress. She appeared in Leslie Howard's tribute to the ATS, *The Gentle Sex* (43) and in Rattigan's comedy, *English Without Tears* (44). She was with her husband, Rex Harrison, in *The Rake's Progress* (45), as a Jewess who is married by the Rake in order to get her out of Germany – and discovers

The Gentle Sex *(43) at war: Lilli Palmer as a refugee girl who joined the women's branch of the army. With (right) Rosamund John.*

sadly that he had done it for money. She then did an inferior version of Stefan Zweig's *Beware of Pity* (46) as the crippled heroine.

Harrison had a Hollywood contract, and Palmer accompanied him. She free-lanced, and made four films: *Cloak and Dagger* (46) with Gary Cooper; *Body and Soul* (47) with John Garfield; the underrated *My Girl Tisa* (48) with Sam Wanamaker; and *No Minor Vices* with Dana Andrews. She looked lovely, and was acting with her usual sensitivity, but none of the films was over-successful. In 1949 she appeared in two plays on Broadway, 'My Name is Aquilon' and as Shaw's Cleopatra; and took a quick trip to France to support Maria Montez in *Hans le Marin*. She and Harrison reappeared together in Britain in *The Long Dark Hall* (50), and it was later that year that their careers picked up, when they did 'Bell Book and Candle' on Broadway. As a result of that they got another chance in Hollywood, in *The Fourposter* (52). Palmer made two more Broadway performances, in 'Venus Observed' and 'The Love of Four Colonels' (53). Then she accepted an offer from Germany to make her first two films there: *Feuerwerk* (54) and *Teufel im Seide* (55) with Curt Jurgens.

The Harrisons took 'Bell Book and Candle' to Britain in 1954, but the marriage came apart during the run, and her part was taken over by Joan Greenwood: the divorce came through in 1957. She returned to Germany where there were film offers: *Anastasia die Letze Zarentochter* (56) with Ivan Desny, which clashed with the 20th-Ingrid Bergman film on the same subject: *Zwischen Zeit und Ewigkeit* with Carlos Thompson, the Argentinian actor whom she married in 1957; *Wie ein Sturmwind* (57); *Der Gläserne Turm* with Peter Van Eyck; *Montparnasse 19*, in France, in a small role, with Gérard Philipe as Modigliani; *Ein Frau Die Weiss Was Sie Will* (58); and the remake of *Mädchen in Uniform*. In France she appeared with Jean Marais in an all-star episoder made as a posthumous tribute to Sacha Guitry, *La Vie à Deux*.

Out of the blue Hollywood recalled Palmer to play opposite Gable, as his ex-wife, in *But Not for Me* (59): mocking and glamorous, she created a firm impression. In Britain she made a revoltingly sentimental nun-film, *Conspiracy of Hearts* (60), and in Germany a version of a Shaw play, *Frau Warren's Gewerbe*–Mrs W.'s Profession, which was, of course, prostitution; but the combination of Shaw and sex got it no more bookings outside Germany than Palmer's earlier German films. World audiences had chances of seeing her in two more films for Paramount: *The Pleasure of His Company* (61) with Fred Astaire and *The Counterfeit Traitor* with William Holden. This was the beginning of a period of intense activity–the suitcases hardly had time to get unpacked: *Leviathan* from Julien Green's novel in France, with Louis Jourdan; with her husband, *Frau Cheney's Ende*, MGM's old warhorse, taken on by the Germans; and in France, Roger Leenhardt's beautiful *Le Rendezvous de Minuit*, in a triple role–as a suicidal woman, as an actress in a film, and for one brief moment, as herself. The Franco-Austrian *Adorable Julia* (62) was something else again–a cheap and badly made version of Somerset Maugham's 'Theatre', which was followed by: *Finden Sie das Constance sich Richtig Verhält?*–more Maugham ('The Constant Wife'); *L'Amore Difficile*; Disney's *The Flight of the White Stallions* (63) with Robert Taylor; *Beta Som*, an Italian film made in English with James Mason; *Das Grosse Liebesspiel*, a corny German rehash of *La Ronde*; *Le Grain de Sable* (64) with Pierre Brasseur; *Operation*

Lilli Palmer never quite got the right breaks in Hollywood and she usually had to make much out of little–as here, in The Pleasure of His Company *(61) with Fred Astaire and Debbie Reynolds.*

Crossbow with Sophia Loren and several British actors; and *The Amorous Adventures of Moll Flanders* (65), rather disheartened as a Madame.

Palmer played opposite Jean Gabin in *Le Tonnerre de Dieu*, and then did *Ces Dames de l'Etoile Rouge* (66), *Jack of Diamonds* and *Le Voyage du Père* with Fernandel. In 1967 she returned to the (British) stage, at the behest of Noël Coward, to appear with him and Irene Worth in his 'Suite in Three Keys'; and remained in Britain to do a dull supporting role in *Sebastian* (67). In 1968 she appeared in *Nobody Runs Forever* and–unsuitably as Jocasta–in *Oedipus the King* with Christopher Plummer. Concurrently in London there was an exhibition of her paintings, done at her home in Switzerland. She said that she and Thompson planned to live there much more in the future. Certainly she might have stayed there instead of making *Hard Contract* (69) and *De Sade* with Keir Dullea; much better was a Spanish horror film *La Residencia* (70).

'The Girl With the Curls'

Mary Pickford

If popularity were the sole criterion of stardom, then Mary Pickford is without doubt the greatest star there has ever been. For most of the 24 years she was on the screen she was the biggest draw of them all–bigger, even, than Chaplin. In the US she was called 'America's Sweetheart', and outside it, less chauvinistically, 'The World's Sweetheart'. Pollsters for 14 years found she was the world's most popular woman. It has to be admitted, as Alexander Walker has pointed out, that she 'profited by the historical accident of launching her film career at exactly the right moment to catch the tide' ('The Celluloid Sacrifice'). She started before players in films were named on the credits or adverts, at that moment when movie-making was becoming big business; and rode to success on the crest of this new industry. In less than 10 years she was, said Benjamin B. Hampton in 'A History of the Movies' (1931), 'the industry's most valuable asset. Woman's place in business has grown enormously in importance in the last three decades, but Mary Pickford is the only member of her sex who ever became the focal point of an entire industry. Her position is unique; probably no man or woman will ever again win so extensive a following.'

Her very success may have contributed to her popularity–an inspiration to the 20th century woman seeking emancipation; at the same time the Pickford character–'Little Mary' of the sub-titles–belonged firmly to the world of Victorian melodrama, and was probably a great consolation to those people who did not care for the changing modern woman. Her public was mainly rural; for millions of people who had never been to a theatre it was an entirely new experience to see a 'star', someone to identify with, to love from a remote distance; it must often have seemed like the incarnation of the heroine from the printed page–more clearly defined, but infinitely more mysterious. She represented purity, innocence and determination. As an actress, contemporary critics never put her in a class with Lillian Gish, and Griffith and Mayer (in 'The Movies', 1957) found it 'increasingly difficult' to assess her appeal. They concluded that she combined idealism with spunk; that she played 'girls in that misty mid-region between sexless childhood and buxom womanliness which seems to have had a strong appeal to many American males of the early century'; but that she was above her rivals because 'her sweetness and light were tempered by a certain realism': she played Pollyanna 'not so much saccharinely as vigorously'.

Even so, she would not go down today. Her films are too remote from our experience in environment or truth, and in industry terms their technical qualities are antediluvian. Whether one holds the old belief that silent screen acting required a range from A to Z, or feels that, with voice withheld, it couldn't go much beyond D, Pickford's range was severely limited. Partly it was limited by type-casting. Certainly the only modern critic to have made an extensive study of her films, Alexander Walker, comes down firmly for her: 'No one seeing these performances today can doubt that she was an actress of manifest talent and imagination – and exciting but unrealized potential. One bitterly regrets that she has never met the right director or found the right story at the same time as she was trying to impress the other part of the Pickford personality, the sexual awareness and worldly toughness, more clearly and uncompromisingly into her performances.' However, contemporary critics didn't think much of her work in the four Talkies she made; everyone agreed that she was dreadful in *Secrets*, a part which should have been well within her range.

She was born in Toronto in 1893; her mother was widowed when Mary was four, but the family income was saved when the child was taken on by a local stock company for such melodramas as 'Uncle Tom's Cabin' and 'The Little Red Schoolhouse'. At nine she was starring in 'The Fatal Wedding', billed as 'Baby Gladys Smith' (her real name). She toured extensively, and at age 13 decided that unless she made Broadway soon she would give up the theatre for good; so she cornered producer David Belasco, who gave her a part in 'The Warrens of Virginia'. Tours of this and the New York run kept her busy 1907–8, but in 1909 family fortunes (now, they all acted – mother, brother, sister) were low and Mary decided to try films. She went to Biograph where D. W. Griffith interviewed her, made her up, and ushered her on to the set of *Pippa Passes*. At the end of the day he asked her to return the following day, offering her $5 per day. She asked for $10, and got it.

The next day they were filming *Her First Biscuits* (often given as her first film; another contender is *The Lonely Villa*) – its stars were Florence Lawrence and William Courtright, both of whom Pickford was to feature in her *My Best Girl*, almost 20 years later. She had a bit part as 'one of those who suffered from a bride's first baking' (remembered Adolph Zukor in 'The Public Is Never Wrong'). Her first star part was *The Violin Maker of Cremona* with Owen Moore (to whom she was married, till drink killed it); after that Griffith offered her a contract with a guarantee of $40 for five days work weekly. She played in *In Old Kentucky*, *The Hessian Renegades*, *To Save Her Soul* (09) and others, often cast as a dusky maiden (*Song of the Wild Wood Flute*, *Ramona*), but it was as herself that she had her first big hit, *The Little Teacher* (10); the sub-titles on that identified her as 'Little Mary', and thus audiences began to refer to her. Exhibitors advertised her as 'Goldielocks' and 'The Girl with the Curls' or – in succession to Florence Lawrence – 'The Biograph Girl'. The film's title was immaterial: 'What Happened to Mary Twice Nightly' was all that was needed when a Pickford pic played in Haddington, Scotland. She had achieved such fame that when she left Biograph for the Independent Motion Picture Co (IMP) her first film for them (with Moore), *Their First Misunderstanding* (10), was advertised thus: 'Little Mary is an Imp now'. IMP paid her $175 a week; a year later Majestic offered $275, and the first picture Pickford and Moore made for that company was called *The Courting of Mary* (11). But soon they returned to Biograph and Griffith, then at the peak of film-making.

Some titles: *The Italian Barber*, *The Way of a Man*, *The One She Loved*, *Wilful Peggy*, *White Roses*, *Home Folks*, *A Feud in the Kentucky Hills* and *In a Sultan's Garden* (IMP). Pickford contributed the scenarios for some of them – *May to December*, *Lena and the Geese* (12). Of *Friends* – with Lionel Barrymore – she says in her memoirs ('Sunshine and Shadow', 1956) that she thinks it was the first film ever to feature a close-up. Her biggest Biograph success was *The New York Hat*, but she had already decided to leave that company, enraged that a newcomer without stage-training – Mae Marsh – was being given the leads in *Man's Genesis* (which she had turned down, because it meant appearing in a grass skirt) and *The Sands of Dee*. She went back to Belasco, and told him she wanted to return to the stage; he cast her as a blind girl, the childhood sweetheart the hero eventually realizes he loves, in 'A Good Little Devil'. When New York learned that this starred 'The Girl with the Curls' the theatre was mobbed. It was the first time in history that film fans had seen an idol in person. At the same time the industry felt honoured that a film player had made it in legit.

The play was filmed (13) and some publicity accrued from the fact that Belasco himself appeared in the prologue – a rare honour for a mere film; and also from the fact that 'Little Mary' was returning to the screen. It was, however, 'a monumental failure' (her memoirs). Famous Players produced, and Zukor, its boss, a few months later offered her a contract to play in his 'B' products at $500 per week; but their success – *Caprice* with Moore, *In a Bishop's Carriage*, where she was a thief, and *Hearts Adrift* especially (in that she was shipwrecked) – was such that early in 1914 it went up to $1,000 a week. Zukor's 'A' pictures ('famous players in famous plays') weren't doing too well, but the 'B' films were doing fine. She had a resounding hit with *Tess of the Storm Country* and lesser ones with *Such a Little Queen*, *The Eagle's Mate* with James Kirkwood, *Behind the Scenes*, *Fanchon the Cricket*, *Cinderella* (14) with Moore, *Mistress Nell* (as Nell Gwyn) and *A Dawn of Tomorrow* (15). Meanwhile, her salary had gone to $2,000 per week – and when an offer came from the American Film Co., to do a serial, *The Diamond in the Sky* at $4,000 a week, Zukor had to match it or lose her (so potent was the Pickford name that her sister, Lotte, was engaged instead). She soon went on to $10,000 a week. Details of her contracts were published, and they are all covered in Terry Ramsaye's 'A Million and One Nights', 1926. He says at one point: 'The fame of all the other famous players was nothing unless it was supported by Mary Pickford. She was the one player really famous to the motion picture exhibitors and their public.'

According to her memoirs, her resolve to get every penny she could from Zukor was due to the fantastic offers from other companies; plus the fact that one evening she had noticed enormous queues for her *Rags*, and none at all for another Famous Players film down the road. Later it became a cause with her that whenever Chaplin's wage got a hike, she got a bigger one. Zukor says in his memoirs: 'There is no doubt about her tremendous drive for success and the cash register nature of a segment of her brain.' *Little Pal*, *The Girl From Yesterday*, *Poor Little Peppina* (16), *Madam Butterfly* (with Marshall Neilan as Pinkerton), *The Foundling*, *The Eternal Grind* and *Hulda from Holland* were the others that kept the public queueing. Eventually, in the summer of 1916 Zukor announced the formation of two new companies, The Mary Pickford Studio and Artcraft (to release its product); for some months she had been flirting with other companies, including Mutual (whose salary to Chaplin grieved her somewhat). The two new companies were both a ruse to keep her and a front to discourage poachers, but she was to get a guarantee of $1,040,000 for two years, plus bonuses, privileges and power.

At the same time Zukor merged Famous Players with Lasky (later to become Paramount); and Pickford soon found that her new bosses wanted to interfere. She let them have their way with *Less Than the Dust*, which was awful, but quarrelled over the next one, *Pride of the Clan* (17). But it was, she says, 'an even more disastrous failure'. So she claimed autonomy when making *A Poor Little Rich Girl* – but no one at the studio liked it; so she buckled under Cecil B. de Mille for *Romance of the Redwoods* and *The Little American*, the latter a propaganda piece about the sinking of the Lusitania (in it, our heroine almost got raped!). But then *A Poor Little Rich Girl* became a big success; and so was *Rebecca of Sunnybrook Farm* which followed the two de Milles; and so was *The Little Princess*, which followed that – so she was able to work with little interference; but these three juvenile parts had typed her. She was irrevocably stuck with 'Little Mary'. In *Stella Maris* (18) she had a dual role, enabling her to play both the angelic crippled title character and the older maid who dotes on her – thus one of the characters could end unhappily but the film still have the required happy ending. She was more conventional in *Amarilly of Clothes Line Alley*, and in *M'liss*, as a 'fearless trusted friend of forest creatures'. (The last five were all directed by Marshall Neilson and written by Frances Marion, who wrote some dozen Pickford vehicles.) Then came the less popular *How Could You Jean?* and *Captain Kidd Junior* (19). Her last picture for Zukor was a short, *Johanna Enlists*.

She had spent much of this period with Chaplin and Douglas Fairbanks encouraging people to buy war bonds. Now she wanted some money for herself. First National offered $250,000 each for three pictures, plus $50,000 to her mother. Zukor couldn't, or wouldn't, meet the price. To prevent her from going to a competitor he offered her $1,000 a week for five years for doing nothing – claiming that she was tired; but she wasn't having any. Her years with Zukor, she has said, were the happiest of her life, implying also that, having 'saved' him at the time of *Tess of the Storm Country*, he might have been more generous. First National were generous – once again her salary was no longer second to Chaplin's and eventually she got an extra $100,000 each for the three pictures she made there – plus complete independence. They were, however, big money-makers for the company: *Daddy Long Legs*, a semi-classic about an 'orphan' adopted by a wealthy benefactor; *The Hoodlum* and *Heart o' the Hills*.

UA was formed in 1919 by Pickford, Griffith, Chaplin and Fairbanks (to whom she was married that year): it was partly a defensive action against rumours that the moguls were going to put a ceiling on star salaries. For UA, as part-owner and

Mary Pickford as Pollyanna *(20), the little orphan girl who won the hearts of all around her, including her crotchety aunt – though she succumbed only after Pollyanna's accident. The film embodied one of Hollywood's cherished themes – that contentment and peace of mind are a surer way to happiness than riches. Also in the still: Helen Jerome Eddy (by the fireplace), Doc Crane (centre) and Herbert Prior (second from right).*

producer, Pickford did very well. *Pollyanna* (20) – the 'glad girl' – was their first film and the first ever sold on a percentage basis (initially exhibitors boycotted the new company, but public opinion forced them to give in). The film put UA on a sound financial basis, though Pickford herself hated it. There followed several like products – *Suds*, as a plain little skivvy; *The Love Light* (21), as an Italian lighthouse keeper betrayed by a German spy; *Through the Back Door*, as a Belgian refugee; *Little Lord Fauntleroy*, in a dual role – awful in drag as the noble lord but good as Dearest, his mother; and a remake of *Tess of the Storm Country* (22). But she yearned to play adult roles.

On the strength of the German *Dubarry*, Pickford brought Ernst Lubitsch to Hollywood to direct her in her 'first' adult role, *Dorothy Vernon of Haddon Hall*; but he didn't like the script, and instead directed her in *Rosita* (23), where she was a fiery señorita – 'the worst picture, bar none, that I ever made' (Pickford). It was a financial failure of large proportions. She then tried *Dorothy Vernon* (24), a drama set in Elizabethan England – 'Mary Pickford as an 18-year-old spitfire' said the ads – but it was little more successful. She felt it was a punishment for ignoring the public's expressed wish – via a contest in Photoplay – that she continue to play parts like Pollyana and Cinderella. Her popularity had begun to diminish a little; in the 1923 'National Star Popularity Contest' she trailed both the Talmadge sisters. There were those who thought that had she been less interested in money she might have persevered and eventually won over the public to a grown-up Mary, but instead she plunged back into the pathos of *Little Annie Rooney* (25) and *Sparrows* (26), her defiantly bobbed hair hidden under a wig of golden curls (she looked older than the other kids but audiences accepted her). One fan-magazine observed that she had drunk deep from the elixir of youth. She did at least play a 17-year-old in *My Best Girl* (27) – a gentle comedy centred on a young girl's romance with the boss's son. Her co-star was Charles

'Buddy' Rogers, whom she married after the famous marriage to Fairbanks ended in 1935.

With the coming of Sound, she hesitated; but wisely chose *Coquette* (29), which had been a success on stage for Helen Hayes; her fans approved and it gained her a Best Actress Oscar. Maybe it was that which persuaded her into doing *The Taming of the Shrew* against her better judgment. For years fans had been clamouring for Doug and Mary, the King and Queen of Hollywood – the palace was called 'Pickfair' – to make a film together; their selection of *The Shrew* betokens perhaps a consciousness of their exalted status, plus a desire to do away with the old era now that Talkies were here. But it was an odd choice in view of both the fans' preference for 'Little Mary' and a complete lack of Shakespearian experience. 'I have no qualms about admitting that Katharine was one of my worst performances' – you can say that again – 'instead of being a forceful tiger-cat, I was a spitting little kitten.' Few people were curious enough to turn up to see it and for years it was remembered only because of a credit: 'Additional dialogue by Sam Taylor'; less generally known is that a Silent version was prepared, in case Talkies were a passing fad. It was the first Talkie to be shown in London with separate performances.

Undeterred, Pickford then decided to get in on the all-talking, all-singing, all-dancing craze, and did all three in *Kiki* (31), playing a Parisian soubrette. She had left it too late to escape from type. Said E. Rossiter Shepherd in Picturegoer: 'It will take another picture to efface from my mind the vision of an over-rouged, under-dressed vamp and replace it with the curly demureness of the real Mary.' She then went back to *Secrets* (33), which she had abandoned before *Kiki* at a loss of $300,000 ($50,000 less than her salary for *Kiki*). Based on a sentimental play which traced a marriage from the teens to old age, it had been a great hit for Norma Talmadge in 1924. But the public didn't want to see Pickford (and Leslie Howard) in it. Having made what she herself called three 'costly and disheartening moving-picture failures' in a row, she retired from the screen. In 1933 she made a vaudeville appearance in New York. In 1934 she published a book entitled 'Why Not Try God' and in 1935 a novel and something called 'My Rendezvous With Life'; and she broadcast frequently for NBC. In 1936 she transferred her talents to CBS; that year she became the first vice-president of UA, and co-produced *One Rainy Afternoon* and produced *The Gay Desperado*. Long after the deaths of Fairbanks and Griffith (who, anyway, had been bought out) Chaplin and Pickford co-owned UA. They finally sold out in 1953. In 1937 was formed the Mary Pickford Cosmetic Co. There were rumours of a comeback in Britain in 1939, and in the early 50s she was definitely set for *Storm Center* – but she changed her mind, and Bette Davis played the part. At least she didn't need the money.

Mary Pickford made only four Talkies, including Kiki *(31), but the public refused to accept her in her new persona as a mature woman. Also, Sound revealed that she really wasn't much of an actress.*

Walter Pidgeon

Walter Pidgeon: 'that handsome piece of screen furniture', as James Agate termed him, but less, surely, because he was wooden than because he seemed to be around in almost every film. He was not (is not) an exciting actor, but was successful at projecting a good masculine dependability – capable, intelligent, honorable. He and Greer Garson together embodied a multitude of the domestic virtues of their time.

He was born in East St John, New Brunswick, Canada, in 1897, and studied at the University of New Brunswick for a year before being commissioned in the Artillery. He was invalided out after an accident, and was sent to Boston for his health. There he became a bank runner and married his childhood sweetheart, who died two years later in childbirth; he also studied singing, and made his stage bow in a local production of 'You Never Can Tell'. Fred Astaire heard him sing at a party and recommended him to friends in New York, but they turned him down after auditioning him. Pidgeon was encouraged to approach Elsie Janis, whom he had met while she was doing troop concerts. She took him as her singing partner and he made his professional debut in 'At Home' with her; they toured with this, in Britain as well as the US, and did vaudeville together. He also had a contract with Victor and was the first artist to record Irving Berlin's 'What'll I Do?' and 'Remember'. Joseph M. Schenck wanted him for a film with Constance Talmadge, and procured his release from his stage contract; but when Pidgeon arrived in Hollywood Schenck had changed his mind and arranged for him to go to Paramount for a supporting role in *Mannequin* (26), which starred Alice Joyce and Dolores Costello.

Pidgeon stayed on and free-lanced: *The Outsider* at Fox; *Miss Nobody*, who was Anna Q. Nilsson in drag; *Old Lives for New*, as the bounder who pinches Lewis Stone's wife, from E. M. Hull's novel 'The Desert Healer' (its British title); *Marriage License*, from a British play, 'The Pelican', with Alma Rubens, again as the Other Man; *The Heart of Salome* (27) again with Rubens, but this time he was the hero; *The Girl From Rio*, as a visiting businessman involved with Carmen Myers; *The Gorilla*, from the old stage comedy-thriller; *Woman Wise* with June Collyer; and *The Thirteenth Juror*, with Anna Q. Nilsson and Francis X. Bushman – Pidgeon on trial for a murder that defending counsel Bushman committed. He had reached the position of leading actor without being a real star, conveying the same qualities as later in his career: nor did he look either different or much younger, except that he was usually moustached. Fox, for whom he had worked on several occasions, made him the male lead in *The Gateway of the Moon* (28), which got him the star role in an indie, *Turn Back the Hours*, stuck with Myrna Loy on a desert island; for Tiffany he made *Clothes Make the Woman*, a poor Hollywood tale; and for Universal, *Melody of Love*, which had Sound sequences – he was a pianist who loses the use of his hands until redeemed by the love of a Good Woman.

The coming of Talkies gave a lift to Pidgeon's career: as an experienced stage artist he was in demand, and of the several offers he accepted one with Warner Bros. Both his first pictures there were made in Silent and Talkie versions: *Her Private Life* (29) – Billie Dove's; and *A Most Immoral Lady* – Leatrice Joy. But Warners wanted Pidgeon for something more spectacular than supporting fading stars in heavy melodramas – for something which couldn't have been done in Silents. They were embarking on a series of Technicolor (two-toned) operettes (the first two had already appeared: *Song of the West* with Vivienne Segal and John Boles; and *Song of the Flame* with Bernice Claire and Noah Beery). Pidgeon and Segal starred in the next: *Bride of the Regiment* (30), adapted from Sigmund Romberg's 'The Lady in Ermine'. Several Pidgeon pictures were released in the fall: *Sweet Kitty Bellairs*, from Belasco's old play about Olde England, with newcomer Claudia Dell; a remake of *The Gorilla*, in the same part he had before; and *Going Wild*, in support of Joe E. Brown, a remake of *Going Up?* which had starred Douglas MacLean. He had a small part in *Renegades* – and it seemed that no month was complete without a Pidgeon picture: in November also *Viennese Nights* was released, 'written specially' for the screen by Romberg and Oscar Hammerstein II. The ads showed Pidgeon kissing Segal, but their names weren't mentioned: a good indication of their standing. In the next one he kissed Bernice Claire, and it was called *Kiss Me Again* (31) after its most popular song: it was from 'Mlle Modiste', and was called in Britain *Toast of the Legion*: American reference books have it under all three titles, a good indication of *its* standing. Indeed, after the first two or three the series was a box-office dud, and *The Hot Heiress* (in support of Ona Munson and Ben Lyon) ended Pidgeon's Hollywood career for the time being.

In fact, illness kept him off the screen. During this period he married for the second time. He returned in a supporting part at RKO, in *Rockabye* (32), starring Constance Bennett; was in James Whales's *The Kiss Before the Mirror* (33), starring Nancy Carroll; and *Journal of a Crime* (34), starring Ruth Chatterton. Jobs were not plentiful,

For almost all of his first twenty years in movies Walter Pidgeon had only leading-man status, as here, in Her Private Life *(29), directed by Alexander Korda (in his pre-British days). Billie Dove was an unhappily married English lady who runs off to the US with young Pidgeon.*

though Pidgeon was offered musicals; he wanted to establish himself as a serious actor, and went to New York and appeared on the stage: 'No More Ladies', taking over from Melvyn Douglas, 'Something Gay' (35) with Tallulah Bankhead, 'The Night of January 16th' and 'There's Wisdom in Women'.

He turned down the lead in Universal's *Show Boat* because he didn't want to be a singer, but returned to Hollywood, under contract to Wanger: had a supporting part in *Big Brown Eyes* (36) starring Joan Bennett, and co-starred with Mary Ellis in *Fatal Lady*. Wanger dropped him and he moved over to Universal: *She's Dangerous* (37) – Tala Birell was; *Girl Overboard* – Gloria Stuart was; *As Good As Married* – John Boles and Doris Nolan were; and *A Girl With Ideas* – Wendy Barrie was. These weren't important parts or pictures and when MGM offered a General Utility contract Pidgeon accepted: to play the hero's friend, the Other Man, etc. He had such parts in *Saratoga*; *My Dear Miss Aldrich* with Edna May Oliver and Maureen O'Sullivan; *Manproof* (38); *The Girl of the Golden West*, as the cold (moustached again) sheriff who loves Jeanette MacDonald until he realizes how much more she loves bandit Nelson Eddy; *The Shopworn Angel*, losing Margaret Sullavan to James Stewart; and *Too Hot to Handle*, Gable's rival in love (Myrna Loy) and business (newsreels). In *Listen Darling* he was the handsome stranger Judy Garland contrives to get married to mother Mary Astor. He was upped to star billing in four programmers: *Society Lawyer* (39), a remake of *Penthouse*, with Virginia Bruce; *6000 Enemies*, as a DA, with Rita Johnson; *Stronger Than Desire*, a domestic drama with Bruce; and *Nick Carter Master Detective* with Johnson. Around this time ads were issued for Hedy Lamarr's *I Take This Woman* with Pidgeon leading the supporting cast; but he wasn't in the film as finally released.

He was loaned to Universal for a similar part to the one in *Listen Darling* – in *Its a Date* (40) he was involved with Deanna Durbin's mother, Kay Francis: at last he was carving a niche as a nice, pipe-smoking mature leading man. He was so easy, so comfortable, so solid (in the best sense) that his way to real stardom was finally going to be short and simple. He was in demand: Republic borrowed him for *Dark Command* with John Wayne, and United Artists for *The House Across the Bay*. MGM put him into two Bs, *Phantom Raiders* and *Sky Murder*, and then into one of those films with which

Their most famous roles: Greer Garson and Walter Pidgeon as Mr and Mrs Miniver *(42). The film won several Oscars, including Best Picture and Best Director – William Wyler. After seeing Britain later in the war Wyler admitted that the film was a basically synthetic portrait of the British at war.*

Hollywood prepared for war, *Flight Command* with Robert Taylor. Twentieth borrowed him for his first lead in years in an A product, *Man Hunt* (41), in which the Nazis are out to get him for once trying to get Hitler: one of Fritz Lang's weakest films. His own studio then co-starred him with Greer Garson, in her first flush of success, in *Blossoms in the Dust*, and there was a strong positive reaction; he had been so convincing as an Englishman in *Man Hunt* that 20th asked for him again for *How Green Was My Valley*, as the priest in the Welsh village that was built on the back lot – Richard Llewellyn's 'trouble at the mine' novel, transformed by John Ford's cheering gift for finding the world in an oyster: a highly popular film and an Oscar winner.

He made a comedy with Rosalind Russell, *Design for Scandal*, and then was with Greer Garson in *Mrs Miniver* (42): and no matter what one thinks of the film or the Minivers he was beautifully cast as Mr. The film put him in the front rank of MGM male stars. *White Cargo* and Hedy Lamarr almost yanked him out again, but two with Garson consolidated the position: *Madame Curie* (43) as Monsieur, and *Mrs Parkington* (44) as Mr. *Weekend at the Waldorf* (45) found him in the arms of Ginger Rogers, and in *Holiday in Mexico* (46) Jane Powell was the daughter trying to match him – with Ilona Massey. *The Secret Heart* with Claudette Colbert and *If Winter Comes* (47) with Deborah Kerr were the sort of films in which women were supposed to like Pidgeon, but *Command Decision* (48), with Gable, was a strong man's film, and one of his best performances. Before it, *Julia Misbehaves* was a misguided attempt to lighten his and Greer's image. *The Red Danube* (49) was anti-Commie drivel; *That Forsyte Woman* and *The Miniver Story* (50) two more English subjects with Garson.

He was a Britisher again in *Soldiers Three* (51) and *Calling Bulldog Drummond*, in the latter as Drummond: business was poor, so it was not the first of a new series. Pidgeon eased back into Bs again: *The Unknown Man* with Ann Harding, *The Sellout* with Audrey Totter; and he was back at being the old reliable standby in *Million Dollar Mermaid* (52), *The Bad and the Beautiful* as the studio boss, *Dream Wife* (53) and *Executive Suite* (54). Betweenwhiles, *Scandals at Scourie* (53) with Garson was an ignominious end to a remarkable partnership. Pidgeon began to specialize in elderly businessmen or serving officers, hiding a heart of gold behind a testy if understanding exterior: *Men of the Fighting Lady* (54); *The Last Time I Saw Paris* as Elizabeth Taylor's father; *Deep in My Heart* as J. J. Shubert to José Ferrer's Sigmund Romberg; *Hit the Deck* (55); *Forbidden Planet* (56) as a mad scientist, with Anne Francis; *The Rack* as Paul Newman's father; and *These Wilder Years* with James Cagney and Barbara Stanwyck, billed below them and indeed below the title. It was the last film of his MGM contract: 19 years ('They were the best,' said Pidgeon later of his years at Metro. 'I'd like to have them all back again. Favourite pictures? Any of the ones with Greer Garson').

Pidgeon returned to Broadway as 'The Happiest Millionaire' (56). In 1959 he did a musical, 'Take Me Along'. He came back to films, top-billed, as Admiral Nelson, a world-famous scientist, making a *Voyage to the Bottom of the Sea* (61), and was top-billed again in Disney's pleasant boy-and-dog picture, *Big Red* (62). His last good part in a good film was as a Senator in *Advise and Consent*. He went to Italy to make *I Due Colonelli*/*The Two Colonels* with Toto, and then wasn't seen on the big screen for five years. Two TV films he had made were shown in British cinemas as features (but not in the US) in 1967: *Deadly Roulette* with

Robert Wagner, which got good notices, and *Casa Nostra An Arch Enemy of the FBI* with Efrem Zimbalist Jr. He was one of several old-time names (Lillian Gish, Keenan Wynn, Joan Collins, Eleanor Parker) supporting David Janssen in *Warning Shot* (67) and was seen briefly as Flo Ziegfeld in *Funny Girl* (68). He returned to Italy to make *A Qualsiasi Prezzo* (69) and then made another TV film, *The House on Green Apple Road.*

Dick Powell

Dick Powell was one of the roundest all-rounders in the history of Hollywood. He was: crooner, film-star, director and producer, TV executive. His most successful manifestation seems to have been as TV executive. It is difficult now to fathom wherein lay his appeal as an actor–but in the 30s he was very popular indeed, as the leading man of innumerable Warner Bros musicals. Cherubically smiling, he chased Ruby Keeler or Priscilla Lane, and was serious only when crossed by the producer who was always putting on the show featuring the songs which Powell was always writing. It was all so predictable; and though many WB musicals had admirable things in them, Powell's performances weren't any of them. He knew it. He fought for years to escape from the inane parts written for him, and finally emerged as a tough guy in the Bogart tradition. But only just.

He was born in 1904 in Mountain View, Arkansas, where he sang in the church choir; and was educated at Little Rock College. He worked for a telephone company for a while but was more interested in bands–he could play most instruments. He got a job with a band, and then toured with several different ones, as instrumentalist and vocalist; finally became emcee at the Stanley and Enright Theatres in Pittsburgh. Here he was spotted by a WB talent scout, who knew the studio was looking for a man to play the title role in *The Crooner*. David Manners got the part but WB cast Powell as another crooner, rather wet–and a small part–in *Blessed Event* (32). Powell indicated qualities beyond mere wetness and was signed to a long-term contract. He was loaned to Fox for *Too Busy to Work* with Will Rogers; back at WB he was in *The King's Vacation* (33), starring George Arliss, and then *42nd Street*: he and Ruby Keeler were the young lovers, fighting and making-up backstage, with Powell emerging now and then to front a lavish and improbable musical number (danced to by her). His warbling wasn't unpleasant, nor was his personality–willing, teasing, amorous; it was neither strong nor individual enough to work against the other elements. It became a staple of Warner musicals and comedies.

He made *Gold Diggers of 1933*; *Footlight Parade*; *College Coach*; *Convention City*; *Wonder Bar* (34)–reputedly the only one of its stars who didn't fight during the making; *Twenty Million Sweethearts* ('I'll string along with you,' he sang to Ginger Rogers); *Dames* ('I only have eyes for you,' he sang endlessly to Keeler); and *Happiness Ahead* (in reality a vehicle for newcomer Josephine E. Hutchinson). There were more of same: *Flirtation Walk* with Keeler, *Gold Diggers of 1935* (35) with Gloria Stuart, *Page Miss Glory* with Marion Davies, *Broadway Gondolier* with Joan Blondell, and *Shipmates Forever* with Keeler, the one about the crooner who enters Annapolis because his dad's an admiral (Lewis Stone)–and is unpopular until he proves himself a hero. Twentieth borrowed him for a band musical with Ann Dvorak and Fred Allen, *Thanks a Million*, whose title tune gave him one of his several hit records. Meanwhile, he was making the box-office top 10 list: he was seventh in 1935, sixth in 1936–a fact which may have influenced his casting in *A Midsummer Night's Dream* to boost it. No other explanation seems probable in the light of his performance (as Lysander), though he was currently fighting with WB over his parts. He returned at once to more typical fare: *Colleen* (36) the last of the seven with Keeler; *Hearts Divided*, a period piece with Marion Davies as a southern belle, Betsy Patterson, and himself as Jerome Bonaparte; and *Stage Struck*, which also starred Joan Blondell, in life now his wife, but not here his romantic interest.

After *Gold Diggers of 1937*, he was loaned to 20th again, to woo Madeleine Carroll *On the Avenue* (37); back at WB, who else could have been *The Singing Marine*? He put on a *Varsity Show* with the Lane sisters and stayed at the *Hollywood Hotel* with Frances Langford and Lola Lane (as a temperamental movie queen) and was *The Cowboy From Brooklyn* (38), as a boosted cowboy crooner afraid of cows. And it was he, not Olivia de Havilland, who was *Hard to Get*, a routine comedy about an heiress being tamed by a gas station attendant. But he refused point-blank to do *Garden of the Moon*, and was replaced by John Payne, then just starting. *Going Places*, with Anita Louise didn't, but a song from it did ('Jeepers Creepers'); then Powell sang for the last time on the screen (he hoped) to Ann Sheridan in *Naughty But Nice* (39).

His contract was up and he had no intention of renewing it. He had loathed playing the same singing ninny, and he signed with Paramount on the understanding that that company would give him more meaty roles. His first there was better than anything he'd done at his old studio, *Christmas in July* (40), a Preston Sturges comedy about a guy who mistakenly thinks he's won a contest and begins to buy out the shops of New York on tick; but *I Want a Divorce* with Blondell was stark enough. He was *In the Navy* (41) with Abbott and Costello and his *Model Wife* was Blondell; both at Universal, and routine; and back at Paramount he was put to singing again, to Mary Martin in *Star Spangled Rhythm* and in *Happy Go Lucky* (43); and then he did a comedy with her, *True to Life*. But *Riding High* with Dorothy Lamour was the last straw: it was precisely the sort of film Powell didn't want to make. He left Paramount, did an interim musical at MGM with Lucille Ball, *Meet the People* (44), and jumped at René Clair's offer of the lead in *It Happened Tomorrow* with Linda Darnell, a comedy/fantasy about a reporter who gets tomorrow's paper a day early – until one day it carries his own obituary. The critics liked it, but public reception was so-so.

Powell eventually persuaded RKO to cast him as a tough guy: Chandler's private eye Marlowe. There were two concurrent Marlowes: Bogart in *The Big Sleep* and George Montgomery in *The High Window* (from 'The Brasher Doubloon'). Powell's *Murder My Sweet* (45) was from 'Farewell My Lovely' and it was a new Powell on display, and vastly different from the old one – but his still cheery face was not Marlowe's, if otherwise the film had a good feel of Chandler. Similarly unshaved, hard-bitten and gun-toting, he appeared in *Cornered*, and there followed several melodramas poised

Hearts Divided *(36) was a lavish historical romance directed by Frank Borzage from a play called 'Glorious Betsy'. Marion Davies was effective in that part, but whoever cast Powell as one of the Bonaparte boys deserved a prize for imagination. Claude Rains was Napoleon.*

The 'new' 'tough' Powell: As Philip Marlowe in Murder My Sweet, *directed by Edward Dmytrick from Chandler's 'Farewell My Lovely' – to which title it reverted for British audiences (the book had already served as the basis of one of the Falcon movies).*

precariously between first- and second-feature level: *Johnny O'Clock* (47) with Evelyn Keyes; *To the Ends of the Earth* (48) with Signe Hasso; *Station West* with Jane Greer; *Pitfall* with Jane Wyatt and Lizabeth Scott; and *Rogue's Regiment* with Marta Toren. There was a sentimental piece with Evelyn Keyes, *Mrs Mike* (49), about a Mountie marriage in the frozen North; and then a couple of minor pieces with his now-wife, June Allyson, *The Reformer and the Redhead* (50) and *Right Cross*. In 1951: *The Tall Target*, *Cry Danger* and *You Never Can Tell*. It was clearly time to quit movies.

Few other washed-up actors ever re-vitalized their careers as astutely as Powell. As far as TV was concerned the time was ripe. In 1952, with David Niven and Charles Boyer, he inaugurated 'Four Star Playhouse' wherein the three of them rotated with a guest star for a TV public mostly starved for big film names. This paved the way for Four Star Television, with numerous series, including 'The Dick Powell Show', a tough-guy drama. Powell became regarded as one of the leaders of TV. Also in 1952 he went into directing, starting with the modestly budgeted *Split Second*, a tense little melo. And he got into a good film, Minnelli's *The Bad and the Beautiful* (52). He appeared in only one more film, *Susan Slept Here* (54), a May–September romantic comedy with Debbie Reynolds; and was 'smug and harassed by turns' (MFB). RKO was the studio, and there were current rumours that he was taking over there as production chief.

But as director or producer/director he

was increasingly in demand – though none of the pictures he directed could be said to have met with a warm critical or public reception: *The Conqueror*, *You Can't Run Away From It*, *The Enemy Below*, *The Hunters*, etc.

He died of cancer in 1963, leaving more than a million dollars.

Eleanor Powell

Eleanor Powell came to the screen as 'The World's Greatest Tap Dancer', a citation from the Dancing Masters of America. She was born in Springfield, Massachusetts, in 1912, and got her professional start dancing in Atlantic City clubs during the summer months. When she was 16, Gus Edwards saw her there, and signed her for his revue at the Ritz Grill in New York. In New York she took dancing lessons from Jack Donahue and got a small role in 'The Opportunists' at the Casino de Paris (28). The following year she was starred in 'Follow Through'; other Broadway shows included 'Fine and Dandy', 'Hot Cha' and 'George White's Scandals'. When Fox made a film called *George White's Scandals* (35) she had a guest spot. She wasn't considered film material.

But an MGM producer, Sam Katz, had seen her on Broadway and wanted her for *Broadway Melody of 1936*. According to Roger Edens, who worked on that and other MGM musicals for 20 years, the studio was unenthusiastic, thinking she lacked femininity. Their beauticians were turned loose on her. Edens said: 'Still, she had a certain unusual quality that was very fresh and appealing and she certainly could dance.' According to contemporary publicity she was signed after *Scandals* for a small role in the *Broadway Melody*, but after some days filming it was given to Una Merkel, and a new, big part was made for her. She was a howling success and MGM signed her to a seven-year contract. After a brief return to Broadway for 'At Home Abroad' (with Beatrice Lillie) Powell settled in at Metro as their dancing equivalent to Jeanette MacDonald. She tapped her way through Cole Porter's *Born to Dance* (36), which had the most grandiose musical finale yet done in Hollywood; through *Broadway Melody of 1938* (37), *Rosalie* with Nelson Eddy, and *Honolulu* (39) with Burns & Allen and Robert Young. The studio then made a bid to co-star her with Fred Astaire because she 'has never quite reached the heights expected of her' (Picturegoer). Thus she became his first dancing partner after leaving Ginger Rogers and RKO, in *Broadway Melody of 1940* (40), but unfortunately their styles didn't jell. *Lady Be Good* (41) and *Ship Ahoy* (42) with Red Skelton were good starring vehicles, but in *I Dood It* (43) she was little more than a foil for Skelton. After a guest stint in *Thousands Cheer* she left Metro: she had said frequently that she wanted to retire – especially now that she had married Glenn Ford.

Fred Astaire and Eleanor Powell in Broadway Melody of 1940: *'The World's Greatest Dancers in the World's Greatest Musical Show!' said MGM with accustomed modesty.*

She decided to make a comeback at UA in *Sensations of 1945* (44) with Dennis O'Keefe, but at the box-office it wasn't one. In the late 40s she was one of the American stars imported by the London Palladium. She danced. She had a guest spot in an Esther Williams vehicle, *The Duchess of Idaho* (50), and in the late 50s a TV series called 'Faith of Our Children', a religious affair. Her marriage broke up in 1959, and in 1961 she made world headlines by starting a night-club act: she danced for an hour nightly in Las Vegas and then New York. It was extraordinarily successful, but it didn't last long. Powell's trouble was, as Gene Kelly once remarked, that she could only do one thing–tap-dance: and that had gone way out of fashion. The other dances she did in her films–like waltzing with high kicks–look ludicrous when seen today. There was little else–a certain charm. William Whitebait once said of Cyd Charisse that when she was acting, he had to keep reminding himself what a good dancer she was: it was equally true of Powell.

William Powell

The suave, moustached appearance of Mr William Powell did not work entirely in his favour. Graham Greene wrote in 1936: 'Mr Powell is a little too immaculate, his wit is too well-turned just as his clothes are too well-made, he drinks hard but only at the best bars; he is rather like an advertisement of a man-about-town in Esquire, he shares some of the irritating day-dream quality of Lord Peter Wimsey.' He was considering Powell's portrait of that sophisticated detective, Nick Charles, pursuer of the 'Thin Man' and he was right about the clothes, except that in some films Powell seemed to alternate only between silk robe and pyjamas and white tie and tails. When he wasn't playing Nick it would be someone similar, a soul-brother, perhaps another detective. Or he had a nice line in shady lawyers, a hangover from his early days of screen skulduggery. His skill and charm disguised somewhat the fact that his screen character was basically unpleasant–that his attitude to most people and especially women was of a refined superiority: it was a character perfected by Noël Coward in 'Private Lives' (what one wouldn't give to have seen Powell play Elyot!).

Later in his career he was able to branch out somewhat and portray genial and ageing businessmen, and right away from type he gave a brilliant performance in *Life With Father*. By this time he was a matchless light comedian, possibly the most polished of all. It was not unusual for his contemporaries to coast along on personality and mannerisms, letting audiences' familiarity with them do the work. Relaxed though he was, Powell never did. His acting, like his clothes, was impeccable.

He was born in Pittsburgh in 1892, the son of a public accountant. The family moved to Kansas City, and Powell was educated at the University there briefly; he withdrew and worked as a clerk in a telephone office, and from there went to New York to study at the AADA for a season. His first stage work was with one-night stands and fit-up companies, but in 1912 he made his New York debut in 'The Ne'er Do Well'; the following year he played an important part in 'Within the Law'. He toured two years with that and then in other plays and he worked in stock. He had his first Broadway success, with 'Spanish Love' (20) and that led to a film offer, that of the villain in John Barrymore's *Sherlock Holmes* (22). It wasn't a big part, but he never looked back. He was cast as François I in Marion Davies's *When Knighthood Was in Flower*; in *Outcast*; in *The Bright Shawl* (23), which he stole from Richard Barthelmess; and in doublet and hose again as the Duke of Orleans in *Under the Red Robe*, starring Robert Mantell and Alma Rubens.

His screen villainy began in earnest in *Romola* (24) as a conniving Italian count, when he wronged both Gish sisters; then he was nasty to Bebe Daniels in *Dangerous Money* at Paramount. Richard Dix at that studio asked for him for *Too Many Kisses* (25), as the Police Chief who ran a gang of bandits on the side, and because of his work in that, Paramount gave him a contract. There followed *Faint Perfume*; *My Lady's Lips*; *The Beautiful City*, on loan to Inspiration; *White Mice* (26), out on loan and sympathetic for once; *Sea Horses*–he was the blackguard who deserts Florence Vidor to go beachcombing; *Desert Gold*, a Western; *The Runaway* and *Aloma of the South Seas*, in both of which he tried to do the dirty on Warner Baxter. He was memorable as the cringing Italian thief in Ronald Colman's *Beau Geste*, after which he did *Tin Gods*, a triangle drama with Thomas Meighan and Aileen Pringle. He was wicked again in a small role in *The Great Gatsby*, and had a good run as the baddie: *New York* (27); *Love's Greatest Mistake*–he blackmailed Evelyn Brent; *Special Delivery* with Eddie Cantor; *Senorita*; *Time to Love* starring Raymond Griffith; Howard Hawks's *Paid to Love* starring Virginia Valli at Fox; *Nevada* and *Beau Sabreur* (28), both with Gary Cooper; and *She's a Sheik*–Bebe Daniels was, and he was an Arab brigand. Between the two he did *Feel My Pulse* with Daniels, and *Partners in Crime*, one of the Beery-Hatton comedies.

He had a part with more substance–though he was still pretty nasty–as the film director in *The Last Command*, directed by von Sternberg, and the 'von' used him again

in *The Dragnet*, as a slimy czar of crime in this underworld drama. He was in *The Vanishing Pioneer* before cuckolding Clive Brook in *Forgotten Faces*; and Brook hardly resented him less in *Interference*, a subtly degenerate performance in Paramount's first all-Talkie. Paramount were pleased with how well Powell's voice recorded: in the shuffle brought about by Sound, they decided to try him in something else, and cast him as A. A. Dine's sleuth Philo Vance in *The Canary Murder Case* (29). The next was Silent, with sound effects only, *The Four Feathers*, from A. E. W. Mason's rousing adventure story set in British Africa during the War. Brook and Richard Arlen starred, and Powell was again on the side of the law. He was the Other Man with Brook and Ruth Chatterton in *Charming Sinners*, demonstrating his ability to play high comedy. Then he was Philo Vance again in *The Greene Murder Case*.

Particularly in the Vance films his stock had risen: he was a surprise asset to his studio, who now put him in his first 'official' star vehicle, *Pointed Heels*, as a theatrical producer, with Fay Wray. His co-star in the next two was Kay Francis, and they became Paramount's top romantic team: *Behind the Make-Up* (30), in which he was a crafty and unscrupulous vaudeville performer, and *Street of Chance*, where he was a gambler. Then he made his last two appearances at Paramount as Vance: *The Benson Murder Case* and a sketch in *Paramount on Parade*. After *Shadow of the Law* he was with Francis again, in *For the Defense*, as a hard-drinking attorney who goes to gaol for love of her. Said Picturegoer: 'What an amazingly good actor William Powell is! His silent screen villains were clever studies in a serio-comic vein, but his Talkie appearances are even better.' Then he did two films with Carole Lombard, who became his wife: *Man of the World* (31), in which he was a blackmailer, and *Ladies' Man*, in which he was a gigolo.

Francis was also in the latter, and she and Powell (and Chatterton) were involved in the deal whereby it was considered that WB filched the three of them from Paramount. Powell, however, felt that he had had too many set parts and was delighted when Warners gave him story approval. That company regarded him as one of their top three male stars (Arliss and Barthelmess were the others, with Edward G. Robinson just behind) – not that they did much with him: *The Road to Singapore* with Doris Kenyon; *High Pressure* (32) with Evelyn Brent in which he was a promoter; *The Jewel Robbery*, as a burglar, and *One-Way Passage*, both with Francis and both welcome box-office gold – indeed, the latter was by far his most successful Warner film. He was an East Side *Lawyer Man* with Joan Blondell; in *Double Harness* (33), with Ann Harding, a drawing-room comedy at RKO; *Private Detective 62*; and Vance again in *The Kennel Murder Case*. There followed *Fashions of 1934* (34) with Bette Davis and *The Key*, a triangle drama with Edna Best and Colin Clive set against the Irish troubles.

Powell, with Chatterton, was now the highest salaried actor on the lot (it had been $6,000 weekly, but was cut to $4,000 during the Depression Economy drive), and WB decided he wasn't worth it. It was announced that he was leaving because he wanted to free-lance, but later it was tacitly agreed that his salary demands were too high. After a short spell Columbia signed him to a four-picture deal and Universal announced that he would play Florenz Ziegfeld for them in a film they were preparing. He then did a picture at MGM, *Manhattan Melodrama*, teamed with Myrna Loy, and its director, W. S. Van Dyke, liked them together enough to try them again in the low-budgeted *The Thin Man*, from Dashiell Hammett's detective story; as a result Powell became a bigger star than ever: MGM secured his release from the Columbia deal, and took over the Ziegfeld project.

The Thin Man was a roaring copper-bottomed success all round: MGM teamed Loy and Powell again in *Evelyn Prentice*, and the two of them became the studio's stock pairing, an adult, worldly, brittle couple, clearly in love, but wise to the other's – manifold – failings. Of the films Powell made at MGM over the next half-dozen years only a couple of them were not originally intended for them as a team – although circumstances in the end saw to it that they were not over-exposed. And although Powell was regarded at once by MGM as a major asset, he at first negotiated for two or three films at a time. However, until he left Metro 13 years later in 1947, he only made four films for other studios. The first of these was the vastly entertaining *Star of Midnight* (35) at RKO, in his stock role of sophisticated detective, with Ginger Rogers. Back at MGM he was in *Reckless*, which co-starred his fiancée, Jean Harlow.

He was in *Escapade* and *Rendezvous*, both intended for Loy, but played by Luise Rainer and Rosalind Russell respectively. Loy did play Mrs Ziegfeld No. 2 in *The Great Ziegfeld* (36), though the project as envisaged by Universal had had the lady as herself (Billie Burke). *Ziegfeld* was a lucky acquisition for the studio, justifying its length and lavishness at the box-office; it

Libelled Lady (*36*). *'Bill Powell, Myrna Loy, Spencer Tracy and Jean Harlow topping their own previous vivid performances in a highly original farce built around Bill's efforts to compromise Myrna who has sued Spencer's paper for libel. A wow.' – Photoplay.*

won that year's Best Picture Oscar and was a big hit especially in Britain (N.B. Powell never quite made the US top 10 stars list, but he was ranked in Britain in 1937 and 1938), and acquired a legendary status among MGM product. He played Ziegfeld in his familiar urbane manner, mocking slightly his own vanity: and with imperiousness added to his asperity. He went to other studios to play with two more delightful comediennes: Jean Arthur in *The Ex-Mrs Bradford*, and Lombard (now the ex-Mrs Powell) in *My Man Godfrey*, in the title role and perfect as the perfect butler. He did another outstanding comedy, *Libeled Lady* with Loy, Harlow and Spencer Tracy ('just about as perfect a comedy foursome as you will encounter anywhere' – Frank S. Nugent in The New York Times); and then *After the Thin Man* which delighted fans by being only a half-strike less than the original one. This completed 1936, making it Powell's *annus mirabilis*.

1937 had to be less happy and it was: with the remake of *The Last of Mrs Cheyney* with Joan Crawford and *The Emperor's Candlesticks*, directed by Von Stroheim from Baroness Orczy's historical novel, with Rainer. However, *Double Wedding*, a farce with Loy, enhanced, and was enhanced by, them. It was now that Powell and MGM came to terms: a seven-year contract *without options* at $155,000 a film. Ill-health intervened. At 20th (unwillingly on loan-out) he and Annabella were *The Baroness and the Butler* (38); he was too ill to play with Garbo in *Ninotchka* and in the light of his decreased activity, MGM sagely cast him with Loy: *Another Thin Man* (39), *I Love You Again* (40), *Love Crazy* (41) and *Shadow of the Thin Man* (which title avoids the ambiguity of the two earlier sequels – the 'Thin Man' himself having been killed off in the original film). His next two co-starred Hedy Lamarr, *Crossroads* (42) and *The Heavenly Body* (44); there were two more with Loy, *The Thin Man Goes Home* and *Song of the Thin Man* (47); between which there was a guest appearance in *Ziegfeld Follies* (45), and a co-starring role with Esther Williams in

Life With Father (*47*) *had been a Broadway hit and both in Britain and the US the movie version was one of the year's top five money-makers. Powell was Father, Irene Dunne was Mother, and most of the fun centred on her efforts to get him baptized.*

The Hoodlum Saint (46).

WB offered Powell the title role in *Life With Father* (47), the big-budgeted version of one of the longest-running and most successful plays in Broadway history, based on Clarence Day's memoirs of his father. Because of the tangled rights situation (no one, according to Variety, knows who owns them) the film cannot be revived; but it is remembered with pleasure by all who saw it–not least for Powell's performance, the best of the crusty-old-curmudgeon-with-the-heart-of-gold breed. Bosley Crowther said that Powell 'so utterly dominates the picture that even when he is not on screen his presence is felt', and Howard Barnes thought this 'the greatest performance of a distinguished career'. The New York Critics as a body voted Powell the year's Best Actor, citing also his performance in a minor comedy for Universal, *The Senator Was Indiscreet*; and Powell did two more duallers for that company, *Mr Peabody and the Mermaid* (48) with Ann Blyth and *Take One False Step* (49) with Shelley Winters. He was somewhat better served by 20th's *Dancing in the Dark*, which found him a Hollywood executive *vis-à-vis* rising star Betsy Drake. Again the notices and the grosses were such a fall from the huge sudden peak of *Life With Father* that he stayed away from films for three years.

He was frankly white-haired and settled (with the good humour, one imagines, of his performances) to playing character parts. In 1951 at Universal he was in *The Treasure of Lost Canyon*, and in a cameo spot in MGM's *It's a Big Country*; and he was again at MGM for *The Girl Who Had Everything* (53)–including him as her father (she was Elizabeth Taylor). He had featured parts in two popular films, *How to Marry a Millionaire* and *Mister Roberts* (55) as Doc, and his genial, cynical presence was as ever an asset above and beyond their other popular ingredients. Due perhaps to the lack of parts such as these, he retired, and though doubtless 'a good one would tempt him back' as the gossip-columnists have it, he is probably more retired than any of the other great male stars.

He lives with his third wife, Diana Lewis, a one-time MGM starlet, in Palm Springs.

Tyrone Power

Darryl F. Zanuck once told Variety: '. . . I think perhaps the greatest contribution I have made to this industry was the discovery of genuine talent. To have been involved in giving the world personalities like Betty Grable, Gene Tierney, Alice Faye, Linda Darnell, Tyrone Power, Marilyn Monroe and Gregory Peck has given me perhaps my deepest satisfaction.' In fact, as a discoverer of talent, 20th has a lower average than any other major studio, and right back to the Fox days it has been a notorious launcher of non-talent. Mr Zanuck is not strictly correct, either, in roping in Peck or Monroe, but the company can certainly claim Tyrone Power as its own.

Whether Power was a 'genuine talent' is debatable. As a young man he was so scrumptious-looking that it hardly seemed to matter, but as he grew older he was simply dull. He was always likeable, and certainly as a young man projected a quality of 'natural modesty' in the same way that James Stewart and Franchot Tone did. He wanted to be a better actor than he was and would perhaps like to be remembered most for his stage-work, which he did to get out of the rut. He didn't care much for most of his films; when his 20th contract expired he said, 'I've done an awful lot of stuff that's a monument to public patience.'

He came from a theatrical family; his father was a matinée idol who had acted with Irving and Tree. The junior Power was born in Cincinatti in 1913, and was always intended to follow in Father's footsteps; in his teens he was put with a Shakespearian company in Chicago and made his debut in 'The Merchant of Venice' (31); and he did some radio work with Don Ameche. He accompanied his father to Hollywood later that year; Father died (while filming) but Power stayed on and got bit parts in such films as *Tom Brown of Culver* (32) and *Flirtation Walk* (34). Discouraged, he tried Broadway and after a small role in 'Romance' was engaged by Guthrie McClintic to understudy Burgess Meredith in 'The Flowers of the Forest', which starred Katharine Cornell. He stayed with the Cornell company and was playing a small role in stock with them, in 'St Joan', when a 20th talent scout saw him and offered a test for a part in *Sing Baby Sing*. He didn't get it, but 20th took him under contract and gave him small parts in *Girls' Dormitory* (36) as Simone Simon's cousin and *Ladies in Love* as Loretta Young's romantic interest.

He had a stronger part in *Lloyds of London*, a period piece, and it made him famous. Twentieth met the demand by rushing him into four films in 1937, three of them with Loretta Young: *Love Is News*; *Café Metropole*, as a playboy posing as a Russian prince; *Thin Ice*, opposite Sonja Henie, as a European prince travelling incognito and giving a good semblance of a playboy; and *Second Honeymoon*. His 1938 films were more sturdy fare. The first two were directed by Henry King, who was responsible for more than a dozen of his films (King's Power films represent a good halfway mark between his early peak, the *Tol'able David* of 1921, and the mediocrity of his later work). In *In Old Chicago* he was one of Mrs O'Leary's boys, a politician corrupt till the fire which her cow started; and in *Alexander's Ragtime Band* he was *the* Alexander, competing with Ameche for Alice Faye. (In life, in 1939, Ameche was best man at his wedding to French actress Annabella, the first of his three wives.) He went to MGM (in exchange for Spencer Tracy) to play Count Fersen in *Marie Antoinette*, but in that overloaded spectacle got swamped: so much so that 20th refused to loan him out again (thus he later lost *King's Row*). His next was 20th's own bid in the historical stakes, *Suez* with Annabella, a \$2 million effort concerned overmuchly with the love-affair between de Lesseps (Power) and the Empress Eugenie (Young), a fiction which hardly endeared the film to critics.

The first two of this quartet were big box-office, and Power was 10th among the stars. In 1939 he had overtaken Gable and Tracy and was runner-up only to Mickey Rooney. He was also voted King of Hollywood (Jeanette MacDonald was Queen); and most of his next films were huge grossers, especially *Jesse James*, an early Technicolor Western with the facts distorted to make him (Power) sympathetic; and *The Rains Came*, from Louis Bromfield's novel about India. There was a lot of spectacle when the rains finally came, and Power was a smiling but improbable Indian prince. Between the two he was merely leading man to Faye in *Rose of Washington Square*–a gambler/gangster, but decent withal–and to Henie in *Second Fiddle*. In any case, beyond the rigging of the script, Power was never able to simulate any sort of villainy: he merely looked perplexed. Lloyd Nolan gave a strong performance as a petty racketeer in Henry Hathaway's *Johnny Apollo* (40), one of the first 'black' forties films, but Power, said

In Old Chicago (*38*): *Alice Faye was a dance-hall singer, and Tyrone Power and Don Ameche were both contenders for her favours. Power, as usual, got her in the end (Ameche was conveniently killed). The film's climax was a spectacular re-creation of the great Chicago fire.*

C. A. Lejeune, 'frequently unlikely on the screen, seems less likely than ever as a "varsity man who puts his soul in hock" to get his father out of prison'. The one before this, *Day-Time Wife* (39), and the one after, *Brigham Young* (Dean Jagger had the title role), gave him few opportunities, but Power did some of his best work in Mamoulian's remake of *The Mark of Zorro* – fop by day and bandit by night – even if his bravado wasn't in the Fairbanks class. At the end of the year he was still up there in the ratings.

He was in another Mamoulian remake, *Blood and Sand* (41), as a bullfighter (the rise and fall of). It was a part he was ideal for, provided that you accepted him as a Spaniard: he gave of his best and the film was a success, aided in no little way by its elegant use of colour. He wanted to return to the stage, but the studio would only spare him for a few weeks in stock (in 'Liliom' with his wife) – nor were they anxious to have him fail on Broadway. He returned to the same old parts in the same old (very different) films: *A Yank in the RAF*, and a popular one, with Betty Grable, *Son of Fury* (42), a Southseaser; *This Above All*, another wartime romance, this time as a Britisher, with Joan Fontaine, from Eric Knight's novel; *The Black Swan*, from Rafael Sabatini's novel, embodying all the clichés of the pirate film, and quite beautifully; and *Crash Dive* (43), a war film. Then 20th had to spare him for somewhat longer as he joined the US Marines for the duration of the war.

His comeback film was the much-touted version of Maugham's *The Razor's Edge* (46): Cukor refused to direct because he didn't like the script and it was, inevitably, not a very good film. Power was as much like a very nice bank clerk as ever (though he smiled less), but as an effective return, it was blunted because his part was impossible. Still, the public turned up in large numbers to see him or the film or both. They stayed away, however, from *Nightmare Alley* (47), received indifferently for being an emasculation of the original novel. Power got the best notices of his career; he had begged to play the part, that of a braggart who climbs to the top of the carny business only to end

The Razor's Edge *(46), directed by Edmund Goulding: Gene Tierney was Isabel and Tyrone Power was Larry in this box-office version of Somerset Maugham's last major novel.*

up alcoholic and an exhibit in the freak house. Twentieth, worried that his star was on the wane, put him into an expensive swashbuckler, *Captain From Castile*, and that, dull as it was, did good business. Then they hurried him into two comedies, *The Luck of the Irish* (48) with Anne Baxter and *That Wonderful Urge* (a remake of *Love Is News*) with Gene Tierney, but neither did much to reassure the company that he still had a following. Two more costume films followed: *Prince of Foxes* (49) – in black and white, a sure sign of faltering confidence – about the Borgias, and the more lavish *The Black Rose* (50), a mediaeval drama from a novel by Thomas B. Costain. Both were tiresome, and the latter was not improved by dialogue like 'Tris! You can't die on me!'

It was made in Britain, and Power stayed in London to play the lead in 'Mister Roberts'; he remained up to his neck in war, as *An American Guerilla in the Philippines* (Fritz Lang made it because, he said, a director has to eat). A Western followed, *Rawhide* (51), with Susan Hayward, and then a romantic drama, *I'll Never Forget You*, with Ann Blyth, a remake of *Berkeley Square*. Variety found Power's performance in the latter 'monotonous' and all these films were indifferently received; Power found, for the first time since 1938, that the top roles at 20th were going to another actor, Gregory Peck. He moved over to Universal for two run-of-the-mill actioners, *The Mississippi Gambler* (53) and *Macdonald of the Canadian Mounties*; then returned to 20th for more of same: *King of the Khyber Rifles* (54), a remake of Ford's *The Black Watch*, and *Untamed* (55), a 'Western' with Hayward set in South Africa. For Ford himself he did *The Long Grey Line*, described by The Spectator critic as 'the longest and greyest film' she had ever seen. At Columbia he did *The Eddie Duchin Story* (56), a rather pleasant biopic about a pianist, and one of the year's top 10 money-takers.

In 1953 he had joined Charles Laughton in a Broadway reading of 'John Brown's Body'; now free of his contract, Power again turned his thoughts to the stage. In London he did 'The Devil's Disciple' (56), but as in his earlier appearance there, was only partially successful; he was much better in a TV 'Miss Julie' with Mai Zetterling, suggesting, virtually for the first time, reserves of talent. In Britain he produced *Seven Waves Away* (57) with Zetterling, a relentlessly grim drama of survivors in a lifeboat; then returned to 20th for the dim film version of Hemingway's *The Sun Also Rises* (58). Billy Wilder cast him as the suspect in *Witness for the Prosecution*, from a play by Agatha Christie, and it seemed he might again push his way to the forefront of Hollywood actors. He then toured the US with Faye Emerson in an abridged version of 'Back to Methuselah'. Towards the end of 1958 he went to Madrid for *Solomon and Sheba* and died there, of a heart attack, after filming a fight with George Sanders. King

The film which shot George Raft (right) to fame: Scarface *(32), produced by Howard Hughes and directed by Howard Hawkes. The others in the foreground: Osgood Perkins, Vince Barnett, Paul Muni (with gun) and Karen Morley.*

Vidor, who directed, says that Power and he himself felt that it was his best part and his best film. He felt that with Power it would have been 'a simply marvellous picture', but without him it turned out to be 'an unimportant, nothing sort of picture'.

George Raft

George Raft was at his most appealing in his early days, be-gloved and be-spatted, a trilby pulled down over his eyes. He was sleek and tough and menaceful (especially when flipping that coin in *Scarface*) – and suitably punished: he reckons he met a violent death in over 80 of his films (i.e. a good 75 per cent of them). Not coincidentally, he knew the background of the shady and sinister character he usually played on the screen.

He was born in New York City in 1903 and brought up in that area known as Hell's Kitchen. By his own confession (his syndicated memoirs, 1957) he was a layabout, though he did some boxing, graduating from gymnasium to the prize-ring. It is reckoned that he lost only seven of his 22 bouts. He also danced, and earned a living at one time as a dance-hall gigolo – again, moving upwards to clubs in London and New York, and thence to the Broadway stage, where he partnered Elsie Pilcer. He danced in such shows as 'City Chap', 'Gay Paree', 'Palm Beach Nights' and 'No Foolin'; but at the same time his cronies were not always on the right side of the law. One was racketeer Owney Maddon who, according to Raft, supported him until he made it big in the movies: 'If I had any ambition it was to be a big shot in my pal Owney Maddon's liquor mob' and 'I had a gun in my pocket and I was cocky because I was working for the gang boss of New York.' It was Maddon who sent him as one of the protection crew to Texas Guinan's night-club, and it was Miss Guinan who suggested that he take a small role in her movie, *Queen of the Night Clubs* (29). This took him to LA, and according to his own report he was sitting in the Brown Derby when director Rowland Brown saw him and told him to report for another bit part in *Quick Millions* (31). He says that he was nervous, though as one of the gang the part shouldn't have been difficult. He had similar parts at other studios: *Hush Money*, *Palmy Days*, *Taxi* (32) as a ballroom contestant, *Scarface*, *Dancers in the Dark* (very nasty as a murderer), *Night World* and *Love Is a Racket*. *Scarface* was the biggest and best of these parts, and it brought attention to Raft and the offer of contracts. He signed with Paramount who starred him in *The Sporting Widow* (Alison Skipworth), *Night After Night* with Mae West, *Madame Racketeer*, and *If I Had a Million* (its weakest episode). He crossed to the other side of the law to be *The Undercover*

Man (33) with Nancy Carroll. Gee, but he was tough, even if he didn't rival Cagney or Robinson in public favour. He was tough with Paramount, too, and was suspended for refusing *The Story of Temple Drake*. He was taken back for *Pick-Up* with Sylvia Sidney, as an ex-gaol bird: he was a taxi-driver and they shacked up together till melodrama intervened. He was a detective out to get Clive Brook in *Midnight Club*; Wallace Beery's rival in *The Bowery* at the newly formed 20th-UA; and an ex-con out to destroy Miriam Hopkins's love for Fredric March in *All of Me* (34). Paramount kept insisting that he was a second Valentino, but the public refused to accept him except as a gangster or something similar; however, he was successful as a hoofer stomping his way to the top in *Bolero* with Carole Lombard. It was popular enough for a follow-up a year later – *Rumba* (35) – after Raft had been a bullfighter in *The Trumpet Blows* and slit-eyed in *Limehouse Blues* with (of course) Anna May Wong.

Stolen Harmony (35) was a gangster-angled musical with Grace Bradley; and *The Glass Key* with Claire Dodd a version of Dashiell Hammett's novel, and a weak one. He did a musical with Alice Faye, *Every Night at Eight*, which was about a radio programme – and the film, alas, looked like one. Columbia borrowed him for *She Couldn't Take It* – Joan Bennett couldn't – and 20th for another comedy, *It Had to Happen* (36) – to Rosalind Russell. Back on his home lot he walked out of a reunion with Lombard because he disliked her choice of cameraman and was replaced by Fred MacMurray (*The Princess Comes Across*). Around this time he said 'I'm not a good enough actor to trust myself to any but the best director, best cameraman, best story.' Paramount to appease him raised his salary to $4,000 a week – even though his box-office was shaky. Photoplay reported that in Texas 'they just don't bother to put Raft's name on the marquee'. His only other film that year was *Yours for the Asking* with Dolores Costello.

Next he objected to his role in *Souls at Sea* (37) with Gary Cooper, and went on suspension until it was more sympathetically written. His salary was raised by another $200. He appeared with Sylvia Sidney again in Fritz Lang's *You and Me* (38) and did an adventure yarn, *Spawn of the North* with Henry Fonda and Dorothy Lamour. Then Paramount and he rowed again when he refused *St Louis Blues*: Lloyd Nolan replaced him, and Paramount were glad to see him go after playing a gambler in *The Lady's From Kentucky* (39) – Ellen Drew.

Warners made a bid for his services: tough-guy films had been a staple of that studio for almost a decade, and they were anxious to add him to their stable of such actors: they put him with Cagney in a prison melo, *Each Dawn I Die*, and with Bogart in *Invisible Stripes* (40); in between which he committed crime at Universal, *I Stole a Million* (39), as a cab-driver, with Claire Trevor. At Wanger-UA he was in Lang's *The House Across the Bay* (40) with Joan Bennett and he was confidently expected to do either or both *The World We Make* and a remake of *A Free Soul* at MGM with Norma Shearer (with whom he was frequently seen socially), but nothing came of either project. His first walk-out at Warners was over *South of Suez*, and George Brent did it; but he was seen, to advantage, in *They Drive By Night* with Bogart. There was reputedly dissension between him and Edward G. Robinson on the set of *Manpower*, his only 1941 film, but Agate said 'their performances have that kind of compulsion which makes you think you're seeing them for the first time'. Warners were much less happy. Raft went to Universal again for *Broadway* (42), supposedly playing himself in this 20s gangster piece, but in fact in the part taken by Glenn Tyron in the 1929 version. He then turned down *Casablanca*. Back in 1937 he had turned down *Dead End* and at WB he had already turned down both *The Maltese Falcon* and *High Sierra*: all four pictures became mighty important ones for Bogart, and now that Bogart was a top draw WB had really no need of Raft. After the totally undistinguished *Background to Danger* (43) his contract was annulled (according to Jack Warner's memoirs the company were prepared to pay him $10,000 in settlement, but due to a misunderstanding on Raft's part he paid that to them: he was equally anxious to be free).

However, having cast himself adrift, Raft found things difficult. After a guest spot in *Stage Door Canteen* he was in another such, *Follow the Boys* (44), though in the story surrounding the revue acts, teamed with the equally somnolent Vera Zorina. He went to 20th to play a Frisco saloon-keeper in *Nob Hill* (45) with Joan Bennett and Vivian Blaine, and then went from one minor melo to another, mostly at UA or RKO: *Johnny Angel*, *Whistle Stop* (46), *Mr Ace* and *Nocturne*. Said Richard Winnington: 'Detective George Raft's approach to recalcitrant citizens, innocent or guilty, is to wreck their rooms, throw hot coffee in their faces, or just plain beat them up, always without a flicker of expression or removing his hat.' More: *Christmas Eve* (47), *Intrigue*, *Race Street* (48), *Outpost in Morocco* (49),

Raoul Walsh's They Drive by Night *(40): Humphrey Bogart and George Raft were truck-driving brothers, and Ann Sheridan was the girl they pick up at a roadside hash-house.*

Johnny Allegro, *Red Light* with Virginia Mayo and *A Dangerous Profession*. Few of them had the upper slot on double bills, and he tried Europe: *Nous Irons à Paris* in France, *Lucky Nick Cain* (50) in Italy (in English) and *I'll Get You for This* in Britain. Back in the US he made a B, *Loan Shark* (52), and then in 1953 did a US-Italo co-production, *The Man From Cairo/Avventura ad Algeri*. There was a revival of interest and he had good parts in Ginger Rogers's *Black Widow* (54) and Robert Taylor's *Rogue Cop*. He co-starred again with Robinson in *A Bullet for Joey* (55), and the MFB observed that Raft's 'familiar' characterization could 'have been taken from almost any of his films during the past 20 years'.

He was one of the many names in *Around the World in 80 Days* (56), and he had a TV series, 'I Am the Law'; but 1957 was an unlucky year for him. He went to Britain to make a B, *Morning Call*, but didn't like the script; then the government refused a work permit for him to do instead *Women of the Night*. He told a reporter (Logan Gourlay in the Sunday Express): 'This is a cruel business if you're sensitive. And Hollywood's a cruel place. The moment you start slipping nobody wants to know you.' But Billy Wilder did want to know and Raft did a guest stint in *Some Like It Hot* (59), as a gang boss. That year he also appeared in *Jet Over the Atlantic*. In 1960 there was another cameo appearance in *Ocean's 11*, and he had bits in two Jerry Lewis films, *Ladies Man* (61) and *The Patsy* (64). In between he was in the British *Two Guys Abroad* (which never appears to have had a showing) and *For Those That Think Young* (63). The US Government came after him for back taxes in 1965, so he accepted an offer of a French movie, *Du Rififi à Paname*, and did something called *The Fat Spy* with Jayne Mansfield. He returned to Britain and worked as host and chairman of a gambling club, but after a trip to the US was refused entry by the British immigration authorities because of alleged 'associations'. He had guest spots in *Casino Royale* (67), *Five Golden Dragons* and *Skidoo* (69).

He has been married once, in 1925.

Luise Rainer

Once, to his intense shame and annoyance, Raymond Chandler found himself keyed-up at the prospect of winning an Oscar. His wife tried to persuade him that the whole thing was merely a lark: 'After all,' she reminded him, 'Luise Rainer won it twice.' She might have added that the second of Rainer's Oscars was won over Garbo's performance in *Camille*. . . . But then,

Hollywood at that time considered Rainer to be of the same stature as Garbo. She arrived in the movie capital in 1935, picked up her two awards in consecutive years, 1936 and 1937, and swiftly departed.

By that time her potential was probably exhausted. She was not without charm or ability, but most of the parts she played required her to be fey, kittenish and long-suffering – a deadly combination, as other middle-European actresses have proved (notably Maria Schell, again briefly, in the 1950s). Failing further evidence, one must assume that MGM did not underestimate Rainer's range (Myrna Loy, looking back on that time, has observed that Louis B. Mayer, for all his faults, really did know what was best for his stars).

She was born in Vienna in 1912 and made her stage debut, after auditioning, in Düsseldorf, when she was 16. She trained with Max Reinhardt and had acted, most successfully, in Vienna, Paris and London (in 'An American Tragedy', 'Measure for Measure' and 'Six Characters in Search of an Author', among other plays) when an MGM talent scout sought her out: he had heard she might be a successor to Garbo. In Hollywood, the studio kept her under wraps, not quite knowing what to do with her. Then at the last minute Myrna Loy walked out of *Escapade* (35) with William Powell: it was a remake of the Austrian *Maskerade* and thus seemed a suitable debut vehicle for Rainer, in the Paula Wessely part. Both film and Rainer's performance were carbon copies of the original and were generally considered inferior.

But it was apparent to the studio after a few days rushes that Rainer gave off a glow to the camera, that she had that quality of which great stars are made; she was cast with Powell again in *The Great Ziegfeld* (36), as the first Mrs Z., Anna Held, a (temperamental) star who loved her impresario-husband very much, but wouldn't countenance his infidelities. The 'telephone scene' at the end of the film has been considered a classic example of great acting – or it is the classic smiling-through-tears bit: at all events this portrayal brought Rainer Oscar No. 1, and the New York Critics Best Actress Award.

Her second Oscar was for *The Good Earth* (37), as O-Lan, in the prestigious screen version of the Pearl S. Buck best-seller.

The Big City *(37): Spencer Tracy was an independent cab-driver involved with a big combine who used gang-warfare to try to destroy him. Luise Rainer as his wife offered encouragement.*

James Agate thought she gave 'an exquisite rendering of what my clever Austrian actress imagines a Chinese peasant woman to be like', but Picturegoer, among others, was scornful of the Oscar, and spoke on different occasions of 'stolid immobility' and 'bovine vacuity'. Max Breen wrote: 'Can it be that the Academy has been dazzled by her stage fame, or is there really something in her two very limited performances, not perhaps apparent to ordinary mortals, which has transcended anything done in those two years by the great Garbo herself?' The film itself, however, drew no adverse reviews and was one of the year's top hits. With Powell she then did a romantic comedy, *The Emperor's Candlesticks*, about spies on different sides who fall in love; and then started battling for more salary. Next, she was the immigrant wife of taxi-driver Spencer Tracy in *The Big City*, and he acted her right off the screen.

For some months there were rumours of temperament and impending retirement; then there turned up *The Toy Wife* (38) with Melvyn Douglas and Robert Young, some melodramatic junk in which she was an unlikely Southern belle; and *The Great Waltz* in which she was on more familiar ground, as the mousy (or kittenish) Mrs Strauss, willing to sacrifice Johannes (Fernand Gravet, with a smirk and a song) to glamorous diva Miliza Korjus. A foreword noted that this was a fiction based on 'the spirit' of Strauss's music, and the ads proclaimed proudly, and more accurately: 'Only MGM could make such a picture.' It was a great success, notably in Russia, where audiences were perhaps impressed by the five-minute revolution in the middle of the plot.

Of *Dramatic School* C. A. Lejeune's sole critical comment was that it was 'designed to accommodate, accentuate, and perpetuate the dewy charms of Luise Rainer': it was by no means a success. Rainer was then given six months leave to visit her husband, Clifford Odets, reputedly to patch up their quickly-failed marriage. MGM did not contradict new rumours of retirement and she was quietly dropped from their contract list. W. H. Mooring wrote later that she had made too many enemies 'living up to Hollywood stardom', but considered, too, that her nerves had been unable to take the stress of studio life plus the break-up of her marriage.

In 1939 she turned up in London in 'Behold the Bride', and then in a dud Broadway revival of 'A Kiss for Cinderella'; she returned to Hollywood determined to try again. She was genuinely embarrassed by her two Oscars and the run of poor films. But Picturegoer reported that no studio was interested. Eventually Paramount signed her for *Hostages* (43) with William Bendix and Arturo de Cordova, just another version of the European underground. Lejeune again: 'Her idea of playing a collaborationist's daughter is to open the eyes very wide, fixing the startled subject with a gaze that would do credit to a passionate Alderney.' There had been talk of two more films at Paramount, but nothing came of it.

Since, she has done occasional stage work in Austria. She lives in London (she is married to a publisher) but has made only two professional appearances in Britain, on TV in 1950, when it was unusual for big stars to appear on TV. She starred in 'By Candlelight' and 'The Seagull': no one who saw her Nina in the latter is likely to ever forget it.

Claude Rains

Claude Rains must be reckoned among the finest actors who ever played in films; he managed to get himself into a score or so of the most enjoyable movies of the 30s and 40s, and they, and weaker efforts, all benefited from his presence. He had a fine speaking voice, like honey with some gravel in it, and that neatly typed him as the most suave and sarcastic of villains, very neat and polished, with a scornful right eyebrow. He encompassed almost every sort of worldly wickedness, though he tended to the artistic rather than executive; and he could go the sympathetic line with ease and authority. His effectiveness depended on his response to his material; he could ham when he felt like it, but he was never lazy and never uninteresting. He was not physically shaped to be a Hollywood leading man, but producers recognized his worth to the extent that he did get star parts throughout his career, and star-billing; and when he didn't, he led the supporting cast.

He was born in 1889 in South London, and made his first appearance on the London stage at the age of 10, when his choir master was asked to provide some boys for a crowd scene in 'Nell of Old Drury' at the Haymarket. It was an experience which convinced him that he was going to be an actor, and he became a call-boy at His Majesty's and subsequently ASM: an engagement that lasted seven years. Finally, in 1911, he got a small part in 'The Gods of the Mountain' by Lord Dunsany at the Haymarket, and later in the year began an Australian tour of 'The Blue Bird' as stage-

Crime Without Passion *(34), the film that established Claude Rains. He was a criminal lawyer who tried to frame an unwanted mistress – and found himself on a murder charge. Esther Dale was his secretary.*

manager, and in Melbourne and Sydney played some small parts; in 1914–15 there he was Granville-Barker's general manager, again playing occasional parts. He returned to Britain to join the army, and served until 1919, when he appeared in 'Uncle Ned' at the Lyceum, Sheffield, in Henry Ainley's company. Then he began to make a name for himself in London: he did an admired 'Government Inspector' and appeared notably at the Everyman in Shaw: Dubedat in 'The Doctor's Dilemma', Napoleon in 'The Man of Destiny', Dick in 'The Devil's Disciple'. He was seldom out of work, and by day taught at RADA (John Gielgud speaks warmly of him as a teacher in his memoir, 'Early Stages'). In 1926 he accompanied his wife, Beatrix Thomson, to New York where she was to star in 'The Constant Nymph': he took a small role, but later played the male lead on a US tour. (He married seven times altogether; his first wife was British stage actress Isabel Jeans.)

He settled in the US and was soon a respected Broadway name: 'And So to Bed' as Samuel Pepys (28), 'Volpone' in the title role, 'Marco's Millions' (on tour), 'The Apple Cart' as Proteus (30), 'The Moon in the Yellow River' (32), 'The Man Who Reclaimed His Head' and 'The Good Earth', among others. He was screen-tested for the role John Barrymore played in *A Bill of Divorcement* but was considered unlikely film material. James Whale, however, saw the test and thought him suitable for his version of H. G. Wells's *The Invisible Man* (33) – where only his voice mattered. The film's success made Rains a film name, and after one more Broadway venture ('They Shall Not Die') he was in demand in Hollywood. The publicity angle on *Crime Without Passion* (34) was that it was his film debut, as he was *seen*: otherwise it was a much admired but pretentious (Hecht and MacArthur) drama about a lawyer (Rains) who, despite the title, becomes unhinged through love. He did his stage role in *The Man Who Reclaimed His Head* (35), going insane again in this anti-war propaganda; and then returned to Britain to play *The Clairvoyant* – a fake music-hall seer who finds he really can. In Hollywood he was mad again as John Jasper in Dickens's *The Mystery of Edwin Drood*, and The New York Times found him 'brilliantly repellent'. And in Paramount's *The Last Outpost* he was a British officer.

Then he signed a long-term contract with Warner Brothers, beginning an association

Rains was one of the few actors who offered stiff competition to Bette Davis. Of their several films together, perhaps the most enjoyable was Mr Skeffington *(44). She marries him for the sake of her brother's reputation, divorces him, and welcomes him back in old age when he is blind and will not know that her beauty is gone.*

which seems to have been happier than that of other top-flight Warner talent. He was mostly the heavy, but in a widely contrasting range of pictures: *Anthony Adverse* (36) as the domineering step-father; *Hearts Divided* as Napoleon; *Stolen Holiday* as a crooked French financier, co-starring with Kay Francis; and *The Prince and the Pauper* (37)–a piece of historical twee by Mark Twain–as the villain. He was then in *They Won't Forget*, a film much admired for its integrity; and though luridly melodramatic, it did attempt to state some of the differences between North and South and did ask its audiences to consider its issues (it never discloses whether the lynched Northerner was guilty or not). But Rains, the film's sole star, as the DA whose kindness comes second to his ambition, was majestically bad (though at the time he was much admired–C. A. Lejeune thought he had 'never done anything quite as good').

He was better as a rancher, Olivia de Havilland's father, in *Gold Is Where You Find It* (38) and superbly right as the wily Prince (later King) John in *The Adventures of Robin Hood*; then was in *White Banners*, beautifully matched, if not outshone, by Fay Bainter in this Lloyd C. Douglas domestic drama; *Four Daughters* as their father; *They Made Me a Criminal* (39) as a relentless detective out to get John Garfield; *Juarez*, hamming as that pocket Caesar, Napoleon III; and *Daughters Courageous*. He got one of his Best Supporting Oscar nominations for his performance as the most corrupt of the Senators in Columbia's *Mr Smith Goes to Washington*. (He was nominated again for *Casablanca*, *Mr Skeffington* and *Notorious* but never won. Contrast Walter Brennan: four nominations, three wins, one performance.) *Four Wives*, *Saturday's Children* (40), *The Sea Hawk* (as a Spaniard), *The Lady With Red Hair* (as David Belasco) and *Four Mothers* (41) kept Rains busy on his home lot; he went outside for a couple–*Here Comes Mr Jordan*, a suave, amiable and deeply unlikeable performance and *The Wolf Man* with Bela Lugosi and Lon Chaney Jr; and returned to Warner Brothers for *King's Row*, back again on the maniacal path. Twentieth Century-Fox then borrowed him to play the intellectual bum for *Moontide* (42); after which he was Bette Davis's kindly psychiatrist in *Now Voyager* and the French police chief with a sinister line in epigrams in *Casablanca*. He was in an

Twilight of Honor (*63*): *Rains's last picture. He was an elderly lawyer befriending a young one.*

episode of *Forever and a Day* (43); then *The Phantom of the Opera* – in a performance verging towards the pathetic, but hugely enjoyable in its obsessions. *Passage to Marseilles* (44) and *Mr Skeffington* gave him sympathetic parts, the latter as Davis's understanding husband.

He was apparently chosen by Shaw himself to play Caesar in *Caesar and Cleopatra* (45) and was notably good in trying circumstances (it was filmed in London during the flying bomb period and he loathed Gabriel Pascal, who produced and directed). On his return to the US he did five in a row: *This Love of Ours* at Universal, a real character part (as an old man); Hitchcock's *Notorious* (46) as the wealthy sophisticate whom Ingrid Bergman marries for the sake of patriotism; a *Mr Jordan*-type fantasy, *Angel on My Shoulder*, with Paul Muni; and his last two for Warner Brothers, *Deception* as an egomaniac composer, and *The Unsuspected* (47) as the villain of the piece again. His free-lance films were less distinguished; though after a very minor piece called *Strange Holiday*, he returned to Britain to star in David Lean's version of H. G. Wells's *The Passionate Friends* (48), playing Ann Todd's cold malevolent husband. After that, *Rope of Sands* (49); *Song of Surrender*, married to Wanda Hendrix in a pointless period melodrama; *The White Tower* (50) as an alcoholic; *Where Danger Lives* with Faith Domergue; and *Sealed Cargo* (51). In 1950 he returned to the stage and scored a New York hit with Sidney Kingsley's adaptation of Koestler's 'Darkness at Noon' and in 1952 did 'Jezebel's Husband' in stock. He returned to films, at his worst, in an unworthy British adaptation of Simenon, *The Man Who Watched Trains Go By* (53). He did T. S. Eliot's 'The Confidential Clerk' in New York in 1954; and another indifferent film, *Lisbon*, in 1956. Ageing, and now white-haired, he was the patriarch in *This Earth Is Mine* (59) with Rock Hudson, and the professor in a new version of *The Lost World* (60). A journey to Italy brought *Il Pianeta degli Uomini/Battle of the Worlds* (61), which played the US in minor situations; after which he brought distinction to small parts in *Lawrence of Arabia* (62) and *Twilight of Honor* (63). His last acting appearance was at the Westport Country Playhouse in 'So Much of Earth, So Much of Heaven' in 1965. He died in May 1967.

Basil Rathbone

Basil Rathbone was, said William K. Everson, 'the best all-round villain the movies ever had . . . adept at any kind of role, including romantic drama and comedy, [he] was at his best in villainy (including modern wife-killers and Nazis) and was absolutely unmatched at playing swaggering scoundrels of other days, where his rich delivery of full-blooded dialogue, while attired in doublets or court finery, made him truly a sight to behold – and to listen to' ('The Bad Guys'). Other commentators occasionally thought that Rathbone, lean and saturnine, was *too* villainous, but he seldom over-weighted his material; he is remembered, too, as a fine Sherlock Holmes.

He was born in 1892 in Johannesburg, South Africa. He was sent to England to be educated (Repton College), after which he went into an insurance office. But he wanted to be an actor and in 1911 got a job with Sir Frank Benson's No. 2 company; he made his debut at Ipswich in 'The Taming of the Shrew' as Hortensio. In 1913 he travelled to the US with Benson's company, still doing small parts. His London debut was in 'The Sin of David' (14), and the same year he played the Dauphin in 'Henry V'. He was called up in 1916, into the Liverpool

Scottish Regiment; was later commissioned and awarded the MC. He returned to the stage at Stratford-upon-Avon, starring as Romeo, Cassius and other parts; in London he played the title role in 'Peter Ibbetson' (20), subsequently playing Hal in 'Henry IV Pt 2' and Iago; he made his film debut in Maurice Elvey's *The Fruitful Vine* (21), followed by a part in the same director's *Innocent*.

In 1922 he made his New York bow in 'The Czarina', returning to London for 'East of Suez' and 'RUR'; and two films: *Loves of Mary Queen of Scots* and a version of Sheridan's *The School for Scandal* (23); in New York again he did 'The Swan', and then accepted Hollywood offers to appear in *Pity the Chorus Girl?* (24), starring Helen Chadwick and Gaston Glass, and *The Masked Bride* (25) with Mae Murray, followed by *The Great Deception* (26) with Aileen Pringle and *The Loves of Sunya* (27) with Gloria Swanson. Simultaneously he was successful with a play of which he was part author, 'Judas'. He acted in San Francisco, London and New York, but mainly in New York: 'Love Is Like That', 'Julius Caesar' (as Cassius) and 'The Command to Love'. His film career began in earnest when MGM imported him to co-star with Norma Shearer in *The Last of Mrs Cheyney* (29), which resulted in a contract. Within the space of a few months he appeared in *Barnum Was Right* at Universal, *The Bishop Murder Case* (30), *A Notorious Affair* with Billie Dove at WB, *Lady of Scandal* (from Frederick Lonsdale's 'The High Road', to which title it reverted in Britain), *This Mad World* and *The Flirting Widow* with Dorothy MacKaill, from a comic novel by A. E. W. Mason. Suddenly leaving MGM, he free-lanced: *A Lady Surrenders* and *Sin Takes a Holiday* (as a philanderer). He returned to Broadway for three plays, and went back to Hollywood for *A Woman Commands* (32) with Pola Negri; then Broadway again ('The Devil Passes').

He was about to start *Reunion in Vienna* for MGM when he got a more attractive offer from Britain. Hollywood, he said, 'is a cruel place–relentless, stern and unforgiving–as I suppose all great industrial centres must be'. The three British pictures hardly enhanced his prestige: *After the Ball* with Esther Ralston, *One Precious Year* and the film of Galsworthy's *Loyalties* (33), over-playing as the wealthy Jew who accuses a British officer of stealing. Said Photoplay: 'An all-British cast, the accent is practically unintelligible for American audiences.' He was in *Just Smith* starring Tom Walls and did 'Tonight or Never' and 'Diplomacy';

The Masked Bride *(25): Basil* Rathbone *as a jewel thief and Mae Murray as one of his gang. He sent her to vamp* Francis X. *Bushman so that they could rob him but–surprise surprise–she fell in love with him. Christy Cabanne directed.*

journeyed to Los Angeles to play Romeo to Katharine Cornell's Juliet, which kept him occupied in various places over the next year. MGM recalled him to play Mr Murdstone in *David Copperfield* (35) and he was, in that, more loathsome than he ever was to be again. But in terms of success, this meant that he was unable to return to the stage for more than 10 years. He was offered more irresistible heavies by a Hollywood that saw everything, metaphorically, in black and white. He was typed. In the autumn of 1935 he was to be seen in six films and he was villainous in five of them: *Anna Karenina*, again at MGM, suave as the hard-done-by Karenin; *The Last Days of Pompeii* at RKO as Pontius Pilate; *A Feather in Her Hat* at Columbia, vaguely sympathetic towards Pauline Lord; *A Tale of Two Cities* briefly seen as the Marquis St Evremonde; *Captain Blood*, unconvincing as a French pirate captain, but in the first of two memorable swordfights with Errol Flynn; and *Kind Lady*,

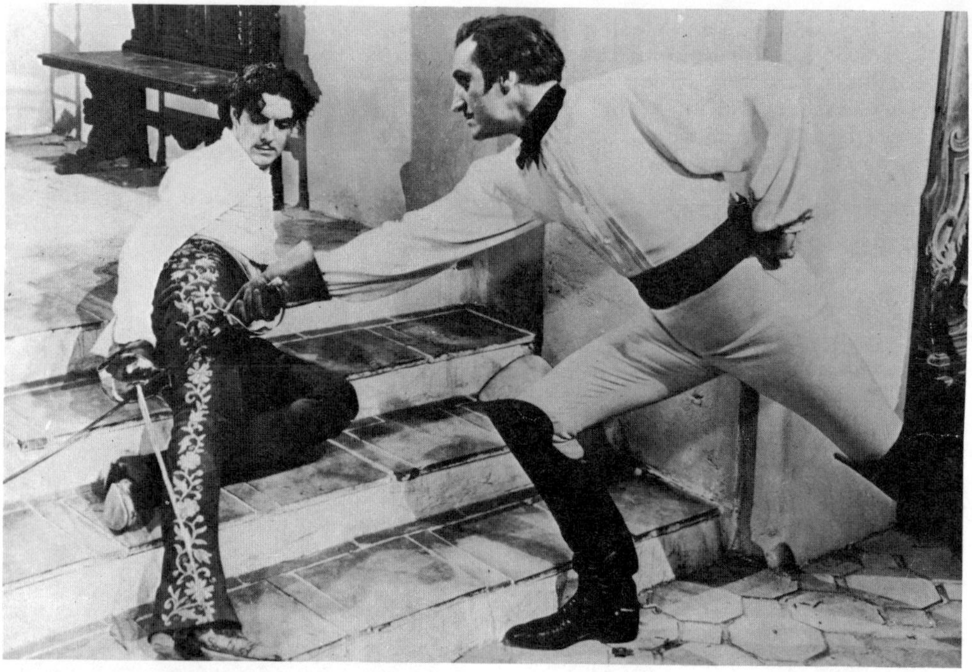

Rouben Mamoulian's The Mark of Zorro *(40) with Basil Rathbone in his familiar role of hero's enemy and pursuer. In this case it's Tyrone Power he's out to kill.*

terrorizing wealthy recluse Aline MacMahon in this fine version of Hugh Walpole's story.

In *Private Number* (36) he was mean to Loretta Young and Robert Taylor; and in *Romeo and Juliet* he was Tybalt. There was a fairly sympathetic role (a suspicious sheik) in *The Garden of Allah*, but he was trying to murder Ann Harding in the British *Love From a Stranger* (37)–after which his chores in Warner Brothers' *Confession* (as a philanderer; with Kay Francis) and *Tovarich* were comparatively light; but what could one make of the one in between, *Make a Wish*, where he was distinctly sympathetic towards child singing star Bobby Breen? He turned down the Raymond Massey role in *The Hurricane* because he was tired of playing heavies but he was then dastardly towards Gary Cooper in *The Adventures of Marco Polo* (38) as the would-be usurper of the throne of Cathay and Flynn again in *The Adventures of Robin Hood* (as Sir Guy); then was in a character role as the sly, hunch-backed Louis XI in *If I Were King* (38), the first of a very loose contract with Paramount. He was with Flynn again in *The Dawn Patrol*.

Son of Frankenstein (39) was him, involved with both Boris Karloff and Bela Lugosi: all the same, thought Howard Barnes in the New York Herald Tribune, 'this latest variation of the original horror tale commits the ultimate sin. It is singularly un-frightening'. Rathbone then had a complete change and played Sherlock Holmes twice for 20th Century-Fox, *The Hound of the Baskervilles* and *The* (unexciting) *Adventures of Sherlock Holmes*. Nigel Bruce was his Watson, and both pictures were well received. At Universal he supported Douglas Fairbanks Jr in *The Sun Never Sets*; starred with Sigrid Gurie in *Rio* as a crooked financier sweating it out in a jungle prison; and did a good Richard III in *The Tower of London* which, *sans élan*, followed the plot line of Shakespeare's play. There was another change when he played an egotistical song-writer ghosted by budding musician Bing Crosby in *Rhythm on the River* (40). He was swashbuckling again in *The Mark of Zorro*–the sworn foe of Tyrone Power–almost his last full-scale excursion into villainy–though he was a wife-murderer and master hypnotist again in *The Mad Doctor* with Ellen Drew. Then, *The Black Cat* with Randolph Scott and Edgar Bergen, *Paris Calling* with Elizabeth Bergner, *International Lady* with George Brent and Ilona Massey, and *Fingers at the Window* (42) as a jack-the-ripper-type doctor, with Lew Ayres: these were duallers. Only half-a-notch up was *Cross Roads* with William Powell.

Universal contracted with Rathbone and Bruce to make a Sherlock Holmes series: these were Bs of uncertain, and deteriorating, quality. The titles: *SH and the Voice of Terror*, *SH and the Secret Weapon*, *SH in*

There is little to be said for any of the Sherlock Holmes films made by Universal in the early 40s: their sole virtue(s) is the playing of Rathbone *and Nigel Bruce (Watson). This one is* Sherlock Holmes and the Secret Weapon *(42).*

Washington (43), *SH Faces Death*, *SH and the Spider Woman* (44), *The Scarlet Claw*, *Pearl of Death*, *The House of Fear* (45), *Pursuit to Algiers*, *The Woman in Green*, *Terror by Night* (46) and *Dressed to Kill*. They were modernized, and bore little resemblance to Conan Doyle. Rathbone, during this period also did *Above Suspicion* (43) with Joan Crawford; *Frenchman's Creek* (44), leching after Joan Fontaine who rejects him: 'You have more conceit of your kisses, m'lord, and less reason for it, than any scoundrel in England'–later she hurls a suit of armour at him; *Bathing Beauty* with Red Skelton; and *Heartbeat* (46) as a modern Fagin with Ginger Rogers. Then, sick of Sherlock, he returned to the stage: on tour and in New York in 1946 he did 'Obsession'; in 1947 he was Dr Sloper in 'The Heiress', in which, at the end of its New York run, he toured. In 1950 he did 'The Winslow Boy' in summer stock and later 'The Gioconda Smile' in New York; he played Sherlock Holmes in a play of that name in 1953, but it didn't run.

Apart from the commentary over the 'Mr Toad' sequence of Disney's *The Adventures of Ichabod and Mr Toad* (49), he had done no film work until he appeared in Bob Hope's *Casanova's Big Night* (54). Times had changed: he was sinister, but in two more comedies, *We're No Angels* (55) and *The Court Jester* (56). He did *The Black Sleep* with Akim Tamiroff; in 1957 he played in 'Hide and Seek'; in 1958 in Spencer Tracy's *The Last Hurrah* (nasty again, as a banker, and one of his best performances) and in 1959 as 'JB'. In 1960–his last stage work–he toured Australia in 'The Marriage-go-Round'; he also did TV ('Criminal at Large'; 'The Lark' and 'Victoria Regina', both with Julie Harris).

Rathbone's films of the 60s are a sorry bunch, and he gave them no more than they were worth. He traded on his reputation and collected his pay packet: the Italian *Ponzio Pilato* (61), *The Magic Sword* (62), Roger Corman's *Tales of Terror*, *The Comedy of Terrors* (63), Curtis Harrington's *Queen of Blood* (66)–a good cut above the others, *Dr Rock and Mr Roll* (67), *Gill Women*, *The Ghost in the Invisible Bikini* and *Hillbillies in a Haunted House* (68). Most of them were not shown in Britain.

Rathbone died in 1967. He had been married twice, the second time to novelist Ouida Bergere.

Michael Redgrave

Michael Redgrave has an eminent position in the British theatre, but his work in the cinema has been relatively less interesting. As a young romantic screen actor he was never quite dashing or fiery enough. He was always too cerebral. This has been a mixed blessing during his career as a whole: at times too much care and thought have compelled him to give a misconceived or dull interpretation, but at others–particularly in less stereotyped roles–he has turned this characteristic to good advantage and manages to be wholly original. Certainly his major performances in both mediums have been men of thought rather than of action.

He was born in Bristol in 1908, of theatrical parents and educated at Cambridge; after an attempt at journalism, he went into teaching (Modern Languages). But his experience of acting at Cambridge and producing school productions warmed him towards a stage career: after three years he changed courses again, and got a job with Liverpool Rep. His first appearance was in 'Counsellor-at-Law' (34), and his first London engagement was with the Old Vic Company in the 1936–7 season, in leads–including Ferdinand in 'Love's Labours Lost', Mr Horner in 'The Country Wife' and Orlando to Edith Evans's Rosalind. By the time war broke out, he was an established West End actor, having, among other activities, played in the famous Gielgud season of 1937–8 (as Bolingbroke, Charles Surface and Tusenbach), and in 'The Family Reunion' as Harry, Lord Monchensey (39).

He was with the Gielgud company when he was offered a long-term film contract by Gaumont-British (later part of the Rank Organization): he accepted reluctantly and was then starred in Hitchcock's *The Lady Vanishes* (38) as the cocky but colourless hero. He was, he recalled later, rather snooty with the film people because he was acting with such a distinguished company during the evening, but Hitchcock brought him down to earth. Hitchcock told the press 'He'll be a second Donat, he can't miss.' It was, of course, a good start. Redgrave has described it as 'quintessential Hitchcock' and mentioned that the director taught him much about screen acting. Success seemed assured when he was assigned two more plum roles before being seen by the film public: Jessie Matthews's love interest in *Climbing High* (39) and Elizabeth Bergner's in *A Stolen Life*; he was also in *A Window in London* with Sally Gray, and Carol Reed's version of A. J. Cronin's best-seller, *The Stars Look Down* (40), somewhat implausibly cast as a coal-miner.

But he was excellent in the title role of *Kipps* (41), perhaps because he looked upon it as a character role; Reed directed this enjoyable version of H. G. Wells's novel, and Redgrave was beautifully partnered by Diana Wynyard and Phyllis Calvert as the two women, from different social spheres. He co-starred with Valerie Hobson in *Atlantic Ferry*, and then took Eric Portman's stage role in *Jeannie*, as the blunt Yorkshireman who brings back to earth the little Scots girl who had come into an inheritance: Barbara Mullen was in the title role, as on the stage, and it was a pleasant sentimental film. He then did a part that he had done on the stage, Robert Ardrey's *Thunder Rock* (42), a notably sincere performance as the misanthropic lighthouse-keeper who had fled society because he had failed to convince Britain of the Nazi menace (ghosts come to persuade him that it is futile to desert causes). And he was a Russian in *The Big Blockade*. By the time both of these were shown he was in the Navy, but he was invalided out in 1942; his contract specified that he must be allowed time off for stage-work, and at this point he took advantage of it. He didn't return to films until *The Way to the Stars* (45), Terence Rattigan's painstaking account of life, love and death on an RAF station. With some reason, it was a fantastic success in Britain, and Daily Mail readers overwhelmingly voted it their favourite movie of the war years; in the same

Kipps (*41*)*: Michael Redgrave in the title role, the haberdasher's assistant who inherits a fortune and is taken up by Society, with Diana Wynyard as that member of Society who is most taken with him. But in the end he chooses scullery maid Phyllis Calvert.*

poll his co-star, John Mills, emerged as the second most popular actor in the country, but Redgrave wasn't among the leaders. He was a little too remote, too cold, he was automatically 'officer-material': it was no surprise to find him as an MP/army officer in the silly *The Years Between* (46), and as one of the higher-ranking prisoners in *The Captive Heart* (even if he was only a Czech impersonating one). This contrived and slushy POW tale was a great success in Britain at the time; it has one of the rare major screen parts played by his wife, Rachel Kempson (and mother of Vanessa, Lynn and Corin; less famous than any of them but their equal in talent).

Earlier, he had had one of his favourite parts, that of the ventriloquist obsessed and then possessed by his dummy in the episoder *Dead of Night* (45), an uneven collection of ghost stories: his was generally considered to be the best. He played a cold-blooded tyrant in a dreary piece about smugglers from Graham Greene's old, first novel *The Man Within* (47); and the 'hero' of *Fame Is the Spur*, an unsuccessful Boulting Brothers movie based on a Howard Spring novel based in turn on the life and times of Ramsay Macdonald. Then he accepted a Hollywood offer for two pictures, neither of which turned out well. One was *Mourning Becomes Electra*, in which he was Orin. It was finally sneaked into Britain where the critics thought him, and not out of chauvinism, the best thing about it. The other, *Secret Beyond the Door* (48), he has described as 'a very bad film', though he liked working with Fritz Lang. He didn't like Hollywood: 'I couldn't take the publicity, the status symbols, and all that foolishness.'

He returned to Britain to play Macbeth, and in 1948 did it in New York. He joined the Old Vic again for the 1949–50 season, and among other parts, played Hamlet. He should have appeared in the film version of Coward's *The Astonished Heart*, but after a couple of days' work he stepped out and Coward stepped in. He did instead another filmed play, Terence Rattigan's *The Browning Version* (51), dangerously inviting comparison with Eric Portman's superb stage performance as the ageing, failed schoolteacher. It was, however, the high point of his film career. Dilys Powell thought him 'beyond praise. In this intimate view of a man who is made to reveal in an hour or so the gradual petrification of a lifetime it is the actor who really counts; at so close a distance the story must be unfolded not simply in actions and words but in tell-tale movements of the eyes, the tightening of the muscles in lips and cheeks. Redgrave puts

The Browning Version (*51*), *Anthony Asquith's film of what is probably Terence Rattigan's best play: Michael* Redgrave *as Crocker-Harris, the failed schoolteacher, and Jean Kent as his contemptuous wife – about to leave him for one of the junior masters.*

an infinity of variation into gestures which are involuntary in the driven human being; and when at a touch of kindness control suddenly gives way the contrast with the hardness and tightness of the earlier scenes is heart-breaking. Screen playing is often a matter less of acting than of being; here for once the player both becomes the character and acts it.'

There is, however, little to be said for his heavy interpretation of John Worthing in *The Importance of Being Earnest* (52), but Anthony Asquith's insistence on a theatrical style could hardly have helped. Redgrave was now letting the theatre take precedence: during two Stratford seasons (51 and 53) he played some of the titanic parts – Hotspur, Richard II, Prospero, Lear, Shylock and Anthony; in the West End he did 'Winter Journey' (52) and in New York 'The Sleeping Prince' (56); in both cities 'Tiger at the Gates' (55). On screen, during this period, he played (not well) an ageing, unsuccessful, and long-bearded French lawyer in *The Green Scarf* (54) with Ann Todd and Leo Genn; and an Air Commodore in *The Sea Shall Not Have Them*, a war film floated on clichés (not the worst of which was the moment when the 'chaps' found out he'd risen from the ranks and was really 'one of us'). He played an Air Commodore again in *The Night My Number Came Up* (55), a neat idea lumberingly done, and was still involved with the RAF in *The Dam Busters*, but as scientist Barnes Wallis, another of his favourite parts. Like most British war films, it was violently over-praised in its country of origin and, briefly, queues reappeared outside British cinemas: and it was much more competent than most. Also in 1955 Orson Welles's *Confidential Report* turned up, with Redgrave as a pussy-loving, antique-dealing old queen, a cameo that was much-liked; but he was embarrassing as an ooh-la-la Frenchman, in *Oh Rosalinda!!*, which was 'Die Fledermaus' modernized by Powell and Pressburger and turned into a morgue.

Following a highly successful TV adaptation of Orwell's '1984', it was hastily filmed (56) with Jan Sterling and Edmund O'Brien: Redgrave was again judged the best thing, as the major representative of Big Brother. Losey's *Time Without Pity* (57) – he was an alcoholic – was more or less ignored at the time, and along with a minor comedy, *Law and Disorder* (58) and a silly melo, *Behind the Mask*, suggests either an indifference on Redgrave's part towards scripts, or lack of better offers. Hollywood, however, came up with a good one – Mankiewicz's remarkable version of Graham Greene's best-selling *The Quiet American* (58): Redgrave, as well as Audie Murphy in the title role, was excellent; the film was literate and faithful to the novel until the last reel, when it brazenly upended Greene's (anti-American) thesis. The resulting brouhaha hurt the box-office.

In 1958 he played Hamlet at Stratford again, as well as Benedick; in 1959 he appeared in his own adaptation of Henry James's 'The Aspern Papers' (he has also written plays and published two volumes on acting and a novel). Also in 1959 he was knighted, but the elevation did nothing for his film career. After a decade of mainly depressing pictures it was hardly surprising that he accepted supporting roles in two that looked okay, both American: *Shake Hands With the Devil* (59) with James Cagney and *The Wreck of the Mary Deare* with Gary Cooper. Then he did an elephantine British comedy, *No My Darling Daughter* (61), only the daughter wasn't one of his own, but one of John Mills's, Juliet; and a brief cameo as the Master of the Household who engages the governess in *The Innocents*. Subsequently, his attitude towards the cinema has been rather that of an elder statesman. He has been: the prison governor in *The Loneliness of the Long Distance Runner* (63); W. B. Yeats, the 'senior' playwright, in *Young Cassidy* (64); the drunken medical officer in *The Hill* (65); and an uncle in *The Heroes of Telemark*. He appeared, but fleetingly, in a silly programmer with Stephen Boyd, *Assignment K* (68), and remarked to an interviewer during its making that the pay was good and the work easy. Unsurprisingly, he played senior officers again in *Oh! What a Lovely War* (69) and *The Battle of Britain*, and was the headmaster in the remake of *Goodbye Mr Chips*, scripted by Rattigan. He was dreadful as Peggotty in *David Copperfield* (70); then was with Bette Davis in *Connecting Rooms*, playing an old man who is a janitor in the school in which he once taught; and did *Goodbye Gemini*. Stage performances during these years have included: Claudius in the National Theatre's 'Hamlet', Uncle Vanya, and Solness in 'The Master Builder', also at the National (63–64), and Ratikin in 'A Month in the Country' (65) with Ingrid Bergman.

Schoolmastering on… Redgrave as the hea… master in the remak… Goodbye Mr Chi… *(69), with Peter O'… as Chips.*

Ralph Richardson

Like the little girl with the curl, there is no happy medium with Sir Ralph: when he is good, he is very, very good, and when he is bad he is horrid. It is a curious talent. Younger cinemagoers (and theatregoers) are sometimes puzzled that he should be considered one of Britain's leading actors; they find him mannered and inflexible, too often the elderly clubman he is in life. But dotted throughout his career are performances of excellence; he has been particularly good at projecting the intellectual 'ordinary' man and the aristocrat 'sicklied o'er with the pale cast of thought', but he is not willowy or aesthetic; he probably would not have been a convincing Hamlet. He is nimble, blunt, trusting, but there is an intelligence which overrides every other quality.

He was born in Cheltenham, Gloucester, in 1902; on leaving school he became an office boy with an insurance company at Brighton, where he lived, but was then left a small legacy. After a few weeks studying art he decided to be an actor and joined a semi-amateur company in Brighton, moving on to a professional company a few months later. This was a group which toured, and he toured with them for three years. In 1926 he joined the Birmingham Rep., with whom he did a two-week London season in 'The Farmer's Wife', which led eventually to a small part in another play by Eden Phillpotts, 'Yellow Sands' (28), with Cedric Hardwicke. He joined the Old Vic in 1930, playing Caliban, Prince Hal and Bolingbroke; in 1931 there he did Petruchio, Bottom and Henry V, and in 1932 Iago, Brutus and Sir Toby. (He returned to the Vic in 1937 and 1938; and was one of its mainstays during its great days, 1944–7–probably the peak of his career.)

The Vic in the early 30s had not attained the exalted status it was to know later, but Richardson had appeared also in the West End, and had achieved a small reputation. It was Hardwicke who recommended him to the makers of *The Ghoul* (33), in a small part; and he then played Jessie Matthews's fiancé in *Friday the Thirteenth*, a good 'cross-section' movie (what has happened before the leading characters are involved in a bus crash). He returned a star in *The Return of Bulldog Drummond*, a poor thing compared with the Ronald Colman Drummond film which turned up a month later. He starred opposite Anna May Wong in *Java Head* and on Hardwicke's recommendation was featured with him in *The King of Paris*; and was the fuzzy-haired maniac/villain of *Bulldog Jack* (35)–Hulbert.

Korda then offered him a contract, with the idea of starring him in *Sanders of the River*, but stage commitments prevented that and the part went to Leslie Banks; in October 1935 Richardson made his American bow as Mercutio in Katharine Cornell's company, touring and later in New York. He was to remain with Korda 21 years (until Korda's death in 1956). During that time he made only a dozen or so films for him, and as many more for other companies–but, as he said in later years, his heart was always in the theatre: 'I don't think films give an actor much satisfaction, when he's making them; but if they go well and they're successful, well, then he's very happy and lucky.' Beyond that, Richardson did not have the matinée idol looks of his friend and colleague, Olivier, and was cast mainly in supporting roles, usually in parts requiring integrity: *Things to Come* (36), H. G. Wells's story written specially for the screen, where he was unbelievably hammy; *The Man Who Could Work Miracles*, Wells again, as a peppery old colonel; *Thunder in the City* (37) for Atlantic, with Edward G. Robinson; and *South Riding* (38), as the squire in Victor Saville's version of Winifred Holtby's Yorkshire novel–perhaps his best part, and played with exact, realistic detail. Earlier he had been cast in the uncompleted *I Claudius*, replacing Raymond Massey, who refused to work with Charles Laughton. Stage plays of the period: 'Bees on the Boat Deck' (36), 'The Amazing Dr Clitterhouse', 'Othello' (38), in the title role, and 'Johnson Over Jordan'.

His parts in *The Divorce of Lady X* and MGM's *The Citadel* were small compared to those of Olivier and Robert Donat respectively, but he was effective, especially in the latter, as a hearty but cynical drunk. He did much better the following year alongside Olivier in *Q Planes* (39), as a devil-may-care SS man, and with John Clements in *The Four Feathers*, from A. E. W. Mason's novel, as the officer who is blinded by the desert sun. He also starred with Merle Oberon in Korda's patriotic *The Lion Has Wings*, and before war broke out, did *On the Night of the Fire*, with Diana Wynyard. He joined the Fleet Air Arm, and was released temporarily for some pictures all about the war: *The Day Will Dawn* (42); *The Silver Fleet*; and *The Volunteer* (43), a documentary extolling the Fleet Air Arm, in which he played himself. Then he was released permanently to help run the Old Vic; and played there Blunschli, Peer Gynt, Uncle Vanya, Falstaff, Cyrano de Bergerac, etc.

His stage work prevented him from accepting a good Hollywood bid–to play the King in *Anna and the King of Siam*, but he returned to films in *School for Secrets* (46), a partially successful picture about boffins; and the following year was knighted. He made his first film for Korda in almost 10 years: *Anna Karenina* (48), where his Karenin–to Vivien Leigh's Anna–is one of its few

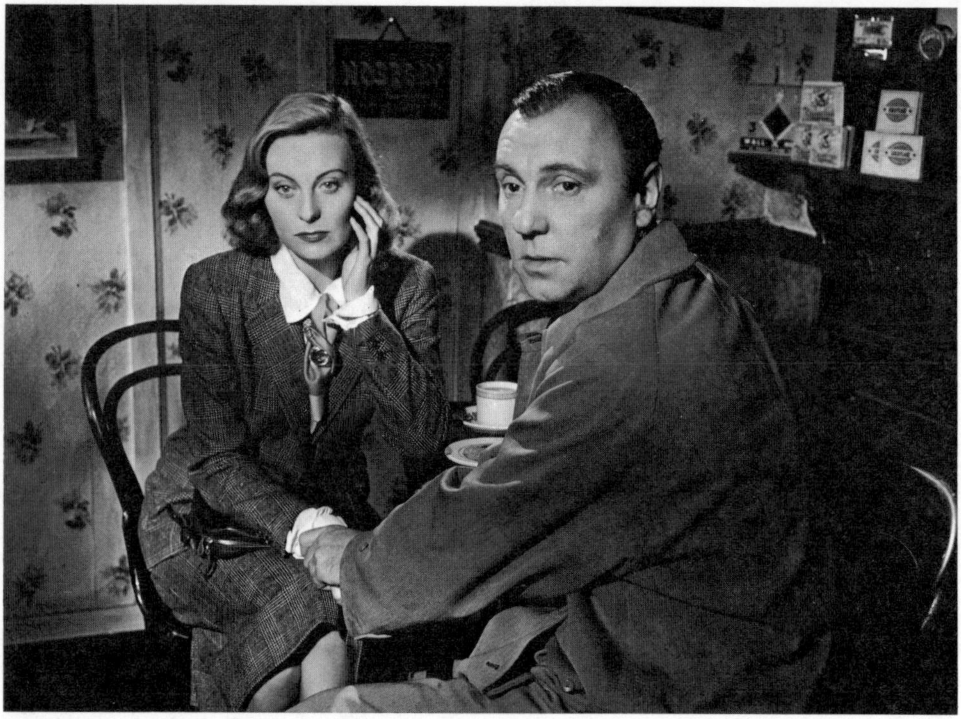

The Fallen Idol (48) remains the best screen version of a Graham Greene work, and it has Ralph Richardson's best screen performance, as Baines, the – married – Embassy butler in love with French typist Michèle Morgan.

satisfactory ingredients. Later that year he was in Carol Reed's film of Graham Greene's *The Fallen Idol*, as the pivotal character, the butler whom the boy thinks betrays him: it is an admirable performance (in one of the best films of that era) and Greene himself thinks it is the best screen delineation of any of his characters. He went to Hollywood to play Dr Sloper in *The Heiress* (50), a part he had played on the London stage, and another domestic tyrant: but it was as different from his Karenin as it was as good. From whence there was a considerable drop to his hammy sea captain in *An Out-Cast of the Islands* (51) and his drear little clerk in *Home at Seven* (which he had also done on the stage, and which he directed. Wisely, he never repeated the experiment). But Lean's *The Sound Barrier* (52) saw him back at his best, and the New York Critics voted him the Best Actor of the year. So did the BFA (Best British Actor).

He continued to see-saw: as the elderly parson in *The Holly and the Ivy* he was dull, but his Buckingham in Olivier's *Richard III* (55) was a brilliant one. Like all his work, the quality has to be explained by direction or casting, because his performances, once conceived, are consistent. No one could have done much with *The Passionate Stranger* (56), a little novelette that seemed to have been run up on a wet afternoon; but in the better *Smiley* earlier the same year, a sentimental Australian 'boy' story, he was better. Stage work during the 50s: 'Three Sisters' (51) as Vershinin; 'A Day by the Sea' (53); 'Separate Tables' and 'The Sleeping Prince' (55), both on tour in Australia; 'The Waltz of the Toreadors' (57) in New York; 'Flowering Cherry' (57); and Graham Greene's 'The Complaisant Lover' (59).

After that, most of his film roles returned to the supporting category: *Our Man in Havana* (59); *Oscar Wilde* (60) as Sir Edward Carson; and Hollywood's *Exodus* and *Long Day's Journey into Night* (62). His role in the latter would seem to be cruel type-casting – the bombastic, ageing, dreamy and vague actor, but Richardson got way under the surface for a memorable portrayal. What he was doing, however, in 20th's silly Greek thing, *The 300 Spartans*, is anybody's guess. His performances in *Woman of Straw* (64) and *Dr Zhivago* (66) were weak, but he got fine notices for his participation in *The Wrong Box*, and was exactly right for his brief stint as Gladstone in *Khartoum*. He was back in the secret service in *The Midas Run/A Run on Gold*, a minor picture, with Fred Astaire and Richard Crenna, one of a run of films in

Sir John Gielgud as Clarence and Sir Ralph Richardson in Richard III *(55), produced and directed by Sir Laurence Olivier. A theatrical knighthood is given rather for service than for achievement, but Gielgud and Richardson qualify on both counts.*

1969. The others: Richard Lester's *The Bed-Sitting Room* in the title role (!); *The Looking Glass War*, from John Le Carré's novel, as the head of the secret service this time; and *Oh! What a Lovely War*, *The Battle of Britain* and *David Copperfield* (70) as Mr Micawber, in each case one of a distinguished cast. He and another theatrical knight, Gielgud, supported Kenneth Haigh playing Napoleon in *Eagle in a Cage*.

His stage work during this decade has remained uneven; he was outstanding in 'Six Characters in Search of an Author' (63), but much of his other work lacked light and shade. He was in, among others: 'The School for Scandal', in London and New York (62–63) and Joe Orton's 'What the Butler Saw' (69). He has appeared from time to time in TV drama. Since 1944 he has been married to actress Meriel Forbes; his first wife died in 1942.

Paul Robeson

Paul Robeson was a moment in time: the wrong moment, perhaps. He was one of the century's great artists, but his skin was the wrong colour. Had he come earlier, few might ever have heard of him. Had he come later he might have been welcomed with the same eagerness as Sidney Poitier and other popular Negro artists. He was successful, but he found the going tough. He had intelligence and fame; was in demand as a concert and recording artist, worked in films and on the stage; but remained always a loner in show business. Even those who admired him often thought it better so. As a great singer, he was clearly qualified to be a solo artist, but his very greatness calls into question the neglect of Robeson by Hollywood. Hollywood, the eternal whipping boy . . . but this same Hollywood did try to make stars out of singers like Lawrence Tibbett. The point is that no singer before or since ever caught the public imagination as Robeson did. To most people the fact that he was Negro was immaterial; no singer before had seemed so real, so unencumbered by artifice, so warm, so sincere: his rich bass-baritone, whether he sang aria or spiritual, 'spoke' to millions. Today we are accustomed to the singer who 'acts' his lyric: Robeson was virtually the first modern singer, in that the emotion conveyed was as true as the voice.

He acted in the same way: powerful, direct, entirely natural. His few film performances were delightful. Most of them were in British films, but even in the British studios there was always conflict between him and the recessionists over whether he should play parts as a human being or as Amos 'n' Andy's second cousin. Marie Seton's biography (1958) movingly portrays his struggles. A note at the front by Alexander Woollcott speaks of his 'greatness as a person . . . his unassailable dignity, and his serene, incorruptible simplicity', and Arthur Bryant in his foreword says that 'no one who has seen him act or heard that wonderful voice is ever likely to forget the experience'. His films were mainly poor, and they were *not* important in the Civil Rights movement which, inevitably, he espoused – nor important in any way except for his presence in them.

He was a remarkable man – indeed, an improbably brilliant one. Born in Princeton, New Jersey, in 1898, the son of a minister of the Church, he graduated from Rutgers University, New Brunswick, NJ, with the highest scholastic average in the history of that institution, then studied Law at Columbia University (he was actually admitted to the Bar in New York). He was excellent at athletics and during his college years was an All-American football player. As an entertainer, he had merely sung as an amateur at parties; but in 1920 he was persuaded to act in 'Simon the Cyrenian' which was being revived by the Harlem YWCA. This was one of the few plays to break away from the Negro stereotype, and Robeson indignantly turned down a consequent offer to play in Eugene O'Neill's 'The Emperor Jones', because that, he felt, didn't. He also did not want a career in professional football; to earn money while studying he sang at the Cotton Club and appeared in a play called 'Taboo' and made his British debut in this, in 1922, in Blackpool. After graduating, he was offered O'Neill's 'All God's Chillun Got Wings' and he also did 'The Emperor Jones', after all because he needed the money. These established him as a force in the New York Theatre; and in the latter play he made his London debut in 1925. In 1926 he was in 'Black Boy' and in 1928 took over the role of Crown in 'Porgy'. Later that year he went to London again to appear in 'Show Boat', and Britain became his adopted home for 13 years: there he did 'Othello' (30) and 'The Hairy Ape' (31) as Yank. He became renowned, internationally, on the concert platform; in 1932 he returned to New York to appear in a revival of 'Show Boat'.

At this point a movie of *The Emperor Jones* (32) was proposed by an independent group: it was made in New York and distributed by United Artists, for whom it did good business – though nominally an 'art film'. Robeson and others, however, considered it a vulgarization of the play (some scenes were added after he had signed the contract, to bring it more in line with the conventional concept of Negro behaviour – cf. King Vidor's *Hallelujah*). The next film offer came from Korda in London: *Sanders of the River* (35), from Edgar Wallace's novel. Robeson was attracted to the idea of playing an African chief as a human being, and by the promise that the film would include much documentary material; but the film was re-worked to make it a hymn to British imperialism in the person of white administrator Sanders: 'Sandy the strong / Sandy the wise / Righter of Wrongs / Hater of Lies' sang Robeson, not insincerely. He loathed the film, and walked out of the London première when asked to make a speech. A British TV company resurrected it in 1959 and there were protests by the representatives of African governments because of the film's prehistoric attitudes. Robeson's cheery performance was its sole, shining, virtue.

Robeson at the time of Sh[ow] Boat *(36)*.

There was less disillusionment with the next, Hollywood's *Show Boat* (36) where his brief was to do little more than sing 'Ol' Man River'. He continued to turn down offers, said director Harry Watt, 'because he felt they did not show the Negro in a sympathetic light', but at the same time felt the onus of taking inferior parts in an attempt to improve the Cinema's usual conception of Negroes. After his experience on *Sanders*, he had a clause in his contract giving him the right to approve the final cut of *Song of Freedom* (36), a melodramatic but not dishonest tale about a London-born Negro – a concert artist – who returns to his African heritage. Robeson himself was fairly enthusiastic (and so was the press), but his attempt to do something with the cardboard character of the chieftain in *King Solomon's Mines* (37) was hardly noticeable. Next was *Jericho* (38) with Henry Wilcoxon, another melodrama, this time about an American Negro who flees from justice and becomes chief of an Arab tribe: some play was made of friendship between black and white and this, Robeson thought, justified its naïvety and the improbabilities of the plot. The same year he did *Big Fella*, a melodrama with songs, set in Marseilles; and then *The Proud Valley* (40), the story of an American Negro who adopts and is adopted by a Welsh mining village and who becomes a hero during a mine disaster. Of course. But at the time this was a significant film, and the only one of which he is proud.

In September 1939 he returned to New

The only one of Paul Robeson's films to be at all worthy of him was Ealing's The Proud Valley *(40), about an American Negro who becomes a miner in Wales. It was directed by Pen Tennyson, of whom great things were expected (he was killed during the war). With Robeson here are Simon Lack, Jack Jones and Charles Williams, all trapped below in a pit disaster.*

York, and three months later starred in 'John Henry' on Broadway. In 1943 he began his record-breaking revival of 'Othello' and toured in it: in 1958 he returned to Britain and played the part with the Royal Shakespeare Company. Between these years he had gradually decreased his activity, due in some measure to the poor press he was receiving in the US because of his Communist affiliations. The State Department indeed had withdrawn his passport so that he was unable to travel to the USSR in 1952 to receive the Stalin Peace Prize. When at last he was able to travel he settled again in Britain, but in 1963, in ill-health, he returned to New York, where he lives in seclusion with his family.

He made one film after *The Proud Valley*, the final episode of 20th's *Tales of Manhattan* (42) with Ethel Waters: folksy and patronizing, it was a negation of everything both artists stood for and was cut by the more discerning of exhibitors.

Edward G. Robinson

'Why did we last?' reiterated Edward G. Robinson in 1963 to an interviewer who asked about the great generation of stars: 'Well, they were people before they were stars. You can have someone new, with a few tricks and a new face and the people will go along with him for a while and then they see through. To last you need to be real. Integrity as a person. And you have to work. I still work as hard, probably harder, at each role I get as I did at the beginning. To my mind, the actor has this great responsibility of playing another human being. It's a great responsibility, you know, it's like taking on another person's life and you have to do as sincerely and honestly as you can.'

He is the least film-starrish of stars. Small, robust, not handsome, he seldom made the fan-magazines. There has never been a Robinson cult nor has he even been *nominated* for an Oscar – which comes, perhaps, of being consistently good and versatile. His standard of playing is as good as anyone's, but the reason he has lasted so long at the top (his physique might have fitted him better to supporting parts) is not simply because he's a fine actor – he is an exciting one. For much of his career he has had to snarl and rant, but he can be very quiet, very placid. He has always seemed to have a great understanding of human

Edward G. Robinson–in spats and grey derby –with his henchmen in Little Caesar *(30), a gangster film that is hardly less exciting today than it was then. It was directed by Mervyn Le Roy, a good director in those days.*

frailties. But, as Raymond Chandler said when discussing him and Bogart, he 'only has to enter a room to dominate it.'

Robinson was born in Bucharest, Rumania, in 1893. The family emigrated to New York when he was nine. After a short spell at Columbia University he moved over to the AADA, and it was there he changed his name from Emmanual Goldenberg (the G in the middle stands for nothing–'God only knows or gangsters,' he said once). His first stage appearance was in Binghampton, New York, in 'Paid in Full' (13); he toured Canada in 'Kismet' and made his Broadway bow in two small parts in 'Under Fire'. After the war (he was in the Navy) he began to make a reputation, notably in 'Banco' (22) which resulted in a film part, as an elderly revolutionary in *The Bright Shawl* (23). Among the plays over the next few years: 'A Royal Fandango' (23), 'Androcles and the Lion' (25) as Caesar, 'The Goat Song', 'Juarez and Maximilian' (as Diaz), 'The Brothers Karamazov' (26), and 'The Racket' (27), his first star role, as a gangster. He was in 'The Man With Red Hair' and in 'Kibitzer' which he wrote with Jo Swerling; then was asked by Paramount to play a gangster in *The Hole in the Wall* (29), starring Claudette Colbert. He played another gangster in *Night Ride* (30) and then was the Italian immigrant in *A Lady to Love*, with Vilma Banky as the mail-order bride in this second of the four film versions of 'They Knew What They Wanted'; he also appeared in the German version (he speaks eight languages). He was a gangster again in Tod Browning's remake of his own *Outside the Law*, an Oriental in *East Is West* with Lupe Velez, and again a gangster in *The Widow From Chicago*.

'Mr Samuel' was his last play for over twenty years; when it folded he went to Hollywood to play *Little Caesar* (30), and his performance as the vicious bragging Al Capone-like killer made him a star: power and style and personality. The film itself, a pungent account of his rise and fall ('Is this the end of Little Rico?') was one of the year's top money-makers and Robinson became at once one of Warners' most important stars. *Smart Money* (31) with James Cagney was more conventional, but it was some years before Warners lost the impetus of these early gangster films, 'torn from today's headlines'. *Five Star Final* still has an impact, the story of a ruthless tabloid editor who finally learns some humanity. It was also one of the top money-makers.

Robinson continued to play bigwigs and bosses, most of them crooked, and all of them wily: he was an Oriental one in *The Hatchet Man*, Wong Low Get. 'There is nothing of the usual theatrical Chinaman,' said Lionel Collier. 'Robinson's performance is a brilliant one.' The film wasn't up to much, though. And he was a murderous one in *Two Seconds* (32), looking back on his career in the electric chair – though the performance itself is a virtual self-parody. *Tiger Shark*, directed by Howard Hawks, gave him a change, but it was a variation on *A Lady to Love* with Zita Johann as the unfaithful wife and Richard Arlen as the lover; Robinson was a one-handed Mexican fisherman. He was a senator in *Silver Dollar* and Collier said 'Once again . . . an outstanding characterization and one which is quite unlike any he has done to date.' It was an impressive film, and so was *Little Giant* (33), a gentle tale about a retired gangster; and he had a third good one in *I Loved a Woman*. The woman was opera-singer Kay Francis and the wife Genevieve Tobin; and it was based on a real-life tycoon, in this case Chicago meat-packer Samuel Insull – though unlike *Citizen Kane* the film showed the fall as well as the rise. *Dark Hazard* (34; the title referred to a greyhound) and *The Man With Two Faces* (he was a murderer) were more conventional but he then did one of his best films, John Ford's Capraesque *The Whole Town's Talking* (35), at Columbia. Presumably cast because of his authority as a gang leader, he was touching in the other part of the dual role, the mild bank clerk mistaken for same. He was back in the big time in Hawks's *Barbary Coast* for Goldwyn.

William Keighley's fine *Bullets and Ballots* (36) found him for the first time on the Right Side of the Law – Bogart was the quarry; *Thunder in the City* (37) in Britain was poor, but back on the Warner lot *Kid Galahad* was well up to standard, with Bette Davis, Bogart, Wayne Morris in the title role and Robinson as his unscrupulous but soft-hearted Italian manager. He went over to MGM to be *The Last Gangster*, then returned to Warners for the last under his contract, *A Slight Case of Murder* (38), another comedy about a retired gangster, but this time rather a black farce in the unmistakable tones of Damon Runyan. A splendid supporting cast included Ruth Donnelly, as his wife, and Allen Jenkins. Graham Greene in his review observed that the funniest film of 1937, *True Confession*, had one corpse and that 'this has four and is four times as funny'. Robinson re-signed with Warners, but the first picture was no cause to celebrate, *The Amazing*

For most of its length Lloyd Bacon's Brother Orchid *(40) was a good crime comedy, and both Robinson and Ann Sothern, as his moll, were at their best.*

Dr Clitterhouse, a silly crime melo. At Columbia *I Am the Law* (he was) and at MGM *Blackmail* (39) were two of the same genre but infinitely superior.

Before the latter Robinson did a hard-hitting 'semi-documentary', *Confessions of a Nazi Spy*, made early in 1939. Granted that he and the Warners were Jewish and director Anatole Litvak a Russian *émigré*, it was a courageous film to make, if only commercially (and in no way comparable to the Iron Curtain films made when Hollywood became politically conscious again 10 years later): it was the first anti-Nazi film and not mealy-mouthed (though by this time only MGM was still releasing in Germany). *Dr Ehrlich's Magic Bullet* (40) also contrived to be anti-Nazi propaganda without much difficulty: Ehrlich was a German Jew whose discoveries benefited mankind, and at the film's climax he prophesied that one day Man would fight diseases of the mind more dangerous than those of the body. . . . The film was timid, however, about Ehrlich's discovery of a cure for syphilis: the word was mentioned fearlessly, but the film managed to suggest that it was some form of TB. In The Spectator Basil Wright paid tribute to Robinson's

It was obvious to even the youngest cinemagoer that this marriage was doomed: Robinson and Marlene Dietrich in Manpower *(41), with George Raft as Best Man and Joyce Compton as Maid of Honour. Raoul Walsh directed this drama of dime-novel dilemmas.*

acting: 'To say that Otto Kruger is almost unrecognizable is an extreme compliment; but to say that Edward G. Robinson is almost unrecognizable is really unbelievable; yet it is true. The star of *Two Seconds* . . . here subordinates himself so completely to the story, and to his make-up, that it is Ehrlich, and Ehrlich only, that we see.'

After which it was quite a descent to *Brother Orchid*, as a crook turned monk, his astringency offset by a painfully holy performance from Donald Crisp. He did another biographical film, also directed by William Dieterle, *A Despatch From Reuters* (the founding of the news agency), then *The Sea Wolf* (41) as the captain. *Manpower* (41) was a remake of *Slim*, with Robinson in his old familiar part as the nice little man who loses his wife (Dietrich) to his buddy (George Raft). He was a newspaper editor again in *Unholy Partners* (the partner was crook Edward Arnold) and an ex-con in *Larceny Inc.* (42), a pleasant comedy and his last film for Warners under his contract. In 1942, in a gesture of friendship, he toured British service installations, which left him time otherwise for only an episode of *Tales of Manhattan*, by sheer, beautiful acting making his the best in the film: the Bowery drunk who dresses up for a college reunion. After a poor war picture, *Destroyer*, he was in Duvivier's other all-star episoder, *Flesh and Fantasy* (43), in a loose adaptation of 'Lord Arthur Savile's Crime'. *Tampico* (44) was wartime melodrama, with Lynn Bari and Victor McLaglen; then he did *Double Indemnity*, as the claims investigator, a role subsidiary to those of Barbara Stanwyck and Fred MacMurray and less showy, but he invested it with great humanity. It was as if he was inspired by his material; he played the elderly soldier in the folksy *Mr Winkle Goes to War* with almost no interest: 'In the Great *Mr Deeds* Tradition' said Columbia's adverts, hopefully. And he was first-rate again as a college professor involved with Joan Bennett and crime in *The Woman in the Window*.

He returned to Britain and broadcast to the European Underground movement, and appeared as a flying instructor in an RAF propaganda film, *Journey Together* (45), for which he took no salary. Then he toured France. Back in Hollywood he played Margaret O'Brien's father in the over-sweet *Our Vines Have Tender Grapes* and then got together with Lang, Bennett and Dan Duryea for a follow-up to *The Woman in the Window*; and *Scarlet Street* is better, if only because it doesn't all turn out to be a dream: a remake of Renoir's *La Chienne*, with Robinson a hen-pecked husband smitten with Bennett. Like the earlier film, it was a

yenne Autumn
is one of John Ford's
nteresting works.
best thing about it
Edward G. Robin-
cameo as Secretary
e Interior Carl
rz.

big success. The next half-dozen alternated between good and bad: *The Stranger* (46), as the representative of the war crimes commission hunting down Nazi Orson Welles in a small New England town; *The Red House* (47), an incredible melo that he produced himself; *All My Sons* (48), a good performance as the paterfamilias in this mediocre version of Arthur Miller's play; Huston's superb *Key Largo*, recreating with affection a gang boss with galloping paranoia; *The Night Has a Thousand Eyes*, a silly thriller about a clairvoyant; and *House of Strangers* (49), a good solid melodrama directed by Joseph L. Mankiewicz, as a Napoleon of East Side finance. Easily the worst was *My Daughter Joy* (50), as a possessive father again (Peggy Cummins's): he made it in Britain, coincidental with his being called before the un-American Activities Commission to explain Communist affiliations. He was cleared, but his film work thereafter was for a while confined to programmers or even Bs: *Actors and Sin* (52), a two-part film by Ben Hecht that had no success at all; *Vice Squad* (53) with Paulette Goddard; *The Big Leaguer*, a baseball story with Vera-Ellen; *The Glass Web*; *Black Tuesday* (54), as a gangster; *The Violent Men* (55), a Western – a species he loathes – with Stanwyck, as a power-hungry cattle-king; *Tight Spot* as a DA with Ginger Rogers; *A Bullet for Joey* with Raft; *Illegal* as a crooked lawyer; *Hell on Frisco Bay* with Alan Ladd; and *Nightmare* (56). It looked as though either he or producers or both were capitalizing on his reputation, re-hatching the great parts of his early career, but in fact some of these modest pictures were better than the As of the time and look excellent now on TV. *Illegal* is particularly good. De Mille's *The Ten Commandments*, at least critically, wasn't worth one of these films: Robinson was a Hebrew leader.

In 1952 he had played in Koestler's 'Darkness at Noon'; now he spent two years, in New York and on tour, in Chayefsky's 'The Middle of the Night'. He returned to films with a stint in Capra's *A Hole in the Head* (59) and then did a good film about a heist, *Seven Thieves* (60). David Robinson took the occasion to observe that he was 'one of the most perfected actors the cinema has produced'. Apart from a British picture, *Sammy Going South* (63), in which he was a diamond smuggler, it was his last lead. He has played various species of executives or men of authority, many of them insubstantial parts: *Pepe* (60, as a film executive); *My Geisha* (62, ditto); *Two Weeks in Another Town* (ditto); *The Prize* (64); *Good Neighbor Sam*; *Robin and the Seven Hoods* (a guest bit as a racketeer); *Cheyenne Autumn*; *The Outrage*; and *The Cincinnati Kid* (65), as the world-weary, experienced poker-player who takes on Steve McQueen. McQueen was good – everyone was good – but Robinson walked off with the film. He was in Disney's *Never a Dull Moment* (67), but more disturbing is his willingness to appear in inferior European pictures, usually as a retired gangster: *The Biggest Bundle of Them All* (66), *Une Blonde de Peking* (67) and *Grand Slam* (68). In 1969 he was in *Mackenna's Gold* and in 1970 *Song of Norway*; he was cast in a big role in *The Angel Levine*, but the brokers wouldn't insure him for such a strenuous part.

Robinson today is bearded, happily married to his second wife. Jean-Claude Brialy, who acted with him in *Une Blonde de Peking*, explained why he goes on working: 'Robinson is marvellous. I can't believe he's 74 – he doesn't seem like an elderly man, but a young man disguised as one. His eyes glint, his mouth is mocking and tender. But what really catches you looking into the famous face, makes you draw up short, is his goodness. He knows the world and people – his experience of humanity is immense. And, he has almost fifty years of career behind him, but there's one thing he has never lost from view – that is to act. To act, for any actor worthy of the name, is *essential* . . . that's why he remains so curious, so warm and so understanding.'

Flora Robson

All great stars have a quality which cannot be exactly pinned down. You can say that Flora Robson has a beautiful speaking voice, but how do you define that stillness, that urgent inner momentum, the flick of humour, the smile that can light up a room – the combination of all four? Perhaps the clue to her art is in the stillness, always an indication of confidence, of an artist having mastered his art. It would have been her wish rather, it is known, to have been beautiful, but she is much more interesting than most of her contemporaries. She has played a wider spectrum of parts than most actresses but is, in the end, better in sympathetic parts.

She was born in South Shields, Durham, in 1902, but was schooled in London; she studied at RADA and was a bronze medallist – which netted her the part of Queen Margaret (one of the 'shadows') in Clemence Dane's 'Will Shakespeare' (21); for the next three years she did rep with Ben Greet and at Oxford, and returned to London in 'Fata Morgana' (24). But she quit the stage suddenly and worked as a welfare officer in a factory for four years. In 1929 she wanted to act again and was in rep in Cambridge for a year (with Robert Donat); in 1931 she did two plays at London's Gate Theatre, including 'Desire Under the Elms' (as Abbie). As a result of these she was offered a part–as a middle-aged Frenchwoman–in *Gentlemen of the Press* (31). She played in *Dance Pretty Lady* (32), Anthony Asquith's version of Compton Mackenzie's 'Carnival' (and as the heroine's mother was the only good thing in the film), and in 1933 in a quota quickie, *One Precious Year*. At the same time her theatrical career was blooming: among others, 'The Anatomist' (her first London hit), 'Six Characters in Search of an Author', 'Dangerous Corner', 'All God's Chillun' and an Old Vic season with Charles Laughton–Varya ('The Cherry Orchard'), Isabella ('Measure for Measure'), Gwendolen ('The Importance of Being Earnest'), Katherine ('Henry VIII'), Lady Macbeth, etc.

It was Laughton who helped put her on the screen map, when he recommended her to Alexander Korda for the Dowager Czarina in *Catherine the Great* (34): apart from the fact that she was too clean, she was the only one of the cast who might have been like the original. She said later that Korda was very good to her: he financed James Bridie's 'Mary Read: Dragoon and Pirate' which she and Robert Donat did and then sent her on holiday. In 1935 she played 'Mary Tudor' and then Korda had her play Mary's sister Elizabeth in *Fire Over England* (37) with a script that included the Tilbury speech (she looked more like the portraits than Bette Davis did two years later, but lacked some of the fire). She did a few weeks as another such, the Empress in the aborted *I Claudius*; and that year also played in a moving World War I story, *Farewell Again*, with Leslie Banks. Stage appearances included 'Anna Christie' and 'Autumn'.

In 1938 she went to Hollywood to play Mrs Read in *Wuthering Heights*, returning to Britain for *Poison Pen* (as a spinster, she of course, writes the offending letters and 'dominates the picture with a performance full of subtle changes'–Photoplay) and *The Lion Has Wings*. She refused the part of Mrs Danvers in *Rebecca* but returned to Hollywood on a two-picture contract for Warner Brothers: *We Are Not Alone* (39) with Paul Muni, and *Invisible Stripes* (40) with Humphrey Bogart. Warner Brothers also asked her to do a supporting part–as Elizabeth I again–in Errol Flynn's *The Sea Hawk* (41), and two years later, before leaving for Britain, she was for them Ingrid Bergman's maid in *Saratoga Trunk*, in a

Flora Robson as the ageing Queen Elizabeth I –she was in her 30s when she played the part–in Fire Over England *(37), from A. E. W. Mason's novel. The lady-in-waiting–and the film's heroine–was Vivien Leigh.*

peculiar dusky make-up. She was also in Paramount's *Bahama Passage* (42). During this American period she did two plays in New York, 'Ladies in Retirement' (40) and 'The Damask Cheek' (42); toured in 'Elizabeth the Queen' in summer theatres (42) and did a season of Grand Guignol in Los Angeles (43).

She returned to the London stage as Thérèse Raquin in a play after Zola; and to British films in Gainsborough's *2000 Women* (44), a few of whom were Phyllis Calvert, Patricia Roc and Jean Kent, all in an internment camp for English women in France. Robson played the understanding, motherly spinster–a role in which she was to be frequently cast in films, particularly in her Rank contract days, just beginning. In 1945 she did *The Years Between*, *Great Day* (a cozy tale about the preparations in an English village for a visit by Mrs Eleanor Roosevelt) and *Caesar and Cleopatra*, as Cleopatra's sinister maid Ftatateetah. She followed with her usual solid supporting chores in three successful ones, *Black Narcissus* (47) as a nun, *Frieda* and *Holiday Camp*; a stage version of

Esma Cannon and Flora Robson as two spinsters at a Holiday Camp *(47). Miss Cannon met death at the hands of Dennis Price, and Miss Robson was a mite luckier: she found merely disillusionment. It was a silly mish-mash, but one of the year's most popular films in Britain.*

Francis Brett Young's novel 'A Man about the House' and two other plays; *Good Time Girl* (48) – Jean Kent, in a supposedly topical story of post-war youth; and *Saraband for Dead Lovers* – an unsympathetic study of one of George I's mistresses.

In 1948 she returned to New York to play Lady Macbeth opposite Michael Redgrave, and she stayed away from films for four years ('Black Chiffon' in London and New York, 'The Winter's Tale', 'The Innocents' – later filmed with Deborah Kerr – and others). She might have stayed away longer: *The Tall Headlines* (52) had no other distinction than her performance. She was an embittered Maltese in *The Malta Story* (53), the Nurse in Castellani's *Romeo and Juliet* (54); then again she concentrated on the stage, returning in 1957 in another unworthy pair, *High Tide at Noon* and *No Time for Tears* (Anna Neagle). Her 'great actress' portrait was almost the only lively feature of *The Gypsy and the Gentleman*, but she just about sank under *Innocent Sinners* (58), a heavy adaptation of Rumer Godden's 'An Episode of Sparrows'. On the stage she had two more big successes – 'Ghosts' and Redgrave's adaptation of 'The Aspern Papers'; she toured South Africa in the latter and in 'Time and Yellow Roses', in 1960 and 1962 respectively, and in 'Time . . . ' appeared in the theatre in Newcastle named after her.

Times, otherwise, weren't very exciting. Two stage ventures were disappointing, and she had only dull roles in *55 Days at Peking* (62) as the Chinese Empress, *Murder at the Gallop* (63), *Guns at Batasi* (64) and *Young Cassidy* (as his mother); and it was sad to see her in a one-line part – as a nun – amid the frantic goings-on of *Those Magnificent Men in their Flying Machines* (65). She was, however, seen to great effect in John Ford's *Seven Women*, made in the United States, but she was not well-served by either the Gig Young-Carol Lynley *The Shuttered Room* (66), as an old crone, or by the Greek-British *Cry in the Wind*, and *Eye of the Devil* (67). However, in 1968 she played Miss Prism in a West End revival of 'The Importance of Being Earnest' and got rave notices. She told an interviewer that she had lost all interest in her craft, but the notices for her Prism had revived it; later, a slated revival of 'Ring Round the Moon' might have damaged her; but in 1969 another revival, the Rodney Ackland-Hugh Walpole

'The Old Ladies', was another success for her. She was also back in big roles in pictures, in *Fragment of Fear* (70) and *The Cellar*, a murder mystery co-starring Beryl Reid.

A biography, 'Flora Robson, by Janet Dunbar, was published in 1960.

Ginger Rogers

When Ginger Rogers went to London to play 'Mame' (69) the ads were in no doubt: 'The legendary Ginger Rogers'. The claim is best justified by her having been one-half of a dancing team – Fred Astaire's most popular and durable partner – than by her later work without him. Not that her own work was undistinguished: she was seldom less than competent and always professional and likeable. Out of her dancing shoes, her flair was for not very high comedy. Time magazine once put her among her peers: 'Less eccentric than Carole Lombard, less worldly-wise than Myrna Loy, less impudent than Joan Blondell, Ginger Rogers had a careless self-sufficiency they lack.' One thinks of her as cheerful, calculating and spunky; attractive in both youth and middle-age.

The driving force, the power behind the throne, has been her mother (right to the present time, as she admits in interviews). Mother gave birth to her in 1911 in Independence, Missouri; there was a divorce and the two girls went to Hollywood, where Mother wrote scripts. Ginger was offered a contract at the age of six, but Mother turned it down. Later Mother was a reporter and theatre critic in Fort Worth, and it was here that Ginger started appearing in local plays and concerts. She substituted as a dancer when Eddie Foy's vaudeville act played the neighbourhood and after she had won a Charleston contest Mother decided it was time she went into vaudeville. She toured Texas and Oklahoma as 'Ginger and her Redheads'; and later, with her first husband, Jack Pepper, had an act called 'Ginger and Pepper'. She starred with Eddie Lowry in Chicago in 1928, then went to New York as a singer with Paul Ash's Orchestra. She appeared in a Rudy Vallee short, *Campus Sweethearts*, and got a part in a Broadway musical, 'Top Speed' (29). The critics noticed her, and so did Paramount, who put her into *The Young Man of Manhattan* (30), as Charles Ruggles's dumb-bell girlfriend. She had a song, 'I've got IT but IT don't do me no good', and became typed as a wise-cracking flapper. Paramount then featured her in: *Queen High*, starring Ruggles and Frank Morgan; *The Sap From Syracuse*, as Jack Oakie's love interest; *Follow the Leader* with Ed Wynn and Ethel Merman – also known as *Manhattan Mary*; and *Honor Among Lovers* (31), comedy relief with Ruggles. But she asked to be released from her contract, claiming that filming and stage work were too much for her (on Broadway she was featured in Gershwin's hit 'Girl Crazy'). In reality she had had a better offer from Pathé, and when her show closed she went to Hollywood. She starred in *The Tip Off* with Robert Armstrong and was also the girl left behind by him, William Boyd and James Gleason – selling candy on Coney Island in *The Suicide Fleet*, an incredible war story. She was then in *Carnival Boat* (32), but the results were less than sensational and Pathé dropped her. She worked around: *The Tenderfoot* with Joe E. Brown; *The Thirteenth Guest* with Lyle Talbot, a thriller at Monogram; *Hat Check Girl* starring Ben Lyon and Sally Eilers; and *You Said a Mouthful* with Brown. She said later: 'I started playing second leads in comedy, then leading women, then second leads in musical comedy – things like . . . *42nd Street*' (33). In that, as Anytime Annie, the chorine with society ambitions and monocled – 'The only time she ever said no she didn't hear the question' – she scored a hit, and after *Broadway Bad* at Fox (as Joan Blondell's pal), Warners put her into another of their musicals, *Gold Diggers of 1933*.

But her best chance came at RKO, as the *Professional Sweetheart*, the Purity Girl of the Air, who deliberately set out to shock a shy suitor, Norman Foster. It wasn't much of a film, but RKO liked her and signed her to a long-term contract. Meanwhile she did *A Shriek in the Night* with Talbot, *Don't Bet on Love* with Lew Ayres (whom she married), and *Sitting Pretty*, as a waitress who helps songwriters Jack Oakie and Jack Haley. Then RKO cast her as the second lead, typically brash, in a musical, *Flying Down to Rio*. She was third-billed, after Dolores del Rio and Raul Roulien, but it was she and partner Fred Astaire, a newcomer from Broadway, who stole the notices. She was a small-town girl in a triangle drama with Joel McCrea, *Chance at Heaven*, and then with Foster again in the unpretentious and enjoyable *Rafter Romance* (34). She went to *Finishing School* with Frances Dee and Billie Burke, which qualified her for three loan-outs, *Change of Heart* at Fox, and two at Warners: *Twenty Million Sweethearts*, opposite Dick Powell, and *Upper World*, where Warren William dallied with her when wife Mary Astor neglected him; she played a chorus girl, at which, by this time, she was more than adept, and got killed at the end.

RKO paired Rogers and Astaire again in

For the first three ye of her film career Gi Rogers was just ano. wise-cracking blona Here she is as one of Gold Diggers of 1 *obviously digging it Warren William.*

Miss Rogers found success and fame from the moment she and Fred Astaire danced together. Their third film together was Roberta *(35), from Jerome Kern's stage hit about some Americans in Paris and a Paris courturier.*

Ginger Rogers was several times successful at impersonating children: this one is Kitty Foyle *(40), her Oscar-winning performance.*

The Gay Divorcee, and they were an even greater success. Rogers did a pointless drama with Francis Lederer, *Romance in Manhattan*, and then another with Astaire (and Irene Dunne), *Roberta* (35). She had not wanted to be a musical star and saw herself becoming successful as such with misgiving. But she said later: 'I loved Fred so, and I mean that in the nicest, warmest way: I had such affection for him *artistically*. I think that experience with Fred was a divine blessing. It blessed me, I know, and I don't think blessings are one-sided.' Financially, RKO were blessed: most of the Astaire-Rogers films were big money-makers and the team went into the top 10. As often as she could, Rogers did 'straight' films: *Star of Midnight*, an enjoyable, polished and typical William Powell vehicle; and after *Top Hat*, *In Person*, as a jaded movie star bullied and wooed by George Brent. She danced in *Follow the Fleet* (36), *Swing Time* and *Shall We Dance?* (37) and as a reward begged to play Elizabeth in *Mary of Scotland*. The studio said no, but did put her to play with Hepburn in *Stage Door*, as the young hopeful whose wisecracks mask her own uncertainty and determination: it was a return to her early screen persona–in her films with Astaire she had become somewhat refined and ladylike. Further, it was a good film and proved that she could be effective without Astaire. She was now getting $3,000 a week. There were two comedies in 1938: *Having Wonderful Time*, a weak one about a holiday camp with Douglas Fairbanks Jr, and *Vivacious Lady*, a good one about professor James Stewart bringing cabaret singer wife to meet his country-club friends.

The break-up of the public's favourite screen team was on the cards for some time. *Carefree* and *The Story of Irene and Vernon Castle* (39) were the last. The official reason was that Rogers wanted to go dramatic, and fans soon accepted the split as inevitable. Fortunately her next film was good (though she had originally turned it down), *Bachelor Mother* with David Niven, a comedy about a salesgirl landed with an abandoned baby. *Fifth Avenue Girl* was less successful in all respects, suggesting that her name alone above the title wasn't strong enough to carry a film. *The Primrose Path* (40) came from a hit play about a girl trying to escape from the wrong side of the tracks by marrying respectability in the person of Joel McCrea: Marjorie Rambeau and Queenie Vasser were a marvellously funny Mother and Grand-mother. And *Lucky Partners* was a dim version of Sacha Guitry's 'Bonne Chance', notable only for her smooth teaming with Ronald Colman, though reputedly there was dissension on the set when she found that his part was bigger than hers.

Then came *Kitty Foyle*, from Christopher Morley's best-seller about a salesgirl who married money (Dennis Morgan) but yearned for a man from her own stratum. 'The result of pounding on the doors of executives was *Stage Door*, *Primrose Path*, *Kitty Foyle*. Those last two are my favourites.' Rogers won an Oscar against stiff competition (Davis in *The Letter*, Fontaine in *Rebecca*, Hepburn in *The Philadelphia Story* and Martha Scott in *Our Town*). She was certainly stunning in Garson Kanin's *Tom Dick and Harry* (41), a comedy about a girl with too many suitors, though the film lost its way. Under the terms of her new contract she was allowed to free-lance, but RKO were making much of her as a Great Actress: they announced dozens of appropriate projects, including *Rain* and *Sister Carrie*. Rogers did a variety of parts, but her hairstyles were more versatile than her performances. In 1942 she had a bubble cut, shoulder-length brunette page-boy, pig-tails of indeterminate colour, and page-boy again in her original blonde. The bubble cut was for the gum-chewing *Roxie Hart*, who takes the rap for a murder her husband committed (a remake of *Chicago*, in which Phyllis Haver had starred, and intermittently amusing). The others: an episode in *Tales of Manhattan*; *The Major and the Minor* with Ray Milland, a Brackett-Wilder comedy about a girl who poses as a child to travel half-fare; and *Once Upon a Honeymoon* at RKO with Cary Grant. *Tender Comrade* (43) was some sentimentality about war wives (of whom Rogers in life was one: she married a marine whom she met while touring for USO), and then Paramount entrusted her with *Lady in the Dark* (44), a Broadway musical they had bought for $285,000, at that time a record sum. W. H. Mooring had a word in Picturegoer on its making: 'Phyllis Brooks almost stole the show. So Ginger got a great deal of it cut out of the film and insisted that Phyllis be given little or no publicity.' As the inhibited magazine editor, Rogers tried for an impersonation of Gertrude Lawrence's original performance. The critics were kind to neither her nor film, but according to the Motion Picture Herald it grossed nearly $4½ million.

Her next films were concoctions of little distinction: *I'll Be Seeing You*, in love with soldier/mental patient Joseph Cotten; *Weekend at the Waldorf* (45) with Walter Pidgeon; *Heartbeat*, a remake of Danielle Darrieux's *Battement de Cœur*, about a pick-pocket who falls for victim Jean-Pierre Aumont; *Magnificent Doll* (46), a dull version of the Dolly Madison story; and *It Had to Be You* (47), a much-too-late attempt to revive screwball comedy. She was off the screen till MGM needed a replacement for Judy Garland in *The Barkleys of Broadway* (49), and the length of the absence may well account for the speed with which she grabbed her dancing shoes: this reunion with Astaire was the first in colour and got a great reception everywhere. It also revived her career: two at WB, *Perfect Strangers* (50) with Dennis Morgan and *Storm Warning*, a dramatic piece with Doris Day about the KKK; and *The Groom Wore Spurs* (51). Then there were three comedies at 20th: *We're Not Married* (52), the best episode, with Fred Allen, about a radio couple whose real marital life is one of mutual aggression; *Monkey Business* with Cary Grant; and the good *Dreamboat* with Clifton Webb, about two Silent stars caught up in the world of TV. There was also a funny film at Paramount, *Forever Female* (53), in which she was delicious as an actress who won't face the fact that she is ageing. She also played an actress (atrociously) in a mild murder mystery, *Black Widow* (54), at 20th.

Like several American stars in the 1950s, she made the mistake of thinking a British film might revitalize her career and brought in tow director David Miller and a brand-new husband, Jacques Bergerac: *Beautiful Stranger*. Better was a programmer at Columbia, *Tight Spot* (55), considerably enlivened by her performance as a gangster's moll and Edward G. Robinson's as the DA. The next three made little impression, but *The First Travelling Saleslady* (56) gave her a delightful sidekick in Carol Channing. *Teenage Rebel*, with Michael Rennie, gave her a teenage daughter; and *Oh Men Oh Women*, a heavy-handed farce, gave her little to do.

In 1951 she had been in a Broadway dud, 'Love and Let Love', and she tried again some years later, with 'The Pink Jungle', but it didn't get even as far as Broadway; in stock she has appeared in, among others, 'Bell Book and Candle', 'The Unsinkable Molly Brown' and 'Annie Get Your Gun' (the film of which she had hoped to do: 'I wanted that role so badly . . . I'd have done it for one dollar'). Her TV debut was in 'Three by Coward' (54) and in Britain she did a musical for the BBC, 'Carissima' (59).

The latter screen work of Ginger Rogers was variable, but she always gave the others lessons in how to be glamorous and soignée. Forever Female (*53*), *a comedy with William Holden.*

She came into her own again in the 60s, first in a TV spectacular in which she sang and danced, and later when she took over from Channing in 'Hello Dolly'. When she and Astaire danced on to the stage to make a presentation at the 1968 Oscar ceremony, they received an ovation such as Hollywood has seldom seen. Her contract for 'Mame' guaranteed her in excess of £250,000, the highest sum ever paid to an artist in London's West End (but she wasn't really up to it).

She has made two more films: in 1965 husband William Marshall, who had earlier been married to Michèle Morgan and Micheline Presle, produced *True Confession* in Jamaica, the first of a new series of Rogers vehicles. It has never been publicly shown and is also presumably the last. She played the Madam of a brothel, and Ray Milland co-starred. The same year she played Mama Jean in the Electrovision *Harlow*, never shown outside the US – where the critics thought she was the best thing about it. Of other films she has said: 'All the roles I refused were unnecessarily vulgar', and of the past: 'I'm most grateful to have had that joyous time in motion pictures... Pictures were talking, they were singing, they were colouring. It was beginning to blossom out: bud and blossom were both present.' And of the future: 'The most important thing in anyone's life is to be giving something. The quality I can give is fun and joy and happiness. This is my gift... I would not like a talent to go to waste.'

Will Rogers

Even in his lifetime it was common to refer to Will Rogers as an American folk-hero; after his untimely death the description was bandied around so often that he dwarfed everyone else in the category. But for many years his pictures were not revived and he is merely a name to most people under 40.

He was born in Colagah, Indian Territory (now Oklahoma), in 1879 of ancestry said to be part Irish, part Cherokee Indian. He was educated in Neosho, Missouri, and at a military academy at Booneville in that state. As a boy he became proficient at riding and lariat throwing and during his time as a ranch hand and later cow-puncher established a battery of tricks. At one point he worked on a ship that plied between Buenos Aires and South Africa, supplying mules to the British engaged in the Boer War, and it was in Johannesburg that he joined his first Wild West Show, billed as 'The Cherokee Kid'. Back in the US he joined another Show and twirled ropes at the St Louis World's Fair of 1904; part of that outfit was engaged to appear at Madison Square Garden the following year during the Annual Horse Fair. He then got on the vaudeville bill at Keiths, Union Square, sitting on a pony, chewing gum and twirling a lasso; he was soon appearing in Hammerstein's Roof Garden and becoming known. He never spoke–until one day one of his tricks went wrong and an ad-lib comment brought a laugh. Gradually, as he toured in vaudeville in the US and overseas, he added dialogue: first he commented on the act that had preceded him; later he was to comment on public figures and the political affairs of the day. He longed to go into a musical comedy and got a part in 'The Wall Street Girl' (12). Later he did 'Hands Up' (15), 'The Passing Show of 1917' and the Ziegfeld 'Midnight Frolic' supper show, which led to appearances in the Follies of 1917 and 1918. His home-spun philosophy and cracker-barrel wit made a surprising hit with New Yorkers: he spoke with seeming sincerity and without malice. He was Mr Everyman–it was soon realized that he spoke for Mr Joe Public. He sauntered shyly on to the stage, pushed back his cowlick and slowly began.

Goldwyn at that time had invested in a unit called Eminent Authors Inc, whose job was to provide films with better scenarios. The boss-man of the outfit was Rex Beach, the most eminent of the eight eminent authors, and when he sold his *Laughing Bill Hyde* (18) to Goldwyn he recommended Rogers as the lead. Rogers, he said, did not need to play the character: he *was* the character. It was not a huge success but Goldwyn signed Rogers to a contract and prepared a series of vehicles which would convert him into a big movie star: *Almost a Husband* (19) with Peggy Wood; *Jubilo*, a popular Saturday Evening Post story about a carefree hobo, that was perhaps the best of this bunch; *Water Water Everywhere* (20); *Jes' Call Me Jim* with Irene Rich; *The Strange Boarder*; *Cupid the Cowpuncher*; *Honest Hutch*; *Guile of Women* (21); *Boys Will Be Boys*; *An Unwilling Hero*; and *Doubling for Romeo*, as a cowhand who falls asleep while reading Shakespeare and dreams he's a glamorous movie star. That one was made in an attempt to kid the Rogers image, which was noticeably cold-shouldered by female audiences. After *A Poor Relation* (22) Goldwyn dropped him. The comedies were slowed down by Rogers's off-screen 'pithy epigrams' which were increasingly incorporated into the sub-titles.

Paramount used Rogers in *One Glorious Day*, which had been intended for Fatty Arbuckle, but it did no better, and an independent, Hodkinson, tried him in a version of Washington Irving's story, *The Headless Horseman*. Also, Rogers tried being his own impresario–and writer and director; but *The Roping Fool*, *Fruits of Faith* and *One Day in 365* were disastrous and he lost all his money. He returned to the Follies in 1922 and 1924, during which time Hal Roach approached him with an offer to make some two-reel comedies. This was not necessarily a comedown after features, as Roach, who specialized in shorts, was at that time ambitious. Rogers made twelve for him, of which the most successful was *Two Wagons Both Covered*, but he was essentially a dialogue comedian and not visually funny. He was clumsy at slapstick. He was offered a lecture tour, and he also began to write humorous pieces for the newspapers: he had already published 'Rogerisms–The Cowboy Philosopher on the Peace Conference' and a similar book on Prohibition. He was sent by the Saturday Evening Post to observe Europe for them and while there appeared at the London Pavilion and accepted an offer from Herbert Wilcox to co-star with Dorothy Gish in *Tip Toes* (27), a story about three broke American vaudevillians in Britain. Paramount released in the US.

In Hollywood First National was anxious to give Rogers another film fling, and selected *A Texas Steer*, about a rancher who is elected to Congress and generally straightens things out, including cynicism and corruption in high places, but the film was not a success (unlike *Mr Smith Goes to Washington* later; not a remake but the same idea). In 1928 he returned to Broadway in 'Three Cheers', and he was one of the stage performers whom Hollywood re-examined when Talkies came in. Fox proposed a new version of *The County Chairman*, already successful as a play and a Silent; Rogers was wary but submitted, though the film they made was *They Had to See Paris* (29) with wife Irene Rich and daughter Marguerite Churchill. It gave him a fine opportunity to show his American-ness, his tolerance of things foreign and contempt for the others who fell for all the pomp frivolity. Now, with Speech, cinema audiences fell for him. He had got $50,000 for it and Fox offered $60,000 for another picture. First he did a

The films Will Rogers *made for Fox were of a good standard, like* A Connecticut Yankee *(31), with Myrna Loy as Morgan La Faye. One of his virtues was his ability to extemporize much of his own dialogue (indeed, few script-writers could write for him): he knew how to play himself superbly, and within those limits was an impressive actor.*

turn in *Happy Days* (30), which was photographed in 'Grandeur', or 'wide film'; then he did *So This Is London*, an old George M. Cohan farce that was much like his first Talkie: Rich was again his wife, but Maureen O'Sullivan the daughter.

Fox put him under contract, and starred him in *Lightnin'* (31). Photoplay said: 'Here's willrogersing at its best. . . . As the shiftless, whimsical, truth-embroidering Bill Jones, he's a nine-reel scream.' Henry King directed, and Louise Dresser was Rogers's wife. Rogers then was Mark Twain's *A Connecticut Yankee* (transported in time to King Arthur's Court) and it was his biggest film hit to date. There followed: *Young As You Feel* with Fifi D'Orsay; *Ambassador Bill*; *Business and Pleasure* (32) with Jetta Goudal; and *Down to Earth*, which was specially written by Homer Croy, the author of *They Had to See Paris*, and was a sequel, set in the US with Rogers giving good advice on coping with the Depression. *Too Busy To Work* was a remake of *Jubilo* and his most serious film to date.

On radio and in the press he was a political figure of some influence. 1932 was the year of the presidential elections and Rogers was considered instrumental in Roosevelt being elected – he seemed to be, at least, the people's spokesman. He now started appearing in film popularity polls and at the end of the year he was ninth at the box-office. The following year he trailed Marie Dressler and in 1934 he supplanted her. The films were above the average among the Fox output: *State Fair*, directed by King, from Phil Strong's novel, a folksy piece with Dressler again and Janet Gaynor; Ford's *Doctor Bull*, as a country doctor; *Mr Skitch* (34) with Zasu Pitts, and the British Florence Desmond doing her impersonations; and *David Harum*, in which he was a small-town banker horse-trading on the side. It had already been a successful novel and Silent and was one of the year's top hits. It didn't matter that most of these were formula pictures: audiences revelled in the situations of *Handy Andy*, in which he was the lackadaisical husband of social climber Peggy Wood: said Photoplay, 'Sophisticated or softie, sixteen or sixty, you'll love this.' Thus he was the ideal interpreter for what are taken to be among John Ford's most

Rogers's – and Janet Gaynor's – best-remembered film is the charming State Fair *(33), directed by Henry King. The two (musical) remakes were both inferior.*

personal works, like *Judge Priest*, set in a Kentucky town where Civil War passions still run high.

His fee had gone to $110,000 per film and a new contract called for $125,000 each, plus 50 per cent of the profits. At last he did *The County Chairman* (35); then *Life Begins at Forty*, as a small-town editor, and *Doubting Thomas* with Billie Burke. Fearing he was slipping at the box-office, he asked for *Steamboat 'Round the Bend* to be released before *In Old Kentucky*. The former was certainly the better; it was John Ford's, with some of the characters from *Judge Priest*, only this time Rogers was a medicine man running a steamboat. But before either was released he was killed in an aircrash (1935), in Alaska, with Wiley Post, the aviator.

He had always had a fondness for flying. The United States was grief-stricken: apart from films his daily press pieces were still widely read. At the end of the year he was still Box Office King – after Shirley Temple. Fox, now 20th, made a couple of films in 1936 with Irvin S. Cobb, who was also a newspaperman and an actor – he had appeared in two of Rogers's films – but after Rogers, he was strictly minor league. In 1952 Warners produced *The Will Rogers Story* with Will Rogers Jr and Jane Wyman as his loving and guiding wife.

During his later career he had finally made an impact on British filmgoers, but he remains a regional figure. None of his comments can be read today with ease, and some are positively thought-stunting, like this to a Picturegoer interviewer in 1926: 'Oh yes, I write. I have done for a long time now. I don't write *good* but I write a lot. My stuff's only for ordinary yappin' rubes. I don't know nothin' about these new movements. You know – the intelligentsia, or whatever they call themselves. Some of them came to see me the other day.' Added the interviewer: 'His look spoke volumes.'

But on the screen he had a genuine charm and was amusing even if he could not be considered an actor of any range. In life he was friendly and, like Gracie Fields, completely unconcerned with and unspoilt by success. Homer Croy was his biographer – 'Our Will Rogers' (53) – and speaks eloquently of Rogers's real meaning to his contemporaries: 'He was the most influential private citizen in the world. He was always hopping off on some air trip; when he arrived in any country in the world (except Russia) he was given an ovation. If there was an earthquake or a disaster of any kind, he would fly to the place; the people would receive him with touching acclaim. He could help them. He was their friend. He was America.'

Mickey Rooney

Like most child stars, Mickey Rooney's misfortune was that he had to grow up – though he was well into his 20s when the decline hit (which made it harder): his small stature had kept him a teenager longer than most teenagers. He says in his autobiography (1967): 'In the year 1938 I had starred in eight pictures. In the years '48 and '49 together, I starred in three. . . . The American public was not clamouring for my work.' Yet for a while he had been the biggest drawing card of them all.

He was born in Brooklyn in 1920, the son of a vaudeville couple: at the age of two he joined their act and three years later he was touring with Sid Gold's dance act. An appearance in a tear-jerker called 'Mr Iron Claw' led him to be cast as a midget in *Not to Be Trusted* (26), followed by a Colleen Moore vehicle, *Orchids and Ermine* (27). He trouped as Joe Yule Jr, his real name, but was now re-christened Mickey McGuire by Radio, who hired him to play in a series of shorts featuring a strip cartoon character of that name, from 1927 onwards: *Mickey's Midnight Frolic*, *Mickey's Mixup*, *Mickey the Romeo*, etc. He made over 40 before the series was dropped in 1933, but in the meantime he was prevented from using Mickey McGuire as a professional name for other work, and someone at Universal suggested Mickey Rooney. He was there to make *My Pal the King* (32) starring Tom Mix. As Rooney he got a featured part in *Fast Companions* and was 'the big surprise' (Photoplay). But fame was a long way off. He had small parts at various studios: *Sin's Pay Day*, *The Beast of the City*, *High Speed*, *The Big Cage* (33, a Clyde Beatty feature), *The Life of Jimmy Dolan* and *The Big Chance*. At MGM he played Eddie Quillan as a boy in *Broadway to Hollywood*, which starred Alice Brady and was an expensive item as most of it was scrapped and filmed again. Still at Metro Rooney was in *The Chief*, and then he moved over to Universal for three: *Beloved* (34), *I Like It That Way* and *The Love Birds*, supporting Zasu Pitts and Slim Somerville. He was also in a serial with Beatty, *The Lost Jungle*.

At MGM Selznick had noticed him and thought his cockiness made him ideal to play Clark Gable as a boy in *Manhattan Melodrama*. They signed him on a week-to-week basis. He was loaned to Universal for *Half a Sinner* with Joel McCrea and to Columbia for *Blind Date*, and then, after *Chained* and *Hide-Out*, MGM put him under long-term contract. His next three were on loan-out: *The County Chairman* (35) at Fox, *The Healer* at Monogram with Ralph Bellamy, and his much-liked Puck in Warners' *A Midsummer Night's Dream*; he then played the kid brother in *Ah Wilderness!*, the first version of Eugene O'Neill's 'happy' family play, and a beautiful film. He supported Jean Harlow in *Riff Raff* and Freddie Bartholomew in Selznick's *Little Lord Fauntleroy* (36): and the contrast of the young English gentleman and the American toughie was so winning that Metro teamed them again in *The Devil Is a Sissy*. He starred for the first time in a B at Warners, *Down the Stretch*, as a jockey, with Patricia Ellis, and gave a beautiful performance as the cabin boy who befriends Bartholomew in *Captains Courageous* (37).

In March 1937 MGM released *A Family Affair*, a very modest version of a minor Broadway play called 'Skidding', about Judge Hardy (Lionel Barrymore), his wife (Spring Byington), their son Andy (Rooney) and their life in the small town of Carvel. Louis B. Mayer (if not the public) liked it so much that a sequel was ordered. Meanwhile, he did *Slave Ship*, again at sea, with Wallace Beery at 20th, *The Hoosier Schoolboy* at

Mickey Rooney as Puck in A Midsummer Night's Dream (*35*).

Monogram, *Live Love and Learn*, *Thoroughbreds Don't Cry* as a jockey – his first co-starring film with Judy Garland, and *Love Is a Headache* (38). *You're Only Young Once* reunited the Hardy family, with Lewis Stone and Sara Haden this time as the parents, and Ann Rutherford coming in as Andy's crush: good wholesome family entertainment, and exhibitors asked a beaming Mayer for another one.... *Judge Hardy's Children*: more money was spent, lifting it from B product to programmer level.

He was featured in *Hold That Kiss* starring Maureen O'Sullivan and Dennis O'Keefe, whom MGM at that point considered would be their next big star, and then opposite Bartholomew in another formula film, *Lord Jeff*; while Garland was added to that other formula, *Love Finds Andy Hardy*. 'The best of it is that love not only finds Andy Hardy but finds him being played by Mickey Rooney . . . he's the perfect composite of everybody's kid brother' (Frank S. Nugent); '. . . an exuberant performance' (Howard Barnes). He gave another good performance, touching if conventional, as the young punk reformed at *Boy's Town*: in this instance he didn't steal the picture, but he took *Stablemates* from Wallace Beery. In this respect he was a threat to all the big stars at MGM, and then, suddenly, after *Out West With the Hardys*, he was a star in his own right: he turned up at third in the top 10; and was awarded a special Oscar.

The studio had already put him into *The Adventures of Huckleberry Finn* (39); he was rushed into *The Hardys Ride High* and *Andy Hardy Gets Spring Fever*, then he and Garland were the *Babes in Arms*, a pleasant musical about a second generation of vaudevillians. It betrayed the Rodgers and Hart original, as James Agate pointed out, adding, 'I am a great admirer of this young gentleman who, when he likes, has more power and pathos than almost anybody else on the screen today.' 'Mickey Rooney can act the legs off a centipede' said The Sunday Times (London). The public agreed: at the end of 1939 Rooney was the biggest attraction in the US and second in Britain; he was top in both countries in 1940 and 1941. In 1940 MGM negotiated a new contract, at $1,000 a week, plus $25,000 per film, plus other moneys reckoned to amount to another $50,000 per year. But after *Judge Hardy and Son* he had his first flop as a star, *Young Tom Edison* (40), a quiet, old-fashioned rural drama; though *Andy Hardy Meets Debutante* soon made up for it. Garland was in the latter, and the two of them continued their calf-love in *Strike Up the Band*. They were a good team, he brash and she wistful and both brimming with vitality and keenness, and they played beautifully together. He did *Andy Hardy's Private Secretary* (41) and *Men of Boy's Town*, and then the two of them were reunited for *Life Begins for Andy Hardy* and *Babes on Broadway*.

Of that one, Dilys Powell wrote: 'It may be argued Mr Rooney, with his extraordinary (though to me not pleasing) talents, has for

Strike Up the Band (*40*). *Said The New York Times: 'Roll out the red carpet, folks, and stand by. That boy is here again, the Pied Piper of the box-office, the eighth or ninth wonder of the world, the kid himself–in short, Mickey Rooney. With a capable assist by Judy Garland. . . .'*

some years now had nothing to learn except, perhaps, reticence', and The New York Times cavilled: 'Mickey doesn't leave much room for anybody else.' He was, indeed, increasingly like a male, adult Shirley Temple: singing, dancing, clowning . . . imitations, always a Big Scene where he cried or made others cry; and it was all increasingly mechanical. Still, in Britain in 1942, the readers of Picturegoer voted him their favourite star (followed by Spencer Tracy, Deanna Durbin, Gary Cooper, Clark Gable and Bette Davis). That year he was in *The Courtship of Andy Hardy*, *A Yank at Eton* (with Bartholomew now supporting him), and *Andy Hardy's Double Life*; then in Clarence Brown's good film of William Saroyan's hokey *The Human Comedy* (43), in *Girl Crazy* with Garland, and he compèred the all-star show which made *Thousands Cheer*. In 1944: *Andy Hardy's Blonde Trouble* and *National Velvet* (conceivably his first adult role). Then he joined the Army.

He returned with *Love Laughs at Andy Hardy* (46), but it wasn't a success; nor was *Killer McCoy* (47), where, as a young boxer (it was a remake of Robert Taylor's *The Crowd Roars*), MGM tried to give him a new image. *Summer Holiday* (48) failed too, and was withdrawn from many cinemas; but the critics had liked it – Rouben Mamoulian's musical version of *Ah Wilderness!* with Rooney as the elder brother this time. He did a less enjoyable musical, *Words and Music*, the story of Rodgers and Hart – 'played with fantastic incompetence by Tom Drake and Mickey Rooney' (The New York Times). And Time: '. . . Mickey Rooney runs his own narrow gamut between the brash and the maudlin, tottering finally to a ludicrous death on the rain-pelted sidewalk.' At UA he did a racing drama, *The Big Wheel* (49) and, then as Bosley Crowther put it (in 'The Lion's Share'), he 'took to complaining about his billing, about his roles. He was angry and particularly caustic because he had not been cast in *Battleground*. Finally, the studio settled his contract.' By his own admission, Rooney was bumptious and big-headed at this time. He appeared at the London Palladium and in night-clubs over the next few years; and again got mixed notices. Part of the trouble was that the qualities which had sat well on him as a youngster now began to look like aggressiveness; and he was the same off-screen as on, which meant that he made enemies.

He set about re-building his career with the expected energy, but the independent company he formed (with backing from an ex-exhibitor) made only a series of duds: *Quicksand* (50), *The Fireball*, *He's a Cockeyed Wonder* and *My Brother the Outlaw* (51), 'woefully miscast' – Variety. He relegated himself to the second feature fold with *The Strip*, and then did three of the early efforts of Richard Quine: *Sound Off* (52), *All Ashore* (53), a musical, and *Drive a Crooked Road* (54), a good one. In 1953 the tide turned a little when he co-starred with Bob Hope in *Off-Limits*, but the same year he was also in *A Slight Case of Larceny* with Eddie Bracken, and then in *The Atomic Kid* (54). He was fourth-billed in a big one, *The Bridges of Toko-Ri* (55); was in the maudlin *The Twinkle in God's Eye*; got good notices for a war picture, *The Bold and the Brave* (56), where he had a very funny crap-playing scene; took over Donald O'Connor's old role with the talking mule, *Francis in the Haunted House*; and co-starred in an old-hat melo about oil-drillers with Jack Carson, *Magnificent Roughnecks*.

Rooney continued to announce plans with himself as producer, star, writer, director or a combination of any of them, but few of them materialized and those that did, did so without éclat (like *My True Story*, which he directed in 1950). He continued to do his Mickey Rooney act in clubs, and went into TV; on TV he had a great success in a play called 'The Comedian' which resulted in a CBS contract. It was clear that he would do almost anything to recover his former glory, but at the same time he began to acquire a nice reputation as a character actor: as the bullet-headed sergeant in *Operation Madball* (57) and as gangster *Baby Face Nelson*, Don Siegel's exciting thriller. But when MGM unaccountably revived the old series, *Andy Hardy Comes Home* (58), nobody welcomed him. There followed: *A Nice Little Bank That Should Be Robbed* with Tom Ewell; *The Last Mile* (59), an unsuccessful remake of the old prison drama that Preston Foster had once done; *The Big Operator*, in the title role; *Platinum High School* and *The Private Lives of Adam and Eve* (60), both Albert Zugsmith junk, the latter co-directed by the two of them; *King of the Roaring Twenties* – Arnold Rothstein, played by David Janssen; *Breakfast at Tiffany's* (61), unconvincing as a Japanese; and *Requiem for a Heavyweight* (62), in a superb performance as Anthony Quinn's buddy. If he had been as good in *Its a Mad Mad Mad Mad World* (63) it might have been that much more bearable. He was fine in Roger Corman's good but little-seen *The Secret Invasion* (64), but there was little to be done with *How to Stuff a Wild Bikini* (65) and little more with the British *24 Hours to Kill* or *Ambush Bay* (66). He then went to Italy to make *The Devil in Love* with Vittorio Gassmann; returned

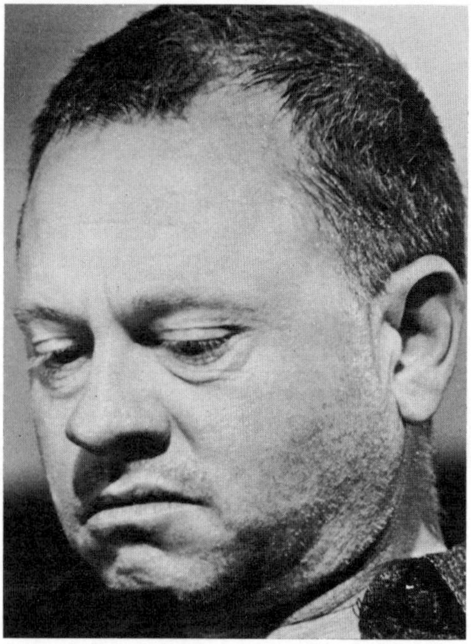

Rooney in one of the several fine, judicious performances he has given since he became a character actor: The Last Mile *(59), a prison drama.*

to the US for *The Extraordinary Seaman* (68), *Skidoo* (69), *The Comic*, *80 Steps to Terror*, as a drunk, and *The Cockeyed Cowboys of Calico County* (70), eighth-billed in this whimsy starring TV favourite Dan Blocker.

Rooney's personal life has been as chequered as his professional one. When he filed a bankruptcy petition in 1962 it was disclosed that he had earned over $12 million – and much of the money he had been paid as a child had been in trust funds; but he had also been married six times. He married for the seventh time in 1969. When MGM were in difficulty in 1970, according to Variety, he offered to take over the reins, promising to make 20 films for $20 million. The offer was refused.

Rosalind Russell

In the musical 'Wonderful Town', in an awkward moment, trying to make conversation, Rosalind Russell said 'I was re-reading "Moby Dick" the other night....' Pause. 'I haven't picked that book up in years....' Still no response. 'It's worth picking up again.' Still no response. Desperately: 'It's about this *whale*.' To anyone who's read 'Moby Dick' the moment was unforgettable; and Russell's delivery as preserved on the Original Cast album is a source of never-ending delight. But then, Russell has an enviable record of stylish and poised light comedy playing, and she has given some neat serious performances. Unfortunately – too often in recent years – she has seemed sometimes to be trying to kill her reputation.

She was born in Waterbury, Connecticut, in 1912, and studied at the AADA in New York. According to some sources she appeared in the 'Garrick Gaieties' of 1926, but her first considerable professional experience was in stock at Saranac Lake in 1930, playing 26 parts in 13 weeks. In 1932 she got a Broadway chance in 'Talent', and that led to an engagement with the Theatre Guild, acting in and around New York. She was in a Broadway revival of 'The Second Man' when Hollywood became interested. Universal paid her fare out to Hollywood, but by the time they got around to thinking about her, MGM had tested her and signed her: not that that studio was very interested until she had scored a hit in LA in 'No More Ladies', put on by the Metro drama coach. She was given a small part as the Other Woman in the Myrna Loy-William Powell *Evelyn Prentice* (34), followed by hardly more important roles in *The President Vanishes* (Paramount, with Edward Arnold), *Forsaking All Others*, *The Night Is Young* (35) and *West Point of the Air*.

Her first chance came when she was given the lead in *The Casino Murder Case*. It was only a B (Paul Lukas as Philo Vance) but drew attention to her, and, after a part the following month in *Reckless*, caused her to be cast as the contrasting woman in Clark Gable's life in *China Seas*: Jean Harlow was the other. Then, when Loy refused to do *Rendezvous* with Powell, Russell replaced her. Picturegoer thought that Loy 'has perhaps more natural charm, but Rosalind Russell is a distinct competitor'. Russell herself said years later: 'I was always the threat, you see, to all the great women stars at Metro and they certainly were legion.' She was loaned to 20th for *It Had to Happen* (36), starring opposite George Raft, and *Under Two Flags* as Claudette Colbert's rival, the upright lady; was featured with Robert Montgomery in *Trouble for Two*; and loaned to Columbia for *Craig's Wife*. She was much too young to play the house-proud Harriet Craig in this adaptation of George Kelly's play, but her performance was much praised.

MGM started giving her better parts: with Montgomery in *Night Must Fall* (37) and in a comedy, *Live Love and Learn*. Both were steps forward, but there was a recession with *Manproof* (38) which starred Loy, and *Four's a Crowd* at Warners, starring Olivia de Havilland. She was then sent to Britain to play Robert Donat's wife in *The Citadel*, an

Rosalind Russell as Craig's Wife *(36)*

His Girl Friday (*40*): *Cary Grant as the editor and Rosalind Russell as his star reporter and ex-wife. She is now on the point of re-marrying– Ralph Bellamy, in the centre of the picture and looking (understandably) worried: he won't get her at the end.*

agreeable performance, correctly accented–and the film's success didn't hurt her either. She was with Montgomery again in *Fast and Loose* (39); then fought the studio to play the catty gossip, Sylvia, in *The Women*. To some observers, she stole the film, though the performance, at Cukor's behest, was remarkably unsubtle–thus anticipating her recent work.

However, her playing in *His Girl Friday* (40) is a really superb piece of work, a lesson to all aspiring actresses. If every artist can give one great performance, that's hers. The film was, under Howard Hawks's direction, an updating of 'The Front Page', with Russell in the formerly male part of Hildy Johnson, ace-reporter. There were reputedly backstage rows at Columbia while her part was beefed up to the size of Cary Grant's, but it doesn't show: a very funny film. There was a whole spate of comedies, most of them above average and all much of a muchness. Here's Russell herself (in two different interviews): 'I played–I think it was 23–career women. I've been every kind of executive and I've owned everything–factories and advertising agencies and pharmaceutical houses. . . . Except for different leading men and a switch in title and pompadour, they were all stamped out of the same Alice in Careerland. The script always called for a leading lady somewhere in the 30s, tall, brittle, not too sexy. My wardrobe had a set pattern: a tan suit, a grey suit, a beige suit, and then a negligee for the seventh reel, near the end, when I would admit to my best friend on the telephone that what I really wanted was to become a dear little housewife.'

The titles: *Hired Wife* with Brian Aherne at Universal; *No Time for Comedy* with James Stewart at WB, a rich and warm performance though the film itself had third-act willies; *This Thing Called Love* (41) at Columbia with Melvyn Douglas; and the last three under her contract: *They Met in Bombay* with Gable (only the first half was intentionally funny), *The Feminine Touch* with Don Ameche and *Design for Scandal* with Walter Pidgeon. At Paramount, Russell did *Take a Letter Darling* (42)–which Katharine Hepburn had turned down–with Fred MacMurray as her secretary; and then she signed a five-year non-exclusive pact with Columbia. She had left MGM because she felt she was swamped by the other ladies, but she was irrevocably typed; and her career went gently downhill. Not, however, with the agreeable *My Sister Eileen* with Aherne and Janet Blair, from a hit Broadway play. *Flight for Freedom* (43) wasn't much, though, a fiction based on the loss of aviatrix Amelia Earhart in the Pacific–but Russell, of course, had a happy ending. *What a Woman!* with Aherne was very ordinary, and she was off the screen after that for more than a year.

She returned with something more serious: *Roughly Speaking* (45) with Jack Carson, a saga of 'an independent woman' (for WB at a fee of $200,000); and *Sister Kenny* (46), a sanctimonious peek at a great figure, played by her in the most obvious way (dewy-eyed and invincible while young, crusty and imperious when old). In between, *She Wouldn't Say Yes* (45) to Lee Bowman, then she was a mixed-up war-widow in *The Guilt of Janet Ames* (47). And then, *Mourning Becomes Electra*, O'Neill's re-telling of Sophocles, reverently filmed by Dudley Nichols with Katina Paxinou, Raymond Massey *et al.* It flopped in the US and sneaked into Britain five years later. Russell, however, was Oscar-nominated (presumably due to her courage). Better was a melo, for her own short-lived independent company, about a Broadway actress, *The Velvet Touch* (48), but it didn't do well. She took another sabbatical, until *Tell It to the Judge* (49): Variety said she flavoured 'the pic with a sophistication that ranges between brashness and sweetness', but her career was really in the doldrums and two more unfunny films didn't help: *A Woman of Distinction* (50) and *Never Wave at a Wac* (52). She could play this stuff blindfolded.

Hollywood had written her off. In 1951 she toured in 'Bell Book and Candle' and in 1953 was invited to do a Broadway musical of *My Sister Eileen*, 'Wonderful Town'. It made her the toast of the Great White Way; she got a Time cover and innumerable awards – and Hollywood wanted her back. Now that she was a *musical* star Paramount constructed *The Girl Rush* (55) for her, but it was a poor film and few went to see it. The other Hollywood bash was her first character part, the spinster aunt in *Picnic*: it was not the sort of performance likely to elicit further offers, so she went back to New York for a play wrought from Patrick Dennis's funny 'Auntie Mame'. Many actresses subsequently played the part, but she was the only choice for the film version (58): it was a huge money-maker in the US but wasn't much liked elsewhere.

Most of the films that followed haven't been liked anywhere, and Russell's overplaying, in mostly character parts, have netted her as poor a set of notices as anyone ever reaped: *A Majority of One* (61), as a Jewish matron; *Five Finger Exercise*, Peter Shaffer's play ruined and – 'Rosalind Russell has never been more campy, a large statement' (Dwight Macdonald); *Gypsy* (62) and *Oh Dad Poor Dad Mama's Hung You in the Closet and I'm Feeling So Sad* (66). Most of these properties were owned by her husband, Frederick Brisson, the theatrical producer. *Gypsy* wasn't, and indeed Russell wasn't bad in it; but it was one of the weakest box-office musicals in years (because audiences resented Ethel Merman not being in her original part?) *Oh Dad Poor Dad* was so bad that it didn't get more than a dozen bookings.

Gypsy (*61*) *was a musical about the early life of stripper Gypsy* Rose Lee (*Natalie Wood*), *and how she was driven by a mother with devouring theatrical ambitions* – *Rosalind Russell in her best late performance. The man is Karl Malden.*

Also in 1966 there was a 'nun' film, *The Trouble With Angels*, and that was successful enough in a modest way to give vent to a sequel, *Where Angels Go Trouble Follows* (68) – but few people heard of that, or of Russell's other 1968 movie, *Rosie*. In 1970 she appeared in a spy spoof, *The Unexpected Mrs Pollifax*, and doubtless she will go on until she gets that elusive Oscar.

George Sanders

Over the past 35 years George Sanders has done a roaring trade in what Stephen Potter called Oneupmanship. On screen, George has seldom stopped sneering. Claude Rains was more dapper, Basil Rathbone more villainous, Clifton Webb more supercilious, Vincent Price more arrogant; but, for an elegant assumption of superiority over the other cast-members, George wins hands down. He has made an extraordinarily successful career out of it, moreover, which isn't easy for even a top supporting actor if you've only one string to your bow. In fact, suave he may always have been, but he has managed a wide variety of parts, including a fair run of romantic leads.

He was born in St Petersburg in 1906; his father was a rope manufacturer, his mother a British horticulturist. The family fled to Britain during the Revolution, and Sanders was educated at Brighton College and at Manchester Technical College, specializing in textiles. He was in the textile business for a while, then became involved in a tobacco venture in South America. This didn't turn out at all well, and on his return to Britain there seemed nothing for it but the stage. He had his voice coached and landed a small role in 'Ballyhoo'; followed by parts in 'Further Horizon' with Edna Best, 'The Command Performance' with Dennis King and Noël Coward's 'Conversation Piece' (34). He finally got a small film part, in *Find the Lady* (36), followed by the lead in *Strange Cargo* – gun-running; he had a brief flash as a Greek god in *The Man Who Could Work Miracles*; and then another good part, moustached, as Eugene Pallette's assistant in *Dishonour Bright*, which starred Tom Walls. He also made *The Outsider*, which wasn't released for a couple of years.

The producers of *Strange Cargo*, British and Dominions, had signed Sanders to a long-term contract, but when their studio burned down they let him go and he went to Hollywood to try his luck there. He was tested by 20th for the role of Madeleine Carroll's unscrupulous foppish husband in *Lloyds of London* (37). It was a small role, but he impressed, and was signed to a long-term contract. There were three feature parts: *Love Is News*, again as a fop; *Slave Ship*; and *The Lady Escapes*, as a French writer, a B starring Gloria Stuart. He was then starred opposite Dolores del Rio: *Lancer Spy* and *International Settlement* (38). Both are war stories, in both he is masquerading as something he isn't, and in both she falls in love with him unwillingly. He did *Four Men and a Prayer* and *Mr Moto's Last Warning*, one of the series which starred Peter Lorre as a Japanese detective. RKO had their eye on Sanders for their own B series, based on Leslie Charteris's 'The Saint', and they negotiated with 20th to share Sanders on a 'featured' basis. 'The Saint' was a smooth adventurer, and Sanders played him well: *The Saint Strikes Back* (39) and *The Saint in London*. The latter was made in London, and there for 20th Sanders appeared in a remake of Will Rogers's, *So This Is London*, but never shown in the US.

In Hollywood he was hunted down, along with Francis Lederer, by Edward G. Robinson, in *Confessions of a Nazi Spy*: already in *Lancer Spy* he had pretended to be a Hun, with Prussian crew-cut and monocle, and until the end of the war this was an impersonation he was to repeat a couple of times a year. He did it again in *Nurse Edith Cavell*. He was in *Allegheny Uprising*, supporting John Wayne; *Green Hell* (40), supporting Douglas Fairbanks Jr; *The Saint's Double Trouble*; *Rebecca*, as that lady's caddish cousin, a small but satisfying part; *The House of Seven Gables*, also at Universal, co-starring with Margaret Lindsay in a cheap version of Nathaniel Hawthorne's novel; *The Saint Takes Over*; *Foreign Correspondent*, as a nice young Englishman, a part that Rex Harrison had turned down; and *Bitter Sweet*, as the Hun-headed Viennese officer who tried to ravish Jeanette MacDonald on the dance floor. He was the baddie again in *Son of Monte Cristo* at UA with Louis Hayward, and it was Hayward who was to take over 'The Saint', after Sanders's last fling, *The Saint at Palm Springs* (41) – and he relinquished the part in turn to Hugh Sinclair.

Before that one, Sanders was in the arms of Ingrid Bergman in *Rage in Heaven* (41), but being nice didn't last and after it he was a nasty Nazi again in *Manhunt*, tracking Walter Pidgeon. RKO then gave him a new series, 'The Falcon', which was heavily indebted to 'The Saint': *The Gay Falcon* and

George Sanders in an unaccustomed role – as romantic hero: in Rage of Heaven *(41) with the young, radiant Ingrid Bergman.*

A Date With the Falcon, both with Wendy Barrie. He was one of the Nazis attempting to take over Africa in *Sundown*, with Gene Tierney, and stayed in the tropics for *Son of Fury* (42) – that was Tyrone Power, and a bit more escapist, but Sanders remained bad. *The Falcon Takes Over*, and then Sanders was more gainfully employed, trying to get Norma Shearer from Robert Taylor in *Her Cardboard Lover*, and in an episode of *Tales of Manhattan*. His first real star part in a real A was in *The Moon and Sixpence*, a good shot at Maugham's novel by director Albert Lewin, with Sanders effective as Strickland-Gauguin.

This put him among Hollywood's more important actors, and RKO reluctantly agreed to release him from 'The Falcon', with *The Falcon's Brother*: his own brother, Tom Conway, was in it, and Sanders got killed during the action ... so Conway took over the series. Sanders supported Tyrone Power again in *The Black Swan*; then starred with Gail Patrick in a B, *Quiet Please Murder*. He was a Nazi again in *This Land Is Mine* (43) – Renoir – from which it was a come-down to *They Came to Blow Up America* with Anna Sten; *Appointment with Berlin*, as an undercover agent; *Paris After Dark* with Brenda Marshall, helping the French underground; and *Action in Arabia* (44), with Virginia Bruce. In the midst of these low-budget actioners on behalf of the war effort he was the nice detective in *The Lodger* (44) with Laird Cregar, and he was now to eschew the B field for some years: it could not be said, however, that the features in which he was top or second-billed were among the best of their time. He seemed to have a compulsive desire to make films; or as he told a reporter years later: 'I am not one of those people who would rather act than eat. Quite the reverse. Larry Olivier was born with the desire to act. I was not. My own desire as a boy was to retire. That ambition has never changed.'

The war was ending and for a change Sanders made three period pieces: *Summer Storm* with Linda Darnell, from a Chekhov story; *The Picture of Dorian Gray* (45) from Wilde's novel, as Lord Henry Wooton – the

Call Me Madam *(53), with Ethel Merman repeating her Broadway success as a Washington hostess appointed ambassadress to a mythological European kingdom (it was based on the real-life Perle Mesta). George Sanders was the country's foreign minister, at whom she set her cap.*

first of his later world-weary, cynical portrayals – in a film about which opinion seems equally divided between terrible and fair; and *Hangover Square*, with Cregar and Darnell at 20th, his last under his contract. *The Strange Affair of Uncle Harry* was almost his only out-and-out sympathetic part, as a mild little man driven to murder when his sisters try to break up his romance. *A Scandal in Paris* (46) and *The Strange Woman* were two more (undistinguished) period pieces and so was *The Private Affairs of Bel Ami* (47), from Guy de Maupassant, with Sanders as Bel Ami, but *The Ghost and Mrs Muir*, supporting Rex Harrison, was better. He did *Lured* with Lucille Ball and was the obvious choice to play Charles II in *Forever Amber*, the film's only decent performance. After an absence he was in an inferior version of a play by Oscar Wilde, *The Fan* (49), as Lord Darlington; and de Mille's *Samson and Delilah*, as the heavy, and a rather jaded one at that. A European trip brought one of the early, misguided 'international' films: *Black Jack* (50), with Herbert Marshall and Patricia Roc, made in Spain by France's Julien Duvivier; Variety thought them all 'ill at ease' and Sanders 'not virile' enough as an action-hero.

Fortunately, a new phase in his career opened with *All About Eve* in which he played 'that venomous fish-wife Addison de Witt', as Bette Davis put it, the cynical drama critic: the dialogue had a bite and he did beautifully, winning a Best Supporting Oscar. He was immediately given two similar roles, in *I Can Get It for You Wholesale* (51) opposite Susan Hayward and *The Light Touch* with Stewart Granger (of the cast Sanders alone had it, but this dialogue defeated even him). Another European trip dissipated what his career had gained through *Eve*: *Ivanhoe* (52), made in Britain, as Robert Taylor's Norman rival, de Bois Guilbert; and a couple more hybrids, *Assignment Paris* with Marta Toren, and even more so, Rossellini's *Viaggio in Italia/Voyage to Italy* (53) with Ingrid Bergman, which Sanders thought a muddle and hated making. However, in Hollywood he landed a plum role, the lead opposite Ethel Merman in *Call Me Madam*, one of the year's big musicals. It was almost his last important leading role.

After *Witness for Murder* (54) he decorated a bevy of historical pieces: *King Richard and the Crusaders*; *Jupiter's Darling*, a musical with Howard Keel; *Moonfleet* (55); *The Scarlet Coat* and *The King's Thief*. Then some indifferent programmers: a sudser with Rock Hudson, *Never Say Goodbye* (56); Fritz Lang's *While the City Sleeps*; *That Certain Feeling* with Bob Hope; *Death of a Scoundrel*, which co-starred his then wife, Zsa Zsa Gabor; and *The Seventh Sin* (57), a dreary remake of *The Painted Veil* with Eleanor Parker. After which he made his career mainly in Britain or on the Continent: *The Whole Truth* (58); *From the Earth to the Moon* and *That Kind of Woman* (59) with Sophia Loren (both in Hollywood); *Bluebeard's Ten Honeymoons*; *A Touch of Larceny*; *Solomon and Sheba* and *The Last Voyage* (60). It has to be said that seldom was Sanders other than his old tired self. During the late 50s there was a TV series called 'The George Sanders Mystery Theatre'. In 1958 Ronald Colman's widow Benita Hume became his third wife; in 1960 he published his 'Memoirs of a Professional Cad'.

And began a series of pictures almost entirely lacking in distinction: *Cone of Silence*; *Village of the Damned*, from John Wyndham's novel 'The Midwich Cuckoos'; *The Rebel*, which was a starring vehicle for Tony Hancock; *Five Golden Hours* (61) with Ernie Kovacs; *Le Rendezvous*; *Operation Snatch* with Terry-Thomas; Disney's *In Search of the Castaways* (62); *Cairo* (63); the unfunny *The Cracksman*, supporting yet another British comic, Charlie Drake; *Dark Purpose* (64); *A Shot in the Dark*; *The Golden Head*, a flop Cinerama adventure made in Hungary; *The Amorous Adventures of Moll Flanders* (65); *The Last of the Secret Agents*; *The Quiller Memorandum* (66); *Good Times* (67) starring Sonny and Cher; *Rey de Africa/One Step to Hell*, an Italian-Spanish melodrama; *The Candy Man*; *Warning Shot*; *The Best House in London* (68) and *The Body Stealers* (69). His career seemed to be on the upgrade slightly with a role in Huston's *The Kremlin Letter* (70), though playing a queer drag queen; and then he went on to make *Rendezvous with Dishonor*.

Norma Shearer

Acting ability is incidental to screen stardom. Says Kirk Douglas playing a film director to star Lana Turner in *The Bad and the Beautiful*: 'You acted badly, you moved clumsily, but the point is however bad you were, every eye in the audience was on you.' It is debatable whether this is true of Turner, but it is supremely true of Norma Shearer, one of her predecessors at MGM ('The Studio of Stars' and 'More stars than there are in Heaven'). Take a film like *Escape*: within minutes of her appearance, you can see it. It's a wet film, and her part is ridiculous, but there it is – the poise, the authority, the extra-something of the real star.

She wasn't beautiful but, to take a line from Noël Coward, she made millions believe she was. Robert Morley recalled in his memoir: 'Shearer reminded me of Marie Tempest.... Both were small women possessed of immense determination, and few illusions about themselves. Both were stars because they had decided that that was what they wanted to be. Shearer had many more obstacles to overcome than Mary [*sic*]. Her voice wasn't particularly pleasing and she was by no means a good actress but her determination was, if anything, the greater. She could leaf through a hundred photographs of herself in a couple of minutes and know exactly which should be passed for publication.... Her knowledge of lighting was as great as the cameraman's, and she could tell from a dozen lights bearing down on her which was likely to cast the wrong shadow.'

This is an assessment considerably at odds with the contemporary image of Shearer: the epitome of glamour, of femininity, of beauty. Fans claimed she was a great actress. She was certainly popular. From 1930 through 1934 she featured prominently in all box-office polls, and only lost her place because of diminished activity. In Britain in 1932, 1934 and 1937 she was voted the top woman star in the Bernstein Questionnaire, and quite incredibly, on the last occasion, had had only one not-too-popular film released since the last poll.

She was born in Montreal in 1904, and trained as a pianist: she began in show business by playing the piano in a music-shop and later in a nickelodeon. When her father's business failed, her mother took her and her sister to New York to try to get them into films. It was a hard grind, but when the girls faltered, Mother was there pushing them. They worked as extras – Norma was somewhere *Way Down East* (20) and a minor member of *The Restless Sex*. Her early credits are confused, but her first film is usually given as *The Flapper*: certainly that year she had a featured part in *The Stealers* – and was noticed by Irving Thalberg, who was to be the major personality in her life and career. She had small parts in Universal's series, *The Leather Pushers*, which led to leads in *The Man Who Paid* (22); *The Devil's Partner*; *Channing of the Northwest* opposite Eugene O'Brien; *A Clouded Name* (23) and *Pleasure Mad*, as a flaming deb.

At this time, while considering a contract offer from Hal Roach, she was offered a better one by Louis B. Mayer (just before the amalgamation with Metro and Goldwyn). Reports vary: either her agent approached Thalberg (Mayer's right-hand man), who remembered her, or a modelling job brought her to Mayer's attention. She was signed at $150 a week, and immediately loaned to First National for *The Wanters* with Marie Prevost. Curiously, she spent her first year

Those of Norma Sh performances most o seen today – her Eliz Barrett Browning, h Juliet and her Marie Antoinette – represe as a demure and suff heroine, but for mos screen career she pla sophisticated woman world, as in A Lady Chance *(29), left, w Johnny Mack Brown*

out on loan: *Lucretia Lombard* with Irene Rich; *The End of the World* (24); *The Wolf Man* at Fox with John Gilbert; *Broadway After Dark* with Adolphe Menjou; *Blue Waters* as a squaw; and *Empty Hands* as a bored socialite, with Jack Holt.

It was a busy year, and the fan-magazines were full of pictures of Shearer: her clothes were *très chic* and her hair bob imitated. And her thesping was beginning to be admired. Her first at MGM was *Broken Barriers* with Menjou and James Kirkwood, but the important one was *He Who Gets Slapped* with Lon Chaney and John Gilbert. Shearer was Consuelo, the bareback rider, and though the part was overlookable, the film was successful enough for Shearer and Gilbert to be re-teamed in *The Snob*, a small-town story centred on a deathbed marriage. MGM decided to build her, mostly in rather soggy dramas. However, *Excuse Me* (25) with Conrad Nagel was a gay comedy about some honeymoon predicaments on a boat-train. There followed: *Lady of the Night*, in a dual role as a society girl and an ex-reform-school girl; *Waking up the Town*, at UA, with Jack Pickford as co-star and director; *Pretty Ladies*, a backstage tale; *A Slave of Fashion* with Lew Cody, as a girl who impersonates another in order to wear glamorous clothes; *The Tower of Lies* with Chaney; *His Secretary* (26) with Cody again, as a plain girl who burgeons into a raving beauty; and *The Devil's Circus*, the first American film directed by Benjamin Christiansen. Then: *The Waning Sex*, a comedy with Nagel; *The Demi-Bride* (27) as a dare-devil French girl, with Cody; *Upstage*, a vaudeville story; and *After Midnight*. She was now a good second-grade star, earning $1,000 a week: she had asked for a revised contract, starting at this figure and rising to $5,000 over a five-year period. Mayer agreed, intending to drop her before then; but early in 1927, after a brief romance, she and Thalberg were married.

Thalberg was the boy wonder of Hollywood, the producer of some of its greatest pictures: his talent for selecting people and properties has become one of Hollywood's enduring legends. His contribution has been downgraded, but the facts are for it: most Thalberg productions, lavish and ambitious, were critical and box-office hits. They had Class. Today many of them seem like empty mansions, but of their time, and of their kind, they were unbeatable. Thalberg was an inveterate believer in the star system, and there was no star he believed in so deeply as his wife. His handling of her career was a triumph.

His plan was to wean Shearer from the ultra-sophisticated parts she had been playing, so she became the gay heroine of Lubitsch's version of *The Student Prince* with Ramon Novarro. Next, she yearned (as of old) for *The Latest From Paris* (28), but was a simple girl again as *The Actress*, Pinero's 'Trelawney of the Wells', following a

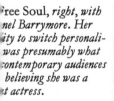

ree Soul, *right, with nel Barrymore. Her ity to switch personali- was presumably what contemporary audiences believing she was a t actress.*

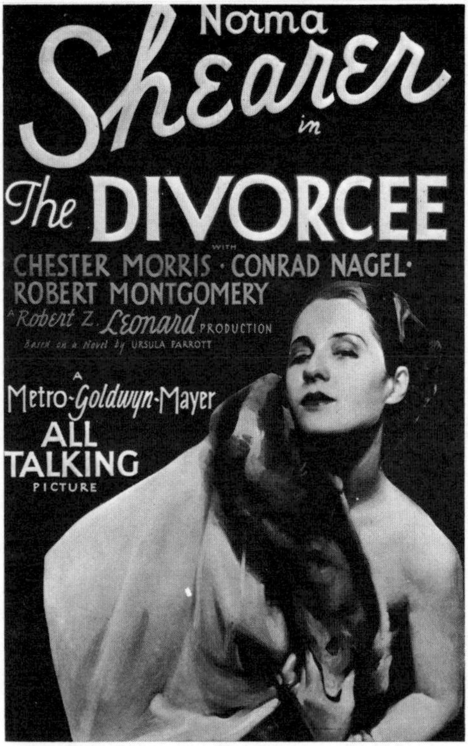

Norma Shearer's popularity was so great and her later appearances so rare that each film was considered a major filmgoing event – and none was more major than Marie Antoinette *(38), made, lavishly, after a two-year absence. She wasn't much like the Queen, but only pedants minded.*

Broadway revival; then again she was a demi-mondaine, *A Lady of Chance* (29), a part-Talkie. But with the coming of the Talkies, the sweet, gentle Shearer was put in abeyance. After some months of uncertainty, Thalberg cast her as a brassy showgirl, the Mary of *The Trial of Mary Dugan* (29): it was a smart move – her voice was *supposed* to be like that. The cast rehearsed beforehand as for a play, and it was photographed like one: Shearer came through with flying colours. She was then the light-fingered Mrs C. in Frederick Lonsdale's *The Last of Mrs Cheyney*, an intelligent performance, and Juliet, to John Gilbert's Romeo, in the balcony scene included in *The Hollywood Revue of 1929* (*not* an intelligent performance).

Her success in her first Talkies launched Shearer into a series of even more ultra-sophisticated parts. For the next couple of years she specialized in restless, over-wealthy, over-sexed (by contemporary standards) women-of-the-world. In the dramas she suffered, in the comedies She Learned the Meaning of True Happiness. The titles tell everything: *Their Own Desire* (30) and *The Divorcee*, both with Robert Montgomery. The latter was strong meat, and it was said that Shearer begged to be allowed to do it: it brought her a Best Actress Oscar. In *Let Us Be Gay* (made and released before *The Divorcee*) she was again a frump who becomes a beauty, and in *Strangers May Kiss* (31) a woman who fails to realize, as Montgomery put it in the film, that 'a man will mix anything else, but takes his women straight'. This was the first under a new contract, at $6,000 a week, one of the highest fees in Hollywood.

The box-office bonanza continued with *A Free Soul*, partly because audiences wanted to see Clark Gable knock her around, after which she and Montgomery knocked each other around, in *Private Lives*, taking on the Coward-Lawrence parts without too heavy a loss – she succeeded in looking entirely wrong and sounding exactly right. She attained screen respectability again in the diluted screen transcription of *Strange Interlude* (32) – even if the role did call for her to have a bastard by lover Gable – and sainthood almost in *Smilin' Through*, an unnecessary but well-done (and popular) version of the lachrymose old warhorse, with Fredric March and Leslie Howard. She was billed unequivocally 'The First Lady of the Screen' a tag the MGM publicity mill hung on her for years to come.

If Shearer aspired to be the Lynn Fontanne of movies she was encouraged by MGM, who even made her up to look as Fontanne had looked in the original production of Idiot's Delight *(39): but it was still a triumph for her – and Gable. The others are Peter Willes and Pat Paterson.*

Her screen appearances became rarer, but Metro ensured that each of them was an event, like Garbo's. *Riptide* (34) was a tense drama with Herbert Marshall as her jealous husband, and Montgomery; *The Barretts of Wimpole Street* another drama that had been a hit in London and New York and was a hit for MGM ('Oh papa, let us get this over and forget it – I can't forgive myself for having made the whole house miserable over a tankard of porter'). Charles Laughton was papa, March was Robert Browning, and Shearer a virginal Elizabeth: her performance – all shining eyes and elegant hand gestures – now makes the film unwatchable.

Since that balcony scene with Gilbert, Shearer had had a hankering to make a film of *Romeo and Juliet* (36). Her husband indulged her, Howard co-starred, and $2 million were spent on it. It didn't make a nickelsworth of profit, but was good enough (Cukor directed) to do MGM some good (i.e. prestige), and it didn't do Shearer any harm. There had been scoffers before the event, but apart from being too old for it, her performance was OK, netting her a fifth Oscar nomination. At this point Thalberg died, and it was thought that she would retire; but she signed a new three-year contract with MGM at $150,000 per picture. It wasn't until 1938, however, that *Marie Antoinette* appeared, and Thalberg had worked on it already for some years before he died. It was reasonably accurate, but the facts were so telescoped to make it appear that the Revolution was caused by the disputed purchase of a diamond necklace. Shearer was charming and sympathetic, at home among MGM's marble halls, but in the wrong film.

Robert Morley, who played Louis XVI, says that rumours were rife that the Front Office wanted to do Shearer in; that this film was to be sabotaged in an attempt to persuade Shearer to sell her large stock in Loew's Inc. (left to her by Thalberg): at the last minute her chosen director, Sidney Franklin, was replaced by W. S. Van Dyke, known as a fast worker. He was allegedly getting a large sum for every day he was under schedule. Thalberg and Mayer had not been friendly for some while before the former's death, and tentative plans had been made for Thalberg to go independent, taking half the stars with him. Whether Shearer knew there was a plan to oust her is not known, but Bosley Crowther ('The Lion's Roar') says that she realized that her regal position was threatened – and was uncertain whether she wanted to continue without Thalberg's aid.

However, she did owe the company five films, and when offered two that had been big Broadway hits, she jumped at them – both comedies: *Idiot's Delight* (39) in a blonde page-boy wig, with Gable, and Clare Boothe Luce's fable about women at Reno, *The Women*. Both were among the year's brightest movies. These followed: *Escape* (40) with Robert Taylor, and two synthetic comedies, *We Were Dancing* (42) from Coward's playlet (she was poor as the Countess), with Melvyn Douglas, and *Her Cardboard Lover* with Taylor. Both flopped. She told Crowther: 'On those two, nobody but myself was trying to do me in.' She also admitted that, whatever unhappiness there was at the studio, those two films – plus her rejection of two others—were fatal. The two she turned down were *Mrs Miniver* and *Gone With the Wind* (she had accepted Scarlett provisionally in 1938, but nixed it when her fan-clubs disapproved).

So she did retire, and married again (a skiing instructor). Offers were made (Bette Davis wanted her for *Old Acquaintance*) and in 1946 the ill-fated Enterprise Studio announced that she had signed with them for two films – which were not made. She lives today, a wealthy woman, among the upper echelons of Hollywood society.

Ann Sheridan

One of the great screen teams was James Cagney and Ann Sheridan. It wasn't written up at the time and, as far as is known, legions of fans didn't write in to ask Warners to reunite them. Indeed, they were only really *teamed* together twice, in two not very notable films, *City for Conquest* and *Torrid Zone*. They complemented each other perfectly, he all bombast and bounce, she more knowing, sharp and disillusioned. The dialogue might have gone something like this: She: 'Why, I don't take no line like that from some jumped-up jerk like you', and Cagney: 'Listen, sister, you take what you can get around here and like it!' She was a good all-rounder but was at her most direct as a Brooklynesque hash-slinger, quick with the wise-cracks, slamming back at Cagney (or George Raft or Pat O'Brien). It wasn't a type that was appreciated too much, when great acting was confused with Greer Garson or Norma Shearer; nor was Sheridan in the same league as Betty Grable as a pin-up. Warner Bros christened her 'The Oomph Girl', and the name stuck, but she really was too warm, too lush and too genuinely glamorous to compete with the other tinny girls. Her singing voice, for instance, a warm contralto, is much more in tune with today's taste. At all events, she never quite received her due.

She was born in Denton, Texas, in 1915, and was completing her studies at the North Texas Teachers' College when, unbeknownst to her (so her studio biographies insisted) her family entered her in a 'Search For Beauty' contest. She won the regional prize, which was a trip to Hollywood and a Paramount test: which resulted in a contract and a small part in a film called, unsurprisingly, *Search for Beauty* (34). She appeared in publicity under her own name, Clara Lou Sheridan, a 'Paramount Star of the Future'. She was photographed for thousands of cheesecake pictures and a few motion-pictures. Some old sources list as many as 20 credits during her Paramount period, but when that studio decided to star her they issued a list of 12, in most of which she was an extra (*Bolero*, *It's a Gift*, etc.). She had bit parts in only *Come on Marines*, *Murder at the Vanities* (that was left on the cutting-room floor) and *Home on the Range* (35), at which point it was decided to build her, and 'Clara Lou' became 'Ann': she was given a featured part (seventh on the cast-list, a big leap) in *Behold My Wife*, followed by co-starring assignments in a couple of unimportant movies, *Car 99* with Fred MacMurray and *Rocky Mountain Mystery* with Randolph Scott. She headed down the cast-list again with *Mississippi*, *The Glass Key* and *The Crusades* and after these Paramount dropped her.

She managed to get a lead in a Grade Z Western, *Red Blood of Courage* with Kermit Maynard, and in a B at Universal, *The Fighting Youth*. She had been out of work a long time and was contemplating returning to Denton when the WB casting director sent for her. He had seen her in something and thought she had possibilities. She signed with Warners. The association began gloomily with *Sing Me a Love Song* (36) starring James Melton and Patricia Ellis, but then she had neat roles in *The Black Legion* (that was the Ku Klux Klan) as a weepy girl; *The Great O'Malley* (37) as star Pat O'Brien's schoolteacher girlfriend; and *San Quentin* as a gangster's moll. She had passed the test, and was starred in a series of Bs: *Wine Women and Horses* with Barton MacLane; *The Footloose Heiress*; *Alcatraz Island* (38) with John Litel; *She Loved a Fireman* with Dick Foran; and *Little Miss Thoroughbred*. She had a featured part in Dick Powell's *A Cowboy From Brooklyn*, then returned to Bs: *The Patient in Room 18* with Patric Knowles, *Mystery House* and *Broadway Musketeers*.

Sheridan after War discovered she had 'oomph'.

But just before that last one two other films had changed things. She had been loaned to Universal for *A Letter of Introduction*, and Universal had discovered she had glamour; and she had done a good gutsy job in Cagney's *Angels With Dirty Faces* (the Angels were the Dead End Kids). Till then WB had seen her as a nice healthy outdoor girl; now they cast her as the girl who started John Garfield on the path to crime in *They Made Me a Criminal* (39) and she was convincing. So she was cast as the saloon floozie in Errol Flynn's *Dodge City*, and on the strength of that was cast opposite Dick Powell in a modest musical, *Naughty But Nice*, converting him, a professor, to swing. At the same time the 'oomph' publicity stunt went into action, and Sheridan was publicized up-hill and down-dale. At the end of the year observers were saying that she had a helluva lot to live up to (Sheridan herself didn't care for the 'oomph' tag, but she had been in Hollywood too long to fight it). Certainly her other 1939 films didn't suggest she was a new Harlow or Clara Bow or whoever: *Winter Carnival* with Richard Carlson, on loan to Wanger; *Indianapolis Speedway* with O'Brien; *Angels Wash Their Faces*; and *Castle on the Hudson* (40) with Garfield.

Her biggest chance came when she was top-starred in *It All Came True*, a pleasant comedy-drama written by Louis Bromfield, with Bogart in support; then she co-starred with Cagney in *Torrid Zone* and (top-billed) with Raft and Bogart in *They Drive By Night*.

Torrid Zone *(40), directed by William Keighley, was a cliché-packed drama set in the tropics, with plantation boss Pat O'Brien scrapping with foreman James Cagney (below) over saloon singer Ann Sheridan. What made it memorable was the playing of the principals and its racy dialogue.*

Here was her waitress, discovered by Raft in a truck-drivers' café and complaining of the boss's hands, 'all ten of 'em'. It was an appealing performance: a young girl, basically innocent, who'd been around too many men to care much, but who'd drop the hard-boiled surface if the smile was the right one. She was equally good, if not very different, in *City for Conquest*, as an ambitious dancer with whom boxer Cagney tries to keep up: disillusionment for them both, and you could see it in the first reel.

Honeymoon for Three (41) co-starred her with George Brent, and in life they had one without a third party – a long one, on Brent's yacht, while waiting for WB to capitulate over Sheridan's salary demands (she was getting only $600 a week despite the 'oomph' publicity, and wanted $2,000). They didn't. Sheridan went back to work anyway, after six months, and did *Navy Blues*, vamping Jack Oakie, and *The Man Who Came to Dinner*, in the part of the actress (based on Gertrude Lawrence). Made and shown simultaneously was *King's Row*, one of the year's big successes: Sam Wood's emotional small-town drama and considered a classic by many (with Ronald Reagan, Robert Cummings, Betty Field and Claude Rains). Now her salary did begin to rise. *Juke Girl* (42) was a dreary piece set among the migratory workers in Florida, and *Wings for the Eagle* was set in California's giant Lockheed aircraft factory (with Dennis Morgan and Jack Carson); much more cheerful was *George Washington Slept Here* with Jack Benny, about a couple settling in a derelict cottage. She didn't have much to do in an Errol Flynn actioner, *Edge of Darkness* (43), and in the all-star *Thank Your Lucky Stars* she had only one song ('Love Isn't Born It's Made') but was pretty sensational doing it.

Her biggest bid for the big time was a musical, *Shine On Harvest Moon* (44), based on the life of Norah Bayes; at last Sheridan was getting the sort of stuff that Grable and Hayworth were getting at their studios – only her musical wasn't in colour except for the finale. It was popular, due perhaps to more plot (too much, in fact) than was usual in backstage musicals, and because Sheridan suggested that old-time magic more convincingly than Grable or Hayworth. She followed with a couple of comedies, *The Doughgirls* from a Broadway success, and *One More Tomorrow* (46), a re-hash of *The Animal Kingdom* with topical references (wartime profiteering). Warners were at that time having great success with their

Ann Sheridan up to her neck in trouble in The Unfaithful *(47): she's just killed – in self-defence – the man with whom she committed one small wartime indiscretion. Now's the time to Confess All to husband Zachary Scott.*

women's fictions (Davis, Crawford) and they passed a couple on to Sheridan, *Nora Prentiss* (47) with Robert Alda and Kent Smith, and *The Unfaithful*: both fulfilled their functions, and were successful. She looked bored throughout *Silver River* (48) – and who could blame her? – an Errol Flynn Western and it completed her contract.

She started free-lancing from a position of strength, and netted co-starring roles opposite Gary Cooper in *Good Sam* (48) – a humorous and compelling performance – and Cary Grant in *I Was a Male War Bride* (49), where she was even better. She said: 'There have been three phases in my career – and the present one, playing comedy and to hell with the oomph, is by far the most satisfying.' Her subsequent films were not, however, prepossessing, and they certainly don't indicate that she had free choice of material. In 1950 she sued RKO for breach of contract, claiming that the lead in *My Forbidden Past* should have gone to her and not Ava Gardner. She had moved to Mexico in 1948, and journeyed to Hollywood for a batch of routine films: *Stella* (50) at 20th, a comedy with Victor Mature; *Woman on the Run* at Universal with Dennis O'Keefe; *Steel Town* (52) with John Lund and Howard Duff; *Just Across the Street* with Lund; and a musical, *Take Me to Town* (53), with Sterling Hayden – 'Ann Sheridan at the peak of her comedy finesse as a dance hall girl' (Steven H. Scheuer). She suffered, along with the other waning stars at Universal, from the fact that their films played double bills and weren't shown to the press.

Somewhat forgotten, she made a B, *Appointment in Honduras*, and another 'little' picture, *Come Next Spring* (56), a bucolic tale which received some attention (her 'mother' performance stood out like a beacon). Later that year she walked away with *The Opposite Sex*: the likes of June Allyson and Joan Collins weren't in her class, but the film was a mess and did nothing for her career. She made only one other film, a useless British safari triangle, *Woman and the Hunter* (57): mercifully, it got few bookings.

She turned to the stage and appeared with Franchot Tone and Dan Dailey in the special presentation of 'The Time of Your Life' which played in Brussels during the 1958 Exposition. She did stock in the US, including a tour of 'Kind Sir' with Scott McKay, who became her third husband. On TV she had two series, an NBC daytime soap opera, 'Another World', and the much more successful (but equally dire) 'Pistols and Petticoats', which was current when she died early in 1967. In London The Times obituary said: 'Without ever quite achieving the mythic status of a super-star, she was always a pleasure to watch, and, as with all true stars, was never quite like anyone else.'

Sylvia Sidney

There were five female stars ruling the roost at Paramount in the early 30s: Dietrich, Miriam Hopkins, Carole Lombard, Claudette Colbert and Sylvia Sidney. Sidney was dark, petite, moist-eyed and an exceptional emotional actress. Unlike the others, she hardly survived leaving the studio, and this would be more understandable had her off-screen personality been anything like the characters she played, which were vulnerable to the hundred and one buffetings that the plots had them heir to. She revolted against these parts by being glamorously groomed in her publicity stills, but even then she hardly conformed to the ideal beauty of the time. She was not a star from the same mould as the other ladies.

She was born in New York City in 1910 of a Rumanian father and Russian mother; studied elocution and dancing as a child and at the age of 15 entered the Theatre Guild School. Her stage debut was in Washington in 'The Challenge of Youth' (26) and the following year she took over a lead in 'The Squall' in New York. There were stock engagements in Denver and more parts in New York (she was once in a play called 'Crime' with the also unknown Kay Francis, Chester Morris and Robert Montgomery). She first attracted major attention in 'Gods of the Lightning' (28) and Fox proposed a featured role in a courtroomer, *Through Different Eyes* (29): an outstanding performance as a murderess, but there were no other offers and she went into stock in Rochester, NY.

She scored in New York in 'Bad Girl', and Paramount offered the lead in *An American Tragedy* which Eisenstein was to direct from Theodore Dreiser's novel; it was postponed and she was offered the role intended first for Clara Bow and then Nancy Carroll in *City Streets* (31), a nice young girl whose nice boy-friend (Gary Cooper) gets caught up in New York racketeering. Paramount offered a contract, seeing her as Bow's successor (for which she was clearly unsuited). She became an unmarried mother in *Confessions of a Co-Ed*, and in a similar plight (pregnant) in *An American Tragedy*, re-activated under Josef Von Sternberg. The author, in common with critics and audiences, disliked the picture (he sued Paramount for infidelity and lost), but it stands up well today – almost as well as the

Sylvia Sidney as the centre of attraction in Mamoulian's City Streets *(31). On the left are boyfriend Gary Cooper and gang boss Paul Lukas; on the right, Stanley Fields, Wynne Gibson and Guy Kibbee.*

1951 remake, *A Place in the Sun*, which seems to be in parts a carbon copy; and just as that was notable for the way Shelley Winters played the slum girl victim, so is this for Sidney's performance in the same part. Phillips Holmes was the boy, and Frances Dee the socialite.

A flop the film may have been, but it doomed Sidney thereafter to a series of waifs in overalls, put-upon girls in back streets. Goldwyn borrowed her for such a role (preferring her to the already announced Carroll) in his stagey Vidor-directed version of Elmer Rice's *Street Scene*; back at Paramount she was one of the *Ladies of the Big House* (32), and in the remake of *The Miracle Man* (Hobart Bosworth had the Chaney part); then suffered in more elegant surroundings in *Merrily We Go to Hell*, a marital drama with Fredric March. In the non-operatic *Madame Butterfly* she had to cope with dialogue like 'Honorable Lieutenant, the most best nice man in all the world' (needless to say, it was a terrible film). Then it was back to rags (she was an ex-con) in *Pick-Up* (33). *Jennie Gerhardt* was a poor version of another Dreiser novel, but the author thought hers 'a beautiful interpretation'. She was promised a film of his 'Sister Carrie' but instead was put into *The Way to Love* with Chevalier–then, because she was ill, had to be replaced by Ann Dvorak (there was some controversy as to whether she was really sick or not). She returned to be a *Good Dame* (34) with March, and the *30 Day Princess*, a welcome (and accomplished) stab at comedy in a dual role, with Cary Grant. After a silly drama in which she was a squaw, *Behold My Wife* (35)–proclaimed Gene Raymond–she did another comedy, *Accent on Youth*, from Samson Raphaelson's play about the boss (Herbert Marshall) with a crush on his secretary. The situation was paralleled in real life according to Norman J. Zierold in 'The Movie Moguls': 'When Schulberg [the head of Paramount] fell unreservedly in love with Sylvia Sidney, it broke up his marriage....'

Nevertheless (or therefore?) Sidney left Paramount and signed an exclusive contract with Walter Wanger (then releasing through Paramount), whose grandiose plans for her included *Ivanhoe* (as Rebecca, with Gary Cooper) and *Wuthering Heights* (with Charles Boyer as Heathcliff to her Cathy). Had either been made, things might have gone differently. She did make as classy a clutch of movies as any artist was ever landed with, but only in what she considered to be constricting parts: *Mary Burns Fugitive* with Melvyn Douglas; the Technicolored *The Trail of the Lonesome Pine* (36); Fritz Lang's *Fury* at MGM as Spencer Tracy's girl-friend; Hitchcock's exciting *Sabotage* in Britain with Oscar Homolka; Lang's *You Only Live Once* (37); and Wyler's *Dead End*. Lang's *You and Me* (38) was summed-up (or put down) thus by Photoplay: 'You have seen Sylvia Sidney and George Raft hounded by the law too many times to find any freshness in this story of two paroled convicts who marry each other. George

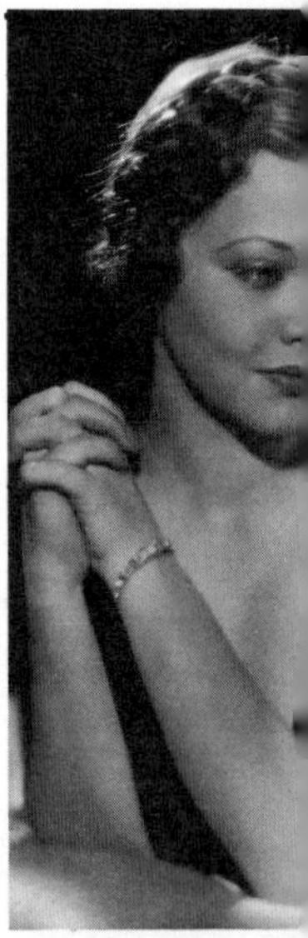

Fritz Lang's Fury *(36): Sylvia Sidney as the worried girlfriend of Spencer Tracy, arrested – wrongly – on a kidnapping charge, and starting off a wave of mob violence – the 'fury' of the title.*

backslides to his old gang, is brought up short by the little woman.'

Wanger then cast her in *Algiers* with Boyer, but she refused to play another weepy, underprivileged heroine, and the part went to Sigrid Gurie. The film, as such, didn't matter to her, because she considered herself an actress and not a star. For some while she had told reporters that she disliked being a property, an investment, and that she disliked Hollywood. She bought up her contract and went to New York to re-establish herself as an actress (she said later that more than anything else Wyler had killed her self-confidence as same). She appeared on the stage with Franchot Tone in 'The Gentle People' and in . . . *One Third of a Nation* (39), an indie dealing with slum problems – the sort of subject she was supposedly running away from, and certainly an inferior film by any standards. It got very few bookings.

She returned to Hollywood to re-establish herself there, but did very few films. She played opposite Humphrey Bogart in *The Wagons Roll at Night* (41), as a fortune-teller in a circus; in 1945 she appeared with James Cagney in *Blood on the Sun*, dressed to the nines as a Eurasian vamp: it looked like a new career for a new Sidney. For Paramount she starred in the interesting film version of Lillian Hellman's *The Searching Wind* (46), but the next two were not quality productions: *Mr Ace* with Raft, and the remake of *Love From a Stranger* (47) as the would-be murder victim of husband John Hodiak. She has since made only three films: *Les Miserables* (52) as Fantine, and also for 20th, *Violent Saturday* (55); and a B for Universal, *Behind the High Wall* (56).

But she has become one of the most hard-working of stage actresses. At the height of her film career she returned to New York to play in 'To Quito and Back' (37) by Ben Hecht; 'Pygmalion' and 'Tonight at 8.30' in stock (38) and Irwin Shaw's 'The Gentle People' (39). In recent years, in stock and on tour (and in New York) she has played in some of the best roles in modern and classical drama, from Auntie Mame to Lady Bracknell. A few of the many titles: 'The Four Poster', 'Enter Laughing', 'Angel Street' ('Gaslight'), 'Joan of Lorraine', 'Anne of a Thousand Days', 'Black Chiffon', 'The Madwoman of Chaillot' and 'The Rivals'; she has also had good parts on TV, in dramas and guesting in series; and has published a book on needlepoint. She was married three times: the first and second husbands were Bennett Cerf and Luther Adler.

Ann Sothern

The title is disputatious, but Ann Sothern had the best claim to the crown of Queen of the Bs. Perhaps she didn't (quite) make the most, but she was easily the best and most popular of the many ladies who toiled in those particular vineyards. The industry thought so well of her that she was given, belatedly, some 'A' chances, recognition long overdue for a star who was warm and direct and versatile. Most of her stills show her as a glycerine-eye-lidded siren, but in her films she was really a friendly, jolly girl.

She was born in 1909 in Valley City, North Dakota, educated in Minneapolis and at the University of Washington. Her mother was a soprano and singing coach, so it wasn't surprising that Sothern decided to go on the stage. She tried Hollywood first and got a bit in *The Show of Shows* (29) at Warners; then MGM tested her and signed her. The fan-magazines of the period carry pictures of her, brunette, under her own name of Harriet Lake, but Metro used her in only one film, *Doughboys* (30), and then dropped her. She went to Broadway, got a small part in 'Smiles' (30) and then the lead in 'America's Sweetheart' (31), the Rodgers and Hart satire on Hollywood; she was in 'Everybody's Welcome' and toured in the Gershwin's 'Of Thee I Sing'. She returned to Hollywood to try again, and considering that she had acquired a small reputation, rather surprisingly changed her name to Ann Sothern: as such she appeared briefly in *Broadway Through the Keyhole* (33), which starred Russ Colombo, Texas Guinan and Blossom Seeley. Lucille Ball – whose early career was similar to Sothern's – was also in it.

Then Columbia signed her to a contract, and starred her opposite Edmund Lowe in *Let's Fall in Love* (34), as a side-show girl promoted to stardom for devious reasons: a minor musical with only one other distinction – it was Harold Arlen's first Hollywood score. Sothern, however, was not quite up to her material. She was loaned to Paramount for the Ruggles-Boland *Melody in Spring*, and then flung into the following Bs: *The Party's Over* with Stuart Erwin; *The Hell-Cat*, a newspaper story with Robert Armstrong; and *Blind Date*, Cinderella-stuff with Neil Hamilton and Paul Kelly. Goldwyn gave her a chance of sorts when he cast her and George Murphy as the juvenile leads in Eddie Cantor's *Kid Millions*: she had little to do except sing, but she scored; as she did in another musical, 20th's *Folies Bergere* (35), as Maurice Chevalier's tempestuous chorine girl-friend.

Columbia put her into *Eight Bells* with Ralph Bellamy, and then into two musicals: *Hooray for Love* at RKO, a poor imitation of *42nd Street*, with Gene Raymond, and notable mainly for a Harlem sequence with Bill Robinson and Fats Waller; and their own *The Girl Friend* with Roger Pryor, which was not the Rodgers and Hart show of that title, but a Napoleonic burlesque. Sothern and Pryor were married in 1936. She then returned to Bs: *Grand Exit* with Lowe; *You May Be Next* (36) with Lloyd Nolan; *Hell-ship Morgan* with George Bancroft; and *Don't Gamble With Love* with Bruce Cabot. Thoroughly dissatisfied with this lot, Sothern left Columbia and signed an exclusive seven-year contract with RKO. They wanted to reunite her and Gene Raymond and did, in *Walking on Air*. They loaned her to Paramount for *My American Wife*, to play an heiress in this sharp satire on snobbery, with European Count Francis Lederer, then cast her with Raymond again, as *The Smartest Girl in Town*. She went to MGM for *Dangerous Number* (37), opposite Robert Young, and to 20th for *Fifty Roads to Town*, where she and Don Ameche played 'with captivating lightness' (Picturegoer). There was: *There Goes My Girl* with Raymond; *Super Sleuth* with Jack Oakie; *Danger Love at Work* at 20th with Jack Haley; *There Goes the Groom* and *She's Got Everything* (38) with Raymond. In reality, she and Raymond didn't get on at all, at all; and

Ann Sothern spent years in B pictures before MGM gave her some good chances, as in Panama Hattie *(42), playing a brassy nightclub singer. Ethel Merman had done it on Broadway.*

she disliked intensely the colourless films they made together. She felt she was being over-exposed and in poor pictures and sought a loophole in her contract.

As a consequence, she was unemployed for most of 1938. Then Wanger cast her in *Trade Winds*, second lead to Joan Bennett, as a Sadie Thompson-like character, wisecracking, a loser, the tart with the heart of gold. She stole the picture, and MGM signed her for a property they had once bought for Jean Harlow and since had been unable to cast, *Maisie* (39): Sothern played a resourceful if scatterbrained blonde always getting in and out of scrapes. Already it was planned as the first of a series, although as a film it was saved only by her performance. MGM signed her to a seven-year exclusive contract. As a B-picture star, it could not be expected that she would rank with their top-rank ladies, but neither was she palmed

Miss Sothern disappeared from the screen for over ten years; returned, with charm, personality and professionalism undimmed, in films such as Sylvia *(65), which starred Carroll Baker.*

off with low-budgeters. Later MGM did give her top vehicles but most of her early films for them were halfway efforts, able to top the bill at smaller situations or play second feature at bigger houses. There were manifold reasons why she could not be catapulted into A pictures at once, for all the respect that filmgoers and critics had for her: other interested parties – exhibitors, leading men, studio executives, etc. – had to be wooed into accepting her as an A-budget talent. She was with Franchot Tone in the inaptly named *Fast and Furious*; and 20th borrowed her for *Hotel for Women*, a melodrama that at one point in its career was known as *Elsa Maxwell's H for W*. She was with William Gargan visiting Lewis Stone in Damon Runyon's hilarious *Joe and Ethel Turp Call on the President*; and then was *Congo Maisie* (40), a loose working-over of *Red Dust*.

At Warners she had a good dramatic part as a wisecracking moll in *Brother Orchid*, and was then *Gold Rush Maisie*. She was also *Dulcy*, a programmer from a Broadway play by George S. Kaufman and Marc Connelly; then *Maisie Was a Lady* (41). Then she was *Ringside Maisie* with George Murphy, called *Cash and Carry* in Britain: all the subsequent films in the series lost the name Maisie in that country, suggesting that there was not a huge popularity for them. They were now Bs: but Sothern got the lead in a big musical, *Lady Be Good*, alongside Eleanor Powell – and it was Sothern's film all the way. There was *Maisie Gets Her Man* (42), and then the coveted lead in another big musical, Cole Porter's *Panama Hattie*, with Red Skelton; but none of the quality of the Broadway original survived, and it was merely a succession of turns. Maybe if it had gone better, she would have got more parts. Instead, she returned to programmers: *Three Hearts for Julia* (43) with Melvyn Douglas; and *Swing Shift Maisie*. In *Thousands Cheer* she did a sketch with Lucille Ball and Frank

Morgan; in *Cry Havoc*, along with Margaret Sullavan and Joan Blondell, she gave a remarkable performance; then *Maisie Goes to Reno* (44)....

Her marriage had ended in divorce in 1942 and in 1943 she had married another B picture star, Robert Sterling; she was away from the screen while daughter Trisha was born, and worked only intermittently thereafter: *Up Goes Maisie* (46) with Murphy, and *Undercover Maisie* (47) with Barry Nelson, the last of the series. She did a big Warner Musical with Dennis Morgan, *April Showers* (48)–and, once again, if this had been a better film it might have opened up a big new career. She looked lovely in colour in MGM's *Words and Music*, guesting and singing–an all too brief appearance. She had then the best film of her career, Mankiewicz's *A Letter to Three Wives*, along with Linda Darnell and Jeanne Crain; but *The Judge Steps Out* (49) at RKO, a romantic drama with Alexander Knox, sent her back a good 10 years (it had been seen in Britain one year earlier, as *Indian Summer*). MGM put her into *Shadow on the Wall* (50) with Zachary Scott, and, pleased with the response to her participation in *Words and Music*, cast her as Jane Powell's mother in *Nancy Goes to Rio*–a fair indication that she was never going to make it, though, in terms of appeal, in that film she left her 'daughter' at the starting-post. In 1953 she made *The Blue Gardenia* and quit Hollywood.

Gratifyingly, she did very nicely in TV: firstly in her own series, 'Private Secretary', and later in 'The Ann Sothern Show'. In 1963 she reappeared on the big screen, stout now and deliberately blowsy, as a vicious old bitch in Olivia de Havilland's *Lady in a Cage*; and she gave neat character studies in *The Best Man* (64), *Sylvia* (65) and *Chubasco* (68).

Barbara Stanwyck

Barbara Stanwyck was never one of the great box-office attractions, but in 1944 she was listed by the US Treasury Dept as the highest paid woman in the country (at over $400,000–Bette Davis was second). At that time she had been in movies over 15 years, and the eminence she had reached was rather the result of slogging than by anything showy in the way of performance or publicity. She was to the public exactly what she was to the film companies–reliable. Right from the start she was a thoroughly professional actress. She was de Mille's favourite actress: 'I have never worked with an actress who was more co-operative, less temperamental, and a better workman, to use my term of highest compliment,' and Fritz Lang has said that 'working with Barbara Stanwyck was one of the greatest pleasures of my career'.

These were exactly the qualities she projected on screen: she was accomplished, down-to-earth and self-assured. She was immediately at home in any milieu and in any costume, though dry and perhaps somewhat cynical. With Bette Davis and Joan Crawford, she makes a Hollywood triumvirate of 'strong' women. Like them, in a couple of films she was menaced, the frightened heroine, but it was unlikely casting. She was in her element running the show, directing the traffic. She was/is an incomparably better actress than Crawford, and if she hardly measures up to Davis at her best, she was never as bad as Davis at her worst. In fact, she never gave a bad performance (something, one feels, she would like as an epitaph).

She was born in Brooklyn in 1907, of Scots-Irish parentage, the youngest of five. They were orphaned while she was young, and she was partly brought up by one of the older girls, who was a showgirl. Stanwyck went to work at 13, wrapping parcels, and did a variety of menial jobs before trying the stage: she wanted to be a dancer, and by sheer grind she made it. At 15, she started in speakeasies, moved on to Broadway and tours; finally landed a straight part–as a dancer–in 'The Noose' (26). The part was enlarged *en route* for Broadway, so that when it reached there she was a 'star'. She became a real star in the next one, 'Burlesque', the classic story of a show-biz marriage on the rocks–she goes up as he, drinking, goes down (a situation she would soon in real life find herself in: but at this time she had just married–comic Frank Fay). She got a small part in a WB Silent, *Broadway Nights* (27), and after her 'Burlesque' long-run she did another film in New York, *The Locked Door* (30), a strong sex drama where she got fourth billing.

'That film was so bad it nearly locked the door of my screen future,' she said later. She accompanied Fay to Hollywood, where he persuaded WB to test her–without result. He went to Columbia (Harry Cohn), offering to pay Stanwyck's salary secretly and the cost of dressing her if they would give her a break: Columbia refused, but did give her a chance in the low-budget *Mexicali Rose*. Fay continued to fight for her, and eventually talked Frank Capra into using her as one of the *Ladies of Leisure* at Columbia. This time the studio liked her and signed her to a contract. Warners borrowed her for *Illicit*, a

Barbara Stanwyck in her first major film role, The Locked Door *(30), with Harry Mestayer, Harry Stubbs and Clarence Burton. They think she's just murdered her husband: she hasn't, but in typical Stanwyck fashion, she sure looks guilty.*

drama about a girl who refuses to marry her lover (James Rennie). Photoplay found it as 'daring as youth' and 'another big triumph for that perfectly grand actress' Stanwyck; but Picturegoer thought 'her accent is unattractive and her acting stilted'. She was a taxi-dancer in the enjoyable *Ten Cents a Dance*, and she was tough and independent. Her reviews now were unanimous: critics found her interpretation refreshing after the 'innocent' way such parts were usually played. With three hits to her credit Stanwyck sued Columbia for more salary, and the matter was settled by sharing her contract with Warners, who wanted her. She divided her time between the two: *Miracle Woman*, as an evangelist, under Capra's direction; William A. Wellman's *Night Nurse*, who was no better than she should be, and *Forbidden* (32), as a librarian in love with a married man (Adolphe Menjou). Picturegoer had changed its mind: 'Barbara Stanwyck is, literally, great. We hear a lot about la Garbo, la Dietrich, la this and la that; but I doubt if any of these publicity-haunted stars could have put so much natural feeling into a part which requires the most sensitive handling and the soul of a true artist.' The film really put Stanwyck on top; when the same magazine listed the top six women stars (Garbo, Constance Bennett, Dietrich, Chatterton, Shearer and Crawford) Menjou himself told the editor that in Hollywood Stanwyck was rated above the last two.

She was then *Shopworn*; was in a remake of Edna Ferber's *So Big*; and in *The Purchase Price*, a marital drama with George Brent, she was a cabaret girl. In *The Bitter Tea of General Yen* (33), which Capra directed, she was an Occidental harboured by lascivious Chinese warlord Nils Asther–and she beautifully conveyed an intrigued sexual repulsion. She was less resistant in *Ladies*

They Talk About, as a hard-boiled gun moll, with Preston Foster; and certainly not at all in *Baby Face*, moving from the stockroom to the executive penthouse. Her image was established: a working girl in recognizable surroundings, but considerably more pushy than the working girls you met in the street. She was much more jaded; she was amoral; and she wasn't, if the crunch came, averse to murder. The Censors saw to it that she suffered at the end, if only by losing her man. The following were mostly melodramas: *Ever in My Heart*, a silly war film with Otto Kruger; *Gambling Lady* (her, with Joel McCrea); a remake of Willa Cather's *A Lost Lady* (34); *The Secret Bride* (35) with Warren William; and *The Woman in Red*, about the girl from the other side of the tracks married into society. During this period she also starred in a stage musical with Fay, 'Tattle Tales' (33), but it didn't save the marriage.

Her two contracts were up, and she made *Red Salute*, as a college girl attracted – temporarily – by Communism. RKO now promised her better things, and she was *Annie Oakley* for them, under George Stevens's direction. The film is negative, as if waiting for Irving Berlin's score, but The Sunday Times (London) thought the original Annie 'had not the personal fascination Barbara Stanwyck brings to the part'. The RKO contract was non-exclusive, and Stanwyck never in her career tied herself to any one studio, but at this time it was a (typically) bold move. She protected herself with multi-pic deals: *A Message to Garcia* (36) at 20th with Wallace Beery; *The Bride Walks Out* at RKO with Gene Raymond; and *His Brother's Wife* at MGM with Robert Taylor: on the last day of shooting, the crew presented Stanwyck with a scroll describing her 'Number One Actress and Swell Person'. *Banjo on My Knee* at 20th was a very serious piece, though set on a Mississippi riverboat and containing some slapstick. John Ford's version of Sean O'Casey's *The Plough and the*

Stanwyck was one of the few serious actresses who consented to do leggy pin-up pictures for GIs during the war: coincidentally she displayed those legs in a couple of films, playing hard-bitten showgirls. This one was Lady of Burlesque *(43), and her performance was fine too.*

Stars was one of his failures (and wasn't helped by the happy ending tacked on); *Internes Can't Take Money* (37) co-starred Joel McCrea; *This Is My Affair* co-starred her with Taylor again, soon to become her second husband. She refused to be typed: she went from the classic weepie *Stella Dallas* (for Goldwyn) to *Breakfast for Two*, a comedy with Herbert Marshall; from another sombre piece, the remake of *Always Goodbye* (38), a mother-love drama with Marshall, to the marvellous madcap comedy of *The Mad Miss Manton* with Henry Fonda.

And she did a Western, de Mille's *Union Pacific* (39) with McCrea and Robert Preston. Preston has said: 'A lot of people feel like I do about Barbara Stanwyck – or Missy, as we all called her. Bill Holden was one newcomer she helped a great deal, and she helped me. She was the first big star with whom I worked, and later, when I got involved with others who were selfish or put on the big star act, I didn't get bugged because Missy had shown me that all stars aren't like that. It's true that nobody else was quite like her. For 20 years I haven't stepped on a stage, or in front of a camera, without wearing the St Genesius medal she gave me. If he was the patron saint of actors, she, in my opinion, is the patroness.' (Quoted in Films in Review.) The film on which she helped Holden was *Golden Boy*. After that she played a shop-lifter, one of her best performances, in *Remember the Night* (40); and she was splendid in *The Lady Eve* (41), again up to no good as a cardsharp cheating Henry Fonda; this was Preston Sturges's funny comedy with, at one point, Stanwyck doing a breath-taking parody of a British socialite. Capra's *Meet John Doe* with Gary Cooper, and *You Belong to Me*, again with Fonda, were weak ones; but then she was in a good one with Cooper, Howard Hawks's *Ball of Fire* (41), in the title role as a gum-chewing, hip-swinging, slangy showgirl who uses and then falls for meek professor Cooper. She did a similar role equally well a couple of years later, William A. Wellman's *Lady of Burlesque* from Gypsy Rose Lee's 'The G-String Murders': they weren't allowed to use that title. Inbetweenwhiles, Wellman's *The Great Man's Lady* (42), with McCrea again, was one of her drearier films, though it gave her a chance to age; and *The Gay Sisters* (Nancy Coleman and Geraldine Fitzgerald were the others) wasn't much better. Then, after the Gypsy Rose Lee film, she co-starred with Charles Boyer in an episode of *Flesh and Fantasy* (43).

Double Indemnity (44) was probably the peak of Stanwyck's career; Billy Wilder directed, Raymond Chandler scripted from a novel by James M. Cain, about a blonde tramp (Stanwyck) in cahoots with an insurance man (Fred MacMurray) to murder her husband and share the loot: perhaps the best of the 40s black dramas. Her insolent, self-possessed wife is one of the screen's definite studies of villainy – and should (it was widely thought) have won an Oscar over Ingrid Bergman's performance in *Gaslight*.

After that, she was mostly nice, but in several of poor quality – mainly for Warners and Hal Wallis, who had her under joint contract (Warners were paying her $225,000 per film). *Christmas in Connecticut* (45) with Dennis Morgan, and *My Reputation* (46) with George Brent were romantic trifles; and *The Bride Wore Boots*, a comedy with Robert Cummings, was completely unworthy of her. She did play a rich bitch in *The Strange Love of Martha Ivers*, a heavy melodrama and probably her best vehicle of the late 40s (to which period it belongs absolutely); had a conventional sturdy part in a coloured Western, *California*; did an Erich Maria Remarque sudser with David Niven, *The Other Love* (47), and was frightened by Humphrey Bogart in *The Two Mrs Carrolls* and by Errol Flynn in *Cry Wolf*. Time magazine said of the former: 'Miss Stanwyck, who does well enough with a tough, worldly kind of part, is baffled by the sleight

Executive Suite *(53), directed by Robert Wise, was about a struggle for power within a corporate structure. Among those involved were Nina Foch and Miss Stanwyck, in a variation of her latterday 'Woman-in-Possession' image.*

Miss Stanwyck is virtually the only major Hollywood talent that Elvis Presley has played with during his film career: Roustabout *(64). The film wasn't worthy of her but she brought style and authority to her role as the carnival boss.*

of hand required for this one.' She was again miscast (but relaxed) in John P. Marquand's story, *B.F.'s Daughter* (48), and then was frightened again by Burt Lancaster in *Sorry Wrong Number*, dubiously extended from a classic short radio thriller: the additions included establishing the Stanwyck character as a typical Stanwyck character – self-willed, wealthy, obstinate and selfish (so who cared if she did get murdered at the end?). This brought her her fourth Oscar nomination.

The next few were no better: *The Lady Gambles* (49); *The File on Thelma Jordan*; *East Side West Side*, though she gave a thoughtful performance in a hackneyed part – the long suffering wife; *No Man of Her Own* (50) with John Lund; and *The Furies*, at her most determined, squabbling with father Walter Huston – whose playing showed up hers as being wildly conventional. That was her last for Wallis and she went to MGM for two: *To Please a Lady* with Clark Gable and *The Man With a Cloak* (51) as a period Mrs Danvers. In Fritz Lang's *Clash By Night* (52) she was a tramp again, and a weary one – with one of Clifford Odets's more memorable lines: 'Home is where you go when you've seen all the other places.' Marilyn Monroe was in it, and co-star Paul Douglas resented the fuss made over her. 'Its this way, Paul,' said Stanwyck, 'she's younger and more beautiful than any of us.' Then there were some programmers: *Jeopardy* (53); *Titanic*; *All I Desire*; *The Moonlighter* with MacMurray; and, better, *Blowing Wild*, with Cooper. Her last good picture was *Executive Suite* (54) and of the all-star boardroom (Holden, Douglas, Fredric March, Walter Pidgeon, Shelley Winters, Nina Foch) hers was the outstanding performance.

She was, as she implied to Douglas, ageing. She had let her hair go grey and perhaps that was the trouble. Maybe she should have stopped working until a good offer came along, or maybe she was realistic enough to realize that with the onset of the 50s good parts for actresses of her generation were hard to come by: but she went on, bossy and managing as ever, in a series of low-budgeters, each more abysmal than the last. She was the only professional thing about most of them: *Witness to Murder* with Gary Merrill; *Cattle Queen of Montana* with

Ronald Reagan; *The Violent Men* (55) as a ranchhouse Regina Giddens carrying on with Brian Keith and killing husband Edward G. Robinson in a fire by withholding his crutches; and a particularly nasty cheapie, *Escape to Burma* with Robert Ryan. *There's Always Tomorrow* (56) found her trying to pinch MacMurray from Joan Bennett; *The Maverick Queen* was a Republic Western; and *These Wilder Years*, though it played B dates, at least saw her measured against James Cagney. *Crime of Passion* (57) with Sterling Hayden, *Trooper Hook* with McCrea and *Forty Guns* were all, to say the most, duallers.

After a five-year absence she returned as the lesbian madame in the film of Nelson Algren's *A Walk on the Wild Side* (62); Laurence Harvey played the lead and it flopped. Two years later she did a low-budget horror film with (ex-husband) Taylor, *The Night Walkers* (64), but it didn't make a ripple; nor was she in her element in an Elvis Presley vehicle, *Roustabout*. In an interview some years ago, she said: 'It isn't that I don't want to work. The trouble is nobody asks me. Some actresses and actors in my position say they can't find the right roles, but I can't fool myself so easily. . . . I don't let it get me down. I'm not made that way. I'm not giving up. . . . Maybe everything hasn't worked out exactly the way I hoped it would, but I've had more than my share of good times.' Hedda Hopper reported that she advised Stanwyck to try Europe, but that she preferred to stay in her Hollywood home, where she lives with a companion.

Ironically, TV brought her a popularity she hadn't dreamt of. She has done much TV over the past decade, including the short-lived 'The Barbara Stanwyck Theatre' in 1960. But in 1965 she was starred in her own Western hour-long series, 'The Big Valley', which ran four seasons and won her a cluster of awards. They could hardy have gone to a more deserving actress.

Anna Sten

Anna Sten must take her unfortunate place in any anthology of the stars as the prime example of those who never made it. She was unlucky, because she was as comely and as talented as many who did. There had been manufactured stars before, and there would be as long as the studio system lasted: many of them cued as little response from the public as she did. Unfortunately, her mentor Sam Goldwyn produced few films, and couldn't hive her off into supporting roles or second features. He brought her to Hollywood in 1932 as his own candidate to oust Garbo and dropped her after three films. She became known as 'Goldwyn's Folly' and was referred to years later as 'The Edsel of the Movie Industry'.

She was born in 1910 in Kiev, Russia. Her father died when she was 12 and, according to Goldwyn publicity, she 'worked as a slavey in a restaurant'. She appeared in an amateur production of Hauptmann's 'Hanneles Himmelfahrt' when she was 15: Stanislavsky saw her and arranged for her to enter the Russian Film Academy; later she joined his company. She appeared in a few Soviet films: *Girl With the Hatbox* (27), *Storm Over Asia*, *Moscow Laughs and Cries* and *The Yellow Ticket* (28). The latter brought her an offer to go to Berlin for *Der Morder Dmitri Karamazov* (29), produced by Fedor Ozep and directed by Eugene Frenke (whom she married). Sten's Grushenka was a magnificent performance, though dominated by Fritz Kortner as Dmitri; she also did the French version. UFA gave her a year's contract and she made *Bomben auf Monte Carlo*, *Salto Mortale* (with Anton Walbrook; directed by E. A. Dupont), *Captain Craddoc* and *Stürme der Leidenschaft* (with Emil Jannings).

Goldwyn, then contemplating his own version of the Dostoevsky novel, saw this *Karamazov* and decided to sign Sten. 'Here was an accomplished actress and a genuinely individual personality quite unlike the imitation Garbos and Dietrichs who were the characteristic imports of the period' (Richard Griffith). Every studio had to have one sooner or later: Lil Dagover at WB, Gwili Andre at RKO, Tala Birell at Universal, Lilian Harvey at Fox. . . . Goldwyn took no chances. His first task was to have Sten taught English. During two years reams of publicity emanated from the Goldwyn studio – as well as some uncomfortable rumours. It was confidently announced that Sten's American bow would be in *Karamazov* opposite Ronald Colman. In the end it turned out to be a lavish production based on Zola's *Nana*, to be directed by Josef Von Sternberg who had done so much for Dietrich; but it was eventually directed by the reliable Dorothy Arzner. It opened in 1934 to unrestrained critical jeers, partly because the original novel had been tailored (i.e. emasculated) for American audiences. In the end, they stayed away and the film was hopefully re-titled *Lady of the Boulevards* for British audiences. Those that did go laughed at Sten's mangling of English and her

The film that Goldwyn chose to launch Anna Sten in was Nana *(34), the story of a nice girl who becomes a tart after her lover goes to war – only to lose him Forever when he discovers the Truth in the last reel. It was a plot that Hollywood filmed endlessly and one could speculate endlessly on why. The wealthy admirer here is Lawrence Grant successfully coercing her into forgetting the said lover.*

coquettish performance. Today both she and the film are silly together, but there was a little something to suggest that if Goldwyn could do anything about her English she might pull through.

He tried again. It was a version of Tolstoy's *Resurrection*, ably directed by Mamoulian, with Fredric March: a much better film, it did no better business. Goldwyn's headache was increased because Sten was feuding with him over publicity – but she became more co-operative when he signed Miriam Hopkins. He persisted: he offered Eugene O'Neill any amount to write anything he wanted for Sten; then a friend, Edwin Knopf, was commissioned to write something which would win audiences over, 'with due respect for her special liabilities and limitations' (Griffith). The result, *The Wedding Night* (35), was directed by King Vidor, but it never amounted to much, the attachment between a peasant girl and a city-soured married writer. The critics liked it, but even Gary Cooper couldn't save it. The five-year contract was dissolved by mutual agreement. Two years later Goldwyn signed Sigrid Gurie. . . .

It was unlikely that a major studio would pick up such a well-publicized failure, and it was a British studio who did: with Frenke directing, from a story by Ozep about the romance of a Russian peasant girl with an army official (Henry Wilcoxon): *A Woman Alone* (36). Its US bookings were so meagre that there was no difficulty when the British *Sabotage* was released under the same title six months later. Sten was then signed to a Grand National contract, but made only one picture for that company, a B, *Exile Express* (39). Then she had supporting parts in *The Man I Married* (40) and *So Ends Our Night* (41). She was in a Resistance drama, *Chetniks* (43) and in a B spy thriller with George Sanders, *They Came to Blow Up America*, and then in *Three Russian Girls* (44). She has worked very occasionally since: in *Let's Live a Little* (48) and *Soldier of Fortune* (55), in minor parts; but she had star roles in two silly Bs, *Runaway Daughters* (56) and *The Nun and the Sergeant* (62). She lives with her husband in New York.

James Stewart

As a young man, James Stewart's gangling figure and modest demeanour qualified him at once for the real all-American boy – the grocer's clerk, the telegraph boy, even the junior college professor; he was 'so unusually usual' said director W. S. Van Dyke in 1939. As he matured he endeared himself to audiences: comfortable, cool-headed, trustworthy, he was (in the 50s, his best period) the ideal Hitchcock hero. He first made the box-office top 10 in 1950 (in Britain as well as the US), and was in the American list from 1952 to 1959 inclusive – in number one position in 1955 (thanks to Hitchcock); and he popped up again in 1965, though by now he was making strictly formula films – and the quality of performance had deteriorated. He has always been variable. His prized performance in *Mr Smith Goes to Washington* now seems over-stuffed with mannerisms – the drawl, the quirky look of astonishment, the shy smile – but the film now also seems like Capra self-parody, with Stewart insufferably idealistic. The more human the character he plays, the better his acting.

He was born in 1908 in the town of Indiana, Pennsylvania, studied civil engineering and then architecture at Princeton, where he met Joshua Logan. After graduation he joined Logan's University Players, whose members included Henry Fonda and Margaret Sullavan. With Fonda he went to New York in 1932 and began getting small parts in plays ('Carrie Nation',

'Yellow Jack', 'Page Miss Glory', etc.). MGM screen-tested him after a recommendation by Hedda Hopper, and signed him to a long-term contract. He started with a bit as a reporter in Spencer Tracy's *The Murder Man* (35), followed by another in *Rose Marie* (36), as the man got at the end by Mountie Nelson Eddy. Better for him was *Next Time We Love* at Universal with Margaret Sullavan, who had requested him for the part of her husband. He was second lead to Ray Milland and he had similar assignments in *Wife vs Secretary* to Clark Gable and *Small Town Girl* to Robert Taylor. His first lead was a B, *Speed*, and he was one of the men who considered Joan Crawford *The Gorgeous Hussy*. His real break came as Eleanor Powell's leading man in *Born to Dance*, a gob who introduced to the world Cole Porter's 'Easy to Love'. 'There is James Stewart,' wrote Alistair Cooke, 'trying to be ingenuous and charming like Gary Cooper but many tricks and light years behind!' He was the baddie in *After the Thin Man* and then got loaned to 20th for the remake of *Seventh Heaven* (37), wildly implausible as a Paris sewer rat, coping with dialogue like 'Don't ever leave me or like a candle I'll go out.'

The Last Gangster with Edward G. Robinson, *Navy Blue and Gold* with Robert Taylor and *Of Human Hearts* (38) with Walter Huston all kept him a bit off-centre, but the next two gave him fine chances: George Stevens's *Vivacious Lady*, a comedy at RKO with Ginger Rogers, and *The Shopworn Angel*, in Gary Cooper's old part, again with Sullavan. So did Capra's *You Can't Take It With You* with Jean Arthur at Columbia, and Selznick's *Made for Each Other* (39), an intense tale of newly-weds with Carole Lombard. His big breaks so far had been away from MGM, who now offered him only *Ice Follies of 1939*. Said Picturegoer: 'James Stewart is becoming rather stereotyped, he needs to watch out that his engaging naturalness which first singled him out does not develop into forced artificiality.'

But then he came up with as fine a run of pictures as any actor ever had, starting with *It's a Wonderful World*, a crazy comedy with Claudette Colbert. Capra borrowed him again for *Mr Smith Goes to Washington* which, like his earlier *Mr Deeds*, was a modern morality tale, with innocence (i.e. good) triumphing over cynicism (i.e. evil). This also co-starred Jean Arthur and it made Stewart almost as big a star as Cooper; it was one of the year's big hits and won Stewart the New York Critics Best Actor award. Also much prized, metaphorically, was his portrait in *Destry Rides Again* of the untypically quiet and gun-shy sheriff who proves to Dietrich and the other townsfolk that words speak louder than actions: Universal made it, and it was a remake of Tom Mix's first Talkie. At last MGM gave him good material: two good ones with Sullavan–Lubitsch's *The Shop Around the Corner* (40), a comedy mainly concerned with a secret pen-pal romance carried on by a couple of shop employees who loathe each other till they learn the truth; and Frank Borzage's *The Mortal Storm*, a very stark tale of the impact of Nazism on a small Bavarian town. The weak one in this batch was Warners' too-well-named *No Time for Comedy*, as a dramatist, with Rosalind Russell as his actress wife; but *The Philadelphia Story* was a peak for most of the people involved and especially Stewart, who got a Best Actor Oscar–though he was second lead (as a reporter) to Cary Grant, who got the girl. His luck suddenly ran out: *Come Live With Me* (41) with Hedy Lamarr, *Pot o' Gold* with Paulette Goddard and *Ziegfeld Girl*.

His war service was distinguished–he remains one of the highest-ranking officers in the US Auxiliary Air Force. He returned to Hollywood, but it was not to MGM, much to their surprise and annoyance. Instead, he joined Liberty Films, the independent company started by Capra and Stevens. Like most of the post-war independent groups, it didn't last long, and Stewart only made one film for them, *It's a Wonderful Life* (46), about a small-town bank manager on the brink of ruin who is taught that life is still worth living by guardian angel Henry Travers; but the war years had taken harsh toll of Capra's rosy view of the scheme of things. Richard Winnington found it 'only really momentous because it brings back to the screen that charmingly gauche actor, James Stewart'. A Capraesque piece directed by William A. Wellman, *Magic Town* (47), did little better. Most of the Hollywood talent who had served during the war returned anxious to make better and more honest films, and there was nothing wrong with the sentiments expressed in either of these–but post-war audiences didn't want sentiment. Stewart's next film, fortunately, was exactly what they did want: *Call Northside 777* (48), a hard-hitting thriller in the 'new' semi-documentary style, though that simply meant location-shooting and other trappings of verisimilitude–factors which audiences now found not only desirable but essential (often under this same director, Henry Hathaway). He played a reporter. He and Henry Fonda were

Lubitsch's The Shop Around the Corner (*40*)*: the scene in the café where James Stewart realizes that fellow-employee Margaret Sullavan is also his pen-pal.*

musicians in the most amusing episode of *On Our Merry Way*, and then he was involved in another technical 'innovation', the ten-minute take devised by Hitchcock for *Rope*. The director made much publicity out of it, but it was basically the technique then used in TV and after this film he dropped it. It certainly didn't improve *Rope*, a version of Patrick Hamilton's play about the Leopold-and-Loeb-like students who murder a friend and give a tea-party in the same room as the corpse. Stewart was the professor who suspected.

You Gotta Stay Happy was a minor comedy with Joan Fontaine; *The Stratton Story* (49) a sentimental baseball biopic which did great business in the US but not elsewhere; and *Malaya* an adventure story that wasted his talents and Spencer Tracy's. Next he did a couple of Westerns, *Winchester 73* (50) for Universal, directed by Anthony Mann, and *Broken Arrow* for 20th, directed by Delmer Daves, and the financial success of both films was to have a far-reaching effect on Stewart's career: for over a decade he was to eschew comedy–in which he had made his name–for movies of like genre. His partnerships with Mann and/or Universal were to be very profitable. His last two comedies were *The Jackpot* with Barbara Hale, which flopped, and *Harvey*, the one about the drunk and his invisible rabbit friend (he had already done this on Broadway for a while). He went to Britain for 20th's *No Highway* (51), from a Nevil Shute novel; returned to play the whole of *The Greatest Show on Earth* under clown make-up.

There are many claimants to the title of first successful free-lance star and the first to have his or her own production company; but almost every permutation of star-studio relationship had already been tried out in the early Silent days. Nor is Stewart's 1952 agreement to work with Universal on a percentage basis the first such deal, as has been claimed, but it *was* the first modern step in a direction which was soon to be stampeded by almost every star in the business. Roughly for 10 years (the 50s) Universal was an assembly line studio, run by accountants, churning out cut-price formula products (the wisest part of the policy was no press-shows). Although the studio manufactured stars, Stewart was the

s Stewart in one of ɪany Westerns he for Anthony ɪ, The Far ɪtry *(55)*

first *big* established star to work there during this period. His pictures had a larger budget than most Universal products, and he worked for less than his usual salary, plus a percentage of the profits. The first, a Western, *Bend of the River* (52), was a hit, and turned up second on the Motion Picture Herald's list of the year's top money-makers.

He then did two for MGM on normal salary conditions, *Carbine Williams* and the Mann-directed *The Naked Spur* (53). Mann directed all but one of the next six films as well: *Thunder Bay*, *The Glenn Miller Story* (54), *The Far Country* (55), *Strategic Air Command* and *The Man From Laramie*. The last two were made for Paramount and Columbia respectively (now that the percentage principle had become generally accepted); they were all successful, but in particular *The Glenn Miller Story*, giving Stewart a great 1954; his non-Mann film, Hitchcock's *Rear Window*, was also a big hit later that year. He was back with Hitch for more revenue in 1956, that director's remake of his own *The Man Who Knew Too Much*, polished, expensive and altogether superior to the 1934 version. But the public wouldn't touch *The Spirit of St Louis* (57), which Jack L. Warner described as 'the most disastrous failure we (i.e. WB) ever had'. It didn't take enough in a week in Lindbergh's birthplace to cover the staff's wages. It was, nevertheless, a gripping Billy Wilder-directed account of the Lindbergh transatlantic flight, with a dedicated performance by Stewart and virtually his last interesting film.

Night Passage was another routine Universal actioner; Hitchcock's *Vertigo* (58) and Quine's *Bell Book and Candle* were both good subjects not improved by Kim Novak's involvement in them; and *Anatomy of a Murder* (59) was an endless courtroomer whose box-office profited from the reputation of the original best-seller and some 'dirty' words. Stewart's performance as the defence attorney brought him another New York Critics citation. He then had three flops in a row: *The FBI Story*, *The Mountain Road* (60) and Ford's *Two Rode Together* (61), but a second consecutive one with Ford, *The Man Who Shot Liberty Valance* (62), did respectably. Stewart, greying and paunchy, seemed old and tired; nor was he any more impressive in some subsequent big Westerns: *How the West Was Won* and Ford's *Cheyenne Autumn* (64). Business was spotty. Interspersed with these were three comedies, with Stewart acting his age as a father: *Mr Hobbs Takes a Vacation* (62), *Take Her She's Mine* (63) – both successful – and *Dear Brigitte* (65) – not. He did a Robert Aldrich adventure melo, *The Flight of the Phoenix* (66),

Hitchcock's The Man Who Knew Too Much *(56), with Doris Day and James Stewart. Hitchcock preferred to work with actors like Stewart and Cary Grant, with whom audiences could identify.*

and then returned to the Western with three directed by Andrew McLaglen, *Shenandoah* (65), *The Rare Breed* (66) and *Bandelero!* (68); and two with Henry Fonda, *Firecreek* (67) and *The Cheyenne Social Club* (70). In 1970 he and Helen Hayes revived 'Harvey' on Broadway.

Stewart married in 1949 and has four children. He has appeared very occasionally on TV.

Margaret Sullavan

Margaret Sullavan's Hollywood career was not very lucrative but she made some good films. So few of them are seen, however, except on The Late Night Movie on TV that her reputation stands less high than it should and seems confined to the people who loved her 'back when'. She was an enchantress pitched, in temperament and magnetism, somewhere (curiously enough) between the two Hepburns. She was warm and winning, honest and independent, playing with an underlying humour the patient and suffering heroines she was most often given. She spoke lightly and quickly, with inflections that enhanced the old drivel thought up for her. Her mastery of both comedy and drama was complete. Yet in life she suffered from a great lack of self-confidence and was – consequently – one of the most temperamental and difficult of stars. Nor did she care for filming, which didn't help matters.

She was born in 1911 in Norfolk, Virginia. She acted with the Baltimore University Players, studied dancing in Boston and then acting. Through a friend she joined the University Players at Cape Cod and made her pro debut with them, in 'The Devil in the Cheese'. She stayed a couple of seasons, and then got a job in a tour of 'Strictly Dishonorable', after which she was offered a Broadway chance in 'A Modern Virgin' (31). It didn't run, but the Shuberts saw her and offered a contract, which took her through several mediocre ventures. Then she took over the ingénue in 'Dinner at Eight', and was seen in that by director John M. Stahl, who offered her a role that Claudette Colbert and Irene Dunne had turned down: inevitably, it was a weepie, *Only Yesterday* (33). She sacrificed Everything for an Hour of Love with John Boles.

After a few days' rushes, Universal knew that they had a radiant new star, and she knew it too. When they offered her a contract, it was on her terms: three-year, non-exclusive, starting at $1,200 a week plus approval rights, a privilege seldom given to an unknown. Nor was she likely to make things easy for Universal, a studio already in (financial) difficulties. On arrival, she had announced: 'Perhaps I'll get used to the bizarre, elaborate theatricalism called Hollywood, but I cannot guarantee it.' Her second film was again awash with sentiment, Frank Borzage's Depression drama, *Little Man What Now?* (34) with Douglass Montgomery; and her third was also sentimental, though it was a comedy: *The Good Fairy* (35), in the title role, from Molnar's comedy about the girl from the orphanage who marries benefactor Herbert Marshall. William Wyler directed, and married her (in succession to Henry Fonda, from whom she'd been divorced for some time).

At Paramount she did a crushingly soppy Civil War drama, *So Red the Rose*, with its phoney portrait of the Old South; then was in *Next Time We Love* (36), an imitation of one of Fannie Hurst's soggier works: James Stewart and Ray Milland helped her form a triangle. Back at Paramount there was a welcome change with *The Moon's Our Home*, even if the title tried to disguise the fact. It does degenerate at the end, but for the most of its length is a slanging match between a temperamental movie queen and a best-selling author, played by Fonda. Still at Paramount she did a few days' shooting on *I Loved a Soldier/Hotel Imperial* before breaking her arm; the film was abandoned. She returned to the stage, scoring a great success in 'Stage Door', playing, not too ironically, a dedicated actress who scorns films. Motherhood (twice) did keep her away from Hollywood for a while; she was married now to agent Leland Hayward.

Hayward arranged a deal for her at MGM for six films; none of these were destined to depart much from the Maggie Sullavan-suffers-so-prettily routine, but they were generally more weighty than what had gone before, and allowed her to extend her range; her touching performance as Robert

One of the lighter moments of Next Time We Love *(36): Margaret Sullavan was a singer who gave up her career to follow reporter-husband James Stewart on a foreign assignment.*

Taylor's tubercular wife in *Three Comrades* (38) brought her the New York Critics Best Actress award and the Picturegoer Gold Medal. Frank Borzage directed from Erich Maria Remarque's novel about post-war Germany. The same year she was *The Shopworn Angel*, the kept woman who falls for another man, a remake of a Nancy Carroll picture intended originally for Joan Crawford. She and Crawford were together in *The Shining Hour* and didn't, despite all predictions, fight. Except on the screen: this is a quadrangle drama – they are sisters-in-law and Robert Young and Melvyn Douglas are their husbands; and then Joan falls for Robert. . . . Then she was in Lubitsch's enchanting comedy *The Shop Around the Corner* (40) – a performance of impish and infinite delicacy – and, again with Stewart, faced *The Mortal Storm* – in Germany again, and anti-Nazi, the story of a family destroyed by Hitler.

She was once more greatly in demand and, though not very interested, flirted: every studio was announcing movies to star Margaret Sullavan. Meanwhile, she wouldn't play ball with Universal, to whom she owed one film, and the battle that had begun when she had signed that contract now culminated in an injunction to prevent her working elsewhere until she had made *The Invisible Woman* for them. They were not entirely joking, and she knew it, so she came to terms. Universal let her go to UA for *So Ends Our Night* (41) – Remarque again and anti-Nazi again, with Fredric March – until they prepared a suitable vehicle, *Back Street*, perhaps the best of the many screen versions of that subject. As (again) a kept woman, she gave a beautiful performance, and Charles Boyer was as good; she stayed on at Universal to do another film with him, a comedy, *Appointment With Love*.

They met, fell in love and were parted by chance; they met again, fell in love again, but he was married now: so she spent the rest of her life as his Back Street *(41) mistress. Margaret Sullavan and Charles Boyer.*

In 1943 she made her last picture for MGM, a terrific performance in a fine war film, *Cry Havoc*, and then it was reported that her terms were too high for any studio to meet. She packed her bags and departed for New York and 'The Voice of the Turtle' by John Van Druten. After a considerable run she went with it to London (47), but it failed to repeat its US success. In 1950 she elected to do another film (for Columbia), a weepie about a woman dying of cancer, *No Sad Songs for Me*. She saved it, said Variety, 'from falling into a maudlin bog . . . by a standout performance that accents intelligence and underplays the agony of her predicament'. But if her reviews might have tempted her to stay on, the film's performance didn't. Her stage work continued to emphasize Hollywood's loss: 'The Deep Blue Sea' (52), 'Sabrina Fair' (53) and 'Janus' (55). In 1956 she walked out of a TV play ('The Pilot') after rehearsing for weeks; and went into a sanatorium.

She was married to a businessman now, and was bringing up her children. In 1959 she decided to return to the stage, in 'Sweet Love Remember'd'; on the tour, on New Year's Day 1960, she died from an overdose of barbiturates. It was disclosed that she was worried by increasing deafness: her doctors said that as long ago as 1948 she was 40 per cent deaf, and that by the time she died, she could only act by lip-reading. Three weeks earlier she had told Theatre Arts: 'I have something of a reputation of not wanting to go to work. . . . I have never been what you call "a dedicated actress". . . .'

Gloria Swanson

Along with Mary Pickford, Gloria Swanson is the only female Silent star whose name still means anything. She has made only one major film, *Sunset Boulevard*, during the last quarter century, but she has only to enter a TV studio or appear on the stage at some charity matinée for audiences to applaud wildly – and apart from that film, few of the younger generation can ever have seen her on the screen. Audiences warm to longevity but the fact is that Swanson remains very much a star. She will answer the questions of even the most doltish TV interviewer with good humour and a dash or two of wisdom, looking chic and still very glamorous. Perhaps one is merely pleased that she appears to be the reverse of the character she played in *Sunset Boulevard* and displays a candour unexpected of stars of her generation; or perhaps she is revered because even those who have never seen her are aware that she was one of the best actresses of Silent pictures, and one of the major personalities of that time.

Philip Hope-Wallace in Sight and Sound (1950) wasn't so certain about the talent: 'Gloria Swanson never struck me as being a particularly good actress: not for example in the same class as Pola Negri. True, she had a face (as she says in *Sunset Boulevard*) and could give most speaking looks which would be effective even in the total silence which sometimes descended if the pianist took time off to rub her chilblains. But they never seemed to me to be subtle speaking looks, seldom in fact imbued with the art of concealing art; in fine, generally self-conscious.'

On the evidence of those of her pictures available today, it is difficult to agree, though she wasn't very good at the outset: she was early on considered the classic example of the actress who 'grew' with her career. She was forbidding (though in life quite a tiny woman) and imperious, with no great gift for distinguishing between the many different sorts of women she played; but she had a considerable gift for comedy–*then*, her looks could be very subtle. Compared with her contemporaries she underplayed: she had a refreshing gaiety and spirit at a time when audiences were accustomed to their heroines being fey and frolicsome. She comes over today better than any other Silent actress apart from Garbo.

She was born in Chicago, probably in 1898 (Time in 1950 reported that the date on the birth certificate had been obliterated), and was brought up on a succession of army camps, both in the US and the Philippines (her father was a civilian employee with the army); she was living in Chicago working as a notions-counter clerk and studying singing when an aunt took her to visit the Essanay Studio–and it all started. She worked as an extra that day and continued to work for Essanay, both as an extra and in bit parts. She was an exceptionally timid child with no ambition towards films, and appears simply to have been flattered that Essanay thought her photogenic. She was tested by Chaplin at this time for his leading lady in *His New Job*, but was uncooperative because she had decided that, if she was going to stay in films, she would be a dramatic actress. The first film on which she had billing appears to have been *The Fable of Elvira and Farina and The Meal Ticket* (15). She also had small parts in *Sweedie goes to College*, *The Broken Pledge* and *A Dash of Courage* (16), all of which featured Wallace Beery. Swanson married him in 1916, and they were divorced three years later; simultaneously they went to Hollywood, where she signed with Mack Sennett: she played in about 10 two-reelers, including *Hearts and Sparks* (16), *Love on Skates*, *Teddy at the Throttle*, *Dangers of a Bride* and *The Sultan's Wife*, as Bobby Vernon's leading lady. At one point she went to Universal when Sennett wouldn't raise her salary, but after one short, *Baseball Madness* (17), she returned to Sennett. She said recently, 'I did my comedies like Duse might have done them. . . . I was funny because I didn't try to be funny. The more serious I got, the funnier the scene became.' She never was a Sennett bathing beauty, though she did appear in a swimsuit in *A Pullman Bride*. It was that film which caused her to leave Sennett: 'He wanted to make me a second Mabel Normand. I told him I didn't want to be a second anybody, so he tore my contract up.'

She followed Bobby Vernon to Triangle, but did not play comedy–and was at last a star. She was the heroine of eight Triangle dramas, all released in 1918: *Society for Sale*, *Her Decision*, *You Can't Believe Everything*, *Everywoman's Husband*, *Shifting Sands*, *Station Content*, *Secret Code* and *Wife or Country*. In most of them she suffered a series of misunderstandings or mischances until reunited at the end with her husband or the man she loved. A couple of them had a strong anti-German bias.

When Triangle went bankrupt she went over to Cecil B. de Mille, who had noticed her in her Sennett days. He released through Paramount, and Swanson stayed with that company until 1926, by which time she was its highest-paid star. The six films which she made for de Mille gave her career a powerful impetus, as the décor and costumes he chose for her began to influence fashion: she was always gowned in styles meant to suggest intrigue and sophistication, and was seen to exist in impeccable luxury. And usually wronged. She was a living demonstration that riches don't bring happiness–until the last reel. De Mille was, of course, incurably moral: it didn't matter what you gave audiences in the way of sex and sin provided that good triumphed in the end. *Don't Change Your Husband* (19) had Swanson doing just that, only to find that the neglect

Gloria Swanson was still in her early 20s when they made her up like this for The Great Moment *(21)–not that it mattered: youth was less highly prized in those days and she was already type-cast as a mature woman.*

by hubby number one was preferable to the womanizing of hubby number two. *For Better For Worse* found her denouncing her sweetheart as a coward only to discover his true worth later. In *Why Change Your Wife?* (20) she was neglected for the more saucy Bebe Daniels, but she won him back by competing on equally glamorous terms.

Before that one, *Male and Female* (19) was an adaptation of Barrie's 'The Admirable Crichton', with Swanson as Lady Mary, chief suitor on the island for Crichton's affections. The title-change was made, apparently, because some exhibitors confused 'Admirable' with 'Admiral', but the new title certainly indicated the slant that de Mille gave to it, including a flashback with Swanson and Thomas Meighan (Crichton) to Babylonian times, on the odd pretext of Crichton recalling W. E. Henley's 'I was a King in Babylon and you were a Christian slave' (a similar idea had been tried in *Don't Change Your Husband*, where Swanson was seduced away from her husband by being described–with appropriate images–as Goddess of Pleasure, Wealth and Love). *Something to Think About* (20) was more sober, a thorough-going melodrama in which she suffered through widowhood, her father's loathing and an unhappy marriage to a cripple. Her last for de Mille was *The Affairs of Anatol* (21) from the Schitzler play. Wallace Reid was the unfaithful Anatol and Swanson the understanding wife who welcomes him back each time. This group of films–and especially *Male and Female*–not only put Swanson on the world map, but influenced other film-makers, who felt they might be as frank about the pleasures of sex as de Mille. Alexander Walker in 'The Celluloid Sacrifice' wonders whether de Mille's favourite theme was responsible to some degree for the breakdown of moral values in the 20s: 'But one can hardly doubt that it helped foster an atmosphere in which traditional values were being questioned and balanced against the alternatives of freedom and pleasure.'

Before *Anatol*, Swanson had made *The Great Moment*, with her name above the title for the first time. Eleanor Glyn wrote the story, the adventures of an English socialite out West before settling down with Milton Sills, who had saved her life in an earlier reel. It was directed by Sam Wood, as were her nine next films: *Under the Lash*, as a drab wife suspected of infidelity by her South African farmer husband; *Don't Tell Everything* with Wallace Reid, an expanded version of some footage left over from *Anatol*; *Her Husband's Trademark* (22)–he throws her into the company of an ex-lover; *Beyond the Rocks* (22) with Valentino; *Her Gilded Cage*, about a publicity stunt that links an actress with a prince until she falls for an American; *The Impossible Mrs Bellew*, as a mother who loses her good name but is compensated by true love with Conrad Nagel; *My American Wife* (23) with Antonio Moreno; *Prodigal Daughters*–she was one of them; and *Bluebeard's Eighth Wife* with Huntley Gordon–in the roles to be taken in the Talkie version by Cooper and Colbert.

Swanson was at this time supposedly feuding with Pola Negri, the studio's new continental star, but it was an invention of the publicity office and seized upon by gossip columnists. She really had no rival on the Paramount lot. She had said: 'I have decided that when I am a star, I will be every inch and every moment the star! Everybody

Swanson often played an unhappy wife, as here in Beyond the Rocks *(22)–and she's still on her honeymoon. About to be a great comfort is Rudolph Valentino.*

from the studio gateman to the highest executive will know it.' The highest executives did: Zukor described her as 'temperamental', but she was also the first film player to be fully aware of the full value of publicity; fans marvelled at a report that she never wore the same dress twice. When a new contract was drawn up in 1923–four pictures a year for three years–her demands were considerable, and included the right to film in Paramount's New York studio as well as a say in the selection of her material–official publicity gave her chief hobby as looking for vehicles for herself. She insisted on playing *Zaza*, which had already seen sterling service with Mrs Leslie Carter (stage) and Pauline Frederick (film): it was to be the first of a series in which she would undergo chameleon changes in order to continually surprise her fans. A star's career in those days was very short and she detected a slight but dangerous public in-difference; she believes that she saved her career by ringing the changes. In *The Humming Bird* (24) she was a French gamine during wartime; in *A Society Scandal* a wronged wife; and in *Manhandled* a shopgirl who is taken up by society, 'a perfect example of her comic art in full flower' (John Russell Taylor in 1968). *Her Love Story* was a Ruritanian romance–in which she wore a bridal outfit reputedly costing $100,000–and *Wages of Virtue* saw her demoted from queen to pride of the Foreign Legion, with Ben Lyon. She actually went to France to make *Madame Sans-Gêne* (25), from the Sardou play about Napoleon's laundress; and she reappeared in the US with the Legion d'Honneur and a brand-new husband, the Marquis de la Falaise de la Coudraye. Earlier, her popularity had suffered when it was announced that she had become a mother–an unwilling reminder to the public that stars were human after all. Now, with the Marquis, she fulfilled every fan's dream of glamour.

De Witt Bodeen detailed in Films in Review some items of her homecoming, with husband and completed film. Her 'billing was the largest ever seen on Times Square up to that time. Her name in electric lights occupied the whole front of the Rivoli Theatre, with the stars and stripes and tricolour flying above.' In Hollywood a brass band met them, and they drove in a motorcade like royalty. At the film's West Coast première the audience rose and sang 'Home Sweet Home'. She made only four more films for Paramount, none of them very interesting: *The Coast of Folly*, a tale of dormant mother-love, in which she played three roles, including mother and daughter; *Stage Struck*, probably the best of the quartet, a comedy in which she was just that;

Gloria Swanson as Maugham's Sadie Thompson (*28*), *the trollop who converted a minister – despite his attempts at vice-versa. It was directed by Raoul Walsh, who doubled up by playing Sergeant O'Hara.*

Swanson became her own producer in order to prolong her career but was dogged by ill-luck, like Queen Kelly *and, above,* Perfect Understanding (*33*)*: her leading man was Laurence Olivier.*

Untamed Lady (26) – a spoiled beauty who meets her match in Lawrence Gray; and *Fine Manners*. Paramount offered to renew her contract at the sensational $18,000 per week, but she refused; nor was she interested in even bigger money. She wanted to go to UA, where she would have the same freedom enjoyed by Chaplin and Co. and produce her own pictures. Now, at UA, she was reputedly earning $20,000 a week (her actual chief backer was Joseph P. Kennedy).

For her first vehicle she chose *The Loves of Sunya* (27) which as *The Eyes of Youth* had once seen service for Clara Kimbell Young. She appeared in several guises, most of them exotic, but it was not a great success. In the next one, *Queen Kelly* (28), she was a convent schoolgirl noticed by the Prince Consort when she loses her knickers and thereafter an object of wrath to his beastly queen, Seena Owen; she escapes from the palace to which the Prince had abducted her, and drowns herself. It was directed by Erich von Stroheim who, said Lotte Eisner, found in Swanson 'recognized star though she was, malleable material, ready to submit to his direction. She makes an adorable Kelly, rogueish and innocent without any affectations.' Von Stroheim, however, was at his most extravagant, and Swanson fired him with the film unfinished and $600,000 down the drain. Her backers would contribute no more money and the film was heavily in debt. She spent $200,000 of her own money on a salvage operation, bringing in as director Edmund Goulding, but it was not, she has said, until 1950 when she made *Sunset Boulevard*, that all the debts incurred by *Kelly* were paid off. A version of it was shown in Europe and South America, but it was never shown commercially in the US. *Sadie Thompson*, in the first year of the Oscars, won for her the first of three nominations. It was, of course, the notorious 'Rain' – the Hays Office wouldn't let the original title be used – and is generally considered to be the most satisfactory of the three attempts to film it: her Sadie, at least, seemed to have stepped straight from the pages of Maugham's story.

She did get back many of her losses with *The Trespasser* (29), a drama of mother-love and her second consecutive smash hit. It was her first Talkie and she sang – 'Love, Your Magic Spell Is Everywhere' – as well as she spoke. She was one of the very few stars without stage training who made an easy transition to Talkies, but it was soon apparent that, accomplished though she was, the public was no longer interested: the great influx of new favourites left room for very few of the old ones. The trouble was, thought Griffith and Mayer, 'to a depression-struck audience, she still symbolized the lost and discredited era of wonderful nonsense'. Further, there were disputes with Goldwyn who, as production head of UA, had to okay the films she wanted to make. Her career ran down through a series of comedies: *What a Widow!* (30), *Indiscreet* (with Ben Lyon), *Tonight or Never* (31) and *Perfect Understanding* (33). The latter, filmed in Britain, ran into difficulties: Swanson's new husband, Michael Farmer, proved inadequate as an actor and was replaced by Laurence Olivier; and the director, Rowland V. Lee, was replaced by the man who had come from Hollywood to cut it. Then the end result was sufficiently poor as to persuade Swanson that she should give up producing and accept the offers she was getting. *The Divine Sarah* and *Twentieth Century* were announced for her, but she did neither. Thalberg at MGM signed her for a remake of *Three Weeks* with Clark Gable, and several other projects (including a life of Lola Montez), but when he died no one else among the executives at MGM was interested and she was quietly dropped.

MGM did loan her to Fox for one film, however, the screen version of the Kern-Hammerstein operetta, *Music in the Air* (34). There was also some interest later at Columbia whose president, Harry Cohn, was always pleased to employ cut-rate talent: first it was announced that she would star in *Maisie Kenyon*; and Swanson brought him a story, *The Second Mrs Draper*, to star herself, but work was abandoned when Cohn disagreed with the screen-writer (it later became *Dark Victory*).

Then it was to be the remake of *Holiday*; while Columbia vacillated, Swanson began certain business enterprises and then undertook some theatre work, beginning with a tour of 'Reflected Glory' by George Kelly. Eventually, she made a film for RKO, the first of her two screen comebacks and quickly forgotten: *Father Takes a Wife* (41), a comedy with Adolphe Menjou. She was paid $35,000 for it. Her second comeback was really something: in the part of Norma Desmond (which Norma Shearer had reputedly turned down) in the Wilder-Brackett *Sunset Boulevard* (50), a bizarre black comedy about an ageing Hollywood queen living in the past ('I'm still big–it's the pictures that got small'). 'Miss Swanson, required to play a hundred per cent grotesque, plays it not just to the hilt, but

Billy Wilder's Sunset Boulevard *(50), a glittering, bitter study of a Hollywood Miss Havisham who dreams of a comeback and still revels in her fan-mail (ghosted by her butler–Von Stroheim). Swanson's great reviews compensated for the later misapprehension that she was somewhat like the star she played.*

right up to the armpits, by which I mean magnificently' (James Agee). 'In a truly outstanding performance she shows us a woman to whom playing a part has become second nature, and an actress to whom acting is life: here is the star of the days when a face had to speak without words' (Dilys Powell). No critic disagreed: Swanson's performance was – and remains – a revelation; but despite the film's brilliance and subsequent fame it was too downbeat for 1950 audiences (now, on TV, it is highly popular).

On the last day of shooting at Paramount the crew gave Swanson a plaque inscribed 'To the Greatest Star of Them All'; Paramount disagreed – or at least hadn't read the eulogies for her performance as Norma; there was some question of putting her in *Darling How Could You!* but they asked her to test, a request which she thought impertinent (Joan Fontaine played the part). Hedda Hopper, however, records that she suggested to Swanson a certain novel as a follow-up to *Boulevard*; Swanson replied, 'I couldn't possibly play the mother of an 18-year-old daughter.' Hopper comments that she was already a grandmother.

WB offered her a B-budget comedy, *Three for Bedroom C* (52) about a movie star travelling to Hollywood, and it was sad to see her trying to cope with such dastardly lines and situations. She has referred to it and the next one – *Mio Figlio Nerone/Nero's Weekend* – as mistakes. The latter was a satire on costume epics, made in Italy in 1956; Alberto Sordi, Brigitte Bardot and de Sica were in the cast, and she played Agrippina. A mistake perhaps; terrible certainly.

There were and still are offers to play parts like Norma Desmond, but Swanson declines them all. She has said often, however, that she would like to film again, should the right part come along. If she feels bitter at the neglect by producers, the warmth of her public reception should dispel it.

Robert Taylor

The assets of Robert Taylor hardly went beyond a good physique and a handsome face, so that with age he faced the career decline inevitable to a matinée idol. He summed up his career adequately in 1967 (quoted in Films in Review): 'I've never been terribly ambitious – simply wanted to do a good job at whatever I did. The reviews usually said I gave an adequate or good performance. I never got raves, but neither did I get pans. I've never had an Oscar and probably never will. I'm content to try to do as well as I can.' He went on: 'My metabolism doesn't lend itself to the Davis-Cagney brand of high-pressure careering. I stayed with one studio for 20 years, took what they gave me to do, did my work. While I wasn't happy with everything, I scored pretty well.'

He was born Spangler Arlington Brough (probably the best remembered 'real name' in show business) in Filley, Nebraska, in 1911, the son of a doctor. There was a plan to follow in Father's footsteps, but instead at college he studied the 'cello, and turned from that to acting after enjoying himself on the amateur stage. He was studying at a Los Angeles (Pomona) drama school when a talent scout saw him in a production of 'Journey's End'. He was screen-tested by Goldwyn without result, but was signed by MGM to a seven-year contract, starting at $35 per week. MGM loaned him to Fox for a Will Rogers's vehicle, *Handy Andy* (34), and then to Universal for a programmer, *There's Always Tomorrow*. He did one film, *Wicked Woman*, on his home lot before getting the part which really started him, in the first of the MGM shorts-series *Crime Does Not Pay* called *Buried Loot*. Some minor roles followed – *Society Doctor* (35), *West Point of the Air* – and leads in a couple of Bs – *Times Square Lady* and *Murder in the Fleet* – before being cast as a theatrical producer in *Broadway Melody of 1936* with Eleanor Powell. 1936 was in fact to make some very sweet music: four Taylor films were released, and at the end of it exhibitors voted him No. 4 box-office attraction. MGM were overjoyed – it was the sort of rise of which studio executives dream – but the film which did it was *Magnificent Obsession*, made on loan-out to Universal, a popular soap opera with Irene Dunne. All the ladies wanted him – Janet Gaynor for *Small Town Girl* (36), Loretta Young for *Private Number* – a remake of *Common Clay*, Barbara Stanwyck for *His Brother's Wife*, Joan Crawford for *The Gorgeous Hussy* – and Garbo. It is more likely, in the case of Garbo, that Taylor was foisted on her, and *Camille* (37), from that point of view, is one of the great mis-matings of the cinema. As James Agate pointed out, he and Lionel Barrymore made a grotesque pair as the Duvals, but Taylor's campus-bred Armand becomes, after several viewings, almost inoffensive; and it should be stressed that as far as MGM were concerned his appeal was much more commercial than hers (he was No. 3 in 1937, No. 6 in 1938).

He was equally at sea in a Jean Harlow comedy *Personal Property* (37), the remake of *The Man in Possession*, but was beginning to

Barbara Stanwyck and Robert Taylor in This Is My Affair *(37): she was a dance-hall singer in with the mob and he a government agent. They fell in love in the film, and in life too.*

find his feet, notably in 20th's *This Is My Affair* with off-screen friend Barbara Stanwyck. Said the ads, unashamed: '*Thrillingly* these real-life sweethearts achieve their true greatness in the most important story either one has ever had . . .', adding 'the picture the whole world is talking about'. There could be much speculation as to what the world could have found to say about this routine romance; but Stanwyck and Taylor were eventually married (in 1939; it lasted till 1952). At least Taylor as a Secret Service agent had a better chance than a re-vamp of an old part, in *Broadway Melody of 1938*, again with Powell. His performance as the breezy, cocky *Yank at Oxford* (38) is quite enjoyable and did much to kill the prevalent image of him as a ladies' man. The filming of it was accompanied by unprecedented publicity for a British film (MGM produced). He was in the popular *Three Comrades*, and then did his image another good turn by playing a boxer in the rip-roaring *The Crowd Roars* and by doing a Western, *Stand Up and Fight* (39), with Wallace Beery. No one was done any good by *Lucky Night*–he was a poet rescued from a park bench by heiress Myrna Loy–or by *Lady of the Tropics*–he was a millionaire in love with dusky Hedy Lamarr; and after the gloom of them *Remember?* with Greer Garson must have been immensely cheering. It was followed by *Waterloo Bridge* (40), with Vivien Leigh, his own favourite film, and the first in which he wore the moustache he was to shave off and grow again with monotonous regularity through the years. He had an impossible role in *Escape* as an American trying to get his mother (Nazimova) out of a Nazi-occupied country, and was an airman in *Flight Command*.

For Warners Errol Flynn had been Robin Hood and other folk-heroes; for 20th Tyrone Power was Jesse James. Now, for MGM, Taylor was *Billy the Kid* (41)–again, considerably romanticized–rather Billy the Kitten. The early Technicolor locations were breathtaking, inevitably dwarfing a good script and Taylor's Kid. He played with panache the fought-over lover in *When Ladies Meet*, but could do little with the role of the 'decent' gang boss in *Johnny Eager*. *Her Cardboard Lover* (42) was a weak comedy, and *Stand By for Action* and *Bataan* (43) were war films–navy/fair and army/fine respectively. His last picture before joining up was the hysterically funny *Song of Russia*, a piece of pop (Tchaikowsky) propaganda about an American orchestra conductor visiting the USSR (not the least funny aspect was its being exhumed and labelled pernicious by the Un-American Activities Committee some years later). Taylor was in the Navy for the last two war years.

There is little to be said about (or for) Taylor's immediate post-war films. *Undercurrent* (46) cast him as a homicidal maniac opposite Katharine Hepburn and he was trampled to death at the end by a horse –for which action it deserved honorary membership of the Critics Circle; in *The High Wall* (47) he was a neurotic war veteran. *The Bribe* (49) and *Conspirator* (made in Britain) were thrillers; *Ambush* and *The Devil's Doorway* (50) were Westerns: each did less well than the one before–Taylor was not to blame–but his standing was rescued by *Quo Vadis?* (51). The Silent version had been a huge grosser for MGM, and the same was hoped for this: it was filmed in Italy with no expense spared, and reaped a gigantic $11 million, at that time the fourth biggest grosser in movie history. Taylor and Deborah Kerr as the Roman centurion and his Christian girl-friend were competent, to say the most, but then talent was less in evidence than money (MGM were inspired

In the 50s MGM jacked-up Taylor's ailing career with a series of mediaeval swashbucklers, following the success of Ivanhoe. *The best of the trio was* Quentin Durward *(55): with Taylor in the title role and lady fair Kay Kendall.*

perhaps by a line spoken in the film by Petronius: 'History will not say the burning of Rome is good but they must say it is collosal'). After a Western, *Westward the Women*, he did a really enjoyable spectacle, *Ivanhoe* (52), from Scott's novel: it was one of the big ones of the year. *Above and Beyond* dealt cursorily with the dropping of the A-bomb; then came another Western, *Ride Vaquero!* (53) and a whaling adventure, *All the Brothers Were Valiant*. *Knights of the Round Table* was an attempt to repeat the success of *Ivanhoe*, but was too much like a children's cut-out book: cut-out figures in front of a cut-out castle.

MGM were very good to Taylor. His box-office star had waned, but they consistently put him into top-budget films – mostly adventure films which wouldn't stretch his resources: *Valley of the Kings* (54), a thriller filmed on location in Egypt; *Rogue Cop*; *Many Rivers to Cross* (55); and *Quentin Durward*, a more exciting film than *Ivanhoe*, and more faithful to Scott (in spirit, at least) – but Taylor himself was more conspicuously out of place. After *The Last Hunt* (56) he did his first outside film in 19 years – 20th's *D-Day the Sixth of June*. There followed: *The Power and the Prize*, *Tip on a Dead Jockey* (57), *Saddle the Wind* (58), *The Law and Jake Wade* and *Party Girl*, the latter an ersatz gangster thriller elevated to classic status by fans of director Nicholas Ray. After a programmer for Paramount, *The Hangman* (59), Taylor did his last under contract for MGM, a thriller, *The House of Seven Hawks*, completing 25 years. His contract had in fact another two years to run: Picturegoer had commented that this would be a record if it went its full term, but it was already a record, beating Gable's 24 years with the same company by a year.

In the early 60s he starred in a TV series, 'The Detectives', and his films became unimportant, degenerating into some Spanish Westerns and some made for TV – but shown outside the US as cinema features. The titles: *Killers of Kilimanjaro* (60), one of the deadly programmers turned out by Warwick-Columbia British; *The Miracle of the White Stallions* (63), a Disney film about the flight of the Lippizaner horses from wartime Vienna; *Cattle King*; *A House Is Not a Home* (64), in a guest part as the backer of Polly Adler's cat-house; *The Night Walker* (65), a low-budget thriller reuniting him with first wife Stanwyck; *The Glass Sphinx* with Anita Ekberg; *Johnny Tiger* (66); *Savage Pampas* (67); *Return of the Gunfighter* (68); *Where Angels Go Trouble Follows*; *Devil May Care* and *The Day the Hot Line Got Hot* (69).

He died in 1969 after a long battle with cancer. Ronald Reagan, the Governor of California, said at his funeral: 'He was more than a pretty boy, an image that embarrassed him because he was a man who respected his profession and was a master of it.'

Shirley Temple

In the 1937 edition of 'Who's Who in America' there were 19 lines devoted to Shirley Temple, only two less than to Mrs Roosevelt and eight more than to Garbo, her Hollywood runner-up. Norman J. Zierold mentions this in his study, 'The Child Stars', and among a host of other extraordinary facts, he says that Shirley, on her eighth birthday, received 135,000 gifts from all over the world. Well, she was officially the biggest-drawing star in the world, and hadn't she already won a special Oscar for bringing 'more happiness to millions of children and millions of grown-ups than any other child of her years in the history of the world'?

She was the infant 'It' girl. It was impossible to escape from her. Apart from films and records, there were Shirley Temple dolls, books and games of all kinds, clothes, items of nursery furniture, etc., and the little girl, smiling broadly, endorsed household goods of which her mother and her studio approved. There was a tremendous upsurge in the popularity of dancing classes for kids, and probably no child within the orbit of Hollywood films was immune from her. Ringlets became popular; children were told to behave 'like Shirley'–and if they didn't, as a punishment they weren't taken to see her. Meanwhile, this dainty object of the world's love sat at home in Hollywood, playing with her dolls and receiving her distinguished visitors. Everyone attested to how completely unspoilt she was (and certainly her mother was an epoch-making watch-dog).

There were two discordant notes: one was the realization that the child had to grow up, and the other (less disturbing in view of their minority) was the sour tone affected by some sections of the press. They were baffled by the phenomenon. Shirley went through the whole bag of tricks in every film, but they remained unimpressed by her many-faceted talent: they found her singing coarse and flat, her dancing merely jigging up and down, her acting nauseatingly cute and her mimicry in a ken with Dr Johnson's lady preacher. They refused to appreciate the technique that others praised, they remained unpersuaded. Only the pessimists would have prophesied that today she would still be famous. She is known to people who have never seen a Shirley Temple film, her name carried forward, living on in the parodies of a hundred music-hall comics. She wasn't, in fact, anywhere near as bad as these imitations would pretend: she had the authentic star's glitter–perhaps in her beaming self-confidence. But, alas, the mockers were right: by any standards prevailing to child performers, talented she wasn't–which makes the whole saga so odd.

It began in Santa Monica in 1928, where Mr and Mrs Temple became the parents of a new baby. He was a bank manager; she, Gertrude Temple, soon perceived in the child the qualities of stardom, and she began hawking her round the studios. At Educational, which specialized in shorts, Shirley was engaged to play in a series called *Baby Burlesks* which were take-offs on movies. She played in *The Incomparable More Legs Sweetrick* (as Dietrich), *The Pie-Covered Wagon*, *Polly-Tix in Washington*. At the same time she began getting small parts in feature

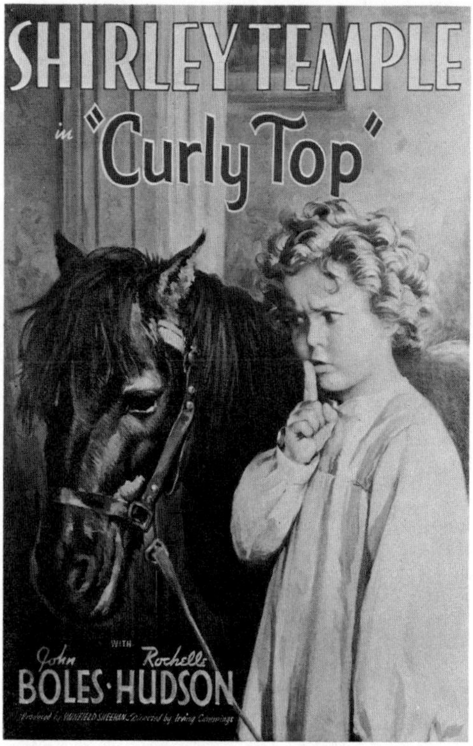

movies: *Red-Haired Alibi* (32), *Out All Night*, *To the Last Man* (33) and *Mandalay* (34). Mrs Temple failed to get Shirley signed on as one of 'Our Gang', and some slight interest by Paramount led to nothing (yet). The child did another series for Educational, *Frolics of Youth*, and was seen in some of these by songwriter Jay Gorney, who was working at Fox on *Stand Up and Cheer*: a tot was needed to sing 'Baby Take a Bow' at the film's climax, and Gorney advised Mrs Temple to have Shirley auditioned. She was chosen and signed at $150 a week. Fox first gave her a bit in *Carolina*, followed by small parts in *Now I'll Tell* and *Change of Heart*. Meanwhile, her song in *Stand Up and Cheer* was receiving much attention, to be followed a couple of weeks later by her performance in *Little Miss Marker*, as the orphan who reforms bookie Adolphe Menjou in Damon Runyan's story. This was made at Paramount, under a two-film deal Mrs Temple had made earlier in the year: and now it was all happening at once. In September Fox released *Baby Take a Bow* (Shirley as the daughter of ex-con going straight James Dunn) and in October Paramount presented *Now and Forever* (Shirley reuniting estranged couple Gary Cooper and Carole Lombard). After her first Paramount film Mr Temple had got Shirley's salary raised to $1,250 weekly: now he started negotiations for a further increase, as

In the good old days before they entered politics: George Murphy and Shirley Temple in Little Miss Broadway *(38): it was all about an orphan taken up by some vaudevillians and the threat that she might be sent back to the orphanage.*

Fox released *Bright Eyes*: she sang 'On the Good Ship Lollipop' and was no longer an adjunct to the plot. Now films were to be built round her. At the end of 1934 she was the eighth draw in the US.

There were four Shirley films in 1935: two Southern tales in which she danced with Bill 'Bojangles' Robinson, *The Little Colonel* (with Lionel Barrymore) and *The Littlest Rebel* ('You're almost nice enough to be a Confederate,' she tells Abraham Lincoln); and sandwiched between them, *Our Little Girl* and *Curly Top* (a version of 'Daddy Long Legs'). Now she was the top box-office star in the US (a position she was to hold steadily over the next three years, in Britain as well). There were four more in 1936: *Captain January* ('Cap! Cap! I don't want to go, I don't want to!' she pleads to Guy Kibbee), the remake of a Baby Peggy vehicle; *Poor Little Rich Girl* with Alice Faye; *Dimples* with Frank Morgan, a weepie with a blackface minstrel finale which even pro-Shirley critics found hard to take; and *Stowaway* with Faye, and impersonating Jolson, Crosby and Cantor. Kipling's hero, *Wee Willie Winkie* (37), changed sex to accommodate Shirley, with Victor McLaglen under John Ford's direction; and Graham Greene's review in the magazine Night and Day brought a libel suit from Fox (now 20th). The review was taken to imply that Shirley was an adult masquerading as a child (Greene spoke of coquetry). The magazine settled out of court (and although the amounts involved were not great, a further libel suit brought bankruptcy).

There was only one other film that year, *Heidi*: 'Dear God,' said the child, 'please make every little boy and girl in the world as happy as I am', and it was seriously considered that the ending of this picture might influence world affairs. The world trembled when, for the new version of *Rebecca of Sunnybrook Farm* (38), 20th cut off her ringlets; but she danced with Bojangles and did her impersonations again. The result was a hit; and so were *Little Miss Broadway* with George Murphy, and *Just Around the Corner* with Bojangles and Joan Davis. Said Film Weekly: 'Shirley Temple has her now unvaried role of good fairy to a lot of bewildered grown-ups. . . .' She was now getting $100,000 per film and was the biggest Hollywood earner after Louis B. Mayer. Her public stayed remarkably faithful: through the lavish, Technicolored *The Little Princess* (39), possibly her best film; *Susannah of the Mounties* with Randolph Scott; and *The Blue Bird* (40), Maeterlinck adapted and in colour. This one did lose money (the first Temple film to do so) but only because it had been so expensive.

Still, the writing was on the wall. Temple had slipped in all the 1939 box-office polls, and clearly the mileage that 20th could get out of her as a child star was circumscribed. Besides, her fee was now $300,000 a picture. She had earned, it was estimated, $3 million (not counting the trust fund the studio had set up for her), a good round sum. Moreover, the never-too-good relationship between the studio and the mother had deteriorated; and when, after *Young People*, co-starring Charlotte Greenwood and Jack Oakie, the Temples offered to buy up the rest of the contract, the studio didn't demur.

The child was 11 (though studio publicity, having from the start taken a year off her age, still insisted she was 10) and Mrs Temple announced that it was time Shirley had some schooling like an ordinary child. She was sent away for an ostensible 18 months, which was an adequate period in which to negotiate a favourable contract at another studio. There was much speculation on the choice (for it was widely believed that the public would want to watch Shirley grow up) and it was expected to be

Shirley Temple with Claudette Colbert in Since You Went Away *(44). Her enormous popularity had almost disappeared overnight, and this was one of the attempted comebacks.*

Universal, where Joe Pasternak was managing Deanna Durbin's career with such success; however, it turned out to be MGM, with its own noted stable of teenage stars. MGM proudly announced that Temple would team with two of them, Mickey Rooney and Judy Garland, in *Babes on Broadway*; she would be supported by Wallace Beery in *Lazy Bones*, and they had bought *Panama Hattie* for her, and *National Velvet*, to co-star Spencer Tracy.... In the end, all they came up with (after a long interval) was a programmer called *Kathleen* (41). Unrecorded, Temple left MGM and turned up at UA in *Miss Annie Rooney* (42), 'overwhelmed by jitterbugs mixed with saccharine' (Picturegoer). There had been an attempt to drum up interest in Temple's first screen kiss (it had worked for Durbin) but the public no longer had time for such frivolities, and war audiences would almost certainly not have wanted to watch an adolescent Temple in the sort of films that Durbin had made. Changing taste partly accounted for the flop of both these films, for, more than Durbin or Garland, Temple belonged firmly to a former era.

But it was also a question of ability. Temple had been off the screen two years – long enough for interest in a comeback to be engendered – when Selznick (who had signed her for seven years) put her into *Since You Went Away* (44), a definite third in interest after Claudette Colbert and Jennifer Jones. She was a typical teenager, and that was the trouble: she was just another Hollywood youngster. Selznick in her only other film for him put her in support of Ginger Rogers and Joseph Cotten in *I'll Be Seeing You*, and then she had a real star part again, in *Kiss and Tell* (46), a distasteful Broadway comedy (she was suspected of being pregnant). It didn't make the circuits. That Temple did have some sort of following was demonstrated by her much-publicized nuptials to an army sergeant, John Agar; and she got herself into the good company of Myrna Loy and Cary Grant in the successful *The Bachelor and the Bobby Soxer* (47). But *Honeymoon* with Guy Madison, and *That Hagen Girl* with Ronald Reagan weren't good ideas, and her part in Ford's *Fort Apache* (48) was small. Her husband, beginning a career as an actor, was in this; but they were divorced in 1949 with the former child star alleging mental cruelty and habitual drunkenness. That year she returned to 20th to play the ingénue in a Clifton Webb vehicle, *Mr Belvedere Goes to College*, and her career petered out ignominiously with *A Kiss for Corliss* (a sequel to *Kiss and Tell*) and a horsey picture, *The Story of Seabiscuit* (49).

In 1950 she was married again, happily, to a non-professional, and declared that she was no longer interested in making movies; however, on TV in the US in 1957 she began a series called 'Shirley Temple's Storybook', as narrator and occasional actress, and three years later had a similar series. She made headlines again when she became involved in politics and ran on the Republican party ticket for Congress (unsuccessfully), and when she protested at the San Francisco Film Festival about a Swedish movie she considered immoral. In 1969 President Nixon appointed her representative to the United Nations.

Franchot Tone

The Cinema has known only two sorts of heroes: the successful and, sometimes, the failures. Apart from some of the characters Bogart played in the 40s there has been no room for the plodders. In the 30s nine out of 10 heroes had stepped straight from the Social Register. The only failures permissible were those hit by the Depression, so heroes were successful: successful lawyers, playwrights, industrialists, detectives, bankers, advertising executives. The male stars of the period were good at playing these confident, worldly people. Franchot Tone's screen character was basically that of the bar-fly, the lounge-lizard; like his confrères he was seldom to be seen actually working, but because he was successful he was never despicable. And of course he had charm and a certain amount of modesty. The war virtually killed the type and Tone was not a good enough actor to survive; his quiet, well-bred assurance went out of fashion. One cannot regret it, but there are few actors today as sympathetic, or who can play comedy with such ease.

He was born in Niagara Falls in 1906, the son of the president of the Carborundum Co. of America. He was educated privately before going to Cornell University, planned to teach languages, but became an actor instead: his first appearance on the stage was in stock in Buffalo in 1927 and later the same year he made his debut in New York City, in 'The Belt'. He worked successively for the New Playwrights Company, the Theatre Guild and the Group Theater, and established himself notably in 'The Age of Innocence' (28) starring Katharine Cornell, 'Green Grow the Lilacs' (31) as Curly, and 'Success Story' (32). He made his film debut for Paramount in *The Wiser Sex* (32) with Claudette Colbert and Lilyan Tashman, while appearing on the stage at nights, but it wasn't until some months later, while playing the lead in 'Success Story' that a studio made a good offer. MGM signed him to a five-year contract.

His first two films for them appeared almost simultaneously: *Gabriel Over the White House* (33), in which he was Walter Huston's secretary, and *Today We Live*, in which he was Joan Crawford's brother (two years later he and Crawford became man and wife). He did normal leading man assignments: opposite Loretta Young in *Midnight Mary*, Miriam Hopkins in King Vidor's *The Stranger's Return*, Maureen O'Sullivan in *Stage Mother* (who was Alice Brady), Jean Harlow in *Bombshell* and Crawford again in *Dancing Lady* (34). His status improved when he was loaned to 20th-UA to co-star with Constance Bennett in *Moulin Rouge*; then again he was just one of several flies around honeypot Crawford in *Sadie McKee*. He was loaned to Fox for *The World Moves On* with Madeleine Carroll; had top billing for the first time in *Straight As the Way*, trying to go like that after a stretch, despite the old mob led by Jack La Rue. He co-starred with Harlow again in *The Girl From Missouri*, and got one of the better parts he wanted in Warners' *Gentlemen Are Born*, a topical tale about four college chums trying to get jobs in these difficult times. 'It has reality' said Photoplay. He was in two of the year's big masculine adventures: *The Lives of a Bengal Lancer* (35), one of his best performances, at Paramount with Gary Cooper, and *Mutiny on the Bounty* in the part that Robert Montgomery turned down, with Gable. Between them he starred in *One New York Night* with Una Merkel and did routine chores in *Reckless* with Harlow and William Powell and *No More Ladies* with Crawford and Montgomery.

Tone was a successful architect who picks up Bette Davis while slumming in *Dangerous*, but his next films were routine: *Exclusive Story* (35) as a newspaperman, with Madge Evans; *The Unguarded Hour* as a barrister, with Loretta Young; *The King Steps Out* as the young Emperor Franz Joseph, with Grace Moore; and *Suzy* as a dashing flyer, with Harlow and Cary Grant, a war film that was set in 1914 but didn't acknowledge it in the costumes. There followed two with Crawford: *The Gorgeous Hussy* and *Love on the Run*. They had been married a year earlier, and during their much publicized romance fan-magazines had noted that in the films they had made together it was some other guy with her in

The Lives of a Bengal Lancer (*35*) *was a popular adventure story glorifying one of the regiments which supported the British Raj. Gary Cooper and Franchot Tone were brother officers, and Tone's devil-may-care performance brought him his best notices to date.*

the final clinch. He did get her in *Hussy*, but it was a minute role; and Gable got her in the other one. Of *Hussy* Crawford says in her memoir that Tone took the part for her sake, that 'it was the breaking point in his career and the breaking point in our marriage'. She speaks tenderly of him while complaining that his late appearance on the set was 'unprofessional and intolerable': perhaps for this reason Variety later described the marriage as 'tempestuous'. Whether or not Tone, like other actors before and after him, found it difficult to be married to a lady who was a bigger star than he was, he did object strenuously to the 'stuffed shirt' parts in which MGM cast him. It was no good reviewers saying he stole *Love on the Run* from Crawford and Gable: these were not the sort of parts he wanted to play.

He had a chance to play period comedy in *Quality Street* (37), an officer of the Regency opposite Katharine Hepburn, and to do stark drama in *They Gave Him a Gun*, as a vicious racketeer and killer, Spencer Tracy's old wartime chum: a good subject that descended to melodrama at the end. He enjoyed both, but then it was back in the old routine: he was a successful surgeon caught *Between Two Women* (Virginia Bruce and Maureen O'Sullivan), a story and screen-play by Von Stroheim, and then was with Crawford again in *The Bride Wore Red*. He was cast as a mere (Austrian) postman, but his usual suave manner was required. In 1937 he appeared among the top 10 male stars in the Bernstein questionnaire, at seventh, beaten only by Gary Cooper, Clark Gable, Charles Laughton, Robert Taylor, Ronald Colman and William Powell. Then he was a playboy in *Manproof* (38) with Myrna Loy. He did *Love Is a Headache* with Gladys George, *Three Comrades* with Margaret Sullavan, Robert Taylor and Robert Young, *Three Loves Has Nancy* with Janet Gaynor and Montgomery, *The Girl Downstairs* (39) with Franciska Gaal, *Thunder Afloat* with

Wallace Beery, and *Fast and Furious* with Ann Sothern. That concluded his contract and the parting between him and MGM was not amicable. That year, too, he and Crawford were divorced. He returned to New York and the Group Theater and appeared in 'The Gentle People' with Sylvia Sidney – and although it didn't impair his work he was by this time drinking heavily.

He returned to Hollywood and signed deals with Universal, Columbia and Paramount: *Trail of the Vigilantes* (40), a good comedy Western; *Nice Girl?* (41) as the older man who captivates Deanna Durbin; *She Knew All the Answers*; *This Woman Is Mine*, a period story with Carol Bruce and John Carroll; and *The Wife Takes a Flyer* (42). He returned to MGM for *Pilot No. 5*, and then appeared in *Star Spangled Rhythm*, in the sketch 'If Men Played Cards As Women Do', with MacMurray, Ray Milland and Lynne Overman. Still at Paramount he did one of his best jobs, the British officer disguised as the waiter in *Five Graves to Cairo* (43), and played with Mary Martin in *True to Life*. He was a successful playwright in *His Butler's Sister* – Durbin in the title role and Pat O'Brien as his butler; and then back at Paramount was in *The Hour Before the Dawn* (44), with Veronica Lake. He followed with two more thrillers, Robert Siodmak's overrated *Phantom Lady*, and the shallow *Deep Waters* at UA with Merle Oberon.

That Night With You (45) was a conventional musical about waitress Susannah Foster becoming a star; and it indicated that it was time Tone returned to the theatre: that year he did 'Hope for the Best' in New York, a title which might well describe his attitude to his film career, but his films were very poor things: *Because of Him* (46) with Durbin again, and again as a successful dramatist; *Lost Honeymoon* (47), a tasteless comedy with Tone uncertain whether or not he's the father of twins; *Honeymoon* playing third fiddle to Shirley Temple and Guy Madison; *Her Husband's Affairs* with Lucille Ball; *I Love Trouble* (48) with Janet Blair; *Every Girl Should Be Married*, supporting Cary Grant and Betsy Drake; and *Jigsaw* (49), a cheap little thriller made by the Danziger Brothers for UA, with Jean Wallace, Tone's wife of seven years – which was as long as the marriage lasted. He got custody of the sons and she later married Cornel Wilde. In 1951 Tone married starlet Barbara Payton, and they divorced a year later; but it was a romance that caused world headlines due to several night-club brawls.

Unhappily, Tone's film career petered out: *The Man on the Eiffel Tower*, made in Europe; *Without Honor* (50), a silly, verbose melodrama with Laraine Day; and *Here Comes the Groom* (51) billed under the title, as the man Jane Wyman doesn't prefer to Bing Crosby. He returned to the stage, where he was sometimes able to appear in stuff of the quality he craved: 'The Second Man' in summer stock in 1950 and 1952; 'Oh Men Oh Women' (53) in New York; a revival of 'The Time of Your Life' (55) at the City Center; 'Uncle Vanya' (56) off-Broadway; and Eugene O'Neill's 'A Moon for the Misbegotten' (57) at the Bijou, New York. He produced and starred in a film of the *Uncle Vanya* (58), but it was a wretched thing, and despite a personal visit by him was unable to get a single public showing in Britain. His fourth marriage ended in divorce in 1959.

In the 60s he continued his occasional stage appearances in New York, notably in a revival of 'Strange Interlude' (63). There were also occasional film parts, of which the most impressive was his ageing and physically sick President in *Advise and Consent* (62). But his wan apparition in one sequence of the Franco-Italian *La Bonne Soupe* (63) with Marie Bell and Annie Girardot sharing the title role, was merely pathetic. He also had small parts in *In Harm's Way* (65) and Arthur Penn's *Mickey One*. At the time of his death, of cancer, in 1969, he was trying to set up a film of Jean Renoir's biography, 'Renoir My Father', with himself in the title role; some months earlier he had relinquished his interest in an off-Broadway theatre that he had hoped to use for experimental work.

Spencer Tracy

During the latter part of his career it became customary for both press and his peers to instance Spency Tracy as one of the greatest – if not *the* greatest – of screen actors. Katharine Hepburn has said so on several occasions ('... he never gussied it up. He just did it, he let it ride along on its enormous simplicity. That's what was absolutely thrilling about Spencer's acting'), but if we dismiss her as partial, there are others. Humphrey Bogart: 'What is a good actor? Spencer Tracy is a good actor, almost the best. Because you don't see the mechanism working, the wheels turning.' Richard Widmark: 'He's the greatest movie actor there ever was. If he had wanted to go the classical route, he could have been as great in that field as Laurence Olivier. I've learned more about acting from watching Tracy than in any other way. He has great truth in everything he does.' Fredric March: 'One of the finest actors of our time. . . . I'm nuts about Spencer.' As this sort of adulation (or appreciation) increased, and Tracy was asked about acting, he would reply gruffly: 'Just know your lines and don't bump into the furniture.' (There is another story that Lee Marvin was having some difficulty with his character and asked Tracy what *his* motivation was. Tracy replied: 'Look, I'm too old, too tired and too goddam rich for all this bull. Let's just get on with the scene.') In fact, Tracy studied his scripts, locked away for days, though the result was – Widmark again – 'so honest and seems so effortless'. And the public liked him: Tracy was one of the few actors whose career went only in an upward curve. Not all his films were hits, but his career had no reversals and he went from being a solid, reliable young actor to Grand Old Man of the movies.

He was born in Milwaukee, Wisconsin, in 1900, of Irish-midwest stock, was educated at Ripon College, where he discovered that he enjoyed debating – which caused him to consider an acting career, and he went to study at the AADA. His first job was as a robot in 'R.U.R.' at $10 a week, and his first real Broadway part was in a comedy starring Ethel Barrymore, 'A Royal Fandango' (23). Later he worked under George M. Cohan in three plays, and by 1929 was well enough known to be able to go from play to play: four of the five were flops, but the fifth, 'The Last Mile', wasn't, and it made Tracy a Broadway name. He played an imprisoned killer. During its run, he made two shorts for Vitaphone (*The Hard Guy* and *Taxi Talks*) and was tested by MGM, Universal, Fox and WB, all of whom considered him unsuitable for films. John Ford, however, saw him in the play and insisted on having him for the lead in *Up the River* (30), another prison story. Fox signed him to a long-term contract.

His second film for them was a hit, *Quick Millions* (31), as a truck driver who becomes a ruthless racketeer. He was thereupon typed as a gangster, though by fighting Fox he managed to get other parts – but mostly as a big-headed tough guy who learns humility in the last reel. He cut his teeth on both comedy and drama, in a series of mainly poor films (most Fox products of this period were clinkers): *Six-Cylinder Love*, a domestic drama with Sidney Fox as his wife; *Goldie* with Warren Hymer, a Flagg and Quirt type comedy, also with Jean Harlow; the poor *Sky Devils* (32) at UA; *She Wanted a Millionaire*, as Joan Bennett's faithful swain; *Disorderly Conduct*, as a demoted cop who goes wrong but reforms; *Young America*, a sentimental domestic piece

Colleen Moore – one of her last films – and Spencer Tracy in The Power and the Glory *(33). When the New Yorker Cinema revived it in 1970 the ads said: 'Famous as the film which influenced the style and content of* Citizen Kane'.

directed by Frank Borzage; *Society Girl* and *Painted Woman*, both of whom were Peggy Shannon (in the latter as a dance-hall girl reformed by pearl-trader Tracy); and *Me and My Gal*, with Bennett and Tracy playing a wisecracking detective.

The film that established him was *20,000 Years in Sing Sing* (33). He was borrowed by WB to replace James Cagney who was feuding with that studio; and his position was consolidated by two other fine movies that year. *The Face in the Sky* with Marion Nixon wasn't one of them, but *The Power and the Glory* was, an epic drama written by Preston Sturges, with a much-publicized 'revolutionary' way of story-telling called 'narratage' – it turned out to be Tracy's voice over the images. Of his performance William Troy wrote in The Nation: 'Spencer Tracy's railroad president is one of the fullest characterizations ever achieved on the screen.' There was *Shanghai Madness*, a poor melodrama in which he was a naval officer cashiered after firing on Chinese communists, and the *Mad Game*, as a boot-legger; and then the other good one, Borzage's *A Man's Castle*, a romance with Loretta Young against a realistic Depression backdrop, with Tracy's acting again the best thing in the film. Fox extended his contract to 1937, four films a year, though he was decidedly not the studio's most popular guy as far as the Front Office were concerned. He was loaned to UA for *Looking for Trouble* (34), teamed with Jack Oakie, as telephone linesmen in a successful comedy, and to MGM to play the title role in *The Show-Off*, George Kelly's play, which was hailed as a personal triumph for him. He and MGM got on well together.

He played a fast-talking promoter in a musical, *Bottoms Up*, and a gambler in *Now I'll Tell*, after which he refused to start *Helldorado* and was replaced by Richard Arlen; then he refused to start *Marie Galante* and was replaced by Edmund Lowe – but he changed his mind after a few days and paid out of his own pocket to have the film restarted with himself. He was right the first time; in any case, it was mainly a showcase for Fox's new discovery, Ketti Gallian. Then there was a small-town comedy, *It's a Small World* (35); at the end of shooting, in Yuma, Arizona, Tracy was arrested for drunkenness and kindred matters (resisting arrest, etc.). This was probably a studio ploy to discipline him, and now another was tried: he was cast in a supporting role (the heavy) in *The Farmer Takes a Wife*. He refused to do it and was fired, though he did do one last film for Fox, a remake of the 1924 *Dante's Inferno*, where he was a dishonest fairground entrepreneur. He was already negotiating with MGM. Mayer didn't want him because they already had one noted roisterer and trouble-maker (Wallace Beery), but Thalberg was enthusiastic.

To be fair to Fox, they had recognized his talent, but hadn't known how to handle it. Also, they had doubted whether he had sex-appeal – and so did MGM. This was somewhat paradoxical because it was hoped that the threat of being supplanted by Tracy would tame Clark Gable, who was playing up. MGM continued to worry about Tracy's lack of appeal to female audiences, even after he had won two Oscars, and for some years they were to give him roles subsidiary to Gable. On the whole, however, the studio did as well by him as he did by them – not that the association began auspiciously: he was featured in *Riff Raff*, as a fisherman. Harlow starred; there was a delay, and MGM hurried him into a quickie, *Murder Man*, as a reporter, and then rushed through *Whipsaw* (36) because Myrna Loy had been off the screen for some time.

The next four, however, pushed him to the forefront of Hollywood stars. He was

Captains Courageous *(37) detailed the adventures of a spoilt child (Freddie Bartholomew) on a Cape Cod fishing smack and specifically with old sea-dog Spencer Tracy: a surprising performance even from this actor. It was fine enough to win him an Oscar.*

disappointed when MGM refused to loan him to John Ford for *The Plough and the Stars* (they thought it would flop), but they did put him in Fritz Lang's noble *Fury*, as an innocent man facing a lynching (though his own performance shifted uneasily from the gentle to the maniacal) and then into their huge-budgeted *San Francisco*, which was shown simultaneously. As the battling (mostly against Gable) priest he received the first of his nine Oscar nominations (a record for a male star). He was one of a quartet of big stars (Loy, Powell, Harlow) in the screwball *Libeled Lady*, and then the Portuguese fisherman in Victor Fleming's version of Rudyard Kipling's *Captains Courageous* (37), uneasy with the accent–or so he claimed: the performance is still by far the best Hollywood attempt at that stock-figure–the earthy, elemental son of the sea/soil (it is Hepburn's favourite Tracy performance). He won an Oscar for it.

After these peaks, he was back at sea level (at least) with *They Gave Him a Gun* (the 'him' was Franchot Tone); *The Big City*, as a taxi-driver; *Mannequin*, as Joan Crawford's love interest–but MGM raised his salary by $1,000 a week; and *Test Pilot* (38), merely as Gable's sidekick–but Time magazine commented that Tracy was 'currently cinema's No. 1 actor's actor'. *Boy's Town* gave him a good part as the crusading Father Flanagan, a performance that was 'perfection itself and the most eloquent tribute to the Nebraska priest' (Frank S. Nugent in The New York Times): this brought him an Oscar for the second year running, and though the movie was little more than cops-and-robbers with social overtones, it was much-praised and a box-office hit (so was *Test Pilot*).

He continued crusading, on loan to his old studio (now called 20th), as the front half of *Stanley and Livingstone* (39), another good one; and, back home, took Hedy Lamarr in *I Take This Woman* (40). He was adventuring again in *Northwest Passage*, 'as impressive as ever' (William Whitebait) in an overlong version of Kenneth Roberts's best-seller (or, rather, the first part of it: MGM abandoned plans to film the rest, either as part of this film or as a sequel, as costs and length of shooting rose). Then, again, he went biographical, in the good *Edison the Man*; buddied and fought Gable again in *Boom Town*; and did another reprise job with *Men of Boy's Town* (41). He essayed *Dr Jekyll and Mr Hyde*: Somerset Maugham visited the set and asked: 'Which one is he supposed to be now?'–both performance and film were considered inferior to Fredric March's version. Tracy agreed; he only played it after several battles with the studio.

He had now overtaken Gable at the box-office. He made his first appearance in the top 10 in 1940, and was to appear again six more times through 1951–and when he was out of it, he was just out of it. These were peak years. He began filming *The Yearling* with Anne Revere, under King Vidor's direction, but difficult locations resulted in postponement (four years later Gregory Peck took over the part). Instead, Katharine Hepburn entered his life as the *Woman of the Year* (42); the following year she was the *Keeper of the Flame*. In between, Tracy was in the film of John Steinbeck's schmaltzy *Tortilla Flat* (42), and then in three war films: *A Guy Named Joe* with Irene Dunne; *The Seventh Cross* (44); and *30 Seconds Over Tokyo*, in a 'special' appearance as Lt Colonel Doolittle. *The Seventh Cross* was infinitely the best but didn't achieve the outstanding success of the other two. There had been too many anti-Nazi chase dramas: this one was set in pre-war Germany and was directed by Fred Zinnemann. Said Tracy's biographer, Larry Swindell: 'The performance illustrated Tracy's sure footing on what Garson Kanin called his plateau beyond greatness, when "the audience is made aware of what a character is saying or thinking no matter what he is doing".' Co-star Signe Hasso said 'I have seldom worked with an actor so engrossed in his role'. While filming, she found him 'intense and withdrawn', and MGM's copywriters were now saying (in the ads): 'The perfect actor'.

After another comedy with Hepburn, *Without Love* (45), Tracy returned to the New York stage, in 'The Rugged Path' by Robert E. Sherwood: its notices were bad, but his weren't. Apart from the ones with Hepburn his late 40s films were unworthy of him: *The Sea of Grass* (47); Sinclair Lewis's *Cass Timberlane* with Lana Turner; *State of the Union* (48); Cukor's uncertain version of a West End success, *Edward My Son* (49), with Deborah Kerr, about an overdose of paternal pride (filmed in Britain); *Adam's Rib*; and *Malaya* with James Stewart, a particularly dull adventure melodrama. The 50s kicked off with the Minnelli-directed *Father of the Bride*, which was a very popular comedy: 'But amidst so much excellence, Spencer Tracy is still outstanding; this is his best playing for years,' said Dilys Powell. There was a sequel, *Father's Little Dividend* (51) and then, after the poor *The People Against O'Hara*, two excellent ones with Cukor directing, *Pat and Mike* (52) with Hepburn, written by Garson Kanin and Ruth Gordon, and *The Actress* (53), written by Gordon, in

Katharine Hepburn and Spencer Tracy on the set of State of the Union *(48). He was an idealist campaigning for the Presidency, and life was complicated by the politically ambitious Angela Lansbury: but there was never any doubt that he would end up back in Hepburn's arms.*

which Tracy was Jean Simmons's pa, and disapproving of her aspirations. It was a critical but not box-office success. In neither category was the one between them, *Plymouth Adventure* (52), a drama of the Mayflower, and described by more than one critic as a 'Thanksgiving Turkey'. It was Sight and Sound who described Tracy as 'a Lear of the Plains', in 20th's heavy Western, *Broken Lance* (54), and it was Gable who said this (to Hedda Hopper): 'Spence *is* the part. The old rancher is mean, unreasonable, and vain. All he has to do is show up and be photographed.'

Tracy got $165,000 plus a percentage for it, his first movie outside MGM in years. For MGM he made a much-praised modern Western, *Bad Day at Black Rock* (55), and he was scheduled to do *The Desperate Hours* with Bogart, but neither would give way on top-billing (though, privately, they were friends). There was started another Western, *Tribute to a Bad Man*, but after some weeks on location director Robert Wise fired Tracy, with MGM's concurrence. The actor never made known publicly his side of the dispute, but the unit's point of view was disclosed in an article in Look in 1962, from which it is clear that Tracy's conduct was unreasonable. In his later years he was

cantankerous and virtually undirectable. The Look piece also made him out to be embittered and sourly conscious of death, which had already taken Bogart and Gable, among many other friends. Tracy was certainly not happy at MGM during the 50s – it had changed too much. It has been acknowledged that few people could handle him during these last years: one was director Stanley Kramer, another was Hepburn, his constant companion. (Tracy had married an actress, Louise Treadwell, in 1923; the marriage endured, though in later years they lived separately.)

MGM and Tracy came to the parting of the ways, 'by mutual agreement', and he moved over to Paramount for *The Mountain* (56), and then to 20th for *The Desk Set* (57), with Hepburn. He was then embroiled in WB's film of Hemingway's *The Old Man and the Sea* (58), but it was hardly worth the considerable effort: he found the location work under Zinnemann arduous – and it was re-done in the studio tank, with John Sturges now directing; then the public stayed away. Said Time magazine on Tracy as the old Mexican fisherman: 'In most roles Tracy plays himself, but usually, out of deference to the part, he plays himself with a difference. This time he plays himself with indifference.' But the same critic thought him Oscar-worthy for his job in John Ford's entertaining *The Last Hurrah*, from Edwin O'Connor's novel, about a wily politician on his last campaign, surrounded by a host of old-time character actors; and also at Columbia, three years later, he did *The Devil at Four O'Clock* (61), playing an alcoholic priest. Both did poorly.

Meanwhile, he had started to work with Kramer, who produced and directed his last films (though he should also have been in *Cheyenne Autumn* and *The Cincinnati Kid*: when at the last moment ill-health caused him to withdraw from them, Edward G. Robinson replaced him in both). Kramer adored Tracy, and Tracy was amenable with him, but the films are a poor reflection of such cordiality, being mainly viewable for Tracy's participation. *Inherit the Wind* (60) was a dreary evocation of the famous 'monkey-trial', with the Tracy character based on Clarence Darrow (the film was taken from a Broadway play): Tracy was pitted against Fredric March. He was at law again, as a judge, in *Judgment at Nuremberg* (61), a specious enactment of the century's most important trial. Neither film did well, though *Nuremberg* had a certain cachet in the US. The last two were giant box-office, however. In *It's a Mad Mad Mad Mad World* (63), he was surrounded by a bevy of some of America's least funny comics, a sledge-hammer comedy on the subject of greed. He was the police chief who (also) finally succumbed.

Spencer Tracy's last four films were made for producer-director Stanley Kramer: perhaps the best of them was Judgment at Nuremburg *(61) with Marlene Dietrich.*

After four years his health improved enough to permit him to do *Guess Who's Coming to Dinner* (67), a facile comedy about a mixed marriage, with Hepburn as his wife and Sidney Poitier as the prospective son-in-law. He died shortly after shooting was concluded, and was awarded a year later the BFA Best Actor Award (the first time a major film prize was given posthumously). Said Penelope Mortimer in her downbeat review in The Observer: 'Which brings me, thank goodness, to Tracy and Hepburn, and while either of them are on screen the most savage criticism is replaced by gratitude. It is odd, looking back at the film reviews of 20 years ago, to find that Spencer Tracy was not always considered the giant that he appears today. There were more giants, it's true. To me, at any rate, that craggy face and burly build, the exploding humour, extra-ordinary gentleness and toughness of old leather, have always represented the ideal man – and that is real film-fan talk. I found it very moving to see him in this, his last picture, talent, presence and personality all unimpaired.'

Claire Trevor

There were certain male stars – George Brent, Herbert Marshall – who made their careers primarily in women's pictures: and there were ladies who specialized in masculine adventures. Every Western had its saloon floozie, every gangster picture its moll – or several. These were the broads, the beaten-up dames (sometimes literally), hand on hip, cigarette dangling from their lips, usually blonde, cynical, warm-hearted and tough. No one was more sure-footed in her portrayal of these ladies than Claire Trevor, who started as an ingénue and got side-tracked into such parts. She was a man's star. She hadn't good enough curves and was too careful an actress to be raised to top stardom by her audiences, and she later considered that she hadn't played the Hollywood game strenuously enough; but most of her work is glowing. It is not gawdy or bright, but has the dark satisfying polish of a piece of amber. Audiences may have taken her for granted, but buffs cherish her.

She was born in New York City in 1909 or 1912 and educated at schools in Larchmont; she took an art course at Columbia and later enrolled with the AADA. Her professional experience began at the Festival Theatre in Ann Arbor, Michigan, after which a Warner talent scout saw her and recommended her for some of the Vitaphone shorts then being made at that company's Flatbush studio. She also played with a stock company that Warners had established at St Louis as a training ground for talent. She was in stock again at Southampton, Long Island, when she was offered a star role in 'Whistling in the Dark' (32), opposite Edward Arnold. The following year she was in 'The Party's Over', and during its run signed a five-year contract with Fox.

Her first film part was in a Western starring George O'Brien, *Life in the Raw* (33), and she performed a similarly innocuous function in another picture with him, *The Last Trail*. She had a good part, as a reporter, in *The Mad Game* with Spencer Tracy, but her chance came when Sally Eilers walked out of *Jimmy and Sally*, one of several slight pictures Eilers had been doing with James Dunn: Trevor replaced her, and Fox teamed her with Dunn again in *Hold That Girl* (34), again as a tabloid newsgal, sharp and full of wisecracks. She was Shirley Temple's mother in *Baby Take a Bow* and a cabaret singer in *Wild Gold*, a poor drama of the ghost towns, with John Boles as a drunken engineer. The pattern was already established. Fox were impressed by the verve of so young a girl and put her into *Elinor Norton* (35), based on a Mary Roberts Rinehart story about a girl who marries a neurotic (Hugh Williams). Photoplay described it as 'unbelievably dull' and 'completely boring', a verdict echoed by the public, and Trevor's chances of becoming a star at this stage receded.

It was, in any case, a B picture, and Trevor now found herself firmly established as a B picture actress: *Spring Tonic* with Lew Ayres; *Black Sheep* with Edmund Lowe; *Dante's Inferno*, an A with Spencer Tracy; *Navy Wife* in the title role, with Ralph Bellamy; *My Marriage* (36) and *Song and Dance Man*, both with Paul Kelly; *Human Cargo* with Brian Donlevy; *To Mary With Love*, supporting Myrna Loy; *Star for a Night*, a mother-love drama; *15 Maiden Lane* with Cesar Romero; and *Career Woman* and *Time Out for Romance* (37), both with Michael Whalen. Paramount borrowed her to play a nightclub singer in a programmer, *King of Gamblers*, starring Akim Tamiroff and Lloyd Nolan, and then Fox–now 20th–made her a reporter again in *One Mile From Heaven*, a timid attempt at a racial drama–about a coloured woman who claims parentage of a white child: its melodramatics were redeemed by Bill Robinson's dancing.

Goldwyn borrowed her for *Dead End*, where she had one showy scene: she was Humphrey Bogart's ex-girlfriend who'd taken to streetwalking. This was a big picture, much praised, and she hoped it would do for her what *Of Human Bondage* had done for Bette Davis; it did bring her an Oscar nomination in the Supporting category, but not better parts. She said later that if Darryl F. Zanuck 'hadn't confidence in a player, said player might just as well up and leave at the outset'. She completed her contract with *Second Honeymoon*, as confidante to Loretta Young; *Big Town Girl* with Donald Woods; and *Walking Down Broadway* (38), a tale of six showgirls that had nothing to do with Von Stroheim's earlier film.

She went to Warners to make a film with Edward G. Robinson (with whom she was doing a radio programme), *The Amazing Dr Clitterhouse*: she was Bogart's moll who in the last reel betrays him. She stayed at Warners for the Technicolor *Valley of the Giants*, as the saloon girl with a past reformed in the last reel by Wayne Morris. Some slight prestige accrued from these two performances, despite the stereotyped parts, but that was dissipated when Trevor unaccountably returned to 20th to play yet another reporter in *Five of a Kind* (39), whose sole purpose was to exploit the Dionne quintuplets. However, *Stagecoach* was on its way, Ford's fine Western with John Wayne, with Trevor expectedly cast as an American *boule de suif*: her reputation and everyone else's rose as a result of the film's success.

At Universal she was George Raft's anxious wife in *I Stole a Million*; then she co-starred with Wayne again in *Allegheny Uprising* and *The Dark Command* (40); she stayed out west for *Honky Tonk* (41), supporting Clark Gable and Lana Turner (but alas, most of Trevor's scenes were cut), and *Texas*, starring with William Holden and Glenn Ford. She starred with Ford again in *The Adventures of Martin Eden* (42), but at MGM again was in support, in *Crossroads*. Then she returned to Bs and programmers: *Street of Chance* with Burgess Meredith; *The Desperadoes* (43) with Randolph Scott and Ford; *Good Luck Mr Yates*; and *The Woman of the Town* with Albert Dekker. She was off the screen for a while, becoming a mother (by her second husband; she married for the third, and last, time in 1948), and returned in a series of thick-ear melodramas, each poorer than the

John Ford's Stagecoach *(39) marked his return to his first love, the Western, after ten years of (mainly) dramas that varied from* The Lost Patrol *to* Mary of Scotland. *It was equally significant for some of its performers, including Claire Trevor and John Wayne.*

last: *Murder My Sweet* (44) with Dick Powell, *Johnny Angel* (45) with George Raft, *Crack-Up* (46) with Pat O'Brien, *Born to Kill* (47) with Lawrence Tierney, and *Raw Deal* (48) with Dennis O'Keefe (the last two were directed by Robert Wise and Anthony Mann, respectively, before they hit the big time). After *Crack-Up* there was a change of pace when she played a hard-boiled shopgirl in *The Bachelor's Daughters* (46). Depressed by this bunch, she had returned to the stage, including a New York appearance in 'The Big Two' (47), which soon folded, though she got nice notices. She said later that this experience finally rid her of the ambition to be a Broadway star, and that she would try to be a movie star instead – at last.

It was too late. Within a year she gave two of her best performances, demonstrated her versatility and won an Oscar: but she didn't thereafter get better parts in better pictures. In *Key Largo* she supported Bogart, Bacall, etc., in a flashy part as Edward G. Robinson's drink-sodden mistress or moll, so desperate for a drink she would croak her way through 'Moanin' Low' to please him: it was a great performance and brought her a Best Supporting Oscar. Then she had one of her rare 'normal' parts in *The Babe Ruth Story*, as Mrs R opposite William Bendix as the baseball player, and was magnificent again as the bitchy Broadway actress in *The Velvet Touch*, supporting Rosalind Russell. And she gave a lively comedy performance in *The Lucky Stiff* (49), but it wasn't a good picture. Nor were these: *Borderline* (50) with Fred MacMurray, *Best of the Badmen* (51) with Robert Ryan, *Hard Fast and Beautiful*, as the ruthless mother of Sally Forrest, *Hoodlum Empire* (52) with Brian Donlevy, and *My Man and I* with Shelley Winters and Wendell Corey.

Stop You're Killing Me (53) was a musical remake of *A Slight Case of Murder*, with Broderick Crawford in the Edward G. Robinson role and Trevor as his wife, played before by Ruth Donnelly. Trevor was inferior, but then, so was the film. *The Stranger Wore a Gun* was a typical Randolph Scott Western, originally made in 3-D, with Trevor 'easy and graceful as the hard, good girl' (the MFB). She could play such parts

Claire Trevor hasn't had all the luck she deserved in films, and she has only made four films in the last decade: but her part in The Stripper *(63) was a good one. With Joanne Woodward as the old friend who seduces her son.*

blindfold: she gave her usual loose-lady performance in *The High and the Mighty* (54), but in a reasonably good film it could stun– and this one brought her third Oscar nomination. *Man Without a Star* (55) was a Western with Trevor propped up against the saloon bar as usual–Jeanne Crain was her rival for Kirk Douglas, and the sweet Crain, of course, got him. She had small parts in *Lucy Gallant* and *The Mountain* (56), the latter with Spencer Tracy; and another good chance in *Marjorie Morningstar* (58), as Natalie Wood's mother. On TV she won an Emmy for her performance as Fran in 'Dodsworth' (56) with Fredric March, and she appears regularly if not frequently in that medium.

Three of her last four films gave her good parts. In *Two Weeks in Another Town* (62) she was Edward G. Robinson's scornful harpy of a wife, and in *The Stripper* (63) she was Richard Beymer's mother, a widow whose generous kindness to old friend Joanne Woodward turns somewhat sour. In *How To Murder Your Wife* (65) she was another man-hating harridan, married to Eddie Mayehoff and anxious that Virna Lisi should start to treat Jack Lemmon in the same way. Her last picture was *The Cape Town Affair* (67), an amateurish South African thriller, where she had a brave stab at playing an old pedlar who is also a police informer.

Lana Turner

Lana Turner has been a film-star for 30 years. She has no other identity than that of film-star–and that in its most obvious sense: a glamour girl from a mould, a fabulous creature who moves, on screen, among beautiful furnishings, and who, off-screen, is primarily noted for a series of love-affairs and marriages. She has been married seven times, and her name has been linked by the fan-magazines with a score of other men. It is presumably due to this that she owes the longevity of her career, which has consistently triumphed over appalling personal notices. Even her admirers would admit that she couldn't act her way out of a paper bag.

Her beginnings seem to be on par for those of a Hollywood glamour queen. She was born in Wallace, Idaho, in 1921. Her parents moved to California, where they separated; the child was partly brought up by cruel foster-parents. Her father was a victim of murder for robbery. When the young Turner was reunited with her mother they often lived in poverty–until she was 15, when she was seen by Billy Wilkerson of The Hollywood Reporter in a Los Angeles drugstore, an event which passed into Hollywood mythology. Wilkerson was struck by her looks and nubile figure. He got her an agent, who got her a contract at WB, with a small part in Mervyn Le Roy's lynching drama, *They Won't Forget* (37) – she was seen sipping soda at a drugstore fountain. She had a bit in *The Great Garrick* and was loaned out to play a Eurasian dancer in *Marco Polo*. She was also in *Four's a Crowd*, but WB weren't impressed, and when Le Roy, who was moving to MGM, requested Turner's release so that she could accompany him, they let her go.

Her new studio made her Mickey Rooney's love interest in *Love Finds Andy Hardy* (38) and then put her in a series of programmers: *Rich Man Poor Girl* with Robert Young, *Dramatic School* and *Calling Dr Kildare* (39). She was starred in *These Glamour Girls*, a campus comedy in which she revenged herself on the socialite likes of Jane Bryan and Anita Louise; and in the weak *Dancing Co-ed*, *Two Girls on Broadway* (40) and *We Who Are Young*. It could not be said that the public response to Turner in these films was enthusiastic, but it was another story with stills. MGM were publicizing her as the 'Sweater Girl', and pictures of the well-stacked Turner were much in demand (she was to come into greater prominence when the US entered the war, and was one of the half-dozen leading pin-ups). There was, therefore, a good reason to star her in the big *Ziegfeld Girl* (41) along with Judy Garland and Hedy Lamarr. Turner was the one whose preference for men and jewellery (over a stage career) led to tragedy and death. She was by no means up to the dramatic demands of an undemanding part, and in *Dr Jekyll and Mr Hyde* was ludicrously mis-cast as an English deb.

MGM saw her as a successor to Joan Crawford: a remake of *Our Dancing Daughters* was contemplated, but instead she was given the accolade of starring opposite Clark Gable in *Honky Tonk*, playing a prim young miss who is wooed by him and converted into something more carnal. The film was so successful that they were re-teamed for *Somewhere I'll Find You* (42). Between these two, Turner found *Johnny Eager*, where the other MGM biggie, Robert Taylor, changed her from sociology student to gangster's moll. *Slightly Dangerous* (43), a comedy, was, after those, a let-down, but after a year's absence (she was in New York with husband Artie Shaw) she did *Marriage Is a Private Affair* (44), one of the myriad films about hasty wartime marriages and totally undistinguished; but she carried it to a certain success – co-star John Hodiak meant little at the box-office. Equally topical was *Keep Your Powder Dry*, in which she joins the WACs – spoilt, selfish and uncooperative, until vouchsafed a vision of what Serving her Country Really Means. *Weekend at the Waldorf* (45) had several other stars – Van Johnson, Ginger Rogers – and was a big success; and *The Postman Always Rings Twice* (46) was the third cinematization of James M. Cain's masterly thriller (already filmed in France in 1939 and Italy in 1942). She was a *femme fatale* who inveigles John Garfield into murdering her elderly husband, probably her most effective performance.

Now entrenched as one of the top ladies on the MGM lot, she had a couple of box-office hits: *Green Dolphin Street* (47) with Van Heflin a period melodrama from a novel by Elizabeth Goudge, set in New Zealand; and *Cass Timberlane*, where she was a girl from the other side of the tracks married to judge Spencer Tracy. Re-teaming with Gable in a war story, *Homecoming* (48), didn't, however, reap the same rewards; and she was unremittingly modern as Milady de Winter in the otherwise enjoyable *The*

Nubile young wife, old husband, and convenient handyman (John Garfield): James M. Cain's The Postman Always Rings Twice *brought some exciting twists to an old situation, and the film version (46) provided Lana Turner with one of her best chances.*

Madame X had been a famous tearjerker for Dorothy Donnelly (16), Pauline Frederick (20), Ruth Chatterton (29) and Gladys George (37): it was silly of Lana Turner (66) to invite comparison (but sillier still of Universal to re-do it at all). With Ricardo Montalban.

Three Musketeers. She was off the screen again for a year before doing *A Life of Her Own* (50) with Ray Milland, one of the least successful of George Cukor's films.

MGM were in a quandary: Turner's box-office was falling rapidly, and she wasn't worth keeping as a prestige item. The solution was to put her into musicals, where acting ability didn't matter. She couldn't sing, but that didn't matter either – she could be (and was) dubbed. *Mr Imperium* (51) co-starred Ezio Pinza, in an attempt to launch him into screen stardom after his success in 'South Pacific'; it was a box-office disaster. Her second musical was altogether in a bigger league – *The Merry Widow* (52) and it was in every way but one entirely worthy of the Lehar score, curtailed though it was. But that one was crucial – Turner herself. Critic after critic cracked that she was the unmerriest widow you ever saw, and she was still out of her depth as the (alcoholic) movie-star in the much-liked *The Bad and the Beautiful* (53), though Richard Winnington thought casting her as 'a star of the genus Lana Turner could be a master stroke!'

In *Latin Lovers* she and Ricardo Montalban were more or less incidental to a camera tour of Brazil. It was a flop, and so was *The Flame and the Flesh* (54), a curious remake of a 1937 French melodrama (*Naples au Baiser du Feu*). The MFB thought some pleasure could be derived from the playing, described as 'intriguingly inept', and added that Turner gave 'a rich display of familiar mannerisms'. Once more she was hopefully teamed with Gable in *Betrayed* – but to no avail; and her own performance, as a Dutch double agent helping the Resistance, was notably useless – though the dialogue didn't help. Not even Garbo could have made much of her role of a high priestress in *The Prodigal* (55), a Biblical effort with Edmund Purdom, but she was competent in *The Sea Chase* with John Wayne – her first outside MGM in over 15 years. Her contract wound up with *Diane* in which, again, she was inappropriate – as Diane de Poitiers. Christopher Isherwood worked on the script. The film was a failure, and Turner's contract was not renewed (but anyway MGM were shuffling off all their contract stars). Picturegoer at this time described her as 'a difficult actress on set'.

Twentieth then signed her to play Myrna Loy's old role in the remake of *The Rains Came*, *The Rains of Ranchipur*. It was another flop. She stayed away again until the modestly budgeted *The Lady Takes a Flyer* (57), with Jeff Chandler, at Universal, and then played a frigid widow in *Peyton Place*, neurotically concerned about her bastard daughter's virginity. The original novel had been one of the most successful ever published, and 'Peyton Place' had become a synonym for any small town with an underground sex-life of bizarre complexity. There was nothing to prevent the film from becoming a giant grosser – nothing, not even script, direction and acting of soporific dullness; and the box-office got a boost from the scandal involving Turner in 1958.

Her daughter (by her second husband) stabbed to death a small-time gangster-gigolo, Johnny Stompanato, who was her lover. The subsequent headlines raked up such items as the letters Turner had written to Stompanato and her not insubstantial love-life. The verdict was justifiable homicide, and Turner emerged from the case as a rather pitiable figure; and despite *Peyton Place*, a dubious bet to continue in films. The British film she had made just before the scandal, *Another Time Another Place* (58), died at the box-office, but more probably of press maulings. However, she was engaged by Ross Hunter of Universal to appear in *Imitation of Life* (59) and that copped some of the year's biggest money. It was a remake of the Fannie Hurst novel that Claudette Colbert had done earlier, centring on an actress's troubles with her daughter. Dated and vulgar, it bore out Hunter's allegation that in the right vehicle, the public (especially the female part of it) would turn out to see the old stars. He thereupon put Turner into a follow-up, *Portrait in Black* (60), and another remake of an old sudser, *Madame X* (65), but the grosses–particularly of the second one, indicated that Turner was one old star the public didn't want to see. (Said Pauline Kael: 'She's not Madame X, she's Brand X; she's not an actress, she's a commodity.') Also, a dim film version of James Gould Cozzens's novel *By Love Possessed* (60) did poorly; so did *Bachelor in Paradise* (61) and *Who's Got the Action?* (62), where Turner was little more than a foil to Bob Hope and Dean Martin respectively. Her only other recent films have been duallers, *Love Has Many Faces* (64) and *The Big Cube* (70) made in Mexico. In 1969 she married for the seventh time, and began a TV series with George Hamilton, 'The Survivors', based on an idea by Harold Robbins. It didn't run long.

Rudolph Valentino

He was born in Castellaneto, in southern Italy, in 1895, and christened Rodolpho Alfonzo Raffaelo Pierre Filibert Guglielmi di Valentina d'Antonguolla, a bizarre start to a life which, like the name, was really too grandiose for him: witnesses speak of his intelligence and sensitivity (as if surprised to find he had these qualities), but he seems to have been an uninteresting man. Certainly today, as an actor, his much-vaunted magnetism is barely discernible–little more than a flashing of the eyes and a flaring of the nostrils. In ardour, he looks most like a vampire about to bite, but he does have a certain panther-like grace in movement. No personality comes through, as–to take a couple of names at random from the same period–it does with William Haines or Antonio Moreno; but if he appears to us today a ridiculous figure, snarling at some heroine while rigged up as if for a camp carnival ball, so indeed did he at the time to large sections of the public–particularly the masculine half, who despised him for his foppishness and resented him for such accoutrement as the slave bracelet he flaunted.

It is unlikely that he would have been a star at any other time–in the unlikely event of his happening at any other time: his life bore a pleasing resemblance to the films and novels of the day, rags-to-riches and fierce, unrequited passions. 'In my country men are the masters–and I believe that women are happier that way' was his creed, but in life he was completely subject to the whims of his second wife, Natacha Rambova (born Winifred Shaunessy in Salt Lake City), even to the extent of allowing her almost to sabotage his film career. Efforts were made to persuade the public that he was a regular two-fisted guy, but it was generally conceded, even among his admirers, that he had been a gigolo of no particular discrimination–rather than starve, of course. (One biographer, Irving Shulman, concludes that Valentino was not homosexual; but if the extracts from his diary printed in Kenneth Anger's 'Hollywood-Babylone' are genuine, he was.) However, much of the truth was not admitted at the time, and some accounts of Valentino's youth are entirely fictitious.

In his birthplace he was regarded as a failure. His father, an army vet, died when he was young. The boy was sent to a military academy at Taranto, and later joined the navy but was unacceptable as officer-material in either service; he did have some success when, as a bleak alternative, he studied agriculture. However, he preferred to squander the family money, and at 18 was packed off to New York. His friends were other Italian immigrants until, according to Adela Rogers St John, he was befriended by three wealthy Frenchmen. When they dropped him, he became a gardener on a Long Island estate; but the occupation he found most congenial was dancing: after a while as a 10¢-a-dancer, he began exhibition dancing with a regular partner, in dance-halls and then in clubs. Then he met Bonnie

Glass, one of Manhattan's favourites, and he replaced Clifton Webb as her partner; he later danced with Joan Sawyer . . . but to the police department he was known as a petty thief and blackmailer. He left New York in the cast of a musical, 'The Masked Model'; it failed in Ogden, and he made his way to San Francisco, where he danced in 'Nobody Home' until it folded. But he made friends easily, and managed to cadge money: one friend recommended him to try the movies and he moved to Los Angeles.

He got a job dancing in a ballroom scene in *Alimony* (18) at the standard 'extra' fee of $5 a day. He danced in a nightclub, and through a friend heard of a likely role in *A Married Virgin*–a good one, as a villainous Italian count. Unfortunately, the film ran into financial difficulties and wasn't released for two years (20). He got small parts in *A Society Sensation* and *All Night*, both with Carmel Myers; and also at Universal, a couple with Mae Murray, whom he had known in New York: *The Delicious Little Devil* (19) and *The Big Little Person*, though she disliked his attempt at an Irishman in the latter. He was now making $100 a week. He was an Apache dancer in *A Rogue's Romance* with Earle Williams, and had a bit in *The Homebreaker* with Dorothy Dalton and Douglas McLean. Then Dorothy Gish chose him for a leading role–more villainy–in a comedy, *Out of Luck*, but this again led nowhere. However, he applied for and got a role in *The Eyes of Youth* starring Clara Kimbell Young, apparently as the hero, but in the final reel revealed to be a professional co-respondent employed by her husband.

Once again, the best he could do afterwards was a bit part in *An Adventuress* (20), which starred female impersonator Julian Eltinge: it was re-issued, after Valentino's success, as *The Isle of Love*. He also had parts, mostly as the villain, in *The Cheater*; *Passion's Playground*, playing the brother of his real-life friend, Norman Kerry; *Once to Every Woman*, as an Italian count, starring Dorothy Phillips; *Stolen Moments*; and *The Wonderful Chance*. He was married during this period, but his wife, Jean Acker, left him on the wedding night.

One of the powers behind Metro's throne was June Mathis, a plump and aggressive spinster: it was she who is regarded as Valentino's discoverer. She picked most of the studio's properties, and insisted on doing *The Four Horsemen of the Apocalypse* (21), a best-seller by Vicente Blasco-Ibañez. She produced and wrote the scenario; and was resolved to have Valentino for a lead role when she saw him in *The Eyes of Youth*. He was a success from the first day of shooting and his part was built up–that of a South American ne'er-do-well in France during World War I who becomes a hero. The première in New York was a sensation: this was another step that made movie-going respectable, and it made $4½ million (only three other films of the 20s figure on the Variety list of top grossers). Valentino had only featured billing, but all prints were soon recalled and the credits altered to make him the star.

His massive new public could see him a month later in *Uncharted Seas*, an Alaska gold-rush adventure directed by Wesley Ruggles; but the new heart-throb's real follow-up was *Camille*, as Armand to the great Nazimova. (It was on the set that he met Rambova, 'the Ice Maiden'; she was the art director.) The film was a success. Then *The Four Horsemen* team–Mathis, director Rex Ingram, co-star Alice Terry–reunited with him to do *The Conquering Power*, a heavy version of Balzac's 'Eugenie Grandet'. During its making, Mathis demanded a salary hike for him, from $350 a week to $450 but the studio offered only $400. So, when the film was completed, they moved together in some dudgeon to Paramount, where he got $500 a week, to increase to $1,000 or more over a three-year period.

Paramount's announcement of their coup was ecstatic, and they had just the property for their new star: *The Sheik*, a rubbishy but best-selling desert charade by E. M. Hull. Valentino, of course, had the title role, the kidnapper of a high-born English girl (Agnes Ayres, who was top-billed). The action, in the words of Griffith and Mayer, consisted of little but 'a menacing Valentino staring at a pleading Agnes Ayres while they warily circled each other for a clinch that was a long time in coming'. Clearly this was as appealing as had been Miss Hull's prose, for within two years it had earned $2 million–Valentino's second most successful film (re-issued in 1938 with a music-track and some success). Susceptible females fainted, and went Sheik-mad; an Arabian influence became noticeable in interior decoration; and a hit song emerged, 'The Sheik of Araby'. Already, Valentino's salary had risen to $1,250. The next was unspectacular, *Moran of the Lady Letty* (22), from a story by Frank Norris about a society sprig shanghaied aboard a yacht and falling for the captain's daughter (Dorothy Dalton). Critics found him unconvincing as a normal young man, so the next one, a modern triangle story, *Beyond the Rocks*, included lots of flashbacks to more romantic eras with him and Gloria Swanson as all the

Stunned by his success in The Sheik *and in other exotic roles, Valentino and his cohorts forced upon Paramount a vehicle called* The Young Rajah (*22*), *ostensibly a tale about a princeling trying to win back his throne, but in reality little but an excuse to present Valentino thus. Public ridicule proved Paramount right – but female fans still queued.*

lovers; it was specially concocted for them by Elinor Glyn.

He was delighted with the next, *Blood and Sand*, from Ibañez's bull-fighting story, co-starring Nita Naldi and directed by Fred Niblo. The New York Times decreed that Valentino was acting again, after just 'slicking his hair and posing' in recent films, and it was a big one at the wickets: but it had been difficult to make, with Valentino, spurred on by Rambova and Mathis, becoming more finicky. Now he demanded choice of properties, and complete control of his career; his films, he told a reporter, 'do not live up to my artistic ambitions'. Paramount unwillingly let him make *The Young Rajah*, written by Mathis, directed by Philip Rosen, but the result – Rudy in little but a jewelled jock-strap and a turban and some pearls – was a fiasco. The studio reasserted their contractual rights and had to take out an injunction to prevent him working elsewhere (his second legal difficulty at that time; earlier, a tangle had caused him to be indicted for bigamy). They offered him new terms, including $7,000 a week provided they had artistic control, but at Rambova's bidding, he refused – despite the fact that they were penniless. To make some money they embarked on a nationwide dancing tour, and he published a book of 'poems' called 'Day Dreams'.

They holidayed in Europe, and at the end of 1923 a compromise was reached: Valentino would make films for an independent, J. D. Williams, and Paramount would distribute. The first, a version of Booth Tarkington's *Monsieur Beaucaire* (24) – French aristocrat disguised as a barber at the court of the Spanish king – was eagerly awaited by fans, and restored Valentino generally to favour: 'Gorgeous is a word we invariably avoid,' said The New York Times, 'but this pictorial effort is thoroughly deserving of such an adjective, as never have such wondrous settings or beautiful costumes been seen in such a photoplay.' James R. Quirk in Photoplay, however, thought it a pity that Valentino was trying to be an actor at the expense of the personality that made him a sensation. In the end, however, the public didn't respond as hoped, and the effeminacy of Valentino's costumes was blamed. He was given a more masculine image in *A Sainted Devil*, an Argentinian tale by Rex Beach ('Rope's End') – entangled

After the débâcle of The Young Rajah *and many highly publicized private misfortunes, Valentino needed a good film, and he got it in* Monsieur Beaucaire (*24*), *the story of a barber who masquerades as a nobleman. The lady whose honour he's defending is Doris Kenyon.*

with two women and getting drunk. And in *Cobra* (25), also with Nita Naldi, there were some prize-fighting sequences. But both films were laughed off the screen – something which Valentino, of all stars, could least surmount.

Rambova was blamed for the downbeat response: willy-nilly, she had had the say-so on all three Williams pictures – designing the costumes on *Beaucaire*, interfering with the scripts of the other two (both, finally, were a mess). Now, Williams refused to back a tale that she had constructed for her husband, *The Hooded Falcon*, and the association was dissolved. But Rambova was out: Valentino was sought by other companies only on that condition – UA offered him the moon ($10,000 per week, plus a percentage) provided that Rambova was kept off it. To console her, he financed *What Price Beauty?* in which, producing and directing, she indulged her taste for outré décor and what looked like lesbian fantasies; when finally released, by Pathé, it was another fiasco. Not long afterwards, she left him.

His first film for UA was *The Eagle*, from Pushkin's 'Dubrovsky', a Russian Robin Hood during the days of Catherine the Great (Louise Closser Hale). Vilma Banky co-starred, and Clarence Brown directed: it was favourably received, and so was *The Son of the Sheik*, from E. M. Hull's new best-seller; Banky was the girl again, and there was a special guest appearance by Agnes Ayres as the hero's mother. Said The Times (London): 'It is impossible to ignore him. He is a personality on the screen, not merely a handsome presence.' Both films did smash business, which went some way towards consoling Valentino for the dreadful publicity he was now getting, culminating in the Chicago newspaper attack headed: 'The Pink Powder Puff' (a men's rest-room had installed a slot-machine with face-powder, supposedly to please him).

In August 1926 he went into a New York hospital with a perforated ulcer . . . the world (the female part of it) held its breath, and much of it gathered outside the hospital. He died ($200,000 in debt; he had earned over $5 million). The lying-in-state and the funeral were both major Happenings, with thousands of women lining the streets and several riots. This was the start of an entirely new form of necrology, and there are today, still, Valentino fan-clubs. Three years after he died, June Mathis died, and was buried beside him. Among the several memoirs published was Rambova's, which included conversations with Valentino from the Beyond. Interest in him hardly abated; in 1938 UA re-issued both its films, with surprisingly successful results. Film producers continually announced plans for a life of Valentino (20th planned one with Tyrone Power) and in 1951 one finally materialized from Columbia called *Valentino*, with Eleanor Parker and Anthony Dexter. It was a flop, and Dexter was soon forgotten. In 1967 Marcello Mastroianni appeared in an Italian stage musical based on Valentino, and doubtless the last has not been heard of him.

Valentino in The Son of the Sheik (*26*)*: most of his acting was like that.*

Conrad Veidt

Robert Morley was, in his early days, Dialogue Director on one of Conrad Veidt's pictures. Veidt, said Morley, 'was a master at delivering lines and had been delivering them in the same way for years. He always spoke them very slowly when everyone else spoke rather fast, and softly when everyone else spoke loudly. On the screen this seemed most effective.' In other words, Veidt was a highly accomplished technician, but not an actor likely to capture the imagination – even if doting fan-magazines spoke of his 'intriguing moodiness and reserve'. His tall, gaunt figure, the broken accent, the command and the haughty face, expressing often an aloofness and a possibility of cruelty: these qualified him to play with great skill a certain type of person – usually, of course, a German person.

He was born in Berlin in 1893 and educated there at the Hohenzollern Gymnasium. In 1912 he began to study under Max Reinhardt; played under his management in Berlin, with the other famous alumni – Werner Krauss, Jannings, Albert Basserman and Paul Weigel. His first big part was in Georg Kaiser's 'Korallen'. He also acted over a period of years in a score of other European cities. He made his film debut in *Das Tagebuch einer Verlorenen* (17), subsequently appearing in *Es Werde Licht*, *Prostitution* (18), *Satanas* (19) and *Der Januskopf* (20), a double role under the direction of Murnau. Next was the famous surrealist film known best as *The Cabinet of Dr Caligari*: Veidt played the maniac, and the success of the film made him internationally known. The next were *Prinz Kuckuck* (21); and *Das Indische Grabmal* in which he was a fanatical Hindu; after which he did some of the historical subjects so popular in Germany: *Danton*, *Lady Hamilton* (22) as Nelson, *Paganini*, *Lucretia Borgia* and *Carlos und Elizabeth* (23). He co-starred in *NJU* (24) with Jannings and Elizabeth Bergner; was in Paul Leni's grotesque *Die Wachsfigurenkabinet* as Ivan the Terrible, and in another evocation of the supernatural, *Orlacs Hände*; was in a Franco-German co-production *Le Comte Kostia/Graf Kostja* (25) and in *Liebe Macht Blind* with Lil Dagover. He was successively *Der Geiger von Florenz* (26), *Die Brüder Schellenberg*, another *doppelrolle*, with Dagover, and *Der Student von Prag*, given unlimited wealth in return for his soul – a film which first made him very famous outside Germany and which was to overshadow all his later work. Just before it, he made *Dürfen wir Schweigen?* with Fritz Kortner, and *Kreuzzug des Weibes* and afterwards *Die Flucht in die Nacht*. He then worked abroad: he played Pirandello's *Enrico IV* (27) in an Italian version of that play; was in the Swedish Ernst Mattson's *Jerusalem* (27); and went to France for *Les Maudits*.

Veidt's association with 'demoniacal' roles led to an offer from Hollywood: to play Louis XI to John Barrymore's Villon in *The Beloved Rogue*. He stayed on to make *A Man's Past*; *The Man Who Laughs* (28), from Victor Hugo's story about a man whose face is scarred into a permanent laugh, directed by Paul Leni; and *The Last Performance* (29), again with Mary Philbin, directed by Paul Fejos, and with a brief Talkie sequence. None of them was very successful, and Veidt's accent, at this stage, precluded a Hollywood career. He returned to Germany and UFA for his first Talkie, and appeared in the English version that was made simultaneously: *Die Letzte Kompagnie/The Last Company* (30), a story of Napoleonic times. He made *Der Mann der den Mord Beging*, set among the diplomatic set in Istanbul; then did the German version only of a UFA/BIP co-production, *Cape Forlorn/Menschen in Kafig* directed by E. A. Dupont. He was in the German version only of *Journey's End*, in the Colin Clive part, made in Hollywood; and in a German *Rasputin*. He made *Der Kongress Tanzt/Congress Dances* (31) in three versions (the third was in French), along with Willy Fritsch and Lilian Harvey and, as Metternich, completely walked away with the film.

Conrad Veidt was probably the most likeable German actor who worked extensively outside his own country, even if some of his performances weren't: but his Metternich in Congress Dances *(31) was in every way admirable.*

There was a British offer: *Rome Express* (32), with Esther Ralston, confidently considered the best British film made up to that time, and then he returned to Deutschland for the spectacular but weak *FP 1 Antwortet Nicht*; *Ich und die Kaiserin* with Harvey; and *Der Schwarz Huzar*. But with the coming of the Nazis he settled in

Britain (his wife was Jewish); he became a naturalized citizen in 1939. Work was not lacking: *I Was a Spy* (33); *The Wandering Jew*, homeless through 2,000 years, a wheezy old melodrama that Matheson Lang had done to death in innumerable stage tours years before; and the equally venerable *Bella Donna* (34), one of several film versions and probably the worst, with Mary Ellis this time as the fatal lady. He went to Germany on a visit and the Nazis held him there because his next film was announced as *Jew Süss* (35), claiming that he was too ill to travel; but his British company, Gaumont British, sent over their doctors and the Nazis let him go rather than cause an international incident. The film was an expensive version of Feuchtwanger's novel about the persecution of the Jews in 18th-century Germany, and, specifically, of the one (Veidt) who survives because of his financial brilliance–until the end, when he dies a Jew, having discovered he is really a Christian. It was not, withal, a distinguished film, and there was a mixed reaction to *The Passing of the Third Floor Back*, from Jerome K. Jerome's popular stage thriller: he was, of course, the mystical stranger who was probably Christ. He was then *King of the Damned* (36), a rebel convict, with Hollywood's Helen Vinson; and a mysterious sea captain in *Dark Journey* (37), with Vivien Leigh. He gave a stylish but unlikeable performance in *Under the Red Robe*, from Stanley J. Weyman's swashbuckling novel; Raymond Massey was Richelieu, and Victor Sjöstrom directed. He made two more in France: *Tempête Sur l'Asie* and *Le Jouer d'Echecs*, in which he killed people via chessmen until he himself was killed. There followed a couple co-starring with Valerie Hobson: *A Spy in Black* (39) and *Contraband* (40), the latter some Powell and Pressburger fun with Veidt and Valerie among Nazi agents in London.

With the outbreak of war he had announced that he would remain in British pictures and not go to Hollywood, and in fact it was a British producer, Alexander Korda, who demanded Veidt's presence in the US. Korda had been filming *The Thief of Bagdad*, but had abandoned it when the war started: he resumed in 1940 in Hollywood and Veidt went to complete his part (the film was of its kind a remarkable achievement, especially visually). Veidt remained there, where there was plentiful employment playing Nazis and other sinister gentlemen; and W. H. Mooring in Picturegoer reported that Veidt gave more of his salary to British War Relief than most British stars in Hollywood (contemporary reports suggest that Veidt was a genuinely nice man and not at all afflicted with that remarkable egotism common to many German actors). He lost, however, the top star status he had had in British films: *Escape* (40) with Norma Shearer; *A Woman's Face* (41) as Joan Crawford's protector (Cukor, who directed, found him 'absolutely charming to work with . . . . really gay and funny'); *Whistling in the Dark*, trying to kill off Red Skelton; *Nazi Agent*, starring in a phoney B with Ann Ayers, and playing a double role; *The Men in Her Life*, an artificial performance as Loretta Young's dancing master; *All Through the Night* (42) as a Nazi agent in New York whose plans are foiled by Humphrey Bogart; *Casablanca*; and *Above Suspicion* (43). Just after completing the latter, in 1942, Veidt died of a heart attack. He left a widow (his third wife).

Erich Von Stroheim

'The Man You Love to Hate.' Erich Von Stroheim's tag is remembered and his appearance, through countless stills, must be familiar even to those who haven't seen him: bull-headed, close-cropped, dark eyes gleaming, sometimes monocled, in a pudgy face; immaculately uniformed in the panoply of a Prussian hussar or a Viennese musical comedy star–helmets, caps, epaulettes, with silk gloves, boots or gaiters, gleamingly polished; brandishing the ultra-long cigarettes or cigarette-holder, the cane or riding whip–an insistence on detail with a consistency which suggests fetishism. He was an adventurer, a tyrant, a parvenue: as with his clothes, there was an element of personal predilection in the parts he played. He was a strong actor, a superb villain–he seldom played anything else–a bizarre and fascinating figure. His work as a director has been much chronicled, and the Silent pictures he made are accepted classics, rich, entirely personal and engrossing. Like Orson Welles he failed to meet Hollywood on its own terms: a great directorial talent went to waste and he enlivened a series of mainly poor pictures with his acting.

He was born in Vienna in 1885, the son of a Prussian merchant and a Czech mother (both Jewish). He was not, as was claimed, of a noble Austrian family, but was an officer in the Austrian army, where his meticulous eye for military detail first became practised. He was also a newspaper man, and this was a trade he followed after he emigrated to the US in 1906. Little is known of his life in the States before he went into films but one source says he became an actor on the

Orpheum Circuit (vaudeville) in a dramatization of one of his own novels. He co-wrote a play, 'The Mask', and was in Los Angeles in 1914 trying to get a job in the new medium, films.

His first screen work appears to have been a bit part in *Captain McLean* (14), which starred Lillian Gish, and he then had a bit part in *Ghosts* (15) with Henry B. Walthall, from Ibsen's play and directed by John Emerson. He had a small part in *The Birth of a Nation*, and he attached himself to D. W. Griffith's company, working variously as technical or military adviser, art director, assistant director or actor. Griffith produced and Emerson directed *Old Heidelberg* (from the play on which 'The Student Prince' is based) and Von Stroheim advised and assisted, as well as playing the Prince's valet, a part for which he was doubtless well qualified. He had minor parts in *His Picture in the Papers* (16) with Douglas Fairbanks, *Intolerance*, *The Social Secretary* starring Norma Talmadge, *Less Than the Dust* with Mary Pickford, *Panthea* (17) with Talmadge, *In Again Out Again* with Fairbanks, *For France*, in which he had his first large part, as a Prussian officer, with Betty Howe, and *Sylvia of the Secret Service* with Irene Castle. He was similarly cast in *The Unbeliever* (18), *Hearts of the World*, *The Hun Within* starring Dorothy Gish, and *The Heart of Humanity* (19). He was also the art director on *Macbeth* with Sir Herbert Beerbohm Tree and Constance Collier.

He was by now well known among film people, but as his entry in the Motion Picture Almanac noted, 'when war was over he was inactive for nine months due to dearth of war pictures'. He wanted to direct, and approached Carl Laemmle of Universal with an original screenplay (some sources suggest it was a novel) called 'The Pinnacle'. Re-titled *Blind Husbands*, Laemmle gave it the go-ahead, with Von Stroheim also directing, designing and playing the lead. It was set in the Tyrol and there were three main characters: an austere surgeon and his bored young wife and an army lieutenant, ostentatiously well-groomed. It is the habit of the officer to seduce whatever serving maid happens to be handy, but he turns his attention to the wife – until foiled by a mountain guide and later punished by the husband. The climax in particular is preposterous, but Lewis Jacobs was able to write: 'Unlike other triangle stories, this one was not in the pulp fashion; it was penetrating and serious, and distinguished in its realistic detail and vivid characterizations.' Universal were delighted with the results, both critical and commercial, and Von Stroheim made for them a similar story, *The Devil's Passkey* (20), in which he did not appear.

He directed and wrote *Foolish Wives* (21), as well as playing its central character, a bogus (uniformed) Count. Again there is an American couple who are to be sundered by his old-world morals – the Ambassador to Monaco and his wife: just as the film is both a condemnation and glorification of frivolous Riviera society, so it remains ambiguous as to the effect of these 'morals' on those encountering them. In the film many people do: almost every woman who crosses the screen is seduced, and one poor soul who proves unwilling gets summarily raped. There is also a snide hint that his female accomplices, 'cousins' and 'maid', are not carnally unknown to him. Von Stroheim brought to the part, said Lotte Eisner, 'a ferocious irony, a kind of sub-conscious love-hate'. The film was originally very long (18 reels) because Von Stroheim wanted to eliminate any supporting programme; but Universal disagreed and cut it by one-third. Inevitably it lost money, but as Joel W. Finler points out in his excellent monograph on Von Stroheim, 'it was a great artistic success and its reputation helped to establish Universal as a major studio'.

The battles of Von Stroheim vs studio chiefs had begun, and Universal (Irving Thalberg) removed him from *The Merry-Go-Round* halfway through filming: they got cold feet over both the rising costs and the

Von Stroheim as The Great Gabbo *(29). Even as a ventriloquist he got into uniform.*

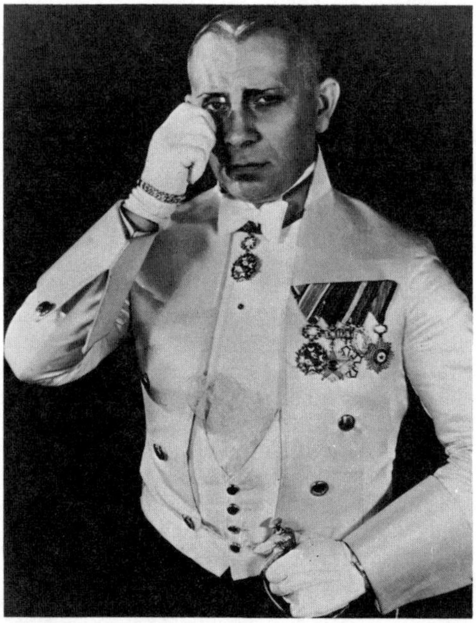

daring of the story. He moved to the Goldwyn Company and made *Greed* (23), directing only, and again its great length was reduced despite his appeals. This same Goldwyn Co. became part of MGM, and Thalberg joined it as producer. It was therefore somewhat surprising when Von Stroheim was invited to direct *The Merry Widow* (25) at that studio: he worked with his own crew and it was a Von Stroheim picture rather than the intended vehicle for John Gilbert and Mae Murray, or even a transcription of the stage success. Again there were erotic scenes which couldn't be used, and again Von Stroheim was removed before filming was completed. The film's enthusiastic reception meant that he would not be workless yet; he did the scenario for John Barrymore's *The Tempest*, and worked for two years at Paramount on *The Wedding March* (28). He acted in this, as the central character, Prince Nicki, an officer torn between the cripple he loves (Fay Wray) and the lame girl he is forced by parental decree to marry (Zasu Pitts). His screen character was now softened and humanized; it could not be called sympathetic, but the rapes, if not the seductions, were left to others. The obligatory orgy sequence went to the fathers of the bride and groom, getting drunker and drunker on the floor of a brothel. Again Von Stroheim had filmed at great length while the studio watched cautiously: eventually, while he was filming what he intended to be Part Two he was again removed. Part One was released, cut, simply as *The Wedding March*; Part Two was released, mutilated, as *The Honeymoon*, but only in Europe: before he died Von Stroheim re-cut both parts – the copies possessed by the Cinematheque Français, but Part Two was subsequently destroyed in a fire. No other copy exists (nor, it seems, does any archive have a copy of *The Devil's Passkey*). Von Stroheim moved on to UA to direct Gloria Swanson in *Queen Kelly*, but that was closed down in mid-production, and with it went his last chance, for the moment, of directing. He was only to find employment as an actor.

Memorably, he was *The Great Gabbo* (29), directed by James Cruze for Sono-Art and written by Ben Hecht, the story of a ventriloquist who becomes his dummy, a macabre study of schizophrenia. Said Cruze of Von Stroheim, off screen: 'He never enters a room; he makes an entrance.' He was a butler in the second of three film versions of *Three Faces East* (30), until unmasked by Constance Bennett as a German spy. He supported Lily Damita, Adolphe Menjou and Laurence Olivier in *Friends and Lovers* (31) at RKO, who kept him on to play a fanatical film director in *The Lost Squadron* (32), a man who knowingly sent men to their deaths for the shots he needed for his 'flying' film. Von Stroheim played it with no apparent sense of self-parody, but from all accounts the character was not unlike him, in its mirthless sarcasm, its rages and its senseless extravagance (e.g. all the soldiers in *The Merry Widow* had been dressed in silk underwear that was never seen). In *As You Desire Me* he was Garbo's protector, exerting a hypnotic influence over her.

He was then given another chance to direct, by Fox: *Walking Down Broadway*. It was done on a reasonable budget, but was never released, and indeed was re-shot by Alfred Werker and released as *Hello Sister*: the trouble this time seems to have been less to do with Von Stroheim himself than a studio feud at executive level. He acted again, in a couple of cheap little independent films: *Crimson Romance* (34) with Ben Lyon, and *Fugitive Road* with Leslie Fenton. On both he was military adviser, and he advised at MGM on *Anna Karenina*. He acted in Republic's *The Crime of Dr Crespi* (35), based on Poe's 'The Premature Burial', and worked at MGM on stories and screenplays. He directed there *The Emperor's Candlesticks* (36) with William Powell. He reputedly cabled Eisenstein for a job in 1935, and although there was a possibility that MGM might have let him direct again, again entirely on their terms, he preferred to return to Europe where he might also return to more autocratic film directing. But bad luck dogged him, and he continued to make his living as an actor.

In France he starred in *Marthe Richard* with Edwige Feuillère, and then in Renoir's great *La Grande Illusion* (37) with Pierre Fresnay and Jean Gabin, with Von Stroheim as the prison camp commandant who unexpectedly sympathizes with fellow aristocrat Fresnay. He was in the English version of Edmond T. Greville's *Mademoiselle Docteur*, a spy story, in the part Louis Jouvet played in the French version directed by Pabst.

Jouvet and Von Stroheim were matched in *L'Alibi* – Jouvet the detective and Von Stroheim his prey, an illusionist in a nightclub. He worked almost without let-up: Christian-Jaque's *Les Pirates de Rail* (38), *L'Affaire Lafarge*, Christian-Jaque's good *Les Disparus de Saint-Agil* with Michel Simon, *Ultimatum* with Dita Parlo, *Gibraltar* as the boss of a beauty parlour, with Viviane Romance, *Derrière la Façade* (39) with Jules Berry and Simon; *Rappel Immédiat* with Mireille Balin, *Pièges* with Maurice

Chevalier, *Le Monde Tremblera* with Claude Dauphin and Madeleine Sologne, *Tempête sur Paris* as a swindler blackmailed by Arletty, *Macao l'Enfer du Jeu* with Balin and Sessue Hayakawa, *Menaces* with Balin and *Paris–New York* with Simon. A directorial project, in cooperation with Renoir, and starring himself and Jouvet, *La Dame Blanche*, came to nothing when war broke out.

He returned to Hollywood, where he played in *I Was an Adventuress* (40), 20th's remake of a French film similarly titled, with Vera Zorina inadequate in the part played by Feuillère; and *So Ends Our Night* (41), expectedly, as the Hun pursuing the Jewish refugees. For the next year or so he was occupied with the part of Jonathan Brewster in a tour of 'Arsenic and Old Lace', but he returned to films with a good one, Wilder's *Five Graves to Cairo* (43): he played Rommel, and though he was like him neither physically nor in any other way, was so powerful that it hardly seemed to matter; and within the limitations of his acting style, it was an excellent performance. He was in Goldwyn's *The North Star*, but his subsequent American films were another matter. He did a quartet at Republic: *The Lady and the Monster* (44), *Storm Over Lisbon*, both with Richard Arlen, *The Great Flammarion* (45), as a vaudeville sharpshooter who murders his wanton assistant Mary Beth Hughes, and *Scotland Yard Investigator* with C. Aubrey Smith. He did Lew Landers's *The Mask of Dijon* (46) with Denise Vernac, then wisely returned to France.

But again, it was mostly formula stuff: *La Foire aux Chimères*, *On ne Meurt pas Comme Ça!*, again as a film director, *La Danse de Mort* (47), Strindberg's bitter play which he helped adapt and script, with Vernac as the wife (in real life she became his wife), *Le Signal Rouge* (48) and *Portrait d'un Assassin* (49). It was Wilder who recalled him to Hollywood for *Sunset Boulevard* (50), his best film by far since his last Wilder film; he was Gloria Swanson's valet-butler. He was full of suggestions for typical Von Stroheim touches, some of which Wilder used. The rest of his films were made in Europe: the remake of *Alraune* (52) with Hildegarde Neff, in Germany, in the part played in the earlier versions by Paul Wegener and Albert Basserman, *Minuit Quai de Bercy* (53) with Madeleine Robinson, *L'Envers du Paradis* with Vernac, *Alerte au Sud* with Jean-Claude Pascal, Sacha Guitry's all-star *Napoléon* (54) as Beethoven, *Série Noire* (55)

Peter Van Eyck, Anne Baxter and Von Stroheim, as Rommel, in Billy Wilder's Five Graves to Cairo *(43). Wilder has recalled that when he told Von Stroheim that his films were ten years before their time Von Stroheim confidently corrected him: 'Twenty'.*

with Robert Hossein, and *La Madone des Sleepings* (55) with Gisele Pascal. He was awarded the Legion d'Honneur not long before he died in 1957.

Anton Walbrook

Anton Walbrook was an actor of authority and persuasive continental charm and, in life, an overweening egotism. This probably prevented his later career from being more prolific. He was born in Vienna in 1900, into a circus family – they had been clowns for 300 years. Walbrook (or Adolf Wohlbruck, the name he used till he went to Hollywood in 1936) preferred the legit stage, and after a varied education won a scholarship to the Max Reinhardt school in Berlin. He acted in Vienna, Dresden and Munich and was well known when he got a part in *Der Fluch der Bösen Tat* (25). However, his first important part on screen was with Anna Sten in *Salto Mortale* (31) which, coincidentally, was about circus life. He was also in *Der Stolz der Drei Kompanie* with Heinz Ruhmann; *Baby* (32); *Die Fünf Verfluchten Gentlemen*; *Drei von der Stempelsti*; *Melodie der Liebe* starring Richard Tauber; *Regine* (33); *Mond über Marokko* with Camilla Horn; *Keine Angst vor Liebe*; *Viktor und Viktoria* and *Walzerkrieg*, both with Renate Muller; *Eine Frau die Weisse was Sie Will* (34); *Die Englische Heirat* and Willy Forst's *Maskerade*. This was the film which first made him known outside German-speaking territories. He did *Die Vertauschte Braut*; the remake of *Der Student von Prag* (35); *Zigeunerbaron*; *Ich War Jack Mortimer* and Forst's *Allotria*. In 1936 he made two pictures which had both French and German versions, *Der Kurier des Zaren/Michel Strogoff*, and *Port-Arthur* with Danielle Darrieux.

With the rise of the Nazis he sought to work abroad and negotiated a contract with Gaumont-British. But he had his first English-speaking screen role when RKO summoned him to Hollywood to remake the *Strogoff* film, now called *The Soldier and the Lady* (37). This time he merely walked through his part, but it brought him a fair degree of renown, and to the attention of Herbert Wilcox, who was looking for a Prince Albert to marry his *Victoria the Great* (37): Walbrook's success opposite Anna Neagle caused him to settle in Britain, though the GB contract had been dissolved when that company temporarily ceased production.

The Courtship of Queen Victoria: Anton Walbrook as Albert and Anna Neagle as Victoria the Great *(37). Walbrook's performance suggested that Albert married beneath him.*

Wilcox put him into the remake of Ivor Novello's Silent vehicle, *The Rat*, and then Albertized him again for *Sixty Glorious Years* (38). In 1939 he made his British stage debut, in the first presentation there of 'Design for Living' with Rex Harrison and Diana Wynyard. In 1940 he starred opposite Wynyard in *Gaslight*, a much praised film version of the stage melodrama (Edwardian husband tries to drive his wife mad in order to pick up her fortune): MGM bought it to remake it and all copies were reputedly destroyed – but it has been shown in both countries since the MGM effort. His next was his biggest success: *Dangerous Moonlight* (41), which introduced the 'Warsaw Concerto'. That was the reason: there was little else to recommend it, a junky story about a Polish pianist-cum-RAF pilot, involved with Sally Gray. Then Powell and Pressburger used him in two of the better British wartime films, *49th Parallel* and *The Life and Death of Colonel Blimp* (43). In 1944 he did a potboiler, *The Man From Morocco*, but its reception proved that he was hardly a name to conjure with at the box-office.

He became a British citizen in 1947; in 1948 he was used by Powell and Pressburger as the dominating impresario of *The Red Shoes*, an expensive project dedicated to The Dance. Rank financed, but when the makers overstepped the budget there was a tentative move to sell the thing to Korda. The film went on to be a huge money-maker and took more money than any other foreign film in the US until then. It was the first intelligent attempt to portray the world of the ballet, and it had assets in Sadlers Wells dancer Moira Shearer and names such as Massine and Helpmann: but as a film it was pretty poor stuff. Walbrook followed it with the less successful *The Queen of Spades* with Edith Evans and then was off the screen till Max Ophuls's *La Ronde* (50), playing the elegant master of ceremonies. This gave his career a new lease of life in Britain, but meanwhile, in Germany he starred in *Wien Tanzt* (51); returning to the London stage in 1952 in 'Call Me Madam'. A while later he was in another, lesser, musical, 'Wedding in Paris'; and in a French picture with Madeleine Robinson, *L'Affaire Maurizius* (54).

He made two more films in 1955, one execrable and one superb. The bad one was *Oh Rosalinda!!* made by Powell and Pressburger. After *Red Shoes* they had attempted the even more ambitious *Tales of Hoffman*, again with Shearer – but it was a box-office failure; they attempted to renew faith in their 'class' musicals by this modernized version of 'Die Fledermaus' – Walbrook had that part and was the only good thing in it – but, warned by the press, the public stayed away in millions. The good one was Max Ophuls's *Lola Montez* (Martine Carol), a typical chiaresco based loosely on that loose lady's life: the unusual narrative form caused difficulties with both distributors and public when it came out, but its status as a 'classic' grew, and it was accepted as such on a highly successful New York showing in 1969. It was made in France; Walbrook returned to Britain for two more films, *Saint Joan* (57) as Cauchon, and *I Accuse* (58), and he was in another couple of stage plays in London. But increasingly he found it easier to get work on the Continent and he was virtually forgotten by his adopted country when he died in 1967.

John Wayne

Future historians of the art of the film will probably pause at the name of John Wayne only because he appeared in some of John Ford's best Westerns; but it is a name which gives pause to everyone interested in the industry. Time in 1967 said he was 'the greatest moneymaker in movie history: the gross comes to nearly $400 million'; he has probably earned more than any other movie actor during a long and always rising career. His popularity has been consistent: during the 20-year period 1949–68 there was only one year (58) when he wasn't one of the USA's 10 top draws; there were four occasions (50, 51, 54, 69) when he was No. 1, and another three when he was No. 2 (56, 57, 63). The British rated him less highly, but as late as 1968 he headed the list of top box-office stars in that country. In 1968, too, a poll was taken among US TV viewers to find out the most popular artists on TV, including stars in films: Wayne headed the list (followed by some more film-stars: (2) Bob Hope, (3) Spencer Tracy, (4) Clark Gable and at No. 8 Gary Cooper and Sydney Poitier tying with some TV performers).

It is true that actors in action pictures do hold their public easily. Wayne's audiences are generally less discriminating than Brando's (there is still an audience for a poor Wayne vehicle, whereas a poor Brando picture will sink without trace). It is significant that the one year he wasn't in the top 10 was the one year he had only one film, and it was a 'straight' one – and a disaster. Yet he offers much more than a 'ride 'em cowboy' image. To justify himself in 1951 he commented: 'Success in films has little to do with acting', and 10 years later he was saying: 'Sometimes I wonder about my career. I don't do much really, I suppose. Just sell sincerity. And I've been selling the hell out of it ever since I got going.' In fact, his hallmark is integrity rather than sincerity. He is never mean and dirty (like Bogart) or possessed of doubts (like Cooper): he is the idealized American, representing, as one writer had it, 'the indomitable spirit which sent our forefathers Westward'. He is leathery, weather-beaten, tough and masculine: hard-drinking, impatient of men, polite towards women. The Galahad image was not harmed by the divorce allegations – cruelty, drunkenness – of his first wife, nor by his rabid right-wing politics. His frequently expressed admiration for the late Senator McCarthy indicates a stubborn and not uncommon mentality, but even his opponents grant him the courage of his convictions. Louis B. Mayer once summed him up: 'John Wayne has an endless face and he can go on forever.'

Wayne was born Marion Morrison in Winterset, Iowa, in 1907, the son of a druggist. For health reasons the family moved to California where they had difficulties in making ends meet. Wayne entered the University of Southern California on a football scholarship, and a USC coach through an old friend (Tom Mix) got him a job in the property department at Fox. He decorated the sets of Ford's *Mother Machree* (28) – sometimes given as his first film – and thus began a life-long friendship with the director. Ford made him a racetrack spectator in *Hangman's House*, and used him and another USC football player, Ward Bond, in a football game in *Salute* (29). He had a bit in Ford's *Men Without Women* (30) and another in *Rough Romance*; then Ford recommended him to Raoul Walsh for *The Big Trail*, which had a big budget and couldn't afford a name star. Wayne starred, with Marguerite Churchill, but the film was one big flop. He made two more for Fox – *Girls Demand Excitement* (31), a college comedy, and *Three Girls Lost* starring opposite Loretta Young – and then signed a five-year contract with Columbia. The first was *Men Are Like That* co-starring Laura La Plante, about a woman's revenge on her lover, but he failed to hold his status. Within two years he was a featured player in important movies or the star of cheap factory-line Westerns.

For 10 years he was a prince of the sage at Saturday matinées, along with Hoot Gibson, Tim McCoy, Johnny Mack Brown, Tom Mix, Buck Jones, Gene Autry, Bob Steele and others. There were so many that Wayne himself is never sure whether he has made 200 or 400 movies, and most of the lists differ. Here's one, year by year, with some other events: 1931: *Range Feud*, *Maker of Men*. 1932: *Texas Cyclone*, *Lady and Gent*, *Two-Fisted Law*; Columbia dropped him and he went to WB. *Ride Him Cowboy*, *The Big Stampede*. Did two serials for Mascot, *Shadow of the Eagle* and *Hurricane Express*. 1933: *Haunted Gold*, *The Telegraph Trail*, *Baby Face* (a Barbara Stanwyck vehicle), *His Private Secretary*, *Somewhere in Sonora*, *The Life of Jimmy Dolan* (which starred Douglas Fairbanks Jr), *The Man From Monterey*. Moved over to Monogram: *Riders of Destiny*, *Sagebrush Trail*. Played a French legionnaire in a Mascot serial, *The Three Musketeers*. 1934: *West of the Divide*, *The Lucky Texan*, *Texas Terror*, *Blue Steel*, *The Man From Utah*, *Randy Rides Alone*, *The Star Packer*, *The Trail Beyond* (much better than the others), *'Neath the Arizona Skies*. 1935: *The Lawless Frontier*, *Rainbow Valley*, *Paradise Canyon*, *The Dawn Rider*, *Desert Trail*. Left Monogram for Republic: *Westward Ho!*, *The New Frontier*. Abandoned an abortive career as a record star under the pseudonym 'Singing Sam'. 1936: nine films released, including several of the non-Western Bs he was to make for Universal over the next three years: *The Lawless Nineties*, *King of the Pecos*, *The Oregon Trail*, *Winds of the Wasteland*, *I Cover Chinatown*, *The Sea Spoilers*, *The Lonely Trail*, *Conflict* (from John London's novel). 1937: *California Straight Ahead*, *I Cover the War*, *Idol of the Crowds*, *Adventure's End*. 1938: *Born to the West* (for Paramount). Started a Western series for Republic, 'The Three Mesquiteers' (made eight in all): *Overland Stage Raiders*, *Pals of the Saddle*, *Santa Fe Stampede*, *Red River Range*. 1939: *The Night Raiders*, *Wyoming Outlaw*, *Three Texas Steers*, *The New Frontier*.

But his first film released in 1939 was *Stagecoach*. Ford had not made a Western for 10 years when he agreed to do this for Wanger/UA. He borrowed Wayne from Republic to join a cast of reliable but not star players; the part, anyway, required little more of Wayne than he usually did, and, wisely, he wasn't given too much dialogue. Few people expected the film to be the success it was (it remains one of the best and most famous of Westerns); and Wayne's name became known to more than the patrons of his Z Westerns. Things began to happen. RKO put in a bid for his services, reuniting him with Trevor, for *Allegheny Uprising*: it wasn't a *Stagecoach*, but its budget was bigger than Wayne had been wont to have.

Republic suddenly had a valuable property under contract. Since its foundation in 1935 that studio had had no aspirations above Bs (most of which turned out to be Ds and

The star of True Grit *meets the star of* Pandora's Box: *John Wayne (left) and Louise Brooks in* Overland Stage Raiders *(38). It was one of the 'Three Mesquiteer' pictures: Ray Corrigan (right) and Max Terhune (front) were the other two.*

Es): now it stood to make a lot by loaning Wayne to other companies: he had signed a new five-year contract just before *Stagecoach* and was now getting $200 a week; he was loaned to Paramount a year later for $1,500 weekly. And so as not to devalue him, his pictures for them had to be better: so *Dark Command* (40) was infused with a big budget (by Republic standards) and the borrowed talents of Trevor, Walter Pidgeon and director Walsh (Roy Rogers had a small role). It was a Civil War story; and was followed by *Three Faces West*, a heavy trek from the dustbowl country, with Charles Coburn and Sigrid Gurie joining Wayne as European refugees. Ford borrowed him again to play a seaman in *The Long Voyage Home*, a beautiful series of vignettes about the merchant marine taken from some plays by Eugene O'Neill, supporting Wilfred Lawson, Thomas Mitchell and Ward Bond. Universal borrowed him to play the nonchalant naval officer whom Dietrich falls for in *Seven Sinners* and he proved that in this particular sort of part–tough and humorous–he was unbeatable. With *A Man Betrayed* (41) co-starring Frances Dee and the period-piece *The Lady From Louisiana* (who was Ona Munson) Republic settled Wayne into a series of double-feature actioners.

Outside he did better–notably in *The Shepherd of the Hills* and as the baddie in de Mille's *Reap the Wild Wind* (42), both at Paramount; fighting Randolph Scott over Dietrich in both *The Spoilers* and *Pittsburgh*; as an escaped pilot in Joan Crawford's idiotic *Reunion in France*; and romancing with Jean Arthur in *The Lady Takes a Chance* (43). The best Republic could do were: *Lady for a Night* (41) with Joan Blondell, *In Old California* (42) and *In Old Oklahoma* (43) with Martha Scott, but at least they were first in getting him properly into World War II, whose battles he was to continue to fight throughout his career. The film was *The Fighting Seabees* (44), and Susan Hayward frequently diverted him from the war. Then it was back to the Old West–*Flame of Barbary Coast* and *Tall in the Saddle*, the latter for RKO, after which he signed a one-picture-a-year contract with that company.

There were two war pictures in 1945, Republic's *Back to Bataan*; and MGM's *They Were Expendable*, which Ford directed. It was not a success, but William Whitebait, reassessing it years later, thought it 'perhaps the most moving and most faithful of all war films'. It was a big drop from that to a film released a few weeks earlier, *Dakota*, which co-starred the wife of Republic's president,

After Stagecoach *Wayne became one of the most sought-after actors in Hollywood, and Universal borrowed him three times to co-star with Marlene Dietrich – for whose favours his rival in two of these films was Randolph Scott (left). This one is* The Spoilers *(42).*

the lovely Vera Hruba Ralston. There was *Without Reservations* (46) at RKO, a peripatetic comedy with Claudette Colbert, and then he became his own producer at Republic – perhaps a reward for his loyalty: *The Angel and the Badman* (47), a Western with Gail Russell. After *Tycoon* with Laraine Day he was in three notable Westerns, Ford's *Fort Apache* (48) with Henry Fonda, a Civil War tale; Howard Hawks's *Red River*, Wayne's biggest commercial success to date by far; and Ford's *Three Godfathers*, the remake of an old fable about three escaping outlaws lumbered with a baby. It was for Ford enthusiasts only, and didn't do well.

But Wayne's six films for Ford during this period of the career provide some of his best work. After producing *The Wake of the Red Witch* – again with Russell and again not much liked – he was in Ford's *She Wore a Yellow Ribbon* (49), a Technicolor tribute to the US Cavalry and an exceptional film by any standards: it is Ford's own favourite among his Westerns and Wayne's favourite role. *The Fighting Kentuckian* didn't do well, despite the presence again of Vera Hruba Ralston, but *Sands of Iwo Jima* was a tremendous hit, though in fact a very ordinary war film. As the tough Sergeant Stryker, Wayne got his first Oscar nomination. There followed Ford's *Rio Grande* (50) and then *Operation Pacific* (51), the first of a non-exclusive pact with WB; Wayne was about to finish with both RKO and Republic. *The Flying Leathernecks* and *Jet Pilot* were the last two for RKO. The latter was made in 1950, produced by Howard Hughes and directed by Joseph von Sternberg – one of Hollywood's *films maudits*: after many trade rumours about cutting and mutilating, it didn't surface until 1957, to be written off quickly as a tedious bore. Wayne left Republic with a bang: that company would fold in the mid-50s, and he and Ford now gave it the biggest box-office hit of its entire life: *The Quiet Man* (52), which wove together a great number of tattered Irish strands – rumbustious humour, sentiment – into an enormously attractive fabric.

Few of the Warner films that he made were a quarter as distinguished: *Big Jim McLain*, in which he was the scourge of the subversive left; *Trouble Along the Way* (53), as a football coach (very sticky); *Island in the Sky*; *Hondo*; *The High and the Mighty* (54), an aviation drama; *The Sea Chase* (55) as a German officer; and *Blood Alley*, a dislikeable mixture of synthetic heroics and Commie-baiting. The last four were particularly strong at the wickets, but *Hondo* was the only one with any real merit. He returned to RKO for *The Conqueror* (56), which Dick Powell produced and directed. An expensive epic about the young Genghis Khan, it was little more than a Western with Wayne dolled up in droopy moustache and slit eyes – and struggling with lines like 'I feel this Tartar woman is for me'. The critics pulled it and him apart, but it did quite well. He was on much more familiar ground with *The Searchers*, another rewarding excursion with Ford. It was also potent at the box-office, but when they reunited again for *The Wings of the Eagles* (57) the magic had very definitely eluded them. *Legend of the Lost* did no better – a protracted adventure story set in the Sahara. Wayne produced. His only 1958 picture achieved the feat of being even worse, although John Huston directed: *The Barbarian and the Geisha*, a dreary account of Townsend Harris's diplomatic descent on the Japanese in 1856. The MFB thought that 'Wayne, now corpulent and ageing, can only achieve a weary monotone sincerity.'

To some, the standard was maintained with an overlong Hawks Western, *Rio Bravo* (59), but it was very popular: it certainly wasn't up to *The Horse Soldiers* with William Holden, even though that was Ford on an off-day. He took no salary (in 1956 he had been the highest-paid actor in the world, at $666,666.66) for *The Alamo* (60), a grandiose flag-waving epic about the struggle of Texas to secede from Mexico. He produced and directed – and really he shouldn't have. Still, it was a labour of love (as it turned out; it did eventually make some money on re-issues). After that he contented himself with appearing in other people's big budgeters: *North to Alaska*; *The Comancheros!* (61); Ford's dull *The Man Who Shot Liberty Valance*; Hawks's *Hatari!* (62) which was particularly successful; *The Longest Day*; *How The West Was Won*, in a brief guest spot; Ford's free-wheeling South Seas story *Donovan's Reef*; *McLintock* (63); *Circus World*, made in Spain (the US title was *The Magnificent Showman*); *The Greatest Story Ever Told* (65) – 10 seconds in long-shot as a Roman centurion and intoning on the soundtrack 'This truly is the Son of God'; *In Harm's Way* and *The Sons of Katie Elder*. About this time he successfully underwent an operation for cancer. It could not be said that he returned to the screen with renewed vigour: for some time now he had been giving a tired parody of his old self. The effect worked in Hawks's *El Dorado* (67), but not in such tiresome pieces as *Cast a Giant Shadow* (66) and *The War Wagon* (67). In 1968 he was involved in a simple-minded defence of the Vietnam war, *The Green Berets*, which aroused the wrath of anti-war demonstrators all over the world. Despite that (and its notices) it achieved a huge domestic gross of over $8 million. The Wayne-plus-war formula still worked, but *The Hellfighters* fought fire – and to the action fans that was nowhere near as alluring.

John Wayne in Rio Grande (*50*)

Kim Darby and John Wayne in True Grit (*69*), *for which he won an Oscar.*

The Undefeated (69) with Rock Hudson was a so-so Western, but *True Grit* was a touching one, about the relationship of an old gunfighter and a determined teenager (Kim Darby). It did good business, made Wayne again the No. 1 box-office star and brought him a Best Actor Oscar and the best notices of his career. Dilys Powell wrote this tribute: 'It is thirty years since in *Stagecoach* as the romantic and touching Ringo Kid he first made a notable appearance. The physical image has changed since then–the figure thickened, the face lined (though still truculently handsome); and the character which fits the actor, that too has changed. The gallant cowboy who addressed every woman as ma'am has given way in *True Grit* to a drunken tough who wants his price. Nevertheless with a director such as Henry Hathaway–another of the old-style spell-binders–he can still re-create for us the golden mythology of the West.'

He followed with two more Westerns, *Chisum* (70) and Hawks's *Rio Lobo*.

Johnny Weissmuller

Of all the screen Tarzans, Johnny Weissmuller remains most identified with the role and it with him. He was neither the first nor last, but he lasted the longest. With the possible exception of the first Tarzan, Elmo Lincoln with his shoulder-length hair, Weissmuller was the most physically right. He was brawny and big-boned, with features that were not entirely unsimian. His face expressed a sort of brooding gentleness which was about all that was required in the way of acting; he seldom looked harried as he swung from branch to branch or outdistanced the crocodiles but, again, a look of contentment in his prowess was not inappropriate. Later in the series when they made him talk–after a fashion–he was no worse or no better than the other Tarzans.

Tarzan was the creation of an American hack-writer called Edgar Rice Burroughs (1875–1950): in the original novel, 'Tarzan of the Apes', published in 1914, Tarzan was an orphaned English milord lost in the African jungle and reared by apes; he eventually learns of his inheritance, outwits the baddies, but returns to the jungle–which, profitably, permitted Burroughs to write a number of sequels. National Pictures filmed the first novel with Lincoln in 1918, and its success spawned an immediate sequel, *The Romance of Tarzan*. Three years later Lincoln did a serial, *The Adventures of Tarzan*. Other Silent Tarzans: Gene Polar in *The Return of Tarzan* (20), P. Dempsey Tabler in *Son of Tarzan* (20, a serial) with Kamuela C. Searle in the title role, James Pierce in *Tarzan and the Golden Lion* (27), and Frank Merrill in *Tarzan the Mighty* (28) and *Tarzan the Tiger* (30). In 1932 MGM revived the character with Weissmuller.

Weissmuller was born in Chicago in 1907, and educated in that city's University. Under the auspices of the Illinois Athletic Club he became renowned as a swimmer long before MGM became interested: in 1924 at the Olympic Games in Paris he broke three swimming records. He was also at the 1928 Games in Amsterdam and when he turned professional in 1929 was unchallenged as the world's finest swimmer. He had made some sport shorts and was on holiday in California when MGM approached him to test for Tarzan after the actor they had signed became ill: the film, *Tarzan the Ape Man* (32), was strictly back-projection stuff and studio jungle, but the schedule couldn't wait: under W. S. Van Dyke's direction Weissmuller played the part and the film was a big success. The heroine was Maureen O'Sullivan, an attractive actress whom MGM restricted to second leads and wishy-washy parts such as these, and together they were *Tarzan and His Mate* (34). They were co-starred again in *Tarzan Escapes* (36), *Tarzan Finds a Son* (39), *Tarzan's Secret Treasure* (41) and *Tarzan's New York*

Maureen O'Sullivan, Cheetah the Chimp and Johnny Weissmuller in the first of the very successful Tarzan films in which they appeared, Tarzan the Ape Man (*32*).

Adventure (42). The son was, literally, found – the survivor of a plane crash – and when relatives came to claim him he too preferred the jungle way of life.

Meanwhile, there were other Tarzans, but most cinemagoers considered them imposters. Sol Lesser at Principal produced *Tarzan the Fearless* (33) with Buster Crabbe, and then at 20th *Tarzan's Revenge* (38) with Glen Morris; while Burroughs himself was involved in a serial with Herman Brix, *New Adventures of Tarzan* (35), later released as two features, one of that title and one called *Tarzan and the Green Goddess*. None of these approached the standard of the MGM pictures, but MGM during the war lost interest, and Lesser, now producing at RKO, took over Weissmuller and son, Johnny Sheffield.

After a guest spot in *Stage Door Canteen* (43), Weissmuller did *Tarzan Triumphs* and *Tarzan's Desert Mystery*, in both of which he was Jane-less. He got a new mate, Brenda Joyce, in *Tarzan and the Amazons* (45), and she stayed with him as long as he was with the series: *Tarzan and the Leopard Woman* (46), *Tarzan and the Huntress* (47) and *Tarzan and the Mermaids* (48). Before the last two, he did his only 'straight' film, a Paramount B, *Swamp Fire* (46). He, or Tarzan, was no longer potent box-office, and Lesser replaced him by the younger Lex Barker, who made five Tarzan pictures between 1948 and 1952. Later Tarzans include Gordon Scott and, again at MGM, Denny Miller (in a remake of *Tarzan the Ape Man*, 60) and Jock Mahoney.

Weissmuller moved over to Columbia where Sam Katzman produced him a series of low-budget actioners featuring one who might have been Tarzan's less sophisticated cousin, Jungle Jim, and including a chimpanzee to replace Tarzan's famous Cheetah. The titles: *Jungle Jim* (48), *The Lost Tribe* (49), *Captive Girl* (50), *Mark of the Gorilla*, *Pygmy Island*, *Fury of the Congo Land* (51), *Jungle Manhunt*, *Jungle Jim and the Forbidden Land* (52), *Voodoo Tiger*, *Savage Mutiny* (53), *Jungle Man-Eaters* (54) and *Cannibal Attack*. These were strictly for the lower half of double bills at less discriminating situations. The MFB waxed indignant over the next one: 'This is a preposterous and in some respects rather distasteful film, which insults the intelligence of the most tolerant spectator.' This was *Jungle Moon Men*, and like Weissmuller's last, *The Devil Goddess* (55), the leading character was called 'Johnny Weissmuller': again he was Tarzan's cousin. 'Jungle Jim' became a TV series in 1958. Weissmuller is now Vice-President of a Swimming Pool Company named after him. He lives in Florida. After a long absence from the screen he appeared in *The Phynx* (70).

He has been married and divorced five times. His third wife (1933–8) was Lupe Velez, a Silent Screen star who faded with the coming of Talkies but kept going in a B series based apparently on her own personality and called 'The Mexican Spitfire'.

Orson Welles

Orson Welles's actual acting achievements (if such they can be called) have been heavily overshadowed by his prowess as a director, and that, in turn, has been usually overrated – due perhaps to one of the best possible reasons: that he did make, at the outset of his career, at least one-and-a-half masterpieces. Not that he is negligible as an actor, far from it: his ebullience and generous authority have given focus to more dull films than seems humanly possible.

As a young man he was known as 'the boy wonder' or the *enfant terrible*: 'There but for the grace of God, goes God' was a famous quip. He came to the cinema with an already strong reputation for the *etonné-moi* bit, and a large ego. He started young. He was born in Kenosha, Wisconsin, in 1915, and educated in Woodstock, Illinois, and for a very short while was an artist and journalist. While on a walking and sketching tour of Ireland in 1931 (he was 16) he bluffed his way into a part at the Gate Theatre, Dublin (as the Duke of Württemberg in 'Jew Süss'). He appeared subsequently at the Abbey as guest star. In 1934, back in the US, he was managing and organizing the Woodstock (Illinois) Theatre Festival; through Alexander Woollcott he met Katharine Cornell and toured with her as Mercutio and Marchbanks. His first New York appearance was with her as Chorus and Tybalt. In 1936 he became director of the Negro People's Theatre and directed a coloured 'Macbeth'; in 1937 he was appointed a director of the Federal Theatre Project, New York, for whom he produced 'Horse Eats Hat' (a version of Labiche's 'An Italian Straw Hat'), 'Doctor Faustus' (he played Faustus) and 'The Cradle Will Rock'. The same year, with John Houseman, he founded the Mercury Theatre, starting with a modern-dress Fascist-orientated 'Julius Caesar', in which he played Brutus; the Mercury's subsequent fame was based on that and only three other productions, the last of which, 'Danton's Death', closed the project. (Most commentators find it difficult to assess how original

Orson Welles in Citizen Kane *(41): his achievements behind the camera on this film have tended to overshadow the fact that his performance in it was one of the most dynamic in the history of films.*

or influential the Mercury was.) At the same time he was broadcasting regularly, and in 1938 was responsible for the radio production 'The War of the Worlds', which is remembered for the panic it caused among those of its listeners who didn't realize it was a play.

By one of those peculiar cracked strokes of genius which are staked throughout the history of Hollywood, RKO invited him to make a movie *carte blanche*. Welles first planned a film of Conrad's 'The Heart of Darkness' and then something called 'The Smiler With the Knife' with Carole Lombard – but she wasn't willing. So he gathered a nucleus of talent from the Mercury, and for $750,000 directed, produced, starred in and co-wrote (with Herman J. Mankiewicz) *Citizen Kane* (41), a thinly disguised study of the career of William Randolph Hearst. The reaction of the Hearst press was only one reason why it was disastrous at the box-office, though the most important: the hammering by Hearst certainly negated the huge critical acclaim. Welles intended it as sociology, but despite its dazzling comments and its technique it is most successful as a study of human relationships. In Leslie Halliwell's words, it is 'often acclaimed as the best film of all time: certainly none has used the medium with more vigour and enthusiasm'. Over the years, as its stature has become assured, it has more than got its money back.

Welles was already at work on a version of *The Magnificent Ambersons* (42), the Booth Tarkington novel, as producer/director/writer only. The film was described by Dilys

Powell as 'part-triumph, part-failure': it was in fact cut about and added to after Welles had left it. It was also a box-office flop. Welles, helped by the enmity of the Hearst press, was now a much less privileged person in the film world. (In Britain no West End cinema and very few others would take it, but those that did played to packed audiences, who applauded at the end.) He only supervised and 'designed' the film version of Eric Ambler's *Journey into Fear*, though he did appear in it as a Turkish colonel of police. He signed a contract with Korda to co-produce, direct and play the lead in *War and Peace* (with Merle Oberon as Natasha) but, like many Korda projects, it came to nothing. That left Welles free to do *Jane Eyre* (44), acting only, but much influenced by the style of *Kane*. Welles's Mr Rochester was curious: he moved and looked the part, darkly romantic, but it was hard to believe that he wasn't as insane as his wife.

During the war he entertained the troops, and in *Follow the Boys* he did a variation of his act–sawing Marlene Dietrich in half. He did a soap opera, *Tomorrow Is Forever* (46), with Claudette Colbert, and in quick succession directed and acted in *The Stranger*, an artificially heightened drama about an ex-Nazi (Welles) settled in a small American town; he directed and acted in *The Lady From Shanghai* (48), starring his then-wife Rita Hayworth: the final cost (reputedly $2 million) and confusion virtually brought about the end of his work as a director in Hollywood. His own performance was weird; the film neither poor nor brilliant but incomprehensible.

He did persuade Republic to let him film–in 21 days–*Macbeth*, which he described as 'a kind of violently sketched charcoal drawing of a great play': it *looked* more like a disused coal-mine serving as a pantomime set, and Welles's own headgear was entertaining. At this point, perhaps wisely, he left Hollywood, and, except briefly, hasn't worked there since. 'I came to Europe because there was not the slightest chance for me (or for anybody, at that) to obtain freedom of action.' His 'European' career began with parts in two minor historical pieces, *Black Magic* (49) as Cagliostro, and *Prince of Foxes*, followed by *The Third Man*: Welles's Harry Lime, the suave, mocking black-marketeer, was his best performance since *Kane* and one of the cinema's most memorable of all. The film itself was Britain's top money-maker in 1949, but it did somewhat less well in the US. He stayed in Britain to play a sort of Genghis Khan in *The Black Rose* (50), a dull swashbuckler with pretensions; and on the London stage appeared as and directed 'Othello'. He made a film (52) of that play after many vicissitudes, including the sinking of all his own money into it. He did not think, he said later, that he was 'particularly good' as Othello: like the *Macbeth*, the film has its adherents, and it is generally better.

When he needed work Herbert Wilcox offered him the part of Manderson in *Trent's Last Case*, the first film of what must have been one of the most dispiriting periods of his career; he played Benjamin Franklin in *Si Versailles m'était Conté* (53); was in *L'Uomo, La Bestia e La Virtu*, the French *Napoléon* (54), none of which had wide showings outside their countries of origin; and was in two feeble British efforts, Wilcox's *Trouble in the Glen* and *Three Cases of Murder* (he played Lord Mountdrago in the episode based on a Maugham short story; the film was never released). Perhaps personally more upsetting to him was the failure of *Confidential Report* (55), a thriller that he wrote and directed. Eagerly awaited, it was something of a shambles, but, again, had been mutilated by other hands.

Another flirtation with Hollywood proved more fruitful. He was paid $20,000 for one day's work on *Moby Dick* (56)–he played Father Mapple; did a thriller, *Man in the Shadow* (57), and was then engaged to direct another, *Touch of Evil* (58), apparently at the insistence of the star, Charlton Heston, who wouldn't believe that Welles was only to co-star. Once again, the gremlins got to work after Welles left the studio, though the changes this time were slight. At least it emerged as recognizably Welles, and, while not perfect, as entertainment it left most of the year's films standing. For 20th he made three: the serviceable version of Faulkner, *The Long Hot Summer*; *The Roots of Heaven* in Africa; and *Compulsion* (59). *Compulsion* jettisoned most of the atmosphere and strength of Meyer Levin's novel based on the Leopold/Loeb murder trial, but Welles's own performance in the Clarence Darrow role was stunning. Dilys Powell was moved to say: 'And it scores–to come down to brass tacks–in having Orson Welles. Mr Welles is among the great solo performers of the screen; more than once his noble organ-voice with its capacity for irony or persuasion, throwaway or thunder, has brought a few remarkable minutes into some unremarkable film.'

Then again, all was dross, starting with the Rank Organization's *n*th attempt to interest the world market, *Ferry to Hong Kong* (his co-stars were Curt Jurgens and Sylvia Syms); a Zanuck-produced-in-Paris *Crack*

Orson Welles in Compulsion *(59)*.

...elles in I Tartari (*60*), ... of the mediocre films ... which he has spent the ... ter days of his career.

in the Mirror (60), and a bunch of European 'spectaculars': *David e Golia*; Abel Gance's *Austerlitz*; *I Tartari* and *La Fayette*. He was perhaps trying to get money to finance the completion of his *Don Quixote*, begun in Spain in 1957, and to this day unfinished. He did get backing for his own version of Kafka's *The Trial* (62), filmed in English and French in Paris. The French reviews were good; the British and American ones were not. A small part (smiling benignly as a film director) in the Pasolini sketch of an unspeakable four-part film, *Rogopag*, was followed by *The VIPs* (63) – again a film director, but foreign, volatile and gross. His figure had become mountainous by this time. And it seemed inevitable that he should be in such international 'all-star' efforts as *La Fabuleuse Aventure de Marco Polo* (65), *Casino Royale* (66) and *Is Paris Burning?* His polished performance in the latter was one of the few satisfying things about it, and he brought the same distinction to his Cardinal Wolsey in a fine film, *A Man for All Seasons*. Simultaneously appeared another venture into Shakespeare, *Chimes at Midnight*, from a stage adaptation he had made of the Falstaff scenes of *Henry IV*, Parts One and Two. His own Falstaff was bemused and a little melancholy, and the film had taken on the character of that part of Spain in which it was filmed: dark, chilled, harsh. But more than anything since *Ambersons* it made one regret the neglect or wastage of his talent. He has announced no new plans to direct, but doubtless has some; and his fertile mind presumably still has ambitious projects to be realized on TV or the stage (he has worked often in both mediums over the past 20 years). Meanwhile, he continues to appear in meretricious stuff like *The Sailor From Gibraltar* (67), *I'll Never Forget Whatsisname* (68), *House of Cards*, *Southern Star* (69) and *12+1*, though 1970 saw an improvement: *Start the Revolution Without Me* (70) in a part tacked on after the film was finished, *The Kremlin Letter*, *The Battle of the River Nevetna*, *Catch-22* and *Waterloo*.

Mae West

Mae West's first appearance in films is perhaps the most famous first appearance of them all. She sidled on to the screen in bejewelled splendour, and the hat-check girl said 'Goodness, what beautiful diamonds!' 'Goodness had nothing to do with it, dearie,' said Mae. She wrote the exchange herself, and she also wrote the following: 'The man I don't like doesn't exist', 'It's better to be looked over than overlooked', 'Opportunity knocks for every man, but give a woman a ring', 'I always say, keep a diary and one day it will keep you', 'I used to be Snow White but I drifted', 'There are no withholding taxes on the wages of sin', 'It's not the men in my life that count, it's the life in my men', 'A man in the house is worth two in the street', 'Beulah, peel me a grape' and 'A man has more character in in his face at 30 than 20 – he has suffered longer'. There are hundreds more, though only 'Come up and see me some time' makes most dictionaries of quotations. However, the RAF named their inflatable life-saving device 'Mae West', to which her response was: 'I've been in "Who's Who", and I know what's what, but it's the first time I've been in a dictionary'.

Her witticisms may seem limp if you have never seen her, but they are irresistibly funny to anyone who has once been exposed to her. Big, blowsy, blonde and bosomy, she sways on to the screen with all the aplomb of a good female impersonator. Frank Marcus wrote once: 'A good drag act should express the assumption that a man makes a better woman than a woman. There are two ways in which this can be achieved: by a display of extravagant glamour, or by caricaturing female characteristics, making them appear ridiculous or even faintly disgusting.' It is as good a description of West as there is, even to the 'disgusting': Mae West caused many temperatures to rise in her time, not least that of William Randolph Hearst, who thought that Congress should do something about her. One critic, Don Herold, opined, 'I think I would rather let my daughters see Mae West's films regularly than see Hearst newspapers regularly. . . . Mae West burlesques sex, kids it, and I prefer that as moral fare for young American junior misses to the over-serious consideration of sex suggested by Garbo, Dietrich, Joan Crawford and others.' But as a tribute it is a trifle serious for an artist who never took herself seriously, a great clown who could put more innuendo in the flicker of an eyelash than seemed possible.

Rather surprisingly, she admits to a birth-date in her memoirs: 1893 in Brooklyn. Her father was a prominent heavyweight boxer, and encouraged her bent for showing off – at five, she was doing public imitations of Eva Tanquay, and a year later she was with Hal Clarendon's stock company at the Gotham Theatre in Bushwick, Brooklyn, playing all the famous kid-parts: Little Eva, Little Willie, Little Lord Fauntleroy. She studied dancing, and went into burlesque as The Baby Vamp. Although others claimed

Rochelle Hudson gets reassured by Mae West in She Done Him Wrong *(32)–and whatever the advice was, it was non-motherly. There were no ingénues in Miss West's later films, and the only women around were there to be scorned and mocked.*

to be, she *was* the originator of the shimmy dance; she also did imitations of George M. Cohan and Eddie Foy. In 1919 she went legit, in a show called 'Sometime' with Ed Wynn. In 1921 Pathé offered her a big part in *Daredevil Jack* (Dempsey), but at the last minute she changed her mind to star on the Pantage's vaudeville circuit (her pianist was Harry Richman, later to be famous in his own right).

She wrote her own material; in 1926 she returned to legit in a show she wrote, produced and directed: 'Sex'. It caused a furore: half of New York–those that had seen it–were at her feet; the other half were after her blood, and finally they got her: she was fined and sent to jail for 10 days for obscenity. She was more careful with 'The Drag', in which most of the characters were fags (she wasn't in it), a novel idea then: it played Paterson, New Jersey, but she was persuaded not to bring it into town. One called 'The Wicked Age' didn't run long, but 'Diamond Lil' in 1928 was a smash. In 'The Pleasure Man' most of the leading characters were female impersonators: the police closed the show and West was hauled into court again. She won her case, but instead of reviving it, went on tour with 'Lil'. Her last play was 'The Constant Sinner', adapted from a novel she had written. Then she accepted a Hollywood offer. (She had already been tested by Charles Walsh, who had tried to 'sell' her to Fox, where he worked, and to WB, but neither studio was interested.)

George Raft had requested her for *Night After Night* (32) and because of her eminence (or notoriety) Paramount offered her $5,000 weekly for 10 weeks' work, a staggering sum for a part which wasn't the biggest in the film (she was fourth-billed)–but she wanted out when she saw the script. Such was the interest engendered that Paramount couldn't let her go and finally she agreed to stay provided that she could write her own lines. Raft said later: 'In this picture, Mae West stole everything but the cameras.' It was hardly a performance. West didn't act, she postured–but whatever it was, it was mighty effective. Paramount begged her to stay, and she agreed on condition the next film was *Diamond Lil*; but because of its notoriety the studio insisted on its being called *She Done Him Wrong* (33). Like many of her subsequent films, it gave her a chance to sashay about in the feathers and sequins of the gay 90s, devouring every man in sight. She never vamped them–nothing so common: she simply let men know she liked them (though she liked diamonds better). Cary Grant was one of the enslaved, as he

I'm No Angel (*33*)*: that fact was clear from the opening number, when Mae sauntered into view and sang 'They Call Me Sister Honky Tonk'.*

was in *I'm No Angel*: she was a lady lion-tamer–'a girl who lost her reputation but never missed it'. The film sprawled somewhat and grossed $3 million. Producer William Le Baron made this statment to exhibitors: 'In the middle of the Depression the Mae West pictures . . . broke box-office records all over the country and attendance records all over the world. In fact, *She Done Him Wrong* must be credited with having saved Paramount at a time when that studio was considering selling out to MGM, and when Paramount theatres–1,700 of them–thought of closing their doors and converting into office buildings. Mae West is a life-saver to the motion picture

industry.' She was voted the eighth biggest draw of 1933. This success saved her too: bluenoses all over the country were up in arms and their counterparts in Hollywood were out to get her. The Hays office brought in a new production code in 1934 to combat the more insidious code of the West; and throughout her career there were influential Hollywood figures waiting for her to fail. Even less biased people considered her a nine-days'-wonder.

Her next vehicle started out as *It Ain't No Sin*, but the Hays office decreed a title change, and it became *Belle of the Nineties* (34). The censor objected, again, to certain scenes and dialogue, but the expurgated version was still a wow–'a triumph of Mae over matter' as Photoplay said–and got West elected the fifth biggest money-maker for 1934 (the only girl to beat her, Janet Gaynor, had several films to her one). Despite the censor, Paramount signed Mae to a new two-year contract at $300,000, including $100,000 for the original story and screenplay, and in 1935 she was the highest-paid woman in the US. Her film that year was *Goin' to Town*, and she was a thoroughly bad lot (a cattle-rustler's widow) who schemed her way into marriage and high society: at her best giving better than she'd got from the socialites who insulted her, and as Delilah in an opera. Her script cleverly scouted the provisions of the Hays Code–and probably contains more memorable quips than any of her films. She was down to 11th on the list of money-making stars but that was still impressive, with only one film released. There was more censor trouble when, as *Klondike Annie* (36), for plot reasons, she impersonated a Salvation Army-type sister. The Hearst press rose to new heights of virulence, though Hollywood gossip claimed that this time this was due to some unflattering remark that West had made about Marion Davies. However, the posters claimed: 'She made the Frozen North . . . Red Hot!' and only prudes were worried. (Another slogan used for Mae was: 'Nothing else matters – here's Mae West/ When she's good she's very good/When she's bad she's better.') Her 1937 film was *Go West Young Man*, adapted from a Gladys George stage success, 'Personal Appearance'; and she was doing radio-work. After one broadcast the Manhattan College magazine launched a broadside: West was 'the very personification of sex in its lowest connotation' polluting 'the sacred precincts of homes with shady stories, foul obscenity, smutty suggestions and horrible blasphemy'. In 1938 *Every Day's a Holiday* and Mae was Peaches O'Day, a con girl who takes refuge in a black wig and disguise as Mlle Fifi. She was allowed no double entendres or salty dialogue, and the film 'was both a bore and a striking illustration of the dangers and follies of trying to harness as explosive and undisciplinable a talent as Mae's' (William K. Everson).

Paramount then made what seems to have been one of the most heinous errors in film history: they turned down Mae's request to play Catherine the Great (Dietrich's version had flopped, and Lubitsch disliked West's script – ironically, he later made a comedy about Catherine which flopped). It was also clear from the receipts of the last couple of West films that her popularity had nose-dived. The novelty had worn off or Puritanism had perhaps triumphed. At that point Universal approached Mae to co-star with W. C. Fields in *My Little Chickadee* (39), a film more notable for promise than achievement. She wrote her own script, and he wrote his, and it was he of course who refused to compromise: the result is messy and unworthy of either of them. Universal made her another offer but they couldn't agree on a script; and there were similar difficulties with some propositions from Columbia. Instead, she let Gregory Ratoff talk her into an independent venture, *The Heat's On* (43); for the first time on screen she was not in the fashions of the nineties and she regretted it.

She returned to Broadway with a revue made from her Catherine material, 'Catherine Was Great' and in 1947–8 was in London and the British provinces, chalking up another triumph for 'Diamond Lil'. She toured in it in the US for four years after that, including New York, and then turned to TV and nightclubs, in an act with a group of muscle-men. For over a decade her only public appearance was in an edition of a vapid TV series, 'Mr Ed', in 1964, although she occasionally attended film society showings of her films. Interviews suggested that she was clinging to a former glory, and photographs indicated a reluctance to look her age. But then, she is Mae West, and the interviewers had got it wrong, because she was as famous as she ever was. Nor had she been neglected: among the many projects she turned down was *The First Travelling Saleslady*, and *Pal Joey* (with Brando co-starring and Wilder directing) was at one time mooted. She did agree to take a smallish part in *The Art of Love* in 1964, as a Madame, but on condition that she wrote her own lines: her offer was rejected, and Ethel Merman played the part.

Myra Breckinridge (*70*). *Raquel Welch had the title role, but Mae West had top billing. Apparently Miss Welch was no more pleased about this than about the clause in Miss West's contract which gave her the exclusive right to wear black or white. Indeed there seems to have been dissension on all sides.*

In 1970 she appeared – miraculously – in a film: as a Hollywood agent in Gore Vidal's sex-change comedy, *Myra Breckinridge*. Raquel Welch played the boy/girl title role, and both castings were a publicity man's dream. Variety commented that West's $350,000 for 10 days' work (plus writing her own dialogue) was worth every cent in publicity to the studio. Her reasons for returning were not disclosed, but were probably not financial. But then her film career is curious: perhaps, like Buster Keaton's, it was a progression from vaudeville rather than an end in itself. When she found that conditions were not ideal, she preferred to go back to the stage, to hear audiences rather than technicians laugh. But it is she who has the last laugh – over the snide interviewers – because she is Mae West. She is unique, a legend, part of American folk-lore.

Diana Wynyard

Had she wanted it, Diana Wynyard might have had a screen career as long and distinguished as that of Davis or Hepburn. As a stage actress she was excellent but seldom outstanding; nor was her later screen work likely to make anybody's eyes pop out. But her early film work is quite, quite stunning. Quiet, cool, gracious, ladylike, she was warmer and more believable than those adjectives imply: either her acting hasn't dated an iota or it was years before its time. In *Rasputin and the Empress* the Barrymores are acting away like mad and about as convincing as a tree-full of parrots, but Wynyard simply exists, in the same naturalistic way that someone like Spencer Tracy existed. In *One More River* the cast are, expectedly, more subdued; the film is still Galsworthy junk: but when Wynyard is on the screen, at any point you might be watching a film made yesterday.

She was born in 1906 in London; was educated in Croydon at a school where she studied dramatics; made her London debut walking-on in 'The Grand Duchess' (25). She went into rep and laid the foundations of her career with William Armstrong's company in Liverpool, 1927–9. London fame came with 'Sorry You've Been Troubled' by Walter Hackett in 1929; Wynyard's biggest success after that was probably in Congreve's 'The Old Bachelor' with Nigel Playfair's company. In 1932 she went to New York to appear in 'The Devil Passes' with Basil Rathbone – and took the place by storm. MGM offered a contract and cast her as a character based on the Princess Youssoupoff in *Rasputin and the Empress* (32).

Fox borrowed her for *Cavalcade* (33), opposite Clive Brook, Noël Coward's jingoistic account of 30 eventful years in the life of a British family. The stage production was filmed, as a guide, and claims were made for the final result – the best 'British' film ever made. It was certainly exquisitely directed (by Frank Lloyd) and authentic (an all-British cast) by the standards of the time; there were rave notices and, surprisingly, in a Depression-torn US it turned out to be the year's biggest grosser – at $3½ million. Coward said he found Wynyard's performance 'entirely entrancing. . . . To her I am immensely grateful. . . . I again repeat, I find her performance magnificent.'

Back at MGM she played in *Men Must Fight*, an interesting mother-love drama with Lewis Stone and Phillips Holmes – instilling pacifist ideas into the latter; the film concluded with an air raid on New York in 1940. It was not a success and, worse, like *Cavalcade*, gave audiences the impression that she was a middle-aged woman. Next she was with John Barrymore again in

Cynics scoffed when the Fox Film Co. poured a small fortune into Noël Coward's very British Cavalcade *(33) – why, it hadn't even been done on Broadway! – but it was a big hit in the US and Britain; Clive Brook and Diana Wynyard.*

Reunion in Vienna, from Robert E. Sherwood's play about old romance in old ditto. She was loaned to RKO for a couple with Clive Brook, *Where Sinners Meet* (34), from A. A. Milne's comedy, 'The Dover Road', and *Let's Try Again*, a marital drama. Of the former Photoplay said 'much, much too talkie' and of the next 'a trifle ponderous' – *One More River* at Universal. It was yet another British subject and again authentic, though with clichés (C. Aubrey Smith as the squire) to match those of the book (it's one of the later volumes of 'The Forsyte Saga'). Wynyard was the unhappy wife whose husband tries to frame her with a man she likes (Frank Lawton).

She had had a London offer to play Charlotte Brontë in 'Wild Decembers' (35) and she didn't return to Hollywood. Neither MGM nor she ever made any public announcement of the break, and observers later concluded that she was homesick and longing to return to the stage. She did say that she didn't care for filming and that she was unhappy in Hollywood. But then she was a failure in Hollywood, by Hollywood's standards: all the films she made after *Cavalcade* did poorly (in Britain as well), and she wasn't prepared to fight the front office for any of the parts earmarked for Crawford or Shearer. In Britain she certainly refused film offers for some years, while having several big stage hits: 'Lean Harvest', 'Sweet Aloes', 'Candida' revived, 'Design for Living' (39) and 'No Time for Comedy'. Producer Joseph Somlo finally talked her into doing a picture with Ralph Richardson, *On the Night of the Fire* (39), about a couple who commit a minor theft and find themselves wading gradually deeper into tragedy. In 1940 she did two which were 'topical': Anthony Asquith's *Freedom Radio*, reuniting her with Brook, and Warners' British remake of an old Arliss film, *The Prime Minister*, as Mrs Disraeli to John Gielgud's unsemitic Dizzy (Fay Compton over-acted as Victoria). In *Gaslight* with Anton Walbrook she was most touching as the frightened wife. In 1941 for Carol Reed (to whom she was married, 1943–7, the second of three husbands) she was the wealthy betrothed of Michael Redgrave *Kipps*. She returned to the stage in 'Watch on the Rhine' (42) and was not seen again on screen until she played Lady Chiltern in *An Ideal Husband* (47).

In 1951 she did a cameo in an inferior *Tom Brown's Schooldays* (Robert Newton was Dr Arnold); in 1956 gave a surprisingly touching performance as a hard matron in a silly nurse drama starring Belinda Lee, *The Feminine Touch*; and made only one more film, the American *Island in the Sun* (57). Her work on the London stage was often memorable. It included: 'Captain Carvallo', 'Much Ado About Nothing' (a perfect Beatrice to Gielgud's Benedick), 'The Seagull' (as Arkadina) and 'Hamlet' (as Gertrude). She was with Britain's National Theatre at its inception, playing Gertrude again; she was in 'Andorra' and was rehearsing a revival of 'Hay Fever' when she died, in 1964.

Loretta Young

As a young woman, Loretta Young was very pretty, with big eyes and apple cheeks, and as she aged she remained lovely to look upon. Her screen presence was crisp and glamorous in the best tradition, and these factors presumably determined her success. She slipped with ease from comedy to drama – especially if her roles required her to dress elegantly. She was known as 'Hollywood's beautiful hack'. She also seems to have been one of those masterly lady stars who know all about lighting and costumes, and keep a mirror beside her on the set. Her first husband, Grant Withers, described her after their separation as 'a steel butterfly', though at this time (the early Talkies), on screen, she was anything but. Later, perhaps, but her early acting can stand with the best: a radiant young woman doing with sensitivity a series of mainly working-class and put-upon heroines.

Loretta Young – epit[...] of 30s glamour – in T[...] Devil To Pay (*30*).

She was born in 1912 in Salt Lake City. Her parents separated when she was four, and Mother moved to Los Angeles where she opened a boarding-house and hired out her four small daughters as film extras whenever possible. For a while Loretta attended a convent; her real film career began by accident, when director Mervyn Le Roy telephoned the household asking for Polly Ann Young to appear in a Colleen Moore vehicle, *Naughty But Nice* (27): she was away, so sister Loretta went instead. After that she had a bit in *Whip Woman* (28) starring Antonio Moreno and Estelle Taylor, and was selected from 50 candidates to play in Lon Chaney's *Laugh Clown Laugh* as the high-wire performer adored by him and loved by Nils Asther. She was in Paramount's *The Magnificent Flirt* starring the magnificent Florence Vidor; then Warners signed her. There were featured roles in *The Head Man* and a Richard Barthelmess starrer, *Scarlet Seas*; then the lead in *The Squall* (29), her first all-Talkie, as a Hungarian girl upset by the advent of gypsy Myrna Loy; plus a fine chance in the minor

The Girl in the Glass Cage–i.e. box-office. *The Careless Age* and *The Fast Life* were grim melodramas with Douglas Fairbanks Jr, and WB liked them together so much that, after she had put in an appearance in *The Show of Shows*, they were teamed together again in the more cheerful *The Forward Pass* and *Loose Ankles* (30), where she was an heiress and he a gigolo who answers her marriage ad. In real life she married Withers, after they had been involved together in *The Second Floor Mystery*. She was the governess in love with John Barrymore in *The Man From Blankleys*; twin sisters in *Road to Paradise*, one a crook trying to heist the other's jewellery; the daughter of Otis Skinner in *Kismet*; and a young girl married to the ageing Conway Tearle in *Road to Paradise*.

Young–epitome
s glamour–at the
of China (*43*).

Goldwyn borrowed her to replace Constance Cummings during the shooting of *The Devil to Pay*, opposite Ronald Colman, but she was less lucky on loan to RKO for a Foreign Legion tale starring Ralph Forbes, *Beau Ideal* (31)–hers wasn't much of a part. She was married to an older man again, Conrad Nagel–while he was suffering from amnesia–in *The Right of Way*, and the film certainly lost its way before the end. Young was loaned to Fox for *Three Girls Lost*, and was then back on the same old theme again, *Too Young to Marry*–Grant Withers. It may have been a successful Broadway comedy ('Broken Dishes') but bore an uncanny relevance to real life, with Mother objecting to her marrying an older man–except in life there was no happy ending as they were divorced not long after the film was released. Then Young was the *Big Business Girl* with Ricardo Cortez. She said *I Like Your Nerve* to Fairbanks; was a reporter and Jean Harlow's rival in *Platinum Blonde* and Walter Huston's daughter in a gangland story, *The Ruling Voice*. Possibly her best work was as James Cagney's wife in the fast-moving *Taxi* (32).

Warners were at last beginning to consider her one of their major assets, but as a divorcee not yet 20 she had to be very carefully cast not to offend cinema-goers. She was too virginal-looking to be anything but an innocent–but her circumstances were usually unfortunate. In William A. Wellman's *The Hatchet Man* she married fellow-Oriental Edward G. Robinson, who had killed her father. Picturegoer thought she had 'never appeared to better advantage . . . she is almost unbelievably different from her normal screen self'. She did a couple of career-vs-marriage stories, *Play Girl*, married to gambler Norman Foster, and, also with Foster, *Weekend Marriage*–called *Working Wives* in Britain. *Life Begins* was never shown in that country, being banned by the censor (Young was a convicted murderess dying in child-birth); while *They Call It Sin* there became *The Way of Life*–neither of which suggests the mild little triangle drama it was. George Brent co-starred. She was a shopgirl in *Employees Entrance* (33), tempted by boss Warren William to be unfaithful to husband Wallace Ford, and then partnered by Paul Lukas in a double sense in *Grand Slam*, a satiric comedy about bridge players. In Fox's *Zoo at Budapest* she was a refugee from an orphanage, loved by zoo-keeper Gene Raymond, and in *The Life of Jimmy Dolan* with Fairbanks she ran one. She, Cortez and Wellman went over to MGM for *Midnight Mary*–she was a murderess again–with Franchot Tone; then Wellman directed her and Richard Barthelmess in *Heroes for Sale*. There was a change from maudlin melodrama with *The Devil's in Love*, but it was just another Foreign Legion story (with Victor Jory, at Fox). There were more tears in her last for Warners, *She Had to Say Yes*; nor was she exactly happy in *A Man's Castle* with Spencer Tracy, but it was by far her best film of the period.

She signed a contract with 20th Century, the new company founded by Darryl F. Zanuck after leaving Warners and releasing through UA; and they started off well with *House of Rothschild* (34), which turned out to be a big hit. Young was George Arliss's daughter, and a good cast included Helen Westley, C. Aubrey Smith, Robert Young, Boris Karloff and Reginald Owen. She was simply Colman's leading lady in *Bulldog Drummond Strikes Back*. *Born To Be Bad* was not her but her son–though she reformed at the end when Cary Grant made her realize that she was responsible for his delinquency. She was loaned to Fox for *Caravan* (a Countess marrying gypsy Charles Boyer) and for *The White Parade* (nurses and John Boles); and was back with Colman in *Clive of India* (35), and with Gable in *Call of the Wild*, a terrible performance, as she later admitted. Twentieth had no plans for her so she went to Paramount for two: Wanger's *Shanghai* with Boyer again, and de Mille's *The Crusades*, as Berengaria, married to Cœur-de-Lion (Henry Wilcoxon) by proxy: a film memorable for a comforting soldier saying 'This is gonna be tough on you baby'. She was hardly less incongruous, but the film was a great grosser. At MGM she did a crime melodrama, *The Unguarded Hour* (36), with Franchot Tone.

In the meantime 20th Century had

As a young woman Loretta Young had a spiritual quality and a sensitivity that were but hinted at in her later performances. She was at her early best in Frank Borzage's A Man's Castle *(33), with Spencer Tracy, left, and Walter Connolly. And Marjorie Rambeau.*

'amalgamated' with Fox, and Young's contract was re-drawn on an exclusive basis, on the understanding that she got the company's plum roles. Already with 20th she had acquired prestige, had left her suffering days way behind. Whether the films were better is doubtful (they were certainly bigger): she seldom was. She did suffer just twice more, in *Private Number* with Robert Taylor, and as the brave *Ramona*: Film Weekly thought 'too much weeping blurs her portrayal'. However, *Ladies in Love* was very funny: in the cast was Janet Gaynor (whose place at the studio Young was taking) plus Tyrone Power–this was the first of several co-starring vehicles. Their *Love Is News* (37) was also delightful and their *Café Metropole* a passable romance. Over to Don Ameche and *Love Under Fire* as a jewel thief; to Warner Baxter in a weak triangle drama, *Wife Doctor and Nurse* with Virginia Bruce; then back to Power for a *Second Honeymoon*.

John Ford directed *Four Men and a Prayer* (38): the prayer was to clear their father, cashiered Colonel C. Aubrey Smith, and to win Loretta. Richard Greene did. She was one of the *Three Blind Mice* (girls after wealthy husbands–a plot 20th were to utilize again at least six times), and the Empress Eugenie in *Suez*. *Kentucky* was an ordinary (if popular) horsey picture, with Greene; and *The Story of Alexander Graham Bell* (39) merely a chore, although the cast included her sisters (one of them, Sally Blane, had some slight Hollywood success). She loathed all these parts, and *Suez* had been the last straw–but it was *Alexander Graham Bell* that broke the camel's back: she had wanted to play Mrs Bell as the deaf-mute she was and had to compromise by being deaf only. After *Wife Husband and Friend* (a comedy with Warner Baxter) she quit the studio. Some sources suggest this Zanuck-Young dispute was over money, that 20th withheld a raise, due to differences with her agent, Myron Selznick.

At all events, after a comedy for Wanger-UA, *Eternally Yours*, she was, according to Bob Thomas in 'King Cohn', black-listed. After months without an offer, Harry Cohn of Columbia agreed to take her at $75,000 each for three films, half her normal fee. She was only too pleased to accept. *The Doctor Takes a Wife* (40) and *He Stayed for Breakfast* were both comedies; then she went to Universal for *The Lady From Cheyenne* (41), hokum directed by the

The Farmer's Daughter *(47) was a comedy about a Minnesota Swedish farm girl (Loretta Young) who wins both the heart of her employer (Joseph Cotten) and a seat in Congress. With them is Charles Bickford. She later played variations of this character on television.*

once-esteemed Frank Lloyd. At Columbia she was the 'Ballerina' of Lady Eleanor Smith's novel, adapted as *The Men in Her Life*, and she stayed on for another mediocre comedy, *Bedtime Story* (42), and a thriller with Brian Aherne, *A Night to Remember*. She did two at Paramount with Alan Ladd, *China* (43) and *And Now Tomorrow* (from Rachel Field's novel about a deaf socialite), and, in between, one of the worst of the women-at-war dramas, Universal's *Ladies Courageous* (44). In 1945 *Along Came Jones*, who was Gary Cooper, and in 1946 *The Stranger*, who was Edward G. Robinson, on the track of Young's husband, Orson Welles. *The Perfect Marriage* was one of the flavourless marital comedies (in this case with David Niven) that Young had already done several times too often.

She had free-lanced with success and presumably reached the peak of her career with *The Farmer's Daughter* (47), a comedy with Joseph Cotten. It wasn't a performance that the press had remarked, except for a good Swedish accent and her blonded hair, but it won a Best Actress Oscar (the competition: Joan Crawford in *Possessed*, Susan Hayward in *Smash-Up*, Dorothy McGuire in *Gentlemen's Agreement* and Young's friend Rosalind Russell in *Mourning Becomes Electra*). Oscar did nothing for her–few of her subsequent films were good, and none of them offered good acting parts: *The Bishop's Wife*, religious whimsy with Cary Grant and Niven; *Rachel and the Stranger* (48), wooed by Robert Mitchum and William Holden; *The Accused* (49), a so-called psychological thriller with Wendell Corey and Robert Cummings; *Mother Is a Freshman*, a comedy at 20th with Van Johnson; and a nun film at same, appropriately called *Come to the Stable*. *Key to the City* (50) cast her agreeably as a lady mayor having a fling with fellow-mayor Gable; and, also at MGM, *Cause for Alarm* (51) was a neat thriller in *Sorry Wrong Number* mould produced and co-written by second husband Ted Lewis. She gave a fine performance, but it played as a B. So did the last four, more or less: *Half Angel* with Joseph Cotten; *Paula* (52), a melo with Kent Smith; *Because of You*, a sudser with Jeff Chandler; and *It Happens Every Thursday* (53) with John Forsythe.

In 1953 she went into TV with 'The Loretta Young Show', a drama series more notable for the *haute couture* of her introduction than for drama. Nevertheless it was highly popular, and won several Emmys over the years–to everyone's surprise it ran until 1961. In that year was settled out of court her (estranged) husband's suit alleging malpractice over the dissolution of their TV company; and she published a book, 'The Things I Had to Learn'. In 1962 she tried 'The New Loretta Young Show', but the only new thing about it was that it was one continuing sudser instead of many different ones. It lasted only one season.

Robert Young

Robert Young was the all-purpose leading man. For over 20 years his fortunes hardly varied: A pictures and B pictures; comedy and drama; lead roles and second leads; co-starring with big stars and little ones; at this studio and that–but mostly MGM, to whom he was under contract during the greater part of this period. Naturally, he was dependable, but he had two qualities, often overlooked: he was amiable, and as a romantic hero he hardly ever aged.

He was born in Chicago in 1907, educated in Seattle and Los Angeles; he worked as a bank teller, reporter and salesman, learning a certain amount of his craft at a small theatre in Carmel. He started in films as an extra, got his chance when he was chosen to assist another artist in a screen test and impressed the director in charge of the test. MGM signed him and loaned him to Fox for a role in *The Black Camel* (31), a Charlie Chan feature with Warner Oland. He played the son of Helen Hayes in *The Sin of Madelon Claudet* and was loaned to Columbia where he (moustached) and Constance Cummings were members of *The Guilty Generation*; and back at MGM he was an ardent prohibitionist in *The Wet Parade* (32) because Dad killed Mommy in a drunken frenzy. His first star role was in *New Morals for Old* opposite Margaret Perry in this version of John Van Druten's 'After All', and he had another good part in *Unashamed*, as a murderer: he shot the lover of sister Helen Twelvetrees to avenge the family honour–though she had deliberately kept the lover with her all night in order to force the family's consent to her marriage. It made an interesting courtroomer. Less noticeable were his stints in *Strange Interlude* and Eddie Cantor's *The Kid From Spain*.

He learned why *Men Must Fight* (33)–a lesson useful in both *Today We Live*, when he lost Joan Crawford to Gary Cooper, and in *Hell Below*, a submarine drama with Walter Huston. He was Marie Dressler's captain son in *Tugboat Annie* and a disillusioned football hero in *Saturday's Millions* at Universal, the first of a string of loan-outs. He was Ann Harding's bounder-husband in *The Right to Romance*, Janet Gaynor's romantic interest in *Carolina*, Katharine Hepburn's in *Spitfire* (34), and Loretta Young's (as one of Wellington's officers) in *House of Rothschild*. On his home lot he was a prodigal son in a Southern drama with Jean Parker, *Lazy River*, and in a *Paris Interlude* he hero-worshipped a shoddy adventurer, Otto Kruger. These were Bs, and Young stayed in Bs for a while: *Whom the Gods Destroy* at Columbia with Walter Connolly; *Death on the Diamond*, a mystery with a baseball setting, with Paul Kelly and Madge Evans; and *The Band Plays On*, collegiate stuff with Betty Furness. He was Wallace Beery's son–and superior officer–in *West Point of the Air* (35), and Evelyn Venable's in Hal Roach's *Vagabond Lady*: 'really coming into his own as the captivating scapegrace son of a too, too dignified family' (Photoplay).

He was an adman in *Calm Yourself* with Madge Evans; a soldier seduced from his duty by commie Barbara Stanwyck in the funny *Red Salute*, made by Reliance; and was involved in Universal's *Remember Last Night?*, an exhilarating comedy thriller directed by James Whale with Edward Arnold and Constance Cummings. At Paramount he competed with Fred MacMurray for Claudette Colbert in *The Bride Comes Home*, and MGM, ever prodigal with his services, then loaned him to Gaumont-British for a couple–neither of them very important roles: Hitchcock's *Secret Agent* (36) and *It's Love Again*, as Jessie Matthews's leading man. He returned to a B, *Three Wise Guys*, and was then with Stanwyck again, at RKO, in *The Bride Walks Out*; there were two more Bs, both with Florence Rice, *Sworn Enemy* and *The Longest Night*; then he was loaned to 20th to support Shirley Temple and Alice Faye in *Stowaway*. He and Ann Sothern did *Dangerous Number* (37) at MGM, and then he was loaned to Paramount again to compete for Claudette Colbert again, this time against Melvyn Douglas: *I Met Him in Paris*. He and Florence Rice were *Married Before Breakfast*; he had a rare historical role in *The Emperor's Candlesticks*; he was Franchot Tone's rival for Joan Crawford in *The Bride Wore Red*; but *Navy Blue and Gold* was one of the few A films in which he was top-billed (over James Stewart and Lionel Barrymore). He was top-billed again in a programmer, *Paradise for Three* (38), with Frank Morgan and old sidekick Rice, but he was the second, or other, man in three pictures released in June that year: 20th's *Josette* with

Robert Young was less a star in his own right than a good leading man: this is one of several appearances opposite Joan Crawford – The Bride Wore Red (37), *directed by Dorothy Arzner.*

Don Ameche and Simone Simon; *The Toy Wife* with Melvyn Douglas and Luise Rainer; and *Three Comrades* with Robert Taylor, Margaret Sullavan, and Tone: he was the one who got killed.

Rich Man Poor Girl was a funny little picture with Young and Ruth Hussey in the title roles and Lew Ayres and Lana Turner in support; *The Shining Hour* was another Crawford opus, with other familiars – Sullavan and Melvyn Douglas; and *Honolulu* (39) was an Eleanor Powell vehicle, with Young in a dual role as a film-star who changes places with an ordinary man. He was a playboy who jilts Virginia Field at the altar and then falls for Annabella in *Bridal Suite*; and a rancher who gets wrongly accused of murder in the goings-on caused by *Maisie* (Ann Sothern). *Miracles for Sale* was a mystery involving magicians, with Rice; and *Florian* (40) was a horse, in Technicolor, from Felix Salten's novel, with Helen Gilbert, and Young's best chance in a long time. He supported Spencer Tracy in *Northwest Passage*, in a role that Robert Taylor turned down; had the minor role, as Margaret Sullavan's fiancé (till he turned Nazi), in *The Mortal Storm*; was in the minor *Sporting Blood*; was wrongly diagnosed by Lew Ayres in *Dr Kildare's Crisis*; and was loaned to 20th for a Randolph Scott film, *Western Union* (41).

He co-starred with Laraine Day in the remake of *The Trial of Mary Dugan*; coped with Powell and Sothern in *Lady Be Good*, as one half of a song-writing team (Sothern was the other); and was a *Married Bachelor* with Ruth Hussey. Then MGM out of the blue gave him the chief part in one of their most important productions, *H. M. Pulham Esq.*, from John P. Marquand's novels. Young seized his chance, encouraging all the people who had been rooting for him for years, gave a fine performance and got superb notices. MGM put him into another B, *Joe Smith American* (42), from a story by Paul Gallico, but after that his position was no longer equivocal: he starred opposite Jeanette MacDonald in *Cairo*, and was top-billed in an important weepie, *Journey for Margaret* (O'Brien), playing an American war correspondent in Britain; he then co-starred with Lana Turner in *Slightly Dangerous* (43).

Twentieth borrowed him for another top role, that of the husband in *Claudia*, opposite Dorothy McGuire, and kept him on to co-star with Betty Grable in *Sweet Rosie O'Grady*, but in that musical he was somewhat out of place. He played a Yank in Britain – 'with naturalness and humour' (Forsyth Hardy) – in *The Canterville Ghost* (44) with young O'Brien and Charles Laughton: his last at MGM after 14 years. Freelancing, he started strong, but as with others in his position, couldn't maintain the

Margaret Sullavan was another actress with whom Young appeared on several occasions: in The Mortal Storm *(40) they were engaged but she later fell for James Stewart.*

impetus: at RKO he appeared with McGuire in *The Enchanted Cottage* (45) and with Laraine Day in a soft-centred romance, *Those Endearing Young Charms*; he went to Paramount for *The Searching Wind* (46), with Sylvia Sidney, and to 20th for *Claudia and David* with McGuire. At RKO he did a minor comedy, *Lady Luck*, with Barbara Hale; *They Won't Believe Me* (47) with Susan Hayward; and *Crossfire*, with Roberts Mitchum and Ryan, a much-praised murder-tale with an anti-semitism plot twist.

After almost a year's absence he turned up in his first Western, *Relentless* (48) at Columbia, not a distinguished picture, though he was quite convincing as a wandering cowboy; then he had a successful comedy, *Sitting Pretty*, with Clifton Webb and Maureen O'Hara. After that his career gently declined: *Adventure in Baltimore* (49) with Shirley Temple; *Bride for Sale* with Claudette Colbert; *That Forsyte Woman* at MGM, as Young Jolyon; *And Baby Makes Three* (50) with Hale; *Goodbye My Fancy* (51) with Joan Crawford; *The Second Woman* with Betsy Drake; *The Half-Breed* (52), a poor Western; and, in a supporting role, *Secret of the Incas* (54).

He disappeared for a while, but returned on TV starring in a successful series, 'Father Knows Best'. In 1967 he toured in 'A Generation' and in 1969 was in another hit TV series, 'Marcus Welby MD'. He married in 1933 and has four daughters.

Roland Young

Roland Young was a short, elderly English-born character actor with two or three expressions. He was somewhat bemused, vaguely quizzical and never surprised at the madness of others. He usually appeared in comedy, where he underplayed with skill and charm. Said Phil Lonergan years ago in Picturegoer: 'Roland Young is very popular with the ladies. His wit and sparkle are more interesting to the fair sex than Adonis figures and clear-cut noses.' One lady he was popular with was Catherine Deneuve, who said in an interview with the Sunday Times in 1968: 'I think the best film performance I've ever seen was given by Roland Young as the Earl in an old Leo McCarey film called *Ruggles of Red Gap*. I love that quiet, easy comedy – that's how I would like to act.' James Agee wrote in 1944 that he 'is able to make anything he appears in seem much more intelligent, human and amusing than it has any intrinsic right to'.

Young was born in London in 1887, the son of an architect. He was educated at Sherborne College, Dorset, and at London University; and then studied at RADA. He made his London debut in 'Find the Woman' in 1908 and in 1912 went to New York to appear in 'Hindle Wakes'. Most of his subsequent career was in the US, and in World War I he served in the US army. By that time he was an established stage name, most notably in three comedies written for him by Clare Kummer: 'Good Gracious Annabelle!' (16), 'A Successful Calamity' (17) and 'Rollo's Wild Oat' (20). He later married Miss Kummer's daughter, Frances (1921–40). Among other stage appearances: 'Luck in Pawn' (19), 'The Devil's Disciple' (23), as General Burgoyne, in London, 'Beggar on Horseback' (24) and 'The Last of Mrs Cheyney' (26). He made two Silent pictures: *Sherlock Holmes* (22) with John Barrymore, and *Moriarty* the same year: in both he was Dr Watson.

With the coming of Talkies MGM signed him to a contract and he made his Talkie debut in *The Unholy Night* (29), a thriller directed by Lionel Barrymore, followed by *Her Private Life* – Billie Dove's, at Warners; *The Bishop Murder Case*; *Wise Girls* (30); de Mille's *Madam Satan* starring Kay Johnson and Reginald Denny; and *New Moon* with Lawrence Tibbett. Fox borrowed him for two farces: *Don't Bet on Women* (31), in which he's the over-trusting husband of Jeanette MacDonald and bets Edmund Lowe he won't be able to kiss her; and *Annabelle's Affairs*, the new film version of 'Good Gracious Annabelle!', between which he was in *The Prodigal* with Tibbett. He was in de Mille's *The Squaw Man*, and in *The Guardsman*, supporting Lynn Fontanne and Alfred Lunt in the only film they made together, a version of the play by Molnar. At Columbia he was a drunken doctor in *The Pagan Lady*, starring Evelyn Brent and Conrad Nagel. At RKO he was featured in Pola Negri's *A Woman Commands* (32), and he then supported Robert Montgomery in *Lovers Courageous*, written specially for the screen by Frederick Lonsdale: it was Young's last for MGM and as he began to free-lance he found himself enormously in demand. At Paramount he did three which benefited greatly from his presence: *One Hour With You*, dallying with Jeanette MacDonald while his wife Genevieve Tobin is courted by her husband, Chevalier; *This Is the Night*, starring, with Charlie Ruggles and Lily Damita; and *Street of Women* with Kay Francis. 'Roland Young's sprightly acting saves this story from gloom' said Photoplay.

He was now, if not a big crowd-puller, an audience favourite and officially a star. It was considered a great coup when Korda persuaded him to return to Britain to appear in *Wedding Rehearsal*, as a guards officer. Back in Hollywood he aided and abetted butler Slim Summerville and maid Zasu Pitts in *They Just Had To Get Married* (33) – only they were trying to make up their minds about a divorce; and co-starred with Alison Skipworth in *A Lady's Profession*, about two British aristocrats unwittingly running a speakeasy. He did: *Pleasure Cruise* at Fox with Genevieve Tobin; *Blind Adventure*, a murder mystery with Robert Armstrong; and *His Double Life*, excellent as the shy artist who impersonates his valet and marries the latter's mail-order bride Lillian Gish, when he himself is supposed to be dead. He went to Broadway to appear in 'His Master's Voice', and returned to Hollywood for a supporting role in Bing Crosby's *Here Is My Heart* (34) and to be a memorable Uriah Heep in *David Copperfield* (35). While there he also did his engaging job in *Ruggles of Red Gap*. There were two more Broadway plays, then some unrewarding supporting stints in films: *The Unguarded Hour* (36) starring Loretta Young; *One Rainy Afternoon* starring Francis Lederer; and *Give Me Your Heart*, as the novelist who acts as a *deus ex machina* to the problems of Kay Francis.

He went to Britain to make *The Man Who Could Work Miracles*, and stayed on to co-star with Chili Bouchier in *Gypsy* (37); in Hollywood he did *Call It a Day*, then was back in Britain for *King Solomon's Mines*. In Hollywood he was Thorne Smith's *Topper*, the mild little man who finds that he is beset by a couple of squabbling ghosts (Constance Bennett and Cary Grant). It is for this series he is best remembered; Billie Burke was Mrs Topper, and in her memoir she said that Young was 'always dry and fun to work with'. They made several more films together. In Eddie Cantor's *Ali Baba Goes to Town* he was an Arab potentate (of sorts); then he crossed the Atlantic once more to play with Jessie Matthews in *Sailing Along* (38). He was married to Billie Burke again in *The Young in Heart* and in *Topper Takes a Trip* (39); then to Fay Bainter in an adequate version of a funny Broadway comedy, *Yes My Darling Daughter* – Priscilla Lane was the daughter. He returned to supporting parts in three weak programmers, *The Night of*

The Philadelphia Story (*40*) *was designed primarily as a showcase for Katharine Hepburn, but another reason it was so good was the supporting cast – like Virginia Weidler and Roland Young, respectively her cynical sister and indulgent uncle.*

Nights with Pat O'Brien and Olympe Bradna; *Here I Am a Stranger* with Richard Dix; and *He Married His Wife* (40) with Joel McCrea and Nancy Kelly, a divorce comedy whose title gave away the denouement, as if anyone cared.

Indeed, Young's parts were now much smaller: *Irene*; *Star Dust*, as a talent scout; *Private Affairs*; *Dulcy*; *The Philadelphia Story*, as Katharine Hepburn's whimsical uncle; and *No No Nanette*. His last star part was in *Topper Returns* (41) with Burke and Joan Blondell, but he brought his genial presence to *The Flame of New Orleans* with Dietrich, *Two-Faced Woman* with Garbo, *The Lady Has Plans* (42), and *They All Kissed the Bride* with Joan Crawford. He had small parts in two all-star episoders, *Tales of Manhattan* and *Forever and a Day* (43), and 'stole' the latter, according to Picturegoer. In 1945 he began a radio series and he later appeared regularly on TV, but his film work diminished: *Standing Room Only* (44) with Paulette Goddard; *And Then There Were None* (46) with Walter Huston, Barry Fitzgerald and Louis Hayward; *Bond Street* (48), a poor British four-part film, with Jean Kent as the inevitable streetwalker; and *You Gotta Stay Happy* with Joan Fontaine. He was a mass murderer in Bob Hope's *The Great Lover* (49), and then he supported Fred Astaire in *Let's Dance* (50); but the last two were hardly worthy of his participation, *St Benny the Dip* (51) with Dick Haymes and Nina Foch, and *The Man From Tangier* (53) with Nils Asther and Nancy Coleman.

He died in 1953. In 1948 he had married for the second time.

Acknowledgment of sources

Grateful acknowledgment is made to the many critics, authors and journalists who are quoted in this book – also to their publishers. The newspapers and magazines that have been helpful are The Times, The Daily Telegraph, The Daily Mail, Daily Mirror, Daily Express, The Guardian, Financial Times, Evening News, The Evening Standard, Daily Herald, The Observer, The Sunday Times, The Sunday Telegraph, Sunday Express, The New York Times, News Chronicle, New York Daily News, New York Herald - Tribune, New York World - Telegram, New York Mirror, The New York American, The Spectator, The New Statesman, New York Magazine, The Nation, The New Republic, The New Yorker, Life, Time, Esquire, Newsweek, Look, Playboy, Vanity Fair, Films in Review, Films and Filming, Cinémonde, The Australian Film Guide, L'Ecran Français, Film Weekly, The National Board of Review Magazine, The Hollywood Reporter, Kine Weekly, The Bioscope, Picturegoer, Photoplay, Picture Show, Motion Picture Herald, Punch, Sequence, Show Magazine, Theatre Arts Magazine, Variety, The Silent Cinema, Sight and Sound and the Monthly Film Bulletin. The Bernstein Questionnaire and the programmes of the National Film Theatre were also most useful.

The books that were used include:

Agate, James: *Around Cinemas*. London: Home and Van Thal, 1946; *Around Cinemas Second Series*. London: Home and Van Thal, 1948.
Agee, James: *Agee on Film*. New York: McDowell, Obolensky, 1958; Grosset and Dunlap, 1969. London: Peter Owen Ltd, 1967.
Alpert, Hollis: *The Barrymores*. New York: Dial Press, 1964. London: W. H. Allen, 1965.
Anger, Kenneth: *Hollywood Babylone*. Paris: Éditions J. - J. Pauvert, 1959.
Anstey, Edgar; Manvell, Roger; Lindgren, Ernest and Rotha, Paul (Eds.): *Shots in the Dark*. London: Allan Wingate, 1951.
Astaire, Fred: *Steps in Time*. New York: Harper and Bros., 1959. London: Heinemann, 1959.
Astor, Mary: *My Story*. New York: Doubleday, 1959.
Bainbridge, John: *Garbo*. New York: Doubleday, 1955. London: Muller, 1955.
Balcon, Sir Michael: *A Lifetime of Films*. London: Hutchinson, 1969.
Barker, Felix: *The Oliviers*. London: Hamish Hamilton, 1953. New York: Lippincott, 1953.
Barr, Charles: *Laurel and Hardy*. London: Studio Vista, 1967. Berkeley: University of California Press, 1968.
Billquist, Fritiof: *Garbo*. New York: G. P. Putnam's Sons, 1960. London: Barker, 1960.
Blesh, Rudi: *Keaton*. New York: Macmillan Co., 1966. London: Secker & Warburg, 1967.
Bogdanovitch, Peter: *Fritz Lang in America*. London: Studio Vista, 1969. New York: Praeger, 1969.
Brownlow, Kevin: *The Parade's Gone By*. New York: Alfred A. Knopf, 1968. London: Secker and Warburg, 1969.
Burke, Billie: *With a Feather on My Nose*. New York: Appleton - Century - Crofts, 1949. London: Peter Davies, 1951.
Burton, Hal (Ed.): *Great Acting*. London: British Broadcasting Corporation, 1967. New York: Hill and Wang, 1968.
Cahn, William: *Harold Lloyd's Funny Side of Life*. New York: Duell, Sloan and Pearce, 1964. London: Allen and Unwin, 1966.
Cantor, Eddie with Jane Kesner Ardmore: *Take My Life*. New York: Doubleday, 1957.
Chandler, Raymond: *Raymond Chandler Speaking*. New York: Houghton Mifflin, 1962. London: Hamish Hamilton, 1962.
Chaplin, Charles: *My Autobiography*. London: The Bodley Head, 1964. New York: Simon and Schuster, 1964.
Chaplin, Charles Jr: *My Father Charlie Chaplin*. New York: Random House, 1960. London: Longmans, 1960.
Chevalier, Maurice: *With Love*. Boston: Little, Brown & Co., 1960. London: Cassell, 1960.
Connell, Brian: *Knight Errant*. London: Hodder and Stoughton, 1955. New York: Doubleday, 1955.
Conway, Michael and Ricci, Mark: *The Films of Jean Harlow*. New York: The Citadel Press, 1965.
Cooke, Alistair: *Douglas Fairbanks*. New York: Museum of Modern Art, 1940.
Cooke, Alistair (Ed.): *Garbo and the Night Watchman*. London: Jonathan Cape, 1937. Thames and Hudson, 1971.
Courtneidge, Cicely: *Cicely*. London: Hutchinson, 1953.
Crawford, Joan with Jane Kesner Ardmore: *Portrait of Joan*. New York: Doubleday, 1962. London: Muller, 1963.
Crichton, Kyle: *The Marx Brothers*. New York: Doubleday, 1950. London: Heinemann, 1951.
Crosby, Bing: *Call Me Lucky*. New York: Simon and Schuster, 1953. London: Muller, 1953.
Crowther, Bosley: *The Lion's Share*. New York: Dutton, 1957.
Croy, Homer: *Our Will Rogers*. New York: Duell, Sloan and Pearce/Boston: Little, Brown & Co., 1953.
Davidson, Bill: *The Real and the Unreal*. New York: Harper and Bros., 1961.
Davis, Bette: *The Lonely Life*. New York: G. P. Putnam's Sons, 1962. London: Macdonald, 1963.
de Mille, Agnes: *Dance to the Piper*. Boston: Little, Brown & Co./New York: Atlantic Monthly Press, 1951. London: Hamish Hamilton, 1951.
de Mille, Cecil B.: *Autobiography*. New York: Prentice - Hall, 1959. London: W. H. Allen, 1960.
Dictionnaire du Cinéma. Paris: Éditions Seghers, 1962.
Dressler, Marie: *The Life Story of an Ugly Duckling*. New York: Robert M. McBride & Co., 1924.
Eells, George: *Cole Porter. The Life That He Led*. New York: G. P. Putnam's Sons, 1967. London: W. H. Allen, 1967.
Essoe, Gabe and Lee, Ray: *Gable: A Complete Gallery of His Screen Portraits*. Los Angeles: Price/Stern/Sloan Publishers Inc., 1967. London: Wolfe Publishing, 1967.
Everson, William K.: *The Bad Guys*. New York: Citadel Press, 1964.
Ewen, David: *Complete Book of the American Musical Theater*. New York: Henry Holt & Co., 1958.
Eyles, Allen: *The Marx Brothers Their World of Comedy*. London: Zwemmer/New Jersey: A. S. Barnes & Co., 1966.
Fields, Gracie: *Sing As We Go*. London: Muller, 1960. New York: Doubleday.
The Film Daily Yearbook (various editions). New York: The Film Daily.
Filmlexicon degli Autori e delli Opere (7 vols.). Rome: Edizione di Bianco e Nero, 1958.
Finler, Joel W.: *Stroheim*. London: Studio Vista, 1967. Berkeley: University of California Press, 1968.

Fowler, Gene: *Goodnight Sweet Prince*. New York: Viking Press, 1944. London: H. Hammond, 1949.
Funke, Lewis and Booth, John E. (Eds.): *Actors Talk About Acting*. New York: Random House, 1961. London: Thames and Hudson, 1962.
Gehman, Richard: *Bogart*. Greenwich, Conn.: Fawcett Publications Inc., 1965. London: Oldbourne, 1967.
Gifford, Denis: *British Cinema An Illustrated Guide*. London: Zwemmer/New York: A. S. Barnes & Co., 1968.
Gish, Lillian with Pinchot, Ann: *The Movies, Mr Griffith and Me*. Englewood Cliffs, N.J.: Prentice-Hall, 1969. London: W. H. Allen, 1969.
Goodman, Ezra: *The Fifty Year Decline and Fall of Hollywood*. New York: Simon and Schuster, 1961.
Graves, Robert and Hodge, Alan: *The Long Weekend*. London: Faber and Faber, 1940.
Griffith, Richard: *Samuel Goldwyn: The Producer and His Films*. New York: Museum of Modern Art Film Library, 1956.
Griffith, Richard and Mayer, Arthur: *The Movies*. New York: Simon and Schuster, 1957. London: Spring Books, 1963.
Halliwell, Leslie: *The Filmgoer's Companion*. London: Macgibbon and Kee, revised edition, 1967. New York: Hill and Wang, revised edition, 1967.
Hampton, Benjamin, B.: *A History of the Movies*. New York: Covici, Friede, 1931.
Hancock, Ralph and Fairbanks, Letitia: *Douglas Fairbanks The Fourth Musketeer*. New York: Henry Holt & Co., 1953. London: Peter Davies, 1953.
Hardwicke, Sir Cedric: *A Victorian in Orbit*. New York: Doubleday, 1961. London: Methuen, 1962.
Hardy, Forsyth: *Filmgoers' Review*. Edinburgh: Albyn Press, 1945.
Higham, Charles and Greenberg, Joel: *The Celluloid Muse: Hollywood Directors Speak*. London: Angus and Robertson, 1969.
Hopper, Hedda and Brough, James: *The Whole Truth and Nothing But*. New York: Doubleday, 1963.
Howard, Leslie Ruth: *A Quite Remarkable Father*. New York: Harcourt Brace, 1959. London: Longmans, 1960.
Huff, Theodore: *An Index to the Films of Ernst Lubitsch*. London: British Film Institute, 1947; *The Early Work of Charles Chaplin*. London: British Film Institute (Index series), revised edition, 1961.
Jacobs, Lewis: *The Rise of the American Film*. New York: Harcourt, Brace, 1939. Teachers College Press, Columbia University, 1970.
Kael, Pauline: *I Lost It at the Movies*. Boston: Atlantic-Little, 1965. London: Jonathan Cape, 1966. *Kiss Kiss Bang Bang*. Boston: Little, Brown & Co., 1968.
Keaton, Buster with Charles Samuels: *My Wonderful World of Slapstick*. New York: Doubleday, 1960. London: Allen and Unwin, 1967.
Knight, Arthur: *The Liveliest Art*. New York: Macmillan, 1957. London: Muller, 1959.
Kobal, John: *Marlene Dietrich*. London: Studio Vista/New York: E. P. Dutton, 1968.
Kyrou, Ado: *Amour-Erotisme et Cinéma*. Paris: Le Terrain Vague, 1957.
Lake, Veronica and Bain, Donald: *Veronica*. London: W. H. Allen, 1969.
Lamarr, Hedy: *Ecstasy and Me*. New York: Bartholomew House, 1966. London: W. H. Allen, 1967.
Lamprecht, Gerhard: *Deutsche Stummfilme 1923–31* (2 vols.). Berlin: Deutsche Kinemathek, 1967.
Lanchester, Elsa: *Charles Laughton and I*. London: Faber and Faber, 1938.
Lejeune, C. A.: *Chestnuts in Her Lap*. London: Phoenix House, 1948 (second edition).
Levant, Oscar: *The Memoirs of an Amnesiac*. New York: G. P. Putnam's Sons, 1965.
Loos, Anita: *A Girl Like I*. New York: The Viking Press, 1966. London: Hamish Hamilton, 1967.
Marx, Arthur: *Life With Groucho*. New York: Simon and Schuster, 1954. London: (*Groucho*) Gollancz, 1954.
Maugham, W. Somerset: *A Writer's Notebook*. London: Heinemann, 1950. New York: Doubleday, 1949.
Mizener, Arthur: *The Far Side of Paradise*. Boston: Houghton Mifflin, 1951. London: Eyre and Spottiswoode, 1951.
Morley, Robert and Stokes, Sewell: *Robert Morley Responsible Gentleman*. London: Heinemann, 1966. New York: (*Robert Morley: A Reluctant Autobiography*) Simon and Schuster, 1967.
Morley, Sheridan: *A Talent to Amuse*. London: Heinemann, 1969.
McCabe, John: *Mr Laurel and Mr Hardy*. New York: Doubleday, 1961. London: Museum Press, 1962.
McWhirter, Norris and McWhirter, Ross (Eds.): *The Guinness Book of Records*, 1969 edition. London: Guinness Superlatives, 1969.
Newquist, Roy: *Showcase*. New York: William Morrow & Co., 1966; *A Special Kind of Magic*. New York: Rand McNally, 1967.
Noble, Peter (Ed.): *The British Film Yearbook*. London: British Yearbooks, 1945, 1946.
Pasternak, Joe: *Easy the Hard Way*. New York: G. P. Putnam's Sons, 1956. London: W. H. Allen, 1956.
Payne, Robert: *The Great Charlie*. London: Pan Books, 1957 (revised edition).
Pickford Mary: *Sunshine and Shadow*. New York: Doubleday, 1955. London: Heinemann, 1956.
Platt, Frank C. (Ed.): *Great Stars of Hollywood's Golden Age*. New York: New American Library, 1966.
Ramsaye, Terry: *A Million and One Nights*. New York: Simon and Schuster, 1926.
Ramsaye, Terry (Ed.): *International Motion Picture Almanack* (various editions). New York: Quigley Publishing Co.
Reed, Rex: *Do You Sleep in the Nude?* New York: New American Library, 1968. London, W. H. Allen, 1969.
Rideout, Eric H.: *The American Film*. London: Mitre Press, 1937.
Ringgold, Gene: *The Films of Bette Davis*. New York: Citadel Press, 1966.
Robinson, David: *Hollywood in the Twenties*. London: Zwemmer/New York, A. S. Barnes & Co., 1968.
Rooney, Mickey: *i.e. an autobiography*. New York: G. P. Putnam's Sons, 1965.
Ross, Lillian and Ross, Helen: *The Player*. New York: Simon and Schuster, 1962.
Rotha, Paul and Griffith, Richard: *The Film Till Now*, revised edition. London: Vision Press, 1960 (Spring Books, 1967).
Samuels, Charles: *The King: A Biography of Clark Gable*. New York: Coward-McCann, 1962. London: (*King of Hollywood; Clark Gable*) W. H. Allen, 1962.
Scheuer, Steven H. (Ed.). *TV Key Movie Reviews and Ratings*. New York: Bantam Books, 1961; revised edition–as *Movies On TV*, 1968.
Schickel, Richard: *The Stars*. New York: Dial Press, 1962.
Sennett, Mack with Cameron Shipp: *King of Comedy*. New York: Doubleday, 1954. London: Peter Davies, 1955.

Seton, Marie: *Paul Robeson*. London: Dennis Dobson, 1958.
Shulman, Irving: *Valentino*. New York: Trident Press, 1967. London: Leslie Frewin, 1968.
Speed, F. Maurice: *Film Review* (annual). London: Macdonald and W. H. Allen. New York: A. S. Barnes & Co.
Swanberg, W. A.: *Citizen Hearst*. New York: Charles Scribner's Sons, 1961.
Swindell, Larry: *Spencer Tracy*. New York and Cleveland: World Publishing/New American Library, 1969. London: W. H. Allen, 1970.
Tabori, Paul: *Alexander Korda*. London: Oldbourne Press, 1959. New York: Heinman, 1959.
Taylor, Deems, with Marcelene Peterson and Bryant Hale: *A Pictorial History of the Movies*, revised and enlarged edition. New York: Simon and Schuster, 1949.
Taylor, Robert Lewis: *W. C. Fields His Follies and Fortunes*. New York: Doubleday, 1949. London: Cassell, 1950.
Thomas, Bob: *King Cohn*. New York: G. P. Putnam's Sons, 1967. London: Barrie and Rockliff, 1967; *Thalberg Life and Legend*. New York: Doubleday, 1969.
Trewin, J. C.: *Robert Donat*. London: Heinemann, 1968.
Tynan, Kenneth: *Curtains*. London: Longmans, 1961. New York: Atheneum, 1961; *Tynan Right and Left*. London: Longmans, 1967. New York: Atheneum, 1967.
Vidor, King: *A Tree Is a Tree*. New York, Harcourt Brace, 1953. London: Longmans, 1954.
Von Sternberg, Joseph: *Fun in a Chinese Laundry*. New York: Macmillan Co., 1965. London: Secker and Warburg, 1966.
Walker, Alexander: *The Celluloid Sacrifice*. London: Michael Joseph, 1966. New York: Hawthorn Books, 1967.
Warner, Jack L. with Dean Jennings: *My First Hundred Years in Hollywood*. New York: Random House, 1965.
Weinberg, Herman G.: *The Lubitsch Touch*. New York: E. P. Dutton, 1968.
West, Mae: *Goodness Had Nothing To Do With It*. New York: Prentice-Hall, 1960. London: W. H. Allen, 1960.
Who's Who in Hollywood, various editions. New York: Dell Publications.
Who's Who in the Theatre, various editions. London and New York: Pitman.
Wilcox, Herbert: *Twenty-Five Thousand Sunsets*. London: The Bodley Head, 1967.
Winnington, Richard: *Drawn and Quartered*. London: Saturn Press, 1948.
Wolfe, Tom: *The Kandy-Kolored Tangerine-Flake Streamlined Baby*. New York: Farrar, Straus and Giroux, 1965. London: Jonathan Cape, 1966.
Zierold, Norman J.: *The Child Stars*. New York: Coward-McCann, 1965. London: Macdonald, 1966; *The Moguls*. New York: Coward-McCann, 1969.
Zolotow, Maurice: *Marilyn Monroe*. New York: Harcourt, Brace, 1960. London: W. H. Allen, 1961.
Zukor, Adolph: *The Public Is Never Wrong*. New York: G. P. Putnam's Sons, 1953. London: Cassell, 1954.

For picture research, grateful acknowledgment is made to The Odhams Periodicals Library, The Kobal Collection, The British Film Institute, and Tracy Lee; and to MGM, Warner Brothers, 20th Century-Fox, Paramount, RKO, Universal, Republic, Columbia, United Artists, UFA. The Rank Organization, London Films, British Lion, Ealing Studios, Woodfall, Cinema Center and Walt Disney.

Index of title changes

As the titles listed in the text are the original titles, this index is arranged alphabetically according to the changed or alternative titles – with the original title, country and date appearing on the right. We have not taken into account those cases where films are re-titled for television.

Abandon Ship, US	*Seven Waves Away*, GB (57)
Abbott and Costello Meet the Ghosts, GB	*Abbott and Costello Meet Frankenstein*, US (48)
Adios, GB	*The Lash*, US (31)
Advance to the Rear (alternative title)	*Company of Cowards?*, US (64)
Affair in Monte Carlo, US	*Twenty-four Hours in a Woman's Life*, GB (53)
Affairs in Versailles, US	*Si Versailles m'était Conté*, F (54)
The Affairs of Sally, GB	*The Fuller Brush Girl*, US (50)
After Midnight, GB	*Captain Carey*, US (50)
All That Money Can Buy, GB	*The Devil and Daniel Webster*, US (41)
All This and Money, Too, GB	*Love Is a Ball*, US (63)
Along Came Sally, US	*Aunt Sally*, GB (34)
Always in My Heart, GB	*Mr Imperium*, US (51)
Angel Street, US	*Gaslight*, GB (40)
Arms and the Girl, GB	*Red Salute*, US (35)
Arms and the Woman, GB	*Mr Winkle Goes to War*, US (44)
Arouse and Beware, GB	*The Man from Dakota*, US (40)
The Avengers, US	*The Day Will Dawn*, GB (42)
Bachelor Bait, GB	*Adventure in Baltimore*, US (49)
Bachelor Girls, GB	*The Bachelor's Daughters*, US (46)
Bachelor's Folly, US	*The Calendar*, GB (31)
Bachelor Knight, GB	*The Bachelor and the Bobby-Soxer*, US (47)
Bad Sister, US	*The White Unicorn*, GB (47)
The Badge of Courage, GB	*Turn Back the Hours*, US (28)
The Bank Detective, GB	*The Bank Dick*, US (40)
The Battle of Austerlitz, US	*Austerlitz*, F (60)
The Battle of the Worlds, US	*Il Pianeta degli Uomini*, It (60)
The Beachcomber, US	*Vessel of Wrath*, GB (38)
The Beautiful Cheat, GB	*What a Woman!*, US (43)
Behold We Live, GB	*If I Were Free*, US (33)
Big Deal at Dodge City, GB	*A Big Hand for the Little Lady*, US (66)
Birds of Prey, GB	*The Ace of Aces*, US (38)
Blackout, US	*Contraband*, GB (40)
Blood Money, GB	*Requiem for a Heavyweight*, US (62)
Blood on my Hands, GB	*Kiss the Blood off My Hands*, US (48)
Bonaventure, GB	*Thunder on the Hill*, US (51)
Borderlines, GB	*The Caretakers*, US (68)
The Boy from Barnardo's, GB	*Lord Jeff*, US (38)
A Boy Is Ten Feet Tall, US	*Sammy Going South*, GB (62)
Breaking the Sound Barrier, US	*The Sound Barrier*, GB (52)
Broadway Singer, GB	*Torch Singer*, US (33)
By Hook or by Crook, GB	*I Dood It*, US (43)
Cadets on Parade, GB	*Junior Army*, US (42)
Café of Seven Sinners, GB	*Seven Sinners*, US (40)
Call Me Genius, US	*The Rebel*, GB (61)
Cardigan's Last Case, GB	*States' Attorney*, US (32)
Cargo of Innocents, GB	*Stand by for Action*, US (42)
Carnival Nights, GB	*Carnival*, US (35)
The Case of Mrs Pembroke, GB	*Two Against the World*, US (36)
Cash and Carry, GB	*Ringside Maisie*, US (41)
Casino de Paree, GB	*Go Into Your Dance*, US (35)
Cast Iron, GB	*The Virtuous Sin*, US (30)
Caught by Television, GB	*Trapped by Television*, US (36)
Chamber of Horrors, US	*The Door With Seven Locks*, GB (40)
Charley's American Aunt, GB	*Charley's Aunt*, US (41)
Choose Your Partner, GB	*Two Girls on Broadway*, US (40)
The City Jungle, GB	*The Young Philadelphians*, US (59)
Clouds over Europe, US	*Q Planes*, GB (39)
College Days, GB	*The Freshman*, US (25)
Compromised GB	*The Sophomore*, US (29)
Concealment, GB	*The Secret Bride*, US (35)
Colonel Blimp, US	*The Life and Death of Colonel Blimp*, GB (43)
The Contact Man, GB	*Alias Nick Beal*, US (49)
Courageous, GB	*A Lost Lady*, US (34)
The Courtney Affair, US	*The Courtneys of Curzon Stre* GB (47)
Crooks in Clover, GB	*Penthouse*, US (33)
Czarina, GB	*A Royal Scandal*, US (45)
Dark Sands, US	*Jericho*, GB (37)
A Date With Destiny, GB	*The Mad Doctor*, US (41)
Daughter of Luxury, GB	*Five and Ten*, US (31)
Daughters of Destiny, US	*Destinées*, F (53)
Dead Image, GB	*Dead Ringer*, US (64)
Deadline, GB	*Deadline USA*, US (52)
Devil on Wheels, GB	*Indianapolis Speedway*, US (3
The Devil Takes the Count, GB	*The Devil Is a Sissy*, US (36)
The Diamond Earrings, US	*Madame de . . .*, F (53)
Die! Die! My Darling, US	*Fanatic*, GB (65)
The Dover Road, GB	*Where Sinners Meet*, US (34)
Drums, US	*The Drum*, GB (38)
East of the Rising Sun, GB	*Malaya*, US (50)
Elephants Never Forget, GB	*Zenobia*, US (39)
Ellen, GB	*The Second Woman*, US (49)
Embassy Girl, GB	*Hat Check Girl*, US (32)
End of the Rainbow, GB	*Northwest Outpost*, US (47)
Enemies of the Public, GB	*Public Enemy*, US (31)
Escape From Yesterday, GB	*Ride a Crooked Mile*, US (38)
Escape to Happiness, GB	*Intermezzo – A Love Story*, U
Eternal Youth, GB	*West Point*, US (28)
Every Other Inch a Lady, GB	*Dancing Co-ed*, US (39)
Every Woman's Man, GB	*The Prizefighter and the Lady*, US (33)
Eye Witness, US	*Your Witness*, GB (49)
The False Idol, GB	*The False Madonna*, US (32)
Farewell My Lovely, GB/US	*Murder My Sweet* (*Farewell M* *Lovely*), US (44)
The Faun, GB	*Bought and Paid For*, US (16)
Female Co-respondent, GB	*Adventure in Washington*, US
The Fifth Chair, GB	*It's in the Bag*, US (45)
Fine and Dandy, GB	*The West Point Story*, US (50
The Flight of the White Stallions, GB	*The Miracle of the White Stall* US (62)
The Flood, GB	*The Johnstown Flood*, US (26)
For Love or Money, US	*Cash*, GB (33)
For You Alone, GB	*When You're in Love*, US (37)
The Forsyte Saga, GB	*That Forsyte Woman*, US (49
Forward March, GB	*The Dough Boys*, US (30)
Four Against Fate, US	*Derby Day*, GB (52)
Fraternally Yours, GB	*Sons of the Desert*, US (34)
Free to Live, GB	*Holiday* (38)
The French They Are a Funny Race, US	*Les carnets de Major Thompso* F (55)
Frou Frou, GB	*Toy Wife*, US (38)
The Gay Divorce, GB	*The Gay Divorcee*, US (34)
The Gay Falcon, GB	*The Falcon Takes Over*, US (4
The Gay Nineties, GB	*The Floradora Girl*, US (30)
The Gay Mrs Trexel, GB	*Susan and God*, US (40)
A Genius in the Family, GB	*So Goes My Love*, US (46)
Gentleman for a Day, GB	*Union Depot*, US (32)
The Girl From Mexico, GB	*Mexicali Rose*, US (29)
The Girl I Made, GB	*Made on Broadway*, US (33)
The Girl in Overalls, GB	*Swing Shift Maisie*, US (43)
The Girl in Room 17, GB	*Vice Squad*, US (53)
Girl in Pawn, GB	*Little Miss Marker*, US (34)
The Girls He Left Behind, GB	*The Gang's All Here*, US (43)
The Golden Hour, GB	*Pot o' Gold*, US (41)
Golden Virgin, US	*The Story of Esther Costello*, GB (57)
Golden Youth, GB	*Just Suppose*, US (26)
Good Girl, GB	*Good Dame*, US (34)
Good Morning Doctor, GB	*You Belong to Me*, US (42)
The Grace Moore Story, GB	*So This Is Love*, US (53)
The Green-eyed Woman, GB	*Take a Letter Darling*, US (4
Guilty As Charged, GB	*Guilty As Hell*, US (32)
Guns in the Afternoon, GB	*Ride the High Country*, US (6
Hallelujah I'm a Tramp, GB	*Hallelujah I'm a Bum*, US (33)
Harmony Parade, GB	*Pigskin Parade*, US (36)